Street by Street

WEST MIDLANDS

PLUS BROMSGROVE, CANNOCK, KIDDERMINSTER, LICHFIELD, NUNEATON, REDDITCH, ROYAL LEAMINGTON SPA, RUGBY, TAMWORTH, WARWICK

Enlarged Areas Birmingham, Coventry, Walsall, Wolverhampton

2nd edition November 2003
© Automobile Association Developments Limited 2003

Original edition printed May 2001

Ordnance Survey® This product includes map data licensed from Ordnance Survey ® with the permission of the Controller of Her Majesty's Stationery Office.
© Crown copyright 2003.
All rights reserved. Licence number 399221.

Published by AA Publishing (a trading name of Automobile Association Developments Limited, whose registered office is Millstream, Maidenhead Road, Windsor, Berkshire SL4 5GD. Registered number 1878835).

Mapping produced by the Cartography Department of The Automobile Association. (A01723)

A CIP Catalogue record for this book is available from the British Library.

Printed in Italy by Printer Trento srl.

Key to map pages	ii-iii
Key to map symbols	iv–1
Enlarged map pages	2-9
Main map pages	10-207
Index – towns & villages	208–209
Index – streets	210-262
Index – featured places	262-272
Acknowledgements	272

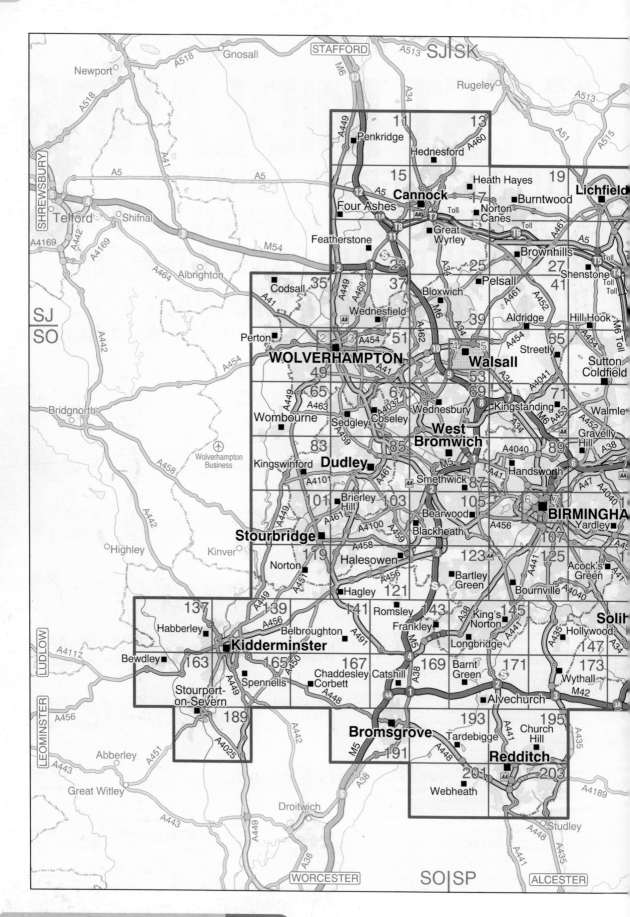

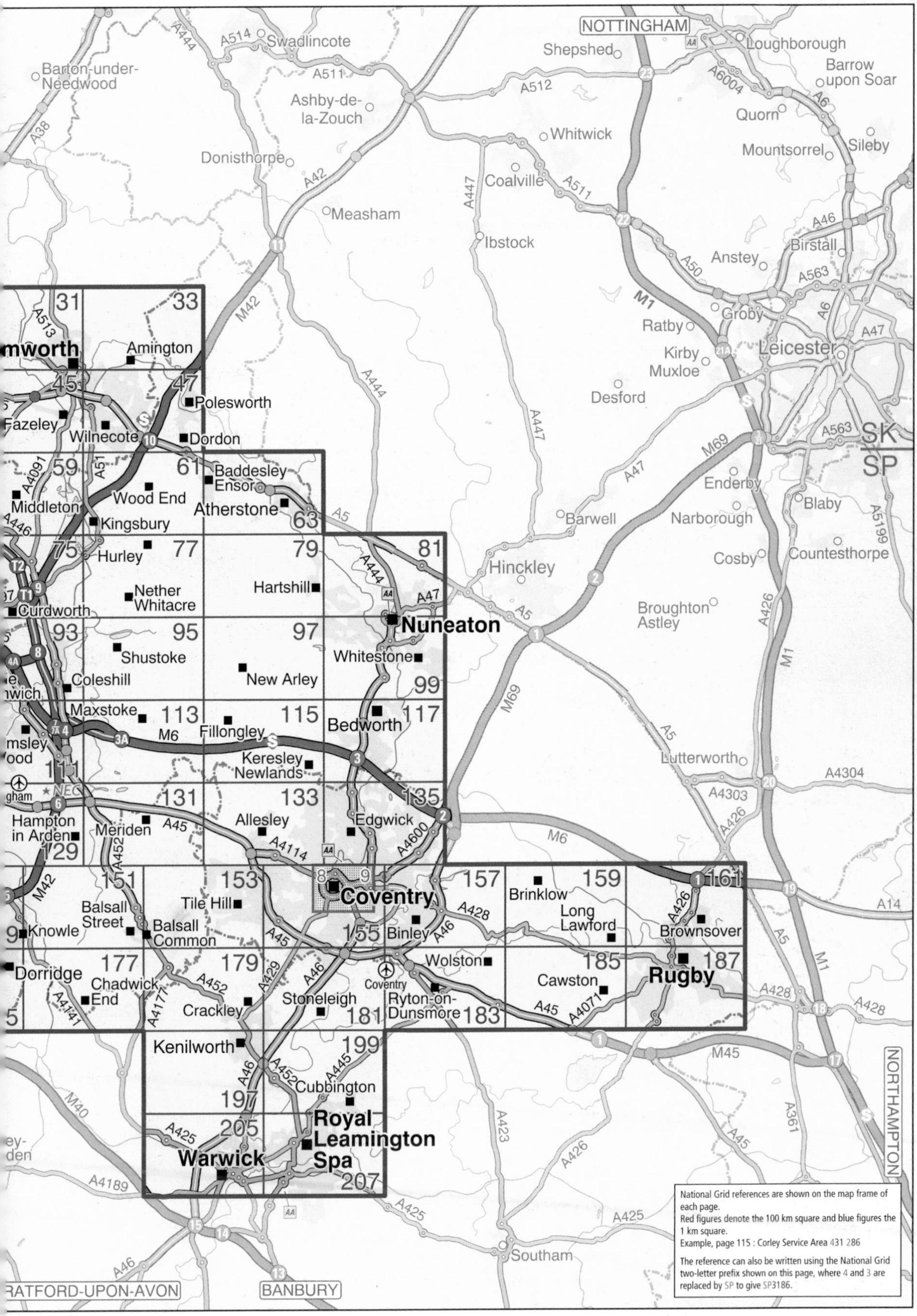

NOTTINGHAM

Swadlincote
Shepshed
Loughborough
Barrow upon Soar
Barton-under-Needwood
Quorn
Sileby
Ashby-de-la-Zouch
Whitwick
Mountsorrel
Donisthorpe
Coalville
Anstey
Birstall
Measham
Ibstock
Desford
Leicester
SK
SP
Enderby
Barwell
Narborough
Bleby
Hinckley
Cosby
Countesthorpe
Broughton Astley
Amington
Polesworth
Baddesley Ensor
Atherstone
Hinckley
Wilnecote
Dordon
Fazeley
Middleton
Wood End
Kingsbury
Hurley
Hartshill
Nuneaton
Nether Whitacre
Curdworth
Shustoke
Whitestone
New Arley
Coleshill
Maxstoke
Fillongley
Bedworth
Keresley
Newlands
Lutterworth
Meriden
Allesley
Edgwick
Hampton in Arden
Coventry
Brinklow
Long Lawford
Brownsover
Tile Hill
Balsall Street
Balsall Common
Binley
Knowle
Wolston
Cawston
Rugby
Dorridge
Chadwick End
Crackley
Stoneleigh
Ryton-on-Dunsmore
Kenilworth
Cubbington
Royal Leamington Spa
Warwick
Southam
STRATFORD-UPON-AVON
BANBURY
NORTHAMPTON

31 33
45 47
59 61 63
75 77 79 81
93 95 97 99
113 115 117
111
131 133 135
129
151 153 157 159 161
155
177 179 185 187
181 183
199
197
205 207

National Grid references are shown on the map frame of each page.
Red figures denote the 100 km square and blue figures the 1 km square.
Example, page 115 : Corley Service Area 431 286

The reference can also be written using the National Grid two-letter prefix shown on this page, where 4 and 3 are replaced by SP to give SP3186.

3.6 inches to 1 mile   **Scale of main map pages 1:17,500**

0   1/2   miles   1
0   1/2   kilometres   1 1/2   2

Motorway/Toll Motorway	Light railway & station
Junction 9 — Motorway junction	Preserved private railway
Services — Motorway service area	LC — Level crossing
Primary road single/dual carriageway	Tramway
Services — Primary road service area	Ferry route
A road single/dual carriageway	Airport runway
B road single/dual carriageway	County, administrative boundary
Other road single/dual carriageway	Mounds
Minor/private road, access may be restricted	93 — Page continuation 1:17,500
One-way street	7 — Page continuation to enlarged scale 1:10,000
Pedestrian area	River/canal, lake
Track or footpath	Aqueduct, lock, weir
Road under construction	465 Winter Hill — Peak (with height in metres)
Road tunnel	Beach
AA — AA Service Centre	Woodland
P — Parking	Park
P+ — Park & Ride	Cemetery
Bus/coach station	Built-up area
Railway & main railway station	Featured building
Railway & minor railway station	City wall
Underground station	

A&E	Hospital with 24-hour A&E department		Castle
PO	Post Office		Historic house or building
	Public library	Wakehurst Place NT	National Trust property
i	Tourist Information Centre	M	Museum or art gallery
i	Seasonal Tourist Information Centre		Roman antiquity
	Petrol station, 24 hour Major suppliers only		Ancient site, battlefield or monument
†	Church/chapel		Industrial interest
	Public toilets		Garden
	Toilet with disabled facilities		Garden Centre Garden Centre Association Member
PH	Public house AA recommended		Garden Centre Wyevale Garden Centre
	Restaurant AA inspected		Arboretum
Madeira Hotel	Hotel AA inspected		Farm or animal centre
	Theatre or performing arts centre		Zoological or wildlife collection
	Cinema		Bird collection
	Golf course		Nature reserve
▲	Camping AA inspected		Aquarium
	Caravan site AA inspected	V	Visitor or heritage centre
	Camping & caravan site AA inspected		Country park
	Theme park		Cave
	Abbey, cathedral or priory		Windmill
			Distillery, brewery or vineyard

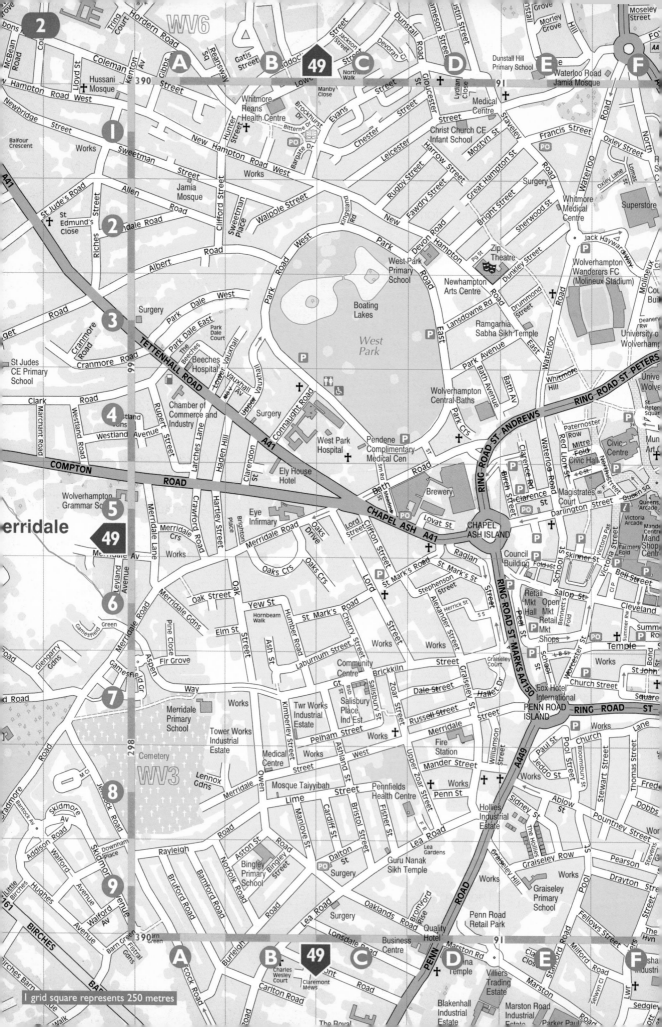

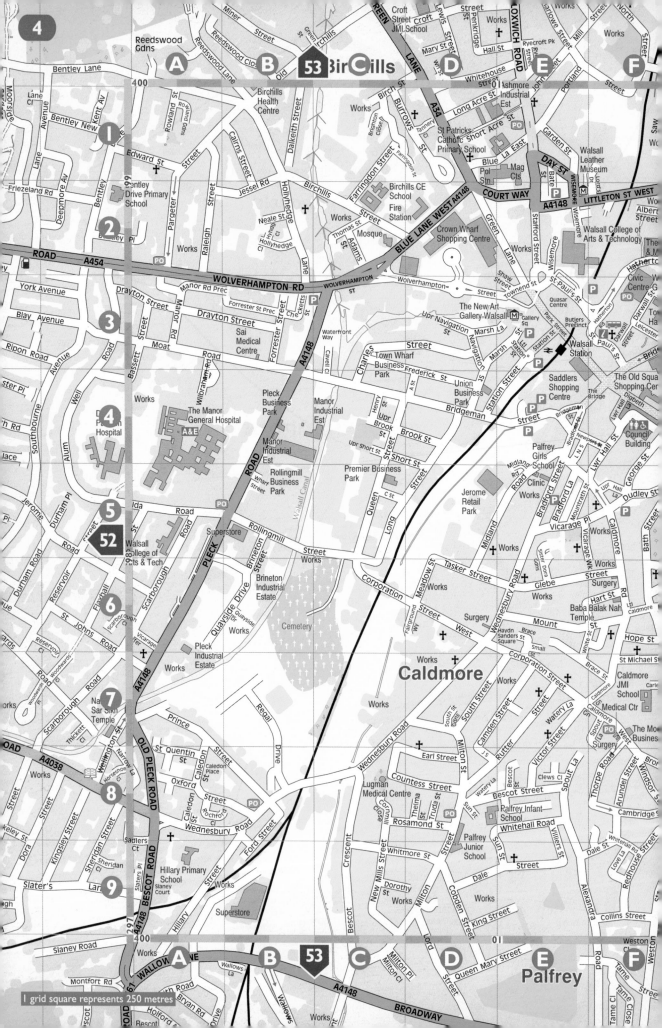

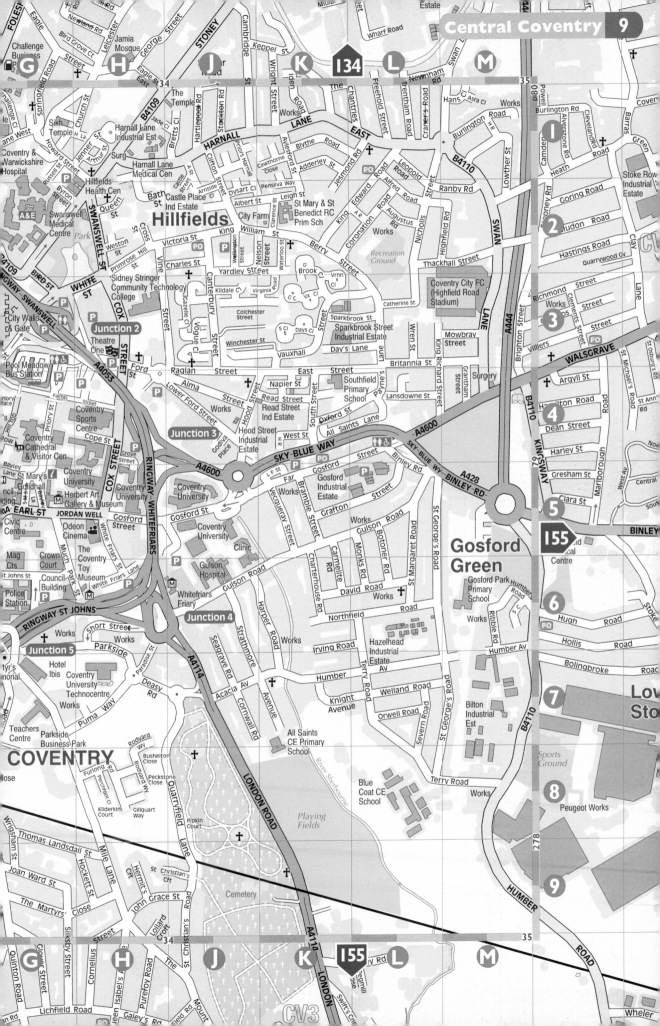

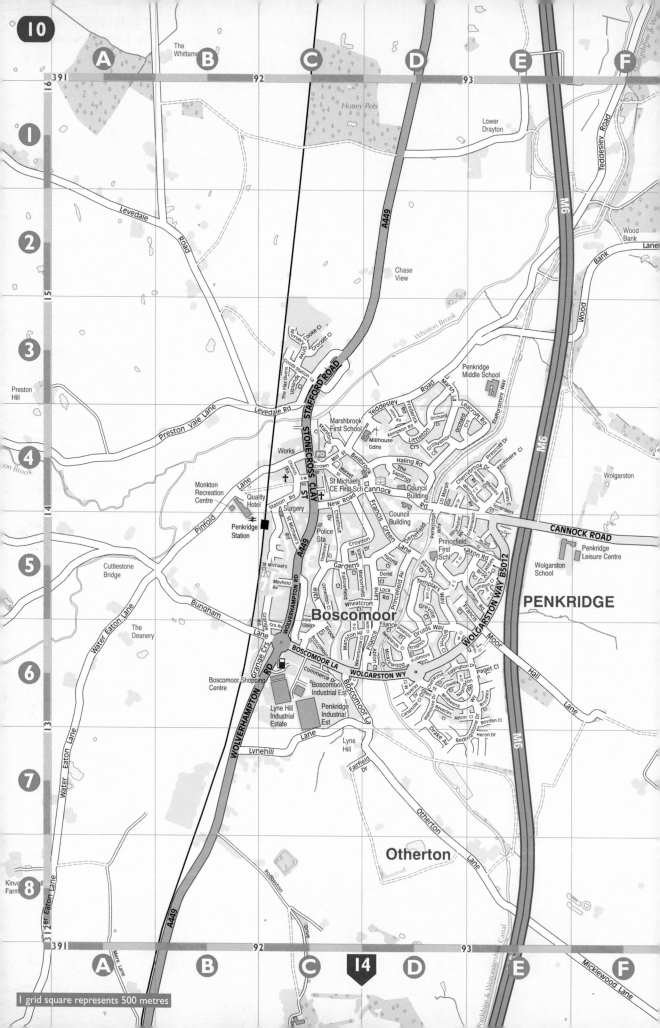

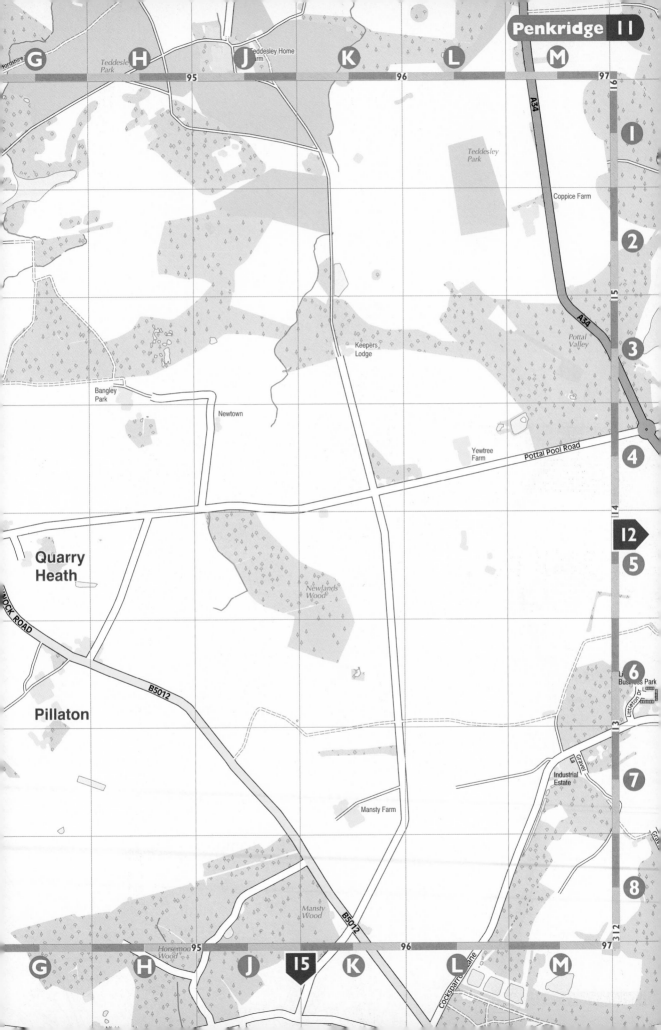

G   H   J   K   L   M

95   96   97

Teddesley Park

Teddesley Home Farm

Teddesley Park

Coppice Farm

A34

A34

Pottal Valley

Keepers Lodge

Bangley Park

Newtown

Yewtree Farm

Pottal Pool Road

12

Quarry Heath

Newlands Wood

Business Park

Littleton Dr

Pillaton

B5012

Gravel La

Industrial Estate

Mansty Farm

Mansty Wood

B5012

HANNOCK ROAD

Cockspare Lane

Horsemoor Wood

95   96   97

G   H   J   15   K   L   M

I

2

3

4

5

6

7

8

A · B · C · 10 · D · E · F

391 · 92 · 93

I

Kinva
Farm

Mere Lane

Mere Lane
Farm

A449

2

Rodbaston

Staffordshire
College of Agriculture

Rodbaston

Staffordshire & Worcestershire Canal

M6

Mickiewood Lane

Garden Centre

3 Gailey

A5

Christ
Church
School

Council
Building

Gailey
Wharf

Harrisons Lane

Gailey Lea
Farm

Gailey Lea Lane

M6

Council
Building

A5

Gailey
Upper
Reservoir

4

Croft Farm

Croft Lane

Calf Heath
Reservoir

Gailey
Lower
Reserv

Junction 12

5

Crateford La

Gravelly
Way

Vicarage Road

Woodlands Lane

i Lane

Heath
Farm

M6

6

Woodside
Farm

Stable Lane

Calf Heath

STAFFORD ROAD

7

Vicarage Road

Straight Mile

Straight Mile

Kings Rd

Kings Rd

Works

Queens

A449

Sprint
Industrial
Estate

**Four
Ashes**

Station Road

Station Drive

Enterprise Drive

Latherford Close

Asbury Cl

PO

Laches Clos

Deepmore
Close

Latherford Lane

308

391

92

93

8

Station Drive

Deepmore
Farm

Latherford

A · B · C · 22 · D · E · F

Standeford

1 grid square represents 500 metres

Lane

Works

Mere Pits

Comberford

Manor Lane   Tollgate Lane

Comberford   Lane

Wigginton

St Leonards
CE Primary
School

Comberford
Hall

LC

Walrand Cl

Main
Street

The Rawlett
School

River Tame

Windmill
Cl

32

Gillway

LC

Windmill
Farm

Coton Lane

Claremont
Rd

Hayworth
Cl

Hill Top Av

Pine
Cl

Mildenhall

Browning
Close

Kipling
Rise

Telford Road

Carlton

Cedar
Dr

Hawthorne Av

Lilac
Cl

Laburnum Av

Cemetery

Ashcroft
County
Infants Sch

B5493

St Elizabeths
Primary School

Cherry Tree

Queensway

Cromwell Rd

Mdox
Close

Coton Green
Primary Sch

Bloomfield Wy

Lark Hall
Infants School

Byron
Cl

Redhill

Chestnut Av

Flax Hill
Junior
School

Coton Hall
Farm

Scimitar Close

Willoughby

Danelagh
Cl

Robert Clifton
Rd

Shelley
Av

Milton
Av

Gillway

Borough Rd

Coton Lane

Kepler

Fontenaye
Rd

Libra
Cl

Faina
Cl

Solway

**Borough
Park**

Highgrove
Close

Helmingham

Chartwell

Mercia Cl

Compton Rd

Crs

Park School

Thackeray Drive

Chesterton

Kensington
Dr

6

Godolphin

Kentwell

Buckingham Road

Meiford

Ariane

Roman
Way

Edgar
Rd

**Tamworth
RUFC**

Masefield

Old Pl

Cope's Dr

Eliot Cl

Windsor

Burton

Coton

Newstead

Gerard

Cavendish

**Wigginton
Park**

Elzbt Dr

LC

Burns
Rd

Chesterton Wy

St Ives
Close

Queen
Elizabeth's
Mercian School

Somerville

Rufford

Swallowfield

Alders
Lane

Neander

Leyfields

Bronte
Cl

Stevenson

Coleridge

Marmion
Junior
School

Keble
Walk

TAMWORT

Oxbridge

LICHFIELD

Wynyates

Lichfield Trading
Est

Lagrange

Mariner

Armstrong

Lovell

Wordsworth Av

Arnold

Shakespeare

Abbottsall

Salter's Lane

Upper
Cungate

Croft St

Tamworth &
Lichfield College

Tamw
Statio

Dunstall Lane

Exeter
Dr

Way

Apollo

Borman

Aiders

Brunel

Freville Cl

Aldergate
Med Cen

ROAD
A51

Gargarin

Lichfield Road Industrial Estate

Lichfield Road
Industrial Est

**The
Leys**

Moorgate
Primary
School

Laurel

Woodcroft

OFFA DRIVE

Bradford Street

Park St

Prospect St

Hospital
Street

Cherry

Youth
Cen

Council
Building

Swanmote

Cygnet

Meadow
Park

Nevill
Street

Barbara
St

Offa
St

Albert Rd

Police

8

Dunstall
Farm

Halford Street

Alfred St

ALDERGATE

Arts

Shop
Prct

LICHFIELD ST

Fire
Station

Med Cen

Council
Building

Market St

**Tamw
Castle**

George St

Broad Meadow

Balfour

45

Lady
Bridge

Fazeley Road

Ankerside
Shopping Cen

TAMEDRIVE

ANKERDRIVE

SAXON

Lady Meadow

Castle
Pleasure
Grounds

Pleasure
Bowl

G H J K L M

25 26 27 08

I

Lonkhills Farm

Staffordshire County
Warwickshire County

B5493

Newton Lane Seck

The Gn

Seckington

2

07

B5493

The Poplars

3

Main Road

Hangman's Lane

atfold Barn
rm

New Road

4

06

The Decoy

Shuttington
Fields Farm

PO

5

Pear Tree Cl

Shuttington

Crnt Crs

School Lane

Milner Drive

Church La

6

05

Shuttington Bridge

Alvecote

7

Coventry Canal

M42

Bramcote Hall

8

Robey's Lane

Potford Bridge

304

25 26 27

G H J ▼**47** K L M

Golf Course

Tamworth
Municipal
Golf Club

R Anker

G H J **27** K L M

Stonnall

Lower Stonnall

Heath Close

Berry

St Peters CE Primary School
Surgery

Main Street

Garnet Close

Westwick Close

Walnut

Wall

Mill Lane

New Barns

1 Footherley

Thornes

Thornes CfK

St Peter's Cl

PO

Church Road

GlenWood Rise

New Barns Lane

Hook

2

Gravelly Lane

Wood Lane

3

Lazy Hill

Birch Lane

Gainsborough Hill Farm

Bosses

4

Hill Top Walk

Bar Walk

Druids Heath

Cotswold Close

Knoll Croft

Kinver Crs

Clifton Av

Ledbury Close

Tenbury Close

Stratford

Malvern

Links Way

Side Way

Drive

Wood Lane

Forge Lane

Forge Farm

42

Druids Av

Emdale Dr

Wyevale Garden Centre

CHESTER ROAD

A452

5

Druids Heath Farm

PH

Druids Heath Golf Club

Holly Lane

Stonnall Road

Mill Green

6

Golf Course

Back Lane

Hobs Hole Lane

Forge Lane

7

WS9

Cemetery

Cooper & Jordan CE J&I School

The Fairlawns at Aldridge Hotel

Gould Firm Lane

Green Lane

Walsall Staffordshire County

A454

ALDRIDGE ROAD

Mill Lane

Lakeside

spinney

Little Aston Hall Drive

WA

Icroft Way

LITTLE **ASTON ROAD**

A452

Fotherley Road

Fotherley Brook

Golf Course

Roman Road

8 Littl

Angels RC

St Francis of Assisi RC School

Branton Hill Lane

Bourne Farm

Beech Gate

300th

Squirrel Walk

Cottage M

A452

dshire County

Walsall

Golf Cou

Little Aston Golf Club

stonehouse

Shrubbery

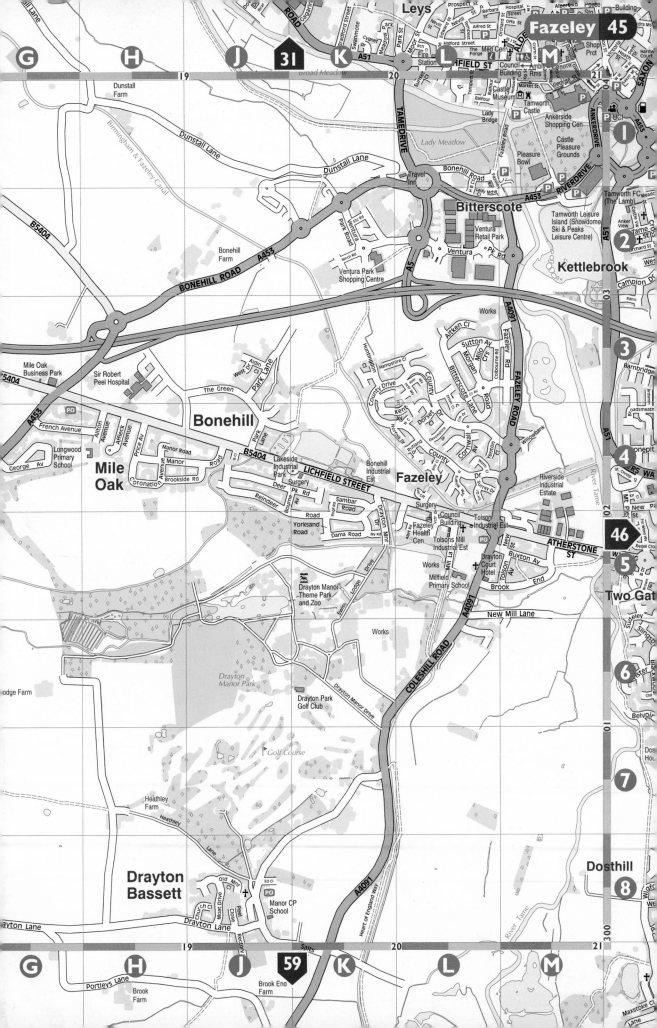

POLESWORTH

St Helena

Birchmoor

Dordon

Hall End

Polesworth Station

Polesworth High School

Birchwood Primary School

Dordon Primary School

Polesworth Nethersole Infant School

The Nethersole School (CE Controlled Primary)

Tamworth Municipal Golf Club

Travelodge

Junction 10

Birch Coppice Industrial Estate

Birch Coppice Industrial Est

TAMWORTH ROAD

GRENDON ROAD

WATLING STREET

Green Lane

Birchmoor Road

Dordon Road

Coventry Canal

R Anker

Golf Course

Warwickshire County / Staffordshire County

Works

Robey's Lane

Pooley Lane

Hermitage Lane

Dark La

B5000

Service Area

M42

Council Building

Surgery

Dordon Farm

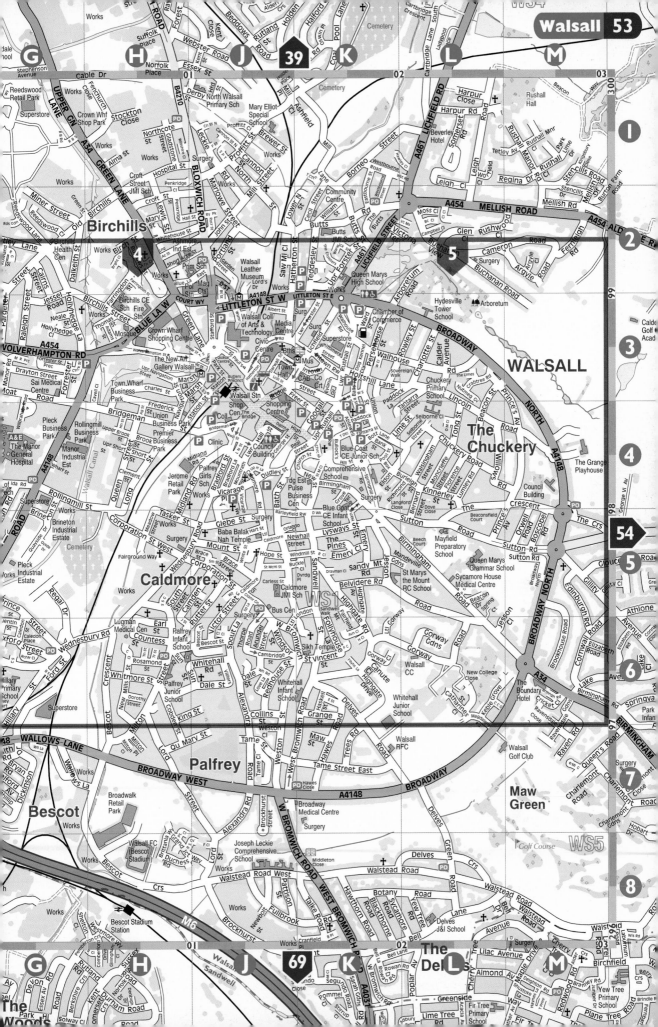

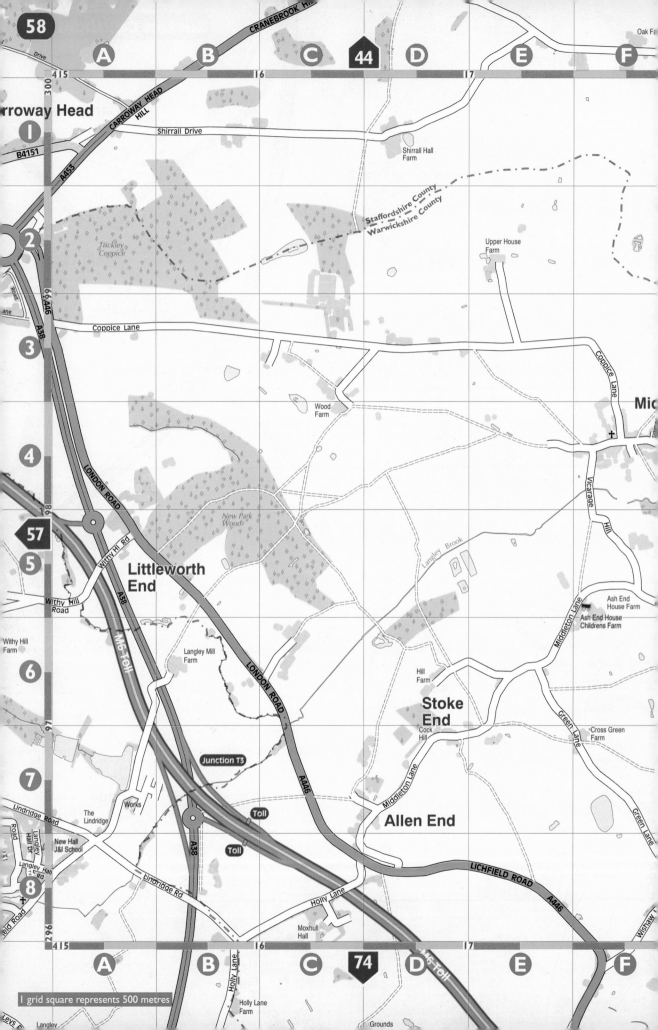

A B C 44 D E F

CRANEBROOK HILL

415 300 16 17

rroway Head

1

B4151

Shirrall Drive

Shirrall Hall
Farm

A453

CARROWAY HEAD HILL

2

Road

A38

B4446

Trickley
Coppice

Staffordshire County
Warwickshire County

Upper House
Farm

Coppice Lane

3

Coppice Lane

Mi

Wood
Farm

4

LONDON ROAD

98

Vicarage Hill

New Park
Wood

Langley Brook

57

5

Littleworth
End

Withy Hl Rd

Ash End
House Farm

Middleton Lane

Ash End House
Childrens Farm

Withy Hill
Road

Withy Hill
Farm

A38

97

Langley Mill
Farm

Hill
Farm

Green Lane

6

M6 Toll

Stoke
End

Cross Green
Farm

Cock
Hill

7

LONDON ROAD

Junction T3

A446

Middleton Lane

Lindridge Road

Works

Toll

Allen End

Green Lane

The
Lindridge

Langley Hall Dr

New Hall
J&I School

Road

A38

Toll

Langley Hall
Rd

8

LICHFIELD ROAD

A446

Wishaw

eld Road

Lindridge Rd

Holly Lane

96

415 16 17

Moxhull
Hall

M6 Toll

A B C 74 D E F

Holly Lane

ey Langley

Holly Lane
Farm

Grounds

Drayton
Bassett

Dosthill

G H J K L M

45

75

60

Portleys Lane

Brook
Farm

Brook End
Farm

Drayton Lane

Salts
La

Gallows Brook

Heart of England Way

River Tame

Maxstoke c

Slade Lane

MWORTH

Church Lane

Middleton
Pool

Middleton
Hall

New House
Farm

B78

Heart of England Way

Birmingham & Fazeley Canal

River Tame

Tame View
Caravan Site

Cliff Hall La

C

ROA

Crowberry
Lane

Hunts
Green

Heart of England Way

Broomey
Croft Farm

M42

Wishaw Lane

Brick Kiln Lane

Bodymoor

Lower
Farm

Heath

Road

Bodymoor
Heath

Kingsbury
Water Park

Middleton House
Farm

Bdymr Hth La

Works

North
Wood

Bodymoor

Centenary Wy

A4091

A4091

300

99

98

97

296

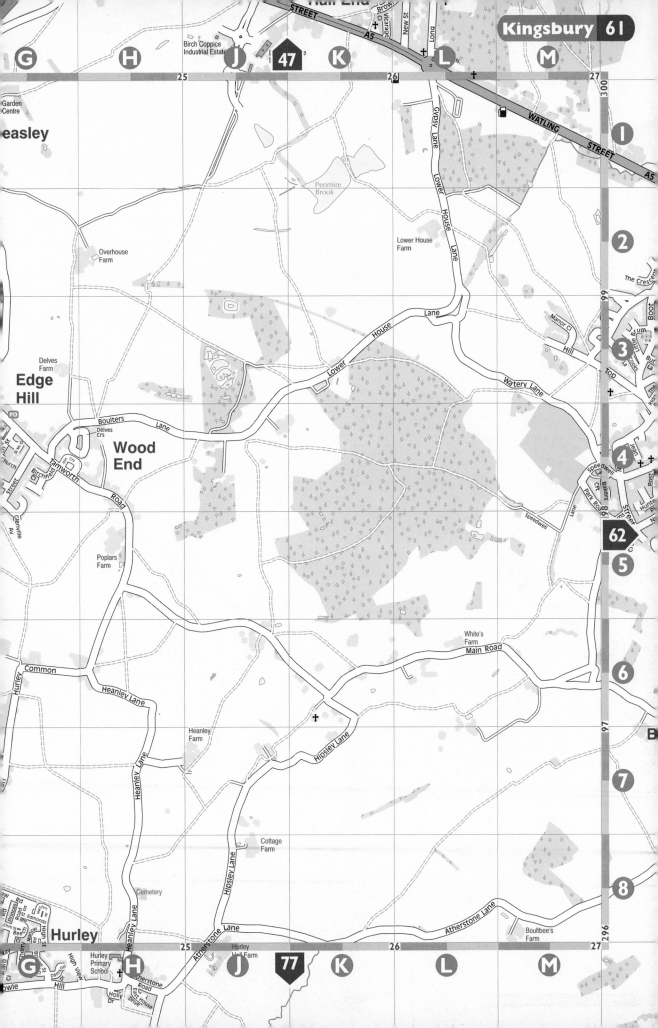

G H J **47** K L M

easley

Garden
Centre

Birch Coppice
Industrial Estate

Penmire
Brook

Lower House
Farm

Cypsy Lane

Lower House Lane

WATLING STREET A5

I

2

The Crescent

3

Overhouse
Farm

Manor Cl

Hill

Little B'um

Delves
Farm

Edge
Hill

Lower House Lane

Watery Lane

Wood
End

PO

Boulters Lane

Delves
Crs

Tamworth Road

Glenville
Av

Church

Birchfield

Speedwell

Park Road

Bakers

Speedwell
Lane

62

4

5

Poplars
Farm

White's
Farm

Main Road

6

Common

Heanley Lane

Heanley
Farm

Hipsley Lane

B

7

Hurley

Heanley Lane

Hipsley Lane

Cottage
Farm

Atherstone Lane

Boultbee's
Farm

8

Hurley
Primary
School

Cemetery

Atherstone Lane

Atherstone
Road

Hurley
Hall Farm

East House
Drive

Holly
Dr

High View

G H **77** J K L M

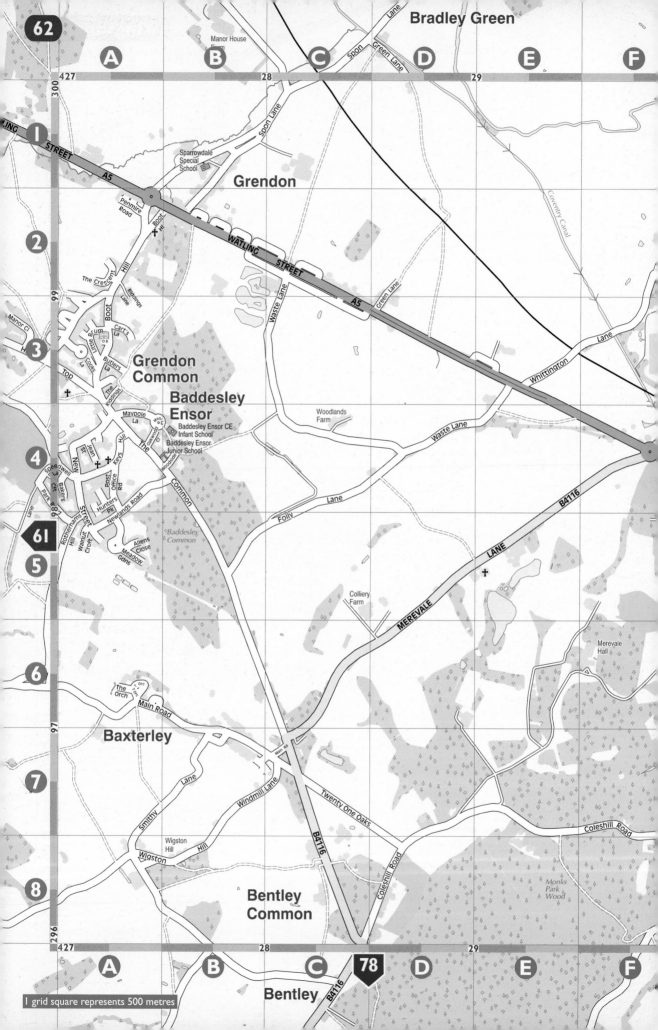

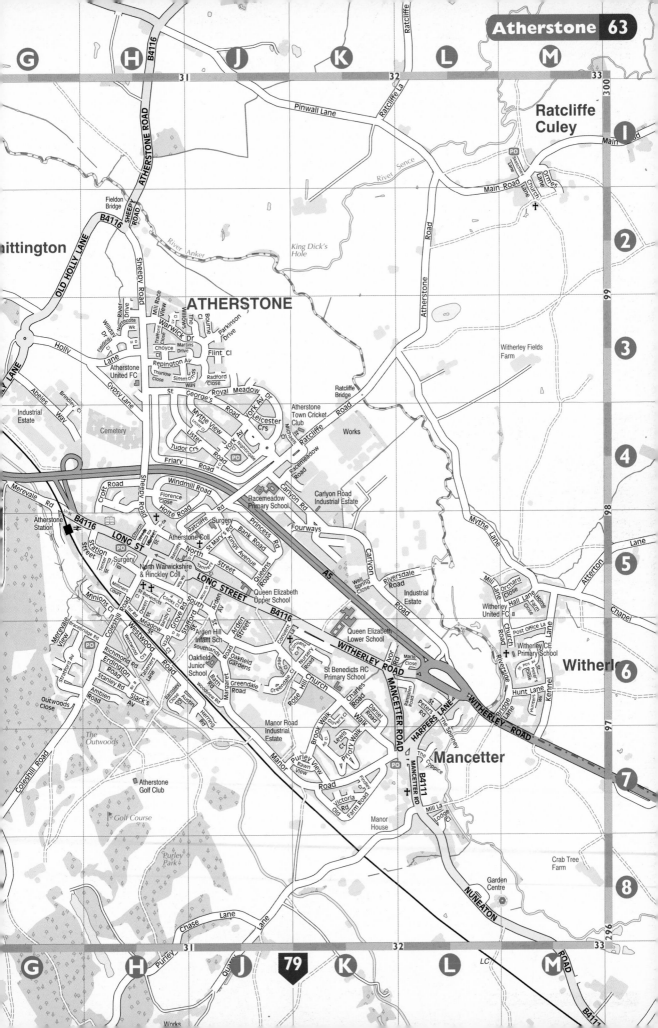

Lower
Penn

Westcroft
Farm

A   B   C   48   D   E   F

385   96   86   87

1

Trysull Holloway

Dirtyfo... Lane

Spring Hill Lane

Greyhound

Dimmingsdale Rd

Ebstree Road

2

95

Penstone Lane

Blackpit Lane

Dene Road

Orton Lane

Showell Lane

Orton

3

Union Lane

Flash Lane

Awbridge
Bridge

Staffordshire & Worcestershire Canal

Monarch's Way

Orton
Hill

4

94

Bell Road

Bell Road

Trysull Road

Trysull

† White RW

Manor
House

All Saints
CE Primary
School

Connaught
Drive

Strathmore Dr

Chequers Av

Strathmore Crs

Bearnett

5

Woodford Lane

Common Road

Bratch Park

The
Bratch

Bratch Lane

Bratch
Hollow

Station Road

Bullmeadow Lane

Victoria Gv

Billy

Meadow Lane

Buns

Bull Lane

6

93

Felashill Road

Felashill Cl

Hillside Wy

Heller Ct

Dalton Ct

Tollhouse

Lockside

Penleigh Gdns

Bullmeadows Way

Aspe Cl

Mount Pleasant
Avenue

Ounsdale Road

Monarch's Way

Churchward Drive

Hatch Heath Close

Mount Road

Westfield
Primary
School

Bramblewood

Hazel Grove

St Benedict
Biscop CE
Primary Sch

Waverley
Gdns

Church Rd

School Road

Póli Stn

Surgery

Wombourne Cricket
Tennis & Bowling Club

Wombrook
Business Cen

Ounsdale
High School

Ounsdale
Sports Centre

Planks Lane

Cannon Rd

Walk Lane

Civic Cen

PO

Rookery

WOMBOURNE

Ounsdale

Wombrook Ind Est

St Bernadettes
RC Primary
School

Lindale Drive

Spines Clinc

Windsor Crs

Bramer Dr

Kirkstone Crs

Rennison Drive

High Street

Gravel Hill

Surg

Redcliffe

7

Smestow Bridge
Industrial
Estate

Works

Pool House Road

The Meadlands

Quendale

Marburn Way

Giggetty Lane

Cherry Trees
Special
School

Brook Road

Woof Hill

Redhill Av

The Longlands

Common Road

High Mdw

Pinewood

Glenside

Greenhill

Copper Beech Dr

Poplar Rd

Beggars Bush

smestow Gate

BRIDGNORTH ROAD

Heathbank

Millfields

Heath House Wy

Swinford Road

Brickbridge

Giggetty

Van Diemans Rd

Jenks Road

Westleigh

Dean Road

Chapel St

Calvin Cl

PO

Blakeley
Heath
Primary Sch

Blakeley

Whites Wood Lane

Woodlands

The Broadway

Sytch Lane

Greenhill Gdns

Greenhill
Farm

8

292

385   86   B4176   NORTH ROAD   87

A   B   C   82   D   E   F

Chapel Lane

Monarch's Way

Heath Mill Road

Works

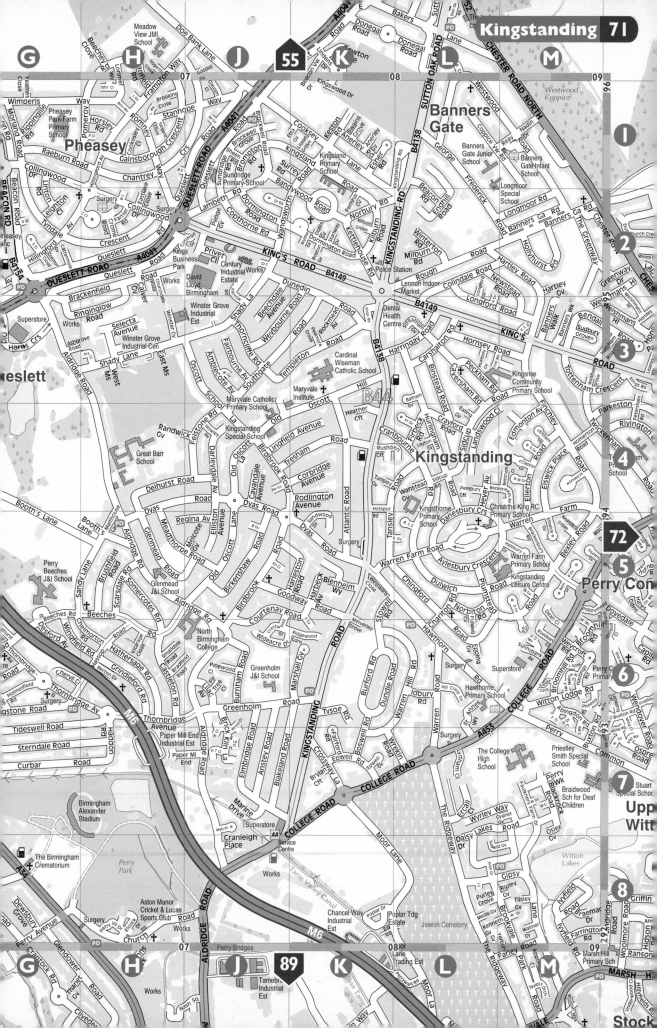

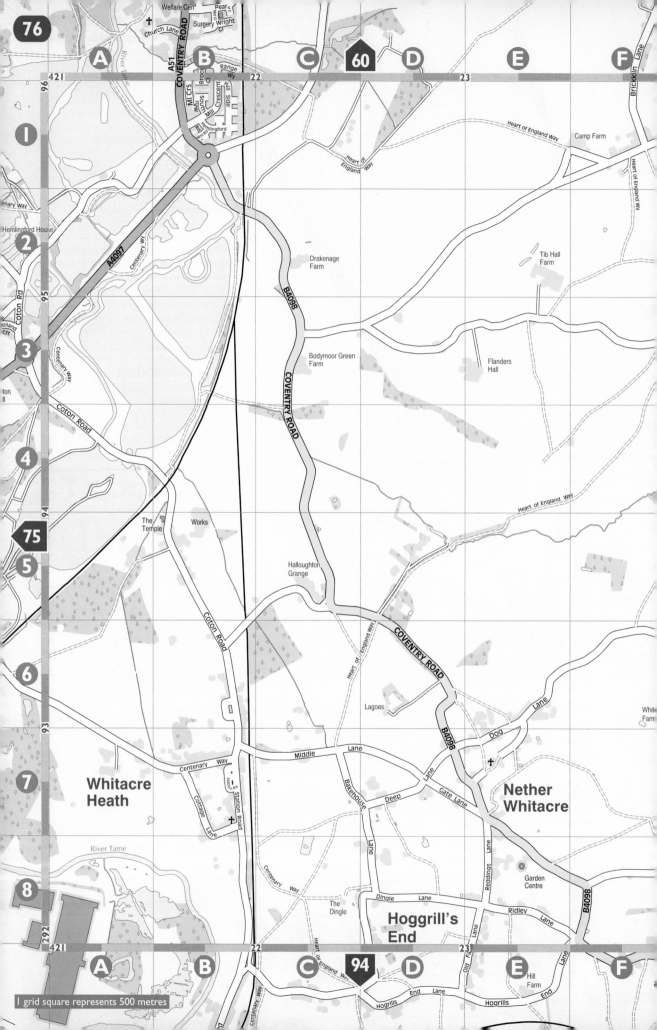

G **Hurley** H J ■ 61 K L M

Cemetery

Hipsley L...

Atherstone Lane

Atherstone La...

Boultbee's Farm

Heanl...

Hurley Primary School

Atherstone Road

Holly Dr

East House Drive

High View

Damson

Cherry

Bridge St

Orchard Rd

High St

W Dr

Chris St St

Bee

Cl

Rd

Rd

owle

Hill

25 26 27

96

Hurley Hall Farm

Kimberley Hall Farm

1

2

95

Foul End

Brook End

Brook End Farm

3

Nightingale's Farm

94

B4116

Manor House Farm

4

78

5

Gospel Oak

B4116

re

Hoar Park

6

93

ATHERSTONE

ROAD

Centenary Way

7

Botts Green

B4116

Holt Hall Farm

Hoar Pa... Farm

8

Botts Green Lane

Hurley Lane

Whitacre Fields

New House Farm

Centenary Way

92

NUNEATON R...

Monwode Lan...

G H J ■ 95 K L M

Pound Lane

Hoar Hall

25 26 27

B4098

San

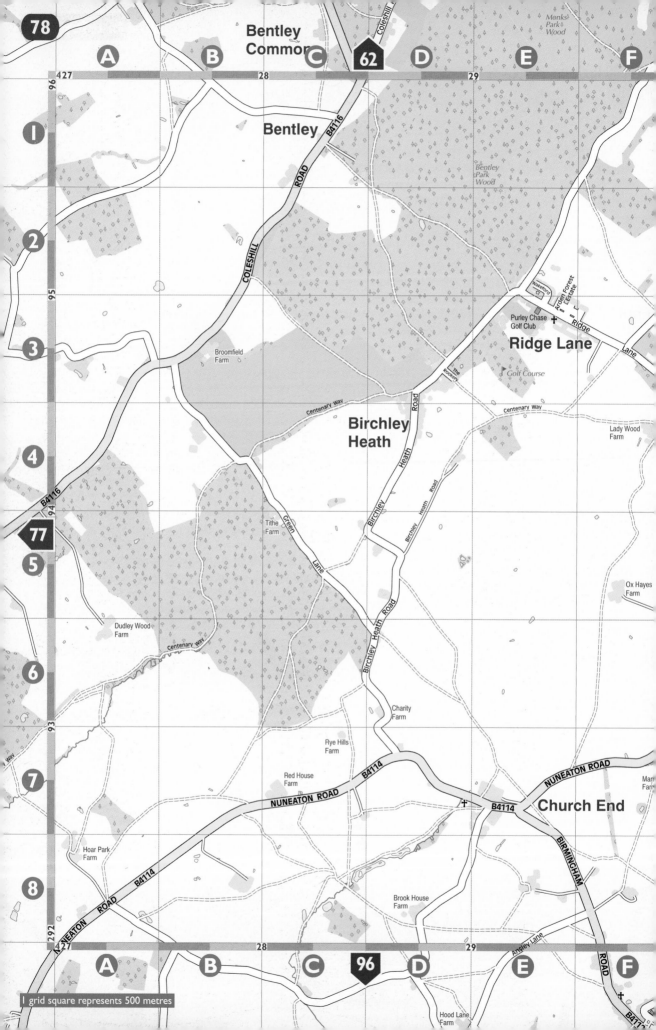

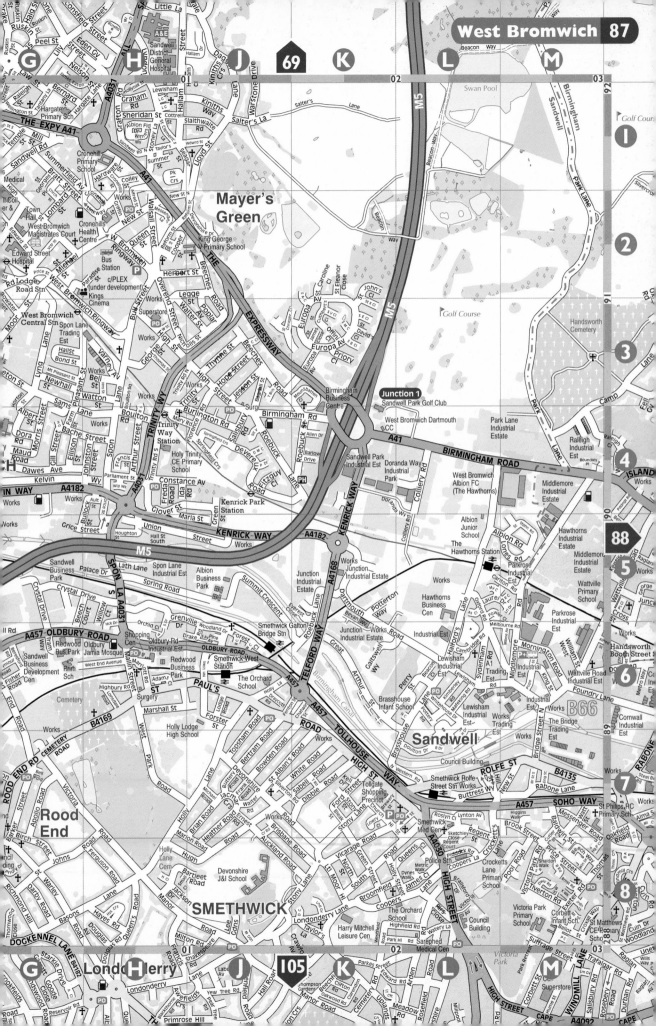

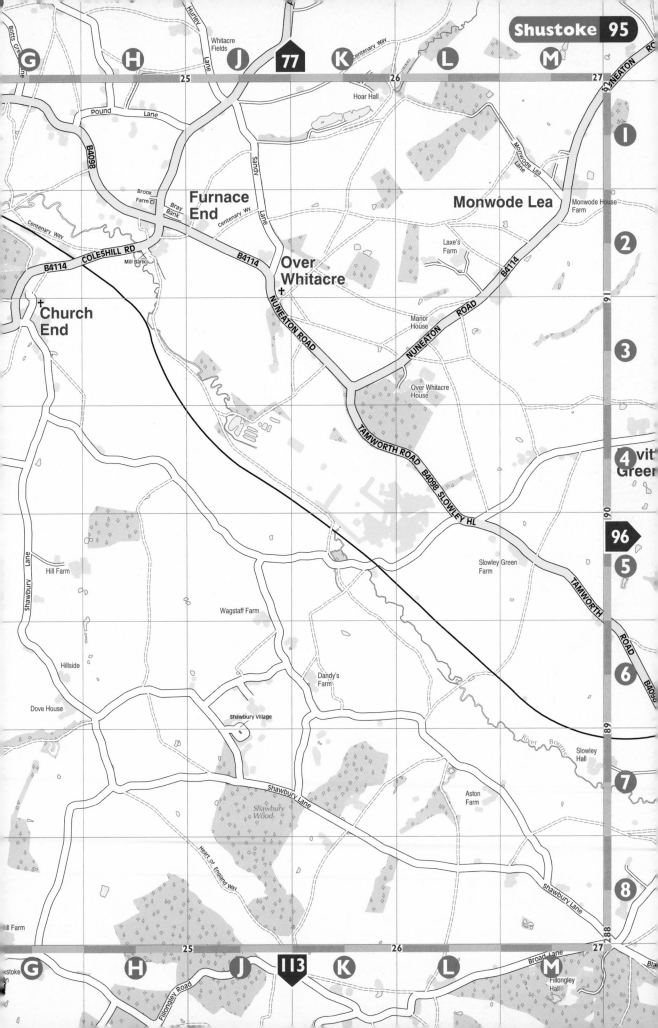

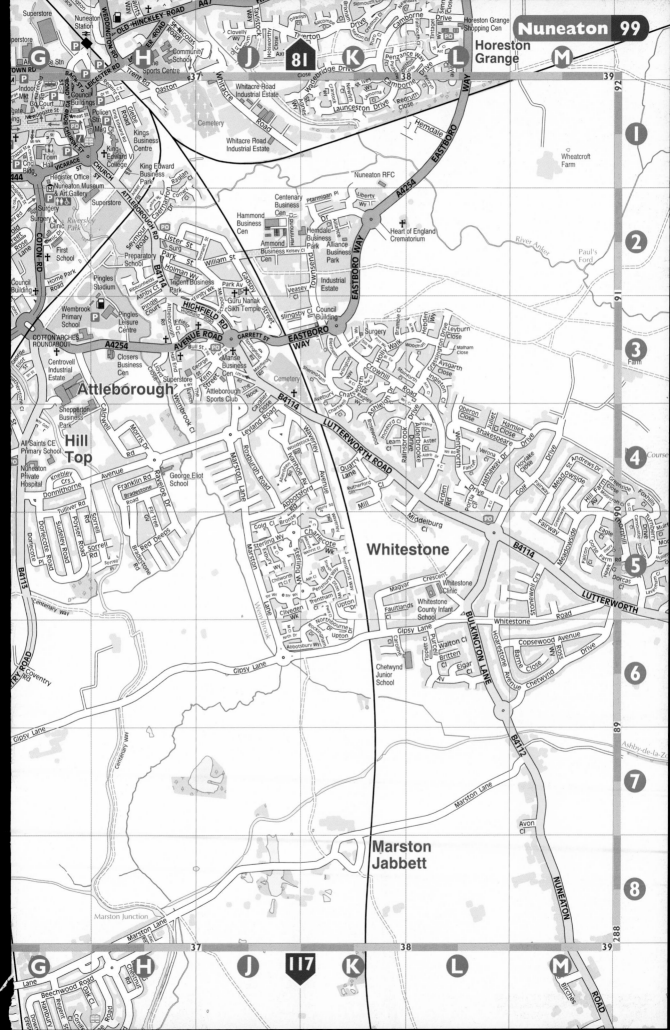

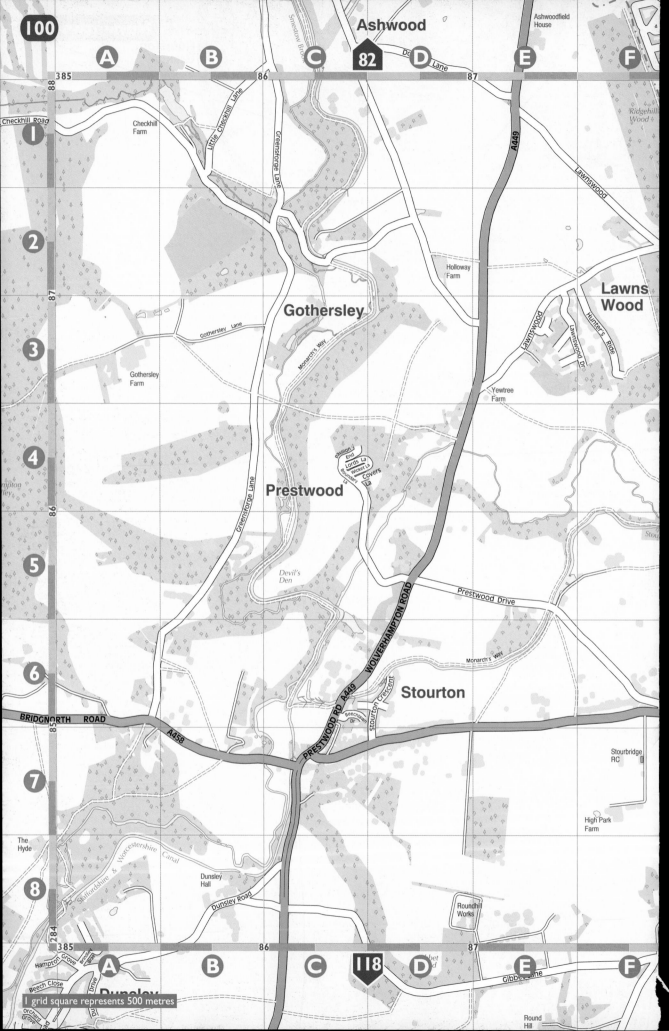

A B C 82 D E F

385 86 87

Checkhill Road

1 Checkhill Farm

Little Checkhill Lane

Greensforge Lane

Smestow Brook

Ashwood

Doctors Lane

Ashwoodfield House

Ridgehill Wood

Lawnswood

2 Holloway Farm

Lawns Wood

Lawnswood

Lawnswood Dr

Hunter's Ride

Gothersley

Gothersley Lane

Monarch's Way

3 Gothersley Farm

Yewtree Farm

4 Pavilion
End
Lords La
Boundary La Wicker La
Covers La

Prestwood

Greensforge Lane

Prestwood Drive

5 Devil's Den

Wolverhampton Road

Monarch's Way

6 A449

Stourton Crescent

Stourton

BRIDGNORTH ROAD A458

PRESTWOOD RD A449

Beechtree Dr

Stourbridge RC

7 The Hyde

High Park Farm

Staffordshire & Worcestershire Canal

Dunsley Hall

8 Dunsley Road

Roundhill Works

Round Hill

284 385 86 118 87

Hampton Grove
Beech Close

A B C D Gibbet Lane E F

Dunsley

Orchard Grove

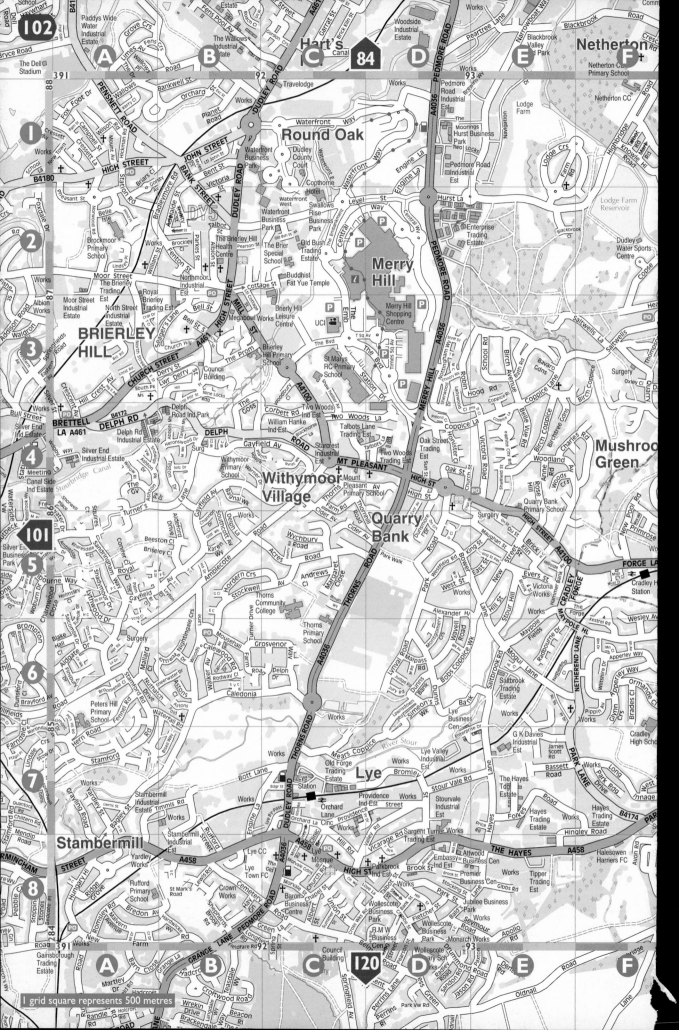

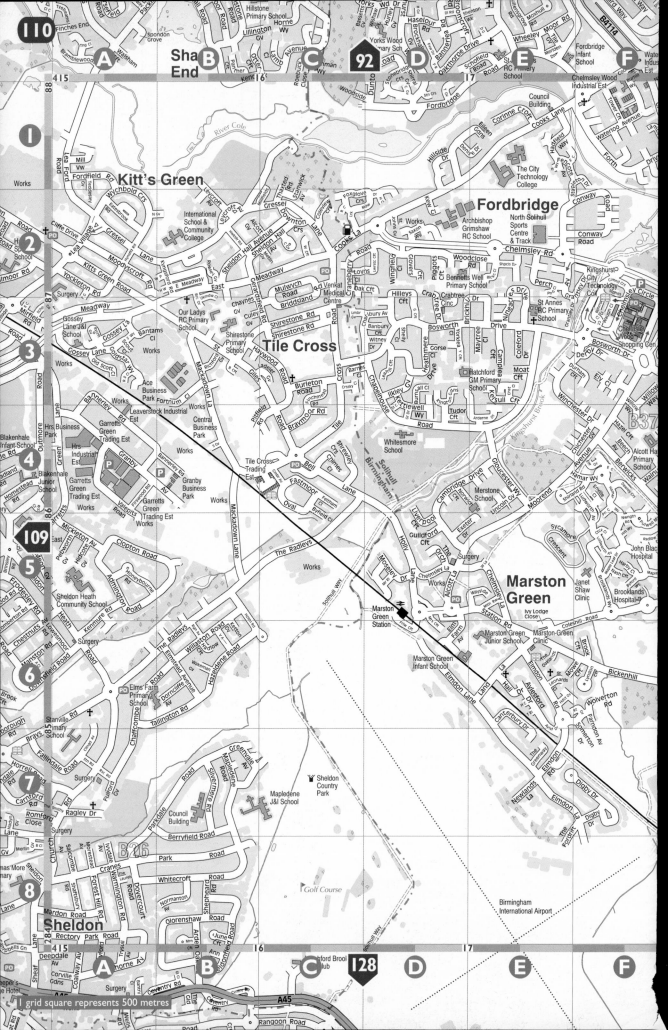

1 grid square represents 500 metres

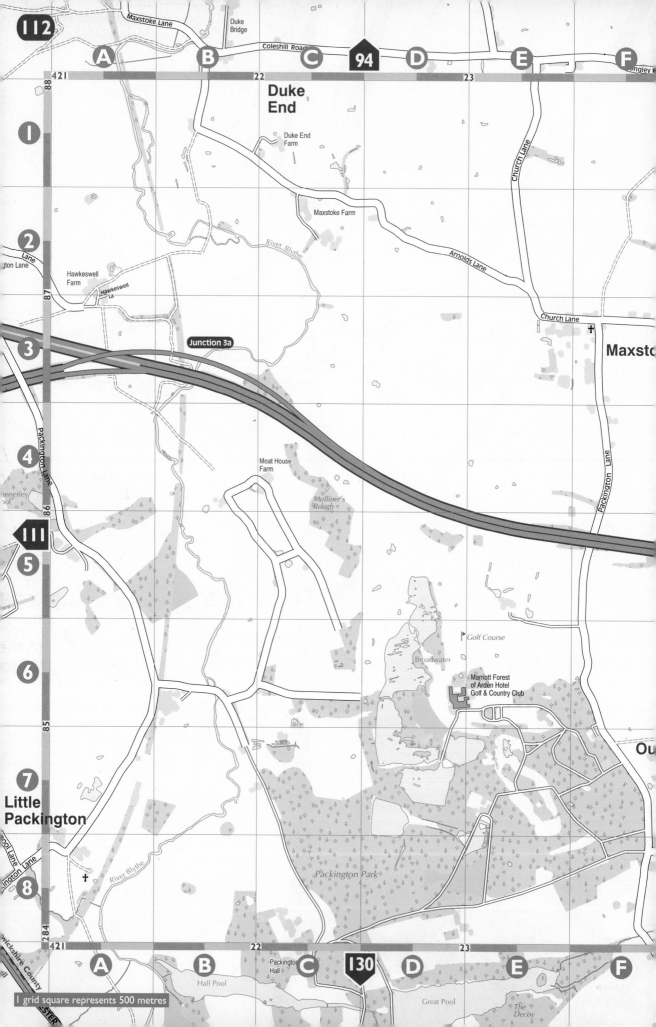

A   B   Coleshill Road   C   **94**   D   E   F

421   22   23

88

Duke End

Duke End Farm

1

87

Duke Bridge

Maxstoke Lane

Church Lane

Maxstoke Farm

Arnolds Lane

River Blythe

2

Hawkeswell Farm

Hawkeswell La

ington Lane

Church Lane

✝

Maxsto

3

Junction 3a

Packington Lane

98

4

Moat House Farm

Mulliner's Rough

annerley Pool

111

5

Golf Course

Broadwater

6

85

Marriott Forest of Arden Hotel Golf & Country Club

Ou

7

Little Packington

284

pol Lane

ington Lane

✝

River Blythe

8

Packington Park

421   22   23

wickshire County

ESTER

A   B   Packington Hall   C   **130**   D   E   F

Hall Pool

Great Pool

The Decoy

1 grid square represents 500 metres

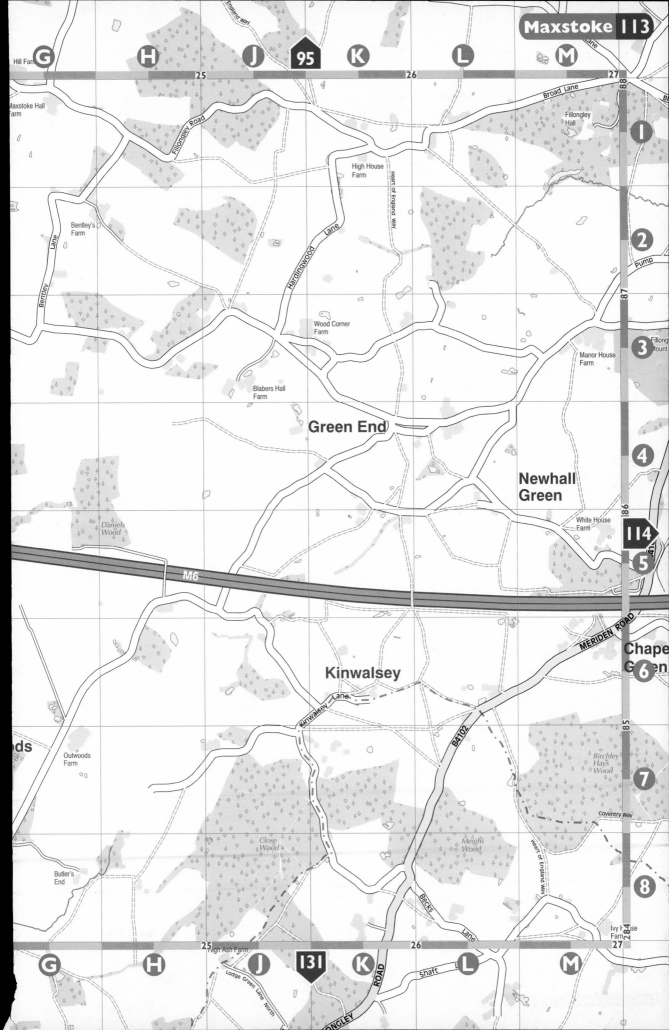

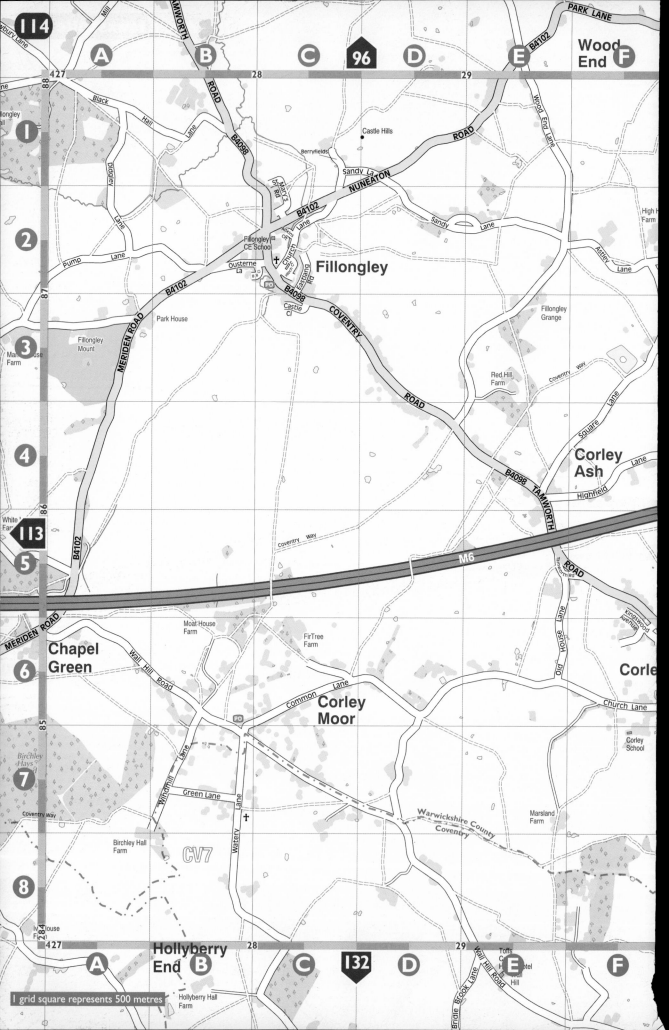

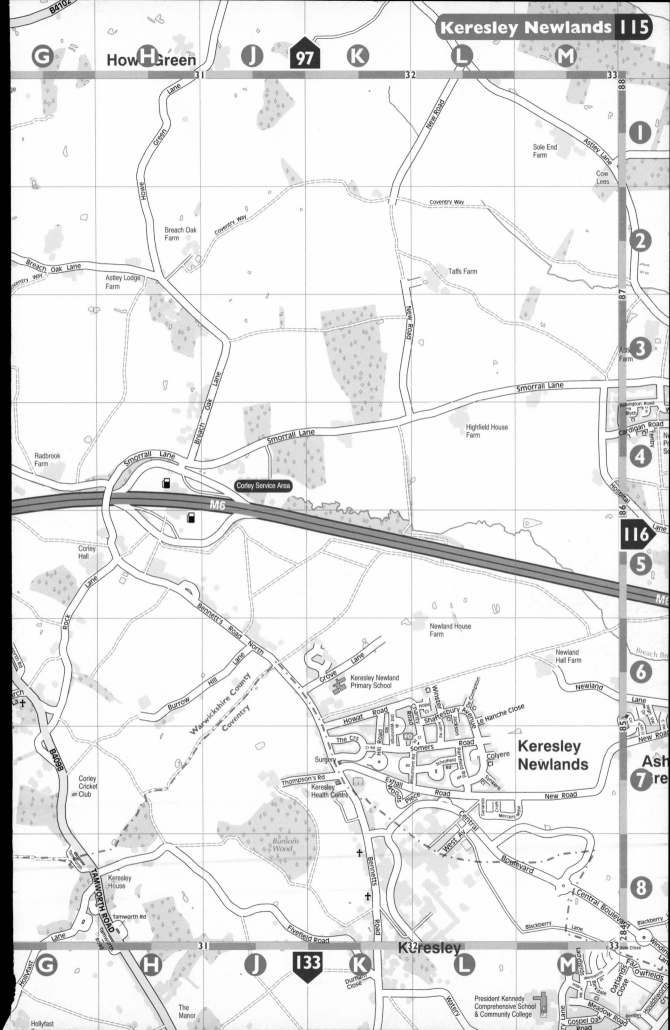

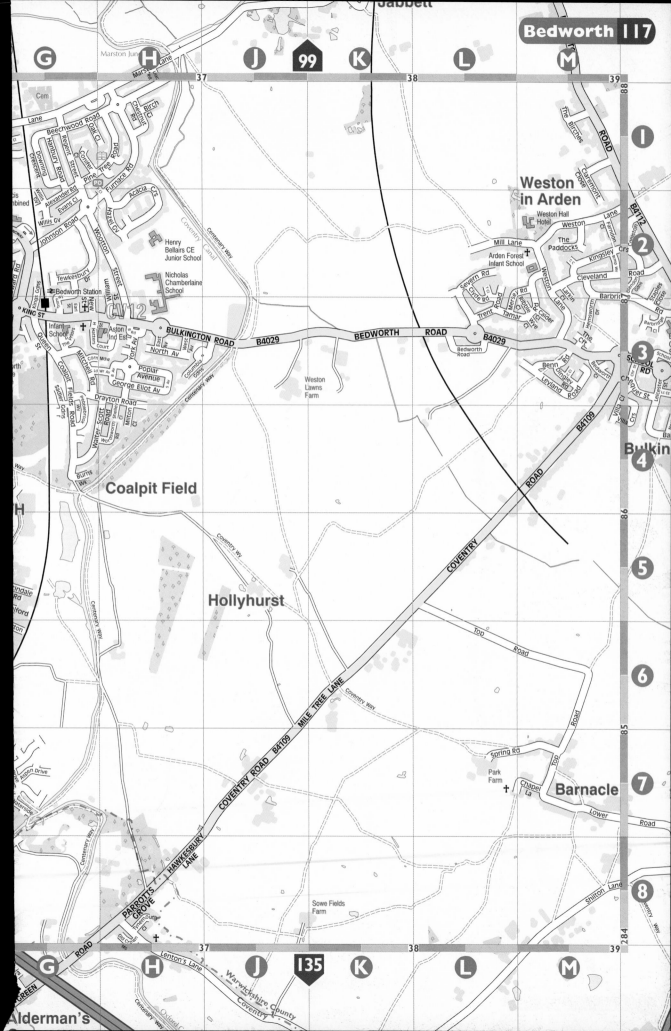

Jabbett

G H J **99** K L M

Weston
in Arden

Cem

Marston Jun

Beechwood Road
Hanbury Road
Downing Crescent
Regent Street
Conifer
Pine Tree Road
Oak Cl
Birch Cl
Chestnut Rd

Alexander Rd
Evans Cl
Acacia Crs
Hazel Gv
Willis Cv

Johnson Road
Wootton Street
William Street

Coventry Canal
Centenary Way

Henry
Bellairs CE
Junior School

Weston Hall
Hotel

Mill Lane

Arden Forest
Infant School

The
Paddocks
Weston Lane
Claremont Close
The Birches
Farndon Close

Kingsley Crs
Temple Way
Cleveland
Barbric
Road
Larkin
Staples Close

Tewkesbury Dr
Bedworth Station
New St
Earl St

Nicholas
Chamberlaine
School

Kings Gdns
CV12

King St

KING ST

Infant School

Hatters
Court

Aston Ind Est

North Av
Corn Mdw
East Av
West Av
York Av

Poplar
Avenue

George Eliot Av

Columbia Gdns
Centenary Way

BULKINGTON ROAD

B4029

BEDWORTH ROAD

B4029

Bedworth
Road

Weston
Lawns
Farm

Severn Rd
Clyde Rd
Trent Road
Mersey Rd
Tamar
Calder
Ribble
Wye

Benn
Dingley Rd
Leyland Road

SCHOOL RD

Villa Crs

Chequer St

Leicester Ct

Mitchell Rd
Coalpit Fields Road
Walter Scott Road
Drayton Road
Sadler Gdns
Shelley
Milton
Odsworth

Burns
Wk

B4109

Coalpit Field

Bulkin

Coventry Wy

Hollyhurst

Centenary Way

COVENTRY

ROAD

Top
Road

Spring Rd

Park
Farm

Chapel
La

Barnacle

Lower
Road

Indale Rd
ilford
ton

COVENTRY ROAD B4109

MILE TREE LANE

Coventry Way

Top Road

Aspen drive
Waterside

Centenary Way

HAWKESBURY
LANE

PARROTTS
GROVE

Tynemouth

Sowe Fields
Farm

Shilton Lane

Old Crown

ROAD

Lenton's Lane

Warwickshire County
Coventry

Centenary Way
Oxford C

SCREEN

Alderman's

I
2
3
4
5
6
7
8

G H J **135** K L M

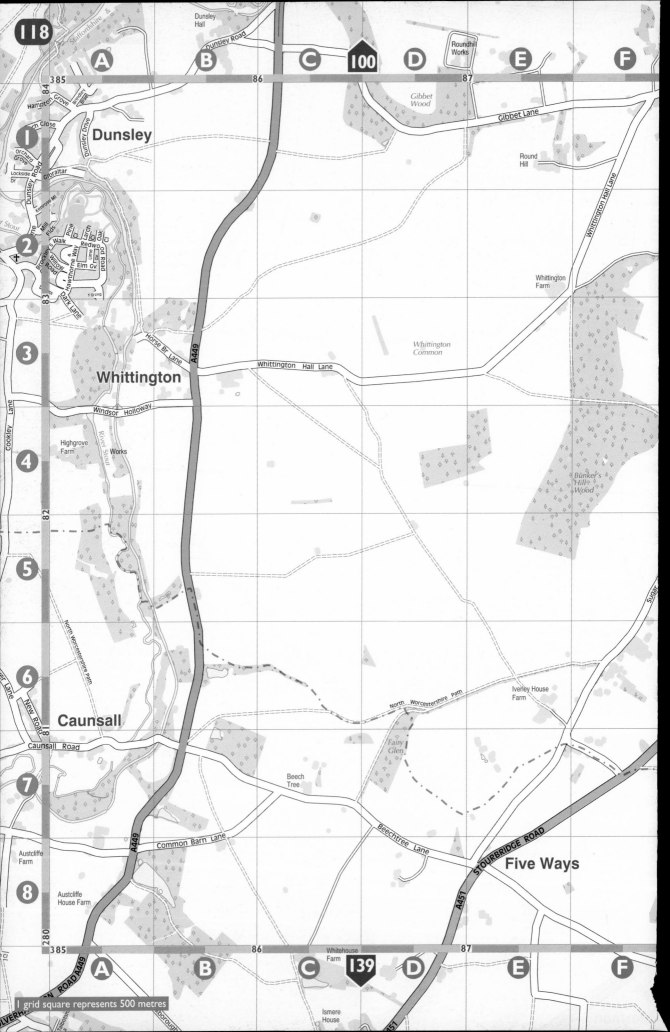

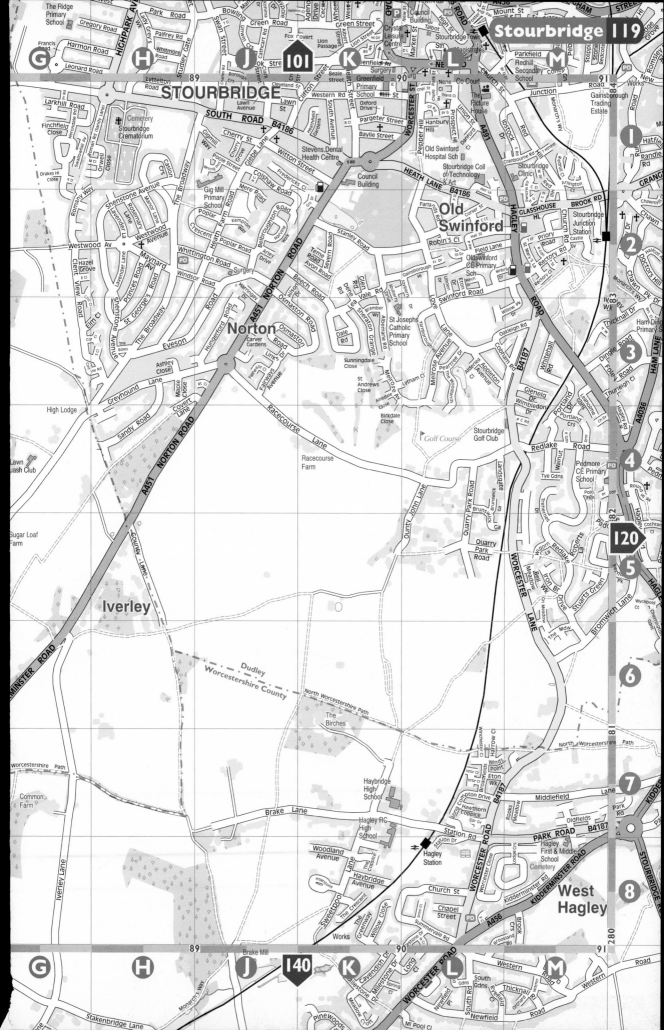

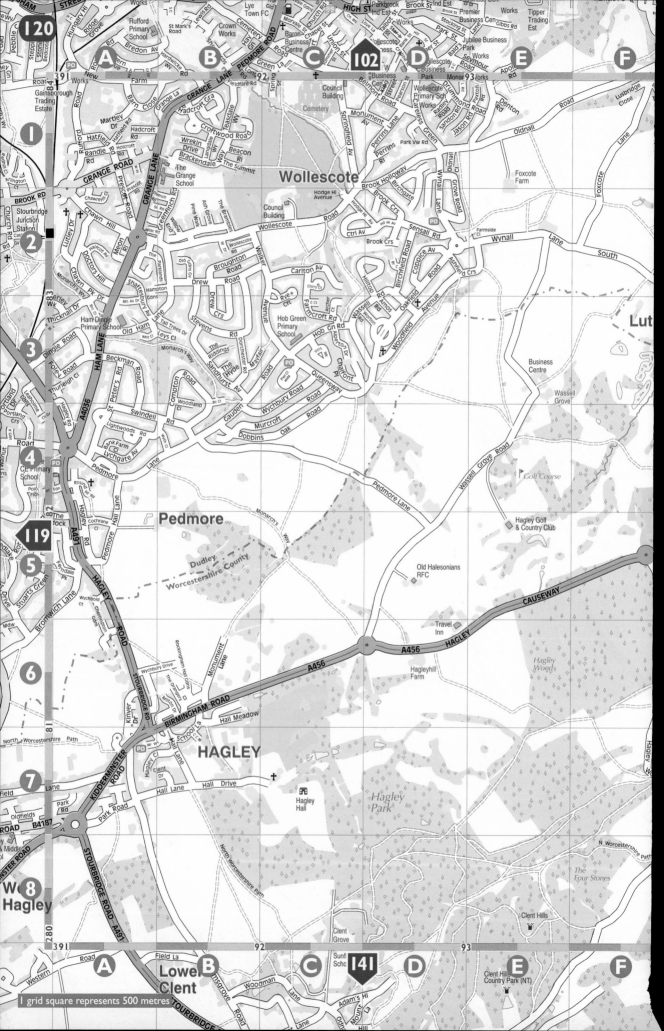

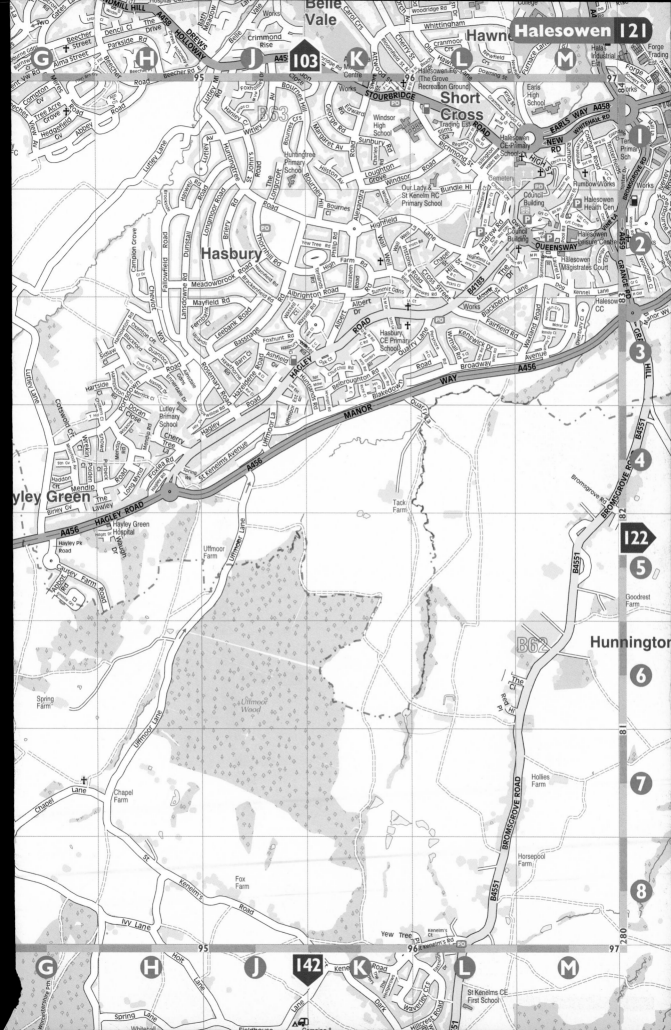

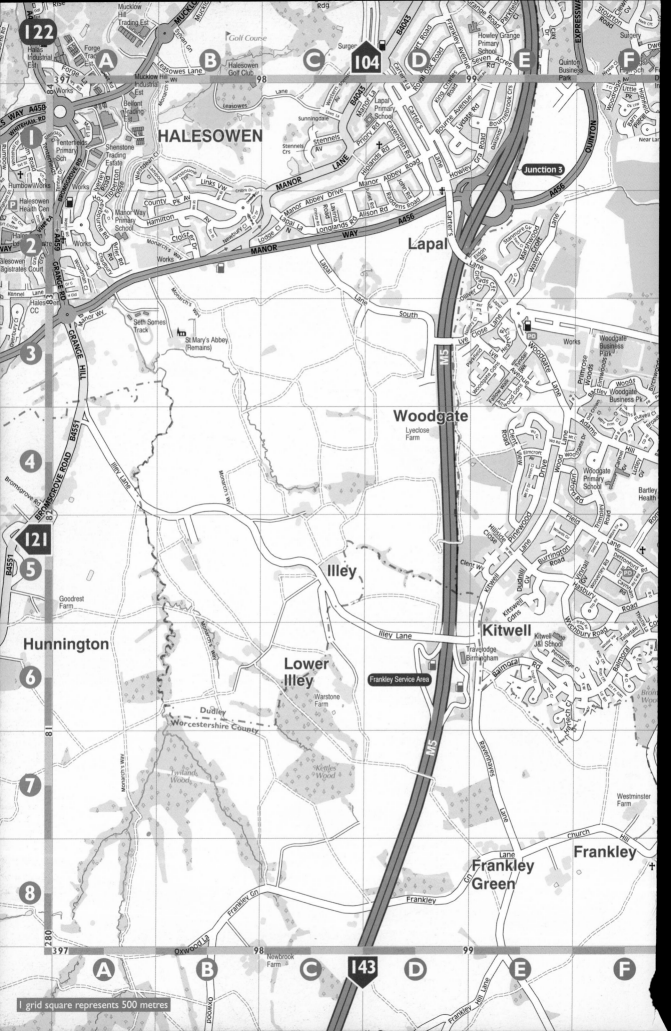

I grid square represents 500 metres

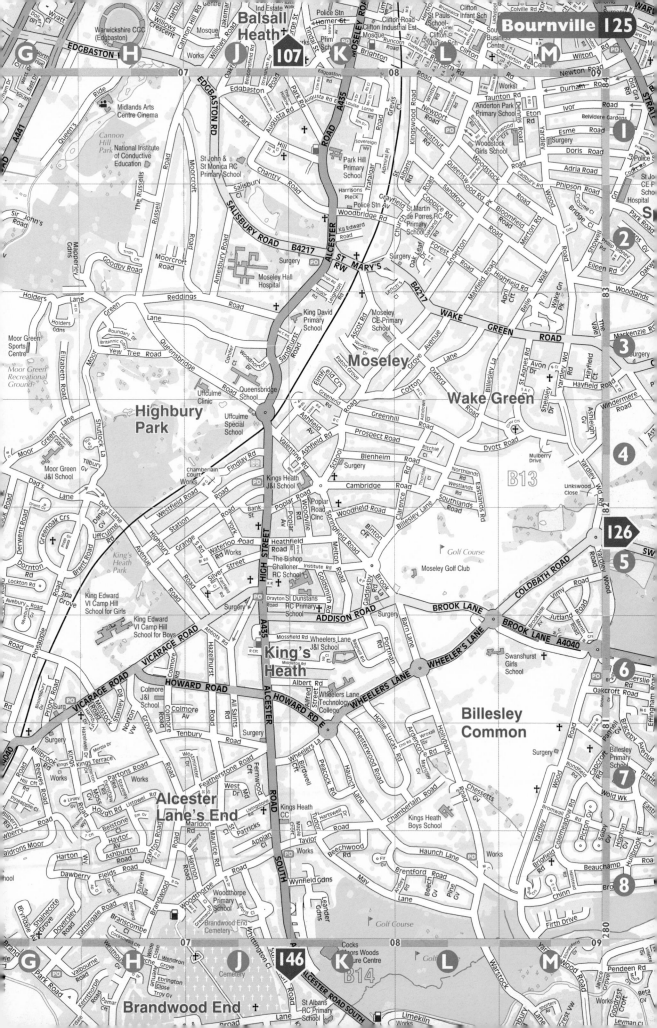

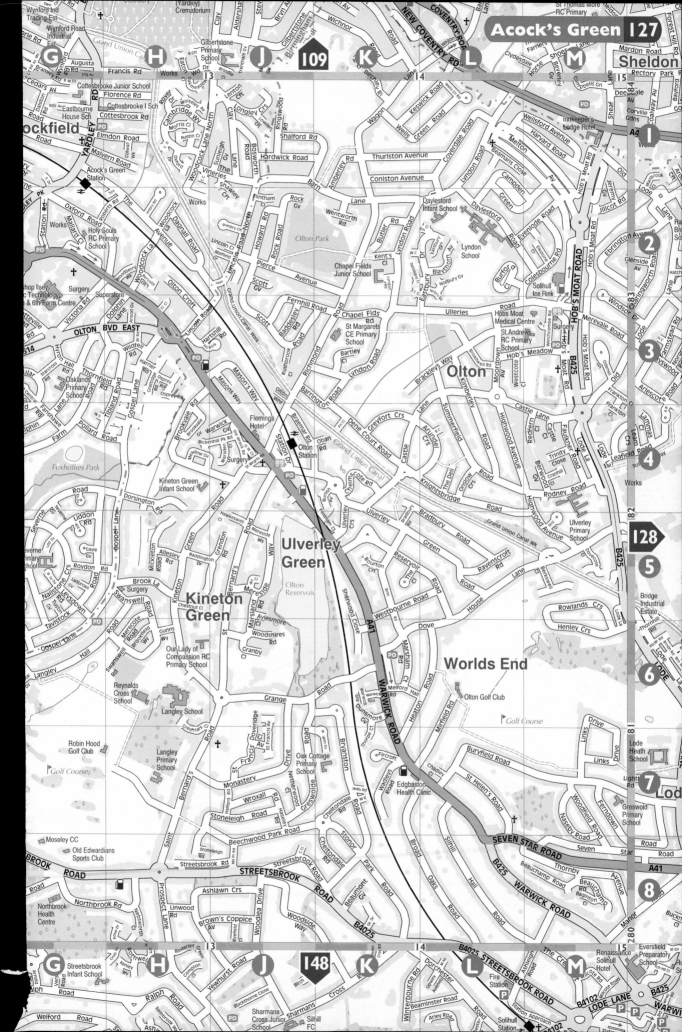

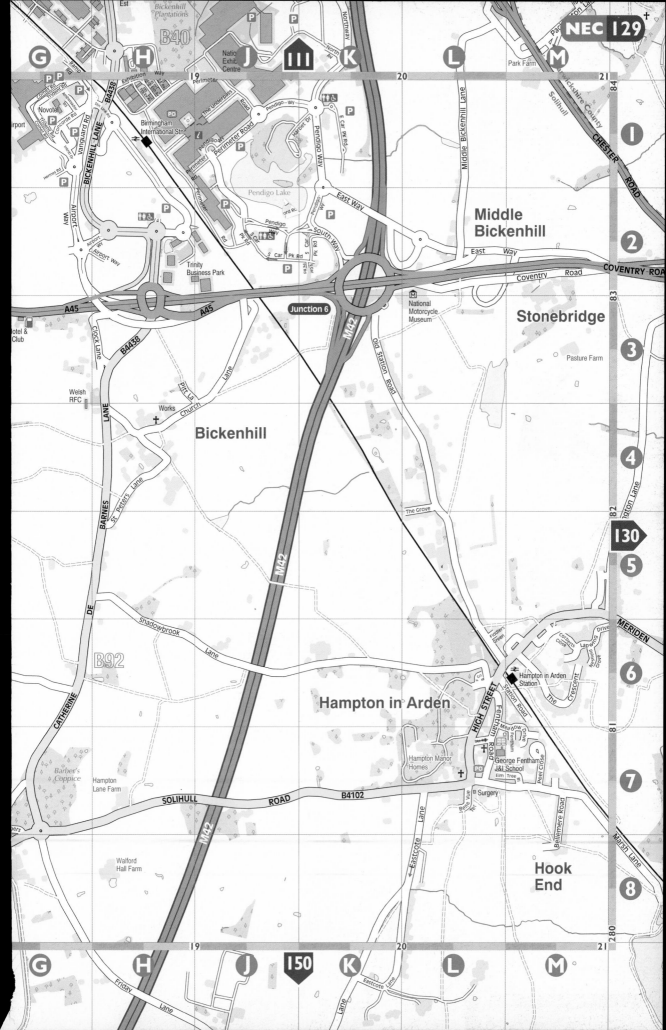

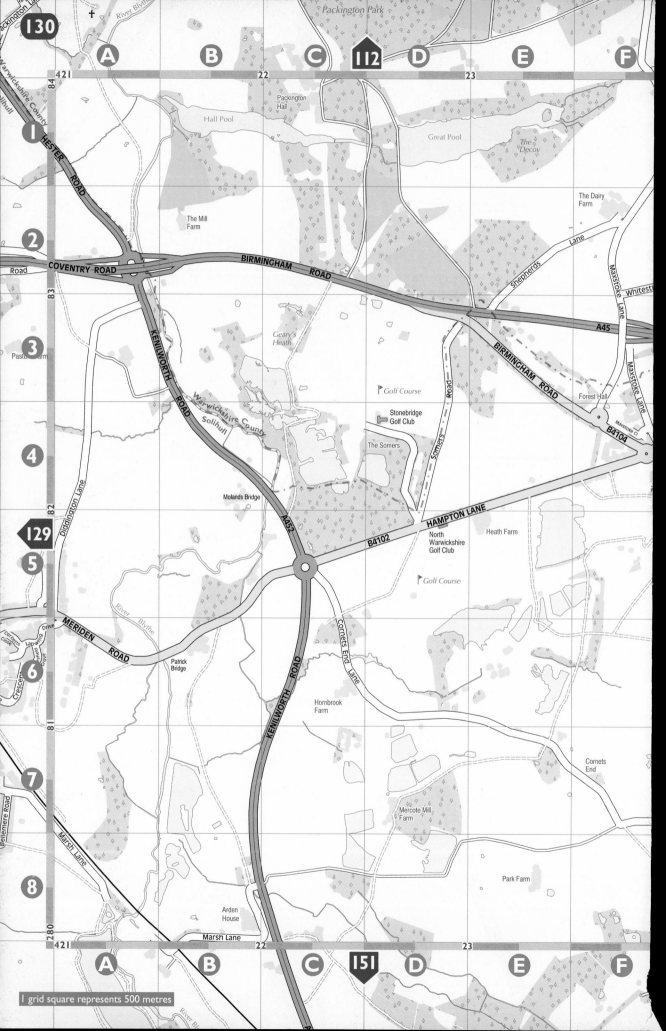

130

A   B   C   112   D   E   F

84 421   22   23

Packington Park

River Blythe

Packington Hall

Hall Pool

Great Pool

The Decoy

1

HESTER ROAD

The Mill Farm

The Dairy Farm

2

Road

COVENTRY ROAD

BIRMINGHAM ROAD

Shepherds Lane

Maxstoke Lane

Whitestt

83

KENILWORTH ROAD

Geary's Heath

A45

3

Pastu Farm

BIRMINGHAM ROAD

Maxstoke Lane

Golf Course

Forest Hall

Warwickshire County

Stonebridge Golf Club

Maxstoke Cl

Solihull

Somers Road

B4104

4

Diddington Lane

A452

Molands Bridge

The Somers

82

HAMPTON LANE

129

B4102

North Warwickshire Golf Club

Heath Farm

5

River Blythe

Golf Course

MERIDEN ROAD

81

Patrick Bridge

Cornets End Lane

6

Crescent

Lapwing

Drive

Grove

Hornbrook Farm

Cornets End

KENILWORTH ROAD

7

Bellemere Road

Mercote Mill Farm

Marsh Lane

8

Park Farm

Arden House

280 421   Marsh Lane   22   23

A   B   C   151   D   E   F

1 grid square represents 500 metres

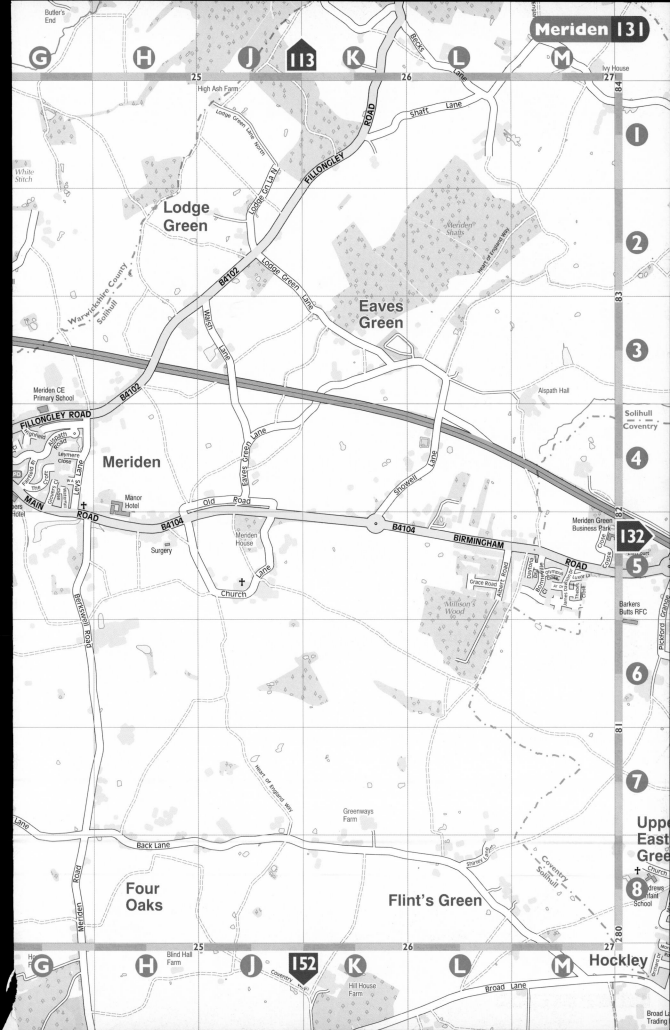

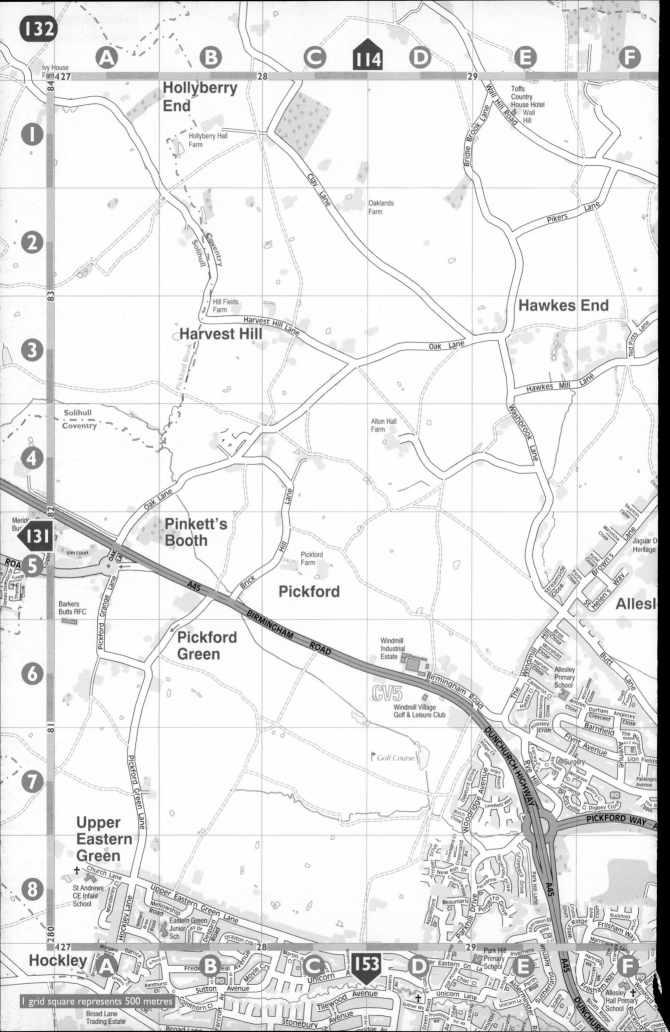

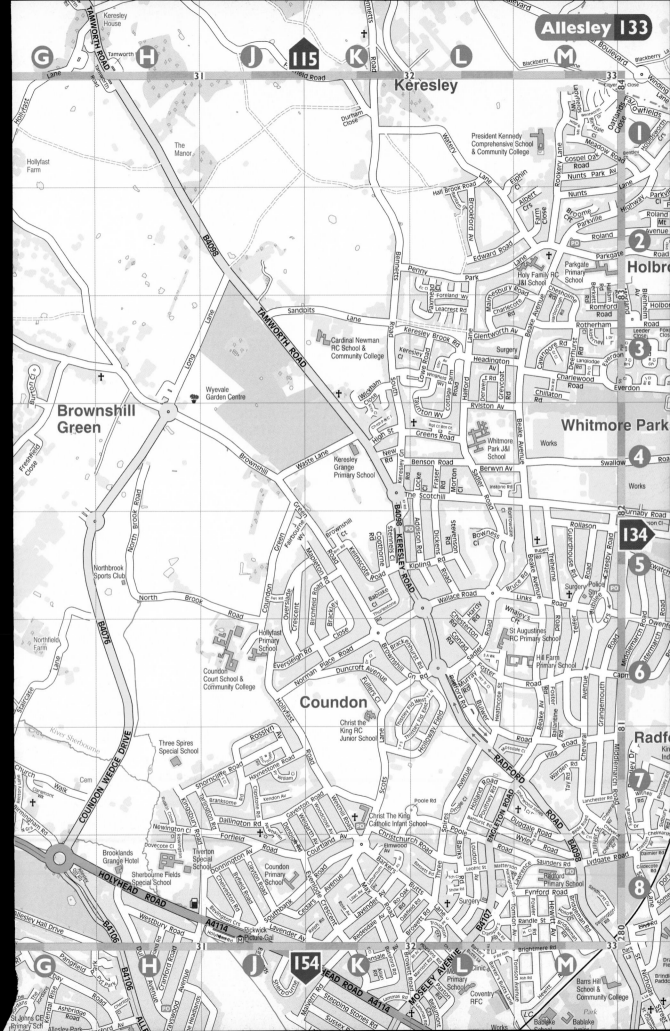

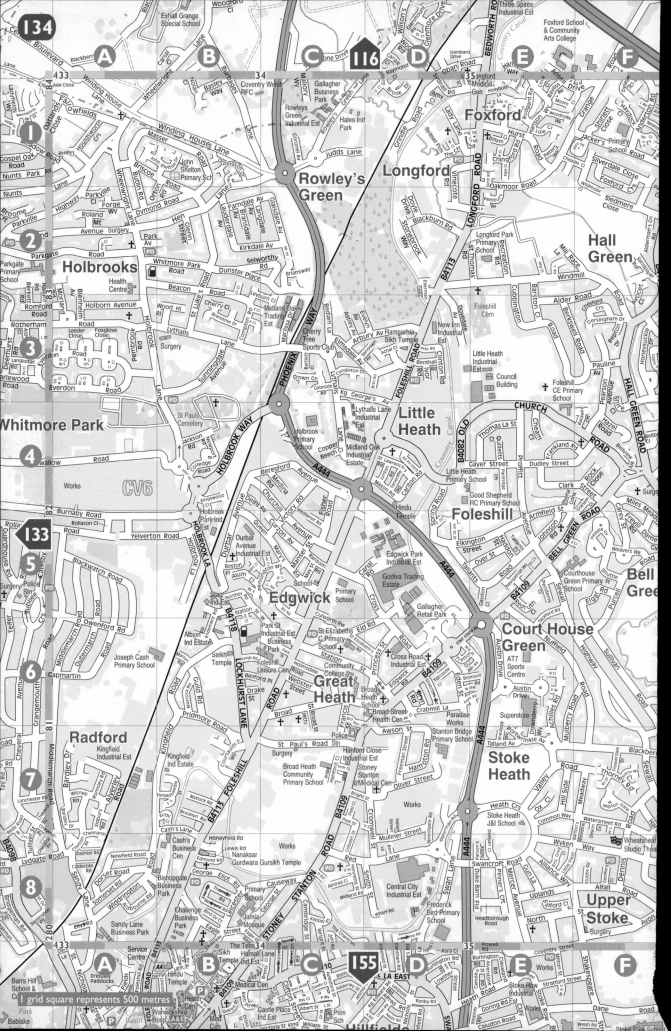

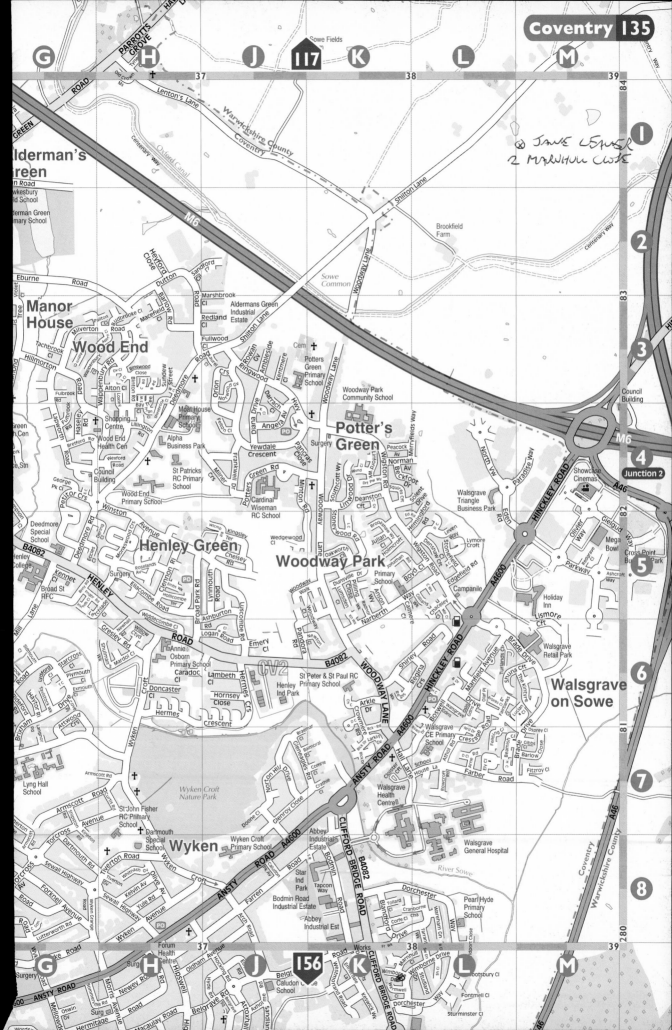

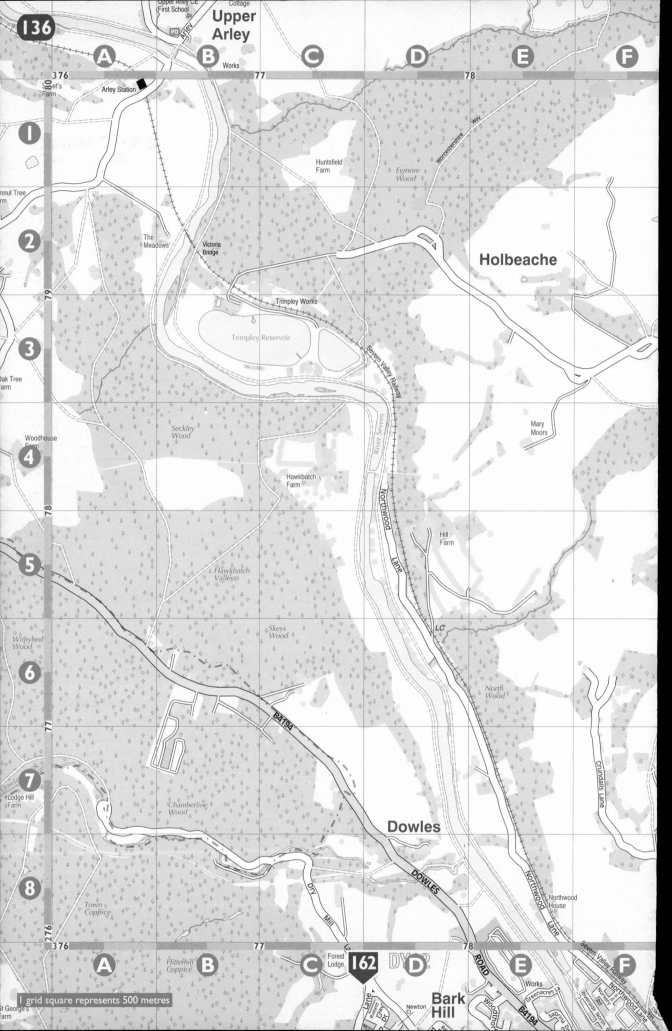

Upper Arley

Upper Arley CE First School

Cottage

PO

ARLEY

Works

B

A

C

D

E

F

80

I

et's Farm

Arley Station

nut Tree rm

Huntsfield Farm

Eymore Wood

Worcestershire Way

79

2

The Meadows

Victoria Bridge

Holbeache

Trimpley Works

Oak Tree arm

3

Trimpley Reservoir

Seckley Wood

Severn Valley Railway

River Severn

Mary Moors

Woodhouse Farm

4

Hawkbatch Farm

78

5

Hawkbatch Valleys

Hill Farm

Northwood Lane

Withybed Wood

6

Skeys Wood

LC

North Wood

77

B4194

7

Chamberline Wood

Dowles

Crundalls Lane

Lodge Hill Farm

DRY MILL

DOWLES

8

Town Coppice

276

Northwood Lane

Northwood House

St George's Farm

A

Hitterhill Coppice

B

Forest Lodge

C

162

DY

D

E

Works

Greenacres La

Severn Valley Railway

Northwood Lane

F

Bark Hill

ROAD

Woodthor

B4194

Lane

Newton Cl

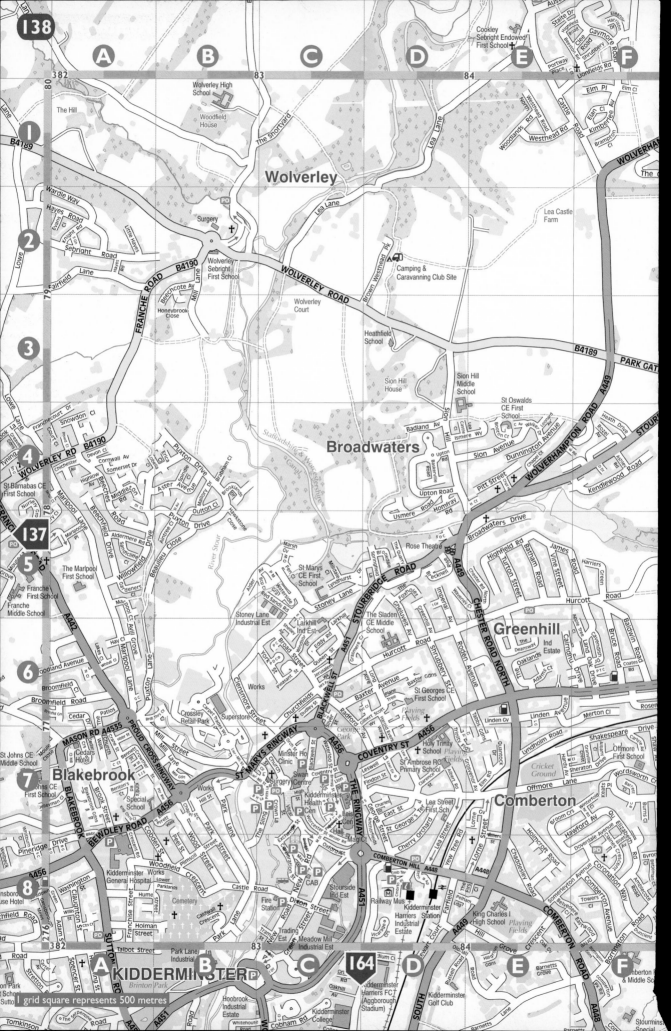

G H J **118** K L M

86 87 88 80

I

iffe Farm

Whitehouse Farm

Ismere House

Axborough Lane

STOURBRIDGE ROAD

A451

Orchard Road

Pemberton Crs

Roseberry Gdns

Clifton Rd

New Rd

Drive

Woodland Grove

The Alexander Patterson Special School

Waggon Lane

Waggon Lane

Churchill Lane

Chur

2

Churchill Lane

Scuthorpe Road

The Croft

79

Wheatmill Cl

Blaked tn

3

Mill Lane

Station

Brookside Way

Elm Dr

Mill Cl

The Av

Lynwood

Royall Cl

BIRMINGHAM

B

A451

Woodhouse Farm

Golf Course

Churchill & Blakedown Golf Club

Wannerton Road

Drive

PO

Blaked First Sc

Kennels

Hurcott Lane

Hurcott Wood

Wannerton Farm

Swan Cl

A456

Forge Lane

4

Hairshire Lane

78

Hurcott

Park Hall

New Wood Lane

140

5

A456

Sandy Lane

BIRMINGHAM ROAD

Deansford Lane

6

77

Bissell Wood

Belling Farm

7

Munro Cl

Rosetti Cl

Little Dunclent Farm

Offmore Farm Close

Offmore Farm

Ruskin Av

Chaucer Crs

Prior Cl

Elmdale

Silver Birch

Mount Segg

Mearse Farm

Ba

8

Deansford Lane

276

86 87 88

G H J **165** K L M

Dunclent

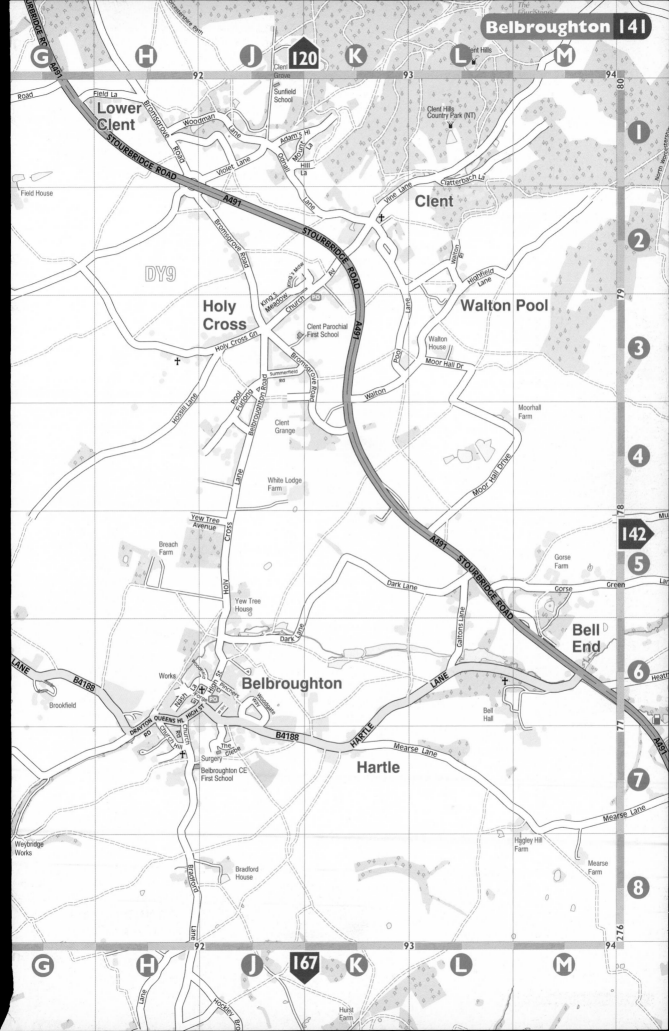

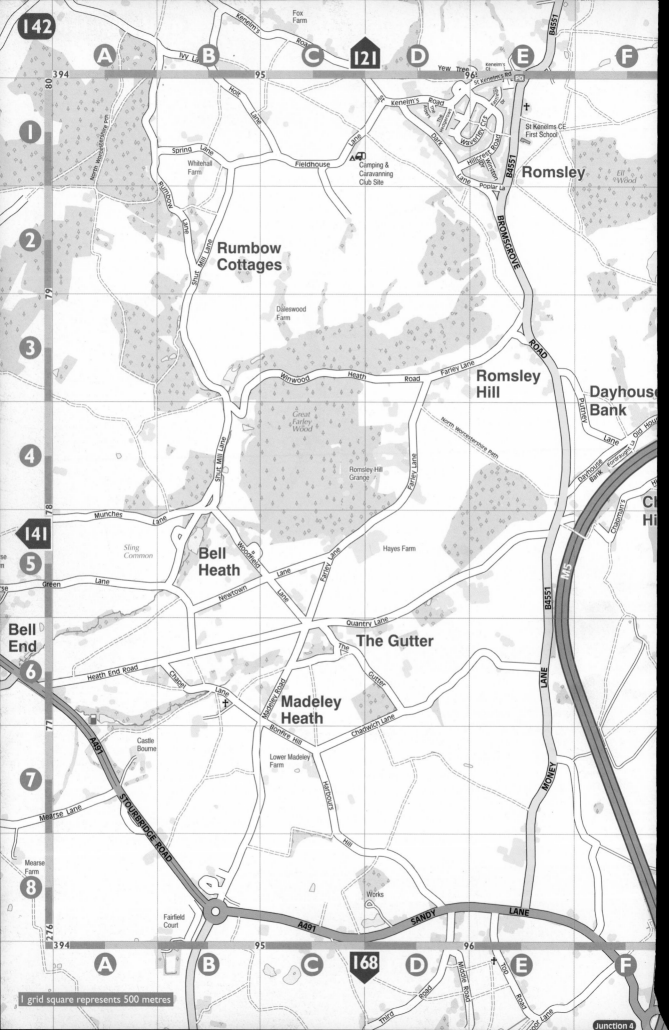

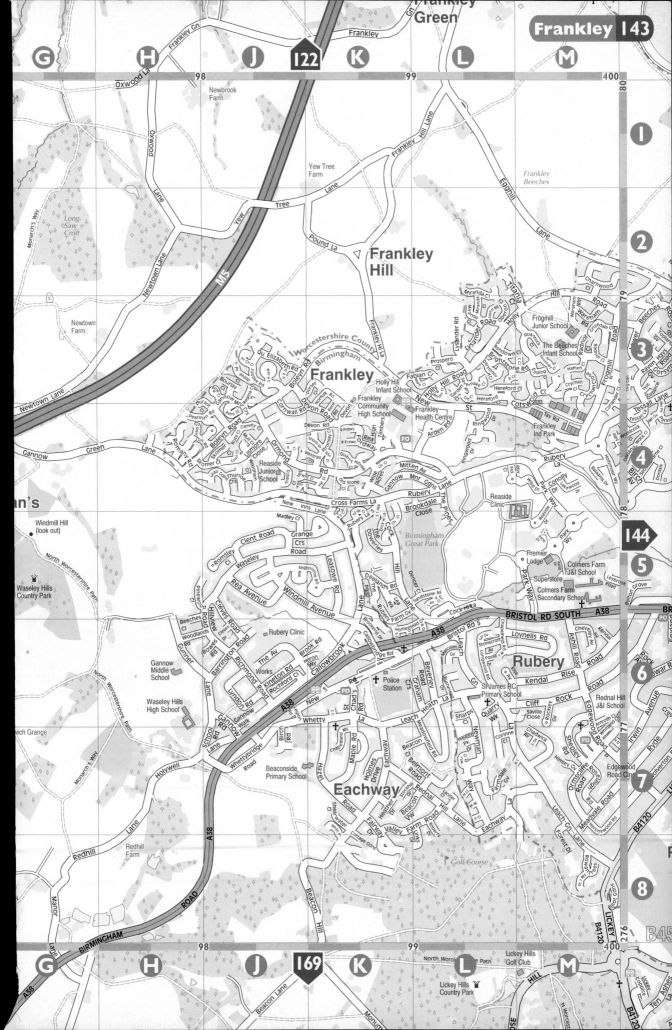

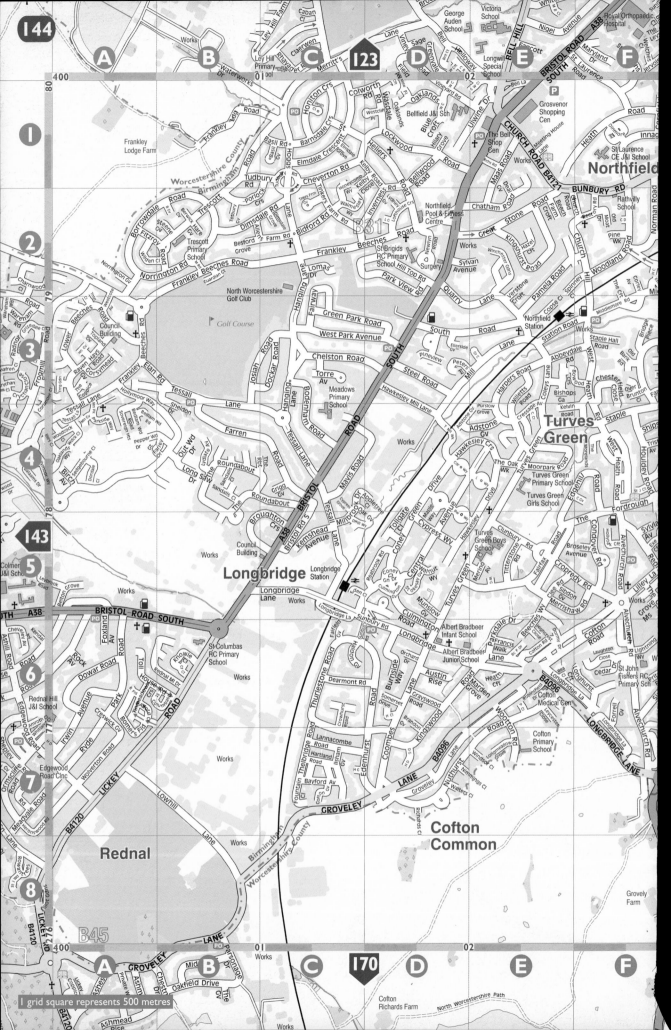

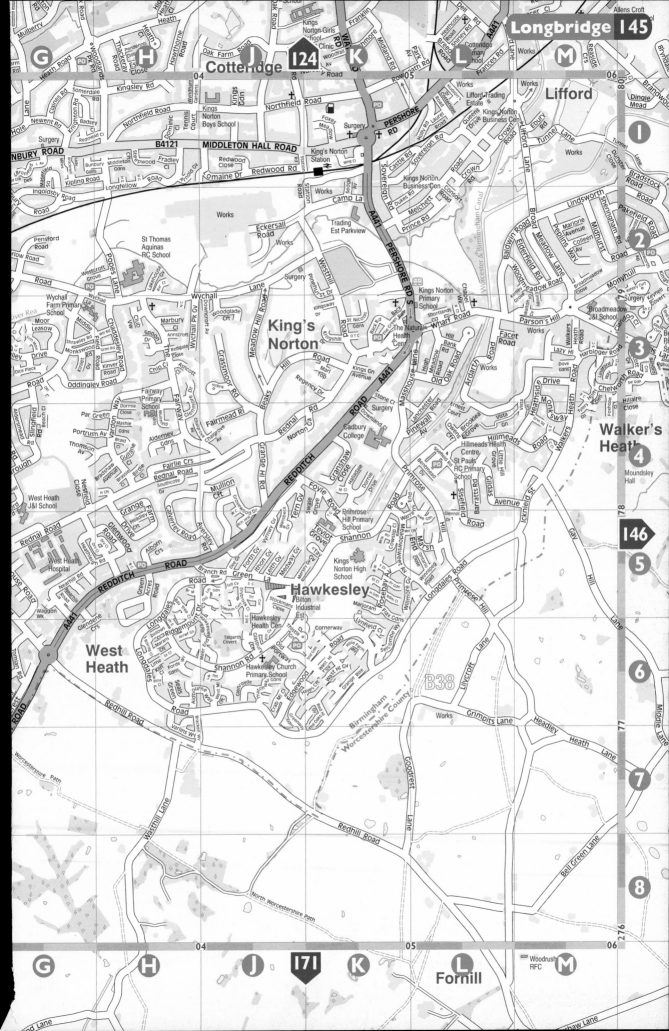

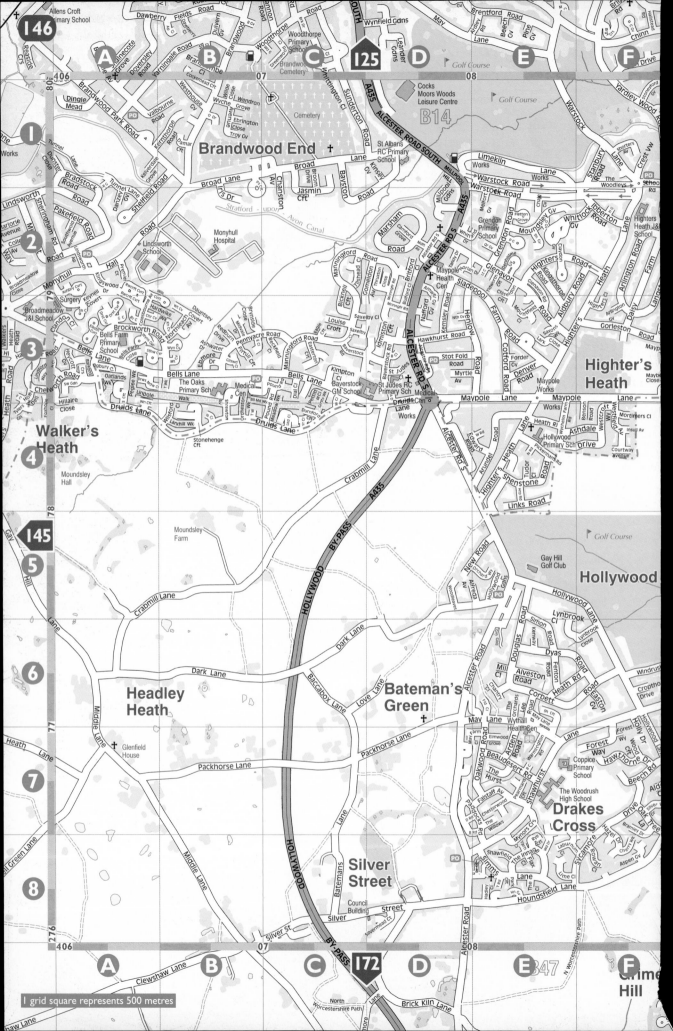

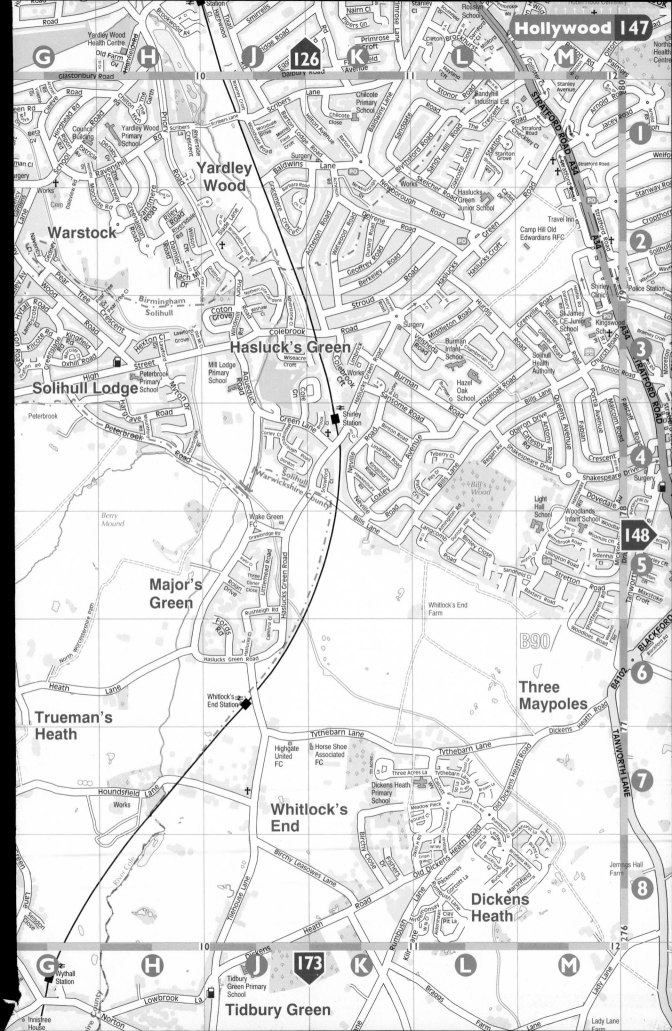

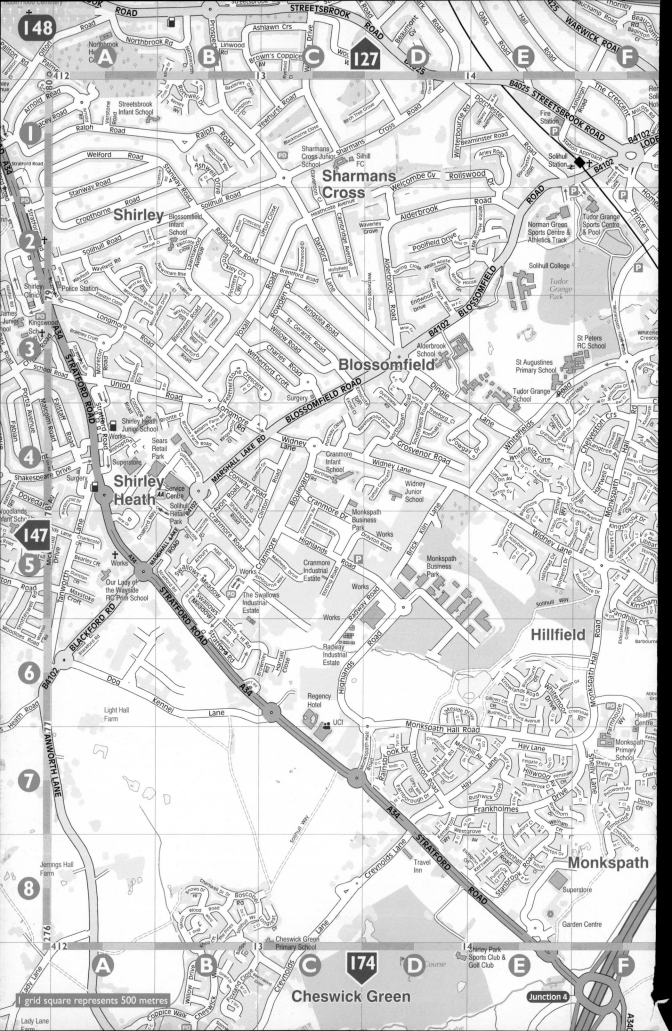

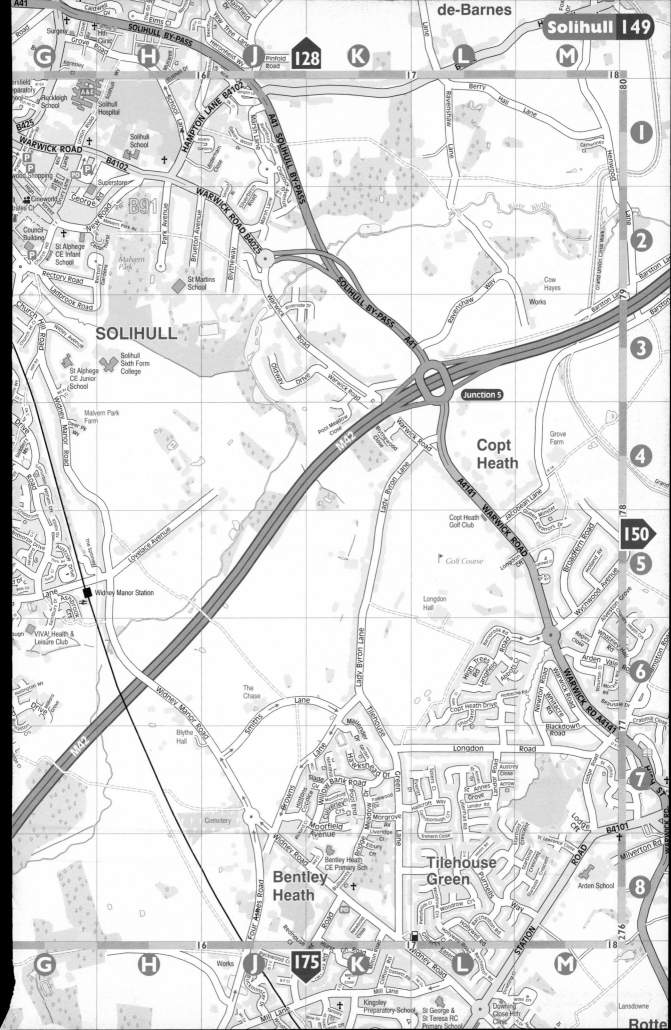

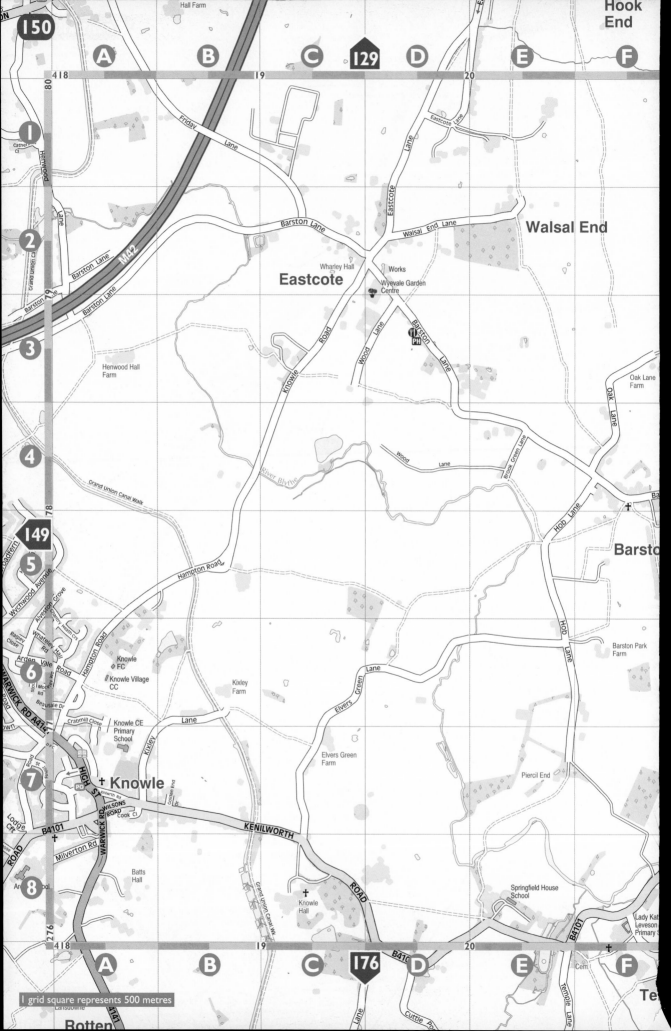

G H J **130** K L M
Park Farm

Marsh Lane 22 23 24

Arden House

I
2
3
4

152

5
6
7
8

River Blythe

Ryton End

Bradnock's Marsh

Business Centre

Garden Centre

KENILWORTH ROAD

A452

Bradnock's Marsh Lane

Wootton Lane

Park Lane

Heart of England Way

Wootton Green

KENILWORTH RD.

Fern Bank

Lavender Hall Lane

Blythe House

Barston Lane

Wootton Green Lane

Travel Inn

Chapel Drive

Hathaway Close

Wilmot Cft
Birch Av
Grovefield
Croveland Crs
Riddings Hill

River Blythe

Grange Farm

Bengate Drive
Finch Cft

Clyde Rd
Holyoak Dr

Clebe Way
Greenfield Avenue
Hayeswood
Copson Cl

Turnpike
Green Lane
Ashley Way
Astley Way

Haigs Hotel

Huggins Cl
Floyd Cft

PO

Balsall Common Health Clinic

Arden Cft
Burnett Rd

Elm Grove
Elm Gv
Sunr

6

BALSALL STREET

Magpie Lane

Saracen Dr

Balsall St

Balsall St

B4101

Fernhill Lane

Magpie Farm

Neerlers

Whitmash Close

Speedwell Dr

Tudor Close

End Lane
Tample Cl
Fern Dale C Rd

Childs Oak Close

Works

Station Road

Burbury

Foxes Way

Tidmarsh Cl

Kemps Green

Dale
Meadow Cl

Wilton Rd

Finford Cft

Stoneton Crescent

Bradley Croft

Cedar Wood Drive

Seat Hills

Laureis

Kenilworth Rd

Kelsey Cl

Leveson Crs

Gipsy Lane

Heart of England School

A452

7

Balsall Street

Frog Lane

BALSALL STREET EAST

Asbury Road

Balsall Common Primary School

ALDER LANE

8

Road 22 23 24

G H J **177** K L M

Balsall **Sedgemere**

Long Brook Lane

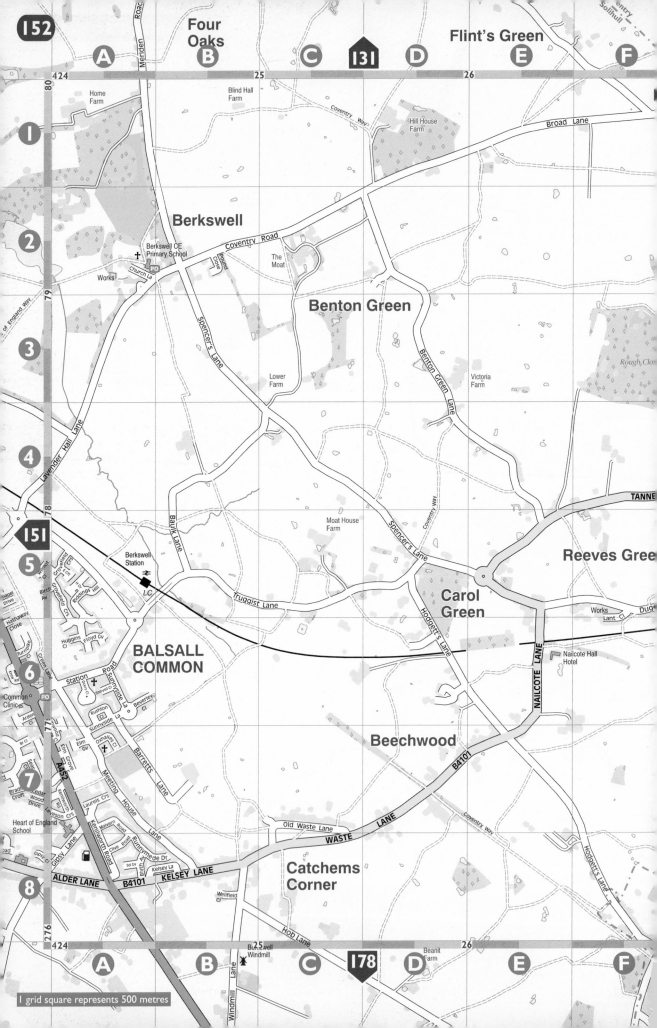

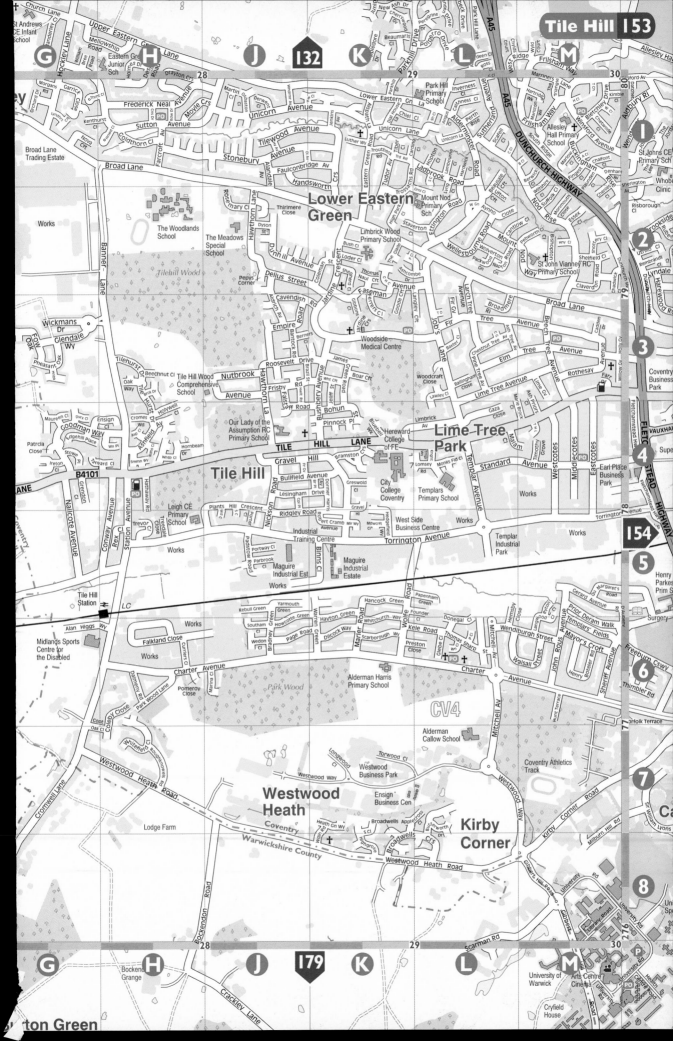

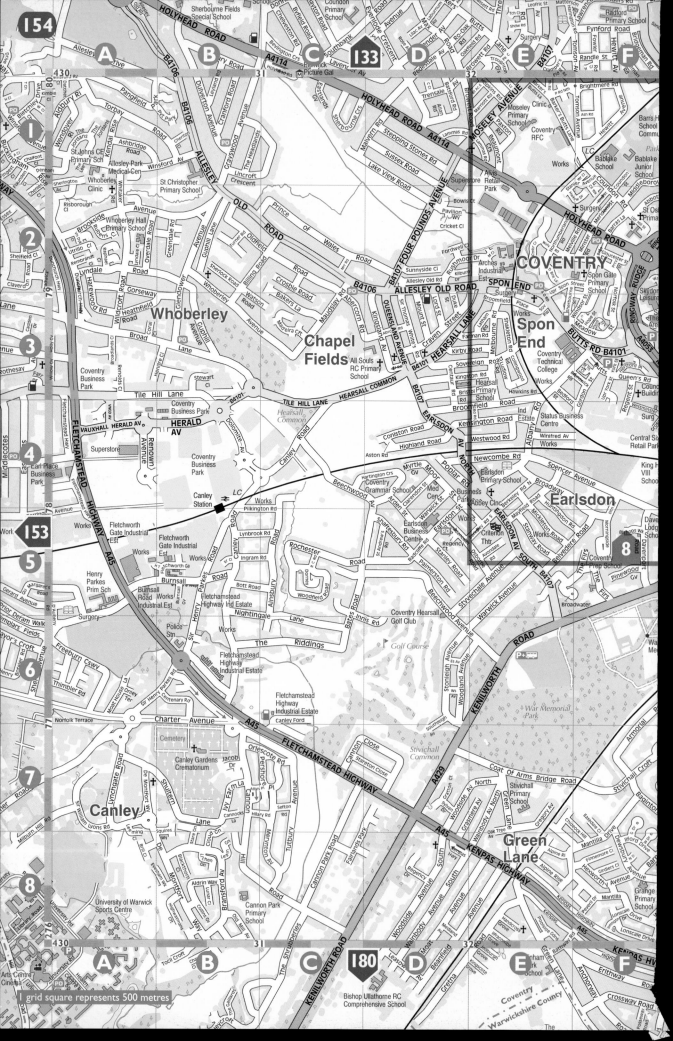

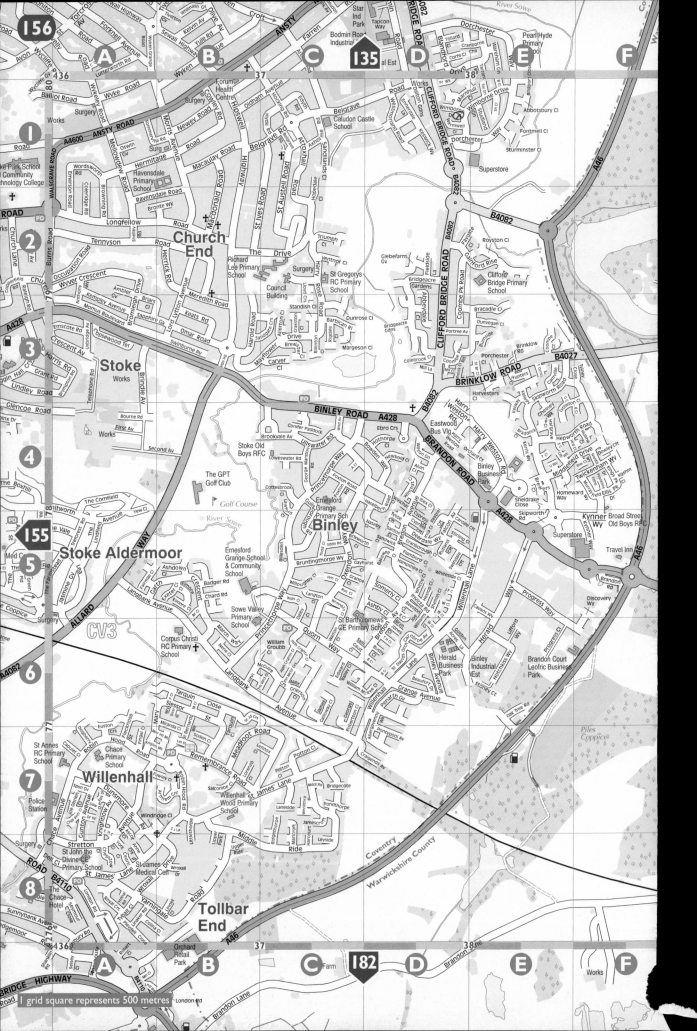

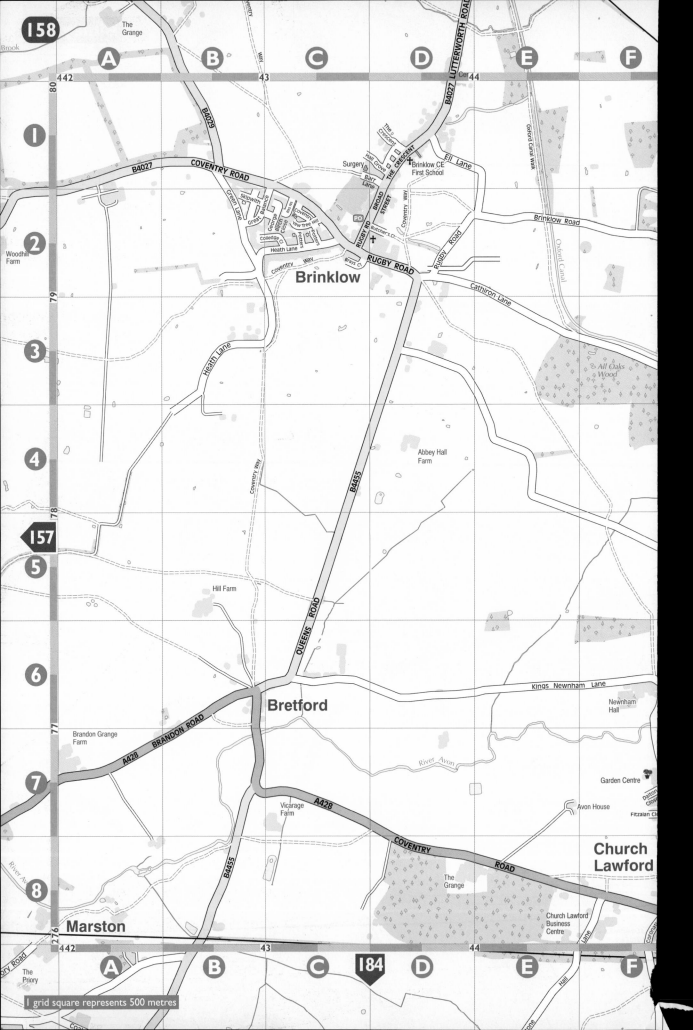

G H J K L M

46 47 48 80

I

Easenhall

Farm Lane

Brinklow Road

Main Street

PH The Golden Lion Inn

Rugby Road

Back Lane

Main Street

Meadow Way

2 rb Magr

Town Thorns Farm

Easenhall Road

Works

PAILTON ROAD

B4112

79

Harbor Parva

3

RUGBY ROAD

Oxford Canal Walk

Cathiron Lane

Cathiron

Cathiron Lane

Cathiron Lane

Works

Cathiron Lane

Oxford Canal

Oxford Canal Walk

4

78

Cathiron Lane

160

B4112

5

HARB

Fennis Fields Farm

Highfields

Little Lawford Lane

Little Lawford Lane

6

King's Newnham

Little Lawford Lane

Clayhill Lane

Little Lawford

River Avon

77

Clayhill Lane

Holbrook Grange

7

Clayhill Farm

Home Farm

ch Road

†

Cemetery

St John's La

Thomas Way

The Spinney

Round Avenue

Ashman Avenue

Holbrook Road

Garratt Close

8

Clayhill Lane

Judge Close

Cross Street

Long Lawford Primary School

Elizabeth Way

Steeping Way

Thirnmill Road

27

48

Long Lawford

Chapel Street

West St

Bailey's

Main Street

Old Street

PO

†

Townsend

Weaver Dr

Cherwell C Lane

46 47

185

A428

COVENTRY ROAD

Livingstone Avenue

South View Road

The Green

Railway Street

Back Lane

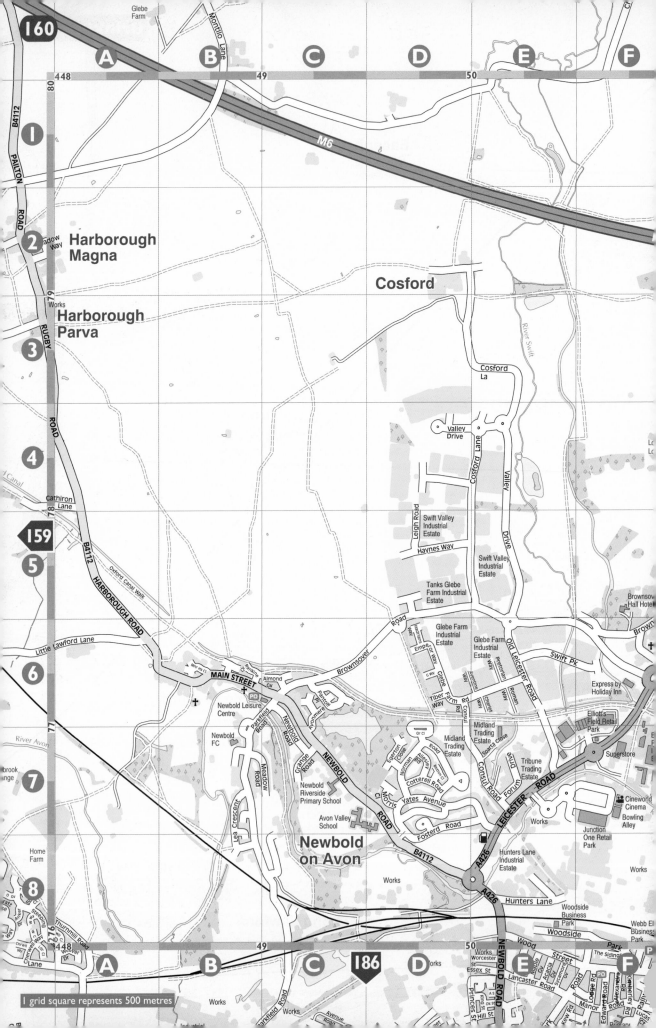

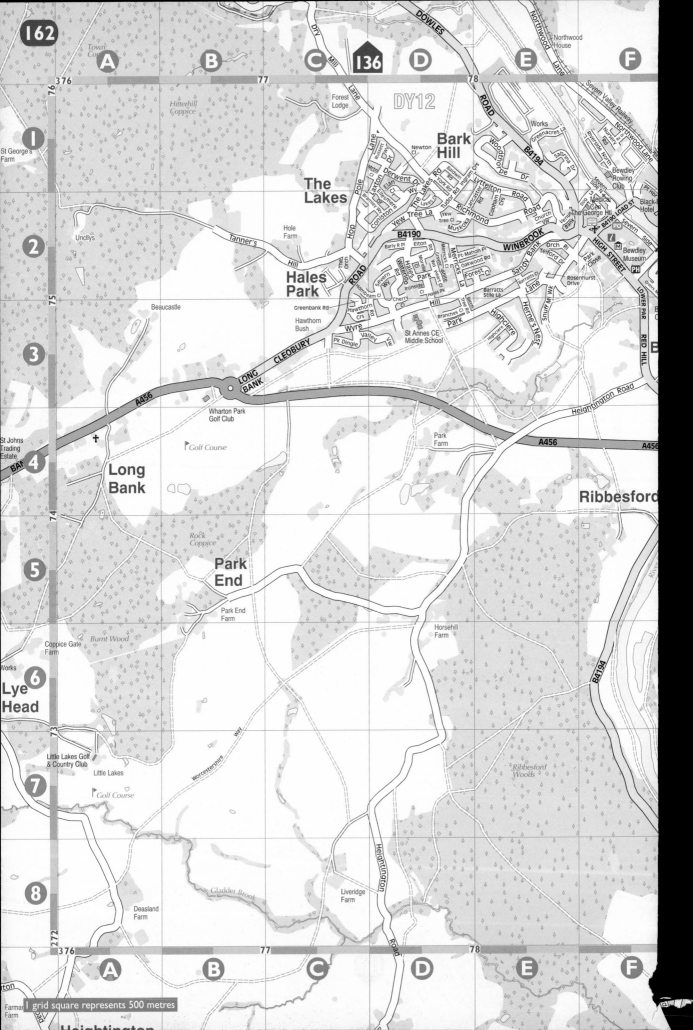

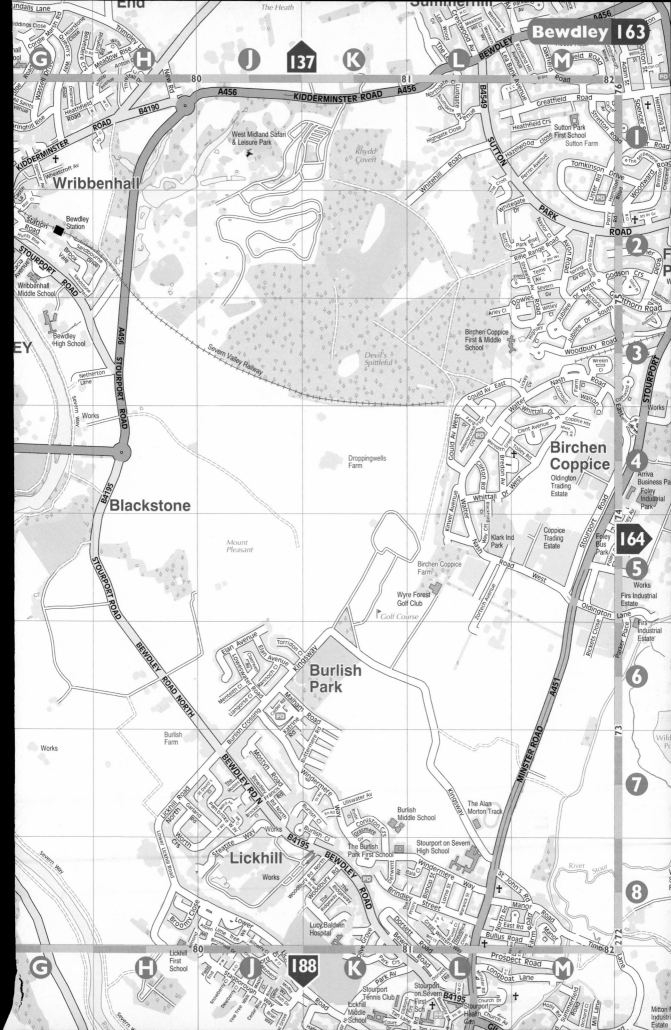

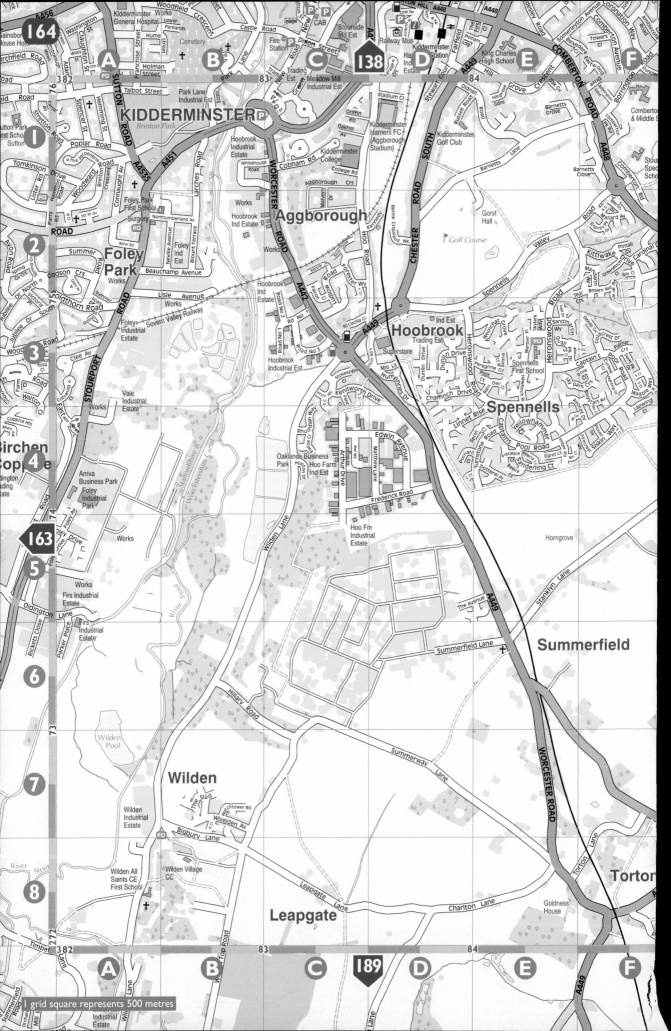

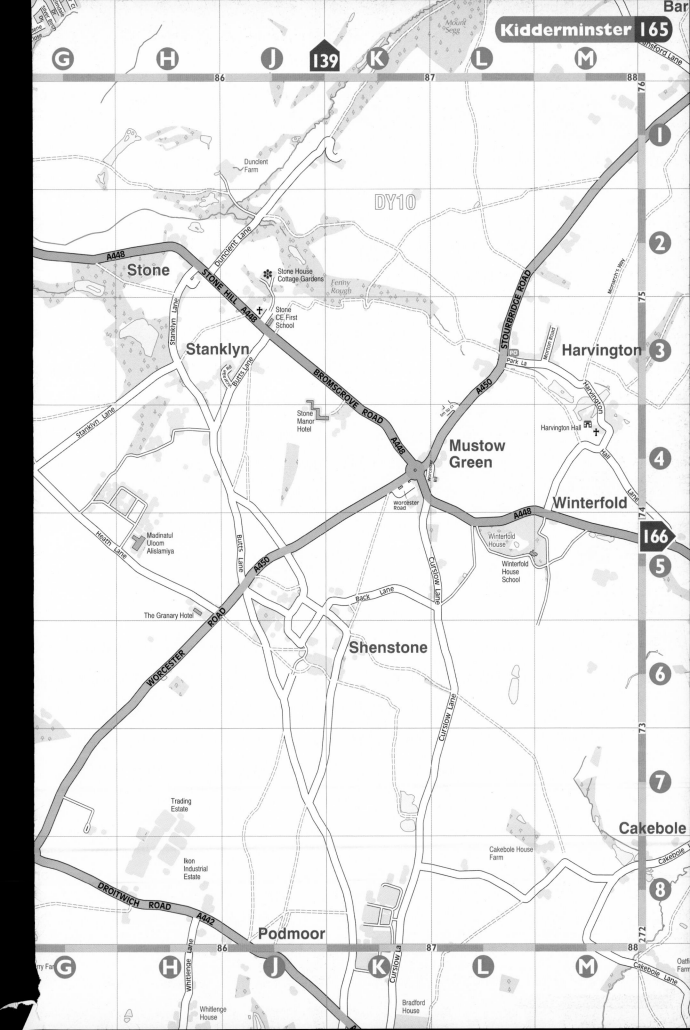

Bar

G H J **139** K L M

Mount Segg

Baxlnsford Lane

86 87 88

1

DY10

2

Dunclent Farm

Dunclent Lane

A448

Stone

Stone House Cottage Gardens

Fenny Rough

STOURBRIDGE ROAD

Morton Road

75

3

Harvington

PO

Park La

Stone Hill A448

Stanklyn Lane

Butts Lane

Scar Rd

✝ Stone CE First School

Stanklyn

BROMSGROVE ROAD

Stone Manor Hotel

A450

Harvington Lane

Harvington Hall ✝

Stanklyn Lane

A448

Sm to Cl

Mustow Green

Worcester Rd

4

Harvington Hall

Heath Lane

Madinatul Uloom Alislamiya

Butts Lane

A450

Worcester Road

Winterfold

A448

Winterfold House

174

166

The Granary Hotel

WORCESTER ROAD

Back Lane

Curslow Lane

Winterfold House School

5

Shenstone

6

Curslow Lane

73

7

Trading Estate

Cakebole

Ikon Industrial Estate

Cakebole House Farm

Cakebole Lane

8

DROITWICH ROAD

A442

Podmoor

Whitlenge Lane

86

Curslow La

87 88

272

Cakebole Lane

G H J K L M

Whitlenge House

Bradford House

Oatfield Farm

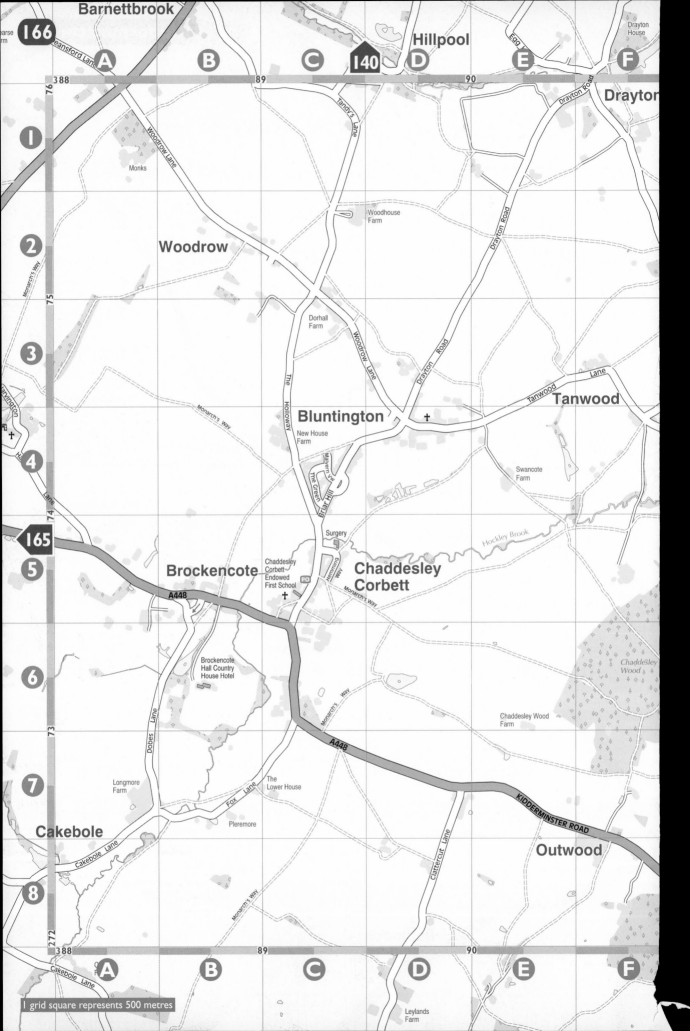

Barnettbrook

A   B   C   140   D   Hillpool   E   F   Drayton House

388   89   90   Drayton

76

1

Woodrow Lane

Monks

Woodhouse Farm

2

Monarch's Way

75

Tandy's Lane

Drayton Road

Woodrow

Dorhall Farm

3

The Holloway

Woodrow Lane

Tanwood Lane   Tanwood

Monarch's Way

Bluntington

New House Farm

†

4

The Green

Malvern Vw

Barley Hill

Swancote Farm

Lane

74

165   Surgery

Hockley Brook

5   Brockencote   Chaddesley Corbett Endowed First School   PO   Hammond Way   Chaddesley Corbett

A448   Monarch's Way

Chaddesley Wood

6   Brockencote Hall Country House Hotel   Monarch's Way   Chaddesley Wood Farm

73   Dobes Lane

A448

7   Longmore Farm   Fox Lane   The Lower House   Clattercut Lane   KIDDERMINSTER ROAD

Pleremore

Cakebole   Monarch's Way   Outwood

8   Cakebole Lane   Leylands Farm

272

388   89   90

Cakebole Lane

A   B   C   D   E   F

1 grid square represents 500 metres

G H J **141** K L M

1
2
3
4
168
5
6
7
8

Bradford House
Mearse Farm

Hurst Farm

Broom Hill

Woodlands Farm

Bournes Green

Hockley Brook

Dordale

Pepper Wood

Waystone Lane

Dordale Road

Hockley Brook Lane

Hockley Brook Lane

Bradford Lane

Monarch's Way

Insetton House

Royal Content Farm

Santery Hill Wood

Woodcote Lane

Works

Warbage Lane

Yarnold Lane Farm

Nutnells Wood

Nature Reserve

Warbage Lane

Road

Woodland Road

Church Road

Victoria Road

Priory Road

Whinfield Road

Niblett Hill

Monarch's Way

Dodford

Randan Wood

Alfreds

Alfreds Well

B61

Woodcote Green

Woodcote Manor House

Priory Road

Dodford First School

Fockbury Road

Monarch's Way

Fockbury Rd

Fockb Farm

Park Farm

Monarch's Way

KIDDERMINSTER ROAD

G H J **190** K L M

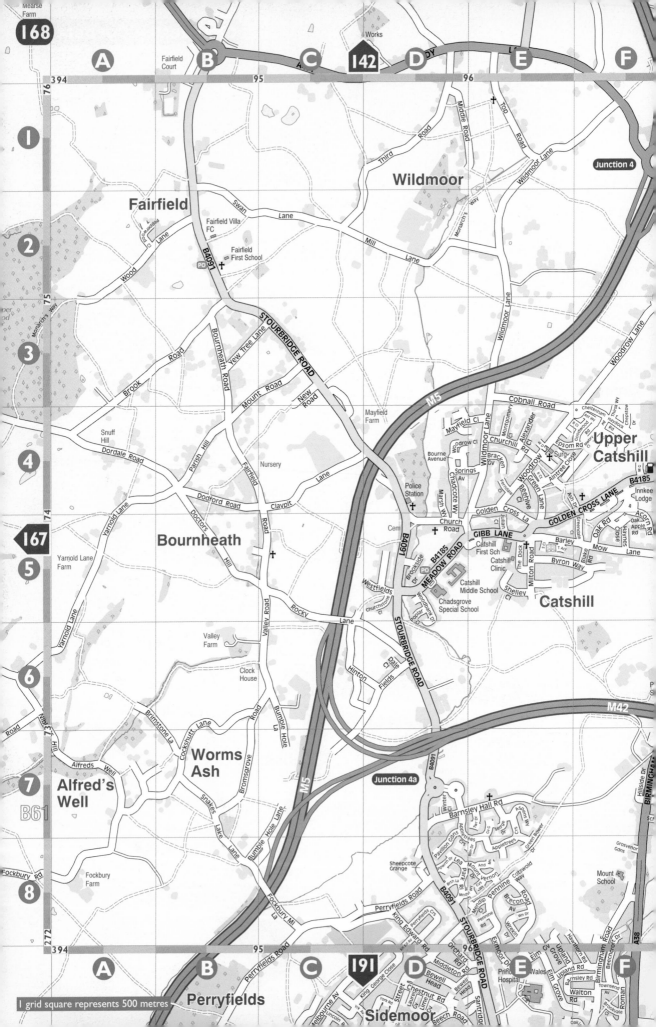

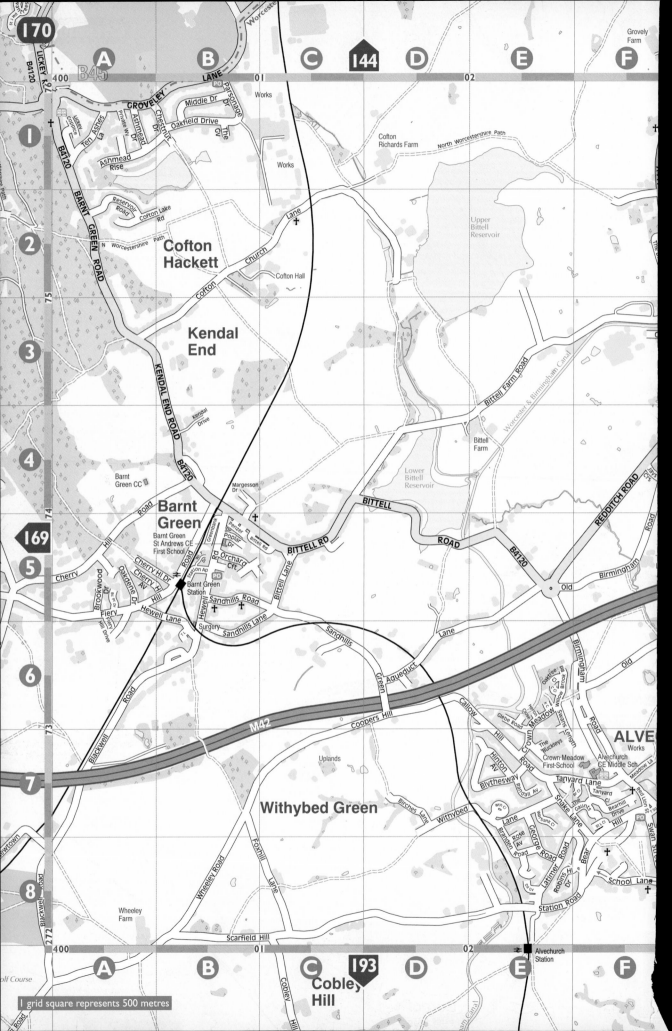

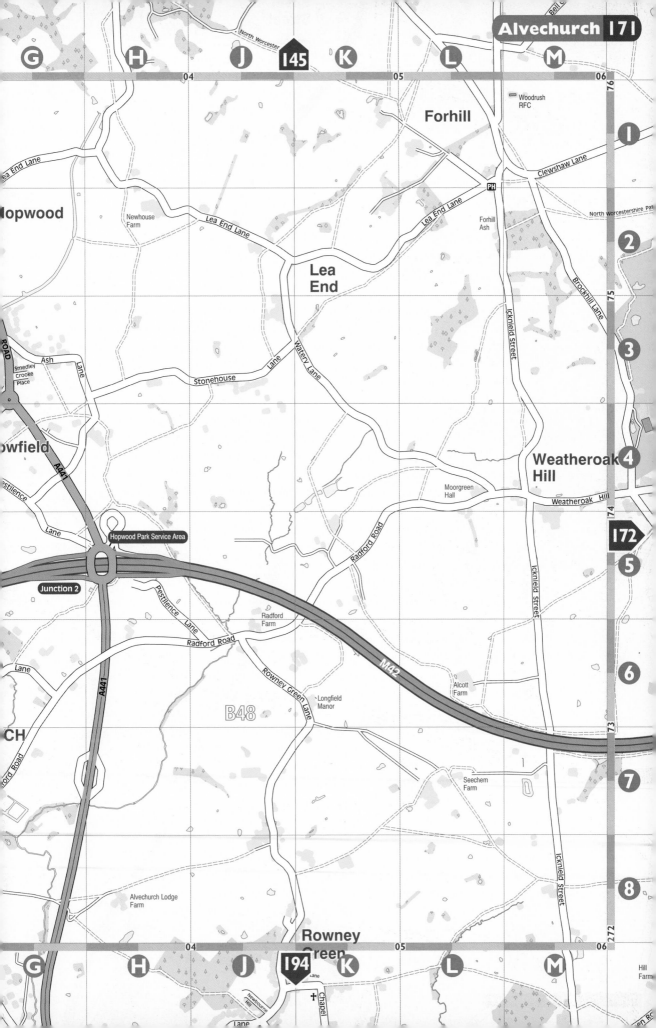

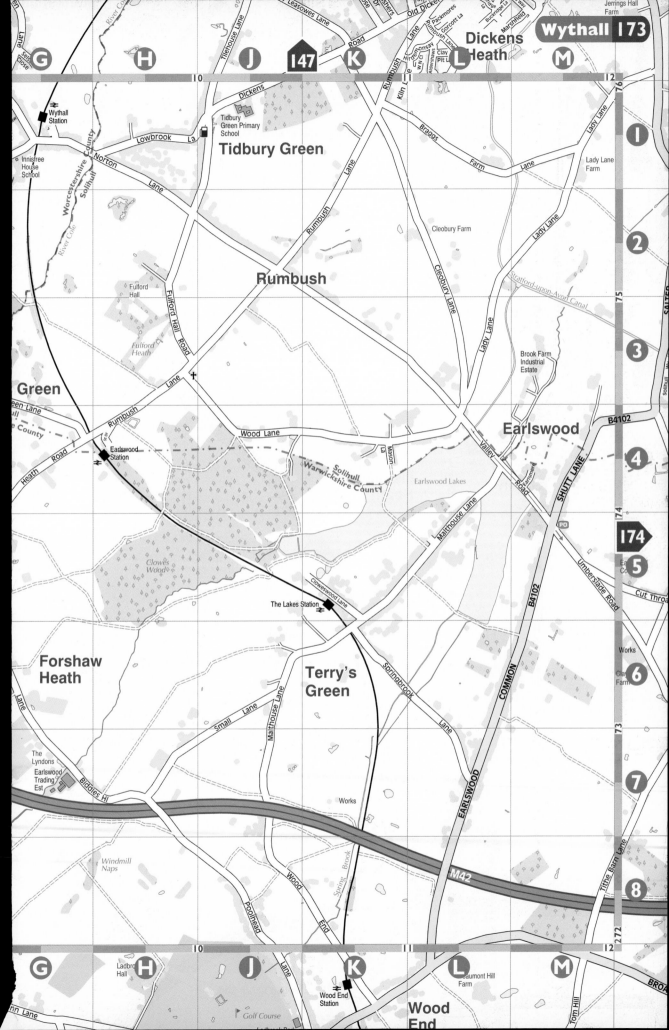

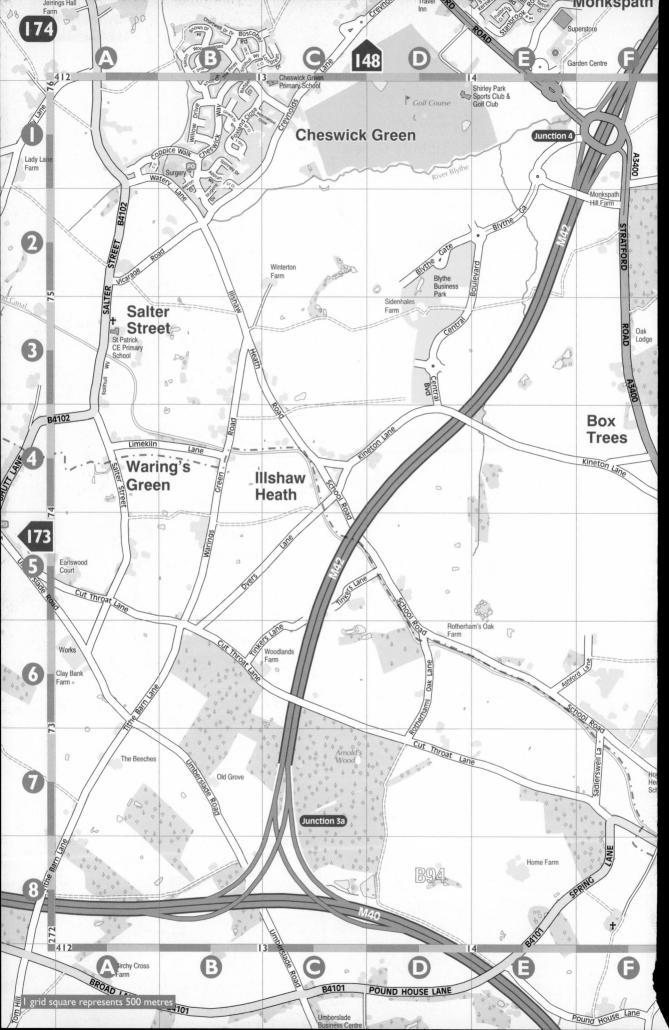

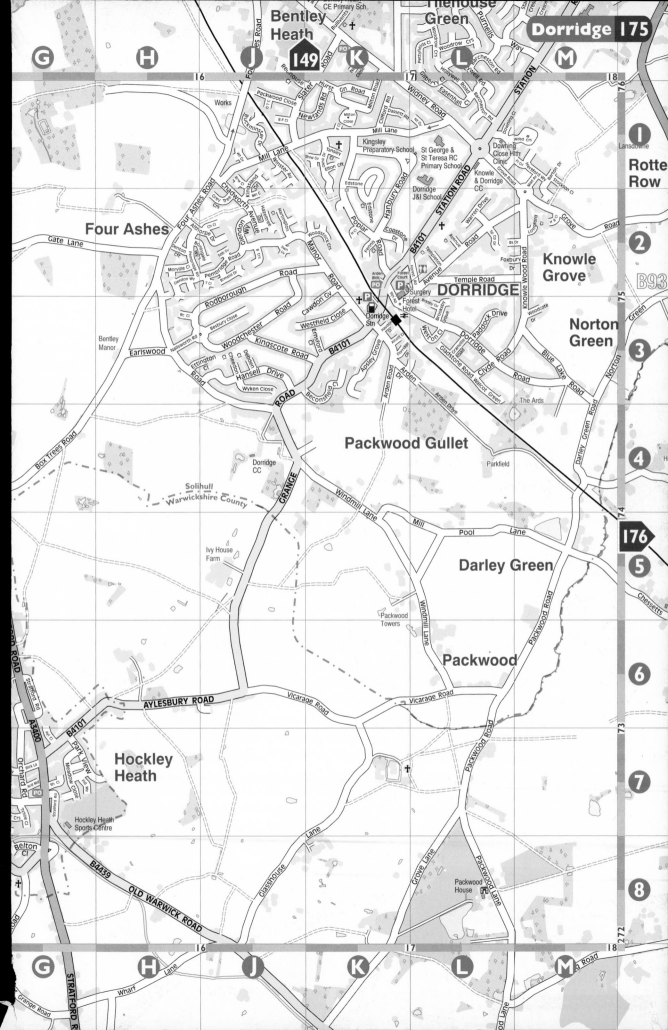

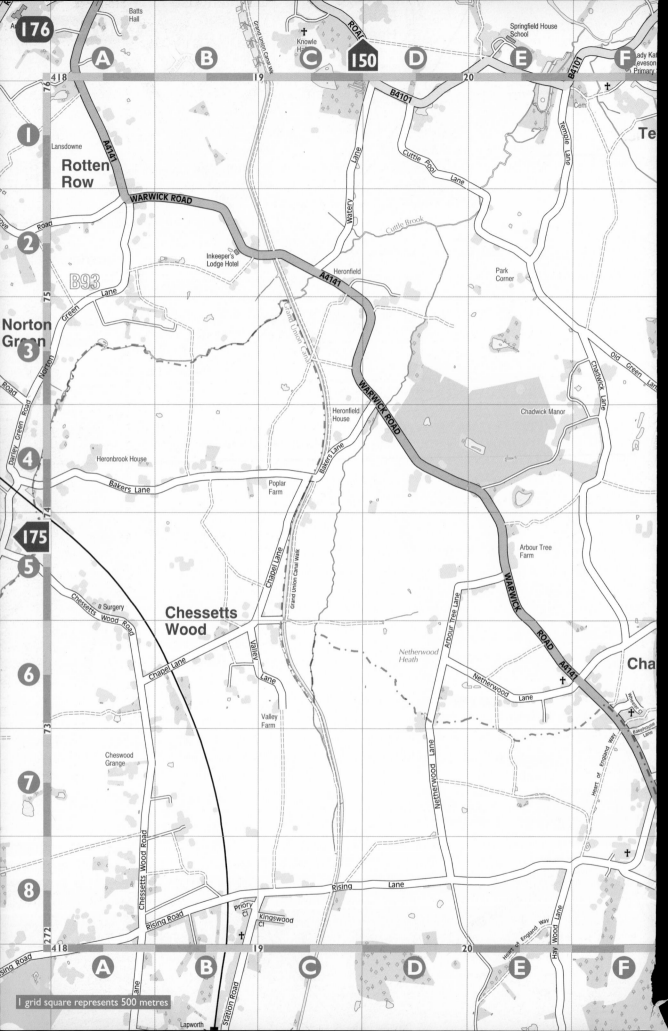

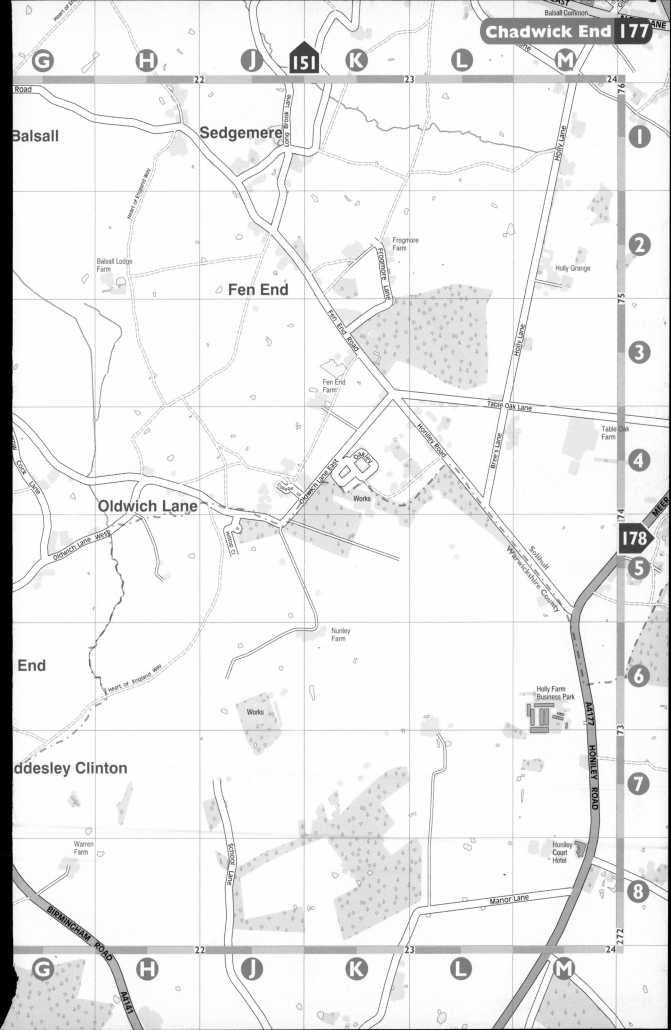

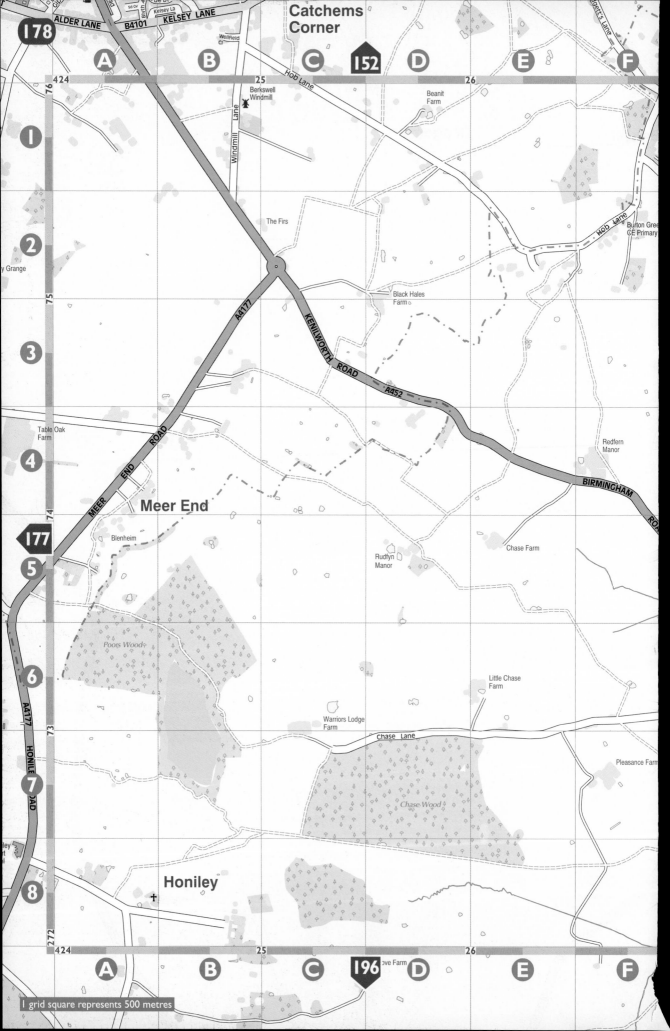

G H J **153** K L M

28 29 30

Bockendon Grange

rton Green

Coventry Way

Crackley Lane

Hurst Farm

South Hurst Farm

University of Warwick

Arts Centre Cinema

Cryfield House

1

2

76

PO

P

75

Long Meadow Barn Farm

Rye Meadow

Crackley Wood

Cryfield Grange

3

4

74

Red Lane

Dunns Pitts Farm

Centenary Way

180

5

A452

Hollis Lane

Camp Farm

Princes Drive Industrial Estate

Princes Dr

Crackley

St Augustines RC Primary School

The Spring

Crackley Lane

Common

Woodland Rd

Leagh Cl

St Josephs School

Ind Est

Inchbrook

6

73

Centenary Wy

Dalehouse L Ind Est Works

Chase Lane

East Chase Farm

Priors Field CP School

BEEHIVE HILL

A452

B4103

Cobbs Rd

Woodcote

Priorsfield Road

Grange Av

Malthouse Lane

Rose Croft

Fernhill Close

Amherst Road

Upper   Spring   Lane

COVENTRY   ROAD

A429

Ladyes Hill

Convent Cl

Alpine Ct

Littleton Cl

Moss Gv

Southmed Dr

Windmill

Northvale Cl

Centenary Way

Dalehouse Rd

Greensward Cl

7

272

De Montfort

Avenue

Clinton

Berkeley Road

Bromley

FIELDGATE LANE

Clarendon House Hotel

NEW   STREET   A429

Tanters   Hill

Hawkesworth

Lower Ladyes

Hills

Manor   Road

Forge

Stoneleigh Rd

Mill End

Webster

Redfern Av

Woodmill Mdw

Finham Road

Tisdale Rise

Sturley

Rawnsley

8

CLINTON LANE

Works

Avenue

Denton Close

Clinton Av

Elmbank Road

Elizabeth Way

PO

PH

High   Street

Pears Cl

Lawrence Cl

Abbotsford School

School   Lane

Hyde Road

Albion Street

Henry Street

Arthur Street

Park   Road

Glendale

Adcock Drive

Hollymead

Villiers Rd

Parkfield Drive

Keeling Road

Park Hill Junior School

Purlieu   Lane

Castle Green

Castle Hill

CASTLE ROAD

Kenilworth Castle

Abbey Fields Swimming Pool

Finham Brook

Priory Thtr

ROSEMARY HILL

ABBEY HILL

A452 PRIORY ROAD

Spring   Lane

The Blundells

St Nicholas CE Combined School

Cherry Orchard

Rosemary Lane

Piper's Lane

Works

Whitemoor Road

Willow Meer

Whitemoor

Tulip Tree Av

Kenilworth School

Leyes   Lane

Courthouse Cft

G H J **197** K L M

28 29 30

Grounds Farm

Montfort

Police Stn

Welfare Clnc

B4105

Mercia Av

Highfield Cl Sth

Brookside Av

Surgery Road

Station   Rd

PO

Council Building

Playbox Theatre

Thorns County Infant

Brooke   Road

B4103

Mingdale   Avenue

Elmdene Road

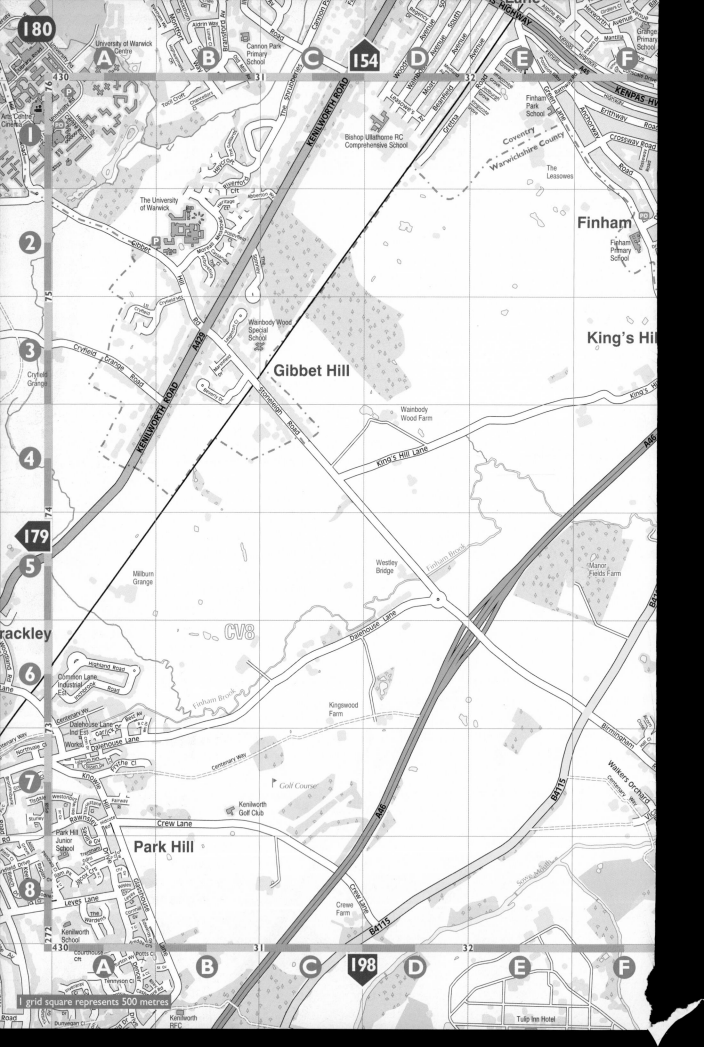

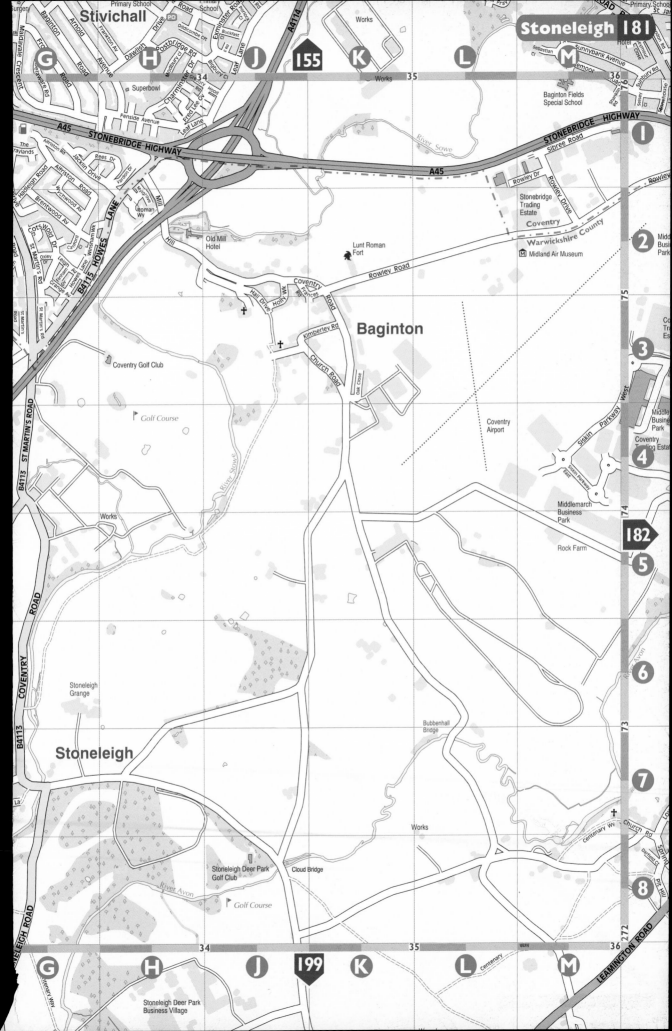

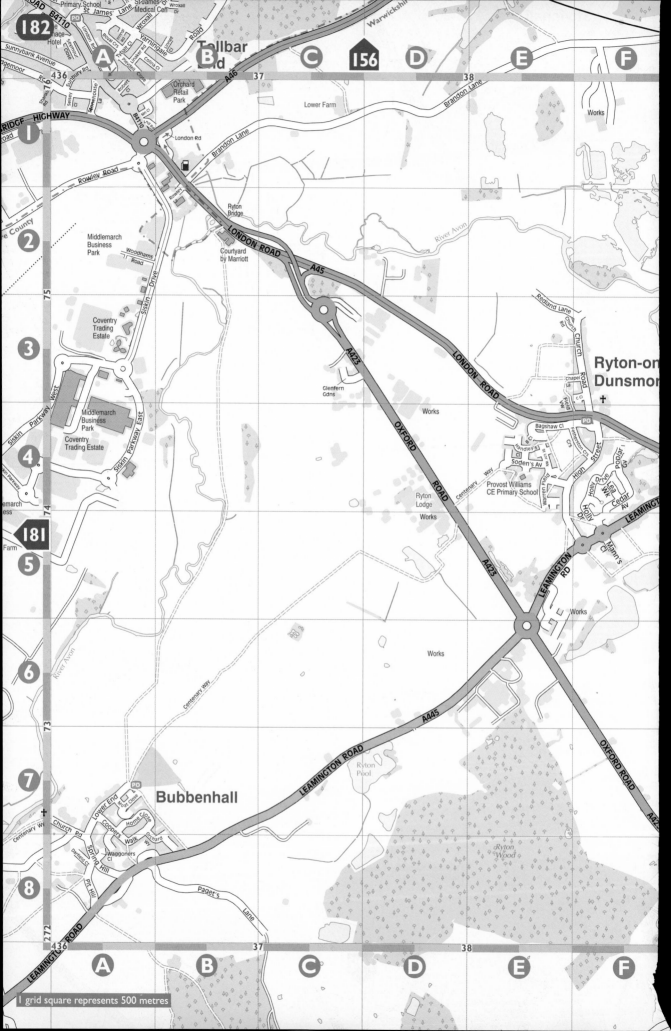

Marston

Lawford

The Grange

Church Lawford Business Centre

158

The Priory

Coalpit Lane

New Farm

Limestone Hall

Coalpit Lane

Heath Business Park

Heath House

Heath Farm

Rookery Hall

Lawford Lodge Farm

183

Coalpit Lane

Manor Farm

Ferry Farm

Wolston Grange

A45

LONDON ROAD

Dunsmore Heath

Home Farm

Coalpit Lane

Avenue House

Rugby Lane

A45

Broomhill Farm

LONDON

Heath Farm

B4453

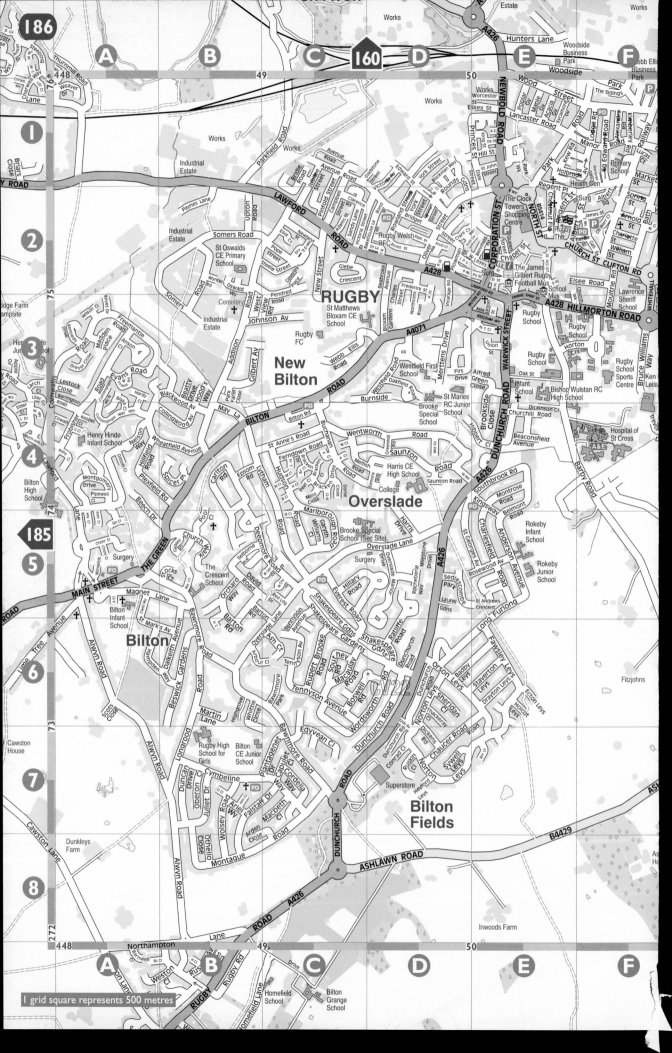

163

STOURPORT-
ON-SEVERN

Areley
Kings

The Walshes

Lower H

Astley
Cross

DY13

190

A · B · C **167** D · E · F

Woodcote Manor House

KIDDERMINSTER R...

391

72

I

2

71

Durrance Farm

3

Risingbridge

4

70

Cooksey Gr...n

5

Green Lane

Cooksey

6

69

Berrylane Farm

Berry Lane

7

Dog Lane

Cooksey Corner

Cooksey Lodge Farm

8

268

Crutch Lane

391

92

Berry Lane

Newhouse Lane

Timberhonger Lane

Timberhonger

Cobbler's Coppice

Swan Lane

West Lodge Farm

93

Bungay Lake Lane

Bungay Lake Farm

Warridge Lodge Farm

Bungay Lake Lane

KIDDERMINSTER ROAD

Park Farm

Monarch's Way

Dodford First School

Fockb...

Road

Monst...

Park Gate

Monsieurs Hall Lane

A448

Puckbur

Foxwalks Farm

Graft... Hous...

M5

Rectory Lane

Upton Warren

...CESTER ROAD

Works

A · B · C · D · E · F

I grid square represents 500 metres

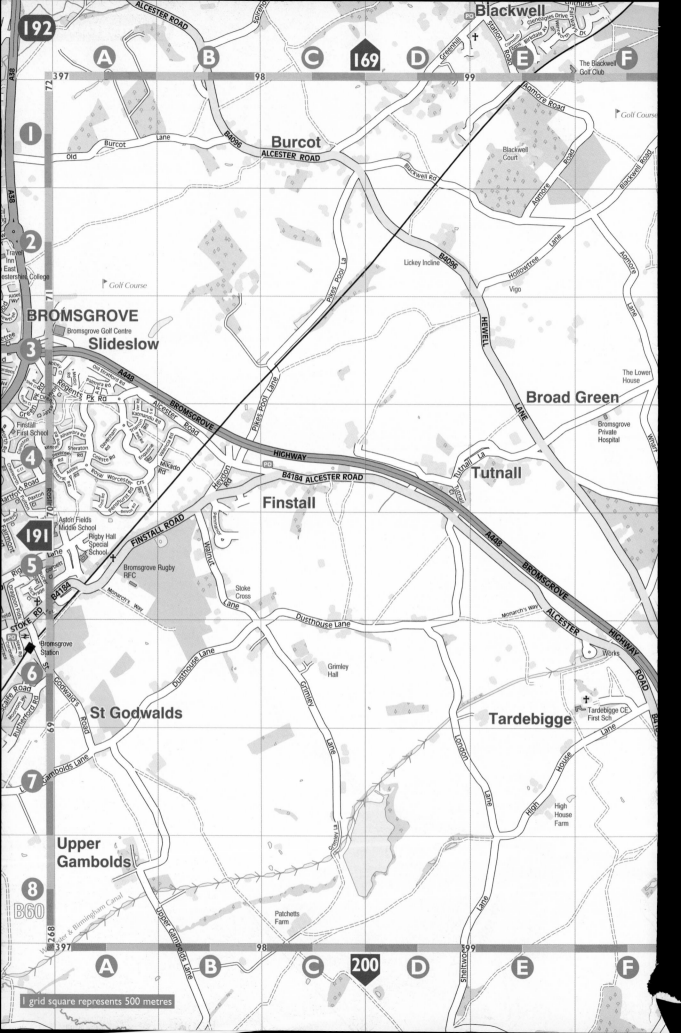

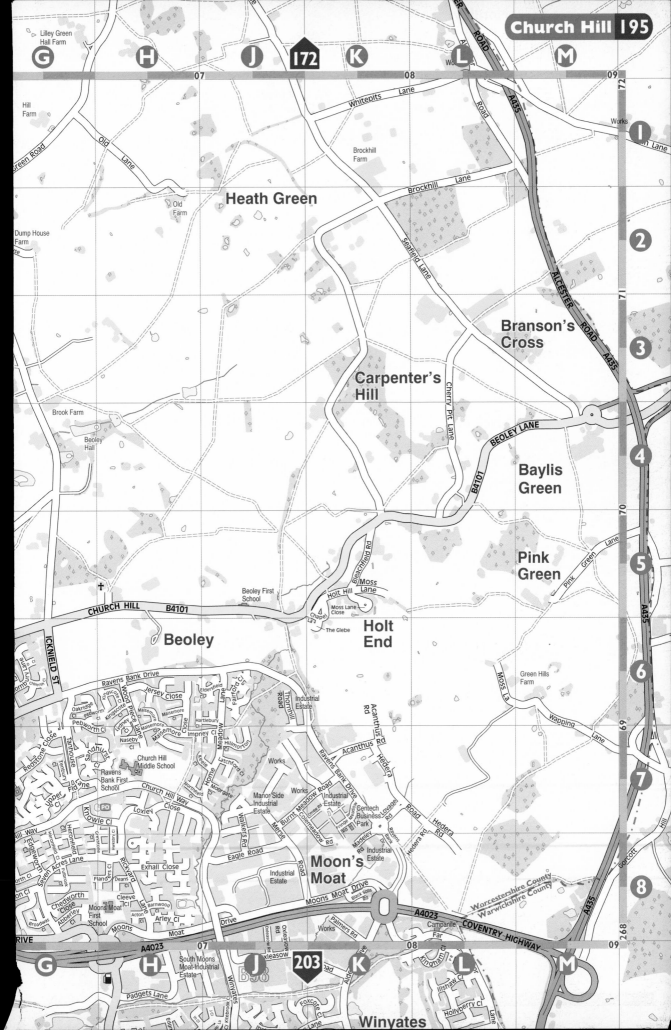

G H J **172** K L M

07 08 09 72

1

Works

Lilley Green Hall Farm

Whitepits Lane

Hill Farm

Old Lane

Green Road

Old Lane

Brockhill Farm

Brockhill Lane

2

Heath Green

Old Farm

Dump House Farm

Searield Lane

Branson's Cross 3

Brook Farm

Carpenter's Hill

Cherry Pit Lane

ALCESTER ROAD A435

Beoley Hall

BEOLEY LANE

B4101

Baylis Green 4

Beoley First School

Bleachfield Rd

Moss Lane

Pink Green 5

CHURCH HILL B4101

Holt Hill

Chapel La

Moss Lane Close

The Glebe

Holt End

Green Hills Farm 6

ICKNIELD ST

Beoley

Ravens Bank Drive

Jersey Close

Eldershield

Fairford Cl

Meadow Lane

Thornhill Road

Industrial Estate

Moss La

Wapping Lane

A435 69

Oakridge Cl
Pebworth Cl
Kingscote Cl
Lydney Cl
Maisemore Cl
Maisemore Close
Hartlebury
Impney Cl
Hillmorton

Redstone Cl

Tanhouse Lane
Tenbury Cl
Sandhurst

Naseby Cl

Church Hill Middle School

Keele

Latchford Cl

Home

Works

Acanthus Rd

Acanthus Rd

Hedera Rd

7

Upper Cl

Ravens Bank First School

Church Hill Way

Northfield

Moorgate

Works

Ravens Bank Drive

Industrial Estate

Centech Business Park

Lovagel Rd

Ravens Bank

Hedera Rd

Hedera Road

Gorcott

Knowle Cl

Loxley

Walkers Rd

Merse Rd

Manor Side Industrial Estate

Colemeadow Rd

Fringe Meadow Rd

Madeley Rd

Industrial Estate

Hedera Rd

Hill Way

Heronfield Cl

Edgeworth Cl

Rickyard

Exhall Close

Eagle Road

Burnt Meadow Road

Moon's Moat

Worcestershire County

Warwickshire County

8

Seven Acres Lane

Flanders Cl

Deans

Cleeve Cl

Industrial Estate

Black Solis Rd

Moons Moat Drive

Campanile

Far

A435 268

Chedworth Close
Abberley Cl
Barnwood Cl
Acton Cl
Arley Cl

Moons Moat First School

Broadway

Moons Moat Drive

A4023

Oxleasow Rd
Drakelow Rd

Palmers Rd

Works

COVENTRY HIGHWAY

DRIVE

G H J **203** K L M

Padgets Lane

South Moons Moat Industrial Estate

Winyates

B98

xleasow

Foxcote

Aldcot

Kingham Cl

Illshaw Rd

Hollyberry Cl

Lane

07 08 09

Winyates

Honiley

A   B   C   178   D   E   F

72 424   25   26

71

1

2

Grove Farm

3 Beausale

Butlers End   Barracks La

Fernwood Farm

Rouncil Lane

Elmwood Farm

Inchford Brook

4

Kites Nest Lane

5
Haseley Green

Beausale Ho

Beausale Lane

Bannerhill Farm

70

Waste Green

6

69

Bulloak Farm

Deer Park Farm

7

Kites Nest Lane

Kingstanding Farm

Old Man Farm

8

Haseley Business Centre

Haseley Manor

424   25   204   26

A   B   C   D   E   F

ale Lane

Turkey

Kenilworth Castle

Abbey Fields Swimming Pool

Priory Thtr

Whiten...

Tinham Brook

G 28 **H** 29 **J** **179** **K** **L** **M** 30

St Nicholas CE Combined School

Council Building

De Montfort Hotel

B4103

B4104

Police

Welfare Clnc

Mercia Av

Greville Rd

Highfield Cl Sth

Surgery

Station Rd

Playbox Theatre

Superstore

Talisman Theatre & Arts Centre

Randall Road

Queen's Road

KENILWORTH

Clinton Combined School

Archer Road

The Mews

Cemetery

Lunn Avenue

Caesar Road

John O'Gaunt

St Nicholas Av

Roseland Road

St John's

St Johns

St Johns Primary School

Windy Arbour

Thorns County Infant School

Blackthorne Road

Thornby Avenue

Brooke Road

Hermitage Way

Worcester Rd

Walnut Tree La

Birches Lane

Leamington Road

A452

A46

Leamington Rd

Percy Road

Oaks

Beauchamp Road

Dudley Road

Essex Cl

Rounds Hill

Beechwood Cft

Castle Sixth Form Centre (Kenilworth School)

Council Lane

Gypsy Lane

Sovereign Cl

Hunt Paddocks

Centenary Way

Rouncil Farm

Little Woodcote

Woodcote

Woodcote

Woodcote Drive

Goodrest Farm

Centenary Way

Home Farm

The Elms

Leek Wootton

Hill Wootton Road

Tidmarsh Road

All Saints Primary School

Wootton Court

The Warwickshire Golf Club

Golf Course

B4115

Warwick Road

G 28 **H** 29 **J** **205** **K** **L** **M** 30

198

Grounds Farm

Oaks Farm

Centenary Way

Cl Lane

1

2

3

4

5

6

7

8

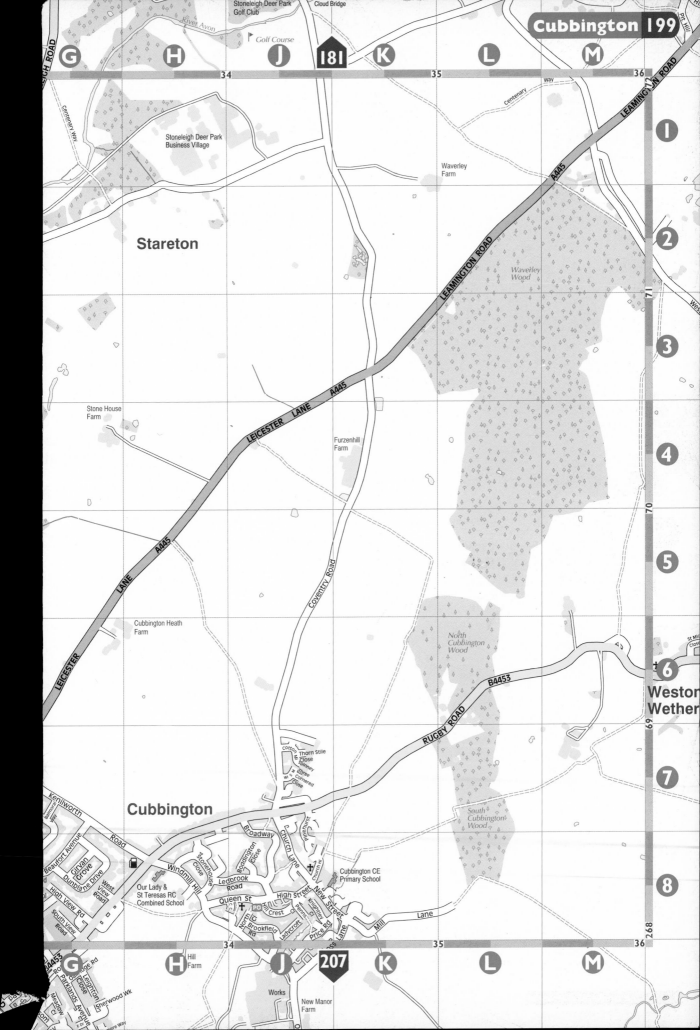

G H J **181** K L M

34 35 36

I

Cloud Bridge

Stoneleigh Deer Park
Golf Club

Golf Course

River Avon

Centenary Way

Stoneleigh Deer Park
Business Village

Waverley
Farm

Centenary Way

LEAMINGTON ROAD

A445

Stareton

2

Waverley
Wood

71

3

Stone House
Farm

LEICESTER LANE A445

Furzenhill
Farm

4

70

5

Cubbington Heath
Farm

North
Cubbington
Wood

LEICESTER LANE

A445

Coventry Road

6

B4453

**Westor
Wether**

St Mi
Close

RUGBY ROAD

69

7

Kenilworth
Road

Cubbington

Cotton Mill
Thorn Stile
Close
Spinney
Three
Cornered
Close

South
Cubbington
Wood

268

8

Beaufort Avenue

Balmoral
Girvan
Grove

Dunblane Drive

West
View
Road

High View Rd

South View
Road

Windmill Hill

Stonehouse
Close

Ledbrook
Road

Our Lady &
St Teresas RC
Combined School

Queen St

North
Brookfield Rd

Broadway

Boddington
Close

Church Lane

Pidehurst

High Street

New Street

PO
Hill
Crest

Ladycroft

Perns

Price Rd

Knighton

Church Rd

Cross Lane

Mill

Lane

Cubbington CE
Primary School

G H J **207** K L M

Hill
Farm

Works

New Manor
Farm

34 35 36

A4453

Leighton Close

Sherwood Wk

Bridge Rd

Parklands Avenue

Meadow

Park

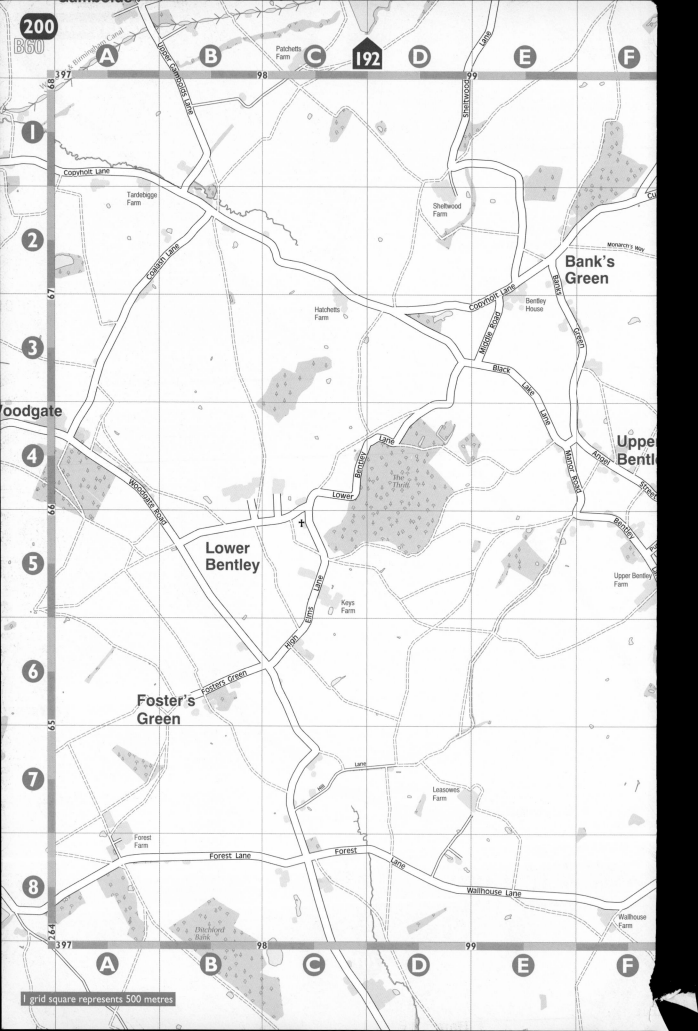

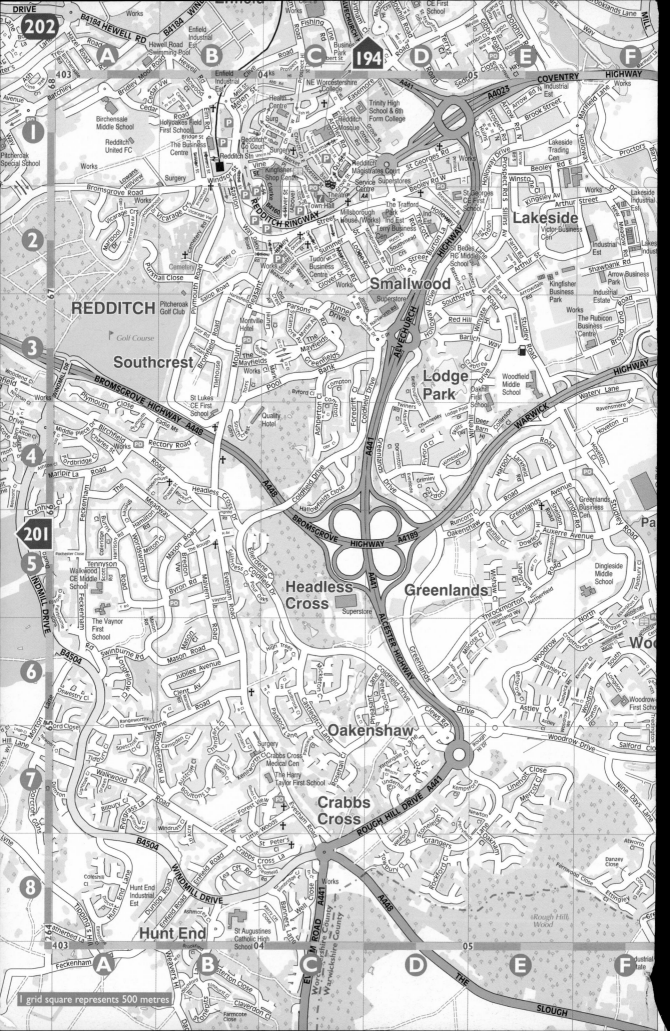

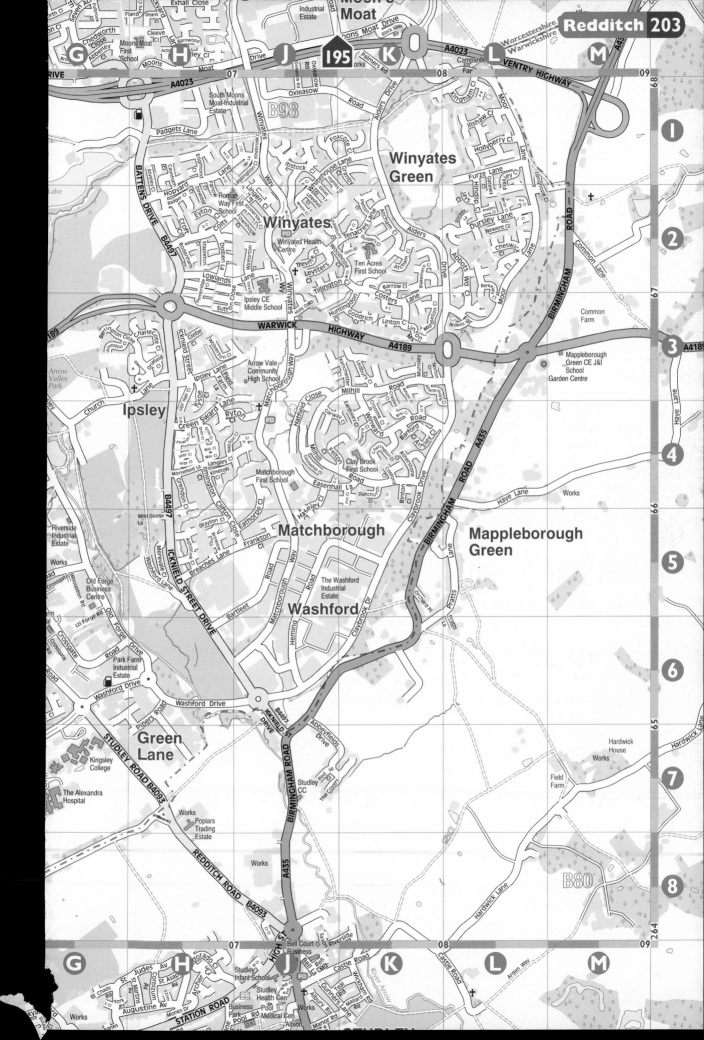

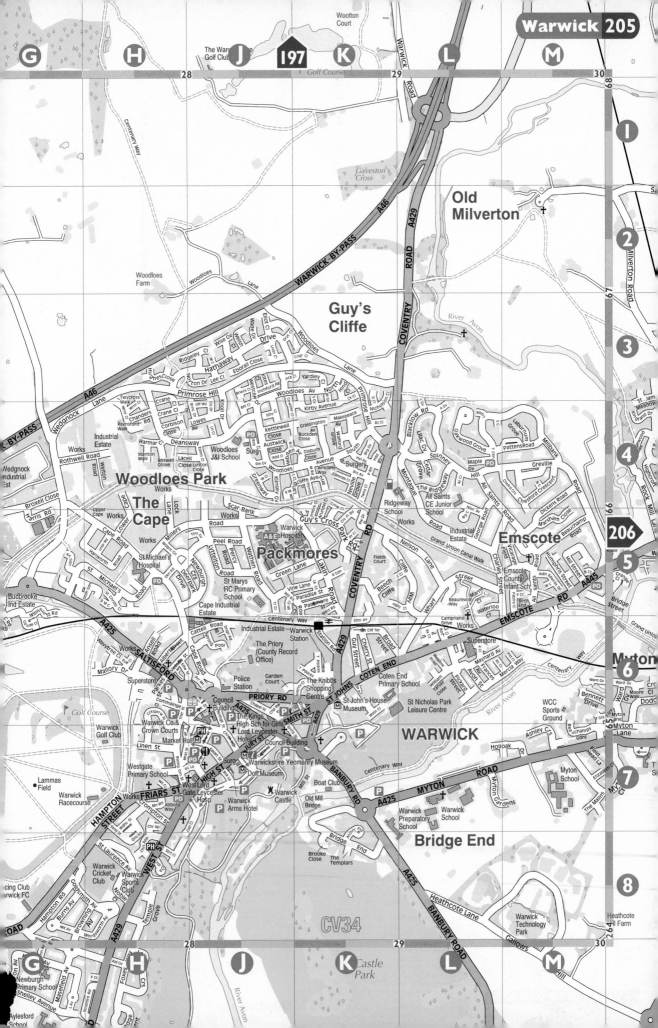

Acock's Green 126 E2
Aggborough 164 C2
Alcester Lane's End 125 H7
Alderman's Green 135 G1
Aldershawe 28 C2
The Alders 31 J7
Aldridge 40 E7
Alfred's Well 168 A7
Allen End 58 D7
Allesley 132 F5
Alum Rock 108 E2
Alvechurch 170 F7
Alvecote 33 H7
Amblecote 101 K6
Amington 32 E8
Ansley 96 F1
Ansley Common 79 K6
Apes Dale 169 K7
Areley Kings 188 A4
Arrowfield Top 170 F4
Ash Green 116 A7
Ashmore Lake 51 M1
Ashmore Park 37 K4
Ashow 198 C4
Ashwood 82 C8
Astley 89 K7
Astley Cross 188 C5
Aston 89 K7
Aston Fields 191 L5
Atherstone 63 J3
Attleborough 99 G3
Bacon's End 111 G1
Baddesley Clinton 177 G7
Baddesley Ensor 62 B3
Baginton 181 K3
Ballard's Green 96 B2
Balls Hill 68 E4
Balsall Common 152 A6
Balsall Heath 107 J8
Balsall Street 151 K8
Bank's Green 200 E2
Banners Gate 71 L1
Baptist End 85 G7
Bark Hill 162 D1
Barnacle 117 M7
Barnettbrook 140 A8
Barnt Green 170 B4
Barr Common 55 C2
Barston 150 F5
Bartley Green 123 H5
Batchley 201 L2
Bateman's Green 146 D6
Baxterley 62 A7
Baylis Green 195 M4
Bearwood 105 L3
Beausale 196 A3
Bedworth 116 F5
Bedworth Heath 116 B3
Beech Lanes 105 J6
Beechwood 93 D7
Belbroughton 141 J6
Belgrave 46 C4
Bell End 141 M6
Belle Vale 103 K8
Bellevue 169 G3
Bell Green 134 F5
Bell Heath 142 B5
Bentley 52 B2
Bentley 78 B1
Bentley Common 62 B8
Bentley Heath 149 J8
Benton Green 152 C3
Beoley 195 H6
Berkswell 152 B2
Bermuda 98 E5
Bescot 53 G7
Bewdley 162 F3
Bickenhill 129 H4
Bilbrook 35 G1
Billesley 126 A7
Billesley Common 125 L6
Bilston 51 G6
Bilton 186 A6
Bilton Fields 186 D7
Binley 156 C5
Binley Woods 157 G6
Birch Acre 172 B6
Birchen Coppice 163 M4
Birch End 69 K6
Birches Green 90 D3
Birchfield 89 H4
Birchills 53 H2
Birchley Heath 78 C4
Birchmoor 47 J6
Birmingham 6 C7
Bitterscote 45 L2
Black Bank 116 A4
Blackdown 198 D8
Blackfords 16 D2
Blackheath 103 M3
Black Lake 68 E6
Blackstone 163 H4
Blackwell 169 L8
Blakebrook 138 A7
Blakedown 140 K4
Blakeley 64 E8
Blakenall Heath 39 G4
Blakenhall 49 M6
Bloomfield 67 K7
Blossomfield 148 C3
Bloxwich 38 E4
Bluntington 166 C4
Blyth End 94 A3
Bodymoor Heath 59 L8
Boldmere 72 E4
Bolehall 46 A1
Boley Park 71 K5
Bonehill 45 J4
Boney Hay 18 F4
Bordesley Green 108 C4
Borough Park 31 M6
Boscomoor 10 C5
Botts Green 77 H8
Bournbrook 124 E3
Bournes Green 167 G3
Bourne Vale 55 G2
Bournheath 168 B5
Bournville 124 D6
Bowling Green 103 H2
Box Trees 174 F4
Brades Village 86 B4
Bradley 67 J5
Bradmore 49 J5
Bradnock's Marsh 151 H2
Bramford 66 E6
Brandon 157 K8
Brandwood End 146 B1
Branson's Cross 195 L3
The Bratch 64 D5
Bretford 158 C6
Bridge End 205 L8
Bridgetown 16 B6
Brierley Hill 102 A3
Brinklow 158 C2
Brinsford 22 B6
Bristnall Fields 104 F2
Broad Green 192 E3
Broadwaters 138 C4
Brockencote 166 B5

Brockmoor 101 M1
Bromford 91 J4
Bromley 83 L8
Bromsgrove 191 M3
Broome 140 E3
Broom Hill 167 H2
Brownhills 26 E5
Brown's Green 88 D1
Brownshill Green 133 G4
Brownsover 161 G6
Bubbenhall 182 B7
Buckland End 91 L6
Buckpool 101 K3
Budbrooke 204 C6
Burcot 192 C1
Burlish Park 163 K6
Burnt Tree 85 K5
Burntwood 18 E6
Burntwood Green 19 H7
Burton Green 179 G1
Bushbury 36 C2
Cakebole 165 M7
Caldecote 80 D3
Caldmore 4 C7
Calf Heath 14 D7
California 123 K3
Camp Hill 80 C8
Campion Hills 207 G4
Canley 154 A7
Cannock 16 A2
The Cape 205 H4
Carol Green 152 D5
Carpenter's Hill 195 K3
Carroway Head 57 M1
Castle Bromwich 92 A5
Castlecroft 48 E5
Castle Vale 91 L2
Catchems Corner 152 C8
Catchems End 137 H8
Catherine-de-Barnes .128 E8
Cathiron 159 K4
Catshill 26 E7
Catshill 168 E5
Caunsall 118 A6
Causeway Green 104 D2
Cawston 185 L6
Chaddesley Corbett ..166 C5
Chadsmoor 16 C1
Chad Valley 106 D6
Chadwick 189 J6
Chadwick End 176 F6
Chapel End 79 M5
Chapel Fields 154 C3
Chapel Green 114 A6
Chapman's Hill 142 F4
Charford 191 J5
Charlemont 69 H6
Charlton 189 H2
Chase Terrace 18 C5
Chasetown 18 D7
Chattle Hill 93 J3
Chelmsley Wood 111 G4
Cheslyn Hay 24 B2
Chessetts Wood 176 B5
Chesterfield 28 C5
Cheswick Green 174 C1
Cheylesmore 155 J6
Chilvers Coton 98 E4
Chorley 19 J3
The Chuckery 5 K4
Churchbridge 16 D8
Church End 78 E7
Church End 95 G3
Church End 156 A2
Churchfield 69 J8
Church Hill 13 H8
Church Hill 68 E1
Church Hill 194 E8
Churchill 140 A2
Church Lawford 158 F8
Cinder Hill 66 D4
Claregate 35 H7
Clayhanger 26 B7
Clent 141 L2
Cliff 59 M5
Clifton upon Dunsmore ..161 L3
Coalpit Field 117 H4
Coal Pool 39 K8
Cobley Hill 193 J1
Codsall 34 D1
Cofton Common 144 D7
Cofton Hackett 170 B2
Cole End 93 K5
Colehall 91 M8
Coleshill 93 L7
Collycroft 116 F1
Colton 65 L2
Colton Hills 65 L2
Comberford 31 J2
Comberton 138 E7
Compton 49 H3
Cooksey Corner 190 B7
Coombeswood 104 A7
Copt Heath 149 L4
Corley 114 F6
Corley Ash 114 F4
Corley Moor 114 C6
Coseley 67 G4
Cosford 160 D2
Coton 31 G7
Cotteridge 124 D8
Coundon 133 J6
Court House Green ...134 E6
Coven Heath 22 A7
Coventry 9 J4
Crabbs Cross 202 C7
Crackley 179 M6
Cradley 103 G7
Cradley Heath 103 G5
Creswell Green 19 J3
Cross Green 22 B4
Crossway Green 189 L7
Cubbington 199 H7
Curdworth 74 E7
Dam Mill 34 F4
Darby End 103 H1
Darby's Hill 85 M6
Darlaston 52 A6
Darlaston Green 52 A6
Darley Green 175 L5
Darnford 21 K7
Daw End 39 M8
Dayhouse Bank 142 F3
Deepfields 66 F4
The Delves 69 L1
Devitts Green 96 A4
Dickens Heath 147 L8
Digbeth 7 J6
Dodford 167 K7
Doe Bank 57 G6
Dogingtree Estate 12 B5
Dordale 167 K3
Dordon 47 K7
Dosthill 45 M8
Dowles 136 D7
Drakes Cross 146 E2
Drayton 166 F1
Drayton Bassett 45 H8
Druids Heath 41 G4

Dudley 85 H3
Dudley Port 86 A1
Dudley's Fields 38 D5
Dudley Wood 103 G3
Duke End 112 C1
Dunsley 118 D4
Dunstall Hill 35 M8
Eachway 143 K7
Earlsdon 8 A8
Earlswood 173 L4
Easenhall 159 J1
Eastcote 150 C2
Eaves Green 131 K3
Edgbaston 106 D7
Edge Hill 61 G3
Edgwick 134 C5
Edial 19 J7
Elcock's Brook 201 H7
Elmdon 128 E2
Elmdon Heath 128 C6
Emscote 205 L5
Enfield 194 B8
Erdington 90 E2
Essington 37 K2
Ettingshall 50 D8
Ettingshall Park 66 B2
Eve Hill 84 E3
Exhall 19 J7
Fairfield 137 M2
Fairfield 168 A2
Falcon Lodge 57 M7
Fallings Heath 52 C8
Farewell 19 L1
Fazeley 45 L4
Featherstone 23 G6
Fen End 177 J2
Fillongley 114 C2
Finham 180 F2
Finstall 192 C4
Fishley 39 G1
Five Ways 118 E8
Flint's Green 131 K8
Foleshill 134 D5
Foley Park 164 A2
Footherley 42 C3
Fordbridge 110 E2
Fordhouses 35 M2
Forhill 171 L1
Forshaw Heath 173 G6
Foster's Green 200 A6
Foul End 77 G3
Four Ashes 14 A7
Four Ashes 175 G2
Four Crosses 15 H6
Four Oaks 56 C2
Four Oaks 131 H8
Four Oaks Park 56 D5
Foxford 134 D1
Foxlydiate 201 J2
Franche 137 M4
Frankley 122 F8
Frankley 143 K5
Frankley Green 122 E8
Frankley Hill 143 K2
Freasley 61 G1
Friar Park 69 H2
Furnace End 95 J2
Gailey Wharf 14 D3
Galley Common 79 L8
Garrets Green 109 L4
Gentleshaw 18 E1
Gibbet Hill 180 C3
Gib Heath 88 E6
Giggetty 64 C8
Gilbertstone 109 K7
Gillway 31 L6
Gilson 93 J4
Glascote 46 A2
Glebe Farm 109 K1
Golds Green 68 C5
Goldthorn Park 66 B1
Goodyers End 116 A4
Gornalwood 84 A2
Gorstey Ley 19 G6
Goscote 39 K5
Gosford Green 9 M5
Gospel End Village 65 K5
Gothersley 100 D3
Gravelly Hill 90 D3
Great Barr 70 D3
Great Bridge 67 M7
Great Heath 134 C6
Great Saredon 15 H7
Great Wyrley 24 E2
Green End 113 J4
Green Heath 12 E6
Greenhill 138 E6
Greenlands 202 D5
Green Lane 154 E8
Green Lane 203 H7
Greensforge 82 B7
Grendon 62 B1
Grendon Common 62 A3
Griff 98 F7
Griffin's Hill 124 B6
Grimes Hill 172 F1
Grove End 74 D2
Grove Vale 70 A4
Gun Hill 96 D6
Guns Village 86 E1
The Gutter 142 C6
Guy's Cliffe 205 K3
Habberley 137 L7
Hackman's Gate 140 D4
Haden Cross 103 L5
Hagley 120 B7
Halesowen 122 A1
Hales Park 162 C2
Hall End 47 K8
Hall Flat 169 G6
Hall Green 69 G5
Hall Green 126 E6
Hall Green 134 F2
Hammerwich 27 H1
Hampton in Arden 129 K6
Hampton Magna 204 D7
Hampton on the Hill ..204 C8
Hamstead 70 C5
Handsworth 88 B3
Handsworth Wood 88 F2
Harborne 105 L7
Harborough Magna ...160 A2
Harborough Parva 160 A3
Harden 39 K6
Hardwick 55 K3
Hartle 141 K7
Hartlebury 189 L3
Hartlebury Common ..189 G3
Hart's Hill 84 C8
Hartshill Green 79 M4
Harvest Hill 132 B5
Harvills Hawthorn 68 B6
Harvington 165 M3
Hasbury 121 J2
Hasluck's Green 147 J3
Hateley Heath 69 G7
Hatherton 15 K4
Hatton 204 A2

Hawkes End 132 E3
Hawkesley 145 J5
Hawks Green 16 E4
Hawne 103 L8
Hayfield Hill 18 D1
Hayley Green 121 G4
Hay Mills 108 F7
Hazelslade 13 L7
Headless Cross 202 C5
Headley Heath 146 A6
Heath End 39 K4
Heath Green 195 J2
Heath Hayes 17 K4
Heath Town 50 E1
Hednesford 12 E8
Henley Green 135 H5
Higham on the Hill 81 K2
Highbridge 25 L7
Highbury Park 125 H4
Highgate 107 K5
High Heath 40 A3
High Heath 57 M5
Highter's Heath 146 F3
High Town 12 D8
Hill 56 E1
Hillfield 148 E6
Hillfields 9 H2
Hill Hook 42 C7
Hillmorton 187 K5
Hillpool 140 D8
Hill Top 68 E5
Hill Top 96 E4
Hill Top 99 G4
Hill Wood 43 G8
Hill Wootton 198 A7
Hilton 27 L5
Himley 82 F7
Hinksford 82 D5
Hints 44 B3
Hobble End 25 G6
Hockley 46 C8
Hockley 152 F1
Hockley Heath 175 H7
Hodgehill 91 H8
Hoggrill's End 76 D8
Holbeache 136 E2
Holbrooks 134 A2
Holly Bank 40 F2
Hollyberry End 132 B1
Hollyhurst 117 J5
Hollywood 146 F5
Holt End 195 K6
Holy Cross 141 J3
Honiley 178 B8
Hoobrook 164 D3
Hook End 129 M8
Hopwas 30 E6
Hopwood 171 G2
Horeston Grange 81 L8
Horsley Heath 68 A3
Howe Green 97 H8
Hunnington 121 M6
Hunt End 202 A8
Huntington 12 B7
Hunts Green 58 C5
Hurcott 139 G5
Hurley 61 G8
Hurley Common 60 F6
Hurst Green 104 D5
Hurst Hill 66 D5
Illey 122 C5
Illshaw Heath 174 B4
Inkford 172 E4
Ipsley 203 G4
Iverley 119 H5
Kates Hill 85 J4
Kendal End 170 B3
Kenilworth 197 J2
Keresley 133 K1
Keresley Newlands ..115 M7
Kettlebrook 45 M2
Kidderminster 164 A4
Kineton Green 127 H5
Kingsbury 60 B7
King's Heath 125 J6
King's Hill 68 D2
Kings Hill 180 F3
Kingshurst 92 E6
King's Newnham 159 G6
King's Norton 145 J3
Kingstanding 71 L4
Kingswinford 82 F7
Kinwalsey 113 K6
Kirby Corner 153 L7
Kitt's Green 110 A1
Kitwell 122 E6
Knowle 150 A7
Knowle Grove 175 M2
The Knowle 85 L8
The Laches 22 D7
Ladies Hill 179 L7
Ladywood 106 E3
Lakeside 202 E2
The Lakes 162 C1
Lambert's End 86 E2
Landywood 24 C3
Lane Green 35 G2
Lane Head 38 A7
Lanesfield 66 E1
Laney Green 23 L3
Langley 86 D8
Langley Green 104 F1
Lapal 122 D2
Lawford Heath 185 H6
Lawns Wood 100 F2
Lea End 171 K2
Lea Hall 109 L3
Lea Marston 75 L6
Leamore 38 E7
Leapgate 164 E3
Lea Bank 6 C9
Lee Wootton 197 J7
Leighswood 40 E5
Leomansley 20 C6
Leyfields 31 K7
Ley Hill 56 E4
The Leys 31 L8
Lichfield 20 D5
Lickey 169 L2
Lickey End 169 H7
Lickhill 163 J8
Lifford 145 M1
Lillington 207 H2
Lime Tree Park 153 L4
Lincomb 189 C7
Linthurst 169 M7
Little Aston 42 A8
Little Bloxwich 39 H2
Little Bromwich 108 D3
Little Hay 43 G3
Little Heath 134 D4
Little Lawford 159 L6
Little Norton 25 M3
Little Packington 111 M7
Little Saredon 23 H2
Littlewood 24 B1
Littleworth 17 K1
Littleworth End 58 A5
Little Wyrley 25 H5

Lode Heath 128
Lodge Green 131
Lodge Hill 123
Lodge Park 202
Londonderry 105
London Fields 84
Long Bank 162
Longbridge 144
Longford 134
Long Lawford 159
Lower Bentley 200
Lower Bradley 67
Lower Clent 141
Lower Eastern Green .153
Lower Gornal 84
Lower Heath 188
Lower Illey 121
Lower Penn 48
Lower Stoke 155
Lower Stonnall 41
Low Habberley 137
Low Hill 36
Lozells 89
The Lunt 51
Lutley 120
Lydiate Ash 169
Lye 103
Lyndon Green 109
Lynn 27
Madeley Heath 142
Major's Green 147
Mancetter 63
Maney 72
Manor House 135
Mappleborough Green ..203
Marlbrook 169
Marston 75
Marston 158
Marston Green 108
Marston Jabbett 99
Matchborough 203
Maw Green 53
Maxstoke 112
Mayer's Green 87
Meer End 178
Mere Green 56
Meriden 131
Merridale 49
Merry Hill 49
Merry Hill 102
Mesty Croft 52
Middle Bickenhill 129
Middle Hill 23
Middle Stoke 155
Middleton 58
Mile Oak 45
Mill Green 41
Milverton 206
Minworth 74
Monkspath 148
Monmore Green 50
Monwode Lea 95
Moon's Moat 203
Moor Hall 57
Moseley 50
Moseley 125
Mount Pleasant 116
Mount Pleasant 201
Moxley 67
Muckley Corner 27
Mushroom Green ...102
Mustow Green 165
Myton 206
Neal's Green 116
Nechells 90
Nechells Green 107
Nether Stowe 21
Netherton 84
Nether Whitacre 76
New Arley 96
New Bilton 186
Newbold on Avon ..160
Newbolds 36
Newbridge 49
Newhall Green 113
New Invention 38
New Oscott 72
Newton 70
Newton 161
Newtown 24
New Town 26
New Town 86
Newtown 89
Norchard 189
Northfield 144
Norton 119
Norton Canes 17
Norton East 17
Norton Green 25
Norton Green 175
Nuneaton 98
Oaken 34
Oakenshaw 202
Oakham 85
Ocker Hill 68
Old Arley 96
Oldbury 79
Oldbury 86
Old Fallings 36
Oldfallow 16
Old Hill 103
Old Milverton 205
Old Perton 48
Old Swinford 119
Oldwich Lane 177
Olton 127
Orton 64
Orton Hill 64
Otherton 15
Ounsdale 64
Outwood 166
Outwoods 112
Overend 103
Over Green 74
Overslade 186
Over Whitacre 95
Oxbarn 49
Oxley 35

Packmores 205
Packwood 175
Packwood Gullet 175
Palfrey 54
Palmers Cross 34
Park End 162
Park Farm 202
Parkfield 39
Park Gate 190
Park Hill 180
Park Village 36
Pedmore 120
Pelsall 39
Pelsall Wood 39
Pendeford 35
Penkridge 10
Penn 49
Pensnett 84
Perry Barr 70
Perry Beeches 70

...y Common ...71 M5	Russell's Hall ...84 C5	Stivichall ...155 G8	Trysull ...64 A4	Whitemoor ...179 L8
...y Crofts ...32 A6	Ryton-on-Dunsmore ...182 F3	Stockfield ...127 G1	Tudor Hill ...56 E7	Whitestone ...99 K5
...yfields ...191 H1	St Godwalds ...192 A6	Stockingford ...97 M3	Turves Green ...144 E2	Whitley ...155 K7
...ton ...48 C1	St Helena ...47 K4	Stockland Green ...90 A1	Tutnall ...192 E4	Whitlock's End ...147 J7
...asey ...71 G1	St Johns ...197 K3	Stockwell End ...35 G8	Two Gates ...46 A5	Whitmore Park ...133 M4
...adilly ...60 D5	St Nicolas Park ...81 L6	Stoke ...156 A3	Tyburn ...91 J2	Whittington ...63 G2
...ford ...132 C5	Salter Street ...174 A3	Stoke Aldermoor ...156 A5	Tyseley ...108 E8	Whittington ...118 A3
...ford Green ...132 B6	Saltley ...108 C1	Stoke End ...58 D6	Ulverley Green ...127 J5	Whoberley ...154 A3
...ton ...11 G6	Sandfields ...20 F8	Stoke Heath ...134 E7	Upper Bentley ...200 F4	Wigginton ...31 M3
...ett's Booth ...132 B5	Sandwell ...87 L7	Stoke Heath ...191 H8	Upper Catshill ...168 F4	Wightwick ...48 C6
...Green ...195 M5	Scotlands ...36 E5	Stone ...165 H2	Upper Eastern Green ...132 A7	Wilden ...168 B7
...155 L6	Seckington ...33 L2	Stonebridge ...129 M3	Upper Gambolds ...192 A8	Wildmoor ...168 D1
...19 M8	Sedgemere ...177 J1	Stone Cross ...69 H4	Upper Gornal ...66 C7	Willenhall ...51 M2
...hill ...52 F7	Sedgley ...66 C5	Stoneleigh ...181 G7	Upper Landywood ...24 C6	Willenhall ...156 A7
...gh Hill ...79 L6	Selly Oak ...124 B4	Stoneydelph ...46 F4	Upper Stoke ...134 F8	Wilnecote ...46 D6
...moor ...165 J8	Selly Park ...124 E4	Stoney Hill ...191 L4	Upper Witton ...72 A7	Wimblebury ...17 K2
...esworth ...47 L4	Shard End ...92 B8	Stonnall ...41 H1	Vauxhall ...107 M2	Windy Arbour ...197 L2
...obello ...51 J3	Shareshill ...23 H3	Stourbridge ...119 H1	Vigo ...40 D3	Winson Green ...88 C8
...way ...86 A7	Sharmans Cross ...148 C1	Stourport-on-Severn ...188 C2	The Village ...83 J6	Winterfold ...165 M4
...tway ...172 E7	Sheldon ...109 M8	Stourton ...100 D6	Wake Green ...125 L4	Winyates ...203 J2
...er's Green ...135 K4	Shelfield ...40 A5	Stow ...21 G4	Walker's Heath ...145 M4	Winyates Green ...203 K1
...stwood ...100 C4	Shenley Fields ...123 J6	Stow Lawn ...51 H5	Walkwood ...201 L7	Wishaw ...74 E3
...stfield ...50 F7	Shenstone ...28 D8	The Straits ...65 M8	Wall ...28 B3	Witherley ...35 M6
...rose Hill ...103 H1	Shenstone ...165 K6	Streethay ...21 L3	Wallbrook ...67 G6	Withymoor Green ...170 C2
...ces End ...65 J4	Shenstone Woodend ...42 E4	Streetly ...55 M4	Wall Heath ...82 F5	Withymoor Village ...102 C4
...pect Village ...17 M1	Shire Oak ...26 D7	Stretton-on-Dunsmore ...183 L8	Wallington Heath ...38 E2	Witton ...89 J2
...Green ...12 D4	Shire Oak Hill ...26 F8	Stubber's Green ...40 C5	Walmley ...73 K5	Wollaston ...101 J1
...e Hayes ...73 H8	Shirley ...148 A2	Summerfield ...164 E6	Walmley Ash ...73 M6	Wollescote ...120 C1
...rry Bank ...102 D5	Shirley Heath ...148 A4	Summerfield ...27 J4	Walsal End ...150 E2	Wolston ...183 M2
...rry Heath ...11 G5	Short Cross ...121 L1	Summer Hill ...67 L4	Walsall ...5 G7	Wolverhampton ...3 J4
...rry Hill ...46 E7	Short Heath ...38 C7	Summerhill ...137 L8	Walsall Wood ...40 D1	Wolverley ...138 C1
...slett ...71 G3	Short Heath ...72 D7	Sutton Coldfield ...57 H8	Walsgrave on Sowe ...135 M6	Wombourne ...64 B7
...nton ...104 E7	Shustoke ...94 D3	Swan Village ...66 D7	The Walshes ...188 E6	Woodcock Hill ...123 J5
...ford ...134 A7	Shuttington ...33 J6	Swindon ...82 D3	Walton Pool ...141 L5	Woodcote ...37 J6
...ford Semele ...207 H4	Sidemoor ...191 K1	Sydenham ...207 G8	Ward End ...90 E8	Woodcote Green ...167 G2
...cliffe Culey ...63 M1	Silver End ...101 M4	Tamworth ...31 M7	Waresley ...189 K5	Wood End ...37 G6
...insley ...13 M8	Silver Street ...146 C8	Tanner's Green ...172 F3	Waring's Green ...174 A4	Wood End ...61 H4
...dican Heath ...73 L1	Slade Heath ...22 C3	Tansley Hill ...85 K6	Warley Woods ...105 J4	Wood End ...96 F8
...dditch ...202 A3	Slideslow ...192 A3	Tanwood ...166 E3	Warstock ...147 G2	Wood End ...135 G3
...nal ...144 A8	Small Heath ...108 A5	Tardebigge ...192 E6	Warstone ...23 M5	Woodgate ...122 D4
...ves Green ...152 E5	Smallwood ...202 D2	Tat Bank ...86 E6	Warwick ...205 L7	Woodgate Valley ...123 G2
...esford ...162 F4	Smestow ...82 A1	Temple Balsall ...176 F1	Washford ...203 J5	Wood Green ...52 E8
...acre ...105 G7	Smethwick ...87 J8	Ten Acres ...124 F5	Washwood Heath ...90 C7	Wood Hayes ...36 F4
...ge Lane ...78 E3	Soho ...88 A7	Terry's Green ...173 K6	Waste Green ...196 A6	Wood Hill ...157 M1
...erside ...194 C7	Solihull ...149 G3	Tettenhall ...55 G8	Water Orton ...92 F2	Woodhouses ...19 L6
...inson's End ...97 J1	Solihull Lodge ...147 G3	Tettenhall Wood ...49 H1	Watford Gap ...42 D6	Woodloes Park ...205 H4
...baston ...14 B1	South Yardley ...109 H7	Thimble End ...73 L4	Weatheroak Hill ...171 M4	Woodrow ...166 B2
...nsley ...142 E1	Sparkbrook ...107 M6	Thornes ...41 J2	Webheath ...201 J4	Woodrow ...202 F6
...nsley Hill ...142 E3	Sparkhill ...126 A2	Three Maypoles ...147 M6	Weddington ...81 G5	Woods Bank ...52 B8
...nd End ...87 G7	Spon End ...8 B5	Tidbury Green ...173 J1	Wednesbury ...68 B3	Woodsetton ...66 C6
...eville ...66 E5	Springfield ...3 K2	Tile Cross ...110 C3	Wednesbury Oak ...67 K4	Woodside ...84 D7
...ten Row ...176 A1	Springfield ...85 K8	Tile Hill ...153 J4	Wednesfield ...37 H7	The Woods ...69 G1
...ton Park ...106 C1	Springfield ...126 A4	Tilehouse Green ...149 L8	Weeford ...43 L1	Woodway Park ...135 J5
...ghley ...57 G2	Springhill ...24 B8	Timberhonger ...190 C4	Weoley Castle ...123 K4	Wootton Green ...151 K4
...nd Oak ...102 C1	Springhill ...27 H6	Tipper's Hill ...96 C7	Wergs ...34 D7	Wordsley ...101 J2
...nd's Green ...86 C5	Spring Hill ...65 G1	Tipton ...67 L6	West Bromwich ...86 F4	Worlds End ...127 L6
...vley Regis ...85 M8	The Spring ...179 K6	Tipton Green ...67 H7	West Chadsmoor ...12 D7	Worms Ash ...168 B7
...vley's Green ...134 C1	Stakenbridge ...140 B2	Titton ...189 H5	Westcroft ...36 F2	Wribbenhall ...163 G1
...vney Green ...171 K8	Stambermill ...102 A8	Tividale ...85 M4	West Hagley ...119 M8	Wyken ...135 H8
...val Leamington Spa ...206 F4	Standeford ...22 A1	Tollbar End ...156 B8	West Heath ...145 G6	Wylde Green ...73 H4
...ery ...143 L6	Stanklyn ...165 H3	Toll End ...67 M7	West Hill ...12 E7	Wythall ...172 C3
...gby ...186 C3	Staple Hill ...169 G5	Torton ...164 F8	Weston in Arden ...117 M1	Yardley ...109 H5
...ton ...84 B1	Stareton ...199 H2	Tower Hill ...70 E7	Westwood Heath ...153 J2	Yardley Wood ...147 J1
...mbow Cottages ...142 B2	Stechford ...109 J2	Trescott ...48 A7	Whateley ...60 C2	Yew Tree ...69 M2
...mbush ...173 J2	Stirchley ...124 E6	Triangle ...26 F1	Whitacre Heath ...76 A7	
...ner Hill ...16 C5		Trimpley ...136 F4	Whiteheath Gate ...104 C1	
...shall ...40 A6		Trueman's Heath ...147 G6	Whitehouse Common ...57 K7	

...SING THE STREET INDEX

...eet names are listed alphabetically. Each street name is followed by its postal town or area locality, the Postcode District,
...page number, and the reference to the square in which the name is found.

...ndard index entries are shown as follows:

...erley Av *STRPT* DY13 ....**188** B5

...eet names and selected addresses not shown on the map due to scale restrictions are shown in the index with an asterisk:

...ey Cottages *COVS* CV3 * **156** D6

...ENERAL ABBREVIATIONS

...ACCESS	CTYD ...COURTYARD	HLS ...HILLS	MWY ...MOTORWAY	SE ...SOUTH EAST
...ALLEY	CUTT ...CUTTINGS	HO ...HOUSE	N ...NORTH	SER ...SERVICE AREA
...APPROACH	CV ...COVE	HOL ...HOLLOW	NE ...NORTH EAST	SH ...SHORE
...ARCADE	CYN ...CANYON	HOSP ...HOSPITAL	NW ...NORTH WEST	SHOP ...SHOPPING
...ASSOCIATION	DEPT ...DEPARTMENT	HRB ...HARBOUR	O/P ...OVERPASS	SKWY ...SKYWAY
...AVENUE	DL ...DALE	HTH ...HEATH	OFF ...OFFICE	SMT ...SUMMIT
...BEACH	DM ...DAM	HTS ...HEIGHTS	ORCH ...ORCHARD	SOC ...SOCIETY
...BUILDINGS	DR ...DRIVE	HVN ...HAVEN	OV ...OVAL	SP ...SPUR
...BEND	DRO ...DROVE	HWY ...HIGHWAY	PAL ...PALACE	SPR ...SPRING
...BANK	DRY ...DRIVEWAY	IMP ...IMPERIAL	PAS ...PASSAGE	SQ ...SQUARE
...BRIDGE	DWGS ...DWELLINGS	IN ...INLET	PAV ...PAVILION	ST ...STREET
...BROOK	E ...EAST	IND EST ...INDUSTRIAL ESTATE	PDE ...PARADE	STN ...STATION
...BOTTOM	EMB ...EMBANKMENT	INF ...INFIRMARY	PH ...PUBLIC HOUSE	STR ...STREAM
...BUSINESS	EMBY ...EMBASSY	INFO ...INFORMATION	PK ...PARK	STRD ...STRAND
...BOULEVARD	ESP ...ESPLANADE	INT ...INTERCHANGE	PKWY ...PARKWAY	SW ...SOUTH WEST
...BYPASS	EST ...ESTATE	IS ...ISLAND	PL ...PLACE	TDG ...TRADING
...CATHEDRAL	EX ...EXCHANGE	JCT ...JUNCTION	PLN ...PLAIN	TER ...TERRACE
...CEMETERY	EXPY ...EXPRESSWAY	JTY ...JETTY	PLNS ...PLAINS	THWY ...THROUGHWAY
...CENTRE	EXT ...EXTENSION	KG ...KING	PLZ ...PLAZA	TNL ...TUNNEL
...CROFT	F/O ...FLYOVER	KNL ...KNOLL	POL ...POLICE STATION	TOLL ...TOLLWAY
...CHURCH	FC ...FOOTBALL CLUB	L ...LAKE	PR ...PRINCE	TPK ...TURNPIKE
...CHASE	FK ...FORK	LA ...LANE	PREC ...PRECINCT	TR ...TRACK
...CHURCHYARD	FLD ...FIELD	LDG ...LODGE	PREP ...PREPARATORY	TRL ...TRAIL
...CIRCLE	FLDS ...FIELDS	LGT ...LIGHT	PRIM ...PRIMARY	TWR ...TOWER
...CIRCUS	FLS ...FALLS	LK ...LOCK	PROM ...PROMENADE	U/P ...UNDERPASS
...CLOSE	FLS ...FLATS	LKS ...LAKES	PRS ...PRINCESS	UNI ...UNIVERSITY
...CLIFFS	FM ...FARM	LNDG ...LANDING	PRT ...PORT	UPR ...UPPER
...CAMP	FT ...FORT	LTL ...LITTLE	PT ...POINT	V ...VALE
...CORNER	FWY ...FREEWAY	LWR ...LOWER	PTH ...PATH	VA ...VALLEY
...COUNTY	FY ...FERRY	MAG ...MAGISTRATE	PZ ...PIAZZA	VIAD ...VIADUCT
...COLLEGE	GA ...GATE	MAN ...MANSIONS	QD ...QUADRANT	VIL ...VILLA
...COMMON	GAL ...GALLERY	MD ...MEAD	QU ...QUEEN	VIS ...VISTA
...COMMISSION	GDN ...GARDEN	MDW ...MEADOWS	QY ...QUAY	VLG ...VILLAGE
...CONVENT	GDNS ...GARDENS	MEM ...MEMORIAL	R ...RIVER	VLS ...VILLAS
...COTTAGE	GLD ...GLADE	MKT ...MARKET	RBT ...ROUNDABOUT	VW ...VIEW
...COTTAGES	GLN ...GLEN	MKTS ...MARKETS	RD ...ROAD	W ...WEST
...CAPE	GN ...GREEN	ML ...MALL	RDG ...RIDGE	WD ...WOOD
...COPSE	GND ...GROUND	ML ...MILL	REP ...REPUBLIC	WHF ...WHARF
...CREEK	GRA ...GRANGE	MNR ...MANOR	RES ...RESERVOIR	WK ...WALK
...CREMATORIUM	GRG ...GARAGE	MS ...MEWS	RFC ...RUGBY FOOTBALL CLUB	WKS ...WALKS
...CRESCENT	GT ...GREAT	MSN ...MISSION	RI ...RISE	WLS ...WELLS
...CAUSEWAY	GTWY ...GATEWAY	MT ...MOUNT	RP ...RAMP	WY ...WAY
...COURT	GV ...GROVE	MTN ...MOUNTAIN	RW ...ROW	YD ...YARD
...CENTRAL	HGR ...HIGHER	MTS ...MOUNTAINS	S ...SOUTH	YHA ...YOUTH HOSTEL
...COURTS	HL ...HILL	MUS ...MUSEUM	SCH ...SCHOOL	

POSTCODE TOWNS AND AREA ABBREVIATIONS

ACGN ....Acock's Green
ALDR ....Aldridge
ALE/KHTH/YWD ....Alcester Lane's End/
    King's Heath/Yardley Wood
ALVE ....Alvechurch
AST/WIT ....Aston/Witton
ATHST ....Atherstone
BDMR/CCFT ......Bradmore/Castlecroft
BDWTH ....Bedworth
BEWD ....Bewdley
BFLD/HDSWWD ....Birchfield/
    Handsworth Wood
BHAMNEC ....Birmingham N.E.C.
BHTH/HG ....Balsall Heath/Highgate
BILS/COS ....Bilston/Coseley
BKDE/SHDE....Buckland End/Shard End
BKHL/PFLD ...Blakenhall/Priestfield
BLKHTH/ROWR ....Blackheath/
    Rowley Regis
BLOX/PEL ....Bloxwich/Pelsall
BNTWD ....Burntwood
BORD ....Bordesley
BRGRVE ....Bromsgrove east
BRGRVW ....Bromsgrove west
BRLYHL ....Brierley Hill
BRWNH ....Brownhills
BTACH/HAR ....Bishop's Tachbrook/
    Harbury
BVILLE ....Bournville
CBHAM ....Central Birmingham
CBHAMNE ......Central Birmingham
    northeast
CBHAMNW ......Central Birmingham
    northwest

CBHAMW .....Central Birmingham west
CBROM ....Castle Bromwich
CDSL ....Codsall
CDYHTH ....Cradley Heath
CHWD/FDBR/MGN ...Chelmsley Wood/
    Fordbridge/Marston Green
CNCK/NC ....Cannock/Norton Canes
COV ....Coventry
COVE ....Coventry east
COVEN ....Coven
COVN ....Coventry north
COVS ....Coventry south
COVW ....Coventry west
CRTAM ....Central & Rural Tamworth
CSCFLD/WYGN ....Central Sutton
    Coldfield/Wylde Green
CSHL/WTROR ..Coleshill/Water Orton
CVALE ....Castle Vale
DARL/WED ....Darlaston/Wednesbury
DIG/EDG ....Digbeth/Edgbaston
DOR/KN ....Dorridge/Knowle
DROIT ....Droitwich
DSYBK/YTR ...Daisy Bank/Yew Tree
DUDN ....Dudley north
DUDS ....Dudley south
DUNHL/THL/PER ....Dunstall Hill/
    Tettenhall/Perton
EDG ....Edgbaston
ERDE/BCHGN ....Erdington east/
    Birches Green
ERDW/GRVHL ......Erdington west/
    Gravelly Hill
ETTPK/GDPK/PENN ..Ettingshall Park/
    Goldthorn Park/Penn

FOAKS/STRLY ......Four Oaks/Streetly
GTB/HAM ....Great Barr/Hamstead
GTWY ....Great Wyrley
HAG/WOL ....Hagley/Wollescote
HALE ....Halesowen
HDSW ....Handsworth
HEDN ....Hednesford
HHTH/SAND ...Hateley Heath/Sandwell
HIA/OLT ....Hampton in Arden/Olton
HLGN/YWD ...Hall Green/Yardley Wood
HLYWD ....Hollywood
HOCK/TIA ....Hockley Heath/
    Tanworth-in-Arden
HRBN ....Harborne
HWK/WKHTH ....Hawkesley/
    Walker's Heath
KGSTG ....Kingstanding
KGSWFD ....Kingswinford
KIDD ....Kidderminster
KIDDW ....Kidderminster west
KINVER ....Kinver
KNWTH ....Kenilworth
LDYWD/EDGR ....Ladywood/
    Edgbaston Reservoir
LGLGYN/QTN ..Langley Green/Quinton
LGN/SDN/BHAMAIR ...Lyndon Green/
    Sheldon/
    Birmingham Airport
LICH ....Lichfield
LICHS ....Lichfield south
LOZ/NWT ....Lozells/Newtown
LUTT ....Lutterworth
MGN/WHC ....Mere Green/
    Whitehouse Common

MKTBOS/BARL/STKG..Market Bosworth/
    Barlestone/Stoke Golding
MOS/BIL ....Moseley/Billesley
NFLD/LBR ....Northfield/Longbridge
NUN ....Nuneaton
NUNW/HART ....Nuneaton west/
    Hartshill
OLDBY ....Oldbury
PBAR/PBCH ..Perry Bar/Perry Beeches
PENK ....Penkridge
POL/KGSB/FAZ ....Polesworth/
    Kingsbury/Fazeley
RBRY ....Rubery
RCOVN/BALC/EX ...Rural Coventry
    north/Baisall Common/Exhall
REDE ....Redditch east
REDW ....Redditch west
RIDG/WDGT ...Ridgacre/Woodgate
RLSN ....Royal Leamington Spa north
RLSS ....Royal Leamington Spa south
RMSLY ....Romsley
RRUGBY ....Rural Rugby
RSTAF ....Rural Stafford
RUGBYN/HIL ....Rugby north/
    Hillmorton
RUGBYS/DCH ....Rugby south/
    Dunchurch
RUGE ....Rugeley
RUSH/SHEL ....Rushall/Shelfield
RWWCK/WEL ...Rural Warwick/
    Wellesbourne
SCFLD/BOLD ....Sutton Coldfield/
    Boldmere
SEDG ....Sedgley

SHHTH ....Short H
SHLY ....Selly
SLYOAK ....Selly
SMHTH ....Small H
SMTHWK ....Smeth
SMTHWKW ....Smethwick
SOLH ....So
SPARK ....Sparkhill/Sparkb
STAFS ....Stafford s
STETCH ....Stetch
STRBR ....Stourbr
STRPT ....Stourport-on-Se
STUD ....Stu
TAM/AM/WIL ....Tamwo
    Amington/Wilne
TLHL/CAN ....Tile Hill/Ca
TPTN/OCK ....Tipton/Ocke
VAUX/NECH ...Walmley/Nec
WALM/CURD ...Walmley/Curdw
WASH/WDE ...Washwood He
    Warc
WBROM ....West Brom
WLNHL ....Willie
WMBN ....Wombo
WNSFLD ....Wednes
WOLV ....Wolverham
WOLVN ......Wolverhampton r
WSL ....Walsall
WSNGN ....Winson G
WWCK ....War
YDLY ....Ya

Index - streets   Aar - Alf

A

Aaron Manby Ct
  TPTN/OCK DY4 * 67 K5
Abberley Av *STRPT* DY13 ....188 B5
Abberley Cl *HALE* B63 ....121 K3
  REDE B98 ....195 G8
Abberley Rd *LGLYGN/QTN* B68 ..104 F5
  SEDG DY3 ....84 A1
Abberley St *DUDS* DY2 ....85 G5
  SMTHWK B66 ....88 B8
Abberton Cl *HALE* B63 ....122 A2
Abberton Gv *SOLH* B91 ....148 F6
Abberton Wy *TLHL/CAN* CV4 ..180 B2
Abbess Gv *YDLY* B25 ....109 J4
Abbey Cl *BRGRVE* B60 ....191 M3
  HHTH/SAND B71 ....68 F8
Abbey Cottages *COVS* CV3 * ..156 D6
Abbey Crs *HALE* B63 ....121 H1
  LGLYGN/QTN B68 ....105 H4
Abbey Cft *POL/KGSB/FAZ* B78 ..47 L3
Abbeydale Cl *COVS* CV3 ....156 D2
Abbeydale Rd *NFLD/LBR* B31 ..144 E3
Abbey Dr *BLOX/PEL* WS3 ....25 L8
Abbey End *KNWTH* CV8 ....197 K1
Abbeyfield Rd *ERDW/GRVHL* B23..72 C5
  WOLVN WV10 ....36 C1
Abbeyfields Dr *STUD* B80 ....203 J6
Abbeygate *NUN* CV11 * 99 C1
Abbey Gn *NUN* CV11 * 80 F8
Abbey Green Ct
  POL/KGSB/FAZ B78 ....47 L4
Abbey Hl *KNWTH* CV8 ....197 K1
Abbey Rd *COVS* CV3 ....155 K7
  DUDS DY2 ....85 H7
  ERDW/GRVHL B23 ....90 B3
  HALE B63 ....121 C1
  HRBN B17 ....106 B8
  KIDDW DY11 ....137 L7
  REDW B97 ....202 C1
  SEDG DY3 ....84 A2
  SMTHWK B67 ....105 H4
  TAM/AM/WIL B77 ....46 B2
Abbey Sq *BLOX/PEL* WS3 ....38 C3
Abbey St *HEDN* WS12 ....12 F6
  NUN CV11 ....80 F8
  RUGBYN/HIL CV21 ....187 G1
  SEDG DY3 ....84 A2
  WSNGN B18 ....88 E8
Abbey St North *WSNGN* B18 ......88 E8
Abbey Vw *POL/KGSB/FAZ* B78 ..47 M5
Abbey Wy *COVS* CV3..................155 K7
  RUSH/SHEL WS4 ....40 A7
Abbots Fld *CNCK/NC* WS11 ....12 C8
Abbotsford Av *POL/KGSB/FAZ* B78..45 L3
Abbotsford Dr *DUDN* DY1 ....84 C4
Abbotsford Rd *LICHS* WS14 ....21 H6
  NUN CV11 ....99 J4
  RLSS CV31 ....206 D6
Abbots Ms *BRLYHL* DY5 ....102 B4
Abbots Rd *ALE/KHTH/YWD* B14..125 J6
Abbots Wy *BDMR/CCFT* WV3 ......49 J4
  WSNGN B18 ....88 F7
  WWCK CV34 ....205 H7
Abbots Wood Cl *REDE* B98 ......203 L2
Abbotts Cl *STRPT* DY13 ....164 B7
Abbotts Fld *CNCK/NC* WS11 ......12 C8
Abbotts La *COV* CV1 * 8 A7
Abbotts Rd *ERDE/BCHGN* B24..90 D4
Abbotts St *BLOX/PEL* WS3 ....39 H3
  RLSS CV31 ....206 D6
Abbotts Wk *COVS* CV3 ....157 G6
Abbotts Wy *RUGBYN/HIL* CV21..187 K4
Abdon Cl *SLYOAK* B29 ....123 M6
Abeles Wy *ATHST* CV9 ....63 G3
Abelia *TAM/AM/WIL* B77 ....46 C2
Abercorn Cl *COVW* CV5 ....154 D3
Aberdeen Cl *COVW* CV5 ....132 B3
Aberdeen Rd *NUN* CV11 ....99 J4
Aberdeen St *WSNGN* B18 ....106 C1
Aberford Cl *WNSFLD* WV11 ....52 B1
Abergavenny Wk *COVS* CV3 ....156 D3
Abigails Cl
  LGN/SDN/BHAMAIR B26 ....109 M6
Abingdon Cl *WOLV* WV1 ....50 F3
Abingdon Rd *BLOX/PEL* WS3 ......38 D3
  DUDS DY2 ....103 H2
  ERDW/GRVHL B23 ....72 A3
  WOLV WV1 ....50 F3
Abingdon Wy *BLOX/PEL* WS3 ......38 D3
  CVALE B35 ....91 L2
  NUN CV11 ....81 K6
Ablewell St *WSL* WS1 ....5 G4

Ablow St *BKHL/PFLD* WV2 ....2 B8
Abnalls Cft *LICH* WS13 ....20 D4
Abnalls La *LICH* WS13 ....20 A5
Abney Dr *BILS/COS* WV14 ....66 D4
Aboyne Cl *DIG/EDG* B5 ....107 H7
Ab Rw *CBHAMNE* B4 ....7 K3
Acacia Av *BEWD* DY12 ....163 G2
  CHWD/FDBR/MGN B37 ....92 D7
  COV CV3 ....9 J7
  DSYBK/YTR WS5..........................69 L1
Acacia Cl *CHWD/FDBR/MGN* B37..92 D7
  DUDN DY1 ....84 E2
  OLDBY B69 ....85 M3
Acacia Crs *BDWTH* CV12 ....117 H2
  CDSL WV8 ....34 C2
Acacia Dr *BILS/COS* WV14 ....66 E6
Acacia Gv *HEDN* WS12 ....17 K2
  RUGBYN/HIL CV21 ....186 E1
Acacia Rd *BVILLE* B30 ....124 C5
  COV CV5 ....8 A1
  RLSN CV32 ....206 A6
Acanthus Rd *REDE* B98 ....195 K7
Acfold Rd *BFLD/HDSWWD* B20 ..70 C8
Achal Cl *COVN* CV6 ....134 D3
Acheson Rd *HLGN/YWD* B28 ....147 K2
Achilees Cl *GTWY* WS6 ....24 C3
Achilles Rd *COVN* CV6 ....134 D4
Ackleton Gdns *BDMR/CCFT* WV3..49 K6
Ackleton Gv *SLYOAK* B29 ....123 K5
Acorn Cl *ACGN* B27 * 108 F3
  BDWTH CV12 ....116 A5
  BNTWD WS7 ....18 E4
  BVILLE B30 ....124 C5
  CNCK/NC WS11 ....17 C3
  GTWY WS6 ....24 E4
  KNWTH CV8 ....180 F6
  WBROM B70 ....86 F3
Acorn Dr *RUGBYS/DCH* CV22 ..185 M4
Acorn Gdns *SLYOAK* B29 ....124 C5
Acorn Gv *CBHAMW* B1 ....6 A4
  CDSL WV8 ....34 C3
  STRBR DY8 ....101 J4
Acorn Rd *BRGRVW* B61 ....168 E5
  RMSLY B62 ....104 A5
  WNSFLD WV11 ....37 L4
The Acorns *BRGRVW* B61 ....168 E5
Acorn St *COVS* CV3 ....155 M5
  WLNHL WV13 ....52 A3
Acre La *REDW* B97 ....201 J3
Acre Ri *SHHTH* WV12 ....37 M8
Acres Rd *BRLYHL* DY5 ....102 C5
Acton Cl *REDE* B98 ....195 H8
Acton Dr *SEDG* DY3 ....83 M2
Acton Gv *BILS/COS* WV14 ....66 F1
  KGSTG B44 ....71 L3
Ada Lewis Ct *GTB/HAM* B43 ......70 C6
Adam Rd *COVN* CV6 ....134 D6
Adams Brook Dr
  RIDG/WDGT B32 ....122 F4
Adams St *SMTHWK* B66 ....87 H6
  TPTN/OCK DY4 ....67 K4
Adams Ct *KIDD* DY10 ....138 E6
Adam's Hi *HAG/WOL* DY9 ....141 J7
  RIDG/WDGT B32 ....122 F4
Adamson Cl *CNCK/NC* WS11 ......15 M4
Adams Rd *BDMR/CCFT* WV3 ......49 G6
  BRWNH WS8 ....26 B8
Adams St *RUGBYN/HIL* CV21 ..186 C2
  VAUX/NECH B7 * 7 K1
  WBROM B70 ....86 E2
  WSL WS2 ....4 C2
Adam St *KIDDW* DY11 ....138 A3
Adare Dr *COVS* CV3 ....155 G7
Ada Rd *HEDN* WS12 ....17 J2
Ada Wrighton Cl *SHHTH* WV12 ..38 A6
Adcock Dr *KNWTH* CV8 ....178 F1
Addenbrooke Crs *KIDDW* DY11..163 L4
Addenbrooke Dr
  SCFLD/BOLD B73 ....72 F3
Addenbrooke Rd
  RCOVN/BALC/EX CV7 ....115 L6
  SMTHWK B67 ....105 K2
Addenbrooke St *BLOX/PEL* WS3..39 G6
  DARL/WED WS10 ....52 B5
Addenbrook Wy *TPTN/OCK* DY4..68 C5
Adderley Park Cl
  WASH/WDE B8 * 108 C1
Adderley Rd *WASH/WDE* B8 ......108 A2
Adderley Rd South
  WASH/WDE B8 ....108 A2
Adderley St *BORD* B9 ....7 L7
  COV CV1 ....9 K1
Addingham Cl *WWCK* CV34 ......205 H5
Addison Cl *CNCK/NC* WS11 ....12 C8
  DARL/WED WS10 ....68 D1
  NUNW/HART CV10 ....79 K8
Addison Gdns *SEDG* DY3 ....65 L8
Addison Gv *WNSFLD* WV11 ....36 F4

Addison Pl *BILS/COS* WV14 ....51 K6
  CSHL/WTROR B46 ....92 F2
Addison Rd
  ALE/KHTH/YWD B14 ....125 K6
  BDMR/CCFT WV3 ....49 K5
  BRLYHL DY5 ....101 M3
  COVN CV6 ....133 L5
  DARL/WED WS10 ....69 J3
  RUGBYS/DCH CV22 ....186 B3
Addison St *DARL/WED* WS10 ......68 D3
Addison Ter *DARL/WED* WS10 * ..68 D3
Adelaide Av *WBROM* B70 ....68 K6
Adelaide Dr *HEDN* WS12 ....17 K2
Adelaide Rd *RLSN* CV32 ....206 C5
Adelaide St *BHTH/HG* B12 ....7 J9
  BRLYHL DY5 ....102 B2
  COV CV1 ....9 J1
  REDW B97 ....202 B1
Adelaide Wk *BKHL/PFLD* WV2 ......3 J8
Adey Rd *WNSFLD* WV11 ....37 K5
Adkins Cft *RCOVN/BALC/EX* CV7..114 C2
Adkins La *SMTHWK* B67 ....105 K4
Admington Dr
  RWWCK/WEL CV35 ....204 C3
Admington Rd *STETCH* B33 ......110 A5
Admiral Gdns *KNWTH* CV8 ......180 A7
Admiral Parker Dr *LICHS* WS14 ..28 D8
Admiral Pl *MOS/BIL* B13 ....125 K1
Admirals Wy
  BLKHTH/ROWR B65 ....103 M3
Adonis Cl *CRTAM* B79 ....32 A7
Adrian Cft *MOS/BIL* B13 ....126 A4
Adrians' Cft *ATHST* CV9 ....63 K7
Adria Rd *SPARK* B11 ....125 M1
Adshead Rd *DUDS* DY2 ....85 G6
Adstone Gv *NFLD/LBR* B31 ......144 D4
Adwalton Rd
  DUNHL/THL/PER WV6 ....48 D2
Affleck Av *POL/KGSB/FAZ* B78 ....45 H4
Agenoria Dr *STRBR* DY8 ....101 K8
Aggborough Crs *KIDD* DY10 ......164 C5
Agincourt Rd *COVS* CV3 ....155 J6
Agmore La *BRGRVE* B60 ....192 F2
Agmore Rd *BRGRVE* B60 ....192 E1
Ainsbury Rd *COVW* CV5 ....153 M2
Ainsdale Cl *COVN* CV6 ....134 F1
  STRBR DY8 ....119 K3
Ainsdale Gdns *HALE* B63 ....121 H3
Ainsworth Rd *WOLVN* WV10 ......36 C1
Aintree Cl *BDWTH* CV12 ....116 F1
  BRGRVW B61 ....168 E4
  COVN CV6 ....134 C8
  HEDN WS12 ....13 K7
  KIDDW DY11 ....138 B5
Aintree Dr *RLSN* CV32 ....207 J2
Aintree Gv *BKDE/SHDE* B34 ......92 B7
Aintree Rd *WOLVN* WV10 ....36 B1
Aintree Wy *DUDN* DY1 ....84 C3
Aire Cft *NFLD/LBR* B31 ....144 F4
Airfield Dr *ALDR* WS9 ....54 C2
Airport Wy *HIA/OLT* B92 ....129 H2
Aitken Cl *POL/KGSB/FAZ* B78 ....45 L3
Ajax Cl *GTWY* WS6 ....24 D4
Akdene Cl *GTWY* WS6 ....24 B3
Akrill Cl *WBROM* B70 * 86 E2
Alamein Rd *WLNHL* WV13 ....51 J4
Alandale Av *COVW* CV5 ....153 J1
Alan Higgs Wy *TLHL/CAN* CV4..153 G6
Alan Bray Cl *KIDD* DY10 ....138 F7
Albany Crs *BILS/COS* WV14 ....51 G7
Albany Dr *HEDN* WS12 ....17 J3
Albany Gdns *SOLH* B91 ....149 H1
Albany Gv *KGSWFD* DY6 ....83 K4
  SHHTH WV12 ....38 A4
Albany Rd *COVW* CV5 ....8 A8
  HRBN B17 ....106 A7
Albany Ter *RLSN* CV32 ....206 C4
Albemarle Rd *STRBR* DY8 ....119 K3
Albermarle Rd *KGSWFD* DY6 ....83 L8
Albert Av *BHTH/HG* B12 ....107 L7
Albert Clarke Dr *SHHTH* WV12 ..38 A4
Albert Cl *CDSL* WV8 ....34 C1
Albert Crs *COVN* CV6 ....133 M2
Albert Davie Dr *HEDN* WS12 ......17 J1
Albert Dr *HALE* B63 ....121 K3
  SEDG DY3 ....82 C2
Albert Fearn Gv *COVN* CV6 ......134 D4
Albert Rd *ALE/KHTH/YWD* B14 ..125 J6
  AST/WIT B6 ....88 F6
  BRGRVW B61 ....191 G5
  COVW CV5 ....131 L5
  CRTAM B79 ....31 M8
  ERDW/GRVHL B23 ....90 B2
  HALE B63 ....88 C4
  HDSW B21 ....88 C4
  HRBN B17 ....105 M8
  KIDD DY10 ....138 D7
  LGLYGN/QTN B68 ....105 G3
  POL/KGSB/FAZ B78 ....45 L5

STETCH B33 ....109 H2
  WOLV WV1 ....2 A2
Albert Sq *RUGBYN/HIL* CV21 ..186 F2
Albert St *BRLYHL* DY5 ....84 B6
  CBHAMNE B4 ....7 H5
  CNCK/NC WS11 ....16 D1
  COV CV1 ....9 J2
  DARL/WED WS10 ....68 C3
  HAG/WOL DY9 ....102 C8
  HEDN WS12 ....13 H8
  KGSWFD DY6 ....83 K5
  NUNW/HART CV10 ....98 C2
  REDE B98 ....194 D8
  RLSN CV32 ....206 A4
  RUGBYN/HIL CV21 ....186 E2
  STRBR DY8 ....101 K8
  TPTN/OCK DY4 ....67 K5
  WBROM B70 ....87 G4
  WSL WS1 ....4 F2
  WWCK CV34 ....205 H6
Albert St East *OLDBY* B69 ....86 F6
Albion Av *WLNHL* WV13 ....52 A3
Albion Field Dr *HHTH/SAND* B71..87 H1
Albion Pl *CNCK/NC* WS11 ....16 C5
Albion Rd *BRWNH* WS8 ....26 C5
  HHTH/SAND B71 ....87 L5
  SPARK B11 ....108 B8
  WBROM B70 ....86 D3
Albion St *BILS/COS* WV14 ....51 J7
  BRLYHL DY5 ....102 B2
  CBHAMW B1 ....6 B3
  CRTAM B79 ....32 A8
  KGSWFD DY6 ....82 F5
  KNWTH CV8 ....179 L8
  OLDBY B69 ....86 D4
  TPTN/OCK DY4 ....67 K8
  WLNHL WV13 ....51 M3
  WOLV WV1 ....3 H5
Alborn Crs *HWK/WKHTH* B38 ....145 H5
Albrighton Rd *HALE* B63 ....121 J2
Albrighton Wk *NUN* CV11 ....99 L3
Albright Rd *LGLYGN/QTN* B68 ..105 H1
Albury Wk *BHTH/HG* B12 ....107 L6
Albutts Rd *CNCK/NC* WS11 ....25 M2
Alcester Hwy *REDE* B98 ....202 D2
Alcester Rd *ALE/KHTH/YWD* B14..125 K2
  ALE/KHTH/YWD B14 ....146 D2
  BHTH/HG B12 ....125 K2
  REDW B97 ....202 C1
Alcombe Gv *STETCH* B33 ....109 J3
Alcott Cl *DOR/KN* B93 ....175 K3
Alcott Gv *STETCH* B33 ....110 B2
Alcott La
  CHWD/FDBR/MGN B37 ....110 D3
The Alcove *BLOX/PEL* WS3 ....39 H3
Aldbourne Cl *NUN* CV11 ....80 D7
Aldbourne Rd *COV* CV1 ....134 A8
Aldbourne Wy
  HWK/WKHTH B38 ....145 H6
Aldbury Ri *COVW* CV5 ....154 A1
Aldbury Rd *ALE/KHTH/YWD* B14..146 E3
Aldeburgh Cl *BLOX/PEL* WS3 ......38 E2
Aldeford Dr *BRLYHL* DY5 ....102 B3
Alden Hurst *BNTWD* WS7 ....18 D5
Alder Av *KIDDW* DY11 ....138 B5
Alderbrook Cl *REDW* B97 * 193 M8
  SEDG DY3 ....65 M4
Alderbrooke Dr *NUN* CV11 ....99 L4
Alderbrook Rd *SOLH* B91 ....148 C2
Alder Cl *HLYWD* B47 ....146 F7
  LICHS WS14 ....21 K6
  WALM/CURD B76 ....73 J6
Alder Coppice *SEDG* DY3 ....65 M4
Alder Crs *DSYBK/YTR* WS5 ....69 M1
Alder Dr *BDMR/CCFT* WV3 ....49 J4
Alderdale Av *SEDG* DY3 ....66 A2
Alderdale Crs *HIA/OLT* B92 ......148 F1
Alder Dr *CHWD/FDBR/MGN* B37..110 F4
Alderflat Pl *VAUX/NECH* B7 ....90 A4
Alderford Cl *CDSL* WV8 ....35 A5
Aldergate *CRTAM* B79 ....31 M8
Alder Gv *RMSLY* B62 ....104 C7
Alderham Cl *SOLH* B91 ....149 J2
Alderhithe Gv *FOAKS/STRLY* B74..55 M2
Alder La *NFLD/LBR* B31 ....124 A7
  RCOVN/BALC/EX CV7 ....114 E3
Alderlea Cl *STRBR* DY8 ....119 L3
Alderley Crs *BLOX/PEL* WS3 ......39 J8
Alderley Rd *BRGRVW* B61 ....191 H5
Alderman's Green Rd *COVE* CV2..134 F2
Alder Meadow Cl *COVN* CV6 ....133 M2
Aldermere Rd *KIDDW* DY11 ......138 A5

Alderminster Gv
  RWWCK/WEL CV35 20
Alderminster Rd *COVW* CV5 15
Aldermoor La *COVS* CV3 ....15[?]
Aldermore Dr *NUNW/HART* B75 *..[?]
Alderney Cl *COVN* CV6 ....13[?]
Alderney Gdns
  HWK/WKHTH B38 ....[?]
Alder Park Rd *SOLH* B91 ....14[?]
Alderpits Rd *BKDE/SHDE* B34 ..9[?]
Alder Rd *BHTH/HG* B12 ....12[?]
  COVN CV6 ....[?]
  DARL/WED WS10 ....[?]
  KGSWFD DY6 ....[?]
Alders Cl *REDE* B98 ....20[?]
Alders Dr *REDE* B98 ....20[?]
Aldersea Dr *AST/WIT* B6 ....[?]
Aldershaw Rd
  DUNHL/THL/PER WV6 ....[?]
Aldershaws *SHLY* B90 ....14[?]
Alders La *CRTAM* B79 ....[?]
  NUNW/HART CV10 ....[?]
Aldersley Av
  DUNHL/THL/PER WV6 ....[?]
Aldersley Cl
  DUNHL/THL/PER WV6 ....[?]
Aldersley Rd
  DUNHL/THL/PER WV6 ....[?]
Aldersmead Rd *NFLD/LBR* B31 ..14[?]
Alderson Rd *WASH/WDE* B8 ......[?]
The Alders *BDWTH* CV12 ....11[?]
  RMSLY B62 ....[?]
Alderton Cl *SOLH* B91 ....14[?]
Alderton Dr *BDMR/CCFT* WV3 ....4[?]
Alderton Ms *RLSS* CV31 ....20[?]
Alder Wy *BRGRVE* B60 ....19[?]
  FOAKS/STRLY B74 ....[?]
  HEDN WS12 ....1[?]
Alderwood Ri *SEDG* DY3 ....6[?]
Aldgate Dr *BRLYHL* DY5 ....10[?]
Aldgate Gv *LOZ/NWT* B19 ....[?]
Aldis Cl *HLGN/YWD* B28 ....12[?]
  WSL WS2 * ....[?]
Aldis Rd *WSLW* WS2 ....[?]
Aldrich Av *TLHL/CAN* CV4 ....15[?]
Aldridge By-Pass *ALDR* WS9 ....[?]
  POL/KGSB/FAZ B78 ....10[?]
  STRBR DY8 ....[?]
Aldridge Rd *FOAKS/STRLY* B74 ..5[?]
  LGLYGN/QTN B68 ....10[?]
  PBAR/PBCH B42 ....[?]
  RUSH/SHEL WS4 ....5[?]
Aldridge St *DARL/WED* WS10 ....[?]
Aldrin Wy *TLHL/CAN* CV4 ....15[?]
Aldwick Cl *RLSN* CV32 ....20[?]
Aldwych Cl *ALDR* WS9 ....[?]
Aldwyche Dr *BDMR/CCFT* WV3 ..4[?]
Alesmore Meadow *LICH* WS13 ..2[?]
Alexander Dr *BRGRVW* B61 ......16[?]
Alexander Gdns *PBAR/PBCH* B42..[?]
Alexander Hl *BRLYHL* DY5 ....10[?]
Alexander Rd *ACGN* B27 ....[?]
  BDWTH CV12 ....11[?]
  CDSL WV8 ....[?]
  SMTHWKW B67 ....[?]
  WSLW WS2 ....[?]
Alexander St *BDMR/CCFT* WV3 ..[?]
Alexander Ter *SMTHWKW* B67 * ..8[?]
Alexandra Av *HDSW* B21 ....[?]
Alexandra Crs *HHTH/SAND* B71 ..[?]
Alexandra Ms *CRTAM* B79 ....[?]
Alexandra Pl *BILS/COS* WV14 ....[?]
Alexandra Rd *BVILLE* B30 ....12[?]
  COV CV1 ....[?]
  DARL/WED WS10 ....[?]
  DIG/EDG B5 ....[?]
  ETTPK/GDPK/PENN WV4 ....[?]
  HALE B63 ....12[?]
  HDSW B21 ....[?]
  RLSS CV31 ....20[?]
  RUGBYN/HIL CV21 ....20[?]
  WSL WS1 ....[?]
Alexandra St *DUDN* DY1 ....[?]
  NUN CV11 ....[?]
Alexandra Wy *ALDR* WS9 ....[?]
  TPTN/OCK DY4 ....[?]
Alex Grierson Cl *COVS* CV3 ......[?]
Alfall Rd *COV* CV2 ....[?]
Alford Cl *RBRY* B45 ....[?]
Alfreda Av *HLYWD* B47 ....[?]
Alfred Green Cl
  RUGBYS/DCH CV22 ....[?]
Alfred Rd *COV* CV1 ....[?]

HDSW B21 ....88 C5
SPARK B11 ....107 H4
red St ALE/KHTH/YWD 125 K6
AST/WIT B6 ....89 H5
BHTH/HG B12 ....107 H8
BLOX/PEL WS3 ....38 F4
CRTAM B79 ....31 L8
DARL/WED 52 A8
RUGBY/HIL CV21 ....186 D6
SMTHWK B66 ....87 M6
WBROM B70 ....87 H1
reds Well BRGRVW B61 ....191 J4
riston Rd COVS CV3 ....155 L4
gernon Rd LDYWD/EDGR B16 ....106 D3
ambra Rd BRGRVE B60 ....192 A4
ce Cl BDWTH CV12 ....116 D4
ce St BILS/COS WV14 ....51 H7
cia Cl RUGBY/DCH CV22 ....185 L5
son Cl TPTN/OCK DY4 ....67 L3
son Dr STRBR DY8 ....119 J3
son Rd RMSLY B62 ....122 C2
son Sq COVE CV2 ....134 F1
an Cl STRBR DY8 ....101 K4
ans Cl COVE CV2 ....154 D1
ans La RRUGBY CV23 ....161 L8
ans Cl RRUGBY CV23 ....161 L8
ard TAM/AM/WIL B77 ....46 C3
ard Wy COVS CV5 ....156 A6
but Cl CDYHTH B64 ....103 H4
cock St BORD B9 ....7 L7
TPTN/OCK DY4 ....68 A5
croft Rd SPARK B11 ....126 D3
enby Cl KGSWFD DY6 ....83 L8
en Cl GTB/HAM B43 ....70 C6
en Gv GTB/HAM B43 ....70 C6
endale Rd WALM/CURD B76 ....73 J5
YDLY B25 ....108 F6
en Dr DARL/WED WS10 ....52 A7
WBROM B70 ....87 K4
en Rd DARL/WED WS10 ....52 B8
DUNHL/THL/PER WV6 ....49 L2
TPTN/OCK DY4 ....67 K4
ens Av WSNGN B18 * 88 D7
ens Cl ATHST CV9 ....62 A5
SHHTH WV12 ....37 M8
ens Croft Rd
ALE/KHTH/YWD B14 ....124 F1
ens Farm Rd NFLD/LBR B31 ....144 B2
ens La BLOX/PEL WS3 ....39 K3
ensmead TAM/AM/WIL B77 ....46 A3
ensmore Rd REDE B98 ....203 L3
ens Rd WSNGN B18 ....88 D7
en St WBROM B70 ....86 B2
erdale Rd BRWNH WS8 ....26 C7
erton Cl COVE CV2 ....156 A6
erton La HHTH/SAND B71 ....69 G5
erton Rd YDLY B25 ....108 F6
esley Cl MGN/WHC B75 ....57 G9
esley Cft COVW CV5 ....132 E7
esley Hall Dr COVW CV5 ....133 G8
esley Old Rd COV CV1 ....133 G8
esley Rd HIA/OLT B92 ....127 H5
RUGBY/HIL CV21 ....160 D7
esley St AST/WIT B6 ....89 J8
eston Rd WOLVN WV10 ....36 B4
eyne Gv ERDE/BCHGN B24 ....90 E4
eyne Rd ERDE/BCHGN B24 ....90 E4
e Alley NUN CV11 ....99 K2
iance Cl NUN CV11 ....99 K2
iance Wy COVN CV6 ....134 E8
ied Cl COVN CV6 ....134 B3
ingham Gv GTB/HAM B43 ....71 H1
ington Cl DSYBK/YTR WS5 ....54 B5
itt Gv KNWTH CV8 ....179 M8
man Rd ERDE/BCHGN B24 ....90 F1
myn Dr FOAKS/STRLY B74 ....55 L7
port Cl CNCK/NC WS11 ....16 C4
port Rd CNCK/NC WS11 ....16 C4
Saints Dr BEWD DY12 ....163 G1
Saints Dr FOAKS/STRLY B74 ....56 D3
Saints La COV CV1 ....9 K4
Saints Rd
ALE/KHTH/YWD B14 ....125 J6
BDWTH CV12 ....116 D4
BKHL/PFLD WV2 ....3 H8
BRGRVW B61 ....191 J4
DARL/WED WS10 ....52 C7
WSNGN B18 ....88 E8
WWCK CV34 ....205 M5
Saints' St WSNGN B18 ....88 E8
sops Cl BLKHTH/ROWR B65 ....103 K1
ton Av POL/KGSB/FAZ B78 ....45 H4
ton Ct TAM/AM/WIL B77 * 46 C2
wood Gdns RIDG/WDGT B32 ....122 E2
na Av TPTN/OCK DY4 ....67 L6
na Crs VAUX/NECH B7 ....107 M1
na Pl DUDS DY2 ....85 G4
na St COV CV1 ....9 K4
DARL/WED WS10 ....52 A7
DARL/WED WS10 ....52 A7
HALE B63 ....103 G8
LOZ/NWT B19 ....89 J7
SMTHWK B66 ....88 A7
WLNHL WV13 ....51 M3
WOLVN WV10 ....3 M5
WSLW WS2 ....52 C1
na Wy LOZ/NWT B19 ....89 H6
mond Av DSYBK/YTR WS5 ....69 L1
KIDD DY11 ....137 L5
NUNW/HART CV10 ....80 A7
RLSN CV32 ....206 D2
WSLW WS2 ....52 C1
mond Cl BLOX/PEL WS3 ....39 K3
CNCK/NC WS11 ....16 C4
SLYOAK B29 ....123 L7
mond Cft PBAR/PBCH B42 ....70 D7
mond Dr
DUNHL/THL/PER WV6 ....50 A1
RUGBY/HIL CV21 ....160 C6
WWCK CV34 ....205 L4
mond Rd HEDN WS12 ....12 B5
KGSWFD DY6 ....83 J5
mond Tree Av COVE CV2 ....135 G3
mond Wy STRPT DY13 ....188 B3
nwick Cl HEDN WS12 ....11 J3
nwick Rd DIG/EDG B5 ....7 K5
pha Cl BHTH/HG B12 ....107 J2
pine Ct KNWTH CV8 ....179 L7
pine Dr DUDS DY2 ....102 F1
HEDN WS12 ....17 H1
pine Rd COVS CV3 ....154 E8
pine Wy BDMR/CCFT WV3 ....49 G3
path Cl TPTN/OCK DY4 ....67 H4
path La COVW CV5 ....153 K1
RCOVN/BALC/EX CV7 ....131 G4
BLH B91 ....128 E7
n Rd BORD B9 ....108 C3
m Rd BORD B9 ....108 F2
OLH B91 ....128 B7

Alston St LDYWD/EDGR B16 ....106 D3
Althorpe Dr RLSN CV31 ....175 H2
Althorpe St RLSS CV31 ....206 E6
Alton Av SHHTH WV12 ....37 M4
Alton Cl COVE CV2 ....135 H3
REDW B97 ....201 M4
WOLVN WV10 ....36 C1
Alton Cottages
ETTPK/GDPK/PENN WV4 * 65 K4
Alton Gv CNCK/NC WS11 ....15 M4
DUDS DY2 ....85 J4
Alton Rd SLYOAK B29 ....124 D2
Alum Cl COVN CV6 ....134 B5
Alum Dr BORD B9 ....88 E8
Alumhurst Rd WASH/WDE B8 ....108 F1
Alum Rock Rd WASH/WDE B8 ....90 B8
Alumwell Cl WSLW WS2 * 52 A1
Alum Well Rd WSLW WS2 ....52 F4
Alvaston Cl BLOX/PEL WS3 ....39 G2
Alvechurch Hwy BRGRVE B60 ....169 G2
Alvechurch Rd HALE B63 ....121 K5
REDE B98 ....194 C8
Alveley Cl REDE B98 ....203 H1
Alverley Cl KGSWFD DY6 ....82 F5
Alverley Rd COVN CV6 ....134 A7
Alverstoke Cl COVEN WV9 ....35 K3
Alverstone Rd COVE CV2 ....155 L1
Alveston Cl TAM/AM/WIL B77 * 60 A1
Alveston Gv BORD B9 ....108 F3
SLYOAK B29 ....149 M6
Alveston Rd HLYWD B47 ....146 E6
Alvin Cl COVS CV3 ....155 L6
RMSLY B62 ....104 D5
Alvington Cl SHHTH WV12 ....52 B3
Alvis Cl CRTAM B79 ....31 K6
Alwen St STRBR DY8 ....101 K4
Alwin Rd BLKHTH/ROWR B65 ....103 M3
Alwold Rd SLYOAK B29 ....123 L3
Alwyn Rd TAM/AM/WIL B77 ....46 C6
Alwyn Cl GTWY WS6 ....24 D2
Alwyn Freeman Ct
RCOVN/BALC/EX CV7 * 115 L6
Alwyn Rd RUGBY/DCH CV22 ....186 A6
Amanda Av
ETTPK/GDPK/PENN WV4 ....65 K1
Amanda Dr
LGN/SDN/BHAMAIR B26 ....109 K4
Ambassador Rd
CHWD/FDBR/MGN B37 ....129 G1
Amber Cl TAM/AM/WIL B77 ....46 G1
Amber Dr OLDBY B69 * 86 E8
Ambergate Cl BLOX/PEL WS3 ....39 G2
Ambergate Dr KGSWFD DY6 ....83 G5
Amberley Cl GTB/HAM B43 ....70 F2
Amberley Gv AST/WIT B6 ....89 L2
Amberley Rd HIA/OLT B92 ....127 K2
Amberley Wy RMSLY B62 ....103 M7
Amberwood Cl SHHTH WV12 ....52 B2
Ambien Rd ATHST CV9 ....63 H6
Amblecote Av KGSTG B44 ....71 J3
Amblecote Cl REDE B98 ....203 L3
RIDG/WDGT B32 ....105 J8
Amblecote Rd BRLYHL DY5 ....102 B5
KIDD DY10 ....138 F8
Ambler Gv COVE CV2 ....156 A2
Amblecote Cl
RIDG/WDGT B32 ....105 J3
RUGBY/HIL CV21 ....161 H6
Ambleside Cl BILS/COS WV14 * 51 J1
Ambleside Dr BRLYHL DY5 ....102 A3
Ambleside Gv SHHTH WV12 ....37 M4
Ambleside Rd BDWTH CV12 ....116 E3
Ambleside Wy BRGRVE B60 ....191 M4
KGSWFD DY6 ....83 H7
NUN CV11 ....81 J7
Ambrose Cl RUGBYN/HIL CV21 ....161 G2
WLNHL WV13 ....51 J3
Ambrose Crs KGSWFD DY6 ....83 G5
Ambury Wy GTB/HAM B43 ....70 B5
Amelas Cl STRBR DY8 ....101 L5
Amersham Cl COVW CV5 ....153 M1
RIDG/WDGT B32 ....105 J8
Amesbury Rd MOS/BIL B13 ....125 J2
Amherst Av BFLD/HDSWWD B20 ....88 E2
Amherst Rd KNWTH CV8 ....197 L5
Amicombe TAM/AM/WIL B77 ....47 G4
Amington Cl MGN/WHC B75 * 57 M3
Amington Rd SHLY B90 ....147 L5
TAM/AM/WIL B77 ....46 A1
YDLY B25 ....108 A7
Amiss Gdns SMHTH B10 ....108 A5
Amity Cl SMTHWK B66 * 87 M8
Amos Av NUNW/HART CV10 ....98 F3
Amos Jacques Rd BDWTH CV12 ....116 E1
Amos La WNSFLD WV11 ....37 H5
Amos Rd HAG/WOL DY9 ....120 D3
Amphlett Cft TPTN/OCK DY4 ....85 M1
Amphletts Cl DUDS DY2 ....103 J2
Ampton Rd EDG B15 ....106 F6
Amroth Cl RBRY B45 ....143 M6
Amroth Ms RLSS CV31 ....207 G7
Amwell Gv ALE/KHTH/YWD B14 ....146 D2
Anchorage Rd DSYBK/YTR WS5 ....54 B5
FOAKS/STRLY B74 ....56 F7
Anchor Cl LDYWD/EDGR B16 ....106 C4
TAM/AM/WIL B77 ....46 C1
Anchorfields KIDD DY10 ....138 D7
Anchor La BILS/COS WV14 ....66 F3
Anchor Rd ALDR WS9 ....40 F7
BILS/COS WV14 ....67 G3
Anchorway Rd COVS CV3 ....180 F1
Anders CRTAM B79 ....31 L7
Andersleigh Dr BILS/COS WV14 ....66 E6
Anderson Av
RUGBY/DCH CV22 ....186 E5
Anderson Crs GTB/HAM B43 ....70 C3
Anderson Rd ERDW/GRVHL B23 ....72 C7
SMTHWK B66 ....105 L4
TPTN/OCK DY4 ....67 L8
Anderton Cl FOAKS/STRLY B74 ....56 F6
Anderton Park Rd MOS/BIL B13 ....125 L2
Anderton Rd BDWTH CV12 ....116 A4
COVN CV6 ....134 B1
SPARK B11 ....108 A7
Anderton St CBHAMW B1 ....6 A4
Andover Crs KGSWFD DY6 ....101 K1
Andover Pl CNCK/NC WS11 ....16 E1
Andover St DIG/EDG B5 ....7 K5
Andressy Ms BRGRVW B61 ....168 E8
Andrew Cl SHHTH WV12 ....38 B7
Andrew Gdns HDSW B21 ....88 C2
Andrew Rd HALE B63 ....121 L3
HHTH/SAND B71 ....87 H2
TPTN/OCK DY4 ....67 L4
Andrews Cl BRLYHL DY5 ....103 G2
Andrews Rd ALDR WS9 ....40 F1
Anerley Gv KGSTG B44 ....71 K1
Anerley Rd KGSTG B44 ....71 K1
Angela Av BLKHTH/ROWR B65 ....104 F1
COVE CV2 ....135 J4
Angela Pl BILS/COS WV14 ....51 H7
Angel Cft BNTWD WS7 ....18 C4

Angelica TAM/AM/WIL B77 ....46 D2
Angelica Cl WSLW WS2 ....69 J2
Angelina St BHTH/HG B12 ....107 H6
Angel Pas STRBR DY8 ....101 L8
Angel St DUDN DY1 ....84 F5
REDW B97 ....200 F4
WOLVN WV10 ....36 C1
Anglesey Av CBROM B36 ....92 F7
Anglesey Cl BNTWD WS7 ....19 G8
COVW CV5 ....132 F6
Anglesey Crs BRWNH WS8 ....26 D3
HEDN WS12 ....13 G8
Anglesey Rd BRWNH WS8 ....26 D5
LICH WS13 ....20 D6
Anglesey St HEDN WS12 ....12 F8
LOZ/NWT B19 ....89 G6
Angless Wy KNWTH CV8 ....197 K2
Anglian Rd ALDR WS9 ....40 B7
Anglia Cl CNCK/NC WS11 ....16 B2
Angorfa Cl LICH WS13 ....20 D6
Angus Cl COVW CV5 ....153 L1
HHTH/SAND B71 ....69 G7
Anita Av TPTN/OCK DY4 ....85 J3
Ankadine Rd STRBR DY8 ....90 C5
Anker Cl BNTWD WS7 ....19 H7
Ankerdine Av STRPT DY13 ....188 B4
Ankerdine Ct HALE B63 ....121 L2
Ankerdine Crt CRTAM B79 ....45 M1
Anker Dr RRUGBY CV23 ....159 M8
Ankermoor Cl TAM/AM/WIL B77 * 60 A1
Ankerside POL/KGSB/FAZ B78 ....47 L2
Anker St NUN CV11 ....99 H2
Anker Vw POL/KGSB/FAZ B78 ....47 L5
TAM/AM/WIL B77 ....46 A2
Annan Av WOLVN WV10 ....36 C6
Ann Crs CNCK/NC WS11 ....15 J3
Ann Cft LGN/SDN/BHAMAIR B26 ....128 B3
Anne Cl WBROM B70 ....86 C2
Anne Crs COVS CV3 ....156 A8
Anne Gv TPTN/OCK DY4 ....67 M4
Anne Rd BRLYHL DY5 ....102 E4
ETTPK/GDPK/PENN WV4 ....49 M8
SMTHWK B66 ....87 M6
Ann Rd HLYWD B47 ....172 E2
Annscroft HWK/WKHTH B38 ....145 H3
Ann St WLNHL WV13 ....51 M2
Ansbro Cl WSNGN B18 ....88 C6
Ansculf Rd STRBR DY8 ....101 M4
Ansell Dr COVN CV6 ....116 E8
Ansell Rd ERDE/BCHGN B24 ....90 D4
SPARK B11 ....108 A7
WWCK CV34 ....205 H6
Ansley Cl REDE B98 ....203 K4
Ansley Common
NUNW/HART CV10 ....79 L6
Ansley La RCOVN/BALC/EX CV7 ....96 D3
Ansley Rd NUNW/HART CV10 ....97 H2
NUNW/HART CV10 ....98 A3
Anslow Gdns WNSFLD WV11 ....38 A3
Anslow Rd ERDW/GRVHL B23 ....72 A3
Anson Av LICH WS13 ....20 E5
Anson Cl GTWY WS6 ....24 C3
RUGBYS/DCH CV22 ....186 A3
Anson Gv ACGN B27 ....127 H3
Anson Rd GTWY WS6 ....24 D4
WBROM B70 ....68 C6
WSLW WS2 ....52 C1
Anstey Cft
CHWD/FDBR/MGN B37 * 110 E1
Anstey Gv ACGN B27 ....126 F4
Anstey Rd KGSTG B44 ....71 J7
Anston Wy WNSFLD WV11 ....37 H6
Anstree Cl GTWY WS6 ....24 B3
Anstruther Rd EDG B15 ....106 C6
Ansty Dr HEDN WS12 ....11 H3
Ansty Rd COVE CV2 ....135 K7
COVE CV2 ....156 A1
Antelope Gdns WWCK CV34 ....204 E3
Anthony Rd WASH/WDE B8 ....108 C2
Anthony Wy COVE CV2 ....156 A3
Anton Cl BEWD DY12 ....137 M8
Anton Dr WALM/CURD B76 ....73 L7
Antony Rd SHLY B90 ....147 M4
Antrim Cl COVW CV5 ....132 E6
Antringham Gdns EDG B15 ....106 B5
Antrobus Rd ACGN B27 ....127 L1
HDSW B21 ....88 C4
Anvil Crs BILS/COS WV14 ....67 G3
Anvil Dr OLDBY B69 ....86 C7
Apex Rd BRWNH WS8 ....26 B8
Apley Rd STRBR DY8 ....101 J6
Apollo CRTAM B79 ....31 K6
Apollo Cl CNCK/NC WS11 ....12 E8
Apollo Rd ERDE/BCHGN B24 ....91 H2
Apollo Rd HAG/WOL DY9 ....102 E8
LGLGN/QTN B68 ....87 G7
Apollo Wy BFLD/HDSWWD B20 ....89 G4
WWCK CV34 ....206 B8
Appian Cl ALE/KHTH/YWD B14 ....125 H8
Appian Wy SHLY B90 ....174 B1

Arbor Wy
CHWD/FDBR/MGN B37 ....111 G3
Arbour Cl KNWTH CV8 ....197 M2
RUGBYS/DCH CV22 ....186 B6
Arbour Ms CNCK/NC WS11 ....17 K7
Arbour Tree La DOR/KN B93 ....176 D6
Arbury Av BDWTH CV12 ....116 B2
COVN CV6 ....134 C3
Arbury Cl RLSN CV32 ....206 D3
Arbury Garth
NUNW/HART CV10 ....98 A2
Arbury Hall Rd SHLY B90 ....148 B5
Arbury Rd NUNW/HART CV10 ....98 B5
Arcal St SEDG DY3 ....66 C6
Archer Cl DARL/WED WS10 ....68 C2
LGLYGN/QTN B68 ....104 F1
Archer Ct HAG/WOL DY9 ....120 C3
Archer Rd ALE/KHTH/YWD B14 ....147 G1
BLOX/PEL WS3 ....39 J7
KNWTH CV8 ....197 J2
REDE B98 ....202 C1
Archers Cl ERDW/GRVHL B23 ....72 A5
Archers Spinney
RUGBYN/HIL CV21 ....187 M5
Archery Flds WWCK CV34 ....205 M3
Archery Rd
RCOVN/BALC/EX CV7 ....130 F4
RLSS CV31 ....206 C5
Arches La RUGBYN/HIL CV21 ....161 G8
Arch Hill St DUDS DY2 ....85 G8
Archibald Rd LOZ/NWT B19 ....89 H5
Arch Rd COVE CV2 ....135 J8
Arcot Rd HLGN/YWD B28 ....126 D3
Ardath Rd HWK/WKHTH B38 ....145 L3
Ardav Rd WBROM B70 ....68 A8
Arden Av ATHST CV9 ....63 J5
Arden Buildings DOR/KN B93 ....175 K2
RCOVN/BALC/EX CV7 ....131 G4
RLSS CV31 ....206 B6
STRBR DY8 ....101 J2
STRBR DY8 ....101 J7
WWCK CV34 ....205 L4
Ardencote Rd MOS/BIL B13 ....125 L8
Arden Cft HIA/OLT B92 ....129 L6
HIA/OLT B92 ....128 A1
Arden Dr DOR/KN B93 ....175 J2
LGN/SDN/BHAMAIR B26 ....109 K6
MGN/WHC B75 ....57 M8
SCFLD/BOLD B73 ....72 F5
Arden Forest Est
NUNW/HART CV10 ....78 D1
Arden Gv LDYWD/EDGR B16 ....106 C4
OLDBY B69 ....86 E8
Arden Meads HOCK/TIA B94 ....175 G7
Arden Oak Rd
LGN/SDN/BHAMAIR B26 ....110 B8
Arden Pl DARL/WED WS10 ....67 M1
Arden Rd ACGN B27 ....126 F1
AST/WIT B6 ....89 H5
DOR/KN B93 ....175 K3
HLYWD B47 ....146 E7
KNWTH CV8 ....197 M2
NUN CV11 ....99 L4
RBRY B45 ....143 L4
SMTHWK B66 ....105 L1
TAM/AM/WIL B77 ....46 D8
WASH/WDE B8 ....108 A2
Ardens Cl REDE B98 ....203 L3
Arden St ATHST CV9 ....63 J6
COVW CV5 ....154 D4
Arden Vale DOR/KN B93 ....149 M6
Arderne Dr
CHWD/FDBR/MGN B37 ....110 E4
Ardgay Dr HEDN WS12 ....12 D6
Ardingley Wk BRLYHL DY5 ....101 M6
Ardley Cl DUDS DY2 ....85 H5
Ardley Rd ALE/KHTH/YWD B14 ....125 L8
Areley Common STRPT DY13 ....188 C5
Areley La STRPT DY13 ....188 C2
Aretha Cl KGSWFD DY6 ....83 J5
Argil Cl RUSH/SHEL WS4 ....5 L1
Argosy Cl BKHL/PFLD WV2 ....49 M7
Argyle Av TAM/AM/WIL B77 ....46 B1
VAUX/NECH B7 ....90 A5
Argyle Cl RUSH/SHEL WS4 ....5 L1
STRBR DY8 ....101 J4
Argyle Rd RUSH/SHEL WS4 ....5 L1
WOLVN WV10 ....35 M3
Argyll St COVE CV2 ....155 L5
Ariane CRTAM B79 ....31 J6
Ariel Wy RUGBYS/DCH CV22 ....186 B6
Arion Cl TAM/AM/WIL B77 ....32 B8
Arkall Cl CRTAM B79 ....32 A4
Arkle TAM/AM/WIL B77 ....60 B1
Arkle Cft BLKHTH/ROWR B65 ....85 K7
CBROM B36 ....92 E6
Arklet Cl NUNW/HART CV10 ....80 A8
Arkley Gv HLGN/YWD B28 ....126 F6
Arkley Rd HLGN/YWD B28 ....126 F6
Arkwright Rd RIDG/WDGT B32 ....105 G8
WSLW WS2 ....38 C6
Arlen Dr GTB/HAM B43 ....70 B4
Arlescote Cl MGN/WHC B75 ....57 G9
Arlescote Rd HIA/OLT B92 ....128 A3
Arleston Wy SHLY B90 ....148 B5
Arley Cl OLDBY B69 ....86 C7
Arley Dr STRBR DY8 ....119 J2
Arley Gv
ETTPK/GDPK/PENN WV4 ....49 H8
Arley La NUNW/HART CV10 ....97 G3
Arley Ms RLSN CV32 ....206 B4
Arley Rd SLYOAK B29 ....124 D2
SOLH B91 ....148 E1
WASH/WDE B8 ....90 B7
Arley Vls WSNGN B18 * 106 B1
Arlidge Cl BILS/COS WV14 ....67 G4
Arlidge Crs KNWTH CV8 ....180 A8
Arlington Av RLSN CV32 ....206 D3
Arlington Ct STRBR DY8 ....119 H1
Arlington Gdns STRBR DY8 * 119 J2
Arlington Gv
ALE/KHTH/YWD B14 ....146 E2
Arlington Ms RLSN CV32 ....206 D3
Arlington Rd
ALE/KHTH/YWD B14 ....146 E2
HHTH/SAND B71 ....69 H7
Arlon Av NUNW/HART CV10 ....99 K3
Armada Cl ERDW/GRVHL B23 ....90 A4
Armarna Dr COVE CV2 ....156 B3
Armfield St COVN CV6 ....134 D4
Armorial Rd COVS CV3 ....154 F7
Armoury Rd SPARK B11 ....108 A5
Armscote Gv
RWWCK/WEL CV35 ....204 E3
Armscott Rd COVE CV2 ....135 G8
Armside Cl BLOX/PEL WS3 ....39 G4

Armson Rd
RCOVN/BALC/EX CV7 ....116 E4
Armstead Rd COVEN WV9 ....35 L2
Armstrong CRTAM B79 ....31 K7
Armstrong Av COVS CV3 ....155 L4
Armstrong Cl
RUGBYS/DCH CV22 ....186 C4
RLSS CV31 ....101 M7
Armstrong Dr CBROM B36 ....92 D4
DUNHL/THL/PER WV6 ....35 L7
WSLW WS2 ....52 E1
Armstrong Wy WLNHL WV13 ....51 M5
Arncliffe Cl NUN CV11 ....99 M3
Arncliffe Wy WWCK CV34 ....205 K4
Arne Rd COVE CV2 ....135 L7
Arnhem Cl DUNHL/THL/PER WV6 ....35 L7
Arnhem Cnr COVS CV3 ....155 J7
Arnhem Rd WLNHL WV13 ....51 M3
Arnhem Wy TPTN/OCK DY4 ....68 A3
Arnold Av COVS CV3 ....155 G8
Arnold Cl CRTAM B79 ....31 L8
WSLW WS2 ....52 D2
Arnold Gv SHLY B90 ....148 A1
SLYOAK B29 ....124 D4
Arnold Rd SHLY B90 ....147 M1
Arnolds La CSHL/WTROR B46 ....112 D2
Arnold St RUGBYS/DCH CV21 ....186 F2
Arnotdale Dr HEDN WS12 ....12 D6
Arnside Cl COVN CV1 ....9 J2
Arnwood Cl WSLW WS2 ....52 D3
Arosa Dr HRBN B17 ....123 M4
Arps Rd CDSL WV8 ....34 E2
Arran Cl CNCK/NC WS11 ....16 E2
GTB/HAM B43 ....70 C2
NUNW/HART CV10 ....98 A3
Arran Dr TAM/AM/WIL B77 ....46 D6
Arran Rd BKDE/SHDE B34 ....91 K7
Arran Wy CBROM B36 ....92 E6
Arras Bvd RWWCK/WEL CV35 ....204 E7
Arras Rd DUDS DY2 ....85 J3
Arrow Cl DOR/KN B93 ....149 L7
Arrowdale Rd REDE B98 ....202 E3
Arrowfield Gn
HWK/WKHTH B38 ....145 H6
Arrowfield Top ALVE B48 * 170 F4
Arrow Rd BLOX/PEL WS3 ....39 J7
Arrow Rd North REDE B98 ....202 E1
Arrow Rd South REDE B98 ....202 E1
Arsenal St BORD B9 ....108 A4
Artemis Dr RLSS CV31 ....206 C8
Arthingworth Cl COVS CV3 ....156 C4
Arthur Dr KIDD DY11 ....164 C4
Arthur Gunby Cl
MGN/WHC B75 * 57 K6
Arthur Harris Cl SMTHWK B66 ....105 M2
Arthur Pl CBHAMW B1 ....6 B4
Arthur Rd EDG B15 ....106 F7
ERDE/BCHGN B24 ....90 E3
HDSW B21 ....88 C2
TPTN/OCK DY4 ....67 L7
YDLY B25 ....108 E7
Arthur St BILS/COS WV14 ....51 H7
BKHL/PFLD WV2 ....50 B7
CNCK/NC WS11 ....16 D1
COV CV1 ....9 H1
HEDN WS12 ....17 H3
KNWTH CV8 ....179 L8
REDE B98 ....202 E2
SMHTH B10 ....107 M4
WBROM B70 ....87 H4
Artillery St BORD B9 ....107 M3
Arton Cft ERDE/BCHGN B24 ....90 D3
Arundel TAM/AM/WIL B77 ....46 A3
Arundel Av DARL/WED WS10 ....67 L3
Arundel Crs HIA/OLT B92 ....128 A3
Arundel Dr OLDBY B69 ....85 K5
Arundel Gv
DUNHL/THL/PER WV6 ....48 E2
Arundel Pl SPARK B11 ....107 L7
Arundel Rd ALE/KHTH/YWD B14 ....146 E4
BRGRVE B60 ....191 M4
COVS CV3 ....155 H7
SHHTH WV12 ....38 A4
STRBR DY8 ....101 G3
WOLVN WV10 ....35 M3
Arundel St WSL WS1 ....5 H5
Arun Wy WALM/CURD B76 ....73 L4
Asbury Rd DARL/WED WS10 ....69 J3
RCOVN/BALC/EX CV7 ....151 M8
Ascot Cl BDWTH CV12 ....116 F1
COVS CV3 ....156 A7
LDYWD/EDGR B16 ....106 D3
LICHS WS14 ....21 H7
OLDBY B69 ....86 C7
Ascot Dr CNCK/NC WS11 ....16 A4
DUDN DY1 ....84 D3
ETTPK/GDPK/PENN WV4 ....65 L1
TAM/AM/WIL B77 ....60 B2
Ascot Gdns STRBR DY8 ....101 G3
Ascot Rd MOS/BIL B13 ....125 K3
Ascot Ride RLSN CV32 ....207 G3
Ascot Wy BRGRVW B61 ....191 L8
Ash Av BHTH/HG B12 ....107 L8
Ashborough Dr SOLH B91 ....149 G6
Ashbourne Cl CNCK/NC WS11 ....16 C1
Ashbourne Gv AST/WIT B6 * 89 J5
Ashbourne Rdg HALE B63 ....103 H8
Ashbourne Rd BLOX/PEL WS3 ....39 G2
ETTPK/GDPK/PENN WV4 ....66 C2
LDYWD/EDGR B16 ....106 B2
WOLV WV1 ....50 E2
Ashbourne Wy SHLY B90 ....148 B5
Ashbridge Rd COVW CV5 ....154 A1
Ashbrook Crs SOLH B91 ....148 F5
Ashbrook Dr RBRY B45 ....143 L5
Ashbrook Gv BVILLE B30 ....125 G5
Ashbrook Ri NUNW/HART CV10 ....79 M5
Ashbrook Rd BVILLE B30 ....125 G5
Ashburn Gv WLNHL WV13 ....52 A3
Ashburton Rd
ALE/KHTH/YWD B14 ....125 H8
COVE CV2 ....135 L2
Ashbury Covert BVILLE B30 ....146 A2
Ashby Cl CBROM B36 ....91 G7
COVS CV3 ....156 D5
Ashby Ct NUN CV11 ....99 H4
SOLH B91 ....148 D3
Ashby Rd CRTAM B79 ....31 M8
Ashcombe Av
BFLD/HDSWWD B20 ....88 C2
Ashcombe Gdns
ERDE/BCHGN B24 ....91 H2
Ashcott Cl HWK/WKHTH B38 ....145 H3
Ash Crs CHWD/FDBR/MGN B37 ....92 D7
KGSWFD DY6 ....83 J7
Ash Cft TPTN/OCK DY4 * 85 L3
Ashcroft Gv BFLD/HDSWWD B20 ....89 H4
Ashcroft La LICHS WS14 ....28 C5
Ashcroft Wy
RCOVN/BALC/EX CV7 ....135 M5
Ashdale Cl COVS CV3 ....157 G3
HEDN WS12 ....11 K3
KGSWFD DY6 ....83 H5

Ashdale Dr *ALE/KHTH/YWD* B14 ..146 E4
Ashdale Gv
 LGN/SDN/BHAMAIR B26 ......109 L5
Ashdale Rd *TAM/AM/WIL* B77 .....32 B8
Ashdene CI *KIDD* DY10 ....139 G8
 KIDDW DY11 ....189 L3
 SCFLD/BOLD B73 ....72 E2
Ashdene Gdns *KNWTH* CV8 ......197 M1
 STRBR DY8 ....101 G3
Ashdown CI *COVS* CV3 ....156 B5
 MOS/BIL B13 ....125 L4
 RBRY B45 ....143 L3
Ashdown Dr *NUNW/HART* CV10 ...98 D3
 STRBR DY8 ....101 J2
Ash Dr *BRGRVW* B61 ....168 E4
 HHTH/SAND B71 ....69 G7
 KNWTH CV8 ....197 L1
 NUNW/HART CV10 ....79 L5
Ashen CI
 ETTPK/GDPK/PENN WV4 ....66 A2
Ashenden Rd *BDMR/CCFT* WV3 ...48 E4
Ashenhurst Rd *DUDN* DY1 ....84 D5
Ashe Rd *NUNW/HART* CV10 ....97 M2
Ashes Rd *OLDBY* B69 ....104 D1
Ashfern Dr *WALM/CURD* B76 ....73 K6
Ashfield Av *ALE/KHTH/YWD* B14..125 K4
 TLHL/CAN CV4 ....153 H4
Ashfield CI *BLOX/PEL* WS3 ....53 J1
Ashfield Crs *DUDS* DY2 ....103 G2
 HAG/WOL DY9 ....120 D2
Ashfield Gv *HALE* B63 ....121 J3
 WOLVN WV10 ....36 A2
Ashfield Rd
 ALE/KHTH/YWD B14 ....125 K4
 BDMR/CCFT WV3 ....49 H3
 BILS/COS WV14 ....67 L3
 KNWTH CV8 ....197 M2
 WOLVN WV10 ....36 A2
Ashford Dr *BDWTH* CV12 ....116 E2
 SEDG DY3 ....66 C6
 WALM/CURD B76 ....73 J8
Ashford La *HOCK/TIA* B94 ....174 E6
Ashfurlong CI
 RCOVN/BALC/EX CV7 ....151 M7
Ashfurlong Crs *MGN/WHC* B75 ....57 J6
Ashfurlong Rd *DUDN* DY1 ....66 E8
Ash Green La
 RCOVN/BALC/EX CV7 ....116 A7
Ashgrove *BNTWD* WS7 ....18 D8
Ash Gv *BHTH/HG* B12 ....107 M8
 BORD B9 ....107 K3
 CNCK/NC WS11 ....16 D1
 HAG/WOL DY9 ....120 B2
 KIDDW DY11 ....137 M6
 LICH WS13 ....21 G5
 POL/KGSB/FAZ B78 ....60 B6
 RCOVN/BALC/EX CV7 ....96 C5
 RCOVN/BALC/EX CV7 ....116 A6
 SEDG DY3 ....84 A3
 STRPT DY13 ....188 C1
 TAM/AM/WIL B77 ....46 D8
Ashgrove CI *BRGRVW* B60 ....169 H4
Ashgrove Rd *KGSTG* B44 ....71 G3
Ash HI *BDMR/CCFT* WV3 ....49 H4
Ashill Rd *RBRY* B45 ....143 H6
Ashington Gv *COVS* CV3 ....155 L8
Ashington Rd *BDWTH* CV12 ....116 A4
Ashlands CI *CRTAM* B79 ....32 A6
Ashland St *WOLV* WV3 ....2 C7
Ash La LA *ALDE* B48 ....171 L3
 GTWY WS6 ....24 E2
Ashlawn Crs *SOLH* B91 ....127 H8
Ashlawn Rd *RUGBYS/HIL* CV21 ...187 K5
 RUGBYS/DCH CV22 ....186 C8
 RUGBYS/DCH CV22 ....186 F7
Ashlea *POL/KGSB/FAZ* B78 ....47 K8
Ashleigh Dr *BFLD/HDSWWD* B20 ...88 F3
 NUN CV11 ....99 K4
 TAM/AM/WIL B77 ....46 C5
Ashleigh Gv *MOS/BIL* B13 ....125 M4
Ashleigh Rd *OLDBY* B69 ....69 H6
 SOLH B91 ....148 F1
Ashley CI *EDG* B15 ....107 G6
 KGSWFD DY6 ....101 G1
 STRBR DY8 ....119 H3
Ashley Ct *RBRY* B45 ....169 L4
Ashley Crs *WWCK* CV34 ....205 M7
Ashley Gdns *CDSL* WV8 ....34 D1
 WASH/WDE B8 ....107 J3
Ashley Mt *DUNHL/THL/PER* WV6 ...35 H8
Ashley Rd *BLOX/PEL* WS3 ....38 D4
 BNTWD WS7 ....18 E3
 ERDW/GRVHL B23 ....90 C2
 ETTPK/GDPK/PENN WV4 ....49 J8
 KIDD DY10 ....138 F4
Ashley St *BILS/COS* WV14 ....51 J7
 BLKHTH/ROWR B65 ....104 A4
Ashley Ter *SLYOAK* B29 * 124 C4
Ashley Wy *RCOVN/BALC/EX* CV7 ..151 M6
Ashmall *BNTWD* WS7 ....27 H1
Ashman Av *RRUGBY* CV23 ....159 M8
Ashmead Dr *RBRY* B45 ....170 A1
Ashmead Gv *ERDE/BCHGN* B24 ...90 E3
Ashmead Rd *BNTWD* WS7 ....18 E3
Ash Ms *ACGN* B27 ....109 C8
Ashmole Av *BNTWD* WS7 ....19 K5
Ashmole CI *LICHS* WS14 ....21 G7
Ashmole Rd *WBROM* B70 ....68 D6
Ashmore Av *WNSFD* WV11 ....37 L4
Ashmore Lake Rd *SHHTH* WV12 ...51 M1
Ashmore Lake Wy *SHHTH* WV12 ..51 M1
Ashmore Rd *BVILLE* B30 ....124 D8
 COVN CV6 ....8 C1
Ashmores CI *REDW* B97 ....202 B8
Ashold Farm Rd
 ERDE/BCHGN B24 ....91 G3
Asholme CI *CBROM* B36 ....91 G6
Ashorne CI *ACGN* B27 ....126 F6
 COVE CV2 ....135 G3
 REDE B98 ....203 H5
Ashover Gv *WSNGN* B18 ....106 C1
Ashow CI *KNWTH* CV8 ....197 M1
Ashperton CI *REDE* B98 ....202 C4
Ash Priors CI *TLHL/CAN* CV4 ......153 M3
Ashridge CI *NUN* CV11 ....99 K5
Ash Rd *DARL/WED* WS10 ....52 D8
 DUDN DY1 ....84 F2
 TPTN/OCK DY4 ....85 J1
 WASH/WDE B8 ....108 B1
Ashstead CI *WALM/CURD* B76 ......73 M7
Ash Ter *OLDBY* B69 ....85 G8
Ashton Ct *REDW* B97 ....201 M4
Ashton Cft *LDYWD/EDGR* B16 ....106 E5
 SOLH B91 ....148 B4
Ashton Dr *RUSH/SHEL* WS4 ....40 A2
Ashton Park Dr *BRLYHL* DY5 ....102 A4
Ashton Rd *YDLY* B25 ....108 F6
Ash Tree Av *TLHL/CAN* CV4 ....153 L3
Ashtree CI *STRBR* DY8 ....101 L5
Ash Tree Dr
 LGN/SDN/BHAMAIR B26 ....109 H6
Ashtree Gv *BILS/COS* WV14 ....67 M2
Ash Tree La *LICH* WS13 ....21 L4

Ash Tree Rd *BVILLE* B30 ....124 E7
 REDW B97 ....201 M1
Ashtree Rd *BLOX/PEL* WS3 ....39 L2
 CDYHTH B64 ....103 K3
 OLDBY B69 ....86 B5
Ashurst CI *COVN* CV6 ....116 F8
Ashurst Rd *WALM/CURD* B76 ....73 K7
Ash Vw *HEDN* WS12 ....12 B5
Ashville Av *BKDE/SHDE* B34 ....91 K6
Ashville Dr *HALE* B63 ....103 L8
Ashwater Dr
 ALE/KHTH/YWD B14 ....146 B3
Ash Wy *ERDW/GRVHL* B23 ....72 A5
 SPARK B11 ....107 M8
Ashwell Dr *SHLY* B90 ....148 B1
Ashwells Gv *COVEN* WV9 ....35 K3
Ashwood Av *COVN* CV6 ....133 K8
 STRBR DY8 ....101 G3
Ashwood CI *FOAKS/STRLY* B74 ....55 J5
Ashwood Ct
 RUGBYS/HIL CV21 * 186 D1
Ashwood Dr
 CHWD/FDBR/MGN B37 ....111 H2
Ashwood Gv
 ETTPK/GDPK/PENN WV4 ....49 L8
Ashwood Lower La
 KGSWFD DY6 * 100 C7
Ashwood Rd *NUNW/HART* CV10 ...80 C7
Ashworth Rd *PBAR/PBCH* B42 .....70 F4
Askew Bridge Rd *SEDG* DY3 * 83 M2
Askew CI *SEDG* DY3 ....66 C8
Aspbury Cft *CBROM* B36 ....92 B4
Aspen CI *ACGN* B27 ....126 E2
 TLHL/CAN CV4 ....153 H4
 WALM/CURD B76 ....73 K3
Aspen Dr *HEDN* WS12 ....13 L7
Aspen Dr
 CHWD/FDBR/MGN B37 ....111 G5
 COVN CV6 ....117 G7
Aspen Gdns *BFLD/HDSWWD* B20 ...88 F4
Aspen Rd *BNTWD* WS7 ....18 D5
 BORD B9 ....108 E2
 HLYWD B47 ....146 F8
 SHHTH WV12 ....38 C6
The Aspens *POL/KGSB/FAZ* B78 ...60 A6
Aspens Wy *BRGRVW* B61 ....168 E7
Aspen Wk *STRPT* DY13 ....163 J8
Aspen Wy *BDMR/CCFT* WV3 ....2 A7
Asplen CI *KNWTH* CV8 ....198 A1
Aspley CI *WOLVN* WV10 ....14 C1
Aspley La *DUNHL/THL/PER* WV6 ...22 B2
 OLDBY B69 ....86 B3
Asquith Dr *CNCK/NC* WS11 ....17 G3
Asra CI *COVE* CV2 ....135 H8
 SMTHWK B66 ....87 G3
Assheton CI *RUGBYS/DCH* CV22 .186 A5
Astbury Av *SMTHWK* B67 ....105 K2
Astbury CI *BLOX/PEL* WS3 ....38 E1
 WOLV WV1 ....50 E4
Aster Av *KIDDW* DY11 ....138 B4
Aster CI *NUN* CV11 ....99 L4
Aster Wk *COVEN* WV9 ....35 L2
Asthill Cft *COVS* CV3 ....8 E3
Asthill Gv *COVS* CV3 ....8 E9
Astley Av *COVN* CV6 ....134 C5
 RMSLY B62 ....104 D7
Astley CI *REDE* B98 ....202 E6
 RLSN CV32 ....206 B3
 TPTN/OCK DY4 ....68 B7
Astley Cft *REDE* B98 ....202 E6
Astley Gdns *STRPT* DY13 ....188 C7
Astley La *NUNW/HART* CV10 ....97 M4
 NUNW/HART CV10 ....97 M4
 RCOVN/BALC/EX CV7 ....114 F2
Astley PI *RUGBYS/HIL* CV21 ......187 M6
 WOLV WV1 ....49 L7
Aston Brook Gn *AST/WIT* B6 * 89 K8
Aston Brook St *AST/WIT* B6 ....89 J7
Aston Brook St East *AST/WIT* B6 ...89 J8
Aston Bury *EDG* B15 ....106 B5
Aston Church Rd *VAUX/NECH* B7 ...90 A6
Aston CI *BILS/COS* WV14 ....67 L1
 LICHS WS14 ....28 D7
 PENK ST19 ....10 D6
Aston Expressway *AST/WIT* B6 .....89 J3
Aston Hall Rd *AST/WIT* B6 ....89 J5
Aston La *BFLD/HDSWWD* B20 ......89 J3
Aston Manor CI
 BFLD/HDSWWD B20 ....89 J3
Aston Rd *AST/WIT* B6 ....7 J1
 BRGRVW B60 ....191 K7
 COVW CV5 ....154 D4
 NUN CV11 ....80 F8
 OLDBY B69 ....85 L4
 WLNHL WV13 ....52 B5
Aston Rd North *AST/WIT* B6 ....89 K7
Astons CI *BRLYHL* DY5 ....102 B6
Astons Fold *BRLYHL* DY5 ....102 B6
Astor Dr *MOS/BIL* B13 ....126 A4
Astoria CI *SHHTH* WV12 ....38 B4
Astor Rd *FOAKS/STRLY* B74 ....55 L4
 KGSWFD DY6 ....83 K8
Atcham CI *REDE* B98 ....203 K2
Athelney Ct *BLOX/PEL* WS3 * 39 L2
Athelstan Ct *PENK* ST19 ....10 E5
Athelstan Gv
 DUNHL/THL/PER WV6 ....34 C8
Athelstan Wy *CRTAM* B79 ....31 K6
Atherstone CI *RLSN* CV32 ....206 B8
Atherstone La *REDE* B98 ....203 K4
 SHLY B90 ....147 J3
Atherstone La *ATHST* CV9 ....73 J1
 ATHST CV9 ....63 H1
 ATHST CV9 ....63 H1
 CSHL/WTROR B46 ....73 H1
 NUNW/HART CV10 ....79 M3
 WOLV WV1 ....50 F3
Atherstone St
 POL/KGSB/FAZ B78 ....45 M5
Atherston PI *TLHL/CAN* CV4 ....54 A5
Athlone Rd *DSYBK/YTR* WS5 ....54 A5
Athol CI *RIDG/WDGT* B32 ....123 H5
Athole St *BHTH/HG* B12 ....107 L6
Athol Crs *NUNW/HART* CV10 ....98 C3
Atlantic Rd *KGSTG* B44 ....71 K5
Atlantic Wy *DARL/WED* WS10 ......68 C4
Atlas Est *AST/WIT* B6 * 89 L3
Atlas Gv *WBROM* B70 ....68 A7
Attenborough CI *LOZ/NWT* B19 ....89 M6
Atterton La *ATHST* CV9 ....63 M5
Attingham Dr *CNCK/NC* WS11 ....16 F4
 GTB/HAM B43 ....70 B3
Attleborough La
 CSHL/WTROR B46 ....92 E4
Attleborough Rd *NUN* CV11 ....99 H3
Attlee CI *OLDBY* B69 ....86 B3
Attlee Crs *BILS/COS* WV14 ....67 J3
Attlee Gv *CNCK/NC* WS11 ....17 G3
Attlee Rd *WSLW* WS2 ....52 C2
Attoxhall Rd *COVE* CV2 ....156 C1

Attwell Pk *BDMR/CCFT* WV3 ....49 H6
Attwell Rd *TPTN/OCK* DY4 ....67 K4
Attwood CI *WASH/WDE* B8 ....90 C7
Attwood Crs *COVE* CV2 ....135 G7
Attwood Gdns
 ETTPK/GDPK/PENN WV4 ....50 C5
Attwood Rd *BNTWD* WS7 ....18 A6
Attwood St *HAG/WOL* DY9 ....102 D8
 HALE B63 ....103 K8
Atworth CI *REDE* B98 ....202 F8
Aubrey Rd *RIDG/WDGT* B32 ....105 J6
 SMHTH B10 ....108 D6
Auchinleck Dr *LICH* WS13 ....21 G4
Auchinleck Sq *EDG* B15 * 6 A4
Auckland Dr *CBROM* B36 ....92 D5
Auckland Rd *KGSWFD* DY6 ....101 J1
 SMTHWK B66 ....87 G5
 SPARK B11 ....107 L6
Auden Ct *NUNW/HART* CV10 ....97 K1
Auden Ct *DUNHL/THL/PER* WV6 ...48 D1
Audley Dr *BRBY* B45 ....169 G1
Audley Rd *STETCH* B33 ....109 J1
Audnam *STRBR* DY8 ....101 J4
Augusta PI *RLSN* CV32 ....206 D5
 MOS/BIL B13 ....125 J1
Augusta Rd East *MOS/BIL* B13 ....125 K1
Augusta Rd *WSNGN* B18 ....6 C1
Augusta St *WSNGN* B18 ....88 D7
Augustine Gv *FOAKS/STRLY* B74 ..42 D8
 WSNGN B18 ....88 D7
Augustus CI *CSHL/WTROR* B46 ....93 K4
Augustus CI *EDG* B15 ....106 D5
Augustus Rd *COV* CV1 ....9 L2
 EDG B15 ....9 G3
Augustus St *WSLW* WS2 ....4 D4
Aulton Rd *MGN/WHC* B75 ....57 J3
Ault St *WBROM* B70 ....87 H4
Austcliff CI *REDW* B97 ....202 B7
Austcliff Dr *SOLH* B91 ....149 G5
Austen CI *NUNW/HART* CV10 ....79 K8
Austen PI *EDG* B15 ....6 E5
Austin CI *DUDS* DY2 ....85 H2
Austin Cote La *LICHS* WS14 ....21 J6
Austin Cft *CBROM* B36 ....92 C4
Austin Dr *COVN* CV6 ....134 E6
Austin Edwards Dr *WWCK* CV34 ..205 M5
Austin Ri *NFLD/LBR* B31 ....144 D6
Austin Rd *BRGRVW* B61 ....191 J5
 HDSW B21 ....88 A4
Austin *DUNHL/THL/PER* WV6 ......49 M1
Austin Wy *PBAR/PBCH* B42 ....70 E6
Austrey CI *HIA/OLT* B92 ....149 L7
Austrey Gv *SLYOAK* B29 * 123 L5
Austrey Rd *BILS/COS* WV14 ....66 E2
Austwick CI *WWCK* CV34 ....205 J4
Austy CI *CBROM* B36 ....91 J5
Autherley Jct *COVEN* WV9 * 35 L1
Autumn Berry Gv *SEDG* DY3 ....66 C7
Autumn CI *RUSH/SHEL* WS4 ....40 A3
Autumn Dr *LICH* WS13 ....21 H9
 RUSH/SHEL WS4 ....40 A3
 SEDG DY3 ....84 B2
Auxerre Av *REDE* B98 ....202 E5
Avalon CI *ERDE/BCHGN* B24 ....90 F1
Avalon Rd *BVILLE* B30 ....124 B6
Avebury CI *NUN* CV11 ....99 K5
Avebury Gv *BVILLE* B30 ....125 G6
Avebury Rd *BVILLE* B30 ....125 G5
Ave Maria CI *CDYHTH* B64 ....103 J4
Avenbury Dr *SOLH* B91 ....149 J1
Avenbury Dr *REDE* B98 ....203 K4
Aventine Wy *RUGBYS/HIL* CV21 ..160 D6
Avenue CI *DOR/KN* B93 ....175 L2
 VAUX/NECH B7 ....89 J4
Avenue Perry *WOLVN* WV10 ....36 D5
Avenue Rd *ALE/KHTH/YWD* B14 ..125 H5
 AST/WIT B6 ....89 K8
 BDMR/CCFT WV3 ....49 J5
 BILS/COS WV14 ....67 G5
 BLKHTH/ROWR B65 ....104 B4
 DARL/WED WS10 ....52 B7
 DOR/KN B93 ....175 L2
 DUDS DY2 ....84 C7
 ERDW/GRVHL B23 ....90 D1
 HDSW B21 ....88 B3
 HEDN WS12 ....17 J3
 KNWTH CV8 ....179 H7
 NUN CV11 ....81 G8
 RLSS CV31 ....206 D6
 RUGBYS/HIL CV21 ....186 C1
Avenue Station Ap *RLSS* CV31 * .206 D6
The Avenue *ACGN* B27 ....127 H2
 BDMR/CCFT WV3 ....48 F5
 BLKHTH/ROWR B65 ....103 L2
 BRGRVW B60 ....191 H6
 COVS CV3 ....155 L7
 ETTPK/GDPK/PENN WV4 ....65 J1
 KIDD DY10 ....139 M3
 KIDDW DY11 ....189 L5
 LOZ/NWT B19 ....89 G5
 RBRY B45 ....143 J6
 WALM/CURD B76 ....73 J4
Averill Rd
 LGN/SDN/BHAMAIR B26 ....109 L5
Avern CI *TPTN/OCK* DY4 ....67 M7
Aversley Rd *HWK/WKHTH* B38 ....145 H5
Avery Dell Ind Est *BVILLE* B30 ....124 F8
Avery Dr *ACGN* B27 ....127 G1
Avery Myers CI *LGLYGN/QTN* B68 ..86 F9
Avery Rd *SCFLD/BOLD* B73 * 72 B5
 SMTHWK B66 ....88 D7
Aviemore CI *NUNW/HART* CV10 ....98 E3
Aviemore Crs *GTB/HAM* B43 ....70 F1
Avill *TAM/AM/WIL* B77 ....46 E8
Avill Gv *KIDDW* DY11 ....138 A6
Avington CI *SEDG* DY3 ....66 B6
Avion CI *WSL* WS1 ....5 G8
Avocet CI *COVN* CV6 ....134 F3
 STETCH B33 ....109 J2
Avocet Dr *KIDD* DY10 ....164 E3
 STRPT DY13 ....188 F5
Avon *TAM/AM/WIL* B77 ....46 E8
Avonbank CI *REDW* B97 ....202 A7
Avon CI *BDWTH* CV12 ....99 M7
 BRGRVW B60 ....191 K7
 BRLYHL DY5 ....83 M6
 DUNHL/THL/PER WV6 ....48 D2
Avon Crs *STRBR* DY8 * 101 G3
Avon Dr *CBROM* B36 ....92 D6
 HLYWD B47 ....125 M3
 MOS/BIL B13 ....125 L1
 WNSFD WV11 ....52 A3
Avonlea Ri *RLSN* CV32 ....206 A3
Avonmere *RUGBYS/HIL* CV21 .....160 C2
Avon Ms *STRBR* DY8 ....101 G3
Avon Rd *BLOX/PEL* WS3 ....39 J4

 BNTWD WS7 ....18 D8
 CNCK/NC WS11 ....15 M6
 CNCK/NC WS11 ....16 B6
 HALE B63 ....102 F8
 KIDDW DY11 ....163 M2
 KNWTH CV8 ....197 J2
 SHLY B90 ....148 B5
 STRBR DY8 ....119 K2
Avon St *COVE* CV2 ....134 F8
 RRUGBY CV23 ....187 J1
 RUGBYN/HIL CV21 ....186 E1
 SPARK B11 ....107 L6
 WWCK CV34 ....205 L6
Awbridge Br *WMBN* WV5 ....64 C3
Awbridge Rd *DUDS* DY2 ....103 G2
Awefields Crs *SMTHWK* B67 ......105 H1
Awlmakers Gv *BLOX/PEL* WS3 .....39 G6
Awson St *COVN* CV6 ....134 D7
Axborough La *KIDD* DY10 ....139 G1
Axholme Rd *COVE* CV2 ....156 C1
Axletree Wy *DARL/WED* WS10 .....52 F8
Axminster CI *NUN* CV11 ....81 J8
Ayala CI *CBROM* B36 ....91 J5
Aylesbury CI *HOCK/TIA* B94 ....175 G7
Aylesbury Crs *KGSTG* B44 ....71 L5
Aylesbury Rd *HOCK/TIA* B94 ......175 H6
 SEDG DY3 ....65 M3
Aylesford CI *HDSW* B21 ....88 B4
Aylesford St *BHTH/HG* B12 ....107 K7
 COV CV1 ....9 K1
 RLSS CV31 ....206 E7
Aynho CI *COVW* CV5 ....153 L2
Ayre Rd *ERDE/BCHGN* B24 ....90 F1
Ayrshire CI *CBROM* B36 ....91 H5
Ayrton CI *DUNHL/THL/PER* WV6 ...48 E1
Aysgarth CI *NUN* CV11 ....99 L3
Azalea CI *DUDN* DY1 ....84 F2
Azalea Gv *BORD* B9 ....108 E2
Aziz Isaac CI *LGLYGN/QTN* B68 * ..87 G7

B

Babbacombe Rd *COVS* CV3 ....155 H8
Babington Rd *HDSW* B21 ....88 C6
Bablake CI *COVN* CV6 ....133 K5
Bablake Cft *HIA/OLT* B92 ....127 L4
Babors Fld *BILS/COS* WV14 ....66 E2
Baccabox La *HLYWD* B47 ....146 C6
Bacchus Rd *WSNGN* B18 ....88 D7
Bachelors Bench *ATHST* CV9 ....63 H6
Bache St *WBROM* B70 ....87 G4
Bach Mill Dr
 ALE/KHTH/YWD B14 ....147 H2
Backcester La *LICH* WS13 ....20 F5
Backcrofts *CNCK/NC* WS11 ....16 C4
Backhouse La *WNSFLD* WV11 ....51 L1
Back La *ALDR* WS9 ....41 K6
 CSHL/WTROR B46 ....94 D3
 KIDD DY10 ....165 K5
 LICHS WS14 ....28 A8
 RCOVN/BALC/EX CV7 ....131 H8
 RUGBY CV23 ....159 L2
 RRUGBY CV23 ....185 L1
 SHLY B90 ....147 L8
 WWCK CV34 ....205 L6
Back St *NUN* CV11 ....81 G8
Badby Leys *RUGBYS/DCH* CV22 ..186 D6
Baddesley CI *RLSS* CV31 ....207 H8
Baddesley Rd *HIA/OLT* B92 ....127 J3
Bader Rd *DUNHL/THL/PER* WV6 ...48 B2
 WSLW WS2 ....52 D3
Bader Wk *CVALE* B35 ....91 K3
Badger CI *HEDN* WS12 ....12 A7
 REDE B98 ....203 H2
 SHLY B90 ....174 B1
Badger Dr *WOLVN* WV10 ....3 H1
Badger Rd *COVS* CV3 ....156 B5
Badgers Bank Rd
 FOAKS/STRLY B74 ....42 D8
Badgers CI *BLOX/PEL* WS3 ....25 L8
Badgers Cft *RMSLY* B62 ....103 M6
The Badgers *RBRY* B45 ....169 L3
Badger St *HAG/WOL* DY9 ....102 C7
 SEDG DY3 ....66 C8
Badgers Wk *STRPT* DY13 * 188 E1
Badgers Wy *HEDN* WS12 ....17 H4
Badger Wy *BRGRVW* B60 ....169 H6
Badland Av *KIDD* DY10 ....138 D4
Badminton CI *DUDN* DY1 ....84 D2
Badsey CI *NFLD/LBR* B31 ....145 G1
Badsey Rd *OLDBY* B69 ....86 B8
Baffin CI *RUGBYS/DCH* CV22 ......186 C4
Baggeridge CI *SEDG* DY3 ....83 G6
Baggott St *BKHL/PFLD* WV2 ....50 A6
Baginton CI *SOLH* B91 ....127 M8
Baginton Rd *COVS* CV3 ....154 F7
 CVALE B35 ....91 M1
Bagley St *HAG/WOL* DY9 ....102 A7
Bagnall CI
 LGN/SDN/BHAMAIR B26 ....109 H7
Bagnall Rd *BILS/COS* WV14 ....51 G7
Bagnall St *BLOX/PEL* WS3 ....39 G6
 TPTN/OCK DY4 ....68 C3
 WBROM B70 ....87 J3
Bagnall Wk *BRLYHL* DY5 ....102 B4
Bagnell Rd *ALE/KHTH/YWD* B14 ..125 K6
Bagot St *CBHAMNE* B4 ....7 H1
Bagridge CI *BDMR/CCFT* WV3 ......48 D5
Bagridge Rd *BDMR/CCFT* WV3 .....48 D5
Bagshaw CI *KNWTH* CV8 ....182 M8
Bagshawe Cft *ERDW/GRVHL* B23 ..72 B6
Bagshaw Rd *STETCH* B33 ....109 J2
Bailey Av *TAM/AM/WIL* B77 ....46 D8
Bailey CI *CNCK/NC* WS11 ....16 C1
Bailey Rd *BILS/COS* WV14 ....50 F6
Bailey's La *RRUGBY* CV23 ....159 L8
Bailey St *WBROM* B70 ....68 C5
 WOLVN WV10 ....3 J4
Bakehouse La *CSHL/WTROR* B46 ..76 C7
 DOR/KN B93 ....176 F7
 RUGBYN/HIL CV21 ....186 D2
Baker Av *BILS/COS* WV14 ....66 D5
 RLSS CV31 ....206 D7
Baker CI *BNTWD* WS7 ....18 D5
Baker House Gv *GTB/HAM* B43 .....70 B6
Baker Rd *BILS/COS* WV14 ....67 G5
Bakers Cft *ATHST* CV9 ....62 A4
Bakers Gdns *CDSL* WV8 ....34 C1
Baker's La *ALDR* WS9 ....40 F7
 COVW CV5 ....154 C3
 DOR/KN B93 ....176 A4
 FOAKS/STRLY B74 ....43 J8
Bakers Ms *DOR/KN* B93 * 176 F7
Baker St *BNTWD* WS7 ....18 D7
 BORD B9 ....108 B4
 COVN CV6 ....116 F7
 HDSW B21 ....88 D5

 SPARK B11 ....126 ...
 TPTN/OCK DY4 ....85 ...
 WBROM B70 ....86 ...
Balaams Dr *NFLD/LBR* B31 ....143 ...
Bala CI *STRPT* DY13 ....125 ...
 ALE/KHTH/YWD B14 ....125 ...
Balcaskie CI *EDG* B15 ....106 ...
Balcombe Rd
 RUGBYS/DCH CV22 ....187 ...
Balden Rd *RIDG/WDGT* B32 ....105 ...
Bald's La *HAG/WOL* DY9 ....72 ...
Baldmoor Lake Rd
 ERDW/GRVHL B23 ....72 ...
Baldwin CI *BILS/COS* WV14 ....86 ...
Baldwin Rd *BEWD* DY12 ....162 ...
 BVILLE B30 ....138 ...
 KIDD DY10 ....138 ...
Baldwins La *HLGN/YWD* B28 ....147 ...
Baldwin St *BILS/COS* WV14 ....67 ...
 SMTHWK B66 ....87 ...
Baldwin Wy *SEDG* DY3 ....84 ...
Balfour *CRTAM* B79 ....45 ...
Balfour Dr *OLDBY* B69 ....69 ...
Balfour Rd *KGSWFD* DY6 ....83 ...
Balfour St *BHTH/HG* B12 ....107 ...
Balham Gv *KGSTG* B44 ....71 ...
Balking CI *BILS/COS* WV14 ....66 ...
Ballantine Rd *COVN* CV6 ....133 ...
Ballarat Wk *STRBR* DY8 ....101 ...
Ballard Crs *DUDS* DY2 ....85 ...
Ballard Rd *DUDS* DY2 ....85 ...
Ballard Wk
 CHWD/FDBR/MGN B37 ....92 ...
Ball Flds *TPTN/OCK* DY4 ....85 ...
Ballingham CI *TLHL/CAN* CV4 .....153 ...
Balliol Rd *COVE* CV2 ....135 ...
Ball La *COVEN* WV9 ....22 ...
Ballot St *SMTHWK* B66 ....87 ...
Balls Hi *WSL* WS1 ....5 ...
Balls St *WSL* WS1 ....5 ...
Balmain Crs *WNSFLD* WV11 ....36 ...
Balmoral CI *COVS* CV3 ....135 ...
 CRTAM B79 ....31 ...
 LICHS WS14 ....21 ...
 RMSLY B62 ....103 ...
 RUSH/SHEL WS4 ....40 ...
Balmoral Dr *HEDN* WS12 ....12 ...
 SHHTH WV12 ....37 ...
 WMBN WV5 ....64 ...
Balmoral Rd *CBROM* B36 ....91 ...
 ERDW/GRVHL B23 ....72 ...
 ETTPK/GDPK/PENN WV4 ....49 ...
 FOAKS/STRLY B74 ....42 ...
 RIDG/WDGT B32 ....122 ...
 STRBR DY8 ....101 ...
Balmoral Vw *DUDN* DY1 ....84 ...
Balmoral Wy
 BLKHTH/ROWR B65 ....104 ...
 RLSN CV32 ....199 ...
 WSLW WS2 ....52 ...
Balsall Heath Rd *DIG/EDG* B5 .....107 ...
Balsall St *RCOVN/BALC/EX* CV7 ..151 ...
Balsall St East
 RCOVN/BALC/EX CV7 ....151 ...
Baltic CI *CNCK/NC* WS11 ....16 ...
Baltimore Rd *PBAR/PBCH* B42 .....70 ...
Balvenie Wy *DUDN* DY1 ....84 ...
Bamber CI *BDMR/CCFT* WV3 ....49 ...
Bamburgh *TAM/AM/WIL* B77 ....46 ...
Bamburgh Gv *RLSN* CV32 ....206 ...
Bamford CI *BLOX/PEL* WS3 ....39 ...
Bamford Rd *BDMR/CCFT* WV3 * .....2 ...
 BLOX/PEL WS3 ....39 ...
Bamford St *TAM/AM/WIL* B77 ....45 ...
Bampfylde PI *PBAR/PBCH* B42 * ...71 ...
Bampton Av *BNTWD* WS7 ....18 ...
Bamville Rd *WASH/WDE* B8 ....90 ...
Banbrook CI *HIA/OLT* B92 ....128 ...
Banbury CI *SEDG* DY3 ....84 ...
Banbury Cft
 CHWD/FDBR/MGN B37 ....110 ...
Banbury Rd *CNCK/NC* WS11 ....15 ...
 WWCK CV34 ....205 ...
Banbury St *DIG/EDG* B5 ....7 ...
Bancroft *TAM/AM/WIL* B77 ....46 ...
Bancroft CI *BILS/COS* WV14 ....67 ...
Bandywood Rd *KGSTG* B44 ....71 ...
Baneberry Dr *WOLVN* WV10 ....22 ...
Banfield Av *DARL/WED* WS10 ....52 ...
Banfield Rd *DARL/WED* WS10 ......68 ...
Banford Rd *WASH/WDE* B8 ....108 ...
Bangham Pit Rd *NFLD/LBR* B31 ..123 ...
Bangley La *POL/KGSB/FAZ* B78 ....44 ...
Bangor Rd *BORD* B9 ....108 ...
Bangor Vls *DARL/WED* WS10 * ....2 ...
Bankdale Rd *WASH/WDE* B8 ....90 ...
Bankes Rd *SMHTH* B10 ....108 ...
Bank Farm CI *HAG/WOL* DY9 ......120 ...
Bankfield Dr *RLSN* CV32 ....206 ...
Bankfield Rd *BILS/COS* WV14 ....67 ...
 TPTN/OCK DY4 ....85 ...
Banklands Rd *DUDS* DY2 ....85 ...
Bank Rd *ATHST* CV9 ....85 ...
 DUDS DY2 ....85 ...
Bankside Crs *FOAKS/STRLY* B74 ...42 ...
Bankside Wy *ALDR* WS9 ....41 ...
Banks Rd *COVN* CV6 ....133 ...
Banks St *WLNHL* WV13 ....51 ...
Bank St *ALE/KHTH/YWD* B14 ......125 ...
 BILS/COS WV14 ....67 ...
 BRLYHL DY5 ....102 ...
 CDYHTH B64 ....103 ...
 HEDN WS12 ....17 ...
 HHTH/SAND B71 ....69 ...
 RUGBYN/HIL CV21 * ....186 ...
 WOLVN WV10 ....36 ...
 WSL WS1 ....5 ...
Bankwell St *BRLYHL* DY5 ....101 ...
Banner La *TLHL/CAN* CV4 ....153 ...
Bannerlea Rd
 SCFLD/BOLD B73 * ....71 ...
Bannerley Rd *STETCH* B33 ....110 ...
Banners Ct *SCFLD/BOLD* B73 * .....71 ...
Banners Ga Rd
 SCFLD/BOLD B73 ....71 ...
Banners Gate Rd
 SCFLD/BOLD B73 ....71 ...
Banners Gv *ERDW/GRVHL* B23 .....72 ...
Banners La *HALE* B63 ....20 ...
 REDW B97 ....202 ...
Banners Wk *KGSTG* B44 ....71 ...
Bannister Rd *DARL/WED* WS10 ...105 ...
Bannister St *CDYHTH* B64 ....103 ...

...nstead Cl BKHL/PFLD WV2 .....50 C6
...ntam Gv COVN CV6 ....133 L2
...ntams Cl STETCH B33 ....118 A1
...nt Mill Rd BRGRVE B60 ......191 L4
...ntock Av BDMR/CCFT WV3 ....49 K5
...ntock Rd TLHL/CAN CV4 .....153 J3
...nton Cl ERDW/GRVHL B23 ....72 B5
...ntry Cl
  LGN/SDN/BHAMAIR B26 ......128 A1
...ptist End Rd DUDS DY2 ....85 G8
...rbara Rd HLGN/YWD B28 .....147 J2
...rbara St CRTAM B79 ....119 J4
...bel Dr WOLV WV1 ....50 F1
...ber Cl HEDN WS12 ....17 J3
...bers La HIA/OLT B92 ....129 G7
...bican Ri COVE CV2 ....156 C3
...bourne Cl SOLH B91 ....148 F6
...bridge Rd BRCTVE CV12 .....187 K6
...by La RUGBYN/HIL CV21 .....187 K6
...by Rd RUGBYS/DCH CV22 ....186 E4
...rcheston Dr
  RWWCK/WEL CV35 ....132 ..
...rclay Rd SMTHWK B67 ....105 J4
...cliff Av TAM/AM/WIL B77 ....46 C2
...croft WLNHL WV13 ....51 M2
...rdell Cl LICH WS13 ....20 F2
...rdfield Cl PBAR/PBCH B42 ....70 D5
...rdley Dr COVN CV6 ....134 A7
...rdon Dr SHLY B90 ....148 B3
...rdon View Rd
  POL/KGSB/FAZ B78 ....47 L6
...rowell Cl CDSL WV8 ....105 K5
...ford Cl COVS CV3 ....156 F5
...DARL/WED WS10 ....52 A5
...REDE B98 ....203 K4
...WALM/CURD B76 ....73 K1
...ford Crs
  ALE/KHTH/YWD B14 ....146 A3
...ford Rd KNWTH CV8 ....197 M3
...SHLY B90 ....148 B3
...WSNGN B18 ....106 C1
...sford St DIG/EDG B5 ....107 J5
...gery Dr DUNHL/THL/PER WV6 .2 B1
...gham Cl SHLY B90 ....148 B3
...ker Rd FOAKS/STRLY B74 .....56 F6
...ker's Butts La COVN CV6 ......8 F1
...kers La HLYWD B47 ....172 D4
...ker St LGLYGN/QTN B68 ....88 F6
...LOZ/NWT B19 ....88 F6
...k Pike RIDG/WDGT B32 ....123 G2
...klands Cft BKDE/SHDE B34 ....91 M7
...le Gv CBROM B36 ....92 D6
...CDSL WV8 ....35 J3
...RUGBYN/HIL CV21 ....187 L5
...SEDG DY3 * 66 D6
...ley Ct RLSN CV32 * 206 D3
...DUNHL/THL/PER WV6 * ....6 ..
...leyfield Ri KGSWFD DY6 ......82 E5
...leyfield Rw WSL WS1 ....4 ..
...ley Mow La BRGRVW B61 .....168 E5
...ley Pl COVS CV3 * 155 M5
...lich Wy REDE B98 ....202 D3
...lling Wy TAM/AM/WIL CV10 ..198 F4
...low Cl LGLYGN/QTN B68 ......104 E2
...RBRY B45 ....143 J3
...TAM/AM/WIL B77 ....46 C1
...low Cl WBROM B70 ....87 K4
...low Rd COVE CV2 ....135 H2
...DARL/WED WS10 ....52 E8
...lows Rd SMHTH WV12... ....38 A7
...mouth Rd ERDW/GRVHL B23 ...90 D1
...nabas Rd ERDW/GRVHL B23 ...90 D1
...maby Sq WOLVN WV10 ....36 B6
...nack Av COVS CV3 ....154 F8
...nack Rd WWCK CV34 ....205 M4
...nard Cl
  CHWD/FDBR/MGN B37 ......111 H4
...RLSN CV32 ....207 G2
...nard Pl BKHL/PFLD WV2 ....50 C7
...nard Rd MGN/WHC B75 ....7 J6
...WNSFLD WV11 ....37 K4
...n Av SEDG DY3 ....66 D3
...nbridge TAM/AM/WIL B77 ......46 A3
...nbrook Rd DOR/KN B93 ....149 L8
...n Ct BRGRVE B60 ....191 J7
...BVILLE B30 ....124 F7
...CDYHTH B64 ....103 J4
...HAG/WOL DY9 ....120 A1
...HALE B63 ....121 J3
...LICH WS13 ....20 F2
...POL/KGSB/FAZ B78 ....47 K7
...n Cft BNTWD WS7 ....26 E1
...GTWY WS6 ....24 E2
...RIDG/WDGT B32 ....123 G2
...ncroft Rd OLDBY B69 ....85 L5
...ncroft St WBROM B70 ....68 E5
...ne Cl NUN CV11 ....99 M6
...nes Cl STETCH B33 ....110 C3
...nes HI SLYOAK B29 ....123 K3
...nes Rd LICHS WS14 ....20 F2
...nesville Cl SMHTH WS10 .....108 E5
...net Rd ERDW/GRVHL B23 ......72 B8
...nett Cl BILS/COS WV14 ....51 H1
...KGSWFD DY6 ....83 H1
...nett Gn KGSWFD DY6 ....83 H8
...nett Rd WLNHL WV13 ....51 H1
...netts Cl KIDD DY10 ....164 E1
...netts Dr KIDD DY10 ....164 E1
...netts La BRWNH WS8 ....26 D5
...KIDD DY10 ....164 E1
...nett St STRBR DY8 ....101 H2
...PTN/OCK DY4 ....85 L1
...ney Cl TPTN/OCK DY4 ....85 L2
...n Farm Ct BILS/COS WV14 ....51 L6
...nfield Av COVN CV6 ....132 F6
...nfield Cl LICHS WS14 ....20 F2
...nfield Dr HIA/OLT B92 ....129 G7
...nfield Gv BFLD/HDSWWD B20.70 C8
...nfield Rd BRGRVW B61 ....191 J4
...RMSLY B62 ....104 B6
...STRPT DY13 ....188 A4
...PTN/OCK DY4 ....67 J7
...nfield Wy HEDN WS12 ....13 L7
...nford Cl SMHTH WS10... ....38 A7
...nford Crs LGLYGN/QTN B68...104 E2

Barn Owl Cl KIDD DY10 ....164 E1
Barn Owl Dr BLOX/PEL WS3 ....39 K1
Barnpark Covert
  ALE/KHTH/YWD B14 ....146 A3
Barn Piece RIDG/WDGT B32 ....122 F1
Barnsbury Av CSCFLD/WYGN B72.73 G7
Barns Cl ALDR WS9 ....40 D1
Barns Cft FOAKS/STRLY B74 ....55 M2
Barnsdale Crs NFLD/LBR B31 ..144 C1
Barns La RUSH/SHEL WS4 ....40 A5
Barnsley Cl ATHST CV9 ....63 H6
Barnsley Hall Rd BRGRVW B61 .168 D7
Barnsley Rd BRGRVW B61 ......191 L1
  HRBN B17 ....105 L4
Barnstaple Cl COVN CV5 * 132 D8
Barnstaple Rd SMTHWK B66 ....87 M8
Barn St DIG/EDG B5 ....7 G4
Barnswood Cl CNCK/NC WS11...15 M5
  HALE B63 ....103 G8
Barnwood Cl REDE B98 ....195 H8
Barnwood Rd CDSL WV8 ....35 J4
  RIDG/WDGT B32 ....123 K1
Baron Cl BNTWD WS7 ....18 E4
Baron Leigh Dr TLHL/CAN CV4 *.153 H7
Barons Cl HRBN B17 ....105 M7
  NUNW/HART CV10 ....98 A1
Baron's Field Rd COVS CV3 ....155 J6
Barpool Rd NUNW/HART CV10 ..98 D1
Barrack Cl MGN/WHC B75 ....57 L7
Barrack La HALE B63 ....102 F7
Barracks Cl BLOX/PEL WS3 .....39 J5
Barracks La BLOX/PEL WS3 .....39 H5
  BRWNH WS8 ....27 G4
  RWWCK/WEL CV35 ....196 A3
Barracks St WALN/NECH B7 .....7 J2
  WBROM B70 ....68 E5
  WWCK CV34 ....205 J6
Barracks Wy COV CV1 * 8 F7
Barrar Cl STRBR DY8 ....101 J5
Barras Gn COVE CV2 ....155 L1
Barras La COV CV1 ....8 C4
Barratts La BEWD DY12 ....162 E2
Barratts Cft BRLYHL DY5 ....84 A4
Barratts Rd HWK/WKHTH B38 ..145 L5
Barratts Stile La BEWD DY12 ..162 E2
Barr Common Cl ALDR WS9 ....54 F2
Barr Common Rd ALDR WS9 ....54 F2
Barrett Cl KIDD DY10 ....138 F7
Barretts La
  RCOVN/BALC/EX CV7 ....152 A2
Barrhill Cl GTB/HAM B43 ....70 D3
Barrie Av KIDD DY10 ....139 G6
Barrington Cl DSYBK/YTR WS5 ..69 L2
  WOLVN WV10 ....36 A4
Barrington Rd HIA/OLT B92 ....127 J3
  RBRY B45 ....143 J6
Barr Lakes La BLOX/PEL WS3 ...54 C6
Barr La
  MKTBOG/BARL/STKG CV13 ....81 M2
  RRUGBY CV23 ....158 C1
Barron Rd NFLD/LBR B31 ......144 F2
Barrow Cl COVE CV2 ....135 M7
  REDE B98 ....203 K2
Barrowfield La KNWTH CV8 ....197 K1
Barrow Hill Rd BRLYHL DY5 .....84 A4
Barrow Rd KNWTH CV8 ....197 K1
Barrows La
  LGN/SDN/BHAMAIR B26 ....109 J5
Barrows Rd SPARK B11 ....108 A7
Barrow Wk DIG/EDG B5 ....107 J6
Barrs Crs CDYHTH B64 ....103 K5
Barrs St CDYHTH B64 ....103 K5
Barrs St LGLYGN/QTN B68 .....104 E1
Barr St LOZ/NWT B19 ....89 G8
  SEDG DY3 ....84 A2
Barry Rd DSYBK/YTR WS5 ....54 A6
Barsby Cl ATHST CV9 ....63 H6
Barsham Dr BRLYHL DY5 ....84 A4
Barston Cl COVN CV6 ....134 E2
Barston La HIA/OLT B92 ....150 D3
  RCOVN/BALC/EX CV7 ....151 H5
  SOLH B91 ....149 M3
Bartestree Cl REDE B98 ....203 K4
Bartholomews La BRGRVW B61 .168 D8
Bartholomew Ct COVS CV3 * ...155 L2
Bartholomew Rw DIG/EDG B5 ....7 J4
Bartholomew St DIG/EDG B5 ....7 J4
Bartic Av KGSWFD DY6 ....101 K1
Bartleet Rd REDE B98 ....203 H6
  SMTHWKW B67 ....87 H8
Bartlett Cl COVN CV6 ....134 C3
  PENK ST19 ....10 D5
  TPTN/OCK DY4 ....67 M4
Bartley Cl HIA/OLT B92 ....127 K3
Bartley Dr NFLD/LBR B31 ......123 J3
Bartley Woods RIDG/WDGT B32.122 F3
Barton Crs RLSS CV31 ....207 G2
Barton Cft HLGN/YWD B28 .....147 K1
Barton Dr DOR/KN B93 ....175 M1
Barton Lodge Rd
  HLGN/YWD B28 ....147 J1
Barton Rd BDWTH CV12 ....116 F1
  COVN CV6 ....134 D3
  ETTPK/GDPK/PENN WV4 .....66 C1
  NUNW/HART CV10 ....99 G4
  RUGBYS/DCH CV22 ....186 B5
Bartons Bank LOZ/NWT B19 ....89 H4
Bartons Ct COVE CV2 * 155 L1
Barton's Meadow COVE CV2 ...134 F8
Barton St WBROM B70 ....86 F3
Bar Wk ALDR WS9 ....41 H1
Barwell Ct DOR/KN B93 ....175 J1
  RLSN CV32 ....206 D2
Barwell Rd BORD B9 ....107 M3
Barwick St CBHAMNW B3 ....6 F4
Basalt Cl WSLW WV2 ....52 E1
Basant Cl WWCK CV34 ....205 L6
Bascote Cft REDW B97 ....201 M4
Basford Brook Dr COVN CV6 ..116 D8
Basil Gv NFLD/LBR B31 ....144 C1
Basil Rd NFLD/LBR B31 ....144 C1
Basin La TAM/AM/WIL B77 ......46 D4
Baskerville Rd KIDD DY10 .....138 D4
Baskeyfield Cl LICHS WS14 ....21 H6
Basley Wy COVN CV6 ....134 B3
Baslow Cl BLOX/PEL WS3 ....38 F2
  STETCH B33 ....109 J1
Baslow Rd BLOX/PEL WS3 ......38 F2
Basons La LGLYGN/QTN B68 ....87 G3
Bassano Rd BLKHTH/ROWR B65.104 A4
Bassenthwaite Ct KGSWFD DY6 .83 H7
Bassett Cl
  ETTPK/GDPK/PENN WV4 .....49 G7
  SHHTH WV12 ....52 B1
  WALM/CURD B76 ....73 J1
Bassett Cft SMHTH B10 ....107 H5
Bassett Rd COVN CV6 ....133 G8
  DARL/WED WS10 ....69 G3
  HALE B63 ....102 E7
Bassetts Gv
  CHWD/FDBR/MGN B37 ....92 C3
Bassett St WSLW WV2 ....4 A4

Bassnage Rd HALE B63 ....121 J3
Batchcroft BILS/COS WV14 .....51 H8
Batchelor Cl STRBR DY8 ......101 K5
Batchley Rd REDW B97 ....201 M3
Bateman Dr SCFLD/BOLD B73 ...72 F4
Bateman's Acre South COVN CV6 .8 A4
Bateman's La HLYWD B47 ......146 C8
Bates Cl WALM/CURD B76 ....73 L6
Bates Gv WNSFLD WV11 ....36 F1
Bates HI REDW B97 * 202 B1
Bates Rd COVW CV5 ....154 C6
Bate St ETTPK/GDPK/PENN WV4 .66 E2
  WOLV WV1 ....4 E1
Batham Rd KIDD DY10 ....138 D5
Bath Av WOLV WV1 ....2 E3
Batheaston Cl
  HWK/WKHTH B38 ....145 H6
Bath Meadow HALE B63 ....103 J8
Bath Pas DIG/EDG B5 ....7 G7
Bath Pl RLSS CV31 ....206 D4
Bath Rw EDG B15 ....6 D8
  OLDBY B69 ....86 B5
Bath St BILS/COS WV14 ....51 J8
  CBHAMNE B4 ....7 G2
  COV CV1 * 9 J7
  DUDS DY2 ....85 G5
  RLSS CV31 ....206 D6
  RUGBYN/HIL CV21 ....186 F2
  SEDG DY3 ....66 B4
  WLNHL WV13 ....51 M4
  WOLV WV1 * 3 J3
  WSL WS1 ....4 F5
Bathurst Cl COVN CV6 ....133 L7
Bathurst Rd SOLH B91 ....129 L5
Bath Wk BHTH/HG B12 ....107 J8
Bathway Rd COVS CV3 ....180 E1
Batmans Hill Rd BILS/COS WV14..67 J3
Batsford Cl REDE B98 ....202 F8
Batsford Rd COVN CV6 ....154 D1
Batson Ri STRBR DY8 ....101 L5
Battalion Ct COVN CV6 ....133 L4
Battenhall Rd HRBN B17 ......105 J4
Battens Cl REDE B98 ....202 D2
Battens Dr REDE B98 ....203 H1
Battery Wy COVE CV2 ....126 C1
Battlefield HI WMBN WV5 ......64 F6
Battlefield La WMBN WV5 ......64 F7
Baulk La RCOVN/BALC/EX CV7 .152 B5
Bavaro Gdns BRLYHL DY5 ......102 B1
Baverstock Rd
  ALE/KHTH/YWD B14 ....146 D3
Bawnmore Ct
  RUGBYS/DCH CV22 ....186 D5
Bawnmore Pk
  RUGBYS/DCH CV22 ....186 D5
Bawnmore Rd
  RUGBYS/DCH CV22 ....186 D5
Baxter Av KIDD DY10 ....138 C6
Baxter Cl TLHL/CAN CV4 ......153 L3
Baxter Ct RLSS CV31 ....206 E6
Baxter Gdns KIDD DY10 ....138 C6
Baxterley La SOLH B91 ....148 E1
  WALM/CURD B76 ....73 K4
Baxters Rd SHLY B90 ....147 M5
Bayer St BILS/COS WV14 ....67 G3
Bayford Av
  LGN/SDN/BHAMAIR B26 ....128 A3
  NFLD/LBR B31 ....144 C7
Bayley Crs DARL/WED WS10 ....52 A5
Bayley La COV CV1 ....9 G5
Bayleys La TPTN/OCK DY4 ......68 A1
Bayley St STRBR DY8 ....119 K1
Baylis Av WNSFLD WV11 ....37 K5
Bayliss Av COVN CV6 ....134 E1
Bayliss Cl BILS/COS WV14 .....51 G6
  NFLD/LBR B31 ....123 M8
Baynton Rd WLNHL WV13 ......38 A6
Bayston Av BDMR/CCFT WV3 ...49 J5
Bayston Rd
  ALE/KHTH/YWD B14 ....146 C1
Bayswater Rd
  BFLD/HDSWWD B20 ....89 H4
  SEDG DY3 ....84 B3
Bayton Rd RCOVN/BALC/EX CV7.116 F5
Bayton Wy
  RCOVN/BALC/EX CV7 ....117 G6
Baytree Av BLOX/PEL WS3 .....38 E6
Bay Tree Cl COVE CV2 ....135 H4
  HWK/WKHTH B38 ....145 J6
Baytree Rd BLOX/PEL WS3 .....38 E3
Baywell Cl SHLY B90 ....148 B6
Beach Av BHTH/HG B12 ....107 M8
  ETTPK/GDPK/PENN WV4 .....66 E2
Beach Brook Cl SPARK B11 ....107 M8
Beachburn Wy
  BFLD/HDSWWD B20 ....88 D2
Beach Cl NFLD/LBR B31 ....145 G4
Beachcroft Rd KGSWFD DY6 ...83 G4
Beach Dr HALE B63 ....103 L8
Beach Rd BILS/COS WV14 ......51 L6
  SPARK B11 ....107 M8
  STRPT DY13 ....188 C4
Beach St HALE B63 ....103 L8
Beachwood Av KGSWFD DY6 ...83 G4
Beacon Cl GTB/HAM B43 ....70 D4
  RBRY B45 ....143 K7
  SMTHWK B66 ....87 L6
Beacon Dr WSL WS1 ....5 L7
Beaconfields LICH WS13 ....20 E5
Beacon Gdns LICH WS13 ....20 E4
Beacon HI ALDR WS9 ....55 G4
  AST/WIT B6 ....89 J5
  RBRY B45 ....143 J8
Beacon La BRGRVE B60 ....169 H2
  SEDG DY3 ....66 C2
Beacon Ri BILS/COS WV14 .....51 M8
  HAG/WOL DY9 ....120 B1
  SEDG DY3 ....66 C4
Beacon Rd ALDR WS9 ....54 F6
  COVN CV6 ....134 B3
  DSYBK/YTR WS5 ....54 C5
  GTB/HAM B43 ....71 G2
  KGSTG B44 ....71 L1
  SCFLD/BOLD B73 ....72 F4
  SHHTH WV12 ....38 A5
Beaconsfield Av
  ETTPK/GDPK/PENN WV4 .....50 B8
  RUGBYS/DCH CV22 ....186 E2
Beaconsfield Ct WSL WS1 ......5 L6
Beaconsfield Crs
  BHTH/HG B12 * 107 H8
Beaconsfield Dr
  ETTPK/GDPK/PENN WV4 .....50 B8
Beaconsfield Rd BHTH/HG B12..125 H3
  COVE CV2 ....155 M3
  FOAKS/STRLY B74 ....56 F6
Beaconsfield St HHTH/SAND B71.69 H8

RLSS CV31 ....206 F5
Beacon St BILS/COS WV14 .....66 D3
  LICH WS13 ....20 E5
  WSL WS1 ....5 L7
Beacon Vw RBRY B45 ....143 K7
Beacon View Dr KGSTG B44 ....71 K1
Beacon View Rd
  HHTH/SAND B71 ....69 K4
Beacon Wy ALDR WS9 ....40 K4
  HEDN WS12 ....17 K2
  RUSH/SHEL WS4 ....53 M1
Beadborough Wk ALDR WS9 ...40 K4
Beake Av COVN CV6 ....133 M7
Beakes Rd SMTHWKW B67 ....105 K2
Beaks Farm Gdns
  LDYWD/EDGR B16 ....106 B3
Beaks Hill Rd HWK/WKHTH B38.145 J4
Beak St CBHAMW B1 ....6 F6
Beale Cl CVALE B35 ....91 L3
Beale St BRGRVE B60 ....169 J8
Beales St AST/WIT B6 ....89 M5
Beales Wy COVE CV2 ....135 J3
Bealeys Av WNSFLD WV11 .....37 G5
Bealeys La BLOX/PEL WS3 .....38 E3
Beaman's Cl HIA/OLT B92 ....127 L1
Beamish Cl COVE CV2 ....135 L7
Bean Cft RIDG/WDGT B32 .....123 G3
Beanfield Av COVS CV3 ....180 D1
Bean Rd DUDS DY2 ....85 H5
  TPTN/OCK DY4 ....67 H7
Beardmore Rd
  CSCFLD/WYGN B72 ....73 G5
Bearhill Dr ALVE B48 ....170 C6
Bear Lane Cl POL/KGSB/FAZ B78..47 L3
Bearley Cft WDGT WV10 ......148 A5
Bearmore Rd CDYHTH B64 ....103 J4
Bearnett Dr
  ETTPK/GDPK/PENN WV4 .....65 G3
Bearwood Rd SMTHWK B66 ...105 L3
Beasley Gv PBAR/PBCH B42 ...70 F3
Beaton Cl WLNHL WV13 ....51 J3
Beaton Rd FOAKS/STRLY B74 ..56 F6
Beatrice St RUGBYS/DCH CV22.186 A4
Beatrice Wk TPTN/OCK DY4 ....85 G7
Beatty Dr RUGBYS/DCH CV22 .186 A6
Beaubrook Gdns STRBR DY8 ..101 H2
Beauchamp Av
  BFLD/HDSWWD B20 ....70 D8
  KIDD DY10 ....164 A2
  RLSN CV32 ....206 D4
Beauchamp Cl
  CHWD/FDBR/MGN B37 ....110 F3
  WALM/CURD B76 ....73 M6
Beauchamp Gdns WWCK CV34.205 M7
Beauchamp Ms RLSN CV32 * .206 D4
Beauchamp Rd KNWTH CV8 ...197 J3
  MOS/BIL B13 ....125 M8
  RLSN CV32 ....206 D4
  SOLH B91 ....127 L8
  TAM/AM/WIL B77 ....46 C1
  WWCK CV34 ....205 M5
Beau Ct CNCK/NC WS11 ....16 C4
Beaudesert BNTWD WS7 ....18 E4
Beaudesert Cl HLYWD B47 ....146 E7
Beaudesert Rd
  BFLD/HDSWWD B20 ....88 F5
  COVW CV5 ....154 B5
  HLYWD B47 ....146 E7
Beaufell Cl WWCK CV34 ....205 J4
Beaufort Av KIDD DY10 ....138 D1
  KIDDW DY11 ....137 L5
  RLSN CV32 ....199 G8
Beaufort Dr COVS CV3 ....156 D6
Beaufort Rd LDYWD/EDGR B16.106 D4
  REDW B97 ....202 D2
Beaufort Wy ALDR WS9 ....54 F1
Beaulieu Av KGSWFD DY6 ....101 K1
Beaulieu Cl KIDDW DY11 ......137 H3
Beaulieu Pk RLSS CV31 ....207 H7
Beaumaris Cl COVW CV5 ......132 D8
  DUDN DY1 ....65 K4
Beaumont Cl GTWY WS6 ....24 D3
  TPTN/OCK DY4 ....67 G8
Beaumont Crs COVN CV6 ....8 A1
Beaumont Dr BRLYHL DY5 ....102 B1
  HRBN B17 ....123 M1
Beaumont Gv SOLH B91 ....127 K8
Beaumont Lawns BRCVE CV12.169 G4
Beaumont Pl NUNW/HART CV10..98 D2
Beaumont Rd BVILLE B30 .....124 C7
  DARL/WED WS10 ....68 D1
  GTWY WS6 ....24 D3
  NUN CV11 ....98 D1
  RCOVN/BALC/EX CV7 ....115 G7
  RMSLY B62 ....104 A4
Beaumont Wy WWCK CV34 ....205 L5
Beaurevoir Wy WWCK CV34 ...205 L5
Beausale Cft COVW CV5 ......153 L2
Beausale Dr DOR/KN B93 .....149 M6
Beausale La RWWCK/WEL CV35.196 A5
Beauty Bank CDYHTH B64 ....103 L5
Beauty Bank Crs STRBR DY8 .101 J7
Beaver Cl WNSFLD WV11 ....37 K8
Bebington Cl COVEN WV9 .....35 K5
Beccles Dr WLNHL WV13 ....51 L3
Beck Cl SMTHWK B66 ....105 L1
Beckenham Av KGSTG B44 .....71 L4
Beckensall Cl DUDN DY1 ....84 F4
Becket Cl MGN/WHC B75 ....42 D7
Beckett Rd REDE B98 ....194 D8
Beckett St BILS/COS WV14 .....51 J7
Beckfield Cl
  ALE/KHTH/YWD B14 ....146 C3
  RUSH/SHEL WS4 ....40 A5
Beckfield Rd RUGBYN/HIL CV21.186 F6
Beckford Dr COVE CV2 ....135 K4
Beckford Cft DOR/KN B93 * ..175 K2
Beckman Rd HAG/WOL DY9 ...120 A3
Becks La RCOVN/BALC/EX CV7.113 J3
Beconsfield Ct DOR/KN B93 ...175 K4
Becton Gv PBAR/PBCH B42 ....71 H6
Bedcote Pl STRBR DY8 ....101 M8
Beddoe Cl TPTN/OCK DY4 .....68 B8
Beddows Rd BLOX/PEL WS3 ....39 L8
Bede Rd BDWTH CV12 ....116 E1
  COVN CV6 ....98 D1
Bede Village BDWTH CV12 * ..116 A5
Bedford Dr MGN/WHC B75 .....57 J7
Bedford Pl HEDN WS12 ....13 G1
  RLSN CV32 ....206 D4
Bedford Rd HHTH/SAND B71 ...57 J6
  MGN/WHC B75 ....57 J8
  SPARK B11 ....107 M8
Bedford St COV CV1 ....8 B9
  RLSN CV32 ....206 D4
  TPTN/OCK DY4 ....67 M4

WOLV WV1 ....50 E6
Bedford Ter LOZ/NWT B19 * ...89 H5
Bedingstone Dr PENK ST19 ....10 D7
Bedlam La COVN CV6 ....134 C3
Bedlam Wood Rd
  NFLD/LBR B31 ....144 A4
Bedworth Cl BDWTH CV12 ....117 H3
Bedworth Cft TPTN/OCK DY4 ..85 M1
Bedworth Gv BORD B9 ....108 C3
Bedworth La BDWTH CV12 ....116 A1
Bedworth Rd BDWTH CV12 ....117 L3
  COVN CV6 ....116 B8
Beebee Rd DARL/WED WS10 ...52 D8
Beecham Cl ALDR WS9 ....40 E5
Beech Av BHTH/HG B12 ....107 L8
  CHWD/FDBR/MGN B37 ....110 F4
  RIDG/WDGT B32 ....105 H7
  RMSLY B62 ....104 A5
  TAM/AM/WIL B77 ....46 C2
Beech Cliffe WWCK CV34 .....205 K5
Beech Cl ATHST CV9 ....61 G8
  MGN/WHC B75 ....56 E1
  NUNW/HART CV10 ....79 L5
  POL/KGSB/FAZ B78 ....47 L6
  SEDG DY3 ....66 C4
  WOLVN WV10 ....35 M5
Beechcote Av KIDDW DY11 ...138 B3
Beech Ct GTWY WS6 * 24 E1
  HEDN WS12 * 12 F6
  SMTHWK B66 ....87 C6
  WSL WS1 ....5 J3
Beechcroft BDWTH CV12 .....116 D4
  DARL/WED WS10 ....52 D8
  TPTN/OCK DY4 ....68 D4
Beechcroft Av HLGN/YWD B28.126 D7
Beechcroft Crs
  FOAKS/STRLY B74 ....55 H4
Beechcroft Dr BRGRVE B60 ...191 H1
Beechcroft Est HALE B63 .....103 G7
Beechcroft Pl WOLVN WV10 ...36 A7
Beechcroft Rd CBROM B36 ....91 M5
  CDYHTH B64 ....103 H4
  KIDD DY11 ....137 L5
Beechdale Av KGSTG B44 ......71 J3
Beechdale Rd BLOX/PEL WS3 ..38 D5
Beech Dene Gv
  ERDW/GRVHL B23 ....72 C8
Beech Dr KNWTH CV8 ....179 M8
  RUGBYS/DCH CV22 ....186 A4
Beecher Pl HALE B63 ....103 H8
Beecher Rd HALE B63 ....103 H8
Beecher Rd East HALE B63 ....103 H8
Beecher St HALE B63 ....103 G8
Beeches Av ACGN CV7 ....127 C1
Beeches Cl KGSWFD DY6 ....83 H8
Beeches Dr ERDE/BCHGN B24 ..91 C1
Beeches Farm Dr
  NFLD/LBR B31 ....144 E6
Beeches Pl BLOX/PEL WS3 .....39 H6
Beeches Rd BLKHTH/ROWR B65.103 M4
  BLOX/PEL WS3 ....39 H7
  HHTH/SAND B71 ....87 J2
  KIDDW DY11 ....138 A4
  LGLYGN/QTN B68 ....105 G2
  PBAR/PBCH B42 ....71 H6
The Beeches BDWTH CV12 ....116 D4
  POL/KGSB/FAZ B78 ....47 L5
  WBROM B70 ....87 J3
  WOLV WV1 ....2 A3
Beeches View Av HALE B63 ...121 G1
Beeches Wy NFLD/LBR B31 ...144 E6
Beechey Cl GTB/HAM B43 ......55 H8
Beechfield Cl RMSLY B62 .....104 A5
Beechfield Dr KIDDW DY11 ....138 A4
Beechfield Gv BILS/COS WV14 ..66 F6
Beechfield Ri LICH WS13 ......21 H5
Beechfield Rd SMTHWK B67 ..105 K1
  SPARK B11 ....107 M7
Beech Gdns CDSL WV8 ....34 C4
  LICHS WS14 ....21 G7
Beech Ga FOAKS/STRLY B74 ....41 M8
Beechglade BFLD/HDSWWD B20..88 D1
Beech Gn DUDN DY1 ....66 B8
Beech Gv ALE/KHTH/YWD B14.125 L8
  HEDN WS12 ....12 B5
  RCOVN/BALC/EX CV7 ....96 C3
  WWCK CV34 ....205 M4
Beech Hill Rd CSCFLD/WYGN B72.73 H7
Beech Hurst HWK/WKHTH B38.145 J5
Beechlawn Dr KINVER DY7 ....100 C6
Beechmore Rd
  LGN/SDN/BHAMAIR B26 ....109 K8
Beechmount Dr
  ERDW/GRVHL B23 ....72 E7
Beechnut Cl SOLH B91 ....128 B8
  TLHL/CAN CV4 ....153 H3
Beechnut La SOLH B91 ....128 C8
Beech Park Dr RBRY B45 ......170 A5
Beech Pine Cl HEDN WS12 ....12 E5
Beech Rd BRGRVW B61 ....191 K1
  BVILLE B30 ....124 C6
  COVN CV6 ....133 M8
  CRTAM B79 ....31 L5
  DARL/WED WS10 ....52 D8
  DUDN DY1 ....85 G1
  ERDW/GRVHL B23 ....72 D6
  HLYWD B47 ....146 F7
  KGSWFD DY6 ....83 H8
  OLDBY B69 ....85 L5
  STRBR DY8 ....101 J8
  WLNHL WV13 ....51 J3
  WOLVN WV10 ....35 M5
Beech Tree Av COVW CV5 .....153 M3
  WNSFLD WV11 ....37 K8
Beech Tree Cl KGSWFD DY6 ....83 J5
  REDW B97 ....201 L4
Beech Tree La CNCK/NC WS11...16 B5
Beechtree Rd ALDR WS9 ....40 D2
Beech Wy HWK/WKHTH B38 ...145 K5
Beech Wy SMTHWK B66 ....105 J5
Beechwood Av COVW CV5 .....156 C4
  WNSFLD WV11 ....37 K8
Beechwood Cl BLOX/PEL WS3 ..38 F2
  SHLY B90 ....174 B1
Beechwood Crs
  TAM/AM/WIL B77 ....32 D8
Beechwood Cft
  FOAKS/STRLY B74 ....56 B4
Beechwood Dr
  DUNHL/THL/PER WV6 ....48 E3
  RUGBYN/HIL CV21 * 186 D1
Beechwood Park Rd SOLH B91.127 L8
Beechwood Rd
  ALE/KHTH/YWD B14 ....125 K8
  BDWTH CV12 ....117 G1
  DUDS DY2 ....85 J4
  GTB/HAM B43 ....70 D7
  NUNW/HART CV10 ....80 B7
  SMTHWKW B67 ....105 J5
  WBROM B70 ....87 F2

Beecroft Av LICH WS13 ....20 F4
Beecroft Rd CNCK/NC WS11 ....16 C4
Beehive CI BRGRVW B61 ....168 C4
Beehive HI KNWTH CV8 ....179 H6
Beehive La WALM/CURD B76 ....75 G7
Bee La WOLVN WV10 ....36 B2
Beeston CI AST/WIT B6 ....89 L6
  BRLYHL DY5 ....102 A5
  COVS CV3 ....156 D5
Beeton Rd WSNGN B18 ....88 C7
Beet St BLKHTH/ROWR B65 ....104 A4
Beever Rd TPTN/OCK DY4 ....68 B6
Beggars Bush La WMBN WV5 ....64 A6
Beighton CI FOAKS/STRLY B74 ....42 C7
Beilby Rd BVILLE B30 ....124 F7
Belbroughton CI REDE B98 ....202 D3
Belbroughton Rd
  HAG/WOL DY9 ....141 J4
  HALE B63 ....121 K3
  KIDD DY10 ....140 A4
  STRBR DY8 ....119 J2
Belchers La BORD B9 ....108 E3
Beldray Pk BILS/COS WV14 * 51 J7
Beldray Rd BILS/COS WV14 ....51 J7
Belfry CI BLOX/PEL WS3 ....38 E2
Belfry Dr STRBR DY8 ....101 J7
The Belfry DUNHL/THL/PER WV6 ..48 B1
Belgrade Rd WOLVN WV10 ....35 M3
Belgrade Sq COV CV1 * 8 C1
Belgrave Ct KGSWFD DY6 ....101 K1
Belgrave Dr RUGBYS/HIL CV21 ....161 H7
Belgrave Int DIG/EDG B5 ....107 H6
Belgrave Middleway
  DIG/EDG B5 ....107 J6
Belgrave Rd BHTH/HG B12 ....107 K7
  COVE CV2 ....156 C1
  RMSLY B62 ....104 B5
  TAM/AM/WIL B77 ....46 C5
Belgrave Sq COVE CV2 ....156 C1
Belgrave Wk WSLW WS2 ....52 F2
Belgrove CI EDG B15 ....106 C7
Belinda CI WLNHL WV13 ....51 K2
Bellairs Av BDWTH CV12 ....116 C4
Bellam Rd RWWCK/WEL CV35 ....204 D6
Bellamy CI SHLY B90 ....148 A4
Bellamy Farm Rd SHLY B90 ....148 A4
Bellamy La WNSFLD WV11 ....37 H6
Bell Barn Rd EDG B15 ....6 D9
Bellbrook PENK ST19 ....10 C4
Bellbrooke CI COVE CV2 ....134 F4
Belle CI BORD B9 ....108 C2
  CBROM B36 ....92 F7
  DARL/WED WS10 ....52 B6
  LICH WS13 ....20 D4
Bell CI RLSN CV32 * 206 D3
Bellcroft LDYWD/EDGR B16 ....6 A6
Bell Dr DSYBK/YTR WS5 ....53 L8
  HEDN WS12 ....13 C6
  RCOVN/BALC/EX CV7 ....116 C4
  WASH/WDE B8 ....108 D2
Bellefield Av WSNGN B18 ....106 C1
Bellefield Rd WSNGN B18 ....106 C1
Belle Isle BRLYHL DY5 ....102 A2
Bellemere Rd HIA/OLT B92 ....129 M8
Bellencroft Gdns
  BDMR/CCFT WV3 ....48 F6
Bell End BLKHTH/ROWR B65 ....104 A2
Belle Orch KIDD DY11 ....137 M8
Belle V HALE B63 ....103 J3
Bellevue DIG/EDG B5 ....107 H6
  STRBR DY8 ....119 J2
Bellevue Av LDYWD/EDGR B16 *..106 B3
Belle Vue CI BRGRVE B60 ....169 G5
Belle Vue Dr RMSLY B62 ....104 B7
Belle Vue Rd
  BLKHTH/ROWR B65 * 104 A2
Belle Vue Rd BILS/COS WV14 ....67 K3
  LGN/SDN/BHAMAIR B26 ....109 L6
Bellevue St BILS/COS WV14 ....51 J8
Belle Vue Ter HIA/OLT B92 ....129 L7
Belle Wk MOS/BIL B13 ....125 M3
Bellfarm Ms CDYHTH B64 * 103 J3
Bellflower CI WOLVN WV10 ....22 E6
Bell Fold LGLGYN/QTN B68 * 87 G7
Bell Green La RWBY/WKHTH B38 ..145 M8
Bell Green Rd COVN WS8 ....134 C5
Bell Heather Rd CNCK/NC WS11 ..26 B3
Bell HI NFLD/LBR B31 ....123 L8
Bell Holloway NFLD/LBR B31 ....123 K8
Bellington TAM/AM/WIL B77 ....47 H4
Bellington Cft SHLY B90 ....148 E7
Bellis St LDYWD/EDGR B16 ....106 D4
Bell La BLOX/PEL WS3 ....38 C1
  DSYBK/YTR WS5 ....69 L1
  NFLD/LBR B31 ....144 A2
  STETCH B33 ....110 C4
Bellman CI DARL/WED WS10 ....52 B6
Bell Meadow Wy
  ALE/KHTH/YWD B14 ....146 B3
Bell PI BKHL/PFLD WV2 * 8 F9
Bell Rd DSYBK/YTR WS5 ....54 B7
  DUDS DY2 ....85 G8
  WMBN WV5 ....64 A6
Bell Rw STRPT DY13 ....188 E2
Bells Farm CI
  ALE/KHTH/YWD B14 ....146 A3
Bellsize CI CNCK/NC WS11 ....17 K3
Bells La BNTWD WS7 ....18 D4
  HWK/WKHTH B38 ....146 A3
  STRBR DY8 ....101 H4
Bells Moor Rd WBROM B70 ....68 E7
Bell St BILS/COS WV14 ....51 J7
  BRLYHL DY5 ....84 B6
  BRLYHL DY5 ....102 B3
  DARL/WED WS10 ....52 B6
  TPTN/OCK DY4 ....67 J8
  WBROM B70 ....87 H3
  WOLV WV1 ....2 F6
Bell St South BRLYHL DY5 ....102 B3
Bell Tower Ms RLSN CV32 ....206 D2
Belle Wy COVN WS8 ....134 C4
Bell Vue Rd BLKHTH/ROWR B65 ..104 A3
Bellwood Rd NFLD/LBR B31 ....144 D1
Belmont Av CNCK/NC WS11 ....16 A3
Belmont CI ALDR WS9 ....40 E6
  GTWY WS6 ....24 E1
  REDW B97 ....201 M4
  TPTN/OCK DY4 ....67 K7
Belmont Covert NFLD/LBR B31 ..123 M7
Belmont Dr RLSN CV32 ....206 E1
Belmont Gdns BILS/COS WV14 ....67 L1
Belmont Ms RLSN CV32 * 206 E1
Belmont Pas CBHAMNE B4 ....7 M5
Belmont Rd BRLYHL DY5 ....84 B7
  COVN CV6 ....134 D4
  ETTPK/GDPK/PENN WV4 ....49 L8
  HAG/WOL DY9 ....120 C3
  HDSW B21 ....88 A5
  RBRY B45 ....143 K7
  RUGBYS/DCH CV22 ....186 E5
  SMTHWK B66 ....105 L3
  TAM/AM/WIL B77 ....46 C7
Belmont Rd East HDSW B21 ....88 A5

Belmont Rw CBHAMNE B4 ....7 K3
Belmont St COV CV1 ....6 C6
Belper DUDN DY1 ....84 F4
Belper Rd BLOX/PEL WS3 ....39 G2
  WBROM B70 ....86 D2
Belper Rw DUDS DY2 ....103 J1
Belsize TAM/AM/WIL B77 ....46 C3
Belstone CI ALE/KHTH/YWD B14..125 H4
Belton Av WNSFLD WV11 ....36 F4
Belton CI HOCK/TIA B94 ....175 G8
Belton Gv RBRY B45 ....144 A5
Belvedere La 12 E8
Belvedere Av
  ETTPK/GDPK/PENN WV4 ....49 M8
Belvedere CI BNTWD WS7 ....18 D8
  CRTAM B79 ....32 A6
  KGSWFD DY6 ....101 K1
  KIDD DY10 ....138 D5
Belvedere Crs BEWD DY12 ....137 G8
Belvedere Dr BRGRVW B61 ....191 L1
Belvedere Gdns
  DUNHL/THL/PER WV6 ....35 H6
Belvedere Rd COVW CV5 ....154 E5
  ERDE/BCHGN B24 ....90 E3
Belvide Gdns CDSL WV8 ....34 D1
Belvide Gv SLYOAK B29 ....123 M5
Belvidere Gdns SPARK B11 ....125 M1
Belvoir TAM/AM/WIL B77 ....46 A6
Belvoir CI DUDN DY1 ....84 C3
Belvoir Rd BRGRVE B60 ....192 A5
Belwell Dr FOAKS/STRLY B74 ....56 E3
Belwell La FOAKS/STRLY B74 ....56 E3
Bembridge CI SHHTH WV12 ....37 H5
Bembridge Rd STETCH B33 ....109 L3
Benacre Dr DIG/EDG B5 ....7 K5
Benbeck Cv TPTN/OCK DY4 ....67 G8
Benches CI BNTWD WS7 ....18 B7
Bendall Rd KGSTG B44 ....71 M3
Benedictine Rd COVS CV3 ....155 G6
Benedon Rd
  LGN/SDN/BHAMAIR B26 ....109 L6
Bengrove CI REDE B98 ....202 E6
Benion Rd CNCK/NC WS11 ....16 D1
Benmore Av DIG/EDG B5 ....107 H7
Bennett Av DUDN DY1 ....66 F7
Bennett CI KNWTH CV8 * 197 L1
Bennett Dr WWCK CV34 ....205 M6
Bennett Rd FOAKS/STRLY B74 ....56 D2
Bennett's Fold BKHL/PFLD WV2 ..2 E6
Bennett's HI CBHAMNW B3 ....6 F5
  DUDS DY2 ....85 J5
Bennetts Rd
  RCOVN/BALC/EX CV7 ....115 K4
  WASH/WDE B8 ....90 B7
Bennetts Rd North
  RCOVN/BALC/EX CV7 ....115 H5
Bennetts Rd South
  RCOVN/BALC/EX CV7 ....133 K2
Bennett St KIDD DY11 ....138 A4
  LOZ/NWT B19 ....89 L6
  RUGBYN/HIL CV21 ....186 D2
Ben Nevis Wy STRBR DY8 ....101 L7
Bennfield Rd RUGBYN/HIL CV21..186 E2
Benn Rd BDWTH CV12 ....117 M3
Benn St RUGBYS/DCH CV22 ....187 G3
Benson Av
  ETTPK/GDPK/PENN WV4 ....50 A8
Benson CI DUNHL/THL/PER WV6 ..34 C8
  LICH WS13 ....21 H4
Benson Rd ALE/KHTH/YWD B14..146 B4
  COVN CV6 ....133 L4
  WSNGN B18 ....88 D7
Benson Vw CRTAM B79 ....32 A5
Bent Av RIDG/WDGT B32 ....105 H7
Benthall Rd COVN CV6 ....134 D3
Bentham Ct NFLD/LBR B31 ....123 K8
Bentley Bridge Pk
  WLNHL WV13 * 50 F1
Bentleybridge Wy WLNHL WV13 ..13 G1
Bentley Brook La HEDN WS12 ....13 L7
Bentley Ct REDW B97 ....202 B2
  RLSN CV32 ....206 F2
Bentley CI COVN CV6 ....134 A1
Bentley Dr CDSL WV8 ....34 D1
  WSLW WS2 ....52 F3
Bentley Farm CI DOR/KN B93 ..175 J1
Bentley Gv SLYOAK B29 ....123 K5
Bentley La RCOVN/BALC/EX CV7..113 G5
  REDW B97 ....200 F3
  SHHTH WV12 ....38 B8
  WSLW WS2 ....52 E1
Bentley Mill CI WSLW WS2 ....52 D4
Bentley Mill La WSLW WS2 ....52 D4
Bentley Mill Wy WSLW WS2 ....52 D4
Bentley New Dr WSLW WS2 ....52 F3
Bentley Rd CBROM B36 ....92 B6
  NUN CV11 ....99 M3
  RCOVN/BALC/EX CV7 ....116 E4
  WOLVN WV10 ....36 B2
Bentley Rd North WSLW WS2 ....52 C4
Bentley Rd South
  DARL/WED WS10 ....52 B6
Bentmead Ov HWK/WKHTH B38..145 L4
Benton Av SPARK B11 ....108 A7
Benton CI SHHTH WV12 ....52 B1
Benton Crs BLOX/PEL WS3 ....39 H3
Benton Green La
  RCOVN/BALC/EX CV7 ....152 D3
Benton Rd SPARK B11 ....108 A7
Benton's CI KIDD DY11 ....138 A7
Benton's La GTWY WS6 ....24 A5
Bentons Mill Cft VAUX/NECH B7 ..90 A5
The Bentree COVS CV3 ....155 M5
Bent St BRLYHL DY5 ....102 B1
Ben Willetts Wk
  BLKHTH/ROWR B65 ....104 A4
Beoley CI CSCFLD/WYGN B72 ....73 G4
Beoley Gv RBRY B45 ....143 L6
Beoley La REDE B98 ....195 L4
Beoley Rd East REDE B98 ....202 E1
Beoley Rd West REDE B98 ....202 D2
Berberry CI BVILLE B30 ....124 D7
Berenska Dr RLSN CV32 ....206 E3
Beresford Av COVN CV6 ....134 C4
Beresford Crs WBROM B70 ....86 F2
Beresford Dr SCFLD/BOLD B73 ..72 E4
Beresford Rd BLOX/PEL WS3 ....39 J5
  OLDBY B69 ....87 G6
The Berets WMBN/WHC B75 * 57 K7
Bericote Cft ACGN B27 ....127 L2
Bericote Rd RLSN CV32 ....198 C5
Berkeley CI
  DUNHL/THL/PER WV6 ....48 D2
  NUNW/HART CV10 ....98 E2
  REDE B98 ....203 J2
Berkeley Crs STRPT DY13 ....188 E5
Berkeley Dr KGSWFD DY6 ....83 G6
Berkeley Rd KNWTH CV8 ....179 J7
  SHLY B90 ....125 M8
  YDLY B25 ....108 E5
Berkeley Rd East YDLY B25 ....108 F5
Berkeley Rd North COVW CV5 ....8 A8
Berkeley St WSLW WS2 ....52 F5
Berkeswell Rd REDE B98 ....194 F6
Berkett Rd COVN CV6 ....133 M2
Berkley Dr BRGRVE B60 ....191 M5

Berkley Crs MOS/BIL B13 ....126 A4
Berkley St CBHAMW B1 ....6 C6
Berkshire CI DARL/WED WS10 ....69 G1
  NUNW/HART CV10 ....98 C2
Berkshire Crs DARL/WED WS10 ..69 G1
The Berkshire BLOX/PEL WS3 * ..38 C2
Berkswell CI DUDN DY1 ....84 C2
  FOAKS/STRLY B74 ....56 E3
  HIA/OLT B92 ....127 M5
Berkswell Rd COVN CV6 ....134 E3
  ERDE/BCHGN B24 ....90 F1
  RCOVN/BALC/EX CV7 ....131 G5
Bermuda CI DUDN DY1 ....66 F7
Bermuda Pk NUNW/HART CV10 ..98 E7
Bermuda Rd NUNW/HART CV10 ..98 E5
Bernard PI WSNGN B18 * 88 D8
Bernard Rd LGLGYN/QTN B68 ..105 C3
  TPTN/OCK DY4 ....67 L6
Bernard St WBROM B70 ....87 H3
  WSL WS1 ....J6
Berners CI TLHL/CAN CV4 ....153 J3
Berners St LOZ/NWT B19 ....89 G6
Bernhard Dr HDSW B21 ....88 C3
Bernie Crossland Wk
  KIDD DY10 * 164 D2
Bernwall CI STRBR DY8 ....119 K1
Berrandale Rd CBROM B36 ....91 K5
Berrington CI REDE B98 ....203 G3
Berrington Dr BILS/COS WV14 ..66 F5
Berrington Rd
  NUNW/HART CV10 ....80 B5
  RLSS CV31 ....206 F7
Berrington Wk DIG/EDG B5 ....107 J6
Berrow Dr EDG B15 ....106 C7
Berrow Hill Rd KIDDU DY11 ....137 M4
Berrowside Rd BKDE/SHDE B34..92 C7
Berrow Vw BRGRVE B60 ....191 H6
Berry Av DARL/WED WS10 ....51 M8
Berrybush Gdns SEDG DY3 ....66 C6
Berry CI LOZ/NWT B19 ....89 H7
Berry Dr ALDR WS9 ....40 C8
  RBRY B45 ....169 L4
  SMTHWK B66 ....87 L7
Berryfield Rd
  LGN/SDN/BHAMAIR B26 ....110 B8
Berryfields ALDR WS9 ....27 J8
  WASH/WDE B8 ....90 C8
  RCOVN/BALC/EX CV7 ....114 C1
Berry Hall La SOLH B91 ....149 L1
Berry HI HEDN WS12 ....13 J8
Berry La BRGRVW B61 ....190 A4
Berry Rd DUDN DY1 ....67 G8
  WASH/WDE B8 ....90 B7
Berry St COV CV1 ....9 K2
  WOLV WV1 ....3 G5
  WSNGN B18 ....88 D7
Bertha Rd SPARK B11 ....108 B8
Bertie CI KNWTH CV8 * 197 L1
Bertie Rd KNWTH CV8 ....197 K1
Bertie Ter RLSN CV32 * 206 C4
Bertram CI TPTN/OCK DY4 ....68 A4
Bertram Rd BORD B9 ....108 B4
  SMTHWK B66 ....87 L7
Berwick CI COVW CV5 ....153 M1
  WWCK CV34 ....205 J3
Berwick Dr CNCK/NC WS11 ....15 M5
Berwick Gv GTB/HAM B43 ....70 F1
  NFLD/LBR B31 ....144 B2
Berwicks La
  CHWD/FDBR/MGN B37 ....110 F4
Berwood Farm Rd
  CSCFLD/WYGN B72 ....73 G7
Berwood Gdns
  ERDE/BCHGN B24 ....73 G7
Berwood La ERDE/BCHGN B24 ....91 J2
Berwood Pk CVALE B35 ....91 L3
Berwood Rd WALM/CURD B76 ....73 H7
Berwyn Av COVN CV6 ....133 L4
Berwyn Gv GTWY WS6 ....24 D2
Berwyn Wy NUNW/HART CV10 ..98 A1
Besant Gv ACGN B27 ....126 E3
Besbury CI DOR/KN B93 ....175 J3
Bescot Crs WSL WS1 ....52 C3
Bescot Ct PBAR/PBCH B42 * 70 E6
Bescot Rd WSLW WS2 ....52 F7
Bescot St WSL WS1 ....4 E3
Besford Gv NFLD/LBR B31 ....144 B2
  SHLY B90 ....148 F7
Besom Wy GTWY WS6 ....24 C3
Bessborough Rd YDLY B25 ....109 H5
Best Av WNWTH CV8 ....180 A6
Best Rd BILS/COS WV14 ....51 H6
Best St CDYHTH B64 ....103 K3
Beswick Gdns
  RUGBYS/DCH CV22 ....186 B6
Beta Gv ALE/KHTH/YWD B14 ....147 G1
Betjeman Ct KIDD DY10 ....138 F8
Betjeman PI WOLVN WV10 ....36 E4
Betley Gv STETCH B33 ....109 L1
Betony CI DSYBK/YTR WS5 ....68 C2
Betsham CI KGSTG B44 ....71 M4
Bettany Gld WOLVN WV10 ....36 C1
Betteridge Dr WALM/CURD B76 ..73 J1
Bettina CI NUNW/HART CV10 ....79 M8
Bettman CI COVS CV3 ....155 J7
Bett Rd BFLD/HDSWWD B20 ....88 C2
Betty's La CNCK/NC WS11 ....25 L1
Bevan Av
  ETTPK/GDPK/PENN WV4 ....66 C1
Bevan CI BILS/COS WV14 ....51 K7
  RUSH/SHEL WS4 ....40 A4
Bevan Lee Rd CNCK/NC WS11 ....16 B2
Bevan Rd BRLYHL DY5 ....101 L3
  TPTN/OCK DY4 ....85 M1
Bevan Wy SMTHWK B66 ....87 K5
Beverley Av NUNW/HART CV10 ..97 M1
Beverley CI CSCFLD/WYGN B72 ..73 G6
  KIDDU DY11 ....137 K7
  PENK ST19 ....10 D6
  RCOVN/BALC/EX CV7 ....152 A6
Beverley Court Rd
  RIDG/WDGT B32 ....104 F7
Beverley Cft ERDW/GRVHL B23 ..90 B4
Beverley Dr KGSWFD DY6 ....83 G6
Beverley Gv
  LGN/SDN/BHAMAIR B26 ....109 M8
Beverley HI HEDN WS12 ....13 H7
Beverley Rd HHTH/SAND B71 ....69 H4
  RBRY B45 ....143 L6
  RLSN CV32 ....206 D4
Beverly Dr TLHL/CAN CV4 ....180 B3
Beverston Rd
  DUNHL/THL/PER WV6 ....48 E1
  TPTN/OCK DY4 ....67 M3
Bevington Crs COVN CV6 ....133 J8
Bevington Rd AST/WIT B6 ....89 K5
Bevin Rd WSLW WS2 ....52 C2
Bewdley Dr WOLV WV1 ....50 F3
Bewdley HI KIDDU DY11 ....137 L8
Bewdley Rd BVILLE B30 ....124 F6
  KIDDW DY11 ....158 A3
  STRPT DY13 ....163 K8

Bewdley Rd North STRPT DY13 ..163 J7
Bewdley Vls WSNGN B18 * 106 B1
Sewell Head BRGRVW B61 ....191 K1
Bewlay CI BRLYHL DY5 ....101 M6
Bewley Rd SHHTH WV12 ....52 B2
Bewlys Av BFLD/HDSWWD B20 ..88 C1
Bexfield CI COVW CV5 ....132 E7
Bexhill Gv EDG B15 ....6 D8
Bexley Gv HHTH/SAND B71 ....69 J6
Bexley Rd KGSTG B44 ....71 M5
Bexmore Dr LICH WS13 ....21 K4
Beyer CI TAM/AM/WIL B77 ....46 E3
Bhylls Crs BDMR/CCFT WV3 ....49 G5
Bhylls La BDMR/CCFT WV3 ....48 F6
Biart PI RUGBYN/HIL CV21 ....187 H2
Bibbey's Gn WOLVN WV10 ....36 D1
Bibsworth Av MOS/BIL B13 ....126 B5
Bibury Rd HLGN/YWD B28 ....126 C6
Bicester Sq CVALE B35 ....91 M1
Bickenhill La
  CHWD/FDBR/MGN B37 ....111 H7
Bickenhill Park Rd HIA/OLT B92..127 H4
Bickenhill Pkwy
  CHWD/FDBR/MGN B37 ....111 H7
Bickenhill Rd
  CHWD/FDBR/MGN B37 ....110 F6
Bickford Rd AST/WIT B6 ....89 L4
  WOLVN WV10 ....36 D8
Bickington Rd RIDG/WDGT B32..123 H4
Bickley Av FOAKS/STRLY B74 ....42 C8
  SPARK B11 * 108 A7
Bickley Gv
  LGN/SDN/BHAMAIR B26 ....109 M8
Bickley Rd BILS/COS WV14 ....51 L7
  RUSH/SHEL WS4 ....40 A4
Bicknell Cft
  ALE/KHTH/YWD B14 ....146 C3
Bickton CI ERDE/BCHGN B24 ....73 G7
Biddings La BILS/COS WV14 ....66 F3
Biddles HI HOCK/TIA B94 ....173 G7
Biddlestone Gv DSYBK/YTR WS5 ..71 M6
Biddlestone PI DARL/WED WS10 ..51 M6
Biddulph Pk BNTWD WS7 * 18 B4
Bideford Dr SLYOAK B29 ....124 A4
Bideford Rd COVE CV2 ....135 G6
  SMTHWK B66 ....87 M8
Bideford Wy CNCK/NC WS11 ....15 M5
Bidford CI SHLY B90 ....148 B3
Bidford Rd NFLD/LBR B31 ....144 C2
Bierton Rd YDLY B25 ....109 G5
Bigbury CI COVS CV3 ....155 J8
Bigbury La STRPT DY13 ....164 B7
Biggin CI CVALE B35 ....91 L2
  DUNHL/THL/PER WV6 ....34 C8
Biggin Hall Crs COVS CV3 ....155 M3
The Big Peg WSNGN B18 * 6 E1
Bigwood Dr MGN/WHC B75 ....57 L7
  RIDG/WDGT B32 ....123 G4
Bilberry CI STRPT DY13 ....163 J8
Bilberry Crs HEDN WS12 ....12 A8
  WALM/CURD B76 ....73 J2
Bilberry Dr RBRY B45 ....143 L7
Bilberry Rd ALE/KHTH/YWD B14..125 C2
  COVE CV2 ....135 H3
Bilboe Rd BILS/COS WV14 ....67 K2
Bilbrook CI CDSL WV8 ....34 C3
Bilbrook Gv CDSL WV8 ....34 C2
  SLYOAK B29 ....123 K3
Bilbrook Rd CDSL WV8 ....34 C2
Bilbury CI REDW B97 ....202 A2
Bilhay La WBROM B70 ....68 E8
Bilhay St WBROM B70 ....68 F8
Billau Rd BILS/COS WV14 ....67 J3
Billesley La ALVE B48 ....172 C1
  MOS/BIL B13 ....125 L5
Billesley La MOS/BIL B13 ....125 L5
Billingham CI SOLH B91 ....148 E5
Billing Rd COVW CV5 ....154 B2
Billingsley Rd
  LGN/SDN/BHAMAIR B26 ....109 L5
Billinton CI COVE CV2 ....156 C3
Bills La SHLY B90 ....147 K5
Billsmore Gn HIA/OLT B92 ....128 A6
Bills St DARL/WED WS10 ....52 C7
Billy Buns La WMBN WV5 ....64 E5
Billy Wright CI
  ETTPK/GDPK/PENN WV4 ....49 H7
Bilport La WASH/WDE B8 ....68 D5
Bilston La WLNHL WV13 ....51 H6
Bilston Rd BKHL/PFLD WV2 ....3 L8
  TPTN/OCK DY4 ....67 M3
  WLNHL WV13 ....51 L6
  WOLV WV1 ....3 H6
Bilston St DARL/WED WS10 ....52 C7
  SEDG DY3 ....66 B5
  WLNHL WV13 ....51 L4
Bilston Street Island WOLV WV1 ..3 H6
Bilton Grange Rd
  LGN/SDN/BHAMAIR B26 ....109 K6
Bilton La RRUGBY CV23 ....185 M3
Bilton Rd RUGBYS/DCH CV22 ..186 B4
Binbrook Rd SHHTH WV12 ....52 B1
Bincomb Av
  LGN/SDN/BHAMAIR B26 ....109 M7
Binfield St TPTN/OCK DY4 ....85 L1
Bingley Av WASH/WDE B8 ....108 F1
Bingley Gv BDMR/CCFT WV3 ....34 F3
Binley CI
  LGN/SDN/BHAMAIR B26 ....109 M7
  SHLY B90 ....147 L5
Binley Gv COVS CV3 ....156 D6
Binley Rd COV CV1 ....9 L4
Binns CI TLHL/CAN CV4 ....153 K5
Binstead Ky KGSTG B44 ....71 L3
Binswood Av RLSN CV32 ....206 D3
Binswood CI COVE CV2 ....135 G1
Binswood Rd RMSLY B62 ....104 E6
Binswood St RLSN CV32 ....206 C3
Binton CI REDE B98 ....203 K4
Binton Cft MOS/BIL B13 ....125 K5
Binton Rd COVE CV2 ....135 H2
  SHLY B90 ....147 K4
Birbeck PI BRLYHL DY5 ....83 M7
Birchall St DGTH/HG B12 ....7 M8
Birch Av BNTWD WS7 ....18 D7
  BRLYHL DY5 ....102 E3
  BRWNH WS8 ....26 C5
  CNCK/NC WS11 ....16 A5
  NFLD/LBR B31 ....144 A4
  RCOVN/BALC/EX CV7 ....151 K5
Birch Brook La LICHS WS14 ....28 C7
Birch Crs OLDBY B69 ....85 M4
Birch Cft
  CHWD/FDBR/MGN B37 ....111 G4
Birch Cft ERDE/BCHGN B24 ....73 G7
Birch Croft Rd MGN/WHC B75 ..57 H6
Birchdale BILS/COS WV14 ....51 H6

Birchdale Av ERDW/GRVHL B23 ..90 B5
Birchdale Rd ERDW/GRVHL B23 ..72 A8
Birch Dr FOAKS/STRLY B74 ....42 C7
  RMSLY B62 ....104 A7
  WMBN WV5 75
Birchensale Rd REDW B97 ....201 M4
Birches Av CDSL WV8 35
Birches Barn Av
  BDMR/CCFT WV3 49
Birches Barn Rd
  BDMR/CCFT WV3 49
Birches Green Rd
  ERDE/BCHGN B24 90
Birches La ALVE B48 197
  KNWTH CV8 197
Birches Park Rd CDSL WV8 34
Birches Ri WLNHL WV13 51
Birches Rd CDSL WV8 34
The Birches BDWTH CV12 117
  STRPT DY13 188
Birchfield Av
  DUNHL/THL/PER WV6
Birchfield CI ATHST CV9
  HALE B63 121
Birchfield Crs HAG/WOL DY9 120
Birchfield Dr STRPT DY13 163
Birchfield Gdns AST/WIT B6 * 104
Birchfield La OLDBY B69 104
Birchfield Rd COVN CV6 133
  HAG/WOL DY9 120
  KIDDW DY11 137
  PBAR/PBCH B42 89
  REDW B97 201
Birchfields Dr HEDN WS12 12
Birchfields Rd SHHTH WV12 51
Birchfield Wy DSYBK/YTR WS5 69
Birchgate HAG/WOL DY9 120
Birchglade BDMR/CCFT WV3 49
Birchgrave CI COVN CV6 134
Birch Gv LGLGYN/QTN B68 105
  LICH WS13 21
  POL/KGSB/FAZ B78 47
Birch Hill Av WMBN WV5 64
Birch Hollow EDG B15 106
Birchills St WSLW WS2 4
Birch La ALDR WS9 41
  LGLGYN/QTN B68 104
  RUSH/SHEL WS4 40
Birchley Heath Rd
  NUNW/HART CV10 78
Birchley Park Av OLDBY B69 86
Birchley Ri HIA/OLT B92 109
Birchmoor CI HLGN/YWD B28 ..126
Birchmoor Rd
  POL/KGSB/FAZ B78 47
Birchover Rd WSLW WS2 52
Birch Rd AST/WIT B6 89
  LGLGYN/QTN B68 105
  RBRY B45 143
  SEDC DY3 66
  WNSFLD WV11 37
Birch Rd East AST/WIT B6 89
Birch St LGLGYN/QTN B68 87
  TPTN/OCK DY4 67
  WOLV WV1 2
Birch Ter BNTWD WS7 18
  DUDS DY2 103
Birch Tree Gdns ALDR WS9 40
Birchtree Gdns BRLYHL DY5 102
Birch Tree Gv SOLH B91 148
Birchtree Hollow SHHTH WV12 ..38
Birch Tree Rd BEWD DY12 162
Birchtree Rd NUNW/HART CV10 ..80
Birchtrees ERDE/BCHGN B24 91
Birchtrees Cft
  LGN/SDN/BHAMAIR B26 109
Birchtrees Dr STETCH B33 110
Birch Wk LGLGYN/QTN B68 105
Birchway CI RLSN CV32 206
Birchwood Av
  POL/KGSB/FAZ B78 47
Birchwood CI KIDDU DY11 137
  WNSFLD WV11 37
Birchwood Crs BHTH/HG B12 ..125
Birchwood Rd BHTH/HG B12 ..125
  COVS CV3 157
  ETTPK/GDPK/PENN WV4 65
  LICHS WS14 21
Birchwoods RIDG/WDGT B32 ..122
Birchy Leasowes La SHLY B90 ..147
Birdbrook Rd KGSTG B44 71
Bird End HHTH/SAND B71 69
Bird Grove Ct COV CV1 9
Birdie CI HWK/WKHTH B38 145
Birdlip Gv RIDG/WDGT B32 104
Birds Bush Rd TAM/AM/WIL B77 ..46
Birds Meadow BRLYHL DY5 83
Bird St COV CV1 9
  LICH WS13 21
  SEDC DY3 66
Birdwell Cft MOS/BIL B13 125
Birkdale Av BRGRVE B60 192
  SLYOAK B29 124
Birkdale CI COVN CV6 133
  NUN CV11 99
  STRBR DY8 119
  WOLV WV1 36
Birkdale Dr OLDBY B69 86
Birkdale Gv SLYOAK B29 124
Birkdale Rd BLOX/PEL WS3 39
Birkenshaw Rd KGSTG B44 71
Birley Gv HALE B63 121
Birmingham New Rd DUDN DY1 ..67
  ETTPK/GDPK/PENN WV4 66
Birmingham Rd ALDR WS9 40
  ALDR WS9 170
  ALVE B48 170
  BKHL/PFLD WV2 2
  BLKHTH/ROWR B65 87
  BRGRVE B60 191
  CBROM B36 92
  CNCK/NC WS11 15
  CSCFLD/WYGN B72 72
  CSHL/WTROR B46 92
  DSYBK/YTR WS5 55
  DUDN DY1 67
  GTB/HAM B43 70
  GTB/HAM B43 71
  HAG/WOL DY9 120
  HALE B63 120
  KIDD DY10 158
  KIDD DY10 178
  KNWTH CV8 179
  LICH WS13 20
  NUNW/HART CV10 99
  OLDBY B69 86
  RCOVN/BALC/EX CV7 115
  RCOVN/BALC/EX CV7 150
  REDW B97 202
  RWWCK/WEL CV35 117
  RWWCK/WEL CV35 203

STUD B80 ....203 J7
WALM/CURD B76 ....75 L6
WBROM B70 ....87 J4
WSL WS1 ....5 H6
WWCK CV34 ....204 F5
ingham St DARL/WED WS10 ...52 H3
DUDS DY2 ....85 H4
HALE B63 ....121 M2
OLDBY B69 ....86 E5
STRBR DY8 ....101 M3
WLNHL WV13 ....51 M3
WSL WS1 ....5 G5
nham CI TPTN/OCK DY4 ....67 H4
stall Dr RRUGBY CV23 ....161 H7
tell Wy BRLYHL DY5 ....102 B7
et Av KIDD DY10 ....138 F8
hbury CI EDG B15 ....106 C5
hop Asbury Crs GTB/HAM B43 ...69 M5
hop CI CNCK/NC CV11 ....143 J4
hop Hall Crs BRGRVE B60 ....191 J6
hops CI DUDS DY2 ....85 J5
hop St COV CV1 ....7 H9
hop's Ct
CHWD/FDBR/MGN B37 ....111 J5
hopsgate Ga NFLD/LBR B31 ...144 E3
hopsgate St EDG B15 ....9 G6
hop's Meadow MGN/WHC B75 ...57 J2
hopstone CI REDE B98 ....203 K3
hop St COV CV1 ....7 H9
STRPT DY13 ....163 L8
hops Wk COW CV5 ....8 C9
HALE B63 ....42 D6
hopton CI COVW CV5 ....153 M2
hopton Rd SMTHWKW B67 .....105 K4
hton Gv DUDS DY2 ....83 H1
sel Dr DARL/WED WS10 ....68 C7
sell CI HLGN/YWD B28 ....126 D2
sell St DIG/EDG B5 ....107 J5
RIDG/WDGT B32 ....104 E7
set Crs RLSS CV32 ....206 F7
set CI BILS/COS WV14 ....51 K8
set Crs RLSS CV32 ....206 F7
ham CI PENK ST19 * 10 C6
on CI HRBN B17 ....105 M6
tell CI WOLVN WV10 ....36 C1
tell Farm Rd RBRY B45 ....170 C5
tell La RBRY B45 ....170 C5
tell Rd RBRY B45 ....170 C5
terne Dr
DUNHL/THL/PER WV6 ....2 B1
tern Wood Rd KIDD DY10 ....164 F2
terscote La
POL/KGSB/FAZ B78 ....45 L3
hill La CSHL/WTROR B46 ....94 D3
ckacre Rd DUDS DY2 ....84 B5
cka-Tree Ct
NUNW/HART CV10 * 80 D8
ck-a-Tree PI
NUNW/HART CV10 * 98 C1
ck-a-Tree Rd
NUNW/HART CV10 ....98 C1
ck Bank
RCOVN/BALC/EX CV7 ....116 F4
ckberry Av BORD B9 ....108 E2
HOCK/TIA B94 ....174 F1
ckberry CI DUDS DY2 ....84 C5
RRUGBY CV23 ....161 H6
ckberry La ALDR WS9 ....40 F1
BLKHTH/ROWR B65 ....85 K8
COVN CV6 ....134 F7
FOAKS/STRLY B74 ....55 J4
HALE B63 ....121 L3
RCOVN/BALC/EX CV7 ....115 M8
ckbird Cft CBROM B36 ....92 E6
ckbrook CI DUDS DY2 ....102 E2
ckbrook La DUDS DY2 ....84 E8
ckbrook Wy WOLVN WV10 ....36 C1
ckburn Av
DUNHL/THL/PER WV6 ....35 J6
ckburne Rd HLGN/YWD B28 ...126 D7
ckburn Rd COVN CV6 ....134 D2
ckbushe CI HRBN B17 ....105 K6
ckcat CI
CHWD/FDBR/MGN B37 ....110 E2
ck Country New Rd
BILS/COS WV14 ....51 L7
ck Country Route
BILS/COS WV14 ....51 L7
ckdown TAM/AM/WIL B77 ....47 G4
ckdown CI RBRY B45 ....143 L3
ckdown Rd DOR/KN B93 ....149 M7
ckfirs La
CHWD/FDBR/MGN B37 ....111 H6
KIDD DY11 ....121 H4
ckford CI HALE B63 ....121 H4
KIDD DY11 ....163 L4
ckford St SHLY B90 ....148 A6
SPARK B11 ....126 A1
ckford St WSNGN B18 ....88 C8
ckfriars CI CRTAM B79 ....31 K6
ckgreaves CI
WALM/CURD B76 ....75 K4
ck Hall La
RCOVN/BALC/EX CV7 ....114 A1
ckhalve La WNSFLD WV11 ....74 F5
ckham Dr SCFLD/BOLD B73 .....72 E6
ckham Rd WNSFLD WV11 ....37 K5
ck Haynes Rd SLYOAK B29 .....123 J2
ckhorse La BRLYHL DY5 ....85 L4
ck Horse La KIDD DY10 ....138 B7
ck Horse Rd COVN CV6 ....116 C1
ck Lake HHTH/SAND B71 ....68 E7
ck Lake La BRGRVE B60 ....200 E8
ck La RLSN CV32 ....206 F3
cklow Rd WWCK CV34 ....205 L4
ckman Wy
RUGBYN/HIL CV21 ....186 D1
ckmoor Cft STETCH B33 ....133 H8
ckmore La BRGRVE B60 ....191 L6
ckpit La WMBN WV5 ....64 C2
ck Prince Av COVS CV3 ....155 J7
ckrock Rd ERDW/GRVHL B23 ...71 H4
ckroot CI BNTWD WS7 ....27 H1
ckroot Rd FOAKS/STRLY B74 ...56 E5
ckshaw Dr COVE CV2 ....135 K7
cksmiths La HOCK/TIA B94 .....175 G7
cksmith Wy WBROM B70 ....87 G3
ck Soils Rd REDE B98 ....195 L4
ckstitch La REDW B97 ....201 L4
ckthorn Av BNTWD WS7 ....26 D3
ckthorn CI BVILLE B30 ....124 A7
LHL/CAN CV4 ....154 B8
ckthorn Rd HEDN WS12 ....13 L7
ckthorne Rd SOLH B91 ....148 L1
ckthorne Rd
SYBK DY2? WS5 ....5 K8
DUDS DY2 ....84 D1
WTH CV7 ....197 L2
SMTHWKW B67 ....105 L4
ckthorn Gv WWCK CV34 ....204 D3
ckthorn Rd BVILLE B30 ....124 A7
B36 ....92 B4
DY8 ....101 K4
ckwater Rd COVN CV6 ....134 A5
ckwater Rd BRLYHL DY5 ....83 L8

Blackwell Rd BRGRVE B60 ....192 D1
COVN CV6 ....134 C5
CSCFLD/WYGN B72 ....73 H4
RBRY B45 ....170 A7
Blackwell St KIDD DY10 ....138 C7
Blackwood Dr
RUGBYS/DCH CV22 ....186 B3
WNSFLD WV11 ....36 F5
Blackwood Dr FOAKS/STRLY B74 ...55 J3
Blackwood Rd BRGRVE B60 ...191 M3
FOAKS/STRLY B74 ....55 J4
TAM/AM/WIL B77 ....46 A6
Blades Rd WBROM B70 ....86 B1
Bladon CI NUN CV11 ....81 K5
Bladon Wk DARL/WED WS10 ...20 D7
Blaenwern Dr HALE B63 ....102 F6
Blagdon Rd HALE B63 ....103 L7
Blair Gv BDWTH CV12 ....116 B4
Blair Gv CHWD/FDBR/MGN B37 ...111 H4
Blakedon Rd DARL/WED WS10 ...68 C2
Blakedown Rd HALE B63 ....121 K3
Blake Hall CI BRLYHL DY5 ....101 M6
Blakeland Rd KGSTG B44 ....71 J7
Blakelands Av RLSS CV31 ......206 F7
Blakelands St BORD B9 ....108 D3
Blake La BORD B9 ....108 D3
Blakeley
DUNHL/THL/PER WV6 ....35 K6
Blakeley Hall Gdns OLDBY B69 ...86 F6
Blakeley Hall Rd OLDBY B69 .....86 F6
Blakeley Heath Dr WMBN WV5 ...64 E8
Blakeley Ri
DUNHL/THL/PER WV6 ....35 K6
Blakeley Wood Rd
TPTN/OCK DY4 ....68 J5
Blakemere Av YDLY B25 ....109 J5
Blakemere Rd REDE B98 ....203 K2
Blakemore CI RIDG/WDGT B32 ...123 K2
Blakemore Dr MGN/WHC B75 ....57 K7
Blakemore Rd ALDR WS9 ....40 F2
WBROM B70 ....86 E3
Blakenall CI BLOX/PEL WS3 ......39 H4
Blakenall Heath BLOX/PEL WS3 ...39 H5
Blakenall La BLOX/PEL WS3 .....39 H5
Blakenall Rw BLOX/PEL WS3 ....39 H5
Blakeney Av HRBN B17 ....105 L6
STRBR DY8 ....101 H7
Blakeney CI SEDG DY3 ....109 M4
Blakenhale Rd STETCH B33 ....133 H4
Blakenhall Gdns BKHL/PFLD WV2 ...50 B6
Blake PI BORD B9 ....108 D3
Blake Rd BRGRVE B61 ....168 F5
Blakesfield Dr RBRY B45 ....169 L4
Blakesley CI WALM/CURD B76 ...73 K8
Blakesley Ms YDLY B25 ....109 H5
Blakesley Rd YDLY B25 ....109 H4
Blake St FOAKS/STRLY B74 ....42 D7
Blakewood CI BKDE/SHDE B34 ...92 A8
Blandford Av CBROM B36 ....92 C4
Blandford Dr COVE CV2 ....135 K8
STRBR DY8 ....101 J3
Blandford Gdns BNTWD WS7 ....19 C7
Blandford Rd RIDG/WDGT B32 ...105 J3
RLSN CV32 ....206 A4
Blandford Wy
RWWCK/WEL CV35 ....204 E6
Blay Av WSLW WS2 ....52 F3
Blaydon Av MGN/WHC B75 ....57 J9
Blaydon Rd COVEN WV9 ....35 L4
Blaythorn Av HIA/OLT B92 ....127 L2
Blaze Hill Rd KGSWFD DY6 ....82 E5
Blaze Pk KGSWFD DY6 ....82 F5
Bleaberry RUGBYN/HIL CV21 ...161 G6
Bleachfield Rd REDE B98 ....195 K5
Bleak Hill Rd ERDW/GRVHL B23 ...72 A8
Bleak House Dr BNTWD WS7 ....18 B5
Bleakhouse Rd
LGLYGN/QTN B68 ....105 C4
Bleak St SMTHWKW B67 ....87 K7
Blenheim CI COVN CV6 ....134 A2
RUSH/SHEL WS4 ....40 B6
Blenheim Crs BRGRVE B60 ......191 L5
RLSS CV32 ....207 G8
Blenheim Dr GTB/HAM B43 ....70 B5
Blenheim Rd BNTWD WS7 ....18 E5
CNCK/NC WS11 ....25 L7
KGSWFD DY6 ....82 D2
MOS/BIL B13 ....125 K4
SHHTH WV12 ....37 M7
SHLY B90 ....148 B3
Blenheim Wy CVALE B35 ....91 J3
DUDN DY1 ....84 C3
KGSTG B44 ....71 K5
Bletchley Dr COVW CV5 ....153 M1
TAM/AM/WIL B77 ....46 A5
Bletchley Rd ERDE/BCHGN B24 ...91 J1
Blewitt CI CBROM B36 ....92 B3
Blewitt St BRLYHL DY5 ....12 F7
Blews St AST/WIT B6 ....89 J8
Blindpit La WALM/CURD B76 .....74 F5
Blithe CI STRBR DY8 ....101 M6
Blithfield Gv BRLYHL DY5 ....101 M6
Blithfield Gv ERDE/BCHGN B24 ...73 G8
Blithfield PI CNCK/NC WS11 .....16 F4
Blithfield Rd BRWNH WS8 ....26 A3
Blockall DARL/WED WS10 ....52 B6
Blockley Rd REDW B97 ....201 J3
Blockley Rd BDWTH CV12 ....116 F4
Blondvil St COVS CV3 ....155 G6
Bloomfield CI WMBN WV5 ....64 B7
Bloomfield Crs LICH WS13 ....20 E3
Bloomfield Dr SHHTH WV12 ......38 B4
Bloomfield Pk TPTN/OCK DY4 ...67 H7
Bloomfield Rd MOS/BIL B13 .....125 L2
TPTN/OCK DY4 ....67 J6
Bloomfield St North HALE B63 ...103 K8
Bloomfield St West HALE B63 ...121 K1
Bloomfield Ter TPTN/OCK DY4 ...67 H7
Bloomfield Wy CRTAM B79 ....31 K6
Bloomsbury Gv
ALE/KHTH/WD B14 ....125 G6
Bloomsbury St BKHL/PFLD WV2 ...2 D3
VAUX/NECH B7 ....89 M8
Bloomsbury Wk
VAUX/NECH B7 * 89 M8
Bloomsbury CI LICHS WS14 * ...124 D3
Blossom Av SLYOAK B29 * 124 D3
Blossom Dr BRGRVW B61 ....168 F8
Blossomfield CI SOLH B91 ....148 D3
Blossom Gv CBROM B36 ....91 H5
Blossom HI ERDE/BCHGN B24 ...90 A4
Blossom HI ERDE/BCHGN B24 ...91 C1
Blossom's Fold WOLV WV1 ....2 D1
Blossomville Wy ACGN B27 .....126 F1
Blount CI PENK ST19 ....10 D6
Blount Ter KIDD DY11 ....164 B2
Blowers Green Crs DUDS DY2 ...84 F6

Blower's Green Rd DUDS DY2 ....84 F6
Bloxam Gdns
RUGBYS/DCH CV22 ....186 D3
Bloxam PI RUGBYN/HIL CV21 ...187 M4
Bloxcidge St LGLYGN/QTN B68 ...86 F3
Bloxwich La WSLW WS2 ....38 E7
WSLW WS2 ....52 E1
Bloxwich Rd BLOX/PEL WS3 ......39 L4
Bloxwich Rd North SHHTH WV12 ...38 B7
Bloxwich Rd South
WLNHL WV13 ....51 L2
Blucher St CBHAMW B1 ....6 E7
Blue Ball La HALE B63 ....103 C7
Bluebell CI HEDN WS12 ....17 J7
RRUGBY CV23 ....161 H5
STRBR DY8 ....101 G3
Bluebell Crs WNSFLD WV11 ......37 H8
Bluebell Dr BDWTH CV12 ....116 C3
CHWD/FDBR/MGN B37 ....111 H3
Bluebell La GTWY WS6 ....24 C3
Bluebell Rd ALDR WS9 ....40 F2
CDYHTH B64 ....103 J2
DUDN DY1 ....84 F2
Bluebell Wk TLHL/CAN CV4 .....153 K4
Bluebellwood CI
WALM/CURD B76 ....73 L2
Bluebird CI LICHS WS14 ....21 H5
Blue Cedars STRBR DY8 ....101 G7
Blue Cft NFLD/LBR B31 ....144 A1
Blue Lake Rd DOR/KN B93 ......175 M4
Blue La East WSLW WS2 ....4 D1
Blue La West WSLW WS2 ....4 C2
Blundell Apart SPARK B11 ....108 B8
Bluestone Av SPARK B11 ....108 A7
SHLY B90 ....148 B8
Blyth Av RCOVN/BALC/EX CV7 ...152 A8
Blyth Br CSHL/WTROR B46 ....94 A5
Blyth CI BDWTH CV12 ....116 A4
Blythe CI BNTWD WS7 ....19 H7
REDW B97 ....202 B6
Blythefield Av GTB/HAM B43 .....70 A4
Blythe Gdns CDSL WV8 ....34 D1
Blythe Ga HOCK/TIA B94 ....174 E2
Blythe Rd COV CV1 ....9 K1
CSHL/WTROR B46 ....93 M3
Blythe St TAM/AM/WIL B77 ....46 A2
Blythesway ALVE B48 ....170 E7
Blytheway SOLH B91 ....149 J2
Blythewood CI DOR/KN B93 .....149 K4
Blythsford Rd HLGN/YWD B28 ...147 K1
Blythswood Rd SPARK B11 ......126 E1
Blyton CI LDYWD/EDGR B16 .....106 D7
Boar Cft TLHL/CAN CV4 ....153 K3
Board School Gdns SEDG DY3 ...66 D7
Boar Hound CI WSNGN B18 * ...106 E1
Boat La ALDR WS9 ....27 K4
Boatman's La ALDR WS9 ....40 C5
Bobbington Wy DUDS DY2 ....85 H8
Bobs Coppice Wk BRLYHL DY5 ...102 D6
Bockendon Rd TLHL/CAN CV4 ...179 H1
Boddington CI RLSN CV32 ....199 J3
Bodenham CI REDE B98 ....203 K2
Bodenham Rd
LGLYGN/QTN B68 ....104 F5
NFLD/LBR B31 ....144 E3
Boden Rd HLGN/YWD B28 ....126 E6
Bodens La ALDR WS9 ....54 E6
Bodicote Gv MGN/WHC B75 ......57 J2
Bodington Rd MGN/WHC B75 ...19 J6
Bodmin CI DYSBK/YTR WS5 ....54 B6
Bodmin Gv NECH B7 * 89 M8
Bodmin Ri DYSBK/YTR WS5 ......54 B6
Bodmin Rd COVE CV2 ....135 K2
DUDS DY2 ....103 H3
Bodnant Wy KNWTH CV8 ....180 A1
Bodymoor Heath La
WALM/CURD B76 ....59 J4
Bodymoor Heath Rd
POL/KGSB/FAZ B78 ....59 J7
Bognop Rd WNSFLD WV11 ....37 H1
Bohun St TLHL/CAN CV4 ....153 K4
Boldmere CI SCFLD/BOLD B73 ...72 E6
Boldmere Dr SCFLD/BOLD B73 ...72 E5
Boldmere Gdns SCFLD/BOLD B73 ...72 D2
Boldmere Ga SCFLD/BOLD B73 * ...72 D2
Boldmere Rd SCFLD/BOLD B73 ...72 E5
Boldmere Ter SLYOAK B29 * 124 C4
Bolebridge St CRTAM B79 ....45 M1
Boley CI LICHS WS14 ....21 G6
Boley Cottage La LICHS WS14 ...21 H6
Boley La LICHS WS14 ....24 B3
Boley CI GTWY WS6 ....24 B3
Boleyn Rd RBRY B45 ....143 J4
Bolingbroke Rd COVS CV3 ....155 L4
Bolney Rd RIDG/WDGT B32 .....105 J8
Bolton CI COVS CV3 ....155 J8
Bolton Rd SMHTH B10 ....107 M4
WNSFLD WV11 ....37 G8
Bolton St BORD B9 ....107 M3
Bolton Wy BLOX/PEL WS3 ....38 D2
Bomers Fld RBRY B45 ....144 A6
Bond Dr CVALE B35 ....91 L3
Bondfield Rd MOS/BIL B13 ......125 M7
Bond Ga NUN CV11 ....99 G1
Bond Gate Chambers
NUN CV11 * 99 G1
Bond Sq WSNGN B18 ....106 E1
Bond St BILS/COS WV14 ....66 F6
BKHL/PFLD WV2 ....2 D5
BLKHTH/ROWR B65 ....104 C3
BVILLE B30 ....124 E6
COV CV1 ....8 E4
LOZ/NWT B19 ....89 J6
NUN CV11 ....81 C8
WBROM B70 ....87 J4
Bondway HEDN WS12 ....12 D5
Bonehill Rd POL/KGSB/FAZ B78 ...45 H7
POL/KGSB/FAZ B78 ....45 J1
Bone Hill La WOLV WV1 ....1 ?
Boney Hay Rd BNTWD WS7 ....18 B1
Bonfire HI HAG/WOL DY9 ....142 C7
Bonham Gv YDLY B25 ....109 H4
Boningale Wy DOR/KN B93 .....175 H2
Bonington Dr BDWTH CV12 ......116 E1
Bonner Dr WALM/CURD B76 ......73 K8
Bonner Gv ALDR WS9 ....40 B1
Bonneville CI COVW CV5 ....131 M5
Bonniksen CI RLSS CV31 ....206 D3
Bonnington CI
RUGBYN/HIL CV21 ....187 M4
Bonnington Wy GTB/HAM B43 ...69 L8
Bonsall Rd ERDW/GRVHL B23 ...72 F2
Bonville Gdns WOLVN WV10 ......36 C1
Booth CI BLOX/PEL WS3 ....39 H5
KGSWFD DY6 ....83 C7
Booth HI ATHST CV9 ....62 A3
Booth St BLOX/PEL WS3 ....39 H5
Booths Farm Rd
PBAR/PBCH B42 ....70 B5
Booth's La PBAR/PBCH B42 ....70 F4
Bowden Rd SMTHWKW B67 ......87 J5
Bowden Wy COVS CV3 ....156 C4
Bowdler Rd BKHL/PFLD WV2 * 3 H9
Bowen Av
ETTPK/GDPK/PENN WV4 ....66 E2
Booton CI KIDD DY10 ....138 C4

Boot Piece La REDW B97 ....193 M8
Bordeaux CI DUDN DY1 ....84 C2
Borden CI CDSL WV8 ....35 K5
Bordesley Circ SMHTH B10 ......107 M4
Bordesley CI BORD B9 ....108 C3
Bordesley Gn BORD B9 ....108 C3
Bordesley Gn East BORD B9 ....109 J3
Bordesley Gn Rd BORD B9 ......108 E3
Bordesley La REDE B98 ....194 C7
Bordesley Middleway
SPARK B11 ....7 M9
Bordesley Park Rd SMTHWKW B10 ...107 M4
Bordesley St DIG/EDG B5 ....7 J5
Bore St LICH WS13 ....20 F6
Borman CRTAM B79 ....31 K8
Borneo St RUSH/SHEL WS4 ....53 K1
Borough Crs OLDBY B69 ....86 C5
Borough Rd CRTAM B79 ....31 M6
Borrington Gdns KIDD DY10 ....164 F1
Borrington Rd KIDD DY10 ....164 F1
Borrowcop La LICHS WS14 ....21 G8
Borrowdale RUGBYN/HIL CV21 ...161 M5
BILS/COS WV14 * 51 M5
Borrowdale CI BRLYHL DY5 ....101 L4
COVN CV6 ....133 L4
Borrowdale Dr RLSN CV32 ....206 A3
Borrowdale Gv NFLD/LBR B31 ...144 B1
Borrowdale Rd NFLD/LBR B31 ...144 B2
Borrow St WLNHL WV13 ....51 L2
Borwick Av WBROM B70 ....86 E2
Boscobel Av TPTN/OCK DY4 ......85 K1
Boscobel CI DUDN DY1 ....84 D2
SHLY B90 ....148 B8
Boscobel Rd GTB/HAM B43 ....70 B3
SHLY B90 ....148 B8
Boscombe Av SPARK B11 * 108 A7
Boscombe Ct PENK ST19 ....10 C6
Boscomoor Ct PENK ST19 ....10 C6
Boscomoor La PENK ST19 ....10 C6
Boston CI HEDN WS12 ....17 J4
Boston Gv KGSTG B44 ....71 M5
Boston PI COVN CV6 ....134 B5
Bosty La ALDR WS9 ....40 B8
Boswell Av DARL/WED WS10 .....52 B8
DARL/WED WS10 ....68 A4
Boswell CI DOVE CV2 ....135 L6
Boswell Gv WWCK CV34 ....205 H4
Boswell Rd BILS/COS WV14 ......16 B1
CNCK/NC WS11 ....16 B1
FOAKS/STRLY B74 ....71 K7
KGSTG B44 ....71 K7
RUGBYS/DCH CV22 ....186 C6
Bosworth CI SEDG DY3 ....66 D7
Bosworth Dr
CHWD/FDBR/MGN B37 ....110 D3
Botany Dr SEDG DY3 ....66 B8
Botany Rd DYSBK/YTR WS5 ....53 K8
Botany Wk LDYWD/EDGR B16 * ...106 E3
Botha Rd BORD B9 ....108 C2
Botoner Rd COV CV1 ....9 L5
Botteley Rd WBROM B70 ....68 E7
Bottetourt Rd HRBN B17 ....123 L2
Botteville Rd ACGN B27 ....127 G3
Bott La HAG/WOL DY9 ....102 B7
WSL WS1 ....5 H4
Bottrill St NUN CV11 ....80 F8
Bott Rd COVW CV5 ....154 B5
Botts Green La
CSHL/WTROR B46 ....77 C8
Boughton Rd
RUGBYN/HIL CV21 ....161 G7
YDLY B25 ....109 G6
Boulevard BRLYHL DY5 ....102 C3
SCFLD/BOLD B73 ....72 C6
Boultbee Rd CSCFLD/WYGN B72 ...73 G6
Boulters La ATHST CV9 ....63 ?
Boulton CI BNTWD WS7 ....18 F5
Boulton Middleway WSNGN B18 ...88 F8
Boulton Retreat HDSW B21 * 88 C6
Boulton Rd HDSW B21 ....88 C6
SOLH B91 ....128 A6
Boulton Rd REDW B97 ....202 B7
WBROM B70 ....87 H4
Boultons Sq WBROM B70 ....87 H4
Boulton St ERDW/GRVHL B23 ...91 M1
Boundary Av
BLKHTH/ROWR B65 ....104 C3
Boundary Crs SEDG DY3 ....66 A2
Boundary Dr MOS/BIL B13 ....125 H3
Boundary HI SEDG DY3 ....66 A1
Boundary PI HDSW B21 ....87 M4
Boundary Rd ALDR WS9 ....40 C5
FOAKS/STRLY B74 ....56 B6
RUGBYN/HIL CV21 ....187 H4
WLNHL WV13 ....51 G4
Boundary Wy
DUNHL/THL/PER WV6 ....48 D3
ETTPK/GDPK/PENN WV4 ....49 G7
Bourn Av RBRY B45 ....143 J5
Bournbrook Rd SLYOAK B29 ....124 D2
Bourne Av BRGRVW B61 ....168 D4
POL/KGSB/FAZ B78 ....45 J5
RMSLY B62 ....122 C1
TPTN/OCK DY4 ....68 C4
Bournebrook CI DUDS DY2 ....85 C8
Bourne Brook CI
RCOVN/BALC/EX CV7 ....114 A1
Bournebrook Vw
RCOVN/BALC/EX CV7 ....96 C4
HEDN WS12 ....17 H3
MOS/BIL B13 ....125 G3
SOLH B91 ....128 C7
Bourne Gn RIDG/WDGT B32 ....105 J8
Bourne Hill CI DUDS DY2 ....103 J1
Bourne Rd AST/WIT B6 ....89 M6
COVS CV3 ....156 A4
Bournes Crs HALE B63 ....102 F7
Bournes HI HALE B63 ....102 F6
Bourne St BILS/COS WV14 ....66 E6
DUDS DY2 ....85 H4
Bourne Wy Gdns SLYOAK B29 ...124 E5
Bournheath Rd BRGRVW B61 ...168 B3
Bourn Mill Dr AST/WIT B6 ....89 J7
Bournville La BVILLE B30 ....124 B6
Bourton CI DYSBK/YTR WS5 ......69 G3
Bourton Cft HIA/OLT B92 ....127 K5
Bourton Dr RLSS CV31 ....206 F5
Bourton Rd HIA/OLT B92 ....127 K5
Bovey Cft WALM/CURD B76 ....73 L6
Bowater Av STETCH B33 ....91 L2
Bowater Ct COVS CV3 * 155 K7
Bowater House
PBAR/PBCH B42 ....70 B6
Bowcroft Gv BKDE/SHDE B34 ...75 J2
Bowden Wy COVS CV3 ....156 C4
Bowdler Rd BKHL/PFLD WV2 * 3 H9
Bowen Av
ETTPK/GDPK/PENN WV4 ....66 E2

Bowen-cooke Av CDSL WV8 ....34 C7
Bowen St
ETTPK/GDPK/PENN WV4 ....50 C8
Bower Bank STRPT DY13 ....188 C3
Bower CI LICH WS13 ....21 H3
Bowercourt CI SOLH B91 ....148 K4
Bower Hill Dr STRPT DY13 ....188 C3
Bower La BRLYHL DY5 ....102 C5
Bowers Cft RLSN CV32 ....198 B3
Bowes Dr CNCK/NC WS11 ....16 D1
Bow Fell RUGBYN/HIL CV21 .....160 M5
Bowfell CI COVW CV5 ....153 M1
Bowker St WLNHL WV13 ....51 C3
Bowlas Av MGN/WHC B75 ....56 F5
Bowling Green Av
TAM/AM/WIL B77 ....46 C4
Bowling Green CI
DARL/WED WS10 ....52 B6
ERDW/GRVHL B23 ....72 C6
Bowling Green La
BFLD/HDSWWD B20 ....88 C5
RCOVN/BALC/EX CV7 ....116 C6
Bowling Green Rd BORD B9 * ...108 A4
DUDS DY2 ....103 H2
STRBR DY8 ....101 J8
Bowls Ct COVW CV5 ....154 C2
Bowman Rd PBAR/PBCH B42 ....70 F4
Bowman's Ri WOLV WV1 ....50 E2
Bowmore Rd BRGRVE B60 ....191 K4
Bowness Ct COVW CV5 ....133 L5
Bowood Ct REDW B97 ....202 B7
Bowood Crs NFLD/LBR B31 .....144 E3
Bowood Dr
DUNHL/THL/PER WV6 ....35 J4
Bowood End WALM/CURD B76 ...73 H2
Bowpatch CI STRPT DY13 ....188 B5
Bowpatch Rd STRPT DY13 ......188 B4
Bowshot CI CBROM B36 ....92 B4
Bowstoke Rd GTB/HAM B43 ....70 A5
Bow St BILS/COS WV14 ....51 J7
CBHAMW B1 ....6 E6
WLNHL WV13 ....51 L4
Bowyer Rd WASH/WDE B8 ....108 B1
Bowyer St BORD B9 ....108 B4
The Boxhill COVS CV3 ....155 M4
Boxnott CI REDW B97 ....201 L3
Box Rd CHWD/FDBR/MGN B37 ...111 C5
Box St WSL WS1 ....5 H5
Box Trees Rd HOCK/TIA B94 ....175 G4
Boyce Wy RRUGBY CV23 ....159 H3
Boyd CI COVE CV2 ....135 K5
Boyden CI CNCK/NC WS11 ....15 M4
PENK ST19 ....10 C6
Boyd Gv ACGN B27 ....126 F3
Boyleston Rd BKHL/PFLD WV2 ...84 D8
Boyleston Rd HLGN/YWD B28 ...126 E7
Boyne Rd
LGN/SDN/BHAMAIR B26 ....109 M5
Boyton Gv KGSTG B44 ....71 K2
Brabazon Gv CVALE B35 ....91 K2
Brabham CI KIDD DY11 ....138 B4
Brabham Crs FOAKS/STRLY B74 ...55 K7
Bracadale Av ERDE/BCHGN B24 ...90 E1
Bracadale CI COVS CV3 ....156 B2
Bracebridge CI
RCOVN/BALC/EX CV7 ....151 M7
ERDE/BCHGN B24 ....90 D4
FOAKS/STRLY B74 ....60 A7
POL/KGSB/FAZ B78 ....60 A7
Bracebridge St AST/WIT B6 ....89 J7
NUN CV11 ....98 F1
Braceby Av MOS/BIL B13 ....126 B4
Braces La BRGRVE B60 ....169 G4
Brace St WSL WS1 ....4 F7
Brackenbury Rd KGSTG B44 ....71 M5
Bracken CI BNTWD WS7 ....19 G6
CDSL WV8 ....35 J4
HEDN WS12 ....21 J7
RUGBYS/DCH CV22 ....186 C4
Brackendale Rd HALE B63 ....121 J2
Bracken Dr MGN/WHC B75 ....57 K7
RUGBYS/DCH CV22 ....186 C4
Brackenfield Vw BRLYHL DY5 .....84 B5
Brackenhill Rd BNTWD WS7 ....18 B8
Brackenhurst Rd COVN CV6 .....133 K6
Bracken Park Gdns STRBR DY8 ...101 K3
HEDN WS12 ....12 A8
Bracken Wy FOAKS/STRLY B74 ...55 K5
HWK/WKHTH B38 ....145 H6
Brackenwood Dr WNSFLD WV11 ...37 K8
Brackelsham Wy
TAM/AM/WIL B77 ....32 E7
Brackley Av BFLD/HDSWWD B20 ...89 C4
Brackley CI COVN CV6 ....133 K4
Brackleys Wy HIA/OLT B92 ....127 K2
Bradburn Rd WNSFLD WV11 .....36 F5
Bradburn Rd HEDN WS12 ....12 E5
Bradbury La HEDN WS12 ....12 E5
Bradbury Rd HIA/OLT B92 ....127 K5
Braddock CI COVE CV2 ....135 M7
Brade Dr COVE CV2 ....135 M7
Braden Rd
ETTPK/GDPK/PENN WV4 ....66 H1
Brades CI HALE B63 ....102 F6
Brades Ri OLDBY B69 ....86 B5
Brades Rd OLDBY B69 ....86 C5
Bradestone Rd NUN CV11 ....99 H4
Bradewell Rd CBROM B36 ....92 B4
Bradfield Rd PBAR/PBCH B42 ...71 C6
Bradford CI GTB/HAM B43 ....70 D6
Bradford La BRLYHL DY5 ....141 H8
WSL WS1 ....4 E5
Bradford Rd BRWNH WS8 ....26 C5
CBROM B36 ....91 L6
DUDS DY2 ....84 D7
CRTAM B79 ....31 K8
DIG/EDG B5 ....4 H7
WSL WS1 ....4 H7
Bradgate CI SHHTH WV12 ....38 A7
Bradgate Dr FOAKS/STRLY B74 ...42 C8
Bradgate Rd NUN CV11 ....85 K3
Bradley Cft
RCOVN/BALC/EX CV7 ....151 M7
Bradley La BILS/COS WV14 ....67 J5
Bradleymore Rd BRLYHL DY5 ...102 A2
Bradley Rd BKDE/SHDE B34 * ...92 E7
BKHL/PFLD WV2 ....50 C6
STRBR DY8 ....101 K7
Bradleys CI CDYHTH B64 ....103 J6
Bradley's La BILS/COS WV14 .....67 J5
Bradley St BILS/COS WV14 ....51 M6
BRLYHL DY5 ....102 A2
TPTN/OCK DY4 ....85 K3

Bradley Thursfield Ct
KIDDW DY11 138 A6
Bradmore Cl SOLH B91 148 E5
Bradmore Gv SLYOAK B29 123 L5
Bradmore Rd BDMR/CCFT WV3 49 K5
Bradney Gn TLHL/CAN CV4 153 J6
Bradnick Pl TLHL/CAN CV4 153 K4
Bradnock Cl MOS/BIL B13 126 A6
Bradnock's Marsh La
HIA/OLT B92 151 J3
Bradshaw Av DARL/WED WS10 51 M8
HWK/WKHTH B38 145 H4
Bradshaw Cl TPTN/OCK DY4 85 L2
Bradshawe Cl
ALE/KHTH/YWD B14 147 H2
Bradshaw St WOLV WV1 * 3 H5
Bradstock Rd BVILLE B30 146 A1
Bradwell Cft MGN/WHC B75 57 J2
Braeburn Cl LICH WS13 21 H4
Braemar Av STRBR DY8 101 G4
Braemar Cl COVE CV2 135 J7
SEDG DY3 66 A4
SHHTH WV12 37 L7
Braemar Dr ERDW/GRVHL B23 71 M8
Braemar Gdns HEDN WS12 12 D6
Braemar Rd CNCK/NC WS11 25 L1
HIA/OLT B92 127 J4
RLSN CV32 206 F1
SCFLD/BOLD B73 72 D3
Braemar Wy NUNW/HART CV10 98 E3
Braeside Cft
CHWD/FDBR/MGN B37 111 H3
Braeside Wy BLOX/PEL WS3 39 K2
Brafield Leys
RUGBYS/DCH CV22 186 E7
Bragg Rd BFLD/HDSWWD B20 89 H3
Braggs Farm La SHLY B90 173 L1
Braham CRTAM B79 31 H7
Braid Cl HWK/WKHTH B38 145 H4
Braids Cl RUGBYN/HIL CV21 187 H1
Brailes Cl HIA/OLT B92 128 C6
Brailes Dr WALM/CURD B76 73 K2
Brailes Gv BORD B9 108 F4
Brailsford Cl WNSFLD WV11 37 J5
Brailsford Dr SMTHWK B66 87 L8
Brain St TAM/AM/WIL B77 46 E3
Braithwaite Cl KGSWFD DY6 83 H7
Braithwaite Rd SPARK B11 107 L6
Brake La STRBR DY8 119 J7
Brakesmead RLSS CV31 206 D8
Bramah Wy TPTN/OCK DY4 68 A7
Bramber Dr WMBN WV5 64 D7
Bramber Wy STRBR DY8 119 K3
Bramble Cl AST/WIT B6 89 J6
BRWNH WS8 26 C8
CDYHTH B64 103 K1
CSHL/WTROR B46 93 L6
NFLD/LBR B31 123 K8
NUN CV11 99 K3
SHHTH WV12 38 A6
Bramble Dell BORD B9 108 E2
Bramble Dr HEDN WS12 13 G6
LGN/SDN/BHAMAIR B26 109 L7
Bramble Gn DUDN DY1 66 D8
Bramble La BNTWD WS7 18 F5
Brambleside STRBR DY8 101 K4
The Brambles CNCK/NC WS11 17 L8
HAG/WOL DY9 120 B2
LICHS WS14 21 H7
WALM/CURD B76 73 L5
Bramble St COV CV1 9 K5
Bramblewood WMBN WV5 64 E6
Bramblewood Dr
BDMR/CCFT WV3 49 J5
Bramblewoods BKDE/SHDE B34 92 A8
Brambling TAM/AM/WIL B77 46 E6
Brambling Cl RRUGBY CV23 161 G4
Brambling Ri KIDD DY10 * 164 F4
Brambling Wk EDG B15 107 G6
Bramcote Dr HIA/OLT B92 128 A6
Bramcote Ri FOAKS/STRLY B74 57 G6
Bramcote Rd RIDG/WDGT B32 105 G8
Bramdean Dr PENK ST19 10 D4
Bramdene Av NUNW/HART CV10 81 G5
Bramerton Cl WNSFLD WV11 36 E7
Bramford Dr DUDN DY1 66 F7
Bramley Cl DSYBK/YTR WS5 54 B5
GTB/HAM B43 71 H2
Bramley Cft SHLY B90 148 A3
Bramley Dr BFLD/HDSWWD B20 88 F2
HLYWD B47 146 F7
Bramley Mews Ct ACGN B27 127 G1
Bramley Rd ACGN B27 109 G8
DSYBK/YTR WS5 69 M1
Bramley Wy BEWD DY12 162 C2
Brampton Av HLGN/YWD B28 126 E7
Brampton Cl KIDD DY10 138 F1
Brampton Crs HIA/OLT B92 126 F7
Brampton Dr HEDN WS12 17 J3
Brampton Wy BDWTH CV12 117 M2
Bramshall Dr DOR/KN B93 175 J2
Bramshaw Cl
ALE/KHTH/YWD B14 146 D3
Bramstead Av
DUNHL/THL/PER WV6 48 F3
Bramston Crs TLHL/CAN CV4 153 K4
Bramwell Dr GTWY WS6 24 B5
Bramwell Gdns
RCOVN/BALC/EX CV7 116 D8
Brancaster Cl TAM/AM/WIL B77 32 E7
Branchal Rd ALDR WS9 41 G4
Branches Cl BEWD DY12 162 D3
Branch Rd HWK/WKHTH B38 145 H5
Branden Rd ALVE B48 170 E7
Brandfield Rd COVN CV6 133 K5
Brandhall La LGLYGN/QTN B68 104 F4
Brandhall Rd LGLYGN/QTN B68 104 F4
Brandon Cl FOAKS/STRLY B74 55 K2
SEDG DY3 66 C6
WBROM B70 86 E3
Brandon Gv NFLD/LBR B31 144 D6
Brandon La KNWTH CV8 157 K8
KNWTH CV8 182 B1
Brandon Pde RLSN CV32 206 E5
Brandon Pk BDMR/CCFT WV3 49 J6
Brandon Pl BKDE/SHDE B34 92 B6
Brandon Rd COVS CV3 156 D4
COVS CV3 156 F5
HLGN/YWD B28 126 C3
KNWTH CV8 158 A7
RMSLY B62 104 C4
SOLH B91 128 A6
Brandon Wy BRLYHL DY5 102 C5
WBROM B70 86 E3
Brandwood Gv
ALE/KHTH/YWD B14 125 H8
Brandwood Park Rd
ALE/KHTH/YWD B14 146 A1
Brandwood Rd
ALE/KHTH/YWD B14 125 H8
Branfield Cl BILS/COS WV14 66 E4
Branksome Av HDSW B21 88 D5
Branksome Rd COVN CV6 133 J7
Branscombe Cl
ALE/KHTH/YWD B14 125 H8
Bransdale Av COVN CV6 134 B2
Bransdale Cl
DUNHL/THL/PER WV6 35 L8
Bransdale Rd BRWNH WS8 26 C6
Bransford Av TLHL/CAN CV4 154 B8
Bransford Ri SOLH B91 128 F8
Branstree Dr COVN CV6 134 B3
Brantford Rd YDLY B25 109 G5
Branthill Cft SOLH B91 148 F4
Brantley Av BDMR/CCFT WV3 49 G4
Brantley Rd AST/WIT B6 89 L3
Branton Hill La ALDR WS9 41 G8
Brantwood Av BNTWD WS7 18 E8
Brasshouse La SMTHWK B66 87 K7
Brassie Cl HWK/WKHTH B38 145 H4
Brassington Av SCFLD/BOLD B73 56 F8
Bratch Cl DUDS DY2 103 G2
Bratch Common Rd WMBN WV5 64 C6
Bratch Hollow WMBN WV5 64 E5
Bratch La WMBN WV5 64 E5
Bratch Pk WMBN WV5 64 C5
Brathay Cl COVS CV3 155 H7
Bratt St WBROM B70 87 G1
Braunston Cl WALM/CURD B76 73 L3
Braunston Pl
RUGBYS/DCH CV22 187 H5
Bray Bank CSHL/WTROR B46 95 H2
Brayford Av BRLYHL DY5 101 M6
COVS CV3 155 G7
Braymoor Rd STETCH B33 110 C4
Brays Cl RRUGBY CV23 158 C2
Bray's La COVE CV2 155 L2
Brays Rd
LGN/SDN/BHAMAIR B26 109 L7
Bray St WLNHL WV13 51 M3
Braytoft Cl COVN CV6 134 A3
Brazil St TLHL/CAN CV4 153 J3
Breaches La REDE B98 203 H5
Breach Oak La
RCOVN/BALC/EX CV7 115 G2
RCOVN/BALC/EX CV7 115 H4
Breakback Rd BRGRVW B61 191 H5
Bream TAM/AM/WIL B77 46 B6
Bream Cl
CHWD/FDBR/MGN B37 111 G3
WOLV WV1 50 F1
Breamore Crs DUDN DY1 84 D2
Brean Av
LGN/SDN/BHAMAIR B26 109 K8
Brearley Cl LOZ/NWT B19 89 H8
Brearley St HDSW B21 88 B5
LOZ/NWT B19 89 H8
Brecknell Ri KIDD DY10 138 D5
Brecknock Rd HHTH/SAND B71 68 E7
Brecon Av BRGRVW B61 168 E8
Brecon Dr STRBR DY8 101 M7
Brecon Rd BFLD/HDSWWD B20 88 F5
Bredon Av COVS CV3 156 D6
HAG/WOL DY9 102 A8
KIDDW DY11 163 L4
Bredon Ct HALE B63 121 L2
Bredon Cft WSNGN B18 88 E8
Bredon Rd BRGRVE B60 191 H6
OLDBY B69 86 B8
STRBR DY8 101 L7
Bredon Vw REDW B97 202 B5
Bredon Wy STRPT DY13 188 B4
Breech Cl FOAKS/STRLY B74 55 J6
Bree Cl COVW CV5 132 E6
Breeden Dr WALM/CURD B76 74 F7
Breedon Rd BVILLE B30 124 E8
Breedon Ter WSNGN B18 * 88 E8
Breedon Wy RUSH/SHEL WS4 40 A4
Breen Rydding Dr
BILS/COS WV14 66 F4
Bree's La KNWTH CV8 177 L4
Breeze Av CNCK/NC WS11 17 M8
Brelades Cl DUDN DY1 84 C2
Brendan Cl CSHL/WTROR B46 93 L8
Brendon TAM/AM/WIL B77 46 F4
Brendon Wy NUNW/HART CV10 97 L2
Brennand Rd LGLYGN/QTN B68 104 F4
Brent TAM/AM/WIL B77 46 C6
Brentford Rd
ALE/KHTH/YWD B14 125 K8
SOLH B91 148 C2
Brentmill Cl WOLVN WV10 36 D1
Brentnall Dr MGN/WHC B75 56 F2
Brenton Rd
ETTPK/GDPK/PENN WV4 65 K1
Brent Rd BVILLE B30 125 G5
Brentwood Av COVS CV3 181 G2
Brentwood Cl SOLH B91 148 C2
Brentwood Gv KGSTG B44 71 J5
Brenwood Cl KGSWFD DY6 82 F6
Brereton Cl DUDS DY2 85 J4
Brereton Rd SHHTH WV12 38 A6
Brese Av WWCK CV34 205 K4
Bretby Gv ERDW/GRVHL B23 72 E7
Bretford Rd COVE CV2 135 G4
Bretshall Cl SHLY B90 148 D8
Brett Dr RIDG/WDGT B32 123 G5
Brettell La STRBR DY8 101 L4
Brettell St DUDS DY2 84 F6
Bretton Rd ACGN B27 127 H3
Bretts Cl COV CV1 9 J1
Bretts Hall Est
NUNW/HART CV10 79 K6
Brett St HHTH/SAND B71 68 F8
Brett Young Cl KIDD DY10 138 F8
Brevitt Rd BKHL/PFLD WV2 50 B7
Brewers Cl COVS CV3 156 E4
Brewers Dr BLOX/PEL WS3 39 L4
Brewer St WSLW WS2 53 J1
Brewery St AST/WIT B6 89 J8
DUDS DY2 85 J4
HDSW B21 88 B5
SMTHWKW B67 87 K7
TPTN/OCK DY4 85 K1
Brewhouse Ct LICH WS13 * 20 D4
Brewins Wy BRLYHL DY5 102 D1
Brewood Rd WOLVN WV10 22 A4
Brewster Cl COVE CV2 156 C3
POL/KGSB/FAZ B78 45 J4
Breydon Gv WLNHL WV13 51 K5
Brian Rd SMTHWKW B67 87 J7
Briansway COVN CV6 134 C2
Briar TAM/AM/WIL B77 46 E2
Briar Av FOAKS/STRLY B74 55 L4
Briarbeck RUSH/SHEL WS4 40 A5
Briar Cl BRGRVE B60 169 G7
ERDE/BCHGN B24 90 E1
HEDN WS12 12 E5
RLSN CV32 206 F3
Briardene Av BDWTH CV12 116 F4
Briarfield Rd SPARK B11 126 E2
Briar Hl KIDD DY10 166 C5
Briars Cl BRLYHL DY5 102 A1
COVE CV2 156 A3
NUN CV11 81 J8
RRUGBY CV23 185 M1
The Briars ERDW/GRVHL B23 72 B7
Briars Wy HEDN WS12 18 A1
Briar Wy STRPT DY13 188 C1
Briar Wood Cl BKHL/PFLD WV2 50 E6
Briarwood Cl SHLY B90 174 B1
Brickbridge La WMBN WV5 64 C8
Brickfield Rd YDLY B25 108 F7
Brickheath Rd WOLV WV1 50 E2
Brickhill Dr
CHWD/FDBR/MGN B37 110 E3
Brick Hill La COVW CV5 132 B5
Brickhouse La WBROM B70 68 D7
Brickhouse La South
TPTN/OCK DY4 68 B7
Brickhouse Rd
BLKHTH/ROWR B65 103 L1
Brickiln St BRWNH WS8 26 D6
Brickkiln La ATHST CV9 76 F1
Brick Kiln La HLYWD B47 172 D1
KGSTG B44 71 J6
POL/KGSB/FAZ B78 59 G7
SEDG DY3 83 L2
SOLH B91 148 D5
Brick Kiln St BRLYHL DY5 84 C8
BRLYHL DY5 102 E5
TPTN/OCK DY4 67 J7
Brickkiln St WLNHL WV13 51 K4
Brick St SEDG DY3 66 B5
Brickworks Rd HEDN WS12 17 H2
Brickyard Rd ALDR WS9 40 D4
The Bridal Pth COVW CV5 132 F7
HLGN/YWD B28 126 F8
Briddsland Rd STETCH B33 110 C3
Bridgeacre Gdns COVS CV3 156 D3
Bridge Av GTWY WS6 16 C8
TPTN/OCK DY4 68 A6
Bridgeburn Rd NFLD/LBR B31 123 J5
Bridge Cl SPARK B11 125 M2
Bridgecote COVS CV3 156 C7
Bridge Cft BHTH/HG B12 107 J7
Bridge Cross Rd BNTWD WS7 18 E6
Bridge End WWCK CV34 205 K8
Bridgeford Rd BKDE/SHDE B34 91 M7
Bridgelands Wy
BFLD/HDSWWD B20 89 H4
Bridge La ATHST CV9 63 L6
Bridgeman Cft CBROM B36 92 A6
Bridgeman Rd COVN CV6 133 M8
Bridgeman St WSLW WS2 4 D4
Bridgemary Cl WOLVN WV10 36 D1
Bridge Meadow Dr
DOR/KN B93 149 K8
Bridgend Cft BRLYHL DY5 83 M7
Bridge Piece NFLD/LBR B31 144 F3
Bridge Rd RUSH/SHEL WS4 39 M4
TPTN/OCK DY4 68 A6
WASH/WDE B8 108 C2
Bridges Crs CNCK/NC WS11 17 K8
Bridgeside TAM/AM/WIL B77 46 A3
Bridges Rd CNCK/NC WS11 17 K8
Bridge St ATHST CV9 77 G1
BILS/COS WV14 51 J8
BILS/COS WV14 67 G5
BRWNH WS8 26 C7
CBHAMW B1 6 D7
CNCK/NC WS11 16 C8
COVN CV6 134 D6
DARL/WED WS10 68 D3
HALE B63 103 G6
KIDD DY10 138 C8
NUN CV11 99 G3
OLDBY B69 86 E5
POL/KGSB/FAZ B78 47 L4
REDW B97 202 B1
RUGBYN/HIL CV21 187 G2
STRBR DY8 101 J4
STRPT DY13 188 D2
TAM/AM/WIL B77 32 C8
WBROM B70 86 F1
WLNHL WV13 51 K4
WOLVN WV10 36 C8
WSL WS1 4 F3
WWCK CV34 206 A5
Bridge St North SMTHWK B66 87 M7
Bridge St South SMTHWK B66 87 M7
Bridge St West LOZ/NWT B19 89 H7
The Bridge WSL WS1 4 E4
Bridget St RUGBYN/HIL CV21 186 D2
Bridge Vw CSHL/WTROR B46 * 93 K6
KNWTH CV8 * 181 H2
Bridge Wk ACGN B27 * 127 H2
Bridgewater Av OLDBY B69 104 E1
Bridgewater Cl PENK ST19 10 D5
Bridgewater Crs DUDS DY2 85 J4
Bridgewater Dr BILS/COS WV14 67 G3
Bridgewater St
TAM/AM/WIL B77 32 C8
Bridge Wy BRWNH WS8 26 C7
Bridgnorth Av WMBN WV5 82 D1
Bridgnorth Gv SHHTH WV12 37 M7
Bridgnorth Rd
DUNHL/THL/PER WV6 49 G3
KIDDW DY11 137 K2
KINVER DY7 101 G7
SEDG DY3 64 A8
Bridgwater Cl ALDR WS9 40 D1
Bridle Brook La COVW CV5 132 D1
Bridle Gv HHTH/SAND B71 69 K5
Bridle La FOAKS/STRLY B74 55 H7
Bridle Md HWK/WKHTH B38 145 H5
Bridle Rd RUGBYN/HIL CV21 186 C1
STRBR DY8 101 H7
Bridlewood FOAKS/STRLY B74 55 K5
Bridley Moor Rd REDW B97 202 A1
Bridport Cl COVE CV2 156 E1
Brierley Hill Rd STRBR DY8 101 J3
Brierley La BILS/COS WV14 67 J3
Brierley Rd COVE CV2 135 G5
Brier Road Rd HALE B63 122 A2
Briertey Hill La RUGE WS15 18 F1
Briery Cl CDYHTH B64 103 K6
Briery Rd HALE B63 121 J2
Brigfield Crs MOS/BIL B13 125 M8
Brigfield Rd MOS/BIL B13 125 M8
Bright Crs TAM/AM/WIL B77 46 A3
Brightmere Rd COVN CV6 8 C1
Brighton Cl WSLW WS2 4 C1
Brighton Pl BDMR/CCFT WV3 2 B5
Brighton Rd BHTH/HG B12 107 K8
Brighton St COVE CV2 9 M3
Bright Rd LGLYGN/QTN B68 86 F8
Brightstone Cl WOLVN WV10 36 D1
Brightstone Rd RBRY B45 143 L3
Bright St COVN CV6 134 C7
DARL/WED WS10 52 B8
STRBR DY8 101 H8
WOLV WV1 2 D2
Brightwalton Rd COVS CV3 155 H6
Brightwell Crs DOR/KN B93 175 J2
Brill Cl TLHL/CAN CV4 154 A8
Brimfield Pl
DUNHL/THL/PER WV6 * 49 K1
Brimstone La BRGRVW B61 168 A6
Brindle Av COVS CV3 156 A3
Brindle Cl
LGN/SDN/BHAMAIR B26 109 J8
Brindlefields Wy TPTN/OCK DY4 85 L3
Brindle Rd DSYBK/YTR WS5 70 A1
Brindley Av WNSFLD WV11 37 L4
Brindley Brae KINVER DY7 118 A1
Brindley Cl ATHST CV9 63 G3
PENK ST19 10 E6
STRBR DY8 101 J4
WMBN WV5 64 B7
WSLW WS2 38 D8
Brindley Ct LGLYGN/QTN B68 * 104 F6
TPTN/OCK DY4 67 J8
Brindley Crs HEDN WS12 13 G6
Brindley Dr CBHAMW B1 6 C5
Brindley Heath Rd HEDN WS12 13 G2
Brindley Paddocks COV CV1 8 E2
Brindley Pl CBHAMW B1 6 B6
Brindley Rd HEDN WS12 12 D4
HHTH/SAND B71 68 E5
RCOVN/BALC/EX CV7 116 F6
RUGBYN/HIL CV21 187 L4
Brindley St STRPT DY13 163 K8
Brindley Wy SMTHWK B66 * 88 A8
Brineton Gv SLYOAK B29 123 L4
Brineton St WSLW WS2 4 B6
Bringewood Gv
RIDG/WDGT B32 122 F5
Brinklow Cl REDE B98 203 H5
Brinklow Cft BKDE/SHDE B34 92 B6
Brinklow Rd COVS CV3 156 E3
RRUGBY CV23 158 E2
SLYOAK B29 123 K3
Brinley Wy KGSWFD DY6 83 G7
Brinsford La WOLVN WV10 22 B6
Brinsford Rd WOLVN WV10 36 A2
Brinsley Cl SOLH B91 148 F3
Brinsley Rd
LGN/SDN/BHAMAIR B26 109 M5
Brinton Cl KIDDW DY11 164 A2
Brinton Crs KIDDW DY11 164 A1
Brisbane Cl COVS CV3 155 J7
Brisbane Rd SMTHWKW B67 87 J7
Brisbane Wy HEDN WS12 17 J2
Briscoe Rd COVN CV6 134 A1
Briseley Cl BRLYHL DY5 102 A5
Bristam Cl OLDBY B69 86 C7
Bristnall Hall La
LGLYGN/QTN B68 105 G2
Bristnall Hall Rd
LGLYGN/QTN B68 105 G3
Bristol Cl CNCK/NC WS11 16 F4
Bristol Rd COVW CV5 154 D3
DIG/EDG B5 124 F2
DUDS DY2 103 H3
ERDW/GRVHL B23 90 C2
SLYOAK B29 124 B5
Bristol Rd South NFLD/LBR B31 123 L8
NFLD/LBR B31 144 C4
RBRY B45 143 L6
Bristol St BDMR/CCFT WV3 2 C8
BILS/COS WV14 51 H8
DIG/EDG B5 107 H5
Briston Cl BRLYHL DY5 102 A5
Britannia Cl REDE B98 202 D2
Britannia Gdns
BLKHTH/ROWR B65 104 A2
STRPT DY13 188 E4
Britannia Pk DARL/WED WS10 * 68 B2
Britannia Rd BILS/COS WV14 67 K2
BLKHTH/ROWR B65 104 A2
Britannia St COVE CV2 9 L3
OLDBY B69 86 A3
Britannia Wy LICHS WS14 21 J5
Britannic Gdns MOS/BIL B13 125 H3
Britford Cl ALE/KHTH/YWD B14 146 D2
Briton Rd COVE CV2 155 L1
Brittan Cl BKDE/SHDE B34 92 C7
Brittania Wy WSL WS1 53 H8
Britten Cl NUN CV11 99 L6
Britten St REDW B97 202 B1
Britton Dr CSCFLD/WYGN B72 73 G5
Britwell Rd SCFLD/BOLD B73 72 E3
Brixfield Wy SHLY B90 147 L8
Brixham Cl NUN CV11 81 K8
Brixham Dr COVE CV2 135 G7
Brixham Rd LDYWD/EDGR B16 106 B1
Brixworth Cl COVS CV3 156 C5
Broach Rd STRPT DY13 188 F4
Broad Acres NFLD/LBR B31 123 J7
Broad Cft TPTN/OCK DY4 68 A7
Broadfern Rd DOR/KN B93 149 M5
Broadfield Cl HHTH/SAND B71 69 K5
KGSWFD DY6 83 H8
Broadfields HAG/WOL DY9 119 L7
Broadfields Rd
ERDW/GRVHL B23 72 F6
Broadfield Wk LDYWD/EDGR B16 6 A7
Broadgate COV CV1 8 F5
Broad Ground Rd REDE B98 202 F3
Broadhaven Cl RLSS CV31 207 G6
Broad Heath Cl REDW B97 * 193 M8
Broadheath Dr RUSH/SHEL WS4 40 B5
Broadhidley Dr
RIDG/WDGT B32 122 F4
Broadhurst Gn HEDN WS12 12 C2
Broadhurst Green Rd
HEDN WS12 12 B3
Broadlands WOLVN WV10 22 B8
Broadlands Cl COVW CV5 154 A3
Broadlands Dr BRLYHL DY5 84 C8
Broadlands Ri LICHS WS14 21 H6
Broad La ALE/KHTH/YWD B14 146 B2
BDMR/CCFT WV3 49 J5
BLOX/PEL WS3 38 F5
COVW CV5 154 A3
LICH WS13 19 M8
LICHS WS14 21 H6
RCOVN/BALC/EX CV7 113 M1
RCOVN/BALC/EX CV7 152 E1
RUSH/SHEL WS4 40 A4
WNSFLD WV11 24 B8
Broad Lane Gdns BLOX/PEL WS3 38 E3
Broad La North SHHTH WV12 37 M7
Broad Lanes BILS/COS WV14 67 G1
Broad La South SHHTH WV12 37 L7
Broadlee TAM/AM/WIL B77 47 H4
Broad Meadow ALDR WS9 40 F5
Broadmeadow Cl BVILLE B30 145 M2
Broadmeadow Gn
BILS/COS WV14 51 G6
Broad Meadow La BVILLE B30 145 M2
GTWY WS6 24 E3
Broadmeadows Rd SHHTH WV12 38 C5
Broadmere Ri COVW CV5 153 L3
Broadmoor Av
LGLYGN/QTN B68 105 H3
Broadmoor Cl BILS/COS WV14 67 G1
Broadmoor Rd BILS/COS WV14 67 G1
Broad Oaks WALM/CURD B76 73 L5
Broadoaks Cl CNCK/NC WS11 17 K7
Broad Oaks Rd SOLH B91 127 K8
Broad Park Rd COVE CV2 135 H6
Broad Rd ACGN B27 126 F2
Broadsmeath TAM/AM/WIL B77 46 A4
Broadstone Av BLOX/PEL WS3 39 H6
HALE B63 120 F1
Broadstone Cl
ETTPK/GDPK/PENN WV4 50 B8
Broadstone Rd
LGN/SDN/BHAMAIR B26 109 K3
Broad St BILS/COS WV14 51 G7
BILS/COS WV14 67 G5
BRGRVW B61 191 K1
BRLYHL DY5 84 A7
CNCK/NC WS11 16 C7
COVN CV6 134 C6
EDG B15 6 B7
KGSWFD DY6 83 H8
KIDD DY10 138 C6
OLDBY B69 86 E8
RRUGBY CV23 158 D2
WOLV WV1 3 G4
WWCK CV34 205 K6
Broad Street Jetty COVN CV6 134 C6
Broad Street Jct WOLV WV1 3 H4
Broadwas Cl REDE B98 195
Broadwater COVW CV5 154
Broadwaters Av
DARL/WED WS10 68
Broadwaters Dr KIDD DY10 138
Broadwaters Rd
DARL/WED WS10 68
Broad Wy RUSH/SHEL WS4 40
Broadway BDMR/CCFT WV3 49
CDSL WV8 34
COVW CV5 8
HEDN WS12 12
LGLYGN/QTN B68 105
RLSN CV32 199
SHLY B90 147
WOLVN WV10 36
WSL WS1 53
Broadway Av BORD B9 108
HALE B63 121
Broadway Cft LGLYGN/QTN B68 105
LGN/SDN/BHAMAIR B26 109
Broadway Man COVW CV5 * 8
Broadway North WSL WS1 5
The Broadway
BFLD/HDSWWD B20 89
DUDN DY1 84
DUDN DY1 85
HHTH/SAND B71 68
STRBR DY8 119
WMBN WV5 64
Broadway West WSL WS1 53
Broadwell Rd HIA/OLT B92 127
OLDBY B69 86
Broadwells TLHL/CAN CV4 153
Broadwells Ct TLHL/CAN CV4 * 153
Broadwells Crs TLHL/CAN CV4 153
Broadyates Gv YDLY B25 109
Broadyates Rd YDLY B25 109
Brobury Cft SHLY B90 148
Broc Cl PENK ST19 10
Brockenhurst Wy COVN CV6 116
Brockeridge Cl SHHTH WV12 38
Brocket Cl STRPT DY13 163
Brockhall Gv
CHWD/FDBR/MGN B37 92
Brockhill Dr REDW B97 193
Brockhill La ALVE B48 171
BRGRVE B60 193
REDE B98 195
REDW B97 193
Brockhurst Crs DSYBK/YTR WS5 53
Brockhurst Dr
DUNHL/THL/PER WV6 2
HLGN/YWD B28 126
TLHL/CAN CV4 153
Brockhurst La MGN/WHC B75 43
SHLY B90 147
Brockhurst Pl DSYBK/YTR WS5 53
Brockhurst Rd CBROM B36 91
MGN/WHC B75 57
Brockhurst St DSYBK/YTR WS5 53
Brockley Cl BRLYHL DY5 102
Brockley Gv MOS/BIL B13 125
Brockley Pl VAUX/NECH B7 90
Brockmoor Cl HAG/WOL DY9 120
Brock Rd TPTN/OCK DY4 85
Brockwell Gv KGSTG B44 71
Brockwell Rd KGSTG B44 71
Brockworth Rd
ALE/KHTH/YWD B14 146
Brocton Cl BILS/COS WV14 66
Brodick Wy NUNW/HART CV10 98
Brogden Cl HHTH/SAND B71 69
Bromage Av POL/KGSB/FAZ B78 60
Bromfield Cl AST/WIT B6 89
Bromfield Ct
DUNHL/THL/PER WV6 * 48
Bromfield Crs DARL/WED WS10 69
Bromfield Rd REDW B97 202
Bromford Cl ERDW/GRVHL B23 72
Bromford Crs ERDE/BCHGN B24 90
Bromford Dl
DUNHL/THL/PER WV6 * 49
Bromford Dell NFLD/LBR B31 145
Bromford Dr CBROM B36 91
Bromford Hl BFLD/HDSWWD B20 89
Bromford La ERDE/BCHGN B24 90
OLDBY B69 86
Bromford Ri BDMR/CCFT WV3 2
Bromford Rd CBROM B36 90
DUDS DY2 84
WBROM B70 86
Bromleigh Dr COVE CV2 156
Bromley BRLYHL DY5 83
Bromley Cl HEDN WS12 12
KNWTH CV8 179
Bromley Gdns CDSL WV8 34
Bromley La KGSWFD DY6 101
Bromley Pl
ETTPK/GDPK/PENN WV4 49
Bromley St BKHL/PFLD WV2 50
BORD B9 7
HAG/WOL DY9 102
Brompton Dr BRLYHL DY5 101
Brompton Lawns
DUNHL/THL/PER WV6 48
Brompton Pool Rd
HLGN/YWD B28 147
Brompton Rd KGSTG B44 71
Bromsgrove Hwy BRGRVE B60 192
REDE B98 202
REDW B97 201
Bromsgrove Rd BRGRVW B61 168
HAG/WOL DY9 141
KIDD DY10 165
REDW B97 201
RMSLY B62 121
Bromsgrove St DIG/EDG B5 6
KIDD DY10 138
Bromwall Rd MOS/BIL B13 125
Bromwich Cl COVS CV3 156
Bromwich Dr MGN/WHC B75 57
Bromwich La HAG/WOL DY9 119
Bromwich Rd
RUGBYN/HIL CV21 187
Bromwynd Cl BKHL/PFLD WV2 49
Bromyard Av WALM/CURD B76 73
Bromyard Rd SPARK B11 126
Bronte Cl NUNW/HART CV10 79
RUGBYN/HIL CV21 187
SHLY B90 148
Bronte Ct CRTAM B79 31
Bronte Dr CNCK/NC WS11 17
KIDD DY10 138
Bronte Farm Rd SHLY B90 148
Bronte Rd BKHL/PFLD WV2 50
Bronte Wk COVE CV2 156
Bronwen Rd BILS/COS WV14 67
Bronwen Vls DARL/WED WS10 * 52
Bronze Cl NUN CV11 99
Brook Av TAM/AM/WIL B77 46
Brookbank Av BKDE/SHDE B34 9
Brookbank Gdns SEDG DY3 8
Brookbank Rd SEDG DY3 8
Brook Cl ALDR WS9 4
COV CV1
LGN/SDN/BHAMAIR B26 10
LICH WS13 2
PENK ST19 1

POL/KGSB/FAZ B78 .....76 B1
SHLY B90 .....147 K4
STETCH B33 .....109 J1
ok Crs HAG/WOL DY9 .....119 M8
HAG/WOL DY9 .....120 D2
KGSWFD DY6 .....83 G6
ok Cft
CHWD/FDBR/MGN B37 .....110 F6
LGN/SDN/BHAMAIR B26 .....109 M6
okdale KIDD DY10 .....138 D5
SEDG DY3 .....84 A2
okdale Cl RBRY B45 .....143 K4
okdale Dr
ETTPK/GDPK/PENN WV4 .....49 H7
okdale Rd NUNW/HART CV10 ..81 H6
ok Dr RIDG/WDGT B32 .....123 H4
oke Cl WWCK CV34 .....205 K8
ok End BNTWD WS7 .....26 E1
POL/KGSB/FAZ B78 .....45 L5
okend Dr RBRY B45 .....143 K6
oke Rd HEDN WS12 .....12 D7
KNWTH CV8 .....197 M1
okes Cl OLDBY B69 .....85 M5
oke St DUDS DY2 .....85 G5
ok Farm Cl CSHL/WTROR B46 ..95 H2
okfield Cl ALDR WS9 .....40 E4
okfield Dr CNCK/NC WS11 .....16 C6
okfield Rd ALDR WS9 .....40 E4
CDSL WV8 .....34 F2
RLSN CV32 .....199 J8
WSNGN B18 .....88 D8
ok Fields Cl BRGRVE B60 .....169 G4
okfields Rd
LGLYGN/QTN B68 .....105 G1
okfield Wy HIA/OLT B92 .....127 H6
TPTN/OCK DY4 .....67 L7
okford Av COVN CV6 .....133 L2
ok Green La HIA/OLT B92 .....150 E4
ok Gv CDSL WV8 .....34 F2
okhill Cl SHHTH WV12 .....38 A4
ok Hill Rd WASH/WDE B8 .....108 E1
ok Holloway HAG/WOL DY9 ..120 C2
ok House Cl WOLVN WV10 .....22 F7
okhouse La WOLVN WV10 .....22 D7
ok House La WOLVN WV10 .....22 E7
okhouse Rd BRGRVE B60 .....169 K5
DSYBK/YTR WS5 .....5 L8
okhus Farm Rd
WALM/CURD B76 .....73 L5
oking Cl GTB/HAM B43 .....71 H1
okland Gv ALDR WS9 .....40 D3
okland Rd ALDR WS9 .....40 D2
HAG/WOL DY9 .....119 L8
oklands STRBR DY8 .....101 K4
oklands Av GTWY WS6 .....24 D1
oklands Cl HLGN/YWD B28 .....126 D4
oklands Dr
ALE/KHTH/YWD B14 .....125 J8
KIDDW DY11 .....138 B4
oklands Gv ALDR WS9 .....40 D3
oklands La REDE B98 .....194 F8
oklands Pde WOLV WV1 .....50 F3
oklands Rd CNCK/NC WS11 .....16 E1
HLGN/YWD B28 .....126 D4
e Brooklands SEDG DY3 .....82 C4
oklands Wy
CHWD/FDBR/MGN B37 .....110 F5
ok La ALDR WS9 .....40 E2
ALE/KHTH/YWD B14 .....125 K5
CDYHTH B64 .....103 J3
GTWY WS6 .....24 E2
HIA/OLT B92 .....127 H5
NUNW/HART CV10 .....81 G7
RIDG/WDGT B32 .....105 K8
oklea BDWTH CV12 .....116 D3
oklea Gv HWK/WKHTH B38 .....145 L4
oklime Dr RRUGBY CV23 .....161 J5
oklyn Av AST/WIT B6 .....89 K6
oklyn Gv BILS/COS WV14 .....67 H5
KGSWFD DY6 .....82 F5
oklyn Rd BNTWD WS7 .....26 E1
COV CV1 .....134 B7
HEDN WS12 .....17 H4
okmans Av RIDG/WDGT B32 ..123 H1
okmeadow Ct
HLGN/YWD B28 .....126 B7
ok Meadow Rd
BKDE/SHDE B34 .....91 L7
RUSH/SHEL WS4 .....40 B5
ok Rd BRGRVW B61 .....168 A3
BRGRVW B61 .....191 J4
EDG B15 .....106 C6
GTWY WS6 .....16 C8
LGLYGN/QTN B68 .....104 E3
RBRY B45 .....143 J6
STRBR DY8 .....119 M2
WLNHL WV13 .....51 J4
WMBN WV5 .....64 D7
oksbank Dr CDYHTH B64 .....103 K1
oksby Gv DOR/KN B93 .....175 L3
oks Cft CVALE B35 .....91 L3
okshaw Wy COVE CV2 .....135 K5
okside DARL/WED WS10 .....68 F2
GTB/HAM B43 .....70 B7
NFLD/LBR B31 .....123 K8
RRUGBY CV23 .....183 K7
SEDG DY3 .....84 B3
okside Av COVW CV5 .....154 A2
KNWTH CV8 .....197 J1
MOS/BIL B13 .....125 M6
okside Cl ALVE B48 .....170 F7
ERDW/GRVHL B23 .....72 A6
HALE B63 .....121 H2
RUGBYS/DCH CV22 .....186 E4
WMBN WV5 .....64 B7
okside Dr BRGRVW B61 .....168 D5
okside Rd POL/KGSB/FAZ B78..45 H4
okside Wy KGSWFD DY6 .....82 F6
KIDD DY10 .....139 M3
TAM/AM/WIL B77 .....46 D7
oks Rd CSCFLD/WYGN B72 .....73 G4
ok St BDWTH CV12 .....98 F8
BILS/COS WV14 .....51 J8
BRLYHL DY5 .....102 E5
CBHAMNW B3 .....6 D3
HAG/WOL DY9 .....102 D8
KGSWFD DY6 .....82 F4
KIDDW DY11 .....138 A7
KNWTH CV8 .....183 L2
REDE B98 .....202 E1
SEDG DY3 .....66 E6
SEDG DY3 .....84 A2
SMTHWK B66 .....87 M7
STRBR DY8 .....101 J8
STRBR DY8 .....101 K4
TPTN/OCK DY4 .....67 J7
WBROM B70 .....86 F1
WSLW WS2 .....4 C4
WWCK CV34 .....205 J7
ok Ter BILS/COS WV14 .....51 J8
okthorpe Dr SHHTH WV12 .....52 A1
ok V BEWD DY12 .....163 G2
CNCK/NC WS11 .....16 D5
kvale Av COVS CV3 .....156 C4
vale Cl BRGRVE B60 .....191 M1
vale Gv HIA/OLT B92 .....127 H4
vale Ms SLYOAK B29 .....124 F3
vale Park Rd
ERDW/GRVHL B23 .....71 M8

Brookvale Rd AST/WIT B6 .....89 L2
HIA/OLT B92 .....127 H4
Brookview SMTHWKW B67 * 105 K2
Brook View Cl LOZ/NWT B19 .....89 G7
Brook Wk ATHST CV9 .....63 K7
RIDG/WDGT B32 .....123 H3
Brookweed TAM/AM/WIL B77 .....46 E2
Brookwillow Rd HALE B63 .....121 H3
Brookwood Av HLGN/YWD B28 ..126 B8
Brookwood Dr RBRY B45 .....170 A5
Broom Cl BRGRVE B60 .....191 M3
RUGBYS/DCH CV22 .....186 C4
Broom Covert Rd LICHS WS14 .....29 J5
Broom Crs KIDD DY10 .....138 E7
Broomcroft Rd
CHWD/FDBR/MGN B37 .....92 D8
Broomdene Av BKDE/SHDE B34 .....91 L6
Broom Dr ALE/KHTH/YWD B14 .....146 C1
Broome Av GTB/HAM B43 .....70 A6
Broome Cl HALE B63 .....121 L2
Broome Cft COVN CV6 .....133 M2
Broome Gdns MGN/WHC B75 .....57 G8
Broomehill Cl BRLYHL DY5 .....102 A6
Broome La HAG/WOL DY9 .....140 C2
Broome Rd WOLVN WV10 .....36 B6
Broomfield SMTHWKW B67 .....87 K8
Broomfield Cl KIDDW DY11 .....137 M6
Broomfield Gn KIDDW DY11 .....137 M6
Broomfield Pl COVW CV5 .....8 A5
Broomfield Ri NUNW/HART CV10..98 D3
Broomfield Rd COVW CV5 .....154 D4
DARL/WED WS10 .....69 G2
ERDW/GRVHL B23 .....90 B3
KIDDW DY11 .....137 M6
Broomfields Cl SOLH B91 .....128 B8
Broomhall Av WNSFLD WV11 .....37 H7
Broom Hall Crs ACGN B27 .....126 F6
Broom Hall Gv ACGN B27 .....127 G6
Broomhill Bank CNCK/NC WS11 .....16 C2
Broomhill Cl CNCK/NC WS11 .....16 C1
GTB/HAM B43 .....70 B5
Broomhill La GTB/HAM B43 .....70 A5
Broomhill Rd ERDW/GRVHL B23 .....71 M6
Broomhurst EDG B15 .....106 C5
Broomie Cl MGN/WHC B75 .....73 H1
Broom La SHLY B90 .....147 L7
Broomlea Cl FOAKS/STRLY B74 .....55 J5
Broom Rd DSYBK/YTR WS5 .....69 M2
DUDN DY1 .....84 E1
Broom St BHTH/HG B12 .....7 L9
Broomybank KNWTH CV8 .....179 M7
Broomy Cl STETCH B33 .....91 L8
STRPT DY13 .....163 H8
Broseley Av NFLD/LBR B31 .....144 E5
Broseley Brook Cl BORD B9 .....108 A4
Brosil Av BFLD/HDSWWD B20 .....88 C2
Brotherton Av REDW B97 .....201 K3
Brougham St LOZ/NWT B19 .....88 F6
Brough Cl
ETTPK/GDPK/PENN WV4 .....66 D2
VAUX/NECH B7 .....89 M7
Broughton Ct
DUNHL/THL/PER WV6 .....48 E2
Broughton Crs NFLD/LBR B31 .....144 B5
Broughton Rd BDMR/CCFT WV3 ..49 G4
BFLD/HDSWWD B20 .....88 E5
HAG/WOL DY9 .....120 B2
Browett Rd COVN CV6 .....133 K8
Brown Av TAM/AM/WIL B77 .....46 A5
Brownfield Rd BKDE/SHDE B34 .....92 A7
Brownhills Rd BRWNH WS8 .....26 D8
CNCK/NC WS11 .....17 M8
Browning Av WWCK CV34 .....205 G8
Browning Cl CRTAM B79 .....31 J5
KIDD DY10 .....138 F7
NUNW/HART CV10 .....79 L8
SHHTH WV12 .....38 C6
Browning Crs WOLVN WV10 .....36 A3
Browning Gv
DUNHL/THL/PER WV6 .....48 C1
Browning Rd BNTWD WS7 .....19 G6
COVE CV2 .....156 A1
RUGBYN/HIL CV21 .....187 M5
SEDG DY3 .....83 L1
Brownley Rd SHLY B90 .....148 C6
Brown Lion St TPTN/OCK DY4 .....67 J6
Brownlow St RLSN CV32 .....206 E3
Brown Rd DARL/WED WS10 .....52 A6
Brown's Coppice Av SOLH B91 .....127 H8
Browns Dr SCFLD/BOLD B73 .....72 D5
Brownsea Cl RBRY B45 .....143 J4
Brownsea Dr CBHAMW B1 .....6 E7
Brownsfield Rd LICH WS13 .....21 H4
Browns Gn BFLD/HDSWWD B20 .....88 D2
Brownshill Ct COVN CV6 .....133 K5
Brownshill Green Rd COVW CV5..133 J4
Brownshore La WNSFLD WV11 .....37 L2
Brown's La COVW CV5 .....132 F5
CRTAM B79 .....32 A5
DOR/KN B93 .....149 J7
POL/KGSB/FAZ B78 .....47 K8
Brownsover Cl CBROM B36 .....91 M4
Brownsover La
RUGBYN/HIL CV21 .....160 F6
Brownsover Rd
RUGBYN/HIL CV21 .....160 C6
Brown St BKHL/PFLD WV2 .....50 B6
Brownswall Rd SEDG DY3 .....65 M6
Brown Westhead Pk KIDD DY10..138 D3
Browsholme CRTAM B79 .....31 H7
Broxell Cl WWCK CV34 .....205 G4
Broxwood Pk
DUNHL/THL/PER WV6 .....48 F2
Bruce Rd COVN CV6 .....133 L5
KIDD DY10 .....138 F6
RCOVN/BALC/EX CV7 .....116 D6
Bruce Williams Wy
RUGBYS/DCH CV22 .....186 F3
Brudenell Cl RUGBYS/DCH CV22 ..185 L5
Brueton Av BRGRVE B60 .....191 L5
SOLH B91 .....149 H2
Brueton Dr ERDE/BCHGN B24 .....90 E2
REDE B98 .....202 E2
Brueton Rd BILS/COS WV14 .....51 L6
Bruford Rd BDMR/CCFT WV3 .....2 A9
Brunel Cl BHTH/HG B12 .....107 L8
BNTWD WS7 .....18 F5
COVE CV2 * 9 L4
CRTAM B79 .....31 L7
STRPT DY13 .....163 L8
Brunel Ct BILS/COS WV14 .....67 J5
Brunel Dr TPTN/OCK DY4 .....67 J4
Brunel Gv CDSL WV8 .....34 C7
Brunel Rd OLDBY B69 .....86 B7
Brunel St CBHAM B2 .....6 E6
Brunel Wk DARL/WED WS10 * 52 D7
POL/KGSB/FAZ B78 .....47 L2
Brunel Wy BKHL/PFLD WV2 .....50 E6
Brunslow Cl WLNHL WV13 .....52 A4
WOLVN WV10 .....36 A4
Brunswick Cl RUGBYN/HIL CV21 ..161 G7
Brunswick Ga STRBR DY8 .....119 L4
Brunswick Park Rd
DARL/WED WS10 .....68 E2
Brunswick Rd BHTH/HG B12 .....107 L8
CNCK/NC WS11 .....16 C3
COV CV1 .....8 C6
HDSW B21 .....88 D4
Brunswick St CBHAMW B1 .....6 B6

RLSS CV31 .....206 E7
WSLW WS2 * 4 B9
Brunswick Ter DARL/WED WS10 .....68 D2
Bruntingthorpe Wy COVS CV3 .....156 C5
Brunton Cl COVS CV3 .....156 F4
Brunton Rd SMHTH B10 .....108 D6
Brushfield Rd PBAR/PBCH B42 .....71 H5
Brutus Dr CSHL/WTROR B46 .....93 J4
Bryan Av
ETTPK/GDPK/PENN WV4 .....65 H1
Bryan Rd WSLW WS2 .....53 G7
Bryanston Cl COVE CV2 .....156 E1
Bryanston Ct SOLH B91 * 127 K6
Bryanston Rd SOLH B91 .....127 K7
Bryans Wy HEDN WS12 .....17 K1
Bryant Rd RCOVN/BALC/EX CV7 ..116 E6
Bryant St WSNGN B18 .....88 C8
Bryce Rd BRLYHL DY5 .....83 M8
Brylan Cft KGSTG B44 .....71 K7
Brympton Rd COVS CV3 .....156 A3
Bryn Arden Rd
LGN/SDN/BHAMAIR B26 .....109 J8
Bryndale Av
ALE/KHTH/YWD B14 .....125 G8
Bryn Jones Cl COVS CV3 .....156 D6
Brynmawr Rd
ETTPK/GDPK/PENN WV4 .....66 D2
Bryn Rd COVN CV6 .....134 D6
Brynside Cl BVILLE B30 .....146 B3
Bryony Cl BDWTH CV12 .....116 C4
Bryony Gdns DARL/WED WS10 .....52 B6
Bryony Rd SLYOAK B29 .....123 M6
Buchanan Cl RUSH/SHEL WS4 .....53 L2
Buchanan Rd
RUGBYS/DCH CV22 .....186 C4
RUSH/SHEL WS4 .....5 K1
Buchanan View RUSH/SHEL WS4 ..53 L2
Buchan Cl NUNW/HART CV10 .....97 K1
Buckbury Cl HAG/WOL DY9 .....120 B4
Buckbury Cft SHLY B90 .....148 F7
Buckden TAM/AM/WIL B77 .....47 G4
Buckden Cl WWCK CV34 .....205 K4
Buckfast Cl BRGRVW B61 .....191 H4
COVS CV3 .....155 J8
Buckhold Dr COVW CV5 .....132 F8
Buckingham Cl DARL/WED WS10 ..69 G1
NUNW/HART CV10 .....98 F4
Buckingham Dr SHHTH WV12 .....37 M6
Buckingham Gdns LICHS WS14 * ..20 F7
Buckingham Gv KGSWFD DY6 .....83 G6
Buckingham Ms
SCFLD/BOLD B73 .....72 E3
Buckingham Pl HEDN WS12 .....17 G4
Buckingham Ri COVW CV5 .....153 M1
DUDN DY1 .....84 C3
Buckingham Rd
BLKHTH/ROWR B65 .....104 B1
CBROM B36 .....92 D6
CRTAM B79 .....31 J6
ETTPK/GDPK/PENN WV4 .....65 L1
Buckingham St LOZ/NWT B19 .....6 E1
Buckland Cl HEDN WS12 .....17 H4
Buckland End BKDE/SHDE B34 .....91 L7
Buckland Rd COVN CV6 .....133 M3
Bucklands End La
BKDE/SHDE B34 .....91 K7
Buckle Cl WSL WS1 .....4 F7
Buckley Rd
ETTPK/GDPK/PENN WV4 .....49 H8
RLSN CV32 .....206 F3
The Buckleys ALVE B48 .....170 E7
Buckminster Dr DOR/KN B93 .....175 J1
Bucknall Rd WNSFLD WV11 .....37 L4
Bucknell Cl SOLH B91 .....128 A8
Bucknill Crs RUGBYN/HIL CV21 .....187 M5
Buckridge Cl HWK/WKHTH B38 .....145 H6
Buckridge La SHLY B90 .....147 L8
Bucks Head Cottages
LICHS WS14 * 30 A7
Bucks Hl NUNW/HART CV10 .....79 M6
Buckthorn Cl HEDN WS12 .....12 D5
Buckton Cl MGN/WHC B75 .....57 J3
Buckwell La RRUGBY CV23 .....161 M7
Budbrooke Cl COVE CV2 .....135 H3
Budbrooke Rd WWCK CV34 .....204 F6
Budbrook Gv BKDE/SHDE B34 .....92 C7
Budden Rd TPTN/OCK DY4 .....67 H6
Bude Rd DSYBK/YTR WS5 .....54 B6
Buffery Rd DUDS DY2 .....85 H6
Bufferys Cl SOLH B91 .....148 F5
Buildwas Cl BLOX/PEL WS3 .....38 D3
Bulford Cl ALE/KHTH/YWD B14 .....146 D3
Bulger Rd BILS/COS WV14 .....51 G6
Bulkington La NUN CV11 .....99 L5
Bulkington Rd BDWTH CV12 .....117 H3
Bullace Cft EDG B15 .....124 B2
Bulldog La LICH WS13 .....20 F4
Buller St
ETTPK/GDPK/PENN WV4 .....50 C8
Bullfield Av TLHL/CAN CV4 .....153 J4
Bullfields Cl BLKHTH/ROWR B65 .....85 K8
Bullfinch Cl DUDN DY1 .....84 C5
Bullimore Gv KNWTH CV8 .....197 L3
Bullivents Cl DOR/KN B93 .....149 K8
Bull La BILS/COS WV14 .....67 M2
WBROM B70 .....86 E2
WMBN WV5 .....64 F6
Bullmeadow La WMBN WV5 .....64 E6
Bullmoor La LICHS WS14 .....27 L4
Bullock's Rw WSL WS1 .....5 G4
Bullock St VAUX/NECH B7 .....89 L8
WBROM B70 .....87 H5
Bullows Rd BRWNH WS8 .....26 A7
Bull Ring HALE B63 .....121 M2
KIDD DY10 .....138 C7
NUNW/HART CV10 .....98 F3
Bull's Head La COVS CV3 .....155 L4
Bull's La WALM/CURD B76 .....74 A3
Bull St BRLYHL DY5 .....101 M4
CBHAM B2 .....7 G4
DARL/WED WS10 .....52 C7
DUDN DY1 .....84 E5
HRBN B17 .....106 B7
NUN CV11 .....99 H3
SEDG DY3 .....84 A3
WBROM B70 .....87 H3
Bullus Rd STRPT DY13 .....188 E1
Bull Yd COV CV1 .....8 E5
Bulrush Cl BRWNH WS8 .....26 C6
Bulwell Cl AST/WIT B6 .....89 L6
Bulwer Rd COVN CV6 .....133 L6
Bulwick Cl COVS CV3 .....156 F4
Bumble Hole La BRGRVW B61 .....168 B8
Bumblehole Mdw WMBN WV5 .....64 D6
Bunbury Gdns NFLD/LBR B31 .....145 G1
Bunbury Rd NFLD/LBR B31 .....145 G1
Bundle Hl HALE B63 .....121 L2
Bungalow Est COVN CV6 * 134 D1
Bungalows GTWY WS6 * 24 E4
The Bungalows WBROM B70 * 68 D7
Bungay Lake La BRGRVW B61 .....190 D3
Bungham La PENK ST19 .....10 B5
Bunker's Hill La BILS/COS WV14 .....51 J5
Bunn's La DUDS DY2 .....85 K4
Buntsford Dr BRGRVE B60 .....191 J7
Buntsford Hl BRGRVE B60 .....191 J8
Buntsford Park Rd
BRGRVE B60 .....191 K8
Bunyan Pl CNCK/NC WS11 .....16 C1

Burbage Cl WOLVN WV10 .....36 C7
Burbages La COVN CV6 .....116 B8
Burberry Gv
RCOVN/BALC/EX CV7 .....151 L7
Burbidge Rd BORD B9 .....108 B2
Burbury Cl BDWTH CV12 .....117 G1
RLSN CV32 .....207 G3
Burbury Ct WWCK CV34 .....205 M5
Burbury St LOZ/NWT B19 .....89 G7
Burbury St South
LOZ/NWT B19 * 89 G7
Burcot Av BRGRVE B60 .....191 M1
WOLV WV1 .....50 E3
Burcote Rd ERDE/BCHGN B24 .....91 H2
Burcot La BRGRVE B60 .....191 M2
Burdock Cl CNCK/NC WS11 .....16 F2
DSYBK/YTR WS5 .....69 L2
Burdock Rd SLYOAK B29 .....123 L7
Burdons Cl STETCH B33 .....91 L8
Bure Gv WLNHL WV13 .....52 B4
Burfield Rd HALE B63 .....103 G7
Burford Cl DSYBK/YTR WS5 .....69 L1
HIA/OLT B92 .....127 L2
Burford Ms RLSS CV31 .....207 G8
Burford Rd HLYWD B47 .....146 D7
KGSTG B44 .....71 K6
Burgage Pl NUN CV11 .....99 G1
Burges COV CV1 .....8 F3
Burges Gv WWCK CV34 .....205 K4
Burgess Cft HIA/OLT B92 .....128 D6
Burghley Cl NUN CV11 .....99 K3
Burghley Dr HHTH/SAND B71 .....69 K3
KIDDW DY11 .....137 M8
Burghley Wk BRLYHL DY5 .....101 M5
Burgh Wy WSLW WS2 .....52 E1
Burgoyne St CNCK/NC WS11 .....12 E8
Burhill Wy
CHWD/FDBR/MGN B37 .....110 F1
Burke Av MOS/BIL B13 .....126 B4
Burkitt Dr TPTN/OCK DY4 .....68 A5
Burland Av
DUNHL/THL/PER WV6 .....35 J6
Burleigh Cl HEDN WS12 .....12 E5
RCOVN/BALC/EX CV7 .....151 M6
SHHTH WV12 .....37 M7
Burleigh Cft BNTWD WS7 .....26 E1
Burleigh Rd BDMR/CCFT WV3 .....49 L6
Burleigh St WSL WS1 .....5 H5
Burleton Rd STETCH B33 .....110 C3
Burley Cl SHLY B90 .....147 K3
Burlington Rd COVE CV2 .....9 M1
NUNW/HART CV10 .....98 F6
SMHTH B10 .....108 D4
WBROM B70 .....87 H4
Burlington St AST/WIT B6 .....89 J7
Burlish Av HIA/OLT B92 .....127 K4
Burlish Cl STRPT DY13 .....163 K7
Burlish Crossing STRPT DY13 .....163 J7
Burltons Ter BEWD DY12 * 162 F2
Burman Cl SHLY B90 .....147 L3
Burman Dr CSHL/WTROR B46 .....93 K8
Burman Rd SHLY B90 .....147 K3
Burmese Wy BLKHTH/ROWR B65 ..85 K7
Burnaby Cl NUNW/HART CV10 .....79 M8
Burnaby Rd COVN CV6 .....134 A5
Burnaston Crs SHLY B90 .....149 G6
Burnaston Rd HLGN/YWD B28 .....126 C5
Burnbank Gv ERDE/BCHGN B24 .....90 F1
Burn Cl SMTHWKW B67 .....105 L1
Burncross Wy WOLVN WV10 .....36 D7
Burnell Gdns BDMR/CCFT WV3 .....49 J5
Burnel Rd SLYOAK B29 .....123 L3
Burnet Gv WOLVN WV10 .....22 F5
Burnett Rd FOAKS/STRLY B74 .....55 M3
Burney La WASH/WDE B8 .....91 G8
Burnfields Cl ALDR WS9 .....40 E6
Burnham Av WOLVN WV10 .....36 A5
YDLY B25 .....109 G7
Burnham Cl KGSWFD DY6 .....101 K1
Burnham Gn CNCK/NC WS11 .....15 M5
Burnham Meadow
HLGN/YWD B28 .....126 E7
Burnham Ri NUN CV11 .....81 L7
Burnham Rd COVS CV3 .....155 L7
KGSTG B44 .....71 J6
Burnhill Gv SLYOAK B29 .....123 L5
Burnlea Gv NFLD/LBR B31 .....145 G4
Burnsall Cl
CHWD/FDBR/MGN B37 .....110 D3
COVEN WV9 .....35 L2
Burnsall Gv COVW CV5 .....154 B5
Burnsall Rd COVW CV5 .....154 B5
Burns Av TPTN/OCK DY4 .....67 L6
WOLVN WV10 .....36 B3
WWCK CV34 .....205 G8
Burns Cl KIDD DY10 .....138 F7
LICHS WS14 .....20 F7
REDW B97 .....202 A5
STRBR DY8 .....101 L5
Burns Dr BNTWD WS7 .....19 G6
Burns Gv SEDG DY3 .....83 L1
Burnside COVS CV3 .....156 E3
RUGBYS/DCH CV22 .....186 C3
Burnside Gdns DSYBK/YTR WS5 .....54 B7
Burnside Wy NFLD/LBR B31 .....144 D6
Burns Pl DARL/WED WS10 .....51 L8
Burns Rd COVE CV2 .....155 M2
CRTAM B79 .....31 L7
DARL/WED WS10 .....51 L8
RLSN CV32 .....206 F1
Burns St CNCK/NC WS11 .....16 E1
Burns Wk BDWTH CV12 .....117 G4
Burnthorne La STRPT DY13 .....188 A4
Burnthurst Crs SOLH B91 .....148 E6
Burnt Meadow Rd REDE B98 .....195 J7
Burnt Oak Dr STRBR DY8 .....101 L8
Burnt Tree TPTN/OCK DY4 .....85 K3
Burntwood Rd BNTWD WS7 .....27 H1
CNCK/NC WS11 .....17 L7
Burrington Rd RIDG/WDGT B32 ..122 E5
Burrowes St WSLW WS2 .....4 D1
Burrow Hill Cl CBROM B36 .....92 A5
Burrow Hill La
RCOVN/BALC/EX CV7 .....115 H6
Burrows Rd KGSWFD DY6 .....101 K1
Burrows St WSLW WS2 .....4 C1
Burslem Cl BLOX/PEL WS3 .....38 E1
Bursnips Rd WNSFLD WV11 .....38 A1
Burton Av RUSH/SHEL WS4 .....39 M6
Burton Cl COVW CV5 .....133 G4
CRTAM B79 .....32 A6
Burton Crs WOLVN WV10 .....3 J3
Burton Farm Rd
RUSH/SHEL WS4 .....53 M2
Burton La REDE B98 .....202 D2
Burton Old Rd LICH WS13 .....21 K4
Burton Old Rd East LICHS WS14 .....21 J5
Burton Old Rd West LICH WS13 .....21 H5
Burton Rd DUDN DY1 .....84 D1
LICH WS13 .....21 K4
WOLVN WV10 .....3 K2
Burton Wood Dr
BFLD/HDSWWD B20 .....89 H3
Buryfield Rd SOLH B91 .....127 L7
Bury Hill Rd OLDBY B69 .....86 B6
Bury Rd RLSS CV31 .....206 C6
Busby Cl COVS CV3 .....156 D6
Bush Av SMTHWK B66 .....88 A8
Bushbery Av TLHL/CAN CV4 .....153 K4

Bushbury Cft
CHWD/FDBR/MGN B37 .....111 G2
Bushbury La WOLVN WV10 .....36 D3
Bushbury Rd STETCH B33 .....91 L8
WOLVN WV10 .....36 E7
Bush Cl TLHL/CAN CV4 .....153 K2
Bushell Dr SOLH B91 .....149 H1
Bushelton Cl COV CV1 .....9 H8
Bushey Cl FOAKS/STRLY B74 .....55 K3
Bushey Fields Rd DUDN DY1 .....84 C6
Bush Gv BLOX/PEL WS3 .....39 L3
HDSW B21 .....88 A4
Bushley Cl REDE B98 .....202 E6
Bushley Cft SOLH B91 .....148 F5
Bushman Wy BKDE/SHDE B34 .....92 C8
Bushmore Rd HLGN/YWD B28 .....126 E7
Bush Rd DUDS DY2 .....103 G3
TPTN/OCK DY4 .....85 J1
Bush St DARL/WED WS10 .....52 B6
Bushway Cl BRLYHL DY5 .....101 L3
Bushwood Dr DOR/KN B93 .....175 L2
Bushwood Rd SLYOAK B29 .....123 M4
Bustleholme Av HHTH/SAND B71..69 K4
Bustleholme Crs
HHTH/SAND B71 .....69 J4
Bustleholme La HHTH/SAND B71 ..69 K3
Butcher's Cl RRUGBY CV23 .....158 D2
Butcher's La COVW CV5 .....133 G7
HALE B63 .....103 G6
Butchers Rd HIA/OLT B92 .....129 L7
Butcroft Gdns DARL/WED WS10 .....52 C7
Bute Cl RBRY B45 .....143 J4
SHHTH WV12 .....37 M7
Butler Cl KNWTH CV8 .....180 A6
Butler Rd HIA/OLT B92 .....127 K2
Butlers Cl BFLD/HDSWWD B20 .....88 E2
ERDW/GRVHL B23 .....72 B4
Butlers Crs
RCOVN/BALC/EX CV7 .....116 E4
Butlers End RWWCK/WEL CV35 ..196 A3
Butler's Hill La REDW B97 .....193 M8
Butlers La ATHST CV9 .....62 A3
FOAKS/STRLY B74 .....56 D2
Butlers Leap RUGBYN/HIL CV21 ..161 H8
Butlers Prec WSL WS1 .....4 E3
Butler's Rd BFLD/HDSWWD B20 .....88 E2
Butler St WBROM B70 .....86 E1
Butlin Rd COVN CV6 .....134 A1
RUGBYN/HIL CV21 .....187 H2
Butlin St VAUX/NECH B7 .....90 A6
Buttercup Cl DSYBK/YTR WS5 .....69 L2
KIDDW DY11 .....138 C5
Buttercup Dr BRGRVE B60 .....169 G7
Butterfield Cl
DUNHL/THL/PER WV6 .....48 B2
Butterfield Rd BRLYHL DY5 .....83 M6
Buttermere RUGBYN/HIL CV21 .....161 H7
TAM/AM/WIL B77 .....46 F6
Buttermere Av NUN CV11 .....81 L7
Buttermere Cl BRLYHL DY5 .....101 M6
CNCK/NC WS11 .....16 E2
COVS CV3 .....156 D6
DUNHL/THL/PER WV6 .....35 H5
Buttermere Ct
DUNHL/THL/PER WV6 .....48 D1
Buttermere Dr RIDG/WDGT B32 ..123 K2
WNSFLD WV11 .....37 L3
Buttermere Gv SHHTH WV12 .....37 M4
Buttermere Rd STRPT DY13 .....163 K7
Butterworth Cl BILS/COS WV14 .....66 E4
Butterworth Dr TLHL/CAN CV4 .....153 L7
Buttery Rd SMTHWKW B67 .....87 J7
Butt La COVW CV5 .....132 F6
Buttons Farm Rd
ETTPK/GDPK/PENN WV4 .....65 H2
Buttress Wy SMTHWK B66 .....87 L7
Butts COV CV1 .....8 C6
Butts Cl CNCK/NC WS11 .....25 J1
Butts La CNCK/NC WS11 .....25 J1
KIDD DY10 .....165 J5
Butts Rd COV CV1 .....8 C5
ETTPK/GDPK/PENN WV4 .....65 K1
RUSH/SHEL WS4 .....53 K2
Butts St RUSH/SHEL WS4 .....53 K2
The Butts LICHS WS14 .....28 B3
RUSH/SHEL WS4 .....53 K2
Buxton Av POL/KGSB/FAZ B78 .....45 M5
Buxton Cl BLOX/PEL WS3 .....39 G2
Buxton Rd BLOX/PEL WS3 .....39 G2
DUDS DY2 .....84 E7
ERDW/GRVHL B23 .....71 M7
SCFLD/BOLD B73 .....72 E4
Byfield Cl STETCH B33 .....110 C4
Byfield Rd COVN CV6 .....133 J8
Byfleet Cl
ETTPK/GDPK/PENN WV4 .....66 E2
Byford Cl REDE B98 .....202 C3
Byford St NUNW/HART CV10 .....98 D1
Byford Wy
CHWD/FDBR/MGN B37 .....110 F5
Byland TAM/AM/WIL B77 .....46 B2
Bylands Cl BRGRVW B61 .....191 J4
Byland Wy BLOX/PEL WS3 .....38 D3
By Pass Rd TAM/AM/WIL B77 .....32 E8
Byrchen Moor Gdns BRLYHL DY5 ..83 M6
Byrne Rd BKHL/PFLD WV2 .....50 B6
Byron Av AST/WIT B6 .....89 M2
BDWTH CV12 .....117 H3
LICHS WS14 .....20 F8
Byron Cl BNTWD WS7 .....18 D4
KIDD DY10 .....138 F8
SMHTH B10 * 108 B6
Byron Crs DUDN DY1 .....66 F8
Byron Cft FOAKS/STRLY B74 .....42 D7
SEDG DY3 .....83 L1
Byron Pl CNCK/NC WS11 .....12 D8
Byron Rd CRTAM B79 .....31 L6
REDW B97 .....202 B5
SHHTH WV12 .....38 C6
SMHTH B10 .....108 B6
WOLVN WV10 .....36 E4
Byron St BRLYHL DY5 .....84 B6
COV CV1 .....9 G2
HHTH/SAND B71 .....68 F8
Byron Wy BRGRVW B61 .....168 E5
Bywater Cl COVS CV3 .....154 F8
Byways BLOX/PEL WS3 .....39 G2

C

Caban Cl NFLD/LBR B31 .....123 J8
Cable Dr WSLW WS2 .....53 G1
Cable St BKHL/PFLD WV2 .....3 K9
Cabot Gv DUNHL/THL/PER WV6 .....48 C1
Cadbury Dr CVALE B35 .....91 K4
Cadbury Rd MOS/BIL B13 .....125 M1
Cadbury Wy HRBN B17 .....105 M8
Cadden Dr COVW CV5 .....153 M3
Caddick Crs HHTH/SAND B71 .....69 H6
Caddick Rd PBAR/PBCH B42 .....70 F4
Caddick St BILS/COS WV14 .....66 E5
Cadet Dr SHLY B90 .....147 L2
Cadgwith Gdns BILS/COS WV14 .....67 L3
Cadine Gdns MOS/BIL B13 .....125 G4

Cadle Rd WOLVN WV10....36 B6
Cadman Cl BDWTH CV12....117 G2
Cadman Crs WOLVN WV10....36 E7
Cadman's La GTWY WS6....25 G5
Cadnam Cl HRBN B17....124 A2
WLNHL WV13....51 M5
Cadogan Rd TAM/AM/WIL B77....46 B8
Caen Cl RWWCK/WEL CV35....204 E6
Caernarfon Dr NUN CV11....99 H2
Caernarvon Cl SHHTH WV12....38 A6
Caernarvon Wy DUDN DY1....84 C3
Caesar Rd KNWTH CV8....197 J2
Caesar Wy CSHL/WTROR B46....93 J4
Cairndhu Dr KIDD DY10....138 E6
Cairn Dr WSLW WS2....52 D3
Cairns St WSLW WS2....4 B1
Caister TAM/AM/WIL B77....32 E7
Caister Dr WLNHL WV13....51 K5
Caistor Cl POL/KGSB/FAZ B78....44 F5
Caithness Cl COVW CV5....153 L1
Cakemore Rd RMSLY B62....104 C3
Cala Dr EDG B15....106 F6
Calcot Dr DUNHL/THL/PER WV6....35 J6
Calcutt Wy SHLY B90....147 L7
Caldecote Cl NUNW/HART CV10....81 G5
Caldecote Gv BORD B9....109 G4
Caldecote Rd COVN CV6....134 A8
Caldecott Pl RUGBYN/HIL CV21....187 G3
Caldecott St RUGBYN/HIL CV21....187 G3
Caldeford Av SHLY B90....148 E6
Calder TAM/AM/WIL B77....46 F3
Calder Av WSL WS1....5 J3
Calder Cl BDWTH CV12....117 M3
COVS CV3....155 J6
Calder Dr WALM/CURD B76....73 L5
Calderfields Cl RUSH/SHEL WS4....53 L2
Calder Gv BFLD/HDSWWD B20....88 D4
Calder Ri DUDN DY1....66 D7
Calder Rd STRPT DY13....163 J6
Calder Wk RLSS CV31....207 G8
Caldmore Gn WSL WS1....4 F7
Caldmore Rd WSL WS1....4 F5
Caldwall Crs KIDDW DY11....138 B8
Caldwell Gv SOLH B91....128 A8
Caldwell Rd BORD B9....108 F2
NUN CV11....99 H4
Caldwell St HHTH/SAND B71....69 H5
Caldy Wk STRPT DY13....163 J7
Cale Cl TAM/AM/WIL B77....46 A3
Caledonia BRLYHL DY5....102 B6
Caledonian TAM/AM/WIL B77....46 D3
Caledonian Cl GTB/HAM B43....70 A2
Caledonia Rd BKHL/PFLD WV2....3 J9
Caledonia St BILS/COS WV14....51 J7
Caledon Pl WSLW WS2....4 A8
Caledon St WSLW WS2....4 B8
Calewood Rd BRLYHL DY5....102 B6
Californian Gv BNTWD WS7....18 D5
California Rd OLDBY B69....85 L4
California Wy RIDG/WDGT B32....123 K2
Callaghan Gv CNCK/NC WS11....17 G3
Callcott Dr BRLYHL DY5....102 B6
Callear Rd DARL/WED WS10....68 B4
Callendar Cl NUN CV11....81 L6
Calley Cl TPTN/OCK DY4....85 K2
Callowbridge Rd RBRY B45....143 K6
Callowbrook La RBRY B45....143 K5
Callow Cl STRPT DY13....188 B4
Callow Hill La REDW B97....201 K7
Callow Hill Rd ALVE B48....170 D6
Callows La KIDD DY10....138 C7
Calmere Cl COVE CV2....135 K5
Calshot Rd PBAR/PBCH B42....70 E5
Calstock Rd SHHTH WV12....52 B1
Calthorpe Cl DSYBK/YTR WS5....54 C7
Calthorpe Man EDG B15 *....6 A8
Calthorpe Rd
BFLD/HDSWWD B20....89 G3
DSYBK/YTR WS5....54 B7
EDG B15....106 E5
Caludon Park Av COVE CV2....135 J8
Caludon Rd COVE CV2....155 L1
Calver Crs WNSFLD WV11....37 K8
Calver Gv KGSTG B44....71 H2
Calverley Rd HWK/WKHTH B38....145 H4
Calvert Cl COVS CV3....155 J6
Calverton Gv GTB/HAM B43....70 C5
Calves Cft WLNHL WV13....51 L2
Calvestone Pl
RUGBYS/DCH CV22 *....185 L6
Calvestone Rd
RUGBYS/DCH CV22....185 L6
Calvestone Sq
RUGBYS/DCH CV22 *....185 M5
Calvin Cl WMBN WV5....64 D8
WOLVN WV10....36 B2
Calving Hl CNCK/NC WS11....16 C3
Camberley Crs
ETTPK/GDPK/PENN WV4....66 C3
Camberley Dr
ETTPK/GDPK/PENN WV4....65 L1
Camberley Gv
ERDW/GRVHL B23....72 C7
Camberley Rd KGSWFD DY6....101 L1
Camberwell Ter RLSS CV31....206 E6
Camborne Cl AST/WIT B6....
Camborne Dr NUN CV11....
Camborne Rd DSYBK/YTR WS5....54 B6
Cambourne Rd
BLKHTH/ROWR B65....104 A2
Cambrai Dr HLGN/YWD B28....126 C5
Cambria Cl SHLY B90....147 J6
Cambrian TAM/AM/WIL B77....46 D3
Cambria St CNCK/NC WS11....16 B2
Cambridge Av SCFLD/BOLD B73....72 F5
SOLH B91....148 C2
Cambridge Cl ALDR WS9....40 E5
Cambridge Crs EDG B15....107 G6
Cambridge Dr
CHWD/FDBR/MGN B37....110 D4
NUNW/HART CV10....98 B2
Cambridge Gdns RLSN CV32 *....206 E4
Cambridge Rd DUDS DY2....84 E6
MOS/BIL B13....125 K4
SMTHWK B66....87 L6
Cambridge St CBHAMW B1....6 D5
COV CV1....134 C8
RUGBYN/HIL CV21....187 G2
WBROM B70....86 F3
WOLVN WV10....3 H1
WSL WS1....4 F8
Cambridge Wy ACGN B27....127 H1
Camden Cl CBROM B36....91 L5
DSYBK/YTR WS5 *....69 L1
Camden Dr CBHAMW B1....6 B3
TAM/AM/WIL B77....46 C2
Camden St ALDR WS9....40 C1
CBHAMW B1....6 B3
COVE CV2....155 L1
WSL WS1....4 D7
WSNGN B18....106 E1
Camden Wy KGSWFD DY6....83 H4
Camellia Gdns COVEN WV9....35 K2
Camelot Cl CNCK/NC WS11....16 D2
Camelot Wy SMHTH B10....108 A5
Cameo Dr STRBR DY8....101 K5
Cameron Cl COVW CV5....132 E6
RLSN CV32....206 E1
Cameron Rd RUSH/SHEL WS4....5 K1
Camford Gv
ALE/KHTH/YWD B14....146 D2
Cam Gdns BRLYHL DY5....83 M6
Camhouses TAM/AM/WIL B77....46 F4
Camino Rd RIDG/WDGT B32....123 K2
Camomile Cl DSYBK/YTR WS5....69 L2
Campbell Cl CRTAM B79....31 K5
NUNW/HART CV10....97 L1
RUSH/SHEL WS4....53 L2
Campbell Pl DARL/WED WS10....52 B7
Campbells Gn
LGN/SDN/BHAMAIR B26....109 M8
Campbell St BRLYHL DY5....102 A1
RUGBYN/HIL CV21....186 C2
Campden Cl REDW B97....202 B7
Campden Gn HIA/OLT B92....127 L2
Campden Gv
RWWCK/WEL CV35....204 C3
Camp Hl BHTH/HG B12....107 L5
Camp Hill Circ BHTH/HG B12....107 L5
Camp Hill Dr NUNW/HART CV10....80 B7
Camphill La DARL/WED WS10....68 D3
Camp Hill Rd NUNW/HART CV10....80 A6
Campian's Av GTWY WS6....24 B3
Campion Cl COVS CV3....155 H7
DSYBK/YTR WS5....69 L2
WMBN WV5....64 C7
Campion Dr TAM/AM/WIL B77....46 A2
WOLVN WV10....22 E6
Campion Gn RLSN CV32....206 E3
Campion Gv HALE B63....121 H2
Campion Rd RLSN CV32....206 E3
Campion Ter RLSN CV32....206 E4
Campion Wy BEWD DY12....137 H8
RRUGBY CV23....161 H5
SHLY B90....147 L8
Camp La HDSW B21....87 M3
HWK/WKHTH B38....145 K2
Camplea Cft
CHWD/FDBR/MGN B37....110 E3
Camplin Crs BFLD/HDSWWD B20....70 C8
Campling Cl BDWTH CV12....117 M3
Campriano Dr WWCK CV34....205 L6
Camp Rd MGN/WHC B75....43 H7
Camp St BORD B9....108 A4
DARL/WED WS10....68 D3
WOLV WV1....2 F2
Campville Crs HHTH/SAND B71....69 J4
Campville Gv
CHWD/FDBR/MGN B37....92 D8
Camp Wood Cl SLYOAK B29....124 C5
Camrose Cft BHTH/HG B12....107 J7
BKDE/SHDE B34....91 M7
Camrose Gdns COVEN WV9....35 L2
Camsey La BNTWD WS7....19 J5
Camville COVS CV3....156 E3
Canal La ERDE/BCHGN B24....90 E4
Canal Rd COVN CV6....134 C5
RWWCK/WEL CV35....204 A3
Canal Side ALVE B48....170 F3
BVILLE B30 *....145 L3
Canalside COVN CV6....116 F7
Canal Side DUDS DY2....103 J1
Canalside Cl BLOX/PEL WS3....39 J4
HHTH/SAND B71....69 J3
PENK ST19....10 D6
Canal St BRLYHL DY5....84 C8
OLDBY B69....86 D6
STRBR DY8....101 K7
Canary Gv LOZ/NWT B19....89 G5
Canberra Rd COVE CV2....135 G1
DSYBK/YTR WS5....54 A8
Canberra Wy BHTH/HG B12 *....107 K5
Canford Cl BHTH/HG B12....107 K6
COVS CV3....181 G2
Canford Crs CDSL WV8....34 C2
Canford Pl CNCK/NC WS11 *....16 D4
Canley Ford COVW CV5....154 C6
Canley Rd COVW CV5....154 C4
Cannas Ct TLHL/CAN CV4 *....154 B7
Cannel Rd BNTWD WS7....18 B6
Canning Cl DSYBK/YTR WS5....54 B7
Canning Gdns WSNGN B18....106 C1
Canning Rd DSYBK/YTR WS5....54 B7
TAM/AM/WIL B77....46 C1
Cannock Rd BNTWD WS7....18 A5
CNCK/NC WS11....16 E1
HEDN WS12....17 L5
SHHTH WV12....38 A6
WOLVN WV10....3 H1
WOLVN WV10....23 G6
WOLVN WV10....36 E5
Cannocks La TLHL/CAN CV4....154 B7
Cannock Wood Rd HEDN WS12....13 M8
Cannock Wood St HEDN WS12....13 L7
Cannon Cl TLHL/CAN CV4....154 C7
Cannon Dr BILS/COS WV14....67 G3
Cannon Hill Gv BHTH/HG B12 *....107 J8
Cannon Hill Pl BHTH/HG B12 *....107 J8
Cannon Hill Rd BHTH/HG B12....107 H8
TLHL/CAN CV4....154 B7
Cannon Park Rd TLHL/CAN CV4....154 C8
Cannon Rd WMBN WV5....64 E7
Cannon St CBHAM B2....7 G5
WLNHL WV13....51 M3
WSLW WS2....53 J1
....North WSLW WS2....53 J1
Canon Dr RCOVN/BALC/EX CV7....116 B7
Canon Hudson Cl COVS CV3....156 A7
Canterbury Av WLNHL WV13....52 B3
Canterbury Cl
BLKHTH/ROWR B65....104 C1
BLOX/PEL WS3....25 L8
HHTH/SAND B71....69 J5
TAM/AM/WIL B77....46 A2
Canterbury Dr BNTWD WS7....19 H6
CHWD/FDBR/MGN B37....110 E6
DUNHL/THL/PER WV6....48 B1
Canterbury Rd
BFLD/HDSWWD B20....89 H4
ETTPK/GDPK/PENN WV4....49 H8
HHTH/SAND B71....69 H5
KIDDW DY11....137 K6
Canterbury St COV CV1....9 J2
Canterbury Wy CNCK/NC WS11....16 F4
NUN CV11....81 L5
Cantlow Cl COVW CV5....153 L2
Cantlow Rd MOS/BIL B13....125 L7
Canton La WALM/CURD B76....75 L8
Canute Cl WSL WS1....5 H8
Canvey Cl RBRY B45....143 J4
Canwell Av
CHWD/FDBR/MGN B37....92 D8
Canwell Dr MGN/WHC B75....43 M8
Canwell Gdns BILS/COS WV14....66 F1
Canwell Ga MGN/WHC B75....57 J1
Capcroft Rd MOS/BIL B13....125 M7
Cape Hl SMTHWK B66....105 M1
Capener Rd GTB/HAM B43....70 E3
Capern Gv RIDG/WDGT B32....105 K8
Cape Rd WWCK CV34....205 H5
Cape St WBROM B70....86 C1
WSNGN B18....106 B1
Capethorn Rd SMTHWK B66....105 L2
Capilano Rd ERDW/GRVHL B23....72 A6
Capmartin Rd COVN CV6....133 M6
Cappers La LICHS WS14....21 J5
Capponfield Cl BILS/COS WV14....66 F2
Capstone Av WOLVN WV10....35 M5
WSNGN B18....106 E1
Captain's Cl BDMR/CCFT WV3....49 H5
Captains Pool Rd KIDD DY10....164 E4
Capulet Cl COVS CV3....156 A7
RUGBYS/DCH CV22....186 C7
Caradoc TAM/AM/WIL B77....46 E3
Caradoc Cl COVE CV2....135 H6
Carcroft Rd YDLY B25....109 G5
Cardale Cft COVS CV3....156 D5
Cardale St BLKHTH/ROWR B65....104 A3
Carden Cl WBROM B70....86 D1
Carder Crs BILS/COS WV14....67 H1
Carder Dr BRLYHL DY5....102 A3
Cardiff St BDMR/CCFT WV3....2 C8
Cardigan Cl HHTH/SAND B71....69 G6
Cardigan Dr SHHTH WV12....37 M7
Cardigan Pl HEDN WS12....13 G8
Cardigan Rd BDWTH CV12....116 A4
Cardigan St CBHAMNE B4....7 K3
Cardinal Crs BRGRVW B61....191 H4
Cardinal Dr KIDD DY10....164 F2
Cardinal Wy CNCK/NC WS11....16 B3
Carding Cl COVW CV5....153 K1
Cardington Av PBAR/PBCH B42....70 F4
Cardoness Pl DUDN DY1....84 D3
Cardy Cl REDW B97....201 L1
Careless Gn HAG/WOL DY9....120 D1
Carey TAM/AM/WIL B77....46 E8
Carey St COVN CV6....134 F4
Carfax CNCK/NC WS11....16 C5
Cargill Cl COVN CV6....116 D8
Carhampton Rd MGN/WHC B75....57 L7
Carillon Gdns
BLKHTH/ROWR B65....104 A2
Carisbrooke TAM/AM/WIL B77....46 E3
Carisbrooke Av
CHWD/FDBR/MGN B37....111 G3
Carisbrooke Cl DARL/WED WS10....69 J3
Carisbrooke Ct
DUNHL/THL/PER WV6....48 E2
Carisbrooke Crs
DARL/WED WS10....69 J2
Carisbrooke Dr RMSLY B62....122 B2
Carisbrooke Gdns WOLVN WV10....36 C2
Carisbrooke Rd
DUNHL/THL/PER WV6....48 E2
HRBN B17....105 M4
WOLVN WV10....36 C2
Carisbrook Rd
NUNW/HART CV10....81 H7
Carlcroft TAM/AM/WIL B77....46 F3
Carless Av HRBN B17....105 M6
Carless St WSL WS1....4 F7
Carlisle Rd CNCK/NC WS11....15 M6
Carlisle St WSNGN B18....88 C8
Carl St WSLW WS2....39 H8
Carlton Av BILS/COS WV14....51 K6
FOAKS/STRLY B74....55 K3
HAG/WOL DY9....120 C2
HDSW B21....88 C4
WNSFLD WV11....36 E6
Carlton Cl BDWTH CV12....117 M2
DUDN DY1....67 G7
HEDN WS12....17 H1
KIDDW DY11....137 L5
MGN/WHC B75....57 H6
REDW B97....201 M4
Carlton Crs BNTWD WS7....18 E5
CRTAM B79....31 K5
Carlton Cft FOAKS/STRLY B74....55 L3
Carlton Gdns COVW CV5 *....154 E5
Carlton Ms CBROM B36....92 A5
Carlton Rd BDMR/CCFT WV3....49 J5
BORD B9....108 B4
COVN CV6....134 D4
RUGBYS/DCH CV22....186 B4
SMTHWK B66....87 L5
Carlyle Av KIDD DY10....138 F7
Carlyle Cl NUNW/HART CV10....79 K8
Carlyle Gv WOLVN WV10....36 C4
Carlyle Rd BLKHTH/ROWR B65....104 A3
BRGRVE B60....191 M5
LDYWD/EDGR B16....106 C4
LOZ/NWT B19....89 G5
WOLVN WV10....36 D5
Carlyon Rd ATHST CV9....63 K5
Carmel Cl HEDN WS12....13 G8
Carmel Gv RIDG/WDGT B32....122 F4
Carmelite Rd COV CV1....9 K5
Carmichael Cl LICHS WS14....21 H6
Carmodale Av PBAR/PBCH B42....70 C4
Carnbroe Av COVS CV3....156 D6
Carnegie Av TPTN/OCK DY4....85 L1
Carnegie Cl COVS CV3....155 M8
Carnegie Dr DARL/WED WS10....68 E2
Carnegie Rd
BLKHTH/ROWR B65....103 M3
Carnford Rd
LGN/SDN/BHAMAIR B26....109 M7
Carnforth Cl KGSWFD DY6....82 F8
Carnforth Rd BRGRVE B60....191 M4
Carnoustie TAM/AM/WIL B77....32 E8
Carnoustie Cl BLOX/PEL WS3....38 E2
BRGRVW B61....191 H5
MGN/WHC B75....57 H5
Carnwath Rd SCFLD/BOLD B73....72 C3
Carol Av BRGRVW B61....191 H2
Carol Crs HALE B63....103 K8
WNSFLD WV11....37 J7
Carol Gdns STRBR DY8....101 K5
Carolina Cl NUN CV11....99 K6
Caroline Rd MOS/BIL B13....125 K1
Caroline St CBHAMW B1....6 D2
DUDS DY2....85 J4
WBROM B70....86 F3
Carpenter Gld HALE B63....103 H8
Carpenter Rd EDG B15....106 F8
Carpenters Ct BHTH/HG B12 *....107 K8
Carpenter's Rd LOZ/NWT B19....89 G6
Carpet Trades Wy KIDDW DY11....138 B6
Carrick Cl BLOX/PEL WS3....25 L8
Carriers Cl WSLW WS2....52 C2
Carriers Fold WMBN WV5 *....64 F6
Carrington Rd DARL/WED WS10....69 H3
Carrisbrooke Rd
DARL/WED WS10....69 H3
Carroway Head Hl
MGN/WHC B75....58 A1
Carrs La CBHAMNE B4....7 H5
Carrs Cl RCOVN/BALC/EX CV7....116 B8
Carshalton Rd KGSTG B44....71 L3
Cartbridge Crs BLOX/PEL WS3....39 L8
Cartbridge La RUSH/SHEL WS4....39 L8
Cartbridge La South
RUSH/SHEL WS4....39 L8
Carter Av CDSL WV8....34 F2
KIDDW DY11....163 M1
Carter Rd COVS CV3....155 J7
DUNHL/THL/PER WV6....35 M8
GTB/HAM B43....70 B1
Carters Cl BRGRVE B60....191 M6
WALM/CURD B76....73 K2
Cartersfield La ALDR WS9....27 H7
Carter's Gn WBROM B70....86 F1
Carters Hurst STETCH B33....109 M4
Carter's La RMSLY B62....104 D8
Carthorse La REDW B97....193 M8
Carthusian Rd COVS CV3....155 G5
Cartland Rd BVILLE B30....124 F6
SPARK B11....108 A6
Cartmel Cl COVW CV5....153 L1
Cart's La ATHST CV9....62 A3
The Cartway
DUNHL/THL/PER WV6....48 B1
Cartwright Gdns OLDBY B69....86 A3
Cartwright Rd MGN/WHC B75....57 G2
Cartwright St BKHL/PFLD WV2....3 G9
Carvell Cl COVW CV5....132 F4
Carver Cl COVE CV2....156 C3
Carver Ct TPTN/OCK DY4 *....67 L4
Carver Gdns STRBR DY8....119 J3
Carver St WSNGN B18....6 A2
Cascade Cl COVS CV3....155 J7
Casern Vw MGN/WHC B75....57 L7
Casewell Rd KGSWFD DY6....83 G5
Casey Av ERDW/GRVHL B23....72 B5
Cash Joynson Av
DARL/WED WS10....52 A5
Cashmore Av RLSS CV31....206 D8
Cashmore Rd BDWTH CV12....116 C4
KNWTH CV8....198 A1
Cash's La COV CV1....134 B7
Casia Gv KNWTH CV8....198 A1
Caslon Crs STRBR DY8....119 H1
Caslon Rd HALE B63....103 G7
Caspian Wy COVE CV2....135 L5
Cassandra Cl BRLYHL DY5....84 A4
TLHL/CAN CV4....180 B2
Cassowary Rd
BFLD/HDSWWD B20....88 D2
Castello Dr CBROM B36....92 B4
The Castings BILS/COS WV14....67 H3
Castlebridge Rd WNSFLD WV11....37 L6
Castle Cl BRWNH WS8....26 D3
CDYHTH B64....103 M4
COVS CV3....155 H7
HIA/OLT B92....127 M4
RCOVN/BALC/EX CV7....114 C3
TAM/AM/WIL B77....46 C1
WWCK CV34....205 H7
Castle Crs CBROM B36....92 A5
Castlecroft CNCK/NC WS11....17 J8
Castle Cft LGLYGN/QTN B68....105 H5
Castlecroft Av BDMR/CCFT WV3....48 E5
Castlecroft Gdns
BDMR/CCFT WV3....48 F5
Castlecroft La BDMR/CCFT WV3....48 D5
Castlecroft Rd BDMR/CCFT WV3....48 D5
BILS/COS WV14....51 J6
Castleditch La REDE B98....202 C6
Castle Dr CSHL/WTROR B46....93 K8
NUNW/HART CV10....97 J6
SHHTH WV12....37 M8
Castle Dyke LICH WS13....20 F6
Castleford Gv SPARK B11 *....126 A1
Castleford Rd SPARK B11....126 A1
Castlefort Rd ALDR WS9....40 E2
Castlegate Dr DUDN DY1....85 J3
Castlegate Wy DUDN DY1....85 J3
Castle Gn KNWTH CV8....179 H8
Castle Grounds DUDN DY1 *....85 H3
Castle Gv STRBR DY8....119 M2
Castlehall TAM/AM/WIL B77....46 E3
Castle Hts CDYHTH B64 *....103 M5
Castle Hl DUDN DY1....85 H3
KNWTH CV8....179 J8
Castlehill Rd ALDR WS9....41 G2
Castlehills Dr CBROM B36....91 L5
Castle La BEWD DY12....163 G2
CSHL/WTROR B46....94 D5
HIA/OLT B92....127 L4
WWCK CV34....205 J7
Castle Ms RUGBYN/HIL CV21....186 F2
Castle Mill Rd DUDN DY1....85 G1
Castle Mound Wy
RRUGBY CV23....161 H3
Castle Pl COV CV1 *....9 J1
Castle Rd ALDR WS9....40 E3
BVILLE B30....145 K1
KIDD DY10....138 E1
KIDDW DY11....138 B8
KNWTH CV8....179 H8
KNWTH CV8....197 J1
NUNW/HART CV10....79 M4
NUNW/HART CV10....81 G6
SLYOAK B29....123 L3
TAM/AM/WIL B77....46 D8
TPTN/OCK DY4....67 K8
Castle Rd East LGLYGN/QTN B68....105 H5
Castle Rd West
LGLYGN/QTN B68....105 G5
Castle St BILS/COS WV14....67 G5
BRWNH WS8....26 D3
COV CV1....9 J2
DARL/WED WS10....52 B5
DUDS DY2....85 H4
RUGBYN/HIL CV21....186 F2
SEDG DY3....66 B5
TPTN/OCK DY4....67 J8
WBROM B70....68 E6
WOLV WV1....3 G5
Castleton Rd BLOX/PEL WS3....39 G2
PBAR/PBCH B42....71 H6
Castleton St DUDS DY2....85 G8
Castle Vw DUDN DY1....84 F3
NUNW/HART CV10....79 M4
TAM/AM/WIL B77....46 A2
Castle View Cl DARL/WED WS10....67 L1
Castle View Rd DARL/WED WS10....67 L1
Caswell Rd RLSS CV31....206 F7
SEDG DY3....66 A5
Cat & Kittens La WOLVN WV10....22 C7
Cater Dr WALM/CURD B76....73 K3
Caterham Dr STRBR DY8....101 K2
Catesby Dr KGSWFD DY6....83 H5
Catesby Rd COVN CV6....133 M5
RUGBYS/DCH CV22....187 H4
SHLY B90....147 M4
Cateswell Rd HLGN/YWD B28....126 D3
Cathcart Rd STRBR DY8....101 J8
Cathedral Av KIDDW DY11....137 L7
Cathedral Ri LICH WS13....20 E5
Cathel Dr PBAR/PBCH B42....70 E6
Catherine Cl BRGRVE B60....191 K5
Catherine De Barnes La
HIA/OLT B92....129 G7
Catherine Dr SCFLD/BOLD B73....56 E7
Catherine Rd BILS/COS WV14....66 E4
Catherines Cl SOLH B91....149 M1
Catherine St AST/WIT B6....89 L6
COV CV1....9 L3
Catherton Cl TPTN/OCK DY4....68 A3
Cathiron La RRUGBY CV23....158 D2
Catholic La SEDG DY3....66 A6
Catisfield Crs CDSL WV8....35 K4
Cat La BKDE/SHDE B34....91 M6
Caton Gv HLGN/YWD B28....126 E6
Cato St VAUX/NECH B7....107 M1
Cato St North VAUX/NECH B7....90 A8
Catsbridge La CNCK/NC WS11....15 J6
Catshill Rd BRWNH WS8....26 E6
Cattell Dr MGN/WHC B75....57 M8
Cattell Rd BORD B9....108 A4
WWCK CV34....205 J6
Cattells Gv VAUX/NECH B7....90 A7
Cattermole Gv GTB/HAM B43....71 G2
Cattock Hurst Dr
CSCFLD/WYGN B72....73 H6
Causeway BLKHTH/ROWR B65....104
Causeway Green Rd
LGLYGN/QTN B68....104
Causeway Rd BILS/COS WV14....67
The Causeway YDLY B25....109
Causey Farm Rd HALE B63....121
Cavalier Circ WOLVN WV10....36
Cavalier Cl NUN CV11....99
Cavandale Av KGSTG B44....71
Cavan's Cl CNCK/NC WS11....16
Cavans Wy COVS CV3....156
Cave Cl RUGBYS/DCH CV22....185
Cavell Closet WSLW WS2....4
Cavell Rd BNTWD WS7....19
DUDS DY2....85
Cavendish CRTAM B79....31
Cavendish Cl BRGRVE B60....169
HWK/WKHTH B38....145
KGSWFD DY6....101
Cavendish Dr HAG/WOL DY9....140
KIDD DY10....138
Cavendish Gdns WSLW WS2....52
Cavendish Rd
LDYWD/EDGR B16....106
RMSLY B62....122
TLHL/CAN CV4....153
WOLV WV1....50
WSLW WS2....38
Cavendish Wy ALDR WS9....40
Caversham Cl NUN CV11....81
Caversham Rd KGSTG B44....71
Cawdon Gv DOR/KN B93....175
Cawdor Crs LDYWD/EDGR B16....106
Cawnpore Rd COVN CV6....133
Cawston La RUGBYS/DCH CV22....185
Cawston Wy
RUGBYS/DCH CV22....186
Cawthorne Cl COV CV1....9
Caxton Gv KGSTG B44....72
Caxton St CNCK/NC WS11....16
Caynham Cl REDE B98....203
Caynham Rd RIDG/WDGT B32....122
Cayton Gv ERDW/GRVHL B23....72
Cecil Dr OLDBY B69....86
Cecil Rd ERDE/BCHGN B24....90
SLYOAK B29....125
Cecil St CBHAMNE B4....7
CNCK/NC WS11....16
RUSH/SHEL WS4....53
STRBR DY8....101
Cecily Rd COVS CV3....155
Cedar Av BILS/COS WV14....66
BRWNH WS8....26
CBROM B36....92
KNWTH CV8....182
Cedar Bridge Cft
FOAKS/STRLY B74....56
Cedar Cl BNTWD WS7....18
BVILLE B30....124
DSYBK/YTR WS5....69
HEDN WS12....16
LGLYGN/QTN B68....105
LICHS WS14....21
POL/KGSB/FAZ B78....60
RLSN CV32....206
STRBR DY8....119
STRPT DY13....188
Cedar Crs KIDDW DY11....138
Cedar Dr BRGRVE B60....191
CRTAM B79....31
ERDE/BCHGN B24....73
FOAKS/STRLY B74....55
KIDDW DY11....138
NFLD/LBR B31....144
Cedar Gv BDMR/CCFT WV3....49
CDSL WV8....34
GTWY WS6....24
HAG/WOL DY9....119
WWCK CV34....205
Cedarhill Dr CNCK/NC WS11....16
Cedarhurst RIDG/WDGT B32....105
SOLH B91....149
Cedar Park Rd REDW B97....202
SHHTH WV12....38
Cedar Ri STRPT DY13....188
Cedar Rd BNTWD WS7....18
BVILLE B30....124
DARL/WED WS10....68
DUDN DY1....84
NUNW/HART CV10....80
REDW B97....202
TPTN/OCK DY4....67
WLNHL WV13....51
Cedars Av ACGN B27....127
COVN CV6....133
KGSWFD DY6....101
WMBN WV5....64
Cedars Rd RCOVN/BALC/EX CV7....116
The Cedars
DUNHL/THL/PER WV6 *....35
DUNHL/THL/PER WV6 *....49
YDLY B25....109
Cedar Ter BRGRVE B60....191
Cedar Vw REDW B97....202
Cedar Wy NFLD/LBR B31....144
WNSFLD WV11....37
Cedarwood FOAKS/STRLY B74....56
Cedarwood Cft PBAR/PBCH B42....70
Cedar Wood Dr
RCOVN/BALC/EX CV7....151
Cedar Wood Rd SEDG DY3....84
Cedric Cl COVS CV3....156
Celandine RRUGBY CV23....161
TAM/AM/WIL B77....46
Celandine Cl STRBR DY8....101
Celandine Rd COVE CV2....135
DUDN DY1....84
The Celandines WMBN WV5....64
Celandine Wy BDWTH CV12....116
Celbury Wy GTB/HAM B43....70
Celeste Rd BRGRVE B60....192
Celtic Rd CNCK/NC WS11....16
Celts Cl BLKHTH/ROWR B65....104
Cemetery La NUNW/HART CV10....79
WSNGN B18....88
Cemetery Rd CNCK/NC WS11....16
HAG/WOL DY9....102
LGLYGN/QTN B68....104
REDW B97....202
SMTHWKW B67....105
WLNHL WV13....51
WSLW WS2....52
Cemetery St BILS/COS WV14....51
GTWY WS6....24
Cemetery Wy BLOX/PEL WS3....39
Centaur Rd COVW CV5....154
Centenary Cl NFLD/LBR B31....144
Centenary Dr HDSW B21....88
Centenary Rd TLHL/CAN CV4....154
Centenary Sq CBHAMW B1....6
Centenary Wy CSHL/WTROR B46....93
KNWTH CV8....17
KNWTH CV8....19
NUNW/HART CV10....
RLSS CV31....
WALM/CURD B76....
WWCK CV34....
Centernary Wy COVS CV3....
Central Ar WOLV WV1....

ntral Av BILS/COS WV14 .....51 J6
BLKHTH/ROWR B65 .....104 A3
CDYHTH B64 .....103 H6
CNCK/NC WS11 .....12 D8
COVE CV2 .....155 L3
HAG/WOL DY9 .....120 C2
NFLD/LBR B31 .....144 D5
NUN CV11 .....80 F8
RLSS CV31 .....206 D7
TPTN/OCK DY4 .....67 K7
ntral Bvd HOCK/TIA B94 .....174 D3
RCOVN/BALC/EX CV7 .....115 M8
ntral Dr BILS/COS WV14 .....67 H6
BLOX/PEL WS3 .....38 E4
SEDG DY3 .....84 B3
ntral Pk DUDS DY2 * 103 J2
ntral Park Dr RRUGBY CV23 .....161 K5
WSNGN B18 .....88 D8
ntral Sq BRGRVE B60 .....191 L4
ntral Sq BEDG/BCHGN B24 * 90 E1
ntre La HALE B63 .....121 M2
ntre Centreway ALE/KHTH/YWD B14 .....147 H1
nturion Cl CSHL/WTROR B46 .....93 K6
nturion Wy TAM/AM/WIL B77 .....46 F7
ntury Pk BORD B9 .....108 A3
ntury Rd OLDBY B69 .....86 E5
olmund Crs CHWD/FDBR/MGN B37 .....110 D3
eaceley Av COVE CV2 .....155 M8
eaceley Cl ERDW/GRVHL B23 * 72 B6
adbury Dr HALE B63 .....148 F5
adbury Rd HALE B63 .....120 C2
adcote Wy BRGRVW B61 .....168 D4
REDE B98 .....202 D4
addesley Cl OLDBY B69 .....86 B8
addesley Dr HAG/WOL DY9 .....119 M4
addesley Rd HALE B63 .....121 K3
HWK/WKHTH B38 .....145 H1
EDG B15 .....138 E8
adley Cl SOLH B91 .....127 L7
ad Rd BILS/COS WV14 .....106 D6
EDG B15 .....107 G5
ad's Ditch HEDN WS12 .....12 C3
adshunt Cl CBROM B36 .....92 B3
adsmoor Ter VAUX/NECH B7 .....89 M7
adstone Cl SOLH B91 .....148 F7
adswell Hts LICH WS13 .....21 H2
ad Valley Tr HRBN B17 .....106 B7
adwell Cl DUDS DY3 .....34 D1
adwick Av HAG/WOL DY9 .....142 C7
adwick Av RBRY B45 .....143 M7
adwick Cl COVW CV5 .....153 M3
ETTPK/GDPK/PENN WV4 .....G7
adwick Cl GTB/HAM B43 * 70 C5
adwick La DOR/KN B93 .....176 F3
STRPT DY13 .....188 D5
adwick Mnr DOR/KN B93 * 176 E4
adwick Ms DOR/KN B93 * 176 E4
adwick Rd MGN/WHC B75 .....57 K8
adwick Wk REDE B98 .....202 E6
adworth Br HIA/OLT B92 .....175 J1
affcombe Rd LGN/SDN/BHAMAIR B26 .....109 A7
SEDG DY3 .....84 A3
affinch Cl HEDN WS12 .....16 F7
affinch Dr CBROM B36 .....92 F6
KIDD DY10 .....164 D3
affinch Rd HAG/WOL DY9 .....120 D3
ainmakers Cl BILS/COS WV14 .....67 C2
alcot Dr HEDN WS12 .....89 H5
alcot Gv BFLD/HDSWWD B20 .....70 D8
aldon Cl COVEN WV10 .....35 L3
ale Gv ALE/KHTH/YWD B14 .....146 E2
alfield CRTAM B79 .....31 H7
alfont Av CNCK/NC WS11 .....16 A5
COVW CV5 .....153 M1
alfont Pl HAG/WOL DY9 .....120 C2
alford Rd ERDW/GRVHL B23 .....72 A5
alford Wy SHLY B90 .....148 A5
algrove Crs SOLH B91 .....148 F4
algrove Gv HWK/WKHTH B38 .....145 L2
allenge Cl COV CV1 .....9 C1
allenge Wy WOLVN WV10 .....36 C8
allenor Av WLNHL WV13 .....51 H3
alybeate Cl RBRY B45 .....143 K4
RLSN CV32 .....199 J8
amberlain Cl OLDBY B69 .....86 B3
RLSN CV32 .....6 C1
amberlain Crs SHLY B90 .....147 J3
amberlain St BDWTH CV12 .....116 F1
amberlain Rd MOS/BIL B13 .....125 K7
RUGBYN/HIL CV21 .....187 M5
amberlain's La ETTPK/GDPK/PENN WV4 .....65 J2
amberlain Sq CBHAMNW B3 .....6 C1
amberlain Wk CSHL/WTROR B46 * 93 K6
SMTHWK B66 * 87 J3
ance Cft ... UN B68 .....104 F5
ance Fld RLSS CV31 .....207 H4
ancellor Cl EDG B15 .....106 C5
ancel Wy RMSLY B62 .....104 A6
ancery Ct HEDN WS12 .....13 C6
ancery La NUNW/HART CV10 .....9 M6
ancery La BRLYHL DY5 .....102 D3
anders Rd WWCK CV34 .....205 H4
andler Dr ETTPK/GDPK/PENN WV4 .....65 J2
andlers Cl COVEN WV10 .....35 L4
REDW B97 .....202 B4
WSNGN B18 .....C1
andlers Dr TAM/AM/WIL B77 .....32 F8
andlers Keep BRWNH WS8 .....26 A2
andos St COVE CV2 .....155 L2
NUN CV11 .....98 C1
RLSN CV32 .....206 F3
ange Brook Cl NUN CV11 .....81 K5
annon Dr BRLYHL DY5 .....102 B5
anston Av ALE/KHTH/YWD B14 .....146 C1
anterelle Gdns ETTPK/GDPK/PENN WV4 .....65 L1
antry Crs BILS/COS WV14 .....51 K6
GTB/HAM B43 .....71 H1
e Chantries COV CV1 * 9 K1
antry Pl BLOX/PEL WS3 .....39 H5
antry Rd HDSW B21 .....88 A2
antry Vw BDWTH B47 * 104 E6
anters Heath Crs DOR/KN B93 .....149 M5
INVER DY7 .....101 G6
MOS/BIL B13 .....125 J1
e Chantry WWCK CV34 .....205 L4
pel Ash WOLV WV1 .....3 C3
pel Ash Island WOLV WV1 * 2 A4
pel Av BRWNH WS8 .....26 C3
pel Cl CDYHTH B64 .....103 M5
WMBN WV5 .....64 D8

Chapel Ct KIDD DY10 .....138 E4
RLSN CV32 * 206 F3
Chapel Dr BRWNH WS8 .....26 A1
HLYWD B47 .....172 D2
RCOVN/BALC/EX CV7 .....151 H3
Chapelfield Ms RBRY B45 .....143 H3
STRBR DY8 .....119 L1
Chapel Fields Rd HIA/OLT B92 .....127 K3
Chapel Gdns WLNHL WV13 .....51 M3
Chapel Hl KIDD DY10 .....138 E4
Chapel House La HALE B63 .....103 G8
Chapel House Rd CHWD/FDBR/MGN B37 .....110 D3
Chapel House St BHTH/HG B12 * 7 K8
Chapel La ALVE B48 .....194 D1
CDSL WV8 .....34 D2
CTB/HAM B43 .....70 D1
HAG/WOL DY9 .....142 B6
HLYWD B47 .....172 C3
HOCK/TIA B94 .....176 A6
KNWTH CV8 .....20 F7
LICHS WS14 .....20 F7
RCOVN/BALC/EX CV7 .....117 M7
REDE B98 .....195 K5
RMSLY B62 .....121 C3
RUGE WS15 .....18 L1
SEDG DY3 .....82 A1
SLYOAK B29 .....124 C3
STRPT DY13 .....188 C3
Chapelon TAM/AM/WIL B77 .....46 E3
Chapel Rw WWCK CV34 .....205 J6
Chapel Sq GTWY WS6 .....24 B3
Chapel St BDWTH CV12 .....116 F2
BILS/COS WV14 .....67 K1
BKHL/PFLD WV2 .....50 B6
BLOX/PEL WS3 .....39 H5
BNTWD WS7 .....18 B5
BRGRVE B60 .....191 L5
BRLYHL DY5 .....84 A6
BRLYHL DY5 .....102 B3
BRWNH WS8 .....26 C3
CBHAMNE B4 .....7 J4
DARL/WED WS10 .....68 C2
DUDS DY2 .....103 H1
HAG/WOL DY9 .....102 C8
HAG/WOL DY9 .....119 L8
HALE B63 .....121 L2
HDSW B21 .....88 B6
HEDN WS12 .....17 J4
KGSWFD DY6 .....82 F5
KIDD DY10 .....138 B7
NUN CV11 .....99 C1
OLDBY B69 .....86 C4
RUGE WS15 * 18 L1
RMSLY B62 .....121 C3
RUGE WS15 .....18 L1
SEDG DY3 .....82 A1
SLYOAK B29 .....124 C3
STRPT DY13 .....188 C3
Chapel Vw SMTHWK B67 .....105 K1
Chapel Wk BRGRVE B60 .....191 L3
BVILLE B30 .....124 C3
SEDG DY3 .....84 A3
Chapelwood Gv PBAR/PBCH B42 * 71 J4
Chapel Yd COVE CV2 * 117 H4
Chaplain Rd HEDN WS12 .....17 J3
Chapman Cl RLSS CV31 .....207 J8
Chapman Rd SMHTH B10 .....108 A5
Chapman's Hi BRGRVW B61 .....142 F5
Chapmans Pas CBHAMW B1 * 6 C6
Chapman St WBROM B70 .....86 F2
Chapter Ho WBROM B70 * 86 F2
Chard Rd COVS CV3 .....156 B5
Charfield Cl BVILLE B30 .....124 C3
Charford Rd BRGRVE B60 .....191 K5
Charingworth Dr RWWCK/WEL CV35 .....204 C3
Charingworth Rd HIA/OLT B92 .....128 A3
Chariot Wy RUGBYN/HIL CV21 .....160 E6
Charity Rd RCOVN/BALC/EX CV7 .....115 M7
Charlbury Av CHWD/FDBR/MGN B37 .....110 D3
Charlbury Crs LGN/SDN/BHAMAIR B26 .....109 K5
Charlbury Ms RLSS CV31 .....207 H7
Charlecote Cft SHLY B90 .....148 A5
Charlecote Dr DUDN DY1 .....84 C2
ERDW/GRVHL B23 .....72 C6
Charlecote Gdns RLSS CV31 .....207 H8
SCFLD/BOLD B73 .....72 E5
Charlecote Ri NUN CV11 .....51 K4
Charlecote Rd COVW CV5 .....153 L3
Charlecote Wk NUN CV11 .....99 K5
Charlecott Cl MOS/BIL B13 .....126 B6
Charlemont Av HHTH/SAND B71 .....69 K5
Charlemont Cl DSYBK/YTR WS5 .....54 A5
Charlemont Crs HHTH/SAND B71 .....69 J5
Charlemonte Cl HEDN WS12 .....17 J2
Charlemont Gdns DSYBK/YTR WS5 .....53 M7
Charlemont Rd DSYBK/YTR WS5 .....53 M7
HHTH/SAND B71 .....69 J5
Charles Av BLKHTH/ROWR B65 .....104 A1
Charles Av ETTPK/GDPK/PENN WV4 .....49 M8
KIDD DY10 .....138 C4
WNSFLD WV11 .....37 K1
Charles Cl BLOX/PEL WS3 .....25 L8
WASH/WDE B8 .....108 A1
Charles Cl CDYHTH B64 .....103 M5
Charlesdale Dr ALDR WS9 .....54 F1
Charles Dr VAUX/NECH B7 .....89 M7
Charles Eaton Rd BDWTH CV12 .....116 C2
Charles Edward Rd LGN/SDN/BHAMAIR B26 .....109 H7
Charlesfield Rd RUGBYS/DCH CV22 .....186 E5
Charles Foster St DARL/WED WS10 .....52 A7
Charles Gardner Rd RLSS CV31 .....206 F7
Charles Henry St DIG/EDG B5 .....107 J3
Charles Holland St WLNHL WV13 .....51 M3
Charles Rd AST/WIT B6 .....89 L4
BRLYHL DY5 .....102 A6
HALE B63 .....121 K1
SMHTH B10 .....108 C5
SOLH B91 .....148 C5
STRBR DY8 .....119 J1
TPTN/OCK DY4 .....67 J4
Charles St ATHST CV9 .....61 G8
COV CV1 .....9 C1
KIDD DY10 .....138 D7
NUN CV11 .....80 D8
RCOVN/BALC/EX CV7 .....96 C5
REDW B97 .....202 A4
RUGBYS/DCH CV22 .....186 D6
SMTHWK B66 .....88 A6
WBROM B70 .....68 D8
WLNHL WV13 .....52 A3

WSLW WS2 .....4 C4
WWCK CV34 .....205 J6
Charles Wk BLKHTH/ROWR B65 .....86 A8
Charles Warren Cl RUGBYN/HIL CV21 .....186 F2
Charles Wesley Ct BDMR/CCFT WV3 * 49 L6
Charlesworth Av SHLY B90 .....148 F7
Charleville Rd LOZ/NWT B19 .....88 F6
Charlewood Rd COVN CV6 .....133 M4
Charlock Gv CNCK/NC WS11 .....17 C2
Charlotte Cl TPTN/OCK DY4 .....67 J7
Charlotte Rd BVILLE B30 .....124 E7
DARL/WED WS10 .....68 A2
EDG B15 .....107 C5
Charlotte St CBHAMNW B3 .....6 C5
DUDN DY1 .....84 F5
RLSS CV31 .....206 F7
RUGBYN/HIL CV21 .....186 F2
Charminster Av YDLY DY25 .....109 H5
Charminster Dr COVS CV3 .....181 H1
Charnley Dr MGN/WHC B75 .....57 J3
Charnwood Av NUNW/HART CV10 .....98 B3
SEDG DY3 .....66 B3
Charnwood Cl BILS/COS WV14 .....67 M2
BRLYHL DY5 .....101 M6
HEDN WS12 .....17 C1
LICH WS13 .....21 J3
RBRY B45 .....143 M2
Charnwood Ct HAG/WOL DY9 .....120 C3
Charnwood Dr DSYBK/YTR WS5 .....69 L3
PBAR/PBCH B42 .....70 D6
Charnwood Wy RLSN CV32 .....207 G2
Charter Appoach WWCK CV34 .....205 H7
Charter Ap WWCK CV34 .....205 H7
Charter Cl CNCK/NC WS11 .....16 C5
Charter Cl CNCK/NC WS11 * 16 C5
Charter Crs CDYHTH B64 .....103 M5
Charterfield Dr HEDN WS12 .....17 C4
KGSWFD DY6 .....83 H5
Charterhouse Dr SOLH B91 .....148 F4
Charterhouse Rd COV CV1 .....9 K5
Charter Rd RUGBYS/DCH CV22 .....187 J5
TPTN/OCK DY4 .....68 A4
Charters Av CDSL WV8 .....34 F4
Charter St BRLYHL DY5 .....84 C8
Chartist Rd WASH/WDE B8 .....90 B7
Chartley Cl DOR/KN B93 .....175 J2
DUNHL/THL/PER WV6 .....48 D1
Chartley Rd ERDW/GRVHL B23 .....90 A4
HHTH/SAND B71 .....69 G2
The Chartway BLOX/PEL WS3 .....39 M1
Chartwell CRTAM B79 .....31 H6
Chartwell Cl DUDN DY1 .....66 F7
NUN CV11 .....81 K4
Chartwell Dr FOAKS/STRLY B74 .....56 B1
SHLY B90 .....148 B8
WMBN WV5 .....64 D8
WOLVN WV10 .....36 C4
Charwelton Dr RUGBYN/HIL CV21 .....161 J7
Chase Av GTWY WS6 .....24 C2
Chase Cl NUNW/HART CV10 .....81 K7
Chase Gv ERDE/BCHGN B24 .....73 H7
Chaselands BNTWD WS7 .....18 A5
Chase La KNWTH CV8 .....178 D7
Chaseley Av CNCK/NC WS11 .....16 A3
Chaseley Cft CNCK/NC WS11 .....15 M3
Chaseley Gdns BNTWD WS7 .....18 C6
The Chase Link BRWNH WS8 .....26 A4
Chasepool Rd SEDG DY3 .....83 M4
Chase Rd BLOX/PEL WS3 .....38 E5
BNTWD WS7 .....18 C6
BRWNH WS8 .....26 A4
SEDG DY3 .....83 M4
Chaseside Dr HEDN WS12 .....16 F2
The Chase DUNHL/THL/PER WV6 .....35 M7
WALM/CURD B76 .....73 H6
Chase Vw BNTWD WS7 .....18 C7
Chasewater Wy CNCK/NC WS11 .....17 K8
Chater Dr WALM/CURD B76 .....73 L4
Chaters Cl TPTN/OCK DY4 .....67 J3
Chatham Cl COVS CV3 .....156 A1
Chatham Rd NFLD/LBR B31 .....144 E7
Chatsworth Cl CSCFLD/WYGN B72 .....73 H6
SHHTH WV12 .....37 M8
SHLY B90 .....148 B8
Chatsworth Crs RUSH/SHEL WS4 .....40 B6
Chatsworth Dr NUN CV11 .....99 K5
Chatsworth Gdns RLSS CV31 .....207 H7
Chatsworth Gv KNWTH CV8 .....180 A8
RLSS CV31 .....207 H7
Chatsworth Ms STRBR DY8 * 101 J3
Chatsworth Ri COVS CV3 .....155 J8
Chatsworth Rd CDYHTH B64 .....103 G5
Chattaway Dr RCOVN/BALC/EX CV7 .....151 M7
Chattaway St VAUX/NECH B7 .....90 A6
Chatterton Av LICH WS13 .....13 J3
Chattle Hl CSHL/WTROR B46 .....93 J3
Chattock Av SOLH B91 .....149 J1
Chattock Cl CBROM B36 .....91 J5
Chatwell Gv SLYOAK B29 .....123 M8
Chatwin Pl BILS/COS WV14 .....67 M3
Chatwin St SMTHWK B66 .....87 K4
Chatwins Whf TPTN/OCK DY4 .....67 K5
Chaucer Av SEDG DY3 .....66 C8
SHHTH WV12 .....37 C5
TPTN/OCK DY4 .....67 M3
Chaucer Cl BILS/COS WV14 .....67 M1
CRTAM B79 .....31 L7
ERDW/GRVHL B23 .....89 M2
LICHS WS14 .....21 C5
STRBR DY8 .....101 L5
Chaucer Crs KIDD DY10 .....139 C2
Chaucer Dr BNTWD WS7 .....18 A2
NUNW/HART CV10 .....97 L1
Chaucer Gv ACGN B27 .....126 F4
Chaucer Rd BLOX/PEL WS3 .....39 J5
BRGRVE B60 .....191 M5
RUGBYS/DCH CV22 .....186 D7
Chauntry Pl COV CV1 .....9 K3
Chauson Gv SOLH B91 .....147 M8
Chavasse Rd CSCFLD/WYGN B72 .....73 C2
Chawner Cl BRLYHL DY5 .....84 B6
Chawn Hl HAG/WOL DY9 .....120 A4
Chawnhill Cl HAG/WOL DY9 .....120 A4
Chawn Park Dr HAG/WOL DY9 .....120 A4
Chaynes Gv STECH B33 .....91 H8
Chaytor Rd POL/KGSB/FAZ B78 .....47 C5
Cheadle Cl COVE CV2 .....134 C1
PENK ST19 * 10 D1
Cheadle Dr ERDW/GRVHL B23 .....72 B5
Cheam Cl COVN CV6 .....134 C4

Cheam Gdns DUNHL/THL/PER WV6 .....35 J5
Cheapside BHTH/HG B12 .....7 K8
STRPT DY13 .....188 D3
WLNHL WV13 .....51 L4
Cheatham St VAUX/NECH B7 .....90 A5
Checketts St WSLW WS2 .....4 B3
Checkley Cl SHLY B90 .....148 F7
Checkley Cft WALM/CURD B76 .....73 K5
Cheddar Rd BHTH/HG B12 .....107 J7
Chedworth Cl REDE B98 .....195 C8
SLYOAK B29 .....123 M6
Cheedon Cl DOR/KN B93 .....175 J3
Chelford Cl NUN CV11 .....81 L4
Chelford Crs KGSWFD DY6 .....101 L2
Chell Cl PENK ST19 .....10 D6
Chells Gv MOS/BIL B13 .....125 M8
Chelmar Cl CBROM B36 .....92 D5
Chelmar Dr BRLYHL DY5 .....83 C7
Chelmarsh COVE CV6 .....134 A8
Chelmarsh Av BDMR/CCFT WV3 .....48 G4
Chelmorton Rd PBAR/PBCH B42 .....71 G5
Chelmscote Rd HIA/OLT B92 .....127 K4
Chelmsley Av CSHL/WTROR B46 .....93 K7
Chelmsley Cir CHWD/FDBR/MGN B37 .....110 C2
Chelmsley La STECH B33 .....110 C1
Chelmsley Rd CHWD/FDBR/MGN B37 .....110 E2
Chelney Wk COVS CV3 .....156 C6
Chelsea Cl NUN CV11 .....81 K6
RIDG/WDGT CV32 .....123 K1
Chelsea Dr FOAKS/STRLY B74 .....56 D1
Chelsea Wy KGSWFD DY6 .....83 C7
Chelsey Rd COVE CV2 .....135 J5
Chelston Dr DUNHL/THL/PER WV6 .....49 J1
Chelston Rd NFLD/LBR B31 .....144 E5
Cheltenham Av BRGRVW B61 .....168 F4
Cheltenham Cl BDWTH CV12 .....116 F1
Cheltenham Cft COVE CV2 .....135 K6
Cheltenham Dr BRGRVE B60 .....191 H5
KGSWFD DY6 .....82 F4
Chelthorn Cl SOLH B91 .....149 G3
Cheltondale Rd SOLH B91 .....127 K8
Chelveston Crs SOLH B91 .....148 F4
Chelveston Rd COVN CV6 .....133 J8
Chelwood Gdns ETTPK/GDPK/PENN WV4 .....50 F8
Chelwood Gv COVE CV2 .....135 K4
Chelworth Rd HWK/WKHTH B38 .....145 M3
Chem Rd BILS/COS WV14 .....50 F8
Chenet Wy CNCK/NC WS11 .....16 C5
Chenies Cl COVW CV5 .....153 M2
Cheniston Rd SHHTH WV12 .....38 A7
Chepstow Cl COVS CV3 .....156 A8
DUNHL/THL/PER WV6 .....48 D1
Chepstow Gv RBRY B45 .....143 M7
Chepstow Rd BLOX/PEL WS3 .....26 A8
WOLVN WV10 .....22 B8
Chepstow Vls BHTH/HG B12 * 107 M8
Chequerfield Dr BDMR/CCFT WV3 .....49 L7
Chequers Av WMBN WV5 .....64 D6
Chequers Cl STRPT DY13 .....188 D5
Chequers Ct CNCK/NC WS11 * 17 L8
The Chequers LICH WS13 * 21 C5
Chequer St BDMR/CCFT WV3 .....49 L7
Cherhill Covert ALE/KHTH/YWD B14 .....146 A3
Cherington Cl REDE B98 .....203 H1
Cherington Rd SLYOAK B29 .....124 C5
Cheriton Cl COVW CV5 .....154 B1
Cheriton Gv DUNHL/THL/PER WV6 .....48 C2
Cherrington Dr GTWY WS6 .....24 D1
Cherrington Gdns DUNHL/THL/PER WV6 .....48 F3
HAG/WOL DY9 .....120 A5
Cherrington Wy SOLH B91 .....148 F4
Cherry Bank HEDN WS12 .....13 G7
Cherrybrook Dr PENK ST19 .....10 D3
Cherrybrook Wy COVE CV2 .....135 G4
Cherry Cl ATHST CV9 .....77 G1
BEWD DY12 .....162 D5
BNTWD WS7 .....18 D7
COVN CV6 .....134 B3
Cherry Crs BRGRVW B61 .....191 J3
ERDE/BCHGN B24 .....90 D2
Cherry Dr BORD B9 .....108 D3
Cherry Gv RUGBYS/DCH CV22 .....186 C5
SMTHWK B66 .....88 A8
STRBR DY8 .....119 J1
Cherry Hill Av RBRY B45 .....170 A5
Cherry Hill Dr RBRY B45 .....170 A5
Cherry Hill Rd RBRY B45 .....170 A5
Cherry La DARL/WED WS10 .....68 E3
RWWCK/WEL CV35 .....204 D7
SCFLD/BOLD B73 .....72 D2
SEDG DY3 .....82 F2
Cherry Lea BLOX/SHDE B34 .....91 M1
Cherry Orch CDYHTH B64 .....103 K4
KIDD DY10 .....138 D8
KNWTH CV8 .....179 L8
LICHS WS14 .....21 G6
Cherry Orchard Av HALE B63 .....103 K8
Cherry Orchard Crs HALE B63 .....103 K8
Cherry Orchard Dr BRGRVW B61 .....191 J2
Cherry Orchard Rd BFLD/HDSWWD B20 .....70 D8
Cherry Pit La REDE B98 .....195 L3
Cherry Rd TPTN/OCK DY4 .....67 K6
Cherry St BDMR/CCFT WV3 .....2 C5
CBHAM B2 .....7 G5
CRTAM B79 .....31 M8
HALE B63 .....103 K8
STRBR DY8 .....119 J1
Cherry Tree Av DSYBK/YTR WS5 .....69 M1
NUNW/HART CV10 .....80 D7
Cherrytree Ct HAG/WOL DY9 .....120 C2
Cherry Tree Gdns CDSL WV8 .....34 F2
Cherry Tree La CDSL WV8 .....34 F2
HALE B63 .....103 J8
Cherry Tree Rd CNCK/NC WS11 .....25 M1
HEDN WS12 .....12 F5
KGSWFD DY6 .....83 J5
Cherry Tree Wk CRTAM B79 .....31 L5
REDW B97 .....202 A7
STRPT DY13 .....188 C6
Cherry Wk HLYWD B47 .....158 B6
Cherry Wy KNWTH CV8 .....179 L8
Cherrywood Crs SOLH B91 .....149 G5
Cherrywood Gn BILS/COS WV14 .....67 M1
Cherrywood Gv COVW CV5 .....132 D5
Cherrywood Rd BORD B9 .....108 D3
WALM/CURD B76 .....73 L2
Cherrywood Wy FOAKS/STRLY B74 .....56 B1
Chervil Cl COVN CV6 .....133 M1
Chervil Ri WOLV WV10 .....3 L2

Cherwell Dr BRWNH WS8 .....25 M3
CBROM B36 .....92 D5
Cherwell Gdns AST/WIT B6 * 89 H5
Cherwell Wy RRUGBY CV23 .....185 M1
Chesford Br KNWTH CV8 .....198 A5
Chesford Crs COVN CV6 .....134 F3
WWCK CV34 .....205 M4
Chesham St RLSS CV31 .....206 F6
Cheshire Av SHLY B90 .....147 L2
Cheshire Cl RUGBYS/DCH CV22 .....186 A5
STRBR DY8 .....101 H5
Cheshire Gv DUNHL/THL/PER WV6 .....48 G3
KIDD DY11 .....137 L6
Cheshire Rd AST/WIT B6 .....89 L3
SMTHWK B67 .....105 L1
WSLW WS2 .....52 D3
Chesholme Rd COVN CV6 .....133 M1
Cheshunt Pl ALE/KHTH/YWD B14 .....125 J5
The Chesils COVS CV3 .....155 G7
Chessetts Gv MOS/BIL B13 .....125 L7
Chessetts Wood Rd HOCK/TIA B94 .....176 A5
Chesshire Av STRPT DY13 .....188 C5
Chesshire Cl STRPT DY13 .....188 C5
Chester Av DUNHL/THL/PER WV6 .....35 K6
Chester Cl CHWD/FDBR/MGN B37 .....110 E3
CNCK/NC WS11 .....16 F4
LICH WS13 .....21 G2
WLNHL WV13 .....52 A4
Chesterfield Ct ALDR WS9 * 40 F3
Chesterfield Rd LICHS WS14 .....20 E8
Chester Gdns SCFLD/BOLD B73 .....72 C4
Chestergate ERDE/BCHGN B24 .....91 H1
Chester Pl WSLW WS2 .....52 F4
Chester Rd LGLYGN/QTN B68 .....105 C5
Chester Rd ALDR WS9 .....41 J4
BRWNH WS8 .....103 C5
CDYHTH B64 .....103 C5
CHWD/FDBR/MGN B37 .....110 F1
CSHL/WTROR B46 .....111 J4
CVALE B35 .....91 K2
FOAKS/STRLY B74 .....55 L2
HHTH/SAND B71 .....68 F4
LICHS WS14 .....30 B2
RCOVN/BALC/EX CV7 .....129 K1
SCFLD/BOLD B73 .....72 B4
Chester Rd North BRWNH WS8 .....26 B4
FOAKS/STRLY B74 .....55 L7
KIDD DY10 .....138 E5
Chester Rd South KIDD DY10 .....164 D2
Chester St AST/WIT B6 .....89 L7
COV CV1 .....2 C1
DUNHL/THL/PER WV6 .....2 C1
RUGBYN/HIL CV21 .....187 C1
Chester Ter BEWD DY12 * 137 H8
Chesterton Cl REDE B98 .....203 H1
Chesterton Cl SOLH B91 .....127 J8
Chesterton Dr NUNW/HART CV10 .....97 K1
RLSS CV31 .....206 F3
Chesterton Rd BHTH/HG B12 .....107 M8
COVN CV6 .....133 L5
WOLVN WV10 .....36 E5
Chesterton Wy CRTAM B79 .....31 L7
Chesterwood ALDR WS9 .....55 J3
HLYWD B47 .....146 E7
Chesterwood Gdns BFLD/HDSWWD B20 .....89 H3
Chesterwood Rd MOS/BIL B13 .....125 L7
Chestnut Av CRTAM B79 .....31 M6
DUDN DY1 .....85 C2
KNWTH CV8 .....197 K2
TPTN/OCK DY4 .....67 K6
Chestnut Cl CDSL WV8 .....34 D1
CNCK/NC WS11 .....17 C3
FOAKS/STRLY B74 .....55 L3
HIA/OLT B92 .....127 H5
POL/KGSB/FAZ B78 .....60 B7
STRBR DY8 .....119 C3
Chestnut Ct CBROM B36 .....92 C6
Chestnut Crs NUNW/HART CV10 .....80 D8
ERDE/BCHGN B24 .....91 L5
GTWY WS6 .....24 B2
LICHS WS14 .....28 D8
RBRY B45 .....170 A1
RUSH/SHEL WS4 .....39 M5
WMBN WV5 .....64 D7
Chestnut Fld RUGBYN/HIL CV21 .....186 E2
Chestnut Gv CSHL/WTROR B46 .....93 L6
HRBN B17 .....106 B3
KGSWFD DY6 .....83 C2
KIDD DY11 .....137 M5
KNWTH CV8 .....183 L2
TLHL/CAN CV4 .....153 L3
Chestnut Pl BLOX/PEL WS3 .....39 H7
BLOX/PEL WS3 .....39 J7
BRGRVW B61 .....191 K1
DARL/WED WS10 .....68 E3
LGLYGN/QTN B68 .....105 C6
MOS/BIL B13 .....125 K5
Chestnuts Av LGN/SDN/BHAMAIR B26 .....109 M6
Chestnut Sq RLSN CV32 .....206 F3
Chestnuts Sdwth BDWTH CV12 .....116 C3
Chestnut Tree Av TLHL/CAN CV4 .....153 J1
Chestnut Wy BDMR/CCFT WV3 .....49 L5
Cheston Rd VAUX/NECH B7 .....89 L7
Cheswell Cl DUNHL/THL/PER WV6 .....48 F3
Cheswick Cl COVN CV6 * 134 E3
REDE B98 .....203 L2
WLNHL WV13 .....51 K5
Cheswick Wy SHLY B90 .....174 B2
Cheswood Dr WALM/CURD B76 .....73 M7
Chesworth Rd BRGRVE B60 .....191 M4
Chetland Cft HIA/OLT B92 .....128 D6
Chettle Rd BILS/COS WV14 .....67 K2
Chetton Av WOLVN WV10 .....36 C6
Chetton Gn WOLVN WV10 .....35 M2
Chetwode Cl COVW CV5 .....153 M1
Chetwood Cl DUNHL/THL/PER WV6 .....35 L8
Chetwynd Av POL/KGSB/FAZ B78 .....47 L5
Chetwynd Cl PENK ST19 .....10 D6
WSLW WS2 .....52 A2
Chetwynd Dr NUN CV11 .....99 C7
Chetwynd Gdns CNCK/NC WS11 * 16 B2
Chetwynd Pk HEDN WS12 .....13 L8
Chetwynd Rd BKHL/PFLD WV2 * 49 M7
WASH/WDE B8 .....90 C5
WNSFLD WV11 .....37 H1
Cheveley Av RBRY B45 .....143 M6
Chevening Cl SEDG DY3 .....66 C8
Cheveral Av COVN CV6 .....133 M8
Cheveral Rd BDWTH CV12 .....116 E1
Cheverel Pl NUN CV11 .....98 F2
Cheverel St NUN CV11 .....98 F2
Cheveridge Cl SOLH B91 .....148 E4

Cheverton Rd NFLD/LBR B31 ....144 C2
Cheviot TAM/AM/WIL B77 ....47 G4
Cheviot Cl NUNW/HART CV10 ....97 M2
STRPT DY13 ....188 B5
Cheviot Ri HEDN WS12 ....17 G1
RLSN CV32 ....207 G2
Cheviot Rd BKHL/PFLD WV2 ....50 D6
STRBR DY8 ....101 L7
Cheviot Wy HALE B63 ....121 H2
Cheylesmore COV CV1 ....8 F6
Cheylesmore Cl SCFLD/BOLD B73 ..72 F1
Cheyne Gdns HLGN/YWD B28 ....147 J2
Cheyne Wk BRLYHL DY5 ....102 A6
Cheyney Cl
DUNHL/THL/PER WV6 ....35 L8
Chichester Av DUDS DY2 ....85 H8
KIDDW DY11 ....138 A4
Chichester Cl NUN CV11 ....81 L6
Chichester Ct SCFLD/BOLD B73 * ..56 F8
Chichester Dr CNCK/NC WS11 ....17 G4
RIDG/WDGT B32 ....104 E8
Chichester Gv
CHWD/FDBR/MGN B37 ....110 F4
Chichester La
RWWCK/WEL CV35 ....204 C7
Chicory Dr RRUGBY CV23 ....161 H5
Chideock Hl COVS CV3 ....154 E7
Chiel Cl COVW CV5 ....153 K1
Chigwell Cl CVALE B35 ....91 L2
Chilcote Cl HLGN/YWD B28 ....147 K1
Childs Av BILS/COS WV14 ....66 E3
Childs Oak Cl
RCOVN/BALC/EX CV7 ....151 L7
Chilgrove Gdns
DUNHL/THL/PER WV6 ....35 G8
Chilham Dr
CHWD/FDBR/MGN B37 ....111 G3
Chillaton Rd COVN CV6 ....133 M3
Chillingham TAM/AM/WIL B77 ....46 A6
Chillinghome Rd CBROM B36 ....91 H5
Chillington Cl GTWY WS6 ....24 C4
Chillington Dr CDSL WV8 ....34 D1
DUDN DY1 ....84 D2
Chillington Flds WOLV WV1 ....50 E4
Chillington Pl BILS/COS WV14 ....51 G8
Chillington Rd TPTN/OCK DY4 ....68 A4
Chillington St WOLV WV1 ....3 L8
Chiltern Cl GTWY WS6 ....24 B4
HALE B63 ....121 G3
SEDG DY3 ....84 B2
STRPT DY13 ....188 B5
Chiltern Dr WLNHL WV13 ....51 H4
Chiltern Leys COVN CV6 ....8 A1
Chiltern Rd STRBR DY8 ....101 M7
TAM/AM/WIL B77 ....47 G4
The Chilterns COVW CV5 ....153 M1
Chilton Rd ALE/KHTH/YWD B14 ..147 H1
Chilwell Cl SOLH B91 ....148 F4
Chilwell Cft LOZ/NWT B19 ....89 J7
Chilworth Av WNSFLD WV11 ....37 K6
Chilworth Cl AST/WIT B6 ....89 K7
NUN CV11 ....99 J5
Chimes Cl STETCH B33 ....110 C4
Chimney Rd TPTN/OCK DY4 ....68 B6
The Chines NUNW/HART CV10 * 81 H6
Chingford Cl STRBR DY8 ....101 C1
Chingford Rd COVN CV6 ....134 E1
KGSTG B44 ....71 L5
Chinley Gv KGSTG B44 ....72 A4
Chinn Brook Rd MOS/BIL B13 ....125 M8
Chip Cl HWK/WKHTH B38 ....145 H3
Chipperfield Rd CBROM B36 ....91 J5
Chipstead Rd ERDW/GRVHL B23 ....72 B6
Chipstone Cl SOLH B91 ....149 G5
Chirbury Gv NFLD/LBR B31 ....144 F4
Chirk Cl KIDDW DY11 ....164 C3
Chirton Gv ALE/KHTH/YWD B14 ..125 H7
Chiseldon Cft
ALE/KHTH/YWD B14 ....146 E2
Chisholm Gv ACGN B27 ....127 G5
Chiswell Rd WSNGN B18 ....106 C1
Chivington Cl SHLY B90 ....148 F7
Chorley Av BKDE/SHDE B34 ....91 K6
Chorley Gdns BILS/COS WV14 ....50 F8
Chorley Rd BNTWD WS7 ....18 D4
Choyce Cl ATHST CV9 ....63 H3
Christchurch Cl EDG B15 ....106 C5
NUNW/HART CV10 ....98 D4
Christ Church Gdns LICH WS13 ....20 D6
Christ Church Gv WSL WS1 * 5 K9
Christchurch La LICH WS13 ....20 D6
Christchurch Rd COVN CV6 ....133 K7
Christine Cl DARL/WED WS10 ....68 A3
Christine Ledger Sq
RLSS CV31 * 206 E7
Christopher Rd BKHL/PFLD WV2 ....3 J9
RMSLY B62 ....122 C2
SLYOAK B29 ....124 A3
Chub TAM/AM/WIL B77 ....46 B6
Chubb St WOLV WV1 ....3 H4
Chuckery Rd WSL WS1 ....5 J4
Chudleigh Gv GTB/HAM B43 ....70 B5
Chudleigh Rd ERDW/GRVHL B23 ....90 C1
Church Av BFLD/HDSWWD B20 * ..89 G4
HAG/WOL DY9 ....141 J3
MOS/BIL B13 * 125 K2
STRBR DY8 ....101 L6
STRPT DY13 ....188 E1
Churchbridge OLDBY B69 ....86 D7
Churchbridge Pk
CNCK/NC WS11 * 16 C8
Church Cl ATHST CV9 ....61 G4
CHWD/FDBR/MGN B37 ....92 E7
HLYWD B47 ....172 D2
KNWTH CV8 ....182 F3
LICHS WS14 ....28 D8
NUNW/HART CV10 ....79 M5
POL/KGSB/FAZ B78 ....45 J8
RCOVN/BALC/EX CV7 ....96 C3
RRUGBY CV23 ....159 M2
Church Cft HALE B63 ....121 L1
HRBN B17 ....123 M1
Church Cross Vw BRLYHL DY5 ....84 B5
Churchdale Cl NUNW/HART CV10 ..98 A1
Churchdale Rd KGSTG B44 ....71 H2
Church Down Cl REDW B97 ....202 B7
Church Dr BVILLE B30 ....124 F6
POL/KGSB/FAZ B78 ....30 F6
STRPT DY13 ....188 E1
Church End RLSS CV31 ....207 J7
Churchfield Av TPTN/OCK DY4 ....67 K5
Churchfield Cl COVEN WV9 ....22 A3
VAUX/NECH B7 ....90 A7
Churchfield Rd WOLVN WV10 ....35 M5
Churchfields BRGRVW B61 ....191 K3
KIDD DY10 ....138 C6
Churchfields Cl BRGRVW B61 ....191 K2
Churchfields Gdns
BRGRVW B61 ....191 K2
Churchfields Rd BRGRVW B61 ....191 K2
DARL/WED WS10 ....68 D2
Churchfield St DUDS DY2 ....85 G5
Church Gdns SMTHWKW B67 * 105 L2
WOLVN WV10 ....50 E1
Church Gn BFLD/HDSWWD B20 ....88 D3
BILS/COS WV14 ....51 G5
Church Gn East REDW B97 ....202 C1
Church Gn West REDW B97 ....202 C1
Church Gv BFLD/HDSWWD B20 * ..88 F4
MOS/BIL B13 ....126 A8
Church Hl BRLYHL DY5 ....102 B3
CSHL/WTROR B46 ....93 L6
DARL/WED WS10 ....68 D2
ETTPK/GDPK/PENN WV4 ....65 J1
HAG/WOL DY9 ....141 H7
HEDN WS12 ....13 G8
NFLD/LBR B31 ....144 E2
REDE B98 ....195 G5
RIDG/WDGT B32 ....122 E8
RLSN CV32 ....199 J8
RLSN CV32 ....206 C5
RRUGBY CV23 ....183 K8
WSL WS1 ....5 G4
Church Hill Cl SOLH B91 ....149 G3
Church Hill Rd
BFLD/HDSWWD B20 ....88 F4
DUNHL/THL/PER WV6 ....35 H7
SOLH B91 ....149 G3
Church Hill St SMTHWKW B67 ....87 K7
Church Hill Wy REDE B98 ....195 G8
Churchill Av COVN CV6 ....134 C4
KNWTH CV8 ....179 L7
Churchill Cl OLDBY B69 ....86 A3
Churchill Dr BLKHTH/ROWR B65 ..103 M3
STRBR DY8 ....101 L6
Churchill Gdns SEDG DY3 ....66 A6
Churchill La KIDD DY10 ....139 M3
Churchill Pl STETCH B33 ....109 M4
Churchill Rd BORD B9 ....108 D3
BRGRVW B61 ....168 E4
HALE B63 ....121 K3
LICHS WS14 ....28 E8
MGN/WHC B75 ....57 L8
RUGBYS/DCH CV22 ....186 E4
SCFLD/BOLD B73 ....72 A3
WSLW WS2 ....52 C2
Church La ALDR WS9 ....41 J1
AST/WIT B6 ....89 L5
ATHST CV9 ....63 M1
BFLD/HDSWWD B20 ....88 D3
BKHL/PFLD WV2 ....2 E7
BNTWD WS7 ....27 H1
BRGRVW B61 ....191 K3
CDSL WV8 ....34 D1
CNCK/NC WS11 ....15 K5
COVE CV2 ....155 M2
COVEN WV9 ....22 A3
COVW CV5 ....132 A8
CRTAM B79 ....31 M8
CRTAM B79 ....33 J6
CSHL/WTROR B46 ....112 E1
HALE B63 ....121 M1
HHTH/SAND B71 ....68 F8
HIA/OLT B92 ....129 H4
KNWTH CV8 ....180 F7
NUNW/HART CV10 ....81 G6
NUNW/HART CV10 ....97 H4
POL/KGSB/FAZ B78 ....59 G4
POL/KGSB/FAZ B78 ....60 A8
RCOVN/BALC/EX CV7 ....96 D3
RCOVN/BALC/EX CV7 ....114 C2
RCOVN/BALC/EX CV7 ....114 F6
RCOVN/BALC/EX CV7 ....115 G6
RCOVN/BALC/EX CV7 ....116 C6
RCOVN/BALC/EX CV7 ....131 J5
RCOVN/BALC/EX CV7 ....152 A2
RLSN CV32 ....199 J7
RLSN CV32 ....206 E2
STETCH B33 ....109 K2
WALM/CURD B76 ....74 D4
WALM/CURD B76 ....74 F7
WALM/CURD B76 ....75 L7
Church Ms
RCOVN/BALC/EX CV7 * 96 C3
Church Moat Wy BLOX/PEL WS3 ..38 F5
Churchover Cl WALM/CURD B76 ..73 H7
Church Park Cl COVN CV6 ....133 K4
Church Pth RWWCK/WEL CV35 ....204 D7
Church Pl BLOX/PEL WS3 ....39 H5
Church Rd ALDR WS9 ....41 J2
AST/WIT B6 ....89 L5
ATHST CV9 ....63 M6
BDMR/CCFT WV3 ....49 J6
BILS/COS WV14 ....67 H4
BLKHTH/ROWR B65 ....104 A2
BLOX/PEL WS3 ....39 L2
BNTWD WS7 ....19 H6
BRGRVW B61 ....167 L6
BRGRVW B61 ....168 D5
BRGRVW B61 ....191 K2
BRWNH WS8 ....26 D6
CDSL WV8 ....34 D1
CNCK/NC WS11 ....15 L4
CNCK/NC WS11 ....25 J1
CSHL/WTROR B46 ....94 E3
DUDS DY2 ....84 F8
DUNHL/THL/PER WV6 ....35 J8
DUNHL/THL/PER WV6 ....48 C1
DUNHL/THL/PER WV6 ....48 F2
EDG B15 ....106 E6
ERDE/BCHGN B24 ....90 E1
HAG/WOL DY9 ....102 C8
HAG/WOL DY9 ....141 H6
HALE B63 ....103 G6
KNWTH CV8 ....181 K3
KNWTH CV8 ....182 A7
KNWTH CV8 ....182 F3
LGN/SDN/BHAMAIR B26 ....109 H7
LGN/SDN/BHAMAIR B26 ....109 J5
LGN/SDN/BHAMAIR B26 ....110 A8
LICHS WS14 ....28 D8
MOS/BIL B13 ....125 L2
NFLD/LBR B31 ....144 E2
NUNW/HART CV10 ....79 M5
NUNW/HART CV10 ....98 A2
PBAR/PBCH B42 ....71 H8
PENK ST19 ....10 C4
POL/KGSB/FAZ B78 ....47 L8
REDW B97 ....201 K3
REDW B97 ....202 C1
RRUGBY CV23 ....159 G8
SCFLD/BOLD B73 ....72 D5
SCFLD/BOLD B73 ....72 F2
SEDG DY3 ....82 C3
SHHTH WV12 ....38 B7
SHLY B90 ....147 M3
SMTHWKW B67 ....105 K1
STETCH B33 ....109 M3
STRBR DY8 ....101 H3
STRBR DY8 ....119 M2
TAM/AM/WIL B77 ....60 A1
WMBN WV5 ....64 F6
WOLVN WV10 ....23 G3
WOLVN WV10 ....36 A4
YDLY B25 ....109 J5
Church Rw ATHST CV9 * 62 A4
Churchside Vw ALDR WS9 ....40 F3
Church Sq OLDBY B69 ....86 E6
Churchstone Cl BRGRVW B61 ....168 D5
Church St ATHST CV9 ....63 H5
BILS/COS WV14 ....51 H8
BKHL/PFLD WV2 ....2 E7
BLOX/PEL WS3 ....38 F5
BLOX/PEL WS3 ....39 G5
BNTWD WS7 ....18 C8
BRGRVW B61 ....191 K3
BRLYHL DY5 ....84 B6
BRLYHL DY5 ....102 A3
BRLYHL DY5 ....102 D4
BRWNH WS8 ....26 C8
CBHAMNW B3 ....6 F4
CDYHTH B64 ....103 J4
CNCK/NC WS11 ....16 B7
CNCK/NC WS11 ....16 C4
CNCK/NC WS11 ....16 E1
COV CV1 ....9 H1
CRTAM B79 ....31 M8
DARL/WED WS10 ....52 B7
DARL/WED WS10 ....67 M1
DUDS DY2 ....85 G5
HAG/WOL DY9 ....119 L8
KIDD DY10 ....138 C7
LICH WS13 ....21 G5
LOZ/NWT B19 ....89 G6
NUN CV11 ....99 H1
OLDBY B69 ....86 E5
RLSS CV31 ....206 E6
RMSLY B62 ....104 B4
RRUGBY CV23 ....161 L8
RUGBYN/HIL CV21 ....186 E2
SEDG DY3 ....84 B2
STRBR DY8 ....101 L8
TPTN/OCK DY4 ....85 L3
WBROM B70 ....87 G1
WLNHL WV13 ....51 M3
WOLVN WV10 ....50 E1
WSL WS1 ....5 G5
WWCK CV34 ....205 J7
Church Ter MGN/WHC B75 * 57 G2
RLSS CV31 ....206 E6
STETCH B33 * 109 J4
Church V BFLD/HDSWWD B20 ....88 F4
CNCK/NC WS11 ....25 J1
HHTH/SAND B71 ....69 H7
Church Vw ALDR WS9 ....40 D2
BEWD DY12 ....162 E2
KNWTH CV8 * 182 F4
SPARK B11 ....108 A7
Church View Cl BLOX/PEL WS3 ....39 G5
Church View Dr CDYHTH B64 ....103 K4
Church Vls HDSW B21 * 88 C3
Church Wk ATHST CV9 ....63 K6
BDMR/CCFT WV3 ....49 K6
COVW CV5 ....133 G7
DUNHL/THL/PER WV6 ....35 J8
KIDDW DY11 ....138 A7
RLSS CV31 ....206 D6
RUGBYN/HIL CV21 ....186 F2
RUGBYS/DCH CV22 ....186 B5
STRPT DY13 ....188 C3
WASH/WDE B8 ....90 E7
Churchward Cl STRBR DY8 ....101 M7
Churchward Gv WMBN WV5 ....64 E5
Church Wy BDWTH CV12 ....116 F2
RUSH/SHEL WS4 ....39 M3
Churchyard Rd TPTN/OCK DY4 ....67 M8
Churnet Gv
DUNHL/THL/PER WV6 ....48 D1
Churn Hill Rd ALDR WS9 ....54 E1
Churns Hill La SEDG DY3 ....82 F2
Churston Cl BLOX/PEL WS3 ....38 E2
Chylds Ct COVW CV5 ....132 E8
Cider Av BRLYHL DY5 ....102 C5
Cinder Bank DUDS DY2 ....85 G7
Cinder Rd BNTWD WS7 ....18 C6
SEDG DY3 ....83 M4
Cinder Wy DARL/WED WS10 ....68 C2
Cinquefoil Leasow
TPTN/OCK DY4 ....68 A7
The Circle NUNW/HART CV10 ....98 C1
Circuit Cl WLNHL WV13 ....51 M2
Circular Rd ACGN B27 ....127 G4
Circus Av
CHWD/FDBR/MGN B37 ....111 G3
Cirencester Cl BRGRVE B60 ....191 M3
City Ar LICH WS13 * 20 F6
City Plaza CBHAM B2 * 7 G5
City Rd LDYWD/EDGR B16 ....106 A3
OLDBY B69 ....85 M6
City Vw WASH/WDE B8 ....108 B1
Civic Cl CBHAMW B1 ....6 C5
Claerwen Av STRPT DY13 ....163 J6
Claerwen Gv NFLD/LBR B31 ....123 J8
Claines Crs KIDD DY10 ....138 F7
Claines Rd HALE B63 ....103 H8
NFLD/LBR B31 ....145 G1
Clandon Cl ALE/KHTH/YWD B14 ..145 M3
Clanfield Av WNSFLD WV11 ....37 K5
Clapgate Gdns
ETTPK/GDPK/PENN WV4 ....66 E2
Clap Gate Gv WMBN WV5 ....64 C7
Clapgate La RIDG/WDGT B32 ....123 G3
Clap Gate Rd WMBN WV5 ....64 C6
Clapham Sq RLSS CV31 ....206 F6
Clapham St RLSS CV31 ....206 F7
Clapham Ter RLSS CV31 ....206 F6
Clapton Gv KGSTG B44 ....71 M4
Clara St COVE CV2 ....155 L3
Clare Av WNSFLD WV11 ....37 K4
Clare Cl RLSN CV32 ....207 G3
Clare Ct RUGBYN/HIL CV21 ....186 D2
Clare Crs
ETTPK/GDPK/PENN WV4 ....66 D3
Clare Dr EDG B15 ....106 D5
Clarel Av WASH/WDE B8 ....108 A2
Claremont Cl BDWTH CV12 ....117 M1
Claremont Ms BDMR/CCFT WV3 ....49 L6
Claremont Pl WSNGN B18 * 88 E8
Claremont Rd BDMR/CCFT WV3 ....49 L6
CRTAM B79 ....31 K5
RLSS CV31 ....206 E7
RUGBYN/HIL CV21 ....187 G2
SEDG DY3 ....66 C5
SMTHWK B66 ....105 M1
SPARK B11 ....107 M6
WSNGN B18 ....88 E7
Claremont St BILS/COS WV14 ....51 G7
CDYHTH B64 ....103 J4
Claremont Wk COVW CV5 ....133 G7
Claremont Wy HALE B63 ....121 L2
Clarence Av HDSW B21 * 88 A5
Clarence Gdns FOAKS/STRLY B74 ..56 D3
Clarence Rd BILS/COS WV14 ....51 J6
DUDS DY2 ....85 H7
ERDW/GRVHL B23 ....90 B2
FOAKS/STRLY B74 ....42 C8
HDSW B21 ....88 A5
HRBN B17 ....106 B7
MOS/BIL B13 ....125 L5
RUGBYN/HIL CV21 ....186 C2
SPARK B11 ....126 A1
WOLV WV1 ....2 E4
Clarence St COV CV1 ....9 K2
KIDD DY10 ....138 D7
NUN CV11 ....98 F1
RLSS CV31 ....206 E7
SEDG DY3 ....66 C8
WOLV WV1 ....2 E5
Clarence Ter RLSN CV32 * 206 D4
Clarence Wy BEWD DY12 ....162 F1
Clarenden Pl HRBN B17 ....106 A8
Clarendon Av RLSN CV32 ....206 D4
Clarendon Cl REDW B97 ....193 M8
Clarendon Ct RLSN CV32 * 206 D4
Clarendon Crs RLSN CV32 ....206 C4
Clarendon Dr TPTN/OCK DY4 ....68 B5
Clarendon Pl BLOX/PEL WS3 ....39 K1
RLSN CV32 ....206 C4
RMSLY B62 ....104 D7
Clarendon Rd KNWTH CV8 ....197 L2
LDYWD/EDGR B16 ....106 C4
MGN/WHC B75 ....57 G2
RUSH/SHEL WS4 ....40 A3
SMTHWKW B67 ....105 K1
Clarendon Sq RLSN CV32 ....206 D4
Clarendon St BDMR/CCFT WV3 ....2 B5
BLOX/PEL WS3 ....38 F4
COVW CV5 ....154 D4
RLSN CV32 ....206 E4
Clare Rd BLOX/PEL WS3 ....39 K7
WOLVN WV10 ....36 C6
Clare's Ct KIDDW DY11 ....138 A7
Clarewell Av SOLH B91 ....148 E4
Clarion Wy CNCK/NC WS11 ....12 C8
Clarke's Av HEDN WS12 ....12 E4
KNWTH CV8 ....197 L2
Clarkes Gv TPTN/OCK DY4 ....68 A7
Clarke's La HHTH/SAND B71 ....69 G6
WLNHL WV13 ....52 A3
Clarke St REDW B97 ....202 C1
Clark Rd BDMR/CCFT WV3 ....49 K3
Clarkson Rd DARL/WED WS10 ....68 E2
Clark St COVN CV6 ....134 E4
LDYWD/EDGR B16 ....106 D3
STRBR DY8 ....101 J8
Clarry Dr FOAKS/STRLY B74 ....56 D5
Clary Gv DSYBK/YTR WS5 ....69 L2
Clatterbach La HAG/WOL DY9 ....141 L1
Clattercut La DROIT WR9 ....166 D8
Claughton Ct KIDDW DY11 ....138 A8
Claughton Rd DUDS DY2 ....85 H4
Claughton Rd North DUDS DY2 ....85 H4
Claughton St KIDDW DY11 ....138 A8
Clausen Cl GTB/HAM B43 ....71 J1
Clavedon Cl NFLD/LBR B31 ....123 J6
Claverdon Cl BRWNH WS8 ....26 E5
SOLH B91 ....148 C1
Claverdon Dr FOAKS/STRLY B74 ....55 M1
GTB/HAM B43 ....70 B5
Claverdon Gdns ACGN B27 ....108 F8
Claverdon Rd COVW CV5 ....153 M2
Claverley Dr
ETTPK/GDPK/PENN WV4 ....49 H8
Clay Av NUN CV11 ....81 K6
Claybrook Dr STUD B80 ....203 K6
Claybrook St DIG/EDG B5 ....7 G8
Claycroft Ter DUDN DY1 ....66 F7
Claydon Gv ALE/KHTH/YWD B14 ..146 E2
RWWCK/WEL CV35 ....204 C2
Claydon Rd KGSWFD DY6 ....83 G4
Clay Dr RIDG/WDGT B32 ....104 E8
Claygate Rd HEDN WS12 ....17 J2
Clayhanger La BRWNH WS8 ....26 B7
Clayhanger Rd BRWNH WS8 ....26 D7
Clayhill La RRUGBY CV23 ....159 K6
Clay La COVE CV2 ....155 L1
COVW CV5 ....132 C1
LGN/SDN/BHAMAIR B26 ....127 J1
OLDBY B69 ....104 E1
Claymore TAM/AM/WIL B77 ....46 B7
Claypit Cl WBROM B70 ....86 E2
Claypit La BRGRVW B61 ....168 C4
Clay Pit La LICHS WS14 ....28 D1
SHLY B90 ....147 L8
Claypit La WBROM B70 ....86 E2
Clay St PENK ST19 ....10 C4
Clayton Cl BKHL/PFLD WV2 ....50 A6
Clayton Dr BRGRVE B60 ....191 M6
CBROM B36 ....92 A5
Clayton Rd BILS/COS WV14 ....66 F6
COVN CV6 ....133 J8
WASH/WDE B8 ....90 B8
Clear Vw KGSWFD DY6 ....82 F7
Clearwell Gdns DUDN DY1 ....84 D2
Cleasby TAM/AM/WIL B77 ....47 G4
Clee Av KIDDW DY11 ....164 A3
Clee Hill Dr BDMR/CCFT WV3 ....48 D4
Clee Hill Rd SEDG DY3 ....84 A1
Clee Rd DUDS DY2 ....84 E6
LGLYGN/QTN B68 ....105 G1
NFLD/LBR B31 ....144 E5
STRBR DY8 ....101 L7
Cleeton St HEDN WS12 ....17 H4
Cleeve TAM/AM/WIL B77 ....46 B2
Cleeve Cl REDE B98 ....195 H8
STRPT DY13 ....188 B5
Cleeve Dr FOAKS/STRLY B74 ....42 D7
Cleeve Rd ALE/KHTH/YWD B14 ....147 G1
BLOX/PEL WS3 ....38 D2
Cleeves Av RLSS CV31 ....206 B7
Cleeve Wy BLOX/PEL WS3 ....38 D3
Clee View Meadow SEDG DY3 ....66 B3
Clee View Rd WMBN WV5 ....64 C8
Clematis TAM/AM/WIL B77 ....46 D2
Clematis Dr COVEN WV9 ....35 K2
Clemens St RLSS CV31 ....206 E6
Clement Pl BILS/COS WV14 * 51 H6
Clement Rd BILS/COS WV14 ....51 H6
RMSLY B62 ....104 B4
Clements Cl OLDBY B69 ....104 D1
Clements Rd YDLY B25 ....109 H5
Clements St COVE CV2 ....155 L2
Clement St CBHAMW B1 ....6 B4
NUN CV11 ....98 F2
WSLW WS2 ....4 C5
Clement Wy RUGBYS/DCH CV22 ..185 L5
Clemson St WLNHL WV13 ....51 L3
Clennon Ri COVE CV2 ....135 H5
Clensmore St KIDD DY10 ....138 B6
Clent Av KIDDW DY11 ....163 M4
REDW B97 ....202 B6
Clent Dr HAG/WOL DY9 ....120 A7
NUNW/HART CV10 ....97 M2
Clent Hill Dr BLKHTH/ROWR B65 ....85 L8
Clent Rd HDSW B21 ....88 B4
LGLYGN/QTN B68 ....105 G5
RBRY B45 ....143 J5
STRBR DY8 ....101 L7
Clent View Rd HALE B63 ....121 G1
RIDG/WDGT B32 ....122 E4
STRBR DY8 ....119 G3
Clent Vls BHTH/HG B12 * 125 M1
Cleobury Cl REDW B97 ....193 M8
Cleobury La HOCK/TIA B94 ....173 L2
Cleobury Rd BEWD DY12 ....162 C3
Cleton St TPTN/OCK DY4 ....85 M2
Clevedon Av CBROM B36 ....92 C4
Clevedon Rd BHTH/HG B12 ....107 J7
Cleveland Cl WLNHL WV13 ....51 H4
WNSFLD WV11 ....37 K4
Cleveland Dr CNCK/NC WS11 ....16 F1
RBRY B45 ....169 L3
Cleveland Pas BKHL/PFLD WV2 ....2 F6
Cleveland Rd BDWTH CV12 ....117 M2
BKHL/PFLD WV2 ....3 H7
COVE CV2 ....155 L1
Cleveland St BKHL/PFLD WV2 ....2 F6
DUDN DY1 ....84 F4
STRBR DY8 ....119 J1
Cleveley Dr NUNW/HART CV10 ....80 B6
Cleves Crs GTWY WS6 ....24 B4
Cleves Dr RBRY B45 ....143 J6
Cleves Rd RBRY B45 ....143 J5
Clewley Dr COVEN WV9 ....35 L2
Clewley Gv RIDG/WDGT B32 ....104 F8
Clews Cl WSL WS1 4
Clewshaw La HWK/WKHTH B38 ..171
Clews Rd REDE B98 202
Cley Cl DIG/EDG B5 107
Clifden Gv KNWTH CV8 180
Cliffe Dr STETCH B33 109
Cliffe Rd RLSN CV32 206
Cliffe Wy WWCK CV34 205
Cliff Hall La POL/KGSB/FAZ B78 59
Clifford Bridge Rd COVE CV2 156
COVS CV3 156
Clifford Rd DOR/KN B93 175
SMTHWKW B67 105
WBROM B70 86
Clifford St DUDN DY1 84
DUNHL/THL/PER WV6 2
LOZ/NWT B19 89
TAM/AM/WIL B77 46
Clifford Wk LOZ/NWT B19 89
Cliff Rock Rd RBRY B45 143
Clift Av SHHTH WV12 38
Clift Cl SHHTH WV12 38
Clifton Av ALDR WS9 41
BRWNH WS8 26
CNCK/NC WS11 16
CRTAM B79 31
Clifton Cl AST/WIT B6 89
OLDBY B69 104
REDE B98 203
Clifton Crs SHLY B90 148
Clifton Gdns CDSL WV8 35
Clifton Gn HLGN/YWD B28 126
Clifton La CRTAM B79 32
HHTH/SAND B71 69
Clifton Rd AST/WIT B6 89
BHTH/HG B12 107
CBROM B36 92
DUNHL/THL/PER WV6 35
KIDD DY10 139
KIDDW DY11 163
NUNW/HART CV10 98
RMSLY B62 104
RUGBYN/HIL CV21 186
RUGBYN/HIL CV21 187
SCFLD/BOLD B73 72
SMTHWKW B67 105
Clifton St BDMR/CCFT WV3 2
BILS/COS WV14 66
CDYHTH B64 103
COV CV1 9
STRBR DY8 119
Clifton Ter ERDW/GRVHL B23 * 90
Clinic Dr HAG/WOL DY9 102
NUN CV11 99
Clinton Av KNWTH CV8 179
RWWCK/WEL CV35 204
Clinton Crs BNTWD WS7 18
Clinton Gv SHLY B90 148
Clinton La KNWTH CV8 179
Clinton Rd BILS/COS WV14 51
COVN CV6 134
CSHL/WTROR B46 93
SHLY B90 148
Clinton St RLSS CV31 206
WSNGN B18 88
Clipper Vw LDYWD/EDGR B16 106
Clipstone Rd COVN CV6 133
Clipston Rd WASH/WDE B8 90
Clissold Cl BHTH/HG B12 107
Clissold Pas WSNGN B18 106
Clissold St WSNGN B18 106
Clive Cl MGN/WHC B75 57
Cliveden Av ALDR WS9 40
PBAR/PBCH B42 89
Cliveden Coppice
FOAKS/STRLY B74 56
Cliveden Wk NUN CV11 99
Clivedon Wy CDYHTH B64 103
Cliveland St CBHAMNE B4 7
Clive Rd BNTWD WS7 18
BRGRVE B60 191
RCOVN/BALC/EX CV7 152
REDW B97 194
RIDG/WDGT B32 105
Clive St HHTH/SAND B71 69
Clockfields Dr STRBR DY8 101
Clock La HIA/OLT B92 129
Clockmill Av BLOX/PEL WS3 39
Clockmill Pl BLOX/PEL WS3 39
Clockmill Rd BLOX/PEL WS3 39
Clodeshall Rd WASH/WDE B8 108
Cloister Cft COVE CV2 135
Cloister Crofts RLSN CV32 206
Cloister Dr RMSLY B62 122
The Cloisters RUSH/SHEL WS4 5
Cloister Wy RLSN CV32 206
Clonmel Rd BVILLE B30 124
Clopton Crs
CHWD/FDBR/MGN B37 111
Clopton Rd STETCH B33 110
The Close DARL/WED WS10 68
HALE B63 103
HIA/OLT B92 127
HLYWD B47 146
HRBN B17 105
KNWTH CV8 157
LICH WS13 20
RLSS CV31 206
RMSLY B62 121
SEDG DY3 82
SEDG DY3 84
SLYOAK B29 * 124
Clothier Gdns WLNHL WV13 51
Clothier St WLNHL WV13 51
Cloud Br KNWTH CV8 181
Cloudbridge Dr HIA/OLT B92 128
Cloud Gn TLHL/CAN CV4 154
Cloudsley Gv HIA/OLT B92 127
Clovelly Gdns COVE CV2 135
Clovelly Rd COVE CV2 134
Clovelly Wy NUN CV11 81
Clover Av
CHWD/FDBR/MGN B37 111
Clover Cl RRUGBY CV23 161
Cloverdale DUNHL/THL/PER WV6 ..48
Cloverdale Cl
RCOVN/BALC/EX CV7 133
Clover Dr RIDG/WDGT B32 123
Clover Hl DSYBK/YTR WS5 54
Clover La KGSWFD DY6 82
Clover Lea Sq WASH/WDE B8 90
Clover Ley WOLVN WV10 3
Clover Mdw HEDN WS12 17
Clover Piece TPTN/OCK DY4 68
Clover Rdg GTWY WS6 24
Clover Rd SLYOAK B29 123
Cloweswood La HOCK/TIA B94 173
Club La WOLVN WV10 22
Club Rw SEDG DY3 66
Club Vw HWK/WKHTH B38 145
Clunbury Cft BKDE/SHDE B34 91
Clunbury Rd NFLD/LBR B31 144
Clun Cl DUDS DY2 8
Clunes Av NUN CV11 8
Clun Rd NFLD/LBR B31 1
Clyde Av RMSLY B62 10
Clyde Ms BRLYHL DY5 8
Clyde Rd BDWTH CV12 1
DOR/KN B93 17

esdale
 GN/SDN/BHAMAIR B26 ....109 L8
esdale Rd RIDG/WDGT B32 ....104 F7
.E BHTH/HG B12 ....7 L8
OYHTH B64 ....103 J4
bourne Gdns HALE B63 ....103 G8
bourn La RUSH/SHEL WS4 ....40 A5
heath La RUSH/SHEL WS4 ....40 A5
pit Fields Rd BDWTH CV12 ......117 G8
pit La KNWTH CV8 ....184 A1
Pool La BLOX/PEL WS3 ....39 K6
port Rd WOLV WV1 ....50 E4
way Av BDMR/CCFT WV3 ....49 L7
way Gdns BDMR/CCFT WV3 ....49 H7
OX/PEL WS3 ....38 E5
bett Rd BNTWD WS7 ....18 A6
Cobbles CSCFLD/WYGN B72 ....75 G8
ole Wk WSNGN B18 * 88 E8
La RD KNWTH CV31 ....179 H7
den Av RLSS CV31 ....207 C8
den Cl DARL/WED WS10 ....52 D7
den St COVN CV1 ....134 C8
ARL/WED WS10 ....52 D7
DDW DY11 ....138 A7
RTBR DY8 ....101 H7
DDW DY11 ....164 C1
TRBR DY8 ....119 L3
nam Cl BRGRVE B60 ....191 K2
ALE B35 ....91 K2
am Court Ms
 JGBYN/HIL CV21 ....187 L5
kermouth Ct RLSN CV32 ....206 B3
.E Hill La RBRY B45 ....143 K6
sheds La RMSLY B62 ....104 A5
kshunt Hl
.LE/KHTH/YWD B14 ....125 H8
ksparrow La CNCK/NC WS11 ....15 L1
ksparrow St W WWCK CV34 ....205 H4
kspur St POL/KGSB/FAZ B78 ......47 J6
kthorpe Cl D HRBN B17 ....105 K6
sall Gdns CDSL WV8 ....34 C1
sall Rd CDSL WV8 ....35 G4
DYHTH B64 ....103 J5
wood Rd BHTH/HG B12 ....35 J6
eld NFLD/LBR B31 ....72 D4
on Church La RBRY B45 ....170 B3
on Ct REDW B97 ....193 M8
on Crs NFLD/LBR B31 ....144 C7
on Lake Rd RBRY B45 ....170 A2
on St WBROM B70 ....86 E8
eland Pl CDYHTH B64 ....103 H5
on Cl NUNW/HART CV10 ....50 C1
kton St WOLVN WV10 ....97 J1
burne Grove Dr
.LSN CV32 ....206 B3
bourne Rd
.OL/KGSB/FAZ B78 ....45 L3
and Gv EDG B15 ....85 L1
hester St COV CV1 ....9 J3
bath Rd MOS/BIL B13 ....125 M5
field Dr REDE B98 ....202 D3
ridge Cl HRBN B17 ....105 G3
PARK B11 ....108 B7
by Cl TLHL/CAN CV4 ....153 H7
Ct CHWD/FDBR/MGN B37 ....110 F3
ford Cl REDW B97 ....201 L3
ford Dr
HWD/FDBR/MGN B37 ....110 E3
Gn SHLY B90 ....147 H3
. Hall La BKDE/SHDE B34 ....92 B7
hill CRTAM B79 ....31 M8
hurst Cft SHLY B90 ....148 D7
man Rd DARL/WED WS10 ....52 E8
man St
UNHL/THL/PER WV6 ....49 K1
.L/CAN CV4 ....153 K6
meadow Rd
SHL/WTROR B46 ....93 K6
OS/BIL B13 ....125 M8
nso Rd SMTHWK B66 ....106 A1
raine Cl BLOX/PEL WS3 * 25 L3
ridge Cl BLOX/PEL WS3 * 25 L2
RDW B97 ....202 A5
HHTH WV12 ....38 C6
ridge Dr
UNHL/THL/PER WV6 ....48 C1
.L/CAN CV4 ....153 K6
B/HAM B43 ....70 C6
sbourne Av
.LE/KHTH/YWD B14 ....146 A3
sbourne Rd HIA/OLT B92 ....127 M2
shill Cl REDW B97 ....202 A8
shill Heath Rd
HWD/FDBR/MGN B37 ....111 G7
shill Rd ATHST CV9 ....62 D8
HST CV9 ....78 D4
/SDE B46 ....91 K6
hill Rd
.L/FDBR/MGN B37 ....110 E8
/SDE B46 ....92 F3
.L/WTROR B46 ....94 B3
/WTROR B46 ....94 C8
/WHC B75 ....57 H8

POL/KGSB/FAZ B78 ....45 L6
WALM/CURD B76 ....75 G8
Coleshill St CBHAMNE B4 ....7 J3
MGN/WHC B75 ....57 G8
Coleside Av MOS/BIL B13 ......126 B6
Coles La CSCFLD/WYGN B72 .....73 G2
HHTH/SAND B71 ....68 A3
The Colesleys CSHL/WTROR B46..93 L7
Cole St DUDS DY2 ....103 J1
Cole Valley Rd HLGN/YWD B28 126 B7
Coleview Crs STETCH B33 ......110 C2
Coleville Rd WALM/CURD B76 ...73 M7
Coleys La NFLD/LBR B31 ....144 E3
Colgrave Av MOS/BIL B13 ......126 B6
Colina Cl COVS CV3 ....156 A8
Colindale Rd KGSTG B44 ....71 K2
Colinwood Cl GTWY WS6 ....24 D4
Colledge Cl RRUGBY CV23 .....158 B2
Colledge Rd COVN CV6 ....134 B4
Colleen Av BVILLE B30 ....145 M2
College Cl DARL/WED WS10 .....68 E3
College Dr BFLD/HDSWWD B20 ...88 D3
RLSN CV32 ....206 D3
College Farm Dr
 ERDW/GRVHL B23 ....72 B5
College Gv BFLD/HDSWWD B20 *...88 C7
College Hl SCFLD/BOLD B73 ....72 F1
College La CRTAM B79 ....31 M8
KNWTH CV8 ....177 M1
College Rd BFLD/HDSWWD B20 ...88 D3
BRGRVE B60 ....191 L5
DUNHL/THL/PER WV6 ....49 H1
KGSTG B44 ....71 J3
MOS/BIL B13 ....126 A5
RMSLY B62 ....104 E7
SCFLD/BOLD B73 ....72 B4
STRBR DY8 ....119 L1
WASH/WDE B8 ....108 C2
College St NUNW/HART CV10 ....98 F3
WSNGN B18 ....106 E1
College Vw
 DUNHL/THL/PER WV6 ....49 K1
College Wk BRGRVE B60 ....191 L5
Collet Rd COV CV2 ....135 K7
Collets Brook MGN/WHC B75 ....57 L3
Collett TAM/AM/WIL B77 ....46 E4
Collett St STRBR DY8 ....101 L7
Colletts Gv
 CHWD/FDBR/MGN B37 ....110 F3
Collett Wk COV CV1 * 8 C2
KNWTH CV8 * 197 K1
Colley Av WOLVN WV10 ....36 E7
Colley La HALE B63 ....103 G2
Colley Orch HALE B63 ....103 G2
Colley St WBROM B70 ....87 H1
Collier Cl BRWNH WS8 ....26 A6
GTWY WS6 ....24 C3
Colliers Cl SHHTH WV12 ....37 M7
Colliers Fold RCOVN/BALC/EX CV7..115 J8
Colliery Dr BLOX/PEL WS3 .....38 D7
Colliery La RCOVN/BALC/EX CV7..116 F4
Colliery Rd HHTH/SAND B71 ....87 L1
WOLV WV1 ....3 M5
Collindale Ct KGSWFD DY6 .....83 H4
Collingbourne Av
 LGN/SDN/BHAMAIR B26 ....110 A7
Colling Wk
 CHWD/FDBR/MGN B37 ....92 B3
Collingwood Av
 RUGBYS/DCH CV22 ....186 A4
Collingwood Dr GTB/HAM B43 ...71 H2
Collingwood Rd COVW CV5 .....133 H4
WOLVN WV10 ....36 C3
Collins Cl RIDG/WDGT B32 ....104 B3
Collins Gv TLHL/CAN CV4 .....154 B8
Collins Hl LICH WS13 ....20 C1
Collinson Cl REDE B98 ....202 E4
Collins Rd BRWNH WS8 ....26 B7
DARL/WED WS10 ....68 F2
WWCK CV34 ....206 B8
Collins St WBROM B70 ....86 C2
WSL WS1 ....4 F9
Collis Cl BRGRVE B60 ....191 M5
Collis St STRBR DY8 ....101 L5
Collister Cl SHLY B90 ....126 F8
Columbine Cl DSYBK/YTR WS5...82 K2
Colly Cft CHWD/FDBR/MGN B37..92 C4
Collycroft Pl ACGN/QTN B68 ...88 A4
Colman Av WNSFLD WV11 ....37 K7
Colman Hl HALE B63 ....103 H8
Colman Hill Av HALE B63 .....103 H8
Colmers Wk NFLD/LBR B31 .....144 B4
Colmore Av
 ALE/KHTH/YWD B14 ....125 H6
Colmore Circus Queensway
 CBHAMNE B4 ....7 G3
Colmore Dr MOS/BIL B13 ......125 M4
Colmore Flats LOZ/NWT B19 * ...6 F1
Colmore Rd
 ALE/KHTH/YWD B14 ....125 H6
Colmore Rw CBHAMNW B3 ....6 F4
Coln Cl NFLD/LBR B31 ....123 K7
Colonial Rd BORD B9 ....108 D3
Colshaw Rd STRBR DY8 ....119 J1
Colston Rd ERDE/BCHGN B24 ...90 F2
Colt Cl FOAKS/STRLY B74 .....55 L6
Coltham Rd SHHTH WV12 ....38 B7
Coltishall Cft CVALE B35 .....91 K3
Coltman Cl LICHS WS14 ....21 H6
Coltsfoot Cl WNSFLD WV11 ....37 J8
Colts La REDE B98 ....203 H2
Columbia Cl DIG/EDG B5 ......107 H7
Columbia Gdns BDWTH CV12 ...117 H7
Columbian Crs BNTWD WS7 .....18 D5
Columbian Dr CNCK/NC WS11 ...16 C2
Columbine Wy BDWTH CV12 ....116 C4

Commainge Cl WWCK CV34 .....205 H6
Commerce Dr PENK ST19 ....10 C6
Commercial Rd WOLV WV1 ....3 K6
WSLW WS2 ....38 E6
Commercial St CBHAMW B1 ......6 D7
WSLW WS2 ....38 E6
Common Barn La KIDD DY10 ....118 B6
Common La CNCK/NC WS11 ....16 E2
KNWTH CV8 ....179 M6
LGN/SDN/BHAMAIR B26 ....109 L8
LICHS WS14 ....20 C3
POL/KGSB/FAZ B78 ....47 L5
RCOVN/BALC/EX CV7 ....114 C6
STUD B80 ....203 M2
WASH/WDE B8 ....90 D7
Common Rd WMBN WV5 ....82 D1
BLOX/PEL WS3 ....84 A7
Commonside BLOX/PEL WS3 ......39 L3
BRLYHL DY5 ....84 A7
Common Side BRWNH WS8 ....26 B8
RUGE 18 E2
The Common ATHST CV9 ....62 A4
Common Vw BNTWD WS7 ....18 B3
HEDN WS12 ....12 F6
Common Wy COVE CV2 ....134 E7
Communication Rw EDG B15 .....6 C8
Compton Cl REDE B98 ....202 C3
RLSN CV32 ....207 C3
SOLH B91 ....148 B5
Compton Cft
 CHWD/FDBR/MGN B37 ....111 H4
Compton Dr DUDS DY2 ....85 J9
FOAKS/STRLY B74 ....55 J6
KGSWFD DY6 ....83 H8
Compton Gv HALE B63 ....120 C1
KGSWFD DY6 ....83 H8
Compton Hill Dr
 BDMR/CCFT WV3 ....49 H3
Compton Rd BDMR/CCFT WV3 ....49 H3
CDYHTH B64 ....103 C4
COVN CV6 ....134 B3
CRTAM B79 ....31 K6
ERDE/BCHGN B24 ....90 C4
HAG/WOL DY9 ....120 B4
RMSLY B62 ....104 D8
Compton Rd West
 BDMR/CCFT WV3 ....49 H3
Comrie Cl COVE CV2 ....135 K7
Comsey Rd CBHAMNE B4 ....70 F2
Comwall Cl BLOX/PEL WS3 .....39 L3
Comyn St RLSN CV32 * 206 F4
Conchar Cl CSCFLD/WYGN B72 73 G2
Conchar Rd CSCFLD/WYGN B72 73 G2
Concorde Rd
 LGN/SDN/BHAMAIR B26 ....129 C1
Condor Gv CNCK/NC WS11 ......17 G4
Condover Cl WALM/CURD B76 ...73 H6
Condover Rd NFLD/LBR B31 ....144 F5
Conduit Rd CNCK/NC WS11 .....15 L1
Coneyford Rd BKDE/SHDE B34...92 A7
Coney Gn STRBR DY8 ....101 M8
Coney Green Dr NFLD/LBR B31..144 F5
Coneygree Rd TPTN/OCK DY4 ...85 L2
Congleton Cl COVN CV6 ....134 C3
Congreve St CBHAMNW B3 ....6 F4
Congreve Wk WWCK CV34 ......205 K3
Conifer Cl BDWTH CV12 ....117 G1
BRLYHL DY5 ....102 A5
HEDN WS12 ....12 E5
Conifer Dr HDSW B21 ....88 C6
NFLD/LBR B31 ....144 F2
Conifer Gv BRGRVW B61 ....191 K2
RLSS CV31 ....206 B8
Conifer Paddock COVS CV3 ....156 C4
RMSLY B62 ....104 D8
Conifer Rd FOAKS/STRLY B74 ..55 J5
Coningsby Cl RLSS CV31 ......207 C7
Coningsby Dr KIDDW DY11 .....137 H5
Coniston TAM/AM/WIL B77 ......46 F6
Coniston Av HIA/OLT B92 .....127 K1
Coniston Cl BRGRVE B60 ......191 M4
HLGN/YWD B28 ....126 D6
RUGBYN/HIL CV21 ....161 H7
Coniston Crs GTB/HAM B43 ....70 D6
STRPT DY13 ....163 K7
Coniston Dr COWW CV5 ....153 H1
KGSWFD DY6 ....82 F6
Coniston Rd COWW CV5 ....154 D4
DUNHL/THL/PER WV6 ....35 H5
ERDW/GRVHL B23 ....72 B3
FOAKS/STRLY B74 ....55 J5
SOLH B91 * 127 L6
WNSFLD WV11 ....37 L4
Coniston Wy BEWD DY12 ....162 D2
CNCK/NC WS11 ....16 C4
NUN CV11 ....81 K6
Connaught Av DARL/WED WS10...69 G2
KIDDW DY11 ....164 A3
Connaught Cl DSYBK/YTR WS5...54 A6
Connaught Dr WMBN WV5 ....64 E4
Connaught Rd BILS/COS WV14...51 K6
BRGRVE B60 ....192 A4
WOLV WV1 ....3 G1
Connops Wy HAG/WOL DY9 .....102 C8
Connor Rd HHTH/SAND B71 .....143 M4
Conolly Dr RBRY B45 ....143 M4
Conrad Cl BHTH/HG B12 ....107 L6
RUGBYS/DCH CV22 ....186 D7
Conrad Rd COVN CV6 ....133 L6
Consort Crs BRLYHL DY5 ......84 A7
Consort Dr DARL/WED WS10 ....52 A5
Consort Rd BVILLE B30 ....145 L2
Constable Cl BDWTH CV12 .....98 E8
GTB/HAM B43 ....71 H3
Constable Rd RUGBYN/HIL CV21..187 M4
The Constables
 LGLYGN/QTN B68 ....104 F3
Constance Av WBROM B70 ......87 H4
Constance Cl
 RCOVN/BALC/EX CV7 ....116 D5
BDWTH CV12 DIG/EDG B5 ....107 H8
Constantine La
 CSHL/WTROR B46 ....93 K4
Constantine Wy BILS/COS WV14..67 L3
Constitution Hl DUDS DY2 ....85 H5
DIG/EDG B5 ....7 G8
Consul Rd RUGBYN/HIL CV21 ..160 E7
Containerbase
 PBAR/PBCH B42 * 71 K3
Convent Cft ATHST CV9 ....63 K6
BKHL/PFLD WV2 ....50 A5
CNCK/NC WS11 ....16 B5
KNWTH CV8 ....179 L6
Convent La ATHST CV9 ....63 J6
Convent Rd DARL/WED WS10 ....68 E2
Conway Av HHTH/SAND B71 .....68 F4
LGLYGN/QTN B68 ....104 F3
RIDG/WDGT B32 ....104 C1
TLHL/CAN CV4 ....153 G1
Conway Cl DUDN DY1 ....67 G7
KGSWFD DY6 ....83 K1
SHLY B90 ....148 B1
Conway Crs BDWTH CV12 ......116 F1
Conway Rd BRGRVE B60 ....191 M4
CHWD/FDBR/MGN B37 ....110 B3
CNCK/NC WS11 ....15 M5
DUNHL/THL/PER WV6 ....48 D4
RLSN CV32 ....206 F3
SHLY B90 ....148 B1

SPARK B11 ....108 A7
Conwy Cl NUN CV11 ....99 H2
WSLW WS2 ....52 E1
Conybere St BHTH/HG B12 .....107 K6
Conyworth Cl ACGN B27 ....127 K1
Cook Cl COVN CV6 ....134 E1
DOR/KN B93 ....150 A7
Cooke Cl DUDS DY2 ....85 H6
DUNHL/THL/PER WV6 ....48 C1
RUGBYN/HIL CV21 ....161 G6
Cooke Ct COV CV2 ....205 A3
WWCK CV34 ....205 K3
Cookes Cl NFLD/LBR B31 ......145 G3
Cookesley Dr GTB/HAM B43 ....71 H1
Cooke St BKHL/PFLD WV2 ......50 B6
Cookley Cl HALE B63 ....121 K3
Cooknell Dr STRBR DY8 ....101 J3
Cook Rd BLOX/PEL WS3 ....39 H3
Cooks Cl ATHST CV9 ....62 A5
Cooksey La KGSTG B44 ....71 K1
Cooksey Rd SMHTH B10 ....107 M5
Cooks La ATHST CV9 ....62 A3
STETCH B33 ....91 J8
Cook St COV CV1 ....9 H2
DARL/WED WS10 ....52 D7
VAUX/NECH B7 ....90 A6
Coombe Av COVS CV3 ....156 A6
Coombe Cl COVEN WV9 * 35 L2
Coombe Dr COVS CV3 ....157 G8
Coombe Hl CDYHTH B64 ....103 K6
Coombe Pk FOAKS/STRLY B74 ...56 D6
Coombe Park Rd COVS CV3 ....156 F6
Coombe Rd
 BFLD/HDSWWD B20 ....89 J4
SHLY B90 ....126 F8
Coombes La NFLD/LBR B31 ....144 D7
Coombe St COVS CV3 ....156 A6
Coombs Rd RMSLY B62 ....103 M7
Co-operative St COVE CV2 ....134 F2
Cooper Av BRLYHL DY5 ....101 L3
Cooper Cl WBROM B70 ....87 J3
Cooper's Bank Rd BRLYHL DY5...84 A4
Coopers Coppice HEDN WS12 *...17 M1
Coopers Hl ALVE B48 ....170 C7
Coopers La SMTHWK B66 ....87 L8
Coopers Rd BFLD/HDSWWD B20...88 E2
Cooper St NUN CV11 ....99 H1
WBROM B70 ....87 H2
WOLV WV1 ....3 M9
Coopers Wk KNWTH CV8 ....182 A1
Cope Arnolds Cl COVN CV6 ...134 D1
Copeland RUGBYS/DCH CV22 ...161 G6
Copeley Hl AST/WIT B6 ....90 A4
Copes Crs WOLVN WV10 ....36 E7
Cope's Dr CRTAM B79 ....31 L6
Cope St BLOX/PEL WS3 ....39 G7
COV CV1 ....9 H4
DARL/WED WS10 ....52 D7
WSNGN B18 ....106 C2
Cophall St TPTN/OCK DY4 .....68 E8
Cophams Cl HIA/OLT B92 .....128 A3
Copland Pl TLHL/CAN CV4 ....153 H1
Coplow Cl RCOVN/BALC/EX CV7..151 L7
Coplow Cottages
 LDYWD/EDGR B16 * 106 D2
Coplow St LDYWD/EDGR B16 ...106 D2
Coplow Ter LDYWD/EDGR B16 ..106 D2
Copnor Gv
 LGN/SDN/BHAMAIR B26 ....110 J7
Copperhall Gv STETCH B33 ...109 J7
Copperas St COVE CV2 ....134 F3
Copper Beech Cl COVN CV6 ...134 C4
Copperbeech Cl
 RIDG/WDGT B32 ....105 K8
Copperbeech Dr
 BHTH/HG B12 ....107 L8
Copper Beech Dr KGSWFD DY6...83 H4
WMBN WV5 ....64 F7
Copper Beech Gdns
 BFLD/HDSWWD B20 ....88 D3
Copperfield Rd COVE CV2 ....155 M2
Copperfields LICHS WS14 .....21 H6
Copperkins Rd HEDN WS12 ....17 H1
Coppermill Rd HEDN WS12 ....12 D4
Coppice Cl BNTWD WS7 ....18 D5
ERDE/BCHGN B24 ....90 D2
GTWY WS6 ....143 A6
RBRY B45 ....143 K6
REDW B97 ....202 A2
SEDG DY3 ....66 A6
SHLY B90 ....174 A1
SOLH B91 * 127 L6
WNSFLD WV11 ....37 L4
Coppice Crs BRWNH WS8 ......26 M6
Coppice Dr ACGN B27 ....126 F3
POL/KGSB/FAZ B78 ....47 K6
Coppice Farm Wy SHHTH WV12..37 M4
Coppice Hts KIDDW DY11 ......21 K6
Coppice Hts KIDDW DY11 .....163 M4
Coppice Hollow
 RIDG/WDGT B32 ....122 F4
Coppice La ALDR WS9 ....40 D1
BNTWD WS7 ....27 L2
BRLYHL DY5 ....26 B5
BRWNH WS8 ....26 B5
CNCK/NC WS11 ....37 G8
DUNHL/THL/PER WV6 ....34 F7
POL/KGSB/FAZ B78 ....58 A3
SHHTH WV12 ....38 A7
Coppice Ri BRLYHL DY5 ......84 A4
Coppice Rd ALDR WS9 ....40 D1
BDMR/CCFT WV3 ....49 H5
BILS/COS WV14 ....66 E5
CDYHTH B64 ....103 J6
HIA/OLT B92 ....125 J2
MOS/BIL B13 ....125 J2
Coppice Side BRWNH WS8 .....26 B5
Coppice St TPTN/OCK DY4 .....86 B6
WBROM B70 ....86 C1
Coppice View Rd
 SCFLD/BOLD B73 ....71 L1
Coppice Wk SHLY B90 ....174 A1
Copplestone Cl BKDE/SHDE B34..91 M7
Copps Rd RLSN CV32 ....206 B3
Copse Cl COV CV2 ....155 M5
NFLD/LBR B31 ....144 A3
Copse Crs BLOX/PEL WS3 .....39 G7
Copse Rd DUDS DY2 ....102 F2
The Copse FOAKS/STRLY B74 ...56 D4
RCOVN/BALC/EX CV7 ....116 C6
Copsewood Av NUN CV11 ......99 M6
Copswood Ter COVS CV3 ......15 M5
Copston Dr DOR/KN B93 ......175 K7
Copston Gv SLYOAK B29 ......123 M6
Copthall Rd HDSW B21 ....88 A3

Copt Heath Cft DOR/KN B93 ...149 M5
Copt Heath Dr DOR/KN B93 ...149 L6
Copthorne Av BNTWD WS7 .....26 D1
Copthorne Rd BDMR/CCFT WV3..49 L6
COVN CV6 ....133 K5
KGSTG B44 ....71 J2
Copt Oak Cl TLHL/CAN CV4 ...153 G6
Copyholt La BRGRVE B60 .....200 A3
Coral Cl COVW CV5 ....154 A3
Coralin Cl
 CHWD/FDBR/MGN B37 ....110 F3
Corbett Cl BRGRVE B60 ......191 M5
Corbett Crs STRBR DY8 ......101 L6
Corbett Rd BRLYHL DY5 ......102 C4
HLYWD B47 ....146 E6
KIDDW DY11 ....137 L5
Corbetts Cl HIA/OLT B92 ....129 M6
Corbett St RUGBYN/HIL CV21..187 G1
SMTHWK B66 ....105 M1
Corbin Rd POL/KGSB/FAZ B78...47 L5
Corbison Cl WWCK CV34 ......205 H4
Corbridge Av KGSTG B44 .....71 K4
Corbridge Rd SCFLD/BOLD B73..72 F2
Corbyn Rd BORD B9 ....108 F2
DUDN DY1 ....84 D5
Corbyns Cl BRLYHL DY5 ......83 M6
Corbyns Hall La BRLYHL DY5...83 M6
Corbyns Hall Rd BRLYHL DY5...83 M6
Cordelia Wy RUGBYS/DCH CV22..186 F5
Cordle Marsh Rd BEWD DY12 ..137 G8
Cordley St WBROM B70 ....86 F1
Corfe Cl COVE CV2 ....135 K8
DUNHL/THL/PER WV6 ....48 D2
Corfe Dr OLDBY B69 ....85 L3
Corfe Rd BILS/COS WV14 .....66 C5
Corfton Dr DUNHL/THL/PER WV6..49 G2
Coriander Cl NFLD/LBR B31 ..143 M4
Corinne Cl RBRY B45 ....143 L3
Corinne Cft
 CHWD/FDBR/MGN B37 ....110 F3
Corinthian Pl COVE CV2 * ...135 H6
Corisande Rd SLYOAK B29 ....124 A3
Corley Av NFLD/LBR B31 .....144 F2
Corley Cl SHLY B90 ....147 G6
Corley Vw RCOVN/BALC/EX CV7..116 A6
Cornbrook Rd SLYOAK B29 ....123 K7
Cornbury Gv SHLY B90 ....146 B1
Corncrake Cl CSCFLD/WYGN B72 73 H5
Corncrake Dr DUDN DY1 ......84 C2
Corncrake Rd DUDN DY1 ......163 M3
Corndon Cl KIDDW DY11 ......163 M3
Cornel TAM/AM/WIL B77 ......46 D3
Cornel Cl
 CHWD/FDBR/MGN B37 ....111 G5
Cornelius St COVS CV3 ......155 H5
Corner La REDW B97 ....201 J3
Cornerway HWK/WKFTH B38 ....145 K6
Cornets End La
 RCOVN/BALC/EX CV7 ....130 C5
Cornfield CDSL WV8 ....35 K3
Cornfield Av BRGRVE B60 ....191 M5
Cornfield Cl KGSWFD DY6 ....82 C5
Cornfield Cft
 CHWD/FDBR/MGN B37 ....111 H2
WALM/CURD B76 ....73 K2
Cornfield Dr LICHS WS14 ....21 H6
Cornfield Rd
 BLKHTH/ROWR B65 ....103 K1
NFLD/LBR B31 ....144 F1
WALM/CURD B76 ....73 K4
The Cornfield COVS CV3 .....156 A4
Cornflower Cl WOLVN WV10 ...22 C6
Cornflower Crs DUDS DY2 ....85 K5
Cornflower Dr RRUGBY CV23 ..161 G5
Cornflower Rd BRWNH WS8 ....26 B7
Cornforth Cl
 POL/KGSB/FAZ B78 * 60 D7
Corngreaves Rd CDYHTH B64 ..103 H5
The Corngreaves
 BKDE/SHDE B34 ....92 A4
Corngreaves Wk CDYHTH B64 ..103 H5
Cornhampton Cl REDW B97 ....193 M8
Cornhill CNCK/NC WS11 ......12 C4
Corn Hl DSYBK/YTR WS5 ......54 C5
WOLV WV1 ....3 H4
Cornhill Gv BVILLE B30 .....125 G7
Cornish Cl NUNW/HART CV10 ..79 K5
Cornish Crs NUNW/HART CV10..98 E3
Corn Mdw BDWTH CV12 ....116 D2
Corn Mill Cl RIDG/WDGT B32..123 J4
WALM/CURD B76 ....73 K4
Cornmill Cl WSL WS1 ....4 C8
Cornmill Gdns BRGRVE B60 ...169 L8
Cornmill Gv
 DUNHL/THL/PER WV6 ....48 D2
Cornovian Cl
 DUNHL/THL/PER WV6 ....34 C8
Corns Gv WMBN WV5 ....64 D8
Cornwall Av KIDDW DY11 .....138 A4
LGLYGN/QTN B68 ....104 F5
POL/KGSB/FAZ B78 ....47 M3
WLNHL WV13 ....52 B3
Cornwall Cl ALDR WS9 ....40 E4
DARL/WED WS10 ....69 L2
KGSWFD DY6 ....83 H5
WWCK CV34 ....205 K4
Cornwall Ga SHHTH WV12 .....37 M8
Cornwallis Rd
 RUGBYS/DCH CV22 ....185 M4
WBROM B70 ....86 F4
Cornwall Pl RLSN CV32 ......206 B3
WSLW WS2 ....52 C2
Cornwall Rd BFLD/HDSWWD B20...9 J7
COV CV1 ....9 J7
DSYBK/YTR WS5 ....5 M8
DUNHL/THL/PER WV6 ....49 G1
HEDN WS12 ....12 F8
RBRY B45 ....143 J3
SMTHWK B66 ....87 H1
STRBR DY8 ....101 H5
Cornwall St CBHAMNW B3 ......6 E4
TPTN/OCK DY4 ....67 J8
Cornyx La SOLH B91 ....128 E7
Coronation Av
 POL/KGSB/FAZ B78 ....45 M3
POL/KGSB/FAZ B78 ....47 M3
WLNHL WV13 ....52 B3
Coronation Crs CRTAM B79 ...33 K5
Coronation Rd ALDR WS9 .....40 D2
ATHST CV9 ....77 C1
BILS/COS WV14 ....51 C7
COV CV1 ....9 G2
DARL/WED WS10 ....69 G2
GTB/HAM B43 ....70 C1
RRUGBY CV23 ....161 M8
RUSH/SHEL WS4 ....39 M4
SLYOAK B29 ....124 D3
TPTN/OCK DY4 ....67 H8
WASH/WDE B8 ....90 D2
WNSFLD WV11 ....36 M8
Coronation St CRTAM B79 ....31 H8
Coronation Ter BRGRVE B60 ..191 M6
Coronel Av COVN CV6 ....134 C1
Corporation Rd DUDS DY2 ....85 K4
Corporation St CBHAMNE B4 ...7 H8
COV CV1 ....8 E5

umbrian Cft HALE B63 .....121 H3
Cumbria Wy WASH/WDE B8 .....90 B7
Cumming St RLSS CV31 .....206 E6
Cundall Cl RLSS CV31 .....206 F7
unningham Rd
  DUNHL/THL/PER WV6 .....48 C1
  WSLW WS2 .....52 C3
unningham Wy North
  RUGBYS/DCH CV22 .....186 A4
upfields Av TPTN/OCK DY4 .....68 A5
upfields Crs TPTN/OCK DY4 .....68 A6
urbar Rd PBAR/PBCH B42 .....71 C7
urdale Rd RIDG/WDGT B32 .....122 F5
urie Cl RUGBYN/HIL CV21 .....187 H2
urla Rd REDW B97 .....200 F2
urlew TAM/AM/WIL B77 .....46 B6
urlew Cl BDWTH DY10 .....164 F3
  LICHS WS14 .....21 J6
urlew Hl CNCK/NC WS11 .....16 C2
urlews Cl ERDW/GRVHL B23 .....72 A5
urlieu Cl RWWCK/WEL CV35 .....204 E7
urral Rd BLKHTH/ROWR B65 .....103 M2
urriers Cl TLHL/CAN CV4 .....153 H6
urslow Cottages KIDD DY10 * 165 K8
urslow La KIDD DY10 * 87 M8
urtin Dr DARL/WED WS10 .....67 M1
urtis Cl SMTHWK B66 .....106 A4
urtis Rd COVE CV2 .....135 H7
urtiss Cl BRGRVE B60 * 192 D5
urzon Av COVN CV6 .....134 C5
urzon Circ CBHAMNE B4 .....7 L3
urzon St RLSS CV31 .....207 G7
urzon St BKHL/PFLD WV2 .....50 B8
  CBHAMNE B4 .....7 K4
uthbert Rd WSNGN B18 .....106 C1
utlers Rough Cl NFLD/LBR B31 .....123 K8
utler St NFLD/LBR B66 .....87 M8
utshill Cl CBROM B36 .....92 A5
ut Throat La HOCK/TIA B94 .....174 A1
he Cutting RUSH/SHEL WS4 .....53 K1
uttle Mill La WALM/CURD B76 .....75 J3
uttle Pool La DOR/KN B93 .....176 D1
utty Sark Dr STRPT DY13 .....188 E3
utworth Cl WALM/CURD B76 .....73 L2
ygnet Cl ALVE B48 .....170 E6
  HEDN WS12 .....13 G6
ygnet Dr BRWNH WS8 .....26 C6
ygnet Gv ERDW/GRVHL B23 .....71 L7
ygnet La BRLYHL DY5 .....84 A6
ygnet Rd WBROM B70 .....68 B8
ygnus Wy WBROM B70 .....68 D8
ymbeline Wy
  RUGBYS/DCH CV22 .....186 B7
ypress Av SEDG DY3 .....66 B3
ypress Cft COVS CV5 .....156 D5
ypress Gdns KGSWFD DY6 .....101 G1
ypress La NFLD/LBR B31 .....144 C3
ypress Ri DSYBK/YTR WS5 .....70 A1
  DUDS DY2 .....85 K4
ypress Sq ACGN B27 .....109 G8
ypress Wy NFLD/LBR B31 .....144 D5
yprus Cl SLYOAK B29 .....123 L6
yprus St BKHL/PFLD WV2 .....49 M7
  OLDBY B69 .....86 E5
vril Gv SMHTH B10 * 108 A5
vril Rd SMHTH B10 .....108 A5

D

ace TAM/AM/WIL B77 .....46 B6
acer Cl BVILLE B30 .....124 E4
ace Rd WOLV WV1 .....50 F1
adford Vw BRLYHL DY5 .....101 M3
adleys Wd
  RCOVN/BALC/EX CV7 * 114 D8
ad's La MOS/BIL B13 .....125 G4
affern Av RCOVN/BALC/EX CV7 .....96 E5
affern Rd
  RCOVN/BALC/EX CV7 .....116 E4
affodil Cl SEDG DY3 .....66 C6
affodil Pl DSYBK/YTR WS5 .....54 B5
affodil Wy NFLD/LBR B31 .....144 C5
agger La HHTH/SAND B71 .....69 J8
agnall Rd COVE CV2 .....127 H2
agnell End Rd REDE B98 .....194 D5
ahlia Cl WOLV WV1 .....51 G4
aimler Cl BRWNH WS8 .....92 D4
aimler Rd ALE/KHTH/YWD 147 G1
  COVN CV6 .....134 A4
aintree Cft COVS CV5 .....155 G6
aintry Dr POL/KGSB/FAZ B78 .....30 F6
airy Cl TPTN/OCK DY4 .....67 M8
airy La REDW B97 .....193 L8
aisy Bank HEDN WS12 .....12 D5
aisy Bank Crs DSYBK/YTR WS5 .....59 M3
aisy Farm Rd
  ALE/KHTH/YWD B14 .....146 F3
aisy Meadow TPTN/OCK DY4 .....68 A2
aisy Rd LDYWD/EDGR B16 .....106 D3
aisy Wk COVEN WV9 .....35 L2
aisy Wk DUNHL/THL/PER WV6 .....49 M1
albeg Cl CDSL WV8 .....35 J5
albury Rd HIA/OLT B92 .....128 C5
alby Cl COVS CV5 .....156 C6
alby Rd BLOX/PEL WS3 .....39 K7
ale Cl BRGRVW B61 .....168 D6
  GTB/HAM B43 .....70 B4
  SMTHWK B67 .....105 L2
  TPTN/OCK DY4 .....68 B8
  WWCK CV34 .....205 L5
alecote Av HIA/OLT B92 .....128 C5
ale Dr BNTWD WS7 .....18 F6
ale End CBHAMNE B4 .....7 H5
  DARL/WED WS10 .....52 B7
ale Hi BRGRVE B60 .....80 C8
alehouse La KNWTH CV8 .....180 A7
ale Meadow Cl
  RCOVN/BALC/EX CV7 * 151 M7
ale Rd REDE B98 .....194 B8
  RMSLY B62 .....103 G8
  SLYOAK B29 .....124 C2
  STRBR DY8 .....119 K3
ales Cl DUNHL/THL/PER WV6 .....35 M7
alesman Cl KGSWFD DY6 .....82 F6
ale St BDMR/CCFT WV3 .....2 D7
  DARL/WED WS10 .....68 C8
  LSN CV32 .....206 D1
  ... CV32 .....186 E1
  ... B66 .....105 L2
eswood Pk RMSLY B62 * 142 D3

Dale Ter OLDBY B69 .....86 A5
Daleview Rd
  ALE/KHTH/YWD B14 .....147 G2
Dalewood Rd COVS CV3 .....180 F2
Dalewood Cft
  LGN/SDN/BHAMAIR B26 .....109 K7
Daley Cl CBHAMW B1 .....6 A1
Daley Rd BILS/COS WV14 .....67 K3
Dalkeith Av RUGBYS/DCH CV22 .....186 B6
Dalkeith Rd SCFLD/BOLD B73 .....72 C3
Dalkeith St WSLW WS2 .....4 E1
Dallas Rd ERDW/GRVHL B23 .....90 A1
Dallimore Cl HIA/OLT B92 .....127 K2
Dallington Rd COVN CV6 .....133 J7
Dalloway Cl DIG/EDG B5 .....107 H7
Dalmeny Rd TLHL/CAN CV4 .....153 H6
Dalston Cl DUDS DY2 .....85 H7
Dalston Rd ACGN B27 .....127 G1
Dalton Cl RRUGBY CV23 .....158 F7
Dalton Ct WMBN WV5 .....64 C8
Dalton Gdns COVE CV2 .....156 D1
Dalton Rd BDWTH CV12 .....116 D3
  COVW CV5 .....8 C9
  WSLW WS2 .....52 E2
Dalton St BDMR/CCFT WV3 .....2 C7
  CBHAMNE B4 .....7 H1
Dalton Wy CBHAM B3 .....7 G4
Dalvine Rd DUDS DY2 .....102 F3
Dalwood Cl BILS/COS WV14 .....66 F6
Daly Av RWWCK/WEL CV35 .....204 D7
Damar Cft ALE/KHTH/YWD B14 .....146 B3
Dama Rd POL/KGSB/FAZ B78 .....45 K5
Dame Agnes Gv COVN CV6 .....134 E1
Damien Cl SMTHWKW B67 .....87 K8
  SHHTH WV12 .....37 L7
Damson Dr ATHST CV9 .....77 C1
Damson La SOLH B91 .....148 D7
Damson Pkwy HIA/OLT B92 .....128 D2
Damson Rd RWWCK/WEL CV35 .....204 D7
Damson Wy BEWD DY12 .....162 F1
Damson Whf TPTN/OCK DY4 .....85 L2
Dam St LICH WS13 .....20 F5
Danbury Cl WALM/CURD B76 .....73 L3
Danbury Rd SHLY B90 .....147 M2
Danby Dr HEDN WS12 .....18 L1
Danby Gv ERDE/BCHGN B24 .....90 F3
Dando Rd DUDS DY2 .....85 H5
Dandy Bank Rd KGSWFD DY6 .....83 J5
Dandy's Wk WSL WS1 .....5 G6
Dane Gv MOS/BIL B13 .....125 H5
Danelagh Cl CRTAM B79 .....31 K6
Danes Cl COVE CV2 .....155 M1
Danesbury Crs KGSTG B44 .....71 L5
  RLSS CV31 .....207 H7
Danes Cl WNSFLD WV11 .....37 K1
Danescourt Rd
  DUNHL/THL/PER WV6 .....35 G7
Danescroft STRPT DY8 .....188 D1
Daneswood Dr ALDR WS9 .....40 D2
Daneswood Rd COVS CV3 .....157 J6
Dane Ter BLKHTH/ROWR B65 .....86 A8
Daneways Cl FOAKS/STRLY B74 .....55 L5
Danford Cl STRBR DY8 .....119 L1
Danford Gdns BDMR/CCFT WV3 .....108 A5
Danford La SOLH B91 .....148 C2
Danford Rd HLYWD B47 .....146 D7
Danford Wy GTB/HAM B43 .....70 B2
Dangerfield La DARL/WED WS10 .....52 A8
Daniel Av NUNW/HART CV10 .....98 A2
Daniel Rd ATHST CV9 .....63 K6
Daniels La ALDR WS9 .....55 G1
Daniels Rd BORD B9 .....108 E3
Danilo Rd CNCK/NC WS11 .....16 B4
Danks St TPTN/OCK DY4 .....85 L2
Danzey Cl REDW B97 .....202 F8
Danzey Green Rd CBROM B36 .....91 M4
Danzey Gv BVILLE B30 .....146 A2
Daphne Cl COVE CV2 .....135 G2
Darby Cl BILS/COS WV14 .....66 E3
Darby End Rd
  BLKHTH/ROWR B65 .....103 J1
Darby Rd DARL/WED WS10 .....68 F7
  LGLYGN/QTN B68 .....87 G8
Darbys Hill Rd OLDBY B69 .....85 M6
Darby St BLKHTH/ROWR B65 .....104 A8
Darell Cft WALM/CURD B76 .....73 J2
Darfield Wk BHTH/HG B12 * 107 K5
Darges La GTWY WS6 .....24 D1
Darkhouse La BILS/COS WV14 .....67 G3
Dark La BDWTH CV12 .....116 B4
  BRGRVE B60 .....191 H7
  COV CV1 .....8 E2
  GTWY WS6 .....25 G4
  HAG/WOL DY9 .....141 J6
  HWK/WKHTH B38 .....146 B3
  KINVER DY7 .....118 A2
  LICH WS13 .....19 L4
  POL/KGSB/FAZ B78 .....47 J5
  RMSLY B62 .....142 D1
  WNSFLD WV11 .....23 H6
  WOLV WV1 .....23 H6
Darlaston La BILS/COS WV14 .....51 L6
Darlaston Rd WSLW WS2 .....52 E5
Darley Av BKDE/SHDE B34 .....91 K7
Darleydale Av KGSTG B44 .....71 L5
Darley Dr DUNHL/THL/PER WV6 .....35 M8
Darley Green Rd DOR/KN B93 .....175 M4
Darley Wy FOAKS/STRLY B74 .....55 K6
Darlington St DARL/WED WS10 .....52 B7
Darlington Yd WOLV WV1 * 2 E5
Darnel Cft SMHTH B10 .....107 H4
Darnel Hurst Rd MGN/WHC B75 .....57 G2
Darnford Cl COVE CV2 .....135 K6
  CSCFLD/WYGN B72 .....73 H6
  HLGN/YWD B28 .....126 E8
Darnford La LICHS WS14 .....21 J7
Darnford Moors LICHS WS14 .....21 J7
Darnford Vw LICH WS13 .....21 J4
Darnick Rd SCFLD/BOLD B73 .....72 B2
Darnley Rd LDYWD/EDGR B16 .....106 D3
Darrach Cl COVE CV2 .....135 J3
Darris Rd SLYOAK B29 .....124 E5
Dartford Rd BLOX/PEL WS3 .....38 D4
Dartington Wy NUN CV11 .....99 K5
Dartmoor Cl RBRY B45 .....143 L3
Dartmouth Av BLOX/PEL WS3 .....39 J4
  CNCK/NC WS11 .....16 A6
  STRBR DY8 .....101 H2
  WSLW WS2 .....51 K3
Dartmouth Circ AST/WIT B6 .....89 K8
Dartmouth Cl BLOX/PEL WS3 .....39 J4
Dartmouth Dr BLOX/PEL WS3 .....16 A5
  CNCK/NC WS11 .....16 A5
Dartmouth Mdw
  HWK/WKHTH B38 .....145 J5
Dartmouth Pl BLOX/PEL WS3 .....39 J7
Dartmouth Rd CNCK/NC WS11 .....16 A6
  COVE CV2 .....135 G2
  SLYOAK B29 .....124 D3
  SMTHWK B66 .....87 K5
Dartmouth Sq BKHL/PFLD WV2 .....3 H8
  WBROM B70 .....86 F2

Dart St BORD B9 .....107 M4
Darvel Rd SHHTH WV12 .....52 B5
Darwall St WSL WS1 .....4 F3
Darwin Cl BNTWD WS7 .....18 F6
  COVE CV2 .....135 L7
  HEDN WS12 .....12 D1
Darwin Ct DUNHL/THL/PER WV6 .....48 C1
Darwin Pl WSLW WS2 .....38 F7
Darwin Rd WSLW WS2 .....38 F7
Dassett Gv BORD B9 .....109 C3
Dassett Rd DOR/KN B93 .....175 K1
Datchet Cl COVW CV5 .....154 A1
Datteln Rd CNCK/NC WS11 .....16 E1
D'Aubeny Rd TLHL/CAN CV4 .....153 M5
Dauntsey Covert
  ALE/KHTH/YWD B14 .....146 B3
Davena Dr SLYOAK B29 .....123 J3
Davena Gv BILS/COS WV14 .....67 K7
Davenham Rd BRGRVE B60 .....192 A4
Davenport Dr BRGRVE B60 .....191 M4
  CVALE B35 .....92 A2
Davenport Rd
  DUNHL/THL/PER WV6 .....34 F8
  WNSFLD WV11 .....37 J7
Daventry Gv RIDG/WDGT B32 .....105 G2
Daventry Rd COVS CV3 .....155 H6
Davey Rd BFLD/HDSWWD B20 .....88 A4
  WBROM B70 .....86 E1
David Peacock Cl TPTN/OCK DY4 .....85 M8
David Rd BFLD/HDSWWD B20 .....88 F3
  RCOVN/BALC/EX CV7 .....116 D5
  RUGBYS/DCH CV22 .....186 B5
  TPTN/OCK DY4 .....67 L6
Davidson Av RLSS CV31 .....206 E6
Davidson Rd LICHS WS14 .....20 F6
Davies Av BILS/COS WV14 .....67 L2
Davies Rd RCOVN/BALC/EX CV7 .....116 D6
Davis Av TPTN/OCK DY4 .....85 J1
Davis Cl RLSN CV32 .....206 B3
Davis Gv
  LGN/SDN/BHAMAIR B26 .....109 H7
Davison Rd SMTHWK B67 .....105 K3
Davis Rd SHHTH WV12 .....38 B5
  TAM/AM/WIL B77 .....46 D1
Davy Rd WSLW WS2 .....38 E8
Dawberry Cl
  ALE/KHTH/YWD B14 .....125 H8
Dawberry Fields Rd
  ALE/KHTH/YWD B14 .....125 G8
Dawberry Rd
  ALE/KHTH/YWD B14 .....125 G8
Daw End RUSH/SHEL WS4 .....40 A7
Daw End La RUSH/SHEL WS4 .....39 M7
Dawes Av WBROM B70 .....87 G4
Dawes Cl COVE CV2 .....155 L4
Dawley Brook Rd KGSWFD DY6 .....83 H6
Dawley Crs
  CHWD/FDBR/MGN B37 .....110 F4
Dawley Rd KGSWFD DY6 .....83 G5
Dawlish Cl NUN CV11 .....81 J8
Dawlish Dr COVS CV3 .....155 H8
Dawlish Rd DUDN DY1 .....66 F8
  SLYOAK B29 .....124 D3
  SMTHWK B66 .....87 M8
Dawn Dr TPTN/OCK DY4 .....68 B8
Dawney Dr MGN/WHC B75 .....56 F1
Dawn Rd NFLD/LBR B31 .....123 J7
Dawson Av BILS/COS WV14 .....66 F6
Dawson Rd BRGRVW B61 .....191 J1
  COVS CV3 .....155 L4
  HDSW B21 .....88 C5
Dawson Sq BILS/COS WV14 * 51 G8
Dawson St BLOX/PEL WS3 .....39 H5
  SMTHWK B66 .....105 J2
Day Av WNSFLD WV11 .....37 J6
Daybrook Cl REDW B97 .....193 M8
Dayhouse Bank RMSLY B62 .....142 F4
Daylesford Rd HIA/OLT B92 .....127 L2
Days Cl COV CV1 .....9 L3
Day's La COV CV1 .....9 K3
Daytona Dr COVW CV5 .....131 M5
Deacon Cl RUGBYS/DCH CV22 .....187 G4
Deacon St NUN CV11 .....99 G2
Deakin Av BRWNH WS8 .....26 B4
Deakin Rd ERDE/BCHGN B24 .....90 C1
  MGN/WHC B75 .....57 J6
Deakins Rd YDLY B25 .....108 F8
Deal Av BNTWD WS7 .....18 E5
Deal Dr DUDS DY2 .....85 K4
Deal Gv NFLD/LBR B31 .....144 E1
Deanbrook Cl SHLY B90 .....162 F6
Dean Cl CSCFLD/WYGN B72 .....72 F6
  KGSTG B44 .....71 L3
Dean Ct CDSL WV8 .....34 F3
Deansway BRGRVW B61 .....191 H4
Deansway WWCK CV34 .....205 H4
The Deansway KIDD DY10 .....138 E6
Dearman Rd SPARK B11 .....107 M6
Dearmont Rd NFLD/LBR B31 .....144 C6
Dearne Ct SEDG DY3 .....66 E7
Deasy Rd COV CV1 .....9 H7
Deavall Wy CNCK/NC WS11 .....16 E1
Debden Crs DOR/KN B93 .....175 J3
Debenham Crs YDLY B25 .....109 H4
Debenham Rd YDLY B25 .....109 H4
Deborah Cl
  ETTPK/GDPK/PENN WV4 .....50 A7
De-Compton Cl
  RCOVN/BALC/EX CV7 .....115 L6
Deedmore Rd COVE CV2 .....135 H4
Deegan Cl COVE CV2 .....134 E7
Dee Gv CNCK/NC WS11 .....16 E1
Deelands Rd RBRY B45 .....143 K5
Deeley TAM/AM/WIL B77 .....46 C5
Deeley Cl DIG/EDG B5 .....107 G6
Deeley Dr TPTN/OCK DY4 .....68 B7
Deeley Pl BLOX/PEL WS3 .....38 F5
Deeley St BLOX/PEL WS3 * 38 F5
Deepdale POL/KGSB/FAZ B78 .....47 H4
Deepdale Av
  LGN/SDN/BHAMAIR B26 .....127 M1

Deepdale La DUDN DY1 .....84 C2
Deepdales WMBN WV5 .....64 C7
Deep La CSHL/WTROR B46 .....76 D7
Deeplow Cl CSCFLD/WYGN B72 * 73 C1
Deepmoor Rd STECH B33 .....109 K2
Deepmore Av WSLW WS2 .....52 F3
Deepmore Rd
  RUGBYS/DCH CV22 .....186 B5
Deepwood Cl RUSH/SHEL WS4 .....39 M5
Deer Barn Hl REDE B98 .....202 E4
Deer Cl BLOX/PEL WS3 .....39 C4
  CNCK/NC WS11 .....17 L6
Deerdale Wy COVS CV3 .....156 D5
Deerfold Crs BNTWD WS7 .....18 F7
Deerhill TAM/AM/WIL B77 .....47 G4
Deerhurst Cl REDE B98 .....195 G6
Deerhurst Ri HEDN WS12 .....13 K7
Deerhurst Rd
  BFLD/HDSWWD B20 .....70 D8
  COVN CV6 .....133 M3
Deerings Rd RUGBYN/HIL CV21 .....187 L5
The Deer Leap KNWTH CV8 .....179 M7
Deer Pk BLOX/PEL WS3 .....39 J4
Deer Pk Rd TAM/AM/WIL B77 .....13 M5
Deerpark Dr WWCK CV34 .....205 H5
Deer Park Rd POL/KGSB/FAZ B78 .....46 F4
Deer Park Wy SOLH B91 .....149 G4
Defford Av ALE/KHTH/YWD B14 .....126 A7
Defford Cl REDW B97 .....201 J4
Defford Dr LGLYGN/QTN B68 .....104 F1
Dehavilland Cl NUN CV11 .....80 F8
De Havilland Dr CVALE B35 .....91 L3
Deighton Rd DSYBK/YTR WS5 .....69 M1
Delage Cl COVN CV6 .....134 F1
Delamere Cl CBROM B36 .....92 B4
Delamere Dr GTB/HAM B43 .....70 A2
Delamere Rd BDWTH CV12 .....116 D3
  BEWD DY12 .....163 G1
  HLGN/YWD B28 .....126 D6
  SHHTH WV12 .....38 A6
Delamere Wy RLSN CV32 .....207 C1
Delancey Keep MGN/WHC B75 .....57 L8
Delaware Rd COVS CV3 .....155 C8
Delhi Av COVN CV6 .....134 B4
Delhurst Av
  ETTPK/GDPK/PENN WV4 .....66 C2
Delhurst Rd KGSTG B44 .....71 H4
Delius St TLHL/CAN CV4 .....153 J2
Della Dr RIDG/WDGT B32 .....123 J5
Dell Cl COVS CV3 .....155 M8
Dell Farm Cl DOR/KN B93 .....149 M1
Dellow Gv ALVE B48 .....170 E6
Dellows Cl HWK/WKHTH B38 .....145 H6
Dell Rd BRLYHL DY5 .....83 M8
  BVILLE B30 .....124 E8
The Dell CRTAM B79 .....31 M7
  HEDN WS12 .....17 K1
  HIA/OLT B92 .....127 L4
  LDYWD/EDGR B16 * 106 D3
  NFLD/LBR B31 .....123 H7
  STRBR DY8 .....101 J7
Delmore Wy WALM/CURD B76 .....73 M7
Delph Dr BRLYHL DY5 .....102 C6
Delphinium Cl BORD B9 .....108 D2
  KIDD DY10 .....138 A4
Delph La BRLYHL DY5 .....102 B5
Delph Rd BRLYHL DY5 .....102 B4
Delrene Rd HLGN/YWD B28 .....147 K2
Delta Wy CNCK/NC WS11 .....16 C6
Deltic TAM/AM/WIL B77 .....46 E4
Delves Crs ATHST CV9 .....61 H4
  DSYBK/YTR WS5 .....53 L8
Delves Green Rd DSYBK/YTR WS5 .....53 L7
Delville Rd DARL/WED WS10 .....68 D2
De Marnham Cl WBROM B70 .....87 J4
De Montfort Rd KNWTH CV8 .....179 J7
De Montfort Wy TLHL/CAN CV4 .....154 B8
De Moram Gv HIA/OLT B92 .....128 D6
Dempster Rd BDWTH CV12 .....116 E1
Demuth Wy OLDBY B69 .....86 E3
Denaby Gv ALE/KHTH/YWD B14 .....147 H1
Denbigh Cl DUDN DY1 .....84 D3
Denbigh Crs HHTH/SAND B71 .....68 F7
Denbigh Dr DARL/WED WS10 .....69 H1
  HHTH/SAND B71 .....68 F7
Denbigh Rd COVN CV6 .....133 J7
  TPTN/OCK DY4 .....68 D8
Denbigh St BORD B9 .....108 B3
Denbury Cl HEDN WS12 .....17 K1
Denby Buildings RLSN CV32 * 206 D5
  VAUX/NECH B7 .....89 M8
Denby Cl SHLY B90 .....148 F7
Dencer Cl RBRY B45 .....143 K5
Dencer Dr KNWTH CV8 .....198 A1
Dencil Cl HALE B63 .....103 H8
Dene Av KGSWFD DY6 .....101 G1
Dene Court Rd HIA/OLT B92 .....127 K4
Denefield Rd PENK ST19 .....10 D5
Denegate Cl WALM/CURD B76 .....73 M7
Dene Hollow MOS/BIL B13 .....126 A6
Denehurst Cl RBRY B45 .....169 L4
Denehurst Wy
  NUNW/HART CV10 .....98 C2
Dene Rd
  ETTPK/GDPK/PENN WV4 .....64 D1
  STRBR DY8 .....119 K2
Denewood Av
  BFLD/HDSWWD B20 .....88 D3
Denewood Wy KNWTH CV8 .....180 A8
Denford Gv
  ALE/KHTH/YWD B14 .....125 H8
Dengate Dr
  RCOVN/BALC/EX CV7 .....151 M6
Denham Av COVW CV5 .....153 M1
Denham Ct ATHST CV9 .....63 J5
Denham Gdns BDMR/CCFT WV3 .....48 F5
Denham Rd ACGN B27 .....108 F8
Denholme Gv
  ALE/KHTH/YWD B14 .....146 E2
Denholm Rd SCFLD/BOLD B73 .....72 B2
Denise Dr BILS/COS WV14 .....66 F5
  CHWD/FDBR/MGN B37 .....110 D4
  HRBN B17 .....124 A1
Denleigh Rd KGSWFD DY6 .....101 J1
Denmark Ri HEDN WS12 .....13 H6
Denmark Vls LICH WS13 * 20 B8
Denmead Dr WNSFLD WV11 .....37 K5
Denmore Gdns WOLV WV1 .....50 F1
Dennett Cl WWCK CV34 .....205 K3
Dennis TAM/AM/WIL B77 .....46 C3
Dennis Hall Rd STRBR DY8 .....101 K4
Dennis Rd BHTH/HG B12 .....125 M1
  COVE CV2 .....135 G1
Dennis St STRBR DY8 .....101 K4
Denshaw Rd
  ALE/KHTH/YWD B14 .....125 H7
Denton Cl KNWTH CV8 .....179 H7
Denton Cft DOR/KN B93 .....174 F4
Denton Gv GTB/HAM B43 .....70 B6
  STECH B33 .....109 H3
Denton Rd HAG/WOL DY9 .....120 D1
Dent St CRTAM B79 .....32 A4

Denver Rd ALE/KHTH/YWD B14 .....146 E3
Denville Cl BILS/COS WV14 .....51 J6
Denville Crs BORD B9 .....108 F2
Denville Rd RLSN CV32 .....206 E2
Depwo Gv RIDG/WDGT B32 .....122 F5
Derby Av DUNHL/THL/PER WV6 .....35 J6
Derby Dr
  CHWD/FDBR/MGN B37 .....110 F3
Derby Rd LICHS WS14 .....30 C7
Derby St DIG/EDG B5 .....7 H2
  WSLW WS2 .....53 H1
Dereham Cl WASH/WDE B8 .....108 A1
Dereham Ct RLSN CV32 .....206 E2
Derek Av DARL/WED WS10 .....67 J3
Derek Av POL/KGSB/FAZ B78 .....47 J3
Dereton Cl DUDN DY1 .....84 C6
Dering Cl COVE CV2 .....135 H5
Deronda Cl BDWTH CV12 .....116 E2
Derrick Burchers Ml
  KIDD DY10 * 138 C7
Derron Av
  LGN/SDN/BHAMAIR B26 .....109 J8
Derry Cl HRBN B17 .....123 L2
  KNWTH CV8 .....183 L2
Derrydown Cl ERDW/GRVHL B23 .....72 A4
Derrydown Rd PBAR/PBCH B42 .....70 D3
Derry St BKHL/PFLD WV2 .....3 G9
  BRLYHL DY5 .....102 A3
Dersingham Dr COVN CV6 .....134 F3
Derwent Av STRPT DY13 .....163 K4
Derwent Cl BRLYHL DY5 .....83 M7
  COVW CV5 .....153 J1
  FOAKS/STRLY B74 .....55 K3
  RLSN CV32 .....206 B3
  RUGBYN/HIL CV21 .....161 G7
  WLNHL WV13 .....52 A3
Derwent Dr BNTWD WS7 .....19 H7
Derwent Gv BEWD DY12 .....162 D1
  HLGN/YWD B28 .....126 D6
  SHHTH WV12 .....38 A6
Derwent Rd BDWTH CV12 .....116 D3
  BVILLE B30 .....125 G5
  CNCK/NC WS11 .....16 B5
  COVN CV6 .....133 L3
  DUNHL/THL/PER WV6 .....35 H5
Derwent Wy BRGRVE B60 .....191 M4
  NUN CV11 .....81 K7
Desford Av PBAR/PBCH B42 .....71 G6
Despard Rd COVW CV5 .....152 F1
Dettonford Rd RIDG/WDGT B32 .....122 F5
Devereux Cl CBROM B36 .....92 A5
  TLHL/CAN CV4 .....153 C4
Devereux Rd MGN/WHC B75 .....57 G4
  WBROM B70 .....87 J4
Devey Dr TPTN/OCK DY4 .....68 B7
Devine Cft TPTN/OCK DY4 .....68 B8
Devitts Cl SHLY B90 .....148 F7
Devon Cl KIDD DY11 .....138 A4
  NUNW/HART CV10 .....98 D2
Devon Crs ALDR WS9 .....40 D2
  DUDS DY2 .....85 G4
  HHTH/SAND B71 .....69 G7
Devon Gv COVE CV2 .....134 F8
Devonport Cl REDW B97 .....202 A8
Devon Rd CNCK/NC WS11 .....16 D5
  DARL/WED WS10 .....69 G1
  RBRY B45 .....143 K4
  SMTHWKW B67 .....105 J6
  STRBR DY8 .....101 H6
  WLNHL WV13 .....52 B4
  WOLV WV1 .....51 G1
Devonshire Av WSNGN B18 .....88 D7
Devonshire Dr HHTH/SAND B71 .....87 J2
  POL/KGSB/FAZ B78 .....45 L4
Devonshire Rd
  BFLD/HDSWWD B20 .....88 D3
  SMTHWK B67 .....87 J7
Devonshire St WSNGN B18 .....88 D7
Devon St VAUX/NECH B7 .....108 A1
Devoran Cl
  DUNHL/THL/PER WV6 .....49 M1
  RCOVN/BALC/EX CV7 .....116 F5
Dewar Gv RUGBYN/HIL CV21 .....188 C1
Dewberry Dr DSYBK/YTR WS5 .....69 L2
Dewberry Rd STRBR DY8 .....101 K4
Dewhurst St STETCH B33 .....109 M2
Dewis Gv ALE/KHTH/YWD B14 .....146 E5
Dewsbury Av COVS CV3 .....154 F8
Dewsbury Cl STRBR DY8 .....101 J2
Dewsbury Dr BNTWD WS7 .....19 G4
  ETTPK/GDPK/PENN WV4 .....65 L2
Dewsbury Gv PBAR/PBCH B42 .....71 J7
Dexter La ATHST CV9 .....77 G2
Dexter Wy POL/KGSB/FAZ B78 .....45 K1
Deykin Av AST/WIT B6 .....89 L3
Deykin Rd AST/WIT B6 .....20 E7
D'Eyncourt Rd WNSFLD WV11 .....36 E1
Dial Cl ALE/KHTH/YWD B14 .....146 C3
Dial House La COVW CV5 .....153 K1
Dial La STRBR DY8 .....101 J5
  WBROM B70 .....68 D7
Diamond Gv CNCK/NC WS11 .....17 G3
Diamond Park Dr STRBR DY8 .....101 J4
Diana Cl ALDR WS9 .....40 F2
Diana Dr COVE CV2 .....135 J4
Dibble Cl SHHTH WV12 .....38 B8
Dibble Rd SMTHWKW B67 .....87 H4
Dibdale Rd DUDN DY1 .....84 D2
Dibdale St DUDN DY1 .....84 D3
Dice Pleck NFLD/LBR B31 .....145 G3
Dickens Cl NUNW/HART CV10 .....97 L1
  SEDG DY3 .....65 M8
Dickens Gv ALE/KHTH/YWD B14 .....146 E2
Dickens Heath Rd SHLY B90 .....147 L8
Dickens Rd BILS/COS WV14 .....67 H3
  RUGBYS/DCH CV22 .....186 D7
  WOLV WV10 .....36 F1
  WWCK CV34 .....205 M5
Dickinson Av WOLV WV10 .....36 D5
Dickinson Ct
  RUGBYS/DCH CV22 .....186 E6
Dickinson Dr WALM/CURD B76 .....73 J1
  WSLW WS2 .....53 C7
Dickinson Rd WMBN WV5 .....82 K1
Dick Sheppard Av
  TPTN/OCK DY4 .....67 M5
Didcot Cl REDW B97 .....202 A8
Diddington Av HLGN/YWD B28 .....126 E8
Diddington La HIA/OLT B92 .....130 A5
Didgley Gv
  CHWD/FDBR/MGN B37 .....92 B8
Didgley La RCOVN/BALC/EX CV7 .....114 A1
Didsbury Rd
  RCOVN/BALC/EX CV7 .....116 E4
Digbeth DIG/EDG B5 .....7 H6
  WSL WS1 .....4 F4
Digbey Cl COVW CV5 .....132 F7
Digby Cft CSHL/WTROR B46 .....92 F2
Digby Dr
  CHWD/FDBR/MGN B37 .....110 F7
Digby Rd CSHL/WTROR B46 .....93 K7
  KGSWFD DY6 .....83 H5
  SCFLD/BOLD B73 .....72 C2
Dilcock Wy TLHL/CAN CV4 .....153 K6
Dilke Rd ALDR WS9 .....40 D8
Dillam Cl COVN CV6 .....134 E1
Dillotford Av COVS CV3 .....155 G6

Dilloways La WLNHL WV13 51 J4
Dilwyn Cl REDE B98 203 K4
Dimbles Hl LICH WS13 20 F4
Dimbles La LICH WS13 20 E3
Dimmingsdale Bank
RIDG/WDGT B32 123 G1
Dimmingsdale Rd
ETTPK/GDPK/PENN WV4 48 B8
Dimminsdale WLNHL WV13 51 L4
Dimmocks Av BILS/COS WV14 67 H5
Dimmock St
ETTPK/GDPK/PENN WV4 50 C8
Dimsdale Gv NFLD/LBR B31 144 C2
Dimsdale Rd NFLD/LBR B31 144 B2
Dinedor Cl REDE B98 203 H2
Dingle Av CDYHTH B64 103 J5
Dingle Cl BVILLE B30 124 B6
COVN CV6 133 L7
DUDS DY2 85 J6
Dingle Hollow OLDBY B69 86 B5
Dingle La CSHL/WTROR B46 76 D8
SOLH B91 148 D3
WLNHL WV13 51 L1
Dingle Md ALE/KHTH/YWD B14 146 A1
Dingle Rd BRWNH WS8 26 C8
DUDS DY2 85 J6
HAG/WOL DY9 119 M3
KGSWFD DY6 101 L1
WMBN WV5 64 D8
Dingle St OLDBY B69 86 B5
The Dingle BDMR/CCFT WV3 49 H4
NUNW/HART CV10 80 C7
OLDBY B69 86 B5
SHLY B90 148 B8
SLYOAK B29 124 C3
Dingle Vw SEDG DY3 66 A6
Dingley Rd BDWTH CV12 117 M3
DARL/WED WS10 52 E8
Dinham Gdns DUDN DY1 84 C2
Dinmore Av NFLD/LBR B31 144 F1
Dinmore Cl REDE B98 203 H2
Dippons Dr
DUNHL/THL/PER WV6 48 E3
Dippons Mill Cl
DUNHL/THL/PER WV6 48 E2
Dirtyfoot La
ETTPK/GDPK/PENN WV4 48 E8
Discovery Cl TPTN/OCK DY4 68 A8
Discovery Wy COVS CV3 156 F5
The Ditch WSL WS1 5 G4
Ditton Cl RUGBYS/DCH CV22 186 A4
Ditton Gv NFLD/LBR B31 144 D7
Dixon Cl CVALE B35 91 L3
TPTN/OCK DY4 68 A7
Dixon Rd SMHTH B10 107 M5
Dixon's Green Rd DUDS DY2 85 J5
Dixon St BKHL/PFLD WV2 50 C7
KIDD DY10 138 C8
Dobbins Oak Rd HAG/WOL DY9 120 B4
Dobbs Mill Cl SLYOAK B29 124 F3
Dobbs St BKHL/PFLD WV2 2 F8
Dobes La KIDD DY10 166 A7
Dockar Rd NFLD/LBR B31 144 C3
Dockers Cl RCOVN/BALC/EX CV7 152 A6
Dock La DUDN DY1 84 F4
Dock Meadow Dr
ETTPK/GDPK/PENN WV4 66 E1
Dock Rd STRBR DY8 101 K3
The Dock BRGRVW B61 168 E5
HAG/WOL DY9 102 D8
Doctors Hl BRGRVW B61 168 B4
HAG/WOL DY9 120 A2
Doctors La KGSWFD DY6 82 D8
Doctor's Piece WLNHL WV13 51 M3
Dodd Av WWCK CV34 206 A6
Doddington Gv
RIDG/WDGT B32 122 F5
Dodds La LICH WS13 19 G2
Dodford Cl RBRY B45 143 K6
Dodford Rd BRGRVW B61 168 B4
Dodgson Cl COVN CV6 134 E1
Doe Bank La ALDR WS9 55 H7
COV CV1 8 B4
Doe Bank Rd TPTN/OCK DY4 68 A4
Dogberry Cl COVS CV3 156 A7
Dogge Lane Cft ACGN B27 126 F3
Dogkennel La LGLYGN/QTN B68 87 G8
Dog Kennel La HALE B63 121 M2
SHLY B90 148 A6
WSL WS1 5 H3
Dog La BEWD DY12 162 F2
BRGRVW B61 190 A7
CSHL/WTROR B46 76 E7
LICHS WS14 43 L1
TAM/AM/WIL B77 32 F7
Dogpool La BVILLE B30 124 F4
Doidge Rd ERDW/GRVHL B23 90 B2
Dolben La REDE B98 203 H2
Dollery Dr DIG/EDG B5 107 G8
Dollis Gv KGSTG B44 71 K2
Dollman St VAUX/NECH B7 107 M2
Dolman Rd AST/WIT B6 89 J5
Dolobran Rd SPARK B11 107 M6
Dolomite Av COVW CV5 154 B4
Dolphin Cl BLOX/PEL WS3 39 K4
Dolphin La ACGN B27 127 G4
Dolphin Rd REDE B98 194 E8
SPARK B11 108 B8
Dolton Wy TPTN/OCK DY4 67 J7
Domar Rd KIDDW DY11 137 M6
Dominic Cl BVILLE B30 145 H1
Doncaster Cl COVE CV2 135 H6
Doncaster Wy CBROM B36 91 G5
Don Cl EDG B15 106 B5
Donegal Cl TLHL/CAN CV4 153 L6
Donegal Rd FOAKS/STRLY B74 55 L8
Dongan Rd WWCK CV34 205 J6
Don Gv CNCK/NC WS11 * 16 B6
Donibristle Cft CVALE B35 91 L1
Donnington Av COVN CV6 133 J8
Donnington Cl REDE B98 195 G8
Donnithorne Av
NUNW/HART CV10 99 G4
Dooley Cl WLNHL WV13 51 J3
Doone Cl COVE CV2 135 J7
Dorado TAM/AM/WIL B77 46 B7
Doran Cl HALE B63 121 H4
Doranda Wy HHTH/SAND B71 87 K4
Dora Rd HDSW B21 88 C6
SMHTH B10 108 C6
WBROM B70 87 G4
Dora St WSLW WS2 52 F6
Dorcas Cl NUN CV11 99 M5
Dorchester Av
RWWCK/WEL CV35 204 D7
Dorchester Cl SHHTH WV12 38 A5
Dorchester Ct SOLH B91 148 E1
Dorchester Dr HRBN B17 123 M1
Dorchester Rd CNCK/NC WS11 15 M4
HAG/WOL DY9 120 B3
SHHTH WV12 38 A5
SOLH B91 148 E1
Dorchester Wy COVE CV2 135 K8
COVE CV2 156 D1
NUN CV11 81 L6
Dordale Cl NFLD/LBR B31 144 A4
Dordale Rd HAG/WOL DY9 167 H2
Dordon Cl SHLY B90 147 J4
Dordon Rd POL/KGSB/FAZ B78 47 K5
Doreen Gv ERDE/BCHGN B24 90 F3
Doris Rd BORD B9 108 B4
CSHL/WTROR B46 93 K5
SPARK B11 125 M1
Dorking Gv EDG B15 6 D8
Dorlcote Rd WASH/WDE B8 108 E1
Dorlecote Pl NUNW/HART CV10 99 G5
Dorlecote Rd
NUNW/HART CV10 99 G5
Dormer Av TAM/AM/WIL B77 32 C8
Dormer Harris Av
TLHL/CAN CV4 153 K4
Dormer Pl RLSN CV32 206 D5
Dormie Cl HWK/WKHTH B38 145 H4
Dormington Rd KGSTG B44 71 K2
Dormston Cl REDE B98 202 D4
SOLH B91 149 G5
Dormston Dr SEDG DY3 66 B5
SLYOAK B29 123 K3
Dormy Dr NFLD/LBR B31 144 E6
Dorncliffe Av STETCH B33 110 B6
Dorney Cl COVW CV5 154 C5
Dornie Dr HWK/WKHTH B38 145 K4
Dornton Rd BVILLE B30 125 G5
Dorothy Powell Wy COVE CV2 135 K4
Dorothy Rd SMTHWKW B67 105 L2
SPARK B11 108 F8
Dorothy St WSL WS1 4 C9
Dorridge Cl REDW B97 201 M4
Dorridge Cft DOR/KN B93 175 K3
Dorridge Rd DOR/KN B93 175 L3
Dorrington Gn PBAR/PBCH B42 70 E8
Dorrington Rd PBAR/PBCH B42 70 E8
Dorset Cl NUNW/HART CV10 98 D2
POL/KGSB/FAZ B78 45 L4
RBRY B45 143 K3
Dorset Dr ALDR WS9 40 E4
Dorset Pl BLOX/PEL WS3 39 G6
Dorset Rd COV CV1 134 A8
HEDN WS12 17 J4
HRBN B17 105 M2
STRBR DY8 101 H6
WASH/WDE B8 90 A7
Dorset Tower WSNGN B18 * 6 A2
Dorsett Rd DARL/WED WS10 52 A7
DARL/WED WS10 69 H3
STRPT DY13 163 K8
STRPT DY13 188 E1
Dorsett Road Ter
DARL/WED WS10 52 A7
Dorsheath Gdns
ERDW/GRVHL B23 90 D1
Dorsington Cl
RWWCK/WEL CV35 204 C2
Dorsington Rd ACGN B27 127 H4
Dorstone Covert
ALE/KHTH/YWD B14 146 A3
Dorville Cl HWK/WKHTH B38 145 H5
Dosthill Rd (Two Gates)
TAM/AM/WIL B77 46 B7
Dotterel Pl KIDD DY10 164 E4
Douay Rd ERDE/BCHGN B24 72 F7
Double Rw DUDS DY2 103 J1
Doughty St TPTN/OCK DY4 68 A8
Douglas Av CBROM B36 91 H7
LGLYGN/QTN B68 87 H8
Douglas Davies Cl SHHTH WV12 52 A1
Douglas Pl WOLVN WV10 36 A7
Douglas Rd ACGN B27 126 F1
BILS/COS WV14 67 H5
CSCFLD/WYGN B72 73 G2
HDSW B21 88 C5
HLYWD B47 146 E6
LGLYGN/QTN B68 105 H1
RMSLY B62 104 C4
RUGBYN/HIL CV21 161 G7
Douglass Rd DUDS DY2 85 H5
Doulton Cl COVE CV2 * 135 J4
RIDG/WDGT B32 123 K2
Doulton Dr SMTHWK B66 87 L7
Doulton Rd BLKHTH/ROWR B65 103 L1
Dovebridge Cl WALM/CURD B76 73 K1
Dove Cl BDWTH CV12 116 C2
BNTWD WS7 19 H7
DARL/WED WS10 68 F1
KIDD DY10 164 E3
WSL WS1 5 J5
YDLY B25 109 J5
Dovecote Cl COVN CV6 133 H8
DUNHL/THL/PER WV6 49 G1
SOLH B91 127 M5
TPTN/OCK DY4 68 A8
Dovecote Rd BRGRVW B61 191 J4
The Dovecotes MGN/WHC B75 56 F2
Dovedale CNCK/NC WS11 12 E8
RUGBYN/HIL CV21 161 G6
Dovedale Av BLOX/PEL WS3 25 L8
COVN CV6 134 D3
SHHTH WV12 51 L1
SHLY B90 147 M4
Dovedale Ct
ETTPK/GDPK/PENN WV4 66 D3
Dovedale Dr HLGN/YWD B28 126 D7
Dovedale Rd ERDW/GRVHL B23 72 A7
ETTPK/GDPK/PENN WV4 66 C2
KGSWFD DY6 83 J5
Dove Dr STRBR DY8 101 L5
Dove Gdns HWK/WKHTH B38 145 M3
Dove Hollow GTWY WS6 24 D4
HEDN WS12 17 J1
Dovehouse Flds LICHS WS14 20 F7
Dove House La HIA/OLT B92 127 K6
Dovehouse Pool Rd AST/WIT B6 89 J5
Dover Cl RIDG/WDGT B32 122 E6
Dovercourt Rd
LGN/SDN/BHAMAIR B26 110 A8
Doverdale Av KIDD DY10 138 F8
Doverdale Cl HALE B63 103 H8
REDE B98 202 F6
Dove Rdg STRBR DY8 101 L6
Doveridge Cl SOLH B91 127 J7
Doveridge Pl WSL WS1 5 G7
Doveridge Rd HLGN/YWD B28 126 C8
Doversley Rd
ALE/KHTH/YWD B14 125 G8
Dover St BILS/COS WV14 51 H7
COV CV1 * 8 D4
WSNGN B18 88 D7
Dovestone POL/KGSB/FAZ B78 47 H4
Dove Wy CBROM B36 92 D5
Dovey Dr WALM/CURD B76 73 L6
Dovey Rd MOS/BIL B13 126 B3
OLDBY B69 86 B5
Dovey Tower VAUX/NECH B7 * 7 M2
Dowar Rd RBRY B45 144 A6
Dowells Gdns STRBR DY8 101 H2
The Doweries RBRY B45 143 K5
Dower Rd MGN/WHC B75 56 F4
Dowler's Hill Crs REDE B98 202 E5
Dowles Cl SLYOAK B29 123 M7
Dowles Rd BEWD DY12 136 D8
KIDDW DY11 163 M3
Dowley Cft COVS CV3 156 F4
Downcroft Av
HWK/WKHTH B38 145 J3
Downderry Wy COVN CV6 134 E7
Downend Cl WOLVN WV10 36 D1
Downes Ct TPTN/OCK DY4 67 J8
Downesway CNCK/NC WS11 16 A3
Downey Cl SPARK B11 107 M6
Downfield Cl BLOX/PEL WS3 * 38 E1
Downfield Dr SEDG DY3 66 C7
Downham Cl DSYBK/YTR WS5 54 C4
Downham Pl BDMR/CCFT WV3 49 K5
Downie Rd CDSL WV8 35 G2
Downing Cl BLKHTH/ROWR B65 104 A4
DOR/KN B93 175 L1
WNSFLD WV11 37 L6
Downing Crs BDWTH CV12 117 G1
Downing Dr CRTAM B79 31 J8
Downing St HALE B63 103 L8
SMTHWK B66 88 A6
Downland Cl HWK/WKHTH B38 145 K4
Downsell Rd REDW B97 201 L3
Downsfield Rd
LGN/SDN/BHAMAIR B26 109 M6
Downside Rd ERDE/BCHGN B24 90 C4
Downs Rd WLNHL WV13 52 A5
The Downs FOAKS/STRLY B74 55 J3
WOLVN WV10 36 A7
Downton Cl COVE CV2 135 L5
Downton Crs STETCH B33 110 C2
Dowty Av BDWTH CV12 116 B4
Dowty Wy COVEN WV9 35 L2
Doyle Dr COVN CV6 134 D2
Dragoon Flds BRGRVE B60 191 M5
Drake Av PENK ST19 10 D6
Drake Cl BLOX/PEL WS3 38 F4
Drake Crs KIDDW DY11 137 L6
Drake Cft LICH WS13 21 G5
Drake Rd BLOX/PEL WS3 39 G4
ERDW/GRVHL B23 90 A2
SMTHWK B66 87 H6
Drakes Cl REDW B97 202 A7
Drakes Cross Pde HLYWD B47 146 E8
Drakes Hill Cl KINVER DY7 119 G1
Drake St COVN CV6 134 B6
HHTH/SAND B71 69 G8
Drancy Av SHHTH WV12 38 B7
Draper Cl KNWTH CV8 198 A1
Draper's Flds COV CV1 8 F2
Drawbridge Rd SHLY B90 147 J5
Draycote Cl HIA/OLT B92 128 B6
Draycott Av ERDW/GRVHL B23 72 B8
Draycott Cl
ETTPK/GDPK/PENN WV4 49 G8
REDW B97 193 M8
Draycott Crs TAM/AM/WIL B77 46 A4
Draycott Dr NFLD/LBR B31 123 J6
Draycott Rd COVE CV2 134 F6
SMTHWK B66 87 J6
Drayman Cl WSL WS1 5 G7
Drayton Cl MGN/WHC B75 56 F2
NUNW/HART CV10 79 L5
REDE B98 203 H5
Drayton Ct BRGRVE B60 191 M5
NUNW/HART CV10 * 79 M3
WWCK CV34 205 J3
Drayton Crs COVW CV5 132 B8
Drayton La POL/KGSB/FAZ B78 44 D8
Drayton Leys
RUGBYS/DCH CV22 186 E6
Drayton Manor Dr
POL/KGSB/FAZ B78 45 K4
Drayton Rd
ALE/KHTH/YWD B14 125 J5
BDWTH CV12 117 G3
HAG/WOL DY9 141 H7
KIDD DY10 166 E2
SHLY B90 148 C5
SMTHWK B66 105 L4
Drayton St BKHL/PFLD WV2 2 F9
WSLW WS2 4 A3
Drayton Wy NUNW/HART CV10 80 A6
Dreadnought Rd BRLYHL DY5 83 M6
The Dreel EDG B15 106 C6
Dreghorn Rd CBROM B36 91 J5
Drem Cft CVALE B35 91 L3
Dresden Cl
ETTPK/GDPK/PENN WV4 66 E1
Drew Crs HAG/WOL DY9 120 B2
KNWTH CV8 197 L1
Drew Rd HAG/WOL DY9 120 B2
Drews Holloway HALE B63 103 H8
Drews Holloway South
HALE B63 103 H8
Drews La WASH/WDE B8 90 E7
Drews Meadow Cl
ALE/KHTH/YWD B14 146 A3
Dreyer Cl RUGBYS/DCH CV22 186 A3
Driffield Cl REDE B98 203 H3
Driffold SCFLD/BOLD B73 72 F2
Driftwood Cl HWK/WKHTH B38 145 H6
Drive Flds
ETTPK/GDPK/PENN WV4 48 F7
The Drive ALVE B48 170 F2
BFLD/HDSWWD B20 88 E3
BLOX/PEL WS3 39 J3
BRLYHL DY5 84 A8
CDSL WV8 34 D2
COVE CV2 156 B2
CSHL/WTROR B46 * 93 L7
DUNHL/THL/PER WV6 * 35 G8
ERDW/GRVHL B23 90 C3
HALE B63 103 H8
HALE B63 121 L2
LICHS WS14 29 J5
REDW B97 193 G7
RUSH/SHEL WS4 40 A4
Droitwich Rd KIDD DY10 165 G8
Dronfield Rd COVE CV2 155 M2
Drovers Wy BRGRVE B60 191 J7
The Droveway COVEN WV9 35 K3
Droylsdon Park Rd COVS CV3 180 F2
Druid Park Rd SHHTH WV12 38 A4
Druid Rd COVE CV2 155 M2
Druids Av ALDR WS9 41 G5
BLKHTH/ROWR B65 104 B1
Druids La ALE/KHTH/YWD B14 146 A4
Druids Wk ALDR WS9 40 E2
Druids Wy PENK ST19 10 D6
Drummond Cl COVN CV6 133 K6
WNSFLD WV11 37 L3
Drummond Gv GTB/HAM B43 71 G2
Drummond Rd BORD B9 108 D3
BRGRVE B60 191 M5
HAG/WOL DY9 120 D1
Drummond St WOLV WV1 2 E3
Drummond Wy
CHWD/FDBR/MGN B37 111 G3
Drury La CDSL WV8 34 D1
RUGBYN/HIL CV21 * 186 E2
SOLH B91 149 G2
STRBR DY8 101 L8
Drybrook Cl HWK/WKHTH B38 145 J5
Drybrooks Cl
RCOVN/BALC/EX CV7 151 M7
Dryden Cl KNWTH CV8 197 K2
NUNW/HART CV10 79 K8
SHHTH WV12 38 C5
TPTN/OCK DY4 67 L6
Dryden Gv ACGN B27 126 F3
Dryden Pl BLOX/PEL WS3 39 J6
RUGBYS/DCH CV22 186 C2
Dryden Rd BLOX/PEL WS3 39 J6
CRTAM B79 31 L6
WOLVN WV10 36 D4
Dryden Wk RUGBYS/DCH CV22 186 C2
Drylea Gv CBROM B36 91 K5
Dry Mill La BEWD DY12 136 C8
Dual Wy HEDN WS12 12 A5
Dubarry Av KGSWFD DY6 83 G6
Duchess Pde WBROM B70 * 87 H2
Duchess Rd LDYWD/EDGR B16 106 E4
WSL WS1 53 H8
Duckhouse Rd WNSFLD WV11 37 H6
Duck La CDSL WV8 34 F3
Duckpen Cottages KIDD DY10 * 139 J5
Duddeston Dr WASH/WDE B8 108 B1
Duddeston Manor Rd
VAUX/NECH B7 7 M1
Duddeston Mill Rd
VAUX/NECH B7 107 M1
Dudding Rd
ETTPK/GDPK/PENN WV4 50 B8
Dudhill Rd CDYHTH B64 103 L2
Dudley Cl BLKHTH/ROWR B65 85 K7
Dudley Crs WNSFLD WV11 37 J7
Dudley Gn RLSN CV32 206 F3
Dudley Park Rd ACGN B27 127 G2
Dudley Port TPTN/OCK DY4 85 L2
Dudley Rd BKHL/PFLD WV2 50 B6
BLKHTH/ROWR B65 85 L8
BRLYHL DY5 102 B1
HALE B63 103 M7
KGSWFD DY6 83 G5
KNWTH CV8 197 K3
OLDBY B69 86 C5
SEDG DY3 66 B6
SEDG DY3 83 G2
TPTN/OCK DY4 67 H8
WSNGN B18 106 B1
Dudley Rd East OLDBY B69 86 A3
Dudley Rd West OLDBY B69 85 M3
Dudley Rw DUDS DY2 85 H4
Dudley Southern By-Pass
DUDS DY2 84 E6
Dudley St ATHST CV9 63 H6
BILS/COS WV14 67 H1
COVN CV6 134 E4
DARL/WED WS10 68 C3
DIG/EDG B5 7 G6
KIDD DY10 138 C6
SEDG DY3 66 B5
WBROM B70 68 D8
WOLV WV1 2 F5
WSL WS1 4 F5
Dudley Wk
ETTPK/GDPK/PENN WV4 50 A8
Dudley Wood Av DUDS DY2 103 G3
Dudley Wood Rd DUDS DY2 103 G4
Dudmaston Wy DUDN DY1 84 C2
Dudnill Gv RIDG/WDGT B32 122 E5
Duffield Cl CDSL WV8 35 K4
Duffy Pl RUGBYN/HIL CV21 187 L5
Dufton Rd RIDG/WDGT B32 105 J8
Dugdale Cl HEDN WS12 17 K2
Dugdale Crs MGN/WHC B75 57 G2
Dugdale Rd COVN CV6 133 L7
Dugdale St NUN CV11 99 G1
WSNGN B18 106 B1
Duggins La
RCOVN/BALC/EX CV7 152 F5
Duke Barn Fld COVE CV2 134 E8
Duke Rd BNTWD WS7 18 C4
Dukes Rd BVILLE B30 145 K2
Duke St BDMR/CCFT WV3 49 L6
BLKHTH/ROWR B65 103 M3
COVW CV5 154 D3
CSCFLD/WYGN B72 72 F1
NUN CV11 98 E1
RLSN CV32 206 E4
RUGBYN/HIL CV21 186 E1
SEDG DY3 66 B8
STRBR DY8 101 L8
WBROM B70 86 F1
WNSFLD WV11 37 H8
WOLV WV1 3 J6
Dukes Wy POL/KGSB/FAZ B78 47 L7
Dulvern Gv ALE/KHTH/YWD B14 125 H8
Dulverton Av COVW CV5 154 B1
Dulverton Rd AST/WIT B6 89 L4
Dulwich Gv KGSTG B44 71 M5
Dulwich Rd KGSTG B44 71 L5
Dumbleberry Av SEDG DY3 66 A6
Dumblederry La ALDR WS9 40 C5
Dumble Pit La HLYWD B47 172 C6
Dumolo's La TAM/AM/WIL B77 46 C2
Dumphouse La ALVE B48 195 G2
Dunard Rd SHLY B90 147 K2
Dunbar Cl KIDD DY10 139 G7
Dunbar Gv GTB/HAM B43 70 F1
Dunblane Dr RLSN CV32 199 G8
Duncalfe Dr MGN/WHC B75 56 F2
Duncan Dr RUGBYS/DCH CV22 186 B7
Duncan Edwards Cl DUDN DY1 84 E5
Duncan St BKHL/PFLD WV2 50 A6
Dunchurch Cl
RCOVN/BALC/EX CV7 151 M6
REDE B98 203 K4
Dunchurch Crs SCFLD/BOLD B73 72 A2
Dunchurch Dr NFLD/LBR B31 123 J6
Dunchurch Hwy COVW CV5 132 E7
Dunchurch Rd
RUGBYS/DCH CV22 186 D7
Dunclent Crs KIDD DY10 138 F8
Dunclent La KIDD DY10 165 H2
Duncombe Gn CSHL/WTROR B46 93 K6
Duncombe Gv HRBN B17 105 K6
Duncombe St STRBR DY8 101 H7
Duncroft Av COVN CV6 133 K6
Duncroft Rd
LGN/SDN/BHAMAIR B26 109 K5
Duncumb Rd MGN/WHC B75 57 L8
Dundalk La GTWY WS6 24 B4
Dundas Av OLDBY B69 85 K5
Dunedin TAM/AM/WIL B77 46 E4
Dunedin Dr RBRY B45 169 L4
Dunedin Rd KGSTG B44 71 J2
Dunhampton Dr KIDD DY10 138 F4
Dunhill Av TLHL/CAN CV4 153 J2
Dunkirk Av WBROM B70 86 C1
Dunkley St WOLV WV1 2 E3
Dunley Cft SHLY B90 148 D7
Dunley Rd STRPT DY13 188 C3
Dunlin Cl ERDW/GRVHL B23 90 A3
KGSWFD DY6 83 L7
Dunlin Dr KIDD DY10 164 D3
WOLVN WV10 22 E6
Dunlop Rd REDW B97 202 A8
Dunlop Wy ERDE/BCHGN B24 91 J4
Dunmore Rd BEWD DY12 137 G8
Dunnerdale RUGBYN/HIL CV21 161 H5
Dunnerdale Rd BRWNH WS8 26 B7
Dunnigan Rd RIDG/WDGT B32 123 K2
Dunnington Av KIDD DY10 138 E4
Dunnose Cl COVN CV6 134 C5
Dunns Bank BRLYHL DY5 102 D6
Dunn's La POL/KGSB/FAZ B78 47 M7
Dunrose Cl COVE CV2 156 C3
Dunsfold Cl BILS/COS WV14 66 E2
Dunsfold Cft AST/WIT B6 89 K7
Dunsford Cl BRLYHL DY5 101 M6
Dunsford Rd SMTHWK B66 105 L3
Dunsink Rd AST/WIT B6 89 K4
Dunslade Crs BRLYHL DY5 102 D5
Dunslade Rd ERDW/GRVHL B23 72 C6
Dunsley Dr KINVER DY7 118
STRBR DY8 101
Dunsley Gv
ETTPK/GDPK/PENN WV4 65
Dunsley Rd KINVER DY7 100
Dunsmore Av COVS CV3 156
RUGBYN/HIL CV21 187
Dunsmore Dr BRLYHL DY5 102
Dunsmore Gv SOLH B91 127
Dunsmore Rd HLGN/YWD B28 126
Dunstall Av
DUNHL/THL/PER WV6 36
Dunstall Cl REDW B97 201
Dunstall Gv SLYOAK B29 123
Dunstall Hl
DUNHL/THL/PER WV6 36
Dunstall La
DUNHL/THL/PER WV6 35
POL/KGSB/FAZ B78 31
Dunstall Rd
DUNHL/THL/PER WV6 49
HALE B63 121
Dunstan Cft SHLY B90 148
Dunster TAM/AM/WIL B77 46
Dunster Cl BVILLE B30 145
Dunster Gv
DUNHL/THL/PER WV6 48
Dunster Pl COVN CV6 134
Dunster Rd
CHWD/FDBR/MGN B37 111
Dunston Cl GTWY WS6 24
KGSWFD DY6 83
Dunston Dr BNTWD WS7 18
Dunsville Dr COVE CV2 135
Dunton Cl MGN/WHC B75 56
Dunton Coppice
WALM/CURD B76 75
Dunton Hall Rd SHLY B90 147
Dunton La WALM/CURD B76 74
Dunton Rd
CHWD/FDBR/MGN B37 110
Dunvegan Cl COVS CV3 156
KNWTH CV8 198
Dunvegan Rd ERDE/BCHGN B24 90
Durant Cl RBRY B45 143
Durban Rd SMTHWK B66 106
Durbar Av COVN CV6 134
D'urberville Rd BKHL/PFLD WV2 50
Durham Av WLNHL WV13 52
Durham Cl BRGRVW B61 191
POL/KGSB/FAZ B78 45
RCOVN/BALC/EX CV7 133
Durham Crs COVW CV5 132
Durham Cft
CHWD/FDBR/MGN B37 110
Durham Dr HHTH/SAND B71 69
Durham Pl WSLW WS2 52
Durham Rd BLKHTH/ROWR B65 104
DARL/WED WS10 69
DUDS DY2 103
SPARK B11 125
STRBR DY8 101
WSLW WS2 52
Durley Dean Rd SLYOAK B29 124
Durley Dr SCFLD/BOLD B73 72
Durley Rd YDLY B25 109
Durlston Cl TAM/AM/WIL B77 32
Durlston Gv HLGN/YWD B28 126
Durnford Cft
ALE/KHTH/YWD B14 146
Durrell Dr RUGBYS/DCH CV22 185
Dursley Cl HIA/OLT B92 127
SHHTH WV12 52
Dursley Dr CNCK/NC WS11 15
Dursley La REDE B98 203
Dursley Rd BNTWD WS7 18
Dusthouse La BRGRVE B60 192
Dutton Rd COVE CV2 135
Dutton's La MGN/WHC B75 57
Duxford Cl REDW B97 201
Duxford Rd PBAR/PBCH B42 70
Dwellings La RIDG/WDGT B32 104
Dyas Av PBAR/PBCH B42 70
Dyas Rd HLYWD B47 146
KGSTG B44 71
Dyce Cl CVALE B35 91
Dyers La HOCK/TIA B94 174
KNWTH CV8 183
Dymoke St BHTH/HG B12 107
Dymond Rd COVN CV6 134
Dynes Wk SMTHWKW B67 87
Dyott Cl LICH WS13 21
Dyott Rd MOS/BIL B13 125
Dysart Cl COV CV1 9
Dyson Cl RUGBYN/HIL CV21 187
WSLW WS2 52
Dysons Gdns WASH/WDE B8 90
Dyson St TLHL/CAN CV4 153

E

Eachelhurst Rd
ERDE/BCHGN B24 91
Eachus Rd BILS/COS WV14 67
Eachway RBRY B45 143
Eachway La RBRY B45 143
Eacott Cl COVN CV6 133
Eadie Ms REDW B97 202
Eadie St NUNW/HART CV10 98
Eagle Cl BLKHTH/ROWR B65 103
DUDN DY1 84
GTWY WS6 24
NUN CV11 99
Eagle Ct BDMR/CCFT WV3 * 49
Eagle Cft ALE/KHTH/YWD B14 146
Eagle Dr TAM/AM/WIL B77 46
Eagle Gdns ERDE/BCHGN B24 90
Eagle Gv CBROM B36 92
HEDN WS12 17
Eagle La TPTN/OCK DY4 68
Eagle Rd REDE B98 195
Eagle St BDMR/CCFT WV3 49
BKHL/PFLD WV2 3
COV CV1 134
RLSS CV31 206
TPTN/OCK DY4 68
Eagle St East COV CV1 134
Ealing Gv KGSTG B44 71
Ealingham TAM/AM/WIL B77 46
Eardisley Cl REDE B98 203
Earl Dr BNTWD WS7 18
Earlsbury Gdns
BFLD/HDSWWD B20 89
Earls Cl REDW B97 201
Earls Court Rd HRBN B17 105
The Earl's Cft COVS CV3 155
Earlsdon Av North COVW CV5 154
Earlsdon Av South COVW CV5 8
Earlsdon St COVW CV5 154
Earls Ferry Gdns
RIDG/WDGT B32 122
Earlsmead Rd HDSW B21 89
Earlsmere HOCK/TIA B94 175
Earls Rd NUN CV11 80

.USH/SHEL WS4 ...40 A6
ston Wy GTB/HAM B43 ...70 B5
st BDWTH CV12 ...117 C3
.ILS/COS WV14 ...51 H8
.ILS/COS WV14 ...67 H5
OV CV1 ...9 C5
.y River Pl BDWTH DY12 ...162 D2
.UGBYN/HIL CV21 ...186 F2
.B70 ...86 F1
.SL WS1 ...4 D8
.y HALE B63 ...121 M1
swood Common
.wood/TIA B94 ...173 L7
swood Ct
FLD/HDSWWD B20 ...88 A3
swood Gv COVEN WV9 ...35 L2
swood Dr MGN/WHC B75 ...57 G6
swood Dr DOR/KN B93 ...175 H3
GSWFD DY6 ...83 J5
WNSFLD WV11 ...37 C7
tboro Wy COVN CV6 ...99 H3
tbourne Av COVW CV5 ...133 J7
tbourne St RUSH/SHEL WS4 ...53 L2
tbrook Cl WALM/CURD B76 ...73 H1
tbury Rd HIA/OLT B92 ...127 L3
t Cannock Rd HEDN WS12 ...17 J1
tcote Crs BNTWD WS7 ...18 D1
tcote La HIA/OLT B92 ...150 D2
tcote Rd ACGN B27 ...126 E4
tcotes Rd WALM/CURD B76 ...73 H1
tcotes Trl TLHL/CAN CV4 ...153 M4
t Croft Rd
ETTPK/GDPK/PENN WV4 ...65 C1
tdean Ct RLSN CV32 ...206 F3
t Dene Dr DIG/EDG B5 ...125 C1
tern Av BRLYHL DY5 ...101 M3
tern Cl DARL/WED WS10 ...68 A2
tern Green Rd COVW CV5 ...153 K2
tern Rd SCFLD/BOLD B73 ...72 F4
SLYOAK B29 ...124 F2
tern Wy CNCK/NC WS11 ...16 D8
terton Cft
ALE/KHTH/YWD B14 ...146 C3
t Farm Cft SMHTH B10 ...108 B5
tfield Cl ALDR WS9 ...40 F7
tfield Dr HIA/OLT B92 ...128 C5
tfield Pl RUGBYN/HIL CV21 ...186 E2
tfield Retreat WOLV WV1 ...3 M5
tfield Rd BORD B9 ...109 G3
tfield Rd BORD B9 ...107 M4
NUNW/HART CV10 ...
RLSN CV32 ...206 F3
TPTN/OCK DY4 ...67 L3
WOLV WV1 ...3 M6
tgate HEDN WS12 ...13 L8
t Ga LDYWD/EDGR B16 ...106 C2
tgate St BNTWD WS7 ...18 E3
t Gv ETTPK/GDPK/PENN WV4 ...49 M7
t Gv RLSS CV31 ...206 E7
tham Rd MOS/BIL B13 ...126 A7
t Holme BORD B9 ...108 A3
thope Rd STETCH B33 ...109 L1
tlake Cl GTB/HAM B43 ...71 H2
tlands Pl RUGBYN/HIL CV21 ...187 K2
tlands Rd MOS/BIL B13 ...125 L4
tlands RUGBYN/HIL CV21 ...187 K2
tlang Rd
RCOVN/BALC/EX CV7 ...114 C2
tleigh SEDG DY3 ...65 M5
tleigh Gv COVN CV6 ...154 D6
tleigh Cft WALM/CURD B76 ...73 J1
tleigh Dr RMSLY B62 ...142 E1
tleigh Gv YDLY B25 ...109 H5
tley Crs WWCK CV34 ...204 F5
tmoor Cl KGSTG B44 ...71 M3
tney Dr CDSL WV8 ...35 G3
tnor Cl KIDDW DY11 ...164 C3
REDE B98 ...202 C4
tnor Gv RLSS CV31 ...206 F6
ston Gdns WNSFLD WV11 ...37 K8
ston Gv ACGN B27 ...126 E3
HLYWD B47 ...146 F6
t Park Wy WOLV WV1 ...50
t Pathway HRBN B17 ...106 A7
tstridge Cft LICHS WS14 ...28 E1
t Ri MGN/WHC B75 ...57 H7
t Rd BRGRVW B61 ...191 M1
STRPT DY13 ...163 J8
TPTN/OCK DY4 ...67 M1
WOLV WV1 ...3 M6
t St BRLYHL DY5 ...102 A5
CNCK/NC WS11 ...16 C7
COV CV1 ...9 J5
KIDD DY10 ...138 D7
RUGBYN/HIL CV21 ...187 H1
WOLV WV1 ...3 J6
WSL WS1 ...5 G9
t Union St
RUGBYS/DCH CV22 ...186 F5
t Vw TAM/AM/WIL B77 ...46 C2
t View Rd WALM/CURD B76 ...73 H2
t Ville NFLD/LBR B31 ...144 C4
tward Gln CDSL WV8 ...35 G3
t Wy BHAMNEC B40 ...129 K2
tway HRBN B17 ...106 A7
twood Av WBROM B70 ...18
twood Dr KIDD DY10 ...138 D7
twood Rd BHTH/HG B12 ...107 H8
GTB/HAM B43 ...70 D7
ton La RUGBYN/HIL CV21 ...186 D2
ton Cl RLSN CV32 ...206 A4
ton Crs SEDG DY3 ...83 J5
KGSWFD DY6 ...83 J5
ton Ri SHHTH WV12 ...37 H2
ton Av WBROM B70 ...86 D1
ton Cl FOAKS/STRLY B74 ...56 F1
OV CV2 ...135 G4
n Wood Dr
LGN/SDN/BHAMAIR B26 ...109 H8

Eaves Court Dr SEDG DY3 ...66 A3
Eaves Green Gdns ACGN B27 ...108 F8
Eaves Green La
RCOVN/BALC/EX CV7 ...131 J4
Ebbw Vale Ter COVS CV3 ...155 H6
Ebenezer St BILS/COS WV14 ...66 F5
HEDN WS12 ...12 E6
WBROM B70 ...68 D7
Ebley Rd BFLD/HDSWWD B20 ...88 E1
Ebmore Dr ALE/KHTH/YWD B14 ...146 B3
Eborall Ct WWCK CV34 ...205 J3
Eborne Cft
RCOVN/BALC/EX CV7 ...152 A5
Ebourne Cl KNWTH CV8 ...197 L1
Ebrington Av HIA/OLT B92 ...127 M2
Ebrington Cl
ALE/KHTH/YWD B14 ...146 B1
Ebrington Dr
RWWCK/WEL CV35 ...204 C3
Ebrington Rd HHTH/SAND B71 ...69 H7
Ebro Crs COVS CV3 ...156 D4
Ebrook Rd CSCFLD/WYGN B72 ...73 G1
Ebstree Rd
ETTPK/GDPK/PENN WV4 ...48 D8
Ebourne Rd COVE CV2 ...135 G2
Ebury Rd BVILLE B30 ...145 M1
Eccles Cl COVE CV2 ...135 G5
Eccleshall Av WOLVN WV10 ...36 A5
Ecclestone Rd WNSFLD WV11 ...37 L5
Echells Ct BRGRVW B61 ...191 H3
Echo Wy
ETTPK/GDPK/PENN WV4 ...66 E1
Eckersall Rd HWK/WKHTH B38 ...145 J2
Eckington Cl REDE B98 ...202 F5
Ecton Leys RUGBYS/DCH CV22 ...186 E6
Edale TAM/AM/WIL B77 ...46 F4
Edale Cl ETTPK/GDPK/PENN WV4 ...48 D8
KGSWFD DY6 ...82 F6
Edale Rd PBAR/PBCH B42 ...71 G6
Edale Wy COVE CV6 ...134 C2
Eddens Cl
POL/KGSB/FAZ B78 ...45 J8
Eddie Miller Ct BDWTH CV12 * ...117 G4
Eddish Rd STETCH B33 ...109 M1
Eddy Rd KIDD DY10 ...138 C6
Edelweiss Cl STETCH/YTR WS5 ...69 H7
Edenbridge Rd HLGN/YWD B28 ...126 F5
Edenbridge Vw DUDN DY1 ...84 C2
Eden Cl HEDN WS12 ...17 J3
NFLD/LBR B31 ...144 D5
OLDBY B69 ...86 B3
Eden Cft KNWTH CV8 ...197 M1
Edendale Dr
LGN/SDN/BHAMAIR B26 ...109 M7
Eden Gv CHWD/FDBR/MGN B37 ...111 H4
HHTH/SAND B71 ...69 H5
Edenhall Rd RIDG/WDGT B32 ...104 F7
Edenhurst Rd NFLD/LBR B31 ...144 D7
Eden Pl CBHAMNW B3 ...6 C6
Eden Rd HIA/OLT B92 ...128 B2
RCOVN/BALC/EX CV7 ...135 L4
RUGBYN/HIL CV21 ...187 K4
Edensor Cl WOLVN WV10 ...3 K1
Eden St COVN CV6 ...134 D6
Edgar Cl CRTAM B79 ...31 K6
Edgbaston Park Rd EDG B15 ...106 E8
Edgbaston Rd BHTH/HG B12 ...125 J1
DIG/EDG B5 ...107 G8
Edgbaston Rd East
BHTH/HG B12 * ...107 J8
Edgcombe Rd HLGN/YWD B28 ...126 A2
Edgcote Cl RUGBYN/HIL CV21 ...187 M4
Edgefield Rd COVE CV2 ...135 L5
Edge Hill Av WOLVN WV10 ...36 A6
Edge Hill Dr
DUNHL/THL/PER WV6 ...48 C2
Edgehill Pl TLHL/CAN CV4 ...153 G6
Edgehill Rd FOAKS/STRLY B74 ...55 J4
NFLD/LBR B31 ...144 E4
Edgemoor Meadow HEDN WS12 ...17 G4
Edge St BILS/COS WV14 ...67 G5
Edgewood Cl
HWK/WKHTH B38 ...145 J4
RBRY B45 ...143 M6
Edgeworth Cl REDE B98 ...195 G8
SHHTH WV12 ...37 K7
Edgmond Cl REDE B98 ...203 H1
Edgware Rd ERDW/GRVHL B23 ...72 B8
Edgwick Rd COVN CV6 ...134 D6
Edinburgh Av WSLW WS2 ...52 C2
Edinburgh Cl KIDD DY10 ...138 C5
Edinburgh Ct ERDW/GRVHL B24 ...91 H1
Edinburgh Crs RLSS CV31 ...206 D7
STRBR DY8 ...101 G4
Edinburgh Dr RUSH/SHEL WS4 ...53 M3
SHHTH WV12 ...37 K7
Edinburgh La WSLW WS2 * ...52 C1
Edinburgh Rd BILS/COS WV14 ...67 K7
DSYBK/YTR WS5 ...5 M7
DUDS DY2 ...85 H7
LGLYGN/QTN B68 ...104 F3
NUN/HART CV10 ...98 D5
Edinburgh Vis KNWTH CV8 * ...181 K7
Edinburgh Wy RUGBY CV23 ...159 M8
Edingale Rd COVE CV2 ...135 J1
Edison Cl HEDN WS12 ...13 G6
Edison Gv RIDG/WDGT B32 ...105 H8
Edison Rd WALM/CURD B76 ...93 L2
WSLW WS2 ...38 C8
Edith Rd SMTHWK B66 ...105 M2
Edith St WBROM B70 ...68 F2
Edmondes Cl WWCK CV34 ...205 M4
Edmonds Cl STETCH B33 ...109 J3
Edmondscote Rd RLSN CV32 ...206 B5
Edmonton Av KGSTG B44 ...71 M4
Edmonton Cl CNCK/NC WS11 ...16 F3
Edmoor Cl SHHTH WV12 ...37 J4
Edmund Rd COVN CV1 ...134 D8
SEDG DY3 ...66 C5
WASH/WDE B8 ...108 B3
Edmund St CBHAMNW B3 ...6 D4
Ednall La BRGRVE B60 ...191 L7
Ednam Cl HHTH/SAND B71 ...69 H4
Ednam Gv WMBN WV5 ...64 A4
Ednam Rd DUDN DY1 ...85 G1
ETTPK/GDPK/PENN WV4 ...50 A1
Edsome Wy CBROM B36 ...92 F6
Edstone Cl DOR/KN B93 ...175 K2
Edward Av ALDR WS9 ...40 E5
Edward Bailey Cl COVS CV3 ...156 F6
Edward Fisher Dr TPTN/OCK DY4 ...67 L8
Edward Rd ALE/KHTH/YWD B14 ...146 C1
BDWTH CV12 ...117 G3
CSHL/WTROR B46 ...93 C2
DIG/EDG B5 ...107 H7
LGN/SDN/BHAMAIR B26 ...109 H8

HALE B63 ...121 K1
LGLYGN/QTN B68 ...105 G5
SMTHWKW B67 ...105 K5
WBROM B70 ...67 L6
Edward St BNTWD WS7 ...18 D3
DUDS DY2 ...103 G1
ERDE/BHCGN B24 ...72 B8
MGN/WHC B75 ...57 H2
CNCK/NC WS11 ...15 M5
COVE CV2 ...134 C8
CRTAM B79 ...31 J3
DARL/WED WS10 ...52 C7
DUDN DY1 ...84 F4
ETTPK/GDPK/PENN WV4 ...50 D7
LGLYGN/QTN B68 ...104 E1
NUN CV11 ...98 F1
REDW B97 ...202 B5
RLSN CV32 ...206 A4
RUGBYN/HIL CV21 ...186 D1
WBROM B70 ...68 D7
WSLW WS2 ...52 F2
WNCK CV34 ...205 H6
Edward Tyler Rd BDWTH CV12 ...116 E4
Edwin Av KIDD DY11 ...164 D6
Edwin Cl PENK ST19 ...10 D5
Edwin Ct BRGRVE B60 ...191 K5
Edwin Crs BRGRVE B60 ...191 K5
Edwin Phillips Dr
HHTH/SAND B71 ...68 F5
Edwin Rd BVILLE B30 ...124 F6
Edyth Rd COVE CV2 ...135 C1
Edyvean Cl RUGBYS/DCH CV22 ...186 C7
Edyvean-Walker Ct NUN CV11 * ...80 F8
Eel St OLDBY B69 ...86 A6
Effingham Rd MOS/BIL B13 ...126 A7
Egbert Cl AST/WIT B6 ...89 J4
Egelwin Cl DUNHL/THL/PER WV6 ...34 C8
Egerton Cl RUGBYN/HIL CV21 ...160 D7
Egerton Rd ERDE/BHCGN B24 ...72 H2
FOAKS/STRLY B74 ...55 K4
WOLVN WV10 ...36 C2
Egghill La RIDG/WDGT B32 ...143 L1
Eggington Dr PENK ST19 ...10 D6
Eggington Rd STRBR DY8 ...101 H6
Eggington Rd HLGN/YWD B28 ...126 C8
Egg La HAG/WOL DY9 ...140 C4
KIDD DY10 ...140 F1
Egmont Gdns WNSFLD WV11 ...37 K8
Egret Ct KIDD DY10 ...164 E4
Eider Cl KIDD DY10 ...164 F4
Eights Cft BNTWD WS7 ...19 G8
Eileen Gdns
CHWD/FDBR/MGN B37 ...110 E1
Eileen Rd SPARK B11 ...125 M2
Elan Av STRPT DY13 ...163 J6
Elan Cl BEWD DY12 ...162 D1
KIDD DY10 ...138 F1
RLSN CV32 ...207 G2
SEDG DY3 ...84 B2
Elan Rd NFLD/LBR B31 ...144 A3
SEDG DY3 ...66 A5
Elborow St RUGBYN/HIL CV21 ...186 E6
Elbow St CDYHTH B64 ...103 K4
Elbury Cft DOR/KN B93 ...149 K8
Elcock Dr PBAR/PBCH B42 ...71 H4
Eldalade Wy DARL/WED WS10 ...69 G4
Elderberry Cl STRBR DY8 ...119 G2
STRPT DY13 ...188 C1
Elderberry Wy COVE CV2 ...134 F7
Elder Cl CNCK/NC WS11 ...17 G3
POL/KGSB/FAZ B78 ...60 B6
RUGBYS/DCH CV22 ...185 M4
Elderfield Cl REDE B98 ...195 H6
Elderfield Rd BVILLE B30 ...145 M2
Elder Gv WMBN WV5 ...64 D7
Elder La BNTWD WS7 ...19 G6
Eldersfield Cl REDE B98 ...195 H6
Elder Wy ERDW/GRVHL B23 ...90 B3
Eldon Dr WALM/CURD B76 ...73 J6
Eldon Rd NFLD/LBR B31 ...144 E4
RIDG/WDGT B32 ...122 C2
Eldon St DARL/WED WS10 ...52 B6
WSL WS1 ...5 H5
Eldridge Cl COVEN WV9 ...35 K3
Eld Rd COVN CV6 ...134 C6
Eleanor Rd BILS/COS WV14 ...67 H7
Electric Av AST/WIT B6 ...89 M4
Elford Cl BILS/COS WV14 ...67 G1
Elford Gv BILS/COS WV14 ...67 G1
CHWD/FDBR/MGN B37 ...110 F4
Elford Rd HHTH/SAND B71 ...69 J4
HRBN B17 ...123 M2
Elgar Cl CNCK/NC WS11 ...20 F3
LICH WS13 ...20 F1
NUN CV11 ...99 L6
Elgar Crs BRLYHL DY5 ...84 B6
Elgar Rd COVN CV6 ...134 C6
Elgin Cl SEDG DY3 ...66 C4
STRBR DY8 ...100 F5
Elgin Ct ERDW/GRVHL B24 ...91 H1
Elgin Gv YDLY B25 ...109 G6
Elgin Rd BLOX/PEL WS3 ...38 F2
WOLVN WV10 ...23 G4
Elias Cl LICHS WS14 ...21 J7
Eliot Cl CRTAM B79 ...31 L6
WWCK CV34 ...205 J3
Eliot Cft BILS/COS WV14 ...67 H3
Eliot Rd RUGBYS/DCH CV22 ...186 C2
Eliot St VAUX/NECH B7 ...90 A5
Eliot Wy NUNW/HART CV10 ...98 F4
Elizabeth Av BILS/COS WV14 ...67 K7
DARL/WED WS10 ...69 G2
ETTPK/GDPK/PENN WV4 ...49 M8
POL/KGSB/FAZ B78 ...47 J6
Elizabeth Ct WWCK CV34 ...205 M7
Elizabeth Crs LGLYGN/QTN B68 ...105 H3
Elizabeth Dr CRTAM B79 ...31 L7
Elizabeth Gv DUDS DY2 ...85 K6
SHLY B90 ...148 A3
Elizabeth Ms OLDBY B69 ...86 C3
Elizabeth Rd CNCK/NC WS11 ...12 C1
DSYBK/YTR WS5 ...5 M8
HALE B63 ...121 K2
MOS/BIL B13 ...126 A7
REDW B97 ...202 B1
RLSN CV32 ...206 F2
Elizabeth Wk TPTN/OCK DY4 ...67 M4
Elizabeth Wy KNWTH CV8 ...179 L7
RLSS CV31 ...206 F4
STETCH B33 ...109 H2
Elkington Cft SHLY B90 ...148 D8
Elkington St AST/WIT B6 ...89 J8
COVN CV6 ...134 D5
Elkstone Cl SOLH B91 ...128 B8
Elkstone Covert
ALE/KHTH/YWD B14 ...146 A3
Ellacombe Rd COVE CV2 ...135 H3
Ellards Dr WNSFLD WV11 ...37 K6
Ellenvale Cl BILS/COS WV14 ...66 E6
Ellerbeck TAM/AM/WIL B77 ...46 F3
Ellerby Gv ERDE/BHCGN B24 ...91 J1
Ellerdene Cl REDE B98 ...203 H1
Ellerman Gdns COVN CV6 ...134 D4
Ellerside Gv BRLYHL DY5 ...102 B5
Ellerslie Gv BRLYHL DY5 ...102 B5

Ellerslie Rd MOS/BIL B13 ...126 A6
Ellerton Rd KGSTG B44 ...71 M4
Ellerton Wk WOLVN WV10 ...36 D3
Ellesboro' Rd HRBN B17 ...105 H5
Ellesmere Dr BEWD DY12 ...162 D2
Ellesmere Rd BDWTH CV12 ...116 E3
CNCK/NC WS11 ...15 M5
WBROM B70 ...68 A3
Ellice Dr CBROM B36 ...92 F6
Elliot Cl RBRY B45 ...143 M8
Elliot Cl CNCK/NC WS11 ...12 C8
Elliott Rd SLYOAK B29 ...124 C3
Elliotts La CDSL WV8 ...34 E2
Elliott's Rd TPTN/OCK DY4 ...67 J8
Ellis Av BRLYHL DY5 ...101 L3
Ellison St WBROM B70 ...87 G4
Ellis Park Dr COVS CV3 ...156 F4
Ellis St CBHAMW B1 ...6 C7
Elliston Av KGSTG B44 ...71 J5
Elliston Gv
ALE/KHTH/YWD B14 ...146 D1
Elliston Wk CNCK/NC WS11 ...15 D5
Ell La RRUGBY CV23 ...158 D1
Ellowes Rd SEDG DY3 ...84 A4
Ellys Rd COVN CV1 ...134 A8
Elm Av BHTH/HG B12 ...107 L8
BILS/COS WV14 ...51 H7
DARL/WED WS10 ...68 D1
WNSFLD WV11 ...36 F5
Elm Bank MOS/BIL B13 ...125 L2
Elm Bank Cl RLSN CV32 ...206 E1
Elmbank Gv BFLD/HDSWWD B20 ...70 C8
Elmbank Rd DSYBK/YTR WS5 ...69 J8
KNWTH CV8 ...179 J7
Elmbridge Cl HALE B63 ...103 H8
Elmbridge Dr SHLY B90 ...148 F7
Elmbridge Rd KGSTG B44 ...71 J7
Elmbridge Wy SEDG DY3 ...66 B8
Elm Cl COVS CV3 ...157 G6
KIDD DY10 ...138 F1
SEDG DY3 ...83 M3
STRBR DY8 ...119 G3
Elm Ct COVW CV5 ...132 A5
ETTPK/GDPK/PENN WV4 ...49 M8
Elm Cft LGLYGN/QTN B68 ...105 G6
Elmcroft Av RIDG/WDGT B32 ...122 E4
Elmcroft Gdns WOLVN WV10 ...36 C2
Elmcroft Rd
LGN/SDN/BHAMAIR B26 ...109 K6
Elmdale RMSLY B62 ...104 E6
Elmdale Crs NFLD/LBR B31 ...144 C1
Elmdale Dr ALDR WS9 ...41 G5
Elmdale Gv NFLD/LBR B31 ...144 C1
Elmdale Rd BILS/COS WV14 ...66 E6
Elm Dale Rd
ETTPK/GDPK/PENN WV4 ...49 L8
Elmdene Cl KNWTH CV8 ...183 L1
Elmdene Rd KNWTH CV8 ...197 M1
Elmdon Cl HIA/OLT B92 ...128 B3
PENK ST19 ...10 E5
WOLVN WV10 ...35 L4
Elmdon Coppice HIA/OLT B92 ...128 C6
Elmdon La
CHWD/FDBR/MGN B37 ...110 D6
LGN/SDN/BHAMAIR B26 ...128 E2
Elmdon Park Rd HIA/OLT B92 ...128 B3
Elmdon Rd ACGN B27 ...127 C1
CHWD/FDBR/MGN B37 ...110 E7
SLYOAK B29 ...124 C3
WOLVN WV10 ...35 L4
Elm Dr GTB/HAM B43 ...70 D7
KIDD DY10 ...139 M3
RMSLY B62 ...104 C4
Elm Farm Av
CHWD/FDBR/MGN B37 ...110 D6
Elm Farm Rd BKHL/PFLD WV2 ...50 B6
Elmfield Av ERDE/BHCGN B24 ...91 J1
Elmfield Rd CBROM B36 ...92 C6
KIDDW DY11 ...189 L4
NUNW/HART CV10 ...81 G6
Elmfield Vw DUDN DY1 ...84 E2
Elm Gdns DUDN DY1 ...66 B8
Elm Gv ATHST CV9 ...71
BRGRVW B61 ...191 L1
CDSL WV8 ...34 E2
CHWD/FDBR/MGN B37 ...92 D7
KINVER DY7 ...118 A2
RCOVN/BALC/EX CV7 ...96 C3
RCOVN/BALC/EX CV7 ...152 A7
STRPT DY13 ...188 D3
Elmhurst Av
BLKHTH/ROWR B65 ...104 A2
Elmhurst Dr BNTWD WS7 ...26 E1
KGSWFD DY6 ...101 K1
Elmhurst Rd COVN CV6 ...134 C1
HDSW B21 ...88 C4
Elmley Cl BILS/COS WV14 ...67 H6
KIDDW DY11 ...163 M2
Elmley Gv BVILLE B30 ...145 M2
DUNHL/THL/PER WV6 ...48 D2
Elm Ldg HIA/OLT B92 * ...129 L6
Elmore Cl
CHWD/FDBR/MGN B37 ...110 E1
COVS CV3 ...156 B5
Elmore Green Cl BLOX/PEL WS3 ...38 E5
Elmore Green Rd BLOX/PEL WS3 ...38 E3
Elmore Rd RUGBYS/DCH CV22 ...186 D6
STETCH B33 ...109 L2
Elmore Rw BLOX/PEL WS3 ...38 F4
Elm Pl KIDD DY10 ...138 F1
Elm Rd BLOX/PEL WS3 ...39 H7
BVILLE B30 ...124 D5
CNCK/NC WS11 ...17 M8
DUDN DY1 ...85 G2
KGSWFD DY6 ...83 J7
KIDD DY10 ...138 E2
REDW B97 ...202 B1
RLSN CV32 ...206 F2
WALM/CURD B76 ...73 J5
Elms Cl SOLH B91 ...128 B8
MOS/BIL B13 ...125 M4
RLSS CV31 ...207 K2
SCFLD/BOLD B73 ...72 A4
STETCH B33 ...109 H2
TPTN/OCK DY4 ...67 L1
Elms Dr CNCK/NC WS11 ...16 A4
RUGBYS/DCH CV22 ...187 G5
WOLVN WV10 ...23 G4
The Elms Paddock
RRUGBY CV23 ...161 K3
Elms Rd CSCFLD/WYGN B72 ...72 F2
Elmstead Av STETCH B33 ...110 B6
Elmstead Cl DSYBK/YTR WS5 ...54 C4
Elmstead Wd DSYBK/YTR WS5 ...54 C4
Elm St BDWTH CV12 * ...116 C3
LDYWD/EDGR B16 * ...106 D2
POL/KGSB/FAZ B78 * ...60 D7
RWWCK/WEL CV35 ...197 L5
Elmstone Cl REDW B97 ...202 A8
Elm St BDMR/CCFT WV3 ...4 A6
WLNHL WV13 ...51 H3
Elm Ter OLDBY B69 ...85 L4
Elm Tree Av COVW CV5 ...153 L4
Elm Tree Cl POL/KGSB/FAZ B78 ...60 D7
WMBN WV5 ...64 D6
Elm Tree Gv HALE B63 ...103 H7

Elm Tree Ri HIA/OLT B92 ...129 L7
Elm Tree Rd BVILLE B30 ...124 F7
HRBN B17 ...105 L7
Elmtree Rd FOAKS/STRLY B74 ...55 H5
Elm Tree Wy CDYHTH B64 * ...103 K4
Elm Wy NUNW/HART CV10 ...79 L5
WNSFLD WV11 ...37 L2
Elmwood Av COVN CV6 ...133 K8
WNSFLD WV11 ...37 L2
Elmwood Cl CNCK/NC WS11 ...16 C1
RCOVN/BALC/EX CV7 ...151 M6
Elmwood Gdns
BFLD/HDSWWD B20 ...88 B2
Elmwood Gv HLYWD B47 ...146 E7
Elmwood Ri SEDG DY3 ...65 M4
Elmwood Rd ERDE/BHCGN B24 ...91 K4
FOAKS/STRLY B74 ...55 L7
STRBR DY8 ...101 G2
Elmwoods RIDG/WDGT B32 ...122 F3
Elphin Cl COVN CV6 ...133 L1
Elphinstone End
CSCFLD/WYGN B72 ...73 G2
Elsee Rd RUGBYN/HIL CV21 ...186 E2
Elston Hall La WOLVN WV10 ...36 C4
Elstree Rd ERDW/GRVHL B23 ...72 B8
Elswick Gv KGSTG B44 ...71 M4
Elswick Pl KGSTG B44 ...71 M4
Elsworth Gv YDLY B25 ...109 G7
Elter Cl RUGBYN/HIL CV21 ...161 M6
Eltham Gv KGSTG B44 ...71 M4
Eltham Rd COVS CV3 ...155 J6
Elton Cl RLSN CV32 ...207 G3
WOLVN WV10 ...36 C1
Elton Cft DOR/KN B93 ...175 K1
Elton Gv ACGN B27 ...126 E3
Eltonia Cft
LGN/SDN/BHAMAIR B26 ...109 M7
Elton Rd BEWD DY12 ...162 D2
Elunda Gv BNTWD WS7 ...18 C3
Elva Cft CBROM B36 ...92 D4
Elvers Green La DOR/KN B93 ...150 C9
Elvetham Rd EDG B15 ...6 C9
Elviron Dr DUNHL/THL/PER WV6 ...34 C8
Elwells Cl
ETTPK/GDPK/PENN WV4 ...66 D1
Elwell St DARL/WED WS10 ...68 C2
WBROM B70 ...68 B5
Elwy Cir RCOVN/BALC/EX CV7 ...116 A6
Elwyn Rd SCFLD/BOLD B73 ...72 C2
Ely Cl BLKHTH/ROWR B65 ...104 C1
CHWD/FDBR/MGN B37 ...110 F3
CNCK/NC WS11 ...16 C4
COVE CV2 ...135 L7
KIDDW DY11 ...137 L7
Ely Crs HHTH/SAND B71 ...68 F7
Ely Gv RIDG/WDGT B32 ...122 E4
Ely Pl WSLW WS2 ...52 F4
Ely Rd WSLW WS2 ...52 F4
Emay Cl WBROM B70 ...68 C9
The Embankment BRLYHL DY5 ...102 C3
Embassy Dr EDG B15 ...6 A9
OLDBY B69 ...86 C5
Embassy Rd OLDBY B69 ...86 C5
Embassy Wk COVE CV2 ...135 J6
Emberton Wy TAM/AM/WIL B77 ...32 C8
Embleton Gv BKDE/SHDE B34 ...91 L7
Emerald Wy RLSS CV31 ...206 D8
Emerson Cl SEDG DY3 ...84 C2
Emerson Gv WOLVN WV10 ...36 C2
Emerson Rd COVE CV2 ...156 A1
HRBN B17 ...106 A7
WOLVN WV10 ...36 C2
Emery Cl COVE CV2 ...135 J6
ERDW/GRVHL B23 ...90 B4
WSL WS1 ...5 H5
Emery St WSL WS1 ...5 H5
Emily Gdns LDYWD/EDGR B16 ...106 D2
Emily Rd
LGN/SDN/BHAMAIR B26 ...109 H7
Emily St BHTH/HG B12 ...107 K6
WBROM B70 ...86 F3
Emmanuel Rd BNTWD WS7 ...18 F6
SCFLD/BOLD B73 ...72 F6
Emmeline St BORD B9 ...107 M4
Emmott Dr RLSS CV31 ...206 F7
Emperor Wy RUGBYN/HIL CV21 ...160 D6
Empire Cl ALDR WS9 ...40 D7
Empire Rd TLHL/CAN CV4 ...153 J3
Empress Ar COVE CV2 * ...155 M3
Empress Wy DARL/WED WS10 ...52 B5
Emscote Dr SCFLD/BOLD B73 ...72 F5
Emscote Gn SOLH B91 ...148 C3
Emscote Rd AST/WIT B6 ...89 K4
COVS CV3 ...156 A3
WWCK CV34 ...205 M5
Emsworth Crs COVEN WV9 ...35 J3
Emsworth Gv
ALE/KHTH/YWD B14 ...125 J4
Ena Rd COV CV1 ...134 B8
Endeavour Pl STRPT DY13 ...188 C3
Enderby Cl DOR/KN B93 ...175 K1
Enderby Dr
ETTPK/GDPK/PENN WV4 ...65 K1
Enderby Rd ERDW/GRVHL B23 ...72 A6
Enderley Cl BLOX/PEL WS3 ...38 F2
Enderley Dr BLOX/PEL WS3 ...38 F2
Enderly Gv WSNGN B18 ...106 C1
End Hall Rd
DUNHL/THL/PER WV6 ...48 D1
Endhill Rd KGSTG B44 ...71 L2
Endicott Rd AST/WIT B6 ...89 J4
Endmoor Gv ERDW/GRVHL B23 ...72 D7
Endsleigh Gdns RLSS CV31 ...207 H1
Endsleigh Gv HLGN/YWD B28 ...126 C5
Endwood Court Rd
BFLD/HDSWWD B20 ...88 B2
Endwood Dr FOAKS/STRLY B74 ...56 H7
SOLH B91 ...148 D3
Enfield Cl ERDW/GRVHL B23 ...72 D7
Enfield Rd BLKHTH/ROWR B65 ...104 B2
COVE CV2 ...155 M3
EDG B15 ...6 B9
REDW B97 ...202 B8
Enford Cl BKDE/SHDE B34 ...92 B7
Engadine Rd BRGRVE B60 ...192 A4
Engine La BRWNH WS8 ...26 A5
DARL/WED WS10 ...67 L1
HAG/WOL DY9 ...102 A3
STRPT DY13 ...188 D2
TAM/AM/WIL B77 ...46 C3
Engine St OLDBY B69 ...86 B3
SMTHWK B66 ...87 M1
England Crs RLSS CV32 ...206 C1
Englestede Cl
BFLD/HDSWWD B20 ...88 B2
Engleton Rd COVN CV6 ...133 L8
Englewood Dr HLGN/YWD B28 ...126 F6
Ennerdale RUGBYN/HIL CV21 ...161 G6
Ennerdale Cl BRWNH WS8 ...26 C6
RLSN CV32 ...206 B3
Ennerdale Crs NUN CV11 ...81 K9
Ennerdale La COVE CV2 ...156 D1
Ennerdale Rd
DUNHL/THL/PER WV6 ...35 H5
HALE B63 ...121 H3

GTB/HAM B43 ....70 C6
STRPT DY13 ....163 K7
Ennersdale Bungalows
CSHL/WTROR B46 ....93 K4
Ennersdale CI CSHL/WTROR B46 .93 K4
Ennersdale Rd CSHL/WTROR B46..93 K4
Enright CI RLSN CV32 ....206 C2
Ensall Dr STRBR DY8 ....101 J4
Ensbury CI SHHTH WV12 ....52 B1
Ensdale Rw WLNHL WV13 ....51 L4
Ensdon Gv KGSTG B44 ....71 M4
Ensford CI FOAKS/STRLY B74....56 C1
Ensign CI TLHL/CAN CV4.........153 G4
Ensor CI NUN CV11 ....81 K7
Ensor Dr POL/KGSB/FAZ B78 .....47 K4
Enstone Rd DUDN DY1 ....84 D5
ERDW/GRVHL B23 ....72 E7
Enterprise Dr
FOAKS/STRLY B74 * 55 J6
HAG/WOL WV9 ....102 D7
WOLVN WV10 ....14 B8
Enterprise Gv BLOX/PEL WS3 ..25 M8
Enville CI BLOX/PEL WS3 ....7 J1
CHWD/FDBR/MGN 110 F4
Enville PI STRBR DY8 ....101 K8
Enville Rd
ETTPK/GDPK/PENN WV4 ....49 G8
KGSWFD DY6 ....82 F5
SEDG DY3 ....84 B1
Enville St STRBR DY8 ....101 K8
RBRY B45 ....143 M5
Epping Gv KGSTG B44 ....71 L6
Epping Wy RLSN CV32 ....207 G1
Epsom CI BLOX/PEL WS3 ....39 J4
DUNHL/THL/PER WV6 ....48 D1
LICHS WS14 ....21 H6
REDW B97 ....201 M5
TAM/AM/WIL B77 ....60 C2
Epsom Dr COVS CV3 ....156 A5
Epsom Gv KGSTG B44 ....71 M4
Epsom Rd BRGRVW B61 ....168 A7
RLSN CV32 ....207 G1
RUGBYS/DCH CV22 ....186 B4
Epwell CI KGSTG B44 ....71 K7
Epwell Rd KGSTG B44 ....71 K7
Equipoint YDLY B25 * 109 H7
Erasmus Rd RLSN CV32 ....107 L6
Ercall CI ERDW/GRVHL B23 .....71 L7
Erdington Hall Rd
ERDE/BCHGN B24 ....90 D3
Erdington Rd ALDR WS9 ....54 F2
ATHST CV9 ....63 H6
Erica CI BDWTH CV12 ....116 C3
Erica CI KIDDW DY11 ....137 H2
SLYOAK B29 ....125 L5
Erica Rd DSYBK/YTR WS5 ....69 K4
Eric Grey CI COVE CV6 ....134 C1
Eringden TAM/AM/WIL B77 .....46 F4
Erithway Rd COVS CV3 ....180 F5
Ermington Crs CBROM B36 .....91 J6
Ermington Rd
ETTPK/GDPK/PENN WV4 ....50 B8
Erneley CI STRPT DY13 ....188 D4
Ernest Clarke CI SMHTH B67 ..52 A1
Ernest Ct HWK/WKHTH B38 ...145 L4
Ernest Richards Rd
BDWTH CV12 ....116 F1
Ernest Rd BHTH/HG B12 ....125 M1
DUDS DY2 ....85 K4
SMTHWKW B67 ....87 J7
Ernest St CBHAMW B1 ....2 F5
Ernsford Av COVS CV3 ....155 K4
Ernsford CI DOR/KN B93 ....175 K3
Erskine St VAUX/NECH B7 .....107 M2
Erwood CI REDW B97 ....201 M3
Esher Dr COVS CV3 ....155 J4
Esher Rd HHTH/SAND B71 .....69 H7
KGSTG B44 ....71 M3
Eskdale RUGBYS/HIL CV21 ....161 G3
Eskdale CI WOLV WV1 ....50 B3
Eskdale Wk BRLYHL DY5 ....101 M6
Eskrett St HEDN WS12 ....12 F8
Esme Rd SPARK B11 ....125 M1
Esmond CI BVILLE B30 ....124 B8
Essendon Rd WASH/WDE B8 ...108 C1
Essex Av DARL/WED WS10 .....69 G1
KGSWFD DY6 ....82 F8
Essex CI COVN CV6 ....153 M2
Essex Dr HEDN WS12 ....16 F1
Essex Gdns STRBR DY8 ....101 H6
Essex Rd DUDS DY2 ....84 D7
MGN/WHC B75 ....57 H4
Essex St DIG/EDG B5 ....6 C1
RUGBYN/HIL CV21 ....186 D1
WSLW WS2 ....39 G3
Essington Rd SHHTH WV12 ...52 M1
Essington CI LDYWD/EDGR B16..16 D7
Essington Wy WOLV WV1 ....50 D1
Este Rd LGN/SDN/BHAMAIR B26..109 G1
Esterton CI COVN CV6 ....134 A3
Estone Wk AST/WIT B6 ....89 K6
Estria Rd EDG B15 ....106 F6
Estridge La GTWY WS6 ....24 E3
Etchell Rd POL/KGSB/FAZ B78...45 K2
Ethelfield Rd COVE CV2 ....155 M4
Ethelred CI FOAKS/STRLY B74 ..56 B1
Ethelfleda Ter DARL/WED WS10..68 D2
Ethelred CI FOAKS/STRLY B74 ..106 D8
Ethel Rd HRBN B17 ....106 D8
Ethel St CBHAM B2 ....2 F5
LGLYGN/QTN B68 ....104 C1
SMTHWKW B67 ....105 K3
Etheridge Rd BILS/COS WV14 ..51 L5
Eton CI SEDG DY3 ....66 D6
Eton Dr STRBR DY8 ....119 L2
Eton Rd BHTH/HG B12 ....125 M1
Eton Wk HAG/WOL WV6 ....119 L7
Etruria Wy BILS/COS WV14 .....51 J6
Etta Gv KGSTG B44 ....71 J1
Ettingley CI REDE B98 ....202 F8
Ettingshall Park Farm La
ETTPK/GDPK/PENN WV4 ....66 B3
Ettingshall Rd BILS/COS WV14..66 E4
BKHL/PFLD WV2 ....50 E6
Ettington CI DOR/KN B93 ....175 H3
Ettington Rd AST/WIT B6 ....89 J5
COVW CV5 ....153 G2
Ettymore CI SEDG DY3 ....66 E6
Ettymore Rd SEDG DY3 ....66 E5
Ettymore Rd West SEDG DY3 ..66 E5
Etwall Rd HLGN/YWD B28 .....126 C8
Euan CI HRBN B17 ....106 C4
Eunal Ct RLSN CV32 ....206 D3
Europa Av WBROM B70 ....87 K5
Europa Wy LICHS WS14 ....21 K5
Euston Crs COVS CV3 ....156 A5
Euston PI RLSN CV32 ....206 D3
Evans CI BDWTH CV12 ....117 G2
KIDDW DY11 ....138 A2
TPTN/OCK DY4 ....67 G2
Evans PI BILS/COS WV14 ....51 L5

Evans Rd RUGBYS/DCH CV22 ..186 A3
Evans St BILS/COS WV14 ....66 C4
DUNHL/THL/PER WV6 ....2 C1
WLNHL WV13 ....51 H4
Eva Rd LGLYGN/QTN B68 ....105 G3
WSNGN B18 ....88 C7
Eve La DUDN DY1 ....66 D8
Evelyn Av COVN CV6 ....134 C3
Evelyn Rd SPARK B11 ....126 A1
Evenlode CI REDE B98 ....202 D4
Evenlode Crs COVN CV6 ....133 J5
Evenlode Gv WLNHL WV13 .....52 B8
Evenlode Rd HIA/OLT B92 ....127 L2
Everard Ct NUN CV11 ....81 H7
Everard CI RRUGBY CV23 ....161 L8
Everdon CI RUGBYS/DCH CV22..187 J5
Everdon Rd COVN CV6 ....133 M3
Everest CI SMTHWK B66 ....87 J5
Everest Rd BFLD/HDSWWD B20..88 E2
RUGBYS/DCH CV22 ....186 C5
Everglade Rd BILS/COS WV14 ..66 F3
Evergreen CI BILS/COS WV14...66 F3
Evergreen Hts HEDN WS12 .....12 E5
Everitt Dr DOR/KN B93 ....149 L7
Eversleigh Rd COVN CV6 ....133 J6
Eversley Av ERDE/BCHGN B24 ..90 E3
Eversley DI SEDG DY3 ....66 A3
WNSFLD WV11 ....37 G7
Eversley Gv BORD B9 ....108 B4
Everton Rd BORD B9 ....102 E5
Eves Cft RIDG/WDGT B32 ....123 G4
Evesham Pas STL PRES B84 ...38 D2
Evesham Ri DUDS DY2 ....105 H2
Evesham Rd REDW B97 ....202 B5
Evesham St REDW B97 ....202 C4
Evesham Wk TLHL/CAN CV4 ..154 A4
Eveson Rd STRBR DY8 ....119 H3
Evington PI YDLY B25 * 108 E6
Evreux Wy RUGBYN/HIL CV21..186 E2
Ewart Rd WSLW WS2 ....52 C2
Ewell Rd ERDE/BCHGN B24 .....90 F1
Ewhurst Av SLYOAK B29 ....124 D4
Ewhurst CI WLNHL WV13 ....51 J5
Ewloe CI KIDDW DY11 ....164 C4
Exbury CI COVEN WV9 ....35 K3
Exbury CI NUN CV11 ....99 J5
Excelsior Gv BRLYHL DY5 ....102 B1
Exchange St BRLYHL DY5 ....102 B1
KIDD DY10 ....138 C8
The Exchange BLOX/PEL WS3 *.38 F4
Exe Cft NFLD/LBR B31 ....144 F5
Exeter CI COVS CV3 ....156 B5
KIDDW DY11 ....137 L7
Exeter Dr
CHWD/FDBR/MGN B37 ....110 D5
CRTAM B79 ....31 J8
Exeter Pas CBHAMW B1 ....8 E8
Exeter PI WSLW WS2 ....52 F4
Exeter Rd CNCK/NC WS11 .....15 M5
DUDS DY2 ....103 H3
SLYOAK B29 ....124 D3
SMTHWK B66 ....87 M8
Exeter St CBHAMW B1 ....6 E8
Exford CI BRLYHL DY5 ....101 M6
Exhall Basin COVN CV6 * 116 F7
Exhall CI REDE B98 ....195 J8
SOLH B91 ....148 C3
Exhall Gn RCOVN/BALC/EX CV7..116 F6
Exhall Rd RCOVN/BALC/EX CV7..115 K7
Exley TAM/AM/WIL B77 ....46 B4
Exminster Rd COVS CV3 ....155 J4
Exmoor Dr BRGRVW B61 ....168 E8
RLSN CV32 ....207 G1
Exmoor Gn WNSFLD WV11 .....37 G6
Exmouth CI COVE CV2 ....135 J3
The Expressway WBROM B70 ..87 C1
Exton CI RCOVN/BALC/EX CV7..116 A6
WNSFLD WV11 ....37 K5
Exton Gdns SMTHWK B66 * 88 B7
Exton Rd WASH/WDE B8 ....90 B4
Eydon CI RUGBYN/HIL CV21...161 J3
Eyffler CI WWCK CV34 ....205 H5
Eyland Gv WSL WS1 ....5 J3
Eymore CI SLYOAK B29 ....123 M7
Eyre St WSNGN B18 ....106 E2
Eyston Av TPTN/OCK DY4 ....68 B5
Eyton CI REDE B98 ....203 H2
Eyton Cft BHTH/HG B12 ....107 H5
Ezekiel La SHHTH WV12 ....38 A7

F

Fabian CI COVS CV3 ....156 B6
RBRY B45 ....143 K3
Fabian Crs SHLY B90 ....147 M4
Facet Rd HWK/WKHTH B38 ....145 L3
Factory La BRGRVW B61 ....191 J4
Factory Rd TPTN/OCK DY4 .....67 J7
WSNGN B18 ....88 D7
Factory St DARL/WED WS10 ...52 A7
Fairbanks CI COVE CV2 ....135 L6
Fairbourne Av
BLKHTH/ROWR B65 ....104 A5
KGSTG B44 ....71 J3
Fairbourne Gdns REDW B97 ...202 A5
Fairbourne Wy COVN CV6 ....133 J5
Fairburn Crs BLOX/PEL WS3 ..25 M8
Faircroft KNWTH CV8 ....197 K6
Faircroft Av WALM/CURD B76 ..73 J1
Faircroft Rd CBROM B36 ....91 H5
Fairfax Rd MGN/WHC B75 ....73 K1
NFLD/LBR B31 ....144 E5
WOLVN WV10 ....36 B2
Fairfax St COV CV1 ....9 G4
Fairfield CI HEDN WS12 ....17 H4
Fairfield Ct COVS CV3 ....155 L6
Fairfield Dr BLOX/PEL WS3 .....39 M1
CDSL WV8 ....35 J3
PENK ST19 ....10 C7
RMSLY B62 ....104 C2
Fairfield Gv RMSLY B62 ....104 C2
Fairfield La KIDDW DY11 ....137 M2
Fairfield Mt WSL WS1 ....5 J7
Fairfield Ri
RCOVN/BALC/EX CV7 ....131 G4
STRBR DY8 ....101 G8
Fairfield Rd
ALE/KHTH/YWD B14 ....125 J5
BRGRVW B61 ....168 B4
DUDS DY2 ....85 H4
HALE B63 ....121 J3
RMSLY B62 ....104 C2
STRBR DY8 ....101 K3
Fairfields HI POL/KGSB/FAZ B78..47 K5
Fairford CI REDE B98 ....195 A6
Fairford Gdns BNTWD WS7 ......19 J7
STRBR DY8 ....101 J2
Fairford Rd KGSTG B44 ....71 K7
Fairgreen Gdns BRLYHL DY5 ..101 H8
Fairgreen Wy FOAKS/STRLY B74..55 L4

Fairground Wy WSL WS1 ....4 D6
Fairhaven Cft RMSLY B62 ....104 C4
Fairhills SEDG DY3 ....66 B5
Fairhill Wy SPARK B11 ....107 M6
Fairholme Rd CBROM B36 ....90 F6
Fair Isle Dr NUNW/HART CV10..98 D2
Fair Lady Rd BNTWD WS7 ....18 B5
Fairlands Pk TLHL/CAN CV4 ..154 C8
Fairlawn EDG B15 * 106 E6
Fairlawn CI SHHTH WV12 ....38 A4
Fairlawn Dr KGSWFD DY6 .....101 H1
Fairlawns
LGN/SDN/BHAMAIR B26 ....109 K4
WALM/CURD B76 ....73 J3
Fairlie Crs HWK/WKHTH B38 ..145 H4
Fairlight Dr RBRY B45 ....169 L4
Fairmead Ri HWK/WKHTH B38 ..145 J4
Fairmile CI COVS CV3 ....156 A5
Fairmile Rd HALE B63 ....103 K7
Fairmont Rd BRGRVE B60 ....191 L4
Fairmount Dr CNCK/NC WS11...16 C5
Fairoak Dr BRGRVE B60 ....191 K7
DUNHL/THL/PER WV6 ....48 E2
Fair Oaks Dr GTWY WS6 ....24 E5
Fairview Av PBAR/PBCH B42 ...67 M7
Fairview CI LGLYGN/QTN B68 ..104 C2
WNSFLD WV11 ....37 G7
Fairview Crs KGSWFD DY6 .....83 K7
WNSFLD WV11 ....37 G7
Fairview Gv WNSFLD WV11 .....36 F6
Fairview Ms CSHL/WTROR B46 *..93 K6
Fairview Rd DUDN DY1 ....84 C5
ETTPK/GDPK/PENN WV4 ....65 G1
WNSFLD WV11 ....37 G7
Fairway CNCK/NC WS11 ....16 B7
NFLD/LBR B31 ....144 C3
NUN CV11 ....99 M5
RUSH/SHEL WS4 ....40 B4
TAM/AM/WIL B77 ....46 C4
Fairway Av RBRY B45 ....85 L5
Fairway Dr RBRY B45 ....143 K7
Fairway Gn BILS/COS WV14 ....51 M8
Fairway Rd LGLYGN/QTN B68 ..104 D4
Fairways Av STRBR DY8 ....119 J8
Fairways CI COVW CV5 ....132 C4
STRBR DY8 ....119 J8
Fairways Dr BRGRVE B60 ....169 L8
The Fairways RLSN CV32 ....206 B3
Fairway The HWK/WKHTH B38 ..145 H3
Fairyfield Av GTB/HAM B43 .....70 B6
Fakenham Cft HRBN B17 ....105 K6
Falcon TAM/AM/WIL B77 ....46 E1
Falcon Av COVS CV3 ....155 J8
Falcon CI CNCK/NC WS11 ....16 A5
GTWY WS6 ....24 A5
KIDD DY10 ....164 C2
Falcon Crs BILS/COS WV14 ....66 D3
Falcondale Rd SHHTH WV12 ....38 A4
Falconhurst Rd SLYOAK B29 ..124 A3
Falcon Lodge Crs MGN/WHC B75..57 L8
Falcon Pl OLDBY B69 ....86 A6
Falcon Ri STRBR DY8 ....101 G7
Falcon Rd LGLYGN/QTN B68 ...104 A5
The Falcons MGN/WHC B75 ....57 M8
Falcon Wy DUDS DY2 ....84 D4
Falfield CI OLDBY B69 ....86 A7
Falfield Gv NFLD/LBR B31 .....144 C6
Falkland CI TLHL/CAN CV4 ....153 H6
Falkland Cft BVILLE B30 ....124 F7
Falklands CI SEDG DY3 ....82 C3
Falkland Wy CBROM B36 ....92 F8
Falkwood Gv DOR/KN B93 .....149 K7
Fallindale Rd
LGN/SDN/BHAMAIR B26 ....109 M7
Fallings Heath CI
DARL/WED WS10 ....52 D6
Fallow Fld CNCK/NC WS11 ....16 C3
FOAKS/STRLY B74 ....55 M2
LICH WS13 ....20 C7
Fallowfield CDSL WV8 ....35 J3
DUNHL/THL/PER WV6 ....48 B1
Fallowfield Av HLGN/YWD B28..126 D8
Fallowfield CI PENK ST19 ....10 C5
Fallow Field Rd
BLKHTH/ROWR B65 ....103 L2
Fallowfield Rd DSYBK/YTR WS5 ..54 C3
HALE B63 ....121 H2
HIA/OLT B92 ....128 A3
Fallowfields COVN CV6 ....134 A1
Fallow Hl RLSS CV31 ....207 G3
Fallows Rd SPARK B11 ....108 A2
Fallow Wk RIDG/WDGT B32 ..122 E3
Falmouth Dr TAM/AM/WIL B77 ..32 D8
Falmouth Rd BKDE/SHDE B34 ..91 J8
DSYBK/YTR WS5 ....54 B3
Falna Crs CRTAM B79 ....31 K6
Falstaff Av HLYWD B47 ....146 E6
Falstaff CI NUN CV11 ....99 L4
Falstaff Rd SHLY B90 ....148 A3
TLHL/CAN CV4 ....153 J3
Falstone Rd SCFLD/BOLD B73 ..72 B3
Fancott Dr KNWTH CV8 ....179 J7
Fancott Rd NFLD/LBR B31 .....123 L8
Fancourt Av
ETTPK/GDPK/PENN WV4 ....49 H8
Fane Rd WNSFLD WV11 ....37 G4
Fanshawe Rd ACGN B27 ....127 G4
Faraday Av RIDG/WDGT B32 ..105 H8
WALM/CURD B76 ....75 J2
Faraday Rd RUGBYS/DCH CV22 ..187 G4
WSLW WS2 ....38 F7
Faraday Whf VAUX/NECH B7 * ..7 K1
Farber Rd COVE CV2 ....135 L7
Farbrook Wy SHHTH WV12 .....37 M7
Farcroft Av WALM/CURD B76 ...73 K7
Farcroft Gv HDSW B21 ....88 B4
Farcroft Rd HDSW B21 ....88 B4
Fardon Wy ERDW/GRVHL B23 ..72 B2
Fareham Av RUGBYS/DCH CV22..187 J5
Fareham Crs
ETTPK/GDPK/PENN WV4 ....49 G8
Farewell La BNTWD WS7 ....19 J7
Farfield KIDD DY10 ....138 D8
Farfield CI NFLD/LBR B31 .....144 F3
Far Gosford St COV CV1 ....9 K5
Far Highfield WALM/CURD B76 ..73 H1
Far Hill CI HHTH/SAND B71 .....69 H1
Faringdon TAM/AM/WIL B77 ...46 D1
Farlands Dr STRBR DY8 ....120 E1
Farlands Gv GTB/HAM B43 ......70 D6
Farlands Rd STRBR DY8 ....120 E1
Farleigh Dr BDMR/CCFT WV3 ..48 E5
Farleigh Rd
DUNHL/THL/PER WV6 ....48 E2
Farley La HAG/WOL DY9 ....142 C5
Farley Rd ERDW/GRVHL B23 ...89 M1
Farley St RLSS CV31 ....207 G2
Farlow CI COVN CV6 ....134 E7

Farlow CI COVN CV6 * 134 E7
REDE B98 ....203 H1
Farlow Cft
CHWD/FDBR/MGN B37 ....110 D6
Farlow Rd NFLD/LBR B31 ....145 G2
Farmacre BORD B9 ....107 M3
Farman Rd COVW CV5 ....154 D3
Farmbridge CI WSLW WS2 ....52 B3
Farmbridge Rd WSLW WS2 .....52 B3
Farmbridge Av WOLVN WV10 ..34 F5
Farm CI CDSL WV8 ....133 M2
COVN CV6 ....133 M2
CRTAM B79 ....32 A6
HEDN WS12 ....17 G2
HIA/OLT B92 ....128 A3
KIDDW DY11 ....163 H3
SEDG DY3 ....65 M6
STETCH B33 ....109 K2
Farmcote Rd COVE CV2 ....134 D1
STETCH B33 ....109 K2
Farm Cft LDZ/NWT B19 ....89 C7
Farmcott Rd HAG/WOL DY9 ...120 C3
Farmdale Gv RBRY B45 ....143 L7
Farmer Rd SMHTH B10 ....108 E6
Farmers Ct HALE B63 ....121 K1
Farmers Fold CBHAMW WV1 * ..2 F5
Farmers Rd BRGRVE B60 ....191 J4
Farmers Wk HDSW B21 ....88 B6
Farmer Ward Rd KNWTH CV8 ..197 G7
Farmer Wy TPTN/OCK DY4 .....67 M4
Farm Gv RUGBYS/DCH CV22 ..187 J4
Farmhouse Rd SHHTH WV12 ...38 B3
Farmhouse Wy SHLY B90 ....148 C1
Farm La RRUGBY CV23 ....159 J1
Far Moor La REDE B98 ....195 L8
Far Moor Wy WOLVN WV10 .....36 C1
Farm Pl COVS CV3 ....155 M5
Farm Rd BDMR/CCFT WV3 .....49 G5
BLKHTH/ROWR B65 ....103 L1
BRLYHL DY5 ....102 C4
HALE B63 ....103 M3
LGLYGN/QTN B68 ....104 E2
REDE B98 ....202 E2
RLSN CV32 ....206 F2
SMTHWKW B67 ....105 J3
SPARK B11 ....107 M1
STRPT DY13 ....188 F1
TPTN/OCK DY4 ....67 M6
Farmside CI HAG/WOL DY9 ...120 C3
Farmside Gn COVEN WV9 ....35 K3
Farmstead CI WSL WS1 ....53 J8
Farmstead Rd HIA/OLT B92 ....128 A3
The Farmstead COVS CV3 .....155 M5
Farm St LOZ/NWT B19 ....89 C7
WBROM B70 ....87 G4
WSLW WS2 ....53 J1
Farnborough Ct MGN/WHC B75..57 G3
Farnborough Rd CBROM B36 ...91 L5
Farnbury Cft HWK/WKHTH B38..145 M3
Farncote Dr FOAKS/STRLY B74 ..56 D2
Farndale Av COVN CV6 ....134 B2
DUNHL/THL/PER WV6 ....35 L8
Farndale CI BRLYHL DY5 ....101 M7
Farndon Av
CHWD/FDBR/MGN B37 ....110 F6
Farndon CI BDWTH CV12 ....117 M2
Farndon Rd WASH/WDE B8 .....90 D3
Farnham CI GTB/HAM B43 ....70 D3
Farnham Rd HDSW B21 ....88 B3
Farnhurst Rd CBROM B36 ....90 F6
Farnol Rd
LGN/SDN/BHAMAIR B26 ....109 K5
Farnworth Gv CBROM B36 ....92 C4
Farquhar Rd EDG B15 ....106 D7
MOS/BIL B13 ....125 K2
Farquhar Rd East EDG B15 ...106 D7
Farr Dr TLHL/CAN CV4 ....153 M3
Farren Rd COVE CV2 ....135 L6
NFLD/LBR B31 ....144 B4
Farrier CI BRGRVE B60 ....191 J6
Farrier Rd GTB/HAM B43 ....71 H2
Farrier MI BLOX/PEL WS3 .....39 J1
The Farriers
LGN/SDN/BHAMAIR B26 ....109 M7
Farriers Wy NUN CV11 ....99 K3
Farrier Wy KGSWFD DY6 ....82 E6
Farrington Rd
ERDW/GRVHL B23 ....71 M8
ETTPK/GDPK/PENN WV4 ....66 C3
Farrow Rd KGSTG B44 ....71 J2
Farthing La CSCFLD/WYGN B72..72 F1
WALM/CURD B76 ....75 C7
Farthing Pools CI
CSCFLD/WYGN B72 ....73 C1
Farthings La DUDS DY2 ....84 E6
The Farthings HRBN B17 ....106 B7
Farvale Rd WALM/CURD B76 ...74 A7
Far Vw ALDR WS9 ....40 F3
Farway Gdns CDSL WV8 ....34 C3
Far Wood Rd NFLD/LBR B31 ..123 J5
Faseman Av TLHL/CAN CV4 ...153 K3
Fashoda Rd SLYOAK B29 ....124 F4
Fasson CI TAM/AM/WIL B77 .....46 A5
Fastlea Rd RIDG/WDGT B32 ..123 H4
Fastmoor Ov STETCH B33 .....109 J3
Fast Pits Rd YDLY B25 ....108 F5
Fatherless Barn Crs HALE B63..121 G1
Faulconbridge Av COVW CV5 ..153 C1
Faulkland Crs WOLV WV1 ....3 G3
Faulkner CI STRBR DY8 ....119 K1
Faulkner Rd HIA/OLT B92 ....127 M4
Faulknor Dr BRLYHL DY5 ....83 H4
Faultlands CI NUN CV11 ....99 K5
Faversham CI CDSL WV8 ....35 J5
WOLV WV2 ....52 B2
Fawdry CI SCFLD/BOLD B73 ....56 F8
Fawdry St DIG/EDG B5 ....7 K3
SMTHWK B66 ....88 B3
WOLV WV1 ....2 D2
Fawley CI COVS CV3 ....156 A1
WLNHL WV13 ....51 K5
Fawley Gv ALE/KHTH/YWD B14..124 F6
Fawn CI TLHL/CAN CV4 ....12 A7
Fawsley Leys
RUGBYS/DCH CV22 ....186 E6
Faygate CI COVS CV3 ....156 D2
Fazeley Rd POL/KGSB/FAZ B78..45 M1
Fazeley St DIG/EDG B5 ....7 K5
Fearings Cottages
REDW B97 * 202 B8
Fearn Pl SMTHWK B66 * 87 L7
Featherbed La LICH WS13 .....20 C7
REDW B97 ....201 M8
RUGBYN/HIL CV21 ....187 L4
Featherstone CI
NUNW/HART CV10 ....99 G3
SHLY B90 ....148 B3
Featherstone Crs SHLY B90 ...148 B3
Featherstone La WOLVN WV10..22 F5

Featherstone Rd
ALE/KHTH/YWD B14 125
Featherston Rd
FOAKS/STRLY B74 55
Feckenham Rd REDW B97 202
Fecknam Wy LICH WS13 21
Feiashill Rd SEDG DY3 64
Feilding CI COVE CV2 135
Feilding Wy NUNW/HART CV10..79
Felbrigg CI BRLYHL DY5 102
The Feldings ERDE/BCHGN B24 ..91
Feldon La RMSLY B62 104
Felgate CI SHLY B90 148
Fellbrook CI STETCH B33 109
Fell Gv HDSW B21 88
RLSN CV32 207
Fellmeadow Rd STETCH B33 ...109
Fellmeadow Wy SEDG DY3 66
Fellows Av KGSWFD DY6 83
Fellows La HRBN B17 105
Fellows Rd BILS/COS WV14 51
Fellows St BKHL/PFLD WV2 2
Fellows Wy RUGBYN/HIL CV21..187
Felspar Rd TAM/AM/WIL B77 ...46
Felstead CI TAM/AM/WIL B77 ...60
Felsted Wy VAUX/NECH B7 7
Felstone Rd KGSTG B44 71
Feltham CI STETCH B33 110
Felton CI COVE CV2 135
REDE B98 203
Felton Cft STETCH B33 109
Felton Gv SOLH B91 148
Fenchurch CI RUSH/SHEL WS4 ..40
Fenchurch CI WSLW WS2 53
Fen CI KIDDW DY11 138
Fencote Av
CHWD/FDBR/MGN B37 110
Fen End Rd
RCOVN/BALC/EX CV7 176
Fenmere CI
ETTPK/GDPK/PENN WV4 50
Fennel CI GTWY WS6 24
Fennel Cft BKDE/SHDE B34 91
Fennis CI DOR/KN B93 175
Fenn RI SHHTH WV12 37
STRBR DY8 101
Fenn St TAM/AM/WIL B77 46
Fens Crs BRLYHL DY5 84
Fenside Av COVS CV3 181
Fens Pool Av BRLYHL DY5 84
The Fensway BKDE/SHDE B34 ..91
Fenter CI MOS/BIL B13 125
Fentham CI HIA/OLT B92 127
Fentham Ct HIA/OLT B92 128
Fentham Gn HIA/OLT B92 127
Fentham Rd AST/WIT B6 89
ERDW/GRVHL B23 90
HIA/OLT B92 127
Fenton CI ACGN B27 108
HLYWD B47 146
Fenton St BRLYHL DY5 84
SMTHWK B66 105
Fenton Wy ACGN B27 126
Fenwick CI REDW B97 201
Fenwick Dr RUGBYN/HIL CV21..187
Fereday Rd ALDR WS9 41
Fereday's Cft SEDG DY3 66
Ferguson Dr KIDDW DY11 163
TPTN/OCK DY4 67
Ferguson Rd LGLYGN/QTN B68..105
Ferguson St WNSFLD WV11 37
Fern Av TPTN/OCK DY4 67
Fernbank CI HALE B63 121
Fernbank Crs DSYBK/YTR WS5 ..70
Fernbank Rd WASH/WDE B8 ...108
Ferncliffe Rd HRBN B17 123
Fern CI BILS/COS WV14 51
COVE CV2 135
RRUGBY CV23 159
RUSH/SHEL WS4 40
Fern Cft LICH WS13 20
Ferndale Av GTB/HAM B43 70
Ferndale CI BNTWD WS7 18
BRGRVW B61 168
HAG/WOL DY9 120
NUN CV11 99
STRPT DY13 189
Ferndale Ct CSHL/WTROR B46 ..93
Ferndale Crs BHTH/HG B12 ...107
KIDDW DY11 137
Ferndale Dr KNWTH CV8 197
Ferndale Ms CSHL/WTROR B46 ..93
Ferndale Pk HAG/WOL DY9 ...120
Ferndale Rd COVS CV3 157
CSHL/WTROR B46 93
FOAKS/STRLY B74 55
HLGN/YWD B28 126
LGLYGN/QTN B68 104
Fern Dale Rd
RCOVN/BALC/EX CV7 151
Ferndale Rd WNSFLD WV11 37
Fern Dell CI CNCK/NC WS11 16
Ferndene Rd SPARK B11 126
Ferndown Av SEDG DY3 65
Ferndown CI BLOX/PEL WS3 ...38
COVW CV5 132
LGN/SDN/BHAMAIR B26 109
Ferndown Ct
RUGBYS/DCH CV22 186
Ferndown Gdns WNSFLD WV11 ..37
Ferndown Rd
RUGBYS/DCH CV22 186
SOLH B91 147
Ferndown Ter
RUGBYS/DCH CV22 186
Fern Dr GTWY WS6 24
Fern Gv BDWTH CV12 116
Fernhill CI KNWTH CV8 179
Fernhill Dr RLSN CV32 206
Fernhill Gv KGSTG B44 71
Fernhill La RCOVN/BALC/EX CV7..130
Fernhill Rd HIA/OLT B92 127
Fernhurst Dr BRLYHL DY5 83
Fernhurst Rd WASH/WDE B8 ...108
Fernleigh Av BNTWD WS7 18
Fernleigh Gdns STRBR DY8 ...101
Fernleigh Rd RUSH/SHEL WS4 ..53
Fern Leys BDMR/CCFT WV3 49
Fern Rd BDMR/CCFT WV3 2
DUDN DY1 85
ERDE/BCHGN B24 90
HEDN WS12 17
Fernside Gdns SPARK B11 125
Fern Vls DARL/WED WS10 * 52
Fernwood CI REDE B98 202
SCFLD/BOLD B73 72
Fernwood Cft
ALE/KHTH/YWD B14 ....12?
TPTN/OCK DY4 ....
Fernwood Rd SCFLD/BOLD B73 ..
Fernwoods RIDG/WDGT B32 ....
Ferrers CI MGN/WHC B75 ....
TLHL/CAN CV4 1

errers Rd TAM/AM/WIL B77 ....46 B1
errie Gv BRWNH WS8 ....26 C5
erris Gv ACGN B27 ....126 E4
estival Av DARL/WED WS10 ....68 A1
estival Ct CNCK/NC WS11 * 12 C8
estival Ms HEDN WS12 ....12 D7
estival Wy
DUNHL/THL/PER WV6 ....35 M8
etherston Crs KNWTH CV8 ....182 E4
etherston Gra HOCK/TIA B94 * ..175 K8
fernfail Ct ERDW/GRVHL B23 ......72 C8
bbersley WLNHL WV13 ....51 K1
bbersley Bank WLNHL WV13 ......51 K1
ddlers Gn HIA/OLT B92 ....129 L6
eld Av NFLD/LBR B31 ....123 K8
eld Barn Rd
RWWCK/WEL CV35 ....204 D6
eld Cl BLOX/PEL WS3 ....39 G5
BLOX/PEL WS3 ....39 M3
KNWTH CV8 ....179 M8
LGN/SDN/BHAMAIR B26 ....109 L7
STRBR DY8 ....101 L3
WWCK CV34 ....205 M6
eld Cottage Dr STRBR DY8 ....119 M2
eld Cottages COVS CV3 * 156 A8
eld End STRPT DY13 ....188 C1
eldfare BNTWD WS7 ....19 H8
eldfare Cl BLKHTH/ROWR B65 ..103 K1
RRUGBY CV23 ....161 G5
eldfare Ct KIDD DY10 ....164 E4
eldfare Cft CBROM B36 ....92 E5
eldfare Rd HAG/WOL DY9 ....120 B1
eld Farm La REDE B98 ....203 H3
eld Farm Rd TAM/AM/WIL B77 ..46 B4
eldgate La KNWTH CV8 ....179 J6
eld Head La WWCK CV34 ....205 M7
eld Head Pl
DUNHL/THL/PER WV6 ....48 F1
eldhead Rd SPARK B11 ....126 E2
eldhouse La RMSLY B62 ....142 C1
eldhouse Rd BNTWD WS7 ....18 E6
ETTPK/GDPK/PENN WV4 ....66 C1
HEDN WS12 ....12 D6
YDLY B25 ....109 G5
elding Cl ATHST CV9 ....63 H3
eld La GTWY WS6 ....24 D2
HAG/WOL DY9 ....141 G1
RIDG/WDGT B32 ....122 E5
RUSH/SHEL WS4 ....39 M3
SOLH B91 ....128 E8
STRBR DY8 ....119 L2
eld Ms DUDS DY2 ....103 J3
eldon Br ATHST CV9 ....63 H2
eldon Cl SHLY B90 ....148 A2
eld Rd BLOX/PEL WS3 ....39 G4
DUDS DY2 ....85 J4
LICH WS13 ....20 F2
TPTN/OCK DY4 ....67 K5
elds Ct WWCK CV34 ....205 K5
eldside La COVS CV3 ....156 D2
he Fields CDSL WV8 ....34 F1
eld St BILS/COS WV14 ....67 J2
CNCK/NC WS11 ....16 D2
WLNHL WV13 ....51 L3
WOLVN WV10 ....3 J2
eld Vw KNWTH CV8 ....182 E3
eldview Cl BILS/COS WV14 ....67 H3
eld View Cl
RCOVN/BALC/EX CV7 ....116 E5
eld View Dr
BLKHTH/ROWR B65 ....104 D3
eld Wk ALDR WS9 ....40 F6
eld Wy HOCK/TIA B94 ....175 G7
eldways Cl HLYWD B47 ....146 E6
ery Hill Dr RBRY B45 ....170 A5
ery Hill Rd RBRY B45 ....170 A5
fe Rd COVW CV5 ....154 D3
fe St NUN CV11 ....98 E1
field Cl NUN CV11 ....99 H3
field Gv STETCH B33 ....109 K2
fth Av BORD B9 ....108 D3
WOLVN WV10 ....36 B6
lance Cl PENK ST19 ....10 D6
lance La PENK ST19 ....10 D6
ley TAM/AM/WIL B77 ....32 D8
ley Cl CNCK/NC WS11 ....16 A5
ley Rd WOLVN WV10 ....35 M3
llingham Cl
CHWD/FDBR/MGN B37 ....111 H4
llongley Rd CSHL/WTROR B46 ....94 F8
RCOVN/BALC/EX CV7 ....131 G4
lton Av BNTWD WS7 ....18 E5
lton Cft CVALE B35 ....91 L1
mbrell Cl STRBR DY8 ....101 L5
nbury Cl HIA/OLT B92 ....127 K4
nchall Cft HIA/OLT B92 ....128 C6
ncham Cl COVEN WV9 ....35 L2
nch Cl BLKHTH/ROWR B65 ....103 K1
nch Cft RCOVN/BALC/EX CV7 ....151 M6
nchdene Gv BDMR/CCFT WV3 ....49 H4
nch Dr FOAKS/STRLY B74 ....55 L8
nches End BKDE/SHDE B34 ....92 A8
nchfield Cl STRBR DY8 ....119 G1
nchfield Gdns
BDMR/CCFT WV3 ....49 J4
nchfield Hl BDMR/CCFT WV3 ......49 H3
nchfield La BDMR/CCFT WV3......49 G5
nchfield Rd BDMR/CCFT WV3 ....49 J4
nchfield Rd West
BDMR/CCFT WV3 ....49 G4
nchley Av LOZ/NWT B19 * 89 G5
nchley Cl SEDG DY3 ....84 B3
nchley Rd KGSTG B44 ....71 M3
nchmead Rd STETCH B33 ....110 C3
nchpath Rd WBROM B70 ....68 E7
nch Rd LOZ/NWT B19 ....89 G5
ndlay Rd ALE/KHTH/YWD B14 ..125 J4
ndley Cl ATHST CV9 ....63 K7
ndon Cl REDW B97 ....193 L8
ndon Rd WASH/WDE B8 ....90 F7
ndon St KIDD DY10 ....138 D7
neacre La RRUGBY CV23 ....183 G8
nford Cft
RCOVN/BALC/EX CV7 ....151 M7
ngal Cl COVS CV3 ....156 A7
nger Post Dr BLOX/PEL WS3 ......25 L8
ngest Cl COVW CV5 ....153 M1
nham Crs KNWTH CV8 ....179 M7
nham Green Rd COVS CV3 ....180 F2
nham Gv COVS CV3 ....181 G2
nham Rd KNWTH CV8 ....179 M7
nings Ct RLSN CV32 * 206 D3
nlarigg Dr EDG B15 ....106 D7
nmere RUGBYN/HIL CV21 ....161 H7
nmere Rd HLGN/YWD B28 ....126 D5
nmere Wy SHLY B90 ....148 B3
nnemore Cl COVS CV3 ....154 F8
nnemore Rd BORD B9 ....108 E3
nney Well Cl BILS/COS WV14 ......66 F2
nsbury Dr BRLYHL DY5 ....102 A6
nsbury Gv ERDW/GRVHL B23 ......72 B7
nstall Cl CSCFLD/WYGN B72 ....73 G4
VAUX/NECH B7 ....7 M2
stall Rd BRGRVE B60 ....192 A5
wood Cl HIA/OLT B92 ....128 C5
Av BHTH/HG B12 ....107 L8
lank Cl BVILLE B30 ....124 C6
nk Wy BLOX/PEL WS3 ....39 K3
Cl WALM/CURD B76 ....73 H2

Firbeck Gv KGSTG B44 ....71 L4
Firbeck Rd KGSTG B44 ....71 L4
Fir Cl HEDN WS12 ....12 B5
Fir Cft BRLYHL DY5 ....102 A5
Fircroft BILS/COS WV14 ....67 L2
NFLD/LBR B31 ....123 K5
POL/KGSB/FAZ B78 ....60 A6
SOLH B91 ....127 K7
Fircroft Cl BRGRVE B60 ....191 H7
CNCK/NC WS11 ....16 E2
Firecrest Cl CNCK/NC WS11 ....17 G3
ERDW/GRVHL B23 ....71 M6
Firecrest Wy KIDD DY10 ....164 F4
Fir Gv ALE/KHTH/YWD B14 ....125 K8
BDMR/CCFT WV3 ....2 A7
STRBR DY8 ....101 G7
TLHL/CAN CV4 ....153 L3
Firhill Cft ALE/KHTH/YWD B14 ....146 B3
Firmstone St STRBR DY8 ....101 J6
Firsbrook Cl
DUNHL/THL/PER WV6 ....35 L8
Firs Cl BRGRVE B60 ....169 G4
SMTHWKW B67 ....87 L8
The Firs Cl KIDD DY10 ....138 E8
Firs Dr RUGBYS/DCH CV22 ....186 D3
SHLY B90 ....147 L4
Firs Farm Dr CBROM B36 ....91 K6
Firsholm Cl SCFLD/BOLD B73 ....72 E6
Firs Rd KGSWFD DY6 ....83 J7
Firs St DUDS DY2 ....85 H4
First Av BORD B9 ....108 C4
BRWNH WS8 ....26 E5
COVS CV3 ....156 A4
KGSWFD DY6 ....83 L5
SLYOAK B29 ....124 F2
WALM/CURD B76 ....73 L8
WOLVN WV10 ....36 C7
First Exhibition Av
BHAMNEC B40 ....129 H1
The Firs BDWTH CV12 ....116 C3
COVW CV5 ....154 F5
POL/KGSB/FAZ B78 ....60 B6
RCOVN/BALC/EX CV7 * 130 F4
SPARK B11 ....108 A7
First Meadow Piece
RIDG/WDGT B32 ....123 J1
Fir St SEDG DY3 ....65 K6
Firsvale Rd WNSFLD WV11 ....37 K8
Firsway DUNHL/THL/PER WV6 ......48 E4
Firswood Rd STETCH B33 ....110 A4
Firth Dr ALE/KHTH/YWD B14 ....125 M8
RMSLY B62 ....104 C5
Firth Park Crs RMSLY B62 ....104 C5
Fir Tree Av TLHL/CAN CV4 ....153 L3
Fir Tree Cl CRTAM B79 ....31 J6
KGSTG B44 ....71 J6
REDW B97 ....202 B1
Fir Tree Dr DSYBK/YTR WS5 ....69 M1
SEDG DY3 ....66 C6
Fir Tree Gv NUN CV11 ....99 H4
SCFLD/BOLD B73 ....72 D4
Firtree La RCOVN/BALC/EX CV7 ....96 E5
Fir Tree Rd BDMR/CCFT WV3 ....49 H6
Firtree Rd ERDE/BCHGN B24 ....90 F3
Fisher Av RUGBYS/DCH CV22 ......187 J5
Fisher Rd BLOX/PEL WS3 ....38 D3
COVN CV6 ....134 C5
OLDBY B69 ....87 G6
Fishers Dr SHLY B90 ....147 K8
Fisher St BDMR/CCFT WV3 ....2 C8
BRLYHL DY5 ....101 M2
DUDS DY2 ....85 H4
HEDN WS12 ....12 D5
TPTN/OCK DY4 ....68 B8
TPTN/OCK DY4 ....85 L2
WLNHL WV13 ....52 A3
Fishers Wk ATHST CV9 * 63 J6
Fish Hl REDW B97 ....202 C1
Fishing Line Rd REDE B98 ....194 C8
Fishley Cl BLOX/PEL WS3 ....39 G1
Fishley La BLOX/PEL WS3 ....39 G1
Fishponds Rd KNWTH CV8 ....197 J2
Fishpool Cl CBROM B36 ....91 G5
Fishpool La
RCOVN/BALC/EX CV7 ....111 M7
Fistral Gdns BDMR/CCFT WV3 ....49 K6
Fitters Mill Cl DIG/EDG B5 * 107 J7
Fitton Av KGSWFD DY6 ....83 L8
Fitton St NUN CV11 ....98 F2
Fitzalan Cl RRUGBY CV23 ....158 F7
Fitzgerald Pl BRLYHL DY5 ....101 M7
Fitzguy Cl WBROM B70 ....87 J4
Fitzmaurice Rd WNSFLD WV11 ......37 K6
Fitz Roy Av HRBN B17 ....105 K6
Fitzroy Cl COVE CV2 ....135 M7
Fitzroy Rd NFLD/LBR B31 ....144 A2
Five Broadway
LDYWD/EDGR B16 * 6 A8
Fivefield Rd
RCOVN/BALC/EX CV7 ....115 J8
Five Fields Rd SHHTH WV12 ....37 L8
Five Oaks Rd WLNHL WV13 ....51 J5
Fives Gv BNTWD WS7 ....18 A5
Five Ways EDG B15 ....6 A8
Flackwell Rd ERDW/GRVHL B23 ....72 C6
Fladbury Cl DUDS DY2 ....103 H2
REDE B98 ....202 F5
Fladbury Crs SLYOAK B29 ....124 B3
Fladbury Gdns
BFLD/HDSWWD B20 * 89 G5
Fladbury Pl LOZ/NWT B19 * 89 G6
Flamboro' Cl COVS CV3 ....156 D5
Flamborough Cl
BKDE/SHDE B34 ....91 L6
Flamborough Wy
BILS/COS WV14 ....66 F6
Flanders Cl REDE B98 ....195 G8
Flanders Dr KGSWFD DY6 ....83 H5
Flanders Hall Cottages
ATHST CV9 * 76 D3
Flash La WMBN WV5 ....64 C3
Flash Rd OLDBY B69 ....86 E6
Flatlea NFLD/LBR B31 ....144 D1
Flats La LICHS WS14 ....29 L7
The Flats BRGRVW B61 ....191 K2
The Flatts DARL/WED WS10 ....52 C6
Flaunden Cl COVW CV5 ....153 M2
Flavel Crs RLSS CV31 ....206 D6
Flavell Av BILS/COS WV14 ....67 H4
Flavell Cl RIDG/WDGT B32 ....122 F4
Flavells La SEDG DY3 ....83 M3
YDLY B25 ....109 G5
Flavell St DUDN DY1 ....66 F7
Flavel Rd BRGRVE B60 ....191 J6
Flax Cl HLYWD B47 ....146 E8
Flax Gdns HWK/WKHTH B38 ....145 K5
Flaxhall St WSLW WS2 ....52 F5
Flaxley Cl REDE B98 ....203 L2
Flaxley Rd STETCH B33 ....109 K2
The Flax Ovens PENK ST19 ....10 C3
Flaxton Gv STETCH B33 ....109 L1
Flecknoe Cl CBROM B36 ....92 A4
Flecknose St COVS CV3 ....156 A7
Fledburgh Dr WALM/CURD B76 ....73 H2
Fleet Crs RUGBYN/HIL CV21 ....187 J3
Fleet St CBHAMNW B3 ....6 D4
COV CV1 ....8 E5
Fleetwood Gv
LGN/SDN/BHAMAIR B26 ....109 L4

Fleming Pl WSLW WS2 ....38 E7
Fleming Rd RIDG/WDGT B32 ....105 H8
WSLW WS2 ....38 E7
Flemmynge Cl CDSL WV8 ....34 C1
Fletchamstead Hwy
TLHL/CAN CV4 ....154 A4
Fletcher Gv DOR/KN B93 ....175 M1
Fletcher Rd SHHTH WV12 ....38 B4
Fletcher's La WLNHL WV13 ....52 A3
Fletcher St HAG/WOL DY9 ....102 D8
Fletchworth Ga COVW CV5 ....154 B5
Fletton Gv ALE/KHTH/YWD B14 ..146 E2
Flinkford Cl DSYBK/YTR WS5 ....54 A7
Flinn Cl LICHS WS14 ....21 H6
Flint Cl ATHST CV9 ....63 J3
KIDDW DY11 ....164 C3
Flint Green Rd ACGN B27 ....126 F2
Flintham Cl ACGN B27 ....127 J2
The Flintway STETCH B33 ....109 J1
Floodgate St DIG/EDG B5 ....7 K7
Flood St DUDS DY2 ....85 H4
Flora Cl CRTAM B79 ....32 A6
Flora Rd YDLY B25 ....108 F6
Florence Av
ETTPK/GDPK/PENN WV4 ....66 D1
SPARK B11 ....107 M8
Florence Cl ATHST CV9 ....63 H4
RCOVN/BALC/EX CV7 ....116 D5
Florence Gv HHTH/SAND B71 ....69 J4
Florence Rd ACGN B27 ....127 H1
ALE/KHTH/YWD B14 ....125 K5
CDSL WV8 ....35 G2
ERDW/GRVHL B23 ....72 F6
HDSW B21 ....88 B5
OLDBY B69 ....86 B6
SMTHWK B66 ....105 M1
TPTN/OCK DY4 ....67 L6
WBROM B70 ....87 J4
Florence St CBHAMW B1 ....6 E8
HEDN WS12 ....12 E6
WSL WS1 ....5 J5
Florence Vls SPARK B11 * 108 A6
Florendine St TAM/AM/WIL B77 ....32 D8
Florian Gv DARL/WED WS10 ....52 C6
Florida Wy KGSWFD DY6 ....83 L8
Flowerdale Cl BILS/COS WV14 ....66 F5
Flowerdale Dr COVE CV2 ....134 F7
Floyd Gv RCOVN/BALC/EX CV7 ....152 A6
Floyds La RUSH/SHEL WS4 ....40 A7
Floyer Rd SMTHH B10 ....108 C4
Flude Rd RCOVN/BALC/EX CV7 ....116 A7
Flyford Cl REDE B98 ....202 D4
Flyford Cft SLYOAK B29 ....123 K3
Flynt Av COVW CV5 ....132 E7
Fockbury Mill La BRGRVW B61 ....168 C8
Fockbury Rd BRGRVW B61 ....167 L8
Foden Cl LICHS WS14 ....28 D7
Foden Rd PBAR/PBCH B42 ....70 E5
Foinavon Cl BLKHTH/ROWR B65 ....85 K7
Fold St WOLV WV1 ....2 E6
The Fold DARL/WED WS10 ....52 B7
ETTPK/GDPK/PENN WV4 ....65 K1
Foldyard Cl WALM/CURD B76 ....73 L5
Foleshill Rd COV CV1 ....8 F2
COVN CV6 ....134 B7
Foley Av DUNHL/THL/PER WV6 ....48 F2
KIDDW DY11 ....164 A5
Foley Church Cl
FOAKS/STRLY B74 ....55 L3
Foley Dr DUNHL/THL/PER WV6 ......49 G2
KIDDW DY11 ....163 M5
Foley Gv KIDDW DY11 ....163 M5
WMBN WV5 ....64 C8
Foley Rd HAG/WOL DY9 ....119 M3
WASH/WDE B8 ....90 F7
Foley Rd East FOAKS/STRLY B74 ....55 K4
Foley Rd West FOAKS/STRLY B74 ..55 H4
Foley St DARL/WED WS10 ....68 E2
Foley Wood Cl FOAKS/STRLY B74 ..55 J4
Foliot Flds YDLY B25 ....109 H5
Folkes Rd HAG/WOL DY9 ....102 E7
Folkestone Cft CBROM B36 ....91 J5
Folliott Rd STETCH B33 ....109 L2
Follyhouse Cl WSL WS1 * 5 G8
Follyhouse La WSL WS1 ....5 G8
Folly La ATHST CV9 ....62 C5
Fontenaye Rd CRTAM B79 ....31 J6
Fontley Cl
LGN/SDN/BHAMAIR B26 ....109 L4
Fontmell Cl COVS CV3 ....156 E1
Fontwell Rd WOLVN WV10 ....36 B1
Footherley La LICHS WS14 ....42 A1
Footherley Rd LICHS WS14 ....28 D8
Fordbridge Cl REDW B97 ....202 A4
Fordbridge Rd
CHWD/FDBR/MGN B37 ....110 D1
Ford Brook La BLOX/PEL WS3 ....39 M4
Forder Gv ALE/KHTH/YWD B14 ....146 E3
Forde Way Gdns
HWK/WKHTH B38 ....145 H6
Fordfield Rd STETCH B33 ....110 A1
Fordham Gv COVEN WV9 ....35 L2
Fordhouse La BVILLE B30 ....124 F7
Fordhouse Rd BRGRVE B60 ....191 L4
WOLVN WV10 ....36 B4
Ford La LICH WS13 ....19 L3
Fordraught La RMSLY B62 ....142 F4
The Fordrift
CHWD/FDBR/MGN B37 ....110 E8
Ford Rd BRGRVW B61 ....191 J4
Fordrough YDLY B25 ....108 D6
Fordrough Av BORD B9 ....108 C2
Fordrough La BORD B9 ....108 C2
The Fordrough
FOAKS/STRLY B74 ....56 E4
NFLD/LBR B31 ....144 F5
SHLY B90 ....147 G6
Fords Rd SHLY B90 ....147 J6
Ford St COV CV1 ....9 H3
NUNW/HART CV10 ....98 C1
SMTHWKW B67 ....87 K7
WSLW WS2 ....4 B9
WSNGN B18 ....88 F8
Fordwater Rd FOAKS/STRLY B74 ..55 K7
Fordwell Cl COVW CV5 ....154 D2
Foredraft Cl RIDG/WDGT B32 ....123 G3
Foredraft St HALE B63 ....103 H8
Foredrift Cl REDE B98 ....202 C4
Foredrove La HIA/OLT B92 ....128 C7
Forelands Gv BRGRVW B61 ....191 H5
Foreland Wy COVN CV6 ....133 L3
Forest Av BLOX/PEL WS3 ....39 H6
Forest Cl BEWD DY12 ....162 D2
BRGRVE B60 ....168 F7
FOAKS/STRLY B74 ....55 J6
SMTHWK B66 ....87 J6
Forest Ct DOR/KN B93 ....175 K2
Forest Dl RBRY B45 ....143 M7
Forest Dr CDYHTH B64 ....103 J3
HRBN B17 ....106 B7
Foresters Pl RUGBYN/HIL CV21....187 M6
Forester's Rd COVS CV3 ....155 J7
Forester Wy KIDD DY10 ....164 C2
Forest Ga SHHTH WV12 ....38 B5
Forest Gld GTWY WS6 * 24 D3
Forest Hill Rd
LGN/SDN/BHAMAIR B26 ....110 A8
Forest La BLOX/PEL WS3 ....39 J8
BRGRVE B60 ....200 C8

Forest Pk WALM/CURD B76 ....73 J1
Forest Pl BLOX/PEL WS3 ....39 J7
Fore St CBHAM B2 ....7 G5
Forest Rd DOR/KN B93 ....175 L2
DUDN DY1 ....85 G1
LGLYGN/QTN B68 ....105 G6
MOS/BIL B13 ....125 L2
YDLY B25 ....109 G7
Forest Vw REDW B97 ....202 B7
Forest Wy GTWY WS6 ....24 E4
HLYWD B47 ....146 F7
NUNW/HART CV10 ....98 C3
Forfield Pl RLSS CV31 ....206 E6
Forfield Rd COVN CV6 ....133 J8
Forge Cl BNTWD WS7 ....19 H8
CDSL WV8 ....35 J4
Forge Cft WALM/CURD B76 ....73 M7
Forge Dr BRGRVW B61 ....191 K2
Forge La ALDR WS9 ....41 K7
BNTWD WS7 ....19 K7
CDYHTH B64 ....102 F5
FOAKS/STRLY B74 ....42 A7
HAG/WOL DY9 ....141 H6
HHTH/SAND B71 ....69 L7
KGSWFD DY6 ....82 E5
KIDD DY10 ....139 M4
LICH WS13 ....20 E4
LICHS WS14 ....41 M5
RMSLY B62 ....104 A8
WALM/CURD B76 ....73 M7
Forge Leys WMBN WV5 ....64 C7
Forge Mill Rd REDE B98 ....194 D8
Forge Rd BLOX/PEL WS3 ....25 K8
CSHL/WTROR B46 ....94 D3
DARL/WED WS10 ....51 M7
KNWTH CV8 ....179 L7
SHHTH WV12 ....52 A1
STRBR DY8 ....101 K7
Forge St DARL/WED WS10 ....68 C1
HEDN WS12 ....17 G1
The Forge CRTAM B79 ....31 L8
HALE B63 ....102 E5
Forge Valley Wy WMBN WV5 ....64 C7
Forge Wy COVN CV6 ....134 A2
OLDBY B69 ....86 C7
Forknell Av COVE CV2 ....135 G8
Formans Rd SPARK B11 ....126 C2
Formby Av
DUNHL/THL/PER WV6 ....48 B1
Formby Wy BLOX/PEL WS3 ....38 E2
Fornside Cl RUGBYN/HIL CV21 ....161 H6
Forrell Gv NFLD/LBR B31 ....144 F6
Forrest Av CNCK/NC WS11 ....16 C6
WNSFLD WV11 ....37 L1
Forrester St WSLW WS2 ....4 B3
Forrester Street Prec WSLW WS2 ..4 B3
Forrest Rd KNWTH CV8 ....197 J1
Forshaw Heath La
HOCK/TIA B94 ....172 E7
Forshaw Heath Rd
HOCK/TIA B94 ....173 G5
Forster St SMTHWKW B67 ....87 J6
VAUX/NECH B7 ....7 L3
Forsythia Cl NFLD/LBR B31 ....123 K5
Forsythia Gv CDSL WV8 ....34 E2
Fort Crs ALDR WS9 ....40 E2
Forth Dr CHWD/FDBR/MGN B37..110 F1
Forth Gv HWK/WKHTH B38 ....145 J5
Forth Wy RMSLY B62 ....104 C5
Forties TAM/AM/WIL B77 ....46 C6
Fort-mahon Pl BEWD DY12 ....162 D2
Fortnum Cl STETCH B33 ....110 A3
Forton Cl DUNHL/THL/PER WV6 ....48 F3
Fort Pkwy ERDE/BCHGN B24 ....90 F5
ERDE/BCHGN B24 ....91 K3
Forum Dr RUGBYN/HIL CV21 ....160 E7
Forward Cottages ALVE B48 * 170 D7
Fosberry Cl WWCK CV34 ....205 M5
Fosbrooke Rd SMHTH B10 ....108 E5
Fossdale Rd TAM/AM/WIL B77 ......46 E5
Fosseway LICHS WS14 ....20 E8
Fosse Wy RRUGBY CV23 ....183 L7
Fosseway Dr ERDW/GRVHL B23 ....72 C5
Fosseway La LICH WS13 ....28 B1
Fosseway Rd COVS CV3 ....180 F1
Fossil Dr RBRY B45 ....143 L6
Foster Av BILS/COS WV14 ....66 F4
HEDN WS12 ....12 D7
Fosterd Rd RUGBYN/HIL CV21 ....160 D8
Foster Gdns WSNGN B18 * 88 D7
Foster Gn DUNHL/THL/PER WV6 ..48 C2
Foster Pl STRBR DY8 ....101 J7
Foster Rd COVN CV6 ....133 M6
WOLVN WV10 ....36 C7
Fosters Gn BRGRVE B60 ....200 B6
Foster St BLOX/PEL WS3 ....39 H5
DARL/WED WS10 ....52 B6
Foster St East STRBR DY8 ....101 L8
Foster Wy DIG/EDG B5 ....107 G8
Fotherley Brook Rd ALDR WS9......41 K8
Founder Cl TLHL/CAN CV4 ....153 K5
Foundry La BLOX/PEL WS3 ....39 J2
SMTHWK B66 ....87 M6
Foundry Rd KGSWFD DY6 ....82 F5
WSNGN B18 ....88 B8
Foundry St BILS/COS WV14 ....67 G4
KGSWFD DY6 ....82 F5
STRPT DY13 ....188 E1
TPTN/OCK DY4 ....67 J5
Fountain Arcade Chambers
DUDN DY1 * 85 G4
Fountain Cl NFLD/LBR B31 ....144 C7
Fountain Ct CBHAMNE B4 * 7 G3
Fountain La BILS/COS WV14 ....67 H5
OLDBY B69 ....86 D4
Fountain Rd HRBN B17 ....105 M4
Fountains Rd BLOX/PEL WS3 ....38 C3
Fountains Wy BLOX/PEL WS3 ....38 C3
Four Acres RIDG/WDGT B32 ....123 G1
Four Ashes Rd DOR/KN B93 ....175 H2
Four Crosses La WOLVN WV10 ......15 H7
Four Crosses Rd
RUSH/SHEL WS4 ....40 A4
Fourfields Wy
RCOVN/BALC/EX CV7 ....96 D6
Fourlands Av CSCFLD/WYGN B72 ..73 H6
Fourlands Rd NFLD/LBR B31 ....123 J7
Four Oaks Cl REDE B98 ....202 B5
Four Oaks Common Rd
FOAKS/STRLY B74 ....56 C2
Four Oaks Rd FOAKS/STRLY B74....56 D3
Four Pounds Av COVW CV5 ....154 D2
Four Stones Cl SOLH B91 ....148 E4
Four Stones Gv DIG/EDG B5 ....107 H7
Fourth Av BORD B9 ....108 D3
BRWNH WS8 ....26 E5
SLYOAK B29 ....125 G2
WOLVN WV10 ....36 B7
Fourways ATHST CV9 ....63 J5
Four Winds Rd DUDS DY2 ....85 J6
Fowey Cl WALM/CURD B76 ....73 L6
Fowey Rd BKDE/SHDE B34 ....91 K7
Fowgay Dr SOLH B91 ....148 D4
Fowler Cl CDSL WV8 ....34 C7
SMTHWK B66 ....87 L5
Fowler Pl STRPT DY13 ....163 L8
Fowler Rd COVN CV6 ....133 M8
MGN/WHC B75 ....57 L8
Fowler St BKHL/PFLD WV2 ....50 A7

VAUX/NECH B7 ....89 M8
Fowlmere Rd PBAR/PBCH B42 ......70 F5
Fownhope Cl REDE B98 ....203 J2
Fow Oak TLHL/CAN CV4 ....153 G3
Fox Av NUNW/HART CV10 ....81 G5
Foxbury Dr DOR/KN B93 ....175 L2
Fox Cl RUGBYN/HIL CV21 ....187 M4
TAM/AM/WIL B77 ....46 A5
Foxcote Av HDSW B21 ....88 C6
Foxcote Cl REDE B98 ....203 J1
SHLY B90 ....148 B5
Foxcote Dr SHLY B90 ....148 B5
Foxcote La HAG/WOL DY9 ....120 F2
Fox Covert STRBR DY8 ....101 J8
Fox Crs SPARK B11 * 126 B1
Foxcroft Cl BNTWD WS7 ....18 E8
Foxdale Dr BRLYHL DY5 ....101 M2
Foxdale Gv STETCH B33 ....110 A3
Foxdale Wk RLSS CV31 ....207 G7
Foxes Cl BRGRVE B60 ....169 M8
Foxes Meadow BVILLE B30 ....145 K1
WALM/CURD B76 ....73 L5
Foxes Rake CNCK/NC WS11 ....16 C2
Foxes Rdg CDYHTH B64 ....103 J5
Foxes Wy RCOVN/BALC/EX CV7 ..151 M7
Foxfield Dr STRBR DY8 ....119 L2
Foxfields Wy HEDN WS12 ....12 A6
Fox Foot Dr BRLYHL DY5 ....102 A1
Foxford Cl CBROM B36 ....92 B4
CSCFLD/WYGN B72 ....73 G6
Foxford Crs COVE CV2 ....134 F1
Foxglove TAM/AM/WIL B77 ....46 E1
Foxglove Cl BDWTH CV12 ....116 C4
BLOX/PEL WS3 ....25 L8
COVN CV6 ....134 A3
LICHS WS14 ....20 E8
RRUGBY CV23 ....161 J5
WNSFLD WV11 ....37 J8
WOLVN WV10 ....22 F6
Foxglove Crs
CHWD/FDBR/MGN B37 ....110 C2
Foxglove Rd DUDN DY1 ....84 D1
Foxglove Wy BRGRVE B60 ....169 G7
ERDW/GRVHL B23 ....71 M6
HDSW B21 ....88 B6
Fox Green Crs ACGN B27 ....126 E3
Fox Gv ACGN B27 ....126 E3
Fox Hl SLYOAK B29 ....124 A5
Foxhill Cl HEDN WS12 ....17 H3
Fox Hill Cl SLYOAK B29 ....124 A5
Foxhill La ALVE B48 ....170 B8
Fox Hill Rd MGN/WHC B75 ....57 K3
Foxhill's Cl BNTWD WS7 ....18 E8
Foxhills Pk DUDS DY2 ....103 G1
Foxhills Rd
ETTPK/GDPK/PENN WV4 ....65 G2
STRBR DY8 ....101 H4
Foxholes La REDW B97 ....201 L7
The Foxholes KIDD DY10 ....138 D5
Foxhollies Dr HALE B63 ....121 J1
Fox Hollies Rd ACGN B27 ....126 F2
WALM/CURD B76 ....73 K5
Fox Hollow
DUNHL/THL/PER WV6 ....49 G3
Foxhope Cl HWK/WKHTH B38 ......145 M4
Foxhunt Rd HALE B63 ....121 J3
Foxland Av GTWY WS6 ....24 E2
RBRY B45 ....144 A6
Foxland Cl
CHWD/FDBR/MGN B37 ....111 H3
SHLY B90 ....174 B1
Foxlands Av
ETTPK/GDPK/PENN WV4 ....65 H2
Foxlands Crs
ETTPK/GDPK/PENN WV4 ....65 G2
Foxlands Dr CSCFLD/WYGN B72 ....73 H6
ETTPK/GDPK/PENN WV4 ....65 G2
SEDG DY3 ....66 B8
Fox La BRGRVW B61 ....191 H5
KIDD DY10 ....166 B7
LICH WS13 ....20 E1
Foxlea Rd HALE B63 ....121 H4
Foxley Dr SOLH B91 ....128 F8
Foxlydiate Crs REDW B97 ....201 L1
Foxlydiate La REDW B97 ....201 K3
Foxlydiate Ms REDW B97 * 201 L1
Foxmeadow Cl SEDG DY3 ....66 C6
Foxoak St CDYHTH B64 ....103 G4
Foxons Barn Rd
RUGBYN/HIL CV21 ....161 G7
Fox's La WOLV WV1 ....36 B8
Fox St CBHAMNE B4 ....7 J4
DUDN DY1 ....67 G7
Foxtail Wy HEDN WS12 ....17 J1
Foxton Rd COVS CV3 ....156 C4
WASH/WDE B8 ....90 D8
Fox Wk ALDR WS9 ....40 F2
Foxwalks Av BRGRVW B61 ....191 H5
Foxwell Gv BORD B9 ....108 F3
Foxwell Rd BORD B9 ....108 F3
Foxwood Av GTB/HAM B43 ....70 F2
Foxwood Gv
CHWD/FDBR/MGN B37 ....92 D8
Foxwood Rd
CHWD/FDBR/MGN B37 ....92 D8
POL/KGSB/FAZ B78 ....47 K5
Foxyards Cl TPTN/OCK DY4 * 67 H8
Foxyards Rd TPTN/OCK DY4 ....67 H8
Foyle Rd HWK/WKHTH B38 ....145 K4
Fozdar Crs BILS/COS WV14 ....66 E4
Fradley Cl BVILLE B30 ....145 H1
Framefield Dr SOLH B91 ....128 C7
Framlingham Gv
DUNHL/THL/PER WV6 ....48 E2
KNWTH CV8 ....180 A7
Frampton Cl BVILLE B30 ....124 B6
CHWD/FDBR/MGN B37 ....111 H2
Frampton Wk COVE CV2 ....156 D1
Frampton Wy GTB/HAM B43 ....71 H1
Frances Av WWCK CV34 ....205 L6
Frances Crs BDWTH CV12 ....116 E2
Frances Dr BLOX/PEL WS3 ....38 F3
Frances Havergal Cl RLSS CV31 ..206 D7
Frances Rd BVILLE B30 ....124 E8
ERDW/GRVHL B23 ....90 B2
KNWTH CV8 ....181 J2
LOZ/NWT B19 ....89 G5
Franchecourt Dr KIDDW DY11 ....137 M4
Franche Rd KIDDW DY11 ....137 M4
Franchise Gdns DARL/WED WS10..52 D7
Franchise St DARL/WED WS10 ......52 C8
KIDDW DY11 ....138 A8
PBAR/PBCH B42 ....89 J3
Franciscan Rd COVS CV3 ....155 G5
Francis Cl FOAKS/STRLY B74 ....55 K5
KGSWFD DY6 ....83 H5
PENK ST19 ....10 D5
POL/KGSB/FAZ B78 ....47 L3
Francis Dr RUGBYS/DCH CV22......185 L4
Francis Green La PENK ST19 ....10 D4
Francis Rd BRGRVE B60 ....191 K6
LDYWD/EDGR B16 ....106 E4
LICH WS13 ....20 E3
SMTHWKW B67 ....87 H8
STETCH B33 ....109 H2
STRBR DY8 ....101 G8
STRPT DY13 ....163 J7
YDLY B25 ....108 E7
Francis St COVN CV6 ....134 C7

VAUX/NECH B7 .... 7 M1
WBROM B70 .... 87 H4
WOLV WV1 .... 2 E1
Francis Wk NFLD/LBR B31 .... 144 L6
Francis Ward Cl HHTH/SAND B71 .... 68 C3
Frankburn Rd FOAKS/STRLY B74 .... 55 J5
Frankfort St LOZ/NWT B19 .... 89 H7
Frankholmes Dr SHLY B90 .... 148 E7
Frankland Rd COVN CV6 .... 134 C4
Frankley Beeches Rd NFLD/LBR B31 .... 144 A3
Frankley Grn RMSLY B62 .... 122 B8
Frankley Green La RIDG/WDGT B32 .... 122 D8
Frankley Hill La RIDG/WDGT B32 .... 143 K1
Frankley La LGLYGN/QTN B68 .... 104 E5
Frankley Lodge Rd NFLD/LBR B31 .... 144 B1
Frankley Rd LGLYGN/QTN B68 .... 104 C5
Frankley Ter Dr BNTWD WS7 .... 18 F7
Franklin Gv TLHL/CAN CV4 .... 153 J4
Franklin Rd BVILLE B30 .... 124 D8
NUN CV11 .... 99 H4
Franklins Gdns COVS CV3 .... 156 F4
Franklin St WSNGN B18 .... 88 C3
Franklin Wy BVILLE B30 .... 124 D8
Franklyn Cl DUNHL/THL/PER WV6 .... 34 C8
Frankpledge Rd COVS CV3 .... 155 J5
Frank St SMTHWK B67 .... 87 J7
Frank St BHTH/HG B12 .... 107 K6
NUN CV11 .... 98 F2
Franks Wy STETCH B33 .... 109 J3
Frank Tommey Cl BLKHTH/ROWR B65 * 104 A4
Frankton Av COVS CV3 .... 155 H8
Frankton Cl HIA/OLT B92 .... 127 K1
REDE B98 .... 203 J3
Frankton Gv BORD B9 .... 108 F3
Frankton La RRUGBY CV23 .... 183 L8
Frankwell Dr COVE CV2 .... 135 K4
Fraser Cl NUNW/HART CV10 .... 79 M7
Fraser Rd COVN CV6 .... 133 L4
SPARK B11 .... 108 A3
Fraser St BILS/COS WV14 .... 51 J7
Frayne Av KGSWFD DY6 .... 83 G9
Freasley Cl SHLY B90 .... 148 B2
Freasley Rd BKDE/SHDE B34 .... 92 B8
Freda Ri OLDBY B69 .... 86 B5
Freda Rd WBROM B70 .... 87 H4
Fredas Gv HRBN B17 .... 123 L1
Frederick Cl STRBR DY8 .... 119 J1
Frederick Neal Av COVW CV5 .... 153 H1
Frederick Rd AST/WIT B6 .... 89 J3
EDG B15 .... 106 F5
ERDW/GRVHL B23 .... 90 C3
KIDDW DY11 .... 164 D4
LGLYGN/QTN B68 .... 105 H6
PENK ST19 .... 10 D3
RCOVN/BALC/EX CV7 .... 96 C5
SCFLD/BOLD B73 .... 72 E4
SLYOAK B29 .... 124 C3
SPARK B11 .... 126 A1
STETCH B33 .... 109 G2
WNSFLD WV11 .... 37 G8
Fredericks Cl STRBR DY8 .... 119 J1
Frederick St BKHL/PFLD WV2 .... 2 F8
CBHAMW B1 .... 6 C4
RUGBYS/DCH CV22 .... 186 D2
WBROM B70 .... 87 G1
WSLW WS2 .... 4 C4
Frederick William St WLNHL WS13 .... 51 M3
Fred Lee Gv COVS CV3 .... 181 H1
Fred Smith Cl DARL/WED WS10 .... 52 F8
Freeboard La KNWTH CV8 .... 183 J6
Freeburn Cswy TLHL/CAN CV4 .... 154 A6
Freeford Gdns LICHS WS14 .... 21 J7
Freehold St COV CV1 .... 155 K1
Freeland Gv KGSWFD DY6 .... 101 K1
Freeman Dr MGN/WHC B75 .... 73 K1
Freeman Pl BILS/COS WV14 .... 51 J5
Freeman Rd DARL/WED WS10 .... 69 G2
VAUX/NECH B7 .... 89 M8
Freeman St COVN CV6 .... 134 D7
DIG/EDG B5 .... 7 H5
WOLVN WV10 .... 3 L4
Freemantle Rd RUGBYS/DCH CV22 .... 186 A3
Freer Dr BNTWD WS7 .... 19 J3
Freer Rd AST/WIT B6 .... 89 H5
Freer St NUN CV11 .... 99 J7
WSL WS1 .... 4 F3
Freesland Ri NUNW/HART CV10 .... 79 M7
Freeth Rd BRWNH WS8 .... 26 K4
Freeth St LDYWD/EDGR B16 .... 106 D5
OLDBY B69 .... 86 D5
Freezeland St BILS/COS WV14 .... 50 F7
Fremantle Dr HEDN WS12 .... 17 J3
Fremont Dr DUDN DY1 .... 66 C7
French Av POL/KGSB/FAZ B78 .... 45 G4
French Rd DUDS DY2 .... 85 J4
Frensham CHWD/FDBR/MGN B37 .... 111 G3
GTWY WS6 .... 24 C1
Frensham Dr NUNW/HART CV10 .... 79 M8
Frenshaw Gv KGSTG B44 .... 71 K5
Frensham Wy HRBN B17 .... 106 B1
Freshwater Dr BRLYHL DY5 .... 101 M4
Freshwater Gv RLSS CV31 .... 207 G7
Fretton Cl COVN CV6 .... 134 D6
Freville Cl DARL/WED WS10 .... 69 H2
Frevill Rd COVN CV6 .... 134 F5
Friardale Cl DARL/WED WS10 .... 69 H2
Friar Park Rd DARL/WED WS10 .... 69 G2
Friars Cl COVS CV3 .... 157 J6
STRBR DY8 .... 101 G2
Friar's Ga ATHST CV9 .... 63 H5
Friars Gorse KINVER DY7 .... 7 K7
Friars Rd COV CV1 .... 6 E7
Friars St WWCK CV34 .... 205 H7
Friar St DARL/WED WS10 .... 68 F2
Friars Wk CRTAM/AM/WIL B77 .... 46 A2
Friary Av LICH WS13 .... 20 C5
SHLY B90 .... 148 E2
Friary Cl RWWCK/WEL CV35 .... 204 D7
Friary Crs RUSH/SHEL WS4 .... 40 A4
Friary Dr FOAKS/STRLY B74 .... 56 D7
Friary Gdns HDSW B21 .... 88 B3
Friary Rd ATHST CV9 .... 63 H4
HDSW B21 .... 88 C3
Friary St NUN CV11 .... 80 F8
The Friary LICH WS13 .... 20 C5
Friary Vw LICH WS13 * 20 C5
Friday Acre LICHS WS14 .... 20 F5
Friday La HIA/OLT B92 .... 150 B1
Friesland Dr WOLV WV1 .... 50 F2
Friezeland Rd NUN CV11 .... 98 F2
Friezland La BRWNH WS8 .... 26 M8
Frilsham Wy COVW CV5 .... 132 F8
Fringe Green Cl BRGRVE B60 .... 191 L6
Fringe Meadow Rd REDE B98 .... 195 K7

Frinton Gv HDSW B21 .... 88 A6
Frisby Rd RIDG/WDGT B32 .... 105 J3
TLHL/CAN CV4 .... 153 J5
Friston Av LDYWD/EDGR B16 .... 6 A7
Friswell Dr COVN CV6 .... 134 D5
Frobisher Cl GTWY WS6 .... 24 C4
Frobisher Rd COVS CV3 .... 155 C8
RUGBYS/DCH CV22 .... 186 A4
Frodesley Rd LGN/SDN/BHAMAIR B26 .... 109 M5
Froggatt Rd BILS/COS WV14 .... 51 H6
Froggatts Ride WALM/CURD B76 .... 73 K2
Frog La LICH WS13 .... 20 F6
RCOVN/BALC/EX CV7 .... 151 L8
Frogmere Cl COVW CV5 .... 132 F7
COVW CV5 * 133 G7
Frogmill Rd NFLD/LBR B31 .... 143 M3
Frogmore La KNWTH CV8 .... 177 K2
Frome Cl DUDN DY1 .... 84 B3
Frome Dr WNSFLD WV11 .... 37 G8
Front Cottages ALVE B48 * 170 D7
Frost St BKHL/PFLD WV2 .... 50 E7
Froxmere Cl SOLH B91 .... 148 F5
Froyle Cl DUNHL/THL/PER WV6 .... 35 G8
Froysell St WLNHL WV13 .... 51 M5
Fryer Av RLSN CV32 .... 206 C3
Fryer Rd NFLD/LBR B31 .... 144 F6
Fryers Cl BLOX/PEL WS3 .... 38 F6
Fryers Rd WSLW WS2 .... 38 E7
Fryer St WOLV WV1 .... 3 G4
Frythe Cl KNWTH CV8 .... 180 A7
Fuchsia Dr COVEN WV9 .... 35 K2
Fugelmere Cl HRBN B17 .... 105 K6
Fulbrook Cl REDE B98 .... 195 G8
Fulbrook Gv SLYOAK B29 .... 123 K5
Fulbrook Rd COVN CV6 .... 135 G4
DUDN DY1 .... 84 E4
Fulford Dr WALM/CURD B76 .... 73 M8
Fulford Gv LGN/SDN/BHAMAIR B26 .... 109 M5
Fulford Hall Rd HOCK/TIA B94 .... 173 H2
Fulham Rd SPARK B11 .... 107 M8
Fullbrook Cl SHLY B90 .... 148 E8
Fullbrook Rd DYSBK/YTR WS5 .... 53 J8
Fullelove Rd BRWNH WS8 .... 26 E7
Fullers Cl COVN CV6 .... 133 K6
Fullerton Cl CDSL WV8 .... 35 J4
Fullmore Cl PENK ST19 .... 10 D6
Fullwood Cl COVE CV2 .... 135 J3
Fullwood Crs DUDS DY2 .... 84 C7
Fullwoods End BILS/COS WV14 .... 51 M7
Fulmar Crs KIDD DY10 .... 164 F3
Fulmer Wk WSNGN B18 * 106 E2
Fulton Cl BRGRVE B60 .... 191 M4
Fulwell Gv KGSTG B44 .... 71 L5
Fulwell Ms CHWD/FDBR/MGN B37 .... 110 F5
Fulwood Av RMSLY B62 .... 104 C5
Furber Pl KGSWFD DY6 .... 83 K7
Furlong La HALE B63 .... 103 G7
Furlong Meadow NFLD/LBR B31 .... 145 G3
Furlong Rd SEDG DY3 .... 66 B7
The Furlongs STRBR DY8 .... 119 M2
WNSFLD WV11 .... 36 F8
The Furlong DARL/WED WS10 .... 52 C8
Furlong Wk SEDG DY3 .... 84 B1
Furnace Cl BDWTH CV12 .... 117 C2
WMBN WV5 .... 64 C8
Furnace Hl HALE B63 .... 103 H7
Furnace La HALE B63 .... 103 H6
Furnace Pde TPTN/OCK DY4 .... 67 J7
Furnace Rd BDWTH CV12 .... 117 H2
DUDS DY2 .... 85 G5
Furness TAM/AM/WIL B77 .... 46 B3
Furness Cl BLOX/PEL WS3 .... 38 C2
RUGBYN/HIL CV21 .... 161 K6
Furnivall Crs LICH WS13 .... 21 H4
Furrow Cl RUGBYN/HIL CV21 .... 187 H1
The Furrows BRGRVE B60 .... 191 H7
Furst St BRWNH WS8 .... 26 E5
Furzebank Wy SHHTH WV12 .... 52 C1
Furze La REDE B98 .... 203 L1
Furze Wy DYSBK/YTR WS5 .... 54 B5
Fynford Rd COVN CV6 .... 133 M8

G

Gable Cft LICHS WS14 .... 21 J7
Gables Cl RUGBYS/DCH CV22 .... 186 B5
The Gables ERDE/BCHGN B24 .... 91 H1
POL/KGSB/FAZ B78 .... 47 L3
Gabor Cl RUGBYN/HIL CV21 .... 161 G7
Gaddesby Rd ALE/KHTH/YWD B14 .... 125 G7
Gadds Dr BLKHTH/ROWR B65 .... 104 B3
Gadsby Av WNSFLD WV11 .... 37 L6
Gadsby St NUN CV11 .... 99 J2
Gads Gn DUDS DY2 .... 85 G7
Gads Green Crs DUDS DY2 .... 85 J7
Gads La DUDN DY1 .... 84 C4
WBROM B70 .... 86 E2
Gadwall Cft ERDW/GRVHL B23 .... 89 M2
Gaelic Rd CNCK/NC WS11 .... 16 B5
Gagarin B79 .... 31 K8
Gaialands Cl LICH WS13 .... 20 F4
Gaialands Crs LICH WS13 .... 20 F4
Gaia La LICH WS13 .... 20 F4
Gail Cl ALDR WS9 .... 40 F1
Gailey Cft KGSTG B44 .... 71 J2
Gailey Lea La PENK ST19 .... 14 F3
Gailey Pk WOLVN WV10 * 22 A7
Gail Pk BDMR/CCFT WV3 .... 49 H6
Gainford Cl COVEN WV9 .... 35 K4
Gainford Ri COVS CV3 .... 156 D2
Gainford Rd KGSTG B44 .... 72 A4
Gainsborough Crs DOR/KN B93 .... 149 L7
GTB/HAM B43 .... 71 H1
RUGBYN/HIL CV21 .... 187 H4
Gainsborough Dr BDWTH CV12 .... 116 E1
DUNHL/THL/PER WV6 .... 48 D1
POL/KGSB/FAZ B78 .... 45 L2
RLSS CV31 .... 207 G5
Gainsborough Hl STRBR DY8 .... 119 K5
Gainsborough Ms KIDDW DY11 .... 137 M8
Gainsborough Pl DUDN DY1 .... 84 C3
Gainsborough Rd PBAR/PBCH B42 .... 70 F6
Gainsbrook Crs CNCK/NC WS11 .... 17 K8
Gainsford Dr RMSLY B62 .... 103 M7
Gainsla La BLOX/PEL WS3 .... 25 J3
Gairloch Rd WNSFLD WV12 .... 37 M4
Gaitskell Ter OLDBY B69 .... 67 G6
Gaitswell Rd SMTHWK B66 .... 87 K6
Galahad Wy DARL/WED WS10 .... 68 E3
STRPT DY13 .... 188 D1
Galbraith Cl BILS/COS WV14 .... 67 H5
Galena Cl TAM/AM/WIL B77 .... 46 A3
Galena Wy AST/WIT B6 .... 89 J7
Gale Wk BLKHTH/ROWR B65 .... 85 K8
Galey's Rd COVS CV3 .... 155 H5
Gallagher Rd BDWTH CV12 .... 116 C3

Gallery Sq WSL WS1 .... 4 E3
The Galliards TLHL/CAN CV4 .... 180 A1
Galliers Cl TAM/AM/WIL B77 .... 46 D8
Galloway Av BKDE/SHDE B34 .... 91 K7
Gallows Hi WWCK CV34 .... 205 M8
Galmington Dr COVS CV3 .... 154 F8
Galton Cl ERDE/BCHGN B24 .... 91 K1
TPTN/OCK DY4 .... 68 A7
Galton Dr DUDS DY2 .... 84 F7
Galton Rd SMTHWKW B67 .... 105 K4
Galtons La HAG/WOL DY9 .... 141 L6
Galway Rd BKHL/PFLD WV2 .... 51 J7
Gamesfield Gn BDMR/CCFT WV3 .... 49 K4
Gammage St DUDS DY2 .... 84 F5
Gamson Cl KIDD DY10 .... 156 C5
Ganborough Cl REDE B98 .... 203 J4
Gandy Rd SHHTH WV12 .... 37 L7
Gannahs Farm Cl WALM/CURD B76 .... 73 K2
Gannow Green La RBRY B45 .... 143 J4
Gannow Manor Crs RBRY B45 .... 143 J4
Gannow Manor Gdns RBRY B45 .... 143 J6
Gannow Rd RBRY B45 .... 143 J6
Gannow Wk RBRY B45 .... 143 J6
Ganton Rd BLOX/PEL WS3 .... 38 C1
Garage Cl TAM/AM/WIL B77 .... 46 E5
Garden Cl DOR/KN B93 .... 148 E7
RBRY B45 .... 143 L3
WASH/WDE B8 .... 90 E8
Garden Crs BLOX/PEL WS3 .... 39 K2
Garden Cft ALDR WS9 .... 40 F6
Gardeners Cl KIDDW DY11 .... 138 A5
Gardeners Wy WMBN WV5 .... 64 C7
Garden Gv COVW CV5 .... 132 B3
Gardenia Dr COVW CV5 .... 132 B3
The Gardens ERDW/GRVHL B23 .... 90 C2
KNWTH CV8 .... 197 G2
RLSS CV31 .... 207 J8
Garden La WSLW WS2 .... 4 E1
Garden Wk BILS/COS WV14 .... 51 K7
SEDG DY3 .... 84 A3
Gardners Meadow BEWD DY12 .... 162 F3
Gardner Wy KNWTH CV8 .... 197 L3
Garfield Rd LGN/SDN/BHAMAIR B26 .... 109 M5
Garganey Cl KIDD DY10 .... 164 D4
Garibaldi Ter BRGRVE B60 .... 191 L4
Garland Crs RMSLY B62 .... 104 C5
Garland Rd STRPT DY13 .... 163 H7
Garlands Cft RCOVN/BALC/EX CV7 .... 115 L7
The Garlands WNSFLD WV11 .... 37 G6
Garland St BORD B9 .... 108 A2
Garland Wy NFLD/LBR B31 .... 144 F1
Garlick Dr KNWTH CV8 .... 180 A7
Garman Cl GTB/HAM B43 .... 70 C3
Garner Cl BILS/COS WV14 .... 67 H2
Garnet Av GTB/HAM B43 .... 70 F2
Garnet Cl ALDR WS9 .... 41 H5
Garnett Dr MGN/WHC B75 .... 57 J7
Garnette Cl NUNW/HART CV10 .... 79 M8
Garrard Gdns SCFLD/BOLD B73 .... 56 F8
Garratt St BRLYHL DY5 .... 84 C8
Garratt La CLGLYGN/QTN B68 .... 105 H2
STRBR DY8 .... 101 K4
Garratt's La BLKHTH/ROWR B65 .... 103 K3
Garretts Wk RUGBYS/DCH CV22 .... 186 A3
Garretts Green La LGN/SDN/BHAMAIR B26 .... 109 L6
Garrett St NUN CV11 .... 99 J7
Garrick Cl COVW CV5 .... 153 G1
DUDN DY1 .... 84 D2
Garrick Ri BNTWD WS7 .... 18 F6
Garrick Rd CNCK/NC WS11 .... 16 B1
Garrick St WOLV WV1 .... 3 G5
Garrigill TAM/AM/WIL B77 .... 46 E4
Garrington St DARL/WED WS10 .... 52 A6
Garrison La BORD B9 .... 107 M3
Garrison St BORD B9 .... 107 M3
Garth Crs COVS CV3 .... 156 A5
The Garth ALE/KHTH/YWD B14 .... 147 H1
LICH WS13 .... 20 F3
RLSN CV32 .... 206 D1
Garway Cl RDWED WS10 .... 53 J5
RLSN CV32 .... 206 D1
Garway Gv YDLY B25 .... 108 F7
Garwood Rd LGN/SDN/BHAMAIR B26 .... 109 K3
Garyth Williams Cl RUGBYS/DCH CV22 .... 186 C5
Gas Sq BRGRVE B60 .... 191 J4
Gas St CBHAMW B1 .... 6 C6
RLSS CV31 .... 206 F6
Gatacre St SEDG DY3 .... 84 B2
Gatcombe Cl WOLVN WV10 .... 36 C1
Gatcombe Rd DUDN DY1 .... 84 B1
Gate Cl WMBN WV5 .... 64 B8
Gatehouse Cft KNWTH CV8 .... 197 L4
Gatehouse Fold DUDS DY2 * 85 H4
Gatehouse La BDWTH CV12 .... 116 E1
Gate La CSHL/WTROR B46 .... 93 J7
HOCK/TIA B94 .... 175 G5
SCFLD/BOLD B73 .... 72 D3
Gateley Cl REDE B98 .... 203 L1
Gateley Rd LGLYGN/QTN B68 .... 105 J6
Gateside Rd COVN CV6 .... 134 C3
Gate St SEDG DY3 .... 66 C6
TPTN/OCK DY4 .... 85 J3
WASH/WDE B8 .... 90 B8
Gatis St DUNHL/THL/PER WV6 .... 35 L8
Gatwick Rd CVALE B35 .... 91 M1
Gauden Rd HAG/WOL DY9 .... 120 B4
Gaulby Wk COVS CV3 .... 156 E4
The Gaunts ALVE B48 .... 170 F7
Gaveston Rd COVN CV6 .... 133 J7
RLSN CV32 .... 206 A1
Gavin Wy PBAR/PBCH B42 .... 89 L5
Gawne La DUDS DY2 .... 103 J1
Gawsworth CRTAM B79 .... 31 H6
Gaydon Cl SLYOAK B29 .... 123 L3
Gaydon Pl SCFLD/BOLD B73 .... 72 F1
Gaydon Rd ALDR WS9 .... 54 E1
HIA/OLT B92 .... 128 B2
Gayer St COVN CV6 .... 134 D4
Gayfield Av BRLYHL DY5 .... 102 B4
Gay Hill La HWK/WKHTH B38 .... 145 M5
Gayhurst Dr YDLY B25 .... 109 J5
Gayle Gv ACGN B27 .... 127 G5
Gayton Rd HHTH/SAND B71 .... 69 H7
Gaza Cl TLHL/CAN CV4 .... 153 L4
Gazelle Cl COV CV1 .... 134 F5
Geach St LOZ/NWT B19 .... 89 H7
Geach Cl ALE/KHTH/YWD B14 * 147 C2
Geeson Cl VALE B35 .... 91 M1
Gee St LOZ/NWT B19 .... 89 H7
Gem Vls SPARK B11 * 108 A6
Geneva Rd TPTN/OCK DY4 .... 67 H4

Genge Av ETTPK/GDPK/PENN WV4 .... 66 C1
Genners La BLKHTH/ROWR B65 .... 104 B3
Genthorn Cl ETTPK/GDPK/PENN WV4 .... 66 D1
Gentian Cl NFLD/LBR B31 .... 123 K7
Gentian Wy RUGBY CV23 .... 161 J5
Geoffery Cl COVE CV2 .... 134 F8
Geoffrey Cl WALM/CURD B76 .... 73 M6
Geoffrey Pl SPARK B11 * 126 A2
Geoffrey Rd SHLY B90 .... 147 K2
SPARK B11 .... 126 A2
George Arthur Rd WASH/WDE B8 .... 108 B1
George Av BLKHTH/ROWR B65 .... 104 B3
POL/KGSB/FAZ B78 .... 45 G4
George Birch Cl RRUGBY CV23 .... 158 C2
George Bird Cl SMTHWK B66 * 87 L7
George Cl DUDS DY2 .... 85 J5
George Dance Cl KIDD DY10 * 138 T7
George Eliot Av BDWTH CV12 .... 117 H3
George Eliot Rd COV CV1 .... 134 B8
George Eliot St NUNW/HART CV10 .... 99 G3
George Frederick Rd SCFLD/BOLD B73 .... 71 L1
George Henry Rd TPTN/OCK DY4 .... 68 C6
George Hodgkinson Cl COVW CV5 .... 153 K2
George La LICH WS13 .... 20 F5
George Marston Rd COVS CV3 .... 156 C4
George Park Cl COVE CV2 .... 135 C4
George Rd ALVE B48 .... 170 C7
BILS/COS WV14 .... 67 H4
CSHL/WTROR B46 .... 93 C2
ERDW/GRVHL B23 .... 90 A2
GTB/HAM B43 .... 70 D3
HALE B63 .... 121 K1
LGN/SDN/BHAMAIR B26 .... 109 K3
SCFLD/BOLD B73 .... 72 B4
SLYOAK B29 .... 124 C3
SOLH B91 .... 149 G2
WWCK CV34 .... 205 L5
YDLY B25 .... 108 E7
George Robertson Cl COVS CV3 .... 156 C4
George Rose Gdns DARL/WED WS10 .... 51 M7
George St BHTH/HG B12 .... 107 K8
BKHL/PFLD WV2 .... 2 F7
BRGRVE B61 .... 191 K3
CBHAMNW B3 .... 6 C3
COV CV1 .... 134 C8
CRTAM B79 .... 45 M1
DUDN DY1 .... 66 F7
HDSW B21 .... 88 B3
HEDN WS12 .... 17 C1
KIDD DY10 .... 138 B6
LOZ/NWT B19 .... 89 H8
NUN CV11 .... 99 H3
RCOVN/BALC/EX CV7 .... 96 C5
RUGBYN/HIL CV21 .... 186 D2
STRBR DY8 .... 101 K4
WBROM B70 .... 87 H3
WLNHL WV13 .... 51 J1
WSL WS1 .... 4 F5
George St Ringway BDWTH CV12 .... 116 F2
George St West WSNGN B18 .... 106 E1
Georgina Av BILS/COS WV14 .... 67 K2
Geraldine Rd YDLY B25 .... 108 F6
Gerald Rd STRBR DY8 .... 101 J4
Geranium Gv LGN/SDN/BHAMAIR B26 .... 109 L6
Geranium Rd DUDS DY2 .... 85 K5
Gerard CRTAM B79 .... 31 J6
Gerard Av TLHL/CAN CV4 .... 153 M1
Gerard Rd RUGBYS/DCH CV22 .... 185 L5
Gerard Rw RUGBYS/DCH CV22 * 185 L5
Gerardsfield Rd STETCH B33 .... 110 B2
Germander Dr DSYBK/YTR WS5 .... 69 L2
Gerrard Cl LOZ/NWT B19 .... 89 H6
Gerrard Rd WLNHL WV13 .... 51 J4
Gerrard St LOZ/NWT B19 .... 89 G7
WWCK CV34 .... 205 J7
Gervase Dr DUDN DY1 .... 84 D1
Geston Rd DUDN DY1 .... 84 B3
Gheluvelt Av KIDD DY10 .... 138 D5
Gheluvelt Ct STRPT DY13 .... 188 D1
Gibbet Hill Rd TLHL/CAN CV4 .... 180 A2
Gibbet La KINVER DY7 .... 118 C1
Gibbins Rd SLYOAK B29 .... 124 A4
Gibb La BRGRVW B61 .... 168 C5
Gibbons Cl TLHL/CAN CV4 .... 153 K3
Gibbons Crs STRPT DY13 .... 188 D1
Gibbons Gv DUNHL/THL/PER WV6 .... 49 J1
Gibbons Hill Rd SEDG DY3 .... 66 B3
Gibbons La BRLYHL DY5 .... 83 J5
Gibbons Rd DUNHL/THL/PER WV6 .... 49 K1
MGN/WHC B75 .... 57 M5
Gibbs Hill Rd NFLD/LBR B31 .... 144 F6
Gibbs Rd HAG/WOL DY9 .... 102 E8
Gibbs St DUNHL/THL/PER WV6 .... 49 L1
Gibb St BORD B9 .... 7 M8
Gibson Crs BDWTH CV12 .... 116 E3
Gibson Dr BFLD/HDSWWD B20 .... 88 F4
RUGBYN/HIL CV21 .... 187 K4
Gibson Rd BFLD/HDSWWD B20 .... 88 F5
DUNHL/THL/PER WV6 .... 48 C2
Gideon Cl LGN/SDN/BHAMAIR B26 .... 109 H7
Gideons Cl SEDG DY3 .... 66 B8
Gielgud Wy RCOVN/BALC/EX CV7 .... 135 M5
Giffard Rd WOLV WV1 .... 50 F6
WOLVN WV10 .... 23 H8
Giffard Wy WWCK CV34 .... 205 J4
Giffords Cft LICH WS13 .... 20 E4
Giggetty La WMBN WV5 .... 64 C7
Gigg La WALM/CURD B76 .... 74 F2
Gigmill Wy STRBR DY8 .... 119 J3
Gilbanks Rd STRBR DY8 .... 101 H6
Gilberry Cl DOR/KN B93 .... 149 L8
Gilbert Av OLDBY B69 .... 85 M6
RUGBYS/DCH CV22 .... 186 B5
Gilbert Cl BRGRVE B60 .... 191 J6
LICH WS13 .... 21 G3
SMTHWK B66 .... 105 M1
Gilbert La WMBN WV5 .... 64 F6
Gilbert Rd BRGRVE B60 .... 191 J6
LICH WS13 .... 21 C3
SMTHWK B66 .... 87 K6
Gilbert Scott Wy KIDD DY10 .... 138 C6
Gilbertstone Av LGN/SDN/BHAMAIR B26 .... 109 J8
Gilbertstone Cl REDE B98 .... 202 C4
Gilbertstone Rd TPTN/OCK DY4 .... 85 G3
Gilbey Cl WALM/CURD B76 .... 74 F2
Gilchrist Dr EDG B15 .... 106 E4
Gildas Av HWK/WKHTH B38 .... 145 L4
Giles Cl COVN CV6 .... 134 A3
HIA/OLT B92 .... 128 D6
STETCH B33 .... 109 G2
Giles Rd LGLYGN/QTN B68 .... 86 F8
LICH WS13 .... 20 E2

Gilfil Rd NUNW/HART CV10 98
Gilgal STRPT DY13 188
Gildown Pl EDG B15 106
Gillespie Cft AST/WIT B6 89
Gillet Cl NUN CV11 99
Gillhurst Rd HRBN B17 105
Gillians Wk COVE CV2 135
Gilling Gv BKDE/SHDE B34 ....
Gillingham Dr DARL/WED WS10 69
Gillity Av DYSBK/YTR WS5 5
Gillity Cl DYSBK/YTR WS5 5
Gilliver Rd SHLY B90 147
Gilman Cl LGN/SDN/BHAMAIR B26 128
Gillott Cl SOLH B91 149
Gillott Rd LDYWD/EDGR B16 106
Gillows Cft SHLY B90 148
Gillquart Wy COV CV1 9
Gillscroft Rd STETCH B33 109
Gill St DUDS DY2 103
WBROM B70 87
Gillway CRTAM B79 31
Gilmorton Cl HRBN B17 149
SOLH B91 149
Gilpin Cl CBROM B36 91
Gilpin Crs BLOX/PEL WS3 39
Gilpins Cft GTWY WS6 24
Gilson Dr CSHL/WTROR B46 93
Gilson Rd CSHL/WTROR B46 93
Gilson St TPTN/OCK DY4 68
Gilson Wy CHWD/FDBR/MGN B37 92
Gilwell Rd BKDE/SHDE B34 92
Gimble Wk HRBN B17 105
Ginkgo Wk RLSS CV31 206
Gipsy Cl RCOVN/BALC/EX CV7 151
Gipsy La ERDW/GRVHL B23 71
NUNW/HART CV10 99
RCOVN/BALC/EX CV7 152
WLNHL WV13 51
Girdlers Cl COVS CV3 154
Girtin Cl BDWTH CV12 116
Girton Rd CNCK/NC WS11 16
Girvan Gv RLSN CV32 199
Gisborn Cl SMHTH B10 * 107
Gisburn Cl REDW B97 193
WWCK CV34 205
Gladeside Cl RUSH/SHEL WS4 40
The Glades ALDR WS9 40
The Glade CDSL WV8 35
CNCK/NC WS11 15
COVW CV5 153
FOAKS/STRLY B74 55
HAG/WOL DY9 102
LGN/SDN/BHAMAIR B26 128
Gladiator Wy RUGBYN/HIL CV21 160
Gladstone Dr OLDBY B69 86
Gladstone Gv KGSWFD DY6 83
Gladstone Rd DOR/KN B93 175
ERDW/GRVHL B23 17
HEDN WS12 ....
LGN/SDN/BHAMAIR B26 109
SPARK B11 109
STRBR DY8 101
Gladstone St AST/WIT B6 89
DARL/WED WS10 52
HHTH/SAND B71 68
RUGBYN/HIL CV21 186
WSLW WS2 5
Gladys Rd SMTHWKW B67 * 105
YDLY B25 109
Gladys Ter SMTHWKW B67 * 105
Glaisdale Av COVN CV6 134
Glaisdale Gdns DUNHL/THL/PER WV6 35
Glaisdale Rd LGN/SDN/BHAMAIR B26 ....
Glaisedale Gv WLNHL WV13 52
Glaisher Dr WOLVN WV10 36
Glamis Rd SHHTH WV12 37
Glanville Dr MGN/WHC B75 56
Claramara Cl RUGBYN/HIL CV21 161
Glasbury Cft HWK/WKHTH B38 145
Glascote Cl SHLY B90 147
Glascote Gv BKDE/SHDE B34 92
Glascote Rd TAM/AM/WIL B77 46
Glascote Rd TAM/AM/WIL B77 46
Glasscroft Cottages BNTWD WS7 19
Glasshouse Hl STRBR DY8 119
Glasshouse La HOCK/TIA B94 175
KNWTH CV8 180
Glastonbury Cl KIDDW DY11 137
Glastonbury Crs BLOX/PEL WS3 38
Glastonbury Rd ALE/KHTH/YWD B14 126
HHTH/SAND B71 69
Glastonbury Wy BLOX/PEL WS3 38
Glaston Dr SOLH B91 148
Gleads Cft RIDG/WDGT B32 122
Gleave Rd SLYOAK B29 124
Glebe Av BDWTH CV12 116
Glebe Cl REDE B98 203
TLHL/CAN CV4 153
Glebe Crs KNWTH CV8 197
RUGBYN/HIL CV21 186
Glebe Dr SCFLD/BOLD B73 72
Glebefarm Gv COVS CV3 156
Glebe Farm Rd RUGBYN/HIL CV21 160
STETCH B33 91
Glebe Flds WALM/CURD B76 74
Glebefields Rd TPTN/OCK DY4 67
Glebe La NUN CV11 99
STRBR DY8 119
Glebe Pl DARL/WED WS10 51
RLSS CV31 206
Glebe Rd ALVE B48 170
NUN CV11 99
SOLH B91 128
WLNHL WV13 51
Glebe St WSL WS1 4
The Glebe HAG/WOL DY9 141
RCOVN/BALC/EX CV7 115
REDE B98 ....
Glebe Wy RCOVN/BALC/EX CV7 151
Gledhill Pk LICHS WS14 21
Gleeson Dr WWCK CV34 205
Glenavon Rd ALE/KHTH/YWD B14 146
Glen Cl HEDN WS12 17
RUSH/SHEL WS4 53
Glencoe Dr CNCK/NC WS11 16
Glencoe Rd COVS CV3 155
SMTHWK B66 106
Glen Ct BDMR/CCFT WV3 49
Glencroft Rd HIA/OLT B92 128
Glendale Av KNWTH CV8 ....
Glendale Cl BDMR/CCFT WV3 49
HALE B63 ....
Glendale Ct TAM/AM/WIL B77 46
Glendale Dr STETCH B33 109
WMBN WV5 64
Glendawn Cl CNCK/NC WS11 16
Glendene Crs HWK/WKHTH B38 145
Glendene Rd HEDN WS12 17
Glen Devon Cl RBRY B45 143
Glendon Rd ERDW/GRVHL B23 90

ndon Wy DOR/KN B93 175 J2
ndower Av COVW CV5 154 B3
ndower Rd ALDR WS9 40 F4
PBAR/PBCH B42 71 G8
neagles TAM/AM/WIL B77 32 F8
neagles Dr BRGRVE B60 169 L8
TB/HAM B43 70 C1
MGN/WHC B75 57 G6
OLDBY B69 85 L6
neagles Rd BLOX/PEL WS3 38 D2
COVE CV2 135 J7
DUNHL/THL/PER WV6 34 B8
LGN/SDN/BHAMAIR B26 109 L5
nelg Dr STRBR DY8 119 M3
nelg Ms DSYBK/YTR WS5 54 B8
nfern Gdns KNWTH CV8 182 C3
nfern Rd BILS/COS WV14 66 E5
nfield CDSL WV8 35 J3
nfield Av NUNW/HART CV10 81 G6
nfield Cl REDW B97 202 B7
SOLH B91 149 G5
WALM/CURD B76 73 J2
nfield Gv SLYOAK B29 124 E4
ngarry Cl RIDG/WDGT B32 122 F6
ngarry Gdns
BDMR/CCFT WV3 49 K4
nhill Dr HWK/WKHTH B38 145 L5
nhurst Cl WSLW WS2 52 B2
nmead Rd KGSTG B44 71 H5
nmore Av BNTWD WS7 18 E7
nmore Cl BDMR/CCFT WV3 49 J6
nmore Dr COVN CV6 116 D8
HWK/WKHTH B38 145 H4
nmount Av COVN CV6 116 D8
nn St COVN CV6 134 B2
n Park Rd SEDG DY3 84 B3
npark Rd WASH/WDE B8 90 C8
nridding Cl COVN CV6 116 D8
n Ri MOS/BIL B13 126 A7
n Rd SEDG DY3 66 C7
STRBR DY8 119 K2
nroy Cl COVE CV2 135 J7
nroyde HWK/WKHTH B38 145 J6
n Side RIDG/WDGT B32 123 H3
nside Av HIA/OLT B92 127 M2
e Glen BRGRVE B60 * 169 M8
nthorne Dr GTWY WS6 24 C2
nthorne Rd ERDE/BCHGN B24 90 E3
nthorne Wy
ERDE/BCHGN B24 90 E3
ntworth Av COVN CV6 133 L3
ntworth Dr WALM/CURD B76 73 L3
ntworth Gdns
DUNHL/THL/PER WV6 35 M8
nville Av ATHST CV9 61 G5
nville Dr ERDW/GRVHL B23 72 C8
nwood Cl BRLYHL DY5 102 B5
nwood Dr SHLY B90 174 B1
nwood Gdns BDWTH CV12 98 E8
nwood Ri ALDR WS9 41 H2
nwood Rd HWK/WKHTH B38 145 H5
be St DARL/WED WS10 68 D4
ster Dr KNWTH CV8 179 K7
ucester Cl LICH WS13 20 F2
NUN CV11 81 L6
ucester Pl WLNHL WV13 52 B3
ucester Rd DARL/WED WS10 69 G2
DSYBK/YTR WS5 5 M7
DUDS DY2 103 H3
ucester St COV CV1 8 C4
DIG/EDG B5 7 G7
DUNHL/THL/PER WV6 49 M1
RLSS CV31 206 D6
ucester Wy BEWD DY12 162 F1
CHWD/FDBR/MGN B37 110 E4
CNCK/NC WS11 16 F4
ver Cl HLGN/YWD B28 126 D7
ver Rd MGN/WHC B75 57 K8
ver's Cl ATHST CV9 63 K6
HEDN WS12 13 L8
RCOVN/BALC/EX CV7 131 G4
vers Cft
CHWD/FDBR/MGN B37 110 D2
vers Field Dr VAUX/NECH B7 90 A6
vers Rd SMHTH B10 108 A5
ver St BORD B9 7 M6
COVS CV3 155 H5
HEDN WS12 17 K2
REDE B98 202 C2
WBROM B70 87 H4
me Dr DUNHL/THL/PER WV6 35 J8
n Av BILS/COS WV14 67 M2
ndebourne CRTAM B79 31 H6
n Dr BILS/COS WV14 67 M2
n Farm Rd RIDG/WDGT B32 105 G8
nn Crs HALE B63 102 F6
nne Av KGSWFD DY6 101 H1
n Rd RIDG/WDGT B32 105 H7
nside Av RIDG/WDGT B32 105 G8
dfrey Cl RLSS CV31 207 J8
diva Pl COV CV1 9 J4
dolphin CRTAM B79 31 H7
dson Crs KIDDW DY11 163 M2
dson Pl KIDDW DY11 164 A2
ffs Cl RIDG/WDGT B32 123 K2
fton TAM/AM/WIL B77 46 E5
d Av RUGBYS/DCH CV22 185 M5
dborough Cl BILS/COS WV14 67 H2
d Cl NUN CV11 99 J5
dcrest TAM/AM/WIL B77 46 E7
dcrest Cl DUDS DY2 103 H3
dcrest Cft CBROM B36 92 E5
dcrest Dr KIDD DY10 164 F3
den Acres La COVS CV3 156 D6
dencrest Dr OLDBY B69 86 C5
den Cft BFLD/HDSWWD B20 88 D4
den Cross La BRGRVW B61 168 E5
den End Dr DOR/KN B93 150 B7
den Hillock Rd DUDS DY2 103 G2
SPARK B11 108 B8
den Hind Dr STRPT DY13 188 E3
dfinch Cl SLYOAK B29 124 B5
dfinch Rd HAG/WOL DY9 * 120 A2
dicroft Rd DARL/WED WS10 68 E1
dieslie Cl SCFLD/BOLD B73 72 F3
dieslie Rd SCFLD/BOLD B73 72 F3
dsborough TAM/AM/WIL B77 46 E4
ds Hill Gdns HDSW B21 88 D6
ds Hill Rd HDSW B21 88 D5
ds Hill Wy TPTN/OCK DY4 68 B6
dsmith Av
RUGBYS/DCH CV22 186 D6
WWCK CV34 205 G8
dsmith Pl CRTAM B79 31 L6
dsmith Rd
ALE/KHTH/YWD B14 125 K5
BLOX/PEL WS3 39 J5
dstar Wy STETCH B33 110 A3
dthorn Av
ETTPK/GDPK/PENN WV4 49 M8
dthorn Cl COVW CV5 153 H1
dthorn Crs
ETTPK/GDPK/PENN WV4 49 L7
dthorne Av CNCK/NC WS11 16 D3
LGN/SDN/BHAMAIR B26 128 A1
thorne Cl REDW B97 202 A4
thorne Wk BRLYHL DY5 102 B5
thorn Hl
ETTPK/GDPK/PENN WV4 49 M7

Goldthorn Pl KIDDW DY11 164 A3
Goldthorn Rd
ETTPK/GDPK/PENN WV4 49 M7
KIDDW DY11 163 M2
Golf Dr NUN CV11 99 M4
Golf La BILS/COS WV14 51 H6
Golson Cl MGN/WHC B75 57 J7
Gomeldon Av
ALE/KHTH/YWD B14 146 D2
Gomer St WLNHL WV13 51 L3
Gomer St West WLNHL WV13 51 L3
Gooch Cl STRBR DY8 101 L7
Gooch St DIG/EDG B5 107 J5
Gooch St North DIG/EDG B5 7 G8
Goodacre Cl RRUGBY CV23 161 L8
Goodall Gv GTB/HAM B43 55 J8
Goodall St WSL WS1 5 G4
Goodby Rd MOS/BIL B13 125 H2
Goode Av WSNGN B18 88 E8
Goode Cl LGLYGN/QTN B68 105 G1
WWCK CV34 205 G6
Goode Cft TLHL/CAN CV4 153 K3
Goodere Av POL/KGSB/FAZ B78 47 L5
Goodere Dr POL/KGSB/FAZ B78 47 L3
Goodeve Wk MGN/WHC B75 57 M8
Goodison Gdns
ERDE/BCHGN B24 72 F8
Goodman Cl HLGN/YWD B28 126 D7
Goodman St CBHAMW B1 6 A4
Goodman Wy TLHL/CAN CV4 153 G4
Goodrest Av RMSLY B62 104 E7
Goodrest Cft
ALE/KHTH/YWD B14 147 G1
Goodrest La HWK/WKHTH B38 145 K7
Goodrich Av
DUNHL/THL/PER WV6 48 E2
Goodrich Cl REDE B98 203 K3
Goodrich Covert
ALE/KHTH/YWD B14 146 A3
Goodrick Wy VAUX/NECH B7 * 89 M7
Goods Station La PENK ST19 10 C3
Goodway Ct CBHAMNE B4 7 G2
Goodway Rd HIA/OLT B92 128 C2
KGSTG B44 71 J5
Goodwin Cl KIDDW DY11 138 A6
Goodwood Cl CBROM B36 91 H5
COVS CV3 156 A7
HEDN WS12 * 13 L8
Goodwood Dr FOAKS/STRLY B74 55 K7
Goodwood Rd BRGRVW B61 168 F4
Goodwyn Av LGLYGN/QTN B68 105 H6
Goodyear Av WOLVN WV10 36 C6
Goodyear Rd SMTHWKW B67 105 H3
Goodyers End La
RCOVN/BALC/EX CV7 116 B5
Goosehill Cl REDE B98 203 J4
Goosemoor La
ERDW/GRVHL B23 72 D6
Goostry Cl TAM/AM/WIL B77 46 B1
Goostry Rd TAM/AM/WIL B77 32 B8
Gopsal St CBHAMNE B4 7 L3
Gorcott La SHLY B90 147 L8
Gordon Av
ETTPK/GDPK/PENN WV4 66 D2
HHTH/SAND B71 69 G5
LOZ/NWT B19 89 H6
Gordon Cl BDWTH CV12 116 F1
OLDBY B69 86 B3
Gordon Crs BRLYHL DY5 84 C8
Gordon Dr TPTN/OCK DY4 68 A8
Gordon Pl BILS/COS WV14 51 G8
Gordon Rd HRBN B17 106 B7
LOZ/NWT B19 89 G5
Gordon St BKHL/PFLD WV2 3 H8
BORD B9 * 107 M3
COV CV1 8 C7
DARL/WED WS10 52 B7
RLSS CV31 206 E6
Gorey Cl SHHTH WV12 37 M5
Gorge Rd SEDG DY3 66 C5
Goring Rd COVE CV2 155 L1
Gorleston Gv
ALE/KHTH/YWD B14 146 F3
Gorleston Rd
ALE/KHTH/YWD B14 146 F3
Gorsebrook Rd
DUNHL/THL/PER WV6 35 M8
Gorse Cl CHWD/FDBR/MGN B37 110 D3
RUGBYS/DCH CV22 186 C4
SLYOAK B29 123 L5
Gorse Dr HEDN WS12 12 B8
Gorse Farm Rd GTB/HAM B43 70 C5
NUN CV11 99 M5
Gorsefield Rd BKDE/SHDE B34 92 A8
Gorse Green La HAG/WOL DY9 141 M5
Gorse La LICHS WS14 21 J7
Gorse Meadow Dr RBRY B45 169 M5
Gorsemoor Rd HEDN WS12 17 H4
Gorsemoor Wy WNSFLD WV11 37 M2
Gorse Rd DUDN DY1 84 E1
WNSFLD WV11 37 L5
Gorseway BNTWD WS7 18 F8
COVW CV5 154 A2
Gorsey La BLOX/PEL WS3 25 K4
CNCK/NC WS11 15 M4
CNCK/NC WS11 25 G3
CSHL/WTROR B46 93 J3
GTWY WS6 24 D5
HLYWD B47 172 E1
Gorsey Wy ALDR WS9 40 C8
Gorsly Piece RIDG/WDGT B32 123 G1
Gorstey Lea BNTWD WS7 19 G6
Gorstie Cft GTB/HAM B43 70 C5
Gorsty Av BRLYHL DY5 102 A1
Gorsty Bank LICHS WS14 21 J5
Gorsty Cl HHTH/SAND B71 69 K5
Gorsty Hayes CDSL WV8 34 D2
Gorsty Hill Rd RMSLY B62 103 M5
Gorsy Bank Rd
TAM/AM/WIL B77 46 D8
Gorsymead Gv NFLD/LBR B31 144 A3
Gorsy Rd RIDG/WDGT B32 123 H1
Gorsy Wy NUNW/HART CV10 80 B8
Gorton Cft
RCOVN/BALC/EX CV7 151 M6
Gorway Cl WSL WS1 5 H8
Gorway Gdns WSL WS1 5 J8
Gorway Rd WSL WS1 5 J8
Goscote Cl BLOX/PEL WS3 39 K6
REDW B97 193 L7
Goscote La BLOX/PEL WS3 39 J3
Goscote Lodge Crs
BLOX/PEL WS3 39 L6
Goscote Pl BLOX/PEL WS3 39 L6
Goscote Rd BLOX/PEL WS3 39 K4
Gosford St BHTH/HG B12 107 K7
COV CV1 9 J5
Gospel End Rd SEDG DY3 65 M5
Gospel End St SEDG DY3 66 B6
Gospel Farm Rd ACGN B27 126 F5
Gospel La ACGN B27 127 G6
Gospel Oak Rd COVN CV6 133 M1
TPTN/OCK DY4 67 M4
Gosport Cl WOLV WV1 50 F6
Gosport Rd COVN CV6 134 C5
Goss Cft SLYOAK B29 124 B4
Gossett La KNWTH CV8 157 K6
Gossey La STETCH B33 110 A3
The Goss BRLYHL DY5 102 B4

Gotham Rd
LGN/SDN/BHAMAIR B26 109 J7
Gothersley La KINVER DY7 100 B3
Goths Cl BLKHTH/ROWR B65 104 A1
Gough Av WNSFLD WV11 36 F5
Gough Rd BILS/COS WV14 67 G4
EDG B15 107 G6
SPARK B11 108 B8
Gough St CBHAMW B1 6 E7
WLNHL WV13 52 A3
WOLV WV1 3 J5
Gould Av East KIDDW DY11 163 L3
Gould Av West KIDDW DY11 163 L4
Gould Firm La ALDR WS9 41 J7
Gould Rd RWWCK/WEL CV35 204 E6
Gowan Rd WASH/WDE B8 108 C1
Gower Av KGSWFD DY6 101 K1
Gower Rd RMSLY B62 104 C7
SEDG DY3 65 M4
Gower St BKHL/PFLD WV2 3 J8
LOZ/NWT B19 89 H6
WLNHL WV13 51 L3
WSLW WS2 52 F6
Gowland Dr CNCK/NC WS11 15 M4
Goya Cl CNCK/NC WS11 17 G3
Gozzard St BILS/COS WV14 51 J8
Gracemere Crs HLGN/YWD B28 147 J1
Grace Rd COVW CV5 131 L5
OLDBY B69 86 A5
SPARK B11 108 A7
TPTN/OCK DY4 67 L6
Gracewell Rd MOS/BIL B13 126 B4
Grafton Cl REDE B98 202 F6
Grafton Ct TLHL/CAN CV4 * 153 M6
Grafton Crs BRGRVE B60 191 J6
Grafton Dr WLNHL WV13 51 H4
Grafton Gdns SEDG DY3 83 M2
Grafton Gv LOZ/NWT B19 * 89 G6
Grafton La BRGRVW B61 191 G6
Grafton Pl BILS/COS WV14 51 J6
Grafton Rd HDSW B21 88 B4
HHTH/SAND B71 87 H1
LGLYGN/QTN B68 104 D3
SHLY B90 147 G3
SPARK B11 107 M6
Grafton St COV CV1 9 K5
Graham Cl COVN CV6 134 F5
TPTN/OCK DY4 67 M4
Graham Crs RBRY B45 143 K6
Graham Rd HHTH/SAND B71 87 H1
RMSLY B62 104 A5
RUGBYN/HIL CV21 187 G1
STRBR DY8 101 H1
WASH/WDE B8 108 D2
YDLY B25 109 G7
Graham St CBHAMW B1 6 C3
LOZ/NWT B19 89 G6
NUN CV11 80 F8
Grainger Cl TPTN/OCK DY4 68 B7
Grainger Ct CNCK/NC WS11 * 16 B3
Grainger's La CDYHTH B64 103 G5
Grainger St DUDS DY2 85 H6
Graiseley Ct BDMR/CCFT WV3 2 D7
Graiseley Hl BKHL/PFLD WV2 2 D9
Graiseley La WNSFLD WV11 37 G8
Graiseley Rw BKHL/PFLD WV2 2 E9
Graiseley St BDMR/CCFT WV3 2 D7
Graith Cl ALE/KHTH/YWD B14 147 J2
Gramer Ct ATHST CV9 * 63 K7
Grammar School La HALE B63 121 L1
Grampian Rd STRBR DY8 101 L7
Granary Cl HEDN WS12 12 F8
KGSWFD DY6 82 E5
Granary La WALM/CURD B76 73 K2
Granary Rd BRGRVE B60 191 J7
CDSL WV8 35 J4
The Granary ALDR WS9 40 F7
Granborough Cl COVS CV3 156 D5
Granbourne Rd SHHTH WV12 52 B1
Granby Av STETCH B33 110 A4
Granby Cl HIA/OLT B92 127 J6
REDE B98 203 K1
Granby Rd NUNW/HART CV10 98 D2
Grandborough Dr SOLH B91 148 E4
Grand Cl SMTHWK B66 105 M2
Grand Junction Wy WSL WS1 53 H8
Grand Union Canal Wk
CBHAMNE B4 6 F2
DOR/KN B93 150 B8
DOR/KN B93 176 C5
RLSS CV31 207 J7
SOLH B91 149 M2
SPARK B11 108 A6
WWCK CV34 205 L5
Grandys Cft
CHWD/FDBR/MGN B37 110 D3
Grange Av ALDR WS9 40 E4
CNCK/NC WS11 16 D3
COVS CV3 156 D6
COVS CV3 181 G2
KNWTH CV8 179 J7
MGN/WHC B75 57 G2
PENK ST19 10 C6
WASH/WDE B8 * 90 F7
Grange Cl NUNW/HART CV10 80 A6
TAM/AM/WIL B77 46 A5
WWCK CV34 206 A5
Grange Ct BDMR/CCFT WV3 * 2 D7
HAG/WOL DY9 * 120 A2
WSLW WS2 * 52 B3
Grange Crs HALE B63 121 M2
PENK ST19 10 B6
RBRY B45 143 J5
RUSH/SHEL WS4 39 M5
Grange Farm Dr
HWK/WKHTH B38 145 H5
Grangefield Cl CDSL WV8 35 K4
Grange Hl RMSLY B62 122 A3
Grange Hill Rd
HWK/WKHTH B38 145 J4
Grange La BRGRVE B60 193 L2
HAG/WOL DY9 120 B1
KGSWFD DY6 101 K1
LICH WS13 20 A7
LICH WS13 20 D3
MGN/WHC B75 57 G2
Grangemouth Rd COVN CV6 133 M7
Grange Ri HWK/WKHTH B38 145 K6
Grange Rd ALE/KHTH/YWD B14 125 H5
AST/WIT B6 89 J5
BILS/COS WV14 66 F6
BKHL/PFLD WV2 49 M7
BNTWD WS7 18 E8
BORD B9 108 B5
CDYHTH B64 103 L4
CNCK/NC WS11 17 M7
COVN CV6 134 F1
DOR/KN B93 175 J4
DUDN DY1 84 F4
DUNHL/THL/PER WV6 35 G8
ERDE/BCHGN B24 72 F8
HAG/WOL DY9 120 A1
HALE B63 121 M2
HIA/OLT B92 127 J6
KIDDW DY11 137 M6
NUNW/HART CV10 79 M3
PENK ST19 10 C5
RCOVN/BALC/EX CV7 151 K6
REDE B98 202 D1

RLSN CV32 206 E2
RUGBYN/HIL CV21 160 C7
SLYOAK B29 124 D2
SMTHWK B66 105 L2
WBROM B70 86 F2
Grangers La REDE B98 202 D8
Grange St DUDN DY1 84 F4
WSL WS1 5 G9
The Grange WMBN WV5 64 E6
WWCK CV34 205 M6
Grange Wk COVN CV6 * 116 F8
Grangewood Ct HIA/OLT B92 * 127 J6
Granhill Cl REDE B98 202 E5
Granoe Cl COVS CV3 156 C5
Granshaw Cl HWK/WKHTH B38 145 K4
Grant Cl HHTH/SAND B71 69 G8
KGSWFD DY6 83 H5
Grantham Cl BRLYHL DY5 101 M6
Grantham Rd SMTHWK B66 105 M2
SPARK B11 107 M7
Grantham St COVE CV2 9 M3
Grantley Crs KGSWFD DY6 83 G6
Grantley Dr
CHWD/FDBR/MGN B37 110 E3
Granton Cl ALE/KHTH/YWD B14 125 H8
Granton Rd
ALE/KHTH/YWD B14 125 H8
Grantown Gv GTWY WS6 38 E1
Grant Rd COVS CV3 155 M3
RCOVN/BALC/EX CV7 116 E5
Grant St BLOX/PEL WS3 38 F5
EDG B15 6 E9
Granville TAM/AM/WIL B77 46 D4
Granville Cl BKHL/PFLD WV2 3 H8
BRGRVE B60 191 M4
Granville Crest KIDD DY10 138 F7
Granville Dr KGSWFD DY6 83 K8
Granville Rd CDYHTH B64 103 M5
DOR/KN B93 175 L3
Granville Sq EDG B15 6 C7
Granville St BKHL/PFLD WV2 3 H8
CBHAMW B1 6 D7
RLSN CV32 206 E3
WLNHL WV13 51 L2
Grasdene Gv HRBN B17 124 A1
Grasmere Av COVS CV3 154 D7
DUNHL/THL/PER WV6 48 D1
FOAKS/STRLY B74 55 L2
Grasmere Cl
DUNHL/THL/PER WV6 35 H5
GTB/HAM B43 70 D6
KGSWFD DY6 82 F6
KIDD DY10 138 C6
RUGBYN/HIL CV21 161 H7
WNSFLD WV11 37 G6
Grasmere Crs NUN CV11 81 K6
Grasmere Gv STRPT DY13 163 K7
Grasmere Pl CNCK/NC WS11 12 C8
Grasmere Rd BDWTH CV12 116 E3
HDSW B21 88 D6
Grasscroft Dr COVS CV3 155 J7
Grassholme TAM/AM/WIL B77 46 E5
Grassington Av WWCK CV34 205 K4
Grassington Dr
CHWD/FDBR/MGN B37 110 D4
NUN CV11 99 L3
Grassmere Ct GTWY WS6 24 B2
Grassmere Dr STRBR DY8 119 K2
Grassmoor Rd
HWK/WKHTH B38 145 J3
Grassy La WOLVN WV10 36 F4
Graston Cl LDYWD/EDGR B16 106 E3
Gratley Cft HEDN WS12 16 A1
Grattidge Rd HIA/OLT B92 127 H3
Gratton Ct COVS CV3 154 D7
Gravel Bank RIDG/WDGT B32 123 H3
Gravel Hl TLHL/CAN CV4 153 K4
WMBN WV5 64 F7
Gravel La HEDN WS12 11 M7
Gravelly Hl ERDE/BCHGN B24 90 C3
Gravelly Hl North
ERDE/BCHGN B24 90 C2
Gravelly La ALDR WS9 41 J3
ERDW/GRVHL B23 72 D8
Gravel Pit La ALVE B48 194 C1
The Gravel WALM/CURD B76 74 F3
Gray Cl KIDD DY10 138 F7
Grayfield Av MOS/BIL B13 125 K2
Grayland Cl ACGN B27 126 F3
The Graylands COVS CV3 181 G1
Grayling TAM/AM/WIL B77 46 B7
Grayling Cl DARL/WED WS10 67 M2
Grayling Rd BRLYHL DY5 102 A7
Grayling Wk
CHWD/FDBR/MGN B37 111 G3
WOLV WV1 50 F1
Gray Rd HEDN WS12 12 D7
Grayshott Cl BRGRVW B61 191 H2
ERDW/GRVHL B23 72 C8
Grays Rd HRBN B17 106 B7
Grayston Av TAM/AM/WIL B77 46 C1
Gray St BORD B9 107 M3
Grayswood Av COVW CV5 154 B1
Grayswood Park Rd
RIDG/WDGT B32 105 G7
Grayswood Rd NFLD/LBR B31 144 D6
Grazebrook Cft
RIDG/WDGT B32 123 H5
Grazebrook Rd DUDS DY2 85 G6
Grazewood Cl SHHTH WV12 37 M6
Grazier Av TAM/AM/WIL B77 46 A5
Grazing La REDW B97 201 J3
The Grazings KINVER DY7 118 A2
Greadier St SHHTH WV12 38 A8
Great Arthur St SMTHWK B66 87 K6
Great Balance RRUGBY CV23 158 B2
Great Barn La REDW B97 201 M4
Great Barr St BORD B9 7 M6
Great Borne RUGBYN/HIL CV21 161 G6
Great Brickkiln St
BDMR/CCFT WV3 2 C7
Great Br TPTN/OCK DY4 68 B8
Great Bridge Rd BILS/COS WV14 67 L1
Great Bridge St WBROM B70 68 C8
Great Brook St VAUX/NECH B7 7 L2
Great Central Wy
RUGBYN/HIL CV21 187 H1
Great Charles St BRWNH WS8 26 D5
Great Charles St Queensway
CBHAMNW B3 6 E4
Great Colmore St EDG B15 6 E9
Great Cornbow HALE B63 121 M2
Great Croft St DARL/WED WS10 52 B7
Great Farley Dr NFLD/LBR B31 144 A4
Greatfield Rd KIDDW DY11 163 M1
Great Francis St VAUX/NECH B7 107 M1
Great Hampton Rw LOZ/NWT B19 6 D1
Great Hampton St WOLV WV1 2 D2
WSNGN B18 89 G8
Greatheed Rd RLSN CV32 206 C4
Great Hockings La REDW B97 201 J3
Great King St LOZ/NWT B19 89 G8
Great Lister St VAUX/NECH B7 7 K1
Greatmead TAM/AM/WIL B77 46 A4
Greatrey Ct HHTH/SAND B71 68 F5
Great Stone Rd NFLD/LBR B31 144 E2
Great Tindal St
LDYWD/EDGR B16 106 E3
Great Western Ar CBHAMNW B3 7 G4

Great Western Cl WSNGN B18 88 C7
Great Western Dr CDYHTH B64 103 L4
Great Western St
DARL/WED WS10 68 C3
WOLV WV1 3 G3
Great Western Wy STRPT DY13 163 L8
TPTN/OCK DY4 68 B7
Great Wood Rd BORD B9 108 A4
Greaves Av DSYBK/YTR WS5 54 A5
Greaves Cl DSYBK/YTR WS5 54 A5
WWCK CV34 206 A7
Greaves Crs SHHTH WV12 38 A5
Greaves Gdns KIDDW DY11 137 M4
Greaves Rd DUDS DY2 85 H8
Greaves Sq HWK/WKHTH B38 145 M4
The Greaves WALM/CURD B76 74 D7
Grebe Cl ERDW/GRVHL B23 89 M2
Greenacre Cl TAM/AM/WIL B77 32 F8
Greenacre Dr CDSL WV8 34 F3
Greenacre Rd TPTN/OCK DY4 67 L4
Green Acres ACGN B27 126 F3
WMBN WV5 64 D8
Greenacres
DUNHL/THL/PER WV6 34 F8
SEDG DY3 65 M4
WALM/CURD B76 73 L5
Greenacres Av WOLVN WV10 36 F4
Greenacres Cl FOAKS/STRLY B74 55 J3
Greenacres La BEWD DY12 162 E1
Greenacres Rd BRGRVW B61 191 J2
Green Acres Rd
HWK/WKHTH B38 145 H5
Greenaleigh Rd
ALE/KHTH/YWD B14 147 H2
Green Av HLGN/YWD B28 126 C4
Greenaway Cl GTB/HAM B43 71 G2
Greenbank RBRY B45 170 B5
Green Bank Av HLGN/YWD B28 126 C4
Greenbank Gdns STRBR DY8 101 J3
Greenbank Rd BEWD DY12 162 C3
RCOVN/BALC/EX CV7 151 K7
Green Barns La LICHS WS14 42 F5
Green Bower Dr BRGRVW B61 168 E8
Greenbush Dr HALE B63 103 L8
Green Cl HLYWD B47 172 E2
RRUGBY CV23 185 K1
Green Ct HLGN/YWD B28 126 D5
Green Cft BORD B9 108 E2
Greencroft BILS/COS WV14 51 H7
KGSWFD DY6 101 H1
LICH WS13 20 E3
Greendale Cl ATHST CV9 63 J6
BRGRVW B61 168 F5
Greendale Rd ATHST CV9 63 J6
COVW CV5 154 B2
Green Dr RIDG/WDGT B32 123 G4
WOLVN WV10 36 A6
Greenend Rd MOS/BIL B13 125 K3
Greenfels Ri DUDS DY2 85 K5
Greenfield Av BRGRVE B60 169 H4
CDYHTH B64 102 F4
RCOVN/BALC/EX CV7 151 L6
STRBR DY8 101 K8
Greenfield Crs EDG B15 106 E5
Greenfield Cft BILS/COS WV14 67 H2
Greenfield La WOLVN WV10 22 B8
Greenfield Rd GTB/HAM B43 70 A6
HRBN B17 106 A8
SMTHWKW B67 105 J1
Greenfields ALDR WS9 40 E6
CNCK/NC WS11 16 C3
REDE B98 202 C3
Greenfields Rd KGSWFD DY6 83 J8
RUSH/SHEL WS4 40 B3
WMBN WV5 64 E8
The Green Fld COVS CV3 155 M5
Greenfield Vw SEDG DY3 65 M6
Greenfinch Cl KIDD DY10 164 F2
Greenfinch Rd CBROM B36 92 E6
HAG/WOL DY9 120 B2
Greenford Cl REDW B97 193 M8
Greenford Rd
ALE/KHTH/YWD B14 146 F2
Green Gables HLYWD B47 146 E6
MGN/WHC B75 * 56 F6
Green Gables Dr HLYWD B47 * 146 E6
Greenheart TAM/AM/WIL B77 46 E1
Green Heath Rd HEDN WS12 12 E6
Greenhill BRGRVE B60 169 K8
WMBN WV5 64 F7
Greenhill Av KIDD DY10 138 D5
Green Hill Cl BRGRVE B60 169 G7
Greenhill Cl SHHTH WV12 37 M8
TAM/AM/WIL B77 46 A8
Greenhill Dr SLYOAK B29 124 A4
Greenhill Gdns GTB/HAM B43 70 B3
RMSLY B62 104 B7
WMBN WV5 64 F8
Greenhill Ms LICH WS13 21 G5
Greenhill Rd CSCFLD/WYGN B72 72 F5
HDSW B21 88 B3
MOS/BIL B13 125 K4
RMSLY B62 104 B6
RUGBYS/DCH CV22 186 D4
SEDG DY3 66 C8
Greenhill Vls WSL WS1 * 5 G7
Greenhill Wy ALDR WS9 40 F4
Green Hill Wy SHLY B90 126 F8
Greenholm Rd KGSTG B44 71 J6
Greenhough Rd LICH WS13 20 D5
Greenhurst RBRY B45 169 M4
Greening Dr EDG B15 106 F6
Greenland Av COVW CV5 132 D8
Greenland Cl KGSWFD DY6 83 J5
Greenland Ct COVW CV5 132 D8
Greenland Ri HIA/OLT B92 128 B6
Greenland Rd SLYOAK B29 124 F4
Greenlands WMBN WV5 64 D6
Greenlands Av REDE B98 202 E5
Greenlands Dr REDE B98 202 D4
Greenlands Rd
CHWD/FDBR/MGN B37 111 G3
Green La ALDR WS9 41 J8
ATHST CV9 62 D3
BLOX/PEL WS3 39 G6
BLOX/PEL WS3 39 L1
BNTWD WS7 19 H4
BNTWD WS7 26 E3
BORD B9 108 A4
BRGRVW B61 168 E4
CBROM B36 92 C5
CNCK/NC WS11 16 C7
COVS CV3 154 E7
CSHL/WTROR B46 93 L8
DUDN DY1 66 D8
DUNHL/THL/PER WV6 35 J6
GTB/HAM B43 70 B6
HAG/WOL DY9 102 B8
HDSW B21 88 A5
HWK/WKHTH B38 145 J5
KGSWFD DY6 83 H6
LICH WS13 19 G2
LICHS WS14 28 B3
NUNW/HART CV10 78 C5
NUNW/HART CV10 80 A6
POL/KGSB/FAZ B78 47 H6
POL/KGSB/FAZ B78 58 E6
RCOVN/BALC/EX CV7 114 B7
RCOVN/BALC/EX CV7 151 M6

REDW B97 201 K4
RIDG/WDGT B32 105 G7
RMSLY B62 104 B4
RRUGBY CV23 158 B2
RRUGBY CV23 158 F8
RUSH/SHEL WS4 40 B2
SHLY B90 147 J4
STUD B80 202 F8
TAM/AM/WIL B77 47 G6
WSLW WS2 4 D2
WWCK CV34 205 J5
Green Lanes BILS/COS WV14 51 G6
SCFLD/BOLD B73 72 F6
Green Lea TAM/AM/WIL B77 46 E5
Greenleaf Cl COVW CV5 153 L2
Greenleas Gdns HALE B63 122 A2
Green Leigh ERDW/GRVHL B23 72 D5
Greenleighs SEDG DY3 66 B2
Greenly Rd
ETTPK/GDPK/PENN WV4 50 B8
Green Meadow HAG/WOL DY9 119 M5
WNSFLD WV11 37 H8
Green Meadow Cl WMBN WV5 64 C7
Green Meadow Rd SHHTH WV12 37 M6
SLYOAK B29 123 K6
Green Mdw HEDN WS12 17 G4
Greenmoor Rd
NUNW/HART CV10 98 E2
Greenoak Crs BVILLE B30 125 G5
SEDG DY3 66 E6
Green Oak Rd CDSL WV8 34 F3
Greenodd Dr COVN CV6 116 D8
Green Park Av BILS/COS WV14 50 F5
Green Park Dr BILS/COS WV14 51 G5
Green Park Rd BRGRVE B60 191 M4
DUDS DY2 85 K4
NFLD/LBR B31 144 C3
Greenridge Rd
BFLD/HDSWWD B20 70 C8
Green Rd DUDS DY2 85 H6
MOS/BIL B13 126 B4
Green Rock La BLOX/PEL WS3 39 H4
Greenroyde HAG/WOL DY9 119 M4
Greensand Dr BILS/COS WV14 67 G3
Greensforge La KINVER DY7 100 B5
Greenside HRBN B17 106 A8
Greenside Cl NUN CV11 99 M4
Greenside Rd ERDE/BCHGN B24 73 G8
Greenside Wy DSYBK/YTR WS5 69 L1
Greensill Av TPTN/OCK DY4 67 K5
Green Slade Crs BRGRVE B60 169 G4
Greenslade Cft NFLD/LBR B31 144 E3
Green Slade Gv HEDN WS12 13 G6
Greenslade Rd DSYBK/YTR WS5 54 A6
SEDG DY3 65 M3
SHLY B90 147 G3
Greensleeves FOAKS/STRLY B74 56 D3
Greensleeves Cl COVN CV6 133 M3
Greens Rd COVN CV6 133 L4
Greenstead Rd MOS/BIL B13 126 B4
The Greens
DUNHL/THL/PER WV6 * 48 C2
Green St BHTH/HG B12 7 K8
BILS/COS WV14 67 G5
KIDD DY10 164 C1
OLDBY B69 86 E6
STRBR DY8 101 K8
WBROM B70 87 J5
WSLW WS2 53 G2
Greensward Cl KNWTH CV8 179 M7
Green Sward La REDE B98 203 H4
The Greensward COVS CV3 156 E3
Greensway WNSFLD WV11 36 F5
Greens Yd BDWTH CV12 * 117 G2
The Green ALDR WS9 41 G7
BLOX/PEL WS3 38 F4
CBROM B36 91 M6
CNCK/NC WS11 16 B4
CRTAM B79 33 L2
CSCFLD/WYGN B72 73 H4
CSHL/WTROR B46 94 D3
DARL/WED WS10 52 B5
HWK/WKHTH B38 145 K3
KIDD DY10 166 C4
LGLYGN/QTN B68 104 F3
NUN CV11 * 99 J3
POL/KGSB/FAZ B78 45 J3
POL/KGSB/FAZ B78 60 A7
POL/KGSB/FAZ B78 60 F1
RIDG/WDGT B32 104 E7
RRUGBY CV23 185 L1
RUGBYS/DCH CV22 186 A5
SOLH B91 128 B8
TAM/AM/WIL B77 32 F8
Greenvale NFLD/LBR B31 123 K8
Greenvale Av
LGN/SDN/BHAMAIR B26 110 B7
Green Wk HRBN B17 105 K6
Greenway ALDR WS9 40 F3
BFLD/HDSWWD B20 70 D7
NUN CV11 99 M5
POL/KGSB/FAZ B78 47 L2
SEDG DY3 66 C4
WWCK CV34 205 J4
Greenway Av STRBR DY8 101 J4
Greenway Dr SCFLD/BOLD B73 72 A2
Greenway Gdns
HWK/WKHTH B38 145 J6
SEDG DY3 66 C4
Greenway Rd BILS/COS WV14 67 J1
Greenways HALE B63 103 G8
NFLD/LBR B31 123 K5
PENK ST19 10 E5
STRBR DY8 101 G4
The Greenways RLSN CV32 206 F2
Greenway St BORD B9 108 A4
The Greenway
CHWD/FDBR/MGN B37 110 E7
HAG/WOL DY9 119 K8
SCFLD/BOLD B73 71 M2
Greenwood YDLY B25 109 H5
Greenwood Av ACGN B27 126 E3
BLKHTH/ROWR B65 104 B3
LGLYGN/QTN B68 86 F8
Greenwood Cl
ALE/KHTH/YWD B14 125 J8
RRUGBY CV23 159 L8
Greenwood Pk ALDR WS9 41 G4
HEDN WS12 12 F5
Greenwood Pl KGSTG B44 71 M4
Greenwood Rd ALDR WS9 40 F3
HHTH/SAND B71 68 F5
WOLVN WV10 36 A6
The Greenwoods STRBR DY8 101 J8
Greethurst Dr MOS/BIL B13 126 A3
Greets Green Rd WBROM B70 86 C1
Greetville Cl STETCH B33 91 L8
Gregory Av COVS CV3 154 E7
SLYOAK B29 123 L5
Gregory Cl DARL/WED WS10 68 D3
Gregory Dr DUDN DY1 84 E3
Gregory Hood Rd COVS CV3 155 H8
Gregory Rd BNTWD WS7 19 J6
STRBR DY8 101 G8
Greig Ct CNCK/NC WS11 17 G3
Grendon Cl REDE B98 203 H4
TLHL/CAN CV4 153 G4
Grendon Dr RUGBYN/HIL CV21 161 J6
SCFLD/BOLD B73 72 B2
Grendon Gdns BDMR/CCFT WV3 49 H7
Grendon Rd
ALE/KHTH/YWD B14 146 E2
HIA/OLT B92 127 J5
POL/KGSB/FAZ B78 47 L4
Grenfell Cl RLSS CV31 207 G7
Grenfell Dr EDG B15 106 D5
Grenfell Rd BLOX/PEL WS3 39 H2
Grenville Av COVE CV2 155 M2
Grenville Cl RUGBYS/DCH CV22 186 A4
WSLW WS2 52 B2
Grenville Dr ERDW/GRVHL B23 89 M2
SMTHWK B66 87 H5
Grenville Pl WBROM B70 86 C7
Grenville Rd DUDN DY1 84 C4
SHLY B90 147 M3
Gresham Av RLSN CV32 206 F3
Gresham Pl RLSN CV32 * 206 F3
Gresham Rd CNCK/NC WS11 16 C2
HLGN/YWD B28 126 D7
LGLYGN/QTN B68 86 F7
NUNW/HART CV10 98 F5
Gresham St COVE CV2 155 L3
Gresley TAM/AM/WIL B77 46 D4
Gresley Cl MGN/WHC B75 56 E1
Gresley Rd COVE CV2 135 H6
Gresley Rw LICH WS13 21 G5
Gressel La STETCH B33 110 A2
Grestone Av BFLD/HDSWWD B20 88 C2
Greswold Cl TLHL/CAN CV4 153 K4
Greswolde Dr ERDE/BCHGN B24 90 F1
Greswolde Park Rd ACGN B27 126 F2
Greswolde Rd SOLH B91 127 J7
SPARK B11 126 A2
The Greswoldes RLSS CV31 207 K7
Greswold Gdns STETCH B33 91 L8
Greswold St HHTH/SAND B71 68 E8
Gretna Rd COVS CV3 180 D1
Gretton Crs ALDR WS9 40 D8
Gretton Rd ALDR WS9 40 D8
ERDW/GRVHL B23 72 B6
Greville Cl PENK ST19 10 D5
Greville Dr EDG B15 106 F7
Greville Rd KNWTH CV8 197 J1
WWCK CV34 205 M4
Grevis Cl MOS/BIL B13 125 K3
Grevis Rd STETCH B33 109 J4
Greycoat Rd COVN CV6 133 L3
Greyfort Crs HIA/OLT B92 127 K4
Greyfriars Cl DUDN DY1 84 C2
HIA/OLT B92 127 H6
Greyfriars Dr CRTAM B79 31 J8
Greyfriars La COV CV1 8 F5
Greyfriars Rd COV CV1 8 E6
Grey Green La BEWD DY12 136 F8
Greyhound La
ETTPK/GDPK/PENN WV4 48 C8
STRBR DY8 119 H3
Greyhurst Cft SOLH B91 148 F5
Grey Mill Cl SHLY B90 148 D7
Greysbrook LICHS WS14 * 28 E8
Greystoke Av CBROM B36 91 H6
Greystoke Dr KGSWFD DY6 83 H7
Greystone Cl REDE B98 195 G7
Greystone Pas DUDN DY1 84 F4
Greystone St DUDS DY2 85 G4
Grey Tree Crs DOR/KN B93 175 J2
Grice St WBROM B70 87 G5
Griffin Cl BNTWD WS7 18 C5
Griffin Gdns HRBN B17 124 B1
Griffin Rd ERDW/GRVHL B23 72 A8
KIDD DY10 164 C1
RLSS CV31 206 A6
Griffins Brook Cl BVILLE B30 124 B7
Griffins Brook La BVILLE B30 124 A7
Griffin St DUDS DY2 103 G1
WBROM B70 87 H2
WOLV WV1 3 M6
Griffiths Dr WMBN WV5 64 E8
WNSFLD WV11 37 K5
Griffiths Rd DUDN DY1 66 E7
HHTH/SAND B71 69 G4
SHHTH WV12 38 B5
Griff La NUNW/HART CV10 98 B7
Grigg Gv NFLD/LBR B31 144 C4
Grimley Cl REDE B98 202 D4
Grimley La BRGRVE B60 192 C6
Grimley Rd NFLD/LBR B31 145 H3
Grimley Wy CNCK/NC WS11 16 D1
Grimpits La HWK/WKHTH B38 145 L6
Grimshaw Rd HLGN/YWD B28 126 E4
Grimstock Hl CSHL/WTROR B46 * 93 J4
Grimston Cl COVS CV3 156 E3
Grimstone St WOLVN WV10 3 H3
Grindleford Rd PBAR/PBCH B42 71 H6
Grindle Rd COVN CV6 134 D1
Grindsbrook TAM/AM/WIL B77 46 E5
Gristhorpe Rd SLYOAK B29 124 E5
Grizebeck Dr COVW CV5 132 E8
Grizedale RUGBYN/HIL CV21 161 G6
Grizedale Cl RBRY B45 143 M3
Grocott Cl PENK ST19 10 C3
Grocott Rd DARL/WED WS10 67 M1
Grosmont Av BHTH/HG B12 107 L7
Grosvenor Av
BFLD/HDSWWD B20 89 G3
FOAKS/STRLY B74 55 K4
KIDD DY10 138 D7
Grosvenor Cl LICHS WS14 21 H7
MGN/WHC B75 57 G4
PENK ST19 10 D4
WOLVN WV10 36 B3
Grosvenor Crs WOLVN WV10 36 B3
Grosvenor Gdns BRGRVW B61 168 F8
Grosvenor Pk
ETTPK/GDPK/PENN WV4 49 K8
Grosvenor Rd AST/WIT B6 89 M5
BFLD/HDSWWD B20 89 G3
COV CV1 8 D7
ETTPK/GDPK/PENN WV4 66 C2
HRBN B17 105 L7
LGLYGN/QTN B68 104 E1
RLSS CV31 206 E8
RUGBYN/HIL CV21 187 G2
SEDG DY3 84 B3
SOLH B91 148 D4
WOLVN WV10 36 B3
Grosvenor Sq HLGN/YWD B28 126 C8
Grosvenor St CBHAMNE B4 7 J4
WOLVN WV10 3 L3
Grosvenor St West
LDYWD/EDGR B16 6 A7
Grosvenor Wy BRLYHL DY5 102 B6
Grosvenor Wd BEWD DY12 162 D2
Grotto La DUNHL/THL/PER WV6 35 J8
Groucutt St BILS/COS WV14 67 G5
Grounds Dr FOAKS/STRLY B74 56 D2
Grounds Rd FOAKS/STRLY B74 56 D2
Grout St WBROM B70 86 C1
Grove Av HALE B63 121 K2
HDSW B21 * 88 D5
MOS/BIL B13 125 L3
SLYOAK B29 * 124 C4
SOLH B91 128 A8
Grove Cl CNCK/NC WS11 17 K8
Grove Cottage Rd BORD B9 108 B3
Grove Ct PBAR/PBCH B42 * 70 D7
Grove Crs BLOX/PEL WS3 39 K2
BRLYHL DY5 84 A8
Grove Cft RWWCK/WEL CV35 204 C8
Grove Farm Dr MGN/WHC B75 57 K8
Grovefield Crs
RCOVN/BALC/EX CV7 152 A5
Grove Flds NUNW/HART CV10 81 G5
Grove Gdns BRGRVW B61 168 E7
HDSW B21 88 D3
Grove Hl DSYBK/YTR WS5 54 C5
Grove Hill Rd HDSW B21 88 D4
Grove House WSL WS1 * 5 G5
Groveland Rd TPTN/OCK DY4 85 L2
Grovelands Crs WOLVN WV10 36 B2
Grove La BFLD/HDSWWD B20 88 D3
BLOX/PEL WS3 25 J4
DUNHL/THL/PER WV6 48 F3
HOCK/TIA B94 175 L8
HRBN B17 124 A1
RCOVN/BALC/EX CV7 115 K6
SMTHWK B66 88 A8
WALM/CURD B76 74 E2
Groveley La NFLD/LBR B31 144 D7
RBRY B45 170 A1
Grove Ms NFLD/LBR B31 144 F5
Grove Pk KGSWFD DY6 83 G5
RWWCK/WEL CV35 204 B7
Grove Pl NUNW/HART CV10 98 B2
RLSS CV31 206 E7
Grove Rd ALE/KHTH/YWD B14 125 H6
ATHST CV9 63 H6
DOR/KN B93 175 M2
HAG/WOL DY9 120 D1
LGLYGN/QTN B68 105 H4
NUNW/HART CV10 98 B2
SOLH B91 128 A8
SPARK B11 126 A2
Groveside Wy BLOX/PEL WS3 25 L8
Grove St COV CV1 9 H4
DUDS DY2 85 J5
REDE B98 202 C2
RLSN CV32 206 C5
WOLVN WV10 3 M2
WSNGN B18 106 B1
Grove Ter WSL WS1 5 G5
The Grove BDWTH CV12 116 F2
BLKHTH/ROWR B65 104 A3
BNTWD WS7 18 B5
BRLYHL DY5 102 A4
CSHL/WTROR B46 111 K1
DSYBK/YTR WS5 69 M2
ETTPK/GDPK/PENN WV4 50 C8
FOAKS/STRLY B74 42 B8
GTB/HAM B43 70 C1
HIA/OLT B92 129 L5
LDYWD/EDGR B16 * 106 D3
NFLD/LBR B31 144 F5
RBRY B45 170 B1
STRPT DY13 189 G2
WASH/WDE B8 108 A1
WNSFLD WV11 36 F7
Grove Vale Av GTB/HAM B43 70 A4
Grove Wy FOAKS/STRLY B74 55 K6
Grovewood Dr
HWK/WKHTH B38 145 J4
Guardhouse Rd COVN CV6 133 M5
Guardian Ct NFLD/LBR B31 144 B2
SOLH B91 149 H2
Guardians Wy NFLD/LBR B31 123 J5
Guernsey Dr CBROM B36 92 F7
Guest Av WNSFLD WV11 37 G5
Guest Gv LOZ/NWT B19 89 G7
Guild Av BLOX/PEL WS3 39 H6
Guild Cl LDYWD/EDGR B16 106 E3
Guild Cft LOZ/NWT B19 89 H7
Guildford Cl KIDDW DY11 137 L7
Guildford Cft
CHWD/FDBR/MGN B37 110 D5
Guildford Dr LOZ/NWT B19 89 H7
Guildford St LOZ/NWT B19 89 H6
Guild Rd BRGRVE B60 191 K4
COVN CV6 134 B6
Guilsborough Rd COVS CV3 156 C4
Guinness Cl REDW B97 202 B5
Guiting Cl REDW B97 201 M4
Guiting Rd SLYOAK B29 123 L6
Gulistan Rd RLSN CV32 206 C4
Gullane Cl HWK/WKHTH B38 145 H4
The Gullet POL/KGSB/FAZ B78 47 K4
Gullick Wy BNTWD WS7 18 B5
Gulliman's Wy RLSS CV31 207 H7
Gullswood Cl
ALE/KHTH/YWD B14 146 B3
Gulson Rd COV CV1 9 J6
Gumbleberrys Cl
WASH/WDE B8 109 G1
Gundry Cl RLSS CV31 206 E6
Gun Hl RCOVN/BALC/EX CV7 96 E5
Gun La COVE CV2 134 E8
Gunmakers Wk LOZ/NWT B19 89 H6
Gunner Gv MGN/WHC B75 57 L7
Gunner La RBRY B45 143 H6
Gunns Wy HIA/OLT B92 127 H6
Guns La WBROM B70 86 F1
Gunstock Cl FOAKS/STRLY B74 55 J6
Gunter Rd ERDE/BCHGN B24 91 J2
Gunton Av COVS CV3 156 A8
Guphill Av COVW CV5 154 B3
Guphill La COVW CV5 154 B2
Gurnard TAM/AM/WIL B77 46 B7
Gurnard Cl SHHTH WV12 37 M4
Gurney Pl WSLW WS2 38 E8
Gurney Rd WSLW WS2 38 E8
Guthrie Cl LOZ/NWT B19 89 H7
Guthrum Cl
DUNHL/THL/PER WV6 34 D8
ERDW/GRVHL B23 72 C5
Gutteridge Av COVN CV6 133 L3
The Gutter HAG/WOL DY9 142 C6
Guy Av WOLVN WV10 36 C7
Guy Pl East RLSN CV32 206 D4
Guy Pl West RLSN CV32 206 D4
Guy Rd KNWTH CV8 197 K3
Guy's Cliffe Av RLSN CV32 206 B4
WALM/CURD B76 73 K4
Guy's Cliffe Rd RLSN CV32 206 C5
Guy's Cliffe Ter WWCK CV34 205 K6
Guys Cl CRTAM B79 31 K6
WWCK CV34 205 K5
Guy's Cross Park Rd
WWCK CV34 205 K5
Guy's La SEDG DY3 83 M3
Guy St RLSN CV32 206 D4
WWCK CV34 205 K6
Guy's Wk BRGRVW B61 168 E8
Gwalia Gv ERDW/GRVHL B23 * 90 D1
Gwendoline Wy ALDR WS9 40 F1
Gypsy La ATHST CV9 63 H3
CSHL/WTROR B46 93 H3
KNWTH CV8 197 K4
POL/KGSB/FAZ B78 61 L1
REDW B97 193 G8

H

Habberley La KIDDW DY11 137 K5
Habberley Rd BEWD DY12 137 J7
BLKHTH/ROWR B65 104 B3
Habberley St KIDDW DY11 138 A7
Habberly Cft SOLH B91 148 F4
Hackett Cl BILS/COS WV14 66 D4
Hackett Dr SMTHWK B66 87 H6
Hackett Rd BLKHTH/ROWR B65 104 C2
Hackett St TPTN/OCK DY4 68 A6
Hackford Rd
ETTPK/GDPK/PENN WV4 66 D1
Hackmans Gate La
HAG/WOL DY9 140 F6
Hack St BORD B9 7 L7
Hackwood Rd DARL/WED WS10 68 F3
Hadcroft Gra HAG/WOL DY9 120 B1
Hadcroft Rd HAG/WOL DY9 120 A1
Haddock Rd BILS/COS WV14 51 G6
Haddon Crs SHHTH WV12 38 A6
Haddon Cft HALE B63 121 G4
Haddon End COVS CV3 155 J7
Haddon Rd PBAR/PBCH B42 71 H6
RLSN CV32 206 F3
Haddon St COVN CV6 134 E5
Haden Circ BHTH/HG B12 107 K6
Haden Cl CDYHTH B64 103 K6
STRBR DY8 101 H3
Haden Crs WNSFLD WV11 37 K7
Haden Cross Dr CDYHTH B64 103 L6
Hadendale CDYHTH B64 103 L6
Haden Hl BDMR/CCFT WV3 2 A5
Haden Hill Rd CDYHTH B64 103 L6
Haden Park Rd CDYHTH B64 103 J6
Haden Rd CDYHTH B64 103 J3
TPTN/OCK DY4 67 L4
Haden St BHTH/HG B12 107 K7
Haden Wy BHTH/HG B12 107 K7
Hadfield Cl ERDE/BCHGN B24 91 J2
RRUGBY CV23 161 L8
Hadfield Cft LOZ/NWT B19 89 G8
Hadfield Wy
CHWD/FDBR/MGN B37 110 E1
Hadland Rd STETCH B33 109 M4
Hadleigh Cft WALM/CURD B76 73 L7
Hadleigh Rd COVS CV3 181 G2
Hadley Cl DUDS DY2 103 J1
HLYWD B47 146 E8
Hadley Cft SMTHWK B66 87 L6
Hadley Pl BILS/COS WV14 51 G6
Hadley Rd BILS/COS WV14 51 G6
WSLW WS2 38 D7
Hadleys Cft POL/KGSB/FAZ B78 60 B8
Hadley St LGLYGN/QTN B68 104 E1
Hadlow Cft STETCH B33 110 B6
Hadrian Cl RLSN CV32 206 F1
Hadrian Dr CSHL/WTROR B46 93 J4
Hadrians Cl TAM/AM/WIL B77 46 B5
Hadrians Wy RUGBYN/HIL CV21 160 D6
Hadyn Gv
LGN/SDN/BHAMAIR B26 109 M7
Hadzor Rd LGLYGN/QTN B68 105 H5
Hafren Cl RBRY B45 143 M3
Hafren Wy STRPT DY13 188 D1
Hafton Gv BORD B9 * 108 B4
Haggar St BKHL/PFLD WV2 50 A7
Hagley Cswy HAG/WOL DY9 120 D6
Hagley Cl HAG/WOL DY9 120 A7
Hagley Park Dr RBRY B45 143 L7
Hagley Rd HAG/WOL DY9 120 A5
HALE B63 121 G5
HALE B63 121 M2
HRBN B17 106 A4
STRBR DY8 119 M2
Hagley Rd West HRBN B17 105 L4
RIDG/WDGT B32 104 E7
Hagley View Rd DUDS DY2 85 G5
Hagley Vls BHTH/HG B12 * 125 M1
Hagley Wood La HAG/WOL DY9 120 F7
Haig Cl CNCK/NC WS11 12 E8
MGN/WHC B75 57 G6
Haig Rd DUDS DY2 85 K4
Haig St HHTH/SAND B71 69 G7
Hailes Park Cl BKHL/PFLD WV2 50 B7
Hailsham Rd ERDW/GRVHL B23 72 D8
Hailstone Cl BLKHTH/ROWR B65 85 L7
Haines Cl TPTN/OCK DY4 85 M1
Haines St WBROM B70 87 H3
Hainfield Dr SOLH B91 128 C8
Hainge Rd OLDBY B69 86 A3
Hainult Cl STRBR DY8 101 H1
Halberton St WSNGN B18 106 B1
Haldon Gv NFLD/LBR B31 144 C6
Hale Ct WSL WS1 * 5 K6
Halecroft Av WNSFLD WV11 37 H8
Hale Gv ERDE/BCHGN B24 91 H1
Hales Crs SMTHWKW B67 105 J1
Halescroft Sq NFLD/LBR B31 123 J7
Hales Gdns ERDW/GRVHL B23 72 A5
Hales La SMTHWKW B67 105 J1
Halesmere Wy HALE B63 * 122 A2
Halesowen Rd BRGRVW B61 169 G3
CDYHTH B64 103 K5
DUDS DY2 85 G8
RMSLY B62 104 C7
Halesowen St OLDBY B69 86 D6
RMSLY B62 104 A5
Hales Pk BEWD DY12 162 D2
Hales Rd DARL/WED WS10 68 E1
HALE B63 121 L1
Hales St COV CV1 8 F3
Hales Wy OLDBY B69 86 D6
Halesworth Rd COVEN WV9 35 K3
Halewood Gv HLGN/YWD B28 126 E6
Haley St SHHTH WV12 38 A8
Halfcot Av HAG/WOL DY9 120 A2
Halford Crs BLOX/PEL WS3 39 K8
Halford Gv RWWCK/WEL CV35 204 C3
Halford La COVN CV6 133 L5
Halford Rd SOLH B91 127 J7
Halford's La SMTHWK B66 87 L6
Halford St CRTAM B79 31 L8
Halfshire La KIDD DY10 139 M4
Halfway Cl KGSTG B44 71 J7
Halifax Cl COVW CV5 132 E6
Halifax Gv WSNGN B18 * 106 C1
Halifax Rd SHLY B90 147 M2
Haling Cl PENK ST19 10 D5
Haling Rd PENK ST19 10 D4
Haliscombe Gv AST/WIT B6 * 89 J5
Halladale HWK/WKHTH B38 145 K4
Hallam Cl HHTH/SAND B71 87 J1
Hallam Crs WOLVN WV10 36 C7
Hallam Dr HHTH/SAND B71 69 H8
Hallam Rd COVN CV6 133 M2
Hallams Cl KNWTH CV8 157 K8
Hallam St BHTH/HG B12 107 J8
HHTH/SAND B71 87 H1
Hallbridge Cl BLOX/PEL WS3 39 K3
Hallbridge Wy OLDBY B69 85 M3
Hall Brook Rd
RCOVN/BALC/EX CV7 133 L2
Hallchurch Rd DUDS DY2 84 D6
Hall Cl KNWTH CV8 180 F7
Hallcourt Cl CNCK/NC WS11 * 16 C5
Hallcourt Crs CNCK/NC WS11 16 C5
Hallcourt La CNCK/NC WS11 16 C5
Hall Crs HHTH/SAND B71 69 G7
Hallcroft Cl CSCFLD/WYGN B72 73 G6
Hallcroft Wy ALDR WS9 41 G8
DOR/KN B93 149 L7
Hall Dale Cl HLGN/YWD B28 126
Hall Dr CHWD/FDBR/MGN B37 110
HAG/WOL DY9 120
KNWTH CV8 181
Hall End DARL/WED WS10 68
NUN CV11 99
Hallens Dr DARL/WED WS10 68
Hallet Dr BDMR/CCFT WV3 2
Hallewell Rd LDYWD/EDGR B16 106
Hallfields RLSS CV31 207
Hall Gdns ATHST CV9 * 63
Hall Green Rd COVE CV2 134
HHTH/SAND B71 69
Hallgreen St BILS/COS WV14 67
Hall Gv BILS/COS WV14 67
RRUGBY CV23 158
Hall Hays Rd BKDE/SHDE B34 92
Hall La ALDR WS9 40
ATHST CV9 63
BILS/COS WV14 66
BLOX/PEL WS3 39
BNTWD WS7 27
COVE CV2 135
GTWY WS6 24
HAG/WOL DY9 120
TPTN/OCK DY4 67
Hall Meadow CNCK/NC WS11 15
HAG/WOL DY9 120
Hallmoor Rd STETCH B33 109
Hallot Cl ERDW/GRVHL B23 72
Halloughton Rd
FOAKS/STRLY B74 56
Hallowfields Cl REDE B98 202
Hall Park St BILS/COS WV14 50
Hall Rd BFLD/HDSWWD B20 88
CBROM B36 91
RLSN CV32 206
SMTHWKW B67 105
WASH/WDE B8 108
Halls Farm La BEWD DY12 137
Hallstead Rd MOS/BIL B13 125
Hall St BILS/COS WV14 51
CDYHTH B64 103
DUDS DY2 85
LGLYGN/QTN B68 86
SEDG DY3 66
STRBR DY8 119
TPTN/OCK DY4 67
WBROM B70 87
WLNHL WV13 51
WNSFLD WV11 37
WSLW WS2 53
WSNGN B18 6
Hall St East DARL/WED WS10 52
Hall St South WBROM B70 87
Hall Wk CSHL/WTROR B46 111
Halsbury Gv KGSTG B44 71
Halstead Gv SOLH B91 148
Halston Rd BNTWD WS7 18
Halswelle Gv GTB/HAM B43 71
Haltonlea TAM/AM/WIL B77 46
Halton Rd SCFLD/BOLD B73 72
Halton St DUDS DY2 85
Hamar Wy
CHWD/FDBR/MGN B37 110
Hamberley Ct WSNGN B18 106
Hamble TAM/AM/WIL B77 46
Hamble Cl BRLYHL DY5 83
Hambledon Cl COVEN WV9 35
Hamble Gv
DUNHL/THL/PER WV6 48
Hamble Rd
ETTPK/GDPK/PENN WV4 49
PBAR/PBCH B42 70
Hambleton Rd HALE B63 121
Hambletts Rd WBROM B70 86
Hambrook Cl
DUNHL/THL/PER WV6 35
Hambury Dr
ALE/KHTH/YWD B14 125
Hamelin St CNCK/NC WS11 16
Hamgreen La REDW B97 201
Hamilton Av HRBN B17 105
RMSLY B62 122
STRBR DY8 101
Hamilton Cl BDWTH CV12 116
BRGRVE B60 169
HEDN WS12 17
SEDG DY3 66
STRBR DY8 101
Hamilton Dr OLDBY B69 86
SLYOAK B29 124
STRBR DY8 101
Hamilton Gdns WOLVN WV10 36
Hamilton Lea CNCK/NC WS11 17
Hamilton Rd COVE CV2 155
HDSW B21 88
KIDDW DY11 163
REDW B97 202
RLSS CV31 207
SMTHWKW B67 105
TPTN/OCK DY4 68
Hamilton St BLOX/PEL WS3 39
Hamilton Ter RLSN CV32 206
Ham La HAG/WOL DY9 120
KGSWFD DY6 83
Hamlet Cl NUN CV11 99
RUGBYS/DCH CV22 186
Hamlet Gdns HLGN/YWD B28 126
Hamlet Rd HLGN/YWD B28 126
The Hamlet CNCK/NC WS11 17
RWWCK/WEL CV35 197
Hammer Bank HALE B63 102
Hammersley Cl HALE B63 103
Hammersley St BDWTH CV12 116
Hammerwich La BNTWD WS7 27
Hammerwich Rd BNTWD WS7 19
Hammond Av WOLVN WV10 36
Hammond Cl NUN CV11 99
Hammond Dr ERDW/GRVHL B23 72
Hammond Rd COVE CV2 9
Hammond Wy STRBR DY8 101
Hampden Cl BRLYHL DY5 102
Hampden Retreat
BHTH/HG B12 107
Hampden Wy
RUGBYS/DCH CV22 186
Hamps Cl BNTWD WS7 19
Hampshire Cl COVS CV3 156
POL/KGSB/FAZ B78 45
Hampshire Dr EDG B15 106
Hampshire Rd HHTH/SAND B71 68
Hampson Cl SPARK B11 107
Hampstead Cl WNSFLD WV11 37
Hampstead Gld HALE B63 122
Hampton Av BRGRVE B60 191
NUNW/HART CV10 97
Hampton Cl CRTAM B79 32
REDE B98 202
SCFLD/BOLD B73 72
Hampton Ct WNSFLD WV11 * 36
Hampton Court Rd HRBN B17 10
Hampton Cft
RWWCK/WEL CV35 2
Hampton Dr FOAKS/STRLY B74
Hampton Gdns HAG/WOL DY9 1
Hampton Gn CNCK/NC WS11
Hampton Gv BLOX/PEL WS3
RLSN CV32 2

mpton La
RCOVN/BALC/EX CV7 130 D5
SOLH B91 128 F8
SOLH B91 149 H1
mpton Rd AST/WIT B6 89 H5
COVN CV6 134 D7
DOR/KN B93 150 A6
ERDW/GRVHL B23 90 B1
RWWCK/WEL CV35 204 C7
WOLVN WV10 35 M4
mpton St BILS/COS WV14 66 F5
CNCK/NC WS11 16 B6
DUDS DY2 84 F8
LOZ/NWT B19 6 E1
WWCK CV34 205 H7
ms La WALM/CURD B76 75 K8
ms Rd WASH/WDE B8 108 B1
mstead Hall Av
BFLD/HDSWWD B20 70 C8
mstead Hall Rd
BFLD/HDSWWD B20 88 C1
mstead Hl
BFLD/HDSWWD B20 88 D1
mstead Rd
BFLD/HDSWWD B20 88 F4
GTB/HAM B43 70 B6
mstead Ter DARL/WED WS10 68 E3
nam Cl MGN/WHC B75 57 K7
nbury Cl BRGRVE B60 191 L5
HALE B63 * 121 K3
nbury Crs BDMR/CCFT WV3 49 J7
nbury Cft ACGN B27 127 J2
nbury Hl STRBR DY8 119 L1
nbury Rd BDWTH CV12 117 C1
BRGRVE B60 191 H8
BRWNH WS8 26 C3
CNCK/NC WS11 17 K8
DOR/KN B93 175 K2
TAM/AM/WIL B77 46 D1
WBROM B70 86 E2
nch Pl WSL WS1 5 H6
ncock Gn TLHL/CAN CV4 153 K5
ncock Rd WASH/WDE B8 108 D1
ncox St LGLYGN/QTN B68 104 F3
ndcross Gv COVS CV3 154 E8
ndel Ct CNCK/NC WS11 17 G3
ndley Gv NFLD/LBR B31 144 A3
ndley's Cl KNWTH CV8 182 E4
ndley St DARL/WED WS10 68 E1
ndsworth Cl HDSW B21 88 B6
ndsworth Crs COVW CV5 153 J1
ndsworth Dr GTB/HAM B43 70 E2
ndsworth New Rd
WSNGN B18 88 C8
ndsworth Wood Rd
BFLD/HDSWWD B20 88 D2
nford Cl COVN CV6 134 C7
nging La NFLD/LBR B31 144 C4
ngleton Dr SPARK B11 108 B7
ngman's La CRTAM B79 33 L3
nley Cl HALE B63 121 J1
nley St LOZ/NWT B19 6 F1
nlith TAM/AM/WIL B77 46 E5
nnaford Wy CNCK/NC WS11 16 D3
nnafore Rd
LDYWD/EDGR B16 106 B2
nnah Rd BILS/COS WV14 67 L2
nney Hay Rd BNTWD WS7 26 F2
nnon Rd ALE/KHTH/YWD B14 125 J8
nover Cl AST/WIT B6 89 J6
nover Ct
DUNHL/THL/PER WV6 49 G1
REDE B98 * 202 B5
WSLW WS2 52 C4
nover Dr VAUX/NECH B7 90 D5
nover Gdns RLSN CV32 * 206 E4
RUGBYN/HIL CV21 186 F1
nover Pl CNCK/NC WS11 16 C3
nover Rd BLKHTH/ROWR B65 104 A1
nover St BRGRVE B61 191 K3
ns Cl COV CV1 9 M1
nsell Dr DOR/KN B93 175 J3
nsom Rd RIDG/WDGT B32 105 G8
nson Gv HIA/OLT B92 109 K8
nson's Bridge Rd
ERDE/BCHGN B24 73 K8
nson Wy COVN CV6 116 E8
nstone Rd STRPT DY13 188 D4
nwell Cl WALM/CURD B76 73 M6
nwood Cl BHTH/HG B12 107 K5
COVW CV5 153 H1
nworth Cl RLSN CV32 206 F2
nworth Rd WWCK CV34 205 H5
rald Cl DUNHL/THL/PER WV6 34 C8
rbeck Av KGSTG B44 71 K5
rberrow Cl HAG/WOL DY9 119 L7
rbet Dr BHAMNEC B40 129 L1
rbinger Rd HWK/WKHTH B38 145 M3
rborne La SLYOAK B29 124 B3
rborne Park Rd HRBN B17 106 A8
rborne Rd EDG B15 106 C7
SMTHWKW B67 105 H4
rborough Dr ALDR WS9 40 E8
CBROM B36 92 B4
rborough Rd COVN CV6 133 M3
RUGBYN/HIL CV21 160 A5
rborough Wk HAG/WOL DY9 119 M3
rbours Cl BRGRVE B60 191 H6
rbours Hl HAG/WOL DY9 142 C7
rbury Cl REDE B98 203 H4
WALM/CURD B76 73 M7
rbury Rd BHTH/HG B12 107 H8
rby Cl CHWD/FDBR/MGN B37 110 F5
rcourt COVS CV3 156 C8
rcourt Dr DUDN DY1 84 B3
FOAKS/STRLY B74 56 C1
rcourt Gdns NUN CV11 99 G2
rcourt Rd CDYHTH B64 103 K5
DARL/WED WS10 68 D1
ERDW/GRVHL B23 72 C7
rden Cl BLOX/PEL WS3 39 J6
rden Gv BLOX/PEL WS3 39 J6
rden Manor Ct HALE B63 * 122 A2
rden Rd BLOX/PEL WS3 39 H6
rden V HALE B63 * 103 J8
rdie Gn CNCK/NC WS11 16 D2
rding St BILS/COS WV14 67 H4
rdingwood La
RCOVN/BALC/EX CV7 113 J2
rdon Rd
ETTPK/GDPK/PENN WV4 50 D8
rdware St WBROM B70 87 H1
rdwick Cl COVW CV5 153 L1
rdwick Ct CRTAM B79 32 A8
rdwick Dr CDYHTH B64 103 L6
rdwicke Wy HAG/WOL DY9 102 B8
rdwick La STUD B80 203 L8
rdwick Rd FOAKS/STRLY B74 55 K3
GN/SDN/BHAMAIR B26 127 J1
rdwike Wk
LE/KHTH/YWD B14 146 A3
rdwyn Cl COVS CV3 156 E4
dy Av KIDD DY10 138 E7
dy Cl NUNW/HART CV10 97 L1
GBYS/DCH CV22 186 A3
y Rd BLOX/PEL WS3 39 J5
VN CV6 133 L5
RL/WED WS10 68 E2
dy Sq BKHL/PFLD WV2 * 50 D7
Hare & Hounds La
NUNW/HART CV10 98 E3
Harebell TAM/AM/WIL B77 46 E1
Harebell Cl DSYBK/YTR WS5 69 L2
HEDN WS12 17 H3
WOLVN WV10 22 E6
Harebell Crs DUDN DY1 84 E1
Harebell Gdns
HWK/WKHTH B38 145 K5
Harebell Wy RRUGBY CV23 161 H5
Harefield La NUNW/HART CV10 98 D5
Harefield Rd COVE CV2 155 M2
NUN CV11 99 G1
Hare Gv NFLD/LBR B31 144 B2
Haresfield Cl REDW B97 202 B3
Hare St BILS/COS WV14 51 K8
Harewell Dr MGN/WHC B75 57 G4
Harewood Av DARL/WED WS10 69 G2
GTB/HAM B43 70 A3
Harewood Cl HLGN/YWD B28 126 C8
Harewood Rd COVW CV5 154 A2
Harford St LOZ/NWT B19 6 D1
Hargate La HHTH/SAND B71 87 G1
Harger Ct KNWTH CV8 197 K1
Hargrave Cl COVS CV3 156 E4
CSHL/WTROR B46 92 F2
Hargrave Rd SHLY B90 147 H3
Hargreave Cl WALM/CURD B76 73 K6
Hargreaves St BKHL/PFLD WV2 50 E6
Harington Rd COVN CV6 133 L8
Harland Cl BRGRVW B61 191 H2
Harland Rd FOAKS/STRLY B74 56 E2
Harlech Cl KNWTH CV8 180 A8
OLDBY B69 85 L4
RIDG/WDGT B32 122 E7
Harlech Rd SHHTH WV12 38 A7
Harlech Wy DUDN DY1 84 D3
KIDDW DY11 164 C3
Harleston Rd KGSTG B44 71 K5
Harley Cl BRWNH WS8 26 E7
Harley Dr BILS/COS WV14 66 F1
Harley St COVE CV2 155 L2
Harlow Gv HLGN/YWD B28 126 E7
Harlstones Cl STRBR DY8 101 L6
Harlyn Cl BILS/COS WV14 67 L3
Harman Rd CSCFLD/WYGN B72 72 F6
Harmar Cl WWCK CV34 205 H4
Harmer Cl COVE CV2 135 L6
Harmer St WSNGN B18 88 E8
Harmon Rd STRBR DY8 101 G8
Harmony Ct NUNW/HART CV10 98 F3
Harnall Cl SHLY B90 148 C6
Harnall La COV CV1 9 H1
Harnall La East COV CV1 9 J1
Harnall La West COV CV1 8 F1
Harnall Rw COV CV1 9 K4
Harness Cl DSYBK/YTR WS5 69 J1
Harold Davies Dr STRPT DY13 188 D3
Harold Evers Wy KIDD DY10 138 D6
Harold Rd COVE CV2 156 B3
LDYWD/EDGR B16 106 D4
SMTHWKW B67 105 J2
Harold St NUN CV11 99 G2
Harold Ter LOZ/NWT B19 * 89 G5
Harpenden Dr COVW CV5 132 E8
Harper Av WNSFLD WV11 37 G6
Harper Rd BILS/COS WV14 51 H7
COV CV1 9 J6
Harpers La ATHST CV9 63 L7
Harpers Rd HLYWD B47 146 E4
NFLD/LBR B31 144 E3
Harper St WLNHL WV13 51 L3
Harport Rd REDE B98 202 E4
Harpur Cl RUSH/SHEL WS4 53 L1
Harpur Rd RUSH/SHEL WS4 53 L1
Harrier Rd ACGN B27 127 H3
Harriers Gn KIDD DY10 138 F5
Harriet Cl BRLYHL DY5 83 M8
Harringay Dr STRBR DY8 119 J2
Harringay Rd KGSTG B44 71 K3
Harrington Wk LICH WS13 20 D4
Harris Dr PBAR/PBCH B42 70 E5
RUGBYS/DCH CV22 186 D5
SMTHWK B66 105 M2
Harrison Cl BLOX/PEL WS3 39 G4
GTWY WS6 24 B4
RUGBYN/HIL CV21 187 M5
Harrison Crs BDWTH CV12 116 E3
Harrison Rd CNCK/NC WS11 16 C6
ERDE/BCHGN B24 90 D1
FOAKS/STRLY B74 42 C8
REDW B97 202 A5
RUSH/SHEL WS4 40 A3
STRBR DY8 101 L4
Harrison's Fold DUDS DY2 85 G8
Harrisons Gn EDG B15 106 C7
Harrisons La PENK ST19 14 C4
Harrisons Pleck MOS/BIL B13 125 K2
Harrison's Rd EDG B15 106 C7
Harrison St BLOX/PEL WS3 39 G4
Harrison Wy RLSS CV31 206 D8
Harris Rd COVS CV3 155 M3
WWCK CV34 205 G5
Harrold Av BLKHTH/ROWR B65 104 C2
Harrold Rd BLKHTH/ROWR B65 104 C2
Harrold St TPTN/OCK DY4 68 A6
Harrold Ter LOZ/NWT B19 89 G5
Harrop Wy STRBR DY8 101 J5
Harrowby Dr TPTN/OCK DY4 85 L1
Harrowby Pl WLNHL WV13 52 A4
Harrowby Rd BILS/COS WV14 67 L1
WOLVN WV10 35 M2
Harrow Cl BRGRVE B60 191 J7
COVN CV6 134 E1
HAG/WOL DY9 119 L7
Harrowfield Rd STETCH B33 109 J1
Harrow Rd KGSWFD DY6 83 H4
SLYOAK B29 124 D2
Harrow St WOLV WV1 2 D1
Harry Perks St WLNHL WV13 51 L2
Harry Rose Rd COVE CV2 156 C2
Harry Truslove Cl COVN CV6 133 L6
Harry Weston Rd COVS CV3 156 E4
Hart Cl RUGBYN/HIL CV21 187 H3
Hart Dr SCFLD/BOLD B73 72 E5
Hartfield Crs ACGN B27 126 E4
Hartford Cl HRBN B17 105 L6
Hartford Rd BRGRVE B60 191 M4
Hartill Rd
ETTPK/GDPK/PENN WV4 65 H2
Hartill St WLNHL WV13 51 M5
Hartington Cl DOR/KN B93 175 J2
Hartington Crs COVW CV5 154 C4
Hartington Rd LOZ/NWT B19 89 H5
Hartland Av BILS/COS WV14 66 E5
COVE CV2 134 F7
Hartland Rd HHTH/SAND B71 69 K6
NFLD/LBR B31 144 C7
TPTN/OCK DY4 67 H8
Hartland St BRLYHL DY5 84 B6
Hartlebury Cl CNCK/NC WS11 17 G2
DOR/KN B93 175 K2
REDE B98 195 H6
Hartlebury Rd HALE B63 121 K3
OLDBY B69 86 B8
STRPT DY13 189 H2
Hartledon Rd HRBN B17 105 M8
Hartle La HAG/WOL DY9 141 K7
Hartlepool Rd COV CV1 9 J1
Hartleyburn TAM/AM/WIL B77 46 E5
Hartley Dr ALDR WS9 54 F1
Hartley Gv KGSTG B44 71 M2
Hartley Pl EDG B15 106 D5
Hartley Rd KGSTG B44 71 L2
Hartley St BDMR/CCFT WV3 2 A5
Harton Wy ALE/KHTH/YWD B14 125 G8
Hartopp Rd FOAKS/STRLY B74 56 D4
WASH/WDE B8 108 C1
Hartridge Wk COVW CV5 153 M1
Hart Rd ERDE/BCHGN B24 72 E8
WNSFLD WV11 51 H1
Hartsbourne Dr RMSLY B62 122 B1
Harts Cl HRBN B17 106 B7
Harts Green Rd HRBN B17 105 L8
Hartshill Rd BKDE/SHDE B34 91 L7
HIA/OLT B92 127 H3
Hartshorn St BILS/COS WV14 51 H8
Hartside Cl HALE B63 121 G3
Hartslade LICHS WS14 21 J7
Harts Rd WASH/WDE B8 90 C8
Hart St WSL WS1 4 F6
Hartswell Dr MOS/BIL B13 125 K7
Hartwell Cl SOLH B91 148 F4
Hartwell La GTWY WS6 24 E2
Hartwell Rd ERDE/BCHGN B24 90 F3
Harvard Cl DUDN DY1 84 D1
Harvard Rd HIA/OLT B92 127 M1
Harvest Cl BRGRVE B60 191 H7
BVILLE B30 124 F8
SEDG DY3 66 C8
Harvesters Cl COVS CV3 156 E3
FOAKS/STRLY B74 55 J3
Harvesters Rd SHHTH WV12 38 B8
Harvester Wy KGSWFD DY6 82 E5
Harvest Fields Wy
MGN/WHC B75 57 J2
Harvest Gdns LGLYGN/QTN B68 104 E1
Harvest Hill Cl RLSS CV31 * 207 G7
Harvest Hill La COVW CV5 132 B3
Harvest Rd BLKHTH/ROWR B65 103 L1
SMTHWKW B67 105 H2
Harvey Cl COVW CV5 132 E6
Harvey Ct STETCH B33 * 110 B2
Harvey Dr MGN/WHC B75 57 G3
Harvey Rd
LGN/SDN/BHAMAIR B26 109 H6
WSLW WS2 38 F8
Harvills Hawthorn WBROM B70 68 D6
Harvine Wk STRBR DY8 119 J2
Harvington Cl KIDDW DY11 137 L5
REDW B97 193 M8
Harvington Dr SHLY B90 148 F7
Harvington Hall La KIDD DY10 165 M3
Harvington Rd BILS/COS WV14 66 F4
BRGRVE B60 191 L5
HALE B63 121 K3
LGLYGN/QTN B68 104 E5
SLYOAK B29 123 L5
Harvington Wy WALM/CURD B76 73 K5
Harwell Cl CRTAM B79 32 A6
Harwin Cl DUNHL/THL/PER WV6 35 K6
Harwood Drive
TAM/AM/WIL B77 60 B1
Harwood Gv SHLY B90 148 A5
Harwood Rd LICH WS13 20 F2
Harwood St WBROM B70 86 F2
Hasbury Cl HALE B63 121 J3
Hasbury Rd RIDG/WDGT B32 122 E5
Haselbech Rd COVS CV3 156 D4
Haselbury Cnr
NUNW/HART CV10 98 D4
Haseley Cl REDE B98 203 J5
RLSS CV31 206 F8
Haseley Rd COVE CV2 135 G4
HDSW B21 88 C6
SOLH B91 127 J7
Haselor Rd SCFLD/BOLD B73 72 C4
Haselour Rd
CHWD/FDBR/MGN B37 92 D8
Hasilwood Sq COVS CV3 155 M3
Haskell St WSL WS1 5 G9
Haslucks Cl SHLY B90 147 J6
Haslucks Cft SHLY B90 147 L2
Haslucks Green Rd SHLY B90 147 J5
Hassop Rd PBAR/PBCH B42 71 H6
Hastang Flds RLSS CV31 207 G8
Hastings Cl TAM/AM/WIL B77 46 D7
Hastings Ct DUDN DY1 84 C3
Hastings Rd BRGRVE B60 191 J6
COVE CV2 155 L1
ERDW/GRVHL B23 71 M6
Haswell Cl RUGBYS/DCH CV22 187 G3
Haswell Rd HALE B63 121 H2
Hatcham Rd KGSTG B44 72 A3
Hatchett St LOZ/NWT B19 89 J8
Hatchford Av HIA/OLT B92 128 A2
Hatchford Brook Rd
HIA/OLT B92 128 A2
Hatch Heath Cl WMBN WV5 64 D6
Hateley Dr
ETTPK/GDPK/PENN WV4 66 C1
Hatfield Cl ERDW/GRVHL B23 72 B6
REDE B98 203 J4
Hatfield Rd HAG/WOL DY9 120 A1
LOZ/NWT B19 89 H5
Hathaway Cl
RCOVN/BALC/EX CV7 151 M6
WLNHL WV13 51 K5
Hathaway Dr NUN CV11 99 L4
WWCK CV34 205 J3
Hathaway Ms STRBR DY8 * 101 G2
Hathaway Rd MGN/WHC B75 56 E1
SHLY B90 147 M4
TLHL/CAN CV4 153 H4
Hatherden Dr WALM/CURD B76 73 L3
Hatherell Rd RLSS CV31 207 J8
Hathersage Rd PBAR/PBCH B42 71 H6
Hatherton Cft CNCK/NC WS11 16 A4
Hatherton Gdns WOLVN WV10 36 C3
Hatherton Gv SLYOAK B29 123 K4
Hatherton Pl ALDR WS9 40 E6
Hatherton Rd BILS/COS WV14 51 K7
CNCK/NC WS11 15 M4
PENK ST19 10 D4
WSL WS1 4 F3
Hatherton St GTWY WS6 24 A3
WSL WS1 4 F2
Hatters Ct BDWTH CV12 117 G3
Hatters Dr ATHST CV9 63 H3
Hattersley Gv SPARK B11 126 E2
Hatton Cl RWWCK/WEL CV35 204 B3
Hatton Crs WNSFLD WV11 36 E6
Hatton Gdns PBAR/PBCH B42 70 F6
Hatton Rd BDMR/CCFT WV3 * 49 K2
CNCK/NC WS11 15 L4
Hattons Gv CDSL WV8 34 F3
Hatton St BILS/COS WV14 67 J1
Haughton Rd
BFLD/HDSWWD B20 89 G4
Haunch La MOS/BIL B13 125 K7
WALM/CURD B76 75 L5
Haunchwood Dr
WALM/CURD B76 73 K6
Haunchwood Park Dr
NUNW/HART CV10 97 J1
Haunchwood Rd
NUNW/HART CV10 98 B1
Havacre La BILS/COS WV14 67 G3
Havefield Av LICHS WS14 21 H6
Havelock Cl BDMR/CCFT WV3 49 J6
Havelock Rd BFLD/HDSWWD B20 89 G3
SPARK B11 126 C1
WASH/WDE B8 90 C8
Haven Ct RUGBYS/DCH CV22 * 186 C2
Haven Cft GTB/HAM B43 70 B5
Havendale Cl COVN CV6 133 M8
Haven Dr ACGN B27 126 F2
The Haven ALE/KHTH/YWD B14 147 H1
BKHL/PFLD WV2 2 F9
STRBR DY8 101 H3
Haverford Dr RBRY B45 143 M7
Havergal Wk HALE B63 120 F1
Haverhill Cl BLOX/PEL WS3 38 E2
Hawbridge Cl SHLY B90 148 F7
Hawbush Rd BLOX/PEL WS3 39 J7
BRLYHL DY5 101 L3
Hawcroft Gv BKDE/SHDE B34 92 A7
Hawes Cl WSL WS1 53 K7
Hawes La BLKHTH/ROWR B65 103 M1
Hawes Rd WSL WS1 53 K7
Haweswater Dr KGSWFD DY6 83 H7
Hawfield Cl OLDBY B69 86 A6
Hawfield Gv CSCFLD/WYGN B72 73 G6
Hawfield Rd OLDBY B69 86 A6
Hawfinch TAM/AM/WIL B77 46 E8
Hawfinch Ri KIDD DY10 164 E3
Hawford Av KIDD DY10 138 E8
Hawk Cl NUN CV11 99 M5
Hawker Dr CVALE B35 91 K3
Hawkesbury Cl REDE B98 195 H8
Hawkesbury La COVE CV2 117 H8
Hawkesbury Rd SHLY B90 147 K4
Hawkes Cl SLYOAK B29 124 E5
Hawkesford Cl CBROM B36 91 L5
FOAKS/STRLY B74 56 F4
Hawkesford Rd STETCH B33 110 B2
Hawkeshead RUGBYN/HIL CV21 161 H6
Hawkes La HHTH/SAND B71 68 E6
Hawkesley Crs NFLD/LBR B31 144 D4
Hawkesley Dr NFLD/LBR B31 144 D5
Hawkesley End
HWK/WKHTH B38 145 H5
Hawkesley Mill La
NFLD/LBR B31 144 D3
Hawkesley Rd DUDN DY1 84 D5
Hawkes Mill La COVW CV5 132 E3
Hawkesmoor Dr LICHS WS14 21 H5
Hawkes St BORD B9 108 B4
Hawkestone Crs WBROM B70 68 D7
Hawkestone Rd SLYOAK B29 123 L6
Hawkeswell Cl HIA/OLT B92 127 J5
Hawkeswell Dr KGSWFD DY6 83 H5
Hawkeswell La
CSHL/WTROR B46 111 M2
Hawkesworth Dr KNWTH CV8 179 L7
Hawkesyard Rd
ERDE/BCHGN B24 90 C4
Hawkhurst Rd
ALE/KHTH/YWD B14 146 D3
Hawkinge Dr CVALE B35 91 L1
Hawkins Cl DIG/EDG B5 107 J7
LICH WS13 20 F3
RUGBYS/DCH CV22 186 C4
Hawkins Cft TPTN/OCK DY4 85 L1
Hawkins Dr CNCK/NC WS11 24 A1
Hawkins Rd COVW CV5 8 A6
Hawkins St WBROM B70 68 E5
Hawkley Cl WOLV WV1 50 F3
Hawkley Rd WOLV WV1 50 F3
Hawkmoor Gdns
HWK/WKHTH B38 145 L5
Hawks Cl GTWY WS6 24 B3
Hawksford Crs WOLVN WV10 36 B6
Hawks Green La CNCK/NC WS11 16 E8
Hawkshead Dr DOR/KN B93 149 K7
Hawkside TAM/AM/WIL B77 46 F5
Hawksmoor Dr
DUNHL/THL/PER WV6 48 B2
Hawkstone Cl KIDDW DY11 138 B4
Hawkstone Ct CDSL WV8 35 K6
Hawkswell Av WMBN WV5 64 E8
Hawkswell Dr WLNHL WV13 51 K5
Hawkswood Dr
DARL/WED WS10 67 M2
RCOVN/BALC/EX CV7 151 M6
Hawkswood Gv
ALE/KHTH/YWD B14 146 F2
Hawksworth TAM/AM/WIL B77 46 D3
Hawksworth Dr COV CV1 8 B3
Hawkyard Ct CNCK/NC WS11 16 E1
Hawlands RUGBYN/HIL CV21 161 H7
Hawley Cl RUSH/SHEL WS4 53 K1
Hawnby Gv WALM/CURD B76 73 L3
Hawne Cl HALE B63 103 J7
The Hawnelands HALE B63 103 K8
Hawne La HALE B63 103 J7
Hawskford Crs WOLVN WV10 36 B6
Hawthorn Av ATHST CV9 61 G8
GTWY WS6 24 E4
Hawthorn Brook Wy
ERDW/GRVHL B23 72 C5
Hawthorn Cl BORD B9 107 M4
ERDW/GRVHL B23 72 D6
LICH WS13 21 H5
Hawthorn Coppice
HAG/WOL DY9 119 L7
Hawthorn Crs BEWD DY12 162 C3
Hawthorn Cft LGLYGN/QTN B68 105 H6
Hawthorne Av CRTAM B79 31 L5
RCOVN/BALC/EX CV7 96 F5
Hawthorne Cl KNWTH CV8 183 L1
Hawthorne Crs BNTWD WS7 18 E7
Hawthorne Dr HLYWD B47 146 F7
Hawthorne Gv SEDG DY3 84 B3
Hawthorne La CDSL WV8 34 D4
Hawthorne Rd BKHL/PFLD WV2 50 D8
BVILLE B30 124 B8
CBROM B36 92 C6
DUDN DY1 85 G1
EDG B15 106 C6
GTWY WS6 24 D3
HALE B63 121 J3
HEDN WS12 12 B5
HEDN WS12 17 K2
SHHTH WV12 38 C5
WNSFLD WV11 37 K8
Hawthorne Ter
NUNW/HART CV10 80 D8
Hawthorne Wy KINVER DY7 118 A2
Hawthorn Gv KIDDW DY11 137 L7
LOZ/NWT B19 * 89 G5
Hawthorn La TLHL/CAN CV4 153 J3
Hawthorn Pk
BFLD/HDSWWD B20 88 C2
Hawthorn Pl WSLW WS2 52 C2
Hawthorn Rd BRGRVW B61 168 E8
BRLYHL DY5 102 C5
CSCFLD/WYGN B72 73 G4
DARL/WED WS10 68 D1
DSYBK/YTR WS5 53 K8
FOAKS/STRLY B74 55 L4
KGSTG B44 71 L6
REDW B97 201 L1
RLSS CV31 206 D7
RUSH/SHEL WS4 39 M5
TPTN/OCK DY4 67 L5
WOLV WV1 50 F5
The Hawthorns KIDD DY10 * 138 E8
MOS/BIL B13 * 125 K2
POL/KGSB/FAZ B78 60 A6
Hawthorn Ter DARL/WED WS10 68 D1
Hawthorn Wy
RUGBYS/DCH CV22 185 M4
Haxby Av BKDE/SHDE B34 91 L7
The Haybarn WALM/CURD B76 73 L4
Haybridge Av STRBR DY8 119 K8
Haybrook Dr SPARK B11 126 D1
Hay Cl KIDDW DY11 138 A6
Haycock Pl DARL/WED WS10 52 A6
Haycroft Av WASH/WDE B8 90 C8
Haycroft Dr MGN/WHC B75 56 E1
Haydn Sanders Sq WSL WS1 4 E6
Haydock Cl CBROM B36 91 G5
COVN CV6 134 F1
DUNHL/THL/PER WV6 35 M8
TAM/AM/WIL B77 60 B1
Haydock Rd BRGRVW B61 168 F4
Haydon Cl DOR/KN B93 175 K3
Haydon Cft STETCH B33 109 L2
Haye House Gv CBROM B36 91 J6
Haye La STUD B80 203 L4
Hayes Cl RUGBYN/HIL CV21 161 H6
Hayes Crs LGLYGN/QTN B68 87 H8
Hayes Cft HWK/WKHTH B38 145 J6
WOLVN WV10 36 F3
Hayes Green Rd
RCOVN/BALC/EX CV7 116 D4
Hayes Gv ERDE/BCHGN B24 73 H7
Hayes La HAG/WOL DY9 102 E7
RCOVN/BALC/EX CV7 116 D5
Hayes Meadow
WALM/CURD B76 73 H6
Hayes Rd KIDDW DY11 137 M2
LGLYGN/QTN B68 87 H8
NUNW/HART CV10 79 L5
Hayes St WBROM B70 86 E1
The Hayes HAG/WOL DY9 102 E8
NFLD/LBR B31 145 G6
SHHTH WV12 37 M7
Hayes Vw LICH WS13 20 D4
Hayes View Dr GTWY WS6 24 C1
Hayes Wy CNCK/NC WS11 16 E4
HEDN WS12 17 G4
Hayfield Ct MOS/BIL B13 125 M3
Hayfield Hl RUGE WS15 18 D1
Hayfield Rd MOS/BIL B13 125 M3
Hayford Cl REDE B98 194 E8
Hay Gn HAG/WOL DY9 102 B8
Hay Green La BVILLE B30 124 A7
Hay Hall Rd SPARK B11 108 D8
Hay Hl DSYBK/YTR WS5 54 C5
Hayland Rd ERDW/GRVHL B23 72 C7
Hay La COV CV1 9 G5
SHLY B90 148 E7
Hayle TAM/AM/WIL B77 46 B3
Hayle Av WWCK CV34 205 K4
Hayle Cl HWK/WKHTH B38 145 M3
NUN CV11 81 L8
Hayley Green Rd
RIDG/WDGT B32 122 F5
Hayley Park Rd HALE B63 121 G5
Hayling Cl RBRY B45 143 K4
Hayling Gv BKHL/PFLD WV2 49 M7
Hayloft Cl BRGRVE B60 191 J7
The Haylofts HALE B63 121 G4
Haymoor LICHS WS14 21 J6
Haynes Cl BRGRVW B61 168 F5
Haynes La DSYBK/YTR WS5 69 M1
Haynestone Rd COVN CV6 133 J7
Haynes Wy RUGBYN/HIL CV21 160 D5
Hay Pk DIG/EDG B5 107 H7
Haypits Cl HHTH/SAND B71 69 J6
Hayrick Dr KGSWFD DY6 82 F6
Hay Rd YDLY B25 108 E6
Hayseech CDYHTH B64 103 L6
Hayseech Rd HALE B63 103 K7
The Hays Kent's Moat
LGN/SDN/BHAMAIR B26 109 L4
Hayton Gn TLHL/CAN CV4 153 K6
Haytor Av ALE/KHTH/YWD B14 125 H8
Haytor Ri COVE CV2 135 G6
Haywain Cl COVEN WV9 * 35 K3
Hayward Cl RWWCK/WEL CV35 204 D7
Hayward Rd MGN/WHC B75 57 G6
Haywards Cl BLOX/PEL WS3 39 K2
ERDW/GRVHL B23 72 C8
Hayward St BILS/COS WV14 66 F5
Haywharf Rd BRLYHL DY5 83 M8
Haywood Dr
DUNHL/THL/PER WV6 49 G1
RMSLY B62 104 A5
Haywood Rd STETCH B33 110 B3
Haywood's Farm
HHTH/SAND B71 69 K3
Hayworth Cl CRTAM B79 31 K5
Hayworth Rd LICH WS13 21 G3
Hazel Av DARL/WED WS10 68 E1
SCFLD/BOLD B73 72 A4
Hazelbank HWK/WKHTH B38 145 J3
Hazelbeach Rd WASH/WDE B8 90 D8
Hazelbeech Rd WBROM B70 86 F3
Hazel Cl NUNW/HART CV10 79 L6
RLSN CV32 206 E3
Hazel Cft
CHWD/FDBR/MGN B37 110 F4
NFLD/LBR B31 144 E2
Hazelcroft POL/KGSB/FAZ B78 60 A6
Hazeldene STRPT DY13 189 G2
Hazeldene Gv AST/WIT B6 * 89 J5
Hazeldene Rd HALE B63 121 J3
STETCH B33 110 B6
Hazel Dr HEDN WS12 13 L7
HLYWD B47 146 F7
Hazeley Cl HRBN B17 105 K6
Hazel Gdns ACGN B27 * 127 G1
CDSL WV8 34 E1
Hazelgarth TAM/AM/WIL B77 46 E5
Hazel Gv BDWTH CV12 117 H2
BILS/COS WV14 51 J6
HOCK/TIA B94 175 G7
LICHS WS14 21 G6
STRBR DY8 119 G2
WBROM B70 87 G4
WMBN WV5 64 E6
Hazelhurst Rd
ALE/KHTH/YWD B14 125 J6
CBROM B36 92 C6
Hazel La GTWY WS6 24 F3
Hazell Wy NUNW/HART CV10 98 E4
Hazelmere Dr BDMR/CCFT WV3 48 E4
BNTWD WS7 26 D1
Hazelmere Rd HLGN/YWD B28 126 D5
Hazeloak Rd SHLY B90 147 L4
Hazel Rd BDMR/CCFT WV3 49 J6
COVN CV6 134 F4
DUDN DY1 85 G3
KGSWFD DY6 83 J8
NUNW/HART CV10 80 B8
RBRY B45 143 K7
REDW B97 194 A8
TPTN/OCK DY4 68 A4
Hazelton Cl BRGRVE B60 169 G5
SOLH B91 148 F4
Hazelton Rd BRGRVE B60 168 F5
Hazeltree Cft ACGN B27 126 F3
Hazeltree Gv DOR/KN B93 175 J2

A/OLT B92 129 L7
RBN B17 106 A8
SWFD DY6 82 F5
SWFD DY6 83 H7
DD DY10 138 C7
WTH CV8 179 J8
WTH CV8 182 F4
Z/NWT B19 89 J6
N CV11 98 F1
L/KGSB/FAZ B78 47 M3
DG/WDGT B32 104 E7
SN CV32 199 J8
SS CV31 206 D6
GBYN/HIL CV21 187 L5
FLD/BOLD B73 57 G7
DG DY3 66 B4
DG DY3 82 C3
LY B90 147 G3
THWK B66 87 L8
LH B91 149 G1
RBR DY8 101 J3
RBR DY8 101 K6
RBR DY8 101 L8
RPT DY13 188 E2
M/AM/WIL B77 60 A1
TN/OCK DY4 67 J8
TN/OCK DY4 67 K5
ASH/WDE B8 90 B8
BROM B70 87 G1
BROM B70 87 J3
MBN WV5 64 F7
NSFLD WV11 37 G8
SL WS1 4 F4
WCK CV34 205 J7
St Bordesley BORD B9 7 L7
St Deritend DIG/EDG B5 7 K7
ters Cl ALE/KHTH/YWD B14 146 F3
ter's Heath La
E/KHTH/YWD B14 146 E4
ters Rd
E/KHTH/YWD B14 146 E2
Timbers RBRY B45 143 K4
Tower VAUX/NECH B7 * 89 M8
tree Cl RIDG/WDGT B32 122 F4
Trees BFLD/HDSWWD B20 88 D2
Trees Cl REDE B98 202 C6
Trees Rd DOR/KN B93 149 L6
Vw ATHST CV9 77 G1
LS/COS WV14 66 D4
view Dr KGSWFD DY6 101 K1
View Dr
COVN/BALC/EX CV7 116 A6
View Rd RLSN CV32 199 G8
view St DUDS DY2 85 J4
waymans Cft
HL/CAN CV4 154 B8
wood Av HIA/OLT B92 127 L4
Wood Cl KGSWFD DY6 83 G7
wood Cft
WK/WKHTH B38 145 H4
r Gv CHWD/FDBR/MGN B37 111 H3
y Bevins Cl
KTBOS/BARL/STKG CV13 81 K1
y Crs DUDN DY1 66 F7
y Dr ALDR WS9 40 E8
DMR/CCFT WV3 49 H6
ALM/CURD B76 73 L2
y Gv NFLD/LBR B31 144 D1
y Rd NUNW/HART CV10 80 C8
HL/CAN CV4 154 B7
en Rd VAUX/NECH B7 7 M2
eric Crs DUDN DY1 84 D6
erstone Rd YDLY B25 109 G7
cks Crs BLOX/PEL WS3 39 K6
cks Pl BLOX/PEL WS3 39 K6
ire Cl HWK/WKHTH B38 146 A4
ries Rd ERDW/GRVHL B23 90 B3
ry Av DARL/WED WS10 69 G2
ry Crest SEDG DY3 * 66 C8
ry Rd RUGBYS/DCH CV22 186 C5
RPT DY13 164 B6
ry St WSLW WS2 4 A9
Av ETTPK/GDPK/PENN WV4 66 D2
Bank HAG/WOL DY9 120 D1
ank OLDBY B69 86 B5
Bank Dr STETCH B33 109 H1
Bank Rd HALE B63 103 H6
WK/WKHTH B38 145 L3
orough Rd HIA/OLT B92 127 H3
rook Gv STETCH B33 109 K2
ury Dr SHHTH WV12 37 M5
Cl NFLD/LBR B31 144 F4
LSN CV32 206 E2
DG DY3 66 C4
Crs RRUGBY CV23 183 K7
Crest RLSN CV32 199 J8
DG DY3 83 M1
Crest Av BRLYHL DY5 102 A4
rest Av GTB/HAM B43 70 C3
ALE B63 102 F6
OLVN WV10 36 C5
rest Cl CRTAM B79 31 M7
UDS DY2 85 G8
Crest Dr LICH WS13 20 E4
rest Gdns SHHTH WV12 38 B8
Crest Gv KGSTG B44 71 L6
rest Ri BNTWD WS7 26 F1
Crest Rd DUDS DY2 85 J4
OS/BIL B13 125 J3
rest Rd CSCFLD/WYGN B72 73 G5
TB/HAM B43 70 C3
UNW/HART CV10 80 B8
OL/KGSB/FAZ B78 47 K6
MSLY B62 142 D1
Croft Rd
E/KHTH/YWD B14 125 G7
roft Rd KGSWFD DY6 83 J6
ross Wk CBROM B36 91 K6
lene Rd KGSWFD DY6 101 G1
itch La KIDDW DY11 189 J3
Dr CNCK/NC WS11 16 E2
rop Gv HRBN B17 124 B2
ys Cft
HWD/FDBR/MGN B37 110 D2
Farm Av NUN CV11 99 M4
eld Ms SOLH B91 148 F5
eld Rd RUGBYS/DCH CV22 186 A4
OLH B91 148 F5
PARK B11 126 B2
elds SMTHWKW B67 105 H2
elds Rd BRLYHL DY5 101 M6
Fray Dr COVS CV3 155 L8
Gv BFLD/HDSWWD B20 * 89 G3
Grove Crs KIDD DY10 138 E8
rove Gdns KIDD DY10 164 E1
Hook Rd FOAKS/STRLY B74 42 C7
House La STETCH B33 109 K2
urst Gv CBROM B36 92 B4
ard Cl BDWTH CV12 116 E1
ards Cft PBAR/PBCH B42 70 E5
ngford Av GTB/HAM B43 71 H1
La BNTWD WS7 18 C4
RGRVE B60 191 K4
RGRVE B60 200 C7
/HAM B43 70 C3
/WOL DY9 141 J1
D B47 172 C4
/WHC B75 57 M3
an TAM/AM/WIL B77 46 C3

Hillman Dr DUDS DY2 85 J6
Hillman Gv CBROM B36 92 C4
Hillmeads Dr DUDS DY2 85 J6
Hillmeads Rd HWK/WKHTH B38 145 L4
Hillmorton Cl REDE B98 195 J7
Hillmorton La RRUGBY CV23 187 L3
Hillmorton Rd COVE CV2 135 G3
DOR/KN B93 149 L8
FOAKS/STRLY B74 56 D1
RUGBYN/HIL CV21 187 H3
Hillmount Cl HLGN/YWD B28 126 C3
Hill Pk ALDR WS9 40 E1
Hill Pas CDYHTH B64 103 J3
Hill Pl WNSFLD WV11 37 L4
Hill Rise Vw BRGRVE B60 169 G7
Hill Rd HAG/WOL DY9 102 C8
OLDBY B69 85 L3
RCOVN/BALC/EX CV7 115 K7
WLNHL WV13 51 H4
Hill Side COVE CV2 134 E7
POL/KGSB/FAZ B78 76 B1
SEDG DY3 84 A1
Hillside BRWNH WS8 26 E7
LICHS WS14 21 H8
NUNW/HART CV10 79 L5
REDE B98 202 B3
WMBN WV5 64 C6
Hillside Av BLKHTH/ROWR B65 103 M5
BRLYHL DY5 102 E5
HALE B63 103 H7
Hillside Cl BNTWD WS7 18 C8
HEDN WS12 12 E6
KIDDW DY11 137 L6
RIDG/WDGT B32 122 E5
STRPT DY13 188 C5
Hillside Crs BLOX/PEL WS3 39 K3
Hillside Cft HIA/OLT B92 128 C1
Hillside Dr BRGRVE B60 168 F7
CHWD/FDBR/MGN B37 110 D1
FOAKS/STRLY B74 55 K6
KIDDW DY11 137 L6
NUNW/HART CV10 80 A6
PBAR/PBCH B42 70 E7
Hillside Gdns
CHWD/FDBR/MGN B37 * 110 D1
WOLV WV1 50 E2
Hillside Gv KIDD DY10 139 G2
Hillside Rd DUDN DY1 84 E1
ERDW/GRVHL B23 90 B3
FOAKS/STRLY B74 56 D1
GTB/HAM B43 70 B3
Hillstone Gdns WOLVN WV10 36 D5
Hillstone Rd BKDE/SHDE B34 92 B8
Hill St BDWTH CV12 98 F8
BILS/COS WV14 67 J2
BNTWD WS7 18 C8
BRLYHL DY5 102 B3
BRLYHL DY5 102 E5
CBHAM B2 6 E5
CNCK/NC WS11 17 K7
COV CV1 8 D4
DARL/WED WS10 52 C7
DUDS DY2 84 F8
GTWY WS6 24 A3
HAG/WOL DY9 102 D8
HALE B63 121 L2
HEDN WS12 17 G2
KIDDW DY11 138 B7
NUNW/HART CV10 98 B1
RLSN CV32 206 E4
RUGBYN/HIL CV21 186 E1
SEDG DY3 66 C8
SMTHWK B66 87 L7
STRBR DY8 101 K5
STRBR DY8 119 K1
TPTN/OCK DY4 85 K1
WNSFLD WV11 37 K2
WSL WS1 5 G5
WWCK CV34 205 M5
The Hill RIDG/WDGT B32 123 H3
Hill Top ATHST CV9 61 M3
COV CV1 9 G4
HHTH/SAND B71 68 E6
REDW B97 201 K4
Hilltop HAG/WOL DY9 120 C2
Hilltop Av BEWD DY12 163 H1
Hill Top Av CRTAM B79 31 M5
RMSLY B62 104 C6
Hill Top Cl KGSTG B44 71 J7
Hilltop Cl KNWTH CV8 177 J5
Hilltop Dr CBROM B36 91 H6
Hilltop Rd DUDS DY2 85 J5
Hill Top Rd LGLYGN/QTN B68 105 G3
NFLD/LBR B31 144 D2
Hill Top Wk ALDR WS9 41 G4
Hill Vw ALDR WS9 40 F3
Hillview Cl BRGRVE B60 169 G7
HALE B63 103 J7
Hillview Rd BRGRVE B60 169 G7
RBRY B45 143 J5
Hill Village Rd MGN/WHC B75 56 E1
Hillville Gdns STRBR DY8 119 M2
Hill Wd BLOX/PEL WS3 39 K3
Hillwood Av SHLY B90 148 E7
Hillwood Cl STRBR DY8 101 G1
Hillwood Common Rd
MGN/WHC B75 42 F8
Hill Wood Rd MGN/WHC B75 43 G8
Hillwood Rd NFLD/LBR B31 123 J6
RMSLY B62 104 A6
Hill Wootton Rd
RWWCK/WEL CV35 197 L7
Hillyfields Rd ERDW/GRVHL B23 90 A1
Hilly Rd BILS/COS WV14 67 J3
Hilmore Wy TAM/AM/WIL B77 46 C5
Hilsea Cl COVEN WV9 35 K4
Hilston Av
ETTPK/GDPK/PENN WV4 65 G1
HALE B63 121 K1
Hilton Av HLGN/YWD B28 147 J1
NUNW/HART CV10 79 M7
Hilton Cl BLOX/PEL WS3 38 D4
Hilton Ct COVW CV5 * 154 D3
Hilton Cross WOLVN WV10 22 F8
Hilton Dr CSCFLD/WYGN B72 73 G5
Hilton La GTWY WS6 24 E3
WOLVN WV10 23 H5
Hilton Pl BILS/COS WV14 51 J8
Hilton Rd BNTWD WS7 18 A5
ETTPK/GDPK/PENN WV4 66 D1
OLDBY B69 86 A5
SHHTH WV12 38 A5
WOLVN WV10 22 F6
Hilton St WBROM B70 86 E2
WOLVN WV10 3 J2
Himbleton Cl REDE B98 202 D4
Himbleton Cft SHLY B90 148 E7
Himley Av DUDN DY1 84 D3
Himley Cl GTB/HAM B43 70 A3
SHHTH WV12 37 L8
Himley Crs
ETTPK/GDPK/PENN WV4 50 A8
Himley Gdns SEDG DY3 83 K1
Himley Gv RBRY B45 143 M7
Himley La SEDG DY3 82 D3
Himley Rd BDWTH CV12 116 B3
DUDN DY1 84 C4
SEDG DY3 83 J2
Himley St DUDN DY1 84 E4

Hinbrook Rd DUDN DY1 84 C4
Hinchliffe Av BILS/COS WV14 66 F3
Hinckes Rd
DUNHL/THL/PER WV6 34 F8
Hinckley Ct LGLYGN/QTN B68 * 104 F6
Hinckley La
MKTBOS/BARL/STKG CV13 81 M2
Hinckley Rd NUN CV11 81 J8
RCOVN/BALC/EX CV7 135 M5
Hinckley St DIG/EDG B5 6 F7
Hincks St BKHL/PFLD WV2 50 E6
Hind Cl WWCK CV34 205 K3
Hinde Cl RUGBYN/HIL CV21 161 G6
Hindhead Rd
ALE/KHTH/YWD B14 147 G1
Hindlip Cl HALE B63 121 K3
REDE B98 203 L1
Hindlow Cl VAUX/NECH B7 107 M1
Hindon Gv ACGN B27 126 F6
Hindon Sq EDG B15 106 D5
Hingeston St WSNGN B18 6 A1
Hingley Cft FOAKS/STRLY B74 55 K2
Hingley Rd HALE B63 102 E7
Hingley St CDYHTH B64 103 H4
Hinksford Gdns SEDG DY3 82 C3
Hinksford La SEDG DY3 82 C4
Hinsford Cl KGSWFD DY6 83 J5
Hinstock Cl
ETTPK/GDPK/PENN WV4 65 L1
Hinstock Rd BFLD/HDSWWD B20 88 D4
Hintlesham Av EDG B15 106 B8
Hinton Av ALVE B48 170 E7
Hinton Flds BRGRVW B61 168 C6
Hinton Gv WNSFLD WV11 37 K8
Hintons Coppice DOR/KN B93 149 J7
Hints Ct POL/KGSB/FAZ B78 44 B3
Hints La POL/KGSB/FAZ B78 44 D2
Hints Rd POL/KGSB/FAZ B78 44 F3
Hipkins St TPTN/OCK DY4 67 J6
Hiplands Rd RMSLY B62 122 C1
Hipsley Cl CBROM B36 92 A4
Hipsley La ATHST CV9 61 J8
Hipsmoor Cl
CHWD/FDBR/MGN B37 110 D2
Hipswell Hwy COVE CV2 156 B1
Hirdemonsay SHLY B90 147 K8
Hiron Cft COVS CV3 155 G5
The Hiron COVS CV3 155 G5
Hirst Cl RRUGBY CV23 159 L8
Histons Dr CDSL WV8 34 D3
Histons Hl CDSL WV8 34 D3
Hitchcock Cl SMTHWKW B67 87 H8
Hitches La EDG B15 106 F6
Hitchman Ms RLSS CV31 206 E8
Hitchman Rd RLSS CV31 206 E7
Hither Green La REDE B98 194 D6
Hitherside SHLY B90 147 M7
Hoarestone Av NUN CV11 99 L6
Hoarstone STRBR DY8 119 K8
Hoarstone Cl BEWD DY12 137 G8
Hoarstone La BEWD DY12 137 G7
Hobacre Cl RBRY B45 143 L5
Hobart Cft VAUX/NECH B7 89 L8
Hobart Dr DSYBK/YTR WS5 54 A7
Hobart Rd HEDN WS12 17 J3
TPTN/OCK DY4 67 J4
Hobble End La GTWY WS6 24 E7
Hobgate Rd WOLVN WV10 3 L1
Hob Green Rd HAG/WOL DY9 120 C3
Hobhouse Cl GTB/HAM B43 70 D6
Hob La HIA/OLT B92 150 E5
RCOVN/BALC/EX CV7 152 C8
Hobley Cl RUGBYS/DCH CV22 186 B6
Hobley St WLNHL WV13 52 A3
Hobmoor Cft YDLY B25 109 H6
Hob Moor Rd
LGN/SDN/BHAMAIR B26 109 H6
SMHTH B10 108 E4
Hobnock Rd WNSFLD WV11 37 L1
Hobs Hole La ALDR WS9 41 H6
Hob's Meadow HIA/OLT B92 127 L3
Hob's Moat Rd HIA/OLT B92 127 M3
Hobson Cl WSNGN B18 88 E8
Hobson Rd SLYOAK B29 124 F4
Hobs Rd DARL/WED WS10 68 E1
LICH WS13 21 J4
Hobstone Hill La BNTWD WS7 19 J4
Hockett St COVS CV3 9 H9
Hocking Rd COVE CV2 156 C1
Hockley Brook Cl WSNGN B18 88 E8
Hockley Brook La
HAG/WOL DY9 167 J1
Hockley Cl LOZ/NWT B19 89 H7
Hockley Hl WSNGN B18 88 F7
Hockley La COVW CV5 132 A8
DUDS DY2 102 F2
Hockley Pool Cl WSNGN B18 88 F8
Hockley Rd BILS/COS WV14 66 E6
ERDW/GRVHL B23 90 B1
TAM/AM/WIL B77 46 D6
Hockley St LOZ/NWT B19 89 G8
WSNGN B18 6 C1
Hodge Hill Av HAG/WOL DY9 120 D2
Hodge Hill Rd BKDE/SHDE B34 91 J8
Hodge La TAM/AM/WIL B77 32 F7
Hodgetts Cl SMTHWKW B67 105 H2
Hodgetts Dr HALE B63 121 G5
Hodgett's La
RCOVN/BALC/EX CV7 152 D5
Hodgkins Cl BRWNH WS8 26 E7
Hodnell Cl CBROM B36 92 A4
Hodnet Cl BILS/COS WV14 50 F8
KNWTH CV8 179 M8
Hodnet Dr BRLYHL DY5 84 A7
Hodnet Gv DIG/EDG B5 7 G9
Hodnet Pl CNCK/NC WS11 16 F3
Hodson Av WLNHL WV13 52 A4
Hodson Cl WNSFLD WV11 37 K5
Hoff Beck Court Ct BORD B9 * 107 M3
Hogarth Cl BDWTH CV12 116 E1
GTB/HAM B43 55 H8
WLNHL WV13 51 J3
Hoggs La NFLD/LBR B31 144 C1
Hogrills End La
CSHL/WTROR B46 94 E1
Holbeache La KGSWFD DY6 83 H4
Holbeache Rd KGSWFD DY6 83 G5
KINVER DY7 100 E1
Holbeach Rd STETCH B33 109 M3
Holbeche Crs
RCOVN/BALC/EX CV7 114 C2
Holbeche Rd DOR/KN B93 149 L6
MGN/WHC B75 73 M1
Holbein Cl BDWTH CV12 116 E1
Holberg Gv WNSFLD WV11 37 K7
Holborn Av COVN CV6 134 A3
Holborn Hl VAUX/NECH B7 89 M5
Holbrook Av RUGBYN/HIL CV21 186 E1
Holbrook La COVN CV6 134 A3
Holbrook Rd RRUGBY CV23 159 M8
Holbrook Wy COVN CV6 134 B4
Holbury Cl COVEN WV9 35 L3
Holcombe Rd SPARK B11 126 E2
Holcot Leys RUGBYS/DCH CV22 186 E6
Holcroft Rd HAG/WOL DY9 120 A1
HALE B63 103 G8
KGSWFD DY6 83 G4
Holcroft St BKHL/PFLD WV2 50 E6
TPTN/OCK DY4 85 L3

Holden Cl ERDW/GRVHL B23 90 C3
Holden Crs BLOX/PEL WS3 39 J8
Holden Cft TPTN/OCK DY4 85 L2
Holden Pl BLOX/PEL WS3 53 J1
Holden Rd DARL/WED WS10 68 E3
ETTPK/GDPK/PENN WV4 65 H2
Holder Dr CNCK/NC WS11 15 M3
Holder Rd SPARK B11 108 A7
YDLY B25 109 G6
Holders Gdns MOS/BIL B13 125 G3
Holders La MOS/BIL B13 125 G3
Holdford Rd AST/WIT B6 89 K3
Holdgate Rd SLYOAK B29 123 M6
Hole Farm Rd NFLD/LBR B31 124 A8
Hole Farm Wy
HWK/WKHTH B38 145 K6
Hole La NFLD/LBR B31 124 A7
Holford Av WSLW WS2 53 G7
Holford Dr PBAR/PBCH B42 89 J1
Holford Wy AST/WIT B6 89 L2
Holifast Rd CSCFLD/WYGN B72 73 G6
Holioak Dr WWCK CV34 205 L7
Holland Av DOR/KN B93 149 M5
LGLYGN/QTN B68 105 G1
Holland Cl LICH WS13 21 L4
Holland Cft WALM/CURD B76 75 M3
Holland Rd BILS/COS WV14 51 J6
COVN CV6 133 L7
CSCFLD/WYGN B72 72 F2
GTB/HAM B43 70 B6
Holland Rd West AST/WIT B6 89 K7
Hollands Pl BLOX/PEL WS3 39 H4
Hollands Rd BLOX/PEL WS3 39 H4
Holland St CBHAMNW B3 6 C4
CSCFLD/WYGN B72 72 F1
DUDN DY1 84 F5
TPTN/OCK DY4 68 A6
Hollemeadow Av BLOX/PEL WS3 39 H6
Holliars Gv
CHWD/FDBR/MGN B37 92 D8
Hollick Crs RCOVN/BALC/EX CV7 96 E5
Hollicombe Ter COVE CV2 135 H5
Holliday Rd ERDE/BCHGN B24 90 E1
HDSW B21 88 D6
Holliday St CBHAMW B1 6 D6
Hollie Lucas Rd MOS/BIL B13 125 K6
Hollies Av CNCK/NC WS11 16 D4
Hollies Cft DIG/EDG B5 107 G8
Hollies Dr DARL/WED WS10 68 D2
RMSLY B62 * 104 C7
Hollies La KIDDW DY11 137 K2
Hollies Park Rd CNCK/NC WS11 16 D4
Hollies Ri CDYHTH B64 103 K5
Hollies Rd OLDBY B69 85 L5
POL/KGSB/FAZ B78 47 M5
Hollies St BRLYHL DY5 84 B6
The Hollies AST/WIT B6 89 M5
BKHL/PFLD WV2 2 E8
RBRY B45 169 L4
RRUGBY CV23 161 K4
SMTHWK B66 * 106 A1
STRPT DY13 163 J7
Hollin Brow Cl DOR/KN B93 175 M2
Hollingberry La
WALM/CURD B76 73 K2
Hollings Gv SOLH B91 148 F5
Hollington Rd WOLV WV1 50 F5
Hollington Wy SOLH B91 149 G6
Hollinwell Cl BLOX/PEL WS3 38 E2
Hollis La KNWTH CV8 179 J5
Hollis Rd COVS CV3 155 L3
Hollister Dr RIDG/WDGT B32 123 K2
Holloway CRTAM B79 45 M1
NFLD/LBR B31 123 J7
Holloway Bank DARL/WED WS10 68 D5
Holloway Circus Queensway
CBHAMW B1 6 F7
Holloway Dr REDE B98 202 D3
WMBN WV5 64 C8
Holloway Fld COVN CV6 133 L7
Holloway Head EDG B15 6 E8
Holloway La REDE B98 202 D2
Holloway Pk REDE B98 202 E2
Holloway St SEDG DY3 84 B1
WOLV WV1 50 E6
Holloway St West SEDG DY3 66 B8
The Holloway ALVE B48 194 A2
DUNHL/THL/PER WV6 48 F3
KIDD DY10 166 C3
SEDG DY3 82 B4
STRBR DY8 101 K6
WWCK CV34 205 H7
Hollow Crs COVN CV6 133 M8
Hollow Cft NFLD/LBR B31 144 F2
Hollow Croft Rd SHHTH WV12 37 M6
Hollowell Wy RUGBYN/HIL CV21 161 G6
The Hollow MOS/BIL B13 125 J1
Hollowtree La BRGRVE B60 192 E2
Holly Av BHTH/HG B12 107 L8
SLYOAK B29 124 F4
Holly Bank COVW CV5 * 8 A9
Hollybank Av WNSFLD WV11 37 L2
Hollybank Cl BLOX/PEL WS3 38 E4
Hollybank Gv HALE B63 121 H4
Hollybank Rd MOS/BIL B13 125 L7
Hollyberry Av SOLH B91 148 E5
Hollyberry Cl REDE B98 203 L1
Hollyberry Cft BKDE/SHDE B34 92 A7
Hollybrow SLYOAK B29 123 L6
Holly Bush Gv RIDG/WDGT B32 105 H6
Hollybush La CDSL WV8 34 B3
COVN CV6 134 E1
ETTPK/GDPK/PENN WV4 65 H1
STRBR DY8 101 K6
Holly Cl CRTAM B79 31 M6
SHHTH WV12 38 A7
WALM/CURD B76 73 K3
Hollycot Gdns BHTH/HG B12 107 K7
Hollycroft Rd HDSW B21 88 B4
Hollydale Rd
BLKHTH/ROWR B65 104 B2
ERDE/BCHGN B24 91 G2
Holly Dell HWK/WKHTH B38 145 M3
Holly Dr ACGN B27 126 F3
ATHST CV9 77 H1
HLYWD B47 146 F6
KNWTH CV8 182 F4
Hollyfaste Rd STETCH B33 109 M4
Hollyfast La
RCOVN/BALC/EX CV7 133 G1
Hollyfast Rd COVN CV6 133 J6
Hollyfield Av SOLH B91 148 C2
Hollyfield Ct MGN/WHC B75 57 J8
Hollyfield Crs MGN/WHC B75 73 J1
Hollyfield Dr MGN/WHC B75 57 J8
RBRY B45 169 L4
Hollyfield Rd MGN/WHC B75 57 J8
Holly Gv BDMR/CCFT WV3 49 K6
BRGRVW B61 191 K2
BVILLE B30 124 D5
LOZ/NWT B19 88 F5
RRUGBY CV23 158 F8
STRBR DY8 101 K8
TLHL/CAN CV4 154 A3
Holly Grove La BNTWD WS7 18 C4
Holly Hall Rd DUDS DY2 84 E7
Hollyhedge Cl NFLD/LBR B31 123 H7
WSLW WS2 4 B2
Hollyhedge La WSLW WS2 4 B1

Hollyhedge Rd HHTH/SAND B71 69 J6
Hollyhill La LICHS WS14 42 C1
Holly Hill Rd LICHS WS14 28 D8
RBRY B45 143 L3
Hollyhock Rd ACGN B27 126 D4
DUDS DY2 85 K4
Hollyhurst BDWTH CV12 116 D4
CSHL/WTROR B46 93 G3
Hollyhurst Dr STRBR DY8 101 J2
Hollyhurst Gv
LGN/SDN/BHAMAIR B26 109 J7
SHLY B90 147 M5
Hollyhurst Rd SCFLD/BOLD B73 71 M2
Hollyland CSHL/WTROR B46 94 D4
Holly La ALDR WS9 40 E1
ALDR WS9 41 K5
ALVE B48 172 D8
ATHST CV9 63 G4
CHWD/FDBR/MGN B37 110 D5
ERDE/BCHGN B24 72 E8
ERDE/BCHGN B24 91 G2
GTWY WS6 24 D5
HEDN WS12 12 A6
KNWTH CV8 177 M3
MGN/WHC B75 56 E2
SMTHWK B66 87 J6
WALM/CURD B76 74 B1
Hollymoor Wy NFLD/LBR B31 143 M4
Hollymount RMSLY B62 104 E6
Hollyoak Cft NFLD/LBR B31 144 F5
Hollyoake LGLYGN/QTN B68 104 E3
Hollyoake Cl LGLYGN/QTN B68 104 E2
Hollyoak Gv SOLH B91 148 E4
Hollyoak Rd FOAKS/STRLY B74 55 K7
Hollyoak St HHTH/SAND B71 87 H1
Hollyoak Wy CNCK/NC WS11 16 D4
Holly Park Dr ERDE/BCHGN B24 90 F2
Holly Pl AST/WIT B6 * 89 J5
SLYOAK B29 * 124 F3
Holly Rd BLKHTH/ROWR B65 103 M4
BRGRVW B61 191 K1
BVILLE B30 145 L1
DARL/WED WS10 52 D8
DUDN DY1 84 E2
HDSW B21 88 D5
HHTH/SAND B71 69 J5
LDYWD/EDGR B16 106 A4
LGLYGN/QTN B68 105 G5
STRPT DY13 188 F1
Holly Stitches Rd
NUNW/HART CV10 80 C7
Holly St CNCK/NC WS11 12 D7
DUDN DY1 84 C6
RLSN CV32 206 E4
SMTHWKW B67 87 K8
Holly Wk KNWTH CV8 181 J3
NUN CV11 99 K3
RLSN CV32 206 E5
Hollywell Rd DOR/KN B93 149 L8
LGN/SDN/BHAMAIR B26 109 M7
Hollywell St BILS/COS WV14 66 E4
Holly Wd GTB/HAM B43 70 E4
Hollywood By-Pass HLYWD B47 146 C8
Hollywood Cft PBAR/PBCH B42 70 D5
Hollywood Gdns HLYWD B47 146 E5
Hollywood La HLYWD B47 146 E5
Holman Cl WLNHL WV13 51 J3
Holman Rd WLNHL WV13 51 H3
Holman St KIDDW DY11 138 A8
Holman Wy NUN CV11 99 H2
Holmbridge Gv RUSH/SHEL WS4 40 B3
Holmcroft COVE CV2 135 K5
Holmcroft Gdns COVEN WV9 22 A3
Holmcroft Rd KIDD DY10 138 E7
Holme Cl RUGBYN/HIL CV21 161 G7
Holme Ml WOLVN WV10 36 B1
Holme Ri PENK ST19 10 E4
Holmes Dr COVW CV5 132 B8
RBRY B45 143 K7
Holmesfield Rd PBAR/PBCH B42 71 G6
Holmes Rd SHHTH WV12 38 B6
The Holmes WOLVN WV10 36 B2
Holme Wy RUSH/SHEL WS4 39 M6
Holmewood Cl KNWTH CV8 179 M8
Holmfield Rd COVE CV2 155 M3
Holmsdale Rd COVN CV6 134 C6
Holm View Cl LICHS WS14 28 D7
Holmwood Av KIDDW DY11 137 L7
Holmwood Dr REDW B97 202 A2
Holmwood Rd BORD B9 108 B4
Holston Cl HEDN WS12 17 K4
Holsworth Cl TAM/AM/WIL B77 46 B4
Holsworthy Cl NUN CV11 81 J8
Holt Ct North VAUX/NECH B7 * 7 K2
Holt Ct South VAUX/NECH B7 * 7 K2
Holt Crs CNCK/NC WS11 16 F3
Holte Dr MGN/WHC B75 57 H3
Holte Rd AST/WIT B6 89 L4
ATHST CV9 63 H4
SPARK B11 108 B8
Holtes Wk AST/WIT B6 * 89 M5
Holt Hl REDE B98 195 K5
Holt La RMSLY B62 142 B1
Holt Rd RMSLY B62 104 C4
Holtshill La WSL WS1 5 H3
Holt St VAUX/NECH B7 7 J1
The Holt RLSN CV32 206 F1
Holt Vls WALM/CURD B76 * 74 F6
Holwick TAM/AM/WIL B77 46 F5
Holy Cross Gn HAG/WOL DY9 141 J3
Holy Cross La HAG/WOL DY9 141 J5
Holyhead Chambers COV CV1 * 8 D4
Holyhead Rd CDSL WV8 34 B5
COVW CV5 8 B3
Holyhead Rd COVW CV5 133 H8
Holyhead Rd COVW CV5 133 J8
DARL/WED WS10 68 A1
DARL/WED WS10 68 C2
HDSW B21 88 A5
Holyhead Wy HDSW B21 88 B5
Holyoak Cl AST/WIT B6 89 K4
BDWTH CV12 116 D4
RUGBYS/DCH CV22 186 A5
Holyoakes La REDW B97 193 G7
Holy Oaks Cl REDE B98 203 J3
Holyrood Gv AST/WIT B6 * 89 J5
Holy Well Cl LDYWD/EDGR B16 106 E3
Holywell Cl TLHL/CAN CV4 153 H4
Holywell La RBRY B45 143 H7
Holywell Ri LICHS WS14 21 H7
Home Cl KNWTH CV8 182 A7
Homecroft Rd YDLY B25 109 J5
Homedene Rd NFLD/LBR B31 123 J6
Home Farm RWWCK/WEL CV35 197 K7
Home Farm Cl ATHST CV9 63 M5
Homefield Rd CDSL WV8 34 F2
Homelands PBAR/PBCH B42 70 F6
The Homelands WOLVN WV10 * 22 A7
Homelea Rd YDLY B25 109 H5
Homemead Gv RBRY B45 143 K6
Home Meadow La REDE B98 195 J7
Home Park Rd NUN CV11 99 G2
Homer Cl RLSS CV31 206 C8
Homer Hill Rd HALE B63 102 F6
Homer Rd MGN/WHC B75 57 G3
SOLH B91 148 F2
Homers Fold BILS/COS WV14 51 H8
Homer St BHTH/HG B12 107 K8
Homerton Rd KGSTG B44 71 M4

Homestead Cl SEDG DY3 ....66 C8
Homestead Dr MGN/WHC B75 ....57 G2
Homestead Rd STETCH B33 ....109 M4
Homeward Wy COVS CV5 ....156 E4
Homewood Cl WALM/CURD B76 ....73 J2
Homfray Rd KIDD DY10 ....138 D5
Honesty Cl BRWNH WS8 ....26 B6
Honeswode Cl
  BFLD/HDSWWD B20 ....88 E5
Honeyborne TAM/AM/WIL B77 ....57 H6
Honeybourne TAM/AM/WIL B77 ....46 B3
Honeybourne Rd COVW CV6 ....153 M2
  HALE B63 ....121 L2
Honeyborne Crs WMBN WV5 ....64 D8
Honeybourne Rd HALE B63 ....122 C2
  STETCH B33 ....110 A5
Honeybrew Wy WLNHL WV13 ....52 A3
Honeybrook Cl KIDDW DY11 ....138 B3
Honeybrook La KIDDW DY11 ....137 M4
Honeychurch Cl REDE B98 ....202 D2
Honeycomb Wy NFLD/LBR B31 ....144 C2
Honeyfield Rd COV CV1 ....134 B8
Honeysuckle Av KGSWFD DY6 ....83 J1
Honeysuckle Cl
  RIDG/WDGT B32 ....104 F8
Honeysuckle Dr COVE CV2 ....134 F3
  DSYBK/YTR WS5 ....69 L2
  WOLVN WV10 ....23 H2
Honeysuckle Gv ACGN B27 ....109 G8
Honeysuckle Wy GTWY WS6 ....24 F1
Honeytree Cl KGSWFD DY6 ....101 K2
Honiley Dr SCFLD/BOLD B73 ....72 A3
Honiley Rd KNWTH CV8 ....177 L4
  STETCH B33 ....109 L3
Honiley Wy COVE CV2 * 135 H4
Honister Cl BRLYHL DY5 ....102 D4
Honiton Cl NFLD/LBR B31 ....144 C1
Honiton Crs NFLD/LBR B31 ....144 C1
Honiton Rd COVE CV2 ....134 F8
Honiton Wk SMTHWK B66 ....87 M8
Honiton Wy ALDR WS9 ....40 D8
Honnington Ct SLYOAK B29 * 123 K4
Honor Av
  ETTPK/GDPK/PENN WV4 ....50 A8
Hood Gv BVILLE B30 ....145 H1
Hood St COV CV1 ....9 H4
Hood's Wy RUGBYS/DCH CV22 ....186 B4
Hook Dr FOAKS/STRLY B74 ....56 C1
Hook La LICHS WS14 ....42 A2
Hooper St WSNGN B18 ....106 D1
Hoo Rd KIDD DY10 ....164 C2
Hoosen Cl RMSLY B62 ....104 E7
Hope Cl RCOVN/BALC/EX CV7 ....115 L6
Hopedale Cl COVE CV2 ....156 C2
Hopedale Rd RIDG/WDGT B32 ....105 G8
Hope Pl SLYOAK B29 * 124 D3
Hope Rd TPTN/OCK DY4 ....68 A7
Hope St COV CV1 ....8 C5
  DIG/EDG B5 ....107 H6
  DUDS DY2 ....85 G5
  RMSLY B62 ....104 E2
  STRBR DY8 ....101 H2
  WSL WS1 ....4 F6
Hopgardens Av BRGRVE B60 ....191 M3
Hopkins Dr HHTH/SAND B71 ....69 J6
Hopkins Rd COVN CV6 ....133 H8
Hopkins St TPTN/OCK DY4 ....85 L3
Hopleys Cl TAM/AM/WIL B77 ....46 C1
Hop Pole La BEWD DY12 ....162 C2
Hopstone Gdns
  ETTPK/GDPK/PENN WV4 ....49 K8
Hopstone Rd SLYOAK B29 ....123 L4
Hopton Cl COVW CV5 ....153 L1
  TPTN/OCK DY4 ....68 A3
Hopton Crs WNSFLD WV11 ....37 J7
Hopton Crofts RLSN CV32 ....206 A3
Hopton Dr KIDDW DY11 ....164 C4
Hopton Gdns DUDN DY1 ....84 E2
Hopton Mdw MOS/BIL B13 ....126 A8
Hopton Meadow HEDN WS12 ....17 G4
Hopwas Gv
  CHWD/FDBR/MGN B37 ....92 D8
Hopwas Rd POL/KGSB/FAZ B78 ....30 E7
Hopwood Cl HALE B63 ....121 L3
Hopwood Gv NFLD/LBR B31 ....144 C7
Hopyard Cl SEDG DY3 ....83 M2
Hopyard Gdns BILS/COS WV14 ....68 E1
Hopyard La REDE B98 ....203 J1
  SEDG DY3 ....83 M3
Hopyard Rd WSLW WS2 ....52 C3
Horace Partridge Rd
  DARL/WED WS10 ....51 L8
Horace St BILS/COS WV14 ....66 E5
Horatio Dr MOS/BIL B13 ....125 K1
Hordern Cl DUNHL/THL/PER WV6 ....35 K8
Hordern Crs BRLYHL DY5 ....102 B5
Hordern Gv
  DUNHL/THL/PER WV6 ....35 K8
Hordern Pk WOLVN WV10 * 22 A7
Hordern Rd
  DUNHL/THL/PER WV6 ....35 K8
Hornbeam TAM/AM/WIL B77 ....46 E1
  SLYOAK B29 ....123 M6
Hornbeam Crs HEDN WS12 ....13 L7
Hornbeam Dr TLHL/CAN CV4 ....153 H4
Hornbeam Wk BDMR/CCFT WV3 ....2 G7
Hornbrook Gv HIA/OLT B92 ....148 C1
Hornby Gv ALE/KHTH/YWD B14 ....147 G1
Hornby Rd
  ETTPK/GDPK/PENN WV4 ....66 A1
Hornchurch Cl COV CV1 ....8 C7
Horndean Cl COVN CV6 ....134 C5
Horne Cl RUGBYN/HIL CV21 ....187 L5
Horne Wy BKDE/SHDE B34 ....92 C8
Horning Dr BILS/COS WV14 ....67 G2
Horninghold Cl COVS CV3 ....156 C5
Hornsey Cl COVE CV2 ....135 K3
Hornsey Gv KGSTG B44 ....71 L3
Hornsey Rd KGSTG B44 ....71 L3
Hornton Cl FOAKS/STRLY B74 ....42 D8
Horobins Yd BDWTH CV12 * 116 F1
Horrell Rd
  LGN/SDN/BHAMAIR B26 ....109 M7
  SHLY B90 ....147 K3
Horse Bridge La KINVER DY7 ....118 A3
Horsecroft Dr HHTH/SAND B71 ....69 L5
Horse Fair KIDD DY10 ....138 C6
Horsehills Dr BDMR/CCFT WV3 ....49 J3
Horselea Cft WASH/WDE B8 ....109 G1
Horseley Flds WOLV WV1 ....3 J5
Horseley Heath TPTN/OCK DY4 ....67 M7
Horseley Rd FOAKS/STRLY B74 ....55 M3
  GTB/HAM B43 ....71 H1
Horseshoe Cl WSLW WS2 ....52 F6
Horse Shoe Rd COVN CV6 ....134 C5
Horse Shoes La
  LGN/SDN/BHAMAIR B26 ....109 M8
The Horseshoe
  LGLYGN/QTN B68 ....105 G3
Horsfall Rd MGN/WHC B75 ....57 J7
Horsford Rd COVS CV3 ....155 J7
Horsham Av STRBR DY8 ....101 J3
Horsley La LICHS WS14 ....28 E5
Horsley Rd FOAKS/STRLY B74 ....55 M3
  GTB/HAM B43 ....71 H1
Horton Cl DARL/WED WS10 ....52 B7

  SEDG DY3 ....66 A5
Horton Crs RUGBYS/DCH CV22 ....186 E3
Horton Gv SHLY B90 ....148 E8
Horton Pl DARL/WED WS10 ....52 B7
Horton St BHTH/HG B12 ....107 J6
Horton St DARL/WED WS10 ....52 B6
  TPTN/OCK DY4 ....68 B8
Hosiery St BDWTH CV12 ....117 G3
Hoskyn Cl RUGBYN/HIL CV21 ....187 K5
Hospital La BDWTH CV12 ....115 M4
  BILS/COS WV14 ....67 G4
  GTWY WS6 ....23 M3
Hospital Rd BNTWD WS7 ....26 F1
Hospital St CRTAM B79 ....31 M8
  LOZ/NWT B19 ....6 E1
  WOLV WV1 ....3 J1
  WSLW WS2 ....53 H1
Hossill La HAG/WOL DY9 ....141 H4
Hotchkiss Cl COVN CV6 ....156 E6
Hothersall Dr SCFLD/BOLD B73 ....72 D5
Hotspur Rd KGSTG B44 ....71 K4
Hotspur Rd KGSTG B44 ....71 K4
Hough Rd ALE/KHTH/YWD B14 * 126 F1
  WSLW WS2 ....52 E6
Houghton Ct HLGN/YWD B28 * 147 H1
Houghton St OLDBY B69 ....86 D7
Houldey Rd NFLD/LBR B31 ....144 F5
Houldsworth Crs COVN CV6 ....134 A1
Houliston Cl DARL/WED WS10 ....52 F3
Houndsfield Cl HLYWD B47 ....147 G7
Houndsfield Gv HLYWD B47 ....146 E8
Houndsfield La HLYWD B47 ....146 E8
Housman Cl BRGRVE B60 ....191 J5
Houston Rd RUGBYN/HIL CV21 ....161 G7
Houting TAM/AM/WIL B77 ....46 B8
The Houx STRBR DY8 ....101 J5
Hove Av COVW CV5 ....153 J1
Hovelands Cl COVE CV2 ....135 G5
Hoveton Cl REDE B98 ....202 F4
Howard Av BRGRVW B61 ....191 J2
Howard Cl COVW CV5 ....153 K1
Howard Crs HEDN WS12 ....13 L5
Howard Rd ALE/KHTH/YWD B14 ....125 H6
  BFLD/HDSWWD B20 ....88 F7
  BILS/COS WV14 ....67 K2
  GTB/HAM B43 ....70 A5
  HIA/OLT B92 ....127 J2
  NUNW/HART CV10 ....98 E2
  REDE B98 ....202 F5
  WNSFLD WV11 ....37 K5
  YDLY B25 ....127 M2
Howard Rd East
  ALE/KHTH/YWD B14 ....125 J6
Howard St COV CV1 ....9 G1
  LOZ/NWT B19 ....6 E1
  TPTN/OCK DY4 ....67 M8
  WBROM B70 ....87 J4
Howard Wk AST/WIT B6 ....89 L6
Howat Rd RCOVN/BALC/EX CV7 ....115 K6
Howcotte Gn TLHL/CAN CV4 ....153 J6
Howden Pl STETCH B33 ....91 J8
Howdle's La BRWNH WS8 ....26 C5
Howe Green La SHHTH WV12 ....38 A7
Howe Green La
  NUNW/HART CV10 ....115 H2
Howell Dr TPTN/OCK DY4 ....67 L8
Howell Rd BKHL/PFLD WV2 ....50 C6
Howells Cl BDWTH CV12 ....116 B5
Howes Cft CVALE B35 ....91 L3
Howe St CBHAMNE B4 * 7 K3
Howford Gv VAUX/NECH B7 ....107 M1
Howkins Rd RUGBYN/HIL CV21 ....161 G7
Howland Cl COVEN WV9 ....35 K3
Howlette Rd TLHL/CAN CV4 ....153 J3
Howley Av KGSTG B44 ....71 J1
Howley Grange Rd RMSLY B62 ....104 D8
Hoylake TAM/AM/WIL B77 ....46 F1
Hoylake Cl BLOX/PEL WS3 ....38 F2
  NUN CV11 ....99 M4
Hoylake Dr OLDBY B69 ....85 L6
Hoylake Rd
  DUNHL/THL/PER WV6 ....34 B8
Hoyland Wy BVILLE B30 ....124 C5
Huband Cl REDE B98 ....194 E8
Hubert Cft SLYOAK B29 ....124 C3
Hubert Rd SLYOAK B29 ....124 D3
Hubert St AST/WIT B6 ....88 K8
The Hub SOLH B91 * 149 G2
Hucker Cl WSLW WS2 ....52 E6
Hucker Rd WSLW WS2 ....52 E6
Huddesford Dr
  RCOVN/BALC/EX CV7 ....152 A5
Huddisdon Cl WWCK CV34 ....205 K4
Huddlestone Cl WOLVN WV10 ....22 E7
Huddocks Vw BLOX/PEL WS3 ....25 K3
Hudson Av CSHL/WTROR B46 ....93 K7
Hudson Cl DARL/WED WS10 ....52 B7
Hudson Dr
  DUNHL/THL/PER WV6 ....34 C8
Hudson Rd BFLD/HDSWWD B20 ....88 E1
  RUGBYS/DCH CV22 ....186 C4
  TPTN/OCK DY4 ....86 A1
Hudson's Dr BVILLE B30 ....145 L1
Hudswell Dr BRLYHL DY5 ....102 B5
Huggins Cl
  RCOVN/BALC/EX CV7 ....152 A6
Hughes Av BDMR/CCFT WV3 ....49 K5
Hughes Cl WWCK CV34 ....205 H3
Hughes Pl BILS/COS WV14 ....51 H6
Hughes Rd BILS/COS WV14 ....51 H6
  DARL/WED WS10 ....51 L8
Hugh Rd COVS CV3 ....155 L3
  SMHTH B10 ....108 C4
  SMTHWK B67 ....87 H8
Hugh Vls SMHTH B10 * 108 C4
Huins Cl REDE B98 ....202 E1
Hulbert Dr DUDS DY2 ....84 F7
Hulland Pl BRLYHL DY5 ....102 A2
Hullbrook Rd MOS/BIL B13 ....126 A8
Humber Av COVS CV3 ....156 F4
  WALM/CURD B76 ....73 L6
Humber Av COV CV1 ....9 K7
Humber Gdns HALE B63 ....102 F8
Humber Gv CBROM B36 ....92 D4
Humber Rd BDMR/CCFT WV3 ....2 B6
  COVS CV3 ....9 M4
Humberstone Rd
  ERDE/BCHGN B24 ....91 J1
Hume St KIDDW DY11 ....138 B4
  SMTHWK B66 ....105 M1
Humpage Rd BORD B9 ....108 C3
Humphrey Burton's Rd
  COVS CV3 ....155 G5
Humphrey-Davy Rd
  BDWTH CV12 ....116 B5
Humphrey Middlemore Dr
  HRBN B17 ....124 E1
Humphrey St SEDG DY3 ....84 B2
Humphries Crs BILS/COS WV14 ....67 K3

Humphries Dr KIDD DY10 ....164 D5
Humphries Rd WOLVN WV10 ....36 A5
Humphris St WWCK CV34 ....205 M5
Hundred Acre Rd
  FOAKS/STRLY B74 ....55 K6
Hungary Cl DUDN DY1 ....102 A3
Hungary Hl HAG/WOL DY9 ....102 A3
Hungerfield Rd CBROM B36 ....92 A4
Hungerford Rd STRBR DY8 ....100 F7
Hungry La SHLY B90 ....43 K1
Hunningham Gv SOLH B91 ....148 F5
Hunnington Cl RIDG/WDGT B32 ....122 E4
Hunnington Crs HALE B63 ....121 M3
Hunscote Cl SHLY B90 ....147 K4
Hunslet Cl RIDG/WDGT B32 ....122 F7
Hunslet Rd BNTWD WS7 ....18 F5
  RIDG/WDGT B32 ....123 K1
Hunstanton Av HRBN B17 ....105 K5
Hunstanton Cl BRLYHL DY5 ....102 A5
Hunt Cl RWWCK/WEL CV35 ....204 D7
Hunt End La REDW B97 ....202 A8
Hunter Av BNTWD WS7 ....18 E4
Hunter Cl LICHS WS14 ....21 H7
Hunter Rd BLOX/PEL WS3 ....39 K7
Hunter Rd CNCK/NC WS11 ....16 C5
  COVS CV3 ....156 E5
Hunters La RUGBYN/HIL CV21 ....160 E8
Hunters Cl RIDG/WDGT B32 ....62 A5
Hunter's Ride LOZ/NWT B19 ....88 F7
Hunter's Ride LOZ/NWT B19 ....100 F5
Hunter St DUNHL/THL/PER WV6 ....2 B1
  RUGBYN/HIL CV21 ....187 G5
Hunters V LOZ/NWT B19 ....89 G7
Hunters Wk ATHST CV9 ....63 H6
Hunter Ter COVW CV5 ....154 A5
Huntingdon Cl
  POL/KGSB/FAZ B78 ....45 K3
  REDE B98 ....203 J1
Huntingdon Gdns HALE B63 ....103 G6
Huntingdon Rd COVS CV3 ....8 A6
  HHTH/SAND B71 ....68 F6
Huntingdon Wy
  NUNW/HART CV10 ....98 C2
Huntington Rd SHHTH WV12 ....38 B6
Huntington Terrace Rd
  CNCK/NC WS11 ....16 D1
Huntingtree Rd HALE B63 ....121 J3
Huntlands Rd HALE B63 ....121 J3
Hunt La ATHST CV9 ....63 J5
Huntley Dr SOLH B91 ....148 F5
Huntly Rd LDYWD/EDGR B16 ....106 E4
Hunton HI ERDW/GRVHL B23 ....90 B2
Hunton Rd ERDW/GRVHL B23 ....90 C2
Hunt Paddocks KNWTH CV8 ....197 L4
Hunt's La SHHTH WV12 ....38 B7
Huntsman Cl BILS/COS WV14 ....67 H3
Huntsmans Ga BNTWD WS7 ....18 F5
Huntsmans Ri HEDN WS12 ....12 A5
Hunts Mill Dr BRLYHL DY5 ....84 A4
Hunts Ri BEWD DY12 ....163 G2
Hunts Rd BVILLE B30 ....124 E6
Hunt Ter TLHL/CAN CV4 ....153 H6
Hurdlow Av NEWD/HART B38 ....88 F8
Hurley Cl CSCFLD/WYGN B72 ....73 G3
  DSYBK/YTR WS5 ....69 J4
  RLSN CV32 ....206 E3
Hurley Common ATHST CV9 ....61 G7
Hurley Gv CHWD/FDBR/MGN B37 ....92 D8
Hurley La CSHL/WTROR B46 ....77 J8
Hurleys Fold DUDS DY2 ....84 F8
Hurlingham Rd KGSTG B44 ....71 L4
Hurn Wy COVN CV6 ....134 F1
Huron Cl CNCK/NC WS11 ....16 F3
Hurricane Wy CVALE B35 ....91 J3
Hursey Dr TPTN/OCK DY4 ....67 L8
Hurstbourne Crs WOLV WV1 ....50 F4
Hurst Cl CBROM B36 ....92 C6
Hurstcroft Rd STETCH B33 ....109 M2
Hurst Green Rd DOR/KN B93 ....175 K1
  RMSLY B62 ....103 M8
  WALM/CURD B76 ....74 B7
Hurst La BKDE/SHDE B34 ....92 B7
  BRLYHL DY5 ....102 D2
  TPTN/OCK DY4 ....67 H8
Hurst La North BKDE/SHDE B34 ....92 C6
Hurst Rd BDWTH CV12 ....116 F2
  BILS/COS WV14 ....66 E4
  COVN CV6 ....134 C1
  SMTHWK B67 ....105 H3
Hurst St DIG/EDG B5 ....6 F7
The Hurst HLYWD B47 ....146 A6
  MOS/BIL B13 ....126 A6
The Hurstway
  ERDW/GRVHL B23 ....72 A5
Hurstwood Rd KGSTG B44 ....72 A5
Hussey Cl PENK ST19 ....10 D6
Hussey Rd BRWNH WS8 ....26 C5
  CNCK/NC WS11 ....17 K8
Husum Wy KIDD DY10 ....139 G6
Hut Hill La GTWY WS6 ....24 E1
Hutton Av WASH/WDE B8 ....90 B8
Hutton Rd BFLD/HDSWWD B20 ....88 F4
  WASH/WDE B8 ....90 B8
Huxbey Dr HIA/OLT B92 ....128 D5
Huxley Cl COVEN WV9 ....35 L2
Hyatt Sq BRLYHL DY5 ....102 A6
Hyde Cl BRGRVE B60 ....191 M3
Hyde Pl RLSN CV32 ....206 E5
Hyde Rd COVE CV2 ....135 G3
  KNWTH CV8 ....179 K8
  WNSFLD WV11 ....37 H7
Hyde Rd DARL/WED WS10 ....68 E2
  HHTH/SAND B71 ....69 G4
The Hyde HAG/WOL DY9 ....120 B3
Hyett Wy TPTN/OCK DY4 ....67 M3
Hylda Rd BFLD/HDSWWD B20 ....88 F4
Hylstone Crs WNSFLD WV11 ....37 H7
Hylton St WSNGN B18 ....6 A2
Hyperion Gdns COVE CV2 * 135 G8
Hyperion Dr
  ETTPK/GDPK/PENN WV4 ....65 L2
Hyperion Rd CBROM B36 ....91 J4
  KINVER DY7 ....101 G5
Hyron Hall Rd ACGN B27 ....127 G3
Hyssop Cl CNCK/NC WS11 ....16 E5
  VAUX/NECH B7 ....89 L8
Hytall Rd SHLY B90 ....147 G3
Hythe Gv YDLY B25 ....109 H5

I

Ibberton Rd
  ALE/KHTH/YWD B14 ....146 F2
Ibex Cl COVS CV3 ....156 D4
Ibis Cl KIDD DY10 ....164 F2
Ibis Gdns KGSWFD DY6 ....83 L7
Ibstock Cl REDE B98 ....203 J1
Ibstock Dr STRBR DY8 ....119 L4
Ibstock Rd COVN CV6 ....116 E8
Icknield Cl FOAKS/STRLY B74 ....55 L4

Icknield Port Rd
  LDYWD/EDGR B16 ....106 C2
Icknield Sq LDYWD/EDGR B16 ....106 C2
Icknield St ALVE B48 ....171 M5
  HWK/WKHTH B38 ....158 F7
  REDE B98 ....195 G6
  WSNGN B18 ....6 A2
Icknield Street Dr REDE B98 ....203 H5
Ida Rd WBROM B70 ....87 H4
Idbury Rd KGSTG B44 ....71 L6
Iden Rd COV CV1 ....134 C8
Idmiston Cft
  ALE/KHTH/YWD B14 ....146 D3
Idonia Rd DUNHL/THL/PER WV6 ....35 L8
Ilam Pk KNWTH CV8 ....180 A8
Ilex Ct WWCK CV34 ....205 L6
Ilford Cl BDWTH CV12 ....116 D2
Ilford Dr COVS CV3 ....154 F8
Ilford Rd ERDW/GRVHL B23 ....72 E7
Ilfracombe Gv COVS CV3 ....154 E8
Iliffe Wy HRBN B17 ....124 C2
Ilkley Gv CHWD/FDBR/MGN B37 ....110 D3
Illey Cl NFLD/LBR B31 ....143 M4
Illey La RMSLY B62 ....122 A4
Illshaw COVEN WV9 ....35 L2
Illshaw Cl REDE B98 ....203 L1
Illshaw Heath Rd HOCK/TIA B94 ....174 D2
Ilmer Cl RUGBYN/HIL CV21 ....160 F7
Ilmington Cl COVS CV3 ....154 F8
  REDE B98 ....203 H4
  RWWCK/WEL CV35 ....204 B2
Ilmington Dr SCFLD/BOLD B73 ....72 B2
Ilsham Rd SLYOAK B29 ....123 K4
Ilsley Rd ERDW/GRVHL B23 ....90 C1
Imber Rd KIDD DY10 ....164 E4
Imperial Av KIDD DY10 ....138 D5
Imperial Gv KIDD DY10 ....138 D5
Imperial Ri CSHL/WTROR B46 ....93 J3
Imperial Rd BORD B9 ....108 C4
Impney Cl REDE B98 ....195 H7
Impsley Cl CBROM B36 ....91 M5
Inca Cl COVS CV3 ....156 D5
Ince Rd DARL/WED WS10 ....52 A5
Incestre Dr GTB/HAM B43 ....70 A4
Inchbrook Rd KNWTH CV8 ....180 A6
Inchcape Av BFLD/HDSWWD B20 ....88 E2
Inchford Cl NUN CV11 ....99 K4
Inchford Rd HIA/OLT B92 ....128 C6
Inchlaggan Rd WOLVN WV10 ....37 G4
Infantry Pl MGN/WHC B75 ....57 L7
Ingatestone Dr STRBR DY8 ....101 G3
Inge St DIG/EDG B5 ....6 F7
Ingestre Cl BLOX/PEL WS3 ....38 D2
  CNCK/NC WS11 ....16 F4
Ingestre Dr GTB/HAM B43 ....70 A4
Inge St HLGN/YWD B28 ....126 D6
  WOLVN WV10 ....36 A4
Ingham Wy HRBN B17 ....105 K6
Ingleby Gdns
  NUNW/HART CV10 ....98 C2
Ingledew Cl WSLW WS2 ....52 B2
Inglefield Rd STETCH B33 ....109 L2
Inglemere Gv SLYOAK B29 ....123 K6
Inglenook Dr
  BFLD/HDSWWD B20 ....88 F3
Ingleside Vls SPARK B11 * 108 A3
Ingleton Cl NUN CV11 ....99 L3
Ingleton Rd WASH/WDE B8 ....90 C6
Inglewood Av BDMR/CCFT WV3 ....49 K5
Inglewood Cl KGSWFD DY6 ....83 H8
  RLSN CV32 ....206 D1
Inglewood Gv FOAKS/STRLY B74 ....56 A1
Inglewood Rd SPARK B11 ....108 A3
Ingoldsby Rd NFLD/LBR B31 ....145 G2
Ingot Cl WSLW WS2 ....38 F7
Ingram Crs BEWD DY12 ....162 D1
Ingram Gv ACGN B27 ....126 E3
Ingram Pit La TAM/AM/WIL B77 ....32 E8
Ingram Pl BLOX/PEL WS3 ....39 H4
Ingram Rd BLOX/PEL WS3 ....39 H4
  COVW CV5 ....154 D5
Inhedge St SEDG DY3 ....66 C8
The Inhedge DUDN DY1 ....85 J5
Inkberrow Rd HALE B63 ....121 K5
Inkerman Gv WOLVN WV10 ....3 L4
Inkerman St VAUX/NECH B7 ....107 M1
  WOLVN WV10 ....36 A4
Inland Rd ERDE/BCHGN B24 ....90 D3
Innage Cl RLSS CV31 ....206 F5
Innage Rd NFLD/LBR B31 ....144 F1
Innage Ter ATHST CV9 * 63 H5
The Innage HLYWD B47 ....146 B8
Innis Rd COVW CV5 ....154 C6
Inn La KIDDW DY11 ....137 H5
Innsworth Dr CVALE B35 ....91 L1
Insetton Cl REDE B98 ....203 H1
Inshaw Cl STETCH B33 ....109 J2
Institute Rd
  ALE/KHTH/YWD B14 ....125 K6
Instone Rd COVN CV6 ....133 L4
  HALE B63 ....121 K2
Instow Cl SHHTH WV12 ....37 M5
Insull Av ALE/KHTH/YWD B14 ....146 E4
Intended St HALE B63 ....103 G6
International Dr
  LGN/SDN/BHAMAIR B26 ....129 C1
International Sq
  CHWD/FDBR/MGN B37 * 111 G7
Intown SOLH B91 ....5 G3
Intown Rw WSL WS1 ....5 G3
Inveraray Cl KNWTH CV8 ....198 A1
Inverclyde Rd
  BFLD/HDSWWD B20 ....88 E2
Inverness Cl COVW CV5 ....153 L1
Inverness Rd NFLD/LBR B31 ....144 D2
Invicta Rd COVS CV3 ....156 D5
  unsworth COVN WV9 ....35 G3
Ipsley Church La REDE B98 ....203 G5
Ipsley La REDE B98 ....203 H5
Ipsley St REDW B97 ....202 C2
Ipstones Av STETCH B33 ....109 K1
Ipswich Crs PBAR/PBCH B42 ....70 E5
Ireland Green Rd WBROM B70 ....86 E2
Ireton Cl TLHL/CAN CV4 ....153 G4
Ireton Rd BFLD/HDSWWD B20 ....88 E1
  WOLVN WV10 ....36 B2
Iris Cl CRTAM B79 ....32 A7
  DSYBK/YTR WS5 ....69 M1
  SLYOAK B29 ....123 M5
Iris Dr ALE/KHTH/YWD B14 ....146 B1
Irnham Rd FOAKS/STRLY B74 ....56 E1
Iron Bridge Wk HAG/WOL DY9 ....119 M5
Ironbridge Cl COVN CV6 ....116 F2
Iron La STETCH B33 ....109 H1
Ironside Cl BEWD DY12 ....162 D2
Ironstone Rd HEDN WS12 ....18 A2
Irvan Av WBROM B70 ....68 D8
Irvine Cl BLOX/PEL WS3 ....38 D5
Irvine Rd BLOX/PEL WS3 ....38 D5
Irving Cl LICH WS13 ....20 C5
  SEDG DY3 ....83 L1
Irving Rd COV CV1 ....9 K7
  HIA/OLT B92 ....127 M2
  TPTN/OCK DY4 ....68 A2
Irving St DIG/EDG B5 ....6 E7

Irwell TAM/AM/WIL B77 46
Irwin Av RBRY B45 ....
Isaac Walton Pl WBROM B70 ....
Isambard Dr COVN CV6 ....
Isbourne Wy BORD B9 ....
Isis Gv CBROM B36 ....
  WLNHL WV13 ....
Island Dr KIDD DY10 ....
Island Rd HDSW B21 ....
Islington Crs ATHST CV9 ....
Islington Rw EDG B15 ....
Ismere Rd ERDE/BCHGN B24 ....
Ismere Wy KIDD DY10 ....
Itchen Gv DUNHL/THL/PER WV6 ....
Ithon Gv HWK/WKHTH B38 ....
Ivanhoe Av NUN CV11 ....
Ivanhoe Rd BKHL/PFLD WV2 ....
  GTB/HAM B43 ....
  LICHS WS14 ....
Ivanhoe St DUDS DY2 ....
Ivatt TAM/AM/WIL B77 ....
Ivatt Cl RUSH/SHEL WS4 ....
Iverley La KIDD DY10 ....
Iverley Rd HALE B63 ....
Iverley Wk HAG/WOL DY9 ....
  COVN CV5 ....
  REDW B97 ....
  SPARK B11 ....
Ivy Av BHTH/HG B12 ....
Ivy Bank ATHST CV9 * ....
Ivybridge Gv PBAR/PBCH B42 ....
Ivybridge Rd COVS CV3 ....
Ivy Cl CNCK/NC WS11 ....
Ivy Cft RUSH/SHEL WS4 ....
Ivydale Av
  LGN/SDN/BHAMAIR B26 ....
Ivy Farm La TLHL/CAN CV4 ....
Ivyfield Rd ERDW/GRVHL B23 ....
Ivy Gv BRWNH WS8 ....
  NUNW/HART CV10 ....
Ivyhouse Cl BILS/COS WV14 ....
Ivyhouse La BILS/COS WV14 ....
Ivyhouse Rd HWK/WKHTH B38 ....
Ivy House Rd OLDBY B69 ....
Ivy La CBHAMNE B4 ....
Ivy Lodge Cl
  RMSLY B62 ....
Ivy Lodge Cl
  CHWD/FDBR/MGN B37 ....
Ivy Rd BVILLE B30 ....
  DUDN DY1 ....
  HDSW B21 ....
  SCFLD/BOLD B73 ....
  TPTN/OCK DY4 ....
Ivy Wy SHLY B90 ....
Izod St REDW B97 ....
Izons La WBROM B70 ....
Izons Rd WBROM B70 ....

J

Jacey Rd LDYWD/EDGR B16 ....
  SHLY B90 ....
Jackdaw Cl SEDG DY3 ....
Jacker Dr CBROM B36 ....
Jacker's Rd COVN CV6 ....
Jack Hayward Wy WOLV WV1 ....
Jack Holden Av BILS/COS WV14 ....
Jacklin Dr COVS CV3 ....
Jackson Cl CNCK/NC WS11 ....
  LGLYGN/QTN B68 ....
  RCOVN/BALC/EX CV7 ....
  RWWCK/WEL CV35 ....
  SPARK B11 * ....
  TPTN/OCK DY4 ....
  WOLVN WV10 ....
Jackson Crs STRPT DY13 ....
Jackson Dr SMTHWK B67 ....
Jackson Rd COV CV1 ....
  LICH WS13 ....
  RUGBYN/HIL CV21 ....
  WASH/WDE B8 ....
Jackson St DUNHL/THL/PER WV6 ....
  LGLYGN/QTN B68 ....
Jackson Wk CVALE B35 ....
Jackson Wy HIA/OLT B92 ....
Jacmar Crs SMTHWK B67 ....
Jacob Dr TLHL/CAN CV4 ....
Jacobean La DOR/KN B93 ....
Jacob's Hall La GTWY WS6 ....
Jacoby Pl EDG B15 ....
Jacox Crs KNWTH CV8 ....
Jade Cl COV CV1 ....
Jade Gv CNCK/NC WS11 ....
Jaffray Crs ERDE/BCHGN B24 ....
Jaffray Rd ERDE/BCHGN B24 ....
Jaguar TAM/AM/WIL B77 ....
Jakeman Cl REDE B98 ....
Jakeman Rd BHTH/HG B12 ....
James Bridge Cl WSLW WS2 * ....
James Cl DARL/WED WS10 ....
  SMTHWK B67 ....
Jamescroft COVS CV3 ....
James Dawson Dr COVW CV5 ....
James Dee Cl BRLYHL DY5 ....
James Eaton Cl HHTH/SAND B71 ....
James Galloway Cl COVS CV3 ....
James Green Rd TLHL/CAN CV4 ....
Jameson Rd AST/WIT B6 ....
Jameson St
  DUNHL/THL/PER WV6 ....
James Rd CSHL/WTROR B46 ....
  GTB/HAM B43 ....
  KIDD DY10 ....
  SPARK B11 ....
James Samuel Pl BHTH/HG B12 ....
James Scott Rd HALE B63 ....
James St BILS/COS WV14 ....
  CBHAMNW B3 ....
  CNCK/NC WS11 ....
  NUN CV11 ....
  RCOVN/BALC/EX CV7 ....
  WLNHL WV13 ....
James Turner St WSNGN B18 ....
James Watt Dr BFLD/HDSWWD B20 ....
James Watt Queensway
  CBHAMNE B4 ....
James Watt St HHTH/SAND B71 ....
  WBROM B70 ....
Jane Lane Cl WSLW WS2 ....
Janice Gv ALE/KHTH/YWD B14 ....
Janine Av WNSFLD WV11 ....
Jaques Cl CSHL/WTROR B46 ....
Jardine Crs TLHL/CAN CV4 ....
Jardine Rd AST/WIT B6 ....
Jarvis Crs OLDBY B69 ....
Jarvis Rd ERDW/GRVHL B23 ....
Jasmin Cft ALE/KHTH/YWD B14 ....
Jasmine Cl COVEN WV9 ....
Jasmine Gv BRGRVW B61 ....
  CDSL WV8 ....

OVS CV3 156 A5
LSN CV32 206 E3
mine Pl COVS CV3 * 156 A5
mine Rd DUDS DY2 85 K4
AM/AM/WIL B77 46 E1
mine Wy DARL/WED WS10 52 B6
on Cl TAM/AM/WIL B77 32 B8
on Rd HAG/WOL DY9 120 D1
ne Cl HHTH/SAND B71 69 J4
/NSFLD WV11 37 H6
Park Crs KIDD DY10 164 E3
Rd KGSWFD DY6 83 H5
s Av TPTN/OCK DY4 85 M1
s Cl REDE B98 203 L2
s Crs ALVE B48 170 F4
shaw Av GTB/HAM B43 70 C5
n Dr TPTN/OCK DY4 68 B7
n St ATHST CV9 62 A4
vons Pl BILS/COS WV14 51 G8
burgh Av
UNHL/THL/PER WV6 48 C1
burgh Gv COVS CV3 180 E1
do St BKHL/PFLD WV2 2 E8
'cock Rd BDMR/CCFT WV3 49 L5
'erson Cl HHTH/SAND B71 68 F5
'rey Av
TTPK/GDPK/PENN WV4 50 D7
'rey Cl BDWTH CV12 116 B5
'rey Rd BLKHTH/ROWR B65 104 C2
's Av BKHL/PFLD WV2 3 H9
'f St TLHL/CAN CV4 153 K4
eyman Cl KIDDW DY11 137 M7
kins Av COVW CV5 153 K1
kins Cl BILS/COS WV14 51 G8
kinson Rd DARL/WED WS10 68 B4
kins Rd RUGBYN/HIL CV21 187 L4
kins St SMHTH B10 108 A5
kinstown Rd HEDN WS12 13 L7
ks Av WOLVN WV10 36 C5
ks Rd WMBN WV5 64 D8
nens Rd CBHAMNE B4 7 K3
ner Cl WSLW WS2 38 D7
ner Rd WSLW WS2 38 D7
ner St BKHL/PFLD WV2 3 J7
OV CV1 9 H1
nings St CDYHTH B64 103 K3
ny Cl BILS/COS WV14 67 J4
ny Walkers La
UNHL/THL/PER WV6 48 B5
sen TAM/AM/WIL B77 46 C3
ton Rd RLSS CV31 206 F7
hcott Rd WASH/WDE B8 108 E2
hson Dr
GN/SDN/BHAMAIR B26 109 K6
hson Pl RLSS CV31 * 206 F6
emy Gv HIA/OLT B92 127 M1
emy Rd
TTPK/GDPK/PENN WV4 50 A8
ome Dr CNCK/NC WS11 17 L8
ome Rd CNCK/NC WS11 17 K8
'SCFLD/WYGN B72 73 H1
VSLW WS2 52 F4
ome Wy BNTWD WS7 18 F6
rard Dr MGN/WHC B75 57 G8
rard Ms MGN/WHC B75 * 57 G8
ry's La ERDW/GRVHL B23 72 B6
ICHS WS14 30 A5
sey Cl REDE B98 195 H6
sey Cft CBROM B36 92 F7
sey Rd WASH/WDE B8 108 B1
usalem Wk KIDD DY10 138 C6
vis Cl BRLYHL DY5 84 A6
vis Crs FOAKS/STRLY B74 56 B2
vis Pk FOAKS/STRLY B74 56 A1
vis Rd TAM/AM/WIL B77 46 D8
vis Ter HDSW B21 * 88 B5
voise Dr NFLD/LBR B31 123 M8
voise La HHTH/SAND B71 69 J4
voise Rd SLYOAK B29 123 K4
voise St WBROM B70 86 E1
mond Cl HEDN WS12 13 L8
mond Gv ERDE/BCHGN B24 91 H1
mond Rd COV CV1 9 K2
sel Rd WSLW WS2 4 B2
sie Rd ALDR WS9 40 E4
son Cl WSL WS1 5 K8
son Rd MGN/WHC B75 57 L8
SEDG DY3 66 E7
VSL WS1 5 H6
son St WBROM B70 87 J3
sop Dr TAM/AM/WIL B77 32 B8
ons Rd SCFLD/BOLD B73 72 A2
on St BILS/COS WV14 * 66 F5
v's La DUDN DY1 84 C1
gins La RIDG/WDGT B32 123 G5
Av GTB/HAM B43 70 A4
cot Rd HIA/OLT B92 127 M2
Forrest Cl COVS CV3 156 D5
nah Cl BHTH/HG B12 107 K5
nah Rd REDE B98 202 C3
nna Dr COVS CV3 181 G1
n St BKHL/PFLD WV2 50 C7
n Ward St COVS CV3 9 G9
's La TLHL/CAN CV4 153 L3
key Fld SEDG DY3 66 C7
key Hl LICHS WS14 * 21 K8
key La DARL/WED WS10 68 E1
key Rd SCFLD/BOLD B73 72 B3
rell St NUN CV11 80 F8
Obrien Cl COVS CV3 156 A7
Williams Cl COVS CV3 156 D6
ys La CDSL WV8 35 G2
n Bosco Cl HHTH/SAND B71 68 F6
n Bright Cl TPTN/OCK DY4 67 K5
n Bright St CBHAM B2 6 F6
ndory TAM/AM/WIL B77 46 B7
n Fletcher Cl
DARL/WED WS10 68 F1
n Grace St COVS CV3 9 H9
n Harper St WLNHL WV13 51 M3
n Kempe Wy BHTH/HG B12 107 L6
n Knight Rd BDWTH CV12 98 F8
n McGuire Crs COVS CV3 156 C6
n Nash Sq KNWTH CV8 197 K2
n O'gaunt Rd KNWTH CV8 197 J2
n Riley Dr SHHTH WV12 38 A5
n Rd RMSLY B62 122 D1
n Rous Av TLHL/CAN CV4 153 M6
ns Gv GTB/HAM B43 70 A5
n Shelton Dr COVN CV6 134 A1
n Simpson Cl KNWTH CV8 183 L2
ns La GTWY WS6 24 D2
OLDBY B69 86 A3
TPTN/OCK DY4 85 M1
nson Av RUGBYS/DCH CV22 186 B3
WNSFLD WV11 37 K6
nson Cl CBROM B36 91 G7
DARL/WED WS10 52 B8
ICH WS13 21 G4
REDE B98 194 E8
PARK B11 108 A8
nson Dr CVALE B35 91 K2
nson Pl BILS/COS WV14 51 K6
nson Rd BDWTH CV12 117 G2
NTWD WS7 18 D5
NCK/NC WS11 16 B1
OVN CV6 134 E5
ARL/WED WS10 52 B8
ARL/WED WS10 69 G3
ERDW/GRVHL B23 72 D8
SHHTH WV12 38 B6
Johnsons Bridge Rd
HHTH/SAND B71 69 G7
Johnsons Gv LGLYGN/QTN B68 105 G5
Johnson St ATHST CV9 61 G4
BILS/COS WV14 66 D4
BKHL/PFLD WV2 3 G9
VAUX/NECH B7 90 A7
Johnstone St LOZ/NWT B19 89 H5
Johnston St WBROM B70 87 H4
John St BDWTH CV12 116 E3
BKHL/PFLD WV2 50 E7
BLKHTH/ROWR B65 104 A4
BRLYHL DY5 102 B1
CNCK/NC WS11 12 D8
HEDN WS12 17 K2
LOZ/NWT B19 88 F6
NUN CV11 99 G3
NUNW/HART CV10 98 C2
OLDBY B69 86 E6
RLSN CV32 206 D5
STRBR DY8 101 K4
TAM/AM/WIL B77 46 C2
WBROM B70 68 D8
WLNHL WV13 51 L4
WSLW WS2 4 E1
John St North HHTH/SAND B71 68 F8
John Thwaites Cl
RUGBYS/DCH CV22 186 E3
Joiners Cft HIA/OLT B92 128 C5
Joinings Bank LGLYGN/QTN B68 104 F1
Jonathan Rd COVE CV2 135 K5
Jones Field Crs WOLV WV1 50 F3
Jones' La BNTWD WS7 19 K6
GTWY WS6 24 F4
Jones Rd RCOVN/BALC/EX CV7 116 E4
SHHTH WV12 38 B4
WOLVN WV10 36 A7
Jones Wood Cl WALM/CURD B76 73 K6
Jonkel Av TAM/AM/WIL B77 46 D8
Jonquil Cl ERDW/GRVHL B23 72 A6
Jordan Cl KNWTH CV8 197 M3
MGN/WHC B75 56 F4
SMTHWK B66 87 M8
Jordan Leys TPTN/OCK DY4 67 M8
Jordan Pl BILS/COS WV14 67 J2
Jordan Rd MGN/WHC B75 56 F4
Jordans Cl REDW B97 202 B7
The Jordans COVW CV5 154 A1
Jordan Wy ALDR WS9 40 F4
Jordan Well COV CV1 9 G5
Jorden's Wk BEWD DY12 163 G1
Joseph Creighton Cl COVS CV3 156 C6
Joseph Dewsbury Cl
BNTWD WS7 18 C5
Joseph Luckman Rd
BDWTH CV12 116 E1
Joseph St OLDBY B69 86 D7
Josiah Houses BILS/COS WV14 * 67 G5
Josiah Rd NFLD/LBR B31 144 B3
Jowett TAM/AM/WIL B77 46 B3
Jowett's La HHTH/SAND B71 68 F5
Joyberry Dr STRBR DY8 119 K2
Joyce Pool WWCK CV34 205 J6
Joyce Wy RUGBYS/DCH CV22 185 L5
Joynson St DARL/WED WS10 52 C8
Jubilee Av HHTH/SAND B71 68 F6
REDW B97 202 B6
Jubilee Cl BLOX/PEL WS3 39 J7
GTWY WS6 24 D4
Jubilee Crs COVN CV6 133 M6
Jubilee Dr North KIDDW DY11 163 M3
Jubilee Dr South KIDDW DY11 163 M3
Jubilee Gdns ERDW/GRVHL B23 71 M6
Jubilee Rd BILS/COS WV14 67 L1
RBRY B45 143 J3
TPTN/OCK DY4 67 L6
Jubilee St HHTH/SAND B71 69 H6
RUGBYN/HIL CV21 186 C2
Jubilee Ter BDWTH CV12 * 116 F1
Judd Cl BDWTH CV12 116 D2
Judds La COVN CV6 134 C1
Judge Cl OLDBY B69 86 E6
RRUGBY CV23 159 L8
Judge Rd BRLYHL DY5 102 D6
Judith Wy RUGBYS/DCH CV22 185 L5
Juggins La HOCK/TIA B94 172 F6
Julia Av ERDE/BCHGN B24 91 K1
Julia Gdns HHTH/SAND B71 69 K5
Julian Cl BRGRVW B61 168 E5
COVE CV2 135 K5
GTWY WS6 24 E2
WOLV WV1 50 F3
Julian Rd WOLV WV1 50 F3
Julie Cft BILS/COS WV14 67 J4
Juliet Cl NUN CV11 99 L4
Juliet Dr RUGBYS/DCH CV22 186 B7
Juliet Rd RMSLY B62 122 C1
Julius Dr CSHL/WTROR B46 93 K4
Junction One
RUGBYN/HIL CV21 * 160 E7
Junction Rd BKHL/PFLD WV2 50 F6
BRGRVW B61 191 J2
HDSW B21 88 A5
STRBR DY8 101 J5
STRBR DY8 119 M1
Junction St DUDS DY2 84 F5
OLDBY B69 86 C4
WSL WS1 4 D8
Junction St South OLDBY B69 86 E8
The Junction STRBR DY8 101 J5
June Crs TAM/AM/WIL B77 32 C8
June Cft
LGN/SDN/BHAMAIR B26 110 B8
Junewood Cl RUGBYN/HIL CV21 161 H6
Juniper TAM/AM/WIL B77 46 E1
Juniper Cl ACGN B27 108 F8
BDWTH CV12 116 B3
HEDN WS12 13 L7
Juniper Dr COVW CV5 132 D8
DSYBK/YTR WS5 69 M1
WALM/CURD B76 73 L6
Juniper Ri HALE B63 103 G8
Jury Rd BRLYHL DY5 102 D6
Jury St WWCK CV34 205 J7
Jutland Rd MOS/BIL B13 125 M6

K

Kalfs Dr RUGBYS/DCH CV22 185 M5
Kanzan Rd COVE CV2 135 G1
Kareen Gv COVS CV3 157 G6
Karen Cl NUNW/HART CV10 80 C6
Karen Wy BRLYHL DY5 102 B5
Karlingford Cl COVW CV5 154 B5
Katherine Rd SMTHWKW B67 105 K3
Kathleen Av BDWTH CV12 116 C4
Kathleen Rd CSCFLD/WYGN B72 73 G1
YDLY B25 109 G6
Katie Rd SLYOAK B29 124 C4
Katmandu Rd BRGRVE B60 192 A4
Katrine Cl NUNW/HART CV10 80 A8
Katrine Rd STRPT DY13 163 J7
Kay Cl RUGBYN/HIL CV21 161 G6
Kayne Cl KGSWFD DY6 83 G6
Kaysbrook Dr RRUGBY CV23 183 L7
Kean Cl LICH WS13 20 C3
Keanscott Dr LGLYGN/QTN B68 105 G1
Keasdon Gv WLNHL WV13 52 A2
Keating Gdns MGN/WHC B75 56 E1
Keats Av CNCK/NC WS11 12 C8
SMHTH B10 108 B6
Keats Cl CRTAM B79 31 K5
FOAKS/STRLY B74 42 D7
NUNW/HART CV10 79 L8
SEDG DY3 65 L8
STRBR DY8 101 L5
Keats Dr BILS/COS WV14 67 H3
Keats Gv ACGN B27 126 F4
WOLVN WV10 36 E5
Keats Pl KIDD DY10 138 F7
Keats Rd BLOX/PEL WS3 39 J6
COVE CV2 156 B3
SHHTH WV12 38 C6
WOLVN WV10 36 E4
Keble Cl BNTWD WS7 19 G6
CNCK/NC WS11 16 C5
Keble Gv
LGN/SDN/BHAMAIR B26 109 M7
WSL WS1 5 K9
Keble Wk CRTAM B79 31 L7
Kebull Gn TLHL/CAN CV4 153 J5
Kedleston Cl BLOX/PEL WS3 * 38 E2
Kedleston Rd HLGN/YWD B28 126 D7
Keel Dr MOS/BIL B13 126 B4
Keele Cl REDE B98 195 H7
Keeley St BORD B9 107 M3
Keeling Dr CNCK/NC WS11 15 M4
Keelinge St TPTN/OCK DY4 67 M8
Keeling Rd KNWTH CV8 179 M8
Keenan Dr BDWTH CV12 116 B4
Keen St SMTHWK B66 106 A1
Keepers Cl ALDR WS9 40 D2
BNTWD WS7 18 E7
CSHL/WTROR B46 111 L1
KGSWFD DY6 82 F5
LICHS WS14 21 J6
Keepers Gate Cl MGN/WHC B75 57 G6
Keepers La CDSL WV8 34 E5
Keepers Rd FOAKS/STRLY B74 42 A8
Keepers Wk BDWTH CV12 * 116 B4
Keer Ct BORD B9 * 107 M2
Kegworth Cl COVN CV6 134 E1
Kegworth Rd ERDW/GRVHL B23 90 A4
Keir Cl RLSN CV32 206 E3
Keir Pl STRBR DY8 101 J5
Keir Rd DARL/WED WS10 69 G3
Keith Rd RLSN CV32 206 F1
Kelby Cl NFLD/LBR B31 144 C2
Kelby Rd NFLD/LBR B31 144 C1
Keldy Cl DUNHL/THL/PER WV6 35 K8
Kele Rd TLHL/CAN CV4 153 K6
Kelfield Av HRBN B17 123 M1
Kelia Dr SMTHWKW B67 87 K7
Kellett Rd VAUX/NECH B7 7 L1
Kelling Cl BRLYHL DY5 * 102 A5
Kellington Cl WASH/WDE B8 108 D1
Kelmarsh Dr SOLH B91 148 F4
Kelmscote Rd COVN CV6 133 K5
Kelmscott Rd HRBN B17 105 M6
Kelsall Cl WOLV WV1 50 F3
Kelsall Cft CBHAMW B1 6 A4
Kelsey Cl NUN CV11 99 J2
VAUX/NECH B7 * 107 M1
Kelsey La RCOVN/BALC/EX CV7 152 B8
Kelsey's Cl KNWTH CV8 183 K2
Kelso Gdns
DUNHL/THL/PER WV6 48 B1
Kelsull Cft
CHWD/FDBR/MGN B37 110 E3
Kelton Ct EDG B15 106 E6
Kelvedon Gv SOLH B91 149 G1
Kelverdale Gv
ALE/KHTH/YWD B14 146 A1
Kelverley Gv HHTH/SAND B71 69 L4
Kelvin Av COVE CV2 135 H8
Kelvin Cl KIDDW DY11 137 L5
Kelvin Dr CNCK/NC WS11 16 E2
Kelvin Pl WSLW WS2 38 F7
Kelvin Rd NFLD/LBR B31 144 E4
RLSN CV32 198 F8
WSLW WS2 38 E7
Kelvin Wy WBROM B70 87 G4
Kelway COVS CV3 156 E4
Kelway Av GTB/HAM B43 70 F2
Kelwood Dr HALE B63 103 K8
Kelynmead Rd STETCH B33 109 L3
Kemberton Cl BDMR/CCFT WV3 49 G4
Kemberton Rd BDMR/CCFT WV3 49 G4
SLYOAK B29 123 L3
Kemble Cl SHHTH WV12 52 B1
Kemble Cft DIG/EDG B5 107 J6
Kemble Dr CVALE B35 91 L2
Kemelstowe Crs HALE B63 121 G5
Kemerton Wy SHLY B90 148 D8
Kemp Cl WWCK CV34 205 L6
Kempe Rd STETCH B33 109 L1
Kempley Av COVE CV2 156 A3
Kempsey Cl HALE B63 121 J1
HIA/OLT B92 127 K2
OLDBY B69 104 B1
REDE B98 202 F6
Kempsey Covert
HWK/WKHTH B38 145 J6
Kempsford Cl REDE B98 202 D7
Kemps Green Rd
RCOVN/BALC/EX CV7 151 M7
Kempson Av CSCFLD/WYGN B72 73 G4
HHTH/SAND B71 68 F8
Kempson Rd CBROM B36 91 K5
PENK ST19 10 D4
Kempsons Gv BILS/COS WV14 66 F2
Kempthorne Av WOLVN WV10 36 C5
Kempthorne Gdns
BLOX/PEL WS3 38 E3
Kempthorne Rd BILS/COS WV14 51 K7
Kempton Cl HEDN WS12 13 L7
Kempton Ct BRGRVW B61 168 E4
Kempton Crs RLSN CV32 207 G1
Kempton Dr GTWY WS6 24 D3
TAM/AM/WIL B77 60 B1
Kempton Park Rd CBROM B36 91 H5
Kempton Wy STRBR DY8 119 J2
Kemsey Dr BILS/COS WV14 67 K1
Kemshead Av NFLD/LBR B31 144 C5
Kemsley Rd
ALE/KHTH/YWD B14 146 D3
Kem St NUN CV11 99 J3
Kenchester Cl REDE B98 203 K3
Kendal Av CSHL/WTROR B46 93 K6
RBRY B45 143 M6
RLSN CV32 206 A3
Kendal Cl BRGRVE B60 191 M4
DUNHL/THL/PER WV6 35 K7
NUN CV11 81 L7
REDE B98 203 L2
Kendal Ct ALDR WS9 * 40 D1
CNCK/NC WS11 15 M5
Kendal Dr RBRY B45 170 B4
Kendal End Rd RBRY B45 170 A3
Kendal Gv HIA/OLT B92 128 D5
Kendall Ri KGSWFD DY6 83 K8
Kendal Ri COVW CV5 154 A1
DUNHL/THL/PER WV6 35 K7
LGLYGN/QTN B68 104 F2
Kendal Rise Rd RBRY B45 143 M6
Kendal Rd SPARK B11 107 M6
Kendlewood Rd KIDD DY10 138 F4
Kendon Av COVN CV6 133 J7
Kendrick Av BKDE/SHDE B34 110 B1
Kendrick Cl COVN CV6 134 E1
HIA/OLT B92 128 D7
Kendrick Pl BILS/COS WV14 67 L1
Kendrick Rd BILS/COS WV14 67 L1
ERDE/BCHGN B24 73 K8
WOLVN WV10 36 C7
Kendricks Rd DARL/WED WS10 52 D6
Kendrick St DARL/WED WS10 68 E2
Kenelm Rd BILS/COS WV14 67 G4
LGLYGN/QTN B68 104 E2
SCFLD/BOLD B73 72 F1
SMHTH B10 108 C5
Kenelm's Ct RMSLY B62 121 L8
Kenilworth Cl FOAKS/STRLY B74 56 E5
PENK ST19 10 E5
REDW B97 202 B7
STRBR DY8 101 H3
TPTN/OCK DY4 85 H1
Kenilworth Ct DUDN DY1 84 D6
EDG B15 * 106 D5
Kenilworth Crs
ETTPK/GDPK/PENN WV4 66 C1
WSLW WS2 52 E1
Kenilworth Dr CNCK/NC WS11 16 B1
KIDDW DY11 164 C3
NUN CV11 98 E2
Kenilworth Rd
BFLD/HDSWWD B20 89 J4
COVS CV3 154 E6
DOR/KN B93 150 B7
DUNHL/THL/PER WV6 48 D1
KNWTH CV8 178 C3
LGLYGN/QTN B68 105 H5
LICHS WS14 20 F7
RCOVN/BALC/EX CV7 130 A3
RLSN CV32 198 C6
RLSN CV32 199 G7
RLSN CV32 206 D4
TAM/AM/WIL B77 46 C1
TLHL/CAN CV4 180 A4
Kenilworth St RLSN CV32 206 D5
Kenley Gv BVILLE B30 145 L3
Kenley Wy SHLY B90 148 B1
Kenmare Wy WNSFLD WV11 51 G1
Kenmore Av HEDN WS12 12 D6
Kenmure Rd STETCH B33 110 A6
Kennan Av RLSS CV31 206 D7
Kennedy Cl KIDD DY10 164 C2
TAM/AM/WIL B77 46 A4
Kennedy Crs DARL/WED WS10 52 A6
SEDG DY3 84 B1
Kennedy Cft
LGN/SDN/BHAMAIR B26 109 L6
Kennedy Dr RUGBYS/DCH CV22 186 A3
Kennedy Gv BVILLE B30 124 F7
Kennedy Rd WOLVN WV10 3 H3
Kennedy Sq RLSN CV32 206 E4
Kennel La ATHST CV9 63 M6
Kennerley Rd
LGN/SDN/BHAMAIR B26 109 H7
Kennet TAM/AM/WIL B77 46 B4
Kennet Cl BRWNH WS8 26 A3
COVE CV2 135 G5
Kennet Gv CBROM B36 92 D5
Kenneth Gv ERDW/GRVHL B23 71 L8
Kennford Cl OLDBY B69 86 A7
Kennington Rd WOLVN WV10 36 D8
Kenpas Hwy COVS CV3 154 E8
Kenrick Cft CVALE B35 91 K3
Kenrick Wy SMTHWK B66 87 K5
Kensington Av BHTH/HG B12 125 L1
Kensington Cl NUNW/HART CV10 80 A7
Kensington Ct
NUNW/HART CV10 80 A7
Kensington Dr CRTAM B79 31 M6
FOAKS/STRLY B74 42 D8
Kensington Gdns STRBR DY8 101 G4
Kensington Rd COVW CV5 8 A7
SHHTH WV12 37 M6
SLYOAK B29 124 E4
Kensington St LOZ/NWT B19 89 H7
Kenswick Dr HALE B63 121 L3
Kent Av POL/KGSB/FAZ B78 45 L4
WSLW WS2 52 F2
Kent Cl ALDR WS9 40 F4
BLOX/PEL WS3 39 J8
COVS CV3 155 J7
HHTH/SAND B71 68 F6
KIDD DY10 164 C2
Kenthurst Cl COVW CV5 153 G1
Kentish Rd HDSW B21 88 A5
Kentmere Cl COVE CV2 135 J3
PENK ST19 10 E4
Kentmere Rd BRGRVE B60 191 M4
Kenton Av DUNHL/THL/PER WV6 49 K1
Kent Pl DUDS DY2 84 E7
HEDN WS12 17 K4
Kent Rd BKHL/PFLD WV2 50 C6
DARL/WED WS10 69 H1
RBRY B45 143 K4
RMSLY B62 104 C7
STRBR DY8 101 H5
Kent's Cl HIA/OLT B92 127 K2
Kent St DIG/EDG B5 7 G9
SEDG DY3 66 C8
WSLW WS2 39 J8
Kent St North WSNGN B18 88 D8
The Kent RUGBYN/HIL CV21 187 L4
Kentwell CRTAM B79 31 H6
Kenward Cft HRBN B17 105 K6
Kenway HLYWD B47 146 E6
Kenwick Rd HRBN B17 123 M1
Kenwood Rd BORD B9 108 F3
Kenyon Cl BRGRVE B60 191 K4
STRBR DY8 101 L7
Kenyon St CBHAMNW B3 6 D2
Kepler CRTAM B79 31 J6
Keppel Cl RUGBYS/DCH CV22 186 A4
Keppel St COV CV1 134 C8
Kerby Rd ERDW/GRVHL B23 90 A1
Keresley Brook Rd COVN CV6 133 K3
Keresley Cl COVN CV6 133 K3
SOLH B91 128 A8
Keresley Green Rd COVN CV6 133 K4
Keresley Gv SLYOAK B29 123 K3
Keresley Rd COVN CV6 133 K5
Kernthorpe Rd
ALE/KHTH/YWD B14 146 A1
Kerr Dr TPTN/OCK DY4 67 J5
Kerria Rd TAM/AM/WIL B77 46 F1
Kerridge Cl COVEN WV9 35 L3
Kerris Wy COVS CV3 156 E4
Kerry Cl BRLYHL DY5 102 A1
NFLD/LBR B31 123 K7
Kerry Croft Cl REDW B97 202 C8
Kerry Hl BRGRVE B60 191 J7
Kersley Gdns WNSFLD WV11 37 K7
Kerswell Cl REDW B97 193 M8
Kerswell Dr SHLY B90 148 E8
Kesterton Rd FOAKS/STRLY B74 42 C8
Kesteven Cl EDG B15 106 F7
Kesteven Rd HHTH/SAND B71 69 G6
Keston Rd KGSTG B44 71 K1
Kestrel TAM/AM/WIL B77 46 E7
Kestrel Av YDLY B25 108 F5
Kestrel Cl ERDW/GRVHL B23 72 B7
KIDD DY10 164 C2
Kestrel Cft COVS CV3 156 D5
Kestrel Dr FOAKS/STRLY B74 42 D8
Kestrel Gv HEDN WS12 17 G4
SHHTH WV12 38 A5
SLYOAK B29 124 B5
Kestrel Ri DUNHL/THL/PER WV6 35 K6
Kestrel Rd DUDN DY1 84 E5
HALE B63 102 F6
LGLYGN/QTN B68 104 D3
Kestrel Wy GTWY WS6 24 A3
Keswick Cl NUN CV11 81 L7
Keswick Dr KGSWFD DY6 83 H7
RUGBYN/HIL CV21 161 G5
Keswick Gn RLSN CV32 206 B4
Keswick Gv FOAKS/STRLY B74 55 K3
Keswick Rd HIA/OLT B92 127 K1
Keswick Wk COVE CV2 156 D1
Ketley Cft BHTH/HG B12 107 K6
Ketley Flds KGSWFD DY6 83 L8
Ketley Hill Rd DUDN DY1 84 D5
Ketley Rd KGSWFD DY6 83 K7
Kettlebrook Rd SHLY B90 148 F7
TAM/AM/WIL B77 46 A1
Kettlehouse Rd KGSTG B44 71 K2
Kettlesbank Rd SEDG DY3 * 84 A3
Kettlewell Cl WWCK CV34 205 J4
Kettlewell Wy
CHWD/FDBR/MGN B37 110 D3
Ketton Gv STETCH B33 110 B6
Keviliok St COVS CV3 155 H7
Kew Cl CHWD/FDBR/MGN B37 110 D2
KNWTH CV8 180 A8
Kew Dr DUDN DY1 84 E3
Kew Gdns STETCH B33 109 H4
Kew Rd RUGBYN/HIL CV21 186 E1
Kewstoke Cl SHHTH WV12 37 M4
Kewstoke Cft NFLD/LBR B31 123 J7
Kewstoke Rd SHHTH WV12 38 A4
Keyes Dr KGSWFD DY6 83 H4
RUGBYS/DCH CV22 186 A3
Key Hl WSNGN B18 88 F8
Key Hill Circ WSNGN B18 88 F8
Key Hill Dr WSNGN B18 89 G8
Keynell Covert BVILLE B30 146 A3
Keynes Dr BILS/COS WV14 51 J7
Keys Crs HHTH/SAND B71 69 G7
Keyse Rd MGN/WHC B75 57 K6
Keys Hl ATHST CV9 62 A4
Keys Park Rd HEDN WS12 17 J2
Keyte Cl TPTN/OCK DY4 67 L8
The Keyway WLNHL WV13 51 L5
Keyworth Cl TPTN/OCK DY4 67 M8
Khyber Cl DARL/WED WS10 52 A5
Kidd Cft DARL/WED WS10 68 A3
Kidderminster Rd BEWD DY12 163 G1
BRGRVW B61 191 J3
HAG/WOL DY9 119 M8
KGSWFD DY6 82 F6
KIDD DY10 119 G6
KIDD DY10 166 E7
Kidderminster Rd South
KIDD DY10 140 C2
Kielder Cl DSYBK/YTR WS5 70 A2
HEDN WS12 17 J3
Kielder Dr NUNW/HART CV10 98 C3
Kielder Gdns HAG/WOL DY9 119 M4
Kier's Bridge Cl TPTN/OCK DY4 85 L2
Kilburn Dr COVW CV5 154 D2
KGSWFD DY6 83 J4
Kilburn Gv KGSTG B44 71 K2
Kilburn Pl DUDS DY2 85 H7
Kilburn Rd KGSTG B44 71 K2
Kilby Av LDYWD/EDGR B16 106 E3
Kilbye Cl TAM/AM/WIL B77 46 D8
Kilby Gv RLSS CV31 207 G8
Kilbys Gv BFLD/HDSWWD B20 88 D3
Kilcote Rd SHLY B90 147 G3
Kildale Cl COV CV1 9 J3
Kilderkin Ct COV CV1 9 H8
Kildwick Wy WWCK CV34 205 J4
Kilmet Wk SMTHWKW B67 * 87 K8
Kilmore Cft CBROM B36 91 J4
Kilmorie Rd ACGN B27 109 G8
CNCK/NC WS11 16 A3
Kiln Cl NUNW/HART CV10 98 C2
RLSN CV32 206 E3
Kiln La SHLY B90 173 K1
YDLY B25 108 F7
Kilnsey Gv WWCK CV34 205 J4
Kiln Wy POL/KGSB/FAZ B78 47 K4
Kilpeck Cl REDE B98 203 K3
Kilsby Gv SOLH B91 149 G5
Kilvert Rd DARL/WED WS10 68 F3
Kilworth Rd RUGBYN/HIL CV21 187 M6
Kimberlee Av KIDD DY10 138 F1
Kimberley TAM/AM/WIL B77 46 D6
Kimberley Av WASH/WDE B8 90 C8
Kimberley Cl COVW CV5 * 153 K1
FOAKS/STRLY B74 55 L3
REDE B98 194 F6
Kimberley Pl BILS/COS WV14 66 F6
Kimberley Rd BDWTH CV12 116 F1
HIA/OLT B92 127 L3
KNWTH CV8 181 J3
RUGBYN/HIL CV21 186 F1
SMTHWK B66 87 L6
Kimberley St BDMR/CCFT WV3 2 B7
Kimble Cl COVW CV5 153 M1
Kimble Gv ERDE/BCHGN B24 91 H2
Kimbley Ri HHTH/SAND B71 68 E6
Kimpton Cl ALE/KHTH/YWD B14 146 C3
Kimsan Cft FOAKS/STRLY B74 55 L6
Kinchford Cl SOLH B91 148 F5
Kineton Cl REDE B98 203 H4
Kineton Cft RIDG/WDGT B32 123 H5
Kineton Green Rd HIA/OLT B92 127 H5
Kineton La HOCK/TIA B94 174 C4
Kineton Ri SEDG DY3 66 A3
Kineton Rd COVE CV2 135 G7
KNWTH CV8 197 M1
RBRY B45 143 J6
SCFLD/BOLD B73 72 C4
Kinfare Dr DUNHL/THL/PER WV6 48 F1
Kinfare Ri SEDG DY3 84 C1
King Charles Av WSLW WS2 52 C3
King Charles Cl KIDDW DY11 138 A7
King Charles Ct KGSTG B44 71 M3
King Charles Rd RMSLY B62 122 D1
King Charles Sq KIDD DY10 * 138 C7
King Edmund St DUDN DY1 84 F3
King Edward Av BRGRVW B61 191 K1
King Edward Rd BRGRVW B61 168 D8
COV CV1 9 K2
MOS/BIL B13 125 K2
NUN CV11 99 H1
RUGBYN/HIL CV21 186 F1
King Edwards Cl
BFLD/HDSWWD B20 * 88 F5
King Edwards Gdns
BFLD/HDSWWD B20 * 88 F6
King Edward's Rd CBHAMW B1 6 B5
King Edward's Rw
BKHL/PFLD WV2 * 2 F9

King Edward's Sq
SCFLD/BOLD B73 ....57 G8
King Edward St
DARL/WED WS10 ....52 B8
Kingfield Rd COVN CV6 ....134 B7
SHLY B90 ....147 G3
Kingfisher TAM/AM/WIL B77 ....46 E7
Kingfisher Av NUNW/HART CV10 ..80 A8
Kingfisher Cl
LGN/SDN/BHAMAIR B26 ....109 L7
SEDG DY3 ....66 A3
Kingfisher Ct ALVE B48 ....170 E6
Kingfisher Dr CBROM B36 ....92 E5
HEDN WS12 ....17 G1
STRBR DY8 ....119 G1
Kingfisher Gv KIDD DY10 ....164 F2
SHHTH WV12 ....37 M5
Kingfisher Rd ERDW/GRVHL B23 ..72 A6
Kingfisher Veiw STETCH B33 ....91 L8
Kingfisher Wk PENK ST19 ....10 D5
Kingfisher Wy SLYOAK B29 ....124 B5
King George Av BRGRVW B61 ....191 K1
King George Cl BRGRVW B61 ....191 J1
King George Crs
RUSH/SHEL WS4 ....39 M7
King George Pl RUSH/SHEL WS4 ..39 M7
King George's Av BDWTH CV12 ....98 F8
COVN CV6 ....134 C3
King George VI Av
DSYBK/YTR WS5 ....54 A5
Kingham Cl REDE B98 ....203 L1
SEDG DY3 ....84 A3
Kingham Covert
ALE/KHTH/YWD B14 ....146 B3
Kingland Dr RLSN CV32 ....206 A4
King Richard St COVE CV2 ....9 L3
Kings Arms La STRPT DY13 ....188 B6
Kings Av ATHST CV9 ....63 J5
HEDN WS12 ....17 G1
OLDBY B69 ....85 M3
Kingsbridge Rd
NUNW/HART CV10 ....81 H7
RIDG/WDGT B32 ....123 H4
Kingsbridge Wk SMTHWK B66 ....87 M8
Kingsbrook Dr SOLH B91 ....148 F5
Kingsbury Av ERDE/BCHGN B24 ....91 H2
Kingsbury Cl RUSH/SHEL WS4 ....53 M1
WALM/CURD B76 ....74 B8
Kingsbury Link
POL/KGSB/FAZ B78 * 60 E3
Kingsbury Rd COVN CV6 ....133 H7
ERDE/BCHGN B24 ....90 C3
TPTN/OCK DY4 ....67 L5
WALM/CURD B76 ....74 A8
WALM/CURD B76 ....75 L3
Kingsclere Wk
ETTPK/GDPK/PENN WV4 ....49 G6
Kingscliff Rd SMHTH B10 ....108 E5
Kings Cl ALE/KHTH/YWD B14 ....125 G7
STUD B80 * 203 L4
Kingscote Cl REDE B98 ....195 H6
Kingscote Gv COVS CV3 ....180 E1
Kingscote Rd DOR/KN B93 ....175 J3
EDG B15 ....106 B6
King's Ct CHWD/FDBR/MGN B37 ..111 J4
NUN CV11 * 98 F1
STRBR DY8 ....101 J8
Kings Cft CBROM B36 ....92 D6
HEDN WS12 ....17 J1
LGN/SDN/BHAMAIR B26 ....109 L8
Kingscroft Cl FOAKS/STRLY B74 ..55 L5
Kingscroft Rd
FOAKS/STRLY B74 ....55 L6
Kingsdene Av STRBR DY8 ....101 G1
Kingsdown Av PBAR/PBCH B42 ....70 D7
Kingsdown Rd BNTWD WS7 ....18 C4
NFLD/LBR B31 ....123 J4
Kingsfield Rd
ALE/KHTH/YWD B14 ....125 J5
Kingsford Cl CBROM B36 ....92 B4
Kingsford Nouveau
KGSWFD DY6 ....83 L8
Kings Gdn BVILLE B30 ....145 J1
Kings Gdns BDWTH CV12 ....117 G3
Kings Green Av
HWK/WKHTH B38 ....145 K3
Kings Gv COVE CV2 ....155 M2
Kingshayes Rd ALDR WS9 ....40 F3
Kingshill Dr HWK/WKHTH B38 ....145 K3
King's Hill Fld DARL/WED WS10 ..52 C8
King's Hill La COVS CV3 ....180 D4
King's Hill Rd LICHS WS14 ....21 G7
Kingsholm Cl COVS CV3 ....156 F4
Kingshurst RLSS CV31 ....207 J7
Kingshurst Rd NFLD/LBR B31 ....144 E2
SHLY B90 ....147 K4
Kingshurst Wy
CHWD/FDBR/MGN B37 ....92 D8
Kingsland Av COVW CV5 ....154 D3
Kingsland Dr DOR/KN B93 ....175 J2
Kingsland Rd KGSTG B44 ....71 J1
WOLV WV1 ....2 C2
Kingslea Rd SOLH B91 ....148 C3
Kingsleigh Cft MGN/WHC B75 ....56 F3
Kingsleigh Dr CBROM B36 ....91 L5
Kingsleigh Rd
BFLD/HDSWWD B20 ....88 F3
Kingsley Av
DUNHL/THL/PER WV6 ....48 F1
HEDN WS12 ....13 G6
REDE B98 ....202 E2
RUGBYN/HIL CV21 ....187 J4
Kingsley Cl CRTAM B79 ....31 L7
Kingsley Ct YDLY B25 * 109 J5
Kingsley Crs BDWTH CV12 ....117 M2
Kingsley Gdns CDSL WV8 ....34 C2
Kingsley Gv SEDG DY3 ....65 M6
Kingsley Rd BHTH/HG B12 ....107 L8
BVILLE B30 ....145 H1
KGSWFD DY6 ....83 G8
Kingsley St DUDS DY2 ....85 G8
WSLW WS2 ....52 F6
Kingsley Ter COVE CV2 ....135 J5
Kingsley Wk COVE CV2 ....135 K5
Kingslow Av
ETTPK/GDPK/PENN WV4 ....49 H7
Kingsmead Ms COVS CV3 ....156 A7
King's Meadow HAG/WOL DY9 ....141 J3
Kingsmere Cl ERDE/BCHGN B24 ....90 C3
Kings Mill Cl DARL/WED WS10 ....52 C8
Kings Newnham La
RRUGBY CV23 ....158 E6
Kings Newnham Rd
RRUGBY CV23 ....158 F7
Kings Park Dr COVS CV3 ....156 F4
Kings Rd ALE/KHTH/YWD B14 ....125 G7
ERDW/GRVHL B23 ....90 A1
KGSTG B44 ....71 J2
KGSTG B44 ....72 A3
KIDDW DY11 ....138 A7
RUSH/SHEL WS4 ....40 A6
SEDG DY3 ....66 C5
SPARK B11 ....108 E8
WOLVN WV10 ....14 F7
Kings Sq BILS/COS WV14 * 66 E5
Kings Street Prec
DARL/WED WS10 ....52 B7
Kingstanding Rd KGSTG B44 ....71 K3
Kings Ter ALE/KHTH/YWD B14 ....125 G7
Kingsthorpe Rd
ALE/KHTH/YWD B14 ....146 E2
Kingston Cl CRTAM B79 ....32 A6
Kingston Ms RLSS CV31 ....207 G7
Kingston Rd BORD B9 ....107 M4
COVW CV5 ....154 D3
Kingston Rw CBHAMW B1 ....6 C5
Kingston Wy KGSWFD DY6 ....83 G6
King St ALDR WS9 ....40 D3
BDWTH CV12 ....117 G3
BILS/COS WV14 ....66 F4
BILS/COS WV14 ....67 J2
BNTWD WS7 ....18 D8
BRLYHL DY5 ....102 D5
CDYHTH B64 ....103 K4
CRTAM B79 ....45 M1
DARL/WED WS10 ....68 C3
DUDS DY2 ....85 G4
HAG/WOL DY9 ....120 D1
HALE B63 ....121 L1
RLSN CV32 ....206 E4
RUGBYN/HIL CV21 ....186 E1
SMTHWK B66 ....87 M6
SPARK B11 ....107 L7
STRBR DY8 ....101 J7
WLNHL WV13 ....51 M3
WOLV WV1 ....2 F5
WSL WS1 ....4 D9
King Street Pas BRLYHL DY5 ....102 E5
DUDS DY2 ....85 H4
Kingsway CNCK/NC WS11 ....16 E1
COVE CV2 ....155 L2
LGLYGN/QTN B68 ....104 F6
NUN CV11 ....98 F1
POL/KGSB/FAZ B78 ....60 A7
RLSS CV31 ....206 D7
RUGBYS/DCH CV22 ....186 E4
STRBR DY8 ....101 H5
STRPT DY13 ....163 J6
WNSFLD WV11 ....37 L1
WOLVN WV10 ....36 E7
Kingsway Av TPTN/OCK DY4 ....67 L5
Kingsway Dr HWK/WKHTH B38 ....145 K3
Kingsway North ALDR WS9 * 40 C7
Kingsway Rd WOLVN WV10 ....36 E7
Kingsway South ALDR WS9 * 40 C7
Kingsway Ter WNSFLD WV11 * 37 L1
Kingswear Av
DUNHL/THL/PER WV6 ....48 D2
Kingswinford Rd BRLYHL DY5 ....84 C6
Kingswood Av CNCK/NC WS11 ....16 A4
RCOVN/BALC/EX CV7 ....114 F5
Kingswood Cl COVN CV6 ....134 B4
HOCK/TIA B94 ....176 C8
SHLY B90 ....148 B4
Kingswood Cft VAUX/NECH B7 ....90 A6
Kingswood Dr BVILLE B30 ....146 A2
CNCK/NC WS11 ....17 K8
FOAKS/STRLY B74 ....71 K1
GTWY WS6 ....24 E1
Kingswood Gdns
BDMR/CCFT WV3 ....49 K7
Kingswood Rd MOS/BIL B13 ....125 L1
NFLD/LBR B31 ....144 D7
NUNW/HART CV10 ....97 M2
STRBR DY8 ....101 G1
Kingswood Ter YDLY B25 * 108 F6
Kington Cl SHHTH WV12 ....37 M5
Kington Gdns
CHWD/FDBR/MGN B37 ....110 D3
Kington Wy STETCH B33 ....109 J4
King William St COV CV1 ....9 J2
STRBR DY8 ....101 K5
Kiniths Crs HHTH/SAND B71 ....87 J1
Kiniths Wy HHTH/SAND B71 ....87 J1
RMSLY B62 ....104 C4
Kinlet Cl BDMR/CCFT WV3 ....48 E5
REDE B98 ....203 J2
Kinlet Gv NFLD/LBR B31 ....145 G3
Kinloch Dr DUDN DY1 ....84 D2
Kinman Wy RUGBYN/HIL CV21 ....161 G7
Kinnerley St WSL WS1 ....5 J5
Kinnersley Cl REDE B98 ....203 J2
Kinnersley Crs OLDBY B69 ....86 B8
Kinnerton Crs SLYOAK B29 ....123 K3
Kinross Av HEDN WS12 ....12 D6
Kinross Cl NUNW/HART CV10 ....98 D3
Kinross Crs GTB/HAM B43 ....70 F1
Kinross Rd RLSN CV32 ....206 F1
Kinsall Gn TAM/AM/WIL B77 ....47 G7
Kinsey Gv ALE/KHTH/YWD B14 ....146 D1
Kinsham Dr SOLH B91 ....148 F5
Kintore Cft RIDG/WDGT B32 ....122 F5
Kintyre Cl RBRY B45 ....143 J4
The Kintyre COVE CV2 ....135 M6
Kinver Av KIDDW DY11 ....163 L5
SHHTH WV12 ....37 M8
Kinver Cl COVE CV2 ....135 J4
Kinver Crs ALDR WS9 ....41 G4
Kinver Cft BHTH/HG B12 ....107 J7
WALM/CURD B76 ....73 K5
Kinver Dr
ETTPK/GDPK/PENN WV4 ....49 G8
HAG/WOL DY9 ....120 A6
Kinver Rd NFLD/LBR B31 ....145 H3
Kinver St STRBR DY8 ....101 H4
Kinwalsey La
RCOVN/BALC/EX CV7 ....113 J7
Kinwarton Cl
LGN/SDN/BHAMAIR B26 ....109 H7
Kipling Av BILS/COS WV14 ....66 F4
Kipling Cl NUNW/HART CV10 ....79 L8
TPTN/OCK DY4 ....67 L5
Kipling Ri CRTAM B79 ....31 K5
Kipling Rd COVN CV6 ....133 K5
NFLD/LBR B31 ....145 G1
SEDG DY3 ....65 L8
SHHTH WV12 ....38 C6
WOLVN WV10 ....36 B3
Kirby Av WWCK CV34 ....205 K4
Kirby Cl BILS/COS WV14 ....67 J2
COV CV1 ....134 B7
KNWTH CV8 ....157 K8
Kirby Corner Rd TLHL/CAN CV4 ..153 M8
Kirby Dr DUDN DY1 ....84 C2
Kirby Rd COVW CV5 ....154 D3
WSNGN B18 ....88 C7
Kirkby Cl RUGBYN/HIL CV21 ....161 J7
Kirkby Gn SCFLD/BOLD B73 ....72 E2
Kirkby Rd RUGBYN/HIL CV21 ....187 K5
Kirkdale Av COVN CV6 ....134 B2
Kirkham Gdns BRLYHL DY5 ....84 A7
Kirkham Gv STETCH B33 ....109 K1
Kirkham Wy TPTN/OCK DY4 ....67 L8
Kirkland Wy POL/KGSB/FAZ B78 ....44 F5
Kirkside Gv BRWNH WS8 ....26 D6
Kirkstall BLOX/PEL WS3 ....38 D3
Kirkstall Crs BLOX/PEL WS3 ....38 D3
Kirkstone RUGBYN/HIL CV21 ....161 H6
Kirkstone Ct BRLYHL DY5 ....101 M5
Kirkstone Crs GTB/HAM B43 ....70 D7
WMBN WV5 ....64 D7
Kirkstone Rd BDWTH CV12 ....116 E3
Kirkstone Wy BRLYHL DY5 ....101 M5
Kirkwall Rd RIDG/WDGT B32 ....123 H4
Kirkwood Av ERDW/GRVHL B23 ....72 D6
Kirstead Gdns
DUNHL/THL/PER WV6 ....48 F2
Kirtley TAM/AM/WIL B77 ....46 C3
Kirton Cl COVN CV6 ....133 K4
Kirton Gv DUNHL/THL/PER WV6 ....49 G1
SOLH B91 ....148 E4
STETCH B33 ....109 L1
Kitchener Rd COVN CV6 ....134 C4
DUDS DY2 ....85 K4
SLYOAK B29 ....124 F4
Kitchener St SMTHWK B66 ....88 B7
Kitchen La WNSFLD WV11 ....37 J5
WNSFLD WV11 ....37 L3
Kitebrook Cl REDE B98 ....203 J1
SHLY B90 ....148 E6
Kite La REDW B97 ....193 L8
Kites Cl WWCK CV34 ....205 J3
Kites Nest La RWWCK/WEL CV35 ..196 A4
Kitsland Rd BKDE/SHDE B34 ....92 C7
Kitswell Gdns RIDG/WDGT B32 ....122 E5
Kittermaster Rd
RCOVN/BALC/EX CV7 ....130 F3
Kittiwake Dr BRLYHL DY5 ....102 A6
KIDD DY10 ....164 F2
Kittoe Rd FOAKS/STRLY B74 ....56 D2
Kitt's Green Rd STETCH B33 ....109 M2
Kitwell La RIDG/WDGT B32 ....122 E5
Kitwood Av POL/KGSB/FAZ B78 ....47 K7
Kitwood Dr HIA/OLT B92 ....128 B6
Kixley La DOR/KN B93 ....150 A7
Klevedon Cl NUN CV11 ....99 L4
Knaresdale Cl BRLYHL DY5 ....102 A5
Knaves Castle Av BRWNH WS8 ....26 D3
Knebley Crs NUNW/HART CV10 ....99 G4
Knebworth Cl KGSTG B44 ....71 J5
The Knibbs WWCK CV34 * 205 J6
Knight Av COV CV1 ....9 K7
Knightcote Dr SOLH B91 ....148 F5
Knightley Cl RLSN CV32 ....199 J8
Knightley Rd SOLH B91 ....148 D3
Knightlow Av COVS CV3 ....156 A8
Knightlow Cl KNWTH CV8 ....198 A2
Knightlow Rd HRBN B17 ....105 M5
Knighton Cl FOAKS/STRLY B74 ....56 D2
Knighton Dr FOAKS/STRLY B74 ....56 D3
Knighton Rd DUDS DY2 ....103 H1
FOAKS/STRLY B74 ....42 B8
HEDN WS12 ....17 J2
NFLD/LBR B31 ....145 G1
Knight Rd BNTWD WS7 ....18 C4
KIDDW DY11 ....138 A2
Knights Av
DUNHL/THL/PER WV6 ....35 J7
Knightsbridge Av BDWTH CV12 ....98 F8
Knightsbridge Cl
FOAKS/STRLY B74 ....56 D1
Knightsbridge La SHHTH WV12 ....37 M7
Knightsbridge Rd HIA/OLT B92 ....127 K4
Knights Cl ERDW/GRVHL B23 ....90 C3
PENK ST19 ....10 D6
Knights Ct
CHWD/FDBR/MGN B37 ....111 J5
CNCK/NC WS11 ....25 L1
Knights Crs
DUNHL/THL/PER WV6 ....35 J6
Knightsfield Cl SCFLD/BOLD B73 ..72 A2
Knightsford Cl REDW B97 ....201 K3
Knights Hl ALDR WS9 ....54 F2
Knights Rd SPARK B11 ....126 E1
Knights Templar Wy
TLHL/CAN CV4 ....153 L4
Knightstone Av WSNGN B18 ....106 E1
Knights Wood Cl MGN/WHC B75 ..57 H6
Knightwick Crs
ERDW/GRVHL B23 ....72 A8
Knipersley Rd ERDW/GRVHL B23 ..72 E7
Knob Hl RRUGBY CV23 ....183 K7
Knoll Cl BNTWD WS7 ....18 E8
Knoll Cft ALDR WS9 ....41 G4
COVS CV3 ....155 G7
LDYWD/EDGR B16 * 106 E3
SHLY B90 ....174 B1
Knoll Dr COVS CV3 ....155 G7
WWCK CV34 ....205 J3
The Knoll KGSWFD DY6 ....83 J8
RIDG/WDGT B32 ....123 G4
Knottsall La LGLYGN/QTN B68 ....104 F2
Knotts Farm Rd KGSWFD DY6 ....101 G1
Knowesley Cl BRGRVE B60 ....191 M3
Knowlands Rd SOLH B91 ....148 E6
Knowle Cl RBRY B45 ....144 B6
REDE B98 ....195 G7
Knowle Hl ATHST CV9 ....77 G1
KNWTH CV8 ....180 A7
Knowle Hill Rd DUDS DY2 ....102 F1
Knowle La LICHS WS14 ....28 F3
Knowle Rd BLKHTH/ROWR B65 ....103 K1
HIA/OLT B92 ....150 C3
SPARK B11 ....126 B2
Knowles Av NUNW/HART CV10 ....98 A1
Knowles Dr FOAKS/STRLY B74 ....56 E6
Knowles Rd WOLV WV1 ....3 L6
Knowles St DARL/WED WS10 ....68 E2
Knowle Wood Rd DOR/KN B93 ....175 M7
Knox Crs NUN CV11 ....81 K6
Knox Rd BKHL/PFLD WV2 ....50 A7
Knox's Grave La LICHS WS14 ....29 M6
Knutswood Cl MOS/BIL B13 * 126 B6
Kohima Dr STRBR DY8 ....101 J8
Kossuth Rd BILS/COS WV14 ....66 E4
Kurtus TAM/AM/WIL B77 ....46 B7
Kyle Cl WOLVN WV10 ....35 M4
Kylemilne Wy STRPT DY13 ....189 G2
Kyles Wy RIDG/WDGT B32 ....122 F6
Kynaston Crs CDSL WV8 ....34 F3
Kyngsford Rd STETCH B33 ....110 B2
Kynner Wy COVS CV3 ....156 F5
Kyotts Lake Rd SPARK B11 ....107 L6
Kyrwicks La BHTH/HG B12 ....107 L6
Kyter La CBROM B36 ....91 M5

L

Laburnham Rd KGSWFD DY6 ....83 J7
Laburnum Av
CHWD/FDBR/MGN B37 ....92 D7
CNCK/NC WS11 ....16 B6
COVN CV6 ....133 K8
CRTAM B79 ....31 M5
KNWTH CV8 ....197 L1
SMTHWK B67 ....105 J1
Laburnum Cl BDWTH CV12 ....116 C3
BLOX/PEL WS3 ....39 K3
CHWD/FDBR/MGN B37 ....92 D7
CNCK/NC WS11 ....16 C6
HLYWD B47 ....146 E8
POL/KGSB/FAZ B78 ....60 B7
REDE B98 ....202 C3
Laburnum Cft OLDBY B69 ....85 M3
Laburnum Dr WALM/CURD B76 ....73 L2
Laburnum Gv BNTWD WS7 ....18 D7
BRGRVW B61 ....191 K1
KIDDW DY11 ....137 L5
MOS/BIL B13 * 125 K2
NUNW/HART CV10 ....80 B7
RUGBYS/DCH CV22 ....186 C5
WSLW WS2 ....52 D2
WWCK CV34 ....205 M4
Laburnum Rd ALDR WS9 ....40 E2
BVILLE B30 ....124 D6
DARL/WED WS10 ....68 F2
DSYBK/YTR WS5 ....54 A8
DUDN DY1 ....84 F1
ETTPK/GDPK/PENN WV4 ....66 C2
TPTN/OCK DY4 ....67 K6
WOLV WV1 ....50 F5
Laburnum St BDMR/CCFT WV3 ....2 B7
STRBR DY8 ....101 J6
Laburnum Vls SPARK B11 * 108 A8
Laburnum Wy NFLD/LBR B31 ....144 E4
Lacell Cl WWCK CV34 ....205 H4
Laches Cl WOLVN WV10 ....14 B8
Laches La WOLVN WV10 ....22 C3
Ladbroke Dr WALM/CURD B76 ....73 K3
Ladbroke Gv ACGN B27 ....127 G5
Ladbroke Pk WWCK CV34 * 205 J5
Ladbrook Cl REDE B98 ....202 C6
Ladbrook Gv SEDG DY3 ....83 L2
Ladbrook Rd COVW CV5 ....153 L1
SOLH B91 ....149 G2
Ladbury Gv DSYBK/YTR WS5 ....69 L1
Ladbury Rd DSYBK/YTR WS5 ....69 L1
Ladeler Gv STETCH B33 ....110 B3
Ladies Wk SEDG DY3 ....66 B5
Lady Bank CRTAM B79 * 45 M1
RIDG/WDGT B32 ....122 F6
Lady Br POL/KGSB/FAZ B78 ....45 L1
Lady Bracknell Ms
NFLD/LBR B31 ....145 G1
Lady Byron La DOR/KN B93 ....149 K6
Ladycroft LDYWD/EDGR B16 ....6 A6
RLSN CV32 ....199 J8
Ladyfields Wy
RCOVN/BALC/EX CV7 ....133 M1
Lady Grey's Wk STRBR DY8 ....101 H8
Ladygrove Cl REDE B98 ....202 E5
Lady Harriet's La REDE B98 ....202 D1
Lady La COVN CV6 ....134 D1
HOCK/TIA B94 ....173 L3
Ladymead Dr COVN CV6 ....133 M3
Lady Meadow Cl
POL/KGSB/FAZ B78 ....45 L2
Ladymoor Rd BILS/COS WV14 ....67 G3
Ladypool Av SPARK B11 * 107 M7
Ladypool Cl RMSLY B62 ....122 A1
Ladypool Pl RUSH/SHEL WS4 ....39 L8
Ladypool Rd BHTH/HG B12 ....107 L8
Ladysmith Rd HALE B63 ....103 G7
Ladysmock RRUGBY CV23 ....161 H5
Lady Warwick Av BDWTH CV12 ..117 G3
Ladywell Cl WMBN WV5 ....64 E5
Ladywell Wk DIG/EDG B5 ....7 G7
Ladywood Circ
LDYWD/EDGR B16 ....106 E3
Ladywood Cl BRLYHL DY5 ....102 D3
Ladywood Middleway
LDYWD/EDGR B16 ....106 E3
Ladywood Rd FOAKS/STRLY B74 ..56 E5
LDYWD/EDGR B16 ....106 D4
Laggan Cl NUNW/HART CV10 ....80 A8
Lagonda TAM/AM/WIL B77 ....46 B2
Lagrange CRTAM B79 ....31 J7
The Lair POL/KGSB/FAZ B78 ....47 K5
Lake Av DSYBK/YTR WS5 ....5 M9
Lake Cl DSYBK/YTR WS5 ....54 A6
Lakedown Cl
ALE/KHTH/YWD B14 ....146 C4
Lakefield Cl HLGN/YWD B28 ....126 F6
Lakefield Rd WNSFLD WV11 ....37 J8
Lakehouse Gv
HWK/WKHTH B38 ....145 H2
Lakehouse Rd ERDW/GRVHL B23 ..72 C5
Lakeland Dr TAM/AM/WIL B77 ....46 E6
Lakenheath CRTAM B79 ....32 A6
Lakes Cl KIDDW DY11 ....138 A6
Lakes Ct BEWD DY12 ....162 D2
Lakeside BDWTH CV12 ....116 E3
CHWD/FDBR/MGN B37 ....111 J5
FOAKS/STRLY B74 ....41 M8
REDW B97 ....193 H6
Lakeside Cl WLNHL WV13 ....51 J2
Lakeside Ct BRLYHL DY5 ....101 M5
Lakeside Dr CNCK/NC WS11 ....17 L7
SHLY B90 ....148 D6
Lakeside Rd WBROM B70 ....68 E7
Lakes Rd ERDW/GRVHL B23 ....71 L7
The Lakes Rd BEWD DY12 ....162 D2
Lake St SEDG DY3 ....84 B2
Lake View Rd COVW CV5 ....154 D1
Lakewood Dr RBRY B45 ....143 M4
Lakey La HLGN/YWD B28 ....126 E5
Lakin Ct WWCK CV34 ....205 K5
Lakin Rd WWCK CV34 ....205 K5
Lambah Cl BILS/COS WV14 ....51 J6
Lamb Cl BKDE/SHDE B34 ....92 C8
Lamb Crs WMBN WV5 ....64 D8
Lambert Cl ERDW/GRVHL B23 ....72 B8
Lambert Ct KGSWFD DY6 ....83 H5
Lambert Dr BNTWD WS7 ....18 E6
Lambert End WBROM B70 ....86 F2
Lambert Fold DUDS DY2 ....85 J5
Lambert Rd WOLVN WV10 ....36 D7
Lambert St WBROM B70 ....86 F2
Lambeth Cl
CHWD/FDBR/MGN B37 ....110 F1
COVE CV2 ....135 J6
Lambeth Rd BILS/COS WV14 ....50 F6
KGSTG B44 ....71 J2
Lambourn Crs RLSS CV31 ....207 G7
Lambourne Cl COVW CV5 ....153 L1
GTWY WS6 ....24 D2
LICHS WS14 ....21 J5
Lambourne Gv STETCH B33 ....110 C3
Lambourne Wy BRLYHL DY5 ....101 M5
CNCK/NC WS11 ....17 L8
Lambourn Rd ERDW/GRVHL B23 ..90 B1
WLNHL WV13 ....52 B4
Lambscote Cl SHLY B90 ....147 G3
Lamb St COV CV1 ....8 E3
Lamerton Cl COVE CV2 ....135 G7
Lamintone Dr RLSN CV32 ....206 A3
Lammas Cl HIA/OLT B92 ....128 A4
Lammas Ct KNWTH CV8 ....183 L2
Lammas House COVN CV6 * 8 A2
Lammas Rd COVN CV6 ....154 D1
STRBR DY8 ....101 G2
Lammermoor Av GTB/HAM B43 ....70 D3
Lamont Av RIDG/WDGT B32 ....123 K2
Lamorna Cl BDMR/CCFT WV3 ....48 F5
NUN CV11 ....99 K1
Lamp La RCOVN/BALC/EX CV7 ....96 D7
Lamprey TAM/AM/WIL B77 ....46 B7
Lanark Cft CVALE B35 ....91 K2
Lancaster Av ALDR WS9 ....40 F5
DARL/WED WS10 ....69 G2
RBRY B45 ....143 L5
Lancaster Circus Queensway
CBHAMNE B4 ....7 H2
Lancaster Cl ATHST CV9 ....63 J4
BVILLE B30 ....124 E7
Lancaster Dr CVALE B35 ....91 M3
Lancaster Gdns
ETTPK/GDPK/PENN WV4 ....49 J8
Lancaster Pl BLOX/PEL WS3 ....39 G3
KNWTH CV8 ....197 J3
Lancaster Rd BEWD DY12 ....162 D2
BRLYHL DY5 10
RUGBYN/HIL CV21 18
Lancaster St CBHAMNE B4 ....
Lance Dr BNTWD WS7 1
Lancelot Cl WASH/WDE B8 10
Lanchester Cl CRTAM B79 3
Lanchester Rd COVN CV6 13
HWK/WKHTH B38 14
Lanchester Wy CBROM B36 9
Lancia Cl COVN CV6 13
Lander Cl RBRY B45 14
Landgate Rd HDSW B21 8
Land La CHWD/FDBR/MGN B37 ..11
Land Oak Dr KIDD DY10 13
Landor Rd DOR/KN B93 14
REDE B98 20
WWCK CV34 20
Landor St WASH/WDE B8 10
Landport Rd WOLV WV1 ....
Landrake Rd KGSWFD DY6 8
Landsdown Pl WSNGN B18 8
Landseer Cl RUGBYN/HIL CV21 18
Landseer Gv GTB/HAM B43 7
Landsgate STRBR DY8 11
Landswood Cl KGSTG B44 7
Landswood Rd
LGLYGN/QTN B68 10
Landywood Gn GTWY WS6 2
Landywood La GTWY WS6 2
Lane Av WSLW WS2 5
Lane Cl WSLW WS2 5
Lane Cft WALM/CURD B76 7
Lane Green Av CDSL WV8 3
Lane Green Rd CDSL WV8 3
Lane Rd ETTPK/GDPK/PENN WV4 ..6
Lanes Cl WMBN WV5 6
Lanesfield Dr
ETTPK/GDPK/PENN WV4 6
Laneside COVS CV3 15
Laneside Av FOAKS/STRLY B74 5
Laneside Gdns WSLW WS2 5
Lane St BILS/COS WV14 6
Langbank Av COVS CV3 15
Langcliffe Av WWCK CV34 20
Langcomb Rd SHLY B90 14
Langdale Av COVN CV6 13
Langdale Cl BRWNH WS8 2
RLSN CV32 20
RUGBYN/HIL CV21 16
Langdale Ct TAM/AM/WIL B77 3
Langdale Cft HDSW B21 8
Langdale Dr BILS/COS WV14 5
CNCK/NC WS11 1
NUN CV11 8
Langdale Rd GTB/HAM B43 7
STRPT DY13 18
Langdale Wy HAG/WOL DY9 12
Langdon St BORD B9 10
Langfield Rd DOR/KN B93 14
Langford Av GTB/HAM B43 7
Langford Cl WSL WS1 ....
Langford Cft SOLH B91 14
Langford Gv HRBN B17 12
Langham Cl
LGN/SDN/BHAMAIR B26 10
Langham Gn FOAKS/STRLY B74 5
Langholm Dr HEDN WS12 1
SCFLD/BOLD B73 7
Langland Dr SEDG DY3 6
Langley Av BILS/COS WV14 6
Langley Cl REDE B98 20
Langley Crs LGLYGN/QTN B68 10
Langley Cft TLHL/CAN CV4 15
Langley Dr CVALE B35 9
Langley Gdns BDMR/CCFT WV3 4
Langley Green Rd OLDBY B69 10
Langley Gv SMHTH B10 * 10
Langley Hall Dr MGN/WHC B75 5
Langley Hall Rd HIA/OLT B92 12
MGN/WHC B75 5
Langley Heath Dr
WALM/CURD B76 7
Langley High St OLDBY B69 8
Langley Ri HIA/OLT B92 12
Langley Rd
ETTPK/GDPK/PENN WV4 4
LGLYGN/QTN B68 10
SMHTH B10 10
Langleys Rd SLYOAK B29 12
Langlodge Rd COVN CV6 13
Langmead Cl WSLW WS2 5
Langnor Rd COVE CV2 13
Langsett Rd WOLVN WV10 3
Langstone Rd
ALE/KHTH/YWD B14 14
DUDN DY1 8
Langton Cl CBROM B36 9
COVS CV3 15
Langton Pl BILS/COS WV14 5
Langton Rd RUGBYN/HIL CV21 18
WASH/WDE B8 10
Langtree Av SOLH B91 14
Langtree Cl HEDN WS12 1
Langwood Cl TLHL/CAN CV4 15
Langwood Ct CBROM B36 9
Langworth Av ACGN B27 10
Lannacombe Rd NFLD/LBR B31 ..14
Lansbury Av DARL/WED WS10 6
Lansbury Dr CNCK/NC WS11 1
Lansbury Gn CDYHTH B64 10
Lansbury Rd CDYHTH B64 10
Lansdale Av HIA/OLT B92 12
Lansdowne Av CDSL WV8 3
Lansdowne Circ RLSN CV32 20
Lansdowne Cl BDWTH CV12 11
BILS/COS WV14 6
DUDS DY2 8
Lansdowne Crs RLSN CV32 * 20
TAM/AM/WIL B77 4
Lansdowne Pl
RUGBYN/HIL CV21 18
Lansdowne Rd BILS/COS WV14 5
ERDE/BCHGN B24 9
HALE B63 12
HDSW B21 8
RLSN CV32 20
RMSLY B62 10
WOLV WV1 ....
Lansdowne St COVE CV2 ....
RLSN CV32 20
WSNGN B18 10
Lansdown Gn KIDDW DY11 13
Lansdown Pl WSNGN B18 * 8
Lant Cl RCOVN/BALC/EX CV7 15
Lantern Rd DUDS DY2 10
Lapal La RIDG/WDGT B32 12
Lapal La North RMSLY B62 12
Lapal La South RMSLY B62 12
Lapley Cl WOLV WV1 5
Lapper Av
ETTPK/GDPK/PENN WV4 6
Lapwing TAM/AM/WIL B77 4
Lapwing Cl GTWY WS6 2
KIDD DY10 16
Lapwing Cft ERDW/GRVHL B23 7
Lapwing Dr HIA/OLT B92 12
Lapwood Av KGSWFD DY6 8
Lapworth Cl REDE B98 * 20
Lapworth Dr SCFLD/BOLD B73 7

...worth Gv BHTH/HG B12 ....107 K7
...worth Rd COVE CV2 ....135 G4
...ci HRBN B17 ....105 M5
...a Gv TPTN/OCK DY4 ....85 L3
...ham Av HDSW B21 ....88 B3
...ch CI KNWTH DY7 ....118 A2
...CHS WS14 ....21 J6
...UGBYS/DCH CV22 ....185 M3
...h Cft
...HWD/FDBR/MGN B37 ....110 F3
...LDBY B69 ....85 M3
...ches Cottage Gdns
...LDDW DY11 *............................164 B2
...ches La BDMR/CCFT WV3 ....2 B1
...ches St SPARK B11 ....107 L2
...Larches POL/KGSB/FAZ B78 ....60 B6
...chfield WS14 ....116 C8
...ch BFLD/HDSWWD B20...88 F2
...chfields KNWTH CV8 ....8 E1
...WCK CV34 ....205 L6
...chmere Dr BRGRVW B61 ....191 H2
...LGN/VWD B28 ....126 D5
...ch Rd KGSWFD DY6 ....83 J4
...d Tree Av COVW CV5 ....153 L2
...chwood Crs
...OAKS/STRLY B74 ....55 G3
...chwood Gn DSYBK/YTR WS5 ....69 J6
...chwood Gn DSYBK/YTR WS5 ....69 J6
...chwood COVN/BALC/EX CV7 ....116 F5
...combe Dr
...TTPK/GDPK/PENN WV4 ....50 B8
...ge Av DARL/WED WS10 ....68 A1
...ci CIE ALE/KHTH/YWD B14 ....146 A3
...kfield Av CBROM B36 ....91 M5
...kfield Wy COVW CV5 ....132 E7
...khill KIDD DY10 ....138 C6
...khill Rd LICHS WS14 ....119 G1
...khill Wk ALE/KHTH/YWD B14 ....146 A3
...kin CI BDWTH CV12 ....117 M2
...VOLVN WV10 ....36 E4
...kin Gv COVE CV2 ....135 K7
...k Meadow Dr
...HWD/FDBR/MGN B37 ....110 C2
...kspur RUGBYS/DCH CV22 ....161 M3
...AM/AM/WIL B77 ....60 C3
...kspur Av WNSFLD WS7 ....18 D5
...kspur Cft CBROM B36 ....91 M4
...kspur Dr WOLVN WV10 ....22 F6
...kspur CI DUDS DY2 ....85 K5
...kspur Wy BRWNH WS8 ....26 D7
...kswood Dr
...TTPK/GDPK/PENN WV4 ....65 G2
...ne Rd
...LGN/SDN/BHAMAIR B26 ....109 L8
...sington CI REDE B98 ....203 J2
...ches CI DARL/WED WS10 ....52 C7
...chford CI REDE B98 ....195 J3
...elow Rd STRETCH B33 ....109 L3
...ham Av GTB/HAM B43 ....70 C6
...ham Crs TPTN/OCK DY4 ....85 L2
...ham Rd COVW CV5 ....8 A5
...herford CI WOLVN WV10 ....14 F8
...herford La WOLVN WV10 ....14 F8
...hom Gv STETCH B33 ....91 M8
...hom Gv STETCH B33 ....91 M8
...imer CI KNWTH CV8 ....197 K3
...imer Gdns EDG B15 ....107 H6
...imer PI WSNGN B18 ....88 C7
...imer St WLNHL WV13 ....51 L1
...der CI SEDG DY3 ....51 H4
...derdale CI ALDR WS9 ....41 J3
...derdale CI BRWNH WS8 ....26 C4
...RUGBYS/DCH CV22 ....185 M1
...ghton CI NFLD/LBR B31 ....144 F4
...AM/AM/WIL B77 ....46 B3
...inceston Dr NUN CV11 ....99 K3
...inceston Rd DSYBK/YTR WS5 ....54 B8
...e Launde
...ALE/KHTH/YWD B14 ....147 H2
...intry Rd SMTHWK B66 ....106 A2
...ral Dr SMTHWK B66 ....87 M5
...reates Wk FOAKS/STRLY B74...56 E4
...POL/KGSB/FAZ B78 ....47 L6
...rel Bank CRTAM B79 ....31 M7
...rel CI COVE CV2 ....135 J3
...LICH WS14 ....21 H5
...REDE B98 ....202 C3
...rel Dr BNTWD WS7 ....19 G6
...OAKS/STRLY B74 ....55 J5
...HEDN WS12 ....17 J1
...NUNW/HART CV10 ....79 J1
...RUGBYS/DCH CV22 ....185 M4
...SMTHWK B66 ....87 C5
...rel Gdns HDSW B21 ....88 C4
...rel Gdns BDMR/CCFT WV3 ....49 J7
...BILS/COS WV14 ....67 L1
...BRGRVW B61 ....191 K4
...rel La HALE B63 ....121 M2
...rel Rd BVILLE B30 ....124 C7
...rel Rd BVILLE B30 ....145 L1
...DSYBK/YTR WS5 ....53 M8
...DUDN DY1 ....84 F2
...HDSW B21 ....88 C3
...TPTN/OCK DY4 ....67 K6
...rels Crs
...RCOVN/BALC/EX CV7 ....152 A7
...e Laurels
...POL/KGSB/FAZ B78 ....60 B6
...SMTHWK B66 * 106 A1
...rence Gv
...DUNHL/THL/PER WV6 ....35 J3
...riston CI DUDN DY1 ....84 D2
...render Av COVN CV6 ....133 G4
...render CI BDWTH CV12 ....116 C4
...COVEN WV9 ....35 K7
...RUGBYS/DCH CV23 ....161 J5
...render Gdns
...ERDW/GRVHL B23 ....71 H6
...render Rd BILS/COS WV14 ....51 L1
...BLOX/PEL WS3 ....39 J8
...render Hall La
...RCOVN/BALC/EX CV7 ....151 M4
...render Rd BDWTH CV12 ....117 H1
...render Rd DUDN DY1 ....84 F2
...AM/AM/WIL B77 ....46 C1
...rendon La PBAR/PBCH B42 ....70 C7
...a RMSLY B62 ....122 C2
...n Cliff Rd PBAR/PBCH B42 ....70 C7
...den Rd SMHTH B10 ....107 H5
...IX/NECH B7 *.................................7 H3
...ford CI COVS CV3 ....156 C4
...EX/NECH B7 ....107 J4

...SHLY B90 ....147 H3
Lawford Heath La
RRUGBY CV23 ....184 F8
Lawford La RUGBYS/DCH CV22...185 M4
Lawford Rd RLSS CV31 ....206 E7
RUGBYN/HIL CV21 ....186 D2
Lawfred Av WNSFLD WV11 ....37 K4
Lawley CI RUSH/SHEL WS4 ....39 M4
TLHL/CAN CV4 ....153 L3
Lawley Middleway
VAUX/NECH B7 ....7 L2
Lawley Rd BILS/COS WV14 ....50 F7
Lawley St DUDN DY1 ....84 E4
WBROM B70 ....86 D2
The Lawley HALE B63 ....121 G4
Lawn Av STRBR DY8 ....119 J1
Lawnoaks CI BRWNH WS8 ....26 B3
Lawn Rd BKHL/PFLD WV2 ....50 C7
Lawnsdale CI CSHL/WTROR B46 ......93 K7
Lawnside Gn BILS/COS WV14 ....51 H5
The Lawns BDWTH CV12 ....116 B3
Lawn St STRBR DY8 ....119 J1
Lawnswood KINVER DY7 ....100 E1
WALM/CURD B76 ....73 L5
The Lawns BDWTH CV12 ....116 B3
Lawnswood Av HEDN WS12 ....17 H4
Lawnswood Dr ALDR WS9 ....40 E2
KINVER DY7 ....100 E1
Lawnswood Gv HDSW B21 ....88 A4
Lawnswood Ri
DUNHL/THL/PER WV6 ....35 K4
Lawnswood Rd DUDS DY2 ....103 H2
Lawnswood CI HEDN WS12 ....17 H4
Lawnswood Gr SEDG DY3 ....66 B8
Lawnwood Rd DUDS DY2 ....103 G2
Lawrence Av WNSFLD WV11 ....37 K7
WOLVN WV10 ....50 A1
Lawrence Ct WALM/CURD B76 ....74 B7
Lawrence Dr WALM/CURD B76 ....74 B7
Lawrence La CDYHTH B64 ....105 G3
Lawrence Rd RUGBYN/HIL CV21...187 H2
Lawrence Saunders Rd
COVN CV6 ....133 M8
Lawrence Sheriff St
RUGBYS/DCH CV22 ....186 E3
Lawrence St HAG/WOL DY9 ....102 A7
WLNHL WV13 ....51 L2
Lawrence Wk GTB/HAM B43 ....71 H1
Lawson CI ALDR WS9 ....54 F1
Lawson St HHTH/SAND B71 ....69 G8
Lawton CI OLDBY B69 ....86 A7
Laxey Rd LDYWD/EDGR B16 ....106 A2
Laxford CI BHTH/HG B12 ....107 J7
Laxton Dr BEWD DY12 ....162 D2
Laxton Dr YDLY B25 ....109 H4
Layamon Wk STRPT DY13 ....188 H3
Lay Gdns RLSS CV31 ....207 J8
Lazy HI ALDR WS9 ....41 C4
HWK/WKHTH B38 ....145 M3
Lazy Hill Rd ALDR WS9 ....41 C4
Lea Av DARL/WED WS10 ....68 B4
Lea Bank Av DARL/WED WV11 ....137 L6
Leabon Gv HRBN B17 ....124 A1
Leabrook
LGN/SDN/BHAMAIR B26 ....109 K5
Leabrook Rd North
DARL/WED WS10 ....68 B4
Lea Castle CI DUDY DY10 ....138 E4
Lea Castle Dr KIDD DY10 ....139 C3
The Lea Cswy KIDD DY11 ....133 L1
Leach Green La RBRY B45 ....143 M7
Leach Heath La RBRY B45 ....143 K6
Leacliffe Wk FOAKS/STRLY B74.......55 K2
Leacote Dr
DUNHL/THL/PER WV6 ....49 G1
Lea Crs RUGBYS/DCH CV22 ....160 E8
Leacrest Rd COVN CV6 ....133 L3
Leacroft SHHTH WV12 ....38 A6
Leacroft Av WOLVN WV10 ....36 C5
Leacroft CI ALDR WS9 ....40 F5
Leacroft Gv HHTH/SAND B71 ....68 F5
Leacroft La CNCK/NC WS11 ....16 D8
Leacroft Rd KGSWFD DY6 ....83 J5
PENK ST19 ....10 C6
Lea Croft Rd REDW B97 ....202 B8
Leadbetter Dr BRGRVW B61 ....191 H3
Lea Dr LGN/SDN/BHAMAIR B26 ......109 J7
Lea End La ALVE B48 ....171 G1
Leafdown CI HEDN WS12 ....17 H1
Leafenden Av BNTWD WS7 ....18 B8
Leafield CI COVE CV2 ....135 J3
Leafield CI STETCH B33 ....91 L1
Leafield Gdns RMSLY B62 ....104 B5
Leafield Rd HIA/OLT B92 ....127 M4
Leaf La COVS CV3 ....155 K7
Lea Ford Rd STETCH B33 ....110 A1
Leaford Wy KGSWFD DY6 ....83 K6
Leafy Gld FOAKS/STRLY B74...55 J5
Leafy Gld SEDG DY3 ....84 A1
Leagh CI KNWTH CV8 ....179 M6
Lea Green Av TPTN/OCK DY4 ....67 K8
Lea Green La HLYWD B47 ....147 C2
Lea Hall Dr BNTWD WS7 ....18 B4
Lea Hall Rd STETCH B33 ....109 L3
Leahill Cft
CHWD/FDBR/MGN B37 ....110 D3
Lea Hill Rd BFLD/HDSWWD B20 ....89 C3
Leaholme Gdns HAG/WOL DY9...119 M3
Leahouse Gdns
LGLYGN/QTN B68 ....104 C4
Lea House Rd BVILLE B30 ....124 C4
Leahouse Rd LGLYGN/QTN B68 ......104 C4
Leahurst Crs HRBN B17 ....124 A1
Lea La GTWY DY9 ....24 E1
Leam CI NUN CV11 ....99 K4
Leam Crs HIA/OLT B92 ....128 A3
Leam Gn TLHL/CAN CV4 ....154 D7
Leamington Rd CNCK/NC WS11...16 A3
Leamington Rd BHTH/HG B12 ....107 M8
COVS CV3 ....155 G6
KNWTH CV8 ....197 L3
RCOVN/BALC/EX CV7 ....161 A7
Leamore CI WSLW WS2 ....38 A5
Leamount Dr KCSTG B44 ....72 A3
Leam Rd RLSS CV31 ....206 A6
Leam St RLSS CV31 ....206 E7
Leam Ter RLSS CV31 ....206 E6
Leander CI BNTWD WS7 ....18 C4
GTWY WS6 ....24 C1
Leander Gdns
ALE/KHTH/YWD B14 ....125 K8
Leander Rd HAG/WOL DY9 ....120 E1

Lea Park Ri BRGRVW B61 ....168 D8
Leapgate La STRPT DY13 ....164 C8
Lea Rd BDMR/CCFT WV3 ....49 L6
SPARK B11 ....126 B1
Lear Rd WMBN WV5 ....64 F6
Leas CI BDWTH CV12 ....116 E2
Leason La WOLVN WV10 ....36 E3
Leasow Dr EDG B15 ....124 B2
Leasowe Av RBRY B45 ....143 H7
Leasowe's Av COVS CV3 ....180 D1
Leasowes Ct HALE B63 ....121 K3
Leasowes Dr BDMR/CCFT WV3 ....48 B1
Leasowes La RMSLY B62 ....104 A8
Leasowes Rd
ALE/KHTH/YWD B14 ....125 K4
The Leasow LICH WS13 ....20 E4
The Leasow ALDR WS9 ....40 C8
The Leasow WOLVN WV10 ....23 G6
The Leasowe KIDD DY11 ....138 D8
The Leas WOLVN WV10 ....23 G6
The Lea KIDD DY11 ....109 L2
STETCH B33 ....109 L2
Leatherhead CI AST/WIT B6 ....89 K7
Leathermill La
NUNW/HART CV10 ....80 D2
Lea Vale Rd STRBR DY8 ....119 K3
Leavesden Gv
LGN/SDN/BHAMAIR B26 ....109 L8
Lea Vw ALDR WS9 ....40 C8
SHHTH WV12 ....37 L8
Lea Village STETCH B33 ....109 M5
Lea Wk KNWTH CV8 ....143 K5
RBRY B45 ....143 K5
Leaward CI NUNW/HART CV10 ....98 C3
Lea Wood Gv KIDDW DY11 ....137 G3
Lea Yield CI SLYOAK B29 ....124 D3
Lebanon Gv BNTWD WS7 ....18 D5
Lechlade CI REDE B98 ....195 C6
Lechlade Rd GTB/HAM B43 ....70 C5
Leckie Rd WSLW WS2 ....52 J1
Ledbrook Rd RLSN CV32 ....199 H8
Ledbury CI ALDR WS9 ....41 G4
LDYWD/EDGR B16 ....106 B3
REDE B98 ....203 K3
Ledbury Dr WOLVN WV1 ....50 F4
Ledbury Rd RLSS CV31 ....207 J3
Ledbury Wy WALM/CURD B76 ....73 L5
Ledsam St LDYWD/EDGR B16 ....106 B3
Ledwell SHLY B90 ....147 L8
Lee Bank Middleway EDG B15 ....6 D9
Leech St TPTN/OCK DY4 ....68 A8
Lee CI WWCK CV34 ....205 C8
Lee Crs EDG B15 ....107 G5
Leeder CI COVN CV6 ....134 A3
Leedham Av TAM/AM/WIL B77 ....32 C8
Lee Gdns SMTHWK B67 ....87 H5
Leeming CI TLHL/CAN CV4 ....154 A7
Lee Mt EDG B15 *...........................107 G5
Lee Rd CDYHTH B64 ....103 K5
HLYWD B47 ....147 E6
RLSS CV31 ....206 C6
Lees Rd BILS/COS WV14 ....67 K2
Lees St WSNGN B18 ....88 D8
Lees Ter BILS/COS WV14 ....67 K2
Lee St WBROM B70 ....68 C5
The Lee COVW CV5 ....154 A1
Legge La BILS/COS WV14 ....67 H3
CBHAMW B1 ....6 B8
Legge St AST/WIT B6 ....7 J1
BKHL/PFLD WV2 ....50 C7
WBROM B70 ....87 H2
Legion CI CNCK/NC WS11 ....17 L7
Legion Rd RBRY B45 ....143 J6
Le Hanche CI
RCOVN/BALC/EX CV7 ....115 L6
Leicester Cswy COV CV1 ....134 B8
Leicester CI SMTHWK B67 ....105 J4
Leicester Crs ATHST CV9 ....63 J4
Leicester PI HHTH/SAND B71 ....68 F6
Leicester Rd RLSN CV32 ....199 G6
NUN CV11 ....99 J4
RUGBYN/HIL CV21 ....160 F6
Leicester Rw COV CV1 ....2 C1
Leicester St BDWTH CV12 ....116 F2
DUNHL/THL/PER WV6 ....2 C1
RLSN CV32 ....206 F4
WSL WS1 ....4 F3
Leigh Av HRBN B17 ....123 J7
Leigh CI RUSH/SHEL WS4 ....53 L1
Leigh Rd MGN/WHC B75 ....57 M7
RUGBYN/HIL CV21 ....160 D5
RUSH/SHEL WS4 ....53 L1
WASH/WDE B8 ....90 C7
Leighs CI RUSH/SHEL WS4 ....40 A4
Leighs Rd RUSH/SHEL WS4 ....39 M4
Leigh St COV CV1 ....9 K2
Leighswood CI RUSH/SHEL WS4 ......40 A4
Leighswood CI CNCK/NC WS11 ....17 K8
Leighswood Gv ALDR WS9 ....40 F7
Leighswood Rd ALDR WS9 ....40 F7
Leighton CI DUDN DY1 ....84 D6
GTB/HAM B43 ....71 G2
RLSN CV32 ....207 G2
TLHL/CAN CV4 ....154 A7
Leighton Rd BDMR/CCFT WV3 ....49 K7
BILS/COS WV14 ....68 B1
MOS/BIL B13 ....125 K3
Leith Gv HWK/WKHTH B38 ....145 J5
Lelant Gv HRBN B17 ....105 H4
Lellow St HHTH/SAND B71 ....69 G5
Le More FOAKS/STRLY B74 ....56 A1
Lemox Rd WBROM B70 ....70 B4
Lench CI REDW B97 ....193 H6
RMSLY B62 ....104 B5
Lench's CI MOS/BIL B13 ....125 K3
Lenchs Gn DIG/EDG B5 ....107 G5
Lench St CBHAMNE B4 ....7 G2
Lenchs Trust Houses
BHTH/HG B12 *............................107 K6
Len Davies Rd SHHTH WV12 ....37 J4
Lennard Gdns SMTHWK B66 *...106 B7
Lennox CI COVS CV3 ....156 B7
Lennox Gdns BDMR/CCFT WV3 ....49 J6
Lennox Gv SCFLD/BOLD B73 ....72 E6
Lennox St AST/WIT B6 ....6 D1
Lenton Cft
LGN/SDN/BHAMAIR B26 ....127 J3
Lenton's La COVN CV6 ....135 H1
Lenwade Rd LGLYGN/QTN B68 ......104 H5
Leofric St COVN CV6 ....133 L5
Leomansley CI LICH WS13 ....20 D6
Leomansley Rd LICH WS13 ....20 C6
Leomansley Vw LICH WS13 ....20 C6
Leominster Rd SPARK B11 ....126 E3
Leonard Gv KIDD DY10 ....138 E4
Leonard Gv LOZ/NWT B19 ....89 G5
LOZ/NWT B19 ....89 G5
Leonard Rd BFLD/HDSWWD B20......88 D5
STRBR DY8 ....101 G8
Leopold Av BFLD/HDSWWD B20.......70 B4
Leopold Rd COV CV1 ....2 L1

Leopold St BHTH/HG B12 ....107 K5
Lepid Gv SLYOAK B29 ....124 D3
Lerryn CI KGSWFD DY6 ....83 K6
Lerwick CI HEDN WS12 ....16 B6
Lesingham Dr TLHL/CAN CV4 ....153 L4
Lesley Dr KGSWFD DY6 ....83 K6
Lesley Rd OLDBY B69 ....86 A5
Leslie Dr TPTN/OCK DY4 ....67 L4
Leslie Ri BFLD/HDSWWD B20 ....89 H3
FOAKS/STRLY B74 ....56 C1
LDYWD/EDGR B16 ....106 C3
WOLVN WV1 ....50 D1
Lesscroft CI COVEN WV9 ....35 L2
Lester Gv ALDR WS9 ....55 J3
Lester St BILS/COS WV14 ....51 K8
Lestock CI RUGBYS/DCH CV22 ....186 A3
Leswell La KIDD DY10 ....138 D7
Leswell St KIDD DY10 ....138 D7
Letchlade CI COVE CV2 ....135 C5
Levante Gdns STECH B33 ....109 K8
Levedale Rd RSTAF ST18 ....10 A2
Level La WLNHL WV13 ....51 M4
Level St BRLYHL DY5 ....102 C2
Leven Cft WALM/CURD B76 ....73 L6
Leven Dr BNSFLD WV11 ....37 M4
Leven Wy COVE CV2 ....135 G5
Levenwick Wy KGSWFD DY6 ....83 L8
The Leverretts HDSW B21 ....88 B3
Lever St BKHL/PFLD WV2 ....3 J6
Leverton Ri WOLVN WV10 ....36 A7
Leveson CI DUDN DY1 ....85 H4
Leveson Crs
RCOVN/BALC/EX CV7 ....151 M7
Leveson Dr TPTN/OCK DY4 ....67 J7
Leveson Rd WNSFLD WV11 ....37 M5
Leveson St WLNHL WV13 ....51 L3
Levett Rd LICHS WS14 ....30 A4
TAM/AM/WIL B77 ....32 F8
Levington CI
DUNHL/THL/PER WV6 ....34 D7
Levy CI RUGBYN/HIL CV21 ....186 D2
Lewis Av WOLVN WV1 ....50 F2
Lewis CI LICHS WS14 ....21 J6
SHHTH WV12 ....38 D8
Lewis Gv WNSFLD WV11 ....37 H7
Lewisham Rd SMTHWK B66 ....87 L6
WOLVN WV10 ....35 M3
Lewisham St HHTH/SAND B71 ....69 G6
Lewis Rd BVILLE B30 ....125 C6
COV CV1 ....9 M1
HAG/WOL DY9 ....102 B8
LGLYGN/QTN B68 ....104 F6
RLSS CV31 ....207 J8
Lewis St BILS/COS WV14 ....51 J7
TPTN/OCK DY4 ....68 B7
WSLW WS2 ....52 H2
Lewthorn Ri
ETTPK/GDPK/PENN WV4 ....66 D1
Lexington Gn BRLYHL DY5 ....102 A5
Leybourne Crs COVEN WV9 ....35 K5
Leybourne Gv YDLY B25 ....108 F7
Leybrook Rd RBRY B45 ....143 M5
Leyburn CI COVN CV6 ....134 B2
NUN CV11 ....99 L3
SHHTH WV12 ....52 B1
WWCK CV34 ....205 H4
Leyburn Rd LDYWD/EDGR B16 ......106 E4
Leycester CI KNWTH CV8 ....144 E6
Leycester Rd KNWTH CV8 ....197 K3
Leycroft Av STETCH B33 ....110 B2
Leyes La KNWTH CV8 ....180 E2
The Leyes RRUGBY CV23 ....161 L4
Leyfields LICH WS13 ....20 F1
Ley Hill Farm Rd NFLD/LBR B31..123 G4
Ley Hill Rd MGN/WHC B75 ....57 G4
Leylan CI MOS/BIL B13 ....126 B6
Leyland Av BDMR/CCFT WV3 ....49 K4
COVW CV5 ....154 B1
NUN CV11 ....99 L3
TAM/AM/WIL B77 ....46 C3
Leyman CI ALE/KHTH/YWD B14...147 G1
Leymere CI
RCOVN/BALC/EX CV7 ....131 C4
Ley Ri SEDG DY3 ....66 A4
Leys CI SEDG DY3 ....66 A4
Leys Crs BRLYHL DY5 ....101 M2
Leysdown Gv ACGN B27 ....127 C5
Leysdown Rd ACGN B27 ....127 C5
Leyside COVS CV3 ....156 C8
Leys La RCOVN/BALC/EX CV7 ....131 C4
Leys Rd BRLYHL DY5 ....101 M2
Leysters CI REDE B98 ....203 J2
The Leys DARL/WED WS10 ....52 A7
NFLD/LBR B31 ....123 M8
Leys Wood Cft
LGN/SDN/BHAMAIR B26 ....109 J2
Leyton CI BRLYHL DY5 ....102 B5
Leyton Gv KGSTG B44 ....71 L4
Leyton Rd HDSW B21 ....88 D5
Libbards Ga SOLH B91 ....149 C5
Libbards Wy SOLH B91 ....148 F5
Liberty Rd TAM/AM/WIL B77 ....46 D8
Liberty Wy NUN CV11 ....99 K2
Libra CI CRTAM B79 ....31 J5
Library Rd TLHL/CAN CV4 ....153 M8
Library Wy RBRY B45 ....143 K6
Lich Av WNSFLD WV11 ....37 J4
Lichen CI HEDN WS12 ....12 A8
Lichen Gdns HWK/WKHTH B38 ....145 J8
Lichfield Av KIDDW DY11 ....137 K5
Lichfield CI NUN CV11 ....81 L8
RCOVN/BALC/EX CV7 ....96 F5
Lichfield Crs POL/KGSB/FAZ B78......40 C1
AST/WIT B6 ....88 E1
BLOX/PEL WS3 ....25 M8
BLOX/PEL WS3 ....39 G3
BNTWD WS7 ....19 H7
BRWNH WS8 ....26 D5
CNCK/NC WS11 ....16 D5
COVS CV3 ....155 H7
CSHL/WTROR B46 ....93 J5
FOAKS/STRLY B74 ....42 G8
LICHS WS14 ....27 C4
POL/KGSB/FAZ B78 ....30 F6
POL/KGSB/FAZ B78 ....58 E8
RUSH/SHEL WS4 ....40 B5
SHHTH WV12 ....38 D1
WALM/CURD B76 ....37 J1
Lichfield Rd BILS/COS WV14 ....51 J7
CRTAM B79 ....31 K5
POL/KGSB/FAZ B78 ....45 K4
STRPT DY13 ....188 G3
TPTN/OCK DY4 ....67 L3
WOLV WV1 ....4 C1
Lichwood Rd WNSFLD WV11 ....37 K6
Lickey Coppice RBRY B45 ....170 A1
Lickey Grange Dr BRGRVE B60 ......169 J4

Lickey Gv KIDDW DY11 ....163 M3
Lickey Rd STRBR DY8 ....143 M8
STRBR DY8 ....101 M7
Lickey Rock BRGRVW B60 ....169 H4
Lickey Sq RBRY B45 ....169 K3
Lickhill Rd STRPT DY13 ....188 D1
Lickhill Rd North STRPT DY13 ....163 M4
Liddon Av ACGN B27 ....127 G5
Liddon Rd ACGN B27 ....127 G5
Lifford CI ALE/KHTH/YWD B14 ....124 E8
Lifford La BVILLE B30 ....124 E8
Lifford Wy COVS CV3 ....156 C6
Lifton Cft KGSWFD DY6 ....83 K8
Light Ash WOLVN WV10 ....22 A2
Lighthorne Av
LDYWD/EDGR B16 ....106 C2
Lighthorne Rd SOLH B91 ....127 M7
Light La COV CV1 ....8 E2
Lightning Wy NFLD/LBR B31 ....144 F6
Lightoak CI REDW B97 ....202 A7
Lightoak Gv DOR/KN B93 ....189 M5
Lightwood Rd DUDN DY1 ....85 K4
Lightwoods HI SMTHWKW B67 ....105 J5
Lightwoods Rd HAG/WOL DY9 ....120 A4
SMTHWKW B67 ....105 K4
Lilac Av BHTH/HG B12 ....107 L8
CNCK/NC WS11 ....16 B5
COVN CV6 ....133 K8
DSYBK/YTR WS5 ....69 J5
FOAKS/STRLY B74 ....54 C1
KGSTG B44 ....71 J6
Lilac CI REDE B98 ....202 C5
Lilac Dr RUGBYS/DCH CV22 ....185 M3
WMBN WV5 ....64 D7
Lilac Gv BNTWD WS7 ....18 C5
DARL/WED WS10 ....52 C2
STRPT DY13 ....188 C1
WSLW WS2 ....52 C2
WWCK CV34 ....205 L4
Lilac La GTWY WS6 ....24 C5
Lilac Rd BDWTH CV12 ....99 H8
CRTAM B79 ....31 L5
DUDN DY1 ....84 F1
SHHTH WV12 ....38 D1
WOLV WV1 ....5 J6
Lilac Wy RMSLY B62 ....104 C5
Lilbourne Rd RUGBY CV23 ....161 L8
Lilian Gv BILS/COS WV14 ....67 J3
Lilleshall Cft REDE B98 ....203 J2
Lilleshall Crs BKHL/PFLD WV2 ....50 B6
Lilleshall Rd
LGN/SDN/BHAMAIR B26 ....109 M6
Lilley CI COVN CV6 ....134 A3
Lilley Green Rd ALVE B48 ....145 C5
Lilley La NFLD/LBR B31 ....144 F5
Lillington Av RLSN CV32 ....206 D3
RLSN CV32 ....206 E2
Lillington Gv BKDE/SHDE B34 ....92 B3
Lillington Rd COVE CV2 ....135 H4
RLSN CV32 ....206 E1
SHLY B90 ....147 M5
Lilycroft La HWK/WKHTH B38 ....145 J4
Lily Green La REDW B97 ....193 L8
Lily St HHTH/SAND B71 ....69 G8
Lily Wd LGN/SDN/BHAMAIR B26 ....109 H7
Limberlost CI
BFLD/HDSWWD B20 ....88 D7
Limbrick Av TLHL/CAN CV4 ....153 L4
Limbrick CI SHLY B90 ....147 K5
Limbury Gv HIA/OLT B92 *..............128 D5
Lime Av RLSN CV32 ....206 D1
SLYOAK B29 * 124 D3
WSLW WS2 ....52 C2
Lime CI HLYWD B47 ....146 E8
TPTN/OCK DY4 ....67 J8
WBROM B70 ....86 D5
WSLW WS2 ....52 C2
Lime Ct SPARK B11 ....126 A1
Lime Gv ATHST CV9 ....76 F1
BHTH/HG B12 ....107 K8
BILS/COS WV14 ....19 G5
BNTWD WS7 ....191 K4
BRGRVW B61 ....191 K4
CHWD/FDBR/MGN B37 ....110 D4
KINVER DY7 ....118 A2
LGN/SDN/BHAMAIR B26 ....109 H7
LICH WS13 ....21 H5
LOZ/NWT B19 ....89 G5
NUNW/HART CV10 ....80 C8
RUSH/SHEL WS4 ....40 A7
SCFLD/BOLD B73 ....72 F6
SMTHWK B66 ....105 M1
TLHL/CAN CV4 ....153 M3
Lime Kiln CI HWK/WKHTH B38 ....145 H6
HOCK/TIA B94 ....174 A4
Lime Kilns POL/KGSB/FAZ B78 ....47 L5
Lime La BLOX/PEL WS3 ....13 G7
Limepit La DUDN DY1 ....84 E2
HEDN WS12 ....12 B5
Lime Rd DARL/WED WS10 ....68 D3
SEDG DY3 ....66 D4
Limes Coppice
NUNW/HART CV10 ....79 J6
Limescroft CI RUSH/SHEL WS4 ....39 M6
Limes Rd DUDN DY1 ....84 F2
DUNHL/THL/PER WV6 ....49 G1
The Limes BDWTH CV12 ....116 C3
ERDE/BCHGN B24 ....90 D2
LDYWD/EDGR B16 * 106 D2
RCOVN/BALC/EX CV7 ....133 K1
SPARK B11 ....108 A7
WSL WS1 ....5 K3
Limestone Hall La
RRUGBY CV23 ....184 E1
Limes Vw SEDG DY3 ....66 B6
Lime St BDMR/CCFT WV3 ....3 B8
BILS/COS WV14 ....66 E5
WSL WS1 ....5 K3
Limes Wk SEDG DY3 ....66 B6
Lime Tree Av
DUNHL/THL/PER WV6 ....48 G2
RUGBYS/DCH CV22 ....185 M1
TLHL/CAN CV4 ....153 L3
Lime Tree Crs REDW B97 ....201 M4
Lime Tree Gdns CDSL WV8 ....34 F2
Lime Tree Gv NFLD/LBR B31 ....145 C5
Lime Tree Rd ACGN B27 ....109 G8
CDSL WV8 ....34 F2
DSYBK/YTR WS5 ....69 L1
WASH/WDE B8 ....90 F5
Limetree FOAKS/STRLY B74 ....55 H4
Lime Tree Wk STRPT DY13 ....163 J8
Linaker Rd COVS CV3 ....156 M4
Linchmere Rd HDSW B21 ....88 B2
Lincoln Av NUNW/HART CV10 ....79 M6
WLNHL WV13 ....37 L4
Lincoln CI ACGN B27 ....127 J2
LICH WS13 ....21 G2
WWCK CV34 ....205 J4
Lincoln Crs KIDDW DY11 ....137 K7
Lincoln Cft LICHS WS14 ....28 D7

Lincoln Dr CNCK/NC WS11 ......16 D5
Lincoln Gn WOLVN WV10 ......36 E5
Lincoln Gv
  CHWD/FDBR/MGN B37 ....110 E5
Lincoln Rd BRGRVW B61 ......191 H1
  DUDS DY2 ......103 H2
  HHTH/SAND B71 ......69 H4
  HIA/OLT B92 ......127 H3
  SMTHWKW B67 ......105 J3
  WSL WS1 ......5 J5
Lincoln Rd North HIA/OLT B92 ..127 J2
Lincoln St BHTH/HG B12 ......107 J7
  COV CV1 ......9 K3
  WOLVN WV10 ......3 K3
Lincoln Wy CRTAM B79 ......31 J7
Lincomb Bank STRPT DY13 ......189 H7
Lincomb La STRPT DY13 ......189 G8
Lincroft Crs COVN CV5 ......154 B1
Lindale Av CBROM B36 ......91 G7
Lindale Crs BRLYHL DY5 ......101 M7
Lindale Dr WMBN WV5 ......64 D7
Linden Av BNTWD WS7 ......18 D5
  GTB/HAM B43 ......70 B5
  KIDD DY10 ......138 E6
  OLDBY B69 ......86 B5
  RMSLY B62 ......104 C4
  STRPT DY13 ......188 C5
Linden Cl TAM/AM/WIL B77 ......46 D1
  WSLW WS2 * 52 B3
  WWCK CV34 ......205 M3
Linden Dr STRBR DY8 ......119 L2
Linden Gdns KIDD DY10 ......138 E6
Linden Gv KIDD DY10 ......138 E6
Linden La WNSFLD WV11 ......38 C6
Linden Lea BDMR/CCFT WV3 ......49 M3
  BDWTH CV12 ......116 F2
Linden Rd DUDN DY1 ......84 F2
  SLYOAK B29 ......124 C5
  SMTHWK B66 ......105 J3
Lindens Dr FOAKS/STRLY B74 ....55 H8
The Lindens
  DUNHL/THL/PER WV6 ......49 J2
  RIDG/WDGT B32 ......105 J6
Linden Vw HEDN WS12 ......16 F1
Lindenwood SCFLD/BOLD B73 ....56 F7
Lindera TAM/AM/WIL B77 ......46 E1
The Lindfield COVS CV3 ......156 A5
Lindford Dr HWK/WKHTH B38 ....145 M3
Lindhurst Dr HOCK/TIA B94 ......174 F8
Lindisfarne TAM/AM/WIL B77 ......46 B3
Lindisfarne Dr KNWTH CV8 ......198 A1
Lindley Av TPTN/OCK DY4 ......85 K2
Lindley Rd BDWTH CV12 ......116 B3
  COVS CV3 ......155 M3
Lindon Cl BRWNH WS8 ......26 E7
Lindon Dr BRWNH WS8 ......26 E7
Lindon Rd BRWNH WS8 ......26 E7
Lindon Vw BRWNH WS8 ......26 E7
Lindrick Cl BLOX/PEL WS3 ......38 D2
Lindridge Cl REDW B98 ......203 L2
Lindridge Dr WALM/CURD B76 ....74 A7
Lindridge Rd ERDW/GRVHL B23 ..72 D6
  MGN/WHC B75 ......57 K6
  SHLY B90 ......147 K4
Lindrosa Rd FOAKS/STRLY B74 ....55 L5
Lindsay Rd PBAR/PBCH B42 ......70 F4
Lindsey Av NFLD/LBR B31 ......145 G1
Lindsey Crs KNWTH CV8 ......197 L4
Lindsey Pl BRLYHL DY5 ......102 A2
Lindsey Rd HHTH/SAND B71 ......69 G2
Lindsworth Ap BVILLE B30 ......146 A2
Lindsworth Rd BVILLE B30 ......145 M2
Lineholt Cl REDE B98 ......202 F7
Linehouse La BRGRVE B60 ......169 H5
Linen St WWCK CV34 ......205 H7
Linfield Gv YDLY B25 ......109 H4
Linford Wk COVE CV2 ......135 K4
Linforth Dr FOAKS/STRLY B74 ....55 L7
Lingard Cl VAUX/NECH B7 ......89 M8
Lingard Rd MGN/WHC B75 ......57 K8
Lingen Cl REDE B98 ......203 J2
Lingfield Av BEWD DY12 ......137 H8
  CNCK/NC WS11 ......17 L8
Lingfield Cl GTWY WS6 ......24 D3
Lingfield Dr GTWY WS6 ......24 D3
Lingfield Gdns BKDE/SHDE B34 ..91 M7
Lingfield Gv
  DUNHL/THL/PER WV6 ......48 D1
  CNCK/NC WS11 ......17 L8
Lingfield Wy KGSWFD DY6 ......83 L7
Lingham Cl HIA/OLT B92 ......128 B6
Ling Rd HEDN WS12 ......12 A8
Lingwood Dr NUNW/HART CV10 ..98 D2
Linhope Dr KGSWFD DY6 ......83 L7
Link Rd ALDR WS9 ......40 F2
  LDYWD/EDGR B16 ......106 C2
  WMBN WV5 ......64 C6
Links Side Wy ALDR WS9 ......41 L5
Links Dr RBRY B45 ......143 L7
  SOLH B91 ......127 M7
  STRBR DY8 ......119 J3
Links Rd COVN CV6 ......133 M5
  ETTPK/GDPK/PENN WV4 ......65 L3
  HLYWD B47 ......146 E4
  LGLYGN/QTN B68 ......104 D5
Links Vw FOAKS/STRLY B74 ......55 H4
  RMSLY B62 ......122 B1
Linkswood Cl MOS/BIL B13 ......125 M4
The Link ACGN B27 ......126 D4
Linkway RLSS CV31 ......206 C7
Linley Av ALDR WS9 ......40 C8
Linley Dr WOLVN WV10 ......36 C4
Linley Gv ALE/KHTH/YWD B14 ..125 G5
  SEDG DY3 ......83 M3
Linley Rd RUSH/SHEL WS4 ......40 C8
Linley Wood Rd ALDR WS9 ......40 C8
Linnell Rd RUGBYN/HIL CV21 ..187 G3
Linnet Cl COVS CV3 ......156 B8
  RMSLY B62 ......103 M7
  SLYOAK B29 ......124 C5
Linnet Gv SHHTH WV12 ......38 A5
Linnet Ri KIDD DY10 ......138 F8
Linpole Wk ALE/KHTH/YWD B14 ..146 A3
Linsey Rd HIA/OLT B92 ......128 A3
Linslade Cl
  ETTPK/GDPK/PENN WV4 ......66 B1
Linstock Wy COVN CV6 ......134 B1
Linthouse La WNSFLD WV11 ......37 J5
Linthouse Newtown
  BRGRVE B60 ......169 L8
Linthurst Rd BRGRVE B60 ......169 L7
Lintly TAM/AM/WIL B77 ......46 F5
Linton Av SOLH B91 ......148 E4
Linton Cl HALE B63 ......103 J7
  REDE B98 ......203 K3
Linton Cft BILS/COS WV14 ......67 H1
Linton Ms REDE B98 ......203 K3
Linton Rd CDYHTH B64 ......103 K2
  ETTPK/GDPK/PENN WV4 ......49 J8
  GTB/HAM B43 ......71 G1
  SPARK B11 ......126 E1
Linwood Dr COVE CV2 ......135 K4
  HEDN WS12 ......12 D6
Linwood Rd DUDN DY1 ......66 F8

HDSW B21 ......88 C5
  SOLH B91 ......127 H8
Lionel St CBHAMNW B3 ......6 E3
Lion Fields Av COVW CV5 ......132 F7
Lion Hl STRPT DY13 ......188 E7
Lion Pas STRBR DY8 ......101 K8
Lion's Den LICHS WS14 ......27 L5
Lion Sq KIDD DY10 ......138 C7
Lion St KIDD DY10 ......138 C7
  STRBR DY8 ......101 K8
Liskeard Cl NUN CV11 ......84 B6
Liskeard Rd DSYBK/YTR WS5 ..54 B6
Lisko Cl STRBR DY8 ......101 L5
Lisle Av KIDDW DY11 ......164 A2
Lismore Cl RBRY B45 ......143 J4
Lismore Cft
  RCOVN/BALC/EX CV7 ......135 M6
Lismore Dr HRBN B17 ......123 J2
Lissadel Gv KGSTG B44 ......71 K1
Listelow Cl CBROM B36 ......91 H5
Lister Cl TPTN/OCK DY4 ......85 L1
  WSLW WS2 ......38 F8
Lister Rd ATHST CV9 ......63 H4
  DUDS DY2 ......85 G6
  KIDDW DY11 ......163 M2
  WSLW WS2 ......38 F8
Lister St NUN CV11 ......99 H2
  VAUX/NECH B7 ......7 J1
  WLNHL WV13 ......51 M4
Listowel Rd
  ALE/KHTH/YWD B14 ......125 H1
Lisures Dr WALM/CURD B76 ......73 H1
Little Acre REDW B97 ......202 B8
Little Albert St WSL WS1 * 4 F2
Little Ann St DIG/EDG B5 * 7 K6
Little Aston Hall Dr
  FOAKS/STRLY B74 ......41 L8
Little Aston La FOAKS/STRLY B74 ..42 B7
Little Aston Park Rd
  FOAKS/STRLY B74 ......55 L1
Little Aston Rd ALDR WS9 ......41 G7
Little Barrow Wk LICH WS13 ......20 F4
Little Barr St BORD B9 * 7 M5
Little Bell Hall Cottages
  HAG/WOL DY9 * 141 H4
Little Birches BDMR/CCFT WV3 ....49 K5
Little Bricklin St BKHL/PFLD WV2 ..2 F7
Little Bromwich Rd BORD B9 ......108 F4
Little Caldmore WSL WS1 * 4 E6
Little Checkhill La KINVER DY7 ..100 B1
Little Church St COV CV1 * 9 G1
  RUGBYN/HIL CV21 ......186 E2
Little Clothier St WLNHL WV13 ....51 L2
Little Clover Cl VAUX/NECH B7 ....90 A7
Little Cornbow HALE B63 ......121 M7
Little Cft CRTAM B79 ......31 H7
Little Green Lanes
  SCFLD/BOLD B73 ......72 F6
Little Gv RUGBYS/DCH CV22 ..187 C4
Little Hall Rd VAUX/NECH B7 ....107 M1
Little Hardwick Rd ALDR WS9 ....55 H3
Little Hay La LICHS WS14 ......44 F1
Little Hayes KIDDW DY11 ......138 C3
Little Heath Cft BKDE/SHDE B34 ..91 M7
Little Heath La BRGRVE B60 ......169 H7
Little Hill DARL/WED WS10 ......68 D5
Little Hill Wy RIDG/WDGT B32 ..123 H5
Little Hill Wy RIDG/WDGT B32 ..123 H5
Little Johnson's La ALDR WS9 ....54 F4
Little John St BRLYHL DY5 ......102 B1
Little La HHTH/SAND B71 ......69 J1
  SHHTH WV12 ......38 B1
Little Lawford La RUGBY CV23 ..159 J4
Little Lawns CL BRWNH WS8 ......26 D8
Little London WSL WS1 * 4 F8
Little London La RUGBY CV23 ..161 L3
Little Marsh Gv PENK ST19 ......10 C4
Littlemead Av NFLD/LBR B31 ..145 G4
Little Meadow Cft
  SCFLD/BOLD B73 ......71 J2
Littlemead Rd SHLY B90 ......147 H5
Little Moor Hl SMTHWKW B67 ....87 K8
Little Newport St WSL WS1 * 4 E4
Little Oaks Rd AST/WIT B6 ......89 J5
Littleover Av HLGN/YWD B28 ..126 D7
Little Pk RIDG/WDGT B32 ......122 F1
Little Park St COV CV1 * 9 G6
  WOLV WV1 * 3 H5
Little Pennington St
  RUGBYN/HIL CV21 ......186 D2
Little Pipe La LICH WS13 ......19 L1
Little Pitts Cl ERDE/BCHGN B24 ..72 F3
Little Potter St BRLYHL DY5 ......102 B3
Little Pountney St
  BKHL/PFLD WV2 * 2 F8
Little Shadwell St CBHAMNE B4 * ..7 G2
Littleshaw Cft HLYWD B47 ......173 G1
Littleshaw La HLYWD B47 ......173 G1
Little's La WOLV WV1 ......3 H3
Little South St COV CV1 * 9 K4
Little Station St WSL WS1 * 4 E5
Little St DUDS DY2 ......85 H4
Little Sutton La MSN/WHC B75 ....57 J2
Little Sutton Rd MGN/WHC B75 ..57 H3
Littlethorpe COVS CV3 ......156 B8
Littleton Cl KNWTH CV8 ......179 L6
  WALM/CURD B76 ......73 L2
Littleton Crs ATHST CV9 ......63 G2
Littleton Dr HEDN WS12 ......12 A6
Littleton Rd SHHTH WV12 ......38 A6
Littleton St East WSL WS1 * 4 F3
Littleton St West WSLW WS2 * 4 E3
Litton TAM/AM/WIL B77 ......47 G4
Litton TAM/AM/WIL B77 ......47 G4
Liverpool Cft
  CHWD/FDBR/MGN B37 ......110 D4
Liverpool St BORD B9 ......7 L6

Livery St CBHAMNW B3 ......6 E2
  RLSN CV32 ......206 D5
Livingstone Av
  DUNHL/THL/PER WV6 ......34 C8
  RRUGBY CV23 ......185 H1
Livingstone Rd
  ALE/KHTH/YWD B14 ......125 J7
  BFLD/HDSWWD B20 ......89 C4
  BILS/COS WV14 ......50 F8
  BLOX/PEL WS3 ......39 J3
  COVN CV6 ......134 B6
  WBROM B70 ......86 F4
Liza Ct RUGBYN/HIL CV21 ......161 G5
Llangorse Cl STRPT DY13 ......163 K6
Llewellyn Rd RLSS CV31 ......206 D7
Lloyd Crs COVE CV2 ......156 C7
Lloyd Dr
  ETTPK/GDPK/PENN WV4 ......65 G3
Lloyd George St ALE/KHTH/YWD ..17 C3
Lloyd Rd BFLD/HDSWWD B20 ....88 C1
  DUNHL/THL/PER WV6 ......35 H8
  HHTH/SAND B71 ......87 J1
Lloyd Sq EDG B15 * 106 C5
Lloyds Rd RMSLY B62 ......104 A6
Lloyd St CNCK/NC WS11 ......16 B4
  DARL/WED WS10 ......68 C2
  DUDS DY2 ......85 H5
  DUNHL/THL/PER WV6 ......49 K1
  HHTH/SAND B71 ......87 J1
  SMTH B10 ......108 B5
Loach Dr COVE CV2 ......134 F1
Load St BEWD DY12 ......162 F2
Lobelia Cl KIDDW DY11 ......138 A4
Locarno Rd TPTN/OCK DY4 ......67 K7
Lochalsh Gv WNSFLD WV11 ......37 J2
Lochmore Cl TAM/AM/WIL B77 ..46 B3
Lochmore Dr HALE B63 ......103 G2
Lochranza Cft GTB/HAM B43 ......70 C3
Lochsong Cl TAM/AM/WIL B77 ....46 B3
Lock Cl REDW B98 ......201 L1
Lock Dr STETCH B33 ......109 H2
Locke Cl COVN CV6 ......133 L4
Locke Pl VAUX/NECH B7 * 7 M1
Locket Cl WSLW WS2 ......52 D1
Lockfield Cl STRBR DY8 ......101 K3
Lockhart Cl KNWTH CV8 ......197 L1
Lockhart Dr MGN/WHC B75 ......57 G4
Lockheed Cl RLSS CV31 ......206 D8
Lockhurst La COVN CV6 ......134 B6
Locking Cft CVALE B35 ......91 M2
Lockington Cft RMSLY B62 ......104 D7
Lock Keepers Cl CNCK/NC WS11 ..17 K8
Lock Keepers Reach ALVE B48 ..170 D7
Lockley Cl WOLVN WV10 ......50 D1
Lock La WWCK CV34 ......205 H4
Lockley Cft WOLVN WV10 ......50 D1
Lockside ALDR WS9 ......40 D6
  WMBN WV5 ......64 C6
Locksmith Cl WLNHL WV13 ......51 M3
The Locks RRUGBY CV23 ......187 M4
Lock St WOLV WV1 ......3 H3
Locks Vw STRBR DY8 ......101 H4
Lockton Rd BVILLE B30 ......124 D7
Lockwood Rd NFLD/LBR B31 ..144 D1
Lockyer La HIA/OLT B92 ......127 M4
Loder Cl TLHL/CAN CV4 ......153 K2
Lodge Cft ATHST CV9 ......63 J7
  BEWD DY12 ......163 H1
  DSYBK/YTR WS5 ......54 B7
  RMSLY B62 ......122 B2
Lodge Dr
  LGN/SDN/BHAMAIR B26 ..109 J5
Lodge Farm Cl WALM/CURD B76 ..73 J4
Lodgefield Rd RMSLY B62 ......103 M6
Lodge Green La
  RCOVN/BALC/EX CV7 ......131 J2
Lodge Green La North
  RCOVN/BALC/EX CV7 ......131 J2
Lodge Gv ALDR WS9 ......40 E8
Lodge Hill Rd SLYOAK B29 ......124 B4
Lodge La KGSWFD DY6 ......82 F7
  LICH WS13 ......19 H2
Lodgepool Cl KGSTG B44 ......71 J7
Lodge Pool Dr REDE B98 ......202 D4
Lodge Rd AST/WIT B6 ......89 K5
  BILS/COS WV14 ......67 K1
  BNTWD WS7 ......18 C4
  COVS CV3 ......155 M4
  DARL/WED WS10 ......52 B8
  DOR/KN B93 ......149 M7
  REDE B98 ......202 B8
  RUGBYN/HIL CV21 ......186 F1
  RUSH/SHEL WS4 ......39 M4
  SMTHWKW B67 ......87 J6
  STRPT DY13 ......188 E2
  WBROM B70 ......86 F2
  WOLVN WV10 ......3 M5
  WSNGN B18 ......88 C8
Lodge St OLDBY B69 ......86 D6
  SHHTH WV12 ......38 A8
Lodge Vw GTWY WS6 ......24 A2
Loeless Rd STETCH B33 ......109 L2
Lofthouse Crs NFLD/LBR B31 ..144 D1
Lofthouse Gv NFLD/LBR B31 ..144 D1
Lofthouse Rd
  BFLD/HDSWWD B20 ......88 C1
Loftus Cl NFLD/LBR B31 ......123 K5
Loftus Ct BNTWD WS7 ......18 D8
Logan Cl WOLVN WV10 ......36 A3
Logan Rd COVE CV2 ......135 H6
Lole Cl COVN CV6 ......134 E1
Lollard Cft COVS CV3 ......155 H5
Lomaine Dr BVILLE B30 ......145 J1
Lomas Dr NFLD/LBR B31 ......144 D1
Lomas St WOLV WV1 ......2 F1
Lomax Cl WED WS10 ......52 E6
Lomax Rd HEDN WS12 ......12 F6
Lombard Av DUDS DY2 ......103 H2
Lombard Gdns LICH WS13 * 20 F5
Lombard St BHTH/HG B12 ......7 J9
  LICH WS13 ......20 F5
  STRPT DY13 ......188 E2
  WBROM B70 ......86 F2
Lombard St West WBROM B70 * ..87 G2
Lombardy Cft RMSLY B62 ......104 E7
Lombardy Gdns SHHTH WV12 ....38 C5
Lomita Crs TAM/AM/WIL B77 ......46 D1
Lomond Cl BKDE/SHDE B34 ......92 C7
  CRTAM B79 ......31 K5
Lomond Rd SEDG DY3 ......66 A4
Lomond Wy NUNW/HART CV10 ..98 D2
Lomsey Cl TLHL/CAN CV4 ......153 L4
Londonderry La SMTHKW B67 ....87 K8
London Hts DUDN DY1 ......84 B5
London La BRGRVE B60 ......192 D7
London Rd BFLD/HDSWWD B20 ..89 J3
  COV CV1 ......9 J8
  COVS CV3 ......155 K6
  KNWTH CV8 ......183 H4

LICHS WS14 ......21 G8
  MGN/WHC B75 ......57 L1
  RRUGBY CV23 ......184 A6
Long Acre CDSL WV8 ......34 C3
  KIDD DY10 ......138 D5
  VAUX/NECH B7 ......89 M7
Longacre WLNHL WV13 ......51 L5
Longacres HEDN WS12 ......13 G8
  WLNHL WV13 ......51 L5
Long Acre St WSLW WS2 * 4 D2
Long Bank BEWD DY12 ......162 B5
Longboat La STRBR DY8 ......101 J5
  STRPT DY13 ......188 E1
Longboat Quay STRPT DY13 ....103 H1
Longbow Rd NFLD/LBR B31 ..144 D6
Longbridge La LICHS WS14 ......21 G8
Long Bridge Rd LICHS WS14 ......21 G8
Long Brook La KNWTH CV8 ......177 J1
Long Cl HAG/WOL DY9 ......140 F1
Long Close Av COVW CV5 ......132 F7
Long Close Wk CVALE B35 ......91 L2
Long Compton Dr
  HAG/WOL DY9 ......119 M8
Long Cft HEDN WS12 ......16 A1
Longcroft Cl CVALE B35 ......91 L2
The Longcroft HALE B63 ......121 J1
  RUSH/SHEL WS4 ......40 C3
Longdales Rd HWK/WKHTH B38 ..145 H6
Longdon Av
  ETTPK/GDPK/PENN WV4 ......50 B8
Longdon Cft DOR/KN B93 ......149 L5
Longdon Dr FOAKS/STRLY B74 ....56 C1
Longfellow Cl REDW B98 ......202 A6
Longfellow Pl CNCK/NC WS11 ..16 A6
Longfellow Rd BNTWD WS7 ......18 D4
  BVILLE B30 ......145 J4
  COVE CV2 ......156 A2
  SEDG DY3 ......65 J3
Longfield Cl HLGN/YWD B28 ..126 D7
  TAM/AM/WIL B77 ......46 C3
Longfield Rd HAG/WOL DY9 ......123 J6
  NFLD/LBR B31 ......123 J8
  RLSS CV31 ......206 F7
Longford Cl DOR/KN B93 ......175 M2
  RIDG/WDGT B32 ......122 F3
  WMBN WV5 ......64 B8
Longford Gn CNCK/NC WS11 ....16 A6
Longford Gv KGSTG B44 ......71 L2
Longford Rd CNCK/NC WS11 ....16 A5
  COVN CV6 ......134 E2
  KGSTG B44 ......71 L2
  RCOVN/BALC/EX CV7 ......116 E7
  WOLVN WV10 ......50 D1
Longford Sq COVN CV6 ......134 D1
Long Furlong
  RUGBYS/DCH CV22 ......186 E3
Longham Cft RIDG/WDGT B32 ..123 J3
Longhope Cl REDE B98 ......203 J1
Longhurst Cft NFLD/LBR B31 ..144 E6
Long Hyde Rd SMTHWKW B67 ..105 H6
Long Innage HALE B63 ......102 F7
Long Knowle La WNSFLD WV11 ..36 F5
Longlake Av
  DUNHL/THL/PER WV6 ......48 D2
Longlands Dr TAM/AM/WIL B77 ..46 D1
Longlands Rd RMSLY B62 ......122 C2
The Longlands RBRY B45 ......170 B6
  WMBN WV5 ......64 E7
Long La BLKHTH/ROWR B65 ......104 D4
  RCOVN/BALC/EX CV7 ......133 H3
  WNSFLD WV11 ......24 D1
Long Leasow SLYOAK B29 ......123 M6
Longleat CRTAM B79 ......31 H4
  GTB/HAM B43 ......70 A4
  SHLY B90 ......148 C8
Longleat Gv RLSS CV31 ......207 G7
Longleat Rd ALDR WS9 ......40 E3
Long Ley WOLVN WV10 ......3 M3
Longley Av WALM/CURD B76 ......74 B8
Longley Crs
  BKDE/SHDE B34 ......92 C7
Longmeadow Crs
  BKDE/SHDE B34 ......92 C7
Long Meadow Dr SEDG DY3 ......65 M4
Longmeadow Gv
  NFLD/LBR B31 ......144 E7
Long Meadow Rd BRGRVE B60 ..169 G7
Longmeadow Rd
  DSYBK/YTR WS5 ......54 C5
Long Mill Av WNSFLD WV11 ......36 F6
Long Mll North WNSFLD WV11 ..36 F6
Long Mll South WNSFLD WV11 ..36 F6
Longmoor Cl REDW B97 ......158 M7
  WNSFLD WV11 ......37 K8
Longmoor Rd HALE B63 ......121 J2
  SCFLD/BOLD B73 ......71 M2
Longmore Cl SCFLD/BOLD B73 ..55 L8
Longmore Hl STRPT DY13 ......188 D7
Longmore Rd SHLY B90 ......148 B3
Longmore St BHTH/HG B12 ......107 G6
  DARL/WED WS10 ......68 C2
Long Mynd HALE B63 ......121 H4
Long Mynd Cl SHHTH WV12 ......37 M4
Long Mynd Rd NFLD/LBR B31 ..123 J7
Longmyndmy WY STRPT DY13 ..188 B4
Long Nuke Rd NFLD/LBR B31 ..123 J6
Longrood Rd
  RUGBYS/DCH CV22 ......186 D2
Long Saw Dr NFLD/LBR B31 ..144 B6
Longshaw Gv BKDE/SHDE B34 ..92 D3
The Long Shoot NUN CV11 ......81 M7
Longstaff Av HEDN WS12 ......18 A1
Longstaff Cft LICH WS13 ......20 D3
Longstone Cl SHLY B90 ......148 F7
Longstone Rd PBAR/PBCH B42 ..71 G4
Long St ATHST CV9 ......63 G4
  POL/KSCB/FAZ B78 ......47 L8
  SPARK B11 ......107 J7
  WOLV WV1 ......3 G4
  WSLW WS2 ......4 F4
Long Wd BVILLE B30 ......124 C8
Longwood Cl TLHL/CAN CV4 ..153 K2
Longwood La RUSH/SHEL WS4 ..54 C1
Longwood Rd RBRY B45 ......143 L6
  ALDR WS9 ......54 F3
Lonicera Cl RUSBYK/YTR WS5 ....69 M2
Lonscale Dr COVS CV3 ......154 F8
Lonsdale Cl SHHTH WV12 ......37 M8
  BILS/COS WV14 ......51 K7
  DSYBK/YTR WS5 ......54 A7
Lonsdale Rd BDMR/CCFT WV3 ..4 F5
  HRBN B17 ......105 M7
  RLSN CV32 ......206 B1
  WSL WS1 ......5 K5
Lord Austin Dr BRGRVE B60 ......169 J4
Lord Cromwell Ct
  CNCK/NC WS11 * 12 E8

Lord Lytton Av COVE CV2 ......156 A2
Lord's Dr WSLW WS2 ......4 C4
Lords La KINVER DY7 ......100 F1
Lordsmore Cl BILS/COS WV14 ....67 K1
  BILS/COS WV14 ......67 K1
  COVW CV5 ......154 F1
  VAUX/NECH B7 ......89 M7
  WSL WS1 ......4 F5
Lord St West BILS/COS WV14 ....67 K1
Lordswood Cl REDW B97 ......201 M7
Lordswood Rd HRBN B17 ......105 L5
Lordswood Sq HRBN B17 * 105 M5
Lorenzo Cl COVS CV3 ......156 C8
Lorimer Wy GTB/HAM B43 ......55 J3
Lorne Gv KIDD DY10 ......138 E6
Lorne St BNTWD WS7 ......18 D5
  KIDD DY10 ......138 E6
  STRPT DY13 ......163 L2
  TPTN/OCK DY4 ......67 L4
Lorrainer Av STRBR DY8 ......101 H7
Lorton CRTAM B79 ......31 J5
Lothersdale TAM/AM/WIL B77 ....46 F5
Lothians Rd BLOX/PEL WS3 ......25 L2
  DUNHL/THL/PER WV6 ......35 H7
Lottie Rd SLYOAK B29 ......124 B3
Lotus TAM/AM/WIL B77 ......46 F5
Lotus Cft HEDN WS12 ......16 A1
Lotus Ct SMTHWK B67 ......105 J3
Lotus Dr CNCK/NC WS11 ......12 E5
Lotus Wy BLKHTH/ROWR B65 ..104 C4
Loudon Av COVN CV6 ......133 K8
Loughshaw TAM/AM/WIL B77 ....47 G4
Loughton Gv HALE B63 ......121 H2
Louisa St CBHAMW B3 ......6 C4
Louise Cft ALE/KHTH/YWD B14 ..146 A3
Louise Lorne Rd MOS/BIL B13 ..125 J2
Louise Rd HDSW B21 ......88 E3
Louise St SEDG DY3 ......83 H1
Lount Wk LOZ/NWT B19 ......89 J8
Lovage Rd REDE B98 ......195 M3
Lovatt St WOLV WV1 ......2 F2
Lovatt Cl TPTN/OCK DY4 ......68 C1
Lovell Pl CNCK/NC WS11 ......12 A8
Lovatt St CNCK/NC WS11 ......12 A8
Loveday Cl ATHST CV9 ......63 G3
  RLSN CV32 ......206 D1
Loveday St CBHAMNE B4 ......7 G2
Lovelace Av SOLH B91 ......149 L2
Love La DUNHL/THL/PER WV6 ..35 K8
  GTWY WS6 ......24 A1
  HAG/WOL DY9 ......140 E8
  HLYWD B47 ......146 F4
  STRBR DY8 ......119 K1
  VAUX/NECH B7 ......7 J1
  WSL WS1 ......4 E4
Lovell CRTAM B79 ......31 J5
Lovell Cl RCOVN/BALC/EX CV7 ..116 E7
  SLYOAK B29 ......123 L6
Lovell Rd BDWTH CV12 ......116 D1
Love Lyne REDW B97 ......201 L5
Loveridge Cl CDSL WV8 ......34 F3
Loverock Crs RUGBYN/HIL CV21 ..187 J4
Lovett Av OLDBY B69 ......86 A6
Lowans Hill Vw REDW B97 ......201 L7
Low Av GTB/HAM B43 ......70 F2
Lowbridge Cl SHHTH WV12 ......38 A3
Lowbrook La SHLY B90 ......173 G7
Lowden Cft
  LGN/SDN/BHAMAIR B26 ......127 J1
Lowdham TAM/AM/WIL B77 ......47 J2
Lowe Av DARL/WED WS10 ......51 M8
Lowe Dr KGSWFD DY6 ......101 J1
  SCFLD/BOLD B73 ......72 D3
Lowe La KIDDW DY11 ......137 G1
Lower Av RLSS CV31 ......206 E4
Lower Beeches Rd
  NFLD/LBR B31 ......144 A4
Lower Bentley La BRGRVE B60 ..200 A6
Lower Cape WWCK CV34 ......205 H2
Lower Chapel St OLDBY B69 ......86 D5
Lower Church La TPTN/OCK DY4 ..67 L4
Lower City Rd OLDBY B69 ......86 D7
Lower Common La REDW B97 ..201 J8
Lower Dartmouth St BORD B9 ..107 L4
Lower Darwin St BRLYHL DY5 ..102 B3
Lower Derry St BRLYHL DY5 ..102 B3
Lower Eastern Green La
  COVW CV5 ......153 G1
Lower End KNWTH CV8 ......182 F7
Lower Essex St DIG/EDG B5 * 6 F8
Lower Farm
  RWWCK/WEL CV35 * 204 B3
Lower Ford St COV CV1 ......9 H3
Lower Forster St WSL WS1 ......4 F3
Lower Gambolds La
  BRGRVE B60 ......191 L4
Lower Gn TPTN/OCK DY4 * 67 L4
Lower Grinsty La REDW B97 ..201 H6
Lower Ground Cl AST/WIT B6 * 89 L2
Lower Gungate CRTAM B79 ......31 H4
Lower Hall La WSL WS1 ......4 E5
Lower High St DEYHTH B64 ......103 J4
  DARL/WED WS10 ......68 C1
  STRBR DY8 ......101 K8
Lower Higley Cl
  RIDG/WDGT B32 ......123 H3
Lower Hillmorton Rd
  RUGBYN/HIL CV21 ......187 G5
Lower Holyhead Rd COV CV1 ......8 E4
Lower Horseley Flds WOLV WV1 ..3 J3
Lower House La ATHST CV9 ......61 L8
Lower Ladies Hills KNWTH CV8 ..179 H5
Lower La LICH WS13 ......20 A1
Lower Leam St RLSS CV31 ......206 F5
Lower Lichfield St WLNHL WS13 ..51 L1
Lower Lickhill Rd STRPT DY13 ..163 H5
Lower Loveday St CBHAMNE B4 * ..6 F1
Lower Mll RLSN CV32 ......206 C1
Lower Mill St KIDD DY10 ......138 C6
Lower Moor SLYOAK B29 ......124 B4
Lower North St RUSH/SHEL WS4 ..53 M7
Lowe Rd COVN CV6 ......133 J6
Lower Pde
  SCFLD/WYGN B72 ......57 H6
Lower Pk BEWD DY12 ......162 F4
Lowerpark TAM/AM/WIL B77 ......46 B3
Lower Parklands KIDDW DY11 ..138 A4
Lower Prec COV CV1 ......9 G5
Lower Prestwood Rd
  WNSFLD WV11 ......37 H3
Lower Queen St
  SCFLD/WYGN B72 ......73 J1
Lower Reddicroft
  SCFLD/WYGN B72 ......57 J6
Lower Rd HHTH/SAND B71 ......69 L4
  RCOVN/BALC/EX CV7 ......132 A1
Lower Rushall St WSL WS1 * 5 G4
Lower Sandford St LICH WS13 ....20 D5
Lower Severn St CBHAMSW B1 ....6 D6
Lower Shepley La BRGRVE B60 ..192 B8
Lowerstack Cft
  CHWD/FDBR/MGN B37 ......110 C4
Lower St DUNHL/THL/PER WV6 ..35 L8
  RUGBYN/HIL CV21 ......187 H4
Lower Temple St CBHAMSW B1 ....6 D5
Lower Tower St LOZ/NWT B19 ....6 F1

...ver Trinity St BORD B9 ....7 L7
...ver Valley Rd BRLYHL DY5 ...101 L1
...ver Vauxhall WOLV WV1 ....2 A4
...ver Villiers St
...BKHL/PFLD WV2 ....50 A5
...RLSN CV32 ....206 E4
...ver Walsall St WOLV WV1 ...3 L6
...ver White Rd
...RIDG/WDGT B32 ....105 H8
...es Av WWCK CV34 ....205 J4
...esmoor Rd
...LGN/SDN/BHAMAIR B26 ...109 M6
...we St BHTH/HG B12 ....7 M9
...DUNHL/THL/PER WV6 ......2 B1
...eswater Rd COVN CV11 ....81 L7
...eswater Dr SEDG DY3 .....84 B2
...ver Av COVS CV3 ....156 C4
...wfield St REDW B97 ....163 J4
...wfield La REDW B97 ....193 M8
...wforce TAM/AM/WIL B77 ...47 G4
...ew Hill Crs COVN CV6 .....36 C5
...whill La RBRY B45 ....144 A7
...wland Cl CDYHTH B64 ....103 K4
...wland Rd HEDN WS12 .....12 A8
...wlands Dr
...LGN/SDN/BHAMAIR B26 ...109 M6
...wlands La
...FOAKS/STRLY B74 ....55 J5
...wlands Rd STRBR DY8 .....101 J7
...wry Cl BDWTH CV12 ....116 C1
...DUNHL/THL/PER WV6 ......48 D1
...WLNHL WV13 ....51 H3
...ew St GTWY WS6 ....24 A2
...w Thatch HWK/WKHTH B38 145 L6
...wther St COVE CV2 ....9 M2
...w Town OLDBY B69 ....86 B6
...w Wood Rd ERDW/GRVHL B23 .72 C8
...wdale Sidings BILS/COS WV14 .67 K1
...wdale St BILS/COS WV14 ...67 K1
...DARL/WED WS10 ....68 D3
...SHLY B90 ....147 M3
...wley Cl COVE CV2 ....135 H5
...NFLD/LBR B31 ....123 J5
...REDE B98 ....195 H7
...wley Rd MGN/WHC B75 .....57 H2
...SMTHWKW B67 ....105 K4
...wley Av RLSN CV32 ....206 E2
...wton Cl CHWD/FDBR/MGN ..110 C2
...wnells Rd RBRY B45 ....143 L6
...zells Rd BILS/COS WV14 ...88 F6
...zells St LOZ/NWT B19 .....89 G6
...zells Wood Cl LOZ/NWT B19 .88 F6
...zas Circ RLSN CV32 ....89 G7
...zas Ct RLSN CV32 ....206 B5
...RUGBYN/HIL CV21 ....186 F1
...ce Cl CVALE B35 ....91 M1
...cerne Cl COVE CV2 ....135 G2
...ce Rd WOLVN WV10 ....36 C7
...cian Cl COVE CV2 ....135 L6
...cknow Rd SHHTH WV12 ......37 M4
...ddington Rd HIA/OLT B92 ..128 C6
...dford Cl MGN/WHC B75 .....57 H9
...NUNW/HART CV10 ....96 F1
...dford Rd NUNW/HART CV10 ..80 A7
...dgate Cl CSHL/WTROR B46 ..92 E4
...dgate Av KIDDW DY11 ......163 G1
...dgate Cl CSHL/WTROR B46 ..92 E2
...OLDBY B69 ....85 M5
...dgate Hl CBHAMNW B3 ....6 E3
...dgate St DUDN DY1 * 84 F4
...d La CRTAM B79 ....31 L8
...llow Cl
...CHWD/FDBR/MGN B37 ......111 G3
...CNCK/NC WS11 ....17 C3
...SHHTH WV12 ....37 M7
...llow La WSLW WS2 ....52 E1
...llow Rd COVW CV5 ....8 A5
...KIDD WY11 ....164 C5
...REDW B97 ....202 B2
...WASH/WDE B8 ....108 C2
...llow Wy DUDN DY1 ....84 C5
...mer Wy BFLD/HDSWWD B20 ..89 G3
...dstone Av
...ETTPK/GDPK/PENN WV4 .....49 H8
...dstone Rd SLYOAK B29 ....123 K4
...dworth Av
...CHWD/FDBR/MGN B37 ......110 F4
...ff Cl COVS CV3 ....155 M5
...dstrout La SOLH B91 ......128 D7
...worth Rd HALE B63 ....103 H1
...worth Pk KNWTH CV8 ......180 A4
...worth Rd BNTWD WS7 ....18 E5
...HLGN/YWD B38 ....126 E5
...ney Cv
...DSYBK/YTR WS5 ....69 M1
...nley Rd DUDS DY2 ....85 K4
...pton Av COVS CV3 ....155 G7
...sbridge Cl HALE B63 ......103 F1
...her Wy COVW CV5 ....153 K1
...scombe Rd COVE CV2 ....135 J5
...her Av HALE B63 ....121 J1
...ey Cl BDMR/CCFT WV3 ......49 A6
...ley Dr HAG/WOL DY9 ......120 A2
...ley Rd RIDG/WDGT B32 ....122 F4
...ley La HALE B63 ....121 G3
...ley Mill Rd HALE B63 .....121 J1
...on Rd SLYOAK B29 ....124 D2
...terworth Rd COVE CV2 .....135 G8
...ton Cl
...DSYBK/YTR WS5 ....69 M1
...trell Rd FOAKS/STRLY B74 .54 D5
...kor La COVN CV6 ....131 M5
...all Gdns RBRY B45 ....143 J4
...all Gv ACGN B27 ....126 E5
...hgate Av HAG/WOL DY9 ....120 A4
...ey Rd RMSLY B62 ....122 D1
...brook Covert
...HWK/WKHTH B38 ....145 J5
...bury La STETCH B33 ......109 H8
...Cl WLNHL WV11 ....36 F8
...d Cft CVALE B35 ....91 M1
...dington Dr RMSLY B62 .....66 D5
...REDE B98 ....195 J8
...ford Cl COVE CV2 ....135 H3
...ford La ERDE/BCHGN B24 ...90 B3
...ford Cl BLOX/PEL WS3 .....38 C5
...ford Rd COVN CV6 ....133 M8
...SGWFD DY6 ....83 H6
...gam Cl BILS/COS WV14 .....66 D2

Lydiate Ash Rd BRGRVW B61 ..169 G2
Lydiate Ash Rd
BLKHTH/ROWR B65 ....104 A3
Lydney Cl REDE B98 ....195 H7
SHHTH WV12 ....52 B1
Lydstep Gv RLSS CV31 ......207 G6
Lye Av NFLD/LBR B31 ....144 D2
Lye By-pass HAG/WOL DY9 ..102 C7
Lye Close La RIDG/WDGT B32 122 D3
Lyecroft Av
CHWD/FDBR/MGN B37 ......111 H3
Lye Cross Rd OLDBY B69 ....85 M6
Lygon Cl REDE B98 ....194 E8
Lygon Gv RIDG/WDGT B32 ...123 J1
Lymedene Rd PBAR/PBCH B42 .70 F8
Lyme Green Rd STETCH B33 .109 K1
Lymer Rd WOLVN WV10 ....36 A4
Lymesy St COVS CV3 ....155 H7
Lymington Cl COVN CV6 .....134 B5
Lymington Rd BNTWD WS7 ...18 D4
WLNHL WV13 ....52 B3
Lymore Cft COVE CV2 ....135 L5
Lymsey Cft STRBR DY8 ......101 J2
Lyn Av LICH WS13 ....20 D4
Lynbrook Cl DUDS DY2 ....85 H7
HLYWD B47 ....146 E5
Lynbrook Rd COVW CV5 .....154 B5
Lynchgate Ct TLHL/CAN CV4 *154 A7
Lynchgate Rd TLHL/CAN CV4 154 A7
The Lynch NUN CV11 ....99 H5
Lyncourt Gv RIDG/WDGT B32 104 F7
Lyncroft Rd SPARK B11 .....126 D3
Lyndale TAM/AM/WIL B77 ....46 D7
Lyndale Cl COVW CV5 ....154 A2
Lyndale Dr WNSFLD WV11 ...37 K8
Lyndale Rd COVW CV5 ....154 A2
DUDS DY2 ....85 J7
SEDG DY3 ....65 M3
Lynden Cl BRGRVW B61 .....191 J7
Lyndenwood REDW B97 ......201 L3
Lyndholm Rd KIDD DY10 ....138 F2
Lyndhurst Cl COVN CV6 .....138 F8
Lyndhurst Cft COVW CV5 ...153 G1
Lyndhurst Rd BDMR/CCFT WV3 .49 L6
ERDE/BCHGN B24 ....90 D3
HEDN WS12 ....17 H4
HHTH/SAND B71 ....69 H6
RUGBYN/HIL CV21 ....187 K4
STRBR DY8 ....101 J2
Lyndon HHTH/SAND B71 .....69 H8
Lyndon Cl BFLD/HDSWWD B20 .89 J4
CBROM B36 ....92 A5
HALE B63 ....103 J8
SEDG DY3 ....66 C4
Lyndon Ct RLSN CV32 * 206 D3
Lyndon Cft
CHWD/FDBR/MGN B37 ......110 F6
Lyndon Gv HHTH/SAND B71 ..87 H1
KGSWFD DY6 ....82 F5
Lyndon Rd HIA/OLT B92 ....127 K3
RBRY B45 ....143 J6
SCFLD/BOLD B73 ....56 B1
STETCH B33 ....109 J2
Lyndworth Rd BVILLE B30 ..125 G6
Lyneham Cl CRTAM B79 .....31 M5
Lyneham Gdns WALM/CURD B76 .73 L7
Lyneham Wy CVALE B35 .....91 K1
Lynfield Cl HWK/WKHTH B38 145 K6
Lynfield Rd LICH WS13 .....20 D4
Lyng Cl COVW CV5 ....153 L2
Lyng La WBROM B70 ....87 G3
Lynmouth Cl NUN CV11 ......99 K4
Lynmouth Rd COVE CV2 .....135 J5
Lynn Av SLYOAK B29 ....124 A2
Lynn La ALDR WS9 ....31 J7
Lynton Av DUNHL/THL/PER WV6 .35 J4
HHTH/SAND B71 ....69 G6
SMTHWK B66 ....87 L7
Lynton Cl WWCK CV34 ......205 J4
Lynton Rd AST/WIT B6 ....89 G6
COVN CV6 ....134 D4
Lynval Rd BRLYHL DY5 .....102 B2
Lynwood Cl KGSWFD DY6 ....82 F5
Lynwood Av SHHTH WV12 ....38 C5
Lynwood Dr KIDD DY10 .....139 M3
Lynwood Wk HRBN B17 .....124 A1
RLSS CV31 ....207 G7
Lyons Gv SPARK B11 ....126 A2
Lysander Cl RBRY B45 .....143 L3
Lysander St COVS CV3 .....156 A7
Lysander Wy CNCK/NC WS11 ..16 C2
Lyster Cl WWCK CV34 ......204 F5
Lysways St WSL WS1 ....5 J7
Lythall Cl RLSS CV31 ......207 K8
Lythalls La COVN CV6 ....134 C3
Lytham TAM/AM/WIL B77 ....33 C8
Lytham Ct STRBR DY8 ......119 L3
WALM/CURD B76 ....73 M7
Lytham Cft EDG B15 ....6 E9
Lytham Rd DUNHL/THL/PER WV6 .48 B1
RUGBYN/DCH CV22 ....186 B4
Lythwood Dr BRLYHL DY5 ...102 A5
Lyttelton Rd BEWD DY12 ...162 E1
LDYWD/EDGR B16 ....106 B4
STETCH B33 ....109 H8
STRBR DY8 ....101 H8
WWCK CV34 ....205 J3
Lyttleton Av BRGRVW B60 ..191 J6
RMSLY B62 ....104 C6
Lyttleton Cl COVS CV3 .....156 E4
Lyttleton St WBROM B70 ....87 G3
Lytton Av
ETTPK/GDPK/PENN WV4 .....65 H1
Lytton Gv ACGN B27 ....126 F4
Lytton La RIDG/WDGT B32 ..123 K2

M

Maas Rd NFLD/LBR B31 .....144 E1
Mabey Av REDE B98 ....194 D8
Macadam Cl BNTWD WS7 .....18 F5
Macarthur Rd CDYHTH B64 ..103 G5
Macaulay Rd COVE CV2 .....156 B1
RUGBYS/DCH CV22 ....186 C1
Macbeth Cl RUGBYN/DCH CV22 ..186 C1
Macdonald Cl OLDBY B69 ...86 B3
Macdonald Rd COVE CV2 ....156 B2
Macdonald St DIG/EDG B5 ...7 H9
Macefield Cl CDYHTH B64 ..103 J4
Mac Gregor Crs
TAM/AM/WIL B77 ....46 D1
Mac Gregor Tithe CRTAM B79 .31 M8
Machin Rd ERDW/GRVHL B23 ..90 F1
Mackadown La STETCH B33 ..110 B3
Mackay Rd BLOX/PEL WS3 ...39 K1

Mackenzie Cl COVW CV5 ....132 E6
Mackenzie Rd SPARK B11 ...126 A3
Mackmillan Rd
BLKHTH/ROWR B65 ....104 A3
Macmillan Cl OLDBY B69 ....86 A3
Macrome Rd
DUNHL/THL/PER WV6 ......35 J5
Madam's Hill Rd SHLY B90 ..148 B6
Madams Hl RUGBYS/DCH CV22 .186 A3
Maddocks Hl CSCFLD/WYGN B72 .73 G5
Madehurst Rd ERDW/GRVHL B23 .72 C7
Madeira Av CDSL WV8 ....34 A5
Madeira Cft COVW CV5 ......154 C3
Madeley Rd HAG/WOL DY9 ...142 C6
KGSWFD DY6 ....101 L1
REDE B98 ....195 K8
SPARK B11 ....108 A8
Madin Rd TPTN/OCK DY4 .....85 J1
Madison Av CBROM B36 ......91 H7
WSLW WS2 ....52 F3
Madley Cl RBRY B45 ....143 J5
Madou Cl CRTAM B79 ....31 J5
Madresfield Dr HALE B63 ...121 M3
Madrona Rd TAM/AM/WIL B77 .46 F1
Maer Cl BLKHTH/ROWR B65 ..104 A3
Mafeking Rd SMTHWK B66 ...87 K1
Mafeking Vls RMSLY B62 * ..103 M6
Magdala St WSNGN B18 ......88 C8
Magdalen Cl DUDN DY1 ......84 E3
Magdalene Rd WSL WS1 ......5 J9
Magna Cl GTWY WS6 ....24 C2
Magness Crs SHHTH WV12 ...38 A8
Magnet La RUGBYS/DCH CV22 .186 A5
Magnolia Cl COVS CV3 .....154 E8
Magnolia Gv CDSL WV8 ......34 E2
Magnolia Wy DSYBK/YTR WS5 .69 K1
Magnum Cl FOAKS/STRLY B74 * .55 K6
Magnus TAM/AM/WIL B77 ....46 C7
Magpie Cl DUDS DY2 ....85 L7
Magpie La RCOVN/BALC/EX CV7 .151 J7
Magpie Wy KIDD DY10 ......164 F3
Magyar Crs NUN CV11 ....99 K5
Maidavale Crs COVS CV3 ...155 G8
Maidendale Rd KGSWFD DY6 ..82 F6
Maidenhair Dr RRUGBY CV23 .161 H5
Maidensbridge Gdns
KGSWFD DY6 ....82 F4
Maidensbridge Rd KGSWFD DY6 .82 F4
Maidstone Dr BNTWD WS7 ...101 J2
STRBR DY8 ....101 J2
Maidstone Rd
BFLD/HDSWWD B20 ....89 J4
Maidwell Dr SHLY B90 .....148 C5
Main Av ATHST CV9 ....61 L6
Main Rd ATHST CV9 ....62 C7
ATHST CV9 ....63 L2
CRTAM B79 ....33 M3
KNWTH CV8 ....183 L1
LICHS WS14 ....28 D7
MKTBOS/BARL/STKG CV13 ...81 K2
RRUGBY CV23 ....159 J1
RRUGBY CV23 ....159 M2
RRUGBY CV23 ....161 K8
RRUGBY CV23 ....161 L3
RRUGBY CV23 ....185 L1
RUGBYN/HIL CV21 ....160 B6
RUGBYS/DCH CV22 ....186 A5
SPARK B11 ....107 L6
Main Ter BHTH/HG B12 * ...107 L6
Mainwaring Dr MGN/WHC B75 .57 J3
Maisemore Cl REDE B98 ....195 H7
Maisonettes CDSL WV8 * 34 F2
The Maisonettes
ERDE/BCHGN B24 * 90 C3
Maitland TAM/AM/WIL B77 ..46 C7
Maitland Rd DUDN DY1 ......84 A4
WASH/WDE B8 ....108 D1
Majestic Wy
BLKHTH/ROWR B65 ....104 A1
Major St BKHL/PFLD WV2 ....50 C6
Majuba Rd LDYWD/EDGR B16 .106 A1
Makepeace Av WWCK CV34 ..205 K4
Malam Cl TLHL/CAN CV4 ....153 L4
Malcolm Av BRGRVW B61 ...191 J7
ERDE/BCHGN B24 ....73 G8
Malcolm Gv RBRY B45 ......143 J5
Malcolm Rd SHLY B90 ......147 M3
Malcolmson Cl EDG B15 ....106 C6
Maldale Rd DUDN DY1 ....47 G4
Malfield Av REDW B97 .....201 K3
Malfield Dr ACGN B27 .....127 J2
Malham Cl NUN CV11 ....99 L3
Malham Rd STRPT DY13 ....163 J6
TAM/AM/WIL B77 ....47 G4
WWCK CV34 ....205 A4
Malins Rd
ETTPK/GDPK/PENN WV4 .....50 B8
HRBN B17 ....106 B8
Malkit Cl WSLW WS2 ....52 C1
Mallaby Cl SHLY B90 ......147 L5
Mallard Cl ERDW/GRVHL B23 .72 B1
Mallard Av NUNW/HART CV10 .80 A8
Mallard Dr KIDD DY10 .....164 F2
Mallard Cl ACGN B27 ....127 G2
BLOX/PEL WS3 * 39 K3
BRLYHL DY5 ....102 A2
REDE B98 ....194 D8
Mallard Cft LICH WS13 .....21 G5
Mallard Rd ERDW/GRVHL B23 .89 M2
OLDBY B69 ....104 D2
Mallender Dr DOR/KN B93 ..149 K6
Mallerin Cft NUNW/HART CV10 .79 M4
Mallets Cnr LICHS WS14 * ..21 J8
Mallicot Cl LICH WS13 .....21 H4
Mallin Gv NUN CV11 ....86 H6
Mallin St CBROM B36 ....91 J3
Mallory Crs BLOX/PEL WS3 ..39 K1
Mallory Dr KIDDW DY11 ....138 B4
WWCK CV34 ....205 A4
Mallory Ri MOS/BIL B13 ...126 A4
Mallory Rd DUNHL/THL/PER WV6 .48 C2
Mallory Wy
RCOVN/BALC/EX CV7 ....116 C8
Mallow Cl DSYBK/YTR WS5 ..69 K2
Mallow Cft
DUNHL/THL/PER WV6 * 35 M4
Mallow Hl ERDW/GRVHL B23 ..71 M6
Mallows Cl DARL/WED WS10 * .52 B7
Mallow Wy RRUGBY CV23 ...133 L3
Malmesbury Rd COVN CV6 ..133 L3
SMHTH B10 ....108 C7
Malpas Dr RIDG/WDGT B32 ..123 G5
Malpas Gdns CDSL WV8 ......34 C1
Malpass Rd BRLYHL DY5 ...102 C6
Malpass Wk WOLVN WV10 ...36 F5
St ED EDG B15 ....106 B6
Malthouse Cl NUNW/HART CV10 .96 F1
Malthouse Cft AST/WIT B6 ..89 J1
Malthouse Dr DUDN DY1 ....84 E3
Malthouse Gdns LOZ/NWT B19 .89 H6

Malthouse Gv YDLY B25 ....109 J4
Malthouse La
DUNHL/THL/PER WV6 ......35 H7
HOCK/TIA B94 ....179 J7
KNWTH CV8 ....179 J7
PBAR/PBCH B42 ....71 H5
WASH/WDE B8 ....90 C7
Malt House La WOLVN WV10 ..14 F8
Malthouse Rd TPTN/OCK DY4 .67 J8
Malthouse Rw
CHWD/FDBR/MGN B37 ......110 C5
The Maltings ALDR WS9 * ...41 G7
NUN CV11 ....81 J8
RLSN CV32 ....206 D3
WMBN WV5 ....64 E7
WOLV WV1 ....3 C2
Malt Mill La RMSLY B62 ...103 M6
Malton Gv MOS/BIL B13 ....125 M6
Malvern Av HAG/WOL DY9 ..102 D8
NUNW/HART CV10 ....97 M2
RUGBYS/DCH CV22 ....187 H4
Malvern Cl HHTH/SAND B71 ..69 H8
SHHTH WV12 ....51 M1
STRPT DY13 ....188 B5
Malvern Ct ACGN B27 ......127 C1
WOLVN WV10 ....36 B5
Malvern Crs DUDS DY2 ......84 D7
Malvern Dr ALDR WS9 ....41 G5
KIDD DY11 ....164 C2
WOLV WV1 ....50 F4
Malvern Hill Rd VAUX/NECH B7 .90 A6
Malvern Vw KIDD DY10 .....166 C4
KIDDW DY11 ....163 M4
Malvern View Rd SEDG DY3 ..84 B1
Mamble Cl STRBR DY8 ......101 J2
Mammoth Dr WOLVN WV10 ...36 B7
Manby Cl DUNHL/THL/PER WV6 .2 C7
Manby Rd CVALE B35 ....91 L1
Manby St TPTN/OCK DY4 ....67 K5
Mancetter Rd ATHST CV9 ...63 C7
NUNW/HART CV10 ....80 B5
SHLY B90 ....148 A2
Manchester St AST/WIT B6 ..89 F6
OLDBY B69 ....86 F6
Mancroft Cl KGSWFD DY6 ...82 F6
Mancroft Gdns
DUNHL/THL/PER WV6 ......35 C8
Mancroft Rd
DUNHL/THL/PER WV6 ......35 C8
Mandale Rd WOLVN WV10 ...36 D7
Mandarin Av KIDD DY10 ....164 F2
Manderley Cl COVW CV5 ...132 A8
Manders Cft BDMR/CCFT WV3 .49 L6
Manor St BDMR/CCFT WV3 ...3 A8
Manderville Gdns KGSWFD DY6 .83 C7
Mandeville Gdns WSL WS1 ...5 H6
Mandeville Wy BRGRVW B61 .168 B8
Maney Cnr CSCFLD/WYGN B72 .72 F7
Maney Hill Rd
CSCFLD/WYGN B72 ....73 G2
Manfield Av COVE CV2 .....135 L6
Manfield Rd WLNHL WV13 ...51 C2
Manifold Cl BNTWD WS7 ....19 H7
Manilla Rd SLYOAK B29 ....124 D2
Manitoba Cft HWK/WKHTH B38 145 K5
Manley Cl WBROM B70 * 86 E2
Manley Rd LICH WS13 ......21 H4
Manlove St BDMR/CCFT WV3 * .2 B8
Manningford Rd
ALE/KHTH/YWD B14 ....146 D3
Mann's Cl KNWTH CV8 ......182 F5
Manor Abbey Dr RMSLY B62 .122 C2
Manor Abbey Rd RMSLY B62 .122 C1
Manor Av CNCK/NC WS11 ...16 A4
GTWY WS6 ....24 C1
KIDD DY11 ....137 H8
Manor Av South KIDDW DY11 137 L7
Manor Cl DOR/KN B93 * 175 J3
KNWTH CV8 ....179 L7
WSLW WS2 ....4 A4
Manor Court Av NUN CV11 ...99 H1
Manor Court Rd BRGRVW B60 .191 J5
NUN CV11 ....98 F1
Manor Dr SCFLD/BOLD B73 ..72 F1
SEDG DY3 ....82 C3
SEDG DY3 ....83 M2
SLYOAK B29 * 123 M6
WOLVN WV10 ....23 H3
Manor Est KNWTH CV8 .....183 K6
Manor Farm Dr SHHTH WV12 .38 B8
Manor Farm Rd SPARK B11 ..10 C5
Manorfield Cl PENK ST19 ...10 D3
Manor Fold CDSL WV8 ....34 B3
Manor Gdns STETCH B33 ...109 H4
WMBN WV5 ....64 E7
Manor Gv NFLD/LBR B31 ...144 A4
Manor Hall Rd COVS CV3 ...156 A4
Manor Hl SCFLD/BOLD B73 ..72 F1
Manor House Cl
RUGBYN/HIL CV21 ....160 B6
SLYOAK B29 ....123 K4
Manor House Dr COV CV1 ....6 E5
Manor House La
CSHL/WTROR B46 ....92 F2
LGN/SDN/BHAMAIR B26 ....109 J7
Manor House Pk CDSL WV8 ..34 C1
Manor House Rd
DARL/WED WS10 ....68 D1
Manor Houses RMSLY B62 * .104 C6
Manor La BRGRVW B61 ......143 G6
CRTAM B79 ....31 J2
KIDD DY11 ....189 M5
RMSLY B62 ....103 H6
STRPT DY13 ....188 C2
Manor Pk KGSWFD DY6 ....83 H7
NFLD/LBR B31 ....144 A4
Manor Park Rd CBROM B36 ..92 A6
NUN CV11 ....98 A1
Manor Ri BNTWD WS7 ....18 E4
LICHS WS14 ....28 C6
Manor Rd AST/WIT B6 ....89 K4
ATHST CV9 ....63 J7
COV CV1 ....8 E7
DARL/WED WS10 ....68 D1
DOR/KN B93 ....175 K2
ETTPK/GDPK/PENN WV4 ....50 D8
FOAKS/STRLY B74 ....55 J5
HLYWD B47 ....146 C6
HRBN B17 ....106 A3
SCFLD/BOLD B73 ....73 C2
WSLW WS2 ....52 C2

POL/KCSB/FAZ B78 ....45 H4
REDW B97 ....200 E4
RLSN CV32 ....206 F2
RUGBYN/HIL CV21 ....186 F1
SCFLD/BOLD B73 ....56 F8
SMTHWKW B67 ....87 H8
SOLH B91 ....128 E1
STETCH B33 ....109 J8
STRBR DY8 ....101 H3
STRPT DY13 ....163 M8
TAM/AM/WIL B77 ....46 D7
TPTN/OCK DY4 ....67 K8
WOLVN WV10 ....36 A6
WSLW WS2 ....4 A3
Manor Rd North
LDYWD/EDGR B16 ....106 B4
Manor Road Prec WSLW WS2 * .4 A4
Manor Stables DOR/KN B93 * 176 C1
Manor St DUNHL/THL/PER WV6 .35 H7
Manor Terrace Flats
KNWTH CV8 * 179 L7
Manor Vw KNWTH CV8 * 183 K2
Manor Wy HALE B63 ....121 K4
RMSLY B62 ....122 A3
Mansard Cl RCOVN/BALC/EX CV7 .116 A4
Manse Rd RCOVN/BALC/EX CV7 116 A4
Mansell Cl HALE B63 ......102 F6
Mansell Rd REDW B97 ......202 B6
TPTN/OCK DY4 ....67 L5
Mansel Rd SMHTH B10 .....108 C5
Mansel St COVN CV6 ....134 C5
Mansfield Cl CRTAM B79 ...31 J7
Mansfield Rd AST/WIT B6 ..89 H5
YDLY B25 ....109 G8
Mansion Cl DUDN DY1 ....84 E2
Mansion Crs SMTHWKW B67 .105 J1
Mansion Dr BNTWD WS7 ....27 H1
TPTN/OCK DY4 ....68 A8
Manston Dr
DUNHL/THL/PER WV6 ......34 C8
Manston Hl PENK ST19 .....10 C1
Manston Rd
LGN/SDN/BHAMAIR B26 ...109 M6
Manston Vw CRTAM B79 .....32 A5
Manta Rd TAM/AM/WIL B77 ..46 B7
Mantilla Dr COVS CV3 ......154 F8
Manton Cft DOR/KN B93 ....175 J3
Manway Cl BFLD/HDSWWD B20 .70 D8
Manwoods Cl
BFLD/HDSWWD B20 ....88 F3
Maple Av DARL/WED WS10 ...69 G8
RCOVN/BALC/EX CV7 ....116 F4
Maple Bank EDG B15 * 106 C6
Maplebeck Ct SOLH B91 * ..128 A8
Maple Cl BILS/COS WV14 ...67 K1
BNTWD WS7 ....18 C6
HDSW B21 ....88 C4
KIDDW DY11 ....137 H5
STRBR DY8 ....119 H3
STRPT DY13 ....188 C1
Mapledene
LGN/SDN/BHAMAIR B26 ...110 B7
HEDN WS12 ....137 M5
KGSTC B44 ....71 H5
POL/KCSB/FAZ B78 ....60 B6
RUSH/SHEL WS4 ....39 K3
SEDG DY3 ....83 M3
Maple Gn DUDN DY1 ....66 E8
Maple Gv BDMR/CCFT WV3 ...67 K1
BILS/COS WV14 ....67 L3
CHWD/FDBR/MGN B37 ......92 D2
KGSWFD DY6 ....83 J7
LICHS WS14 ....21 H5
LOZ/NWT B19 ....89 G5
RUGBYN/HIL CV21 ....186 E5
WWCK CV34 ....205 L4
Maple Leaf Dr
CHWD/FDBR/MGN B37 ......110 F5
Maple Leaf Rd DARL/WED WS10 68 A4
Maple Ri LGLYCN/QTN B68 ..105 C3
TAM/AM/WIL B77 ....46 D8
Maple Rd BDMR/CCFT WV3 ...49 J5
BLOX/PEL WS3 ....39 K3
BVILLE B30 ....124 C5
CSCFLD/WYGN B72 ....73 C2
DUDN DY1 ....85 G2
NUNW/HART CV10 ....80 C8
RBRY B45 ....143 K7
RLSS CV31 ....206 D7
RMSLY B62 ....104 C6
The Maples BDWTH CV12 ...116 C3
Maple St BLOX/PEL WS3 .....39 K3
Mapleton Gv HLGN/YWD B28 126 F6
Mapleton Rd COVN CV6 ....133 K5
HLGN/YWD B28 ....126 F7
Maple Tree La HALE B63 ...103 G7
Maple Wy NFLD/LBR B31 ...144 D5
Maplewood WALM/CURD B76 ..75 J5
Mapperley Gdns MOS/BIL B13 125 G2
Mapperley Gdns MOS/BIL B13 125 G2
Marans Cft HWK/WKHTH B38 145 H6
Marbury Cl HWK/WKHTH B38 145 H3
Marbury Ms BRLYHL DY5 ...102 B3
Marchant Rd BDMR/CCFT WV3 .49 K3
BILS/COS WV14 ....51 C6
March Cl GTWY WS6 ....24 B1
March End Rd WNSFLD WV11 ..37 H4
Marchfont Cl NUN CV11 .....99 K3
March Gv BEWD DY12 ....162 F1
Marchmont Rd BORD B9 ....108 C3
Marchmount Rd
CSCFLD/WYGN B72 ....73 C5
Marsh Wy ALDR WS9 ....41 G4
COVS CV3 ....156 B6
Marcwood Cl REDW B97 ....193 L8
Marcliff Crs SHLY B90 ....147 C3
Marcos Dr CBROM B36 ....92 D4
Marcot Rd HIA/OLT B92 ....109 K8
Marcroft Pl RLSS CV31 ....207 H4
Marden Cl WLNHL WV13 .....51 K4
Marden Gv NFLD/LBR B31 ..144 E6
Mardol Cl COVE CV2 ....135 H6
Mardon Rd
LGN/SDN/BHAMAIR B26 ...109 H8
Maree Gv WNSFLD WV11 ....37 L3
Marfield Cl WALM/CURD B76 .73 L7
Margam Crs BLOX/PEL WS3 ..38 C3
Margam Ter BLOX/PEL WS3 ..38 D3
Margaret Av BDWTH CV12 ..116 E2
HALE B63 ....121 K1
Margaret Cl BRLYHL DY5 ...102 C5
Margaret Dr CNCK/NC WS11 ..119 H1
STRBR DY8 ....101 H8
Margaret Gdns SMTHWKW B67 .87 J5
Margaret Rd DARL/WED WS10 .52 C2
Margaret Rd ATHST CV9 .....63 J6
DARL/WED WS10 ....106 A3
HRBN B17 ....106 A3
SCFLD/BOLD B73 ....56 B3
WSLW WS2 ....52 C2
Margaret St CBHAMNW B3 ....6 C1

dip Av WASH/WDE B8 ....90 C8
dip Cl BKHL/PFLD WV2 ....50 D7
RGRVW B61 ....168 E8
EDG DY3 ....84 B2
dip Dr NUNW/HART CV10 ....97 M2
dip Rd HALE B63 ....121 H4
TRBR DY8 ....101 H7
THWK B67 ....12 E4
WDE B8 ....108 C1
nin Crs MOS/BIL B13 ....125 M6
nin Rd MOS/BIL B13 ....125 M6
PTN/OCK DY4 ....67 H8
teith Cl STRPT DY13 ....163 J6
on Gv DUNHL/THL/PER WV6 ...48 C1
STETCH B33 ....109 M5
on Ri HAG/WOL DY9 ....120 A2
on Wy WNSFLD WV11 ....37 K6
ranti Cl SHHTH WV12 ....38 A5
CSHL/WTROR B46 ....92 E2
rcer Ct RUGBYN/HIL CV21 ...187 K5
rcer Gv WNSFLD WV11 ....37 H6
rcers Meadow
RCOVN/BALC/EX CV7 ....115 L7
rchants Wy ALDR WS9 ....40 E4
cia Cl KNWTH CV8 ....197 J1
cia Cl BRGRVE B60 ....191 J6
RTAM B79 ....31 J6
cia Dr ALE/KHTH/YWD B14 ...125 H7
DUNHL/THL/PER WV6 ....34 C4
cia Wy WWCK CV34 ....205 L6
rcot Cl REDE B98 ....202 E7
cury Av CVALE B35 ....91 L2
e Av SHHTH WV12 ....37 L8
rcote Rd CNCK/NC WS11 .....127 H6
e Cft CNCK/NC WS11 ....17 K8
edith Gn KIDDW DY11 ....163 L4
edith Pool Cl WSNGN B18 * 88 D7
edith Gn CL COVE CV2 ....156 B3
e Cl CDSL WV8 ....65 L8
WNSFLD WV11 ....37 L8
edith St CDYHTH B64 ....103 H4
re Dr MGN/WHC B75 ....56 F3
re Green Cl MGN/WHC B75 ......56 F3
re Green Gn MGN/WHC B75 ....56 F3
re La PENK ST19 ....14 A1
re Oak Rd
DUNHL/THL/PER WV6 ....34 C8
re Pool Rd MGN/WHC B75 ......57 H3
re Rd ERDW/GRVHL B23 ....90 D3
STRBR DY8 ....119 J1
reside Wy HIA/OLT B92 ....127 J5
re Rd HALE B63 ....103 G8
revale Av NUN CV11 ....98 B7
revale Cl REDE B98 ....203 H1
revale La ATHST CV9 ....62 D6
revale Rd ATHST CV9 ....63 G5
HIA/OLT B92 ....127 M3
revale Vw ATHST CV9 ....63 G5
re Wy RUSH/SHEL WS4 ....40 A5
rganser Wy KIDD DY10 ....164 F2
rganser La Av STRBR DY8 ......101 H7
riden Cl CNCK/NC WS11 ....16 A1
REDE B98 ....203 L2
riden Dr
CHWD/FDBR/MGN B37 ....92 E8
riden Rd HIA/OLT B92 ....128 B2
riden Rd HIA/OLT B92 ....130 A6
RCOVN/BALC/EX CV7 ....113 H6
WOLVN WV10 ....35 L5
ride St COV CV1 ....7 J3
EDG/EDG B5 ....7 H9
ridian Pl BRGRVE B60 * 191 L4
rino Av NFLD/LBR B31 ....144 E5
rlin Cl CNCK/NC WS11 ....16 A1
CVALE B35 ....91 L2
DUDN DY1 ....84 D1
RRUGBY CV23 ....161 G5
TAM/AM/WIL B77 ....46 E7
rlin Gv
LGN/SDN/BHAMAIR B26 ....109 M8
rrick Cl HALE B63 ....121 H3
rricks Rd WNSFLD WV11 ....37 L7
rricks La BEWD DY12 ....162 D2
rrington Cl SOLH B91 ....149 G5
rrion's Ct GTB/HAM B43 ....7 A5
rrishaw Rd NFLD/LBR B31 ....144 E4
rritts Brook Cl SLYOAK B29 ...123 J8
rritt's Brook La
JFLD/LBR B31 ....123 J8
rritt's Hl HIA/OLT B92 ....123 J7
rrivale Rd COVW CV5 ....154 C2
RMSLY B62 ....104 A5
MTHWK B66 ....105 L3
rryfield Rd HIA/OLT B92 ....128 A6
rryfield Gv HRBN B17 ....124 B1
rry Hl DUDN DY1 ....84 B4
rryhill Dr WSNGN B18 ....108 B7
rse Rd REDE B98 ....195 J7
rsey Gv HWK/WKHTH B38 .....123 J5
rsey Rd BDWTH CV12 ....117 L3
BLOX/PEL WS3 ....39 J4
rstal Dr HIA/OLT B92 ....128 C8
rstone Cl BILS/COS WV14 .....155 L2
rstowe Cl ACGN B27 ....126 F2
rton Cl BEWD DY12 ....162 C1
IDD DY10 ....138 F6
GLYGN/QTN DY8 ....104 F3
rton Rd MOS/BIL B13 ....125 M2
rvyn Pl BILS/COS WV14 ....67 K2
rvyn Rd BILS/COS WV14 ....67 K2
rstall Cl BNTWD WS7 ....19 G5
reif Cl BNTWD WS7 ....19 G5
rvey Cl HRBN B17 ....124 B1
rvey Rd HDSW B21 ....124 E1
rvey Dr SHLY B90 ....162 A1
rvey Dr HRBN B17 ....106 J9

Metchley La EDG B15 ....124 B1
HRBN B17 ....106 B8
Metchley Park Rd EDG B15 ....124 B1
Metfield Cft HRBN B17 ....124 B1
KGSWFD DY6 ....83 K7
Metlin Gv STETCH B33 ....110 C2
Metric Wk SMTHWKW B67 ......87 H7
Metro Triangle VAUX/NECH B7 * ...90 B6
Metro Wy SMTHWK B66 ....87 J7
Mews Rd RLSN CV32 ....206 B5
The Mews BDWTH CV12 ....116 F3
BLKHTH/ROWR B65 ....103 M3
KNWTH CV8 ....197 J2
RLSN CV32 * 206 C5
Meyrick Rd WBROM B70 ....68 E7
Meyrick Wk LDYWD/EDGR B16 ...106 D4
Miall Park Rd SOLH B91 ....127 J8
Miall Rd HLGN/YWD B28 ....126 E5
Mica Cl TAM/AM/WIL B77 ....46 F3
Michael Blanning Pl
RCOVN/BALC/EX CV7 * 151 M6
Michael Dr EDG B15 ....107 G6
Michaelmas Rd COVS CV3 ....8 E8
Michael Rd DARL/WED WS10 ...51 M6
SMTHWK B67 ....87 J7
Michaelwood Cl REDW B97 ....201 K3
Michell Cl COVS CV3 ....155 M5
Michelle Cl MOS/BIL B13 ....125 L8
Michigan Cl CNCK/NC WS11 ....16 F3
Micklehill Dr SHLY B90 ....147 M5
Mickle Meadow
RWWCK/WEL CV35 ....204 B3
Mickleover Rd WASH/WDE B8 ...91 G1
Mickleton Cl REDE B98 ....202 C6
Mickleton Av STETCH B33 .....110 A5
Mickleton Rd COVW CV5 ....8 B3
Mickleton Dr
RWWCK/WEL CV35 ....204 B3
Micklewood Cl COVW CV5 ....8 B3
HIA/OLT B92 ....127 H5
Micklewood La PENK ST19 .....10 D6
Mickley Av WOLVN WV10 ....36 C8
Midacre WLNHL WV13 ....51 L4
Middleburg Ct NUN CV11 ....99 L5
Middle Acre Rd
RIDG/WDGT B32 ....123 J3
Middle Av WLNHL WV13 ....51 J5
Middle Bickenhill La
COVE CV2 ....134 F2
HLYWD B47 ....146 E6
KIDD DY10 ....139 M3
KNWTH CV8 ....183 K2
NUN CV11 ....99 J4
SEDG DY3 ....66 B7
STRPT DY13 ....188 F2
Mill Crs BILS/COS WV14 ....66 B6
POL/KGSB/FAZ B78 ....76 D1
Milldale Crs WOLVN WV10 ....36 B1
Milldale Rd WOLVN WV10 ....36 B1
Mill Dr SMTHWK B66 ....87 M8
Mill End KNWTH CV8 ....179 J7
Millennium Pk WBROM B70 * 68 E8
Millennium Cl BILS/COS WV14 ...51 J1
Millennium Gdns CDYHTH B64 ...103 K3
Millennium Pk WBROM B70 * 68 E8
Millennium Wy CDSL WV8 ....34 L1
KNWTH CV8 ....183 K2
Miller Cl BRGRVE B60 ....191 J7
Miller Crs BILS/COS WV14 ....66 B6
Millers Cl WSLW WS2 ....52 D4
Millers Dale Cl
RUGBYN/HIL CV21 ....161 G6
Millers Green Dr KGSWFD DY6 ...82 E5
Millers Rd WWCK CV34 ....205 H5
Miller St AST/WIT B6 ....89 J8
Millers V HEDN WS12 ....17 H4
WMBN WV5 ....64 B8
Millers Wk BLOX/PEL WS3 ....39 J2
Mill Farm Rd HRBN B17 ....124 A2
Millfield NFLD/LBR B31 * 144 E1
RUSH/SHEL WS4 ....39 M4
Millfield Av BLOX/PEL WS3 ....39 H3
RUSH/SHEL WS4 ....39 M4
Millfield Rd BFLD/HDSWWD B20 ...70 D8
BRGRVW B61 ....191 H4
BRWNH WS8 ....26 E6
Millfields STETCH B33 ....110 C2
Millfields Av RUGBYN/HIL CV21 ...187 K5
Millfields Rd BKHL/PFLD WV2 ...50 D8
HHTH/SAND B71 ....68 F8
Millfields Wy WMBN WV5 ....64 B8
Millfield Vw HALE B63 ....121 J1
Millford Cl HLGN/YWD B28 .....126 E5
Mill Gdns SMTHWKW B67 * 105 K5
Mill Gn WOLVN WV10 ....36 C2
Mill Gv CDSL WV8 ....35 G2
Millhaven Av BVILLE B30 ....125 J4
Mill Hill COVS CV3 ....181 H7
SMTHWKW B67 ....105 K2
Millhouse Ct COVN CV6 ....134 C6
Mill House Dr RLSN CV32 ......206 A5
Millhouse Gdns PENK ST19 .....10 D4
Millhouse Rd YDLY B25 ....108 F5
Millicent Cl HEDN WS12 ....12 F7
Millichip Rd WLNHL WV13 ....51 J4
Milliners Ct ATHST CV9 ....63 G5
Millington Rd CBROM B36 ....91 J5
TPTN/OCK DY4 ....67 J4
WOLVN WV10 ....36 C2
Million La ALDR WS9 ....41 K1
ALDR WS9 ....41 J1
ATHST CV9 ....63 L5
BDWTH CV12 ....117 L2
BNTWD WS7 ....27 H7
BRGRVW B61 ....191 H3
BRGRVW B61 ....191 H3
COVS CV3 ....156 D5
CRTAM B79 ....32 A8
DIG/EDG B5 ....7 J7
DOR/KN B93 ....175 J1
DUNHL/THL/PER WV6 ....48 B7
HOCK/TIA B94 ....167 H1
KIDD DY10 ....139 M3
KIDD DY10 ....138 D3
KIDDW DY11 ....138 D7
LICHS WS14 ....28 E7
NUN CV11 ....98 A2
WSL WS1 ....4 E5
Midland St WASH/WDE B8 ......108 B1
Midpoint Pk WALM/CURD B76 * ...74 A3
Midvale Dr ALE/KHTH/YWD B14 ...146 B8
Mikado Rd BRGRVW B60 ....192 B4
Milburn TAM/AM/WIL B77 ....47 J7
Milburn Hill Rd TLHL/CAN CV4 ...153 M8
Milburn Rd KGSTG B44 ....71 L2
Milby Dr NUN CV11 ....99 J4
Milcote Cl REDE B98 ....202 D6
Milcote Dr SCFLD/BOLD B73 ...72 A2
WLNHL WV13 ....51 H4
Milcote Rd SLYOAK B29 ....123 J5
SMTHWKW B67 ....105 K3
SOLH B91 ....149 G1
Milcote Wy KGSWFD DY6 ....82 F6
Mildenhall CRTAM B79 ....31 M7
Mildenhall Rd PBAR/PBCH B42 ...70 E4

Mildred Rd CDYHTH B64 ....103 J3
Mildred Wy OLDBY B69 ....86 A9
Milebrook Gv RIDG/WDGT B32 ...122 F5
Milebush Av CBROM B36 ....92 B4
Mile Flat KGSWFD DY6 ....82 D6
Miles Gv DUDS DY2 ....85 K6
Miles Meadow COVN CV6 ......134 C4
Miles Meadow Cl SHHTH WV12 ...38 A5
Milestone Dr HAG/WOL DY9 ...140 E1
RUGBYS/DCH CV22 ....88 A5
Milestone La HDSW B21 ....88 B3
Milestone Wy SHHTH WV12 .....37 L8
Mile Tree La COVE CV2 ....117 J7
Milford Av BHTH/HG B12 ....107 L7
SHHTH WV12 ....37 L8
STRPT DY13 ....163 J7
Milford Cl COVW CV5 ....132 F7
REDW B97 ....201 M6
STRBR DY8 ....118 D7
Milford Copse HRBN B17 ....105 M8
Milford Cl LOZ/NWT B19 ....89 H8
Milford Cft BLKHTH/ROWR B65 ...85 K7
Milford Gv SHLY B90 ....149 G6
Milford Pl ALE/KHTH/YWD B14 * ...125 J3
Milford Rd BKHL/PFLD WV2 .....50 A6
HRBN B17 ....105 M8
Milford St NUNW/HART CV10 ...98 F6
Milholme Gn HIA/OLT B92 ......128 B6
Milking Bank DUDN DY1 ....84 C3
Mill St DIG/EDG B5 ....7 K7
Millais Cl BDWTH CV12 ....116 E1
Millard Rd BILS/COS WV14 ......66 H4
Mill Bank Dr
SEDG DY3 ....66 B5
Millbank WWCK CV34 ....205 M4
Mill Bank Ms KNWTH CV8 ......179 M7
Millbeck RUGBYN/HIL CV21 ....161 H6
Millbrook Cl CNCK/NC WS11 ....16 D3
Millbrook Dr LICHS WS14 ....28 D7
NFLD/LBR B31 ....144 C5
Millbrook Rd
ALE/KHTH/YWD B14 ....125 G7
Millbrook Wy BRLYHL DY5 ......101 M5
Mill Burn Wy BORD B9 ....107 M3
Mill Cl BRGRVE B60 ....191 K7
COVE CV2 ....134 F2
HLYWD B47 ....146 E6
KIDD DY10 ....139 M3
KNWTH CV8 ....183 K2
NUN CV11 ....99 J4
SEDG DY3 ....66 B7
STRPT DY13 ....188 F2
Mill Crs BILS/COS WV14 ....66 B6
POL/KGSB/FAZ B78 ....76 D1
Milldale Crs WOLVN WV10 ....36 B1
Milldale Rd WOLVN WV10 ....36 B1
Mill Dr SMTHWK B66 ....87 M8
Mill End KNWTH CV8 ....179 J7
Millennium Pk WBROM B70 * 68 E8
Millennium Cl BILS/COS WV14 ...51 J1
Millennium Gdns CDYHTH B64 ...103 K3
Millennium Pk WBROM B70 * 68 E8
Millennium Wy CDSL WV8 ....34 L1
KNWTH CV8 ....183 K2
Miller Cl BRGRVE B60 ....191 J7
Miller Crs BILS/COS WV14 ....66 B6
Millers Cl WSLW WS2 ....52 D4
Millers Dale Cl
RUGBYN/HIL CV21 ....161 G6
Millers Green Dr KGSWFD DY6 ...82 E5
Millers Rd WWCK CV34 ....205 H5
Miller St AST/WIT B6 ....89 J8
Millers V HEDN WS12 ....17 H4
WMBN WV5 ....64 B8
Millers Wk BLOX/PEL WS3 ....39 J2
Mill Farm Rd HRBN B17 ....124 A2
Millfield NFLD/LBR B31 * 144 E1
RUSH/SHEL WS4 ....39 M4
Millfield Av BLOX/PEL WS3 ....39 H3
RUSH/SHEL WS4 ....39 M4
Millfield Rd BFLD/HDSWWD B20 ...70 D8
BRGRVW B61 ....191 H4
BRWNH WS8 ....26 E6
Millfields STETCH B33 ....110 C2
Millfields Av RUGBYN/HIL CV21 ...187 K5
Millfields Rd BKHL/PFLD WV2 ...50 D8
HHTH/SAND B71 ....68 F8
Millfields Wy WMBN WV5 ....64 B8
Millfield Vw HALE B63 ....121 J1
Millford Cl HLGN/YWD B28 .....126 E5
Mill Gdns SMTHWKW B67 * 105 K5
Mill Gn WOLVN WV10 ....36 C2
Mill Gv CDSL WV8 ....35 G2
Millhaven Av BVILLE B30 ....125 J4
Mill Hill COVS CV3 ....181 H7
SMTHWKW B67 ....105 K2
Millhouse Ct COVN CV6 ....134 C6
Mill House Dr RLSN CV32 ......206 A5
Millhouse Gdns PENK ST19 .....10 D4
Millhouse Rd YDLY B25 ....108 F5
Millicent Cl HEDN WS12 ....12 F7
Millichip Rd WLNHL WV13 ....51 J4
Milliners Ct ATHST CV9 ....63 G5
Millington Rd CBROM B36 ....91 J5
TPTN/OCK DY4 ....67 J4
WOLVN WV10 ....36 C2
Mill La Ar SOLH B91 * 149 G2

Millmead Rd SLYOAK B29 ......123 J7
Mill Pk CNCK/NC WS11 ....16 E3
Mill Pl CNCK/NC WS11 ....53 L7
Mill Pool Cl HAG/WOL DY9 .....140 E1
WMBN WV5 ....64 C8
Millpool Gdns
ALE/KHTH/YWD B14 ....146 D2
Millpool Hill Alcester Rd South
ALE/KHTH/YWD B14 ....146 D2
Mill Pool La DOR/KN B93 ....175 G8
Mill Pool Rd HEDN WS12 ....12 F7
Mill Race La COVN CV6 ....134 E2
STRBR DY8 ....101 J7
Millrace Rd REDE B98 ....194 D8
Mill Race Vw ATHST CV9 ....63 H3
Millridge Wy KIDDW DY11 ......189 L4
Mill Rd BRWNH WS8 ....26 A6
CDYHTH B64 ....103 J4
RLSS CV31 ....206 E5
RUGBYN/HIL CV21 ....187 C1
RUSH/SHEL WS4 ....39 M4
STRPT DY13 ....188 F1
Mills Av WALM/CURD B76 ....73 J1
Millsborough Rd REDE B98 .....202 C2
Mills Cl WNSFLD WV11 ....36 F5
Mills Crs BKHL/PFLD WV2 ....3 J9
Millside HLGN/YWD B28 ....147 J2
WMBN WV5 * 64 C8
Mills Rd BKHL/PFLD WV2 ....3 J9
Millstone Cl WALM/CURD B76 ...73 J4
Mill St AST/WIT B6 ....89 J8
BDWTH CV12 ....116 F2
BILS/COS WV14 ....51 G8
BRLYHL DY5 ....102 B3
CDYHTH B64 ....103 G6
CNCK/NC WS11 ....16 C4
COV CV1 ....8 D7
CSCFLD/WYGN B72 ....57 G8
DARL/WED WS10 ....52 A7
KIDDW DY11 ....138 A7
NUN CV11 ....99 C5
REDW B97 ....202 B3
RLSS CV31 ....206 E6
STRBR DY8 ....101 J3
TPTN/OCK DY4 ....68 D8
WBROM B70 ....87 G1
WLNHL WV13 ....52 A3
WSLW WS2 ....53 J2
WWCK CV34 ....205 H4
Mill Ter BDWTH CV12 ....98 F8
Mill Vw STETCH B33 ....110 A1
Mill Wk NUN CV11 ....99 J4
Millwalk Dr COVEN WV9 ....35 L2
The Mill Wk NFLD/LBR B31 ....144 D4
Millward Cl TPTN/OCK DY4 ......67 M8
WBROM B70 ....86 E2
Millwright Cl TPTN/OCK DY4 ....67 M8
Milner Crs COVE CV2 ....135 K4
Milner Dr CRTAM B79 ....33 J6
Milner Rd SLYOAK B29 ....124 E4
Milner Wy MOS/BIL B13 ....126 B5
Milo Crs POL/KGSB/FAZ B78 ...45 L3
Milrose Wy TLHL/CAN CV4 .....153 K5
Milsom Gv BKDE/SHDE B34 ....92 B7
Milstead Rd
LGN/SDN/BHAMAIR B26 ....109 L4
Milston Cl ALE/KHTH/YWD B14 ...146 C2
CRTAM B79 ....31 L6
WWCK CV34 ....205 M4
Milton Av BDWTH CV12 ....117 H4
DOR/KN B93 ....175 K1
KIDD DY10 ....137 L7
REDW B97 ....202 A3
SHHTH WV12 ....38 C6
STRBR DY8 ....101 L6
WSL WS1 ....53 H7
Milton Crs SEDG DY3 ....65 L9
YDLY B25 ....109 H6
Milton Dr HAG/WOL DY9 ....120 B6
Milton Gv HDSW B21 ....88 A5
Milton Pl WSL WS1 ....53 H7
Milton Rd BILS/COS WV14 ....67 H6
CNCK/NC WS11 ....16 C1
DOR/KN B93 ....175 K1
ERDW/GRVHL B23 ....72 C9
SMTHWKW B67 ....87 H6
WOLVN WV10 ....36 B1
Milton St BRLYHL DY5 ....84 B6
COVE CV2 ....155 L1
HHTH/SAND B71 ....68 F8
LOZ/NWT B19 ....89 J7
WSL WS1 ....53 H7
Milverton Cl HALE B63 ....103 L7
WALM/CURD B76 ....73 K6
Milverton Crs RLSN CV32 ......206 C1
Milverton Crs West RLSN CV32 ...206 C1
Milverton Hl RLSN CV32 ....206 D1
Milverton Lawn RLSN CV32 ....206 B5
Milverton Rd COVE CV2 ....135 K4
DOR/KN B93 ....150 A8
ERDW/GRVHL B23 ....72 C9
Milverton Ter RLSN CV32 ....206 C5
Mimosa Cl SLYOAK B29 ....123 H6
Mimosa Wk KGSWFD DY6 ....83 J5
Mincing La BLKHTH/ROWR B65 ...104 A3
Mindelsohn Wy EDG B15 ....124 D1
Minden Gv SLYOAK B29 ....123 H6
Minehead Rd DUDN DY1 ....84 B5
WOLVN WV10 ....35 M3
Miner St WSLW WS2 ....53 G2
Miners Wk POL/KGSB/FAZ B78 ...47 K4
Minerva Cl SHHTH WV12 ....52 C1
TAM/AM/WIL B77 ....32 M3
Minewood Cl BLOX/PEL WS3 ...38 C2
Minions Cl ATHST CV9 ....63 H5
Minith Rd BILS/COS WV14 ....67 H5
Miniva Dr WALM/CURD B76 .....73 L3
Minivet Dr BHTH/HG B12 ....107 K6
Minley Av HRBN B17 ....105 M6
The Minories CBHAMNW B3 .....7 H5
DUDS DY2 ....85 L4
Minors Hl LICHS WS14 ....21 H7
Minstead Rd ERDE/BCHGN B24 ...90 M4
Minster Cl BLKHTH/ROWR B65 ...104 C3
DOR/KN B93 ....149 M5
RWWCK/WEL CV35 ....204 C1
Minster Ct MOS/BIL B13 * 125 L1
Minster Dr SMHTH B10 ....108 A4
Minsterley Cl BDMR/CCFT WV3 ...49 G5
Minster Rd COVN CV6 ....133 L5
STRPT DY13 ....188 C1
The Minster BDMR/CCFT WV3 ...49 G6
Mintern Rd YDLY B25 ....109 H7
Minton Cl WOLV WV1 ....50 M4
Minton Rd COVE CV2 ....135 K4
RIDG/WDGT B32 ....123 K1
Minworth Cl REDW B97 ....201 M6
Minworth Rd CSHL/WTROR B46 ...91 M3
Mira Dr
MKTBOS/BARL/STKG CV13 .....92 D4
Miranda Cl COVS CV3 ....156 B6
RBRY B45 ....143 L3
Mirfield Cl COVEN WV9 ....35 L2

Mirfield Rd SOLH B91 ....127 L7
STETCH B33 ....109 M3
Mission Cl CDYHTH B64 ....103 L4
Mission Dr TPTN/OCK DY4 ....85 L1
Mistletoe Dr DSYBK/YTR WS5 ...69 G2
Mitcham Cl HEDN WS12 ....12 D6
Mitcham Gv KGSTG B44 ....71 K4
Mitchel Cl REDE B98 ....202 C6
Mitcheldean Covert
ALE/KHTH/YWD B14 ....146 B3
Mitchell Av BILS/COS WV14 .....66 F4
TLHL/CAN CV4 ....153 L7
Mitchell Rd BDWTH CV12 ......117 G3
Mitchel Rd KGSWFD DY6 ....101 K1
Mitchells Ct CRTAM B79 * 31 M8
Mitford Dr HIA/OLT B92 ....128 B3
Mitre Cl SHHTH WV12 ....38 B6
WNSFLD WV11 ....37 L2
Mitre Fold WOLV WV1 ....2 D3
Mitre Rd CTWY WS6 ....24 E3
HAG/WOL DY9 ....102 C8
Mitten Av RBRY B45 ....143 K4
Mitton Cl STRPT DY13 ....188 E3
Mitton Gdns STRPT DY13 ......188 D1
Mitton Rd BFLD/HDSWWD B20 ...88 C3
Mitton St STRPT DY13 ....188 E2
Moat Av COVS CV3 ....180 C5
Moat Brook Av COVS CV3 ......155 H8
Moatbrook La CDSL WV8 ....34 B1
Moat Cl KNWTH CV8 ....182 A7
Moat Coppice RIDG/WDGT B32 ...122 C6
Moat Cft
CHWD/FDBR/MGN B37 ....110 C3
Moat Dr HAG/WOL DY9 ....120 A6
RMSLY B62 ....104 D4
Moat Farm Dr BDWTH CV12 ...116 A5
RIDG/WDGT B32 ....122 C4
RUGBYN/HIL CV21 ....187 G6
Moat Farm Wy BLOX/PEL WS3 ...25 J2
Moatfield Ter DARL/WED WS10 ...68 E2
Moat Green Av WNSFLD WV11 ...37 J6
Moat Green Cl CSHL/WTROR B46 ...94 F4
TLHL/CAN CV4 ....154 A6
Moat House La East
WNSFLD WV11 ....37 H6
Moathouse La West
WNSFLD WV11 ....37 H6
Moat House Rd WASH/WDE B8 ...108 E1
Moat La DIG/EDG B5 ....7 H7
GTWY WS6 ....24 E3
LGN/SDN/BHAMAIR B26 ....109 J6
SOLH B91 ....128 A7
Moat Mdw RIDG/WDGT B32 ...123 J1
Moat Rd AST/WIT B6 ....89 J9
Moat Rd LCLYGN/QTN B68 .....104 F2
TPTN/OCK DY4 ....67 L6
WSLW WS2 ....52 D4
Moatside Cl BLOX/PEL WS3 .....25 L3
Moat St WLNHL WV13 ....51 L3
Mobberley Rd BILS/COS WV14 ...66 E4
Mob La RUSH/SHEL WS4 ....40 A5
Mockley Wood Rd DOR/KN B93 ...149 H6
Modbury Av RIDG/WDGT B32 ...123 H4
Modbury Cl COVS CV3 ....155 H8
Moden Cl SEDG DY3 ....66 B8
Moden Hl SEDG DY3 ....66 A7
Moffit Wy STRPT DY13 ....188 C1
Mogul La HALE B63 ....102 E6
Moira Crs
ALE/KHTH/YWD B14 ....147 G1
Moises Hall Rd WMBN WV5 .....64 F7
Molands Br
RCOVN/BALC/EX CV7 ....130 B4
Moland St AST/WIT B6 ....7 H1
Mole St SPARK B11 ....107 H7
Molesworth Av COVS CV3 ......155 L4
Molineux St WOLV WV1 ....2 F3
Mollington Crs SHLY B90 ....148 A2
Mollington Cv
RWWCK/WEL CV35 ....204 B3
Molyneux Rd DUDS DY2 ....103 J3
Momus Bvd COVE CV2 ....156 A3
Monarch Dr TPTN/OCK DY4 .....68 A7
Monarch's Wy
BLKHTH/ROWR B65 ....103 K1
BRGRVW B60 ....192 A5
HAG/WOL DY9 ....120 A2
KGSWFD DY6 ....82 C7
KIDD DY10 ....166 B8
OLDBY B69 ....86 A3
REDW B97 ....201 K3
WNSFLD WV11 ....37 H2
WSLW WS2 ....52 E2
Monarch Wy DUDS DY2 ....102 F7
Mona Rd ERDW/GRVHL B23 .....72 D8
Monastery Dr SOLH B91 ....127 J7
Monckton Rd LGLYGN/QTN B68 ...104 D8
Moncrieffe Cl DUDS DY2 ....85 J5
Moncrieffe St WSL WS1 ....5 J5
Mondrian Rd BRGRVE B60 .....192 A4
Money La BRGRVW B61 ....142 F7
Monica Rd SMHTH B10 ....108 D5
Monins Av TPTN/OCK DY4 ....85 M2
Monk Cl TPTN/OCK DY4 ....85 M2
Monk Rd WASH/WDE B8 ....90 F4
Monks Cl RUGBYS/DCH CV22 ...185 L5
WMBN WV5 ....64 C7
The Monk's Cft COVS CV3 ......155 G6
Monkseaton Rd
CSCFLD/WYGN B72 ....72 F3
Monksfield Av GTB/HAM B43 ...70 B4
Monks Field Cl TLHL/CAN CV4 ...153 L4
Monkshood Ms
ERDW/GRVHL B23 ....71 M4
Monkshood Retreat
HWK/WKHTH B38 ....145 K5
Monks Kirby Rd
WALM/CURD B76 ....73 K2
Monks Pth REDW B97 ....201 K1
Monkspath SHLY B90 ....148 D7
WALM/CURD B76 ....73 K1
Monkspath Cl SHLY B90 ....148 B6
Monkspath Hall Rd SHLY B90 ...148 D7
Monks Rd COV CV1 ....9 L5
COVS CV3 ....157 G8
Monksway Rd
HWK/WKHTH B38 ....145 M3
Monks Wy TAM/AM/WIL B77 ....32 C6
WWCK CV34 ....205 H7
Monkswell Cl BRLYHL DY5 ......102 B4
SMHTH B10 ....108 B6
Monkswood Crs COVE CV2 .....135 L5
Monkswood Rd NFLD/LBR B31 ...145 G3
Monkton Rd SLYOAK B29 ....123 L2
Monmer Cl WLNHL WV13 ....51 M2
Monmer La WLNHL WV13 ....51 M2
Monmore Rd WOLV WV1 ....50 D9
Monmouth Cl COVW CV5 ....153 M2
KNWTH CV8 ....179 K7
Monmouth Dr HHTH/SAND B71 ...68 A7
SCFLD/BOLD B73 ....72 A2
Monmouth Gdns
NUNW/HART CV10 ....98 C1
Monmouth Rd BFLD/HDSWWD B32 ...123 H5
SMTHWKW B67 ....104 F4
WSLW WS2 ....52 C2
Monsal Av WOLVN WV10 ....36 C1

Monsaldale Cl *BRWNH* WS8 ......26 B7
Monsal Rd *PBAR/PBCH* B42......71 G6
Monsieurs Hall La *BRGRVW* B61 ..190 F2
Mons Rd *DUDS* DY2..................85 J4
Montague Rd *ERDE/BCHGN* B24 ..90 B4
    HDSW B21.................................88 D5
    LDYWD/EDGR B16 ....106 C4
    RUGBYS/DCH CV22 ....186 B8
    SMTHWK B66.........................105 M2
    WWCK CV34.........................205 L4
Montague St *AST/WIT* B6...........89 M5
    DIG/EDG B5............................7 M5
Montalt Rd *COVS* CV3................155 J6
Montana Av *PBAR/PBCH* B42 .....70 C5
Montana Wk *NUNW/HART* CV10..98 C2
Montcrieff Dr *RLSS* CV31.........207 G8
Monteagle Dr *KGSWFD* DY6........83 H4
Montfort Gv *SEDG* DY3 *...........66 B6
    WSLW WS2.............................52 F7
Montgomery Av *RWWCK/WEL* CV35 ..204 C7
Montgomery Cl *BRCRVW* B61.....168 E4
    COVS CV3.............................182 A1
Montgomery Ct *WWCK* CV34 * ..205 K6
Montgomery Crs *BRLYHL* DY5....102 D6
Montgomery Cft *SPARK* B11.....108 A6
Montgomery Dr *RUGBYS/DCH* CV22 ..186 A4
Montgomery Rd *WSLW* WS2........52 C3
Montgomery St *SPARK* B11.......107 M6
Montgomery Wy *WASH/WDE* B8.......108 L1
Montjoy Cl *COVS* CV3...............156 D6
Montley *TAM/AM/WIL* B77...........47 C5
Montpelier Rd *ERDE/BCHGN* B24........90 B4
Montpellier Cl *COVS* CV3..........155 D7
Montpellier Gdns *DUDN* DY1 ......84 C3
Montpellier St *BHTH/HG* B12 ....107 F1
Montrose Av *RLSN* CV32............206 E1
Montrose Dr *CVALE* B35..............91 L2
    DUDN DY1.............................84 B5
    NUNW/HART CV10...................98 D2
Montrose Rd *RUGBYS/DCH* CV22 ..186 B4
Montsford Cl *SHLY* B90.............149 K7
Monument Av *HAG/WOL* DY9 .....120 C1
Monument Dr *WOLVN* WV10.........23 C5
Monument La *HAG/WOL* DY9......120 B6
    RBRY B45...............................169 K1
    SEDG DY3...............................66 C4
Monument Rd *LDYWD/EDGR* B16 ..106 D4
Monway Ter *DARL/WED* WS10 ....68 C2
Monwode Lea La *CSHL/WTROR* B46...........95 M1
Monwood Gv *SOLH* B91.............148 D3
Monyhull Hall Rd *BVILLE* B30 ....145 M2
Moodyscroft Rd *STECH* B33......110 A2
Moon's La *GTWY* WS6 ....24 B3
Moons Moat Dr *REDE* B98.........195 J8
Moorbrooke *NUNW/HART* CV10..79 L6
Moor Cl *BNTWD* WS7..................18 F6
Moorcroft Cl *NUN* CV11..............99 M4
Moorcroft Dr *DARL/WED* WS10 ...68 B3
Moorcroft Gdns *REDW* B97........201 M7
Moorcroft Pl *VAUX/NECH* B7 ....7 L2
Moorcroft Rd *MOS/BIL* B13.......125 H2
Moordown Av *HIA/OLT* B92........127 L3
Moore Cl *COVN* CV6.................134 E1
    DUNHL/THL/PER WV6..............48 D1
    FOAKS/STRLY B74 ....42 D7
    WWCK CV34.........................205 J3
Moorend Av *CHWD/FDBR/MGN* B37 ..110 E4
Moor End La *ERDE/BCHGN* B24 ...90 E1
Moore Rd *SHHTH* WV12...............38 B5
Moore's Rw *DIG/EDG* B5.............7 J7
    WOLV WV1.................................3 L6
Moore Wk *WWCK* CV34.............206 A6
Moor Farm Cl *RUGBY* CV23.......183 K7
Moorfield Av *DOR/KN* B93..........149 K7
Moorfield Dr *BRGRVW* B61........191 K2
    HALE B63..............................103 L8
    SCFLD/BOLD B73.....................72 D5
Moorfield Rd *BKDE/SHDE* B34 ....91 L7
    BKHL/PFLD WV2......................50 A6
The Moorfield *COVS* CV3...........155 L5
Moorfoot Av *HALE* B63.............121 G4
Moorgate *CRTAM* B79.................31 L8
Moorgate Cl *REDE* B98.............195 J7
Moor Green La *MOS/BIL* B13.....125 C4
Moor Hall Dr *HAG/WOL* DY9......141 L4
    MGN/WHC B75.........................57 J4
Moorhall La *STRPT* DY13...........188 C2
Moor Hill Dr *STRPT* DY13..........188 D1
Moorhills Cft *SHLY* B90.............149 G4
The Moorings *BRLYHL* DY5.......102 D1
    COVEN WV9 *...........................35 K3
    OLDBY B69.............................86 C5
    RLSS CV31.............................206 F6
Moorland Av *WOLVN* WV10.........36 A7
Moorland Rd *BLOX/PEL* WS3.......38 A7
    CNCK/NC WS11.........................12 C8
    LDYWD/EDGR B16 ....106 B4
Moorlands Dr *SHLY* B90.............148 A3
Moorlands Rd *HHTH/SAND* B71 ...69 K4
The Moorlands *FOAKS/STRLY* B74 ..56 D5
Moor La *AST/WIT* B6...................71 K7
    BLKHTH/ROWR B65.................103 L4
    CRTAM B79.............................32 E7
    LICHS WS14.............................42 C4
    TAM/AM/WIL B77.....................32 B8
Moor Leasow *NFLD/LBR* B31.....145 G3
Moor Meadow Rd *MGN/WHC* B75...........57 H6
Moor Pk *BLOX/PEL* WS3.............38 F2
    DUNHL/THL/PER WV6................34 A8
Moorpark Rd *NFLD/LBR* B31.....144 E4
Moor Pool Av *HRBN* B17...........106 A7
Moor Rd *NUNW/HART* CV10........79 L5
Moors Av *KIDDW* DY11..............189 M3
Moors Cft *RIDG/WDGT* B32.......122 F4
Moorside Gdns *WSLW* WS2.........52 F2
Moorside Rd *ALE/KHTH/YWD* B14 ..147 L5
Moors La *NFLD/LBR* B31...........123 J5
Moors Mill La *TPTN/OCK* DY4.....68 A6
Moorsom St *AST/WIT* B6.............89 J8
Moorsom Wy *BRCRVE* B60........191 M6
The Moors *CBROM* B36..............91 L5
Moor St *BRLYHL* DY5................101 L2
    CBHAMNE B4...........................7 H5
    COVW CV5.............................154 D4
    CRTAM B79.............................31 L8
    DARL/WED WS10......................68 F3
    WBROM B70.............................87 H2
Moor St South *BKHL/PFLD* WV2..50 A6
The Moor *WALM/CURD* B76.........73 L5
Moorville Wk *SPARK* B11...........107 L6
Moorwood Crs *NUNW/HART* CV10 ..79 L5

Moorwood La *NUNW/HART* CV10..79 L5
Morar Cl *CVALE* B35...................91 M1
Moray Cl *RMSLY* B62.................104 C5
Morcom Cl *SPARK* B11.............108 C8
Morcroft *BILS/COS* WV14............67 L2
Mordaunt Dr *MGN/WHC* B75........57 H3
Moreall Mdw *TLHL/CAN* CV4.....180 D2
Moreland Cft *WALM/CURD* B76 ...73 M7
The Morelands *NFLD/LBR* B31 ...144 F4
Morelia Cl *BEWD* DY12..............162 D2
Morestead Av *LGN/SDN/BHAMAIR* B26 ....110 A8
Moreton Av *ETTPK/GDPK/PENN* WV4 ..66 C1
    GTB/HAM B43...........................71 C3
Moreton Cl *RIDG/WDGT* B32.....105 K8
    TPTN/OCK DY4.........................67 M3
Moreton Rd *SHLY* B90...............148 A3
    CNCK/NC WS11..........................16 D1
Morford Rd *ALDR* WS9................40 E6
Morgan Cl *OLDBY* B69................86 B5
    RCOVN/BALC/EX CV7................96 D5
    WLNHL WV13............................51 M1
Morgan Gv *CBROM* B36...............92 D4
Morgan Rd *POL/KGSB/FAZ* B78...45 L3
Morgrove Av *DOR/KN* B93.........149 K7
Morillon Cl *KIDD* DY10..............164 E4
Morjon Dr *GTB/HAM* B43.............70 D3
Morland Rd *COVN* CV6..............134 A2
    GTB/HAM B43...........................71 C1
Morley Gv *DUNHL/THL/PER* WV6..50 A1
Morley Rd *BNTWD* WS7...............18 F6
    WASH/WDE B8.........................90 F7
Morlich Ri *BRLYHL* DY5.............101 M5
Morlings Dr *BNTWD* WS7............18 F5
Morning Pines *STRBR* DY8........119 J1
Morningside *COVW* CV5..............8 C9
    SCFLD/BOLD B73.....................72 D3
Mornington Rd *SMTHWK* B66.....87 M6
Morpeth *TAM/AM/WIL* B77..........46 A6
Morrell St *RLSN* CV32...............206 C3
Morris Av *COVE* CV3.................156 B1
    WSLW WS2.............................52 C3
Morris Cl *ACGN* B27.................127 H1
    RUGBYN/HIL CV21...................160 D7
Morris Cft *CBROM* B36................92 C4
Morris Field Cft *HLGN/YWD* B28 ..147 J1
Morris Hl *POL/KGSB/FAZ* B78.....47 K6
Morrison Av *WOLVN* WV10..........36 B5
Morrison Rd *TPTN/OCK* DY4.......86 A1
Morris Rd *WASH/WDE* B8............90 F7
Morris St *WBROM* B70.................87 C4
Morsefield La *REDE* B98............203 H4
Morson Crs *RUGBYN/HIL* CV21...187 J3
Morston *TAM/AM/WIL* B77............60 B1
Mortimer Rd *KNWTH* CV8...........197 K3
Mortimers Cl *ALE/KHTH/YWD* B14 ...146 F4
Morton Cl *COVN* CV6.................133 L4
Morton Gdns *RUGBYS/DCH* CV21..186 F3
Morton Rd *REDW* B97................201 M7
Morton Rd *BRLYHL* DY5............102 B6
    KIDD DY10.............................165 M3
Morton St *RLSN* CV32...............206 D4
Morvale Gdns *HAG/WOL* DY9....102 C8
Morvale St *HAG/WOL* DY9.........102 C8
Morven Rd *SCFLD/BOLD* B73......72 D3
Morville Cl *DOR/KN* B93............175 H2
Morville Cft *ETTPK/GDPK/PENN* WV4 ..66 F1
Morville Rd *DUDS* DY2..............103 H1
Morville St *LDYWD/EDGR* B16 .....6 A6
Mosborough Crs *LOZ/NWT* B19 ...89 C8
Mosedale *RUGBYN/HIL* CV21.....161 H6
Mosedale Dr *WNSFLD* WV11........37 K8
Moseley Av *COVN* CV6..................8 A1
Moseley Ct *WNSFLD* WV11..........37 K2
Moseley Dr *CHWD/FDBR/MGN* B37 ..110 D5
Moseley Old Hall La *WOLVN* WV10 ..22 E8
    KNWTH CV8.............................197 M2
    WLNHL WV13............................51 H4
    WOLVN WV10............................23 M6
Moseley St *DIG/EDG* B5...............7 J8
    DUNHL/THL/PER WV6................50 A1
    TPTN/OCK DY4.........................68 A6
Mossbank Av *BNTWD* WS7..........18 E7
Moss Cl *ALDR* WS9.....................40 E8
    HEDN WS12.............................12 A8
    RUGBYS/DCH CV22.................186 C4
    RUSH/SHEL WS4.......................53 L2
Mossdale *TAM/AM/WIL* B77..........47 C5
Mossdale Cl *COVN* CV6.............133 C7
Mossdale Crs *NUNW/HART* CV10 ..98 D3
Mossdale Wy *SEDG* DY3..............66 C6
Moss Dr *CSCFLD/WYGN* B72.......73 G2
Mossfield Rd *ALE/KHTH/YWD* B14 ..125 J6
Moss Gdns *BILS/COS* WV14.........66 F2
Moss La *ALE/KHTH/YWD* B14.....125 H7
    KGSWFD DY6............................83 H6
    KNWTH CV8.............................179 M6
Moss House Cl *EDG* B15...............6 A8
Moss La *REDE* B98...................195 K5
Moss Lane Cl *REDE* B98...........195 K5
Mossley Cl *BLOX/PEL* WS3.........38 D4
Mossley La *BLOX/PEL* WS3.........38 D3
Mosspaul Cl *RLSN* CV32...........206 B3
Moss St *CNCK/NC* WS11..............16 E2
Moss St *CNCK/NC* WS11..............16 E1
    RLSS CV31.............................206 E6
Mossvale Cl *CDYHTH* B64.........103 J4
Mossvale Gv *WASH/WDE* B8........90 D8
Moss Wy *FOAKS/STRLY* B74........55 K6
Mostyn Crs *HHTH/SAND* B71......68 B6
Mostyn Rd *HDSW* B21.................88 D4
    LDYWD/EDGR B16 ....106 D4
    STRPT DY13...........................163 J7
Mostyn St *WOLV* WV1...................2 D1
Mott Cl *TPTN/OCK* DY4 *............68 A5
Mottistone Cl *COVS* CV3...........155 H7
Mottram Cl *WBROM* B70..............86 E3
Mottrams Cl *CSCFLD/WYGN* B72..73 G3
Mott St *LOZ/NWT* B19..................6 E1
Mott's Wy *CSHL/WTROR* B46.......93 L7
Moule Cl *KIDDW* DY11..............137 M7
Moultrie Rd *RUGBYN/HIL* CV21...186 F5
Moundsley Gv *ALE/KHTH/YWD* B14 ..146 E4
Mountain Ash Dr *HAG/WOL* DY9..120 A3
Mountain Ash Rd *WALM/CURD* B8 ..26 C8
Mountain Pine Cl *HEDN* WS12 * ...12 E5
Mount Av *BRLYHL* DY5..............102 A1
    HEDN WS12.............................12 F6
Mountbatten Av *KNWTH* CV8.....198 A2
Mountbatten Cl *BNTWD* WS7.......18 D4
Mountbatten Rd *WSLW* WS2........52 D3
Mount Cl *GTWY* WS6..................24 B3
    MOS/BIL B13...........................125 L1

SEDG* DY3................................84 A3
    WMBN WV5..............................64 E6
Mount Cottages *ETTPK/GDPK/PENN* WV4 * ..65 K2
Mount Ct *DUNHL/THL/PER* WV6 * 48 F2
Mount Dr *BDWTH* CV12.............116 E2
    WMBN WV5..............................64 E6
Mountfield Cl *ALE/KHTH/YWD* B14 ..146 E3
Mountford Cl *BLKHTH/ROWR* B65 ..104 A2
Mountford Crs *ALDR* WS9............40 G5
Mountford Dr *MGN/WHC* B75.......57 C5
Mountford La *BILS/COS* WV14......51 H6
Mountford St *SHLY* B90.............147 H4
Mountford St *SPARK* B11..........108 B8
Mount Gdns *CDSL* WV8................34 D1
Mountjoy Crs *HIA/OLT* B92........128 A2
Mount La *HAG/WOL* DY9............141 J1
    SEDG DY3................................84 A3
Mount Nod Wy *COVW* CV5.........153 L2
Mount Pleasant *ALE/KHTH/YWD* B14 ..125 J7
    BILS/COS WV14.........................51 J7
    BKHL/PFLD WV2 *.....................50 D6
    BRLYHL DY5...........................102 C4
    ETTPK/GDPK/PENN WV4 *.......65 K2
    GTWY WS6...............................24 C3
    KGSWFD DY6..........................100 F1
    LGLYGN/QTN B68 *.................104 F1
    REDE B98..............................202 B3
    SMTH B10..............................107 M4
Mount Pleasant Av *HDSW* B21.....88 C4
    WMBN WV5..............................64 D6
Mount Pleasant Rd *BDWTH* CV12 ......116 E2
Mount Pleasant St *BILS/COS* WV14 ..66 F5
    WBROM B70.............................87 C3
Mount Pleasant Ter *NUNW/HART* CV10 ..80 D7
Mountrath St *WSL* WS1.................4 E5
Mount Rd *BLKHTH/ROWR* B65 ...104 C2
    BLOX/PEL WS3..........................39 L1
    BNTWD WS7.............................18 F7
    BRGRVW B61..........................168 B4
    DUNHL/THL/PER WV6................48 E3
    ETTPK/GDPK/PENN WV4..........65 L1
    ETTPK/GDPK/PENN WV4..........66 D3
    HDSW B21................................88 C4
    OLDBY B69...............................86 A5
    STRBR DY8.............................101 H4
    STRBR DY8.............................101 M8
    WLNHL WV13............................51 H4
    WMBN WV5..............................64 D6
Mountserrat Rd *BRGRVE* B60....191 M4
Mountside St *HEDN* WS12...........12 F6
Mounts Rd *DARL/WED* WS10.......68 D3
Mount St *COVW* CV5.................154 D3
    HALE B63..............................121 L3
    HEDN WS12.............................12 G6
    NUN CV11................................98 F1
    REDE B98..............................202 C2
    STRBR DY8.............................101 L8
    TPTN/OCK DY4.........................68 A7
    VAUX/NECH B7.........................90 A7
    WSL WS1..................................4 E6
Mounts Wy *VAUX/NECH* B7.........90 A7
The Mount *CDYHTH* B64............103 L4
    COVS CV3.............................155 H5
Mount Vernon Dr *BRGRVW* B61 ..168 D8
Mount Vw *MGN/WHC* B75...........73 J1
Mount Wd Covert *DUNHL/THL/PER* WV6 ....48 F2
Mousehall Farm Rd *BRLYHL* DY5 ..102 B6
Mouse Hl *BLOX/PEL* WS3............39 K2
Mouse La *KIDDW* DY11.............137 M5
Mousesweet Cl *DUDS* DY2.........103 J1
Mousesweet La *DUDS* DY2.........103 J1
Mousesweet Wk *CDYHTH* B64...102 F3
Mowbray Cl *RBRY* B45..............143 L3
Mowbray Cft *BNTWD* WS7..........18 C4
Mowbray St *COVE* CV3................9 M3
    DIG/EDG B5............................107 J5
Mow Cft *CHWD/FDBR/MGN* B37 ..110 E6
Moxhull Cl *SHHTH* WV12............38 A4
Moxhull Dr *WALM/CURD* B76 ......73 J5
Moxhull Gdns *SHHTH* WV12.........38 A4
Moxhull Rd *CHWD/FDBR/MGN* B37 ..92 E8
Moxley Rd *DARL/WED* WS10........67 M1
Moyeady Av *RUGBYN/HIL* CV21 ..187 J4
Moyle Crs *COVW* CV5................153 H1
Moyle Dr *HALE* B63...................102 F6
Moyses Cft *SMTHWK* B66............87 L5
Mozart Ct *CNCK/NC* WS11..........12 G3
Muchall Rd *ETTPK/GDPK/PENN* WV4 ..49 G3
Much Park St *COV* CV1.................9 A4
Mucklow Hl *RMSLY* B62.............104 B8
Muirfield *TAM/AM/WIL* B77...........32 F8
    SOLH B91................................90 B8
    WASH/WDE B8.........................90 D8
Muirfield Cl *BLOX/PEL* WS3.........38 E2
Muirfield Crs *OLDBY* B69.............85 L6
Muirfield Gdns *HWK/WKHTH* B38 ..145 H4
Muirville Cl *STRBR* DY8.............101 H2
Mulberry Cl *RLSN* CV32............206 E3
Mulberry Dr *MOS/BIL* B13.........125 M4
    WWCK CV34.........................205 K4
Mulberry Gn *DUDN* DY1..............84 C2
Mulberry Pl *BLOX/PEL* WS3.........38 D4
Mulberry Rd *BLOX/PEL* WS3........38 D4
    CNCK/NC WS11.........................16 D2
    COVN CV6..............................134 E7
    NFLD/LBR B31.........................124 A4
    RUGBYS/DCH CV22.................185 M8
Mulberry Wy *NUNW/HART* CV10...79 K5
Muldoon Cl *CNCK/NC* WS11........16 E1
Mulehouse Rd *COVN* CV6..............8 D5
Mull Cft *CBROM* B36...................92 E6
Mullensgrove Rd *CHWD/FDBR/MGN* B37 ..92 E8
Mullett Rd *WNSFLD* WV11...........36 F6
Mullett St *BRLYHL* DY5...............83 M8
Mulliners Cl *CHWD/FDBR/MGN* B37 * ..111 H3
Mulliner St *COVN* CV6...............134 D8
Mullion Cft *HWK/WKHTH* B38.....145 J4
Mulroy Rd *FOAKS/STRLY* B74......56 F7
Mulwych Rd *STECH* B33............110 C2
Munches La *HALE* B63...............121 J8
Munro Cl *KIDD* DY10.................139 G7
Munsley Cl *REDE* B98...............203 K3
Munslow Gv *NFLD/LBR* B31......144 D5
Muntz Crs *HOCK/TIA* B94...........175 C7
Muntz St *SMHTH* B10................109 K1
Murcroft Rd *HAG/WOL* DY9.......120 B4
Murdock Gv *HDSW* B21...............88 B4
Murdock Rd *SMTHWK* B66..........88 B7
Murdock Wy *WSLW* WS2.............38 B7
Murray Cl *SCFLD/BOLD* B73........72 E2
Murrayfield Wy *COVS* CV3.........156 F4

Murrayian Cl *RUGBYN/HIL* CV21 ..186 F2
Murray Rd *COVN* CV6................133 L6
    RUGBYN/HIL CV21..................187 G1
Murrell Cl *DIG/EDG* B5..............107 H6
Murton *TAM/AM/WIL* B77.............47 C5
Musborough Cl *CBROM* B36.........92 A4
Muscott Gv *HRBN* B17..............105 L8
Muscovy Rd *ERDW/GRVHL* B23...90 A2
Musgrave Cl *WALM/CURD* B76 ....73 M7
Musgrave Rd *WSNGN* B18...........88 D8
Mushroom Hall Rd *LGLYGN/QTN* B68 ..86 F8
Musk La *SEDG* DY3....................83 M2
Musk La West *SEDG* DY3............83 M2
Muskoka *BEWD* DY12................162 D2
Muswell Cl *SOLH* B91...............128 B8
Muxloe Cl *BLOX/PEL* WS3..........38 C2
Myatt Av *ALDR* WS9....................40 D8
    BKHL/PFLD WV2........................50 C7
    BNTWD WS7.............................18 E6
Myatt Cl *BKHL/PFLD* WV2............50 C7
Myddleton St *WSNGN* B18.........106 F1
Myers Cft *BRLYHL* DY5..............102 E1
Myhing Dr *BKHL/PFLD* WV2.........50 D6
Mylgrove *COVS* CV3..................181 H1
Mynors Crs *HLYWD* B47.............146 E8
Myring Dr *MGN/WHC* B75...........57 K8
Myrtle Av *ALE/KHTH/YWD* B14...146 D3
    BHTH/HG B12.........................107 L8
    REDE B98..............................202 C3
Myrtle Cl *WLNHL* WV13...............51 H4
Myrtle Gv *BDMR/CCFT* WV3........49 J3
    COVW CV5.............................154 D4
    LOZ/NWT B19 *........................89 C5
Myrtle Pl *SLYOAK* B29 *............124 F3
Myrtle Rd *DUDN* DY1..................84 E2
Myrtle St *BKHL/PFLD* WV2..........50 D7
Myrtle Ter *TPTN/OCK* DY4...........67 M3
Mythe La *ATHST* CV9...................63 L5
Mythe Vw *ATHST* CV9..................63 J4
Myton Crs *WWCK* CV34..............206 A7
Myton Crofts *RLSS* CV31...........206 B8
Myton Dr *SHLY* B90...................147 H3
Myton Gdns *WWCK* CV34..........205 L7
Myton La *WWCK* CV34...............206 A7
Mytton Cl *DUDS* DY2...................85 J4
Mytton Gv *TPTN/OCK* DY4...........67 J2
Mytton Rd *BVILLE* B30...............124 A8
    CSHL/WTROR B46.....................92 D2
Myvod Rd *DARL/WED* WS10........52 E8

N

Naden Rd *LOZ/NWT* B19...............88 F7
Nadin Rd *SCFLD/BOLD* B73..........72 E5
Naesby Rd *DUNHL/THL/PER* WV6 ..48 B8
Nafford Gv *ALE/KHTH/YWD* B14..146 D3
Nagersfield Rd *BRLYHL* DY5.......101 L2
Nagington Dr *PENK* ST19...........10 D6
Nailcote Av *TLHL/CAN* CV4........153 C4
Nailcote La *RCOVN/BALC/EX* CV7 ..152 E6
Nailers Cl *BRGRVE* B60.............191 J7
    RIDG/WDGT B32....................122 D3
Nailers Dr *BNTWD* WS7...............19 C7
Nailers Fold *BILS/COS* WV14........67 C3
Nailors Rw *WMBN* WV5 *.............64 D8
Nailstone Crs *ACGN* B27...........127 C5
Nailsworth Rd *DOR/KN* B93.......175 H3
    REDE B98..............................202 D3
Nairn Cl *HLGN/YWD* B28............126 D8
    NUNW/HART CV10...................98 E3
    REDE B98..............................203 J2
Nairn Rd *BLOX/PEL* WS3.............38 E1
Naily Dr *BILS/COS* WV14.............66 E3
Nanaimo Wy *KGSWFD* DY6........101 L1
Nansen Rd *SPARK* B11..............126 A2
    WASH/WDE B8.........................90 F7
Nantmel Gv *RIDG/WDGT* B32....123 C5
Naomi Wy *ALDR* WS9...................40 F1
Napier *TAM/AM/WIL* B77..............47 C2
Napier Dr *TPTN/OCK* DY4............68 A7
Napier Rd *BKHL/PFLD* WV2..........50 B7
    WSLW WS2.............................38 E2
Napier St *COV* CV1......................9 A4
Naples Rd *BDWTH* CV12............116 H1
Napton Cl *REDE* B98.................203 H4
Napton Dr *RLSN* CV32...............206 E5
Napton Gn *COVW* CV5...............153 C2
Napton Gv *SLYOAK* B29............123 K3
Narberth Wy *COVE* CV3.............135 K6
Nares Cl *RUGBYS/DCH* CV22.....186 C4
Narraway Gv *RUGBYN/HIL* CV21 ..187 J3
Narrowboat Wy *DUDS* DY2...........84 E8
Narrow La *BRWNH* WS8...............26 D5
    RMSLY B62............................104 A8
    WSLW WS2.............................52 F6
Naseby Cl *COVS* CV3.................156 D5
    REDE B98..............................195 H1
Naseby Dr *HALE* B63.................121 H3
Naseby Rd *RUGBYS/DCH* CV22 ..187 M7
    SOLH B91................................90 B8
    WASH/WDE B8.........................90 D8
Nash Av *DUNHL/THL/PER* WV6....48 C2
Nash Cl *BLKHTH/ROWR* B65......104 A4
Nash Cft *CHWD/FDBR/MGN* B37 ..110 F5
Nashe Cl *KIDD* DY10.................139 G8
Nash La *HAG/WOL* DY9.............141 H6
Nash Rd *REDE* B98...................202 C2
Nash Sq *PBAR/PBCH* B42...........89 H1
Nash Wk *SMTHWK* B66 *.............88 A8
Nately Gv *SLYOAK* B29..............123 M2
Nathan Cl *MGN/WHC* B75............57 C5
Naunton Cl *WSLW* WS2...............52 E2
Naunton Rd *WSLW* WS2..............52 E2
Navenby Cl *ALE/KHTH/YWD* B14..147 G2
Navigation Dr *BRLYHL* DY5........102 E1
Navigation La *DARL/WED* WS10...69 K3
Navigation St *CBHAMW* B1...........6 E3
    WOLV WV1.................................3 J7
    WSLW WS2.............................52 C3
Nayland Cft *HLGN/YWD* B28......126 D8
Nayler Cl *RUGBYN/HIL* CV21.....161 J4
Naylor Cl *KIDDW* DY11..............163 M2
Naylors Gv *SEDG* DY3.................84 B2
Neachells Ct *WLNHL* WV13.........51 J4
Neachells La *WLNHL* WV13..........51 H2
    WNSFLD WV11.........................37 H8
Neachless Av *WMBN* WV5...........64 D8
Neachley Gv *STECH* B33...........109 K1
Neal Cl *COVE* CV3 *...................135 L5
Neale Av *COVW* CV5..................132 E7
Neale St *WSLW* WS2...................4 B2
Neander *CRTAM* B79...................31 L8
Nearhill Rd *HWK/WKHTH* B38.....145 G5
Near Lands Cl *RIDG/WDGT* B32..122 F1
Nearmoor Rd *BKDE/SHDE* B34....92 B8
Neasden Gv *KGSTG* B44..............71 M5
Neath Rd *BLOX/PEL* WS3.............38 F1
    SEDG DY3................................66 E7

Nebsworth Cl *SHLY* B90.............127
Nechells Park Rd *VAUX/NECH* B7 ..89
Nechells Pkwy *VAUX/NECH* B7 *....7
Nechells Pl *VAUX/NECH* B7...........7
Needham St *VAUX/NECH* B7........89
Needhill Cl *DOR/KN* B93............149
Needle Mill La *REDE* B98..........194
Needlers End La *RCOVN/BALC/EX* CV7 ..151
Needles House *STUD* B80 *.........203
Needless Aly *CBHAM* B2 *..............7
Needwood Cl *ETTPK/GDPK/PENN* WV4 ..66
Needwood Gv *HHTH/SAND* B71....69
Needwood Hl *LICHS* WS13............20
Neighbrook Cl *REDW* B97...........201
Neilston St *RLSS* CV31..............206
Nelson Av *BILS/COS* WV14...........51
    WWCK CV34.........................205
Nelson Dr *HEDN* WS12................17
Nelson La *WWCK* CV34..............205
Nelson Rd *AST/WIT* B6................89
    DUDN DY1...............................84
    STRPT DY13...........................188
Nelson St *CBHAMW* B1................6
    COV CV1..................................9
    HHTH/SAND B71......................69
    OLDBY B69.............................86
    WLNHL WV13............................51
Nelson Wy *RUGBYS/DCH* CV22...186
Nemesia *TAM/AM/WIL* B77...........156
Nene Cl *COVS* CV3....................156
Nene Wy *CBROM* B36...................92
Neptune St *TPTN/OCK* DY4..........67
Nesbit Gv *BORD* B9...................108
Nesfield Cl *HWK/WKHTH* B38.....145
Nesfield Gv *HIA/OLT* B92...........129
Nesscliffe Gv *ERDW/GRVHL* B23 ..90
Nest Common *BLOX/PEL* WS3.......25
Neston Gv *STECH* B33...............109
Netheravon Cl *ALE/KHTH/YWD* B14 ..146
Nether Beacon *LICH* WS13...........20
Netherbridge Av *LICHS* WS14.......21
Netherby Rd *SEDG* DY3................66
Nethercote Gdns *SHLY* B90.........147
Netherdale Cl *CSCFLD/WYGN* B72 ..73
Netherdale Rd *ALE/KHTH/YWD* B14 ..146
Netherend Cl *HALE* B63.............102
Netherend La *HALE* B63.............102
Netherend Sq *HALE* B63.............102
Netherfield Gdns *ACGN* B27.......126
Nethergate *SEDG* DY3.................66
Nether La *BNTWD* WS7.................19
Nethermill Rd *COVN* CV6...........133
Nethersole St *POL/KGSB/FAZ* B78 ..47
Netherstone Gv *FOAKS/STRLY* B74 ..42
Netherstowe *LICH* WS13..............21
Netherstowe La *LICH* WS13..........21
Netherton Gv *STECH* B33...........110
Netherton La *BEWD* DY12..........163
Netherwood Cl *SOLH* B91...........127
Nethy Dr *DUNHL/THL/PER* WV6....34
Netherwood La *DOR/KN* B93........94
Netley Gv *BNTWD* WS7.................19
Netley Rd *BLOX/PEL* WS3............38
Netley Wy *BLOX/PEL* WS3............38
Nevada Wy *CHWD/FDBR/MGN* B37 ..111
Neve Av *WOLVN* WV10.................36
Nevill Cl *RLSS* CV31.................207
Neville Av *ETTPK/GDPK/PENN* WV4 ..50
    KIDDW DY11...........................164
Neville Cl *REDE* B98.................194
Neville Ct *WWCK* CV34 *............205
Neville Gv *WWCK* CV34..............205
Neville Rd *CBROM* B36................92
    ERDW/GRVHL B23.....................90
    SHLY B90..............................127
Neville St *TAM/AM/WIL* B77.........46
Nevill St *CRTAM* B79...................31
Nevin Gv *PBAR/PBCH* B42...........71
Nevis Ct *BDMR/CCFT* WV3...........37
Nevis Gv *SHHTH* WV12................37
Nevison Gv *GTB/HAM* B43............70
Newall Cl *RUGBY* CV23..............161
Newark Cft *LGN/SDN/BHAMAIR* B26 ..110
Newark Rd *DUDS* DY2................103
    SHHTH WV12...........................132
New Ash Dr *COVW* CV5.............132
Newbank Gv *BORD* B9...............108
New Barns La *LICHS* WS14..........41
New Bartholomew St *DIG/EDG* B5 ..7
New Birmingham Rd *OLDBY* B69 ..85
Newbold Cl *COVS* CV3...............156
    DOR/KN B93..........................149
Newbold Cft *VAUX/NECH* B7........89
Newbold Pl *RLSN* CV32.............206
Newbold Rd *RUGBYN/HIL* CV21 ..160
Newbolds Rd *WOLVN* WV10.........36
Newbold St *RLSN* CV32.............206
Newbold Ter *RLSN* CV32...........206
Newbold Ter East *RLSN* CV32.....207
Newbolt Rd *BILS/COS* WV14.........51
Newbolt St *DSYBK/YTR* WS5........89
New Bond St *BORD* B9...............107
    DUDS DY2.............................101
Newborough Gv *HLGN/YWD* B28 ..147
Newborough Rd *HLGN/YWD* B28...147
Newbourne Hl *ALVE* B48............194
Newbridge Av *DUNHL/THL/PER* WV6 ..49
Newbridge Crs *DUNHL/THL/PER* WV6 ..49
Newbridge Gdns *DUNHL/THL/PER* WV6 ..49
Newbridge Ms *DUNHL/THL/PER* WV6 * ..49
Newbridge Rd *BORD* B9.............108
    KGSWFD DY6............................83
Newbridge St *DUNHL/THL/PER* WV6 ..49
New Brook St *RLSN* CV32..........206
New Buildings *COV* CV1..............9
    WOLVN WV10............................10
Newburgh Crs *WWCK* CV34.......205
Newbury Cl *RIDG/WDGT* B32.....106
Newbury Dr *BRGRVW* B61..........166
    GTWY WS6...............................24
    RLSS CV31.............................207
    RMSLY B62.............................104
Newbury La *OLDBY* B69..............85
Newbury Rd *CNCK/NC* WS11........16
    STRBR DY8.............................119
    WOLVN WV10............................10
Newby Cl *COVS* CV3...................155
Newby Gv *CHWD/FDBR/MGN* B37 ..110

RBRY B45 ....170 B1
Oakfield Gdns ATHST CV9 ....63 J6
CDSL WV8 ....34 F3
COVN CV6 ....133 K8
ERDE/BCHGN B24 ....90 D3
HAG/WOL DY9 ....120 D3
KIDDW DY11 ....137 M8
RUGBYS/DCH CV22 ....186 C6
SLYOAK B29 ....124 E2
SMTHWK B66 ....88 A8
Oakfields Wy SOLH B91 ....101 L4
Oakford Dr COVW CV5 ....132 D7
Oak Gn DUDN DY1 ....66 E8
DUNHL/THL/PER WV6 ....48 F2
NFLD/LBR B31 ....144 G2
Oak Gv KIDD DY10 ....138 E8
WNSFLD WV11 ....36 F6
Oakhall Dr DOR/KN B93 ....175 K1
Oakham Av DUDS DY2 ....85 J6
Oakham Crs REDE B98 ....202 E8
Oakham Crs DUDS DY2 ....85 J6
Oakham Dr DUDS DY2 ....85 K5
Oakhampton Rd STRPT DY13 ....188 C5
Oakham Rd DUDS DY2 ....85 J6
HRBN B17 ....105 M6
Oak HI BDMR/CCFT WV3 ....49 C5
Oakhill Av KIDD DY10 ....164 C5
Oakhill Cl HRBN B17 ....105 M5
Oakhill Crs ACGN B27 ....126 F5
Oakhill Dr BRLYHL DY5 ....101 M6
Oak Hill Dr EDG B15 ....106 C6
Oakhill Rd CNCK/NC WS11 ....16 D3
Oakhurst LICHS WS14 ....21 G6
Oakhurst Rd ACGN B27 ....126 F4
CSCFLD/WYGN B72 ....72 F5
Oakland Cl SOLH B91 ....149 J1
Oakland Dr SEDG DY3 ....83 M3
Oakland Gv BRGRVW B61 ....191 L1
Oakland Rd BLOX/PEL WS3 ....39 L1
HDSW B21 ....88 C5
MOS/BIL B13 ....125 L2
Oaklands NFLD/LBR B31 ....144 D1
RMSLY B62 ....122 E1
WALM/CURD B76 ....74 F2
Oaklands Av HRBN B17 ....105 L8
Oaklands Cl HEDN WS12 ....12 A7
Oaklands Cft CSHL/WTROR B46 ....73 M6
Oaklands Dr BFLD/HDSWWD B20 ....88 D3
Oaklands Gn BILS/COS WV14 ....51 C5
Oaklands Rd BDMR/CCFT WV3 ....2 C5
FOAKS/STRLY B74 ....56 F5
The Oaklands BDMR/CCFT WV3 ....2 D3
CHWD/FDBR/MGN B37 ....110 E6
KIDD DY10 ....138 E6
TLHL/CAN CV4 ....153 L3
Oaklands Wy NFLD/LBR B31 ....144 D1
NFLD/LBR B31 ....144 G4
Oak La BNTWD WS7 ....18 D4
COVW CV5 ....132 A5
HIA/OLT B92 ....150 F3
KGSWFD DY6 ....83 J1
PENK ST19 ....15 C5
WBROM B70 ....86 F2
Oaklea Dr CDYHTH B64 ....103 K3
Oakleaf Cl RIDG/WDGT B32 ....125 L2
Oak Leaf Dr MOS/BIL B13 ....125 L2
Oak Leasow RIDG/WDGT B32 ....122 E1
Oakleigh NFLD/LBR B31 ....145 G3
Oakleigh Dr CDSL WV8 ....34 E2
SEDG DY3 ....66 M4
Oak Leigh Rd STRBR DY8 ....119 L3
Oakleighs STRBR DY8 ....101 L4
Oakley KNWTH CV8 ....177 K4
TPTN/OCK DY4 ....67 L7
Oakley Av ALDR WS9 ....40 E4
Oakley Cl PENK ST19 ....10 E4
Oakley Gv
ETTPK/GDPK/PENN WV4 ....49 H8
Oakley Rd BVILLE B30 ....124 F3
ETTPK/GDPK/PENN WV4 ....49 H8
SMTHB10 ....108 A6
Oak Leys REDW B97 ....202 B2
Oakley Wood Dr SOLH B91 ....149 J1
Oakly Rd REDW B97 ....202 B2
Oakmeadow Cl
LGN/SDN/BHAMAIR B26 ....109 H8
STETCH B33 ....110 B3
Oakmeadow Wy
ERDE/BCHGN B24 ....91 G2
Oakmoor Rd COVN CV6 ....134 D7
Oakmount Cl BLOX/PEL WS3 ....39 K2
Oakmount Rd FOAKS/STRLY B74 ....55 L6
Oak Park Rd STRBR DY8 ....101 K4
Oak Pl RLSS CV31 * 206 F7
Oakridge Cl REDE B98 ....195 C6
SHHTH WV12 ....52 A1
Oakridge Dr GTWY WS6 ....24 C3
SHHTH WV12 ....52 A1
Oakridge Rd RLSN CV32 ....207 C1
Oak Ri CSHL/WTROR B46 ....93 K8
Oak Rd ALDR WS9 ....40 F5
BLOX/PEL WS3 ....25 K8
BRGRVW B61 ....168 F5
DUDN DY1 ....85 C2
LGLGYN/QTN B68 ....105 C6
RUSH/SHEL WS4 ....40 A5
TPTN/OCK DY4 ....67 J4
WBROM B70 ....86 F3
WLNHL WV13 ....51 J3
Oakroyd Crs NUNW/HART CV10 ....80 DC
Oaks Cnr RLSN CV32 * 206 D3
Oaks Crs BDMR/CCFT WV3 ....2 B5
Oaks Dr BDMR/CCFT WV3 ....2 B5
CNCK/NC WS11 ....16 A4
WMBN WV5 ....64 B1
WOLVN WV10 ....22 D7
Oakslade Dr HIA/OLT B92 ....128 C5
Oaks Pl COVN CV6 ....134 C2
Oaks Rd KNWTH CV8 ....197 J3
The Oaks BDMR/CCFT WV3 * 2 A7
BDWTH CV12 ....116 D4
BKDE/SHDE B34 ....91 M8
BLOX/PEL WS3 ....38 E4
HWK/WKHTH B38 ....145 K7
RLSN CV32 * 206 B5
SMTHWKW B67 * 87 K8
Oak St BDMR/CCFT WV3 ....2 B5
BILS/COS WV14 ....66 F6
BRLYHL DY5 ....102 A4
CDYHTH B64 ....103 H4
DUDS DY2 ....103 J1
KGSWFD DY6 ....83 C8
RUGBYS/DCH CV22 ....186 E8
Oakthorpe Dr
CHWD/FDBR/MGN B37 ....92 D8
Oakthorpe Gdns OLDBY B69 ....85 L3
Oak Tree Av COVS CV3 ....154 D6
REDW B97 ....201 M1
Oak Tree Cl DOR/KN B93 ....175 J1
RLSN CV32 ....206 E3
Oaktree Cl ALVE B48 ....170 E6
POL/KGSB/FAZ B78 ....60 B7
Oak Tree Gdns STRBR DY8 ....101 L4
Oak Tree Gv KIDD DY10 ....164 C3
Oak Tree La HLYWD B47 ....146 F7
SLYOAK B29 ....124 E4

Oak Tree Rd COVS CV3 ....156 E6
WASH/WDE B8 ....90 B7
Oaktree Rd DARL/WED WS10 ....68 F2
The Oak Wk NFLD/LBR B31 ....144 F3
Oak Wy TLHL/CAN CV4 ....153 H3
WALM/CURD B76 ....73 K3
Oakwood Cl ALDR WS9 ....40 C1
ATHST CV9 ....62 A4
LICHS WS14 ....28 E7
WNSFLD WV11 ....37 M7
Oakwood Crs DUDS DY2 ....84 D7
Oakwood Cft SOLH B91 ....149 G4
Oakwood Dr
ALE/KHTH/YWD B14 ....146 B1
FOAKS/STRLY B74 ....55 J5
Oakwood Gv WWCK CV34 ....205 L4
Oakwood Rd BEWD DY12 ....162 D2
BLOX/PEL WS3 ....39 J6
HLYWD B47 ....146 E7
SCFLD/BOLD B73 ....72 C4
SMTHWK B66 ....87 J8
SPARK B11 ....126 A2
Oakwoods CNCK/NC WS11 ....16 A5
Oakwood St WBROM B70 ....86 F5
Oakworth Cl COVE CV2 ....135 K5
Oasthouse Cl BRGRVW B60 ....191 H7
KGSWFD DY6 ....82 E6
Oaston Rd CBROM B36 ....92 B5
NUN CV11 ....99 H1
Oatfield Cl BNTWD WS7 ....26 E1
Oatlands Cl COVN CV6 ....133 M1
Oatlands Wk
ALE/KHTH/YWD B14 ....146 A3
Oatlands Wy
DUNHL/THL/PER WV6 ....48 B2
Oatmill Cl DARL/WED WS10 ....52 C3
Oban Dr NUNW/HART CV10 ....98 E3
Oban Rd COVN CV6 ....116 D8
HIA/OLT B92 ....127 K4
Oberon Cl NUN CV11 ....99 J3
RBRY B45 ....143 L3
RUGBYS/DCH CV22 ....186 D7
Oberon Dr SHLY B90 ....147 L4
Occupation Rd BRWNH WS8 ....40 E1
COVE CV2 ....156 A2
Occupation St DUDN DY1 ....84 E3
Ocean Gn DARL/WED WS10 ....68 A2
Ockam Cft NFLD/LBR B31 ....145 G3
Ocker Hill Rd TPTN/OCK DY4 ....67 M4
O'Connor Dr TPTN/OCK DY4 ....68 A4
Oddicombe Cft COVS CV3 ....155 H8
Oddingley Rd NFLD/LBR B31 ....145 G5
Odell Crs BLOX/PEL WS3 ....39 G6
Odell Pl DIG/EDG B5 ....107 G8
Odell Rd BLOX/PEL WS3 ....38 F6
Odensil Gn HIA/OLT B92 ....127 M3
Odiham Cl CRTAM B79 ....32 A5
Odin Cl HEDN WS12 ....11 M8
Odnall La HAG/WOL DY9 ....141 J1
Offa Gr CRTAM B79 ....31 M8
Offa Rd RLSS CV31 ....206 F7
Offa's Dr DUNHL/THL/PER WV6 ....34 F8
Offa St CRTAM B79 ....31 M8
Offchurch La RLSS CV31 ....207 K7
Offchurch Rd RLSN CV32 ....207 J1
Offenham Cl REDE B98 ....194 F7
Offenham Covert
NFLD/LBR B31 ....145 J5
Offini Cl WBROM B70 ....87 K3
Offmoor Rd RIDG/WDGT B32 ....122 F5
Offmore Farm Cl KIDD DY10 ....138 E7
Offmore La KIDD DY10 ....138 E7
Offwell Rd REDE B98 ....203 H4
Ogbury Cl ALE/KHTH/YWD B14 ....146 A3
Ogley Crs BRWNH WS8 ....26 E6
Ogley Dr MGN/WHC B75 ....57 L8
Ogley Hay Rd BNTWD WS7 ....18 E3
BNTWD 26 E3
Ogley Rd BRWNH WS8 ....26 E6
Ogley V BNTWD WS7 ....18 E3
O'Keeffe Cl SPARK B11 ....107 M7
Okehampton Dr
HHTH/SAND B71 ....69 G7
Okehampton Rd COVS CV3 ....155 J8
Okement Gv WNSFLD WV11 ....36 F8
Okement Rd RRUGBY CV23 ....159 M8
Oken Ct WWCK CV34 * 205 H6
Olaf Pl COVE CV2 ....135 L6
Old Abbey Gdns HRBN B17 ....124 D1
Old Acre Cl WALM/CURD B76 ....73 H7
Old Acre Dr HDSW B21 ....88 C6
Oldacre Rd LGLYGN/QTN B68 ....104 E6
Oldany Wy NUNW/HART CV10 ....98 D3
Old Bank Rd NFLD/LBR B31 ....144 F3
Old Barn Rd BVILLE B30 ....124 A6
STRBR DY8 ....101 L4
Old Beeches ERDW/GRVHL B23 ....72 A5
Old Bell Rd ERDW/GRVHL B23 ....72 F3
Olderberrow Cl SHLY B90 ....148 E7
Old Birchills WSLW WS2 ....53 G2
Old Birmingham Rd ALVE B48 * 170 E5
BRGRVE B60 ....169 C6
Old Bridge St LOZ/NWT B19 ....88 F7
Old Bridge Wk
BLKHTH/ROWR B65 ....85 K8
Old Bromford La CBROM B36 ....90 F7
Old Brookside STETCH B33 ....109 J3
Old Budbrooke Rd
RWWCK/WEL CV35 ....204 D7
Old Burcot La BRGRVE B60 ....192 B3
Oldbury Cl REDE B98 ....194 F7
Oldbury Ct CRTAM B79 ....31 M8
Oldbury Ring Wy OLDBY B69 ....86 B7
Oldbury Rd BLKHTH/ROWR B65 ....104 B5
NUNW/HART CV10 ....79 G4
SMTHWK B66 ....86 D2
WBROM B70 ....86 D2
Oldbury St DARL/WED WS10 ....68 F2
Oldbury Wy NUNW/HART CV10 ....79 M4
Old Bush St BRLYHL DY5 ....102 C2
Old Camp HI SPARK B11 ....7 M9
Old Cannock Rd WOLVN WV10 ....23 H4
Old Castle Gv BRWNH WS8 ....26 D3
Old Chapel Rd SMTHWKW B67 ....105 K3
Old Chester Rd South
KIDDW DY11 ....164 C3
Old Church Gn STETCH B33 ....109 J3
Old Church Rd COVN CV6 ....134 D4
CSHL/WTROR B46 ....92 F2
HRBN B17 ....105 M8
Old Crest Av REDE B98 ....202 C2
Old Croft La CBROM B36 ....91 M6
Old Cross St TPTN/OCK DY4 ....67 J8
Old Crown Cl RIDG/WDGT B32 ....122 F4
Old Crown Ms COVE CV2 ....117 M8
Old Damson La HIA/OLT B92 ....128 D3
Old Dickens Heath Rd
SHLY B90 ....147 L8
Olde Hall Ct WOLVN WV10 * 23 H1
Olde Hall La WOLVN WV10 * 23 H1
Old End La BILS/COS WV14 ....67 G6
Old Fallings Crs WOLVN WV10 ....36 E5
Old Fallow Av CNCK/NC WS11 ....16 D5
Old Fallow Rd CNCK/NC WS11 ....16 C5
The Old Falls Cl CDSL WV8 ....34 D2
Old Farm Dr CDSL WV8 ....34 F1

Old Farm Gv
ALE/KHTH/YWD B14 ....126 A8
Old Farm La CSHL/WTROR B46 ....94 E1
Old Farm Meadow
BDMR/CCFT WV3 ....49 G5
STETCH B33 ....109 H3
Oldfield Dr STRBR DY8 ....119 L2
BILS/COS WV14 ....66 F5
COVW CV5 ....154 B2
Oldfields CDYHTH B64 ....103 H5
HAG/WOL DY9 ....119 M7
Old Fordrove WALM/CURD B76 ....73 H2
Old Forest Wy BKDE/SHDE B34 ....91 M7
Old Forge Gdns REDE B98 ....189 L3
Old Grange Rd SPARK B11 ....126 A1
Old Green La DOR/KN B93 ....176 F3
Old Grove Gdns HAG/WOL DY9 ....120 B2
Old Hall La ALDR WS9 ....54 F8
CNCK/NC WS11 ....16 E3
GTWY WS6 ....24 D2
Old Hall St WOLV WV1 ....5 J5
Oldham Av COVE CV2 ....156 B1
Old Ham La HAG/WOL DY9 ....120 A3
Old Hampton La WNSFLD WV11 ....37 G3
Old Hawne La HALE B63 ....103 L8
Old Heath Crs WOLV WV1 ....50 E4
Old Heath Rd WOLV WV1 ....50 E3
Old Hedging La
TAM/AM/WIL B77 ....46 B8
Old Hednesford Rd
CNCK/NC WS11 ....16 E3
Old HI DUNHL/THL/PER WV6 ....35 H8
Old Hinckley Rd
NUNW/HART CV10 ....81 H8
Old Hobicus La LGLYGN/QTN B68 ....86 F8
Old Holly La ATHST CV9 ....63 J3
Old Horns Crs PBAR/PBCH B42 ....71 G3
Oldhouse Farm Cl
HLGN/YWD B28 ....126 D7
Old House La
RCOVN/BALC/EX CV7 ....142 F4
RMSLY B62 ....142 F4
Oldington La SOLH B91 ....148 E5
Oldington La STRPT DY13 ....163 M5
Old Kingsbury Rd
WALM/CURD B76 ....74 A8
Oldknow Rd SMHTH B10 ....108 C7
Old Landywood La
WNSFLD WV11 ....24 A7
Old La ALVE B48 ....195 H1
BLOX/PEL WS3 ....39 G6
DUNHL/THL/PER WV6 ....48 D3
WOLVN WV10 ....23 G6
Old Leicester Rd
RUGBYN/HIL CV21 ....160 E6
Old Level Wy DUDS DY2 ....103 H1
Old Lime Gdns
HWK/WKHTH B38 ....145 J5
Old Lindens Cl FOAKS/STRLY B74 ....55 J5
Old Lode La HIA/OLT B92 ....127 M3
Old London Rd LICHS WS14 ....29 H4
Old Manor Cl POL/KGSB/FAZ B78 ....48 J5
The Old Mnr
DUNHL/THL/PER WV6 * 35 H8
Old Masters Cl WSL WS1 ....5 J4
Old Meadow Rd NFLD/LBR B31 ....144 F6
Old Meeting Rd BILS/COS WV14 ....67 G5
Old Meeting St HHTH/SAND B71 ....68 F8
Old Meeting Yd BDWTH CV12 * 116 F2
Old Mill Av TLHL/CAN CV4 ....154 B8
Old Mill Br WWCK CV34 ....205 K7
Old Mill Cl SHLY B90 ....147 H3
Old Mill Gdns RUSH/SHEL WS4 ....40 A3
Old Mill Gv BFLD/HDSWWD B20 * 89 C3
Old Mill Rd CSHL/WTROR B46 ....93 K6
Old Milverton La RLSN CV32 ....206 C1
Old Milverton Rd RLSN CV32 ....206 A2
Old Moat Dr NFLD/LBR B31 ....144 F2
Old Moat Wy WASH/WDE B8 ....90 F7
Oldnall Cl HAG/WOL DY9 ....120 D1
Oldnall Rd HAG/WOL DY9 ....120 E1
KIDD DY10 ....164 D1
Old Oak Cl ALDR WS9 ....40 F5
Old Oak Rd HWK/WKHTH B38 ....145 J5
Old Oscott HI KGSTG B44 ....71 J4
Old Oscott La KGSTG B44 ....71 J5
Old Pk SLYOAK B29 ....123 L8
Old Park Cl ASTON B6 * 89 L3
Old Park La OLDBY B69 ....86 B8
Old Park Rd DARL/WED WS10 ....52 C7
DUDN DY1 ....85 H3
HEDN WS12 ....13 G8
Old Park Wk LOZ/NWT B19 ....89 J6
Old Penkridge Rd
CNCK/NC WS11 ....16 A3
Old Pleck Rd WSLW WS2 ....4 A7
HLYWD B47 ....146 E6
KIDDW DY11 ....137 M4
RUGBY CV23 ....161 K4
SHLY B90 ....174 B1
Old Portway HWK/WKHTH B38 ....145 J4
Old Postway LOZ/NWT B19 * 89 J6
Old Quarry Cl RBRY B45 ....143 K5
Old Quarry Dr SEDG DY3 ....66 B3
Old Rectory Gdns ALDR WS9 ....41 G7
Old Rd RCOVN/BALC/EX CV7 ....131 J4
Old School Cl WLNHL WV13 ....51 L3
Old School Dr
BLKHTH/ROWR B65 ....103 M2
Old School Ms RLSN CV32 ....206 F2
Old Scott Cl STETCH B33 ....110 A3
Old Smithy Pl WSNGN B18 ....88 E8
Old Snow HI CBHAMNW B3 ....6 F2
Old Stables Wk VAUX/NECH B7 ....90 A6
Old Stafford Rd WOLVN WV10 ....22 A1
Old Station Rd BRGRVE B60 ....191 L5
HIA/OLT B92 ....129 K3
STETCH B33 ....109 H3
Old Stone Cl RBRY B45 ....143 K4
Old Stow Heath La
WLNHL WV13 ....51 G4
Old Stratford Rd BRGRVE B60 ....192 A3
Old Tokengate HRBN B17 ....106 A3
Old Town La BLOX/PEL WS3 ....39 K2
Old Town La WSNGN B18 * 88 D4
Old Vicarage Cl WOLVN WV10 ....22 A1
Old Walsall Rd GTB/HAM B43 ....70 D5
Old Warstone La WNSFLD WV11 ....23 M5
Old Warwick Ct HIA/OLT B92 ....127 J4
Old Warwick Rd HIA/OLT B92 ....127 J4
HOCK/TIA B94 ....175 H8
RLSS CV31 ....206 C6
Old Waste La
RCOVN/BALC/EX CV7 ....152 C7
Oldway Dr SOLH B91 ....149 J3
Old Well Ct RUSH/SHEL WS4 ....39 M6
Old Wharf Rd STRBR DY8 ....101 K7
Oldwich La East KNWTH CV8 ....177 J4
Oldwich La West DOR/KN B93 ....177 J3
Old Winnings Rd
RCOVN/BALC/EX CV7 ....115 K6
Olga Dr TPTN/OCK DY4 ....67 K1
Olinthus Av WNSFLD WV11 ....37 H3
Olive Av COVE CV2 ....156 B1
ETTPK/GDPK/PENN WV4 ....50 C5
Olive Gv STRPT DY13 ....188 D1

Olive Hill Rd RMSLY B62 ....104 B5
Olive La RMSLY B62 ....104 A5
Olive Pl ALE/KHTH/YWD B14 * 125 J6
Oliver Cl DUDS DY2 ....85 J5
Oliver Ct BLKHTH/ROWR B65 ....103 M3
Oliver Crs BILS/COS WV14 ....67 J3
Oliver Rd ERDW/GRVHL B23 ....72 D7
SMTHWK B66 ....106 A2
Oliver St COVN CV6 ....134 D7
RUGBYN/HIL CV21 ....186 D2
VAUX/NECH B7 ....89 L7
Olivier Wy RCOVN/BALC/EX CV7 ....135 M5
Ollerton Rd
LGN/SDN/BHAMAIR B26 ....109 K6
Ollison Dr FOAKS/STRLY B74 ....55 K3
Olliver Cl RIDG/WDGT B32 ....122 D3
Olorenshaw Rd
LGN/SDN/BHAMAIR B26 ....110 B3
Olton Av COVW CV5 ....153 J1
Olton Bvd East ACGN B27 ....127 G3
Olton Bvd West SPARK B11 ....126 D2
Olton Cft ACGN B27 ....127 H2
Olton Mere HIA/OLT B92 * 127 H3
Olton Pl NUNW/HART CV10 ....98 D1
Olton Rd HIA/OLT B92 ....126 F8
Olton Whf HIA/OLT B92 ....127 J3
Olympus Av RLSS CV31 ....206 B7
Olympus Cl COVW CV5 ....131 M5
Olympus Dr TPTN/OCK DY4 ....68 A3
Olympus Gdns STRPT DY13 ....189 G2
Omar Rd COVE CV2 ....156 B3
Ombersley Cl OLDBY B69 * 86 B8
REDE B98 ....202 F7
Ombersley Rd BHTH/HG B12 ....107 L2
HALE B63 ....121 K3
Onley Rd HDSW B21 ....88 B4
Onley La RUGBYS/DCH CV22 ....187 H8
Onley Ter TLHL/CAN CV4 ....153 J3
Onslow Crs HIA/OLT B92 ....127 L4
Onslow Rd SPARK B11 ....126 E1
Ontario Cl HWK/WKHTH B38 ....145 L5
Oozells Sq CBHAMW B1 * 6 A6
Oozells St CBHAMW B1 ....6 C6
Open Field Cl NFLD/LBR B31 ....144 E5
Openfield Cft CSHL/WTROR B46 ....93 G2
The Orangery HAG/WOL DY9 ....120 B6
Oratory Dr COVS CV3 ....156 A7
Orbital Wy CNCK/NC WS11 ....16 A3
Orchard Av CNCK/NC WS11 ....16 A3
SOLH B91 ....128 B8
Orchard Cl ATHST CV9 ....63 K5
BLKHTH/ROWR B65 ....103 J2
CSHL/WTROR B46 ....93 K3
GTWY WS6 ....24 D4
HAG/WOL DY9 ....140 F1
HALE B63 ....103 C7
HDSW B21 ....88 D4
LICH WS13 ....20 C4
NUNW/HART CV10 ....79 L6
PENK ST19 ....10 D4
POL/KGSB/FAZ B78 ....47 L2
RUSH/SHEL WS4 * 40 A5
STRPT DY13 ....188 D1
TAM/AM/WIL B77 ....46 A8
WALM/CURD B76 ....74 F7
WLNHL WV13 ....51 M4
Orchard Ct ATHST CV9 ....63 K6
BDMR/CCFT WV3 ....48 F6
COVS CV3 ....156 D4
KGSWFD DY6 ....83 H7
Orchard Crs COVS CV3 ....8 E3
PENK ST19 ....10 C4
Orchard Cft RBRY B45 ....170 B5
Orchard Dr COVW CV5 ....153 C1
NFLD/LBR B31 ....144 D6
Orchard Gv ALDR WS9 ....54 F1
ETTPK/GDPK/PENN WV4 ....65 L1
FOAKS/STRLY B74 ....56 D2
SEDG DY3 ....83 M2
Orchard La CDSL WV8 ....34 F2
HAG/WOL DY9 ....102 C7
WOLVN WV10 ....23 C2
Orchard Meadow Wk
CVALE B35 ....91 M2
Orchard Pl STUD B80 ....203 B5
Orchard Ri ATHST CV9 ....62 A3
BEWD DY12 ....162 E2
LGN/SDN/BHAMAIR B26 ....109 C6
Orchard Rd BPBAR/PBCH B61 ....191 K1
DSYBK/YTR WS5 ....69 M2
DUDS DY2 ....103 G3
ERDE/BCHGN B24 ....72 F3
HOCK/TIA B94 ....175 C7
KIDD DY10 ....139 G1
WLNHL WV13 ....51 M4
WNSFLD WV11 ....37 G6
The Orchards FOAKS/STRLY B74 ....56 B4
HLYWD B47 ....146 E6
KIDDW DY11 ....137 M4
RUGBY CV23 ....161 K4
SHLY B90 ....174 B1
Orchards Wy BHTH/HG B12 ....107 J2
The Orchard ATHST CV9 ....62 A6
BEWD DY12 ....162 C2
BILS/COS WV14 ....51 J8
BLOX/PEL WS3 ....39 J3
BNTWD WS7 * 18 C7
BRGRVW B61 ....191 J1
CHWD/FDBR/MGN B37 ....110 D5
DUNHL/THL/PER WV6 ....35 J7
Orchard Vls HLYWD B47 * 172 D4
Orchard Wy ACGN B27 ....126 F1
GTB/HAM B43 ....70 D4
HLYWD B47 ....146 E6
NUNW/HART CV10 ....80 A7
RUGBYS/DCH CV22 ....186 K1
Orchestan Wk
ALE/KHTH/YWD B14 ....146 B4
Orchid Cl SMTHWK B66 ....87 H6
Orchid Dr LOZ/NWT B19 ....89 H7
Orchid Wy RRUGBY CV23 ....161 K5
Ordnance Rd COVE CV2 ....134 C0
Oregon Cl KGSWFD DY6 ....83 K7
Oregon Dr SHHTH WV12 ....38 C6
Oregon Gdns BNTWD WS7 ....18 D5
Orford Gv HDSW B21 ....88 A4
Oriel Cl CNCK/NC WS11 ....16 A5
DUDN DY1 ....84 C3
Oriel Dr WOLVN WV10 ....36 B2
Orient Ct NUNW/HART CV10 ....97 J1
Orion Cl GTWY WS6 ....24 D4
WASH/WDE B8 ....108 A1
Orion Crs COVE CV2 ....135 J3
Orion Wy ACGN B27 ....127 G1
Oriole Gv KIDD DY10 ....164 F3

Orkney Av BKDE/SHDE B34 9
Orkney Cl NUNW/HART CV10 9
Orkney Cft CBROM B36 9
Orlando Cl RUGBYS/DCH CV22 18
WSL WS1 9
Orlescote Rd TLHL/CAN CV4 15
Ormande Cl HALE B63 10
Orme Cl STRBR DY8 9
Ormes La ATHST CV9 ....
DUNHL/THL/PER WV6 4
Ormond Pl BILS/COS WV14 6
Ormond Rd RBRY B45 16
Ormonds Cl LICH WS13 2
Ormsby Gv ACGN B27 12
Ormscliffe Rd RBRY B45 14
Orphanage Rd
CSCFLD/WYGN B72 7
ERDE/BCHGN B24 7
Orpington Dr COVN CV6 1
Orpington Rd KGSTG B44 7
Orpwood Rd STETCH B33 11
Orson Leys RUGBYS/DCH CV22 18
Orton Cl CSHL/WTROR B46 9
Orton Gv
ETTPK/GDPK/PENN WV4 4
Orton La
ETTPK/GDPK/PENN WV4 4
Orton Rd COVN CV6 13
Orton Wy CVALE B35 9
Orwell Cl NUNW/HART CV10 7
RUGBY CV23 16
STRBR DY8 9
WNSFLD WV11 3
Orwell Dr HHTH/SAND B71 6
NFLD/LBR B31 14
Orwell Pas DIG/EDG B5 ....
Orwell Rd COV CV1 ....
WSL WS1 ....
Osbaston Cl COVW CV5 15
Osberton Dr DUDN DY1 8
Osborne CRTAM B79 * ....
BRLYHL DY5 ....
KIDD DY10 ....
Osborne Dr DARL/WED WS10 6
Osborne Gv LOZ/NWT B19 * 8
Osborne Rd COVW CV5 ....
ERDW/GRVHL B23 7
ETTPK/GDPK/PENN WV4 ....
HDSW B21 8
WBROM B70 8
Osborn Rd SPARK B11 10
Osbourne Cft SHLY B90 14
Oscott Rd PBAR/PBCH B42 7
Oscott School La KGSTG B44 7
Osier Gv ERDW/GRVHL B23 7
Osier Pl WOLV WV1 ....
Osier St WOLV WV1 ....
Osler St LDYWD/EDGR B16 10
Oslo Gdns COVE CV2 1
Osmaston Rd HRBN B17 12
STRBR DY8 10
Osmington Gv HALE B63 10
Osprey TAM/AM/WIL B77 4
Osprey Cl COVE CV2 13
NUN CV11 9
Osprey Dr DUDN DY1 1
Osprey Gv HEDN WS12 1
Osprey Park Dr KIDD DY10 1
Osprey Rd ERDW/GRVHL B23 7
HIA/OLT B92 12
Ostler Cl KGSWFD DY6 8
Oswald Rd RLSN CV32 20
Oswald St REDW B97 20
Oswestry Cl REDW B97 20
Oswin Gv COVE CV2 15
Oswin Pl BLOX/PEL WS3 3
Oswin Rd BLOX/PEL WS3 3
Othello Cl RUGBYS/DCH CV22 18
Other Rd REDE B98 20
Otherton Cl PENK ST19 1
Otherton La PENK ST19 1
Otley Gv BORD B9 10
Otterburn Cl HEDN WS12 1
Otter Cft BKDE/SHDE B34 9
Otters Rest RLSS CV31 20
Otterstone Cl SEDG DY3 ....
Ottery TAM/AM/WIL B77 4
Oughton Rd BHTH/HG B12 1
Oulton Cl KIDDW DY11 13
Oundle Rd KGSTG B44 7
Ounsdale Crs WMBN WV5 6
Ounsdale Dr DUDS DY2 10
Ounty John La STRBR DY8 11
Ousterne La
RCOVN/BALC/EX CV7 11
Outermarch Rd COVN CV6 13
Outmore Rd STETCH B33 10
Outwood Cl REDE B98 20
Out Wood Dr NFLD/LBR B31 14
Outwoods ATHST CV9 ....
Oval Rd ERDE/BCHGN B24 9
RUGBYS/DCH CV22 18
TPTN/OCK DY4 6
The Oval DARL/WED WS10 6
DUDN DY1 ....
SMTHWKW B70 8
Overberry Cl COVE CV2 13
Overbrook Cl SEDG DY3 ....
Over Brunton Cl NFLD/LBR B31 14
Overbury Cl NFLD/LBR B31 14
RMSLY B62 ....
Overbury Rd NFLD/LBR B31 14
Overdale Av WALM/CURD B76 7
Overdale Cl SHHTH WV12 5
Overdale Dr WSLW WS2 5
Overdale Rd COVW CV5 ....
RIDG/WDGT B32 ....
Overend Rd HALE B63 10
Overend St WBROM B70 8
Overfield Dr BILS/COS WV14 6
Overfield Rd DUDN DY1 ....
RIDG/WDGT B32 ....
Over Green Dr
CHWD/FDBR/MGN B37 9
Overhill Rd BNTWD WS7 1
Overlea Av ACGN B27 12
Over Mill Dr SLYOAK B29 12
Overmoor Cl LOZ/NWT B19 8
Over Pool Rd WASH/WDE B8 9
Overseal Rd WNSFLD WV11 3
Overslade Crs COVN CV6 13
Overslade La
RUGBYS/DCH CV22 18
Overslade Manor Dr
RUGBYS/DCH CV22 18
Overslade Rd SOLH B91 14
Oversley Rd WALM/CURD B76 7
Overstrand WOLVN WV10 ....
Over St COVN CV6 ....
Overton Cl HLGN/YWD B28 12
Overton Dr CSHL/WTROR B46 ....
Overton Gv ACGN B27 12
Overton La BNTWD WS7 1

erton Pl HHTH/SAND B71 ....69 H7
AUX/NECH B7 ....7 L2
erton Rd ACGN B27 ....126 F5
ertons Cl RLSS CV31 ....207 K8
erwood Cft WASH/WDE B8 ....108 C2
erwoods Rd TAM/AM/WIL B77 ..46 D8
enford Rd COVN CV6 ....134 A6
en Pl BILS/COS WV14 ....51 H7
en Rd BDMR/CCFT WV3 ....2 B8
ILS/COS WV14 ....51 H6
VLNHL WV13 ....51 M4
ens Cft HWK/WKHTH B38 ....145 L4
en St ATHST CV9 ....63 H5
ARL/WED WS10 ....52 B6
UDS DY2 ....85 J5
PTN/OCK DY4 ....67 J8
ens Wy CDYHTH B64 ....103 L4
nall Rd BKDE/SHDE B34 ....92 A7
barn Av BDMR/CCFT WV3 ....49 J6
bow Wy KIDDW DY11 ....138 C5
bridge Wy CRTAM B79 ....31 H7
Cl COVE CV2 ....134 E7
endon Wy COVS CV3 ....156 C5
enton Cft HALE B63 ....121 H3
ord Canal Pth
RUGBYN/HIL CV21 ....160 F6
ord Canal Wk RRUGBY CV23 ..158 E1
ord Cl GTWY WS6 ....24 D2
UN CV11 ....81 K5
VASH/WDE B8 ....90 F8
ord Dr ACGN B27 ....127 H1
TRBR DY8 ....119 K1
ord Gn CNCK/NC WS11 ....16 D5
ord Pl RLSN CV32 ....206 E4
ord Rd ACGN B27 ....127 G2
NCK/NC WS11 ....16 D5
RDW/GRVHL B23 ....90 D1
NWTH CV8 ....182 D4
MOS/BIL B13 ....125 L3
RUGBY CV23 ....183 G8
MTHWK B66 ....87 L5
VBROM B70 ....86 F2
ord Rw RLSN CV32 ....206 D4
ord St BILS/COS WV14 ....51 J8
VILLE B30 ....124 E6
OV CV1 ....9 K4
ARL/WED WS10 ....68 F3
IG/EDG B5 ....7 J7
UDN DY1 ....84 F4
IDD DY10 ....138 C8
LSN CV32 ....206 D4
UGBYN/HIL CV21 ....187 G2
VOLV WV1 ....3 H6
VSLW WS2 ....4 A8
hayes Cl
COVN/BALC/EX CV7 ....152 A7
ill Cl REDE B98 ....203 J4
ill Rd HDSW B21 ....88 B3
HLY B90 ....147 G3
Leasow RIDG/WDGT B32 ....123 G3
easow Rd REDE B98 ....195 J8
ey Av WOLVN WV10 ....36 A7
ey Cl DUDS DY2 ....102 F3
TWY WS6 ....24 D4
ey Dr COVS CV3 ....181 G2
ey Gv SLYOAK B29 ....123 L5
ey La WOLV WV1 ....2 F2
ey Links Rd WOLVN WV10 ....35 M5
ey Moor Rd COVEN WV9 ....35 L5
Leys Rd MGN/WHC B75 ....73 M1
ey St WOLV WV1 ....2 F1
p Cl DSYBK/YTR WS5 ....69 L2
piece Dr CBROM B36 ....91 H5
tall Cl WALM/CURD B76 ....74 B8
St SEDG DY3 ....66 B8
ed Cl WNSFLD WV11 ....37 K8
ed Cft ERDW/GRVHL B23 ....90 C2
vood La RMSLY B62 ....143 H1
gen St VAUX/NECH B7 ....7 J1

P

e Crs BILS/COS WV14 ....67 K3
ific Av DARL/WED WS10 ....68 B4
kenham Dr WALM/CURD B76 ..73 K5
khorse La HWK/WKHTH B38 ..146 B7
kington Av BKDE/SHDE B34 ....92 A8
OVW CV5 ....132 F7
kington La
SHL/WTROR B46 ....111 L1
OL/KGSB/FAZ B78 ....30 D8
COVN/BALC/EX CV7 ....112 F4
kington Pl RLSS CV31 ....206 E6
kmores SHLY B90 ....147 L8
kmore St WWCK CV34 ....205 K5
kwood Av
UGBYN/HIL CV21 ....187 M5
kwood Cl
FLD/HDSWWD B20 ....88 E3
OR/KN B93 ....175 J1
UN CV11 ....99 K5
EDW B97 ....201 K4
LSS CV31 ....207 G8
LNHL WV13 ....51 K5
kwood Cottages
OR/KN B93 * 175 K4
kwood Ct SLYOAK B29 ....123 K4
kwood Dr GTB/HAM B43 ....70 B4
kwood Gn COVW CV5 ....153 L2
kwood La HOCK/TIA B94 ....175 L8
kwood Ms WWCK CV34 * 205 M5
kwood Rd HOCK/TIA B94 ....175 L7
GN/SDN/BHAMAIR B26 ....109 M5
LDBY B69 ....85 L4
arn Cl SEDG DY3 ....66 A4
bury COVEN WV9 ....35 M2
bury La BNTWD WS7 ....19 H4
diford Pl NUNW/HART CV10 ....98 A2
dington Rd HDSW B21 ....88 A4
dock Dr DOR/KN B93 ....175 L3
GN/SDN/BHAMAIR B26 ....109 L6
dock La ALDR WS9 ....40 E8
TWY WS6 ....24 E2
EDE B98 ....202 C6
SL WS1 ....5 H4
docks Cl KNWTH CV8 ....183 L2
OL/KGSB/FAZ B78 ....47 K4
docks Gn WSNGN B18 ....88 E8
docks Rd HLYWD B47 ....146 D7
Paddocks BDWTH CV12 ....117 M2
RUGBY CV23 ....183 K8
WCK CV34 ....205 K6
Paddock BILS/COS WV14 ....67 H4
RGRVE B60 ....191 H7
DSL WV8 ....34 E3
UNHL/THL/PER WV6 ....48 B1
G/WOL DY9 ....119 M5
HS WS14 ....21 G8
UGBY CV23 ....161 K4
DY3 ....66 C8
V WV5 ....64 C7
k Vw
L/THL/PER WV6 ....35 M8
x Cl RUGBYN/HIL CV21 ....187 K5
Paddys Rw WALM/CURD B76 * 75 L6
Padgate Cl CVALE B35 ....91 M2
Padgets La REDE B98 ....203 H1
Padmore Ct RLSS CV31 ....206 F7
Padstow TAM/AM/WIL B77 ....32 D8
Padstow Cl NUN CV11 ....81 K8
Padstow Rd ERDE/BCHGN B24 ....91 H1
TLHL/CAN CV4 ....153 J5
Padua Rd BRGRVE B60 ....192 A4
Paganal Dr WBROM B70 ....87 J4
Paganel Dr DUDN DY1 ....85 G2
Paganel Rd SLYOAK B29 ....123 L3
Page Rd TLHL/CAN CV4 ....153 J6
Pages Cl MGN/WHC B75 ....57 G8
Pages La GTB/HAM B43 ....70 C4
Paget Cl BILS/COS WV14 * 66 F5
BRGRVW B61 ....191 J3
LICH WS13 ....20 F3
PENK ST19 ....10 E6
Paget Ct COVE CV2 ....134 F2
Paget Dr BNTWD WS7 ....18 C4
Paget Rd DUNHL/THL/PER WV6 ....49 K2
ERDE/BCHGN B24 ....91 H2
Pagets Cha HEDN WS12 ....18 A1
Paget's La KNWTH CV8 ....182 B8
Paget St WOLV WV1 ....2 D2
Pagham Cl COVEN WV9 ....35 K3
Pagnell Gv MOS/BIL B13 ....126 A7
Paignton Rd LDYWD/EDGR B16 ..106 B2
Pailton Cl COVE CV2 ....135 G3
Pailton Gv SLYOAK B29 ....123 L4
Pailton Rd RRUGBY CV23 ....159 M1
SHLY B90 ....126 F8
Painswick Cl DSYBK/YTR WS5 ....69 M2
REDE B98 ....202 C7
Painswick Rd HLGN/YWD B28 ....126 C6
Paint Cup Rw DUDS DY2 ....103 G3
Painters Cft BILS/COS WV14 ....67 J4
Pakefield Rd BVILLE B30 ....145 M2
Pakenham Cl WALM/CURD B76 ....73 K5
Pakenham Rd EDG B15 ....107 G6
Pake's Cft COVN CV6 ....133 L8
Pakfield Wk AST/WIT B6 * 89 K4
Palace Cl BLKHTH/ROWR B65 ....104 B1
Palace Dr SMTHWK B66 ....87 G5
Palace Rd BORD B9 ....108 C4
Palefield Rd SHLY B90 ....148 D7
Pale La HRBN B17 ....105 K5
Palermo Av COVS CV3 ....155 J7
Pale St SEDG DY3 ....66 C8
Palethorpe Rd TPTN/OCK DY4 ....67 L5
Palfrey Rd STRBR DY8 ....101 H8
Pallett Dr NUN CV11 ....81 L6
Palmcourt Av HLGN/YWD B28 ....126 C6
Palm Cft BRLYHL DY5 ....102 A5
Palmer Cl WNSFLD WV11 ....37 K4
Palmer La COV CV1 ....8 F4
Palmers Cl CDSL WV8 ....35 G3
RUGBYN/HIL CV21 ....187 M5
SHLY B90 ....126 F8
Palmers Gv CBROM B36 ....91 J5
Palmers Rd REDE B98 ....195 K8
Palmerston Dr OLDBY B69 ....86 B3
Palmerston Rd COVW CV5 ....154 D5
SPARK B11 ....107 M7
Palmer St BORD B9 ....7 M6
Palmers Wy CDSL WV8 ....35 G4
Palm Tree Av COVE CV2 ....135 G3
Palmvale Cft
LGN/SDN/BHAMAIR B26 ....109 L7
Palmyra Rd BRGRVE B60 ....192 A3
Palomino Pl LDYWD/EDGR B16 ....106 D3
Pamela Rd NFLD/LBR B31 ....144 E3
Pancras Cl COVE CV2 ....135 J4
Pan Cft CBROM B36 ....91 G6
Pandora Rd COVE CV2 ....135 J6
Pangbourne Rd COVE CV2 ....135 G5
Pangfield Pk COVW CV5 ....154 A1
Panjab Gdns SMTHWKW B67 * 87 K7
Pannel Cft LOZ/NWT B19 ....89 H7
Panther Cft BKDE/SHDE B34 ....92 B8
Pantolf Pl RUGBYN/HIL CV21 ....160 C6
Papenham Gn TLHL/CAN CV4 ....153 L5
Paper Mill Dr REDE B98 ....194 F7
Paper Mill End PBAR/PBCH B42 ....71 H7
Papworth Dr BRGRVW B61 ....168 D8
Papyrus Wy CBROM B36 ....91 K4
Parade RLSN CV32 ....206 D5
The Parade BRWNH WS8 ....26 C4
CDYHTH B64 ....103 J5
DUDN DY1 ....84 F3
KGSWFD DY6 ....82 F6
KIDD DY10 * 138 D5
NUN CV11 ....99 G2
WNSFLD WV11 * 36 E5
Paradise DUDS DY2 ....85 H5
Paradise Circus Queensway
CBHAMNW B3 ....6 D5
Paradise Gv BLOX/PEL WS3 ....39 K2
Paradise La BLOX/PEL WS3 ....39 K2
HLGN/YWD B28 ....126 C7
WOLVN WV10 ....22 C4
Paradise Pl CBHAMNW B3 * 6 E5
Paradise Rw BRGRVE B60 ....191 K4
Paradise St CBHAM B2 ....6 E5
COV CV1 ....9 H7
RUGBYN/HIL CV21 ....187 G2
WBROM B70 ....87 H2
WWCK CV34 ....205 K5
Paradise Wy
RCOVN/BALC/EX CV7 ....135 L4
Paragon Wy
RCOVN/BALC/EX CV7 ....116 F5
Parbrook Cl TLHL/CAN CV4 ....153 J5
Parbury TAM/AM/WIL B77 ....46 B8
The Parchments LICH WS13 ....20 F4
Pardington Cl HIA/OLT B92 ....128 C5
Pargeter Rd SMTHWKW B67 ....105 K3
Pargeter St STRBR DY8 ....119 K1
WSLW WS2 ....4 A2
Par Gn NFLD/LBR B31 ....145 G4
Parish Gdns HAG/WOL DY9 ....119 M4
Parish Hl BRGRVW B61 ....168 B4
Park Aly BEWD DY12 * 162 F2
Park Ap ERDW/GRVHL B23 ....90 A3
Park Av BLKHTH/ROWR B65 ....104 A2
BNTWD WS7 ....18 F8
BVILLE B30 ....124 E8
CNCK/NC WS11 ....17 L8
COVN CV6 ....134 A2
CSHL/WTROR B46 ....93 K7
ETTPK/GDPK/PENN WV4 ....50 A8
LGLYGN/QTN B68 ....104 F2
NUN CV11 ....99 J2
POL/KGSB/FAZ B78 ....47 M5
SMTHWKW B67 * 105 K1
SOLH B91 ....149 H2
STRPT DY13 ....188 D1
TPTN/OCK DY4 ....67 J8
WLNHL WV13 ....51 K3
WMBN WV5 ....64 D8
WOLV WV1 ....2 D4
WSNGN B18 ....88 E6
Park Cl BEWD DY12 ....162 F2
BILS/COS WV14 ....66 F6
BRWNH WS8 ....26 D5
ERDE/BCHGN B24 ....73 H8
GTWY WS6 ....24 C2
HIA/OLT B92 ....128 B3
KNWTH CV8 ....179 M8
OLDBY B69 ....86 A6
Park Ct REDE B98 ....202 E2
RUGBYN/HIL CV21 * 186 E1
Park Crs HHTH/SAND B71 ....87 H1
STRPT DY13 ....188 D1
WOLV WV1 ....2 D4
Park Cft BNTWD WS7 ....18 A5
HLYWD B47 ....146 E8
Parkdale Av DARL/WED WS10 ....68 E1
Parkdale Cl ERDE/BCHGN B24 ....90 D3
Park Dale Ct WOLV WV1 ....2 A3
Parkdale Dr NFLD/LBR B31 ....144 E6
Park Dl East WOLV WV1 ....2 A3
Parkdale Rd
LGN/SDN/BHAMAIR B26 ....110 A7
Park Dl West WOLV WV1 ....2 A3
Park Dingle BEWD DY12 ....162 C3
Park Dr ETTPK/GDPK/PENN WV4 ..50 A8
FOAKS/STRLY B74 ....56 A1
FOAKS/STRLY B74 ....56 D3
RLSS CV31 ....206 C6
Park Edge HRBN B17 ....106 A6
Park End LICHS WS14 ....21 J6
Parkend RUGBYN/HIL CV21 ....160 F6
Park End Dr RIDG/WDGT B32 ....123 H4
Parker Pl STRPT DY13 ....164 A6
Parker Rd WNSFLD WV11 ....37 K4
Parkers Ct COVEN WV9 ....22 A4
Parker St BLOX/PEL WS3 ....38 E4
LDYWD/EDGR B16 ....106 D4
Parkes Av CDSL WV8 ....34 F3
Parkes Crs WNSFLD WV11 ....37 L1
Parkes Hall Rd DUDN DY1 ....66 E8
Parkes La SEDG DY3 ....66 E6
TPTN/OCK DY4 ....67 K5
Parkes Pas STRPT DY13 ....188 E2
Parkes Quay STRPT DY13 ....188 E2
Parkes St BRLYHL DY5 ....102 B2
SMTHWKW B67 ....105 K1
WLNHL WV13 ....51 M4
WWCK CV34 ....205 H6
Parkeston Crs KGSTG B44 ....71 M4
Park Farm Cl
RUGBYS/DCH CV22 ....186 B3
Park Farm Rd GTB/HAM B43 ....70 F2
TAM/AM/WIL B77 ....46 A4
Parkfield RIDG/WDGT B32 ....122 D3
Parkfield Av TAM/AM/WIL B77 ....46 A5
Parkfield Chalet Land
BKHL/PFLD WV2 * 50 B7
Parkfield Cl EDG B15 ....107 G6
KIDDW DY11 ....189 L3
REDE B98 ....194 F7
RMSLY B62 ....104 E8
TAM/AM/WIL B77 ....46 A5
Parkfield Colliery
ETTPK/GDPK/PENN WV4 ....50 D8
Parkfield Crs BKHL/PFLD WV2 ....50 C7
TAM/AM/WIL B77 ....46 A4
Parkfield Dr CBROM B36 ....92 A4
KNWTH CV8 ....179 M8
Parkfield Gv BKHL/PFLD WV2 ....50 C7
Parkfield Rd CSHL/WTROR B46 ....93 K6
DUDS DY2 ....85 H7
ETTPK/GDPK/PENN WV4 ....50 C7
LGLYGN/QTN B68 ....104 E2
RCOVN/BALC/EX CV7 ....115 L7
RUGBYN/HIL CV21 ....160 B7
STRBR DY8 ....101 M8
WASH/WDE B8 ....108 C2
Parkgate Rd COVN CV6 ....133 M2
Park Gate Rd KIDD DY10 ....138 F3
Park Gv CSHL/WTROR B46 ....93 G2
SMHTH B10 * 108 B5
Park Hall Cl DSYBK/YTR WS5 ....54 A7
Park Hall Crs CBROM B36 ....91 M5
Parkhall Cft CBROM B36 ....92 A6
Park Hall Rd DSYBK/YTR WS5 ....54 A7
ETTPK/GDPK/PENN WV4 ....66 B1
Park Head Crs DUDS DY2 * 84 F5
Parkhead Locks DUDS DY2 * 84 E7
Park Head Rd DUDS DY2 ....84 F5
Park Hl BLKHTH/ROWR B65 ....103 M4
DARL/WED WS10 ....69 G1
KNWTH CV8 ....179 M8
MOS/BIL B13 ....125 J1
Park Hill Dr BFLD/HDSWWD B20 ....88 D1
Parkhill Dr COVW CV5 ....132 D8
Park Hill La COVW CV5 ....132 E8
Park Hill Rd HRBN B17 ....106 A7
SMTHWKW B67 ....87 K8
Parkhill Rd BNTWD WS7 ....18 E5
WALM/CURD B76 ....73 K7
Park Hill St DUDS DY2 ....85 J5
Parkhouse Av WNSFLD WV11 ....36 F7
Parkhouse Dr ERDW/GRVHL B23 ..71 L8
Parkhouse Gdns SEDG DY3 ....84 A1
Parkinson Dr ATHST CV9 ....63 J3
Parkland Av KIDDW DY11 ....137 M8
Parkland Cl COVN CV6 ....134 A2
Parklands Av RLSN CV32 ....207 G1
Parklands Cl REDW B97 ....193 L8
Parklands Dr FOAKS/STRLY B74 ....56 D5
Parklands Gdns WSL WS1 ....5 K7
Parklands Rd BILS/COS WV14 ....67 H2
DARL/WED WS10 ....52 C8
WOLV WV1 ....50 E4
The Parklands BDMR/CCFT WV3 ..49 H3
ERDW/GRVHL B23 ....72 B7
HAG/WOL DY9 ....120 B2
Park La AST/WIT B6 ....89 J6
BEWD DY12 ....162 D3
CVALE B35 ....73 M8
DARL/WED WS10 ....52 D7
GTWY WS6 ....24 D2
HALE B63 ....102 E7
HHTH/SAND B71 ....87 M1
KGSWFD DY6 ....83 J6
KIDD DY10 ....165 L3
KIDDW DY11 ....138 B8
LICHS WS14 ....28 E8
LICHS WS14 ....43 G1
NUNW/HART CV10 ....97 G8
NUNW/HART CV10 ....97 K1
OLDBY B69 ....86 E7
POL/KGSB/FAZ B78 ....45 J4
RCOVN/BALC/EX CV7 ....96 E8
RCOVN/BALC/EX CV7 ....151 M3
WOLVN WV10 ....36 C8
Park La East TPTN/OCK DY4 ....85 M1
Park La West TPTN/OCK DY4 ....85 J1
Park Lime Dr RUSH/SHEL WS4 ....53 M1
Park Meadow Av BILS/COS WV14 ..51 G5
Park Ms SLYOAK B29 * 123 M4
The Park Paling COVS CV3 ....155 J7
Park Pl VAUX/NECH B7 ....90 A6
Park Retreat SMTHWK B66 ....105 M1
Park Rdg FOAKS/STRLY B74 ....56 E6
Park Ridge Dr HALE B63 ....102 F7
Park Ri BDMR/CCFT WV3 ....49 J3
Park Rd AST/WIT B6 ....89 L6
ATHST CV9 ....61 M4
BDWTH CV12 ....116 F3
BILS/COS WV14 ....51 G8
BLOX/PEL WS3 ....38 F4
BNTWD WS7 ....18 C5
BNTWD WS7 ....18 F8
BRLYHL DY5 ....102 D5
CNCK/NC WS11 ....16 B4
CNCK/NC WS11 ....17 L8
COV CV1 ....8 F7
CSHL/WTROR B46 ....93 K7
DARL/WED WS10 ....51 M7
DSYBK/YTR WS5 ....54 B8
DUDN DY1 ....66 F7
DUDS DY2 ....85 G7
ERDW/GRVHL B23 ....90 A3
HAG/WOL DY9 ....119 M8
HALE B63 ....102 F7
KNWTH CV8 ....179 L7
MOS/BIL B13 ....125 K1
OLDBY B69 ....86 A5
POL/KGSB/FAZ B78 ....47 M5
RLSN CV32 ....206 D1
RUGBYN/HIL CV21 ....186 E1
RUSH/SHEL WS4 ....40 A8
SCFLD/BOLD B73 ....56 F8
SEDG DY3 ....83 M1
SMTHWKW B67 ....105 K4
SPARK B11 ....126 A2
STRBR DY8 ....101 H8
TAM/AM/WIL B77 ....46 A8
WLNHL WV13 ....51 K2
WOLVN WV10 ....23 H5
WSNGN B18 ....88 D6
Park Rd East WOLV WV1 ....2 C2
Park Rd South WSNGN B18 ....88 F8
Park Rd West STRBR DY8 ....101 G8
WOLV WV1 ....2 B3
Parkside COV CV1 ....9 H6
RIDG/WDGT B32 ....123 G4
TAM/AM/WIL B77 ....46 C4
WWCK CV34 * 205 K6
Parkside Av WLNHL WV13 ....51 J3
Parkside Cl DARL/WED WS10 ....68 F2
Parkside La CNCK/NC WS11 ....15 L2
Parkside Rd BFLD/HDSWWD B20 ..70 C8
HALE B63 ....103 H8
Parkside Wy FOAKS/STRLY B74 ....55 L4
NFLD/LBR B31 ....144 A4
Park Sq CHWD/FDBR/MGN B37 ..111 H5
Parkstone Av BRGRVW B61 ....191 H5
Parkstone Cl RUSH/SHEL WS4 ....40 A4
Parkstone Rd COVN CV6 ....134 D3
Park St AST/WIT B6 ....89 L6
BLKHTH/ROWR B65 ....104 B4
CDYHTH B64 ....103 H3
CNCK/NC WS11 ....16 C7
COVN CV6 ....134 C6
CRTAM B79 ....31 L8
DARL/WED WS10 ....52 A8
DARL/WED WS10 ....68 D2
DIG/EDG B5 ....7 J5
GTWY WS6 ....24 C2
HAG/WOL DY9 ....102 D8
KGSWFD DY6 ....83 H7
KIDDW DY11 ....138 B7
NUN CV11 ....99 H2
OLDBY B69 ....86 D7
RLSN CV32 ....206 D5
STRBR DY8 ....101 K5
STRBR DY8 ....119 L1
TPTN/OCK DY4 ....67 L8
WBROM B70 ....87 H2
WSL WS1 ....4 E3
Park St South BKHL/PFLD WV2 ....50 A7
Park Ter DARL/WED WS10 ....51 M7
HDSW B21 ....88 C5
The Park REDW B97 ....193 G6
Park Vw DARL/WED WS10 ....52 A7
HOCK/TIA B94 ....175 G7
SCFLD/BOLD B73 ....56 E7
Park View Cl
RCOVN/BALC/EX CV7 ....116 E6
Parkview Ct KGSWFD DY6 ....82 F5
Parkview Crs WSLW WS2 ....52 E1
Parkview Dr WASH/WDE B8 ....90 E7
Parkview Rd BILS/COS WV14 ....51 G5
Park View Rd FOAKS/STRLY B74 ....56 B2
HAG/WOL DY9 ....120 D1
NFLD/LBR B31 ....144 D2
Park Vls BORD B9 * 107 M3
Parkville Av HRBN B17 ....123 M2
Parkville Cl COVN CV6 ....134 A2
Parkville Hwy COVN CV6 ....133 M2
Park Wk BRLYHL DY5 ....102 D5
RUGBYN/HIL CV21 ....186 E1
Park Wy RBRY B45 ....143 M5
REDE B98 ....194 E8
WNSFLD WV11 ....37 L4
Parkway RCOVN/BALC/EX CV7 ....135 M5
WASH/WDE B8 ....90 E8
Parkway Rd DUDN DY1 ....84 E3
The Parkway CDSL WV8 ....34 B7
DUNHL/THL/PER WV6 ....48 B1
RUSH/SHEL WS4 ....40 A5
Parkwood Cl BRWNH WS8 ....26 E8
Parkwood Cft PBAR/PBCH B42 ....70 F4
Parkwood Dr SCFLD/BOLD B73 ....72 A3
Park Wood La TLHL/CAN CV4 ....153 H6
Parkwood Rd BRGRVW B61 ....191 J2
Parkyn St BKHL/PFLD WV2 ....3 J9
Parliament St AST/WIT B6 ....89 K7
SMHTH B10 ....108 A5
WBROM B70 ....87 H4
Parlows End HWK/WKHTH B38 ....145 H6
Parmington Cl REDW B97 ....201 M7
Parnell Cl RUGBYN/HIL CV21 ....186 D2
Parr Cl RLSS CV31 ....206 B7
Parrotts Gv COVE CV2 ....117 H8
Parry Rd COVE CV2 ....134 F6
KIDDW DY11 ....163 M2
WNSFLD WV11 ....37 L5
Parsonage Dr HALE B63 ....102 E6
RBRY B45 ....170 B1
Parsonage St HHTH/SAND B71 ....69 H7
OLDBY B69 ....86 F7
Parson's Hl BVILLE B30 ....145 M3
LGLYGN/QTN B68 ....104 F4
Parsons Hollow
TAM/AM/WIL B77 ....46 C6
Parsons La STRPT DY13 ....189 K4
Parson's Nook COVE CV2 ....134 E8
Parsons Rd REDE B98 ....202 C3
Parsons St DUDN DY1 ....85 G4
Parson St TAM/AM/WIL B77 ....46 C6
Partons Rd ALE/KHTH/YWD B14 ..125 H7
Partridge Av DARL/WED WS10 ....51 M7
Partridge Cl
CHWD/FDBR/MGN B37 ....111 G2
HEDN WS12 ....12 B6
Partridge Cft COVN CV6 ....134 E4
LICH WS13 ....21 G5
Partridge Gv KIDD DY10 ....164 E3
Partridge La REDW B97 ....201 L7
Partridge Ml BLOX/PEL WS3 ....39 J2
Partridge Rd
LGN/SDN/BHAMAIR B26 ....109 L4
STRBR DY8 ....119 G1
Passey Rd MOS/BIL B13 ....126 B3
Passfield Av HEDN WS12 ....13 G6
Passfield Rd STETCH B33 ....109 K2
Pasture Ga CNCK/NC WS11 ....16 A3
The Pastures
DUNHL/THL/PER WV6 ....48 B1
Pasture Vw BLOX/PEL WS3 ....39 K4
Patch La REDE B98 ....202 D7
Pat Davis Ct KIDD DY10 ....138 C6
Patent Dr DARL/WED WS10 ....68 A3
Paternoster Rw DIG/EDG B5 * 7 H5
KIDDW DY11 ....138 B7
WOLV WV1 ....2 E4
Paterson Pl BRWNH WS8 ....26 F8
Pathlow Crs SHLY B90 ....147 L4
The Patios KIDDW DY11 ....138 A6
Paton Gv MOS/BIL B13 ....125 K3
Patrcia Cl TLHL/CAN CV4 ....153 G4
Patricia Av ALE/KHTH/YWD B14 ..147 G1
ETTPK/GDPK/PENN WV4 ....50 A8
Patricia Crs DUDN DY1 ....66 F7
Patricia Dr TPTN/OCK DY4 ....85 L3
Patrick Br HIA/OLT B92 ....130 B6
Patrick Gregory Rd
WNSFLD WV11 ....37 K6
Patrick Ms LICH WS13 ....20 D4
Patrick Rd
LGN/SDN/BHAMAIR B26 ....109 J6
Patriot Cl WSL WS1 ....53 H8
Patshull Av WOLVN WV10 ....35 M2
Patshull Cl GTB/HAM B43 ....70 B4
Patshull Gv WOLVN WV10 ....35 M2
Patshull Pl LOZ/NWT B19 * 89 G6
Pattens Rd WWCK CV34 ....205 M4
Patterdale RUGBYN/HIL CV21 ....161 H6
Patterdale Rd CNCK/NC WS11 ....16 E1
ERDW/GRVHL B23 ....90 B1
Patterdale Wy BRLYHL DY5 ....101 M5
Patterton Dr WALM/CURD B76 ....73 K5
Pattingham Rd
DUNHL/THL/PER WV6 ....48 A3
Pattison Gdns ERDW/GRVHL B23 ..90 B3
Pattison St DSYBK/YTR WS5 ....53 J8
Paul Byrne Ct
BFLD/HDSWWD B20 ....88 F4
Pauline Av COVN CV6 ....134 F3
Paul Pursehouse Rd
BILS/COS WV14 ....67 H2
Pauls Coppice BRWNH WS8 ....26 D8
Paul St BILS/COS WV14 ....66 E4
BKHL/PFLD WV2 ....2 E8
DARL/WED WS10 ....68 E3
Paul V TPTN/OCK DY4 ....67 M8
Pavenham Dr DIG/EDG B5 ....125 G1
Pavilion Av SMTHWKW B67 ....105 J2
Pavilion Dr PBAR/PBCH B42 ....89 K2
Pavilion End KINVER DY7 ....100 C4
Pavilion Gdns BRGRVW B61 ....168 D8
DUDS DY2 ....103 G3
Pavilion Rd PBAR/PBCH B42 ....89 K2
The Pavilions CBHAMNE B4 * 7 H5
CHWD/FDBR/MGN B37 ....111 H5
Pavilion Wy COVW CV5 ....154 D2
Pavillion Cl ALDR WS9 ....40 F5
Pavior's Rd BNTWD WS7 ....26 C1
Paxford Cl REDE B98 ....194 F7
Paxford Wy NFLD/LBR B31 ....123 K7
Paxmead Cl COVN CV6 ....133 L3
Paxton Av DUNHL/THL/PER WV6 ..48 C2
Paxton Cl BRGRVE B60 ....191 M4
Paxton Rd COVN CV6 ....8 A1
HAG/WOL DY9 ....120 E1
WSNGN B18 ....88 E8
Payne Cl RLSN CV32 ....206 E3
Paynell Cl COVN CV6 ....133 M3
Payne's La COVE CV2 ....9 L4
RUGBYN/HIL CV21 ....186 B2
Payne St BLKHTH/ROWR B65 ....104 A4
Payton Cl OLDBY B69 ....86 C4
Payton Rd HDSW B21 ....88 B5
Peace Cl GTWY WS6 ....24 C2
Peach Av DARL/WED WS10 ....52 A7
Peachley Cl HALE B63 ....121 M3
Peach Ley Rd SLYOAK B29 ....123 K6
Peach Rd SHHTH WV12 ....37 L7
Peacock Av COVE CV2 ....135 K4
WNSFLD WV11 ....37 L6
Peacock Cl TPTN/OCK DY4 ....85 M1
Peacock Ms KIDDW DY11 ....138 C5
Peacock Rd DARL/WED WS10 ....51 M6
MOS/BIL B13 ....125 K7
Peacocks Est CDYHTH B64 * 103 G4
Peak Cft CBROM B36 ....91 H5
Peak Dr SEDG DY3 ....84 B2
Peake Av NUN CV11 ....81 J5
Peake Crs BRWNH WS8 ....26 D8
Peake Dr TPTN/OCK DY4 ....85 M1
Peake Rd BRWNH WS8 ....26 D8
Peak House Rd GTB/HAM B43 ....70 C2
Peakman Cl RBRY B45 ....143 L7
Peakman St REDW B97 ....202 C1
Peak Rd STRBR DY8 ....101 M7
Peal St WSL WS1 ....5 G4
Pearce Cl DUDN DY1 ....84 C5
Pearl Gv ACGN B27 ....126 F2
Pearl La STRPT DY13 ....188 B5
Pearman Rd RBRY B45 ....143 H4
SMTHWK B66 ....105 L2
Pearmans Cft HLYWD B47 ....146 E7
Pearsall Dr OLDBY B69 ....86 C5
Pears Cl KNWTH CV8 ....179 K8
Pearson Av COVN CV6 ....134 F4
Pearson St BKHL/PFLD WV2 ....2 F9
BRLYHL DY5 ....102 B2
CDYHTH B64 ....103 J4
HAG/WOL DY9 ....120 D1
WBROM B70 ....86 F1
Pear Tree Av NUNW/HART CV10 ....80 C7
POL/KGSB/FAZ B78 ....60 B8
TPTN/OCK DY4 ....67 K8
Peartree Av WLNHL WV13 ....51 M4
Pear Tree Cl CRTAM B79 ....33 J6
GTB/HAM B43 ....69 M4
HEDN WS12 ....12 A6
KIDD DY10 ....138 F6
SHLY B90 ....147 H3
STETCH B33 ....109 H3
Pear Tree Ct
BLKHTH/ROWR B65 ....104 B2
Pear Tree Crs SHLY B90 ....147 G2
Pear Tree Dr
BLKHTH/ROWR B65 ....104 B2
GTB/HAM B43 ....70 A4
Peartree Dr STRBR DY8 ....119 L3
Pear Tree Gv SHLY B90 ....147 H3
Pear Tree La BILS/COS WV14 ....67 H5
BRWNH WS8 ....26 A3
WNSFLD WV11 ....36 F4
Peartree La CDYHTH B64 ....103 J4
DUDS DY2 ....84 D8
Pear Tree Rd BKDE/SHDE B34 ....92 A7
GTB/HAM B43 ....69 M4
SMTHWKW B67 ....105 J1
Pear Tree Wy
RUGBYS/DCH CV22 ....185 M4
Peascroft La BILS/COS WV14 ....51 J7
Peasefield Cl HDSW B21 ....88 A5
Peat Cl RUGBYS/DCH CV22 ....186 C4
Pebblebrook Wy BDWTH CV12 ....117 G3
Pebble Cl STRBR DY8 ....101 M8
TAM/AM/WIL B77 ....46 F2
Pebble Island Wy RLSS CV31 ....207 G8
Pebble Mill Cl CNCK/NC WS11 ....16 D3
Pebble Mill Dr CNCK/NC WS11 ....16 D3
Pebble Mill Rd DIG/EDG B5 ....124 F1
Pebworth Av SHLY B90 ....148 F7
Pebworth Cl COVW CV5 ....153 M2

REDE B98 ....195 G6
SLYOAK B29 ....124 F2
Pebworth Dr
RWWCK/WEL CV35 ....204 C2
Pebworth Dr DUDN DY1 ....84 E2
STECH B33 ....110 A5
Peckham Rd KGSTG B44 ....71 L3
Peckover CI BLKHTH/ROWR B65...103 M4
Peckstone CI COV CV1 ....9 H8
Peddimore La WALM/CURD B76...74 B7
Pedmore CI REDE B98 ....202 F6
Pedmore Court Rd STRBR DY8..119 M4
Pedmore Gv KGSTG B44 ....71 K3
Pedmore Hall La HAG/WOL DY9 ..120 A5
Pedmore La HAG/WOL DY9 ......120 A4
Pedmore Rd BRLYHL DY5 ....102 D1
HAG/WOL DY9 ....102 B8
Peel CI COVN CV6 ....134 C7
DARL/WED WS10 ....129 M7
HIA/OLT B92 ....129 M7
POL/KGSB/FAZ B78 ....43 J8
WLNHL WV13 ....51 L4
Peel Dr HEDN WS12 ....12 E5
Peelers Wy TAM/AM/WIL B77 * ...45 M4
Peel La COVN CV6 ....134 D8
Peel Rd WWCK CV34 ....205 J5
Peel St BDMR/CCFT WV3 ....2 E1
COVN CV6 ....134 D7
DUDS DY2 ....85 J5
HHTH/SAND B71 ....69 G8
KIDDW DY11 ....138 B8
TPTN/OCK DY4 ....51 L1
WLNHL WV13 ....51 L4
WSNGN B18 ....88 C8
Peel Wk HRBN B17 ....105 K6
Peel Wy OLDBY B69 ....86 A3
Pegasus Wk SLYOAK B29 ....124 E4
Peglee Wk ALE/KHTH/YWD B14 ..146 A4
Pegmill CI COVS CV3 ....155 K5
Pelham Dr DUDN DY1 ....84 E3
Pelham Rd WASH/WDE B8 ....108 F1
Pelham St BDMR/CCFT WV3 ....2 B7
Pelsall La BLOX/PEL WS3 ....39 H2
RUSH/SHEL WS4 ....39 M6
Pelsall Rd BRWNH WS8 ....26 B5
Pemberly Av ACGN B27 ....126 E4
Pemberton CI SMTHWK B66 ....105 M2
Pemberton Crs DARL/WED WS10..69 G1
KIDD DY10 ....139 G2
Pemberton Rd BILS/COS WV14 ....67 H4
WBROM B70 ....68 E7
Pemberton St WSNGN B18 ....6 B2
Pembridge CI BRLYHL DY5 ....102 D4
REDE B98 ....203 H5
RIDG/WDGT B32 ....122 E6
Pembridge Rd DOR/KN B93 ....175 J2
Pembroke Av WKNL/PFLD WV2 ....50 B6
CRTAM B79 ....31 H7
SHHTH WV12 ....37 M7
WWCK CV34 ....205 K5
Pembroke CI BDWTH CV12 ....116 A4
Pembroke Cft HLGN/YWD B28 ..126 E8
Pembroke Gdns STRBR DY8 ....101 G3
Pembroke Rd BHTH/HG B12 .....125 L1
HHTH/SAND B71 ....68 F4
Pembroke Wy HHTH/SAND B71 ...68 F6
HLGN/YWD B28 ....126 E8
NUN CV11 ....99 H2
STRPT DY13 ....163 J7
Pembrook Rd COVN CV6 ....134 A3
Pembury Av COVN CV6 ....134 D4
Pembury CI FOAKS/STRLY B74 ....55 K7
Pembury Cft KGSTG B44 ....71 L4
Penarth Gv COVS CV3 ....156 D6
Pencombe Dr
ETTPK/GDPK/PENN WV4 ....50 B8
Pencraig Ct KNWTH CV8 ....179 M8
Pencroft Rd BKDE/SHDE B34 ......91 M6
Penda Gv DUNHL/THL/PER WV6...34 D8
Pendeen Rd
ALE/KHTH/YWD B14 ....147 G1
Pendeford Av
DUNHL/THL/PER WV6 ....35 J5
Pendeford Dr
DUNHL/THL/PER WV6 ....35 L1
Pendeford La COVEN WV9 ....35 L1
Pendeford Mill La CDSL WV8 ....35 G2
Pendennis CI COVN CV6 ....134 C5
Pendennis Dr BVILLE B30 ....124 B8
Pendennis Rd OLDBY B69 ....85 L5
Penderel CI BLOX/PEL WS3 ....39 G4
Penderel St BLOX/PEL WS3 ....39 G4
Pendigo Wy BHAMNEC B40 ....129 K2
Pendinas Dr CDSL WV8 ....34 F2
Pendle HI HEDN WS12 ....17 C1
Pendleton Gv ACGN B27 ....126 C6
Pendragon Rd RUGBYS/DCH CV22 ..186 C5
Pendred Rd GTWY WS6 ....24 C5
Pendrell CI
CHWD/FDBR/MGN B37 ....110 E2
Pendrell Ct CDSL WV8 * 34 C7
Pendrill Rd WOLVN WV10 ....36 D2
Penfields Rd STRBR DY8 ....101 L7
Penge Gv KGSTG B44 ....71 J2
Penhallow Dr
ETTPK/GDPK/PENN WV4 ....50 C8
Penhurst Av BFLD/HDSWWD B20..89 H4
Penk Dr BNTWD WS7 ....19 H7
Penkridge Bank HEDN WS12 ....12 D2
Penkridge CI WSLW WS2 ....53 H1
Penkridge Gv STECH B33 ....109 K1
Penkridge St WSLW WS2 ....53 H2
Penkridge Whf PENK ST19 ....10 D5
Penk Ri DUNHL/THL/PER WV6 .....48 F1
Penleigh Gdns WMBN WV5 ....64 D1
Penley Gv WASH/WDE B8 ....90 F7
Penmanor BRGRVE B60 ....192 B5
Penmire Rd ATHST CV9 ....62 A2
Pennant Gv SLYOAK B29 ....123 M2
Pennant Rd BLKHTH/ROWR B65..103 M2
CDYTH B64 ....103 K5
Pennard Gv RIDG/WDGT B32 .....123 K1
Penn CI BLOX/PEL WS3 ....39 G4
Penn Common Rd
ETTPK/GDPK/PENN WV4 ....65 J4
Penncricket La
BLKHTH/ROWR B65 ....104 C2
Penn Croft La
ETTPK/GDPK/PENN WV4 ....65 L4
Pennhouse Av
ETTPK/GDPK/PENN WV4 ....49 K8
Pennine Dr CNCK/NC WS11 ....16 C3
SEDG DY3 ....84 B2
Pennine Rd BRGRVE B60 ....168 C8
Pennine Wy NUNW/HART CV10 ....97 M3
SHHTH WV12 ....52 B1
STRBR DY8 ....101 L7
TAM/AM/WIL B77 ....46 F5
WASH/WDE B8 ....90 A8
Pennington CI WBROM B70 ....86 B3
Pennington Ms
RUGBYN/HIL CV21 ....186 D2
Pennington St
RUGBYN/HIL CV21 ....186 E2
Pennington Wy COVN CV6 ....134 C5
Penn Rd BKHL/PFLD WV2 ....7 G6
Penrith CI COVW CV5 ....153 L1
Perth Rd SHHTH WV12 ....37 M7

BLKHTH/ROWR B65 ....104 C2
ETTPK/GDPK/PENN WV4 ....65 J1
ETTPK/GDPK/PENN WV4 ....65 K1
Penn Rd Island BDMR/CCFT WV3 ...2 E7
Penn Rd CI RLSN CV32 ....199 J8
Penns Lake Rd WALM/CURD B76 ..73 H6
Penns La CSCFLD/WYGN B72 ....73 H6
Penn St BDMR/CCFT WV3 ....2 D8
CBHAMNE B4 ....39 L1
CDYHTH B64 ....103 K5
Penns Wood CI SEDG DY3 ....66 A3
Penns Wood Dr
WALM/CURD B76 ....73 K6
Pennwood La
ETTPK/GDPK/PENN WV4 ....65 K2
Pennyacre Rd
ALE/KHTH/YWD B14 ....146 B3
Pennycress Gdns WOLVN WV10 ...22 F6
Penny Cress Gn CNCK/NC WS11 ...25 K1
Pennyfield Cft STECH B33 ....109 J2
Pennyford CI REDW B97 ....193 L8
Pennyhill La HHTH/SAND B71 ......69 J6
Pennymoor Rd
TAM/AM/WIL B77 ....46 F6
Penny Park La COVN CV6 ....133 K4
Pennyroyal CI DSYBK/YTR WS5 ....69 L2
Penny Royal CI SEDG DY3 ....84 B5
Pennystone CI RLSS CV31 ....207 H7
Penrice Dr DUDS DY2 ....85 J7
Penrith CI BRLYHL DY5 ....101 M5
RLSN CV32 ....206 A3
Penrith Cft RIDG/WDGT B32 ....123 H5
Penrith Gv
CHWD/FDBR/MGN B37 ....111 G3
Penrose CI TLHL/CAN CV4 ....153 L6
Penryhn CI KNWTH CV8 ....180 A8
Penryn CI DSYBK/YTR WS5 ....54 B6
NUN CV11 ....81 L8
Penryn Rd DSYBK/YTR WS5 ....54 B6
Pensarn Vis DARL/WED WS10 * 52 B7
Pensby CI MOS/BIL B13 ....126 A5
Pensford Rd NFLD/LBR B31 ....145 G2
Pensham Cft SHLY B90 ....148 E7
Penshaw CI WOLVN WV10 ....35 L3
Penshaw Gv MOS/BIL B13 ....126 B4
Penshurst Rd BRGRVE B60 ....192 A5
Penshurst Wy NUN CV11 ....99 K5
Pensilva Wy COV CV1 ....9 K2
Pensnett Rd BRLYHL DY5 ....102 A1
DUDN DY1 ....84 C6
Penstock Dr OLDBY B69 ....104 D1
Penstone La
ETTPK/GDPK/PENN WV4 ....64 C1
Pentire CI NUN CV11 ....81 J8
Pentire Rd LICHS WS14 ....21 H7
Pentland Ct BHTH/HG B12 ....107 K6
Pentlands Gdns
BDMR/CCFT WV3 ....49 J3
Pentos Dr SPARK B11 ....126 B2
Pentridge CI WALM/CURD B76 .....73 K8
Penzance Wy NUN CV11 ....81 K8
Penzer Dr RBRY B45 ....170 B5
Penzer St KGSWFD DY6 ....83 H6
Peolsford Rd BLOX/PEL WS3 ....39 L1
Peplins Wy BVILLE B30 ....145 M2
Peplow Rd STECH B33 ....109 L1
Pepperbox Dr TPTN/OCK DY4 * 67 L8
Pepper Hl STRBR DY8 ....119 L1
Pepper La COV CV1 ....8 F5
Pepperwood CI BRGRVE B61 .....168 B2
Pepper Wood Dr NFLD/LBR B31...144 A4
Pepys Cnr TLHL/CAN CV4 ....153 J2
Perch Av
CHWD/FDBR/MGN B37 ....110 E2
Perch CI WOLV WV1 ....50 F1
Perchfoot CI COV CV1 ....9 H8
Perch Rd WSLW WS2 ....52 E1
Percival Rd COVN CV6 ....134 E1
RUGBYS/DCH CV22 ....187 H5
Percy Crs KNWTH CV8 ....197 J3
Percy Rd KNWTH CV8 ....197 J3
SPARK B11 ....126 B2
WWCK CV34 ....205 J5
Percy St COV CV1 ....8 C4
Peregrine CI DUDN DY1 ....84 D4
Peregrine Dr COVW CV5 ....152 E8
Peregrine Gv KIDD DY10 ....164 E3
Pereira Rd HRBN B17 ....106 A4
Perimeter Rd BHAMNEC B40 ......129 H1
Perivale Gv BILS/COS WV14 ....67 J7
Perivale Wy STRBR DY8 ....101 L5
Periwinkle CI BRWNH WS8 ....26 B7
Perkins CI DUDN DY1 ....67 G7
Perkins Gv RUGBYN/HIL CV21 ....187 K4
Perks Rd WNSFLD WV11 ....37 L4
Permian CI RUGBYN/HIL CV21 ....161 G7
Perott Dr MGN/WHC B75 ....57 H4
Perrett Wk KIDDW DY11 ....138 A7
Perrin Av KIDDW DY11 ....163 M1
Perrins Gv WASH/WDE B8 ....90 E7
Perrins La HAG/WOL DY9 ....120 D1
Perrins Ri HAG/WOL DY9 ....120 D1
Perrott Gdns STRBR DY8 ....101 M4
Perrott St WSNGN B18 ....88 B7
Perry Av PBAR/PBCH B42 ....89 G1
Perry Barr Locks
PBAR/PBCH B42 * 70 F7
Perry CI DUDS DY2 ....85 H5
Perry Common Rd
ERDW/GRVHL B23 ....71 M7
Perry Ct LGLYGN/QTN B68 ....104 F5
Perrycrofts Crs CRTAM B79 ....32 A6
Perryfields CI REDE B98 ....202 D7
Perryfields Crs BRGRVW B61 ......191 H2
Perryfields Rd BRGRVW B61 ....191 H2
Perryford Dr SOLH B91 ....148 F5
Perry Hall Dr SHHTH WV12 ....37 M8
Perry Hall Rd WNSFLD WV11 ....37 K7
Perry Hill Crs LGLYGN/QTN B68 ..104 F6
Perry Hill La LGLYGN/QTN B68 * ..104 F6
Perry Hill Rd LGLYGN/QTN B68 ...105 G6
Perry La BRGRVW B61 ....191 K5
KIDD DY10 ....164 F8
Perryman Dr POL/KGSB/FAZ B78 ..78 D5
Perry Park Crs PBAR/PBCH B42 ...70 F7
Perry Park Rd CDYHTH B64 ....104 M4
Perry St BILS/COS WV14 ....67 M4
DARL/WED WS10 ....52 B5
DARL/WED WS10 ....52 B5
SMTHWK B66 ....87 L6
TPTN/OCK DY4 ....52 A8
Perry Villa Dr PBAR/PBCH B42 .....71 H8
Perry Wk ERDW/GRVHL B23 ....71 M7
Perrywell Rd PBAR/PBCH B42 ......89 L1
Perry Wood Rd PBAR/PBCH B42 ..70 E5
Persehouse St WSL WS1 ....5 H3
Pershore CI BLOX/PEL WS3 ....38 C3
Pershore PI TLHL/CAN CV4 ....154 C7
Pershore Rd BLOX/PEL WS3 ....38 D3
BVILLE B30 ....124 E6
DIG/EDG B5 ....107 H7
HALE B63 ....103 J4
KIDDW DY11 ....137 L2
SMTHWK B66 ....87 J6
Pershore Rd South BVILLE B30 ....145 K2
Pershore St DIG/EDG B5 ....7 G7
Pershore Wy BLOX/PEL WS3 ....38 D3
Perth Ri COVW CV5 ....153 L1
Perth Rd SHHTH WV12 ....37 M7

Perton Brook V
DUNHL/THL/PER WV6 ....48 D3
Perton Gv DUNHL/THL/PER WV6 ..48 D3
SLYOAK B29 ....123 L4
Perton Rd DUNHL/THL/PER WV6 ..48 D3
Pestilence La ALVE B48 ....171 H5
Petard CI TAM/AM/WIL B77 * 46 A5
Petchells CI BRLYHL DY5 ....83 M8
Peter Av BILS/COS WV14 ....67 K3
Peterborough Dr CNCK/NC WS11..17 G4
Peterbrook CI REDE B98 ....202 D6
Peterbrook Ri SHLY B90 ....147 H4
Peterdale Dr
ETTPK/GDPK/PENN WV4 ....65 K2
Peterhead TAM/AM/WIL B77 ....32 D8
Peters Av NFLD/LBR B31 ....144 D5
Petersfield CNCK/NC WS11 ....16 D1
Petersfield Ct HLGN/YWD B28 * ..126 D5
Petersfield Dr
BLKHTH/ROWR B65 ....104 C2
Petersfield Rd HLGN/YWD B28 ....126 C6
Peter's Finger BRGRVE B61 ....191 K4
Petersham PI EDG B15 ....106 C7
Petersham Rd KGSTG B44 ....72 A8
Peter's Hill Rd BRLYHL DY5 ....102 A6
Petershouse Dr
FOAKS/STRLY B74 ....42 D8
Peter's La BNTWD WS7 ....19 L8
Peters St WBROM B70 ....68 E6
Petford St CDYHTH B64 ....103 J4
Petitor Crs COVE CV2 ....135 C4
Pettitt CI ALE/KHTH/YWD B14 .....146 C4
Pettiver Crs RUGBYN/HIL CV21 ...187 K4
Petton CI REDE B98 ....203 K2
Pettyfield CI
LGN/SDN/BHAMAIR B26 ....109 L7
Pettyfields CI DOR/KN B93 ....149 L8
Petworth CI WLNHL WV13 ....51 K5
Petworth Gv
LGN/SDN/BHAMAIR B26 ....109 J7
Pevensey CI DUDS DY2 ....85 K5
Pevensey Rd BRGRVE B60 ....192 A4
Peverell Dr HLGN/YWD B28 ....126 D6
Peveril Gv WALM/CURD B76 ....73 J1
Peveril Rd DUNHL/THL/PER WV6..48 D1
ETTPK/GDPK/PENN WV4 ....66 C2
Pevril Wy GTB/HAM B43 ....70 D3
Peyto CI COVN CV6 ....134 A3
Pheasant CI BDWTH CV12 ....116 B4
Pheasant Cft CBROM B36 ....92 E5
Pheasant La REDE B98 ....202 D6
Pheasant Oak TLHL/CAN CV4 .....153 G3
Pheasant Rd SMTHWKW B67 ....105 H3
Pheasant St BRLYHL DY5 ....102 A2
Philip Gv CNCK/NC WS11 ....12 C7
Philip Rd HALE B63 ....121 K2
TPTN/OCK DY4 ....68 B8
Philip Sidney Rd SPARK B11 ....125 M2
Philip St BILS/COS WV14 ....67 H4
Philip Victor Rd
BFLD/HDSWWD B20 ....88 D4
Phillimore Rd WASH/WDE B8 ....90 B8
Phillippes Rd WWCK CV34 ....205 K4
Phillip Rd WLSW WV11 ....37 K4
Phillips Av WNSFLD WV11 ....37 K4
Phillips St AST/WIT B6 ....89 J7
Phillips Ter REDE B98 ....202 D1
Phipps Av RUGBYN/HIL CV21 .....187 K4
Phipson Rd SPARK B11 ....125 M2
Phoenix Gn EDG B15 ....106 C6
Phoenix Pk BLKHTH/ROWR B65 ..104 B4
Phoenix Ri DARL/WED WS10 ....68 B1
ERDW/GRVHL B23 ....71 K6
TPTN/OCK DY4 ....67 K7
WLNHL WV13 ....51 H2
Phoenix St BKHL/PFLD WV2 ....50 B7
WBROM B70 ....68 D8
Phoenix Wy COVN CV6 ....134 C3
Picasso CI CNCK/NC WS11 ....17 H3
Piccadilly CI POL/KGSB/FAZ B78 ..60 D5
Piccadilly Ar CBHAM B2 ....6 F5
Piccadilly CI
CHWD/FDBR/MGN B37 ....111 G4
Piccadilly Crs POL/KGSB/FAZ B78..60 D5
Pickard CI RUGBYN/HIL CV21 .....161 A6
Pickard St WLNHL WV13 ....205 L6
Pickenham Rd
ALE/KHTH/YWD B14 ....146 E4
Pickering Rd RIDG/WDGT B32 .....123 C4
Pickering Rd WNSFLD WV11 ....37 H8
Pickersleigh CI HALE B63 ....121 J2
Pickford CI NUN CV11 ....99 L4
Pickford Grange La COVW CV5 ....132 A6
Pickford Green La COVW CV5 .....132 A7
Pickford St DIG/EDG B5 ....7 K6
Pickford Wy COVW CV5 ....132 F7
Pickrell Rd BILS/COS WV14 ....66 F4
Pickwick Gv MOS/BIL B13 ....126 A3
Pickwick PI BILS/COS WV14 ....67 J1
Picton Cft
CHWD/FDBR/MGN B37 ....111 H4
Picton Gv MOS/BIL B13 ....125 M8
Picturedrome Wy
DARL/WED WS10 ....52 B7
Piddock Rd SMTHWK B66 ....87 L8
Pierce Av HIA/OLT B92 ....127 J2
Piercy St WBROM B70 ....86 E2
Piers CI WWCK CV34 ....205 K5
Piers Rd WSNGN B18 ....88 B4
Piggots Cft
CHWD/FDBR/MGN B37 ....110 D2
Pike CI BFLD/HDSWWD B20 ....88 D4
Pike Dr CHWD/FDBR/MGN B37 ...111 G2
Pikehelve St TPTN/OCK DY4 ....68 A8
Pike HI BRGRVE B60 ....169 L7
Pikehorne Cft CBROM B36 ....92 B3
Pike Rd WSLW WS2 ....52 E1
Pikers La COVW CV5 ....132 E2
Pikes Pool La BRGRVE B60 ....192 B4
The Pikes RBRY B45 ....143 K5
Pilgrims La RUGBY CV23 ....161 K4
Pilkington Av WALM/CURD B76 .....73 G2
Pilkington Rd COVW CV5 ....154 B5
Pillaton CI PENK ST19 ....10 C6
Pillaton Dr HEDN WS12 ....12 A7
Pilling CI COVE CV2 ....135 K5
Pimbury Rd SHHTH WV12 ....38 B6
Pimlico CI CBROM B36 ....91 M5
Pimbury Rd SHHTH WV12 ....38 B6
Pimpernel Dr DSYBK/YTR WS5 .....69 L2
Pinbury Cft
CHWD/FDBR/MGN B37 ....110 F5
Pinchers CI HAG/WOL DY9 ....141 M4
Pinders La RUGBYN/HIL CV21 * ...186 F1
Pineapple CI
ALE/KHTH/YWD B14 ....125 G7
Pineapple Gv BVILLE B30 ....125 G5
Pineapple Rd BVILLE B30 ....125 G6
Pine Av DARL/WED WS10 ....52 D9
SMTHWK B66 ....87 J6
Pine CI BDMR/CCFT WV3 ....2 A5
CRTAM B79 ....31 M5
GTWY WS6 ....24 D1
KGSWFD DY6 ....83 H7

KINVER DY7 ....118 A2
SOLH B91 ....148 A3
Pinedene STRPT DY13 ....188 F2
Pine Gn DUDN DY1 ....66 E8
Pine Gv ALE/KHTH/YWD B14 ......175 H3
BNTWD WS7 ....18 D5
RBRY B45 ....169 K3
RUGBYN/HIL CV21 ....187 L4
Pinehurst Dr HWK/WKHTH B38...145 K2
Pinehurst RLSN CV32 ....199 J3
Pine Leigh FOAKS/STRLY B74 ......56 F4
Pineneedle Cft SHHTH WV12 ....52 C1
Pineridge Dr KIDDW DY11 ....137 M8
Pine Rd DUDN DY1 ....67 G8
OLDBY B69 ....85 L5
The Pines BDMR/CCFT WV3 ....49 H4
BDWTH CV12 ....116 C3
LICHS WS14 ....21 H7
RBRY B45 ....143 L4
SHLY B90 ....148 B8
TLHL/CAN CV4 * 153 H6
WSL WS1 ....5 G6
Pine St BLOX/PEL WS3 ....39 G4
Pine Tree Av TLHL/CAN CV4 ....153 L3
Pine Tree CI HEDN WS12 ....12 E4
REDW B97 ....201 K2
Pinetree Dr FOAKS/STRLY B74 .....55 H4
Pine Tree Rd BDWTH CV12 ....117 L2
Pinetree Rd BEWD DY12 ....162 D3
Pineview NFLD/LBR B31 ....144 D3
Pine Wk CDSL WV8 ....34 D5
HAG/WOL DY9 ....120 B2
NFLD/LBR B31 ....144 D3
STRPT DY13 ....188 C1
Pinewall Av HWK/WKHTH B38 ....146 C4
Pineways FOAKS/STRLY B74 ....56 A2
STRBR DY8 ....101 G3
Pineways Dr
DUNHL/THL/PER WV6 ....49 J2
The Pineways OLDBY B69 ....86 A8
Pinewood Av BILS/COS WV14 ....67 H4
CNCK/NC WS11 ....16 E1
Pinewood CI BDMR/CCFT WV3 ....48 D5
BRWNH WS8 ....26 C3
DSYBK/YTR WS5 ....69 M1
KGSTG B44 ....71 J6
KIDDW DY11 ....138 A4
RBRY B45 ....143 H5
SHHTH WV12 ....38 B6
WMBN WV5 ....64 E7
Pinewood Dr COVS CV3 ....157 G6
RIDG/WDGT B32 ....122 E5
Pinewood Gv COVW CV5 ....154 B5
SOLH B91 ....148 D3
Pine Woods RIDG/WDGT B32 .....122 E5
Pinewoods RMSLY B62 ....104 E6
SLYOAK B29 ....123 K5
Pinewoods Av HAG/WOL DY9 .....140 D5
Pinewoods CI HAG/WOL DY9 .....140 D5
Pinfield Dr RBRY B45 ....169 M4
Pinfold Ct DARL/WED WS10 * 52 A8
Pinfold Crs
ETTPK/GDPK/PENN WV4 ....49 K8
Pinfold Gdns WNSFLD WV11 ....37 H8
Pinfold Gv BDMR/CCFT WV3 ....49 K8
Pinfold HI LICHS WS14 ....28 D7
Pinfold La ALDR WS9 ....54 F6
CNCK/NC WS11 ....25 J1
ETTPK/GDPK/PENN WV4 ....49 K8
GTWY WS6 ....24 A3
PENK ST19 ....10 E5
Pinfold Rd LICH WS13 ....20 D4
SOLH B91 ....128 C8
Pinfold St BILS/COS WV14 ....51 H8
CBHAM B2 ....6 D5
DARL/WED WS10 ....52 A8
OLDBY B69 ....86 E5
RUGBYN/HIL CV21 ....186 C5
Pingle CI HHTH/SAND B71 ....69 K4
Pingle Ct NUN CV11 ....99 H3
Pingle La BNTWD WS7 ....27 H1
Pink Green La REDE B98 ....195 M6
Pinkney PI LGLYGN/QTN B68 ......105 G2
Pinley Flds COVS CV3 ....155 K5
Pinley CI ALDR WS9 ....70 F7
Pinley Gv GTB/HAM B43 ....69 L1
Pinley Wy SOLH B91 ....148 E5
Pinner Gv RIDG/WDGT B32 ....123 J1
Pinner's Cft COVE CV2 ....134 E8
Pinnock PI TLHL/CAN CV4 ....153 K4
Pinson Rd WLNHL WV13 ....51 K4
Pinta Dr STRPT DY13 ....188 F2
Pintail Dr ERDW/GRVHL B23 ....90 A3
Pintail Gv KIDD DY10 ....164 F2
Pinto CI LDYWD/EDGR B16 ....106 D3
Pinwall La ATHST CV9 ....63 K1
Pinza Cft CBROM B36 ....91 J1
Pioli PI WSLW WS2 * 39 H8
Pioneer CI REDW B97 ....202 B1
Piper CI DUNHL/THL/PER WV6 .....48 D1
Piper PI STRPT DY13 ....101 K5
Piper Rd BDMR/CCFT WV3 ....48 D5
Pipers CI BRGRVE B60 ....191 H5
Pipers Cft LICH WS13 ....20 E3
Pipers Gn HLGN/YWD B28 ....126 D8
Piper's La KNWTH CV8 ....197 L5
NUNW/HART CV10 ....79 G5
Pipers Rd REDE B98 ....203 H2
Pipers Rw WOLV WV1 ....3 H5
Pipes Meadow BILS/COS WV14 ....51 J5
Pipewell CI RUGBYS/DCH CV22 ..186 A4
Pipit Ct KIDD DY10 ....164 E3
Pipkin Ct COV CV1 ....9 J8
Pippin Av HALE B63 ....102 D1
Pirbright CI BILS/COS WV14 ....67 J2
Pirrey CI BILS/COS WV14 ....67 J5
Pitcairn CI BVILLE B30 ....124 F7
Pitcairn Dr RMSLY B62 ....103 H1
Pitcairn Rd SMTHWK B67 ....105 H4
Pitcheroak Cottages
REDW B97 * 201 K4
Pitclose Rd NFLD/LBR B31 ....144 F4
Pitfield Rd STECH B33 ....110 B4
Pitfield Rw DUDN DY1 * 84 F4
Pitfields CI LGLYGN/QTN B68 .....104 E5
Pitfields Rd LGLYGN/QTN B68 ....104 E5
Pitfield St DUDN DY1 * 84 F4
Pithall Rd BKDE/SHDE B34 ....92 B8
Pit HI KNWTH CV8 ....182 A4
Pit Leasow CI BVILLE B30 ....124 F5
Pitman Rd RIDG/WDGT B32 ....105 G8
Pitmaston Rd HLGN/YWD B28 ....126 E7
Pitsford St HSW WSNGN B18 ....6 B1
Pitt La HIA/OLT B92 ....129 H3
Pitts Farm Rd ERDE/BCHGN B24 ..73 G8
Pitts La KIDD DY10 ....138 C2
Pitt St CBHAMNE B4 * 7 L3
KIDD DY10 ....138 C2
Pixall Dr EDG B15 ....106 F6
Pixhall Wk CVALE B35 ....91 H1
Plainview CI FOAKS/STRLY B74 ....55 J3
Plaistow Av CBROM B36 ....91 G4
Planetary Rd WLNHL WV13 ....50 F1
Planetree CI BRGRVE B60 ....191 M3
Plane Tree CI KIDD DY10 ....138 D6
Plane Tree Rd DSYBK/YTR WS5 ....69 M1
Planetree Rd FOAKS/STRLY B74 ...55 H5

Planet Rd BRLYHL DY5 ....102 ...
Plank La CSHL/WTROR B46 ....92 ...
Planks La WMBN WV5 ....64 ...
Plantagenet Dr
RUGBYS/DCH CV22 ....186 ...
Plantation Dr MGN/WHC B75 ....57 ...
Plantation La POL/KGSB/FAZ B78..78 ...
SEDG DY3 ....66 ...
Plantation Rd DSYBK/YTR WS5 ....69 ...
HEDN WS12 ....13 ...
The Plantation BRLYHL DY5 ....83 ...
Plant CI RUGBYS/DCH CV22 ....185 ...
Plant La BNTWD WS7 ....18 ...
Plants Brook Rd
WALM/CURD B76 ....73 ...
Plants CI GTWY WS6 ....24 ...
SCFLD/BOLD B73 ....72 ...
Plants Gv ERDE/BCHGN B24 ....73 ...
Plants Hill Crs TLHL/CAN CV4 .....153 ...
Plants Hollow BRLYHL DY5 ....102 ...
Plant St CDYHTH B64 ....101 ...
STRBR DY8 ....101 ...
Platt Wy BLOX/PEL WS3 ....39 ...
Plascom Rd WOLV WV1 ....50 ...
Plato CI WWCK CV34 ....206 ...
Platts Crs STRBR DY8 ....101 ...
Platts La STRBR DY8 ....101 ...
Platts Rd STRBR DY8 ....101 ...
Platt St CNCK/NC WS11 ....12 ...
DARL/WED WS10 ....52 ...
Playdon Gv
ALE/KHTH/YWD B14 ....146 ...
Pleasant CI KGSWFD DY6 ....101 ...
Pleasant Harbour BEWD DY12 ....162 ...
Pleasant Md ALDR WS9 ....40 ...
Pleasant St WBROM B70 ....68 ...
Pleasant Vw SEDG DY3 ....66 ...
Pleasant Wy RLSN CV32 ....206 ...
Pleck Rd WSLW WS2 ....5 ...
Plestowes CI SHLY B90 ....126 ...
Plexfield Rd RUGBYS/DCH CV22 ..186 ...
Pleydell CI COVS CV3 ....156 ...
Plimsoll Gv RIDG/WDGT B32 ....123 ...
Plimsoll St KIDDW DY11 ....138 ...
Plomer CI RUGBYS/DCH CV22 ....186 ...
Plott La RUGBY CV23 ....183 ...
Plough & Harrow Rd
LDYWD/EDGR B16 ....106 ...
Plough Av RIDG/WDGT B32 ....123 ...
Plough Hill Rd
NUNW/HART CV10 ....79 ...
Ploughmans PI MGN/WHC B75 .....57 ...
Ploughmans Wk BRGRVE B60 ....191 ...
KGSWFD DY6 ....83 ...
LICH WS13 ....21 ...
Plover CI WOLVN WV10 ....21 ...
Ploverdale Crs KGSWFD DY6 ....83 ...
Plover Gv KIDD DY10 ....164 ...
Plowden Rd STECH B33 ....109 ...
Plowman St RUGBYN/HIL CV21 ..186 ...
Plume St VAUX/NECH B7 ....89 ...
Plumstead Rd KGSTG B44 ....71 ...
Plym CI WNSFLD WV11 ....37 ...
Plymouth CI COVE CV2 ....135 ...
NFLD/LBR B31 ....202 ...
REDW B97 ....202 ...
Plymouth Dr RBRY B45 ....169 ...
Plymouth PI RLSS CV31 ....207 ...
Plymouth Rd BVILLE B30 ....124 ...
RBRY B45 ....202 ...
REDW B97 ....202 ...
Pochard CI KIDD DY10 ....164 ...
Pocklington PI NFLD/LBR B31 * ...126 ...
Pointon CI BILS/COS WV14 ....66 ...
Poitiers Rd COVS CV3 ....155 ...
Polden CI HALE B63 ....121 ...
Polesworth Gv BKDE/SHDE B34 ...91 ...
Police Cottages
CSHL/WTROR B46 * ....92 ...
Pollard Rd ACGN B27 ....126 ...
The Pollards ERDW/GRVHL B23 ....73 ...
Polo Flds HAG/WOL DY9 ....119 ...
Polperro Dr COVW CV5 ....132 ...
Pomeroy CI TLHL/CAN CV4 ....153 ...
Pomeroy Rd GTB/HAM B43 ....69 ...
RIDG/WDGT B32 ....122 ...
Pommel CI DSYBK/YTR WS5 ....69 ...
Pond Crs BKHL/PFLD WV2 ....50 ...
Pond Gv BKHL/PFLD WV2 ....50 ...
Pond La BKHL/PFLD WV2 ....50 ...
Pondthorpe COVS CV3 ....156 ...
Ponesfield Rd LICH WS13 ....20 ...
Ponesgreen LICH WS13 ....20 ...
Pontypool Av COVS CV3 ....156 ...
Pool Av CNCK/NC WS11 ....16 ...
Pool Bank REDE B98 ....203 ...
Pool Bank St NUN CV11 ....99 ...
Pool CI RUGBYS/DCH CV22 ....186 ...
WOLVN WV10 ....21 ...
Pool Cottages KNWTH CV8 * ......181 ...
Poole Crs BILS/COS WV14 ....67 ...
BRWNH WS8 ....9 ...
HRBN B17 ....124 ...
Poolehouse Rd GTB/HAM B43 ......69 ...
Pool End CI DOR/KN B93 ....148 ...
Pooles CI COVW CV5 ....132 ...
Pooles La SHHTH WV12 ....38 ...
Poole St STRBR DY8 ....119 ...
Poole's Wy BNTWD WS7 ....19 ...
Pooley Vw POL/KGSB/FAZ B78 .....47 ...
Pool Farm Rd ACGN B27 ....127 ...
Poolfield Av SOLH B91 ....148 ...
Poolfield Rd LICH WS13 ....20 ...
Pool Furlong HAG/WOL DY9 ....141 ...
Pool Gn DARL/WED WS10 ....52 ...
Pool Hall Crs BDMR/CCFT WV3 ....48 ...
Pool Hall Rd BDMR/CCFT WV3 ....48 ...
Pool Hayes La SHHTH WV12 ....37 ...
Poolhead La HOCK/TIA B94 ....173 ...
Pool House Rd WMBN WV5 ....64 ...
Pool La OLDBY B69 ....85 ...
Pool Meadow GTWY WS6 ....24 ...
WALM/CURD B76 ....74 ...
Pool Meadow CI MOS/BIL B13 .....125 ...
SOLH B91 ....148 ...
Pool Rd BRWNH WS8 ....9 ...
HALE B63 ....103 ...
NUNW/HART CV10 ....97 ...
SMTHWK B66 ....87 ...
WNSFLD WV11 ....37 ...
Poolside Gdns COVS CV3 ....154 ...
Pool St AST/WIT B6 ....89 ...
BKHL/PFLD WV2 ....7 ...
DUDN DY1 ....84 ...
WSL WS1 ....5 ...
Pool Vw GTWY WS6 ....24 ...
RUSH/SHEL WS4 ....40 ...
Pope Rd WOLVN WV10 ....37 ...
Popes La HWK/WKHTH B38 ....145 ...
OLDBY B69 ....85 ...
Pope St CBHAMW B1 * ....6 ...
RUGBYS/DCH CV22 ....186 ...

Racecourse Rd
DUNHL/THL/PER WV6 35 L8
Racemeadow Rd ATHST CV9 63 K4
Rachael Gdns DARL/WED WS10 69 G1
Rachel Cl TPTN/OCK DY4 68 A4
Rachel Gdns SLYOAK B29 124 B3
Radbourn Dr FOAKS/STRLY B74 57 G7
Radbourne Dr HALE B63 102 E6
Radbourne Rd SHLY B90 148 B2
Radbrook Wy RLSS CV31 207 H7
Radcliffe Dr RMSLY B62 104 C7
Radcliffe Gdns RLSS CV31 * 206 E7
Radcliffe Rd COVW CV5 154 D5
Raddens Rd RMSLY B62 122 D2
Raddington Dr HIA/OLT B92 127 H5
Raddlebarn Farm Dr
SLYOAK B29 124 D4
Raddlebarn Rd SLYOAK B29 124 D4
Radford Av KIDD DY10 138 C6
Radford Cl ATHST CV9 63 J3
DSYBK/YTR WS5 69 L2
Radford Cottages RLSS CV31 * 206 F6
Radford Dr RUSH/SHEL WS4 40 A3
Radford La
ETTPK/GDPK/PENN WV4 48 D6
Radford Ri SOLH B91 128 C8
Radford Rd ALVE B48 171 G7
COVN CV6 133 L7
RLSS CV31 206 F6
SLYOAK B29 123 L6
Radley Dr NUNW/HART CV10 98 E4
Radley Gv SLYOAK B29 123 L3
Radley Rd HAG/WOL DY9 120 D1
RUSH/SHEL WS4 40 A7
The Radleys STETCH B33 110 B6
Radlow Crs
CHWD/FDBR/MGN B37 110 F5
Radmore Cl BNTWD WS7 18 B5
Radnor Cl RBRY B45 143 M3
Radnor Cft DSYBK/YTR WS5 70 A2
Radnor Dr NUNW/HART CV10 98 C3
Radnor Gn HHTH/SAND B71 69 G6
Radnor Ri HEDN WS12 16 F1
Radnor Rd BFLD/HDSWWD B20 88 F5
LGLYGN/QTN B68 104 F6
SEDG DY3 66 A5
Radnor St WSNGN B18 88 E7
Radnor Wk COVE CV2 135 K5
Radstock Av CBROM B36 91 G6
Radstock Rd SHHTH WV12 38 A4
Radway Cl REDE B98 194 F7
Radway Rd SHLY B90 148 C6
Raeburn Rd GTB/HAM B43 71 G1
Raford Rd ERDW/GRVHL B23 72 B7
Ragees Rd STRBR DY8 101 K2
Raglan Av DUNHL/THL/PER WV6 48 D2
SMTHWK B66 106 A1
Raglan Cl FOAKS/STRLY B74 55 K2
NUN CV11 99 H1
SEDG DY3 65 M6
Raglan Gv KNWTH CV8 179 M8
Raglan Rd DIG/EDG B5 107 H7
HDSW B21 88 A5
SMTHWK B66 106 A1
Raglan St BDMR/CCFT WV3 2 D5
BRLYHL DY5 102 A1
COV CV1 9 J4
Raglan Wy
CHWD/FDBR/MGN B37 111 H3
Ragley Cl BLOX/PEL WS3 38 E4
DOR/KN B93 149 M6
Ragley Crs BRGRVE B60 191 L5
Ragley Dr GTB/HAM B43 70 B3
LGN/SDN/BHAMAIR B26 110 A7
WLNHL WV13 51 K5
Ragley Wy NUN CV11 99 K3
Raglis Cl REDW B97 201 L3
Ragnall Av STETCH B33 110 B6
Raikes La LICHS WS14 27 M7
Railswood Dr BLOX/PEL WS3 39 L2
Railway Dr BILS/COS WV14 51 J8
WOLV WV1 3 H4
Railway La BNTWD WS7 18 C4
WLNHL WV13 51 L4
Railway Rd BFLD/HDSWWD B20 89 K3
SCFLD/BOLD B73 56 F8
Railwayside Cl SMTHWK B66 87 J6
Railway St BILS/COS WV14 51 J8
CNCK/NC WS11 16 C5
CNCK/NC WS11 17 L8
RRUGBY CV23 185 L1
TPTN/OCK DY4 68 A8
WBROM B70 86 F1
WOLV WV1 3 H4
Railway Ter ATHST CV9 * 63 H5
BDWTH CV12 * 117 G3
DARL/WED WS10 68 D3
PBAR/PBCH B42 * 70 D7
RUGBYN/HIL CV21 186 F1
VAUX/NECH B7 89 M6
Railwharf Sidings DUDS DY2 103 H1
Rainbow St BILS/COS WV14 67 H2
BKHL/PFLD WV2 3 G9
Rainham Cl TPTN/OCK DY4 67 H8
Rainsbrook Av
RUGBYS/DCH CV22 187 J5
Rainsbrook Dr NUN CV11 99 L4
SHLY B90 148 D7
Rainscar TAM/AM/WIL B77 46 F6
Raison Av NUN CV11 81 K5
Rake Hl BNTWD WS7 18 F5
Rake Wy EDG B15 6 B7
Raleigh Cl HDSW B21 87 M4
Raleigh Cft GTB/HAM B43 70 C2
Raleigh Rd BILS/COS WV14 67 K2
BORD B9 108 B3
COVE CV2 155 M2
Raleigh St HHTH/SAND B71 87 G1
WSLW WS2 4 A2
Ralph Crs POL/KGSB/FAZ B78 60 A7
Ralph Rd COVN CV6 133 K8
SHLY B90 148 B1
WASH/WDE B8 108 B1
Ralphs Meadow
RIDG/WDGT B32 123 H3
Ralston Cl BLOX/PEL WS3 38 E1
Ramillies Crs GTWY WS6 24 D4
Ramp Rd
CHWD/FDBR/MGN B37 111 G8
Ramsay Cl HHTH/SAND B71 69 K5
Ramsay Crs COVW CV5 132 F6
Ramsay Rd LGLYGN/QTN B68 105 G4
TPTN/OCK DY4 67 J6
WSLW WS2 38 E8
Ramsden Av NUNW/HART CV10 80 A6
Ramsden Cl SLYOAK B29 123 M6
Ramsden Ct NUNW/HART CV10 * 80 A6
Ramsden Rd ATHST CV9 63 L6
Ramsey Cl RBRY B45 143 J4
Ramsey Rd RLSS CV31 206 F7
VAUX/NECH B7 90 A6
Ranby Rd COVE CV2 9 L2
Randall Av ALVE B48 170 E7
Randall Cl KGSWFD DY6 101 K1
Randall Rd KNWTH CV8 197 K2
Randle Dr MGN/WHC B75 57 G2
Randle Rd HAG/WOL DY9 120 A1
NUNW/HART CV10 98 B1
Randle St COVN CV6 133 M8
Randolph Cl RLSS CV31 207 G7
Randwick Gv KGSTG B44 71 H4
Ranelagh Rd BKHL/PFLD WV2 50 A7
Ranelagh St RLSS CV31 206 E7
Ranelagh Ter RLSS CV31 206 D7
Range Meadow Cl RLSN CV32 206 A2
Range Wy POL/KGSB/FAZ B78 60 B8
Rangeways Rd KGSWFD DY6 101 K2
KIDDW DY11 137 L5
Rangeworthy Cl REDW B97 202 A6
Rangifer Rd POL/KGSB/FAZ B78 45 K5
Rangoon Rd HIA/OLT B92 128 C1
Rankine Cl RUGBYN/HIL CV21 160 B6
Ranleigh Av KGSWFD DY6 101 K1
Rann Cl LDYWD/EDGR B16 106 E4
Rannoch Cl BRLYHL DY5 101 M5
STRPT DY13 163 J6
Rannoch Dr NUNW/HART CV10 80 A8
Rannock Cl COVS CV3 156 D3
Ranscombe Dr SEDG DY3 84 A3
Ransome Rd
RCOVN/BALC/EX CV7 96 E5
Ransom Rd COVN CV6 134 C5
ERDW/GRVHL B23 90 A1
Ranulf Cft COVS CV3 155 G6
Ranworth Ri
ETTPK/GDPK/PENN WV4 66 B1
Raphael Cl COVW CV5 154 A2
Rashwood Cl HOCK/TIA B94 174 F7
Ratcliffe Br ATHST CV9 63 K3
Ratcliffe Cl SEDG DY3 66 D6
Ratcliffe La ATHST CV9 63 K1
Ratcliffe Rd ATHST CV9 63 K4
SOLH B91 128 A6
WNSFLD WV11 37 L7
Ratcliffe St ATHST CV9 63 H5
Ratcliff Wk OLDBY B69 * 86 D6
Ratcliff Wy TPTN/OCK DY4 68 A7
Rathbone Cl BILS/COS WV14 51 H8
DIG/EDG B5 107 J6
RCOVN/BALC/EX CV7 115 L7
RUGBYN/HIL CV21 187 L5
Rathbone Rd SMTHWKW B67 105 K3
Rathlin Cl COVEN WV9 35 L2
Rathlin Cft CBROM B36 92 F8
Rathmore Cl STRBR DY8 119 J3
Rathwell Cl COVEN WV9 35 L3
Ratliffe Rd RUGBYS/DCH CV22 186 D6
Rattle Cft STETCH B33 109 J2
Raveloe Dr NUN CV11 99 H4
Ravenall Cl BKDE/SHDE B34 91 M6
Raven Cl GTWY WS6 24 B3
HEDN WS12 12 A6
HEDN WS12 17 J1
Raven Cragg Rd COVW CV5 154 C5
Raven Crs WNSFLD WV11 37 K5
Ravenfield Cl WASH/WDE B8 90 D8
Ravenglass RUGBYN/HIL CV21 161 H6
Ravenhayes La RIDG/WDGT B32 122 E7
Raven Hays Rd NFLD/LBR B31 144 A3
Ravenhill Dr CDSL WV8 34 E2
Ravenhurst Dr GTB/HAM B43 70 C2
Ravenhurst Ms
ERDW/GRVHL B23 90 C2
Ravenhurst Rd HRBN B17 106 A6
Ravenhurst St BHTH/HG B12 7 L9
Raven Rd DSYBK/YTR WS5 53 M7
Ravens Bank Dr REDE B98 195 H6
Ravensbourne Gv WLNHL WV13 52 A3
Ravenscroft STRBR DY8 101 G7
Ravenscroft Rd HIA/OLT B92 127 L5
SHHTH WV12 37 M8
Ravensdale Av RLSN CV32 206 A3
Ravensdale Cl DSYBK/YTR WS5 5 L9
Ravensdale Gdns
DSYBK/YTR WS5 53 M7
Ravensdale Rd COVE CV2 156 A2
SMHTH B10 108 D6
Ravenshaw La SOLH B91 149 L1
Ravenshaw Rd
LDYWD/EDGR B16 106 A3
Ravenshaw Wy SOLH B91 149 L3
Ravenshill Rd
ALE/KHTH/YWD B14 147 G1
Ravensholme
DUNHL/THL/PER WV6 48 D3
Ravensholst TLHL/CAN CV4 * 154 B7
Ravensitch Wk BRLYHL DY5 102 C4
Ravensmere Rd REDE B98 202 F4
Ravensthorpe Cl COVS CV3 156 C5
Ravenstone TAM/AM/WIL B77 46 F5
Raven St STRPT DY13 188 D2
Ravenswood EDG B15 106 C5
Ravenswood Cl
FOAKS/STRLY B74 56 F5
Ravenswood Dr SOLH B91 148 C4
Ravenswood Hl
CSHL/WTROR B46 93 K6
Raven Wy NUN CV11 99 K3
Rawdon Gv KGSTG B44 71 M5
Rawlings Rd SMTHWKW B67 105 L3
Rawlins Cft CVALE B35 91 M2
Rawlinson Rd RLSN CV32 206 F3
Rawlins St LDYWD/EDGR B16 106 E4
Rawnsley Dr KNWTH CV8 180 A7
Rawnsley Rd HEDN WS12 13 J6
Rawn Vw ATHST CV9 63 K7
Raybolds Bridge Rd WSLW WS2 53 G1
Raybolds Bridge St WSLW WS2 53 G1
Raybon Cft RBRY B45 * 143 L7
Raybould's Fold DUDS DY2 85 G8
Rayford Dr HHTH/SAND B71 69 K3
Raygill TAM/AM/WIL B77 46 F5
Ray Hall La GTB/HAM B43 69 M5
Rayleigh Rd BDMR/CCFT WV3 2 A9
Raymond Av PBAR/PBCH B42 70 F7
Raymond Cl COVN CV6 116 D8
WSLW WS2 39 H8
Raymond Gdns WNSFLD WV11 37 J8
Raymond Rd WASH/WDE B8 108 C1
Raymont Gv GTB/HAM B43 70 F1
Rayners Cft
LGN/SDN/BHAMAIR B26 109 K3
Raynor Crs BDWTH CV12 116 B4
Raynor Rd WOLVN WV10 36 D7
Raynsford Wk WWCK CV34 205 H4
The Raywoods
NUNW/HART CV10 98 D2
Rea Av RBRY B45 143 J5
Reabrook Rd NFLD/LBR B31 144 D5
Rea Cl NFLD/LBR B31 144 E6
Readers Wk GTB/HAM B43 70 D4
Reading Av NUN CV11 81 K5
Reading Cl COVE CV2 134 F2
Read St COV CV1 9 K4
Rea Fordway RBRY B45 143 K4
Reansway Sq
DUNHL/THL/PER WV6 49 L1
Reapers Cl SHHTH WV12 38 B8
Reardon Ct WWCK CV34 205 J4
Reaside Crs
ALE/KHTH/YWD B14 124 F8
Reaside Cft BHTH/HG B12 * 107 J7
Reaside Dr RBRY B45 143 M5
Rea St DIG/EDG B5 7 J8
Rea St South DIG/EDG B5 7 H9
Rea Ter DIG/EDG B5 7 K6
Rea Valley Dr NFLD/LBR B31 144 F3
Reaview Dr SLYOAK B29 124 F3
Reaymer Cl WSLW WS2 38 F6
Reay Nadin Dr SCFLD/BOLD B73 71 M1
Rebecca Dr SLYOAK B29 124 C3
Rebecca Gdns
ETTPK/GDPK/PENN WV4 65 K1
Recreation Rd BRGRVW B61 191 K2
COVN CV6 134 E2
Recreation St DUDS DY2 85 H8
Rectory Av DARL/WED WS10 52 B7
Rectory Cl COVW CV5 133 G7
POL/KGSB/FAZ B78 45 J8
RCOVN/BALC/EX CV7 116 E4
STRBR DY8 119 M2
Rectory Cottages
RCOVN/BALC/EX CV7 * 96 C4
Rectory Dr
RCOVN/BALC/EX CV7 116 E4
Rectory Gdns KIDDW DY11 189 L2
SOLH B91 149 H2
STRBR DY8 119 M2
Rectory Gv WSNGN B18 88 C7
Rectory La CBROM B36 91 L5
COVW CV5 133 G7
KIDDW DY11 189 L2
STRPT DY13 188 B3
Rectory Park Av MGN/WHC B75 73 J1
Rectory Park Cl MGN/WHC B75 73 J1
Rectory Park Rd
LGN/SDN/BHAMAIR B26 110 A8
Rectory Rd MGN/WHC B75 57 G8
NFLD/LBR B31 144 F2
RCOVN/BALC/EX CV7 96 C4
REDW B97 202 A4
SOLH B91 149 G2
STRBR DY8 119 M2
Rectory St STRBR DY8 101 H2
Redacre Rd SCFLD/BOLD B73 72 D3
Redacres DUNHL/THL/PER WV6 35 J7
Redbank Av ERDW/GRVHL B23 90 A2
Redbourn Rd BLOX/PEL WS3 38 E1
Red Brick Cl CDYHTH B64 * 103 H6
Redbrook Cl HEDN WS12 17 H4
Redbrook Covert
HWK/WKHTH B38 145 J6
Red Brook Rd WSLW WS2 38 E8
Redbrooks Cl SOLH B91 148 E4
Redburn Dr
ALE/KHTH/YWD B14 146 B3
Redcap Cft COVN CV6 * 134 B1
Redcar Cl BRGRVW B61 168 E4
RLSN CV32 206 F1
Redcar Cft CBROM B36 91 G5
Redcar Rd COV CV1 155 J1
WOLVN WV10 36 B1
Redcliff TAM/AM/WIL B77 32 D8
Redcliffe Dr WMBN WV5 64 F7
Redcotts Cl WOLVN WV10 36 E6
Redcroft Dr ERDE/BCHGN B24 73 G8
Redcroft Rd DUDS DY2 85 J7
Reddal Hill Rd CDYHTH B64 103 J4
Red Deeps NUN CV11 99 H5
Reddicap Heath Rd
MGN/WHC B75 73 K1
Reddicap Hl WALM/CURD B76 73 H1
Reddicroft SCFLD/BOLD B73 57 G8
Reddings La CSHL/WTROR B46 76 E8
HLGN/YWD B28 126 C3
Reddings Rd MOS/BIL B13 125 H3
The Reddings HLYWD B47 146 E8
Redditch Ringway REDW B97 202 B2
Redditch Rd ALVE B48 170 F2
ALVE B48 170 F5
BRGRVE B60 191 H8
HWK/WKHTH B38 145 J4
STUD B80 203 H8
Redesdale Av COVN CV6 133 K8
Redfern Av KNWTH CV8 179 L7
Redfern Cl HIA/OLT B92 127 M4
Redfern Dr BNTWD WS7 18 F8
Redfern Park Wy SPARK B11 108 E8
Redfern Rd SPARK B11 108 E8
Redfly La BRLYHL DY5 84 A7
Redford Cl MOS/BIL B13 125 M3
Redgate Cl HWK/WKHTH B38 145 H3
Redgrave Cl
RCOVN/BALC/EX CV7 135 M5
Redhall Rd LGLYGN/QTN B68 105 J6
SEDG DY3 84 A3
Red Hl BEWD DY12 162 F3
REDE B98 202 D3
STRBR DY8 119 M1
Redhill Av WMBN WV5 64 E7
Redhill Cl CRTAM B79 31 L6
STRBR DY8 119 M1
Red Hill Cl STUD B80 203 J7
Red Hill Gv HWK/WKHTH B38 145 K6
Redhill La BRGRVW B61 143 G8
Red Hill Pl RMSLY B62 121 L6
Redhill Rd CNCK/NC WS11 16 D1
HWK/WKHTH B38 145 H6
NFLD/LBR B31 144 F5
YDLY B25 108 E7
Red Hill St WOLV WV1 2 F2
Red House Av DARL/WED WS10 68 F2
Redhouse Cl DOR/KN B93 149 J8
Red House La ALDR WS9 40 C8
Red House Park Rd
GTB/HAM B43 70 C3
Redhouse Rd
DUNHL/THL/PER WV6 34 F8
Red House Rd STETCH B33 109 J2
STRPT DY13 188 B5
Redhouse St WSL WS1 4 F9
Redhurst Dr WOLVN WV10 35 M2
Redlake TAM/AM/WIL B77 46 C5
Redlake Dr HAG/WOL DY9 119 M5
Redlake Rd STRBR DY8 119 M4
Redland Cl BRGRVE B60 169 G4
COVE CV2 135 H3
Redland La KNWTH CV8 182 E2
Redland Rd RLSS CV31 206 F8
Redlands Cl SOLH B91 128 B8
Redlands Rd SOLH B91 128 A8
Redlands Wy FOAKS/STRLY B74 55 L4
Red La COVN CV6 134 C8
KNWTH CV8 178 F1
KNWTH CV8 179 H5
NUNW/HART CV10 97 J6
SEDG DY3 65 M5
WNSFLD WV11 38 A3
Red Leasowes Rd HALE B63 121 K2
Redliff Av CBROM B36 92 B4
Red Lion Av CNCK/NC WS11 25 L1
Red Lion Cl OLDBY B69 85 L4
Red Lion Crs CNCK/NC WS11 25 L1
Red Lion La CNCK/NC WS11 25 L1
Red Lion St ALVE B48 170 F7
REDE B98 202 C1
WOLV WV1 2 E4
Redlock Fld LICHS WS14 20 E8
Red Lodge Dr
RUGBYS/DCH CV22 186 C5
Redmead Cl NFLD/LBR B31 145 G1
Redmoor Gdns
ETTPK/GDPK/PENN WV4 49 L8
Redmoor Rd RUGE WS15 18 D2
Redmoor Wy WALM/CURD B76 74 B7
Rednal Hill La RBRY B45 143 L7
Rednall Dr MGN/WHC B75 57 G2
Rednal Mill Dr RBRY B45 144 A6
Rednal Rd HWK/WKHTH B38 145 G5
Redpine Crest SHHTH WV12 52 B1
Red River Rd WSLW WS2 38 E8
Red Rock Dr CDSL WV8 34 D3
Redruth Cl COVN CV6 134 E5
DSYBK/YTR WS5 54 B6
KGSWFD DY6 83 H5
NUN CV11 99 K1
Redruth Rd DSYBK/YTR WS5 54 B6
Red Sands Rd KIDDW DY11 138 C5
Redstart Av KIDD DY10 164 F3
Redstone Cl REDE B98 195 G7
Redstone Dr WNSFLD WV11 37 K8
Redstone Farm Rd
HLGN/YWD B28 126 F7
Redstone La STRPT DY13 188 C5
Redthorn Gv STETCH B33 109 H2
Redvers Rd BORD B9 108 C4
Redwell Cl TAM/AM/WIL B77 32 B8
Redwing TAM/AM/WIL B77 46 E7
Redwing Cl BNTWD WS7 19 H8
Redwing Ct KIDD DY10 164 E4
Redwing Dr HEDN WS12 12 A6
Redwing Gv ERDW/GRVHL B23 71 M6
Redwood Av DUDN DY1 66 D8
Redwood Cl BVILLE B30 145 J1
FOAKS/STRLY B74 55 K3
Redwood Cft
ALE/KHTH/YWD B14 125 J6
NUNW/HART CV10 98 E3
Redwood Dr BNTWD WS7 18 D5
CNCK/NC WS11 16 D2
OLDBY B69 85 M3
POL/KGSB/FAZ B78 60 B6
Redwood Gdns ACGN B27 * 108 F8
Redwood Rd BILS/COS WV14 67 H3
BVILLE B30 145 J1
DSYBK/YTR WS5 69 M1
KINVER DY7 118 A2
Redwood Wy SHHTH WV12 37 M5
Reedham Gdns
ETTPK/GDPK/PENN WV4 49 H7
Reedly Rd SHHTH WV12 38 A4
Reedmace TAM/AM/WIL B77 46 A3
Reedmace Cl HWK/WKHTH B38 145 K5
Reedswood Cl WSLW WS2 53 G2
Reedswood Gdns WSLW WS2 53 G2
Reedswood La WSLW WS2 53 G2
Reedswood Wy WSLW WS2 52 E1
Rees Dr COVS CV3 181 G1
WMBN WV5 64 F6
Reeve Ct KIDD DY10 164 E4
Reeve Dr KNWTH CV8 197 L1
Reeve La LICH WS13 20 F5
Reeves Gdns CDSL WV8 34 E1
Reeves Rd ALE/KHTH/YWD B14 125 G7
Reeves St BLOX/PEL WS3 38 F5
Reform St HHTH/SAND B71 87 H2
Regal Cl TAM/AM/WIL B77 46 A5
Regal Cft CBROM B36 90 F5
Regal Dr WSLW WS2 4 B7
Regan Av SHLY B90 147 L4
Regan Crs ERDW/GRVHL B23 72 C7
Regan Dr OLDBY B69 86 B5
Regency Cl BORD B9 108 B4
NUNW/HART CV10 81 H7
Regency Ct COVW CV5 154 D5
Regency Dr COVS CV3 154 D8
HWK/WKHTH B38 145 J3
KNWTH CV8 197 K2
Regency Gdns
ALE/KHTH/YWD B14 147 G2
Regency Ms RLSN CV32 * 206 E5
Regency Wk FOAKS/STRLY B74 42 B8
Regent Av OLDBY B69 85 L4
Regent Cl DIG/EDG B5 107 H7
HALE B63 121 L1
KGSWFD DY6 83 G7
OLDBY B69 85 L5
Regent Ct SMTHWK B66 87 L8
Regent Dr OLDBY B69 85 L4
Regent Gv RLSN CV32 206 D5
Regent Ms BRGRVW B61 * 191 J5
Regent Pde CBHAMW B1 6 C2
Regent Park Rd SMHTH B10 108 A5
Regent Pl CBHAMW B1 6 C2
OLDBY B69 85 M3
RLSS CV31 206 E6
RUGBYN/HIL CV21 186 E1
Regent Rd
ETTPK/GDPK/PENN WV4 49 J8
HDSW B21 88 B5
HRBN B17 106 A7
OLDBY B69 85 L4
Regents Ct BKHL/PFLD WV2 * 2 F7
Regents Park Rd BRGRVE B60 192 A3
Regent St BDWTH CV12 117 G1
BILS/COS WV14 51 H7
BVILLE B30 124 E6
CBHAMW B1 6 C2
CDYHTH B64 103 K3
COV CV1 8 C7
DUDN DY1 67 G7
NUN CV11 99 H1
RLSN CV32 206 D5
RUGBYN/HIL CV21 186 E2
SMTHWK B66 87 L7
TPTN/OCK DY4 67 J5
WLNHL WV13 51 L2
Regiment Ct COVN CV6 133 L4
Regina Av KGSTG B44 71 H5
Regina Cl RBRY B45 143 J4
Regina Crs COVE CV2 135 L6
DUNHL/THL/PER WV6 48 F1
Regina Dr PBAR/PBCH B42 89 H2
RUSH/SHEL WS4 53 L1
Reginald Rd SMTHWKW B67 105 K3
WASH/WDE B8 108 B1
Regis Beeches
DUNHL/THL/PER WV6 * 35 G8
Regis Gdns BLKHTH/ROWR B65 104 A4
Regis Heath Rd
BLKHTH/ROWR B65 104 B3
Regis Rd BLKHTH/ROWR B65 104 A3
DUNHL/THL/PER WV6 34 F8
Regis Wk COVE CV2 135 K6
Reid Av SHHTH WV12 38 B7
Reid Rd LGLYGN/QTN B68 105 G4
Reigate Av WASH/WDE B8 109 G1
Reindeer Rd POL/KGSB/FAZ B78 45 J4
Relay Dr TAM/AM/WIL B77 47 G6
Relko Dr CBROM B36 91 G6
Rembrandt Cl COVW CV5 154 A2
HEDN WS12 17 H3
Remburn Gdns WWCK CV34 205 K5
Remembrance Rd COVS CV3 156 B7
DARL/WED WS10 69 G2
Remington Dr CNCK/NC WS11 16 D5
Remington Pl WSLW WS2 39 G8
Remington Rd WSLW WS2 38 F7
Rendermore Cl PENK ST19 10 C6
Rene Rd TAM/AM/WIL B77 32 C8
Renfrew Cl STRBR DY8 101 G2
Renfrew Gdns KIDDW DY11 138 A8
Renfrew Sq CVALE B35 91 M1
Renison Rd BDWTH CV12 116 C4
Rennie Gv RIDG/WDGT B32 105 H8
Rennison Dr WMBN WV5 64 E7
Renolds Cl COVW CV5
Renown Av COVW CV5
Renown Cl BRLYHL DY5
Renton Gv WOLVN WV10
Renton Rd WOLVN WV10
Repington Av ATHST CV9
Repington Rd North
TAM/AM/WIL B77
Repington Rd South
TAM/AM/WIL B77
Repington Wy MGN/WHC B75
Repton Av DUNHL/THL/PER WV6
Repton Cl CNCK/NC WS11
Repton Dr COVN CV6
Repton Gv BORD B9
Repton Rd BORD B9
Reservoir Cl WSLW WS2
Reservoir Dr CSHL/WTROR B46
Reservoir Pas DARL/WED WS10
Reservoir Pl WSLW WS2
Reservoir Retreat
LDYWD/EDGR B16
Reservoir Rd
BLKHTH/ROWR B65
ERDW/GRVHL B23
HEDN WS12
HIA/OLT B92
KIDDW DY11
LDYWD/EDGR B16
LGLYGN/QTN B68
RBRY B45
RUGBYN/HIL CV21
SLYOAK B29
Reservoir St WSLW WS2
Resolution Wy STRPT DY13
Retallack Cl SMTHWK B66
Retford Dr WALM/CURD B76
Retford Gv YDLY B25
Retreat Gdns SEDG DY3
The Retreat CDYHTH B64
Revesby Wk VAUX/NECH B7
Revival St BLOX/PEL WS3
Rex Cl TLHL/CAN CV4
Reyde Cl REDW B97
Reynard Cl REDW B97
Reynards Cl REDW B97
SEDG DY3
Reynolds Cl LICH WS13
RUGBYN/HIL CV21
SEDG DY3
Reynolds Gv
DUNHL/THL/PER WV6
Reynolds Rd BDWTH CV12
HDSW B21
Reynoldstown Rd CBROM B36
Reynolds Wk WNSFLD WV11
Rhayader Rd NFLD/LBR B31
Rhodes Cl SEDG DY3
Rhone Cl SPARK B11
Rhoose Cft CVALE B35
Rhuddlan Wy KIDDW DY11
Rhys Thomas Cl SHHTH WV12
Ribbesford Av WOLVN WV10
Ribbesford Cl HALE B63
Ribbesford Crs BILS/COS WV14
Ribbesford Dr STRPT DY13
Ribbesford Rd STRPT DY13
Ribble Cl BDWTH CV12
Ribble Rd COVS CV3
Ribblesdale TAM/AM/WIL B77
Ribblesdale Rd BVILLE B30
Ribbonfields NUN CV11
Richard Cooper Rd LICHS WS14
Richard Joy Cl COVN CV6
Richard Pl DSYBK/YTR WS5
Richard Rd DSYBK/YTR WS5
Richards Cl KNWTH CV8
NFLD/LBR B31
OLDBY B69
Richards Gv RLSS CV31
Richardson Cl WWCK CV34
Richardson Dr STRBR DY8
Richards Rd TPTN/OCK DY4
Richards St DARL/WED WS10
Richard St VAUX/NECH B7
WBROM B70
Richard St South WBROM B70
Richard St West WBROM B70
Richard Williams Rd
DARL/WED WS10
Richborough Dr DUDN DY1
Rich Cl WWCK CV34
Riches St DUNHL/THL/PER WV6
Richford Gv STETCH B33
Richmond Aston Dr
TPTN/OCK DY4
Richmond Av BDMR/CCFT WV3
BHTH/HG B12 *
Richmond Cl
BFLD/HDSWWD B20
CNCK/NC WS11
CRTAM B79
Richmond Cft PBAR/PBCH B42
Richmond Dr BDMR/CCFT WV3
DUNHL/THL/PER WV6
LICHS WS14
Richmond Gdns WMBN WV5
Richmond Gv STRBR DY8
Richmond Hl LGLYGN/QTN B68
Richmond Hill Gdns EDG B15
Richmond Hill Rd EDG B15
Richmond Pk KGSWFD DY6
Richmond Pl
ALE/KHTH/YWD B14
Richmond Rd ATHST CV9
BDMR/CCFT WV3
BEWD DY12
DUDS DY2
HIA/OLT B92
HLYWD B47
NUN CV11
RBRY B45
RUGBYN/HIL CV21
SCFLD/BOLD B73
SEDG DY3
SMTHWK B66
WSNGN B18
YDLY B25
Richmond St COVE CV2
HALE B63
WBROM B70
WSL WS1
Richmond St South WBROM B70
Richmond Wy
CHWD/FDBR/MGN B37
Rickard Cl DOR/KN B93
Rickets Cl STRPT DY13
Ricketts Pl BEWD DY12
Rickman Dr EDG B15
Rickyard Cl POL/KGSB/FAZ B78
SLYOAK B29
YDLY B25
Rickyard La REDE B98
Rickyard Piece RIDG/WDGT B32
Riddfield Rd CBROM B36
Ridding Gdns POL/KGSB/FAZ B7
Ridding La DARL/WED WS10
Riddings Cl BEWD DY12
Riddings Crs BLOX/PEL WS3

Riddings Hl
RCOVN/BALC/EX CV7 .....152 A5
Riddings La ATHST CV9 .....62 A3
COVW CV5 .....154 B6
HAG/WOL DY9 .....120 B3
STETCH B33 .....109 J1
TAM/AM/WIL B77 .....32 C8
WOLVN WV10 .....36 E6
Ridgacre La RIDG/WDGT B32 .....105 G8
RIDG/WDGT B32 .....104 F7
Ridgacre Rd West
RIDG/WDGT B32 .....104 E7
MOS/BIL B13 .....126 A7
WSLW WS2 .....52 B2
Ridge Ct COVW CV5 .....132 E7
Ridge Dr RUGBYN/HIL CV21 .....187 L4
Ridgefield Rd RMSLY B62 .....104 A5
Ridge La HAG/WOL DY9 .....102 A8
Ridge La NUNW/HART CV10 .....78 D3
WNSFLD WV11 .....37 H6
Ridgemount Dr
WK/WKHTH B38 .....145 H6
Ridge Rd KGSWFD DY6 .....83 C8
Ridge St STRBR DY8 .....101 C7
Ridgethorpe COVS CV3 .....156 C8
Ridgewater Cl RBRY B45 .....143 M7
Ridge Wy ALDR WS9 .....54 F1
Ridgeway HRBN B17 .....105 M3
DY3 .....66 B6
Ridgeway Av COVS CV3 .....155 C7
RMSLY B62 .....104 C7
Ridgeway Ct WSLW WS2 .....52 D4
Ridgeway Dr
ETTPK/GDPK/PENN WV4 .....65 K2
Ridgeway Rd STRBR DY8 .....101 K3
TPTN/OCK WV4 .....67 L5
The Ridgeway BNTWD WS7 .....18 B3
ERDW/GRVHL B23 .....71 L7
STRPT DY13 .....163 K8
WWCK CV34 .....205 H3
Ridgewood Av STRBR DY8 .....101 C7
Ridgewood Dr MGN/WHC B75 .....56 F4
Ridgewood Gdns KGSTG B44 .....71 K6
Ridgewood Ri TAM/AM/WIL B77 .....32 E8
Ridgley Rd TLHL/CAN CV4 .....153 J5
Ridgmont Cft RIDG/WDGT B32 .....105 J4
Ridgl Cl HHTH/SAND B71 .....69 H4
Ridings Brook Dr CNCK/NC WS11 .....16 E3
Ridings La REDE B98 .....194 F6
Ridings Pk CNCK/NC WS11 .....16 E3
Ridley La CSHL/WTROR B46 .....76 E8
Ridley St DIG/EDG B5 .....
Ridleys Cross STRPT DY13 .....188 C7
WNSFL WV11 .....
Ridleywood Dr MGN/WHC B75 .....57 H8
Ridley TAM/AM/WIL B77 .....46 C2
Ridge Crs BDMR/CCFT WV3 .....
Rifle Dr CBROM B36 .....92 E4
Riley Rd ALD/KHTH/YWD B14 .....147 H2
Riley St WLNHL WV13 .....51 M3
Rilstone Rd RIDG/WDGT B32 .....105 K8
Rindleford Av
ETTPK/GDPK/PENN WV4 .....49 C7
Ringhills Rd CDSL WV8 .....34 F3
Ringinglow Rd KGSTG B44 .....71 C3
Ringmere Av CBROM B36 .....91 M5
Ring BNTWD WS7 .....18 B6
Ring Road St Andrews WOLV WV1 .....2 D5
Ring Road St Davids WOLV WV1 .....3 H4
Ring Road St Georges
BKHL/PFLD WV3 .....3 C7
Ring Road St Johns
BKHL/PFLD WV3 .....2 E7
Ring Road St Marks
BDMR/CCFT WV3 .....2 D6
Ring Road St Patricks WOLV WV1 .....3 C3
Ring Road St Peters WOLV WV1 .....3 G3
Ringswood Rd ERDW/GRVHL B23 .....127 J1
Ring YDLY B25 .....109 G5
Ringway CNCK/NC WS11 .....16 C4
Ringway Hill Cross COV CV1 .....8 E5
Ringway Queens COV CV1 .....8 E5
Ringway Rudge COV CV1 .....9 C5
Ringway St Johns COV CV1 .....9 C6
Ringway St Nicholas COV CV1 .....8 F7
Ringway St Patricks COV CV1 .....8 F7
Ringway Swansewell COV CV1 .....9 C2
Ringway Ringway KIDD DY10 .....138 C2
Ringway Whitefriars COV CV1 .....9 H3
Ringwood Av ALDR WS9 .....40 F8
Ringwood Dr RBRY B45 .....143 J4
Ringwood Hwy COVE CV2 .....135 J3
Ringwood Rd WOLVN WV10 .....36 B4
Ripley Gv ERDW/GRVHL B23 .....71 M8
Ripon Cl COVS CV3 .....155 C5
Ripon Dr HHTH/SAND B71 .....69 H4
Ripon drive TAM/AM/WIL B77 .....45 J8
Ripon field Gv TAM/AM/WIL B77 .....32 B8
Risborough Cft TLHL/CAN CV4 .....180 B2
Rischale Lee Rd SPARK B11 .....108 C4
Risdale Gdns
JNHL/THL/PER WV6 .....34 F8
Rising La HOCK/TIA B94 .....176 C8
Risington Av SLYOAK B29 .....124 C5
Ritchie Cl MOS/BIL B13 .....125 L4
Cft COV CV1 .....8 C4
Rd ATHST CV9 .....63 H5

RLSS CV31 * 206 C5
Riverside Cl BRGRVE B60 .....169 C7
COVS CV3 .....169 L5
Riverside Ct WK/WKHTH B38 .....145 H2
Riverside Crs HLGN/YWD B28 .....147 H1
Riverside Dr SOLH B91 .....149 J3
STETCH B33 .....109 H1
Riverside North BEWD DY12 .....162 F1
Riversleigh Dr STRBR DY8 .....101 J3
Riversley Rd NUN CV11 .....99 G2
River St DIG/EDG B5 .....7 L6
Riverway DARL/WED WS10 .....68 F3
Riverway Dr BEWD DY12 .....162 F1
Rivington Cl STRBR DY8 .....119 J1
Rivington Crs KGSTG B44 .....72 A6
Roach TAM/AM/WIL B77 .....46 B7
Roach Cl BRLYHL DY5 .....84 B8
CHWD/FDBR/MGN B37 .....111 G2
Roach Crs WNSFLD WV11 * 37 K5
Road Eastwood DUDS DY2 .....85 J7
Road No 1 KIDDW DY11 .....164 C3
Road No 2 KIDDW DY11 .....164 C3
Road No 3 KIDDW DY11 .....164 C3
Roanne Ringway NUN CV11 .....98 F7
Robbins Ct RUGBYN/HIL CV21 .....187 K5
Robert Av ERDW/GRVHL B23 .....72 C7
CRTAM B79 .....31 K6
Robert Cl COVS CV3 .....182 A1
Robert Cramb Av
TLHL/CAN CV4 .....153 K5
Robert Hill Cl RUGBYN/HIL CV21 .....187 L4
Robert Rd BFLD/HDSWWD B20 .....88 F4
RCOVN/BALC/EX CV7 .....116 D5
TPTN/OCK DY4 .....67 K7
Roberts Cl ALDR WS9 .....40 F7
RRUGBY CV23 .....183 K7
Roberts Green Rd SEDG DY3 .....84 C1
Roberts La HAG/WOL DY9 .....119 M5
Robertson Cl RRUGBY CV23 .....161 L8
Robertson Knoll CBROM B36 .....91 K6
Robertsons Gdns VAUX/NECH B7 .....90 A6
Roberts Rd ACGN B27 .....127 G2
BLOX/PEL WS3 .....39 K8
DARL/WED WS10 .....69 J3
Robert St SEDG DY3 .....84 C1
Robert Wynd BILS/COS WV14 .....66 D4
Robeson Cl TPTN/OCK DY4 .....67 M4
Robey's La POL/KGSB/FAZ B78 .....33 H4
POL/KGSB/FAZ B78 .....47 H3
Robin Cl CBROM B36 .....92 E5
HEDN WS12 .....12 A1
KGSWFD DY6 .....83 L7
Robin Ct KIDD DY10 .....164 F5
Robin Gv WNSFLD WV11 .....37 L8
Robin Hood Crs HLGN/YWD B28 .....126 D8
Robin Hood Cft HLGN/YWD B28 .....126 D8
Robin Hood La HLGN/YWD B28 .....126 C8
Robin Hood Rd BRLYHL DY5 .....102 D3
COVS CV3 .....156 B7
Robinia TAM/AM/WIL B77 .....46 E1
Robinia Cl RLSN CV32 .....206 F3
Robin Rd ERDW/GRVHL B23 .....90 C1
Robins Cl GTWY WS6 .....24 B3
STRBR DY8 .....119 L2
Robinsfield Dr NFLD/LBR B31 .....144 E6
Robins Hill Dr ALVE B48 .....170 B4
Robinson Cl CRTAM B79 .....31 J6
Robinson Rd BDWTH CV12 .....116 B5
BNTWD WS7 .....18 B7
Robinson's Wy WALM/CURD B76 .....74 B8
Robins Rd BNTWD WS7 .....18 B7
Robins Wy NUNW/HART CV10 .....98 F2
Robotham Cl RUGBYN/HIL CV21 .....160 D7
Robottom Cl WSLW WS2 .....38 F7
Rocester Av WNSFLD WV11 .....37 L3
Rochdale Wy SMHTH B10 .....108 A6
Rocheberie Wy
RUGBYS/DCH CV22 .....186 D5
Roche Rd BLOX/PEL WS3 .....38 D4
Rochester Av BNTWD WS7 .....18 E8
Rochester Cl NUNW/HART CV10 .....98 F2
REDW B97 .....202 A5
Rochester Cft WSLW WS2 .....4 C7
NFLD/LBR B31 .....144 E1
Rochester Wy HEDN WS12 .....17 L5
The Roche BNTWD WS7 .....19 L5
Roche Wy BLOX/PEL WS3 .....38 D4
Rochford Cl HALE B63 .....121 K3
RBRY B45 .....143 K4
WALM/CURD B76 .....73 L5
WSLW WS2 .....4 A8
Rochford Ct SHLY B90 .....148 E7
Rochford Gv
ETTPK/GDPK/PENN WV4 .....49 H8
Rock Av RBRY B45 .....144 A6
Rock Cl COVN CV6 .....134 F4
NUNW/HART CV10 .....97 K1
Rocken End COVN CV6 .....134 E4
Rocket Pool Dr BILS/COS WV14 * 66 F3
Rockford Cl REDE B98 .....202 F2
Rockford Rd PBAR/PBCH B42 .....70 E6
Rock HI BRGRVE B60 .....191 H6
LICHS WS14 .....21 H6
Rockingham Cl BLOX/PEL WS3 * 38 F4
DOR/KN B93 .....175 H3
SEDG DY3 .....83 M2
Rockingham Dr
DUNHL/THL/PER WV6 .....48 D2
NUN CV11 .....99 K6
Rockingham Gdns
FOAKS/STRLY B74 .....56 F7
Rockingham Hall Gdns
HAG/WOL DY9 .....120 B8
Rockingham Rd YDLY B25 .....109 H5
Rockland Dr STETCH B33 .....109 J1
Rocklands Crs LICH WS13 .....21 H5
Rocklands Dr MGN/WHC B75 .....56 F5
Rockley Gv RBRY B45 .....143 M6
Rockley Rd BLKHTH/ROWR B65 .....87 L7
Rockmead Av KGSTG B44 .....71 K3
Rock Mill La RLSN CV32 .....206 A4
Rockmoor Cl STETCH B33 .....110 C2
Rockrose Gdns WOLVN WV10 .....22 E6
Rock St SEDG DY3 .....66 C8
The Rock DUNHL/THL/PER WV6 .....35 H8
Rockville Rd WASH/WDE B8 .....108 C1
Rockwell La ALVE B48 .....194 C1
Rockwood Rd ACGN B27 .....126 F1
Rocky La AST/WIT B6 .....89 L7
BRGRVW B60 .....168 C5
KNWTH CV8 .....198 B3
PBAR/PBCH B42 .....70 D7
Rodbaston Dr PENK ST19 * .....
Rodborough Rd DOR/KN B93 .....175 J3
LGN/SDN/BHAMAIR B26 .....109 M7
Rodbourne Rd HRBN B17 .....124 A2
Roddis Cl ERDW/GRVHL B23 .....72 C7
Roden Av LICH WS13 .....21 G4
Roderick Dr WNSFLD WV11 .....37 H1
Roderick Rd SPARK B11 .....108 A1
Rodhouse Cl TLHL/CAN CV4 .....153 L6

Rodman Cl EDG B15 .....106 B5
Rodney Cl HIA/OLT B92 * 127 M4
LDYWD/EDGR B16 .....106 C3
RUGBYS/DCH CV22 .....186 A4
Rodney Rd HIA/OLT B92 .....127 M4
Rodway Cl BRLYHL DY5 .....102 B6
ETTPK/GDPK/PENN WV4 .....66 D2
LOZ/NWT B19 .....89 H6
Rodway Dr COVW CV5 .....153 H1
Rodyard Wy COV CV1 .....9 H8
Roebuck Cl BKDE/SHDE B34 .....110 C1
Roebuck Gld SHHTH WV12 .....52 C1
Roebuck La WBROM B70 .....87 J4
Roebuck Pl BLOX/PEL WS3 .....39 J7
Roebuck St WBROM B70 .....87 K4
Roe Cl WWCK CV34 .....205 K5
Roedean Cl KGSTG B44 .....71 M6
Rogerfield Rd ERDW/GRVHL B23 .....72 E7
Rogers Cl WNSFLD WV11 .....37 L4
Rogers Rd WASH/WDE B8 .....90 F4
Rokeby Cl WALM/CURD B76 .....73 J1
Rokeby Rd GTB/HAM B43 .....70 D3
Rokeby St RUGBYN/HIL CV21 .....187 G2
Rokewood Cl KGSWFD DY6 .....83 H4
Rokholt Crs CNCK/NC WS11 .....16 A4
Roland Av COVN CV6 .....133 M2
Roland Gdns LOZ/NWT B19 .....89 G5
Roland Mt COVN CV6 .....134 A2
Rolan Dr SHLY B90 .....147 J5
Roland Ter LOZ/NWT B19 .....89 G5
Rolfe St SMTHWK B66 .....87 L7
Rollason Cl COVN CV6 .....134 A5
Rollason Rd COVN CV6 .....133 M5
DUDS DY2 .....85 H5
ERDW/GRVHL B24 .....90 E2
Rollasons Yd COVN CV6 * 134 E2
Rollesby Dr WLNHL WV13 .....51 K5
Rolling Mill Cl DIG/EDG B5 * 107 J6
Rollingmill St WSLW WS2 .....4 B5
Rollswood Dr SOLH B91 .....148 D1
Roman Cl BRWNH WS8 .....26 C5
Roman Ct TAM/AM/WIL B77 .....46 C1
Roman La FOAKS/STRLY B74 .....55 M2
Roman Pk FOAKS/STRLY B74 .....55 M2
Roman Rd COVE CV2 .....155 M2
FOAKS/STRLY B74 .....42 A8
Roman Rd (Sandy La)
COVE CV2 .....119 G1
Roman Vw CNCK/NC WS11 .....16 D8
Roman Wy BLKHTH/ROWR B65 .....104 A2
BRGRVE B60 .....191 M1
COVS CV3 .....181 H2
CRTAM B79 .....31 M1
CSHL/WTROR B46 .....93 J3
EDG B15 .....124 B2
LICHS WS14 .....21 H6
POL/KGSB/FAZ B78 .....47 L7
RUGBYN/HIL CV21 .....160 E6
Romany Wy STRBR DY8 .....119 G2
Roma Rd SPARK B11 .....108 C8
Romford Cl
LGN/SDN/BHAMAIR B26 .....109 M7
Romford Rd COVN CV6 .....133 M3
Romilly Av BFLD/HDSWWD B20 .....88 F3
Romilly Cl STRBR DY8 .....101 J7
WALM/CURD B76 .....73 L1
Romney TAM/AM/WIL B77 .....46 D1
Romney Cl HLGN/YWD B28 .....126 D6
Romsey Av NUNW/HART CV10 .....81 H5
Romsey Gv WOLVN WV10 .....36 A2
Romsey Wy BLOX/PEL WS3 .....38 D2
Romsley Cl RBRY B45 .....143 J5
REDE B98 .....203 K2
RMSLY B62 .....121 M3
RUSH/SHEL WS4 .....40 A3
Romsley Rd COVN CV6 .....134 A7
HAG/WOL DY9 .....102 A8
LGLYGN/QTN B68 .....85 G6
RIDG/WDGT B32 .....122 F5
Romulus Cl BFLD/HDSWWD B20 .....88 F2
Ronald Gv CBROM B36 .....92 B4
Ronald Pl BORD B9 .....108 D3
Ronald Rd BORD B9 .....108 B3
Ron Davis Cl SMTHWK B66 * 87 M8
Ro-oak Rd COVN CV6 .....133 K8
Rood End Rd LGLYGN/QTN B68 .....87 G1
Rooker Av WOLV WV2 .....50 C7
Rookery Av BRLYHL DY5 .....101 L3
ETTPK/GDPK/PENN WV4 .....66 C4
Rookery Cl REDW B97 .....202 B4
Rookery La BKHL/PFLD WV2 .....49 L7
COVN CV6 .....133 M2
POL/KGSB/FAZ B78 .....44 A3
Rookery Pk BRLYHL DY5 .....84 A8
Rookery Ri WMBN WV5 .....64 F7
Rookery Rd
ETTPK/GDPK/PENN WV4 .....66 C4
HDSW B21 .....88 C4
SLYOAK B29 .....124 D3
WMBN WV5 .....64 F7
Rookery St WNSFLD WV11 .....37 G3
The Rookery NUNW/HART CV10 .....78 D3
NUNW/HART CV10 .....79 J8
RIDG/WDGT B32 .....122 E3
Rooks Meadow HAG/WOL DY9 .....119 M7
Rooks Nest RRUGBY CV23 .....158 C2
Rookwood Dr
DUNHL/THL/PER WV6 .....48 D4
Roosevelt Dr TLHL/CAN CV4 .....153 J5
Rooth St DARL/WED WS10 .....68 F1
Roper Cl RUGBYN/HIL CV21 .....187 L5
Roper Wy SEDG DY3 .....66 B7
Rosafield Av RMSLY B62 .....104 D7
Rosalind Av DUDN DY1 .....67 G7
Rosalind Gv WNSFLD WV11 .....37 L8
Rosamond St WSL WS1 .....4 C8
Rosary Rd ERDW/GRVHL B23 .....90 B3
Rosary Vls SPARK B11 * 108 A3
Rosaville Crs COVW CV5 .....152 E7
Rose Av ALVE B48 .....170 E8
COVN CV6 .....133 M6
KGSWFD DY6 .....83 K8
Rose Bank FOAKS/STRLY B74 .....55 L5
Rose Bank Dr BLOX/PEL WS3 * 53 J1
Rosebay Av WK/WKHTH B38 .....145 K5
Rose Bay Meadow
CNCK/NC WS11 .....17 G3
Roseberry Av COVE CV2 .....134 F4
Roseberry Gdns KIDD DY10 .....139 G2
Roseberry Rd SMTHWK B66 .....87 M1
TAM/AM/WIL B77 .....60 A1
Rosebery St BDMR/CCFT WV3 .....2 C7
WSNGN B18 .....106 C1
Rose Cottages
RUGBYN/HIL CV21 * 186 C5
SLYOAK B29 .....124 D3
Rose Cft KNWTH CV8 .....179 J7

Rosecroft Rd
LGN/SDN/BHAMAIR B26 .....110 A7
Rosedale Av ERDW/GRVHL B23 .....90 C2
SMTHWK B66 .....88 A8
Rosedale Cl YDLY B25 .....109 G5
Rose Dene STRPT DY13 .....188 C7
Rosedene Dr
BFLD/HDSWWD B20 .....88 D3
Rose Dr BRWNH WS8 .....26 C8
Rosefield Cft AST/WIT B6 .....89 K6
Rosefield Pl RLSN CV32 .....206 B5
Rosefield Rd SMTHWKW B67 .....105 L1
Rosefield St RLSN CV32 .....206 B5
Rosegreen Cl COVS CV3 .....155 J7
Rosehall Cl SOLH B91 .....148 D4
Rose HI ATHST CV9 .....63 H3
BRLYHL DY5 .....85 K8
RBRY B45 .....169 L1
WLNHL WV13 .....51 L5
Rosehill HEDN WS12 .....12 D5
Rose Hill Gdns WLNHL WV13 .....51 L4
Rose Hill Rd HDSW B21 .....88 E6
Rosehip Cl DSYBK/YTR WS5 .....69 L2
Roseship Dr COVE CV2 .....134 F7
Roseland Av DUDS DY2 .....85 K4
Roseland Rd KNWTH CV8 .....197 K6
Roselands Av COVE CV2 .....135 H5
Rose La BNTWD WS7 .....19 G6
NUN CV11 .....99 G2
Roseleigh Rd RBRY B45 .....143 M7
Rosemary Av BILS/COS WV14 .....51 K7
ETTPK/GDPK/PENN WV4 .....50 A8
GTWY WS6 .....24 B2
Rosemary Crs DUDN DY1 .....66 D7
ETTPK/GDPK/PENN WV4 .....50 A8
Rosemary Crs West
ETTPK/GDPK/PENN WV4 .....49 M8
Rosemary Dr FOAKS/STRLY B74 .....56 A2
HEDN WS12 .....12 D8
Rosemary HI KNWTH CV8 .....179 K8
Rosemary Hill Rd
FOAKS/STRLY B74 .....56 A3
Rosemary La STRBR DY8 .....119 H2
Rosemary Nook
FOAKS/STRLY B74 .....42 B8
Rosemary Rd GTWY WS6 .....24 B2
HALE B63 .....121 H3
KIDD DY10 .....138 F2
STETCH B33 .....109 K3
TAM/AM/WIL B77 .....46 C1
TPTN/OCK WV4 .....67 L8
Rosemoor Dr BRLYHL DY5 .....101 M4
Rosemullion Cl COVE CV2 .....135 J2
Rosemullion Cl
RCOVN/BALC/EX CV7 .....116 F5
Rosenhurst Dr BEWD DY12 .....162 E2
Rose Rd CSHL/WTROR B46 .....93 K5
HRBN B17 .....105 K7
Rose St BILS/COS WV14 .....67 K3
Rosetti Cl KIDD DY10 .....139 G7
Rose Vls YDLY DY5 .....108 E6
Roseville Gdns CDSL WV8 .....34 D1
Roseville Prec BILS/COS WV14 * 67 G5
Rosewood NUN CV11 .....99 K4
Rosewood Cl TAM/AM/WIL B77 .....46 B1
Rosewood Ct TAM/AM/WIL B77 .....46 B1
Rosewood Crs RLSN CV32 .....206 F3
Rosewood Dr ERDW/GRVHL B23 .....90 B3
SHHTH WV12 .....37 M5
Rosewood Gdns WNSFLD WV11 .....37 M2
Rosewood Pk GTWY WS6 .....24 B2
Rosewood Rd DUDN DY1 .....66 F8
Roshven Rd BHTH/HG B12 .....125 L1
Roslin Cl BRGRVE B60 .....191 M4
Roslin Gv LOZ/NWT B19 .....89 G6
Roslyn Cl SMTHWK B66 .....87 L7
Ross BLKHTH/ROWR B65 .....103 M3
Ross Cl BDMR/CCFT WV3 .....49 J3
COVW CV5 .....132 E8
Ross Dr KGSWFD DY6 .....83 G6
Rosse Ct HIA/OLT B92 .....128 C3
Rossendale Cl HALE B63 .....103 H7
Rossendale Wy
NUNW/HART CV10 .....98 B3
Ross Hts BLKHTH/ROWR B65 .....103 M2
Rosslyn Av COVN CV6 .....133 J7
Rosslyn Rd WALM/CURD B76 .....73 K7
Ross Rd BLOX/PEL WS3 .....39 K7
Ross Wy NUN CV11 .....99 M6
Rostrevor Rd WASH/WDE B8 .....108 D4
Rosy Cross CRTAM B79 .....31 M8
Rothay TAM/AM/WIL B77 .....46 D5
Rothbury Gn HEDN WS12 .....17 J3
Rotherby Gv
CHWD/FDBR/MGN B37 .....110 F6
Rotherfield Cl RLSS CV31 .....206 C8
Rotherfield Rd
LGN/SDN/BHAMAIR B26 .....109 M5
Rotherham Rd COVN CV6 .....133 M4
Rotherhams HI ATHST CV9 .....62 A3
Rotherhams Oak La
HOCK/TIA B94 .....174 D7
Rothesay Av TLHL/CAN CV4 .....153 M4
Rothesay Cl NUNW/HART CV10 .....98 E3
Rothesay Cft RIDG/WDGT B32 .....122 F6
Rothesay Dr STRBR DY8 .....101 G2
Rothesay Wy SHHTH WV12 .....37 M7
Rothley Dr RUGBYS/DCH CV22 .....161 J6
Rothwell Dr SHLY B90 .....127 H8
Rothwell Rd WWCK CV34 .....205 G4
Rotten Rw LICH WS13 .....21 G5
Rotton Park Rd
LDYWD/EDGR B16 .....106 C3
Rotton Park St
LDYWD/EDGR B16 .....106 C3
Rough Hay Pl DARL/WED WS10 .....52 A6
Rough Hay Rd DARL/WED WS10 .....52 A6
Rough Hill Dr
BLKHTH/ROWR B65 .....85 K7
REDE B98 .....202 C8
Rough Hills Rd BKHL/PFLD WV2 .....50 D7
Roughknowles Rd
TLHL/CAN CV4 .....153 H7
Roughlea Av CBROM B36 .....91 K6
Roughley Dr MGN/WHC B75 .....57 G3
Roughley Farm Rd
MGN/WHC B75 .....57 J2
Rough Rd KGSTG B44 .....71 L2
The Rough REDW B97 .....202 B5
Round Cl HIA/OLT B92 .....128 B2
The Roundabout
NFLD/LBR B31 .....144 B4
Round Av RRUGBY CV23 .....159 L8
Round Cl SHLY B90 .....147 K7
Round HI SEDG DY3 .....66 C5
Round Hill Av HAG/WOL DY9 .....120 A4
Roundhill Cl WALM/CURD B76 .....73 J1
Roundhills Rd RMSLY B62 .....104 D3
Roundhill Ter RMSLY B62 .....104 C4
Roundhill Wy BRWNH WS8 .....26 E3
Round House Rd COVS CV3 .....155 H5
SEDG DY3 .....84 C1
Roundlea Cl SHHTH WV12 .....37 M6
Roundlea Rd NFLD/LBR B31 .....123 G8
Round Rd ERDE/BCHGN B24 .....90 F3
Round Saw Cft RBRY B45 .....143 K5
Rounds Gdns
RUGBYN/HIL CV21 .....186 D2
Rounds Green Rd OLDBY B69 .....86 C6
Rounds HI KNWTH CV8 .....197 J8
Rounds Hill Rd BILS/COS WV14 .....67 H5
Round St DUDS DY2 .....67 G4
Roundway Down
DUNHL/THL/PER WV6 .....48 C2
Rounton Cl FOAKS/STRLY B74 .....56 B1
Rousay Cl RBRY B45 .....143 K4
Rousdon Gv GTB/HAM B43 .....70 B2
Rover Dr ACGN B27 .....127 H1
CBROM B36 .....92 A2
Rover Cl COV CV1 * 8 C7
Rowallan Rd MGN/WHC B75 .....57 H3
Rowanberry Cl STRPT DY13 .....188 C7
Rowan Cl BRGRVW B61 .....191 J5
COVS CV3 .....157 M6
HLYWD B47 .....146 F8
LICH WS13 .....21 H5
POL/KGSB/FAZ B78 .....60 B7
WALM/CURD B76 .....73 K3
Rowan Cl BVILLE B30 .....145 L3
Rowan Crs BDMR/CCFT WV3 .....49 J6
BILS/COS WV14 .....66 F4
REDW B97 .....201 L1
Rowan Dr HLGN/YWD B28 .....126 E6
RUGBYS/DCH CV22 .....185 M3
WNSFLD WV11 .....37 M2
WWCK CV34 .....205 M4
Rowan Gdns POL/KGSB/FAZ B78 .....47 M8
COVE CV2 .....135 J3
Rowan Gv BNTWD WS7 .....18 D7
Rowan Ri KGSWFD DY6 .....83 J7
Rowan Rd CNCK/NC WS11 .....16 A3
CSCFLD/WYGN B72 .....73 G3
DSYBK/YTR WS5 .....69 K1
NUNW/HART CV10 .....80 A7
REDW B97 .....201 L1
SEDG DY3 .....66 D4
The Rowans BDWTH CV12 .....116 C3
Rowantrees RBRY B45 .....143 M8
Rowan Wy
CHWD/FDBR/MGN B37 .....111 G4
NFLD/LBR B31 .....144 D4
Roway La OLDBY B69 .....86 C4
Rowborough Cl
RWWCK/WEL CV35 .....204 C3
Rowbrook Cl SHLY B90 .....147 J5
Rowchester Ct CBHAMNE B4 * 7 J3
Rowcroft Covert
ALE/KHTH/YWD B14 .....146 A2
Rowcroft Rd COVE CV2 .....135 K7
Rowdale Rd PBAR/PBCH B42 .....71 G6
Rowden Dr ERDW/GRVHL B23 .....72 E7
SOLH B91 .....148 C3
Rowena Gdns SEDG DY3 .....66 C4
Rowheath Rd BVILLE B30 .....145 K1
Rowington Av
BLKHTH/ROWR B65 .....104 B2
Rowington Cl COVW CV5 .....133 H7
Rowington Rd BKDE/SHDE B34 .....92 C7
Rowington Ter YDLY B25 * 108 F6
Rowland Av RCOVN/BALC/EX CV7 .....96 E4
Rowland Ct RCOVN/BALC/EX CV7 .....96 E4
Rowland Gdns WSLW WS2 .....4 A3
Rowland Hill Av KIDDW DY11 .....137 M8
Rowland Hill Dr TPTN/OCK DY4 * 86 A1
Rowlands Av WOLV WV1 .....51 J2
WSLW WS2 .....52 C2
Rowlands Crs SOLH B91 .....127 M5
Rowlands Rd
LGN/SDN/BHAMAIR B26 .....109 J4
Rowland St RUGBYN/HIL CV21 .....186 D2
WSLW WS2 .....4 A1
Rowland Wy KIDDW DY11 .....164 C4
Rowley Cl COVS CV3 .....181 M1
Rowley Cl STETCH B33 .....110 B2
Rowley Hall Av
BLKHTH/ROWR B65 .....104 B2
Rowley Hill Vw CDYHTH B64 .....103 K5
Rowley La COVS CV3 .....181 M2
Rowley PUSH/SHEL WS4 .....39 M6
Rowley Rd KNWTH CV8 .....181 K2
Rowley's Green La COVN CV6 .....134 C1
Rowley Rw WSL WS1 .....5 H3
Rowley Vw BILS/COS WV14 .....67 L2
WBROM B70 .....86 F2
Rowley Village
BLKHTH/ROWR B65 .....104 A2
Rowney Cft HLGN/YWD B28 .....147 J1
Rowney Green La ALVE B48 .....194 B2
Rowood Dr HIA/OLT B92 .....128 A6
Rowse Cl RUGBYN/HIL CV21 .....186 B3
The Row KNWTH CV8 .....181 K5
Rowthorn Cl FOAKS/STRLY B74 .....55 L6
Rowthorn Dr SHLY B90 .....148 E7
Rowton Av
DUNHL/THL/PER WV6 .....48 C2
Rowton Dr FOAKS/STRLY B74 .....55 K8
Roxall Cl KIDD DY10 .....140 F4
Roxburgh Cft RLSN CV32 .....198 F8
Roxburgh Gv GTB/HAM B43 .....71 G1
Roxburgh Rd NUN CV11 .....99 J4
CSCFLD/BOLD B73 .....72 E2
Roxby Gdns
DUNHL/THL/PER WV6 .....35 L8
Royal Cl BLKHTH/ROWR B65 .....86 A8
BRLYHL DY5 .....102 A5
Royal Ct RUGBYN/HIL CV21 * 186 D2
Royal Crs COVS CV3 .....156 A8
Royal Mail St CBHAMW B1 .....6 C4
Royal Meadow Dr ATHST CV9 .....63 J3
Royal Oak La
RCOVN/BALC/EX CV7 .....116 A6
Royal Oak Rd
BLKHTH/ROWR B65 .....85 K7
RMSLY B62 .....122 D1
Royal Oak Yd BDWTH CV12 * 116 C3
Royal Priors RLSN CV32 * 206 D4
Royal Rd MGN/WHC B75 .....57 G8
Royal Scot Gv WSL WS1 .....53 H5
Royal Star Cl STETCH B33 .....110 A3
Royal Worcester Crs
BRGRVE B60 .....192 A4
Roydon Rd ACGN B27 .....127 G5
Royston Cl COVS CV3 .....156 E2
Royston Cha FOAKS/STRLY B74 .....55 L2
Royston Cft BHTH/HG B12 .....107 K7
Royston Wy SEDG DY3 .....66 B5
Rozel Av KIDD DY10 .....138 F4
Rubens Cl COVW CV5 .....154 A2
SEDG DY3 .....66 D4
Rubery Farm Gv RBRY B45 .....143 K5
Rubery Field Cl RBRY B45 .....143 L4
Rubery La RBRY B45 .....143 K4

Rubery La South *RBRY* B45 143 K5
Rubery St *DARL/WED* WS10 52 B5
Ruckley Av *LOZ/NWT* B19 * 89 G6
Ruckley Rd *SLYOAK* B29 123 L5
Rudd Gdns *WOLV* WV1 50 F1
Ruddington Wy *LOZ/NWT* B19 89 J8
Rudgard Rd *COVN* CV6 134 E1
Rudge Av *WOLV* WV1 50 F2
Rudge Cl *SHHTH* WV12 52 A1
Rudge Cft *STETCH* B33 109 L1
Rudge Wk *WSNGN* B18 * 106 E2
Rudgewick Cft *AST/WIT* B6 89 K7
Rudyard Cl *WOLVN* WV10 36 C1
Rudyard Gv *STETCH* B33 109 M2
Rudyngfield Dr *STETCH* B33 109 K2
Rufford *CRTAM* B79 31 J7
Rufford Cl *ERDW/GRVHL* B23 72 B5
Rufford Rd *HAG/WOL* DY9 120 A1
Rufford St *HAG/WOL* DY9 102 B7
Rufford Wy *ALDR* WS9 40 C6
Rugby La *RRUGBY* CV23 183 L7
Rugby Rd *BTACH/HAR* CV33 199 K7
COVS CV3 157 G5
RLSN CV32 206 B5
RRUGBY CV23 158 D2
RRUGBY CV23 158 F8
RRUGBY CV23 159 K2
RRUGBY CV23 159 M3
RRUGBY CV23 185 G1
RRUGBY CV23 185 M1
STRBR DY8 101 H6
Rugby St *WOLV* WV1 2 C2
Rugeley Av *SHHTH* WV12 38 B5
Rugeley Cl *TPTN/OCK* DY4 67 J8
Rugeley Rd *BNTWD* WS7 18 D5
BNTWD WS7 19 G3
HEDN WS12 13 G7
Ruislip Cl *CVALE* B35 91 L1
Ruiton St *SEDG* DY3 84 B1
Rumbow *HALE* B63 121 M1
Rumbow La *RMSLY* B62 142 B1
Rumbush La *HOCK/TIA* B94 173 H4
Rumer Hill Rd *CNCK/NC* WS11 16 C6
Runcorn Cl
CHWD/FDBR/MGN B37 111 G1
REDE B98 202 D5
Runcorn Rd *BHTH/HG* B12 107 K8
Runneymede Gdns
NUNW/HART CV10 98 D2
Runnymede Dr
RCOVN/BALC/EX CV7 152 A8
Runnymede Rd *SPARK* B11 126 C2
Rupert Brooke Rd
RUGBYS/DCH CV22 186 C6
Rupert Rd *COVN* CV6 133 M5
Rupert St *BDMR/CCFT* WV3 2 A4
VAUX/NECH B7 89 L8
Rushall Cl *RUSH/SHEL* WS4 53 M1
STRBR DY8 101 J5
Rushall Manor Cl
RUSH/SHEL WS4 53 M1
Rushall Manor Rd
RUSH/SHEL WS4 53 M1
Rushall Rd *WOLVN* WV10 36 C3
Rushbrook Cl *BRWNH* WS8 26 C7
HIA/OLT B92 127 J3
Rushbrooke Cl *MOS/BIL* B13 125 K1
Rushbrooke Dr *SCFLD/BOLD* B73 72 A1
Rushbrook Gv
ALE/KHTH/YWD B14 146 A2
Rushbury Cl *BILS/COS* WV14 50 F8
SHLY B90 148 B1
Rushden Cft *KGSTG* B44 71 K4
Rushes Ml *BLOX/PEL* WS3 39 J2
Rushey La *SPARK* B11 108 E8
Rushford Av *WMBN* WV5 64 E7
Rushford Cl *SHLY* B90 148 E6
Rush Gn *RIDG/WDGT* B32 123 J3
Rush La *REDE* B98 194 F7
TAM/AM/WIL B77 60 B2
Rushleigh Rd *SHLY* B90 147 J5
Rushmead Gv *RBRY* B45 143 L6
Rushmere Rd *TPTN/OCK* DY4 67 L5
Rushmoor Cl *FOAKS/STRLY* B74 56 F7
Rushmoor Dr *COVW* CV5 8 A4
Rushmore St *RLSS* CV31 206 F6
Rushmore Ter *RLSS* CV31 206 F7
Rushock Cl *REDE* B98 203 G7
Rushton Cl
RCOVN/BALC/EX CV7 152 A6
Rushwater Cl *WMBN* WV5 64 C7
Rushwick Gv *SHLY* B90 148 E7
Rushwood Cl *RUSH/SHEL* WS4 53 L2
Rushy Piece *RIDG/WDGT* B32 123 H2
Rusina Ct *RLSS* CV31 * 206 D7
Ruskin Av *BLKHTH/ROWR* B65 104 B3
ETTPK/GDPK/PENN WV4 66 D3
KIDD DY10 139 G7
SEDG DY3 65 L8
Ruskin Cl *AST/WIT* B6 89 K6
COVN CV6 133 H7
NUNW/HART CV10 79 L8
RUGBYS/DCH CV22 186 D7
Ruskin Gv *ACGN* B27 126 F3
Ruskin Hall Gv *AST/WIT* B6 89 K6
Ruskin Rd *WOLVN* WV10 36 D5
Ruskin St *HHTH/SAND* B71 69 G8
Russel Cft *BRGRVE* B60 191 L6
Russell Bank Rd
FOAKS/STRLY B74 56 C1
Russell Cl *OLDBY* B69 86 B3
TPTN/OCK DY4 68 A4
WNSFLD WV11 37 K4
Russell Rd *BILS/COS* WV14 51 K6
HLGN/YWD B28 126 C3
KIDD DY10 164 D1
MOS/BIL B13 125 H2
Russell's Hall Rd *DUDN* DY1 84 C4
The Russells *MOS/BIL* B13 125 H2
Russell St *BDMR/CCFT* WV3 2 D7
COV CV1 9 G2
DARL/WED WS10 68 D3
DUDN DY1 84 F4
RLSN CV32 206 D4
WLNHL WV13 51 M3
Russell St North *COV* CV1 * 9 G1
Russell Ter *RLSS* CV31 206 E6
Russelsheim Wy
RUGBYS/DCH CV22 186 E3
Russet Gv *TLHL/CAN* CV4 * 180 B2
Russett Cl *BNTWD* WS7 18 E7
DSYBK/YTR WS5 54 B5
Russett Wy *BEWD* DY12 162 D1
BRLYHL DY5 83 L6
Russet Wy *NFLD/LBR* B31 123 J7
Ruston St *LDYWD/EDGR* B16 106 E4
Ruthall Cl *SLYOAK* B29 124 A6
Ruth Cl *DARL/WED* WS10 68 A3
Rutherford Gln *NUN* CV11 99 K4
Rutherford Rd *BRGRVE* B60 191 M7
ERDW/GRVHL B23 72 C6
WSLW WS2 38 E7
Rutherglen Av *COVS* CV3 155 L7
Rutland Av
ETTPK/GDPK/PENN WV4 65 H1
NUNW/HART CV10 98 D1
Rutland Crs *ALDR* WS9 40 F4
BILS/COS WV14 51 H6
Rutland Cft *COVS* CV3 156 D5
Rutland Dr *BRGRVE* B60 191 L5
LGN/SDN/BHAMAIR B26 109 J6
POL/KGSB/FAZ B78 45 L4
Rutland Pl *STRBR* DY8 101 H5
Rutland Rd *DARL/WED* WS10 69 G1
HEDN WS12 17 J4
HHTH/SAND B71 69 G6
SMTHWK B66 105 L4
Rutland St *BLOX/PEL* WS3 39 J8
Rutland Ter *WSNGN* B18 * 88 E8
Rutley Gv *RIDG/WDGT* B32 123 K1
Rutters Meadow
RIDG/WDGT B32 122 F1
Rutter St *WSL* WS1 4 E8
Ryan Av *WNSFLD* WV11 37 L6
Ryan Pl *DUDS* DY2 85 G7
Rycroft Gv *STETCH* B33 110 A3
Rydal *TAM/AM/WIL* B77 46 E6
Rydal Av *NUN* CV11 81 L7
Rydal Cl *COVW* CV5 132 F5
FOAKS/STRLY B74 55 K3
HEDN WS12 12 E5
RUGBYN/HIL CV21 161 H7
STRPT DY13 163 K7
WNSFLD WV11 37 G6
Rydal Dr *DUNHL/THL/PER* WV6 48 D1
Rydding La *HHTH/SAND* B71 69 G5
Rydding Sq *HHTH/SAND* B71 68 F5
Ryde Av *NUNW/HART* CV10 81 H7
Ryde Gv *ACGN* B27 126 E4
Ryde Park Rd *RBRY* B45 144 A7
Ryder Cl *RWWCK/WEL* CV35 204 D7
Ryder Rw *RCOVN/BALC/EX* CV7 96 E5
Ryders Green Rd *WBROM* B70 86 D1
Ryders Hayes La *BLOX/PEL* WS3 39 L1
Ryders Hill Crs
NUNW/HART CV10 80 A6
Ryder St *CBHAMNE* B4 * 7 H3
STRBR DY8 101 H3
WBROM B70 68 D8
Ryebank Cl *BVILLE* B30 124 A8
Ryeclose Cft
CHWD/FDBR/MGN B37 111 H2
Rye Cft *ACGN* B27 109 G8
HAG/WOL DY9 120 C3
HLYWD B47 146 E8
Ryecroft Av
ETTPK/GDPK/PENN WV4 49 M8
Ryecroft Cl *SEDG* DY3 66 A5
Ryecroft Dr *BNTWD* WS7 18 E5
Ryecroft Pk *WSLW* WS2 53 J2
Ryecroft Pl *BLOX/PEL* WS3 39 K7
Ryecroft St *WSLW* WS2 53 J2
Ryefield *CDSL* WV8 35 J4
Ryefield Cl *HAG/WOL* DY9 140 E1
SOLH B91 127 J8
Ryefield La *WALM/CURD* B76 74 F4
Ryegrass La *REDW* B97 202 A7
Rye Grass Wk *CVALE* B35 91 M2
Rye Gv *SPARK* B11 126 D1
Rye Hl *COVW* CV5 132 E7
The Ryelands *RRUGBY* CV23 185 G6
Rye Meadow *KNWTH* CV8 179 J3
Rye Piece Ringway
BDWTH CV12 116 F2
Ryhope Cl *BDWTH* CV12 116 A4
Ryknild Cl *FOAKS/STRLY* B74 42 C7
Ryknild St *LICHS* WS14 21 J7
Ryland Cl *HALE* B63 121 J3
RLSS CV31 206 F7
TPTN/OCK DY4 67 M8
Ryland Rd *EDG* B15 107 G6
ERDE/BCHGN B24 90 D4
SPARK B11 126 B1
Rylands Dr
ETTPK/GDPK/PENN WV4 65 L1
Ryland St *LDYWD/EDGR* B16 6 A7
Ryle St *BLOX/PEL* WS3 39 H3
Rylston Av *COVN* CV6 133 L4
Rylstone Wy *WWCK* CV34 * 205 J4
Rymond Rd *BKDE/SHDE* B34 91 J7
Ryton *TAM/AM/WIL* B77 46 D5
Ryton Br *KNWTH* CV8 182 B2
Ryton Cl *REDE* B98 203 H4
SCFLD/BOLD B73 56 F8
TLHL/CAN CV4 153 M5
WNSFLD WV11 36 E8
Ryton Gv *BKDE/SHDE* B34 92 B6
Ryvere Cl *STRPT* DY13 188 D3

S

Sabell Rd *SMTHWKW* B67 87 K7
Sabrina Dr *BEWD* DY12 162 E1
Sabrina Rd
DUNHL/THL/PER WV6 48 C4
Saddington Rd *COVS* CV3 156 C5
Saddlers Cl *HALE* B63 102 F8
LICHS WS14 21 J5
Saddlers Ms *SOLH* B91 149 G4
The Saddlestones
DUNHL/THL/PER WV6 48 B1
Saddleworth Rd *GTWY* WS6 38 E1
Sadler Gdns *BDWTH* CV12 117 G3
Sadler Rd *BRWNH* WS8 26 E5
COVN CV6 133 L4
MGN/WHC B75 57 K6
Sadlers Ct *WSLW* WS2 52 F6
Sadlers Ml *BRWNH* WS8 * 26 E6
Sadlers Wk *LDYWD/EDGR* B16 106 E4
Sadlerswell La *HOCK/TIA* B94 174 F7
Saffron *TAM/AM/WIL* B77 46 F1
Saffron Cl *RRUGBY* CV23 161 J5
Saffron Gdns
ETTPK/GDPK/PENN WV4 65 L1
Sage Cft *NFLD/LBR* B31 123 K8
St Agatha's Rd *COVE* CV2 155 L2
WASH/WDE B8 90 F8
St Agnes Cl *MOS/BIL* B13 125 M3
St Agnes La *COV* CV1 * 8 F3
St Agnes Rd *MOS/BIL* B13 125 M3
St Agnes Wy *NUN* CV11 99 K1
St Aidan's Rd *CNCK/NC* WS11 16 C1
St Aidans Wk *SMHTH* B10 * 108 A5
St Alban's Av *KIDDW* DY11 137 L6
St Albans Cl *RLSN* CV32 206 A3
SMTHWKW B67 * 87 J7
WNSFLD WV11 37 L5
St Albans Rd *MOS/BIL* B13 125 L1
SMTHWKW B67 87 J7
St Alphege Cl *SOLH* B91 * 149 G2
St Ambrose Cl *RMSLY* B62 104 A5
St Andrew Cl *HEDN* WS12 13 L8
St Andrews *TAM/AM/WIL* B77 46 F1
St Andrews Av *BLOX/PEL* WS3 25 L8
St Andrews Cl *HRBN* B17 123 L2
SEDG DY3 83 L2
STRBR DY8 119 K3
St Andrews Crs
RUGBYS/DCH CV22 186 E5
St Andrews Dr
DUNHL/THL/PER WV6 34 B8
NUN CV11 99 M4
OLDBY B69 85 M6
St Andrew's Rd *BORD* B9 107 M3
COVW CV5 154 D5
MGN/WHC B75 57 G6
RLSN CV32 198 F8
St Andrew's St *BORD* B9 107 M3
DUDS DY2 85 G8
St Andrews Wy
BRGRVW B61 191 H5
St Annes Cl *BFLD/HDSWWD* B20 88 D1
BNTWD WS7 26 C1
St Anne's Ct *MOS/BIL* B13 125 J1
St Annes Gv *DOR/KN* B93 149 L7
St Anne's Rd *CDYHTH* B64 103 G4
LICH WS13 20 F2
RUGBYS/DCH CV22 186 C4
WLNHL WV13 51 M2
WOLVN WV10 35 M4
St Annes Wy *KGSTG* B44 71 L6
St Ann's Rd *COVE* CV2 155 L2
St Anthonys Dr *BLOX/PEL* WS3 25 M8
St Athan Cft *CVALE* B35 91 M2
St Augustine's Rd
LDYWD/EDGR B16 106 B4
St Augustine's Wk *COVN* CV6 133 L6
St Augustus Cl *HHTH/SAND* B71 87 K2
St Austell Cl *CRTAM* B79 31 L7
NUN CV11 81 L8
St Austell Rd *COVE* CV2 156 C2
DSYBK/YTR WS5 54 B6
St Bartholemews Cl *COVS* CV3 156 E3
St Bartholomew's Rd
STRPT DY13 188 C3
St Bartholomew Ter
DARL/WED WS10 68 D2
St Benedicts Cl *ATHST* CV9 63 H5
WBROM B70 87 K3
St Benedict's Rd *BNTWD* WS7 18 F7
SMHTH B10 108 D5
WMBN WV5 64 E6
St Bernards Cl *HEDN* WS12 18 A1
St Bernards Rd
CSCFLD/WYGN B72 73 G3
SOLH B91 127 H8
St Bernards Wk *COVS* CV3 156 B7
St Blaise Av *CSHL/WTROR* B46 92 F3
St Blaise Rd *MGN/WHC* B75 57 H2
St Brades Cl *OLDBY* B69 86 A6
St Brides Cl *SEDG* DY3 66 A5
WMBN WV5 64 D7
Saintbury Dr *SOLH* B91 149 G6
St Caroline Cl *WBROM* B70 87 K2
St Catharines Cl *WSL* WS1 5 J9
St Catherine's Cl *COVS* CV3 155 M5
DUDS DY2 * 85 L4
MGN/WHC B75 57 K6
St Catherine's Crs
ETTPK/GDPK/PENN WV4 65 K1
St Catherine's Rd *BRGRVE* B60 169 K7
LICH WS13 20 F2
St Cecilia Cl *KIDD* DY10 164 C3
St Chad's Circus Queensway
CBHAMNW B3 6 F3
St Chad's Cl *CNCK/NC* WS11 16 E1
SEDG DY3 83 M2
St Chads Queensway
CBHAMNE B4 7 G2
St Chad's Rd *BILS/COS* WV14 51 K6
LICH WS13 20 F4
MGN/WHC B75 57 J8
RBRY B45 143 K6
WOLVN WV10 36 D5
St Christian's Cft *COVS* CV3 9 H9
St Christian's Rd *COVS* CV3 155 J5
St Christopher Cl *HEDN* WS12 13 L8
WBROM B70 87 J3
St Christophers
BFLD/HDSWWD B20 88 D1
St Christopher's Cl *WWCK* CV34 205 H5
St Christopher's Dr
TAM/AM/WIL B77 46 A4
St Clement's Av *BLOX/PEL* WS3 39 G6
St Clement's La *HHTH/SAND* B71 87 H1
St Clements Rd *VAUX/NECH* B7 90 A7
St Columba's Cl *COV* CV1 8 E2
St Columbas Dr *RBRY* B45 144 B6
St Cuthbert's Cl *WBROM* B70 87 K3
St David Cl *HEDN* WS12 13 L7
St Davids Cl *BLOX/PEL* WS3 25 M8
STRPT DY13 163 J7
WBROM B70 87 K3
St Davids Dr *RIDG/WDGT* B32 104 F8
St Davids Gv *BFLD/HDSWWD* B20 88 D1
St Davids Orch *COVS* CV3 156 D6
St Davids Pl *BLOX/PEL* WS3 39 H3
St Davids Wy *NUNW/HART* CV10 98 E7
St Denis Rd *SLYOAK* B29 123 L7
St Dominic's Rd
ERDE/BCHGN B24 90 C4
St Edburghs Rd *STETCH* B33 109 J4
St Editha's Cl *CRTAM* B79 31 M8
St Edithas Rd *POL/KGSB/FAZ* B78 47 L5
St Ediths Gn *WWCK* CV34 * 205 M5
St Edmonds Rd *ATHST* CV9 61 G8
St Edmund's Cl
DUNHL/THL/PER WV6 * 49 K2
WBROM B70 87 K3
St Edward's Rd *SLYOAK* B29 124 D3
Sainte Foy Av *LICH* WS13 20 E8
St Eleanor Cl *WBROM* B70 87 K2
St Elizabeth's Rd *COVN* CV6 134 C6
St Francis Av *SOLH* B91 127 J7
St Francis Cl *BLOX/PEL* WS3 25 M8
HEDN WS12 13 L8
St Fremund Wy *RLSS* CV31 207 G8
St George Dr *HEDN* WS12 13 L8
SMTHWK B66 * 87 L6
St Georges Av *ERDW/GRVHL* B23 72 E8
RUGBYS/DCH CV22 186 D5
St Georges Cl *EDG* B15 106 E6
MGN/WHC B75 57 K7
St Georges Ct *FOAKS/STRLY* B74 42 C8
St Georges Ml *KIDD* DY10 * 138 C7
St Georges Pde *BKHL/PFLD* WV2 3 G6
St Georges Pl *WBROM* B70 87 G1
St George's Rd *ATHST* CV9 63 H3
COV CV1 9 M7
DUDS DY2 85 H7
REDE B98 202 D1
RLSS CV31 206 D7
SHLY B90 148 B5
STRBR DY8 119 H3
St George's St *DARL/WED* WS10 52 B6
LOZ/NWT B19 6 E1
St George's Ter *KIDD* DY10 138 D7
St Georges Wy
NUNW/HART CV10 98 F5
TAM/AM/WIL B77 46 C1
St Gerards Rd *SOLH* B91 148 C3
St Giles Av *BLKHTH/ROWR* B65 103 M1
St Giles Cl *BLKHTH/ROWR* B65 103 M1
St Giles Crs *WOLV* WV1 50 E3
St Giles Rd *BNTWD* WS7 18 F7
RCOVN/BALC/EX CV7 116 B7
STETCH B33 110 B3
WLNHL WV13 51 M4
WOLV WV1 50 E3
St Giles Rw *STRBR* DY8 * 101 L7
St Giles St *DUDS* DY2 85 G8
St Godwald's Crs *BRGRVE* B60 191 M5
St Godwald's Rd *BRGRVE* B60 191 M6
St Helens Av *TPTN/OCK* DY4 68 A8
St Helens Rd *LICH* WS13 20 F2
RLSS CV31 206 D8
SOLH B91 127 L7
St Helen's Wy *COVW* CV5 132 F5
St Heliers Rd *NFLD/LBR* B31 144 C1
St Ives Cl *CRTAM* B79 31 M7
St Ives Rd *COVE* CV2 156 B2
DSYBK/YTR WS5 54 B6
St Ives Wy *NUN* CV11 99 K1
St James Av *BLKHTH/ROWR* B65 103 L1
St James Cl *BLOX/PEL* WS3 * 25 M8
WBROM B70 87 K3
St James' La *COVS* CV3 156 B7
St James Meadow Rd
RLSN CV32 206 A4
St James Pk *WOLVN* WV10 * 22 D4
St James Pl *SHLY* B90 147 M3
VAUX/NECH B7 7 M3
St James Rd *CNCK/NC* WS11 16 A5
CNCK/NC WS11 17 M8
EDG B15 6 A9
HDSW B21 88 B5
MGN/WHC B75 57 G3
OLDBY B69 86 B5
St James's Rd *DUDN* DY1 84 F3
St James's Ter *DUDN* DY1 84 E3
St James St *DARL/WED* WS10 68 C3
SEDG DY3 84 B2
WOLV WV1 3 J6
St James Wk *BRWNH* WS8 26 D6
St John Cl *MGN/WHC* B75 57 H1
St Johns *WWCK* CV34 205 K6
St Johns Av *BLKHTH/ROWR* B65 103 M1
KIDDW DY11 137 L7
KNWTH CV8 197 L2
RUGBYS/DCH CV22 187 J5
St John's Cl *ALDR* WS9 40 D2
CNCK/NC WS11 16 B5
DOR/KN B93 149 M7
LICH WS13 * 20 F7
NUNW/HART CV10 79 J5
SEDG DY3 82 B3
WBROM B70 87 K3
St John's Ct *HEDN* WS12 17 J4
LICHS WS14 * 20 F6
NFLD/LBR B31 144 F4
St John's Dr *LICHS* WS14 28 D8
St Johns Gv
CHWD/FDBR/MGN B37 110 D2
St John's Hl *LICHS* WS14 28 D8
St John's La *RRUGBY* CV23 159 L8
St Johns Rd *BLOX/PEL* WS3 25 M8
BRWNH WS8 26 E8
CNCK/NC WS11 16 B5
DARL/WED WS10 52 A8
DUDS DY2 85 H5
HALE B63 121 J1
HRBN B17 106 B7
LGLYGN/QTN B68 87 G8
RLSS CV31 206 E7
SPARK B11 108 A8
STRBR DY8 101 L7
STRPT DY13 163 L8
TPTN/OCK DY4 67 K6
WNSFLD WV11 37 L2
WSLW WS2 52 F5
St John's Sq *BKHL/PFLD* WV2 2 F7
St Johns St *COV* CV1 9 G6
DUDS DY2 85 G8
KIDDW DY11 138 A7
KNWTH CV8 197 K2
St Johns Ter *RLSS* CV31 * 206 E7
St John St *BRGRVW* B61 191 K3
CRTAM B79 31 M8
RUGBYN/HIL CV21 186 E1
St Johns Wk *PBAR/PBCH* B42 89 H1
St Johns Wd *RBRY* B45 143 M8
St Josephs Av *NFLD/LBR* B31 123 M8
St Josephs Cl *BLOX/PEL* WS3 39 L1
St Josephs Rd *WASH/WDE* B8 90 F8
St Joseph St *DUDS* DY2 85 H4
St Judes Cl *ALE/KHTH/YWD* B14 146 D3
MGN/WHC B75 57 K7
St Jude's Crs *COVS* CV3 156 B6
St Jude's Pas *DIG/EDG* B5 * 6 F7
St Jude's Rd
DUNHL/THL/PER WV6 49 K2
St Jude's Rd West
DUNHL/THL/PER WV6 49 K2
St Katherine's Rd
LGLYGN/QTN B68 105 G3
St Kenelms Av *HALE* B63 121 H4
St Kenelm's Cl *WBROM* B70 87 K3
St Kenelm's Rd *RMSLY* B62 121 H8
St Kilda's Rd *WASH/WDE* B8 * 90 C8
St Laurence Av *WWCK* CV34 205 H8
St Laurence Cl *ALVE* B48 170 F7
St Laurence Rd *NFLD/LBR* B31 123 L8
St Lawrence Cl *DOR/KN* B93 149 M8
St Lawrence Dr *CNCK/NC* WS11 16 F3
St Lawrence Rd
NUNW/HART CV10 96 F1
NUNW/HART CV10 97 G1
St Lawrence's Rd *COVN* CV6 134 D4
St Lawrence Wy
DARL/WED WS10 52 B7
St Leonards Cl
CHWD/FDBR/MGN B37 110 E6
St Leonards Vw
POL/KGSB/FAZ B78 47 L5
St Leonard's Wk *KNWTH* CV8 182 E4
St Loye's Cl *RMSLY* B62 104 B6
St Lukes Cl *BLKHTH/ROWR* B65 103 M1
CNCK/NC WS11 16 A5
St Luke's Rd *BNTWD* WS7 19 G7
COVN CV6 134 B3
Saint Luke's Rd *DARL/WED* WS10 68 F2
St Luke's Rd *DIG/EDG* B5 107 J6
St Lukes St *CDYHTH* B64 103 H4
St Lukes Wy *NUNW/HART* CV10 98 A2
St Margaret Rd *COV* CV1 9 L6
St Margaret's *FOAKS/STRLY* B74 56 A2
St Margarets Av *WASH/WDE* B8 90 F7
St Margarets Dr *HALE* B63 121 K3
St Margarets Rd *BLOX/PEL* WS3 39 L1
CRTAM B79 31 M6
GTB/HAM B43 70 D3
HIA/OLT B92 127 J4
LICH WS13 20 F2
RLSS CV31 206 E8
WASH/WDE B8 90 E7
St Mark's Av *RUGBYS/DCH* CV22 186 A6
St Marks Cl *NUNW/HART* CV10 98 A1
St Marks Crs *CBHAMW* B1 106 E2
St Mark's Ms *RLSN* CV32 206 C4
St Mark's Rd *BDMR/CCFT* WV3 2 C6
BLOX/PEL WS3 39 L1
BNTWD WS7 19 G7
BRWNH WS8 26 E8
DUDS DY2 85 K4
HAG/WOL DY9 102 B8
RLSN CV32 206 B4
SMTHWKW B67 105 H2
TPTN/OCK DY4 67 L5
St Mark's St *BDMR/CCFT* WV3 2 D6
CBHAMW B1 6 A3
St Martin's Cl *BKHL/PFLD* WV2 50 C7
WBROM B70 8
St Martin's Dr *TPTN/OCK* DY4 6
St Martin's Rd *COVS* CV3 18
MGN/WHC B75 5
St Martin's St *EDG* B15
St Martin's Ter *BILS/COS* WV14 6
St Marys Cl *ACGN* B27 12
BILS/COS WV14 6
ERDE/BCHGN B24 9
WOLVN WV10 2
WWCK CV34 20
St Marys Ct *WLNHL* WV13 * 5
St Mary's Crs *RLSS* CV31 20
St Mary's La *STRBR* DY8 11
St Marys Ringway *KIDDW* DY11 13
St Mary's Rd *ATHST* CV9 6
DARL/WED WS10 6
HRBN B17 10
LICH WS13 2
NUN CV11 8
RCOVN/BALC/EX CV7 11
RLSS CV31 20
St Mary's Rw *CBHAMNE* B4
MOS/BIL B13 12
St Mary's Ter *RLSS* CV31 20
St Mary St *COV* CV1
St Mary's Wy *ALDR* WS9 4
TAM/AM/WIL B77 4
St Matthew Cl *HEDN* WS12 1
St Matthew's Av *BNTWD* WS7 1
St Matthews Cl *BLOX/PEL* WS3 * 2
WSL WS1
St Matthew's Rd *BNTWD* WS7 1
LGLYGN/QTN B68 10
SMTHWK B66 8
St Matthew St *WOLV* WV1
St Mawes Rd
DUNHL/THL/PER WV6 4
St Mawgen Cl *CVALE* B35 9
St Michael Rd *LICH* WS13 2
St Michael's Cl *ATHST* CV9 6
ATHST CV9 6
BLOX/PEL WS3 3
PENK ST19 1
RCOVN/BALC/EX CV7 9
STRPT DY13 18
St Michael's Ct
DUNHL/THL/PER WV6 3
St Michael's Crs *OLDBY* B69 10
St Michaels Dr *HEDN* WS12 1
St Michael's Gv *DUDS* DY2 8
St Michael's Rd *COVE* CV2 15
PENK ST19 1
SCFLD/BOLD B73 7
SEDG DY3 6
WSNGN B18 8
WWCK CV34 20
St Michael's Sq *PENK* ST19 1
St Michael St *WBROM* B70 8
WSL WS1
St Michael's Wy
NUNW/HART CV10 9
TPTN/OCK DY4 8
St Modwena Wy *PENK* ST19 1
St Nicholas Av *KNWTH* CV8 19
St Nicholas Church St
WWCK CV34 20
St Nicholas Cl *BLOX/PEL* WS3 3
St Nicholas Ct *WWCK* CV34 * 20
St Nicholas St *COV* CV1
St Nicolas Gdns
HWK/WKHTH B38 14
St Nicolas Park Dr *NUN* CV11 8
St Nicolas Rd *NUN* CV11 8
St Osburg's Rd *COVE* CV2 15
St Oswalds Cl *KIDD* DY10 13
St Oswalds Rd *SMHTH* B10 10
St Patrick Cl *HEDN* WS12 1
St Patricks Cl
ALE/KHTH/YWD B14 12
St Paul's Av *BHTH/HG* B12 10
KIDDW DY11 13
St Paul's Cl *CNCK/NC* WS11 1
COVEN WV9 2
WWCK CV34 * 20
St Paul's Ct *TAM/AM/WIL* B77 * 6
St Pauls Crs *BLOX/PEL* WS3 2
CSHL/WTROR B46 9
WBROM B70 6
St Pauls Dr *RMSLY* B62 10
TPTN/OCK DY4 8
St Paul's Rd *BHTH/HG* B12 10
BNTWD WS7 1
COVN CV6 13
DARL/WED WS10 5
DUDS DY2 8
HEDN WS12 1
NUNW/HART CV10 9
SMTHWK B66 8
St Paul's Sq *CBHAMNW* B3
St Paul's St *WSL* WS1
St Pauls Ter *WWCK* CV34 * 20
St Peter's Av *ATHST* CV9 6
St Peter's Cl *ALDR* WS9 4
ATHST CV9 6
CSCFLD/WYGN B72 7
CSHL/WTROR B46 9
HLGN/YWD B28 12
REDW B97 20
TAM/AM/WIL B77 4
TPTN/OCK DY4 8
St Peters Ct *BLOX/PEL* WS3 3
COV CV1 *
St Peters Cft *SCFLD/BOLD* B73 * 7
St Peters Dr *BLOX/PEL* WS3 3
NUNW/HART CV10 9
St Peters La *HIA/OLT* B92 12
St Peters Rd *ATHST* CV9 6
BFLD/HDSWWD B20 8
BNTWD WS7 1
DUDS DY2 8
HAG/WOL DY9 12
HEDN WS12 1
HRBN B17 10
RUGBYN/HIL CV21 18
St Peters Sq *WOLV* WV1
St Peters Ter *WSLW* WS2 5
St Philips Av *BDMR/CCFT* WV3 4
St Philips Pl *CBHAMNW* B3
St Phillips Av *BDMR/CCFT* WV3 4
St Phillip's Gv *BDMR/CCFT* WV3 4
St Quentin St *WSLW* WS2
St Saviour's Cl *BKHL/PFLD* WV2 5
St Saviour's Rd *WASH/WDE* B8 10
St Silas' Sq *LOZ/NWT* B19 8
St Simons Cl *MGN/WHC* B75 5
St Stephen's Av *WLNHL* WV13 5
St Stephens Ct *HEDN* WS12 * 1
St Stephens Gdns *REDE* B98 19
WLNHL WV13 *
St Stephen's Rd *BNTWD* WS7 1
HHTH/SAND B71
SLYOAK B29 1
St Stephens St *AST/WIT* B6
Saints Wy *NUNW/HART* CV10
St Thomas' Cl *ALDR* WS9
BLOX/PEL WS3
MGN/WHC B75
St Thomas Ct *COV* CV1 *

homas Dr HEDN WS12 ...13 L8
homas Cl COVN CV6 ...134 D2
 RDW/GRVHL B23 ...90 B3
homas Ct NUNW/HART CV10..98 A2
homas's Ct COVN CV1 ...8 E3
homas St DUDS DY2 ...85 G8
incent Cr WBROM B70 ...68 D7
incent Crs WBROM B70 ...87 K3
incent St LDYWD/EDGR B16...6 E3
incent St West
 DYWD/EDGR B16 ...106 E3
ilfreds Cottages
 *COVN/BALC/EX CV7 * ...96 C3
adin Av OLDBY B69 ...86 C8
combe Av
 MOS/BIL B13 * ...125 K1
sbury Cl DUDN DY1 ...84 D2
 NWTH CV8 ...183 K2
 OVS CV3 ...156 B7
sbury Dr BRLYHL DY5 ...102 A5
combe Dr BRLYHL DY5 ...102 A5
combe Cl CNCK/NC WV14 ...5 H4
combe Rd SMTHWK B66 ...87 M8
be St TPTN/OCK DY4 ...68 B8
EDE B98 ...202 F7
ford St AST/WIT B6 ...90 A5
sbury Av COVS CV3 ...155 C7
sbury Chambers
 MOS/BIL B13 * ...125 K1
sbury Cl DUDN DY1 ...84 D2
 NWTH CV8 ...183 K2
 OVS CV3 ...156 B7
 MOS/BIL B13 ...125 J2
sbury Dr CNCK/NC CV11 ...16 F5
 SHL/WTROR B46 ...93 G2
 IDDW DY11 ...137 K7
 NUNW/HART CV10 ...79 M6
sbury Cr CSCFLD/WYGN B72 ...73 C6
sbury Rd LOZ/NWT B19 ...89 H5
 MOS/BIL B13 ...125 J2
 MTHWK WDE B8 ...90 C8
 WASH/WDE B8 ...87 J4
 WBROM B70 ...87 J4
sbury St BDMR/CCFT WV3 ...2 C7
 ARL/WED WS10 ...26 D4
ow Cu BRWNH WS8 ...
y Ward Dr ALDR WS9 ...40 F1
p Cl HHTH/SAND B71 ...68 F6
p Dr CNCK/NC WS11 ...16 D1
LCLYGN/QTN B68 ...105 C3
p Rd LCLYGN/QTN B68 ...105 C2
EDW B97 ...202 B3
p St BHTH/HG B12 ...107 K5
KHL/PFLD WV2 ...67 J1
ILS/COS WV14 ...51 C5
UDN DY1 ...84 E3
star Cl AST/WIT B6 ...89 J7
ash Gv YDLY B25 ...109 G4
brook Rd HAG/WOL DY9 ...102 E6
er Rd TPTN/OCK DY4 ...67 K6
er's La CRTAM B79 ...31 M7
HTH/SAND B71 ...87 J1
EDW B97 ...201 L1
er's Rd ALDR WS9 ...40 E2
er St HOCK/TIA B94 ...87 M4
ers V WBROM B70 ...87 J4
isford WWCK CV34 ...205 H6
isford Gdns WWCK CV34 ...205 H5
a Cl COV CV1 ...8 F5
ley Cottages
 RDE/BCHGN B24 * ...90 D4
ley Rd VAUX/NECH B7 ...89 MH
ley Viad VAUX/NECH B7 ...90 A3
ney El ERDE/BCHGN B24 ...73 H8
rs La POL/KGSB/FAZ B78 ...59 L3
wells La DUDS DY2 ...102 E3
wells Rd DUDS DY2 ...102 F3
warpe Gv SLYOAK B29 ...123 K3
n Barber Ct WBROM B70 * ...17 M3
nbar Rd POL/KGSB/FAZ B78 ...45 M4
nbourn Cl SOLH B91 ...128 C7
nbourne Dr BKDE/SHDE B34 ...92 B6
nbrook Rd WOLVN WV10 ...36 E7
n Gault Cl COVS CV3 ...156 C6
mons La TLHL/CAN CV4 ...153 H4
mpson Cl COVE CV2 ...134 F2
 LDBY B69 ...86 A6
mpson Rd SPARK B11 ...107 M4
mpson Rd North SPARK B11 ...107 M5
mpson St DARL/WED WS10 ...68 F7
ns La WBROM B70 ...87 C3
n Spencer Ct KIDD DY10 ...165 L1
n Wk LICHS WS13 ...21 C3
uels Rd NFLD/LBR B31 ...144 B4
uels Rd RIDG/WDGT B32 ...104 E8
by Cl BDWTH CV12 ...116 E1
dia Cft CBROM B36 ...92 F7
dals Cl NFLD/LBR B31 ...144 B4
dals Ri RMSLY B62 ...122 B2
daiwood Cl SHHTH WV12 ...37 MH
d Bank BLOX/PEL WS3 ...38 F4
dbarn Cl SHLY B90 ...148 D7
dbeds Rd SHHTH WV12 ...52 A1
dbourne Dr BEWD DY12 ...163 G2
dbourne Rd WASH/WDE B8 ...108 L1
derling Cl WOLVN WV10 ...22 F6
derling Rd KIDD DY10 ...164 E4
derling Ri BNTWD WS7 ...19 K5
 RLYHL DY5 ...83 L7
ders La ATHST CV9 ...63 J4
 UDS DY2 ...85 G8
ders Rd BRGRVW B61 ...191 J4
 COVE CV2 ...116 F7
dfield Cl SHLY B90 ...147 L5
dfield Gv SEDG DY3 ...83 M3
dfield Ri HHTH/SAND B71 ...69 J4
 TRBR DY8 ...101 K3
dfields Av SMTHH B10 ...107 M5
dfields Rd LCLYGN/QTN B68 ...105 C3
dford Av
 LKHTH/ROWR B65 ...104 A3
dford Ri
 UNHL/THL/PER WV6 ...35 J7
dford Rd DUDN DY1 ...84 C4
dford St LICHS WS13 ...20 F7
dgate Crs COVE CV2 ...156 B3
dgate Rd HLGN/YWD B28 ...147 K1
 PTN/OCK DY4 ...67 K8
dhills Crs SOLH B91 ...148 F5
dhills Gn RBRY B45 ...170 E4
dhills La RBRY B45 ...170 E6
dhills Rd RBRY B45 ...170 E6
dhill St BLOX/PEL WS3 ...38 C4
dhurst Av CBROM B36 ...91 H7
 AG/WOL DY9 ...120 B7
dhurst Cl REDE B98 ...195 G7
 WSFLD DY6 ...101 J2

MOS/BIL B13 ...125 J3
Sandcliffe Cl KIDDW DY11 ...138 A5
Sandilands Cl COVE CV2 ...156 A5
Sandland Cl BILS/COS WV14 ...51 K1
Sandland Rd SHHTH WV12 ...38 A5
Sandmartin Cl DUDS DY2 ...103 G3
Sandmartin Wy KIDD DY10 ...164 G3
Sandmere Gv
 ALE/KHTH/YWD B14 ...147 H3
Sandmere Rd
 ALE/KHTH/YWD B14 ...147 H3
Sandon Cl REDE B98 ...202 E2
Sandon Gv ERDE/BCHGN B24 ...90 E1
Sandon Rd HAG/WOL DY9 ...120 D1
 HRBN B17 ...105 L4
 NUN CV11 ...80 F8
 WOLVN WV10 ...35 M3
Sandown TAM/AM/WIL B77 ...32 D8
Sandown Av COVN CV6 ...134 C3
 GTWY WS6 ...24 B2
Sandown Cl BNTWD WS7 ...18 D4
 HEDN WS12 ...13 J8
 RLSN CV32 ...207 G1
Sandown Dr BRGRVW B61 *...168 F4
 DUNHL/THL/PER WV6 ...48 D1
Sandown Rd CBROM B36 ...91 H5
 RUGBYN/HIL CV21 ...187 G1
Sandpiper TAM/AM/WIL B77 ...46 D7
Sandpiper Cl HAG/WOL DY9 ...102 D8
 HEDN WS12 ...13 G6
 KIDD DY10 ...164 F3
 RRUGBY CV23 ...161 G4
Sandpiper Gdns
 HWK/WKHTH B38 ...145 K6
Sandpiper Rd COVE CV2 ...134 F2
Sandpiper Wy ERDW/GRVHL B23..72 A7
Sandpit SLYOAK B29 * ...124 C5
Sandpits Cl WALM/CURD B76 ...74 F7
Sandpits La
 RCOVN/BALC/EX CV7 ...133 J3
Sand Pits Pde CBHAMW B1 ...6 A4
Sandra Cl ALDR WS9 ...40 F8
Sandringham Av SHHTH WV12 ...37 M7
Scar Bank WWCK WS34 ...205 J4
Sandringham Cl BNTWD WS7 ...18 C4
 TLHL/CAN CV4 ...153 K8
Sandringham Dr ALDR WS9 ...40 F4
 BLKHTH/ROWR B65 ...104 A1
Sandringham Pl STRBR DY8 ...101 C4
Sandringham Rd
 ETTPK/GDPK/PENN WV4 ...65 J3
 PBAR/PBCH B42 ...70 F7
 RMSLY B62 ...103 M6
 STRBR DY8 ...101 C4
 WMBN WV5 ...64 D7
Sandringham Wy BRLYHL DY5 ...102 A5
Sandstone Av RBRY B45 ...143 L5
Sandstone Rd BEWD DY12 ...163 G2
Sand St WBROM B70 ...86 C1
Sandway Gdns WASH/WDE B8 ...90 A7
Sandway Gv MOS/BIL B13 ...126 A6
Sandwell Av DARL/WED WS10 ...51 M4
Sandwell Pl SHHTH WV12 ...38 B6
Sandwell Rd HDSW B21 ...88 B4
 WBROM B70 ...87 C1
 WOLVN WV10 ...35 M4
Sandwell Rd North
 HHTH/SAND B71 ...87 H1
Sandwell St WSL WS1 ...5 L6
Sandwell Wk WSL WS1 ...5 L6
Sandwick Cl COVS CV3 ...156 D5
Sandwood Dr KGSTG B44 ...71 K5
Sandyacre Wy STRBR DY8 ...101 M8
Sandy Bank BEWD DY12 ...162 E2
Sandy Crs WNSFLD WV11 ...37 L5
 MOS/BIL B13 ...126 A6
Sandyfields Rd SEDG DY3 ...65 KB
Sandy Gv BRWNH WS8 ...26 D4
Sandy Hill Ri SHLY B90 ...147 L1
Sandy Hill Rd SHLY B90 ...147 L1
Sandy Hollow
 DUNHL/THL/PER WV6 ...49 C3
Sandy La AST/WIT B6 ...89 L6
 BRGRVW B61 ...142 D8
 CDSL WV8 ...34 D1
 CNCK/NC WV11 ...15 L4
 COVN CV6 ...134 A8
 CSHL/WTROR B46 ...95 J1
 DARL/WED WS10 ...69 K2
 DUNHL/THL/PER WV6 ...35 J7
 KIDD DY10 ...139 M5
 KIDDW DY11 ...137 L4
 LICHS WS14 ...30 A1
 PBAR/PBCH B42 ...71 H5
 RCOVN/BALC/EX CV7 ...114 D2
 RLSN CV32 ...206 A2
 STRPT DY13 ...188 F4
 WOLVN WV10 ...36 C4
Sandy Mt WMBN WV5 ...64 F6
Sandy Rd STRBR DY8 ...119 H4
Sandys Gv TPTN/OCK DY4 ...67 J8
Sandy Wy EDG B15 ...7 K8
 TAM/AM/WIL B77 ...46 F3
Sangwin Rd TPTN/OCK DY4 ...67 C6
Sankey Rd CNCK/NC WS11 ...16 D2
Sansome Ri SHLY B90 ...147 K3
Sansome Rd SHLY B90 ...147 K3
Sanstone Rd BLOX/PEL WS3 ...39 G2
Santa Maria Wy STRPT DY13 ...188 F4
Santolina Dr DSYBK/YTR WS5 ...69 L2
Santos Cl COVS CV3 ...156 D5
Santridge La BRGRVW B61 ...191 L1
Sant Rd NFLD/LBR B31 ...144 F2
Sapcote Gv COVN CV6 ...134 F1
The Saplings PENK ST19 ...10 D5
Sapphire Ct
 RCOVN/BALC/EX CV7 * ...135 M4
Sapphire Dr CNCK/NC WS11 ...17 G2
 RLSS CV31 ...206 D8
Sapphire Ga COVE CV2 ...156 A3
Saracen Dr MGN/WHC B75 ...57 K7
 RCOVN/BALC/EX CV7 ...151 J7
Sara Cl FOAKS/STRLY B74 ...56 F2
Sarah Cl BILS/COS WV14 ...68 A1
Sarah Gdns DSYBK/YTR WS5 ...69 K1
Sarah Seager Cl STRPT DY13 * ...188 A1
Saredon Cl BORD DY13 ...107 M3
Saredon Cl BLOX/PEL WS3 ...39 L4
Saredon Rd CNCK/NC WS11 ...23 M1
 WOLVN WV10 ...23 H3
Sarehole Rd HLGN/YWD B28 ...126 B6
Sargeaunt St RLSS CV31 ...206 D1
Sargent Cl RLSN CV32 ...206 D4
Sark Dr CBROM B36 ...92 F7
Satchwell Ct RLSN CV32 ...206 D5
Satchwell Pl RLSS CV31 ...206 E1
Saturn Rd CNCK/NC WS11 ...16 C3
Saumur Wy RLSN CV32 ...206 A7
Saunders Av BDWTH CV12 ...116 F3
Saunders Ho WBROM B70 * ...13 M1
Saunton Cl COVW CV5 ...132 C4

Saunton Rd RUGBYS/DCH CV22 ...186 D4
Saunton Wy SLYOAK B29 ...124 B5
Saveker Dr WALM/CURD B76 ...73 J1
Savernake Cl RBRY B45 ...143 L3
Saville Gv KNWTH CV8 ...180 A7
Scotland La RIDG/WDGT B32 ...122 F5
Savoy Cl RIDG/WDGT B32 ...105 K8
Saw Mill Cl RUSH/SHEL WS4 ...4 F1
Saxelby Cl ALE/KHTH/YWD B14..146 E3
Saxilby Pl STRPT DY13 ...188 F1
Saxon Cl COVS CV3 ...157 H6
 GTWY WS6 ...24 E3
 POL/KGSB/FAZ B78 ...47 K4
 RUGBYS/DCH CV22 ...185 L5
 STUD B80 ...203 J8
Saxoncourt
 DUNHL/THL/PER WV6 ...35 G8
Saxondale Av
 LGN/SDN/BHAMAIR B26 ...109 K1
Saxon Dr BLKHTH/ROWR B65 ...104 A1
 CRTAM B79 ...46 A1
Saxonfields
 CHWD/FDBR/MGN B37 ...110 D2
Saxon Mill La CRTAM B79 ...46 A1
Saxon Rd COVE CV2 ...155 M1
 PENK ST19 ...10 D5
Saxons Wy ALE/KHTH/YWD B14..146 F4
Saxon Wk WSL WS13 ...20 C7
Saxon Wood Cl NFLD/LBR B31 ...144 E1
Saxon Wood Rd SHLY B90 ...148 B5
Saxton Dr FOAKS/STRLY B74 ...42 D7
Scafell RUGBYN/HIL CV21 ...161 H6
Scafell Cl COVW CV5 ...153 L1
Scafell Dr BILS/COS WV14 ...51 K6
 ERDW/GRVHL B23 ...72 A3
Scafell Rd STRBR DY8 ...101 M7
Scaife Rd BRGRVE B60 ...191 M7
Scammerton TAM/AM/WIL B77 ...46 A6
Scampton Cl
 DUNHL/THL/PER WV6 ...34 C8
Scampton Wy CRTAM B79 ...32 A5
Scar Bank WWCK WS34 ...205 J4
Scarborough Cl WSLW WS2 ...52 F5
Scarborough Rd WSLW WS2 ...4 A6
Scarborough Wy TLHL/CAN CV4..153 K6
Scarecrow La MGN/WHC B75 ...57 J1
Scarfield Hl ALVE B48 ...170 B8
Scarman Rd KNWTH CV8 ...179 L1
Scarsdale Rd PBAR/PBCH B42 ...71 H5
Scartho Cl NUN CV11 ...99 L8
Schofield Av HHTH/SAND B71 ...68 F5
Schofield Rd
 CHWD/FDBR/MGN B37 ...92 D8
Scholars Ga BNTWD WS7 ...19 H4
 STETCH B33 ...109 M3
Scholefield Rd
 RCOVN/BALC/EX CV7 ...115 L7
Scholarcare Ri FOAKS/STRLY B74...15 J4
Scholarcare Rd BKDE/SHDE B34 ...91 M7
School Av BRWNH WS8 ...26 D5
School Bells Ms KNWTH CV8 *...180 E7
School Cl BDMR/CCFT WV3 ...67 G4
 BILS/COS WV14 ...51 C5
 BRGRVE B60 ...191 M2
 HLYWD B47 ...172 E2
 STRBR DY8 ...101 K5
The School Dr DUDS DY2 ...85 H6
Schoolfield Gv
 RUGBYN/HIL CV21 ...186 E2
Schoolfields Rd LICHS WS14 ...28 E8
School Gdns RUGBYN/HIL CV21 ...187 L4
Schoolgate Cl RUSH/SHEL WS4 ...40 B4
 WASH/WDE B8 ...90 E7
School Gn BILS/COS WV14 ...51 C5
School Hl BTACH/HAR CV33 ...207 M5
 NUNW/HART CV10 ...79 L6
Schoolhouse Cl
 HWK/WKHTH B38 ...145 M3
School House La COVE CV2 ...135 L7
School La ALVE B48 ...170 F8
 BKDE/SHDE B34 ...91 M6
 BLOX/PEL WS3 ...39 K1
 BNTWD WS7 ...18 B5
 BRGRVE B60 ...168 F7
 BRLYHL DY5 ...101 M1
 CRTAM B79 ...33 K6
 HAG/WOL DY9 ...120 B7
 HALE B63 ...121 K3
 KNWTH CV8 ...177 J8
 KNWTH CV8 ...177 K8
 NUNW/HART CV10 ...79 J8
 POL/KGSB/FAZ B78 ...30 F6
 POL/KGSB/FAZ B78 ...44 B2
 RCOVN/BALC/EX CV7 ...116 C6
 RLSS CV31 ...207 J3
 SOLH B91 ...149 H1
 STETCH B33 ...109 K4
 TAM/AM/WIL B77 ...46 A4
 WALM/CURD B76 ...75 L2
 WOLVN WV10 ...35 B3
 WOLVN WV10 ...36 D7
School Rd ALE/KHTH/YWD B14..146 E8
 BRLYHL DY5 ...101 M1
 CNCK/NC WS11 ...17 C7
 DARL/WED WS10 ...69 C6
 DUNHL/THL/PER WV6 ...48 E1
 HLGN/YWD B28 ...126 D5
 HOCK/TIA B94 ...170 C7
 RBRY B45 ...143 J7
 SEDG DY3 ...84 C8
 SHLY B90 ...147 M3
 WMBN WV5 ...64 C6
 WMBN WV5 ...64 F6
 WNSFLD WV11 ...36 F7
School St BRLYHL DY5 ...101 H4
 CDYHTH B64 ...103 H4
 DARL/WED WS10 ...52 A7
 DARL/WED WS10 ...52 B8
 DUDN DY1 ...84 F3
 KNWTH CV8 ...183 L1
 RRUGBY CV23 ...185 L1
 RUGBYN/HIL CV21 ...187 H1
 RUSH/SHEL WS4 ...40 B1
 SEDG DY3 ...84 C5
 STRBR DY8 ...101 C5
 TAM/AM/WIL B77 ...46 A4
 WNLHL WV13 ...51 K3
School St West
 BILS/COS WV14 ...51 C5
School Ter SLYOAK B29 * ...124 D5
School Wk BILS/COS WV14 ...51 C5
 BNTWD WS7 ...18 B5
 NUN CV11 ...99 J3

Selston Rd AST/WIT B6 ...89 J6
Selvey Av GTB/HAM B43 ...70 F2
Selworthy Rd CBROM B36 ...92 B8
 COVN CV6 ...134 B2
Selwyn Cl BKHL/PFLD WV2 ...50 A6
Selwyn Rd BILS/COS WV14 ...19 K6
 LDYWD/EDGR B16 ...106 B2
Selwyn Wk FOAKS/STRLY B74 ...56 F1
Semele Cl RLSS CV31 ...207 J8
Seneschal Rd COVS CV3 ...155 J6
Senneleys Park Rd
 NFLD/LBR B31 ...123 J5
Sennen Cl NUN CV11 ...81 J6
 WLNHL WV13 ...51 K4
Sensall Rd HAG/WOL DY9 ...120 D2
Sentry Wy MGN/WHC B75 ...57 L7
Sephton Dr COVN CV6 ...117 G7
Serin Cl KIDD DY10 ...164 D4
Serpentine Rd AST/WIT B6 ...89 L4
 HRBN B17 ...106 A3
 SLYOAK B29 ...124 E2
The Serpentine KIDDW DY11 ...164 A3
Settle Av BKDE/SHDE B34 ...91 K7
Settle Cft
 CHWD/FDBR/MGN B37 ...110 D4
Setton Dr SEDG DY3 ...66 C6
Seven Acres ALDR WS9 ...40 F8
Seven Acres La REDE B98 ...195 G8
Seven Acres Rd NFLD/LBR B31 ...145 G4
 RMSLY B62 ...104 E8
Sevendwellings Vw
 BRLYHL DY5 ...102 A4
Sevenhills Dr STRPT DY13 ...188 B3
Sevens Rd HEDN WS12 ...18 A2
Seven Star Rd SOLH B91 ...127 L8
Seven Stars Rd OLDBY B69 ...86 E7
Severn Cl BRGRVW B61 ...168 B6
 CBROM B36 ...92 B6
 RLSN CV32 ...207 G2
 SHHTH WV12 ...37 L6
 TPTN/OCK DY4 ...67 K8
Severn Dr BNTWD WS7 ...19 H7
 BRLYHL DY5 ...83 M6
 DUNHL/THL/PER WV6 ...48 C1
Severne Gv ACGN B27 ...127 C4
Severne Rd ACGN B27 ...127 G5
Severn Gv KIDDW DY11 ...163 M2
 LOZ/NWT B19 ...89 G6
 SPARK B11 * ...107 J8
Severn Rd BDWTH CV12 ...117 J2
 BLOX/PEL WS3 ...39 H5
 BRWNH WS8 ...26 A3
 COV CV1 ...9 L7
 HALE B63 ...102 F8
 STRBR DY8 ...119 K2
Severn Side STRPT DY13 ...188 E3
Severn Side North BEWD DY12 ...162 E1
Severn Side South BEWD DY12 ...162 F2
Severn St CBHAMW B1 ...6 E7
Severn Wy BNTWD WS7 ...19 H7
 HLYWD B47 ...172 C2
Sevington Cl SOLH B91 ...149 G5
Sewage Cottages
 NUNW/HART CV10 * ...80 A2
Sewall Hwy COVN CV10 ...134 E5
Seward Cl LICHS WS14 ...21 H4
Seymour Cl COVS CV3 ...156 A8
 GTWY WS6 ...24 D4
 RWWCK/WEL CV35 ...204 D7
 SLYOAK B29 ...124 F3
Seymour Dr REDE B98 ...194 E8
Seymour Gdns FOAKS/STRLY B74..5 J4
Seymour Cl RLSS CV31 ...206 B7
Seymour Rd HAG/WOL DY9 ...102 D8
 KIDDW DY11 ...137 M5
 NUN CV11 ...99 H2
 OLDBY B69 ...87 C6
 RUGBYN/HIL CV21 ...161 G7
 TPTN/OCK DY4 ...68 A7
Shackleton Dr
 DUNHL/THL/PER WV6 ...34 B8
Shackleton Rd BLOX/PEL WS3 ...39 H3
Shadowbrook La HIA/OLT B92 ...129 H6
Shadowbrook Rd COVN CV6 ...133 L8
Shadwell Dr SEDG DY3 ...84 B3
Shadwell St CBHAMNE B4 ...7 G3
Shady La KGSTG B44 ...71 H3
Shadymoor Dr BRLYHL DY5 ...102 A3
Shaftesbury Av HAG/WOL DY9 ...120 A2
 RCOVN/BALC/EX CV7 ...115 L7
Shaftesbury Cl BRGRVE B60 ...191 M3
Shaftesbury Dr HEDN WS12 ...13 C6
Shaftesbury Rd COWW CV5 ...154 D5
 DARL/WED WS10 ...68 F3
Shaftesbury Sq HHTH/SAND B71..87 J4
Shaftesbury St HHTH/SAND B71..87 J4
 WBROM B70 ...86 F1
Shaft La RCOVN/BALC/EX CV7 ...131 L1
Shaftmoor La HLGN/YWD B28 ...126 C3
Shaftsbury Av HALE B63 ...102 F6
Shaftsbury Cl BILS/COS WV14 ...51 K6
Shaftsbury Dr BNTWD WS7 ...19 K6
Shaftsbury Rd
 LGN/SDN/BHAMAIR B26 ...110 A3
Shahjalal Rd WASH/WDE B8 ...90 B8
Shakespeare Av BDWTH CV12 ...117 H3
 LICHS WS14 ...21 J4
 REDE B98 ...202 E3
 WWCK CV34 ...205 G8
Shakespeare Cl BILS/COS WV14 ...67 H3
 CRTAM B79 ...33 J7
Shakespeare Crs BLOX/PEL WS3 ...39 J4
Shakespeare Dr KIDD DY10 ...138 F7
 NUN CV11 ...99 J4
 SHLY B90 ...147 M4
Shakespeare Gdns
 RUGBYS/DCH CV22 ...186 C6
Shakespeare Pl BLOX/PEL WS3 ...39 J4
Shakespeare Rd AST/WIT B6 ...89 M2
 BNTWD WS7 ...18 D5
 SEDG DY3 ...83 L1
 SMTHWKW B67 ...105 H1
 TPTN/OCK DY4 ...67 H7
Shakespeare St COVE CV2 ...155 M1
 SPARK B11 ...108 A8
 WOLV WV1 ...3 J5
Shakespear Gv CNCK/NC WS11 ...16 D1
Shakleton Rd COVW CV5 ...8 A5
The Shales WMBN WV5 * ...64 C8
Shale St BILS/COS WV14 ...51 G6
Shalford Rd HIA/OLT B92 ...127 J1
Shallcross La SEDG DY3 ...84 B2
Shalnecote Gv
 ALE/KHTH/YWD B14 ...125 G8
Shambles DARL/WED WS10 ...68 D3
Shandon Cl RIDG/WDGT B32 ...123 K2
Shanklin Cl GTWY WS6 ...24 D2
Shanklin Dr NUNW/HART CV10 ...81 H7
Shanklin Rd COVS CV3 ...155 J8
Shannon TAM/AM/WIL B77 ...46 D5
Shannon Dr BRWNH WS8 ...26 A3
Shannon Rd HWK/WKHTH B38 ...145 K5
Shapfell RUGBYN/HIL CV21 ...161 H6
Shapinsay Dr RBRY B45 ...143 K4
Shard End Crs BKDE/SHDE B34 ...92 A8
Shardlow Rd WNSFLD WV11 ...37 J5

The Shardway BKDE/SHDE B34 ....92 A8
Sharesacre Cl WLNHL WV13 ......51 M2
Sharington Cl DUDS DY2 ....85 H5
Sharman Rd WOLVN WV10 ....6 C5
Sharmans Cross SOLH B91 ....148 C5
Sharon Cl
  ETTPK/GDPK/PENN WV4 ....50 C3
Sharon Wy HEDN WS12 ....17 H2
Sharp Cl COVN CV6 ....134 A3
Sharpe Cl WWCK CV34 ....205 J5
Sharpe St TAM/AM/WIL B77 ......32 E8
Sharpley Ct COVE CV2 * 135 L3
Sharps Cl RBRY B45 ....143 L6
Sharrat Fld MGN/WHC B75 ....57 H3
Sharratt Rd BDWTH CV12 ....116 D3
Sharrocks St WOLV WV1 ....3 J7
Shaw Cl KIDD DY10 ....138 F7
Shawbank Rd REDE B98 ....202 F2
Shawberry Av CVALE B35 ....91 L2
Shawberry Rd
  CHWD/FDBR/MGN B37 * 92 D8
Shawbrook La
  ALE/KHTH/YWD B14 ....146 C6
Shawbury Cl REDE B98 ....203 J2
Shawbury Gv BHTH/HG B12 ....107 K5
  DUNHL/THL/PER WV6 ....4 C8
Shawbury La CSHL/WTROR B46 .....95 C5
Shawbury Rd WOLVN WV10 ....36 D8
Shawbury Village
  CSHL/WTROR B46 ....95 J6
Shaw Dr BNTWD WS7 ....18 A4
  STETCH B33 ....109 J3
Shawe Av NUNW/HART CV10 ......97 G8
Shaw Hall La COVEN WV9 ....8 D2
Shaw Hedge Rd BEWD DY12 ......163 G1
Shaw Hellier Av BRLYHL DY5 ......102 C3
Shaw Hill Rd WASH/WDE B8 ......108 E1
Shawhurst Cft HLYWD B47 ....146 E6
Shawhurst La HLYWD B47 ....146 E6
Shaw La DUNHL/THL/PER WV6 ......4 B7
  LICH WS13 ....20 E5
  RUGE WS15 ....18 E1
Shawley Cft ACGN B27 ....127 J1
Shaw Rd BILS/COS WV14 ....66 F4
  BKHL/PFLD WV2 ....50 A7
  DUDS DY2 ....84 F6
  TPTN/OCK DY4 ....86 A1
  WOLVN WV10 ....36 B7
Shaws Cl REDW B97 ....201 K3
Shawsdale Rd CBROM B36 ....91 K6
Shaw's La GTWY WS6 ....24 E3
Shaw's Pas DIG/EDG B5 ....7 J5
Shaw St WBROM B70 ....68 C5
  WSLW WS2 ....4 E2
Shayler Gv BKHL/PFLD WV2 ....50 B6
Sheaf La
  LGN/SDN/BHAMAIR B26 ....127 M1
  RBRY B45 ....143 L7
Shearwater Wk
  ERDW/GRVHL B23 ....71 M7
Sheaves Cl
  ETTPK/GDPK/PENN WV4 ....66 E2
Shedden St DUDS DY2 ....85 H5
Sheddington Rd
  ERDW/GRVHL B23 ....72 B6
Sheen Rd KGSTG B44 ....71 J1
Sheepclose Dr
  CHWD/FDBR/MGN B37 ....110 C2
Sheepcote La RLSN CV32 ....206 E4
Sheepcote Gra BRGRVW B61 ......168 D8
Sheepcote La TAM/AM/WIL B77 ....46 D2
Sheepcote St LDYWD/EDGR B16 ....6 A5
Sheepcroft Cl REDW B97 ....201 K3
Sheepfold Cl
  BLKHTH/ROWR B65 ....103 L1
Sheepmoor Cl HRBN B17 ....105 K5
Sheepwash La TPTN/OCK DY4 ......85 H4
Sheepy Rd ATHST CV9 ....63 H2
Sheerwater Dr BRLYHL DY5 ....102 A6
Sheffield Rd SCFLD/BOLD B73 ......72 E6
Sheffield St BRLYHL DY5 ....102 E4
Shefford Rd AST/WIT B6 ....89 K8
Sheila Av WNSFLD WV11 ....37 J6
Shelah Rd HALE B63 ....103 L7
Shelbourne Cl OLDBY B69 ....86 B3
Sheldon Cl BILS/COS WV14 ....67 H2
Sheldon Dr NFLD/LBR B31 ....144 B4
Sheldonfield Rd
  LGN/SDN/BHAMAIR B26 ....128 B1
Sheldon Gv
  LGN/SDN/BHAMAIR B26 ....109 M8
  WWCK CV34 ....205 K3
Sheldon Hall Av STETCH B33 ......110 D1
Sheldon Heath Rd STETCH B33 ...109 L3
Sheldon Rd HHTH/SAND B71 ....69 J5
  REDE B98 ....202 F4
  WOLVN WV10 ....35 L4
Sheldrake Cl COVS CV3 ....156 E4
Shelduck Cl KIDD DY10 * 164 F2
Shelfield Cl CHWD/FDBR/MGN B37 110 D3
  HOCK/TIA B94 ....175 G7
Shelfield Rd
  ALE/KHTH/YWD B14 ....146 A4
Shelley Av KIDD DY10 ....138 C6
  TPTN/OCK DY4 ....67 L5
Shelley Cl BDWTH CV12 ....117 H4
  BRGRVW B61 ....168 A3
  REDW B97 ....202 A4
  SEDG DY3 ....65 J3
  STRBR DY8 ....101 L5
Shelley Dr AST/WIT B6 ....89 M2
  FOAKS/STRLY B74 ....55 M5
Shelley Rd BNTWD WS7 ....18 E4
  CNCK/NC WS11 ....12 B5
  COVE CV2 ....156 A2
  CRTAM B79 ....31 K6
  SHHTH WV12 ....38 C6
  WOLVN WV10 ....36 B7
Shellon Cl COVS CV3 ....156 D5
Shelly Cl CHWD/FDBR/MGN B37 ..110 D3
Shelly Crs SHLY B90 ....148 F7
Shelly Cft STETCH B33 ....109 L2
Shelly La SHLY B90 ....148 F7
Shelsley Av OLDBY B69 ....86 B8
Shelsley Cl PENK ST19 ....10 C1
Shelsley Dr MOS/BIL B13 ....125 M4
Shelsley Wy SOLH B91 ....148 F4
Shelton Cl DARL/WED WS10 ....53 G8
Shelton La HALE B63 ....103 J8
Shelton Sq COV CV1 ....6 E6
Shelton St TAM/AM/WIL B77 ....46 D6
Sheltwood La BRGRVE B60 ....200 D1
Shelwick Gv DOR/KN B93 ....175 K1
Shenley Av DUDN DY1 ....66 F3
Shenley Fields Dr
  NFLD/LBR B31 ....123 L6
Shenley Fields Rd SLYOAK B29 ...123 L6
Shenley Gdns SLYOAK B29 ....123 L6
Shenley Hl NFLD/LBR B31 ....123 L7
Shenley La SLYOAK B29 ....123 L5
Shenstone Av RMSLY B62 ....122 C1
  RUGBYS/HIL CV21 ....187 J4
  STRBR DY8 ....119 H3
Shenstone Ct BRGRVE B60 ....191 G2
  FOAKS/STRLY B74 ....42 F1

Shenstone Ct BDMR/CCFT WV3 .....49 L7
Shenstone Dr ALDR WS9 ....40 E5
  RCOVN/BALC/EX CV7 ....151 L7
Shenstone Rd
  ALE/KHTH/YWD B14 ....146 E4
  GTB/HAM B43 ....70 C5
  LDYWD/EDGR B16 ....106 A2
Shenstone Valley Rd
  RMSLY B62 ....104 D7
Shenton Wk
  CHWD/FDBR/MGN B37 ....92 D8
Shepheard Rd
  LGN/SDN/BHAMAIR B26 ....110 B8
Shepherd Cl LICH WS13 ....21 G3
  TLHL/CAN CV4 ....153 K2
Shepherd Dr SHHTH WV12 ....37 M8
Shepherds Brook Rd
  HAG/WOL DY9 ....102 B8
Shepherds Fold
  BLKHTH/ROWR B65 ....103 M3
Shepherds Gdns EDG B15 ....6 B8
Shepherds Green Rd
  ERDE/BCHGN B24 ....90 D3
Shepherds La
  RCOVN/BALC/EX CV7 ....130 C3
Shepherds Pool Rd
  MGN/WHC B75 ....57 J3
Shepherds Standing
  BKDE/SHDE B34 * 91 M7
Shepherds Wk
  ERDW/GRVHL B23 ....72 A5
  RBRY B45 ....143 M7
Shepley St NUN CV11 ....99 G3
Sheppey Dr CBROM B36 ....92 F8
Shepwell Gdns WOLVN WV10 ......23 C5
Shepwell St WLNHL WV13 ....52 A4
Sherard Cft CBROM B36 ....92 F7
Sheraton Cl ALDR WS9 ....40 F7
  HEDN WS12 ....12 D6
Sheraton Dr KIDD DY10 ....138 E7
Sheraton Gra STRBR DY8 ....119 H3
Sheraton Rd BRGRVE B60 ....192 A4
Sherborne Cl BLOX/PEL WS3 ....39 G6
  CSHL/WTROR B46 ....111 L1
Sherborne Gdns CDSL WV8 ....34 E2
Sherborne Gv CBHAMW B1 ....106 E2
Sherborne Rd WOLVN WV10 ....36 B4
Sherborne St LDYWD/EDGR B16 ....6 A6
Sherbourne Ar COV CV1 * 8 D3
  HEDN WS12 ....17 J1
  NUNW/HART CV10 ....79 M8
Sherbourne Cl REDE B98 ....203 H3
Sherbourne Crs COVS CV3 ....154 C1
Sherbourne Dr ACGN B27 ....127 G1
Sherbourne Pl RLSN CV32 * 206 E4
Sherbourne Rd ACGN B27 ....126 F1
  BHTH/HG B12 ....107 J6
  CDYHTH B64 ....103 L5
  STRBR DY8 ....119 M1
Sherbourne St COV CV1 ....8 B5
Sherbourne Ter RLSN CV32 * 206 D4
Sherbrook Av TAM/AM/WIL B77 ....46 D1
Sherbrook Rd CNCK/NC WS11 ......16 A4
Sherbrooke Cft SHLY B90 ....148 D2
Sheridan Cl NUNW/HART CV10 ......79 K8
  WSLW WS2 ....52 F6
Sheridan Gdns SEDG DY3 ....65 K8
Sheridan St HHTH/SAND B71 ......87 H1
  WSLW WS2 ....52 F6
Sheridan Wk CVALE B35 * 91 L2
Sheriff Av TLHL/CAN CV4 ....153 M6
Sheriff Dr BRLYHL DY5 ....102 D3
Sheriff Rd RUGBYN/HIL CV21 .....187 H3
Sheriffs Cl LICHS WS14 ....21 L3
Sheriffs Orch COV CV1 ....8 E6
Sheriffoot La MGN/WHC B75 ....56 F7
Sheringham EDG B15 ....106 C5
Sheringham Dr BLYN CV11 ....99 K3
Sheringham Rd BVILLE B30 ....145 M2
Sherington Av COVN CV6 ....134 A2
Sherington Dr
  ETTPK/GDPK/PENN WV4 ....50 B8
Sherlock Cl SHHTH WV12 ....38 B8
Sherlock Rd COVW CV5 ....134 B2
Sherlock St DIG/EDG B5 ....107 J5
Sherrans Dell
  ETTPK/GDPK/PENN WV4 ....66 B2
Sherratt Cl WALM/CURD B76 ....73 K5
Sherringham Dr SHHTH WV12 ......38 A4
Sherron Gdns BHTH/HG B12 ....107 K8
Sherston Covert BVILLE B30 ....146 A3
Shervale Cl
  ETTPK/GDPK/PENN WV4 ....49 L7
Sherwin Av BILS/COS WV14 ....51 G6
Sherwood Av TPTN/OCK DY4 ....85 K1
Sherwood Cl ATHST CV9 ....60 F4
  HIA/OLT B92 ....126 D8
  HLGN/YWD B28 ....126 D8
Sherwood Dr BRLYHL DY5 ....102 D4
Sherwood Jones Cl COVN CV6 ....133 M7
Sherwood Ms HLGN/YWD B28 ....126 C7
Sherwood Rd BRGRVE B60 ....191 L1
  HLGN/YWD B28 ....126 C6
  SMTHWKW B67 ....105 L4
  STRBR DY8 ....101 J6
Sherwood St WOLV WV1 ....2 E1
Sherwood Wk RLSN CV32 ....207 H1
  RUSH/SHEL WS4 ....41 G3
Shetland Av TAM/AM/WIL B77 ......46 D6
Shetland Cl COVW CV5 ....153 L1
  DUNHL/THL/PER WV6 ....35 M7
  LDYWD/EDGR B16 ....106 D3
Shetland Dr NUNW/HART CV10 ....98 D5
SMTHWK B66 ....87 H6
Shevlock Wy COVN CV6 ....134 E7
Shidas La OLDBY B69 ....86 C6
Shifnal Wy MGN/WHC B75 ....57 K6
Shillcock Gv LOZ/NWT B19 ....89 J7
Shillingstone Cl COVE CV2 ....155 M2
Shillingstone Dr
  NUNW/HART CV10 ....98 E4
Shilton Cl SHLY B90 ....148 D7
Shilton Gv SLYOAK B29 ....123 K5
Shilton La COVE CV2 ....135 L6
Shinwell Crs OLDBY B69 ....86 B3
Shipbourne Cl RIDG/WDGT B32 ...105 K8
Shipley Fdls ERDE/BCHGN B24 .....90 D3
Shipley Gv SLYOAK B29 ....123 L5
Shipston Rd COVE CV2 ....135 G2
  NFLD/LBR B31 ....144 F4
Shipton Cl DUDN DY1 ....84 C2
Shipton Rd CSCFLD/WYGN B72 ....73 G2
Shipway Rd YDLY B25 ....108 E6
Shire Brook Cl AST/WIT B6 ....89 J1
Shirebrook Cl COVE CV2 ....135 H4
Shire Cl COVN CV6 ....134 F5
  LDYWD/EDGR B16 ....106 D3
  LGLYGN/QTN B68 ....104 F3
Shirehall Pl CNCK/NC WS11 ....16 F3
Shireland Brook Gdns
  WSNGN B18 * 106 B1
Shireland Cl ERDE/BCHGN B24 .....90 B3
Shireland La REDW B97 ....201 L1
Shireland Rd SMTHWK B66 ....105 M5
Shirelea Cl BNTWD WS7 ....18 F5

Shire Rdg ALDR WS9 ....40 E3
The Shires RRUGBY CV23 * 158 F7
Shirestone Rd STETCH B33 ....110 C3
Shireview Gdns BLOX/PEL WS3 * ..39 M1
Shireview Rd BLOX/PEL WS3 ....39 M1
Shirewood CNCK/NC WS11 ....15 M3
Shirland Rd
  CHWD/FDBR/MGN B37 ....110 C4
Shirlett Cl COVN CV6 ....134 F1
Shirley Dr CSCFLD/WYGN B72 ......73 G1
Shirley La RCOVN/BALC/EX CV7 ..131 L8
Shirley Park Rd SHLY B90 ....147 M3
Shirley Rd BVILLE B30 ....146 C1
  COVE CV2 ....135 K6
  DUDS DY2 ....85 J5
  HLGN/YWD B28 ....126 E5
  LGLYGN/QTN B68 ....87 G7
Shirral Gv CHWD/FDBR/MGN B37 ..92 D8
Shirrall Dr POL/KGSB/FAZ B78 ......58 B1
Shoal Hill Cl CNCK/NC WS11 ....15 M4
Sholing Cl COVW CV5 ....35 K4
Shooters Cl DIG/EDG B5 ....107 H6
Shooters Hl CSCFLD/WYGN B72 ....73 H3
Shop La CDSL WV8 ....34 E4
Shopton Rd BKDE/SHDE B34 ....91 L8
Shoreham Cl WLNHL WV13 ....51 H4
Shorncliffe Rd COVN CV6 ....133 J7
Short Acre St WSLW WS2 ....4 D1
Shortbutts La LICHS WS14 ....20 F8
Shorters Av
  ALE/KHTH/YWD B14 ....146 F1
Shortfield Cl
  RCOVN/BALC/EX CV7 ....151 M6
Short Heath Rd
  ERDW/GRVHL B23 ....72 C7
Shortland Cl DOR/KN B93 ....149 L7
Shortlands
  RCOVN/BALC/EX CV7 ....116 B2
Shortlands Cl BVILLE B30 ....145 L3
Shortlands La BLOX/PEL WS3 ....39 L1
Short La GTWY WS6 ....24 C2
Shortley Rd COVS CV3 ....155 J5
Short Rd SMTHWKW B67 ....105 H2
  WOLVN WV10 ....36 C4
Short St BILS/COS WV14 ....51 H7
  BLKHTH/ROWR B65 ....104 A4
  BRWNH WS8 ....26 C6
  CNCK/NC WS11 ....16 C5
  COV CV1 ....9 H6
  DARL/WED WS10 ....52 D6
  DARL/WED WS10 ....68 C2
  DUDN DY1 ....84 E3
  HALE B63 ....121 K1
  NUNW/HART CV10 ....98 A1
  SHHTH WV12 ....38 A3
  STRBR DY8 ....101 K8
  WOLV WV1 ....3 G4
  WSLW WS2 ....2 D3
The Shortwoods
  POL/KGSB/FAZ B78 ....47 L8
The Shortyard KIDDW DY11 ....138 B1
Shorwell Pl BRLYHL DY5 ....102 A4
Shottery Cl COVW CV5 ....153 M2
Shottery Gv WALM/CURD B76 ......73 K4
Shottery Rd SHLY B90 ....147 M4
Shotteswell Rd SHLY B90 ....147 M6
Showell Circ WOLVN WV10 ....36 C6
Showell Green La SPARK B11 ......125 M2
Showell La
  ETTPK/GDPK/PENN WV4 ....64 C2
  RCOVN/BALC/EX CV7 ....131 K1
Showell Rd WOLVN WV10 ....36 B6
Showells Gdns VAUX/NECH B7 .....90 A6
Shrawley Av KIDDW DY11 ....163 M2
Shrawley Cl HALE B63 ....121 L3
  RBRY B45 ....143 K6
Shrawley Rd NFLD/LBR B31 ....145 G3
Shrewley Crs STETCH B33 ....110 C4
Shrewsbury Cl BLOX/PEL WS3 ......38 D4
Shrewton Av
  ALE/KHTH/YWD B14 ....146 B3
The Shrubberies TLHL/CAN CV4 ..180 C1
Shrubbery Av TPTN/OCK DY4 ......67 H8
Shrubbery Cl WALM/CURD B76 .....73 H7
Shrubbery Rd BRGRVE B61 ....191 J4
Shrubbery St KIDD DY10 ....138 D6
The Shrubbery DUDN DY1 ....84 F3
Shrubbery St KIDD DY10 *..........138 E6 *
Shrublands Av
  LGLYGN/QTN B68 ....104 F6
Shrub La ERDE/BCHGN B24 ....90 E1
Shuckburgh Crs
  RUGBYS/DCH CV22 ....187 H5
Shuckburgh Cl RLSN CV32 ....206 E3
Shugborough Dr DUDN DY1 ....84 C3
Shugborough Wy
  CNCK/NC WS11 ....16 F4
Shulman's Wk COVE CV2 ....135 K4
Shultern La TLHL/CAN CV4 ....154 B7
Shuna Cft COVE CV2 ....135 L6
Shustoke La DSYBK/YTR WS5 ......69 M1
Shustoke Rd BKDE/SHDE B34 ......92 A7
  SOLH B91 ....128 B4
Shuttock La MOS/BIL B13 ....125 H4
Shut Mill La RMSLY B62 ....142 B4
Shuttington Dr CRTAM B79 ....33 H6
Shuttington Rd CRTAM B79 ....32 F7
Shutt La HOCK/TIA B94 ....173 M4
Shuttle St COVN CV6 ....134 F5
Shuttleworth Rd RRUGBY CV23 ..161 K6
Shyltons Cft LDYWD/EDGR B16 ...106 E3
Sibdon Gv NFLD/LBR B31 ....144 E5
Sibree Rd COVS CV3 ....181 M1
Sibton Cl COVE CV2 ....135 J1
Sidaway Cl OLDBY B69 ....86 A7
Sidaway St CDYHTH B64 ....103 J4
Sidbury Gv DOR/KN B93 ....175 J2
Sidbury Rd COVN CV6 ....134 A7
Sidcup Cl BILS/COS WV14 ....66 F2
Sidcup Rd KGSTG B44 ....71 L4
Siddeley Av COVS CV3 ....155 L4
  KNWTH CV8 ....197 J2
Siddons Cl LICH WS13 ....20 D3
Siddons Rd BILS/COS WV14 ....67 H3
Siddons Wy HHTH/SAND B71 ....68 E6
Sidenhill Cl SHLY B90 ....147 M5
The Sidings RUGBYS/HIL CV21 ...187 G4
Sidlaw Cl HALE B63 ....121 H3
  WOLVN WV10 ....35 M7
Sidmouth Cl COVE CV2 ....135 G4
  NUN CV11 ....81 K8
Sidney St WOLV WV1 ....2 D4
Signal Gv BKHL/PFLD WV2 ....50 B7
Sidon Hill Wy CNCK/NC WS11 .....17 G2
Sidwick Crs BKHL/PFLD WV2 ....50 F2
Sigmund Cl WOLV WV1 ....50 F2
Signal Gv BKHL/PFLD WS3 ....38 E7
Signal Hayes Rd
  WALM/CURD B76 ....73 L4
Signal Wk TAM/AM/WIL B77 ....46 E3
Silesbourne Cl CBROM B36 * 92 A4
Silhill Hall Rd SOLH B91 ....127 L8
Silica Rd TAM/AM/WIL B77 ....46 F3
Silksby St COVS CV3 ....9 G9
Sillins Av REDE B98 ....202 E2
Sillins Rd REDE B98 ....202 E2
Silva Av KGSWFD DY6 ....101 K1

Silver Birch Av BDWTH CV12 ......116 C3
Silverbirch Cl NUNW/HART CV10 ..79 L6
Silver Birch Cl WASH/WDE B8 ......90 B7
Silver Birch Coppice
  FOAKS/STRLY B74 ....42 B3
Silver Birch Dr HLYWD B47 ....146 F7
  KIDD DY10 ....139 G8
Silver Birch Gv RLSS CV31 ....206 D8
  CHWD/FDBR/MGN B37 ....92 D7
  CNCK/NC WS11 ....25 M1
  ERDE/BCHGN B24 ....72 F7
  FOAKS/STRLY B74 ....55 K4
  HEDN WS12 ....12 E5
Silverbirch Rd SOLH B91 ....149 G2
Silvercroft Av HDSW B21 ....88 A1
Silverdale BRGRVW B61 ....191 K1
Silverdale Cl COVE CV2 ....134 F1
Silverdale Dr WOLVN WV10 ....50 C1
Silverdale Gdns STRBR DY8 ....101 G2
Silverdale Rd ERDE/BCHGN B24 ...91 H1
Silverfield Cl
  ALE/KHTH/YWD B14 ....125 J5
Silver Fir Cl HEDN WS12 ....12 E5
Silver Innage HALE B63 ....103 G6
Silverlands Av LGLYGN/QTN B68 .104 F2
Silverlands Cl HLGN/YWD B28 ....126 D4
Silver Link Rd TAM/AM/WIL B77 ..46 D4
Silvermead Ct HLYWD B47 ....146 E6
Silvermead Rd SCFLD/BOLD B73 ..72 E4
Silvermere Rd
  LGN/SDN/BHAMAIR B26 ....110 B7
Silver's Cl BLOX/PEL WS3 ....25 K8
Silverstone Av KIDDW DY11 ....138 B5
Silverstone Dr COVN CV6 ....134 F1
Silverstone Dr TLHL/CAN CV4 .....52 B2
Silverstone Dr FOAKS/STRLY B74 .55 K7
  RCOVN/BALC/EX CV7 ....116 C8
Silver St ALE/KHTH/YWD B14 .....125 J5
  BRLYHL DY5 ....101 M3
  BRWNH WS8 ....26 C5
  COV CV1 ....8 F3
  DARL/WED WS10 ....52 D6
  DARL/WED WS10 ....68 C2
  DUDN DY1 ....84 E3
  HALE B63 ....121 K1
  NUNW/HART CV10 ....98 A1
  SHHTH WV12 ....38 A3
  STRBR DY8 ....101 K8
  WOLV WV1 ....3 G4
  WSLW WS2 ....5 G4
Silver St (Above) REDW B97 ....202 E2
Silverthorne Av TPTN/OCK DY4 ....67 K8
Silverthorne La CDYHTH B64 ......102 F4
Silverton Crs MOS/BIL B13 ....126 B4
Silverton Hts SMTHWKW B67 * 87 K7
Silverton Rd COVN CV6 ....134 D6
  SMTHWKW B67 ....87 J7
Silverton Wy WNSFLD WV11 ....37 M6
Silvertrees Rd NFLD/LBR B31 .....147 K8
Silvester Rd BILS/COS WV14 ....51 J7
Silvester Wy STRBR DY8 ....101 M4
Silvington Cl SLYOAK B29 ....124 A6
Simcox Gdns RIDG/WDGT B32 ....123 H3
Simcox Rd DARL/WED WS10 ....52 D8
Simcox St HEDN WS12 ....12 D6
Simeon Bissell Cl TPTN/OCK DY4 ..67 J8
Simeon's Wk BRLYHL DY5 ....102 D6
Simmonds Cl BLOX/PEL WS3 ....39 H2
Simmonds Pl DARL/WED WS10 ....52 D6
Simmonds Rd BLOX/PEL WS3 ......39 H2
Simmonds Wy ATHST CV9 ....63 H3
  BRWNH WS8 ....26 C6
Simmons Cl POL/KGSB/FAZ B78 ...58 F4
Simmons Dr RIDG/WDGT B32 ....123 H1
Simmons Leasow
  RIDG/WDGT B32 ....123 H3
Simmons Rd WNSFLD WV11 ....37 M6
Simms La DUDS DY2 ....85 G8
  HLYWD B47 ....146 E8
Simon Cl HHTH/SAND B71 ....69 J4
Simon Rd HLYWD B47 ....146 K6
Simon Stone St COVN CV6 ....134 D5
Simpkins Cl ALDR WS9 ....40 E7
Simpson Gv COVS CV3 ....156 K7
  WOLVN WV10 ....36 C7
Simpson Rd CSCFLD/WYGN B72 ...73 G4
  LICH WS13 ....20 F2
  WOLVN WV10 ....36 C7
  WSLW WS2 ....38 F8
Simpson St OLDBY B69 ....86 C6
Singer Cl COVN CV6 ....134 E5
Singer Cft CBROM B36 ....92 D4
Sion Av KIDD DY10 ....138 E4
Sion Gdns STRPT DY13 ....188 D2
Sion Hl KIDD DY10 ....138 E4
Sir Alfreds Wy WALM/CURD B76 ...73 L4
Sir Harrys Rd DIG/EDG B5 ....107 G7
  EDG B15 ....106 F7
Sir Henry Parkes Rd COVW CV5 ..154 C1
Sir Hilton's Rd NFLD/LBR B31 ....144 F6
Sir John's Rd SLYOAK B29 ....125 G2
Sir Richards Dr HRBN B17 ....105 K6
Sir Thomas White's Rd
  COVW CV5 ....154 D3
Sir William Lyons Rd
  TLHL/CAN CV4 ....154 A7
Sir Winston Churchill Pl
  COVS CV3 ....157 G6
Sisefield Rd HIWK/WKHTH B38 ...145 L4
Siskin Cl BNTWD WS7 ....19 H8
  RRUGBY CV23 ....165 G5
Siskin Dr BHTH/HG B12 ....107 J7
  KNWTH CV8 ....182 A3
Siskin Pkwy East KNWTH CV8 ....181 M3
Siskin Pkwy West KNWTH CV8 ....181 M4
Siskin Rd HAG/WOL DY9 ....120 A2
Siskin Wy KIDD DY10 ....164 F4
Sister Dora Av BNTWD WS7 ....19 K6
Sister Dora Buildings WSL WS1 * ...4 F4
Sister Dora Gdns WSL WS1 ....4 F4
Siviter's Cl BLKHTH/ROWR B65 ...103 M2
Siviter's La BLKHTH/ROWR B65 ...104 A2
Siviter St HALE B63 ....121 M1
Six Acres RIDG/WDGT B32 ....123 G1
Skelcher Rd SHLY B90 ....147 L1
Skelwith Ri NUN CV11 ....81 L7
Skemp Cl BILS/COS WV14 ....67 L1
Sketchley Cl SMTHWK B66 ....87 J4
Sketchley La ATHST CV9 ....63 K1
Skidmore Av BDMR/CCFT WV3 .....49 K5
Skidmore Dr WBROM B70 ....86 E2
Skidmore Rd BILS/COS WV14 ....67 J4
Skilts Av REDE B98 ....202 D4
Skinner La DIG/EDG B5 ....7 H8
Skinner St WOLV WV1 ....2 E4
Skip La DSYBK/YTR WS5 ....69 M1
Skipness TAM/AM/WIL B77 ....32 C8
Skipton Gn
  DUNHL/THL/PER WV6 ....35 L8
Skipton Pl CNCK/NC WS11 ....15 M6
Skipton Rd LDYWD/EDGR B16 ....106 E4
Skipwith Cl RRUGBY CV23 ....158 B2
Skipworth Rd COVS CV3 ....156 C5
Skomer Cl RBRY B45 ....143 L6
Sky Blue Wy COV CV1 ....9 K4
Skye Cl CBROM B36 ....92 A6
  NUNW/HART CV10 ....98 D1
  TAM/AM/WIL B77 ....46 F1
Skye Wk CDYHTH B64 ....103 J4
Skylark Cl BRLYHL DY5 ....84 A4
  ERDW/GRVHL B23 ....72 A6

  HEDN WS12 1
Skylark Wy KIDD DY10 1
Slack La HDSW B21 ....
Slack's Av ATHST CV9 ....
Slacky La BLOX/PEL WS3 ....
Sladd La KIDDW DY11 1
Slade Av BNTWD WS7 ....
Sladefield Rd WASH/WDE B8 1
Slade Gdns CDSL WV8 ....
Slade Gv DOR/KN B93 1
Slade HI DUNHL/THL/PER WV6 ....
  RWWCK/WEL CV35 ....
Slade La HLGN/YWD B28 1
  MGN/WHC B75 ....
  TAM/AM/WIL B77 ....
Slade Lanker BKDE/SHDE B34 .....
Slade Meadow RLSS CV31 2
Sladepool Farm Rd
  ALE/KHTH/YWD B14 1
  HALE B63 ....
  MGN/WHC B75 ....
  RUGBYN/HIL CV21 1
  WOLVN WV10 ....
Slade View Ri HEDN WS12 ....
The Slad STRPT DY13 1
Slaithwaite Rd HHTH/SAND B71 ...
Slaney Ct WSLW WS2 ....
Slaney Rd WSLW WS2 ....
Slatch House Rd
  SMTHWKW B67 1
Slateley Crs SHLY B90 1
Slater Rd DOR/KN B93 1
Slater's La WSLW WS2 ....
Slaters Pl WSLW WS2 ....
Slater St BILS/COS WV14 ....
  TPTN/OCK DY4 ....
  WLNHL WV13 ....
Sleaford Gv HLGN/YWD B28 1
Sleaford Rd HLGN/YWD B28 1
Sleath's Yd BDWTH CV12 1
Sledmere Cl COVE CV2 ....
Sledmore Rd DUDS DY2 ....
Sleets Yd BDWTH CV12 1
Slideslow Av BRGRVE B60 1
Slideslow Dr BRGRVE B60 ....
The Slieve BFLD/HDSWWD B20 ...
Slim Av BILS/COS WV14 ....
Slimbridge Cl REDW B97 1
  SHLY B90 1
Slim Rd WSLW WS2 ....
Slims Ga HALE B63 1
Slingfield Rd NFLD/LBR B31 1
Slingsby TAM/AM/WIL B77 ....
Slingsby Cl NUN CV11 ....
The Sling DUDS DY2 ....
  KIDD DY10 1
Sloane St CBHAMW B1 ....
Slowley Hl RCOVN/BALC/EX CV7 ..
Smallbrook La WMBN WV5 ....
Smallbrook Queensway
  DIG/EDG B5 ....
Small Cl SMTHKW B67 ....
Smalldale Rd PBAR/PBCH B42 ....
Smalley Cl CNCK/NC WS11 ....
Small Heath Br SPARK B11 1
Small Heath Hwy SMTHH B10 1
  YDLY B25 ....
Smallridge LICH WS13 ....
Smallshire Vw WNSFLD WV11 ......
Smallshire Wy STRBR DY8 1
Small St HHTH/SAND B71 ....
  WSL WS1 ....
Smallwood Cl ERDE/BCHGN B24 ...
  WALM/CURD B76 ....
Smallwood Rd CDSL WV8 ....
Smallwood St REDE B98 2
Smarts Av LICHS WS14 ....
Smarts Rd BDWTH CV12 1
Smeaton Gdns WSNGN B18 1
Smedley Crooke Pl ALVE B48 1
Smercote Cl BDWTH CV12 1
Smestow La SEDG DY3 ....
Smestow St WOLVN WV10 ....
Smillie Pl CNCK/NC WS11 ....
Smirrells Rd HLGN/YWD B28 1
Smith Av DARL/WED WS10 ....
  SMTHWKW B67 ....
Smithfield Ri LICH WS13 ....
Smithfield Rd BLOX/PEL WS3 ....
Smithford Wy COV CV1 ....
Smithmoor Crs HHTH/SAND B71 ...
Smith Pl TPTN/OCK DY4 ....
Smith Rd DARL/WED WS10 ....
  WSLW WS2 ....
Smiths Cl BNTWD WS7 ....
  RIDG/WDGT B32 ....
Smiths La DOR/KN B93 ....
Smiths Orch RUGBYN/HIL CV21 ..1
Smith St ATHST CV9 ....
  BDWTH CV12 ....
  BILS/COS WV14 ....
  COVN CV6 ....
  DUDS DY2 ....
  LOZ/NWT B19 ....
  RLSS CV31 2
Smiths Wy CSHL/WTROR B46 ......
Smiths Yd BDWTH CV12 * ....
Smithy Dr BLOX/PEL WS3 ....
Smithy La ATHST CV9 ....
  BRLYHL DY5 ....
  LICH WS13 ....
  RUGBYS/DCH CV22 1
  TAM/AM/WIL B77 ....
The Smithy
  LGN/SDN/BHAMAIR B26 1
Smorrall La BDWTH CV12 1
  BDWTH CV12 1
Smout Crs BILS/COS WV14 ....
Smythe Gv WWCK CV34 2
Snake La ALVE B48 ....
Snakes Lake La BRGRVW B61 1
Snapdragon Dr DSYBK/YTR WS5 ...
Snape Rd COVE CV2 1
  WNSFLD WV11 ....
Sneyd Hall Cl BLOX/PEL WS3 * ....
Sneyd Hall Rd BLOX/PEL WS3 .....
Sneyd La BLOX/PEL WS3 ....
  WNSFLD WV11 ....
Snipe Cl WOLVN WV10 ....
Snowberry Dr BRLYHL DY5 ....
Snowberry Gdns ACGN B27 * ....
Snowdon Cl KIDDW DY11 1
  NUNW/HART CV10 ....
Snowdon Gv HALE B63 1
Snowdon Ri SEDG DY3 ....
Snowdon Rd CNCK/NC WS11 1
Snowdon Wy SHHTH WV12 ....
  WOLVN WV10 ....
Snowdrop Cl BRWNH WS8 ....
Snowford Cl SHLY B90 1
Snow HI BKHL/PFLD WV2 ....

...Hill Jct BKHL/PFLD WV2 .....3 G7
...HAMNE 6 F3
...vs Drive HI SHLY B90.....148 M5
...DE B98 .....194 F7
...shill Gdns DUDN DY1.....84 D1
...Mill Wk BEWD DY12.....162 E3
...rson Cl WNSFLD WV11.....37 K6
...CO CV3.....156 B7
...n's Av KNWTH CV8.....182 E4
...CI SMTHWK B66.....88 E6
...us Av WSNCN B18.....88 A7
...HI WSNCN B18.....88 C5
...Pool Wy WSNGN B18.....88 C5
...ry SMTHWK B66.....87 M7
...t Rd HDSW DY1.....88 C5
...ull La HLGN/YWD B28.....126 E7
...ull Pkwy
...WD/FDBR/MGN B37.....111 J5
...ull Rd HIA/OLT B92.....129 H7
...ARK B11.....126 B2
...ull Wy CBROM B36.....91 M4
...OLT B92.....128 A4
...TIA CV9.....174 A3
...ay Cl SOLH B91.....148 E5
...rcotes Rd PBAR/PBCH B42..71 H5
...rdale Rd NFLD/LBR B31.....145 C1
...erfield CI RUSH/SHEL WS4..40 A4
...erfield Dr GTWY WS6.....24 C4
...erfield Rd BLOX/PEL WS3..54 C5
...erford Gdns WOLVN WV10..36 C3
...erford Pl WLNHL WV13.....51 K4
...erford Wy BILS/COS WV14..66 F5
...erland Rd
...V/SDN/BHAMAIR B26.....109 L4
...erleyton Av KIDD DY10.....138 A8
...erly Cl COVS CV3.....156 D5
...erset Rd POL/KGSB/FAZ B78..45 L4
...erset Crs DARL/WED WS10..69 H1
...erset Dr KIDDW DY11.....138 A4
...LD/LBR B31.....144 D6
...UNW/HART CV10.....98 C1
...DBR DY8.....101 H6
...erset Rd
...HDSWWD B20.....88 D3
...LY B15.....106 C7
...DW/GRVHL B23.....72 C1
...HHTH/SAND B71.....69 H7
...SH/SHEL WS4.....53 L1
...LNHL WV13.....52 B3
...ers Rd
...erton Dr
...WD/FDBR/MGN B37.....110 F6
...WOLV WV2.....72 E7
...erville Ct CRTAM B79.....31 H7
...erville Rd SCFLD/BOLD B73..72 E1
...era Rd BRGRVE B60.....192 A4
...erton Cl COVW WV9.....35 K3
...with Cft CVALE B35.....91 J1
...us TAM/AM/WIL B77.....46 F1
...dale Cft COVS CV3.....156 A4
...el TAM/AM/WIL B77.....32 F8
...el CI OLDBY B69.....85 M3
...OAK B29.....123 L3
...ery Rd DUDN DY1.....85 G2
...erwold Cft B32.....123 L3
...mmerton Rd
...WOLV WV2.....72 E1

Southfield Av CBROM B36.....91 M5
LDYWD/EDGR B16.....106 A2
Southfield Dr ALDR WS9.....40 E8
NUNW/HART CV10.....81 H7
Southfield Dr HLGN/YWD B28..126 E8
KNWTH CV8.....179 L7
Southfield Gv BDMR/CCFT WV3..49 G5
Southfield Rd
LDYWD/EDGR B16.....106 A2
RUGBYS/DCH CV22.....187 C4
WNSFLD WV11.....37 K6
Southfields Cl CSHL/WTROR B46..93 L8
Southfields Rd SOLH B91.....148 D4
Southgate CDYHTH B64.....103 H5
CNCK/NC WS11.....15 M6
WOLV WV1.....2 D4
Southgate Cl KIDDW DY11.....163 L1
Southgate End CNCK/NC WS11..15 M6
Southgate Rd KGSTG B44.....71 J3
South Gn
ETTPK/GDPK/PENN WV4.....49 H8
South Gv ERDW/GRVHL B23.....72 D8
LOZ/NWT B19.....88 F5
South Holme BORD B9.....108 A4
Southlands ATHST CV9.....63 J6
RLSS CV31.....206 F6
Southlands Rd MOS/BIL B13.....125 L4
Southlea Av RLSS CV31.....206 C7
Southlea Cl RLSS CV31.....206 C7
Southleigh Av COVW CV5.....154 D7
Southmead Crs REDE B98.....202 D2
Southmead Dr BRGRVE B60.....168 F7
Southminster Dr
ALE/KHTH/YWD B14.....125 J7
Southorn Ct RLSN CV32 *.....207 H2
South Ov SEDG DY3.....66 C8
South Pde BLOX/PEL WS3 *.....57 C8
South Park Ms BRLYHL WS5.....102 A3
Southport Cl COVS CV3.....155 M8
South Range SPARK B11.....107 M7
South Rdg COVW CV5.....153 M1
South Rd ALE/KHTH/YWD B14..125 J5
BRGRVE B60.....191 M6
ERDW/GRVHL B23.....90 D1
HAG/WOL DY9.....140 E1
NFLD/LBR B31.....144 D3
RRUGBY CV23.....161 K8
SMTHWKW B67.....87 K8
SPARK B11.....107 M6
STRBR DY8.....119 K1
TPTN/OCK DY4.....67 M5
WSNCN B18.....88 C7
South Road Av WSNCN B18.....88 C7
South Roundhay STECH B33.....109 L2
South St ATHST CV9.....63 H5
BRLYHL DY5.....102 A3
COV CV1.....9 J1
HRBN B17.....106 B7
KIDD B10.....138 D7
REDE B98.....202 C2
RUGBYN/HIL CV21.....187 H1
WLNHL WV13.....51 J3
WOLVN WV10.....36 A7
WSL WS1.....4 D7
South Street Gdns WSL WS1.....5 G5
South Tower VAUX/NECH B7 *..107 H1
South Vw GTB/HAM B43.....70 C6
POL/KGSB/FAZ B78.....45 K6
RRUGBY CV23 *.....158 D1
RWWCK/WEL CV35 *.....204 E7
South View B CDSL WV8.....34 F7
South View Rd RLSN.....199 C3
RRUGBY CV23.....185 K1
SEDG DY3.....65 M7
Southville Bungalows
ALE/KHTH/YWD B14 *.....146 F1
Southwark Cl LICH WS13.....21 G2
South Wy BHAMNEC B40.....109 L8
Southway RLSS CV31.....206 E8
Southway Cl KGSTG DY6.....101 K1
Southwick Pl BILS/COS WV14..51 H6
Southwick Rd RMSLY B62.....104 B5
Southwold Av BVILLE B30.....146 A2
Southwood Av BKDE/SHDE B34..91 M6
Southwood Cl KGSWFD DY6..83 J8
Southwood Covert
ALE/KHTH/YWD B14.....146 A3
Sovereign Cl KNWTH CV8.....197 K4
Sovereign Dr DUDN DY1.....84 D3
Sovereign Hts NFLD/LBR B31..144 A4
Sovereign Rd BVILLE B30.....145 K1
COVW CV5.....154 D3
Sovereign Rw WSL WS1 *.....8 B5
Sovereign Wk WSL WS1.....5 H3
Sovereign Wy MOS/BIL B13..125 K1
Sowerby March
ERDE/BCHGN B24.....91 H1
Sowers Cl SHHTH WV12.....38 B1
Sowers Ct MGN/WHC B75.....57 H1
Sowers Gdns SHHTH WV12.....38 B8
Spade Gn LICH WS13.....21 J5
Spadesbourne Rd BRGRVE B60..169 C7
Spa Gv BVILLE B30.....125 G5
Sparkbrook St COV CV1.....9 M3
Spark St SPARK B11.....107 L1
Sparrey Dr SLYOAK B29.....124 E5
Sparrow Cl DARL/WED WS10..52 F7
Sparrow Cock La DOR/KN B93..177 G4
Sparta Cl RUGBYN/HIL CV21..160 E7
Speakers Cl OLDBY B69.....85 M6
Spearhill LICHS WS14.....21 L6
Speed Rd TPTN/OCK DY4.....67 J7
Speedway La KNWTH CV8.....40 D8
Speedwell Cl ALDR WS9.....40 D8
ALE/KHTH/YWD B14 *.....125 H7
Speedwell Dr
RCOVN/BALC/EX CV7.....151 L7
Speedwell Gdns BRLYHL DY5..101 M1
WOLVN WV10.....22 F5
Speedwell La ATHST CV9.....61 M5
Speedwell Rd DIG/EDG B5.....107 J7
YDLY B25.....108 E7
Spencer Av BEWD DY12.....163 C1
BILS/COS WV14.....67 C5
COVW CV5.....8 A4
Spencer Cl HHTH/SAND B71..69 K5
OLDBY B69.....85 M5
SEDG DY3.....83 L1
Spencer Dr BNTWD WS7.....18 E5
Spencer Rd COVW CV5.....8 D6
LICHS WS14.....20 F7
Spencer's La
RCOVN/BALC/EX CV7.....152 B3
Spencer St KIDDW DY11.....164 A1
RLSS CV31.....206 D6
WSNCN B18.....6 C1
Spencer Yd RLSS CV31.....206 D6
Spennells Valley Rd KIDD DY10..164 E2
Spenser Av
DUNHL/THL/PER WV6.....48 C1
Spenser Cl CRTAM B79.....31 J7
Spernall Gv SLYOAK B29.....123 L4
Spetchley Rd REDW B97.....202 A7
Spey Cl DIG/EDG B5.....107 H7

Sphinx Dr COVS CV3.....155 M4
Spiceland Rd NFLD/LBR B31..123 K7
Spicer Pl RUGBYS/DCH CV22..186 B6
Spiers Cl DOR/KN B93.....149 L7
Spies Cl RMSLY B62.....104 D7
Spies La RMSLY B62.....104 D8
Spills Meadow SEDG DY3.....66 C8
Spilsbury Cl RLSN CV32.....206 C3
Spilsbury Cft SOLH B91.....148 E8
Spindle Cl KIDDW DY11.....138 B4
Spindle La SHLY B90.....147 L7
Spindle St COV CV1.....134 B7
Spindlewood Cl HEDN WS12..17 M4
Spinners End Dr CDYHTH B64..103 H4
Spinney Cl BLOX/PEL WS3.....39 L3
BNTWD WS7.....18 E4
COVS CV3.....157 J6
KIDDW DY11.....137 L7
NFLD/LBR B31.....144 E2
POL/KGSB/FAZ B78.....47 K5
RCOVN/BALC/EX CV7.....96 C5
STRBR DY8.....99 K6
Spinney Dr SHLY B90.....174 B1
Spinney Farm Rd CNCK/NC WS11..15 M6
Spinney HI WWCK CV34.....205 L4
Spinney La BNTWD WS7.....18 D4
NUNW/HART CV10.....98 A1
The Spinney ATHST CV9.....63 L6
BDMR/CCFT WV3.....49 H4
BFLD/HDSWWD B20.....88 C1
FOAKS/STRLY B74.....41 M7
HLYWD B47.....172 F1
RLSN CV32.....206 B4
RRUGBY CV23.....159 L8
SEDG DY3.....65 M8
SOLH B91.....149 C5
TLHL/CAN CV4.....180 C2
Spinning School La CRTAM B79..31 M8
Spiral Cl RMSLY B62.....104 C5
Spiral Gn ERDE/BCHGN B24..91 C1
Spirehouse La BRGRVE B60..169 H8
Spires Cft WOLVN WV10.....23 H4
The Spires LICHS WS14.....21 J1
NUNW/HART CV10.....98 A1
Spire Vw BRGRVE B61.....191 K2
Spitfire Rd ERDE/BCHGN B24..91 C3
Spitfire Wy CVALE B35.....91 J1
Splash La HEDN WS12.....17 C2
Spode Pl CNCK/NC WS11.....16 F3
Spon End COV CV1.....8 C3
Spon La ATHST CV9.....62 B1
WBROM B70.....87 H4
Spon La South SMTHWK B66..87 H5
Spon St COV CV1.....8 C3
Spooner Cft DIG/EDG B5.....107 J5
Spooners Cl HIA/OLT B92.....128 D6
Spottiswood Cl
RUGBYS/DCH CV22.....185 L5
Spouthouse La GTB/HAM B43..70 C6
Spout La WSL WS1.....5 J6
Spreadbury Cl HRBN B17.....105 K5
Sprengers Cl PENK ST19.....10 E4
Sprig Cft BDMR/CCFT WV3..36 C5
Spring Av BLKHTH/ROWR B65..104 D3
Springavon Cft HRBN B17.....105 M7
Springbank BORD B9.....107 C6
Springbank Rd EDC B15.....107 C6
Springbrook Cl CBROM B36.....92 A2
Springbrook La HOCK/TIA B94..173 H1
Spring Cl COV CV1.....9 K3
HAG/WOL DY9.....140 D1
RUSH/SHEL WS4.....40 A3
SOLH B91.....148 D2
Spring Coppice Dr DOR/KN B93..175 L2
Spring Crs CDYHTH B64.....103 K6
Springcroft Rd SPARK B11.....126 D3
Springdale Ct NUN CV11 *.....99 C7
Springfield ERDW/GRVHL B23..90 D2
BRGRVE B60.....191 M6
HAG/WOL DY9.....120 C1
LICH WS13.....21 H3
Springfield Av BHTH/HG B12..107 J7
BRGRVE B60.....191 M6
HAG/WOL DY9.....120 C1
Springfield Cl
BLKHTH/ROWR B65.....85 L8
Springfield Ct HLGN/YWD B28 *..126 D2
Springfield Crs BDWTH CV12..116 F3
DUDN DY1.....85 K5
HIA/OLT B92.....128 D5
WALM/CURD B76.....73 L1
WBROM B70.....87 J7
Springfield Dr
ALE/KHTH/YWD B14 *.....125 J4
BILS/COS WV14.....51 J6
CBROM B36.....92 B5
COV CV1.....134 B4
MOS/BIL B13.....126 A4
NUN CV11.....99 J3
RMSLY B62.....104 B6
TAM/AM/WIL B77.....46 E6
WALM/CURD B76.....73 L2
Springfields CSHL/WTROR B46..93 K8
RUSH/SHEL WS4.....38 M1
Springfields Rd BRLYHL DY5..101 M3
LGLGYGN/QTN B68.....105 J2
Springfield St WSNGN B18.....106 C1
Springfield Ter
BLKHTH/ROWR B65.....85 K8
Spring Gdns DUDS DY2.....85 K8
HDSW B21 *.....88 D6
Spring Gv BEWD DY12 *.....163 C1
LOZ/NWT B19 *.....88 F7
Spring Grove Crs KIDDW DY11..163 M2
Spring Grove Gdns WSNCN B18..88 D7
Spring Grove Rd KIDDW DY11..163 M2
Spring Head DARL/WED WS10..68 D3
Spring HI ERDE/BCHGN B24.....90 E2
KNWTH CV8.....182 A8
RCOVN/BALC/EX CV7.....96 D2
WSNCN B18.....106 C1
Springhill Av ETTPK/GDPK/PENN WV4..65 C1
Spring Hill La WSNCN B18 *.....106 C1
Springhill Gdns REDW B97.....201 M3
Springhill La ETTPK/GDPK/PENN WV4..64 F7
Spring Hill Pas WSNCN B18.....106 C1

Springhill Ri BEWD DY12.....163 C1
Spring Hill Rd NUNW/HART CV10..80 A7
Spring Hill Rd BNTWD WS7.....18 A7
BRWNH WS8.....9 C1
WNSFLD WV11.....37 H5
WSL WS1.....4 A5
Spring La ERDE/BCHGN B24.....90 E2
HOCK/TIA B94.....174 E8
KNWTH CV8.....179 L8
RLSS CV31.....207 J8
RMSLY B62.....142 A3
RUSH/SHEL WS4.....40 A3
SHHTH WV12.....51 M1
Spring Meadow CDYHTH B64..103 K4
GTWY WS6.....24 B4
HALE B63.....120 E8
TPTN/OCK DY4.....68 A7
Springmeadow Gv LOZ/NWT B19..89 H7
Spring Meadow Rd DUDS DY2..103 C3
Spring Meadows CI CDSL WV8..34 A2
Spring Parklands DUDN DY1..84 E5
Spring Pool WWCK CV34.....205 J6
Spring Rd COVN CV6.....133 C6
DUDS DY2.....85 H7
EDG B15.....107 H6
ETTPK/GDPK/PENN WV4.....50 E8
LICH WS13.....21 H3
RCOVN/BALC/EX CV7.....117 J7
RUSH/SHEL WS4.....40 A3
SMTHWK B66.....87 H5
SPARK B11.....126 D2
Springs Av BRGRVE B61.....168 D4
Springslade RIDG/WDGT B32..105 K8
The Springs HHTH/SAND B71..91 G1
The Springs CRTAM B79.....14 C5
Spring St CNCK/NC WS11.....16 C5
EDG B15.....107 H5
HAG/WOL DY9.....120 C1
HALE B63.....103 C7
RUGBYN/HIL CV21.....186 F2
TPTN/OCK DY4.....68 A7
Springthorpe Gn ERDE/BCHGN B24..91 G1
Springthorpe Rd ERDE/BCHGN B24..91 G1
Springvale Av BILS/COS WV14..66 F1
DSYBK/YTR WS5.....54 A6
Spring Vale Cl BILS/COS WV14..66 E4
Spring Vale Rd BLKHTH/ROWR B65 *..85 L8
Springvale St WLNHL WV13..51 K4
Springvale Wy BILS/COS WV14..67 C1
Spring Wk HALE B63.....121 H4
SMTHWK B66.....86 E8
WSLW WS2.....4 A5
Springwell Rd RLSS CV31.....207 H1
Sproat Av DARL/WED WS10.....52 A8
Spruce TAM/AM/WIL B77.....46 F1
Spruce Gv ERDE/BCHGN B24..91 G3
RLSS CV31.....206 D8
Spruce Rd DSYBK/YTR WS5..54 A6
HEDN WS12.....12 C4
Spruce Wy ETTPK/GDPK/PENN WV4..49 C1
Spur Tree Av BDMR/CCFT WV3..48 E4
Squadron Cl CVALE B35.....92 A1
Square La RIDG/WDGT B32.....123 C2
Square La RCOVN/BALC/EX CV7..114 F4
The Square ALVE B48.....170 F7
BKHL/PFLD WV2 *.....3 H9
COVE CV2 *.....135 L6
HRBN B17.....105 M7
KNWTH CV8.....197 K1
NUN CV11.....99 J3
SHHTH WV12 *.....38 D5
SOLH B91.....149 G2
TPTN/OCK DY4.....68 B8
Squires Cft COVS CV3.....135 K4
WALM/CURD B76.....73 L4
Squires Ga BNTWD WS7.....18 E5
Squires Rd RRUGBY CV23.....183 K7
Squires Wy TLHL/CAN CV4..154 B8
Squirhill Pl RLSS CV31 *.....206 F6
Squirrel Hollow WALM/CURD B76..73 L4
Squirrels Hollow BNTWD WS7..18 E4
LGLGYGN/QTN B68.....105 H6
Squirrel Wk ETTPK/GDPK/PENN WV4..65 L1
FOAKS/STRLY B74.....42 A8
Stable Ct SEDG DY3.....66 C8
Stable Cft HHTH/SAND B71.....69 K6
Stableford Cl REDW B97.....202 B6
Stable La WOLVN WV10.....14 C1
The Stables SLYOAK B29.....124 E3
Stable Wk NUN CV11.....99 K5
Stable Wy BRGRVE B60.....191 J7
Stacey Cl KNWTH CV8 *.....181 J3
Stacey Grange Gdns RBRY B45 *..143 J7
Stackhouse Cl WALM/CURD B76..40 E1
Stackhouse Dr BLOX/PEL WS3..39 L1
Stadium Cl COVN CV6.....134 D3
KIDD DY10.....164 D1
Stafford Cl BLOX/PEL WS3.....39 L1
Stafford Crs CNCK/NC WS11..30 B2
Stafford Dr HHTH/SAND B71..68 F6
Stafford La CDSL WV8.....34 B4
Stafford Rd CNCK/NC WS11..16 E1
COVEN WV9.....22 A1
DARL/WED WS10.....51 M7
GTWY WS6.....24 B8
HDSW B21.....88 E5
HEDN WS12.....17 J4
LICH WS13.....20 C4
WOLV WV1.....36 A5
Staffordshire Pool Cl AST/WIT B6..89 K4
Staffordshire Wy PENK ST19..10 E4
Stafford St ATHST CV9.....63 H6
CBHAMNE B4.....3 H3
DARL/WED WS10.....51 M7
DUDN DY1.....84 D3
HEDN WS12.....17 J4
WOLV WV1.....3 F3
Stafford Street Jct WOLV WV1..3 F3
Stafford Wy GTB/HAM B43.....70 C6
Stagborough Wy HEDN WS12..17 C2
STRPT DY13.....188 C2
Stag Crs BLOX/PEL WS3.....39 J6
Stag Hill Rd BLOX/PEL WS3..39 J6
Stag Wk WALM/CURD B76.....73 H4
Staines Cl NUN CV11.....81 K6
Stainforth Cl NUN CV11.....99 K5
Stainsby Av LOZ/NWT B19.....89 C3
Stainsby Cft SHLY B90.....148 F8

Staircase La COVW CV5.....133 C6
Stakenbridge La KIDD DY10..140 A1
Staley Cft HEDN WS12.....16 A1
Stalling's La KGSWFD DY6.....83 H5
Stambermill Cl HAG/WOL DY9..102 B8
Stamford Av COVS CV3.....155 C7
Stamford Cl NUN CV11 *.....80 F8
Stamford Crs BNTWD WS7.....18 C5
Stamford Cft SOLH B91.....148 F3
Stamford Gdns RLSN CV32..206 C4
Stamford Gv
BFLD/HDSWWD B20..89 C3
Stamford Rd
BFLD/HDSWWD B20..89 C4
BRLYHL DY5.....102 A7
STRBR DY8.....101 M8
Stamford St STRBR DY8.....101 K6
Stanbrook Rd SHLY B90.....148 E8
Stanbury Av DARL/WED WS10..51 M7
Stanbury Rd
ALE/KHTH/YWD B14..146 F1
Stancroft Gv
LGN/SDN/BHAMAIR B26..109 L5
Standard Av TLHL/CAN CV4..153 L4
Standard Wy VAUX/NECH B7..90 C5
Standbridge Wy TPTN/OCK DY4..67 L3
Standedge TAM/AM/WIL B77..46 E6
Standhills Rd KGSWFD DY6.....83 K8
Standish Cl COVE CV2.....156 C3
Standlake Av CBROM B36.....91 M6
Standlake Ms RLSS CV31.....207 G8
Stand St WWCK CV34.....205 H7
Stanfield Rd GTB/HAM B43.....55 H8
RIDG/WDGT B32.....
Stanford Av PBAR/PBCH B42..70 E6
Stanford Cl PENK ST19.....10 C4
Stanford Dr
REDW B97.....201 M7
Stanford Rd NUN CV11 *.....99 H3
Stanhope Cl BRLYHL DY5.....102 B5
Stanhope Rd SMTHWKW B67..87 K2
Stanhope St BDMR/CCFT WV3..2 K6
BHTH/HG B12.....103 J1
Stanhope Wy GTB/HAM B43..71 H1
Stanhurst Wy HHTH/SAND B71..69 L3
Stanier Av COV CV1.....8 B3
Stanier Cl RUSH/SHEL WS4..39 M6
Stanier Gv BFLD/HDSWWD B20..88 F3
Staniforth St AST/WIT B6.....7 H1
Stanklyn La KIDD DY10.....164 E5
Stanley Av MGN/WHC B75.....73 K1
RIDG/WDGT B32.....
SHLY B90.....147 M1
Stanley Cl HLGN/YWD B28.....126 E6
REDE B98.....194 E8
WNSFLD WV11.....37 K5
Stanley Ct ALE/KHTH/YWD B14 *..125 H6
ATHST CV9.....63 H6
COVW CV5.....154 C7
DARL/WED WS10.....52 F7
HHTH/SAND B71.....69 J6
LGLGYGN/QTN B68.....105 L6
NUN CV11.....80 E8
RUGBYN/HIL CV21.....187 J4
RUSH/SHEL WS4.....39 M7
STRBR DY8.....119 K2
VAUX/NECH B7.....90 A6
WOLVN WV10.....36 B4
Stanley St BLOX/PEL WS3.....39 C5
Stanmore Gv RIDG/WDGT B32..122 C2
Stanmore Rd LDYWD/EDGR B16..106 A4
Stansfield Gv KNWTH CV8.....198 B1
Stanton Av DUDN DY1.....84 D7
Stanton Gv
LGN/SDN/BHAMAIR B26..109 K5
SHLY B90.....147 L1
TPTN/OCK DY4.....67 L8
Stanton Rd GTB/HAM B43.....70 D6
RLSN CV32.....207 C7
SHLY B90.....147 L1
WOLV WV1.....3 H4
Stanville Rd
LGN/SDN/BHAMAIR B26..110 A7
Stanway Gdns HHTH/SAND B71..69 H7
Stanway Gv KGSTG B44.....71 K2
Stanway Rd COVW CV5.....8 B9
HHTH/SAND B71.....69 H7
SHLY B90.....148 B1
Stanwell Gv ERDW/GRVHL B23..72 C7
Stanwick Av STETCH B33.....110 C3
Stapenhall Rd SHLY B90.....148 B8
Staple Flat BRGRVE B60.....169 C5
Stapleford Cft ALE/KHTH/YWD B14..146 A3
Stapleford Gdns BNTWD WS7..19 H7
Stapleford Gv STRBR DY8.....101 J3
Staple Hall Rd NFLD/LBR B31..144 F3
Staplehurst Rd HLGN/YWD B28..126 D5
Staple Lodge Rd NFLD/LBR B31..144 F4
Stapleton Cl REDE B98.....203 H2
WALM/CURD B76.....
Stapleton Dr
CHWD/FDBR/MGN B37..110 E2
Stapleton Rd ALDR WS9.....40 B6
Stapylton Av HRBN B17 *.....105 M8
Starbank Rd SMTHH B10.....108 F1
Starbold Crs DOR/KN B93.....149 M8
Star Cl TPTN/OCK DY4.....68 A8
WSLW WS2.....52 D1
Starcross Cl COVE CV2.....135 C4
Starcross Rd ACGN B27.....127 C3
Stare Gn TLHL/CAN CV4.....154 B8
Stareton Cl TLHL/CAN CV4..154 C8
Star HI EDG B15.....106 F5
Starkey Cft
CHWD/FDBR/MGN B37..111 C3
Starkie Dr LGLGYGN/QTN B68..105 L6
Starley Rd COV CV1.....8 D5
Starley Wy
CHWD/FDBR/MGN B37..111 G7
Star St BDMR/CCFT WV3.....49 C5
HAG/WOL DY9.....102 B8
Startin Rd RCOVN/BALC/EX CV7..116 C2
Statham Dr LDYWD/EDGR B16..106 A3
Station Ap DOR/KN B93.....175 K2
FOAKS/STRLY B74.....
Station Av LDYWD/EDGR B16..105 M4
TLHL/CAN CV4.....153 H5
WWCK CV34.....205 K6
Station Buildings
DUNHL/THL/PER WV6 *..49 J1
Station Cl BLOX/PEL WS3.....39 F5

CDSL WV8 ....34 C2
Station Dr BRLYHL DY5..............101 M4
FOAKS/STRLY B74 ....56 F5
HAG/WOL DY9 ....119 L8
HIA/OLT B92 ....127 J4
HOCK/TIA B94 ....173 H4
KIDD DY10............................139 M3
TPTN/OCK DY4 ....85 M1
WOLVN WV10 ....14 A8
Stationfields CRTAM B79 ....32 A3
Station Hl KIDD DY11.............189 M3
Station Link Rd
CHWD/FDBR/MGN B37..........129 H1
Station Pl BLOX/PEL WS3 ....38 E5
Station Rd ACGN B27.............127 G2
ALDR WS9 ....40 E8
ALE/KHTH/YWD B14 ....125 H5
ALVE B48.............................170 E8
AST/WIT B6...........................89 K4
BEWD DY12 ....163 G2
BILS/COS WV14 ....85 J3
BLKHTH/ROWR B65 ....104 B3
BLOX/PEL WS3 ....39 L2
BNTWD WS7 ....27 J2
BRGRVE B60 ....169 L8
BRLYHL DY5 ....102 A1
BVILLE B30..........................124 C8
CDSL WV8 ....34 C2
CDYHTH B64 ....103 K5
CHWD/FDBR/MGN B37..........110 D5
CSHL/WTROR B46 ....93 K4
CSHL/WTROR B46 ....94 B2
DOR/KN B93.........................175 L2
ERDW/GRVHL B23 ....72 D8
GTWY WS6............................24 D1
HAG/WOL DY9 ....102 C7
HAG/WOL DY9 ....119 L7
HDSW B21.............................88 A5
HEDN WS12 ....13 G7
HIA/OLT B92 ....129 L6
HLYWD B47 ....172 E2
HRBN B17 ....106 A7
HWK/WKHTH B38 ....145 K1
KIDDW DY11.........................189 L6
KNWTH CV8 ....197 K1
LICH WS13 ....21 D6
LICHS WS14 ....28 D1
MKTBOS/BARL/STKG CV13 ....81 K1
NFLD/LBR B31 ....144 E3
OLDBY B69 ....86 E8
PENK ST19.............................10 C4
POL/KGSB/FAZ B78 ....47 M2
RCOVN/BALC/EX CV7 ....96 B5
RCOVN/BALC/EX CV7 ....151 L7
RCOVN/BALC/EX CV7 ....96 B5
RRUGBY CV23........................161 K8
RUSH/SHEL WS4 ....59 L7
SCFLD/BOLD B73 ....72 E4
SOLH B91 ....148 F1
STECH B33 ....109 H2
WMBN WV5 ....65 C4
WOLVN WV10 ....3 M1
WOLVN WV10 ....14 B8
WWCK CV34 ....205 K6
Station Sq COV CV1.................6 E4
Station St ATHST CV9...............63 H5
BLOX/PEL WS3 ....38 F5
BRGRVE B60 ....191 K3
CDYHTH B64 ....103 C5
DARL/WED WS10 ....52 C7
DIG/EDG B5 ....24 C2
GTWY WS6............................24 C2
TPTN/OCK DY4 ....67 M8
WSL WS1 ....4 E3
Station St East COVN CV6.........134 C6
Station St West COVN CV6.........134 C6
Station Tower COV CV1 * 8 B2
Station Wy REDW B97 ....202 B2
Staunton Rd BLOX/PEL WS3 ....38 E2
RLSS CV31............................206 E4
Staveley Rd
ALE/KHTH/YWD B14 ....125 H7
DUNHL/THL/PER WV6 ....2 D1
Staveley Ri RUGBYN/HIL CV21 ...161 H7
Staverton Cl COWW CV5 ....153 M4
Staverton Leys
RUGBYS/DCH CV22 ....186 E6
Stead Cl TPTN/OCK DY4 ....68 E4
WSLW WS2 ....39 G8
Steadman Cft TPTN/OCK DY4 * ...68 B5
Stealtite Wy STRPT DY13 ....163 J8
Stechford La WASH/WDE B8 ....91 G8
Stechford Rd BKDE/SHDE B34 ......91 H8
Steel Dr WOLVN WV10 ....36 B5
Steele St RUGBYS/DCH CV22 ......186 C5
Steel Gv YDLY B25 ....109 G6
Steelhouse La BKHL/PFLD WV2 ......3 J8
CBHAMNE B4 ....7 H3
Steelpark Rd RMSLY B62 ....105 M6
Steel Rd NFLD/LBR B31 ....144 D3
Steene Gv NFLD/LBR B31 ....144 D2
Steeping Rd RRUGBY CV23 ....159 M8
Steeplefield Rd COVN CV6 * 133 L8
The Steeples STRBR DY8 ....119 M2
Steepwood Cft BVILLE B30 ....145 H1
Steere Av CRTAM B79 ....32 A6
Stella Cft
CHWD/FDBR/MGN B37............111 G3
Stella Gv GTB/HAM B43 ....70 A3
Stella Rd TPTN/OCK DY4 ....67 K7
Stencills Dr WOLVN WV10 ....50 D1
Stencills Rd RUSH/SHEL WS4 ......53 M2
Stennels Av RMSLY B62 ....122 C1
Stennels Cl COVN CV6.............133 C5
Stennels Crs RMSLY B62 ....122 C1
Stephens Av WSLW WS2 ....38 F8
Stephens Cl TAM/AM/WIL B77 .....46 E3
Stephenson Dr
CHWD/FDBR/MGN B37............110 F3
DUNHL/THL/PER WV6 ....34 C8
Stephenson Rd BEWD DY12 ....163 G2
Stephenson Rd
RCOVN/BALC/EX CV7 ....116 F6
Stephenson Sq WSLW WS2...........38 F8
Stephenson St BDMR/CCFT WV3 ....2 F6
CBHAM 2 F6
Stephenson Wy HEDN WS12 ....12 F8
Stephens Rd MGN/WHC B75........73 L1
Stephen St RUGBYN/HIL CV21 .....186 D2
Stepney Rd COVE CV2...............155 L1
Stepping Stone Cl WSLW WS2.......52 F7
Stepping Stones STRBR DY8 ......101 M8
Stepping Stones Rd COVW CV5 ....154 D1
Steppingstone St DUDN DY1 ....84 F7
Sterling Pk BRLYHL DY5 * 102 A3
Sterling Wy NUN CV11 ....99 J5
Sterndale Rd PBAR/PBCH B42 .....71 M1
Steven Dr BILS/COS WV14 ....67 J4
Stevens Av RIDG/WDGT B32 ......123 H3
Stevens Dr HEDN WS12 ....13 H7
Stevens Ga BKHL/PFLD WV2 ....2 F9
Stevenson Av REDE B98 ....202 D2
Stevenson Dr COVN CV6 ....133 L5
Stevenson St LICHS WS14 ....31 L7
Stevenson Wk LICHS WS14 ....20 F7

Stevens Rd HAG/WOL DY9 ....120 B3
Steward St WSNGN B18 ....106 E2
Stewart Cl COVW CV5 ....154 B3
Stewart Ct TPTN/OCK DY10 ....164 D1
RCOVN/BALC/EX CV7 ....96 E5
Stewart Rd WSN WV9 ....40 C2
KGSWFD DY6 ....101 H1
Stewarts Rd RMSLY B62 ....104 B6
Stewart St BKHL/PFLD WV2 ....2 F1
NUN CV11 ....98 F2
Stewkins STRBR DY8 ....101 J5
Steyning Rd
LGN/SDN/BHAMAIR B26 ....109 J3
Stickley La SEDG DY3 ....84 A1
Stidfall Gv YDLY CV31 ....207 H7
Stilehouse Crs
BLKHTH/ROWR B65 ....104 A3
Stilthouse Gv RBRY B45 ....143 F6
Stiper's Hl CRTAM B79 ....47 M3
Stirling Av RLSN CV32 ....198 F8
Stirling Cl BVILLE B30.............124 C8
Stirling Crs SHHTH WV12 ....37 M8
Stirling Dr N CNCK/NC WS11 ......15 M5
Stirling Rd BILS/COS WV14 ....67 K2
DUDS DY2 ....85 J7
LDYWD/EDGR B16 ....106 D4
SCFLD/BOLD B73 ....72 B3
SHLY B90 ....148 C5
Stirrup Cl DSYBK/YTR WS5 ....69 K1
Stivichall Cft COVS CV3 ....154 F7
Stockbridge Cl
DUNHL/THL/PER WV6 ....48 D3
Stockdale Pl EDG B15...............106 B5
Stock Exchange Buildings
CBHAMNW B3 * ....2 ..
Stockfield Rd ACGN B27...........126 F1
Stockhay La BNTWD WS7............19 H8
Stockhill Dr RBRY B45 ....143 F7
Stocking St HAG/WOL DY9 ....102 D8
Stockland Rd ERDW/GRVHL B23....90 A1
Stockley Crs SHLY B90 ....148 B2
Stockmans Cl HWK/WKHTH B38 ...145 J5
Stocks Cl RUGBYS/DCH CV22 .....186 B5
Stockton Cl DOR/KN B93 ....175 M1
WALM/CURD B76 ....74 A8
Stockton Gv RLSN CV32 ....206 E3
STETCH B33 ....110 B4
Stockton Rd COV CV1................9 J1
Stockwell Av BRLYHL DY5 ....102 B5
Stockwell End
DUNHL/THL/PER WV6 ....35 H7
Stockwell Ri HIA/OLT B92 ....128 D6
Stockwell Rd
DUNHL/THL/PER WV6 ....35 H6
HDSW B21............................88 C3
Stoke Gn COVS CV3................155 L3
Stoke La
MKTBOS/BARL/STKG CV13 ....81 M1
REDE B98 ....194 F6
Stoke Park Ms COVE CV2 * 155 L2
Stoke Rw COVE CV2 ....155 L1
Stokes Av TPTN/OCK DY4...........67 L5
Stokesay Av
DUNHL/THL/PER WV6 ....48 D2
Stokesay Cl KIDDW DY11 ....164 C5
NUNW/HART CV10 ....98 E2
OLDBY B69 ....85 L5
Stokesay Gv NFLD/LBR B31 ....144 D5
Stokesay Ri DUDN DY1 ....84 C2
Stoke's La LICH WS13 ....17 J6
Stokes St BLOX/PEL WS3 ....38 F5
Stoke Wy EDG B15 ....50 F8
Ston Rd BILS/COS WV14 ....50 F8
Stoneacre Cl BDMR/CCFT WV3 ....48 E4
Stone Av MGN/WHC B75 ....57 L8
Stonebow Av SOLH B91............148 F5
Stonebridge Crs
CHWD/FDBR/MGN B37............110 D1
Stonebridge Hwy COVS CV3 ......181 G1
Stonebrook Wy COVN CV6 ....134 D2
RIDG/WDGT B32 ....123 K3
Stonechat Cl KIDD DY10 ....164 F3
Stonechat Dr ERDW/GRVHL B23...90 A3
Stone Cl HWK/WKHTH B38..........145 K3
Stonecroft Av RBRY B45...........143 L6
Stonecrop Cl BRWNH WS8 ....9 J5
HWK/WKHTH B38 ....145 K5
Stone Cross PENK ST19 ....10 C4
Stonedown Cl
ETTPK/GDPK/PENN WV4 ....66 D2
Stonefield Cl COVE CV2 ....135 L5
Stonefield Dr BRLYHL DY5 ....83 L6
Stonefield Rd BILS/COS WV14 * ...51 H8
Stoneford Rd SHLY B90 ....147 L1
Stonehall Rd
RUGBYS/DCH CV22 ....185 L5
Stonehaven TAM/AM/WIL B77 ......32 D8
Stonehaven Dr COVS CV3 ....181 G2
Stonehaven Gv HLGN/YWD B28 ...126 F5
Stonehenge Cft
ALE/KHTH/YWD B14 ....146 B4
Stone Hl KIDD DY10.................165 H1
Stonehill Cft SHLY B90 ....148 D7
Stonehills RUGBYN/HIL CV21 .....161 G6
Stonehouse Av WLNHL WV13 ....51 K2
Stonehouse Cl REDW B97 ....202 A4
RLSN CV32 ....199 H8
Stonehouse Crs
DARL/WED WS10 ....68 F3
Stonehouse Dr
FOAKS/STRLY B74 ....55 M1
Stonehouse Hl SLYOAK B29 ....123 L3
Stonehouse La ALVE B48............171 J3
COVS CV3............................182 A1
RCOVN/BALC/EX CV7 ....182 A1
RIDG/WDGT B32 ....123 H3
SCFLD/BOLD B73 ....72 D2
Stonehouse Rd BRGRVE B60........191 L5
SCFLD/BOLD B73 ....71 G2
Stonehurst Rd GTB/HAM B43 ......71 G1
Stonelea ALDR WS9.................40 F8
Stonelea Cl HHTH/SAND B71 ....69 J5
Stoneleigh Av KNWTH CV8 ....179 L1
Stoneleigh Cl FOAKS/STRLY B74 ...56 D5
KNWTH CV8 ....180 F7
NUNW/HART CV10 ....79 M3
REDE B98 ....202 D8
Stoneleigh Gdns CDSL WV8.........34 D1
Stoneleigh Rd
BFLD/HDSWWD B20 ....89 J4
KNWTH CV8 ....179 L7
RLSN CV32 ....198 D7
SOLH B91 ....127 H8
TLHL/CAN CV4 ....180 B3
Stoneleigh Wy SEDG DY3............66 B7
Stone Pine Cl HEDN WS12 ....12 D5
Stonepit La TAM/AM/WIL B77 ......46 A4
Stone Rd EDG B15...................107 H6
Stonerwood Av HLGN/YWD B28...126 C6
Stones Gn ERDW/GRVHL B23.........72 D7
Stones St DUDN DY1 ....85 G4
OLDBY B69 ....85 H3
Stoneton Crs
RCOVN/BALC/EX CV7 ....151 L7
Stoneton Gv SLYOAK B29 ....123 L5

WASH/WDE B8 ....90 F7
Stretton Pl BILS/COS WV14.........66 E4
DUDS DY2 ....103 H1
Stretton Rd KIDDW DY11 ....163 H1
NUNW/HART CV10 ....98 E2
SHHTH WV12 ....38 A5
SHLY B90 ....147 M5
Stretton St TAM/AM/WIL B77 ....46 C2
Strettons Rd MGN/WHC B75 ....15 H6
Stringers Hl MOS/BIL B13 ....15 M2
Stringes Cl WLNHL WV13 ....51 M3
Stringes La WLNHL WV13 ....51 M3
Strode Rd BKHL/PFLD WV2 ....50 A7
Stronsay Cl RBRY B45 ....143 K4
Stroud Av SHHTH WV12 ....38 A8
Stroud Cl SHHTH WV12 ....52 A1
Stroud Rd SHLY B90 ....147 K3
Strutt Cl EDG B15 ....106 B5
Stuart Cl WWCK CV34 ....205 H8
Stuart Ct COVN CV6 ....134 E5
RLSN CV32 ....206 C4
Stuart Crs DUDS DY2 ....85 J2
Stuart Dr BLKHTH/ROWR B65 .....104 A1
RMSLY B62 ....104 D8
Stuart's Dr STECH B33 ....109 H4
Stuarts Gn HAG/WOL DY9 ....119 M5
Stuarts Rd STECH B33 ....109 H3
Stuart St BLOX/PEL WS3 ....38 F5
VAUX/NECH B7 ....90 A6
Stuarts Wy RIDG/WDGT B32 ......122 F6
Stubbers Green Rd ALDR WS9 ......40 B5
Stubbington Cl WLNHL WV13 ....51 H4
Stubbs Cl BDWTH CV12 ....116 E1
Stubbs Gv COVE CV2...............134 F8
Stubbs Rd BDMR/CCFT WV3 ....49 G5
Stubby La WNSFLD WV11 ....37 L7
Stubley Dr WOLVN WV10 ....36 B8
Studland Av RUGBYN/HIL CV21 ...187 K4
Studland Gn COVE CV2.............156 E1
Studland Rd HLGN/YWD B28 ......126 E5
Stud La STETCH B33.................109 K2
Studley Cft HIA/OLT B92 ....128 A2
Studley Dr BRLYHL DY5 ....102 A5
Studley Ga STRBR DY8 ....101 H8
Studley Rd BDMR/CCFT WV3 ....49 G5
REDE B98 ....202 E3
Studley St BHTH/HG B12 ....107 L7
Sturgeon's Hl LICHS WS14 ....21 G6
Sturley Cl KNWTH CV8 ....179 M7
Sturman Dr BLKHTH/ROWR B65 ...103 M4
Sturminster Cl COVS CV3 ....156 E1
Stychbrook Gdns LICH WS13 ....20 F3
Styles Cl RLSS CV31 ....206 E7
RWWCK/WEL CV35 ....204 D6
Styvechale Av COVW CV5 ....153 M6
Suckling Green La CDSL WV8 ....34 D3
Sudbury Cl RLSN CV32 ....206 E7
WNSFLD WV11 ....37 J5
Sudbury Gv NUNW/HART CV10 ......80 A5
Sudeley TAM/AM/WIL B77 ....46 A3
Sudeley Cl CBROM B36.............91 M4
Sudeley Gdns SEDG DY3 ....84 B3
Sudeley Rd NUNW/HART CV10 ......80 A5
Suffield Gv ERDW/GRVHL B23 ....71 L8
Suffolk Cl BDWTH CV12 ....116 D2
COVW CV5...........................153 G8
LGLYGN/QTN B68 ....104 F1
NUNW/HART CV10 ....98 C2
WNSFLD WV11 ....37 G7
Suffolk Dr BRLYHL DY5 ....102 A6
Suffolk Gv ALDR WS9 ....40 F5
Suffolk Pl CBHAMW B1 * 6 C7
WSLW WS2 ....39 H8
Suffolk Rd DARL/WED WS10 ....68 E6
DUDS DY2 ....84 E6
Suffolk St Queensway
CBHAMW B1 ....6 E6
Suffolk Wy POL/KGSB/FAZ B78 .....45 L4
Suffrage St SMTHWK B66............87 M4
Sugarbrook La BRGRVE B60 ....191 K8
Sugarbrook Rd BRGRVE B60 ....191 L5
Sugar Loaf La KINVER DY7 ....118 F5
Sugden Gv DIG/EDG B5 ....7 G9
Sulgrave Cl DUDN DY1 ....84 C2
Sullivan Rd COVN CV6.............134 F6
Sumburgh Cft CVALE B35 ....91 L1
Summercourt Dr KGSWFD DY6 ......83 G8
Summercourt Sq KGSWFD DY6 ......83 G8
Summer Cft LOZ/NWT B19............89 H7
Summercroft STRPT DY13 ....188 F1
Summer Dr SEDG DY3 ....83 L4
Summerfield Av KGSWFD DY6 ....83 G6
WBROM B70 ....87 G5
Summerfield Cl
TAM/AM/WIL B77 ....46 B1
Summerfield Crs
LDYWD/EDGR B16 ....106 C2
Summerfield Dr SLYOAK B29 ......123 L6
Summerfield La SLYOAK B29 * 123 L6
Summerfield Rd BNTWD WS7 ....18 E8
DUDS DY2 ....85 H5
HAG/WOL DY9 ....141 H3
HIA/OLT B92 ....127 L4
LDYWD/EDGR B16 ....106 C2
STRPT DY13 ....188 F1
TAM/AM/WIL B77 ....46 B1
Summerfields Av RMSLY B62 ......104 D5
**Summergate SEDG DY3 ....83 M5
Summer Gv LICH WS13 ....21 H3
Summer Hl HALE B63 ....121 M2
KGSWFD DY6 ....83 G7
Summerhill Av KIDDW DY11 ....137 L7
Summerhill Rd BILS/COS WV14 ......67 H4
Summer Hill St CBHAMW B1..........6 A3
Summer Hill Ter CBHAMW B1 ....6 B4
Summerhouse La LICH WS13 ....19 H2
Summerhouse Rd BHTH/HG B12 ...107 L7
BILS/COS WV14 ....66 E4
Summer La LOZ/NWT B19 ....6 F1
RUSH/SHEL WS4 ....39 M3
SEDG DY3 ....84 A2
WALM/CURD B76 ....74 D7
Summerlee Rd
ERDE/BCHGN B24 ....90 D3
Summer Rd ACGN B27...............126 E3
BLKHTH/ROWR B65 ....104 B2
DUDN DY1 ....84 E1
EDG B15.............................107 G6
ERDW/GRVHL B23 ....72 D8
KIDDW DY11.........................189 L6
Summer Rw BKHL/PFLD WV2 ....2 D4
CBHAMNW B1 ....6 D4
Summerside Av WNSFLD WS12........18 A1
Summer St HAG/WOL DY9 ....102 C8
HHTH/SAND B71 ....71 G7
KGSWFD DY6 ....83 G7
REDE B98 ....202 C2
STRBR DY8 ....101 K8
WLNHL WV13 ....51 K3
Summerton Rd OLDBY B69 ....86 B5
Summervale Cl HALE B63 ....120 E2
Summervale Rd HAG/WOL DY9 ....119 L7

Summerville Ter HRBN B17 * ....
Summerway La KIDDW DY11 ....
Summit Crs SMTHWK B66 ....
Summit Gdns HALE B63 ....
Summit Pl SEDG DY3 ....
The Summit HAG/WOL DY9 ....
Sumner Cl RWWCK/WEL CV35 ....
Sumner Rd CSHL/WTROR B46 ....
Sunart Wy NUNW/HART CV10 ....
Sunbeam TAM/AM/WIL B77 ....
Sunbeam Cl CBROM B36 ....
Sunbeam Dr GTWY WS6 ....
Sunbeam St BKHL/PFLD WV2 ....
Sunbeam Wy STETCH B33 ....
Sunbury Cl BILS/COS WV14 ....
Sunbury Rd COVS CV3 ....
HALE B63 ....
NFLD/LBR B31 ....
Suncliffe Dr KNWTH CV8 ....
Suncroft RIDG/WDGT B32 ....
Sunbury Ri NFLD/LBR B31 ....
Sunderland Dr STRBR DY8 ....
Sunderton Rd
ALE/KHTH/YWD B14 ....
Sundew Cft CBROM B36 ....
Sundew St COVE CV2 ....
Sundial La GTB/HAM B43 ....
Sundorne Cl COVW CV5 ....
Sundour Crs WNSFLD WV11 ....
Sundridge Rd KGSTG B44 ....
Sunfield Rd CNCK/NC WS11 ....
Sunfields Cl POL/KGSB/FAZ B78 ....
Sunleigh Gv ACGN B27 ....
Sunley Dr HEDN WS12 ....
Sunningdale RMSLY B62 ....
TAM/AM/WIL B77 ....
Sunningdale Av COVN CV6 ....
DUNHL/THL/PER WV6 ....
KNWTH CV8 ....
Sunningdale Cl
BFLD/HDSWWD B20 ....
NUN CV11 ....
SCFLD/BOLD B73 ....
STRBR DY8 ....
Sunningdale Dr OLDBY B69 ....
Sunningdale Rd BRGRVW B61 ....
SEDG DY3 ....
SPARK B11 ....
Sunningdale Wy BLOX/PEL WS3 .....
Sunny Av BHTH/HG B12 ....
Sunnybank Av COVS CV3 ....
KGSTG B44 ....
Sunnybank Cl ALDR WS9 ....
Sunny Bank Rd
LGLYGN/QTN B68 ....
Sunnybank Rd SCFLD/BOLD B73 * ...
SEDG DY3 ....
Sunnydene WASH/WDE B8 ....
Sunny Hill Cl WMBN WV5 ....
Sunnymead BRGRVE B60 ....
Sunnymead Rd
LGN/SDN/BHAMAIR B26 ....
Sunnymead Wy
FOAKS/STRLY B74 ....
Sunnymede Rd KGSWFD DY6 ....
OLDBY B69 ....
Sunnyside ERDW/GRVHL B23 ....
Sunnyside Cl COVW CV5 ....
RCOVN/BALC/EX CV7 ....
Sunnyside Ct
NUNW/HART CV10 * ....
Sunnyside Gdns KIDDW DY11 ....
Sunnyside La
RCOVN/BALC/EX CV7 ....
Sunridge Av LOZ/NWT B19 ....
WMBN WV5 ....
Sunrise Hl HEDN WS12 ....
Sunset Cl CRTAM B79 ....
GTWY WS6 ....
POL/KGSB/FAZ B78 ....
Sunset Pl
ETTPK/GDPK/PENN WV4 ....
Sunshine Cl KNWTH CV8 ....
Sun St BRLYHL DY5 ....
RUGBYN/HIL CV21 ....
WOLVN WV10 ....
WSL WS1 ....
Sunway Gv COVS CV3 ....
Surfeit Hl CDYHTH B64 ....
Surfeit Hill Rd CDYHTH B64 ....
Surrey Cl CNCK/NC WS11 ....
NUNW/HART CV10 ....
Surrey Crs HHTH/SAND B71 ....
Surrey Dr BDMR/CCFT WV3 ....
POL/KGSB/FAZ B78 ....
STRBR DY8 ....
Surrey Rd DUDS DY2 ....
KGSTG B44 ....
Surrey Wk ALDR WS9 ....
Sussex Av ALDR WS9 ....
DARL/WED WS10 ....
HHTH/SAND B71 ....
Sussex Cl NUNW/HART CV10 ....
Sussex Dr BDMR/CCFT WV3 ....
HEDN WS12 ....
Sussex Rd COVW CV5 ....
SHLY B90 ....
Sutherland Cl GTB/HAM B43 ....
WWCK CV34 ....
Sutherland Dr BDWTH CV12 ....
MOS/BIL B13 ....
WMBN WV5 ....
Sutherland Gv
DUNHL/THL/PER WV6 ....
Sutherland Pl BKHL/PFLD WV2 ......
Sutherland Rd CDYHTH B64 ....
ETTPK/GDPK/PENN WV4 ....
GTWY WS6 ....
Sutherland St AST/WIT B6 ....
Sutton Ap WASH/WDE B8 ....
Sutton Cl REDE B98 ....
Sutton Ct
ETTPK/GDPK/PENN WV4 ....
MGN/WHC B75 ....
Sutton Crs WBROM B70 ....
Sutton New Rd
ERDW/GRVHL B23 ....
Sutton Oak Rd SCFLD/BOLD B73 .....
SCFLD/BOLD B73 ....
Sutton Park Gv KIDDW DY11 ....
Sutton Park Rd KIDDW DY11 ....
Sutton Park Rd KIDDW DY11 ....
Sutton Rd DARL/WED WS10 ....
DSYBK/YTR WS5 ....
ERDE/BCHGN B24 ....
KIDDW DY11 ....
POL/KGSB/FAZ B78 ....
Sutton's Dr GTB/HAM B43 ....
Sutton Stop COVN CV6 ....
Sutton St AST/WIT B6 ....
EDG B15.............................
STRBR DY8 ....
Swadling St RLSS CV31 ....
Swain Crofts RLSS CV31 ....

ins Gv *KGSTG* B44 .....71 K1
edale La *BRGRVE* B60 .....191 J7
ne Gv *HWK/WKTH* B38 .....145 K5
LNHL WV13 .....52 B3
ne Rd *WALM/CURD* B76 .....73 L4
ARL/WED WS10 .....68 F1
UDS DY2 .....103 H3
llow Dr *WOLVN* WV10 .....36 D5
llow Cl *BHTH/HG* B12 .....107 M8
JNHL/THL/PER WV6 .....48 D3
llowdean Rd *COVN* CV6 .....133 J5
llowdale *ALDR* WS9 .....40 E1
JNHL/THL/PER WV6 .....48 D3
llowfall Av *STRBR* DY8 .....119 G1
llowfield *CRTAM* B79 .....31 J7
llowfields Dr *HEDN* WS12 .....16 F2
llowfields Rd *SEDG* DY3 .....66 A2
llow Cl *BLOX/PEL* WS3 .....25 L8
llows' Meadow *SHLY* B90 .....148 B5
llow St *CBHAM* B5 .....4 E4
BROM B70 .....86 E1
nage Cl *COVE* CV2 .....156 E1
nage Rd *SMHTH* B10 .....108 B5
n Av *SMTHWK* B66 .....87 J6
n Bank
TTPK/GDPK/PENN WV4 .....65 K1
way *COVS* CV3 .....24 A3
DD DY10 .....139 M4
n Copse *YDLY* B25 .....109 G8
ncote Dr
TTPK/GDPK/PENN WV4 .....65 K1
ncote Rd *DUDN* DY1 .....84 E5
ETCH B33 .....109 K2
n Ctyd
GN/SDN/BHAMAIR B26 * 109 H7
n Crs *OLDBY* B69 .....104 D1
ncroft Rd *COVE* 134 C5
PTN/OCK DY4 .....67 K5
nfield Dr *BRWNH* WS8 .....26 C6
nfields *BNTWD* WS7 .....19 G7
n Gdns *ERDW/GRVHL* B23 .....90 E1
n La *BRGRVW* B61 .....168 B2
CRRVW B61 .....190 C9
OVE CV2 .....9 M4
RBR DY9 .....101 J3
WOLVN WV10 .....23 G4
nsbrook Gdns
WK/WKTH B38 .....146 A3
nshurst La *MOS/BIL* B13 .....126 A5
ns Length *ALVE* B48 .....170 F7
n St *ALVE* B48 .....170 F7
DRLYHL DY5 .....84 A7
UDS DY2 .....85 G7
LSN CV32 .....206 E4
RBR DY9 .....101 J8
WCK CV34 .....3 L5
nswell Rd *ACGN* B27 .....127 C5
nswell St *COV* CV1 .....9 H2
nswood Gv
HWD/FDBR/MGN B37 * 111 G2
rthmore Rd *SLYOAK* B29 .....123 M6
etbriar La *SHHTH* WV12 .....38 B8
etbriar Rd *BKHL/PFLD* WV2 .....50 E5
etbriar Wy *HEDN* WS12 .....17 J1
etbrier Dr *STRBR* DY8 .....101 J4
etman Pl
UNHL/THL/PER WV6 .....2 B2
etman St
UNHL/THL/PER WV6 .....49 L1
etmoor Cl *CBROM* B36 .....92 A5
etpool La *HWK/WKTH* B38 .....145 J6
et TAM/AM/WIL B77 .....46 C2
et La *BRGRVW* B61 .....191 J5
BROM B36 .....92 E5
WTH CV8 .....197 L3
et Pk *RUGBYN/HIL* CV21 .....160 E6
et Park Gv *KIDD* DY10 .....164 F3
et La *COVS* CV3 .....155 J5
llington Rd *COVN* CV6 .....133 M4
nbrook Cv *KGSTG* B44 .....71 J4
nbrook Wy *SHLY* B90 .....148 B3
nburne Cl
UNW/HART CV10 .....79 L8
nburne Rd *REDW* B97 .....202 A6
ncross Rd *WOLVN* WV10 .....119 M2
ndale *TAM/AM/WIL* B77 .....46 F6
dale *COVS* CV3 .....156 D5
ndell Rd *HAG/WOL* DY9 .....120 A4
ndon Rd *HRBN* B17 .....105 M2
GSWFD DY6 .....82 D5
nfen Broun Rd *LICH* WS13 .....20 E5
nford Gv *DOR/KN* B93 .....175 J2
nford Leys *WMBN* WV5 .....64 B1
nford Rd *SLYOAK* B29 .....123 L2
RBR DY9 .....119 L3
WOLVN WV10 .....36 C8
n Forge Wy *SEDG* DY3 .....82 C3
ss Dr *STRBR* DY8 .....101 K3
ss Hts *STRPT* DY13 .....188 C4
ss Lodge Dr
OL/KGSB/FAZ B78 .....45 K5
nerton Dr *WNSFLD* WV11 .....37 L7
nesmore *TAM/AM/WIL* B77 .....46 C6
ss La *BRGRVW* B61 .....191 J5
OL/KGSB/FAZ B78 .....47 L5
EDE B98 .....202 C3
amore Cl *ERDE/BCHGN* B24 .....90 D2
USH/SHEL WS4 .....39 M5
RBR DY9 .....119 H3
ALM/CURD B76 .....73 K1
amore Crs
HWD/FDBR/MGN B37 .....110 C5
ERDE/BCHGN B24 .....90 D2
COVN/BALC/EX CV7 .....96 F5
LYWD B47 .....146 F8
amore Gn *CNCK/NC* WS11 .....12 C7
UDN DY1 .....66 D8
LLE B30 .....124 D6
/RBR DY9 .....101 L4
amore Pl *BILS/COS* WV14 .....67 L2
amore Rd *AST/WIT* B6 .....89 L1
/WED WS10 .....68 C1
/GRVHL B23 .....72 D6
HAM B43 .....70 C2
SW WS1 .....88 B5

HEDN WS12 .....17 K1
KGSWFD DY6 .....83 J7
NUNW/HART CV10 .....80 B7
OLDBY B69 .....104 L1
POL/KGSB/FAZ B78 .....60 D5
RUSH/SHEL WS4 .....39 M5
SMTHWK B66 .....105 M2
TPTN/OCK DY4 .....67 K6
The Sycamores *BDWTH* CV12 .....116 C3
Sycamore Ter
ALE/KHTH/YWD B14 * 125 G6
Sycamore Wy *ACGN* B27 .....127 C1
HEDN WS12 .....12 B5
Sydenham Dr *STRPT* DY13 .....206 F7
Sydenham Rd *SMTHWK* B66 .....87 H1
SPARK B11 .....108 A7
WOLV WV1 .....50 F5
Sydnall Cl *REDW* B97 .....201 K3
Sydnall Flds *WNSFLD* WV11 .....37 K3
Sydnall Rd *COVS* CV6 .....116 D8
Sydney Cl *WBROM* B9 .....68 C8
BRGRVW B61 .....191 J2
CDYHTH B64 .....102 F4
SMTHWK B67 .....105 J3
Syerscote La *CRTAM* B79 .....32 B2
Sykesmoor *TAM/AM/WIL* B77 .....46 F6
Sylvan Av *NFLD/LBR* B31 .....144 C2
Sylvan Dr *COVS* CV3 .....154 D7
Sylvan Gn *RMSLY* B62 .....104 B8
Sylvia Av *NFLD/LBR* B31 .....144 F5
Symphony Ct *CBHAMW* B1 .....6 B6
Synkere Cl
RCOVN/BALC/EX CV7 .....115 L7
Sytch La *WMBN* WV5 .....64 E8
Sywell Leys *RUGBYS/DCH* CV22 .....186 D1

T

Tabbs Gdns *KIDD* DY10 .....138 E6
Tabeners La *ATHST* CV9 .....63 H6
Table Oak La *KNWTH* CV8 .....177 L3
Tachbrook Cl *COVE* CV2 .....135 G3
Tachbrook Park Dr *RLSS* CV31 .....206 C7
Tachbrook Rd *RLSS* CV31 .....206 C7
Tachbrook St *RLSS* CV31 .....206 E7
Tack Farm Rd *STRBR* DY8 .....101 H4
Tackford Cl *CBROM* B36 .....92 A4
Tackford Rd *COVN* CV6 .....134 C6
Tackley Cl *SHLY* B90 .....147 M5
Tadmore Cl *BILS/COS* WV14 .....51 G8
Tadworth Cl *WOLV* WV1 .....50 D2
Tainters Hl *KNWTH* CV8 .....179 K7
Tait Cft *HIA/OLT* B92 .....128 D5
Talaton Cl *COVEN* WV9 .....35 L3
Talbot *TAM/AM/WIL* B77 .....46 F2
Talbot Av *FOAKS/STRLY* B74 .....55 M2
Talbot Cl *ERDW/GRVHL* B23 .....72 E5
KIDDW DY11 .....189 L4
WSLW WS2 .....39 G5
Talbot Pl *BILS/COS* WV14 .....51 G7
Talbot Rd *BKHL/PFLD* WV2 .....50 A7
BROM B70 .....191 J6
DUDS DY2 .....85 G7
SMTHWK B66 .....105 J4
Talbotshill La *KIDD* DY10 .....139 G1
Talbots La *BRLYHL* DY5 .....102 C4
Talbot St *BRLYHL* DY5 .....102 B2
HAG/WOL DY9 .....102 B3
HALE B63 .....103 G7
KIDDW DY11 .....164 B5
STRBR DY8 .....101 L8
WSNGN B18 .....88 D7
Talfourd St *WOLV* WV10 .....108 D6
Talford St *AST/WIT* B6 .....89 J7
Talfourd St *BORD* B9 .....108 B4
Talgarth Covert
HWK/WKTH B38 .....145 J6
Talisman Cl *KNWTH* CV8 .....197 K2
Talke Rd *DSYBK/YTR* WS5 .....53 K8
Talladale *RIDG/WDGT* B32 .....122 F6
Talland Av *COVN* CV6 .....134 C4
TAM/AM/WIL B77 .....32 C8
Tallants Cl *COVN* CV6 .....134 C5
Tallants Rd *COVN* CV6 .....134 D5
Tallington Rd
LGN/SDN/BHAMAIR B26 .....110 A3
Tall Trees Cl *BRGRVW* B61 * 168 D5
FOAKS/STRLY B74 .....56 B1
SHHTH WV12 .....38 B7
Tall Trees Dr *HAG/WOL* DY9 .....120 B3
Talton Cl *SHLY* B90 .....148 B5
Tamar Cl *BRWNH* WS8 .....26 A3
RRUGBY CV23 .....159 M8
Tamar Dr *CBROM* B36 .....92 D5
SEDG DY3 .....66 D7
WALM/CURD B76 .....73 L3
Tamar Gv *DUNHL/THL/PER* WV6 .....48 C1
WLNHL WV13 .....52 A3
Tamarisk Cl *SLYOAK* B29 .....123 M5
Tamar Rd *BDWTH* CV12 .....117 G3
TAM/AM/WIL B77 .....46 F6
DARL/WED WS10 .....52 A8
Tame Av *BNTWD* WS7 .....19 G7
DARL/WED WS10 .....67 M2
Tame Bank *POL/KGSB/FAZ* B78 .....60 A7
Tame Br *DSYBK/YTR* WS5 .....69 K1
Tame Cl *WSL* WS1 .....53 J7
Tame Dr *BLOX/PEL* WS3 .....39 L4
Tamedrive *POL/KGSB/FAZ* B78 .....45 L1
Tame Gv *CNCK/NC* WS11 .....16 B5
Tame Ri *LGLYGN/QTN* B68 .....104 C3
Tame Rd *AST/WIT* B6 .....89 L3
LGLYGN/QTN B68 .....104 C3
TPTN/OCK DY4 .....68 A8
Tamerton Rd *RIDG/WDGT* B32 .....123 H6
Tameside Dr *CVALE* B35 .....91 L4
PBAR/PBCH B42 .....89 K1
Tame St *BILS/COS* WV14 .....51 K8
TAM/AM/WIL B77 .....46 B1
WBROM B70 .....68 D5
WSL WS1 .....53 J7
Tame St East *WSL* WS1 .....53 K7
Tamhorn House Br *LICHS* WS14 .....34 D7
Tamworth Br *BRWNH* WS8 .....26 D3
Tamworth Rd *ATHST* CV9 .....61 G4
LICHS WS14 .....21 G1
MGN/WHC B75 .....57 H6
POL/KGSB/FAZ B78 .....47 J4
POL/KGSB/FAZ B78 .....60 A4
RCOVN/BALC/EX CV7 .....95 K4
TAM/AM/WIL B77 .....46 A5
Tamworth Rd (Amington)
TAM/AM/WIL B77 .....32 C8
Tamworth Rd (Dosthill)
TAM/AM/WIL B77 .....46 A7
Tamworth St *LICH* WS13 .....20 F5
Tanacetum Dr *DSYBK/YTR* WS5 .....69 M7
Tancred Cl *RLSS* CV31 .....206 D8
Tandy Dr *HEDN* WS12 .....16 D2
Tandy's La *KIDD* DY10 .....166 C1

Tanfield Cl *DUNHL/THL/PER* WV6 .....48 F2
Tanfield Rd *DUDS* DY2 .....84 F6
STETCH B33 .....109 K2
Tanford Rd *HIA/OLT* B92 .....128 A2
Tanglewood Cl *BKDE/SHDE* B34 .....92 A8
BRGRVW B60 .....169 L7
RIDG/WDGT B32 .....122 F1
Tanglewood Gv *SEDG* DY3 .....66 A3
Tangmere Cl
RCOVN/BALC/EX CV7 .....34 C8
Tangmere Dr *CVALE* B35 .....91 L2
Tanhouse Av *TLHL/CAN* CV4 .....46 F6
Tanhouse Farm Rd
HIA/OLT B92 .....128 A3
Tanhouse La *HALE* B63 .....103 G8
REDE B98 .....195 C2
Tan La *STRPT* DY13 .....188 E1
Tanners Cl *MGN/WHC* B75 .....57 J6
Tanners Green La *HLYWD* B47 .....172 E3
Tanners' Hl *BEWD* DY12 .....162 B2
Tanners' La
RCOVN/BALC/EX CV7 .....152 F4
Tannery Cft *ATHST* CV9 .....63 J5
WSLW WS2 .....4 D1
Tansey Green Rd *BRLYHL* DY5 .....83 M5
Tansley Cl *DOR/KN* B93 .....175 K1
Tansley Gv *KGSTG* B44 .....71 K4
Tansley Hill Av *DUDS* DY2 .....85 K5
Tansley Hill Rd *DUDS* DY2 .....85 J5
Tansley Rd *KGSTG* B44 .....71 J5
Tansley Vw *BKHL/PFLD* WV2 .....50 C6
Tansy *TAM/AM/WIL* B77 .....46 A2
Tantany La *WBROM* B70 .....87 G1
Tantarra St *WSL* WS1 .....5 H7
Tanwood Cl *REDW* B97 .....201 L7
SOLH B91 .....148 F5
Tanworth Gv *BHTH/HG* B12 .....107 K7
Tanworth La *SHLY* B90 .....147 M7
Tanyard *LICH* WS13 .....21 G5
Tanyard Cl *ALVE* B48 .....170 F7
TLHL/CAN CV4 .....153 G4
Tanyard La *ALVE* B48 .....170 F7
Tanyards *ACGN* B27 .....127 H2
Tapcroft *COVE* CV2 .....135 K8
Tapestries Av *WBROM* B70 .....86 E1
Taplow Pl *CNCK/NC* WS11 .....16 C1
Tappinger Gv *KNWTH* CV8 .....180 A1
Tapton Cl *BLOX/PEL* WS3 .....39 G2
Tardebigge Cl *REDW* B97 * 193 C7
Tarlington Rd *COVN* CV6 .....133 H7
Tarmac Rd
ETTPK/GDPK/PENN WV4 .....50 F8
Tarn Cl *BDWTH* CV12 .....116 E3
Tarquin Cl *COVS* CV3 .....156 B7
Tarragon Cl *COVE* CV2 .....135 H4
Tarragon Gdns *HLGN/YWD* B28 .....144 A3
Tarrant Gv *RIDG/WDGT* B32 .....105 J4
Tarrant Wk *COVE* CV2 .....135 L8
Tarrington Covert
HWK/WKTH B38 .....145 J5
Tarry Hollow Rd *BRLYHL* DY5 .....83 M5
Tarry Rd *WASH/WDE* B8 .....108 C3
Tarvin Ms *BRLYHL* DY5 .....102 B4
Taryn Dr *DARL/WED* WS10 .....52 B6
Tasker St *WBROM* B70 .....86 C1
WSL WS1 .....4 D6
Tasman Gv
DUNHL/THL/PER WV6 .....34 C8
Tat Bank Rd *OLDBY* B69 .....86 F7
Tatnall Gv *WWCK* CV34 .....205 J5
Taunton Av *WOLVN* WV10 .....36 B1
Taunton Cl *NFLD/LBR* B31 .....144 A2
Taunton Rd *BHTH/HG* B12 .....125 L1
Taunton Wy *COVN* CV6 .....133 L3
Taverners Cl *WLNHL* WV13 .....38 A4
Taverner's Gn
BFLD/HDSWWD B20 .....88 D2
Tavistock Cl *CRTAM* B79 .....32 A6
Tavistock Rd *ACGN* B27 .....127 G6
Tavistock St *RLSN* CV32 .....206 D4
Tavistock Wy *NUN* CV11 .....81 J8
Taw Cl *CBROM* B36 .....92 D6
Tay Cft *CHWD/FDBR/MGN* B37 .....111 G2
Tay Gv *HWK/WKTH* B38 .....145 K5
RMSLY B62 .....104 C5
Taylor Av *RLSN* CV32 .....206 A1
Taylor Cl *KNWTH* CV8 .....179 M7
Taylor Ct *WWCK* CV34 .....205 J5
Taylor Rd *ALE/KHTH/YWD* B14 .....125 K8
DUDS DY2 .....103 J3
ETTPK/GDPK/PENN WV4 .....50 D3
Taylor's La *HHTH/SAND* B71 .....87 H1
OLDBY B69 .....86 C5
Taylors Orch *ERDW/GRVHL* B23 .....89 M1
Taylor Wy *OLDBY* B69 .....85 M5
Tay Rd *COVN* CV6 .....133 M7
Taysfield Rd *NFLD/LBR* B31 .....123 J7
Taywood Dr *SMHTH* B10 .....108 C6
Teachers Cl *COVN* CV6 .....133 L8
The Tea Gdn
RCOVN/BALC/EX CV7 .....116 C5
Tealby Gv *SLYOAK* B29 .....124 E4
Teal Crs *KIDD* DY10 .....164 E4
Teal Dr *ERDW/GRVHL* B23 .....89 M2
Teal Gv *DARL/WED* WS10 .....67 M2
Teall Rd *RUSH/SHEL* WS4 .....90 C3
Team Cl *BNTWD* WS7 .....19 H7
SPARK B11 .....126 C2
Teasdale Wy *HAG/WOL* DY9 .....120 B1
Teasel Cl *RRUGBY* CV23 .....161 M5
Teasel Gv *WNSFLD* WV11 .....37 K3
Teazel Av *BVILLE* B30 .....124 D7
Tebworth Cl *COVEN* WV9 .....35 K3
Tedbury Crs *ERDW/GRVHL* B23 .....72 C7
Tedder Rd *WSLW* WS2 .....52 D3
Teddesley Ct *CNCK/NC* WS11 .....16 B7
Teddesley Gv *PBAR/PBCH* B42 .....89 G2
Teddesley Rd *PENK* ST19 .....15 H4
Teddesley St *RUSH/SHEL* WS4 .....5 G1
Teddesley Wy *HEDN* WS12 .....12 A7
Teddington Gv *PBAR/PBCH* B42 .....89 G2
Ted Pitts La *COVW* CV5 .....132 F3
Tedstone Rd *RIDG/WDGT* B32 .....105 K3
Teesdale Av *BKDE/SHDE* B34 .....91 K4
Teesdale Cl *WOLV* WV1 .....51 H3
Tees Gv *HWK/WKTH* B38 .....145 K5
Teeswater Cl *BRGRVE* B60 .....191 J7
Teign *TAM/AM/WIL* B77 .....60 C1
Teignmouth Rd *SLYOAK* B29 .....124 D1
Telephone Rd *COVS* CV3 .....155 M4
Telfer Rd *COVN* CV6 .....133 M6
Telford Av *GTWY* WS6 .....24 D2
RLSN CV32 .....198 F3
Telford Cl *BNTWD* WS7 .....18 E5
HHTH/SAND B71 .....68 E5
SMTHWK B67 .....105 H4
WSLW B67 .....38 A3
Telford Dr *BRLYHL* DY5 .....102 B2
Telford Gdns *BDMR/CCFT* WV3 .....49 H6
Telford Gv *HEDN* WS12 .....12 D6
Telford Rd *CRTAM* B79 .....31 K5
RLSN CV32 .....198 F3

RCOVN/BALC/EX CV7 .....117 G5
WSLW WS2 .....38 E8
Teme Gv *KIDDW* DY11 .....163 M2
Teme Gv *WLNHL* WV13 .....52 B3
Teme Rd *HALE* B63 .....102 F8
STRBR DY8 .....119 K2
Tempest St *BKHL/PFLD* WV2 .....5 F5
CRTAM B79 .....31 L8
Templar Av *TLHL/CAN* CV4 .....153 G4
Templar's Flds *TLHL/CAN* CV4 .....153 M6
The Templars *DSYBK/YTR* WS5 .....69 M6
WWCK CV34 .....205 K8
Templars Wk *WLNHL* WV13 .....51 L3
Templars Wy *PENK* ST19 .....10 D5
Temple Av *HLGN/YWD* B28 .....126 C2
RCOVN/BALC/EX CV7 .....151 K7
Temple Bar *WLNHL* WV13 .....51 L2
Temple Cl *REDE* B98 .....202 F5
Templefield Gdns *BORD* B9 .....108 A4
Templefield Sq *CBHAM* B12 .....6 F5
Templefield St *BORD* B9 .....108 A4
Temple La *DOR/KN* B93 .....176 E1
Temple Meadows Rd
HHTH/SAND B71 .....69 J8
Templemore Dr *GTB/HAM* B43 .....70 C6
Temple Pas *DOR/KN* B93 .....175 J2
WLNHL WV13 .....51 L2
Temple Rw *CBHAM* B2 .....7 G2
Temple Rw West *CBHAMNW* B3 .....6 F4
Temple Sq *WLNHL* WV13 .....51 L2
Temple St *BILS/COS* WV14 .....51 J8
CBHAM B2 .....6 F5
RUGBYN/HIL CV21 .....187 G3
SEDG DY3 .....66 D6
WBROM B70 .....87 G1
Templeton Cl *DOR/KN* B93 .....175 L2
Templeton Rd *KGSTG* B44 .....71 J3
Temple Wy *CSHL/WTROR* B46 .....93 K4
OLDBY B69 .....86 C5
Tenacre La *SEDG* DY3 .....66 C8
Ten Acres End *BVILLE* B30 .....124 F5
Ten Ashes La *REDE* B98 .....203 K2
Ten Ashes La *RBRY* B45 .....170 A1
Tenbury Cl *ALDR* WS9 .....41 G5
REDE B98 .....195 D1
WSLW WS2 .....52 B2
Tenbury Ct
ETTPK/GDPK/PENN WV4 .....49 H8
Tenbury Gdns
ETTPK/GDPK/PENN WV4 .....65 K1
Tenbury Rd
ALE/KHTH/YWD B14 .....125 H7
Tenby Cl *BDWTH* CV12 .....116 A4
Tenby Gv *MOS/BIL* B13 .....126 B3
Tenby St *CBHAMW* B1 .....6 C2
Tenby St North *CBHAMW* B1 .....6 B2
Tenby Wy *STRPT* DY13 .....188 E1
Teneriffe Rd *COVN* CV6 .....134 D4
Tenlands Rd *HALE* B63 .....103 G1
Tenlons Rd *NUNW/HART* CV10 .....98 D3
Tennal Dr *RIDG/WDGT* B32 .....105 K5
Tennal Gv *RIDG/WDGT* B32 .....105 K5
Tennal La *RIDG/WDGT* B32 .....105 J6
Tennal Rd *RIDG/WDGT* B32 .....105 J5
Tennant St *EDG* B15 .....6 B8
NUN CV11 .....81 H5
Tennis Ct *BVILLE* B30 .....145 H1
Tennis Ct *EDG* B15 * 106 E8
Tennscore Av *GTWY* WS6 .....24 C2
Tennyson Av *BNTWD* WS7 .....18 E6
CRTAM B79 .....31 L7
FOAKS/STRLY B74 .....42 F7
RUGBYS/DCH CV22 .....186 C4
Tennyson Cl *KNWTH* CV8 .....198 A1
COVE CV2 .....156 A2
REDW B97 .....202 A5
SEDG DY3 .....65 L8
SHHTH WV12 .....38 C6
SMTHWK B10 .....108 C6
WOLVN WV10 .....36 A4
Tennyson Gdns
SMTHWK B67 .....105 K1
Tennyson Rd *LCLYGN/QTN* B68 .....104 F1
SMTHWK B67 .....105 K1
Tennyson's Rd
RCOVN/BALC/EX CV7 .....115 J7
Thompson Av *BILS/COS* WV14 .....51 H8
WLNHL WV13 .....51 L2
Thompson Av *NFLD/LBR* B31 .....145 G4
Thompson Dr *VAUX/NECH* B7 .....90 D5
Thompson Gdns
SMTHWK B67 .....105 K1
Thompson Rd *LCLYGN/QTN* B68 .....104 F1
SMTHWK B67 .....105 K1
Thomson's Rd
RCOVN/BALC/EX CV7 .....115 J7
Thompson Av *BILS/COS* WV14 .....51 H8

Thelma Rd *TPTN/OCK* DY4 .....67 J7
Thelma St *WSL* WS1 .....4 D7
Thelsford Wy *HIA/OLT* B92 .....128 B3
Thena Gdns *COVN* CV6 .....134 L4
Theodore Cl *HRBN* B17 .....124 D7
OLDBY B69 .....86 C6
The Pavilions *CSHL/WTROR* B46 .....111 H8
Theresa Rd *SPARK* B11 .....107 M6
Thetford Cl *TPTN/OCK* DY4 .....67 H8
Thetford Gdns *WNSFLD* WV11 .....37 H7
Thetford Rd *PBAR/PBCH* B42 .....70 E6
Thetford Wy *RUSH/SHEL* WS4 .....70 A2
Thickett Cl *WSLW* WS2 .....52 C1
Thicknall Dr *HAG/WOL* DY9 .....119 M3
Thicknall La *HAG/WOL* DY9 .....140 F2
Thicknall Ri *HAG/WOL* DY9 .....140 E1
Thickthorn Cl *KNWTH* CV8 .....197 M3
Thimble End Rd
WALM/CURD B76 .....73 L3
Thimble Mill La *AST/WIT* B6 .....89 M1
Thimblemill Rd *SMTHWK* B67 .....105 H1
Thimbler Rd *TLHL/CAN* CV4 .....154 A6
Thimble Rd *BORD* B9 .....108 B4
Third Av *BORD* B9 .....108 B5
BRWNH WS8 .....26 E4
KGSWFD DY6 .....83 K5
SLYOAK B29 .....125 G2
WOLVN WV10 .....36 A3
Third Exhibition Av
BHAMNEC B40 .....111 H8
Third Rd *BRGRVW* B61 .....168 D1
Thirlestane Cl *KNWTH* CV8 .....180 A1
Thirlmere *RUGBYN/HIL* CV21 .....161 G6
Thirlmere Av *NUN* CV11 .....81 K7
Thirlmere Cl *CNCK/NC* WS11 .....16 C4
COVW CV5 .....133 G5
DUNHL/THL/PER WV6 .....35 H5
WNSFLD WV11 .....37 J3
Thirlmere Gv
DUNHL/THL/PER WV6 .....48 D1
Thirlmere Rd *BDWTH* CV12 .....116 E3
STRPT DY13 .....163 K7
Thirlmere Wk *BRLYHL* DY5 .....101 M6
Thirsk Cft *CBROM* B36 .....91 G5
Thirsk Rd *COVS* CV3 .....155 G8
Thirsk Wy *BRGRVW* B61 .....168 B8
Thirston Cl *WNSFLD* WV11 .....37 L8
Thistle Cl *SEDG* DY3 .....66 D7
Thistle Cft *WNSFLD* WV11 .....37 M3
Thistledown Av *BNTWD* WS7 .....18 E3
Thistle Down Cl
FOAKS/STRLY B74 .....55 L3
Thistledown Dr *HEDN* WS12 .....17 G4
WOLVN WV10 .....36 C4
Thistledown Rd *BKDE/SHDE* B34 * 92 A6
Thistle Gn *HWK/WKTH* B38 .....145 J6
Thistlegreen Cl
BLKHTH/ROWR B65 .....85 K8
Thistlegreen Rd *DUDS* DY2 .....103 J1
Thistle Wy *RRUGBY* CV23 .....161 H5
Thistlewood Gv *DOR/KN* B93 * 176 F2
Thistley Fld East *COVN* CV6 .....133 K7
Thistley Fld North *COVN* CV6 .....133 K6
Thistley Fld South *COVN* CV6 .....133 K7
Thistley Fld West *COVN* CV6 .....133 K7
Thistley Nook *LICH* WS13 * 20 E4
Thomas Crs *SMTHWK* B66 .....88 A8
Thomas Guy Rd *WBROM* B70 .....68 B8
Thomas Landsdail St *COVS* CV3 .....9 G8
Thomas Lane St *COVN* CV6 .....134 E4
Thomas Mason Cl *WNSFLD* WV11 .....37 H4
Thomas Naul Cft *TLHL/CAN* CV4 .....153 K2
Thomas Sharp St
TLHL/CAN CV4 .....153 L1
Thomas St *AST/WIT* B6 .....89 K7
BDWTH CV12 .....116 E3
BKHL/PFLD WV2 .....5 F2
COV CV1 .....8 D5
RLSN CV32 .....206 D4
SMTHWK B66 .....87 M8
TAM/AM/WIL B77 .....46 B1
WBROM B70 .....87 H3
WSLW WS2 .....4 C1
Thomas Wy *RRUGBY* CV23 .....159 L8
Thompson Av *BKHL/PFLD* WV2 .....50 B6
Thompson Cl *DUDS* DY2 .....102 F3
WLNHL WV13 .....51 L2
Thompson Dr *VAUX/NECH* B7 .....90 D5
Thompson Gdns
SMTHWK B67 .....105 K1
Thompson Rd *LCLYGN/QTN* B68 .....104 F1
SMTHWK B67 .....105 K1
Thomson Av *NFLD/LBR* B31 .....145 G4
Thomson Cl *RUGBYN/HIL* CV21 .....160 F7
Thor Cl *CNCK/NC* WS11 .....12 B8
Thoresby *CRTAM* B79 .....31 J7
Thoresby Cft *DUDN* DY1 .....84 D2
Thornberry Dr *DUDN* DY1 .....84 A3
Thornberry Wk *VAUX/NECH* B7 .....90 A7
Thornbridge Av *PBAR/PBCH* B42 .....71 G6
Thornbridge Gv *ALDR* WS9 .....40 D2
Thornbury Ct
DUNHL/THL/PER WV6 .....48 D3
Thornbury La *REDE* B98 .....195 D6
Thornbury Rd
BFLD/HDSWWD B20 .....89 H3
SOLH B91 .....127 M8
TAM/AM/WIL B77 .....46 C5
Thornby Av *KNWTH* CV8 .....197 L3
TAM/AM/WIL B77 .....46 C6
Thornby Rd *ERDW/GRVHL* B23 .....72 C4
Thorncliffe Cl *REDW* B97 .....201 J3
Thorncliffe Wy
NUNW/HART CV10 .....79 L8
Thorn Cl *DARL/WED* WS10 .....68 C1
RUGBYN/HIL CV21 .....161 G7
Thorncroft Wy *DSYBK/YTR* WS5 .....69 M7
Thorne Av *WOLVN* WV10 .....36 C5
Thorne Rd *WLNHL* WV13 .....51 L1
Thornes Cft *ALDR* WS9 .....41 J1
Thorne St *BKHL/PFLD* WV2 .....51 G5
Thorneycroft La *WOLVN* WV10 .....36 D8
Thorneycroft Rd *BILS/COS* WV14 .....67 L2
Thorney Rd *COVS* CV3 .....134 F7
FOAKS/STRLY B74 .....55 K4
Thornfield Cft *SEDG* DY3 .....66 D7
Thornfield Rd *ACGN* B27 .....127 G3
Thorngrove Av *SOLH* B91 .....149 G5
Thornham Wy
ALE/KHTH/YWD B14 .....146 A3
Thornhill Cft *COV* CV1 * 134 D8
Thornhill Dr *NUN* CV11 .....99 H5
Thornhill Gv *HDSW* B21 .....88 D5
Thornhill Pk *FOAKS/STRLY* B74 .....55 L5
Thornhill Rd *BRLYHL* DY5 .....102 B4
COV CV1 .....134 B8
DUDN DY1 .....85 G1
FOAKS/STRLY B74 .....55 L5
HALE B63 .....121 J2
HDSW B21 .....88 D5
HEDN WS12 .....12 D6
REDE B98 .....195 A6
SOLH B91 .....128 A6

U

moor La RMSLY B62 ....121 H7
on Cl SHLY B90 ....148 C2
on Crs SHLY B90 ....148 B2
on Cft COWV CV5 ....153 L2
pool Cl REDW B97 * 202 B8
enhall Rd DOR/KN B93 ....149 L7
eries Rd HIA/OLT B92 ....127 L3
rwood Rd HIA/OLT B92 ....127 K5
rk Gn ERDE/BCHGN B24 ....90 D3
swater Av NUN CV11 ....81 K7
RLSN CV32 ....206 A3
STRPT DY13 ....163 K7
swater Cl RIDG/WDGT B32 ....123 K3
swater Gdns KGSWFD DY6 ....83 H7
swater Ri BRLYHL DY5 ....84 B8
swater Rd BDWTH CV12 ....116 E5
COVS CV3 ....156 C4
SHHTH WV12 ....37 M4
ter Cl CNCK/NC WS11 ....16 C4
ter Dr KGSWFD DY6 ....101 J7
verley Crs HIA/OLT B92 ....127 K5
verley Green Rd HIA/OLT B92 ....127 K5
erscroft Rd COVS CV5 ....155 G5
erston RUGBYN/HIL CV21 ....161 H6
vine Dr NFLD/LBR B31 ....144 E1
berslade Rd HOCK/TIA B94 ....173 M5
SLYOAK B29
derhill Cl REDE B98 ....202 D7
derhill La WOLVN WV10 ....36 C2
derhill Rd TPTN/OCK DY4 ....68 A7
WASH/WDE B8 ....108 D2
derhill Rd OLDBY B69 ....86 B4
derley Cl REDE B98 ....82 F6
e Underpass BHAMNEC B40 ....129 J1
derwood Cl EDG B15 ....124 B2
ERDW/GRVHL B23 ....90 A1
REDW B97 ....201 L6
derwood Rd
BFLD/HDSWWD B20 ....70 C8
ett St LOZ/NWT B19 ....89 G8
SMTHWK B66 ....106 A4
ett Wk LOZ/NWT B19 ....89 G8
icorn Av COWV CV5 153
icorn Hl REDW B97 ....202 B1
icorn La COWV CV5 ....153 K1
ion Cl TAM/AM/WIL B77 ....46 A2
ion La WMBN WV5 ....64 B4
ion Mill St WOLV WV1 ....3 J5
ion Pl COVN CV6 ....134 C1
ion Rd AST/WIT B6 ....89 M5
OLDBY B69 ....86 C4
RLSN CV32 ....206 C4
ion Rw WNSFLD WV11 ....88 D5
ion St BILS/COS WV14 ....51 L8
BLKHTH/ROWR B65 ....104 A4
BNTWD WS7 ....18 C8
CBHAM B2 ....7 G5
CNCK/NC WS11 ....16 C1
DARL/WED WS10 ....68 D3
DUDS DY2 ....102 C8
HAG/WOL DY9 ....138 C6
KIDD DY10 ....138 C6
REDE B98 ....202 D2
RUGBYS/DCH CV22 ....186 E3
STRBR DY8 ....119 L8
TPTN/OCK DY4 ....67 K4
WBROM B70 ....87 H5
WLNHL WV13 ....51 L3
WOLV WV1 ....3 H3
WSL WS1 5
ity Cl DARL/WED WS10 ....68 A1
ity Pl OLDBY B69 * 86 E5
SLYOAK B29 * 124 D3
iversity Rd TLHL/CAN CV4 ....153 M8
ketts Rd SMTHWK B67 ....105 J3
win Crs STRBR DY8 ....101 J8
avon Cl CVALE B35 ....91 L1
land Gv BRGRVW B61 ....191 L1
land Rd BRGRVW B61 ....191 L1
SLYOAK B29 ....124 E3
lands COVE CV2 ....134 E8
lands Av BDMR/CCFT WV3 ....49 H5
BLKHTH/ROWR B65 ....104 B2
WLNHL WV13 ....51 L4
lands Cl DUDS DY2 ....85 J6
PENK ST19 ....10 C3
lands Dr BDMR/CCFT WV3 ....49 J5
SEDG DY3 ....66 B5
lands Gv WLNHL WV13 ....51 G4
lands Rd DUDS DY2 ....85 K6
HDSW B21 ....88 B3
e Uplands SMTHWK B67 ....105 H1
leadon Cl REDW B97 ....201 L7
pper Abbey St REDW B97 ....80 F8
pper Ashley St RMSLY B62 ....104 A4
pper Balsall Heath Rd
BHTH/HG B12 ....107 K7
pper Brook St WSLW WS2 ....4 C4
pper Cape WWCK CV34 ....205 H5
pper Church La TPTN/OCK DY4 ....67 K6
pper Clifton Rd
SCFLD/BOLD B73 ....56 F8
pper Conybere St
BHTH/HG B12 ....107 K6
pper Crossgate Rd REDE B98 ....203 G5
pper Dean St DIG/EDG B5 ....7 G7
pper Eastern Green La
COWV CV5 ....132 A8
pper Ettingshall Rd
BILS/COS WV14 ....66 E5
pper Field Cl REDW B98 ....195 G7
perfield Wy COVS CV5 ....156 A4
pper Forster St RUSH/SHEL WS4 ....5 G1
pper Gambols La
BRGRVW B60 ....192 B4
pper Gough St CBHAMW B3 ....6 D8
pper Gn DUNHL/THL/PER WV6 ....35 M3
pper Green La WSLW WS2 ....3 G7
pper Grosvenor Rd
BFLD/HDSWWD B20 ....88 D3
pper Grove St RLSN CV32 ....206 D4
pper Gungate CRTAM B79 ....31 M7
pper Hall La REDE B98 ....203 H4
pper Hall La WSL WS1 ....4 F5
pper Highgate St
BHTH/HG B12 ....107 K6
pper High St CDYHTH B64 ....103 H4
DARL/WED WS10 ....68 D3
pper Hill St COV CV1 ....2 A2
RLSN CV32 * 206 B3
per Holly Wk RLSN CV32 * 206 D3
per Landywood La GTWY WS6 ....24 D3
e Lea Cottages
DY10 * 138 D2
per Lichfield St WLNHL WV13 ....51 L3
per Mdw RLSN CV32 * 206 D3
per Marshall St CBHAMW B1 ....6 E7

Upper Meadow Rd
RIDG/WDGT B32 ....105 G8
Upper Navigation St WSLW WS2 ....4 C3
Upper Pk COVS CV3 ....156 B8
Upper Prec COV CV1 ....8 E4
Upper Ride COVS CV3 ....156 B8
Upper Rosemary Hl
KNWTH CV8 ....179 K8
Upper Rushall St
DARL/WED WS10 ....68 D3
Upper Russell St
SMTHWK B67 * 20 F7
Upper St John St LICHS WS14 ....20 F7
Upper St Mary's Rd
SMTHWK B67 ....105 K4
Upper Short St WSLW WS2 ....4 C4
Upper Sneyd Rd WNSFLD WV11 ....37 M3
Upper Spon St COV CV1 ....8 B5
Upper Spring La KNWTH CV8 ....179 K6
Upper St DUNHL/THL/PER WV6 ....35 H8
Upper Sutton St AST/WIT B6 ....89 L5
Upper Thomas St AST/WIT B6 ....89 K7
Upper Trinity St BORD B9 ....7 L7
Upper Vauxhall St
ETTPK/GDPK/PENN WV4 ....49 M7
Upper Villiers St
ETTPK/GDPK/PENN WV4 ....49 M7
Upper Well St COV CV1 ....8 E3
Upper William St CBHAMW B1 ....6 C7
Upper York St COV CV1 ....8 C6
Upper Zoar St BDMR/CCFT WV3 ....2 B5
Upton Cl REDE B98 ....203 K2
Upton Dr NUN CV11 ....99 K6
Upton Gdns BILS/COS WV14 ....51 G8
Upton Gv YDLY B25 ....109 G4
Upton Rd KIDD DY10 ....138 D4
RUGBYS/DCH CV22 ....186 B2
STETCH B33 ....109 G3
Upton St DUDS DY2 ....85 G8
Upwey Av SOLH B91 ....148 L1
Usk Wy KIDD DY10 ....138 D5
Usmere Rd KIDD DY10 ....138 D5
Utrillo Ct COVW CV5 ....154 A2
Uxbridge Cl
DUNHL/THL/PER WV6 ....35 M8
Uxbridge Av COVS CV3 ....156 A3
Uxbridge St BNTWD WS7 * 18 D8
Uxbridge Ct BNTWD WS7 * 18 D8
Uxbridge St HEDN WS12 ....17 G1
LOZ/NWT B19 ....89 H8

V

Valbourne Rd
ALE/KHTH/YWD B14 ....146 A1
Vale Av ALDR WS9 ....55 H3
Vale Cl LICH WS13 ....20 F4
Vale Gns RIDG/WDGT B32 ....123 K2
RUGBYN/HIL CV21 ....187 L5
Vale Ct CDYHTH B64 * 103 H6
Vale Gdns LICHS WS14 ....10 C6
Valencia Cft CVALE B35 ....91 M1
Valencia Rd BRGRVW B60 ....192 B4
Valentine Cl FOAKS/STRLY B74 ....55 K6
Valentine Rd
ALE/KHTH/YWD B14 ....125 J4
LGLYGN/QTN B68 ....105 J3
Valepits Rd STETCH B33 ....110 A4
Valerie Gv GTB/HAM B43 ....70 A5
Vale Ri PENK ST19 ....10 C5
Vale Rd DUDS DY2 ....103 J1
STRPT DY13 ....188 E2
Vale Rw SEDG DY3 ....66 B8
Vales Cl WALM/CURD B76 ....73 J6
Vale St BKHL/PFLD WV2 ....50 E7
HHTH/SAND B71 ....69 J7
SEDG DY3 ....66 B8
STRBR DY8 ....101 K5
The Vale COV CV3 ....155 M5
SPARK B11 ....125 M3
Vale Vw ALDR WS9 ....54 F2
NUNW/HART CV10 ....98 C1
Valley Cl KIDDW CV11 ....137 J5
REDW B97 ....201 L7
Valley Dr RUGBYN/HIL CV21 ....160 E4
Valley Farm Rd RBRY B45 ....143 K7
Valley Gn GTWY WS6 ....24 C3
Valley La HOCK/TIA B94 ....176 B6
LICH WS13 ....21 H5
TAM/AM/WIL B77 ....46 C6
Valley Rd BLOX/PEL WS3 ....39 K5
BRGRVW B61 ....168 C6
CDYHTH B64 ....103 J6
COVE CV2 ....134 E7
FOAKS/STRLY B74 ....55 K6
GTB/HAM B43 ....70 A6
HAG/WOL DY9 ....102 D8
HEDN WS12 ....13 H7
HIA/OLT B92 ....128 A1
HOCK/TIA B94 ....173 L4
NUNW/HART CV10 ....97 K1
RLSN CV32 ....206 F3
RMSLY B62 ....104 A5
SEDG DY3 ....66 C6
SMTHWK B67 ....105 K2
WOLVN WV10 36
Valley Side BLOX/PEL WS3 ....39 K3
The Valley BNTWD WS7 * 18 B5
Valley Vw BEWD DY12 ....162 C3
BRWNH WS8 ....26 C5
Vallian Cft CBROM B36 ....91 K6
Vanborough Wk DUDN DY1 ....84 E3
Van Diemans Rd WMBN WV5 ....64 B8
Van Dyke Cl COVW CV5 ....154 A2
Van Gogh Cl CNCK/NC WS11 ....17 H3
Vanguard TAM/AM/WIL B77 ....46 B7
Vanguard Av COVW CV5 ....154 A4
Vanguard Cl CBROM B36 ....91 J5
Vanguard Rd
LGN/SDN/BHAMAIR B26 ....129 J3
Vann Cl SMHTH B10 ....108 A5
Vantage Point WBROM B70 * 87 G3
Varden Cft DIG/EDG B5 ....7 H8
Vardon Dr COVS CV3 ....181 H1
Vardon Wy HWK/WKHTH B38 ....145 H4
Varley V ERDE/BCHGN B24 ....91 H1
Varlins Wy HWK/WKHTH B38 ....145 H7
Varney Av WBROM B70 ....87 H3
Vaughan Cl FOAKS/STRLY B74 ....42 D7
Vaughan Gdns CDSL WV8 ....21 J7
Vaughan Rd WLNHL WV13 ....51 L5
Vaughton Dr MGN/WHC B75 ....57 J7
Vaughton St AST/WIT B6 ....89 K7
Vaughton St South DIG/EDG B5 ....107 J6
Vauxhall Av COVW CV5 ....153 M1
WOLV WV1 ....2 A2
Vauxhall Crs CBROM B36 ....92 D4
Vauxhall Gdns DUDS DY2 ....85 J6
Vauxhall Pl VAUX/NECH B7 ....107 M2
Vauxhall Rd STRBR DY8 ....101 L8
VAUX/NECH B7 ....7 M3

Vauxhall St COV CV1 ....9 K3
DUDN DY1 ....84 F5
Vawdrey Cl STRPT DY13 ....188 C4
Vaynor Dr REDW B97 ....202 B5
Veasey Cl NUN CV11 ....99 J2
Vecqueray St COV CV1 ....9 K5
Velsheda Rd SHLY B90 ....147 L3
Venetia Rd BORD B9 ....108 A3
Venning Gv GTB/HAM B43 ....70 B6
LOZ/NWT B19 ....89 H6
Ventnor Cl CBROM B36 ....91 H6
Ventnor Cl COVE CV2 ....156 C2
LGLYGN/QTN B68 ....105 G6
Ventnor Rd HIA/OLT B92 ....128 A2
Ventnor St NUNW/HART CV10 ....81 G7
Ventura Park Rd
POL/KGSB/FAZ B78 ....45 L2
Venture Centre CNCK/NC WS11 * 16 C7
Venture Wy VAUX/NECH B7 ....7 K1
Venus Bank BEWD DY12 ....162 E2
Vera Rd
LGN/SDN/BHAMAIR B26 ....109 J6
Vera Roberts Wy KIDDW DY11 ....163 M2
Verbena Gdns VAUX/NECH B7 ....7 M2
Verbena Rd NFLD/LBR B31 ....123 L8
Vercourt FOAKS/STRLY B74 ....55 M2
Verdi Ct LICH WS13 ....21 G3
Verdon Ct HIA/OLT B92 ....187 K4
Vere Rd RUGBYN/HIL CV21 ....187 K4
Vere St DIG/EDG B5 ....107 H5
Verity Wk STRBR DY8 ....101 J4
Vermont Gn CNCK/NC WS11 ....16 E2
Vermont Gv RLSS CV31 ....207 H7
Verney Av STETCH B33 ....110 B6
Vernier Av KGSWFD DY6 ....83 L8
Vernolds Cft DIG/EDG B5 ....7 G9
Vernon Av BFLD/HDSWWD B20 ....88 D1
BRWNH WS8 ....26 A6
RUGBYS/DCH CV22 ....187 J5
TPTN/OCK DY4 ....85 J1
Vernon Cl COV CV1 ....9 K3
FOAKS/STRLY B74 ....42 C8
REDE B98 ....194 D8
RLSN CV32 ....206 C2
RMSLY B62 ....104 A5
WLNHL WV13 ....51 J4
WNSFLD WV11 ....37 K1
Vernon Ct LDYWD/EDGR B16 ....106 C4
LGLYGN/QTN B68 ....105 G6
Vernon Rd BILS/COS WV14 ....51 K7
LDYWD/EDGR B16 ....106 B4
LGLYGN/QTN B68 ....87 G7
RMSLY B62 ....104 A5
STRPT DY13 ....188 E5
Vernons La NUNW/HART CV10 ....98 C1
Vernons Pl WOLVN WV10 ....23 H4
Vernon St WBROM B70 ....86 C2
Vernon Wy BLOX/PEL WS3 ....38 C4
Verona Cl NUN CV11 ....99 L4
Verona Rd BRGRVW B60 ....192 A4
Veronica Av
ETTPK/GDPK/PENN WV4 ....50 C8
Veronica Cl SLYOAK B29 ....123 K7
Verona Rd KGSWFD DY6 ....83 L7
Verstone Cft NFLD/LBR B31 ....144 E3
Verstone Rd SHLY B90 ....148 A1
Verwood Cl WLNHL WV13 ....51 H4
FOAKS/STRLY B74 ....56 D3
Vesey Cl CSHL/WTROR B46 ....92 F3
FOAKS/STRLY B74 ....56 D3
Vesey St CBHAMNE B4 ....7 H2
Vestry Cl CDYHTH B64 ....103 K4
Vestry Ct STRBR DY8 ....101 J7
Viaduct Dr DUNHL/THL/PER WV6 ....35 M7
Viaduct St VAUX/NECH B7 ....7 M4
Vibart Rd
LGN/SDN/BHAMAIR B26 ....109 J5
Vicarage Ct ATHST CV9 ....63 J6
BRGRVE B60 ....191 M5
BRLYHL DY5 ....102 A6
BRWNH WS8 ....26 E5
BVILLE B30 ....124 F6
PBAR/PBCH B42 ....71 H6
POL/KGSB/FAZ B78 ....45 K8
TPTN/OCK DY4 ....67 J8
Vicarage Crs KIDD DY10 ....138 D8
Vicarage Fld WWCK CV34 ....205 M5
Vicarage Gdns KNWTH CV8 * 197 L3
RMSLY B62 ....104 B4
WALM/CURD B76 ....73 K6
Vicarage Hl POL/KGSB/FAZ B78 ....58 F4
RUGBYN/HIL CV21 ....187 J1
Vicarage La BRLYHL DY5 ....84 B5
CSHL/WTROR B46 ....92 F3
RCOVN/BALC/EX CV7 ....116 B6
Vicarage Pl WSL WS1 ....4 E5
Vicarage Prospect DUDN DY1 ....84 F4
Vicarage Rd
ALE/KHTH/YWD B14 ....125 G6
AST/WIT B6 ....89 L6
BILS/COS WV14 ....67 G6
BKHL/PFLD WV2 ....3 H5
BLOX/PEL WS3 ....39 L3
BRWNH WS8 ....26 D6
DARL/WED WS10 ....68 D2
EDG B15 ....106 D5
ETTPK/GDPK/PENN WV4 ....49 M7
HAG/WOL DY9 ....102 D8
HHTH/SAND B71 ....69 H7
HOCK/TIA B94 ....174 A2
HOCK/TIA B94 ....175 J6
HRBN B17 ....105 M8
KIDD DY10 ....165 J3
KNWTH CV8 ....180 F7
LGLYGN/QTN B68 ....104 F1
RLSN CV32 ....206 E2
RMSLY B62 ....104 A5
RUGBYS/DCH CV22 ....186 D3
SEDG DY3 ....66 C8
SMTHWK B67 ....87 K8
STETCH B33 ....109 J4
STRBR DY8 ....101 H4
WNSFLD WV11 ....36 F7
WOLVN WV10 ....14 C7
WSNGN B18 ....88 D6
Vicarage Rd West DUDN DY1 ....67 G7
Vicarage St LGLYGN/QTN B68 ....86 F8
NUN CV11 ....99 J2
Vicarage Vw REDW B97 ....202 B2
Vicar St DARL/WED WS10 ....68 D2
WSL WS1 ....4 F5
Vicar St DARL/WED WS10 ....68 D4
DUDS DY2 ....85 G5
KIDD DY10 ....138 C7
SEDG DY3 ....66 D5
Vicars Wk HAG/WOL DY9 ....120 C5
Viceroy Cl EDG B15 ....107 G7
KGSWFD DY6 ....83 L8
Victor Cl HAG/WOL DY9 ....141 J1
Victor Dr BHTH/HG B12 ....107 K7
Victoria Av BLOX/PEL WS3 ....39 G4
RMSLY B62 ....104 A5
RUGBYN/HIL CV21 ....186 E6
SMHTH B10 ....108 B6
SMTHWK B66 ....87 L8
Victoria Br BEWD DY12 ....136 B2
RLSS CV31 ....206 D5
Victoria Ct COVW CV5 * 154 B1

SMTHWK B66 ....88 B7
Vivian Cl HRBN B17 ....106 A8
Vivian Rd HRBN B17 ....106 A8
Vixen Cl WALM/CURD B76 ....73 H6
Vogue Cl COV CV1 ....9 J3
Voyager Dr CNCK/NC WS11 ....16 C7
Vulcan Rd BILS/COS WV14 ....51 K8
LICH WS13 ....21 H3
SOLH B91 ....128 A7
Vyrnwy Gv HWK/WKHTH B38 ....145 J5
Vyse St AST/WIT B6 ....89 M5
WSNGN B18 ....6 C1

W

Wackrill Dr RLSN CV32 ....207 G2
Waddell Cl BILS/COS WV14 ....66 D4
Waddens Brook La
WNSFLD WV11 ....37 J8
Waddington Av GTB/HAM B43 ....70 C4
Wade Av COVS CV3 ....154 F6
Wadebridge Dr NUN CV11 ....99 K1
Wade Gv WWCK CV34 ....205 J3
Wadesmill Lawns WOLVN WV10 ....36 C1
Wade St LICH WS13 ....21 G3
Wadham Cl OLDBY B69 ....86 A7
Wadhurst Rd HRBN B17 ....105 M3
Wadleys Rd SOLH B91 ....127 K7
Waen Cl TPTN/OCK DY4 ....67 M5
Waggoners Cl BRGRVE B60 ....191 J7
KNWTH CV8 ....182 A8
Waggoner's La
POL/KGSB/FAZ B78 ....44 C5
Waggon La KIDD DY10 ....139 J2
Waggon Sq STRPT DY13 ....188 C4
Waggon Wk HWK/WKHTH B38 ....145 G5
Wagoners Cl WASH/WDE B8 ....90 F3
Wagon La HIA/OLT B92 ....127 K1
Wagstaff Cl BILS/COS WV14 ....67 H5
Wainbody Av North COVS CV3 ....154 C8
Wainbody Av South COVS CV3 ....180 D1
Wainwright Cl KGSWFD DY6 ....82 F6
Wainwright St AST/WIT B6 ....89 L6
Waite Rd WLNHL WV13 ....51 J5
Wakefield Cl ATHST CV9 ....76 F1
COVS CV3 ....156 D6
SCFLD/BOLD B73 ....56 C5
Wakefield Ct MOS/BIL B13 * 125 M3
Wakefield Gv CSHL/WTROR B46 ....92 F2
Wakeford Rd NFLD/LBR B31 ....145 G3
Wakeford Rd NFLD/LBR B31 ....145 G4
Wake Gn Pk MOS/BIL B13 ....125 M3
Wake Green Rd MOS/BIL B13 ....125 L3
TPTN/OCK DY4 ....67 L4
Wake Gv WWCK CV34 ....204 F8
Wakelam Gdns CNCK/NC WS11 ....99 K5
Wakelam Gdns GTB/HAM B43 ....70 A4
Wakeley HI
ETTPK/GDPK/PENN WV4 ....65 L2
Wakelin Rd SHLY B90 ....147 M6
Wakeman Dr WNSFLD WV11 ....37 M3
Wakeman Dr OLDBY B69 ....85 M5
Wakeman Gv STETCH B33 ....110 B6
Wakes Cl WLNHL WV13 ....51 M4
Wakes Rd DARL/WED WS10 ....68 E3
Walcot Cl MGN/WHC B75 ....56 F2
Walcot Dr GTB/HAM B43 ....70 C7
Walcot Gdns BILS/COS WV14 ....50 F8
Walcot Gn DOR/KN B93 ....175 J3
Waldale Cl SHHTH WV12 ....38 A4
Walden Gdns
ETTPK/GDPK/PENN WV4 ....49 J7
Walden Rd SPARK B11 ....126 C2
Waldeve Gv HIA/OLT B92 ....128 D5
Waldley Gv ERDE/BCHGN B24 ....91 G2
Waldron Av BRLYHL DY5 ....101 M3
Waldron Cl DARL/WED WS10 ....52 D7
Waldrons Moor
ALE/KHTH/YWD B14 ....125 G8
Walford Av BDMR/CCFT WV3 ....49 K5
Walford Gv HIA/OLT B92 ....128 B2
Walford Gv WWCK CV34 ....205 K4
Walford Rd RUGBYN/HIL CV21 ....187 K5
Walford Rd SPARK B11 ....108 A7
Walford St OLDBY B69 ....85 K3
Walhouse Cl WSL WS1 ....5 G5
Walhouse Dr PENK ST19 ....10 C2
Walhouse Rd WSL WS1 ....5 G5
Walker Av BRLYHL DY5 ....102 B6
HAG/WOL DY9 ....120 E8
OLDBY B69 ....86 A6
WOLVN WV10 ....22 E5
Walker Dr KIDD DY10 ....138 C4
VAUX/NECH B7 ....90 C5
Walker Pl BLOX/PEL WS3 ....39 J5
Walker Rd BLOX/PEL WS3 ....39 J5
Walkers Cft LICH WS13 ....21 G3
Walkers Fold SHHTH WV12 ....38 B7
Walkers Heath Rd
HWK/WKHTH B38 ....145 M4
Walkers Orch KNWTH CV8 ....180 F7
Walkers Ri HEDN WS12 ....13 H5
Walker St DUDS DY2 ....103 G1
TPTN/OCK DY4 ....67 G4
Walkers Wy CSHL/WTROR B46 ....93 L2
RCOVN/BALC/EX CV7 ....116 D4
Walk La WMBN WV5 ....64 C7
Walkmill La CNCK/NC WS11 ....16 C5
The Walk SEDG DY3 ....66 B4
Walkwood Crs REDW B97 ....202 A7
Walkwood Rd REDW B97 ....202 A7
Wallace Cl CNCK/NC WS11 ....17 K8
OLDBY B69 ....86 B7
Wallace Ct CGTWY WS6 ....24 D4
Wallace Rd BDWTH CV12 ....116 A3
BILS/COS WV14 ....67 L2
BRWNH WS8 ....26 C5
COVN CV6 ....133 L7
OLDBY B69 ....86 A6
SLYOAK B29 ....124 C3
Wall Av CSHL/WTROR B46 ....93 K8
Wallbank Rd WASH/WDE B8 ....90 F1
Wallbrook St BILS/COS WV14 ....67 G6
Wall Cft ALDR WS9 ....55 H1
Wall Dr FOAKS/STRLY B74 ....56 D1
Wall End Cl WSLW WS2 ....4 B1
Waller St RLSN CV32 ....206 E3
Wallface HHTH/SAND B71 ....68 D4
Wall Heath La ALDR WS9 ....27 J8
Wall Hill Rd
RCOVN/BALC/EX CV7 * 96 C3
RCOVN/BALC/EX CV7 ....114 A6
Wallhouse Cl REDW B97 ....
REDW B97 ....202 B7
Walling Cft BILS/COS WV14 ....66 F2
Wallingford Av NUN CV11 ....81 H5
Wallington Cl BLOX/PEL WS3 ....38 F3

Wallington Heath
BLOX/PEL WS3 .....38 F3
Wall Island LICHS WS14 * 28 E4
Wall La LICHS WS14 .....28 C2
Wallows Pl BRLYHL DY5 .....53 D7
Wallows Pl BRLYHL DY5 .....84 A8
Wallows Rd BRLYHL DY5 .....102 A1
Wallows Wd SEDG DY3 .....83 L1
Wallsgrove Cl RLSN CV32 .....206 D2
Wall St WOLV WV1 .....50 E3
Wall Well HALE B63 .....121 K2
Wall Well La HALE B63 .....121 K2
Walmead Cft HRBN B17 .....105 K6
Walmer Gv ERDW/GRVHL B23 .....71 M8
Walmer Meadow ALDR WS9 .....40 F6
The Walmers ALDR WS9 .....40 F6
Walmer Wy
CHWD/FDBR/MGN B37 .....111 G2
Walmesley Wy WALM/CURD B76 .....73 K6
Walmley Ash Rd
WALM/CURD B76 .....73 K6
Walmley Cl HALE B63 .....102 F6
Walmley Rd MGN/WHC B75 .....73 K5
Walnut Av CDSL WV8 .....34 F2
Walnut Cl
CHWD/FDBR/MGN B37 .....110 F4
CNCK/NC WS11 .....16 D2
HAG/WOL DY9 .....119 M4
NUNW/HART CV10 .....79 L5
NUNW/HART CV10 .....80 C7
Walnut Cft ATHST CV9 .....62 A5
Walnut Dr BDMR/CCFT WV3 .....49 H4
CNCK/NC WS11 .....16 D3
RLSN CV32 .....206 D2
SMTHWK B66 .....87 M8
Walnut Gv LICHS WS14 .....21 K6
STRPT DY13 .....189 G1
Walnut La BRGRVE B60 .....192 B5
DARL/WED WS10 .....68 C5
Walnut Rd DSYBK/YTR WS5 .....69 L2
Walnut St COVE CV2 .....134 F1
Walnut Tree Cl KNWTH CV8 .....197 L2
NFLD/LBR B31 .....144 C5
RUGBYS/DCH CV22 .....185 M4
Walpole St DUNHL/THL/PER WV6 .....2 D7
Walpole Wk WBROM B70 .....87 H4
Walrand Cl CRTAM B79 .....31 M4
Walsal End La HIA/OLT B92 .....150 D2
Walsall Rd ALDR WS9 .....54 D1
ALDR WS9 .....54 D1
BLOX/PEL WS3 .....39 L3
CNCK/NC WS11 .....16 C5
DARL/WED WS10 .....52 C7
DSYBK/YTR WS5 .....69 K1
FOAKS/STRLY B74 .....42 A7
GTWY WS6 .....24 E1
HHTH/SAND B71 .....69 J3
LICH WS13 .....20 C7
LICHS WS14 .....27 J5
PBAR/PBCH B42 .....70 E5
WLNHL WV13 .....51 H4
Walsall St DARL/WED WS10 .....51 H8
DARL/WED WS10 .....52 B7
TLHL/CAN CV4 .....153 L6
WBROM B70 .....87 H2
WLNHL WV13 .....51 M4
WOLV WV1 .....3 J6
Walsall Wood Rd ALDR WS9 .....40 F4
Walsgrave Gdns COVE CV2 .....135 L6
Walsgrave Rd DHIA/OLT B92 .....128 B6
Walsh Dr WALM/CURD B76 .....73 K1
Walsh Gv ERDW/GRVHL B23 .....72 B5
Walsh La RCOVN/BALC/EX CV7 .....131 J3
Walsingham Dr
NUNW/HART CV10 .....98 E7
Walsingham St WSL WS1 .....5 J5
Walstead Rd DSYBK/YTR WS5 .....53 K8
Walstead Rd West
DSYBK/YTR WS5 .....53 J8
Waltdene Cl GTB/HAM B43 .....70 D2
Walter Cobb Dr SCFLD/BOLD B73..72 E4
Walter Nash Rd East
KIDDW DY11 .....163 L4
Walter Nash Rd West
KIDDW DY11 .....163 L4
Walter Rd BILS/COS WV14 .....67 J2
SMTHWK B66 .....87 J7
Walters Cl NFLD/LBR B31 .....144 B7
Walter Scott Rd DARL/WED CV12..117 G4
Walters Rd LGLYGN/QTN B68 .....104 E6
Walters Rw DUDN DY1 .....84 E4
Walters St BLOX/PEL WS3 .....39 L7
VAUX/NECH B7 .....89 M7
WBROM B70 .....87 H3
Waltham Cl BRGRVW B61 .....191 J4
Waltham Crs NUNW/HART CV10...79 J2
Waltham Gv KGSTG B44 .....71 M4
Walthamstow Ct BRLYHL DY5 .....102 B4
Walton Av BLKHTH/ROWR B65 .....103 H4
Walton Cl BLKHTH/ROWR B65 .....103 J1
COVS CV3 .....156 C6
HALE B63 .....121 K3
KIDDW DY11 .....163 M3
NUN CV11 .....99 K1
REDE B98 .....203 J2
STRPT DY13 .....188 B4
Walton Crs
ETTPK/GDPK/PENN WV4 .....50 C8
Walton Cft SOLH B91 .....148 F4
Walton Dr HAG/WOL DY9 .....102 A8
Walton Gdns CDSL WV8 .....34 D1
Walton Gv BVILLE B30 .....145 M3
Walton Heath BLOX/PEL WS3 .....38 D2
Walton Pool La HAG/WOL DY9 .....141 K3
Walton Rd ALDR WS9 .....40 E3
BRGRVW B61 .....191 J4
DARL/WED WS10 .....69 G3
ETTPK/GDPK/PENN WV4 .....50 B8
LGLYGN/QTN B68 .....105 G4
STRBR DY8 .....101 J2
Walton St TPTN/OCK DY4 .....67 K8
Wanderers Av BKHL/PFLD WV2 .....50 A7
Wanderer Wk ERDE/BCHGN B24 ...91 J2
Wandle Gv SPARK B11 .....126 E3
Wandsworth Rd KGSTG B44 .....71 J2
Wanley Rd COVS CV3 .....155 H7
Wannerton Rd KIDD DY10 .....139 M4
Wansbeck Wk SEDG DY3 .....66 D1
Wansell Ct TLHL/CAN CV4 .....153 L6
Wanstead Gv KGSTG B44 .....71 L4
Wantage Rd CSHL/WTROR B46 .....91 J4
Wappenbury Cl COVE CV2 .....135 G3
Wappenbury Rd COVE CV2 .....135 H4
Wapping La REDE B98 .....195 M6
Warbank Cl ALVE B48 .....170 F3
Warbler Pl KIDD DY10 .....164 E3
Ward Cl WASH/WDE B8 .....90 E8
Warden Av SCFLD/BOLD B73 .....72 D5
Ward End Cl WASH/WDE B8 .....90 D7
Ward End Hall Gv WASH/WDE B8..90 E7
Ward End Park Rd
WASH/WDE B8 .....90 D8

Wardend Rd WASH/WDE B8 .....90 E7
Warden Rd COVN CV6 .....133 M7
SCFLD/BOLD B73 .....72 D5
The Wardens Av COVW CV5 .....132 F7
The Wardens KNWTH CV8 .....180 A8
Ward Gv
ETTPK/GDPK/PENN WV4 .....66 D2
WWCK CV34 .....205 M6
Wardle Cl MGN/WHC B75 .....56 E1
Wardle Pl HEDN WS12 .....12 B8
Wardles La GTWY WS6 .....24 D3
Wardle St CRTAM B79 .....31 L8
Wardlow Rd VAUX/NECH B7 .....89 L8
Wardour Dr
CHWD/FDBR/MGN B37 .....111 G3
Wardour Gv KGSTG B44 .....72 A5
Wardour Rd COVN CV6 .....50 B8
STRPT DY13 .....188 F4
Ward St BILS/COS WV14 .....66 F5
BKHL/PFLD WV2 .....50 F4
HEDN WS12 .....12 D7
LOZ/NWT B19 .....7 G1
WLNHL WV13 .....51 M2
WOLV WV1 .....3 J5
WSL WS1 .....5 H2
Wareham Gn COVE CV2 .....135 L8
Wareham Rd RBRY B45 .....143 J3
Wareing Dr ERDW/GRVHL B23 .....72 B5
Waresley Court Rd
KIDDW DY11 .....189 L4
Waresley Pk KIDDW DY11 .....189 L5
Waresley Rd KIDDW DY11 .....189 L4
Warewell Cl WSL WS1 .....5 G3
Warewell St WSL WS1 .....5 G3
Waring Cl TPTN/OCK DY4 .....67 J3
Waring Rd TPTN/OCK DY4 .....67 L5
Warings Green Rd
HOCK/TIA B94 .....174 B5
The Warings WMBN WV5 .....82 D1
War La HRBN B17 .....105 M8
Warley Cft LGLYGN/QTN B68 .....105 H5
Warley Hall Rd
LGLYGN/QTN B68 .....105 H4
Warley Rd LGLYGN/QTN B68 .....87 G8
Warmington Cl COVS CV3 .....156 C5
Warmington Dr
SCFLD/BOLD B73 .....72 F1
Warmington Gv
RWWCK/WEL CV35 .....204 F5
Warmington Rd HLYWD B47 .....146 E2
LGN/SDN/BHAMAIR B26 .....110 A8
Warmley Cl
DUNHL/THL/PER WV6 .....35 M8
SOLH B91 .....128 B8
Warmwell Cl COVE CV2 .....156 D1
Warneford Ms RLSS CV31 * 206 E6
Warner Cl WWCK CV34 .....205 H4
Warner Dr BRLYHL DY5 .....102 B4
Warner Pl BLOX/PEL WS3 .....39 L7
Warner Rd COVN CV6 .....134 D6
CDSL WV8 .....34 D2
DARL/WED WS10 .....69 G3
WOLV WV1 .....36 D1
Warners Wk SMHTH B10 .....108 A5
Warple Rd RIDG/WDGT B32 .....105 G8
Warren Av WOLV WV10 .....36 D8
Warren Cl HEDN WS12 .....13 L8
LICHS WS14 .....21 J7
RLSN CV32 .....206 D2
TPTN/OCK DY4 .....67 K6
Warren Dr BLKHTH/ROWR B65 ...85 K8
DOR/KN B93 .....175 L2
SEDG DY3 .....66 A3
Warren Farm Rd KGSTG B44 .....71 K5
Warren Fld HWK/WKHTH B38 .....145 K5
Warren Gdns KGSWFD DY6 .....83 G1
Warren Gn TLHL/CAN CV4 .....153 K5
Warren Gv WASH/WDE B8 * 90 C7
Warren Hall Rd DUDS DY2 * 85 J6
Warren House Wk
WALM/CURD B76 .....73 K4
Warren La RBRY B45 .....169 M2
Warren Pl BRWNH WS8 .....26 E6
Warren Rd BNTWD WS7 .....18 B8
BVILLE B30 .....124 C6
KGSTG B44 .....71 L7
RUGBYS/DCH CV22 .....187 H4
WASH/WDE B8 .....90 C7
Warrens Cft DSYBK/YTR WS5 .....54 D8
Warrens End HWK/WKHTH B38 ...145 K5
Warrens Hall Rd DUDS DY2 .....85 J6
Warrington Ct WALM/CURD B76...73 L4
Warrington Dr
ERDW/GRVHL B23 .....72 B6
Warsash Cl WOLV WV1 .....50 F5
Warstock La
ALE/KHTH/YWD B14 .....146 E1
Warstock Rd
ALE/KHTH/YWD B14 .....146 E1
Warston Av RIDG/WDGT B32 .....123 H2
Warstone Cl BKDE/SHDE B34 .....163 H1
Warstone Dr HHTH/SAND B71 .....87 J1
Warstone La CBHAMW B1 * 6 C2
Warstone Ms WSNGN B18 * 6 C1
Warstone Pde East WSNGN B18...6, 6 F1
Warstone Rd WOLVN WV10 .....23 M4
Warstones Crs
ETTPK/GDPK/PENN WV4 .....49 M8
Warstones Dr
ETTPK/GDPK/PENN WV4 .....49 L8
Warstones Gdns
ETTPK/GDPK/PENN WV4 .....49 M7
Warstones Rd
ETTPK/GDPK/PENN WV4 .....65 M1
Warstone Ter HDSW B21 .....88 C5
Wartell Bank KGSWFD DY6 .....83 H4
Warton Cl KNWTH CV8 .....198 A1
Warwards La SLYOAK B29 .....124 E4
Warwell La
LGN/SDN/BHAMAIR B26 .....109 H7
Warwick Av BRGRVE B60 .....191 L5
COVW CV5 .....154 A5
DARL/WED WS10 .....69 G2
DUNHL/THL/PER WV6 .....48 D2
WLNHL WV13 .....52 B3
Warwick Cl CNCK/NC WS11 .....15 H7
LGLYGN/QTN B68 .....104 E3
WBROM B70 .....68 C6
Warwick Ct RLSN CV32 * 206 D4
Warwick Crest EDG B15 .....106 F6
Warwick Dr ATHST CV9 .....63 H3
CDSL WV8 .....34 C1
Warwick Gdns
NUNW/HART CV10 .....98 C1
OLDBY B69 .....86 A3
Warwick Gra SOLH B91 .....127 K6
Warwick Grange SOLH B91 .....127 K6
Warwick Hall Gdns BRGRVE B60..191 L5
Warwick Hwy REDE B98 .....202 D1
Warwick La COV CV1 .....8 F5
Warwick New Rd RLSN CV32 .....206 B5
Warwick Pas CBHAM B2 * 7 G5
Warwick Pl RLSN CV32 .....206 B5
Warwick Rd ACGN B27 .....126 E1

COVS CV3 .....8 D9
DOR/KN B93 .....149 M6
DUDS DY2 .....103 J2
KNWTH CV8 .....183 L2
KNWTH CV8 .....197 K2
LGLYGN/QTN B68 .....104 C2
SCFLD/BOLD B73 .....72 A5
SOLH B91 .....127 K6
SOLH B91 .....149 L2
SPARK B11 .....108 A8
STRBR DY8 .....101 H4
TAM/AM/WIL B77 .....46 C1
Warwick Rw COV CV1 .....8 E6
Warwick St BHTH/HG B12 .....7 L8
BILS/COS WV14 .....67 J1
COVN CV6 .....154 D5
RLSN CV32 .....206 D4
RUGBYS/DCH CV22 .....186 E5
RUSH/SHEL WS4 .....5 K1
STRPT DY13 .....163 L8
WOLV WV1 .....3 J6
Warwick Ter RLSN CV32 .....206 C4
Warwick Wy ALDR WS9 .....40 F4
Wasdale Cl RLSN CV32 .....206 A3
Wasdale Dr KGSWFD DY6 .....83 J7
Wasdale Rd BRWNH WS8 * 26 A3
NFLD/LBR B31 .....144 C2
Weseley Rd RBRY B45 .....143 J3
Washbrook La CNCK/NC WS11 ...25 H1
COVW CV5 .....132 E4
Washbrook Rd DE REDE B98 .....203 H6
Washford Gv YDLY B25 .....108 F5
Washford La REDE B98 .....203 H5
Washington Dr
BFLD/HDSWWD B20 .....88 E2
DUDS DY2 .....103 H7
Washington St CBHAMW B1 * 6 D7
Washington Whf CBHAMW B1 * 6 C7
Wash La YDLY B25 .....109 G5
Washwood Heath Rd
WASH/WDE B8 .....90 B8
Wasperton Cl CBROM B36 .....91 M5
COVS CV3 .....156 D5
Wassell Ct HALE B63 .....121 J3
Wassell Dr BEWD DY12 .....163 G1
Wassell Grove Rd
HAG/WOL DY9 .....120 D4
Wassell Rd BILS/COS WV14 .....51 H6
HAG/WOL DY9 .....120 C3
HALE B63 .....121 J3
Waste La ATHST CV9 .....62 D4
COVN CV6 .....133 J4
RCOVN/BALC/EX CV7 .....152 C8
Wast Hill Gv HWK/WKHTH B38...145 K6
Wasthill La HWK/WKHTH B38 .....145 H8
Wastwater Ct
DUNHL/THL/PER WV6 .....48 D1
Watchbury Cl CBROM B36 .....92 A4
Watch Cl COV CV1 .....8 A4
Watchman Av BRLYHL DY5 .....102 D6
Watchtower Rd STRPT DY13 .....164 B7
Watcombe Cl COVE CV2 .....135 L7
Waterbrook Cl PENK ST19 .....10 C6
Water Dl BDMR/CCFT WV3 .....49 J3
Waterdale SHLY B90 .....148 B8
WMBN WV5 .....64 C8
Waterfall Cl
RCOVN/BALC/EX CV7 .....131 G4
SMTHWK B66 .....87 J6
Waterfall La CDYHTH B64 .....103 L4
Waterfall Rd BRLYHL DY5 .....102 A6
Waterfield Cl TPTN/OCK DY4 .....67 G8
Waterford Pl STETCH B33 .....110 A2
Waterford Rd KGSWFD DY6 .....83 H6
Waterfront East BRLYHL DY5 * ...102 C1
Waterfront Wy BRLYHL DY5 .....102 C1
WSLW WS2 * 4 C3
Waterfront West BRLYHL DY5 .....102 C1
Waterglade La WLNHL WV13 .....51 L4
Waterhaynes Cl RBRY B45 .....143 J7
Waterhead Cl WOLVN WV10 .....36 E3
Waterhead Dr WOLVN WV10 .....36 F3
Waterlade Cl KIDDW DY11 .....189 L3
Waterlaide Rd KIDDW DY11 .....189 L3
Water La HHTH/SAND B71 .....69 G6
Waterlinks Bvd AST/WIT B6 .....89 L6
Waterloo Av
ALE/KHTH/YWD B14 .....125 J5
BEWD DY12 .....162 D2
SMTHWK B66 .....105 L2
WOLV WV1 .....3 G2
YDLY B25 .....108 F7
Waterloo Bvd HEDN WS12 .....17 J1
Waterloo Pl RLSN CV32 * 206 D4
Waterloo Rd
ALE/KHTH/YWD B14 .....125 J5
COV CV1 .....9 K5
DUDN DY1 .....84 E5
KIDD DY10 .....138 C7
RLSS CV31 .....206 F6
TPTN/OCK DY4 .....67 J4
Waterloo St East TPTN/OCK DY4...67 K8
Waterman Rd COVN CV6 .....134 D8
Watermead Gra BRWNH WS8 .....26 C6
Watermeadow Dr
RUSH/SHEL WS4 .....40 B4
Watermere RUSH/SHEL WS4 .....40 B5
Water Mill Cl SLYOAK B29 .....124 D2
Watermill Cl WOLVN WV10 .....36 A6
Water Mill Crs WALM/CURD B76...73 K4
Watermint Cl HEDN WS12 .....17 J2
Water Orton La
CBROM B36 .....92 A5
Water Orton Rd CBROM B36 .....92 A5
Water Rd SEDG DY3 .....83 A3
Watersbridge Gdns
NUNW/HART CV10 .....99 G4
The Waters Edge CBHAMW B1 * ...6 B6
Waterside COVN CV6 .....117 C7
Waterside Cl TAM/AM/WIL B77...23 G7
ERDE/BCHGN B24 .....91 L1
WOLVN WV10 .....22 C3
Waterside Dr RUGBYN/HIL CV21..161 G7
WSNGN B18 .....88 D8
Waterside Gra KIDD DY10 * 138 C5
Waterside Orch ALVE B48 .....170 F3
Waterside Pk TPTN/OCK DY4 * ...68 B6
Waterside Vw BRLYHL DY5 .....101 M3
WSNGN B18 .....88 D8
Waterside Wy BRWNH WS8 .....26 A3
Water Side Wy COVEN WV9 .....35 L3
Watersmead Cl HEDN WS12 .....17 J1
Watersmeet Gv COVE CV2 .....134 C1
Watersmeet Rd COVE CV2 .....134 F7
Waterson Cft
CHWD/FDBR/MGN B37 .....111 H2
Water St BNTWD WS7 .....18 C5
CBHAMNW B3 .....6 D3
KGSWFD DY6 .....83 H6
WBROM B70 .....87 H3
WOLVN WV10 .....3 H2

Waters Vw BLOX/PEL WS3 .....25 M8
Water Tower La KNWTH CV8 .....179 K7
Waterward Cl HRBN B17 .....106 A8
Waterways Dr OLDBY B69 .....86 C4
Waterways Gdns STRBR DY8 .....101 J4
Waterworks Dr NFLD/LBR B31 ...123 H8
Waterworks Rd
LDYWD/EDGR B16 .....106 D4
Watery La ALVE B48 .....171 J3
ALVE B48 .....172 A5
ATHST CV9 .....61 M3
CSHL/WTROR B46 .....94 B3
DOR/KN B93 .....176 C2
HAG/WOL DY9 .....140 D6
LICH WS13 .....18 F2
LICHS WS14 .....21 G2
RCOVN/BALC/EX CV7 .....114 B8
RCOVN/BALC/EX CV7 .....133 L1
REDE B98 .....202 F3
RIDG/WDGT B32 .....122 E2
SHLY B90 .....174 A1
SMTHWK B67 .....87 L8
STRBR DY8 .....101 J3
WLNHL WV13 .....51 J2
Watery La Middleway BORD B9...107 M3
Watford Gap Rd MGN/WHC B75...42 C6
Watford Rd BVILLE B30 .....124 D8
Wathan Av BILS/COS WV14 .....66 C1
Wathen Rd RLSN CV32 .....206 E3
WWCK CV34 .....205 J4
Watkins Gdns NFLD/LBR B31 .....144 F2
Watkins Rd SHHTH WV12 .....38 A8
Watland Gn BKDE/SHDE B34 .....91 L8
Watling Dr KNWTH CV8 .....179 M7
Watling St ATHST CV9 .....62 B2
BNTWD WS7 .....18 E5
BRWNH WS8 .....26 A7
CNCK/NC WS11 .....16 A7
NUN CV11 .....81 M5
POL/KGSB/FAZ B78 .....47 J8
TAM/AM/WIL B77 .....46 A5
WWCK CV34 .....205 J4
Watney Gv KGSTG B44 .....72 A3
Watson Cl CSCFLD/WYGN B72 ...72 F3
WWCK CV34 .....205 J4
Watson Rd BILS/COS WV14 .....66 D3
COVW CV5 .....154 B3
DARL/WED WS10 .....51 L8
VAUX/NECH B7 .....90 C5
WOLVN WV10 .....35 M3
Watsons Cl DUDS DY2 .....85 L8
Watson's Green Flds DUDS DY2 ...85 L5
Watson's Green Rd DUDS DY2 ...85 J5
Watson Wy
RCOVN/BALC/EX CV7 * 152 A6
Watt Cl STRPT DY13 .....163 L8
Wattisham Sq CVALE B35 .....91 J1
Wattis Rd SMTHWK B67 .....105 L3
Wattle Rd WBROM B70 .....86 D2
Watton Cl BILS/COS WV14 .....66 E4
Watton La CVALE B35 .....91 L3
Watton Ln CSHL/WTROR B46 * ...91 L3
Watton St WBROM B70 .....87 G3
Watt Rd ERDW/GRVHL B23 .....90 C1
TPTN/OCK DY4 .....67 M5
Watts Cl TPTN/OCK DY4 .....67 G8
Watts La RUGBYN/HIL CV21 .....187 H5
Watt's Rd SMHTH B10 .....108 B5
Watt St SMTHWK B66 .....87 M7
Wattville Av HDSW B21 * 88 A5
Wattville Rd HDSW B21 .....88 A5
Watwood Rd SHLY B90 .....147 K2
Waugh Cl
CHWD/FDBR/MGN B37 .....110 F3
Waugh Dr HALE B63 .....121 H5
Wavebeck Ct RRUGBY CV23 .....159 H4
Waveley Rd COV CV1 .....8 A3
Wavell Rd BRLYHL DY5 .....102 D6
WASH/WDE B8 .....90 C8
WSLW WS2 .....52 C3
Wavendon Cl COVE CV2 .....135 K4
Waveney Av
DUNHL/THL/PER WV6 .....48 D1
Waveney Cl CNCK/NC WS11 .....15 M4
Waveney Cv CNCK/NC WS11 .....15 M4
Waverhill Rd HDSW B21 .....88 D6
Waverley Av GTB/HAM B43 .....70 F1
NUN CV11 .....99 K5
Waverley Cl KIDD DY10 .....138 D5
Waverley Crs
ETTPK/GDPK/PENN WV4 .....49 M7
ETTPK/GDPK/PENN WV4 .....66 D2
RMSLY B62 .....142 D1
Waverley Gdns WMBN WV5 .....64 F6
Waverley Gv SOLH B91 .....148 B3
Waverley Rd BLOX/PEL WS3 .....38 D3
DARL/WED WS10 .....52 B7
KNWTH CV8 .....197 L2
RLSS CV31 .....206 F7
RUGBYN/HIL CV21 .....187 H4
SMHTH B10 .....108 B6
Waverley Sq NUN CV11 .....99 K5
Waverley St DUDS DY2 .....85 J5
Waverley Wk LICHS WS14 * 20 F7
Waverton Ms RLSS CV31 * 207 G8
Wavytree Cl WWCK CV34 .....205 H6
Waxland Rd HALE B63 .....121 L5
Wayт Cft KIDDW DY11 .....163 L5
Wayfield Cl SHLY B90 .....148 A2
Wayfield Rd SHLY B90 .....148 A2
Wayford Dr CSCFLD/WYGN B72...73 G6
Wayford Gv CVALE B35 .....91 L3
Waynecroft Rd GTB/HAM B43 .....70 C3
Wayside CHWD/FDBR/MGN B37..110 D5
Wayside Acres CDSL WV8 .....34 D3
Wayside Dr FOAKS/STRLY B74 .....56 A2
Wayside Gdns SHHTH WV12 .....38 C8
Wayside Wk WSLW WS2 * 52 A1
Waystone La HAG/WOL DY9 .....167 H2
Wealden Hatch WOLVN WV10 ...36 C1
Wealdstone Dr SEDG DY3 .....84 B3
Weale Gv WWCK CV34 .....205 K3
Weaman St CBHAMNE B4 .....7 G2
Weather La STRPT DY13 .....188 F2
Weatheroak Cl REDW B97 .....201 L4
Weatheroak Hi ALVE B48 .....171 M4
Weatheroak Rd SPARK B11 .....108 A8
Weather Oaks HRBN B17 .....105 M8
Weatheroaks ALDR WS9 .....40 E1
RMSLY B62 .....104 F3
Weaver Av
LGN/SDN/BHAMAIR B26 .....109 M7
WALM/CURD B76 .....73 L4
Weaver Cl BRLYHL DY5 .....83 M7
Weaver Dr RUGBYN/HIL CV21 ...186 A1
Weavers Ri DUDS DY2 .....103 H2
Weavers Wk COVN CV6 .....134 F5
Weaving Gdns CNCK/NC WS11 * ..16 C4
Webb Av DUNHL/THL/PER WV6 ...34 C8
Webbcroft Rd STETCH B33 .....109 J1
Webb Dr RRUGBY CV23 .....161 H5
Webb Ellis Rd
RUGBYS/DCH CV22 .....186 D5
Webb La HLGN/YWD B28 .....126 C2
Webb Rd TPTN/OCK DY4 .....68 A6
Webb St BILS/COS WV14 .....67 J3
NUNW/HART CV10 .....98 A2

WLNHL WV13 51
Webley Ri WOLVN WV10 36
Webster Av WLNHL WV10 * 179
Webster Cl CSCFLD/WYGN B72 ...72
SPARK B11 107
Webster Rd WLNHL WV13 51
WSLW WS2 39
Webster St COVN CV6 5
Webster Wy WALM/CURD B76 73
Weddell Wynd BILS/COS WV14...67
Weddington Rd
NUNW/HART CV10 80
Weddington Ter
NUNW/HART CV10 81
Wedgbury Wy BRLYHL DY5 101
Wedge St WSL WS1 5
Wedgewood Av WBROM B70 68
Wedgewood Cl BNTWD WS7 19
COVE CV2 135
Wedgewood Dr
BFLD/HDSWWD B20 88
Wedgewood Pl WBROM B70 68
Wedgewood Rd
RIDG/WDGT B32 105
Wednesbury Oak Rd
TPTN/OCK DY4 67
Wednesbury One
DARL/WED WS10 * 68
Wednesbury Rd WSLW WS2 4
Wednesfield Rd WLNHL WV13 51
WOLV WV1 3
Wedon Cl TLHL/CAN CV4 153
Weeford Dell WLNHL WV13 51
Weeford Dr BFLD/HDSWWD B20 ...88
Weeford Rd MGN/WHC B75 57
Weights La REDW B97 194
Welbeck Av WOLVN WV10 36
Welbeck Cl RMSLY B62 104
Welbeck Dr KIDDW DY11 137
RUSH/SHEL WS4 53
Welbeck Gv ERDW/GRVHL B23 71
Welbury Gdns
DUNHL/THL/PER WV6 35
Welby Ga RCOVN/BALC/EX CV7...151
Welby Rd HLGN/YWD B28 126
Welches Cl NFLD/LBR B31 123
Welcombe Dr WALM/CURD B76...73
Welcombe Gv SOLH B91 148
Welcome Dr BRGRVW B61 168
Welcome St ATHST CV9 63
Welford Av
LGN/SDN/BHAMAIR B26 109
Welford Cl REDE B98 202
Welford Cv FOAKS/STRLY B74 56
RWWCK/WEL CV35 204
Welford Pl COVN CV6 134
Welford Rd BFLD/HDSWWD B20...88
RUGBYN/HIL CV21 187
SCFLD/BOLD B73 72
SHLY B90 148
TAM/AM/WIL B77 46
Welgarth Av COVN CV6 133
Welham Cft SHLY B90 148
Welland Cl CSHL/WTROR B46 91
RUGBYN/HIL CV21 159
Welland Dr STRBR DY8 101
Welland Gv ERDE/BCHGN B24....91
WLNHL WV13 52
Welland Rd COV CV1 9
HALE B63 121
Welland Wy WALM/CURD B76....73
Well Cl CBROM B36 * 92
Wellcroft Rd BKDE/SHDE B34 91
Wellcroft St DARL/WED WS10 68
Wellesbourne CRTAM B79 32
Wellesbourne Cl
BDMR/CCFT WV3 48
REDE B98 202
Wellesbourne Dr BILS/COS WV14..51
Wellesbourne Rd
BFLD/HDSWWD B20 88
COVW CV5 132
Wellesley Dr TPTN/OCK DY4 67
Wellesley Gdns MOS/BIL B13 126
Wellesley Rd LGLYGN/QTN B68 ...86
Wellfield Cl CNCK/NC WS11 15
Wellfield Gdns DUDS DY2 * 85
Wellfield Rd ALDR WS9 40
HLGN/YWD B28 126
Wellhead La PBAR/PBCH B42 89
Wellington Av BDMR/CCFT WV3 ...49
Wellington Cl KGSWFD DY6 101
Wellington Crs LICH WS13 21
Wellington Dr CNCK/NC WS11 15
Wellington Gdns COVW CV5 8
Wellington Gv SOLH B91 127
Wellington Pl WLNHL WV13 51
Wellington Rd
BFLD/HDSWWD B20 88
BILS/COS WV14 51
BRGRVE B60 191
DSYBK/YTR WS5 53
DUDN DY1 84
EDG B15 107
RLSN CV32 206
SMTHWKW B67 105
TPTN/OCK DY4 68
Wellington Rd South
WBROM B70 .....
Wellington Ter LOZ/NWT B19 * 88
WLNHL WV13 * 51
Wellington Wy CVALE B35 91
Well La BLOX/PEL WS3 39
BNTWD WS7 18
DIG/EDG B5 7
GTWY WS6 24
WNSFLD WV11 .....
Wellman's Rd WLNHL WV13 51
Well Meadow RBRY B45 143
Well Pl BLOX/PEL WS3 39
Wells Av DARL/WED WS10 51
Wells Cl CNCK/NC WS11 15
DUNHL/THL/PER WV6 35
HHTH/SAND B71 69
KIDDW DY11 .....
TPTN/OCK DY4 .....
Wellsford Av HIA/OLT B92 127
Wells Green Rd HIA/OLT B92 127
Well Spring Cl ATHST CV9 .....
Wells Rd BILS/COS WV14 51

BLKHTH/ROWR B65 ....104 C2
BRLYHL DY5 ....101 M2
LGN/SDN/BHAMAIR B26 ....128 A1
lls St COV CV1 ....8 C7
OLDBY B69 ....2 D7
LGN/NWT B19 ....89 G8
iney Gdns COVEN WV9 ....35 L2
lsby Av GTB/HAM B43 ....70 C6
lsh Cl WWCK CV34 ....205 J3
lsh House Farm Rd
RIDG/WDGT B32 ....123 K1
lshmans HI SCFLD/BOLD B73...71 M3
lsh Rd COVE CV2 ....155 M1
RLSN CV32 ....207 K2
lwyndale Rd
CSCFLD/WYGN B72 ....73 G7
mbley Av YDLY B25 ....109 G5
mbley La BRWNH WS7 ....18 A5
mbrook Cl NUN CV11 ....99 H3
mbury TAM/AM/WIL B77 ....32 C8
m Gdns WNSFLD WV11 ....37 H7
ndell Crest WOLVN WV10 ....36 D2
ndiburgh St TLHL/CAN CV4 ....153 L6
ndover Ri COVW CV5 ....154 A1

ndron Gv
BLKHTH/ROWR B65 ....85 L7
ERDW/GRVHL B23 ....72 A6
ETTPK/GDPK/PENN WV4 ....66 C3
ndron Gv BRGRVE B60 ....191 M3

ALE/KHTH/YWD B14 ....146 B1
nlock Av CBROM B36 ....91 M5
nlock Cl BNTWD WS7 ....19 C6
nlock Dr
SEDG DY3 ....66 A6
nlock Dr BDMR/CCFT WV3 ....49 J5
nlock La HALE B63 ....121 H3
SEDG DY3 ....66 A6
nlock Dr BFLD/HDSWWD B20 ...88 J4
nlock Gdns BLOX/PEL WS3 ....39 J8
nlock Rd BFLD/HDSWWD B20 ...101 M7
STRBR DY8 ....101 M7
nlock Wy NUNW/HART CV10 ....97 M1
STRPT DY13 ....188 C4
nman St BHTH/HG B12 ....107 K7
nsley Cft HIA/OLT B92 ....126 F7
nsleydale Rd PBAR/PBCH B42..70 F7

nsley Rd
LGN/SDN/BHAMAIR B26 ....109 K7
ntbridge Rd WLNHL WV13 ....51 G4
ntworth Av CBROM B36 ....91 M5
ntworth Ri BNTWD WS7 ....19 C6
ntworth Rd BLOX/PEL WS3 ....38 D1
FOAKS/STRLY B74 ....56 F5
HIA/OLT B92 ....127 K2
HRBN B17 ....105 M7
RLSS CV37 ....207 H7
RUGBYS/DCH CV22 ....186 D1
STRBR DY8 ....101 H6
WOLVN WV10 ....36 D3
ntworth Gv
DUNHL/THL/PER WV6 ....34 B8
ntworth Park Av HRBN B17 ...105 M7
ntworth Ri RMSLY B62 ....122 B2
ntworth Rd BLOX/PEL WS3 ....38 D1
FOAKS/STRLY B74 ....56 E5
HIA/OLT B92 ....127 K2
HRBN B17 ....105 M7
RLSS CV37 ....207 H7
RUGBYS/DCH CV22 ....186 D1
STRBR DY8 ....101 H6
WOLVN WV10 ....36 D3
ntworth Wy
RIDG/WDGT B32 ....123 K2
nyon Ci TPTN/OCK DY4 ....85 M1
ooley Av SLYOAK B29 ....124 A3
ooley Castle Rd SLYOAK B29 ..123 L4
ooley HI SLYOAK B29 ....124 A5
ooley Park Rd SLYOAK B29 ....123 M4
ergs Dr DUNHL/THL/PER WV6 ..34 A6
ergs Gdns CDSL WV8 * 34 A4
ergs Hall Rd CDSL WV8 ....34 A4
erneth Gv DUNHL/THL/PER WV6..34 F7
rneth Gv BLOX/PEL WS3 ....38 C1
esley Av CDSL WV8 ....34 F3
TMY WS6 ....24 B8
HALE B63 ....102 F6
STRPT DY13 ....188 C4
esley Cl DARL/WED WS10 ....68 C2
CDYHTH B64 ....103 K4
esley Pl HEDN WS12 ....13 G6
TPTN/OCK DY4 ....84 E4
esley Rd BRLYHL DY5 ....83 M8
STRBR DY8 ....34 F3
ERDW/GRVHL B23 ....72 D4
RUGBYS/DCH CV22 ....187 L1
esley's Fold DARL/WED WS10 ...52 B3
esley St BILS/COS WV14 ....67 J3
BKHL/PFLD WV2 ....50 E7
OLDBY B69 ....86 E5
WBROM B70 ....86 F2
esley Wy TAM/AM/WIL B77 ......46 C1
essenden TAM/AM/WIL B77 ......46 E1
BRWNH WS8 ....26 D6
essex Cl BDWTH CV12 ....116 A1
essex Dr CNCK/NC WS11...........16 B3
esson Rd DARL/WED WS10 ....52 A6
esson Rd DARL/WED WS10 ....52 A6
st Acre WLNHL WV13................51 L4
stacre Crs BDMR/CCFT WV3....48 F5
stacre Rd BRLYHL DY5 ....102 C5
stacre Gdns STETCH B33 ....109 K3
st Av BDWTH CV12 ....117 H3
BFLD/HDSWWD B20 ....88 D1
CBROM B36 ....92 B5
COVE CV2 ....155 L3
OLDBY B69 ....85 M5
RCOVN/BALC/EX CV7 ....115 L8
REDE B98 ....202 C2
WNSFLD WV11 ....37 G7
stbook Wy WMBN WV5 ....64 D8
st Brook RIDG/WDGT B32 ....105 J8
estbourne Cl BKDE/SHDE B34 ..91 J7
CNCK/NC WS11 ....16 B3
GTWY WS6 ....24 C1
estbourne Cl BRGRVE B61 ......191 J4
estbourne Cl BNTWD WS7 ....18 C5
EDG B15 ....106 C5
estbourne Gdns EDG B15 ....106 C6
estbourne Gv HDSW B21 * 88 D6
RUGBYS/DCH CV22 ....186 D1
estbourne Rd
DARL/WED WS10 ....52 D6
EDG B15 ....106 C5
ETTPK/GDPK/PENN WV4 ....49 H8
HDSW B21 ....88 D6
HIA/OLT B92 ....127 K6
RMSLY B62 ....104 C1
RUSH/SHEL WS4 ....53 L1
VBROM B70 ....86 F2
estbourne Ter BERW DY12 ......162 F2
estbourne Ter BRGRVW B61 *..191 J4
WolKB/YTR WS5 ....53 K2
st Bromwich Ringway
WBROM B70 ....87 G6
st Bromwich Rd
WOLKB/YTR WS5 ....69 K1

WSL WS1 ....53 J7
West Bromwich St OLDBY B69 ....86 D4
Westbrook Av ALDR WS9 ....40 D8
Westbury Av WOLVN WV10 ....52 D7
Westbury Ms COVE CV2 * 133 H8
Westbury Rd COVW CV5 ....133 H8
DARL/WED WS10 ....52 D7
HRBN B17 ....105 M2
WOLVN WV10 ....98 B1
West Cannock Wy HEDN WS12 ...13 H4
Westcliff Dr WWCK CV34 ....205 J3
Westcliff Dr COVS CV3 ....154 F8
Westcliff Pl NFLD/LBR B31 ....144 D1

Westcott Rd
LGN/SDN/BHAMAIR B26 ....109 L5
Westcote Av WOLVN WV10 ....36 A4
Westcote Cl HIA/OLT B92 ....127 L3
Westcote Cl STRBR DY8 ....101 K2

Westcott Gv
LGN/SDN/BHAMAIR B26 ....109 L5
Westcoft Cl NFLD/LBR B31 ....145 G2
Westcott Rd CDSL WV8 ....34 D7
SEDG DY3 ....65 M3
Westcroft Wy
ALE/KHTH/YWD B14 ....146 F4
Westdean Cl RMSLY B62 ....122 A1
West Dr BFLD/HDSWWD B20 ......88 F5
DIG/EDG B5 ....125 G1
POL/KGSB/FAZ B78 ....45 J3
West End Av SMTHWK B66 ....87 H6
West End St COVW CV5 * 205 H7
Westerdale Cl SEDG DY3 ....66 A6
Westerham Cl KNWTH B93 ....56 A6
Westeria Cl CBROM B36 ....92 A5
Westering Pkwy WOLVN WV10 ...36 A3
Westerings BFLD/HDSWWD B20...89 G1
Western Av BRLYHL DY5 ....101 M3
RMSLY B62 ....122 C1
SEDG DY3 ....65 M5
WSLW WS2 ....52 B2
Western By-Pass LICH WS13 ......20 D5
Western Cl WSLW WS2 ....52 B2
Western Rd CDYHTH B64 ....103 H5
ERDE/BCHGN B24 ....90 E2
HAG/WOL DY9 ....177 H1
HEDN WS12 ....12 F7
OLDBY B69 ....86 B6
SCFLD/BOLD B73 ....72 E4
STRBR DY8 ....119 K1
WSNGN B18 ....106 D7
Western Wy DARL/WED WS10 ....68 A2
KIDDW DY11 ....137 L8

Westfield Av
ALE/KHTH/YWD B14 ....146 F3
Westfield Cl DOR/KN B93 ....175 J3
NUNW/HART CV10 ....81 H7
Westfield Dr ALDR WS9 ....40 E7
WOLVN WV10 ....64 D6
Westfield Gra
ALE/KHTH/YWD B14 ....146 J4
Westfield Gv BDMR/CCFT WV3 ..49 G5
Westfield Mnr MGN/WHC B75 ....56 E1
Westfield Rd ACGN B27 ....126 F2
ALE/KHTH/YWD B14 ....146 J4
BILS/COS WV14 ....50 F6
BRLYHL DY5 ....85 H6
DUDS DY2 ....85 G5
EDG B15 ....106 B5
RMSLY B62 ....104 C4
RUGBYS/DCH CV22 ....186 D3
SEDG DY3 ....66 B4
SMTHWK B67 ....87 K8
WLNHL WV13 ....51 J5
Westfields BRGRVW B61 ....168 C5
Westford Gv HLGN/YWD B28 ....147 J2
HEDN WS12 ....13 K7
Westgate ALDR WS9 ....40 C6
CRTAM B79 ....4 F2
WWCK CV34 ....205 H7
West Gn
ETTPK/GDPK/PENN WV4 ....49 G8
West Green Cl EDG B15 ....106 F5
Westgrove Av SHLY B90 ....148 D7
Westgrove Ter RLSN CV32 ....B5
Westhaven Dr NFLD/LBR B31 ...123 J4
Westhaven Rd FOAKS/STRLY B74..57 G7
Westhay Rd ACGN B27 ....126 F6
Westhead Rd KIDD DY10 ....138 E4
Westhead Rd North KIDD DY10..138 E1
West Heath Rd COVN CV6 ....14 F4
WNSGN B18 ....106 B1
Westhill BDMR/CCFT WV3 ....49 G5
West Hill Av HEDN WS12 ....12 F6
Westhill Cl HIA/OLT B92 ....127 J5
Westhill Rd COVN CV6 ....133 K7
RUSH/SHEL WS4 ....54 B1
West Holme BORD B9 ....108 A3
Westholme Cft BVILLE B30 ......124 C6
Westhouse Gv
ALE/KHTH/YWD B14 ....146 B1
Westland Av BDMR/CCFT WV3 ...49 K3
Westland Cl ERDW/GRVHL B23 ...72 D8
Westland Gdns BDMR/CCFT WV3..49 K3
STRBR DY8 ....101 K5
Westlands Rd MOS/BIL B13 ......125 L4
WALM/CURD B76 ....73 K7
Westlea Rd RLSS CV31 ....206 C7
Westleigh Av COVW CV5 ....154 D6
Westleigh Rd WMBN WV5 ....64 D8
Westley Cl HLGN/YWD B28 ......126 F7
West Leyes RUGBYN/HIL CV21 ..186 B3
Westley Rd ACGN B27 ....126 F2
Westley St BORD B9 ....7 M6
DUDN DY1 ....84 F5
West Mead Dr
ALE/KHTH/YWD B14 ....125 J7
Westmead Dr LGLYGN/QTN B68 ..104 F1
West Ms KGSTG B44 ....71 H3
West Midlands Freeport
LGN/SDN/BHAMAIR B26 ....128 D2
West Mill Cft HWK/WKHTH B38 ..145 J4
Westminster Av
ETTPK/GDPK/PENN WV4 ....49 M8
Westminster Cl BRGRVW B61 ...191 H4
DUDN DY1 ....84 E3
Westminster Dr
ALE/KHTH/YWD B14 ....125 J7
NUNW/HART CV10 ....79 M7
Westminster Rd
BFLD/HDSWWD B20 ....89 G3
CNCK/NC WS11 ....12 C7
HDSW B21 ....88 A1
HIA/OLT B92 ....127 K6
RMSLY B62 ....104 C1
RUSH/SHEL WS4 ....53 L1
VBROM B70 ....86 F2
WSHEL WS4 ....53 L2

Westmore Wy DARL/WED WS10..53 H8

Westmorland Av
NUNW/HART CV10 ....98 C1
Westmorland Ct
POL/KGSB/FAZ B78 ....45 L4
Westmorland Rd COVE CV2 .....156 D1
HHTH/SAND B71 ....69 G7
OLDBY B69 ....86 A7
SPARK B11 ....108 A7
Westonbirt Cl KNWTH CV8 ....180 A7
Weston Cl CNCK/NC WS11 ....17 G4
DOR/KN B93 ....175 L3
RLSS CV31 ....207 L3
WSL WS1 ....53 J7
WWCK CV34 ....205 K6
Weston Crs ALDR WS9 ....54 F1
Weston Dr BILS/COS WV14 ....67 G1
GTWY WS6 ....24 C5
Weston La BDWTH CV12 ....117 M2
SPARK B11 ....109 G1
Weston Rd LICH WS13 ....20 E3
LOZ/NWT B19 ....88 F6
SMTHWKW B67 ....105 K3
Weston St COV CV1 ....9 H2
WSL WS1 ....53 J7
Weston Ter LOZ/NWT B19 * 89 H5
Westover Rd
BFLD/HDSWWD B20 ....88 C1
West Park Av NFLD/LBR B31 ....144 C3
West Park Rd SMTHWKW B67 ....87 H6
West Pathway HRBN B17 ....106 A7
Westport Crs WNSFLD WV11 ......37 K8
Westray Cl RBRY B45 ....143 J4
West Rdg COVW CV5 ....132 E8
Westridge SEDG DY3 ....66 A5
Westridge Rd MOS/BIL B13 ......126 A7
West Ri MGN/WHC B75 ....57 G7
West Rd BRGRVE B60 ....191 L3
GTB/HAM B43 ....70 C6
HALE B63 ....102 F7
REDW B97 ....202 C2
TPTN/OCK DY4 ....67 M5
West Rd South HALE B63 ....102 F7
Westside Dr RIDG/WDGT B32 ...123 H4
West St BLKHTH/ROWR B65 .....104 A4
BLOX/PEL WS3 ....39 G6
BRLYHL DY5 ....83 M8
CNCK/NC WS11 ....16 C1
COV CV1 ....9 K4
CRTAM B79 ....4 F2
DUDN DY1 ....84 F3
DUNHL/THL/PER WV6 ....202 C2
REDW B97 ....202 C2
RRUGBY CV23 ....185 L1
STRBR DY8 ....101 M3
TAM/AM/WIL B77 ....46 A2
VAUX/NECH B7 * 7 J2
WWCK CV34 ....205 M8
Westthorpe Gv LOZ/NWT B19 ....89 G6
West Vw NUNW/HART CV10 ....79 J5
WASH/WDE B8 ....90 F5
WOLVN WV10 ....22 F6
West View Dr KGSWFD DY6 ....83 J8
West View Rd MGN/WHC B75 ....57 J7
RLSN CV32 ....199 G8
RUGBYS/DCH CV22 ....186 B3
Westville Av KIDDW DY11 ....137 L8
Westville Rd WSLW WS2 ....52 E2
Westward Cl KGSTG B44 ....71 K5
West Wy RUSH/SHEL WS4 ....39 M3
Westwick Cl ALDR WS9 ....41 J1
West Winds WOLVN WV10 ....23 C6
Westwood Av SPARK B11 ....126 C1
STRBR DY8 ....119 J2
Westwood Crs ATHST CV9 ....63 H6
Westwood Dr RBRY B45 ....143 J7
SCFLD/BOLD B73 ....71 L1
Westwoods Hollow BNTWD WS7..18 F5
Westwood St BRLYHL DY5 ....101 J1
Westwood Vw
ERDE/BCHGN B24 ....91 G2
Westwood Wy TLHL/CAN CV4 ...153 J7
Wetherby Rd WOLVN WV10 ....36 B1
Wetherby Rd ACGN B27 ....127 G3
BLOX/PEL WS3 ....38 E1
Wetherell Wy
RUGBYN/HIL CV21 ....161 K8
Wetherfield Rd SPARK B11 ......126 E2
Wexford Cl DUDN DY1 ....84 D3
Wexford Rd COVE CV2 ....135 H4
Weybourne Rd KGSTG B44 ....71 J3
Weycroft Rd ERDW/GRVHL B23..71 M6
Weyhill Cl COVEN WV9 ....35 J3
Weymoor Rd HRBN B17 ....123 L2
Weymouth Dr
FOAKS/STRLY B74 ....56 D1
Whaley's Cft COVN CV6 ....133 L5
Wharf Ap ALDR WS9 ....40 D6
Wharf Cl LICHS WS14 * 21 G6
Wharf Cottages ATHST CV9 * 62 F4
Wharfdale Rd SPARK B11 ....108 B8
Wharfedale Cl KGSWFD DY6 ......82 F6
Wharfedale St DARL/WED WS10..68 D3
Wharf La BRGRVE B60 ....192 F4
SOLH B91 ....128 B7
WSNGN B18 ....106 B6
Wharf Rd BVILLE B30 ....145 L3
COV CV1 ....134 D2
YDLY B25 ....108 F8
Wharfside OLDBY B69 ....86 D6
Wharfside St CBHAMW B1 ....6 D7
Wharf St AST/WIT B6 ....89 L6
WOLV WV1 ....4 B3
WSLW WS2 ....4 B1
WSNGN B18 ....88 E7
WWCK CV34 ....205 L5
Whar Hall Rd HIA/OLT B92 ....128 C5
Wharrington Cft REDE B98 ....202 E5
Wharrington HI REDE B98 ....202 E5
Wharton Av HIA/OLT B92 ....128 C6
Wharton St VAUX/NECH B7 ....90 B5
Wharwell La GTWY WS6 ....25 J3
Whatcote Gn HIA/OLT B92 ....128 B5
Whateley Av BLOX/PEL WS3 ......39 K7
Whateley Crs CBROM B36 ....92 B5
Whateley Gn FOAKS/STRLY B74..56 E5
Whateley Hall Cl DOR/KN B93 * .150 A4
Whateley Hall Rd DOR/KN B93...149 M6
Whateley La TAM/AM/WIL B77 ....60 D1
Whateley Pl BLOX/PEL WS3 * 39 K7
Whateley Rd BLOX/PEL WS3 ......39 K7
HDSW B21 ....88 D5
Whateley's Dr KNWTH CV8 ....197 L1
Whatecroft Av BEWD DY12 ......163 G1
Whatecroft Cl BNTWD WS7 ....18 C5
MGN/WHC B75 ....57 J2
PENK ST19 ....10 D5
RMSLY B62 ....104 D5
Wheatcroft Dr
CHWD/FDBR/MGN B37 ....111 G4
Wheatcroft Gv DUDS DY2 ....85 K4
Wheatcroft Rd STETCH B33 ......109 K3
Wheate Cft TLHL/CAN CV4 ....153 K3

Wheaten Cl
CHWD/FDBR/MGN B37 ....111 H2
Wheatfield Av
RUGBYS/DCH CV22 ....186 A6
Wheatfield Cl CBROM B36 ....92 E6
Wheatfield Vw NFLD/LBR B31 ...123 H8
Wheat HI DSYBK/YTR WS5 ....54 C5
Wheathill Cl
ETTPK/GDPK/PENN WV4 ....65 J2
RLSN CV32 ....206 C3
Wheatlands Cl HEDN WS12 ....17 G4
Wheatlands Cft STETCH B33 ....110 C2
The Wheatlands
DUNHL/THL/PER WV6 ....48 B2
Wheatley Cl HIA/OLT B92 ....128 C5
LGLYGN/QTN B68 ....105 G5
MGN/WHC B75 ....57 G2
Wheatley Rd LGLYGN/QTN B68..105 G5
Wheatley St BKHL/PFLD WV2 .....50 C7
WBROM B70 ....86 E1
Wheatmill Cl KIDD DY10 ....139 M3
Wheatmoor Ri MGN/WHC B75 ...57 K6
Wheaton Cl WOLVN WV10 ....36 A6
Wheatridge Cl KGSWFD DY6 ......82 E6
Wheatridge Rd BRGRVE B60 .....191 H7
Wheats Av HRBN B17 ....123 M2
Wheatsheaf Rd CDSL WV8 ....35 J4
LDYWD/EDGR B16 ....106 B3
OLDBY B69 ....85 J5
Wheatstone Cl SEDG DY3 ....66 C7
Wheatstone Gv STETCH B33 ......91 K8
Wheat St NUN CV11 ....99 G1
Wheel Av CDSL WV8 ....34 D2
Wheeler Cl DOR/KN B93 ....176 F6
Wheeler Rd WNSFLD WV11 ....37 G5
Wheeler's Fold WOLV WV1 ....3 G5
Wheeler's La MOS/BIL B13 ....125 K6
Wheeler St LOZ/NWT B19 ....89 H7
STRBR DY8 ....101 K8
Wheeley Moor Rd
CHWD/FDBR/MGN B37 ....92 B3
Wheeley Rd ALVE B48 ....170 B8
HIA/OLT B92 ....128 B6
Wheeley's Cl EDG B15 ....6 C8
Wheeley's La EDG B15 ....6 C8
Wheeley's Rd EDG B15 ....106 F6
Wheel La LICH WS13 ....20 F1
Wheelock Cl FOAKS/STRLY B74...55 K6
Wheelwright Cl BRGRVE B60 .....191 J6
Wheelwright La COVN CV6 ....134 C2
Wheelwright Rd
ERDE/BCHGN B24 ....90 C3
Wheldrake Av BKDE/SHDE B34 ...92 A8
Wheler Rd COVS CV3 ....155 L5
Whernside RUGBYN/HIL CV21 ...161 K8
Whernside Dr
DUNHL/THL/PER WV6 ....35 L8
Wherretts Well La SOLH B91 .....128 C5
Whetstone Cl EDG B15 * 106 D8
Whetstone Dr
RUGBYN/HIL CV21 ....161 J6
Whetstone Gn WOLVN WV10 * ...36 B4
Whetstone Gv WOLVN WV10 ......36 B5
Whetstone La ALDR WS9 ....40 E6
Whetstone Rd WOLVN WV10 ......36 B5
Whettybridge Rd RBRY B45 ......143 J7
Whetty La RBRY B45 ....143 J6
Whichcote Av
RCOVN/BALC/EX CV7 ....131 G4
Whichford Cl WALM/CURD B76 ...73 H7
Whichford Gv BORD B9 ....108 C3
While Rd CSCFLD/WYGN B72 .....72 F1
Whiley Cl RRUGBY CV23 ....161 K8
Whilmot Cl WOLVN WV10 ....22 F7
Whimbrel Cl KIDD DY10 ....164 C5
Whinberry Ri BRLYHL DY5 ....84 A4
Whinchat Gv KIDD DY10 ....164 E3
Whinfield Rd BRGRVE B60 ....167 M7
Whinyates Ri CNCK/NC WS11 .....16 D5
Whisley Brook La
HLGN/YWD B28 ....126 D3
Whiston Av WNSFLD WV11 ....37 J3
Whiston Gv SLYOAK B29 ....123 M5
Whitacre La LICHS WS14 ....27 J8
Whitacre Rd BORD B9 ....108 C2
DOR/KN B93 ....149 M6
NUN CV11 ....81 J8
RLSN CV32 ....206 C5
Whitaker Rd COVW CV5 ....154 A1
Whitbourne Cl BHTH/HG B12 ....107 M8
Whitburn Av PBAR/PBCH B42.....35 C3
Whitburn Cl COVEN WV9 ....35 J5
KIDDW DY11 ....137 M7
Whitburn Rd BDWTH CV12 ....116 A4
Whitby Cl BLOX/PEL WS3 ....38 D7
Whitby Rd BHTH/HG B12 ....125 L1
Whitby Wy CNCK/NC WS11 ....16 D5
Whitchurch Cl REDE B98 ....202 D7
Whitchurch Wy TLHL/CAN CV4..153 H6
Whitcot Gv NFLD/LBR B31 * 144 D5
White Bark Cl HEDN WS12 ....12 E5
Whitebeam Cl BRWNH WS8 ....26 A7
SEDG DY3 ....66 A4
TLHL/CAN CV4 ....153 H4
Whitebeam Cft
HWK/WKHTH B38 ....145 J3
White Beam Rd
CHWD/FDBR/MGN B37 ....111 G3
White City Rd BRLYHL DY5 ....102 A4
White Cl HAG/WOL DY9 ....120 A3
Whitecrest GTB/HAM B43 ....70 D5
Whitecroft Rd
LGN/SDN/BHAMAIR B26 ....110 B8
White Farm Rd
FOAKS/STRLY B74 ....56 C1
Whitefield Cl CDSL WV8 ....34 F3
TLHL/CAN CV4 ....153 H7
Whitefields Crs SOLH B91 ....148 F5
Whitefields Rd SOLH B91 ....148 E4
Whitefriars Dr HALE B63 ....121 H4
White Friars La COV CV1 ....9 H6
White Friars St COV CV1 ....9 J5
Whitegate Dr KIDDW DY11 ....163 L2
Whitegates Rd BILS/COS WV14...67 H3
Whitehall Cl NUNW/HART CV10 ..79 J3
Whitehall Dr DUDN DY1 * 84 E1
HALE B63 ....121 H4
Whitehall Rd BORD B9 ....108 B4
CDYHTH B64 ....103 J4
ETTPK/GDPK/PENN WV4 ....65 M1
HALE B63 ....121 H4
HDSW B21 ....88 C6
KGSWFD DY6 ....83 G7
RUGBYS/DCH CV22 ....119 H3
STRBR DY8 ....119 H3
TPTN/OCK DY4 ....68 B3
WBROM B70 ....87 G3
WSL WS1 ....53 H2
Whitehead Dr KNWTH CV8 ....180 A7
WALM/CURD B76 ....74 B7
Whitehead Gv
RCOVN/BALC/EX CV7 ....151 M6
Whitehead Rd AST/WIT B6 ....89 J4
Whiteheads Ct RLSN CV32 * 206 D4

White Heart Cl BEWD DY12 ......162 D2
Whitehill La SLYOAK B29 ....123 L8
Whitehill Rd KIDDW DY11 ....163 L2
White Hollies BLOX/PEL WS3 .....39 J1
Whitehouse Av COVN CV6 ....116 F7
DARL/WED WS10 ....51 M6
DARL/WED WS10 ....68 D2
Whitehouse Av WNSFLD WV11 ...37 K6
Whitehouse Common Rd
MGN/WHC B75 ....57 J6
Whitehouse Crs BNTWD WS7 * ..18 F5
MGN/WHC B75 ....57 G2
NUNW/HART CV10 ....98 B2
Whitehouse Dr SMTHWK B66 .....87 L6
Whitehouse La CDSL WV8 ....35 K7
Whitehouse Pl RBRY B45 ....143 K7
Whitehouse Rd KIDDW DY11 ....164 B1
POL/KGSB/FAZ B78 ....47 K6
White Houses La WOLVN WV10 * .22 E7
Whitehouse St AST/WIT B6 ....89 K7
BILS/COS WV14 ....67 J2
TPTN/OCK DY4 ....85 L3
WSLW WS2 ....53 H2
Whitehouse Wy ALDR WS9 ....54 D1
White House Wy SOLH B91 ....148 E2
Whitelaw Crs COVW CV5 ....132 F7
Whitemoor Dr SHLY B90 ....149 L6
Whitemoor Rd KNWTH CV8 ......197 L3
White Oak Dr BDMR/CCFT WV3..49 G4
KGSWFD DY6 ....83 G7
Whitepits La ALVE B48 ....195 K1
White Rd RIDG/WDGT B32 ....105 H7
SMTHWK B67 ....87 K7
SPARK B11 ....108 A6
Whites Dr SEDG DY3 ....66 C5
Whiteside Cl COVS CV3 ....156 D5
Whiteslade Cl DOR/KN B93 ....149 L6
Whitesmith Cl SEDG DY3 ....66 B5
White's Rd HHTH/SAND B71 ....69 G7
Whites Rw KNWTH CV8 ....197 L3
Whitestitch La
RCOVN/BALC/EX CV7 ....130 F3
Whitestone Rd HALE B63 ....103 L7
NUN CV11 ....99 L6
White St BHTH/HG B12 ....107 L8
COV CV1 ....9 G3
WSL WS1 ....53 J1
Whites Wd WMBN WV5 ....64 E8
Whitethorn Cl HEDN WS12 ....12 E5
Whitethorn Crs
FOAKS/STRLY B74 ....55 H4
Whitethorn Rd STRBR DY8 ....101 L4
Whitfield Gv EDG B15 ....107 H5
Whitford Cl HEDN WS12 ....13 C6
Whitford Dr SHLY B90 ....148 F6
Whitford Gdns BRGRVW B61 ....191 H3
Whitford Rd BRGRVW B61 ....191 H3
Whitgreave Av WOLVN WV10 * ...22 F7
Whitgreave St WBROM B70 ....86 C2
Whiting TAM/AM/WIL B77 ....46 B6
Whitland Cl RBRY B45 ....143 M7
Whitland Dr
ALE/KHTH/YWD B14 ....146 B2
Whitley Av TAM/AM/WIL B77 ....32 C8
Whitley Cl DUNHL/THL/PER WV6..48 F3
Whitley Court Rd
RIDG/WDGT B32 ....105 G2
Whitley Dr FOAKS/STRLY B74 .....55 L3
Whitley St DARL/WED WS10 ......68 C2
Whitley Village COVS CV3 ....155 K6
Whitlock Gv
ALE/KHTH/YWD B14 ....146 E2
Whitminster Av
ERDE/BCHGN B24 ....90 F2
Whitminster Cl SHHTH WV12 ......52 A1
Whitmore Hl WOLV WV1 ....2 C6
Whitmore Park Rd COVN CV6 ...134 A2
Whitmore Rd SMHTH B10 ....108 A5
STRBR DY8 ....101 H8
Whitmore St WOLV WV1 ....4 C1
WSNGN B18 ....88 F7
Whitnash Cl
RCOVN/BALC/EX CV7 ....151 L7
Whitnash Gv COVE CV2 ....135 H8
Whitney Av STRBR DY8 ....101 H7
Whittaker St BKHL/PFLD WV2 ....50 C6
Whittall Dr East KIDDW DY11 ...163 L4
Whittall Dr West KIDDW DY11 ...163 L4
Whittall St CBHAMNE B4 ....7 C3
Whittimere St WSL WS1 ....5 G3
Whittingham Av WNSFLD WV11 ..37 K7
Whittingham Rd HALE B63 ....103 L8
Whittington Cl
ALE/KHTH/YWD B14 ....125 J8
HHTH/SAND B71 ....69 K5
WWCK CV34 ....205 M5
Whittington Common Rd
LICHS WS14 ....29 L1
Whittington Gv STETCH B33 .....109 K3
Whittington Hall Cottages
KINVER DY7 * 118 C3
Whittington Hall La
KINVER DY7 ....118 C3
Whittington Ov STETCH B33 .....109 K3
Whittington Rd STRBR DY8 ......119 H2
Whittle Cl COVS CV3 ....156 F5
RUGBYS/DCH CV22 ....186 B6
Whittle Cft CVALE B35 ....91 K2
Whittleford Gv CBROM B36 ....92 A4
Whittleford Rd
NUNW/HART CV10 ....98 A2
Whitton St DARL/WED WS10 ......52 C7
Whitville Cl KIDDW DY11 ....138 A4
Whitwell Cl SHLY B90 ....148 E7
Whitworth Av COVS CV3 ....155 M4
Whitworth Cl DARL/WED WS10 ...52 D6
Whitworth Dr HHTH/SAND B71 ...69 J4
Whoberley Av COVW CV5 ....154 B2
Whoberley Ct COVW CV5 * 154 A2
Whyley St WBROM B70 ....86 E8
Whyley Wk OLDBY B69 ....86 E6
Whynot St HALE B63 ....102 F6
Wibert Cl SLYOAK B29 ....124 E4
Wichnor Rd HIA/OLT B92 ....109 K8
Wicket La KINVER DY7 ....100 C4
Wickham Cl COVN CV6 ....133 K3
Wickham Rd RLSN CV32 * 206 E7
Wickham Gdns WNSFLD WV11 ...36 E4
Wicklow Cl HALE B63 ....121 H4
Wickmans Dr TLHL/CAN CV4 ....153 G3
Wiclif Wy NUNW/HART CV10 ......97 M2
Widdecombe Cl COVE CV2 ....135 H5
Widdrington Rd COVN CV6 ....134 A4

Woodchurch Gra
SCFLD/BOLD B73 ....72 D5
Wood CI CSHL/WTROR B46 .....93 K6
Woodclose Av COVN CV6 ....133 K7
Woodclose Rd
CHWD/FDBR/MGN B37 ....110 D2
Woodcock CI NFLD/LBR B31 .....144 A4
Woodcock Gdns WOLVN WV10 ....22 F6
Woodcock La ACGN B27 ....127 H2
NFLD/LBR B31 ....144 C3
Woodcock La North ACGN B27 ....127 H1
Woodcock St VAUX/NECH B7 ....7 K2
Woodcombe CI BRLYHL DY5 ....101 M6
Wood Common Gra
BLOX/PEL WS3 ....39 J1
Woodcote Av KNWTH CV8 ....179 H7
NUN CV11 ....81 K5
Woodcote Dr DOR/KN B93 ....195 J7
RWWCK/WEL CV35 ....197 K6
WASH/WDE B8 ....90 D8
Woodcote La KIDD DY10 ....167 H7
KNWTH CV8 ....179 H8
Woodcote PI LOZ/NWT B19 * 89 G6
Woodcote Rd
DUNHL/THL/PER WV6 ....49 G1
ERDE/BCHGN B24 ....73 H8
RLSN CV32 ....206 D2
WWCK CV34 ....205 K5
Woodcote Wy FOAKS/STRLY B74 .....55 K7
WSNGN B18 ....106 E1
Wood Ct BHTH/HG B12 * 88 C8
Woodcraft CI TLHL/CAN CV4 ....153 L3
Wood Cft HLYWD B47 ....146 F7
Woodcroft Av
BFLD/HDSWWD B20 ....88 E3
CRTAM B79 ....31 M7
TPTN/OCK DY4 ....67 G8
Woodcroft CI BRGRVE B60 ....168 K8
CDYHTH B64 ....103 H5
Woodcross La BILS/COS WV14 .....66 D3
Woodcross St BILS/COS WV14 .....66 D3
Woodend BFLD/HDSWWD B20 ....70 D4
Wood End Dr REDW B97 ....201 M3
HOCK/TIA B94 ....173 J8
RCOVN/BALC/EX CV7 ....114 E1
Woodend PI
DUNHL/THL/PER WV6 ....48 F1
Wood End Rd DSYBK/YTR WS5 .....90 D2
ERDE/BCHGN B24 ....90 D2
WNSFLD WV11 ....37 H6
Woodfall Av BVILLE B30 ....124 D8
Woodfield Av HAG/WOL DY9 ....141 H6
Woodfield Av BRLYHL DY5 ....83 M6
CDYHTH B64 ....103 H5
ETTPK/GDPK/PENN WV4 ....65 K7
HAG/WOL DY9 ....120 D3
OLDBY B69 ....69 L4
Woodfield CI CNCK/NC WS11 .....17 K6
DSYBK/YTR WS5 ....54 C8
MGN/WHC B75 ....56 F5
REDE B98 ....198 F4
Woodfield Crs BHTH/HG B12 ....107 L7
KIDD DY11 ....138 A8
Woodfield Dr CNCK/NC WS11 ....17 K6
Woodfield Hts
DUNHL/THL/PER WV6 ....49 H1
Woodfield La RMSLY B62 ....142 E3
Woodfield Rd
ALE/KHTH/YWD B14 ....125 K5
BHTH/HG B12 ....107 L7
COVW CV5 ....154 C5
SEDG DY3 ....84 A1
SOLH B91 ....127 M7
Woodfields Dr LICHS WS14 ....21 J7
Woodfield St KIDD DY11 ....138 A7
Woodfold Cft ALDR WS9 ....40 F6
Woodford Av CBROM B36 ....91 L5
Woodford CI COVEN WV9 ....35 K3
NUNW/HART CV10 ....98 A4
RCOVN/BALC/EX CV7 ....116 B8
Woodford Crs BNTWD WS7 ....18 F6
Woodford End CNCK/NC WS11 .....16 D1
Woodford Green Rd
HLGN/YWD B28 ....126 E5
Woodford La NUNW/HART CV10 ...79 M2
WMBN WV5 ....64 B5
Woodford Wy HEDN WS12 ....17 G4
Woodfort Rd GTB/HAM B43 ....70 C6
Woodgate Dr RIDG/WDGT B32 ...122 E4
Woodgate Gdns
RIDG/WDGT B32 ....122 E3
Woodgate Rd RIDG/WDGT B32 ...122 E3
Woodgate Rd BRGRVE B60 ....200 A4
Woodgate Wy HAG/WOL DY9 ....141 J6
Woodglade Cft
HWK/WKHTH B38 ....145 J3
Woodgreen GTWY WS6 ....16 C8
Woodgreen CI REDW B97 ....201 M7
Woodgreen Cft
LGLYGN/QTN B68 ....105 G6
Wood Green Rd
DARL/WED WS10 ....68 D2
WSNGN B18 ....106 B1
Woodgreen Rd
LGLYGN/QTN B68 ....105 G6
Woodhall CI NUN CV11 ....99 K3
TPTN/OCK DY4 ....67 L3
Woodhall Cft HIA/OLT B92 ....127 K2
Woodhall Rd
ETTPK/GDPK/PENN WV4 ....65 J1
Woodham CI RBRY B45 ....143 J4
Woodhams Rd KNWTH CV8 ....182 A2
Woodhaven CNCK/NC WS11 ....15 M7
RUSH/SHEL WS4 ....40 B6
Wood Hayes Rd WOLVN WV10 ....36 F3
Woodhill CI WMBN WV5 ....64 D7
Wood Hill Dr WMBN WV5 ....64 D7
Wood Hill RI COVW CV5 ....156 C5
Woodhouse CI COVS CV3 ....156 C5
Woodhouse Fold WNSFLD WV11 ..37 M8
Woodhouse La TAM/AM/WIL B77 .32 E8
Woodhouse Orch
HAG/WOL DY9 ....141 J6
Woodhouse Rd
DUNHL/THL/PER WV6 ....48 F2
RIDG/WDGT B32 ....105 J7
Woodhouse Rd North
DUNHL/THL/PER WV6 ....48 F1
Woodhouses La BNTWD WS7 ....19 J1
Woodhouse St BNTWD WS7 ....19 L8
Woodhouses Rd BNTWD WS7 ....19 K8
Woodhurst Rd BDMR/CCFT WV3 .105 H7
Woodhurst Rd MOS/BIL B13 ....125 L1
Woding Crs TPTN/OCK DY4 ....67 M4
Wodland Av BRLYHL DY5 ....102 E4
Woden CI WMBN WV5 ....64 C6
Woden Crs WNSFLD WV11 ....37 H8
Woden Pas DARL/WED WS10 .....68 D2
Woden Rd DARL/WED WS10 ......137 M6
Woden Rd East
DARL/WED WS10 ....68 F2
Woden Rd North
DARL/WED WS10 ....137 M4
Woden Rd South DARL/WED WS10.68 E4
Woden Rd West DARL/WED WS10 .68 B2
Woden Wy WNSFLD WV11 * 37 H8

SHHTH WV12 ....38 B7
Woodland Cottages
ETTPK/GDPK/PENN WV4 * 65 K1
Woodland Ct HEDN WS12 ....16 A1
LICHS WS14 ....42 E6
Woodland Crs BDMR/CCFT WV3 ..49 H6
Woodland Dr RBRY B45 ....169 L3
SMTHWK B66 ....87 J6
Woodland Gv GTB/HAM B43 ....70 C2
WOLVN WV10 ....139 G2
SEDG DY3 ....83 M2
Woodland Rd CDYHTH B64 ....103 K5
SCFLD/BOLD B73 ....72 F1
Woodland Rd BDMR/CCFT WV3 ...49 H6
BRGRVW B61 ....167 M6
HDSW B21 ....88 A5
KNWTH CV8 ....179 M6
NFLD/LBR B31 ....144 F2
REDW B97 ....201 M2
RMSLY B62 ....104 B5
TAM/AM/WIL B77 ....46 C1
Woodland Wy CSHL/WTROR B46..92 F3
DSYBK/YTR WS5 ....54 C8
Woodlands CI KIDDW DY11 ....189 M5
POL/KGSB/FAZ B78 ....47 L8
Woodlands Cottages
ETTPK/GDPK/PENN WV4 * 65 K1
Woodlands Ct COVW CV5 * 8 A9
Woodlands Crs BLOX/PEL WS3 ...25 K8
Woodlands Farm Rd
ERDE/BCHGN B24 ....91 K1
Woodlands La BDWTH CV12 .....116 C1
SHLY B90 ....147 M5
WOLVN WV10 ....14 F6
Woodlands Paddock
ETTPK/GDPK/PENN WV4 * 65 K1
Woodlands Park Rd BVILLE B30 .124 B8
Woodlands Rd BDWTH CV12 .....116 C2
COVS CV3 ....157 H6
KIDD DY10 ....138 E1
RBRY B45 ....143 H6
SPARK B11 ....126 A2
WASH/WDE B8 ....108 D1
WOLVN WV10 ....64 B8
Woodlands St SMTHWK B66 ....88 A1
The Woodlands ATHST CV9 ....103 L6
CDYHTH B64 ....103 L6
LICH WS13 ....21 H5
MGN/WHC B75 ....57 L7
NUNW/HART CV10 ....79 L4
STRBR DY8 ....119 L3
Woodlands Wy
CHWD/FDBR/MGN B37 ....111 H2
Woodland Wy BNTWD WS7 ....18 F2
POL/KGSB/FAZ B78 ....47 K5
Wood La ALDR WS9 ....41 L5
BFLD/HDSWWD B20 ....88 F3
BLOX/PEL WS3 ....25 L8
BRGRVW B61 ....168 A2
CHWD/FDBR/MGN B37 ....110 C5
ERDE/BCHGN B24 ....90 F4
FOAKS/STRLY B74 ....55 J4
HEDN WS12 ....17 L1
HIA/OLT B92 ....150 D4
HOCK/TIA B94 ....173 J4
HRBN B17 ....105 L7
MKTBOS/BARL/STKG CV13 ....81 H2
NUNW/HART CV10 * 79 L5
RCOVN/BALC/EX CV7 ....79 L5
RIDG/WDGT B32 ....122 E4
SHHTH WV12 ....38 C6
WBROM B70 ....86 E2
WOLVN WV10 ....15 K7
WOLVN WV10 ....36 E1
Wood Lane CI SHHTH WV12 * 38 C6
Woodlawn Gv KGSWFD DY6 ....83 H3
Woodlea Dr ERDE/BCHGN B24 ....90 D3
SOLH B91 ....127 J8
Wood Leasow RIDG/WDGT B32 ..123 H5
Woodleaves HLYWD B47 ....146 D5
Woodleigh Av HRBN B17 ....124 B1
Woodleigh CI HALE B63 ....103 L7
Woodleigh Rd
CSCFLD/WYGN B72 ....72 F4
TLHL/CAN CV4 ....153 K8
The Woodleys
ALE/KHTH/YWD B14 ....146 F1
Woodloes Av North
WWCK CV34 ....205 J3
Woodloes Av South
WWCK CV34 ....205 J4
Woodloes La
RWWCK/WEL CV35 ....205 J2
Woody Bank GTWY WS6 ....24 C3
Woody Bank GTWY WS6 ....24 C3
Woodman CI DARL/WED WS10 ....68 F1
HALE B63 ....122 A2
Woodman La GTWY WS6 ....24 C1
HAG/WOL DY9 ....141 H1
Woodman Rd
ALE/KHTH/YWD B14 ....146 E4
HALE B63 ....122 A2
Woodmeadow Rd BVILLE B30 ...145 L2
Woodmill Meadow KNWTH CV8 ..179 L7
Woodnorton Dr MOS/BIL B13 ....125 J3
Woodnorton Rd
BLKHTH/ROWR B65 ....104 D3
Woodpecker Gv CBROM B36 ....92 A6
KIDD DY10 ....138 F1
Woodpecker Wy CNCK/NC WS11 .17 G2
Woodperry Av SOLH B91 ....148 B3
Wood Piece La REDE B98 ....195 H6
Woodridge AST/WIT B6 ....89 J4
Woodridge Av COVW CV5 ....132 D7
RIDG/WDGT B32 ....122 F1
Woodridge Rd HALE B63 ....103 L8
Wood Ridings LICH WS13 ....20 E4
Wood Rd CDSL WV8 ....34 B1
DUNHL/THL/PER WV6 ....48 F2
SEDG DY3 ....84 A2
WMBN WV5 ....64 B5
Woodroffe Wk COVN CV6 ....134 C1
Woodrow Dr MOS/BIL B13 ....125 K5
Woodrow CI BRGRVW B61 ....168 D4
Woodrow Crs DOR/KN B93 ....149 L8
Woodrow Dr REDE B98 ....202 E2
Woodrow La BRGRVW B61 ....168 A1
KIDD DY10 ....165 K7
Woodrow North REDE B98 ....202 E6
Woodrow North Ter
REDE B98 * 202 F5
Woodrow South REDE B98 ....202 E6
Woodrow Wk REDE B98 ....202 F6
Woodruff Wy DSYBK/YTR WS5 ....69 K1
Woodrush Dr HLYWD B47 ....146 E8
Woods Bank Ter
DARL/WED WS10 ....52 A8
Woods Crs BRLYHL DY5 ....102 E4
Woods Cft LICH WS13 ....20 E4
Woodsetton CI DUDN DY1 ....66 F7
Woodshill Av RBRY B45 ....169 L3
Woodshires Rd COVN CV6 ....116 D8
HIA/OLT B92 ....127 H6
Woodsia CI RUGBY CV23 ....161 H5
Woodside ATHST CV9 ....62 A4
CHWD/FDBR/MGN B37 ....110 C1
FOAKS/STRLY B74 ....56 C3
RCOVN/BALC/EX CV7 ....96 B4
Wood Side WNSFLD WV11 ....37 L5
Woodside Av North COVS CV3 ...154 D7

Woodside Av South COVS CV3 ...154 D8
Woodside CI ATHST CV9 ....61 G4
DSYBK/YTR WS5 ....54 B8
Woodside Crs DOR/KN B93 ....175 L1
Woodside Dr FOAKS/STRLY B74 ..42 A8
RBRY B45 ....169 M5
Woodside Pk HOCK/TIA B94 * ...172 F6
KNWTH CV8 * 182 F7
RUGBYN/HIL CV21 ....160 E8
Woodside PI HEDN WS12 ....12 B8
Woodside Rd DSYBK/YTR WS5 ....54 C7
DUDS DY2 ....84 D7
SLYOAK B29 ....124 E4
Woodsome Gv
ERDW/GRVHL B23 ....72 A6
Woodsorrel Rd DUDN DY1 ....84 D1
Woods Piece
RCOVN/BALC/EX CV7 ....115 K7
Woodstile BKDE/SHDE B34 ....91 H7
Woodstock CI DSYBK/YTR WS5 ...69 L2
DUDN DY1 ....84 D5
STRBR DY8 ....101 G4
Woodstock Crs DOR/KN B93 .....175 K2
Woodstock Dr FOAKS/STRLY B74 .56 B2
HEDN WS12 ....12 A5
STRBR DY8 ....101 G3
Woodstock Rd COVS CV3 ....155 H6
HDSW B21 ....88 D5
MOS/BIL B13 ....125 L1
NUN CV11 ....99 J3
WOLV WV1 ....50 F4
Woodston Gv SOLH B91 ....149 G5
Wood St ATHST CV9 ....61 G5
BDWTH CV12 ....116 E1
BILS/COS WV14 ....51 H8
DARL/WED WS10 ....52 D7
DUDS DY2 ....84 D7
ETTPK/GDPK/PENN WV4 ....64 E2
HAG/WOL DY9 ....102 D2
KIDDW DY11 ....138 D7
NUN CV11 ....98 D1
RLSN CV32 ....206 E2
RUGBYN/HIL CV21 ....160 E3
TPTN/OCK DY4 ....67 J7
WLNHL WV13 ....51 L3
WOLVN WV10 ....36 C8
Woodthorne CI PENK ST19 ....10 D6
Woodthorne CI SEDG DY3 ....84 B3
Woodthorne Rd
DUNHL/THL/PER WV6 ....34 E7
Woodthorne Rd South
DUNHL/THL/PER WV6 ....34 E8
Woodthorpe Dr BEWD DY12 ....162 E1
HAG/WOL DY9 ....120 B2
Woodthorpe Gdns
ALE/KHTH/YWD B14 ....125 J8
Woodthorpe Rd
ALE/KHTH/YWD B14 ....125 H8
Woodvale Rd HLGN/YWD B28 ...147 J1
Woodvale Rd HLGN/YWD B28 ...147 J1
RIDG/WDGT B32 ....122 E4
Woodview Dr EDG B15 ....107 G6
Woodville Gdns SEDG DY3 ....66 D4
Woodville Rd
ALE/KHTH/YWD B14 ....125 K4
HRBN B17 ....105 L7
WWCK CV34 ....205 G8
Woodward CI COV CV1 ....134 C8
HALE B63 ....121 M1
Woodward Rd KIDDW DY11 .....164 A2
Woodwards CI WSLW WS2 ....52 F5
Woodwards PI WSLW WS2 ....52 F5
Woodwards Rd WSLW WS2 ....52 F5
Woodway ERDE/BCHGN B24 ......72 B7
Woodway Av
RWWCK/WEL CV35 ....204 D7
Woodway CI COVE CV2 ....135 J3
Woodway La COVE CV2 ....135 K2
Woodway Wk COVE CV2 ....135 J5
Woodwells Rd WASH/WDE B8 ....90 E8
Woolacombe Lodge Rd
SLYOAK B29 ....124 A3
Woolaston CI REDE B98 ....203 G5
Woolgrove St COVN CV6 ....134 E2
Woolhope CI REDE B98 ....203 J2
Woolmore Rd
ERDW/GRVHL B23 ....90 A1
Woolpack CI
BLKHTH/ROWR B65 ....103 L1
The Woolpack WWCK CV34 * ...205 H7
Woolpack Wy ATHST CV9 ....61 G5
Wootton CI REDW B97 ....201 L1
Wootton Gv KGSTG B44 ....71 M3
Wootton La
RCOVN/BALC/EX CV7 ....151 K1
Wootton Rd BDMR/CCFT WV3 ...49 G6
NFLD/LBR B31 ....144 E6
Woottons Ct CNCK/NC WS11 .....16 D4
Wootton St BDWTH CV12 ....117 G2
Worcester Bar CBHAMW B1 * 6 C6
Worcester CI CNCK/NC WS11 .....16 D5
COVW CV5 ....132 F6
HAG/WOL DY9 ....119 L8
LICH WS13 ....20 F7
MGN/WHC B75 ....57 H2
Worcester Ct BDMR/CCFT WV3 ..49 L7
Worcester Gn HHTH/SAND B71 ...69 G6
Worcester Gv
DUNHL/THL/PER WV6 ....48 B1
Worcester La MGN/WHC B75 .....57 H2
STRBR DY8 ....119 M3
Worcester Ri BRGRVW B61 ....191 K4
Worcester Rd BRGRVW B61 ....191 K4
DUDS DY2 ....103 J2
HAG/WOL DY9 ....119 L8
KIDD DY10 ....138 C5
KIDD DY10 ....165 H6
LCLYGN/QTN B68 ....104 E5
LICHS WS14 ....21 J7
STRPT DY13 ....188 F3
WLNHL WV13 ....51 K1
Worcestershire Wy BEWD DY12.136 D5
BEWD DY12 ....162 B7
Worcester St BKHL/PFLD WV2 .....2 E7
KIDD DY10 ....138 C7
RUGBYN/HIL CV21 ....186 A1
STRBR DY8 ....119 L1
STRPT DY13 ....188 B1
Worcester Wk CBHAM B2 * 7 G6

Word HI HRBN B17 ....105 K6
Wordsley CI REDE B98 ....194 F6
Wordsworth Av CRTAM B79 ....31 L2
ETTPK/GDPK/PENN WV4 ....66 C1
REDW B97 ....202 A5
WWCK CV34 ....205 G8
Wordsworth CI CNCK/NC WS11 ...20 F8
LICHS WS14 ....20 F8
TPTN/OCK DY4 ....67 J8
Wordsworth Ct
DUNHL/THL/PER WV6 ....48 C1
Wordsworth Crs KIDD DY10 .....133 F7
Wordsworth Dr KNWTH CV8 .....198 A1
Wordsworth Rd BDWTH CV12 ...117 H4
BLOX/PEL WS3 ....39 J5
BNTWD WS7 ....31 G5
COVE CV2 ....156 A1
RUGBYS/DCH CV22 ....186 C7
SEDG DY3 ....65 M8
SHHTH WV12 ....38 B6
SMTHWK B10 ....108 B6
WOLVN WV10 ....36 C6
Wordsworth St HHTH/SAND B71 .69 G8
Worfield CI RUSH/SHEL WS4 ....53 L1
Worfield Gdns BDMR/CCFT WV3 .49 K7
World's End Av
RIDG/WDGT B32 ....105 H8
World's End La RIDG/WDGT B32 .105 H8
Worlds End Rd
BFLD/HDSWWD B20 ....88 E2
Worleys Wharf Av
DARL/WED WS10 ....69 J3
Worsdell CI COV CV1 ....8 C2
Worsey Dr TPTN/OCK DY4 ....68 B7
Worsfold CI COVW CV5 ....132 E6
Worth Crs STRPT DY13 ....188 C5
Worthen Gv NFLD/LBR B31 ....144 E5
The Worthings BVILLE B30 ....124 E7
Worthy Down WNSFLD WV11 .....37 K8
Wortley Av WOLVN WV10 * 36 C7
Worton Rd HAG/WOL DY9 ....120 C3
Wragby CI COVN WV9 ....35 M2
Wrekin CI HALE B63 ....121 G8
KIDDW DY11 ....163 H3
Wrekin Dr BDMR/CCFT WV3 ....49 J5
BRGRVW B61 ....168 E8
DUNHL/THL/PER WV6 ....34 E8
HAG/WOL DY9 ....120 D1
Wrekin Gv SHHTH WV12 ....37 M4
Wrekin La DUNHL/THL/PER WV6 .34 E8
Wrekin Rd KGSTG B44 ....71 K7
SCFLD/BOLD B73 ....72 E4
Wrekin Vw BRWNH WS8 ....26 E8
Wrekin View Rd SEDG DY3 ....66 A5
Wrekin Wk STRPT DY13 ....188 B4
Wren Av DUNHL/THL/PER WV6 ....48 B2
Wrenbury Dr COVN CV6 ....134 E1
Wrens Av KGSWFD DY6 ....101 L1
TPTN/OCK DY4 ....67 G8
Wrens Hill Rd DUDN DY1 ....66 F8
Wren's Nest CI SHLY B90 ....147 L8
Wrens Nest Rd DUDN DY1 ....66 E8
Wrens Park Av WALM/CURD B76 ..73 J6
Wren St COVE CV2 ....9 L3
DUDN DY1 ....66 F7
DUDS DY2 ....84 F7
Wrentham St DIG/EDG B5 ....6 E7
Wretham Rd LOZ/NWT B19 ....88 F7
Wrexham Av WSLW WS2 ....52 D4
Wright Av WNSFLD WV11 ....37 H6
Wright CI POL/KGSB/FAZ B78 .....60 B8
Wrighton CI SHHTH WV12 ....38 A5
Wrighton Dr SEDG DY3 ....84 A4
Wright's Av CNCK/NC WS11 ....16 D1
Wright's La CDYHTH B64 ....103 K3
Wright St BILS/COS WV14 ....67 J1
COV CV1 ....134 C8
HALE B63 ....121 M1
SMHTH B10 ....108 C6
WOLVN WV10 * 50 B1
Wrigsham St COVS CV3 ....9 G8
Wrottesley Park Rd CDSL WV8 ....34 B7
Wrottesley Rd
DUNHL/THL/PER WV6 ....34 D7
GTB/HAM B43 ....70 B4
Wrottesley Rd West
DUNHL/THL/PER WV6 ....34 D7
Wrottesley St DIG/EDG B5 * 7 G7
Wroxall CI BRLYHL DY5 ....101 M5
Wroxall Dr COVS CV3 ....156 B8
Wroxall Gv MOS/BIL B13 ....125 L7
Wroxall Rd SOLH B91 ....127 J7
Wroxham Gln WLNHL WV13 ....51 K5
Wroxton Rd YDLY B25 ....109 J5
Wulfric CI PENK ST19 ....10 E5
Wulfruna Gdns BDMR/CCFT WV3 .49 K4
Wulfruna St WOLV WV1 ....2 C3
Wulfrun Sq WOLV WV1 ....3 G6
Wyatt CI DIG/EDG B5 ....107 G8
Wyatt CI BDWTH CV12 * 116 F2
Wyatt Rd MGN/WHC B75 ....57 M7
Wychall Dr WOLVN WV10 ....15 L5
Wychall La HWK/WKHTH B38 ...145 H3
Wychall Park Gv
HWK/WKHTH B38 ....145 H3
Wychbold CI REDW B97 ....201 L7
Wychbold Crs STETCH B33 ....110 A2
Wychbury WALM/CURD B76 .....73 L4
Wychbury CI HALE B63 ....121 L2
Wychbury Rd BDMR/CCFT WV3 ..49 G6
HAG/WOL DY9 ....120 A6
RIDG/WDGT B32 ....122 E5
Wyche Av ALE/KHTH/YWD B14 ..146 B1
Wychelm Farm Rd
ALE/KHTH/YWD B14 ....146 E4
Wych Elm Rd BRWNH WS8 ....26 D8
Wychnor Gv HHTH/SAND B71 ....69 J3
Wychwood Av COVS CV3 ....181 G1
DOR/KN B93 ....149 M5
Wychwood Crs
LGN/SDN/BHAMAIR B26 .....109 L7
Wychwood Dr REDW B97 ....202 B7
Wyckham CI HRBN B17 ....123 L1
Wyckham Rd CBROM B36 ....92 D6
Wycliffe Rd COVE CV2 ....155 M1
Wycliffe Rd West COVE CV2 ....134 F8
Wycome Rd HLGN/YWD B28 ....126 D7
Wye Cliff Rd BFLD/HDSWWD B20 .88 F7
Wye CI BDWTH CV12 ....117 M3
DUNHL/THL/PER WV6 ....48 B2
RLSN CV32 ....207 J2
WALM/CURD B76 ....73 M4
Wyemanton CI GTB/HAM B43 ....70 A4
Wye Rd BLOX/PEL WS3 ....39 J4
Wykeham Gv
DUNHL/THL/PER WV6 ....48 B2
Wykeley Rd COVE CV2 ....156 A1
Wyken Av COVE CV2 ....135 M8

Wyken CI DOR/KN B93 ....175 J3
Wyken Cft COVE CV2 ....135 M8
Wyken Grange Rd COVE CV2 ....135 G8
Wyken Wy COVE CV2 ....134 E8
Wyke Rd COVE CV2 ....156 A1
Wyld CI HHTH/SAND B71 ....68 C5
Wyld Ct COVW CV5 ....132 E8
Wylde Crs BLKHTH/ROWR B65 ..104 A1
Wylde Green Rd
CSCFLD/WYGN B72 ....73 G4
Wyley Rd COVN CV6 ....133 M8
Wymering Av WNSFLD WV11 .....37 K6
Wynall La SHLY B90 ....148 E7
Wynall La South
HAG/WOL DY9 ....120 E2
Wynbrook Gv SHLY B90 ....148 E7
Wynchcombe Av
ETTPK/GDPK/PENN WV4 ....65 J1
Wyncote CI KNWTH CV8 ....197 L1
Wyndcliff Rd BORD B9 ....108 B4
Wyndham Gdns BVILLE B30 .....145 K1
Wyndham Rd
LDYWD/EDGR B16 ....106 D4
Wyndhurst Rd STETCH B33 ....109 J1
Wyndley Dr SCFLD/BOLD B73 ....72 F1
Wyndley La SCFLD/BOLD B73 ....72 E1
Wyndmill Crs HHTH/SAND B71 ...69 L4
Wynds Covert
ALE/KHTH/YWD B14 ....146 B3
Wyndshiels CSHL/WTROR B46 ....93 J1
Wynds Point NFLD/LBR B31 .....123 M8
The Wynd SEDG DY3 ....66 B4
Wynfield Gdns
ALE/KHTH/YWD B14 ....125 J8
Wynford Rd ACGN B27 ....109 G8
Wyn-Griffith Dr TPTN/OCK DY4 ...85 L2
Wynn CI BEWD DY12 ....137 H8
Wynn Rd
ETTPK/GDPK/PENN WV4 ....65 G2
Wynne Crs
ETTPK/GDPK/PENN WV4 ....65 G2
Wynn Rd
ETTPK/GDPK/PENN WV4 ....49 K3
Wynn St EDG B15 ....6 E9
Wynstead Covert
ALE/KHTH/YWD B14 ....146 A3
Wynter Rd RUGBYS/DCH CV22 ..186 B2
Wyntor La HHTH/SAND B71 ....68 F5
Wynyates CRTAM B79 ....31 J7
Wyre CI ALDR WS9 ....40 F1
Wyre Ct BEWD DY12 * 162 D3
Wyre HI BEWD DY12 ....162 C3
Wyre Rd STRBR DY8 ....101 J6
Wyrley Brook Pk
CNCK/NC WS11 * 16 B7
Wyrley CI BRWNH WS8 ....26 D2
LICHS WS14 ....20 E8
SHHTH WV12 ....38 A6
Wyrley La BLOX/PEL WS3 ....25 J4
Wyrley Rd AST/WIT B6 ....89 L2
MGN/WHC B75 ....57 J1
WNSFLD WV11 ....37 L7
Wyrley St WOLVN WV10 ....3 L4
Wyrley Wy ERDW/GRVHL B23 .....71 L7
Wythall Green Wy HLYWD B47 ...172 C2
Wythall Rd HALE B63 ....121 L3
Wythburn Wy
RUGBYN/HIL CV21 ....161 H6
Wythwood Gv HLYWD B47 ....147 G2
TPTN/OCK DY4 ....67 L5
Wythwood Rd HLYWD B47 ....146 F7
Wyton Av LGLYGN/QTN B68 .....105 G3
Wyver Crs COVE CV2 ....9 L3
Wyvern TAM/AM/WIL B77 ....46 D2
Wyvern CI FOAKS/STRLY B74 .....56 F6
LGLYGN/QTN B68 ....104 F1
SHHTH WV12 ....37 L6
Wyvern Gv HHTH/SAND B71 ....12 B8
SLYOAK B29 ....124 A3
Wyvern Rd FOAKS/STRLY B74 .....56 F6
Wyvis CI BDMR/CCFT WV3 ....49 J3

Y

Yale Dr WNSFLD WV11 ....37 J8
Yardley Cl LGLYGN/QTN B68 ....104 F4
REDE B98 ....203 J2
WWCK CV34 ....205 K3
Yardley Fields Rd STETCH B33 ..109 H3
Yardley Green Rd BORD B9 ....108 D4
Yardley Rd ACGN B27 ....127 G1
Yardley St BRLYHL DY5 ....102 A7
COV CV1 ....9 J2
DARL/WED WS10 ....52 A6
Yardley Wood Rd
ALE/KHTH/YWD B14 ....146 C4
MOS/BIL B13 ....125 M3
Yare Gv WLNHL WV13 ....52 B4
Yarmouth Gn TLHL/CAN CV4 ....153 J3
Yarnborough HI STRBR DY8 .....119 J4
Yarningale CI
ALE/KHTH/YWD B14 ....125 G8
COVS CV3 ....156 A8
Yarnold La BRGRVW B61 ....168 A6
Yarranton CI STRPT DY13 ....188 C5
Yarrow CI BLOX/PEL WS3 ....25 L8
RRUGBY CV23 * 161 H5
WNSFLD WV11 ....37 K8
Yarrow Dr HWK/WKHTH B38 ....145 K5
Yarwell CI WOLVN WV10 ....3 H1
Yateley Av PBAR/PBCH B42 ....70 E6
Yateley Crs PBAR/PBCH B42 ....70 E6
Yateley Rd EDG B15 ....106 B6
Yates Av RUGBYN/HIL CV21 .....160 D7
Yatesbury Av CVALE B35 ....91 K2
Yates Cft FOAKS/STRLY B74 ....56 C3
Yates La RMSLY B62 ....104 C3
Yeadon Gdns BDMR/CCFT WV3 ..48 H5
Yeames CI GTB/HAM B43 ....55 G8
Yellowhammer Ct KIDD DY10 ...164 E4
Yelverton CI BLOX/PEL WS3 ....25 L8
Yelverton Dr EDG B15 ....106 C6
Yeman Rd COVN CV6 ....115 M1
Yemscroft Flats
RUSH/SHEL WS4 * 39 L7
Yenton CI POL/KGSB/FAZ B78 .....45 L4
Yeoman CI CSCFLD/WYGN B72 ....72 F1
Yeoman Cl KIDD DY10 ....164 C2
Yeomanry CI MGN/WHC B75 ....57 L1
WWCK CV34 ....205 K6
Yeomans Wy MGN/WHC B75 ....57 H1
Yeovilton CRTAM B79 ....31 J8
Yerbury Gv ERDW/GRVHL B23 ....71 L8
Yew CI COVS CV3 ....156 B8
Yew Croft Av HRBN B17 ....105 L7
Yewdale HRBN B17 ....124 A1

Yewdale Crs COVE CV2.................135 J4
Yewhurst Rd SOLH B91 ....148 B1
The Yews BDWTH CV12 ....116 C3
Yew St BDMR/CCFT WV3 2
Yew Tree Av HAG/WOL DY9 ....141 H5
  LICHS WS14 ....21 J6
Yew Tree Cl BEWD DY12 ....162 D2
  CNCK/NC WS11 ....17 L8
  REDW B97 ....201 L1
Yew Tree Ct RLSS WV31 * 206 D8
Yewtree Dr BRGRVW B60 ....191 H5
Yew Tree Gdns CDSL WV8 ....34 E1
Yew Tree HI RRUGBY CV21 ....158 C2
Yew Tree Hills DUDS DY2 ....103 G2
Yewtree La BLKHTH/ROWR B65 ..103 M3
Yew Tree La BEWD DY12 ....162 D2
  BILS/COS WV14 ....67 H4
  BRGRVW B61 ....168 B3
  DARL/WED WS10 ....68 E3
  DUNHL/THL/PER WV6 ....34 D7
  LGN/SDN/BHAMAIR B26 ....109 J6
  RMSLY B62 ....143 J2
  SOLH B91 ....128 C8

Yew Tree PI RMSLY B62 ....121 K8
Yew Tree Ri WALM/CURD B76 ......73 K2
Yewtree Rd FOAKS/STRLY B74 ....55 F6
  SCFLD/BOLD B73 ....72 E6
Yew Tree Rd AST/WIT B6 ....89 L4
  CBROM B36 ....92 C5
  DSYBK/YTR WS5 ....53 L8
  DUDS DY2 ....103 G1
  EDG B15 ....6 C9
  HALE B63 ....121 J2
  KIDD DY10 ....138 D8
  MOS/BIL B13 ....125 H3
  RUSH/SHEL WS4 ....39 M4
Yew Tree Vls SCFLD/BOLD B73 * ..72 E6
Yew Tree Wk STRPD DY13 ....188 C1
Yockleton Rd STECH B33 ....110 A2
York Av ATHST CV9 ....63 J4
  BDMR/CCFT WV3 ....49 J4
  BDWTH CV12 ....117 H3
  BRGRVW B61 ....191 H1
  WLNHL WV13 ....52 B3
  WSLW WS2 ....52 F3

Yorkbrooke Dr
  LGN/SDN/BHAMAIR B26 ....109 M8
York CI BVILLE B30 ....124 E7
  COVS CV5 ....156 A8
  LICH WS13 ....21 G2
  TPTN/OCK DY4 ....85 H1
York Crs BDMR/CCFT WV3 ....49 H4
  DARL/WED WS10 ....52 B7
  STRBR DY8 ....101 H6
  WBROM B70 ....68 E7
Yorkdale CI SEDG DY3 ....84 B2
York Dr ERDE/BCHGN B24 ....90 F5
Yorke Av BRLYHL WV5 ....101 L4
York Gdns BDMR/CCFT WV3 ....49 J4
Yorklea CI
  CHWD/FDBR/MGN B37 ....110 D3
Yorklea Cft
  CHWD/FDBR/MGN B37 ....110 D3
Yorkminster Dr
  CHWD/FDBR/MGN B37 ....111 C2
York PI KIDD DY10 * 138 C6
York Rd ALE/KHTH/YWD B14 ....125 J5
  BDMR/CCFT WV3 ....48 F5

BEWD DY12 ....162 D1
BLKHTH/ROWR B65 ....104 C2
BRGRVW B61 ....191 K1
CNCK/NC WS11 ....16 D5
DUDS DY2 ....103 J2
ERDW/GRVHL B23 ....90 D1
HDSW B21 ....88 D5
HLGN/YWD B28 ....126 D4
LDYWD/EDGR B16 ....106 B4
RLSS CV31 ....206 D5
RUSH/SHEL WS4 ....40 B6
Yorksand Rd POL/KGSB/FAZ B78 ..45 K5
York St COV CV1 ....8 C5
  HRBN B17 ....106 B7
  KIDD DY10 ....138 C6
  NUN CV11 ....98 E1
  RUGBYN/HIL CV21 ....186 D2
  STRPT DY13 ....188 D2
  WOLV WV1 ....3 J6

Young St WBROM B70 86
Yoxall Gv STECH B33 109
Yoxall Rd SHLY B90 148
Yule Rd COVE CV2 135
Yvonne Rd REDW B97 202

Z

Zion CI GTWY WS6 24
Zions CI CDYHTH B64 103
Zoar St BDMR/CCFT WV3 2
  SEDG DY3 84
Zorrina CI NUNW/HART CV10 79
Zortech Av STRPT DY13 163
Zouche CI STRBR DY8 101

Index - featured places

The 3b Business Village
  HDSW B21 ....88 B6
A1 Trading Estate
  SMTHWK B66 ....87 L6
A1 Trading Estate
  SMTHWKW B67 ....105 L4
Abberley Industrial Centre
  SMTHWK B66 ....88 B8
Abbey CE Infant School
  NUN CV11 ....80 F8
Abbey Clinic
  COVW CV5 ....8 A8
Abbey CP School
  BLOX/PEL WS3 ....38 C2
Abbey Fields Swimming Pool
  KNWTH CV8 ....179 J8
Abbeygate Shopping Centre
  NUN CV11 ....99 G5
The Abbey Hotel
  Golf & Country Club
  REDE B98 ....194 D6
Abbey Industrial Estate
  COVE CV2 ....135 J8
Abbey Infant School
  SMTHWKW B67 ....105 J3
Abbey Junior School
  SMTHWKW B67 ....105 J4
Abbey Stadium
  REDE B98 ....194 C6
Abbey Trading Centre
  REDE B98 ....194 C8
Abbey Tutorial College
  CBHAMNW B3 ....6 E3
Abbots Farm Infant School
  RUGBYN/HIL CV21 ....187 K3
Abbots Farm Junior School
  RUGBYN/HIL CV21 ....187 K3
Abbotsford School
  KNWTH CV8 ....179 K7
Ace Business Park
  STECH B33 ....110 A3
Acocks Green J & I School
  ACGN B27 ....126 F2
Acton Business Park
  NUNW/HART CV10 ....80 D8
Acupoint Magneto Clinic
  SMHTH B10 ....108 C6
Adams Hotel
  RLSS CV31 ....206 D5
Adderley Primary School
  WASH/WDE B8 ....108 B2
Adderley Trading Estate
  WASH/WDE B8 ....108 A1
Advance Business Park
  CNCK/NC WS11 ....16 F2
The Alan Morton Track
  STRPT DY13 ....163 L7
Albert Bradbeer Infant School
  NFLD/LBR B31 ....144 D6
Albert Bradbeer Junior School
  NFLD/LBR B31 ....144 D6
Albert Pritchard Infant School
  DARL/WED WS10 ....52 E8
Albion Business Park
  SMTHWK B66 ....87 J5
Albion Industrial Estate
  COVW CV6 ....134 B6
Albion Industrial Estate
  WBROM B70 ....86 C3
Albion Junior School
  HHTH/SAND B71 ....87 L5
Albion Road Junior School
  WLNHL WV13 ....51 M3
Alcott Hall Primary School
  CHWD/FDBR/MGN B37 ....110 F4
Alderbrook School
  SOLH B91 ....148 B1
Alder Coppice Primary School
  SEDG DY3 ....66 A4
Aldergate Medical Centre
  CRTAM B79 ....31 M7
Alderman Callow School
  TLHL/CAN CV4 ....153 L7
Alderman Green
  Primary School
  COVE CV2 ....135 G2
Alderman Harris
  Primary School
  TLHL/CAN CV4 ....153 K6
Aldermans Green Industrial Est
  COVE CV2 ....135 J3
Alderman Smith School
  NUNW/HART CV10 ....98 B3
Aldermoor Farm
  Primary School
  COVS CV3 ....155 M6
Aldermoor Lane Welfare Clinic
  COVS CV3 ....155 L4
Aldersley High School
  CDSL WV8 ....35 J4
Aldersley Leisure Village
  DUNHL/THL/PER WV6 ....35 K7
Aldersley Stadium
  DUNHL/THL/PER WV6 ....35 K7
Aldridge & Brownhills
  Magistrates Court
  ALDR WS9 ....40 F7
Aldridge School
  ALDR WS9 ....40 E8
Alexander Industrial Park
  BILS/COS WV14 ....67 G1
The Alexander Patterson
  Special School
  KIDD DY10 ....139 G2
Alexandra High School &
  Sixth Form Centre
  TPTN/OCK DY4 ....67 M7

The Alexandra Hospital
  REDE B98 ....203 G7
Alexandra Industrial Estate
  TPTN/OCK DY4 ....67 K7
Alexandra Medical Centre
  HALE B63 ....103 K8
Alexandra Theatre
  DIG/EDG B5 ....6 F6
Al-Furqan Community College
  SPARK B11 ....126 E1
Al-Furqan Primary School
  SPARK B11 ....126 D1
Al Hijrah School
  BORD B9 ....108 C3
Al Huda Girls School
  WASH/WDE B8 ....90 B8
Alice Stevens Special School
  COVS CV3 ....155 L8
Allens Croft Primary School
  ALE/KHTH/YWD B14 ....124 F4
Allens Rough JMI School
  SHHTH WV12 ....38 A4
Allesley Hall Primary School
  COVW CV5 ....153 M1
Allesley Hotel
  COVW CV5 ....132 F7
Allesley Park Medical Centre
  COVW CV5 ....154 A1
Allesley Primary School
  COVW CV5 ....132 E6
Alliance Business Park
  NUN CV11 ....99 K2
All Saints CE Infant School
  BDWTH CV12 ....117 G3
All Saints CE J & I School
  HHTH/SAND B71 ....69 G7
All Saints CE Junior School
  WWCK CV34 ....205 L4
All Saints CE Primary School
  COV CV1 ....9 K7
All Saints CE Primary School
  NUNW/HART CV10 ....99 G4
All Saints Industrial Estate
  WSNGN B18 ....88 E8
All Saints Primary School
  RWWCK/WEL CV35 ....197 L5
All Souls RC Primary School
  COVW CV5 ....154 C3
Alma Industrial Estate
  DARL/WED WS10 ....52 A7
Alpha Business Park
  COVE CV2 ....135 H4
Alston Primary School
  BORD B9 ....108 C2
Althorpe Industrial Estate
  RLSS CV31 ....206 E6
Alumrock Medical Centre
  WASH/WDE B8 ....108 C1
Alumwell Community School
  WSLW WS2 ....52 E4
Alumwell Infant School
  WSLW WS2 ....52 E5
Alumwell Junior School
  WSLW WS2 ....52 E5
Alvechurch CE Middle School
  ALVE B48 ....170 F7
Alvis Retail Park
  COVW CV6 ....8 A3
Amblecote Primary School
  STRBR DY8 ....101 K5
AMC Cinema
  LDYWD/EDGR B16 ....106 F4
Amington Industrial Estate
  TAM/AM/WIL B77 ....46 E2
Amington Industrial Estate
  TAM/AM/WIL B77 ....47 G3
Ammond Business Centre
  NUN CV11 ....99 J2
Amptronik Trading Estate
  SEDG DY3 ....82 B1
Anchor Brook Industrial Park
  ALDR WS9 ....40 F7
Anderton Park
  Primary School
  BHTH/HG B12 ....125 L1
Angel Croft Hotel
  LICH WS13 ....20 F1
Angel Hotel
  RLSN CV32 ....206 E5
Anglesey Business Park
  HEDN WS12 ....17 J1
Anglesey Primary School
  LOZ/NWT B19 ....89 G6
Anglo African Industrial Park
  OLDBY B69 ....86 C3
Anita Myatt Health Centre
  ETTPK/GDPK/PENN WV4 ....65 H1
Ankermoor Primary School
  TAM/AM/WIL B77 ....32 C8
Ankerside Shopping Centre
  CRTAM B79 ....45 M1
Annie Lennard Infant School
  SMTHWK B67 ....105 J2
Annie Osborn Primary School
  COVE CV2 ....135 H6
Apex Business Park
  CNCK/NC WS11 ....17 L8
Apollo Cinema
  RLSN CV32 ....206 C5
Arboretum
  RUSH/SHEL WS4 ....5 K2
Arbury Hall
  NUNW/HART CV10 ....98 A6
Arbury Medical Centre
  NUNW/HART CV10 ....98 C2
Arcadian Shopping Centre
  DIG/EDG B5 ....7 G7

Archbishop Grimshaw
  RC School
  CHWD/FDBR/MGN B37 ....110 D2
Archbishop Ilsey Catholic
  Technology College &
  6th Form Centre
  ACGN B27 ....127 C2
Arches Business Centre
  RUGBYN/HIL CV21 ....161 C8
Arches Industrial Estate
  COVW CV5 ....8 A4
Arches Industrial Estate
  RUGBYN/HIL CV21 ....161 C8
Arden Forest Infant School
  BDWTH CV12 ....117 L2
Arden Hill Infant School
  ATHST CV9 ....63 J6
Arden Hotel & Leisure Club
  HIA/OLT B92 ....129 G3
Arden Industrial Estate
  WASH/WDE B8 ....90 F6
Arden Primary School
  SPARK B11 ....108 A8
Arden School
  DOR/KN B93 ....149 M8
Areley Common First School
  STRPT DY13 ....188 C4
Areley Kings the Windmill
  First School
  STRPT DY13 ....188 C4
The Arena
  COV CV1 ....8 D5
Argyle Street Clinic
  TAM/AM/WIL B77 ....46 C1
Arley Industrial Estate
  RCOVN/BALC/EX CV7 ....96 D5
Arley Sports Centre
  RCOVN/BALC/EX CV7 ....96 C3
Armoury Trading Estate
  SPARK B11 ....108 B7
Arnold Lawn School
  RLSN CV32 ....206 D3
Arran Medical Centre
  CBROM B36 ....92 E6
Arriva Business Park
  KIDDW DY11 ....164 A4
Arrow Business Park
  REDE B98 ....202 F2
Arrow Industrial Estate
  SHHTH WV12 ....37 M6
Arrow Vale Community
  High School
  REDE B98 ....203 J3
Arthur Terry School
  FOAKS/STRLY B74 ....56 E3
Arts Centre
  CRTAM B79 ....31 M8
  LICH WS13 ....20 E5
  NUN CV11 ....98 F1
Arts Centre Cinema
  TLHL/CAN CV4 ....179 M1
Ashbourne Centre
  ERDW/GRVHL B23 ....90 C2
Ashcroft County
  Infants School
  CRTAM B79 ....32 A6
Ash End House Childrens Farm
  POL/KGSB/FAZ B78 ....58 F6
Ashford Industrial Estate
  BKHL/PFLD WV2 ....50 D6
Ashfurlong Health Centre
  MGN/WHC B75 ....57 J5
Ash Green School
  RCOVN/BALC/EX CV7 ....116 B7
Ashlawn School
  RUGBYS/DCH CV22 ....187 J6
Ashmore Industrial Estate
  WSLW WS2 ....4 E1
Ashmore Park Clinic
  WNSFLD WV11 ....37 L5
Ashmores Industrial Estate
  DUDN DY1 ....85 H2
Ashtree Medical Centre
  BVILLE B30 ....124 E7
Ashwood Park Primary School
  STRBR DY8 ....101 H4
Astley Castle
  NUNW/HART CV10 ....97 J5
Astley CE Primary School
  STRPT DY13 ....188 A8
Astley CE Primary School
  NUNW/HART CV10 ....97 J6
Aston Cross Business Park
  AST/WIT B6 ....89 L7
Aston Expressway
  Industrial Estate
  AST/WIT B6 ....89 J8
Aston Fields Industrial Estate
  BRGRVW B60 ....191 L7
Aston Fields Middle School
  BRGRVW B60 ....192 A5
Aston Fields Trading Estate
  BRGRVW B60 ....191 K7
Aston Hall
  AST/WIT B6 ....89 K5
Aston Health Centre
  AST/WIT B6 ....89 J4
Aston Industrial Estate
  AST/WIT B6 ....117 H3
Aston Manor Cricket &
  Lucas Sports Club
  PBAR/PBCH B42 ....71 H8
Aston Manor School
  AST/WIT B6 ....89 K7
Aston Newtown Pool
  & Fitness Centre
  LOZ/NWT B19 ....89 J6

Aston Park Industrial Estate
  NUN CV11 ....80 F7
Aston Science Park
  VAUX/NECH B7 ....7 K1
Aston Tower Primary School
  AST/WIT B6 ....89 K6
Aston University
  CBHAMNE B4 ....7 J2
Aston University
  (Institute of Art & Design)
  CBHAMNE B4 ....7 J1
Aston Villa FC (Villa Park)
  AST/WIT B6 ....89 K4
Aston Wood Golf Club
  LICHS WS14 ....42 C7
Astoria Hotel
  LDYWD/EDGR B16 ....106 B4
AT7 Sports Centre
  COVN CV6 ....134 E6
Atherstone College
  ATHST CV9 ....63 H5
Atherstone Golf Club
  ATHST CV9 ....63 H7
Atherstone Town Cricket Club
  ATHST CV9 ....63 H4
Atherstone United FC
  ATHST CV9 ....63 H3
Atlas Trading Estate
  BILS/COS WV14 ....67 K3
Atlas Trading Estate
  SPARK B11 ....108 B8
Attleborough Fields
  Industrial Estate
  NUN CV11 ....99 K2
Attleborough Sports Club
  NUN CV11 ....99 J3
Attock Community
  Sports & Cricket Club
  MOS/BIL B13 ....126 A4
Attwood Business Centre
  HAG/WOL DY9 ....102 D8
Audley J & I School
  STECH B33 ....109 L1
Autobase Industrial Estate
  TPTN/OCK DY4 ....85 M2
Avenue Clinic
  NUN CV11 ....80 E8
Avery Dell Industrial Estate
  BVILLE B30 ....124 D7
Avon Business Park
  CNCK/NC WS11 ....16 A3
Avoncroft Museum of
  Historic Buildings
  BRGRVE B60 ....191 G4
Avon Industrial Estate
  RUGBYN/HIL CV21 ....161 G8
Avon Valley School
  RUGBYN/HIL CV21 ....160 C7
Axcess 10 Business Park
  WSLW WS2 ....52 C4
Bablake Junior School
  COV CV1 ....8 D2
Bablake School
  COV CV1 ....8 C2
Baddesley Ensor CE
  Infant School
  ATHST CV9 ....62 B4
Baddesley Ensor Junior School
  ATHST CV9 ....62 B4
Bageridge Country Park
  SEDG DY3 ....65 J7
Baginton Fields Special School
  COVS CV3 ....181 M1
Bagley Industrial Park
  DUDS DY2 ....103 H1
Balliol Business Park
  COVEN WV9 ....35 J2
Balsall Common Health Clinic
  RCOVN/BALC/EX CV7 ....151 M6
Balsall Common Primary School
  RCOVN/BALC/EX CV7 ....151 M8
Banners Gate Infant School
  SCFLD/BOLD B73 ....71 M1
Banners Gate Junior School
  SCFLD/BOLD B73 ....71 L1
Bantock House Museum
  BDMR/CCFT WV3 ....49 J4
Barber Institute of Fine Arts
  EDG B15 ....124 D1
Barford Primary School
  LDYWD/EDGR B16 ....106 C2
Barkers Butts RFC
  COVW CV5 ....132 A5
Barnfield Trading Estate
  TPTN/OCK DY4 ....67 J6
Barnt Green Cricket Club
  RBRY B45 ....170 A4
Barnt Green St Andrews
  CE First School
  RBRY B45 ....170 A5
Baron Business Centre
  HAG/WOL DY9 ....102 C8
Barons Court Industrial Estate
  ALDR WS9 ....40 C3
Barons Court Trading Estate
  ALDR WS9 ....40 C3
The Barr Beacon School
  ALDR WS9 ....54 F8
Barrs Hill School &
  Community College
  COV CV1 ....8 D1
Bartley Green FC
  RIDG/WDGT B32 ....123 G4
Bartley Green Health Centre
  RIDG/WDGT B32 ....122 F4
Bartley Green Technology College
  RIDG/WDGT B32 ....123 G4

Barton Industrial Estate
  BILS/COS WV14 51
Baskerville Special School
  HRBN B17 105
Batchley First School
  REDW B97 201
Bath Walk Industrial Estate
  BHTH/HG B12 107
Baverstock Gm School
  ALE/KHTH/YWD B14 146
Baxter College
  KIDDW DY11 137
Bayer Hall Clinic
  BILS/COS WV14 67
Bayton Road Industrial Estate
  RCOVN/BALC/EX CV7 116
Beacon CP School
  SHHTH WV12 38
Beacon Hill Cemetery
  ETTPK/GDPK/PENN WV4 66
Beaconside Primary School
  RBRY B45 143
Beacon Trading Estate
  ALDR WS9 40
Bean Road Industrial Estate
  TPTN/OCK DY4 67
Bearwood Medical Centre
  SMTHWKW B67 105
Bearwood Primary School
  SMTHWK B66 105
Bearwood Shopping Centre
  SMTHWK B66 105
Beauchamp Industrial Park
  TAM/AM/WIL B77 46
Beau Desert Golf Club
  HEDN WS12 13
Beaufort Special School
  CBROM B36 91
Beauty Bank Primary School
  STRBR DY8 101
Bede Shopping Arcade
  BDWTH CV12 116
Bedworth Health Centre
  BDWTH CV12 116
Bedworth Leisure Centre
  BDWTH CV12 117
Bedworth RFC
  BDWTH CV12 117
Beechdale CP School
  WSLW WV1 39
Beeches Hospital
  WOLV WV1 38
The Beeches Infant School
  RBRY B45 143
Beeches Pool & Fitness Centre
  PBAR/PBCH B42 70
Beechwood Business Park
  HEDN WS12 16
Beecroft Hill Special School
  CNCK/NC WS11 16
Belbroughton CE First School
  HAG/WOL DY9 141
Belfont Trading Estate
  RMSLY B62 122
Belgrade Theatre
  COV CV1 8
Belgrave High School
  TAM/AM/WIL B77 46
Belgrave Recreation Centre
  TAM/AM/WIL B77 46
Bell Barn Shopping Centre
  EDG B15 6
Belle Vue Medical Centre
  EDG B15 107
Belle Vue Primary School
  STRBR DY8 101
Bellfield J & I School
  NFLD/LBR B31 144
Bell Green Health Centre
  COVE CV2 135
Bells Farm Primary School
  ALE/KHTH/YWD B14 146
The Bell Shopping Centre
  NFLD/LBR B31 144
Bennetts Well
  Primary School
  CHWD/FDBR/MGN B37 110
Benick Trading Estate
  CNCK/NC WS11 16
Benson Community School
  WSNGN B18 88
Benson Industrial Estate
  WSNGN B18 88
Bentley Bridge Business Park
  WNSFLD WV11 37
Bentley Drive
  Primary School
  WSLW WS2 52
Bentley Heath CE
  Primary School
  DOR/KN B93 149
Bentley Lane Industrial Park
  WSLW WS2 52
Bentley Mill Industrial Estate
  WSLW WS2 52
Bentley West Primary School
  WSLW WS2 52
Beoley First School
  REDE B98 181
Berkswell CE Primary School
  RCOVN/BALC/EX CV7 152
Berkswell Windmill
  RCOVN/BALC/EX CV7 ....
Bermuda Business Park
  NUNW/HART CV10 ....

muda Park
Industrial Estate
NUNW/HART CV10 ...98 D4
cot Hotel
SLW WV8 ...52 F7
an Industrial Estate
ARL/WED WS10 ...68 D2
RLYHL DY5 ...101 L2
erley Hotel
JSH/SHEL WS4 ...53 L1
dley CC
EWD DY12 ...162 F3
dley High School
EWD DY12 ...163 G3
dley Medical Centre
EWD DY12 ...162 F2
dley Museum
EWD DY12 ...162 F2
dley Rowing Club
EWD DY12 ...162 F1
dley Tennis Club
EWD DY12 ...163 G2
y Business Park
RGRVE B60 ...191 K7
ls Acre Primary School
OMR/CCFT WV3 ...48 F6
enhill Trading Estate
HWD/FDBR/MGN B37 ...111 H8
ford Road
dustrial Estate
ST/WIT B6 ...89 L4
rook CE Middle School
DSL WV8 ...34 F1
rook Medical Centre
DSL WV8 ...34 F2
esley Primary School
MOS/BIL B13 ...126 A7
ton Central
Industrial Estate
LS/COS WV14 ...51 J8
ton CE Primary School
LS/COS WV14 ...50 F7
ton Health Centre
LS/COS WV14 ...51 H7
ton Industrial Estate
LS/COS WV14 ...67 L1
ton Key Industrial Estate
LS/COS WV14 ...51 L8
ton Leisure Centre
LS/COS WV14 ...51 H7
t Gallery &
LS/COS WV14 ...51 J7
ton Town FC
LS/COS WV14 ...51 K7
n CE Junior School
UGBYS/DCH CV22 ...186 B7
n High School
UGBYS/DCH CV22 ...185 M4
n Industrial Estate
OVS CV3 ...9 M7
n Industrial Estate
UGBYS/DCH CV22 ...186 A5
ley Primary School
OMR/CCFT WV3 ...2 B9
ey Business Park
OVS CV3 ...156 E4
ey Industrial Estate
OVS CV3 ...156 E6
y Woods Primary School
NWTH CV8 ...157 J6
hbrook Industrial Park
CHS WS4 ...28 C7
n Business Park
NCK/NC WS11 ...16 D7
t Coppice Industrial Estate
OL/KGSB/FAZ B78 ...47 J8
en Coppice F & M School
DDW DY11 ...163 L3
hensale Middle School
B97 ...202 A1
hes First School
SLW WS2 ...34 F4
hes Green J & I School
RDE/BCHGN B24 ...90 F2
nfield Independent
ls School
ST/WIT B6 ...89 J5
nfield Primary School
ST/WIT B6 ...89 H4
hills CE School
SLW WS2 ...4 C3
hills Health Centre
SLW WS2 ...4 B1
ey Industrial Estate
LDBY B69 ...86 C8
h Road East
dustrial Estate
ST/WIT B6 ...89 M3
hwood Primary School
OL/KGSB/FAZ B78 ...47 K6
s Bush County
rimary School
AM/AM/WIL B77 ...46 C5
ingham Alexander Stadium
BAR/PBCH B42 ...71 G7
Birmingham and Midland
ospital for Woman
PARK B11 ...126 A2
ingham Area Civil
ervice Sports Club
HA/OLT B92 ...128 E3
ingham Botanical Gardens
Glasshouses
DG B15 ...106 D6
ingham Business Centre
BROM B70 ...87 K3
ingham Business Park
HL/WTROR B46 ...111 J5
ingham City FC
Andrews Stadium)
ORD B9 ...107 M4
ingham Community
ollege
BHAMNW B3 ...6 E3
SCFLD/WYGN B72 ...57 C8
ingham Conservatoire
CE)
BHAMNW B3 ...6 D5
Birmingham Crematorium
BAR/PBCH B42 ...71 L2
ingham Crown Court
BHAMNE B4 ...7 G2
ingham Heartlands
ospital
ORD B9 ...108 F3
ingham International
rport
N/SDN/BHAMAIR B26 ...110 E8
ingham Marriott Hotel
DYWD/EDGR B16 ...6 A8
Birmingham Mint
WGN B18 ...6 B1
rmingham Nuffield
ospital
G B15 ...106 D8

Birmingham One
Industrial Estate
CBHAMW B1 ...6 B4
Birmingham Repertory Theatre
CBHAMW B1 ...6 D5
Birmingham Wheels
Adventure Park
BORD B9 ...108 A3
Birmingham Womens Hospital
EDG B15 ...106 B8
Birmingham (Yardley)
Crematorium
LGN/SDN/BHAMAIR B26 ...109 H8
Bishop Ashbury's Cottage
GTB/HAM B43 ...69 M4
The Bishop Challoner
RC School
ALE/KHTH/YWD B14 ...125 J1
Bishopgate Business Park
COV CV1 ...134 B8
Bishop Milner RC
Secondary School
DUDN DY1 ...84 E2
Bishop Ullathorne
RC Comprehensive School
COVS CV3 ...180 C1
Bishop Veseys
Grammar School
FOAKS/STLY B74 ...57 C7
Bishop Walsh
Catholic School
WALM/CURD B76 ...73 H3
Bishop Wilson CE
Primary School
CHWD/FDBR/MGN B37 ...111 L2
Bishop Wulstan RC
High School
RUGBYS/DCH CV22 ...186 E5
Bi-tec Industrial Park
WOLV WV1 ...3 M6
Black Boy Hotel
BEWD DY12 ...162 F2
Blackbrook Valley
Industrial Estate
DUDS DY2 ...84 E7
Blackbrook Valley
Industrial Park
DUDS DY2 ...84 E8
Black Country Living Museum
DUDN DY1 ...85 H1
Blackheath Primary School
BLKHTH/ROWR B65 ...103 M4
Blackheath Trading Estate
BLKHTH/ROWR B65 ...104 C3
Black Lake Industrial Estate
WBROM B70 ...68 E7
The Blackwell Golf Club
BRGRVE B60 ...169 M8
Blackwood School
ALDR WS9 ...55 H3
Blakebrook Special School
KIDDW DY11 ...138 A7
Blakedown CE First School
KIDD DY10 ...140 A4
Blake High School
HEDN WS12 ...12 E7
Blakeley Heath Primary School
WMBN WV5 ...64 E8
Blakenall FC
BLOX/PEL WS3 ...39 G8
Blakenall Heath Junior School
BLOX/PEL WS3 ...39 G5
Blakenhale Infant School
STETCH B33 ...109 M4
Blakenhale Junior School
STETCH B33 ...109 M4
Blakenhall Industrial Estate
BKHL/PFLD WV2 ...49 M6
Blakesley Hall & Museum
YDLY B25 ...109 H4
Blakesley Hall Primary School
YDLY B25 ...109 H4
Blanford Mere Primary School
KGSWFD DY6 ...83 J6
Bleakhouse Clinic
LGLYGN/QTN B68 ...105 C4
Bleakhouse Junior School
LGLYGN/QTN B68 ...105 C4
Blossomfield Infant School
SHLY B90 ...148 B2
Blowers Green Primary School
DUDS DY2 ...84 F5
Bloxwich Business Park
WSLW WS2 ...38 C5
Bloxwich CE Primary School
BLOX/PEL WS3 ...38 F4
Bloxwich Golf Club
BLOX/PEL WS3 ...38 F1
Bloxwich Hospital
BLOX/PEL WS3 ...38 F5
Bloxwich Lane
Industrial Estate
WSLW WS2 ...52 C2
Bloxwich Leisure Centre
BLOX/PEL WS3 ...39 G5
Blue Coat CE
Comprehensive School
WSL WS1 ...5 L5
Blue Coat CE Infant School
WSL WS1 ...5 L5
Blue Coat CE Junior School
WSL WS1 ...5 H5
Blue Coat CE School
COV CV1 ...9 L8
The Blue Coat School
EDG B15 ...106 C7
Blythe Business Park
HOCK/TIA B94 ...174 D2
Blythe Special School
CSHL/WTROR B46 ...111 L1
BMI Priory Hospital
EDG B15 ...106 F8
Boat Club
WWCK CV34 ...205 K7
Boating Lakes
WOLV WV1 ...2 C3
Boddis Industrial Park
CDYHTH B64 ...103 L3
Bodmin Road Industrial Estate
COVE CV2 ...135 J8
Boldmere Clinic
SCFLD/BOLD B73 ...72 C2
Boldmere Golf Club
SCFLD/BOLD B73 ...72 C2
Boldmere J & I School
SCFLD/BOLD B73 ...72 D4
Boldmere St Michaels FC
SCFLD/BOLD B73 ...72 D5
Bond's Hospital &
Bablake Old School
COV CV1 ...8 D4
Bonehill Industrial Estate
POL/KGSB/FAZ B78 ...45 K4
Boney Hay Primary School
BNTWD WS7 ...18 E4
Bordesley Abbey (remains of)
REDE B98 ...194 D7
Bordesley Abbey Visitors Centre
REDE B98 ...194 D7

Bordesley Green Girls School
WASH/WDE B8 ...108 C2
Bordesley Green
Primary School
BORD B9 ...108 E3
Bordesley Green
Trading Estate
WASH/WDE B8 ...108 B2
Borough Cemetery
DUDS DY2 ...84 F5
Boscomoor Industrial Estate
PENK ST19 ...10 C6
Boscomoor Shopping Centre
PENK ST19 ...10 B6
Boswells Monument
LICH WS13 ...20 C5
Bosworth Wood
Primary School
CBROM B36 ...92 D4
Boughton Leigh
County Junior School
RUGBYN/HIL CV21 ...161 G6
Boughton Leigh
Infant School
RUGBYN/HIL CV21 ...161 H6
Boughton Road
Industrial Estate
RUGBYN/HIL CV21 ...160 F7
Boulton Industrial Centre
WSNGN B18 ...88 F8
The Boundary Hotel
WSL WS1 ...5 L9
Boundary Industrial Estate
WOLVN WV10 ...22 A4
Bourneville Infant School
BVILLE B30 ...124 C6
Bourneville Junior School
BVILLE B30 ...124 C6
Bournville College of FE
NFLD/LBR B31 ...124 A6
Bournville School of
Art & Craft
BVILLE B30 ...124 C6
Bournville School &
Sixth Form Centre
NFLD/LBR B31 ...124 A7
Bowling Alley
BRLYHL DY5 ...102 B3
Bowling Alley
COVS CV3 ...181 H1
Bowling Alley
LDYWD/EDGR B16 ...106 E4
Bowling Alley
POL/KGSB/FAZ B78 ...45 M1
Bowling Alley
RCOVN/BALC/EX CV7 ...135 M5
Bowling Alley
RLSS CV31 ...206 B7
Bowling Alley
RUGBYN/HIL CV21 ...160 F7
Brackendale Shopping Centre
SHHTH WV12 ...52 B1
Bradford Street Clinic
WSL WS1 ...4 E5
Braidwood School for
Deaf Children
ERDW/GRVHL B23 ...71 M7
Bramford Primary School
DUDN DY1 ...66 E7
Brandhall Clinic
LGLYGN/QTN B68 ...104 F5
Brandhall Golf Club
LGLYGN/QTN B68 ...104 E3
Brandhall Primary School
LGLYGN/QTN B68 ...104 F4
Brandon Court Leofric
Business Park
COVS CV3 ...156 E6
The Brandon Hall Hotel
KNWTH CV8 ...157 J8
Brandon Way Industrial Estate
WBROM B70 ...86 D2
Brandwood End Cemetery
ALE/KHTH/YWD B14 ...125 J8
Brasshouse Infant School
SMTHWK B66 ...87 K6
Brays Special School
LGN/SDN/BHAMAIR B26 ...109 L7
Breener Industrial Estate
STRBR DY8 ...101 M4
Briars Country Club
KIDDW DY11 ...137 L6
Brickhouse J & I School
BLKHTH/ROWR B65 ...103 L2
Bridge Industrial Estate
HIA/OLT B92 ...128 A5
The Bridge Medical Centre
STRPT DY13 ...188 D3
Bridgeside Industrial Estate
TAM/AM/WIL B77 ...46 A2
Bridgeside Trading Estate
TAM/AM/WIL B77 ...46 A3
Bridge Special School
ERDW/GRVHL B23 ...90 C1
Bridge Street Industrial Estate
DARL/WED WS10 ...68 D4
The Bridge Trading Estate
DARL/WED WS10 ...68 D4
Bridge Street
Industrial Estate
SMTHWK B66 ...87 M6
Bridge Works Industrial Estate
KNWTH CV8 ...197 L1
Bridgtown Business Centre
CNCK/NC WS11 ...16 C7
Bridgtown County
Primary School
CNCK/NC WS11 ...16 C7
The Brierley Hill Health Centre
BRLYHL DY5 ...102 B2
Brierley Hill Primary School
BRLYHL DY5 ...102 B3
The Brierley Trading Estate
BRLYHL DY5 ...102 A2
Bierly Hill Leisure Centre
BRLYHL DY5 ...101 M4
The Brier Special School
BRLYHL DY5 ...102 C3
Brindley Business Park
CNCK/NC WS11 ...16 C7
Brindley Place
CBHAMW B1 ...6 C5
Brineton Industrial Estate
WSLW WS2 ...4 B6
Brinklow CE First School
RRUGBY CV23 ...158 D1
Bristnall Hall High School
LGLYGN/QTN B68 ...105 H2
Britannia High School
BLKHTH/ROWR B65 ...104 D3
Broadcott
Industrial Estate
CDYHTH B64 ...103 L4
Broad Heath Community
Primary School
COVN CV6 ...134 C7
Broad Heath School
COVN CV6 ...134 C7
Broad Lane Trading Estate
COVW CV5 ...153 G2
Broadmeadow J & I School
BVILLE B30 ...145 M3

Broad Street Gallery
WOLV WV1 ...3 G4
Broad Street Health Centre
COVN CV6 ...134 D6
Broad Street Old Boys RFC
COVS CV3 ...156 F5
Broad Street RFC
COVE CV2 ...135 G5
Broadwalk Retail Park
WSL WS5 ...53 H7
Broadway Medical Centre
DSYBK/YTR WS5 ...53 K7
Broadway Plaza
LDYWD/EDGR B16 ...106 E4
Broadway School
BFLD/HDSWWD B20 ...89 J3
Broadfield Industrial Park
OLDBY B69 ...86 D5
Broadwyn Trading Estate
CDYHTH B64 ...103 L4
Brockencote Hall
Country House Hotel
KIDD DY10 ...166 B6
Brockmoor
Industrial Estate
KGSWFD DY6 ...101 L2
Brockmoor Primary School
BRLYHL DY5 ...102 A2
Bromford J & I School
CBROM B36 ...91 H6
Bromford Road
Industrial Estate
OLDBY B69 ...86 E4
Bromley Hills Primary School
KGSWFD DY6 ...101 K1
Bromley Primary School
BRLYHL DY5 ...83 M8
Bromsgrove Business Centre
BRGRVW B61 ...191 K3
Bromsgrove Clinic
BRGRVW B61 ...191 K2
Bromsgrove Golf Centre
BRGRVE B60 ...192 A3
Bromsgrove Lower School
BRGRVE B60 ...191 K4
Bromsgrove Museum &
Tourist Information Centre
BRGRVW B61 ...191 L2
Bromsgrove Private Hospital
BRGRVE B60 ...192 F4
Bromsgrove RFCi
BRGRVE B60 ...192 A5
Bromsgrove Rovers FC
BRGRVW B61 ...191 L2
Bromsgrove Upper School
BRGRVE B60 ...191 K4
Brooke Special School
RUGBYS/DCH CV22 ...186 C4
Brooke Special School
(Sec Site)
RUGBYS/DCH CV22 ...186 C5
Brook Farm Industrial Estate
HOCK/TIA B94 ...173 M3
Brookfields Primary School
WSNGN B18 ...6 A1
Brookhurst Primary School
RLSN CV32 ...206 B4
Brooklands Grange Hotel
COVW CV5 ...133 H8
Brooklands Hospital
CHWD/FDBR/MGN B37 ...110 F3
The Brook Primary School
STRBR DY8 ...101 K4
Brookside Industrial Estate
DARL/WED WS10 ...68 F2
Brook Street Business Centre
TPTN/OCK DY4 ...67 J7
Brookvale Primary School
ERDW/GRVHL B23 ...89 M1
Brookvale Trading Estate
AST/WIT B6 ...89 L2
Broomfield Park Surgery
COVW CV5 ...8 B4
Brownhills Business Park
BRWNH WS8 ...26 D8
Brownhills Clinic
BRWNH WS8 ...26 D6
Brownhills Comprehensive
School
BRWNH WS8 ...26 D4
Brownhills West JMI School
BRWNH WS8 ...26 A3
Browning Street
Industrial Estate
LDYWD/EDGR B16 ...6 A6
Brownmead Primary School
BKDE/SHDE B34 ...91 M7
Brownsover Community
School
RRUGBY CV23 ...161 H5
Brownsover Hall Hotel
RUGBYN/HIL CV21 ...160 F7
Brunswick Park Trading Estate
ARL/WED WS10 ...68 F1
Brymill Industrial Estate
TPTN/OCK DY4 ...67 H6
BSA Business Park
SPARK B11 ...108 B7
BT Tower
CBHAMW B3 ...6 E3
Budbrooke Industrial Estate
WWCK CV34 ...205 G5
Budbrooke Medical Centre
RWWCK/WEL CV35 ...204 D6
Budbrooke Primary School
RWWCK/WEL CV35 ...204 D7
Bullring Shopping Centre
DIG/EDG B5 ...7 H6
Bull Ring Trading Estate
BORD B9 ...7 K7
Bull Street Trading Estate
BRLYHL DY5 ...101 M4
Buntsford Hill Business Park
BRGRVE B60 ...191 K7
The Burlington Hotel
CBHAM B2 ...6 F5
Burlish Middle School
STRPT DY13 ...163 K8
The Burlish Park First School
STRPT DY13 ...163 K8
Burman Infant School
SHLY B90 ...147 L3
Burnsall Road Industrial Estate
COVW CV5 ...154 A5
Burnt Tree Industrial Estate
TPTN/OCK DY4 ...85 M3
Burnt Tree J & I School
OLDBY B69 ...85 L3
Burntwood
BNTWD WS7 ...18 D7
Burntwood Health Centre
BNTWD WS7 ...19 G7
Burntwood Town
Shopping Centre
BNTWD WS7 ...18 C7
Burton Green CE Primary
KNWTH CV8 ...178 F2
Burton Industrial Estate
CDYHTH B64 ...103 J5

Bushbury Baths
WOLVN WV10 ...36 C4
Bushbury Health Centre
WOLVN WV10 ...36 C3
Bushbury Hill J & I School
WOLVN WV10 ...36 D4
Busill Jones JMI School
BLOX/PEL WS3 ...38 D5
Butlers Leap
Industrial Estate
RUGBYN/HIL CV21 ...187 H1
Butts JMI School
RUSH/SHEL WS4 ...5 G1
Cadbury College
HWK/WKHTH B38 ...145 K4
Cadbury World
BVILLE B30 ...124 D6
Calderfields Golf Club &
Academy
RUSH/SHEL WS4 ...54 A3
Caldmore JMI School
WSL WS1 ...4 F7
Caldmore Medical Centre
WSL WS1 ...4 F7
Calthorpe Special School
BHTH/HG B12 ...107 L5
Caludon Castle School
COVE CV2 ...156 C1
Cambrian Wharf
CBHAMW B1 ...6 C5
Cambridge Tutorial College
SMHTH B10 ...108 B5
Campanile Hotel
AST/WIT B6 ...89 K8
COVE CV2 ...135 L5
REDE B98 ...195 L8
Camp Hill Clinic
NUNW/HART CV10 ...80 B7
Camp Hill Old Edwardians RFC
SHLY B90 ...147 M2
Camp Hill Primary School
NUNW/HART CV10 ...80 C7
Camping & Caravanning Club Site
KIDD DY10 ...138 D2
RMSLY B62 ...142 C1
Campion School
RLSS CV31 ...207 G8
Canal Side Industrial Estate
BRLYHL DY5 ...101 M4
Canal View Industrial Estate
BRLYHL DY5 ...101 L4
Canley Gardens Crematorium
TLHL/CAN CV4 ...154 B7
Canning Wharf
CBHAMNW B3 ...6 D4
Cannock Centre
CNCK/NC WS11 ...16 B4
Cannock Chase Country Park
HEDN WS12 ...13 H3
Cannock Chase FC
HEDN WS12 ...12 F5
Cannock Chase High School
CNCK/NC WS11 ...16 C3
Cannock Chase Hospital
CNCK/NC WS11 ...16 C3
Cannock Chase
Technical College
CNCK/NC WS11 ...16 B4
Cannock Chase
Technical College
CNCK/NC WS11 ...16 C6
Cannock Industrial Centre
CNCK/NC WS11 ...16 B8
Cannock Motor Racing Stadium
HEDN WS12 ...13 K8
Cannock Park Golf Club
HEDN WS12 ...16 B3
Cannock & Rugeley Cricket Club
HEDN WS12 ...13 L8
Cannock Sports Stadium
CNCK/NC WS11 ...12 D4
Cannon Business Park
BILS/COS WV14 ...67 G4
Cannon Park Primary School
TLHL/CAN CV4 ...154 B8
Canon Evans CE Infant School
BDWTH CV12 ...116 E3
Canon Maggs CE Junior School
BDWTH CV12 ...116 F3
Canterbury Cross
Primary N School
BFLD/HDSWWD B20 ...89 H3
Cape Hill Medical Centre
SMTHWK B66 ...106 A1
Cape Industrial Estate
WWCK CV34 ...205 J5
Cape Primary School
SMTHWK B66 ...106 A1
Cardinal Griffin RC School
CNCK/NC WS11 ...16 B2
Cardinal Newman RC School &
Community College
COVN CV6 ...133 K3
Cardinal Wiseman
Catholic School
KGSTG B44 ...71 K1
Cardinal Wiseman RC School
COVE CV2 ...135 J4
Carlton Business Centre
VAUX/NECH B7 ...90 A8
Carlyle Business Park
WBROM B70 ...68 D8
Carlyon Road Industrial Estate
ATHST CV9 ...63 K4
Carters Green Medical Centre
WBROM B70 ...87 G1
Cash's Business Centre
COV CV1 ...134 B8
Caslon Primary School
HALE B63 ...120 F1
Castle Bromwich
Business Park
CVALE B35 ...91 K4
Castle Bromwich CC
CBROM B36 ...92 A5
Castle Bromwich Hall Gardens
CBROM B36 ...91 L5
Castle Bromwich Infant School
CBROM B36 ...92 C5
Castle Bromwich Junior School
CBROM B36 ...92 B6
Castlecroft J & I School
BDMR/CCFT WV3 ...48 F4
Castle High School
DUDN DY1 ...84 F3
Castle Hills
RCOVN/BALC/EX CV7 ...114 D1
Castle Museum
CRTAM B79 ...45 L1
Castle Place Industrial Estate
COV CV1 ...9 J2
Castle Pleasure Grounds
TAM/AM/WIL B77 ...45 M1
The Castle Pool & Adventure
Play Centre
CVALE B35 ...91 M3
Castle Sixth Form Centre
(Kenilworth School)
KNWTH CV8 ...197 K3

Castle Special School
BLOX/PEL WS3 ....38 F6
Castle Vale Health Centre
CVALE B35 ....91 K2
Castle Vale Industrial Estate
WALM/CURD B76 ....73 L8
Castle Vale School
CVALE B35 ....91 M2
Castle Vale Shopping Centre
CVALE B35 ....91 K2
Castle View Industrial Estate
TPTN/OCK DY4 ....85 K2
Cathedral Lanes
Shopping Centre
COV CV1 ....8 E3
Catshill Clinic
BRGRVW B61 ....168 E5
Catshill First School
BRGRVW B61 ....168 E5
Catshill Middle School
BRGRVW B61 ....168 D5
Causeway Green
Primary School
LGLYGN/QTN B68 ....104 D2
Cedars Business Centre
CNCK/NC WS11 ....16 A6
Cedars Hotel
KIDDW DY11 ....138 A7
Centech Business Park
REDE B98 ....195 K7
Centenary Business Centre
NUN CV11 ....99 J2
Central Business Park
STECH B33 ....110 B4
Central City Industrial Estate
COVN CV6 ....134 D8
Central Clinic
DUDS DY2 ....85 H4
Central Hall
CBHAMNE B4 ....7 H3
Central Industrial Estate
BKHL/PFLD WV2 ....50 D6
Central Park Industrial Estate
BRLYHL DY5 ....102 D3
DUDS DY2 ....103 J1
DUDS DY2 ....103 J2
Central Six Retail Park
COV CV1 ....8 D7
Central Trading Estate
KGSWFD DY6 ....83 H2
Centre Link Industrial Estate
VAUX/NECH B7 ....89 M7
Centrovell Industrial Estate
NUN CV11 ....99 G3
Century Industrial Estate
KGSTG B44 ....71 J2
The Chace Hotel
COVS CV3 ....155 M8
Chace Primary School
COVS CV3 ....156 A7
Chaddesley Corbett
Endowed First School
KIDD DY10 ....166 C1
Chadsgrove Special School
BRGRVW B61 ....168 D5
Chadsmead Primary School
LICH WS13 ....20 E4
Chadsmoor CE Junior School
CNCK/NC WS11 ....16 E1
Chadsmoor Infants School
CNCK/NC WS11 ....16 E1
Chad Vale Primary School
EDG B15 ....106 B6
Chadwick Bank
Industrial Estate
STRPT DY13 ....189 H5
Chadwick Business Park
STRPT DY13 ....189 H5
Chadwick Industrial Estate
STRPT DY13 ....189 H5
Challenge Business Park
COV CV1 ....134 B8
Chamber of Commerce
WSL WS1 ....5 J4
Chamber of Commerce
& Industry
BDMR/CCFT WV3 ....2 A4
Chancel Industrial Estate
DARL/WED WS10 ....52 B8
KGSWFD DY6 ....83 H4
WLNHL WV13 ....51 M3
WOLV WV1 ....50 D4
Chancel Way Industrial Estate
PBAR/PBCH B42 ....71 L4
Chandos Primary School
DIG/EDG B5 ....107 J4
Chantry Industrial Estate
WALM/CURD B76 ....74 F6
Chapel Fields Junior School
HIA/OLT B92 ....127 K2
Chapel Street
Industrial Estate
DUDS DY2 ....103 H1
Charford First School
BRGRVE B60 ....191 K6
Charlemont Primary School
HHTH/SAND B71 ....69 J5
Charles Street Industrial Estate
TPTN/OCK DY4 ....68 C3
Charnwood Business Park
BILS/COS WV14 ....51 K8
Charnwood County
Primary School
LICH WS13 ....21 G2
Charterfield Shopping Centre
KGSWFD DY6 ....83 H5
Chase Leisure Centre
CNCK/NC WS11 ....16 B3
Chase Park Industrial Estate
BNTWD WS7 ....18 B6
Chaseside Business Park
HEDN WS12 ....16 F2
Chase Terrace High School
BNTWD WS7 ....18 C5
Chase Terrace High School
BNTWD WS7 ....18 E6
Chase Terrace Primary School
BNTWD WS7 ....18 D5
Chase Terrace
Technology College
BNTWD WS7 ....18 D5
Chase Town CP School
BNTWD WS7 ....18 C8
Chase Town High School
BNTWD WS7 ....26 C1
Chasetown Industrial Estate
BNTWD WS7 ....18 C6
Chasewater Country Park
BNTWD WS7 ....18 A8
Chasewater Heaths
Business Park
BNTWD WS7 ....18 A6
BNTWD WS7 ....18 D4
Chasewater Industrial Estate
BNTWD WS7 ....18 C4
Chasewater Light Railway
CNCK/NC WS11 ....26 A2
Chase Watersports Centre
BRWNH WS8 ....26 A2

Chasewood Park
Business Centre
HEDN WS12 ....17 J4
Cheapside Industrial Estate
DIG/EDG B5 ....7 K8
Chelmsley Wood
Industrial Estate
CHWD/FDBR/MGN B37 ....92 E8
Chelmsley Wood
Shopping Centre
CHWD/FDBR/MGN B37 ....110 F3
Chelsea Trading Estate
AST/WIT B6 ....89 L7
Cherry Oak Special School
SLYOAK B29 ....124 B3
Cherry Orchard
Primary School
BFLD/HDSWWD B20 ....88 C2
Cherry Tree Sports Club
COVN CV6 ....134 C3
Cherry Trees Special School
WMBN WV5 ....64 D7
Cherrywood Industrial Estate
WASH/WDE B8 ....108 B2
Chesford Grange Hotel
KNWTH CV8 ....198 A5
Cheslyn Hay High School
GTWY WS6 ....23 M2
Cheslyn Hay Primary School
GTWY WS6 ....23 M2
Cheston Industrial Estate
AST/WIT B6 ....89 M6
Cheswick Green
Primary School
SHLY B90 ....148 C8
Chetwynd Junior School
NUN CV11 ....99 K6
Cheylesmore Welfare Clinic
COVS CV3 ....155 J7
Chilcote Primary School
HLGN/YWD B28 ....147 K1
Chillington Works
Industrial Estate
WOLV WV1 ....3 M7
Chilvers Coton Community
Infant School
NUNW/HART CV10 ....98 F2
Chinese Quarter
DIG/EDG B5 ....7 G7
The Chiropody Surgery
YDLY B25 ....109 H4
Chivenor Primary School
CVALE B35 ....91 L3
Christ Church CE Infant School
DUNHL/THL/PER WV6 ....2 D1
Christ Church CE Junior School
DUNHL/THL/PER WV6 ....49 G1
Christ Church CE
Primary School
BLOX/PEL WS3 ....39 H6
LICH WS13 ....20 D6
OLDBY B69 ....86 E5
SPARK B11 ....107 M6
Christ Church Infant School
DUNHL/THL/PER WV6 ....48 E2
Christ Church Junior School
BILS/COS WV14 ....67 H4
Christ Church School
PENK ST19 ....14 A3
Christ the King Catholic
Infant School
COVN CV6 ....133 K7
Christ the King RC
Junior School
COVN CV6 ....133 K6
Christ the King RC
Primary School
KGSTG B44 ....71 L4
Chuckery Primary School
WSL WS1 ....5 J4
Churchbridge Industrial Estate
OLDBY B69 ....86 D7
Churchfield Industrial Estate
DUDS DY2 ....85 G5
Church Hill Middle School
REDE B98 ....195 H7
Churchill & Blakedown
Golf Club
KIDD DY10 ....139 L3
Churchill Precinct
DUDS DY2 ....85 H4
Church Lane Health Centre
STECH B33 ....109 K2
Church Lane Industrial Estate
HHTH/SAND B71 ....69 G7
Church Lawford
Business Centre
RRUGBY CV23 ....158 E8
Church of Ascension CE
Primary School
COVS CV3 ....82 F5
Cineworld Cinema
RUGBYN/HIL CV21 ....160 F7
Cineworld Cinema
SOLH B91 ....149 G2
City Arcade
COV CV1 ....8 E5
City College Coventry
TLHL/CAN CV4 ....153 K4
City College East Birmingham
STECH B33 ....109 M5
City Estate
CDYHTH B64 ....103 H5
City Farm
COV CV1 ....9 J2
City Hospital NHS Trust
WSNGN B18 ....106 D1
City of Coventry-
Brandon Wood Golf Club
KNWTH CV8 ....157 G8
City Plaza Shopping Centre
CBHAM B2 ....6 F5
City Road Primary School
DIG/EDG B16 ....106 B2
The City Technology College
CHWD/FDBR/MGN B37 ....110 E1
City Trading Estate
LDYWD/EDGR B16 ....106 D2
City Walls & Gate
COV CV1 ....9 G3
Clapham Terrace County
Primary School
RLSS CV31 ....206 E6
Claregate Primary School
DUNHL/THL/PER WV6 ....35 K6
Clarendon House Hotel
KNWTH CV8 ....179 K7
Clarkes Industrial Estate
SCFLD/BOLD B73 ....72 E4
Clay Brook First School
REDE B98 ....203 K4
Clearwater Industrial Estate
BKHL/PFLD WV2 ....50 D6
Clent Hills
HAG/WOL DY9 ....120 E8
Clent Parochial First School
HAG/WOL DY9 ....141 J3
Cleton Street Business Centre
TPTN/OCK DY4 ....85 M2

Clifford Bridge Primary School
COVS CV3 ....156 E2
Clifton Infant School
BHTH/HG B12 ....107 L8
Clifton Junior School
BHTH/HG B12 ....107 L8
Clifton Road Industrial Estate
BHTH/HG B12 ....107 K8
Clifton upon Dunsmore CE
Primary School
RRUGBY CV23 ....161 M8
Clinton Combined School
KNWTH CV8 ....197 J2
The Clock Towers
Shopping Centre
RUGBYN/HIL CV21 ....186 E2
Closers Business Centre
NUN CV11 ....99 H3
Clothier Street Primary School
WLNHL WV13 ....51 L2
Cmt Industrial Estate
OLDBY B69 ....86 E5
Coach House Evening
Prep School
SCFLD/BOLD B73 ....72 D3
Coach House Special School
BRGRVE B60 ....190 F8
Coalpool Clinic
BLOX/PEL WS3 ....39 K7
Cobham Business Centre
WASH/WDE B8 ....108 C8
Cockshut Hill Technology
College
LGN/SDN/BHAMAIR B26 ....109 L5
Cocks Moors Woods
Leisure Centre
ALE/KHTH/YWD B14 ....146 D1
Codsall Clinic
CDSL WV8 ....34 E2
Codsall High School
CDSL WV8 ....34 E2
Codsall Middle School
CDSL WV8 ....34 D2
Cofton Medical Centre
NFLD/LBR B31 ....144 E6
Cofton Primary School
NFLD/LBR B31 ....144 E7
Coldland Colts FC
SOLH B91 ....128 D7
Colebourne Primary School
BKDE/SHDE B34 ....91 J8
Coleshill CE Primary School
CSHL/WTROR B46 ....93 K7
Coleshill Clinic
CSHL/WTROR B46 ....93 L7
Coleshill Heath Primary School
CHWD/FDBR/MGN B37 ....111 G4
Coleshill Industrial Estate
CSHL/WTROR B46 ....93 K3
Coleshill Leisure Centre
CSHL/WTROR B46 ....93 K5
Coleshill School
CSHL/WTROR B46 ....111 L2
Coleshill Town FC
CSHL/WTROR B46 ....111 L2
The College High School
ERDW/GRVHL B23 ....71 L7
College of Adult Education
WOLV WV1 ....3 G6
College of Continuing
Education
BLOX/PEL WS3 ....39 H7
Colley Lane Health Clinic
HALE B63 ....103 G7
Colley Lane Primary School
HALE B63 ....102 F7
Collingwood Primary School
WOLVN WV10 ....36 C3
Colmers Farm J & I School
RBRY B45 ....143 M5
Colmers Farm
Secondary School
RBRY B45 ....143 M5
Colmore J & I School
ALE/KHTH/YWD B14 ....125 H6
Colonial Industrial Park
CDYHTH B64 ....103 H6
Colton Hills School
ETTPK/GDPK/PENN WV4 ....65 M1
Combe Abbey Country Park
COVS CV3 ....156 F2
Comberton F & M School
KIDD DY10 ....164 F1
Combined Courts
WOLV WV1 ....3 H5
Comfort Inn
LDYWD/EDGR B16 ....106 B4
Common Lane
Industrial Estate
KNWTH CV8 ....180 A6
Community Leisure Centre
TPTN/OCK DY4 ....67 H7
Conduit Road Industrial Estate
CNCK/NC WS11 ....25 L1
Coneygre Industrial Estate
TPTN/OCK DY4 ....85 K2
Connect Business Park
WASH/WDE B8 ....108 A3
Conway Primary School
SPARK B11 ....107 M7
Cookley Wharf
Industrial Estate
BRLYHL DY5 ....101 L2
Cooper & Jordan CE
J & I School
ALDR WS9 ....41 G7
Copperfield House Hotel
SLYOAK B29 ....124 C2
Coppice High
Community School
WNSFLD WV11 ....37 L6
Coppice Junior School
HIA/OLT B92 ....128 C6
Coppice Primary School
HLYWD B47 ....146 K7
Coppice Primary School
MGN/WHC B75 ....57 G4
Coppice Side Industrial Estate
BRWNH WS8 ....26 B6
Coppice Trading Estate
KIDDW DY11 ....163 M5
Copt Heath Golf Club
DOR/KN B93 ....149 L5
Copthorne Hotel
BRLYHL DY5 ....102 C1
Copthorne Hotel
CBHAMNW B3 ....6 D5
Corbett Hospital
STRBR DY8 ....101 L6
Corbett Industrial Estate
DUDS DY2 ....85 G7
Corbett Infant School
SMTHWK B66 ....87 M8
Corley Cricket Club
RCOVN/BALC/EX CV7 ....115 G7
Corley School
RCOVN/BALC/EX CV7 ....114 F7
Corngreaves Hall Golf Club
CDYHTH B64 ....103 K5

Corngreaves J & I School
CDYHTH B64 ....103 H4
Corngreaves Trading Estate
CDYHTH B64 ....103 H6
Cornwall Industrial Estate
SMTHWK B66 ....88 A6
Cornwall Industrial Estate
WASH/WDE B8 ....108 A1
Cornwall Road Industrial Estate
SMTHWK B66 ....88 A6
Corpus Christi RC
Primary School
COVS CV3 ....156 B6
STECH B33 ....109 H3
WNSFLD WV11 ....37 L5
Coseley Medical Centre
BILS/COS WV14 ....67 G5
The Coseley School
BILS/COS WV14 ....66 F4
Coseley Swimming Pool &
Supachute
BILS/COS WV14 ....67 G5
Coten End Primary School
WWCK CV34 ....205 K6
Coton Green Primary School
CRTAM B79 ....31 K6
Cotteridge Primary School
BVILLE B30 ....124 C8
Cottesbrooke Infant School
ACGN B27 ....127 H1
Cottesbrooke Junior School
ACGN B27 ....127 G1
Cotwall End Primary School
SEDG DY3 ....66 A4
Coundon Court School &
Community College
COVN CV6 ....133 J8
COVN CV6 ....134 C6
Coundon Primary School
COVN CV6 ....133 J8
County Bridge
Primary School
WALW WS2 ....52 C4
Courtfarm Primary School
ERDW/GRVHL B23 ....72 C7
Courthouse Green
Primary School
COVN CV6 ....134 E5
Courtyard by Marriott
KNWTH CV8 ....182 B2
WWCK CV34 ....206 B8
Coventry Airport
COVS CV3 ....181 L4
Coventry Athletics Track
TLHL/CAN CV4 ....153 M7
Coventry Business Park
COVW CV5 ....154 B4
COVW CV5 ....154 D4
Coventry Cathedral &
Visitor Centre
COV CV1 ....9 G4
Coventry City FC
(Highfield Road Stadium)
COVE CV2 ....9 L3
Coventry Golf Club
KNWTH CV8 ....181 K6
Coventry Grammar School
COVW CV5 ....154 D4
Coventry Hearsall Golf Club
COVW CV5 ....154 D5
Coventry Muslim School
COVN CV6 ....134 C4
Coventry Preparatory School
COVW CV5 ....154 F5
Coventry RFC
COVN CV6 ....8 B2
Coventry Sports Centre
WOLVN WV10 ....9 H4
Coventry Technical College
COV CV1 ....8 B6
The Coventry Toy Museum
COV CV1 ....9 H5
Coventry Trading Estate
KNWTH CV8 ....182 A3
Coventry University
COV CV1 ....9 H5
Coventry University
Technocentre
COV CV1 ....9 G7
Coventry & Warwickshire
Hospital
COV CV1 ....9 G1
Coventry Welsh RFC
COVN CV6 ....134 B1
c/PLEX (Under Development)
WBROM B70 ....87 H2
Crabbs Cross Medical Centre
REDW B97 ....202 C7
Crabtree Clinic
CHWD/FDBR/MGN B37 ....110 D3
Cradley CE Primary School
HALE B63 ....103 G6
Cradley Heath Community
Recreation Centre
DUDS DY2 ....103 J4
Cradley High School
HALE B63 ....102 F7
Cradley Town FC
HALE B63 ....121 G1
Craig Croft Child Health Clinic
CHWD/FDBR/MGN B37 ....111 G4
Craig Croft Medical Centre
CHWD/FDBR/MGN B37 ....111 G3
Cranmore Industrial Estate
SHLY B90 ....148 C5
Cranmore Infant School
SOLH B91 ....148 C4
Crescent Industrial Park
DUDS DY2 ....84 F6
The Crescent School
RUGBYS/DCH CV22 ....186 B5
Crescent Theatre
LDYWD/EDGR B16 ....6 B6
Crescent Works Industrial Park
DARL/WED WS10 ....52 B4
Crestwood Park
Primary School
KGSWFD DY6 ....83 L8
The Crestwood
Secondary School
KGSWFD DY6 ....83 K8
Criterion Theatre
COVW CV5 ....8 A9
Crocketts Lane Primary School
SMTHWK B66 ....87 L8
Croft Foundry Industrial Estate
WLNHL WV13 ....51 L3
Croft Industrial Estate
CHWD/FDBR/MGN B37 ....110 D3
Croft Industrial Estate
CHWD/FDBR/MGN B37 ....111 H4
Croft Junior School
NUNW/HART CV10 ....98 C2
Croft Medical Centre
RLSS CV31 ....207 G8
Croft Street JMI School
WSLW WS2 ....53 H1
Cromwell Primary School
VAUX/NECH B7 ....89 L7

Cronehill Primary School
WBROM B70 ....[..]
Cronehills Health Centre
WBROM B70 ....[..]
Crossfield Industrial Estate
LICH WS13 ....[..]
Crossley Retail Park
BLOX/PEL WS3 ....[..]
Crossley Retail Park
KIDDW DY11 13
Cross Quays Business Park
OLDBY B69 ....[..]
Cross Road Industrial Estate
COVN CV6 ....[..]
Cross Street Health Centre
DUDN DY1 ....[..]
Crossways Shopping Centre
CBHAMW B1 ....[..]
Crowne Plaza Hotel
CBHAMW B1 ....[..]
Crown Meadow First School
ALVE B48 17
Crown Wharf Shopping Centre
WSLW WS2 ....[..]
Crown Wharf Shopping Park
WSLW WS2 ....[..]
Crystal Leisure Centre
STRBR DY8 10
Cubbington CE Primary School
RLSN CV32 15
Culwell Industrial Park
WOLVN WV10 ....[..]
Culwell Trading Estate
WOLVN WV10 ....[..]
Curdworth Primary School
WALM/CURD B76 ....[..]
Dadsford Bridge
Industrial Estate
STRBR DY8 ....[..]
Dalehouse Lane
Industrial Estate
KNWTH CV8 18
Dame Elizabeth Cadbury
School
BVILLE B30 ....[..]
Dame Ellen Pinsent School
HRBN B17 ....[..]
Damson Wood Infant School
HIA/OLT B92 ....[..]
Danesmore Park
Primary School
WNSFLD WV11 ....[..]
Darlaston Central
Trading Estate
DARL/WED WS10 ....[..]
Darlaston Clinic
DARL/WED WS10 ....[..]
Darlaston Community School
DARL/WED WS10 ....[..]
Darlaston FC
DARL/WED WS10 ....[..]
Darlaston Road
Industrial Estate
DARL/WED WS10 ....[..]
Dartmouth Golf Club
HHTH/SAND B71 ....[..]
Dartmouth High School
GTB/HAM B43 ....[..]
Dartmouth Special School
COVE CV2 13
Davenport Lodge School
COVW CV5 ....[..]
David Lloyd Birmingham
KGSTG B44 7
Daw End School
RUSH/SHEL WS4 ....[..]
Dawley Brook Primary School
KGSWFD DY6 ....[..]
Dawley Trading Estate
KGSWFD DY6 ....[..]
Daylesford Infant School
HIA/OLT B92 ....[..]
Days Inn
CBHAMW B1 ....[..]
Deanery CE Primary School
WALM/CURD B76 ....[..]
Deansfield High School
WOLV WV1 ....[..]
Deedmore Special School
COVE CV2 13
Deeleys Industrial Estate
WSLW WS2 ....[..]
Deepdale Industrial Estate
DUDN DY1 ....[..]
The Dell Stadium
BRLYHL DY5 ....[..]
Delph Road Industrial Park
BRLYHL DY5 10
Delta Business Centre
CNCK/NC WS11 ....[..]
Delta Trading Estate
BKHL/PFLD WV2 ....[..]
Delves J & I School
DSYBK/YTR WS5 ....[..]
De Montfort Hotel
KNWTH CV8 19
Dental Health Centre
KGSTG B44 ....[..]
Dental Hospital
CBHAMNE B4 ....[..]
Department of Art (UCE)
CBHAMNW B3 ....[..]
The De Vere Belfry Hotel
WALM/CURD B76 ....[..]
Devonshire J & I School
SMTHWKW B67 ....[..]
Deykin Avenue J & I School
AST/WIT B6 ....[..]
D'Eyncourt Primary School
WNSFLD WV11 ....[..]
Diana Princess of Wales
Hospital (for Children)
CBHAMNE B4 ....[..]
Dickens Heath
Primary School
SHLY B90 ....[..]
Digbeth Coach Station
DIG/EDG B5 ....[..]
Dingle Primary School
KGSWFD DY6 ....[..]
Dingleside Middle School
REDE B98 20
Dock Lane Industrial Estate
DUDN DY1 ....[..]
Dock Meadow Drive
Industrial Estate
ETTPK/GDPK/PENN WV4 ....[..]
Dodford First School
BRGRVW B61 ....[..]
Dolphin Sports Centre
BRGRVE B60 ....[..]
Doranda Way Industrial Park
HHTH/SAND B71 ....[..]
Dordon Primary School
POL/KCSB/FAZ B78 ....[..]
Dormston Secondary School
SEDG DY3 ....[..]
Dormston Trading Estate
DUDN DY1 ....[..]

othy Pattison Hospital
/SLW WS2 ... 52 F4
othy Purcell Junior School
ILS/COS WV14 ... 67 M2
ridge Cricket Club ... 175 J4
ridge J & I School
OR/KN B93 ... 175 J4
rington Primary School
BAR/PBCH B42 ... 70 E7
thill Primary School
AR/WIL B77 ... 46 A8
lton Trading Estate
LKHTH/ROWR B65 ... 103 K1
recote J & I School
DSL WV8 ... 35 J4
Dovecote Surgery
GLYGN/OTN B68 ... 105 H6
ning Close Health Clinic
OR/KN B93 ... 175 L1
yton Court Hotel
OL/KGSB/FAZ B78 ... 45 L5
yton Manor
heme Park & Zoo
OL/KGSB/FAZ B78 ... 45 K5
yton Park Golf Club
OL/KGSB/FAZ B78 ... 45 K6
amwell Industrial Estate
DLY B25 ... 108 D7
fold Gallery
CFLD/BOLD B73 ... 72 F8
s Monument
icon Industrial Estate
LKHTH/ROWR B65 ... 85 M8
Dr Phillips
hopping Centre
OVE CV2 ... 135 H4
ids Heath Golf Club
LDR WS9 ... 41 G5
ddeston Mill Trading Estate
WASH/WDE B8 ... 108 A1
ley Central Trading Estate
UDS DY1 ... 84 F5
ley College
UDN DY1 ... 84 F3
ley College
(mons Hill Campus)
UDN DY1 ... 84 F1
ley Golf Club
RLYHL DY5 ... 102 C1
ley Golf Club
LKHTH/ROWR B65 ... 85 K1
ley Kingswinford RFC
GSWFD DY6 ... 82 E6
ley Leisure Centre
UDN DY1 ... 84 F4
ley Museum & Art Gallery
UDN DY1 ... 85 G4
ley Town Hall
UDN DY1 ... 85 G4
ley Water Sports Centre
UDS DY2 ... 102 F2
ley Wood Primary School
UDS DY3 ... 103 G3
ley Zoo & Castle
UDN DY1 ... 85 H3
nstall Hill Industrial Estate
UHL/THL/PER WV6 ... 36 A4
nstall Hill Primary School
UHNL/THL/PER WV6 ... 50 A1
nton Trading Estate
VAUX/NECH B7 ... 90 B6
rbar Avenue
Industrial Estate
OVN CV6 ... 134 B5
rberville Road
Industrial Estate
BKHL/PFLD WV2 ... 50 D6
le Industrial Estate
VBROM B70 ... 68 C5
le Trading Estate
VALE B63 ... 121 L1
Place Business Park
LHL/CAN CV4 ... 153 M4
lsdon Business Centre
OVW CV5 ... 154 D5
lsdon Primary School
OVW CV5 ... 8 A1
ls High School
OVW CV5 ... 121 M1
iswood School
RDW/GRVHL B23 ... 90 C3
iswood Trading Estate
HOCK/TIA B94 ... 173 G7
tbourne House School
ACGN B27 ... 127 G1
st Cannock
Industrial Estate
HEDN WS12 ... 16 F2
stern Green Junior School
OVW CV5 ... 132 B8
stfield Primary School
WOLV WV1 ... 3 M5
stlands County
Primary School
RUGBYN/HIL CV21 ... 187 H3
stlands Court
Business Centre
RUGBYN/HIL CV21 ... 187 G2
st Park J & I School
WOLV WV1 ... 50 F5
st Park Trading Estate
WOLV WV1 ... 3 M8
stwood Business Village ... 156 D4
on Wood Medical Centre
RDE/BCHGN B24 ... 91 H2
ook Adult Training Centre
SCFLD/WYGN B72 ... 73 H2
pse Industrial Estate
TPTN/OCK DY4 ... 67 J8
pse Trading Estate
TPTN/OCK DY4 ... 67 J8
gar Stammers J & I School
BLOX/PEL WS3 ... 39 K6
gbaston Golf Club
EDG B15 ... 106 F2
gbaston Health Clinic
EDG B15 ... 106 C8
gbaston Health Clinic
SOLH B91 ... 127 M3
gbaston High School for Girls
& Prep Department
EDG B15 ... 106 D1
gbaston Shopping Centre
EDG B16 ... 106 E5
gewick Community
Primary School
COVN CV6 ... 134 C5
gewood Road Clinic
RBRY B45 ... 143 M7
wick Park
Industrial Estate
OVN CV6 ... 134 D5
ndscote Track
OV CV32 ... 206 B6
rd Street Hospital
BROM B70 ... 87 G2

Electra Park Industrial Estate
AST/WIT B6 ... 89 M4
Electric Cinema
DIG/EDG B5 ... 6
Elgar House Surgery
REDW B97 ... 202 C1
Elliott's Field Retail Park
RUGBYN/HIL CV21 ... 160 F6
The Ellowes Hall School
SEDG DY3 ... 66 A8
Elmdon Trading Estate
CHWD/FDBR/MGN B37 ... 111 G7
Elmore Green JMI School
BLOX/PEL WS3 ... 38 E4
Elms Farm Primary School
LGN/SDN/BHAMAIR B26 ... 110 A4
Elms Health Centre
HALE B63 ... 102 F7
Elm Street Infant School
WLNHL WV13 ... 52 A2
Elm Terrace Clinic
OLDBY B69 ... 85 M4
Elston Hall Primary School
WOLVN WV10 ... 36 B3
Ely House Hotel
BDMR/CCFT WV3 ... 2
Embassy Industrial Estate
HAG/WOL DY9 ... 102 D8
Empire Industrial Park
ALDR WS9 ... 40 D4
Emscote County
Infant School
WWCK CV34 ... 205 M5
Emscote House School
RLSN CV32 ... 206 B5
Enfield Industrial Estate
REDW B97 ... 194 B8
English Martyrs RC
Primary School
RUGBYN/HIL CV21 ... 187 K6
SPARK B11 ... 126 A1
Ensign Business Centre
TLHL/CAN CV4 ... 153 K7
Enterprise Industrial Park
LICHS WS13 ... 21 K5
Erasmus Darwin Centre
LICH WS13 ... 20 E5
Erdington Hall Primary School
ERDE/BCHGN B24 ... 90 D3
Erdington Industrial Park
ERDE/BCHGN B24 ... 91 K1
Erdington Medical Centre
ERDE/BCHGN B24 ... 90 C3
Erdington Pool & Turkish Suite
ERDW/GRVHL B23 ... 90 C1
Ernesford Grange
Primary School
COVS CV3 ... 156 C4
Ernesford Grange School &
Community School
COVS CV3 ... 156 B5
Essington Light
Industrial Estate
WNSFLD WV11 ... 37 L1
Etone Community School
NUN CV11 ... 81 H8
Etone Sports Centre
NUN CV11 ... 81 H8
Ettingshall Primary School
BILS/COS WV14 ... 50 F1
Euro Business Park
OLDBY B69 ... 86 C4
European Business Park
OLDBY B69 ... 86 C6
Eversfield Preparatory School
SOLH B91 ... 149 G1
Exchange Industrial Estate
CNCK/NC WS11 ... 16 C7
Exhall Business Park
RCOVN/BALC/EX CV7 ... 116 F5
Exhall Cedars Infant School
RCOVN/BALC/EX CV7 ... 116 F5
Exhall Grange Special School
RCOVN/BALC/EX CV7 ... 116 E3
Express by Holiday Inn
COVS CV3 ... 180 F1
CSHL/WTROR B46 ... 111 K6
CVALE B35 ... 91 L4
GTB/HAM B43 ... 70 C1
HLGN/YWD B28 ... 126 E7
LICHS WS14 ... 28 E7
RUGBYN/HIL CV21 ... 160 F5
Express by Holiday Inn
(Birchley Park)
OLDBY B69 ... 86 C2
Expressway Industrial Estate
AST/WIT B6 ... 89 J7
Eye Infirmary
BDMR/CCFT WV3 ... 2
Fairey Industrial Estate
TAM/AM/WIL B77 ... 46 B8
Fairfax School
MGN/WHC B75 ... 57 M4
Fairfield First School
BRGRVW B61 ... 168 B3
Fairfield Villa FC
BRGRVW B61 ... 168 B3
Fairhaven Primary School
STRBR DY8 ... 101 M2
The Fairlawns at Aldridge
Hotel
ALDR WS9 ... 41 J7
Fair View Industrial Estate
WALM/CURD B76 ... 74 F4
Fairway Primary School
HWK/WKHTH B38 ... 145 H3
Falcon Lodge Clinic
MGN/WHC B75 ... 57 L8
Fallings Park
Industrial Estate
WOLVN WV10 ... 36 D8
Fallings Park Primary School
WOLVN WV10 ... 36 E6
Falstaff Hotel
RLSN CV32 ... 206 D4
Fazeley Health Centre
POL/KGSB/FAZ B78 ... 45 L3
Fazeley Industrial Estate
DIG/EDG B5 ... 7 K5
Featherstone Health Centre
WOLVN WV10 ... 22 H4
Featherstone Primary School
ERDW/GRVHL B23 ... 90 C1
Feldon Lane Clinic
RMSLY B62 ... 104 C6
Fernbank Medical Centre
WASH/WDE B8 ... 108 E1
Ferndale Primary School
GTB/HAM B43 ... 70 C6
Field Road Industrial Estate
BLOX/PEL WS3 ... 39 G4
Fillongley CE School
RCOVN/BALC/EX CV7 ... 114 B2
Finham Park School
COVS CV3 ... 180 E1
Finham Primary School
COVS CV3 ... 180 E4
Finstall First School
BRGRVE B60 ... 191 M4

Firs Industrial Estate
STRPT B33 ... 164 A6
Firs Primary School
CBROM B36 ... 91 J5
Fir Tree Primary School
DSYBK/YTR WS5 ... 69 L1
Five Ways Primary School
HEDN WS12 ... 17 H3
Five Ways Shopping Centre
EDG B15 ... 6 A8
Flax Hill Junior School
LBR B79 ... 31 M6
Flemings Hotel
HIA/OLT B92 ... 127 J4
Fletchamstead Highway
Industrial Estate
COVW CV5 ... 154 B6
Fletchworth Gate
Industrial Estate
COVW CV5 ... 154 A5
Florendine Primary School
TAM/AM/WIL B77 ... 32 D8
Foleshill Cemetery
COVN CV6 ... 134 E3
Foleshill CE Primary School
COVN CV6 ... 134 E3
Foleshill Leisure Centre
COVN CV6 ... 134 B6
Foley Business Park
KIDDW DY11 ... 163 M5
Foley Industrial Estate
KIDDW DY11 ... 164 A3
Foley Industrial Park
KIDDW DY11 ... 164 A4
Foley Park First School
KIDDW DY11 ... 164 A2
The Foot Clinic
CBHAMNW B3 ... 6 E4
Fordbridge Infant School
CHWD/FDBR/MGN B37 ... 92 F8
Fordhouse Road
Industrial Estate
WOLVN WV10 ... 36 A5
Fordhouses Cricket Club
WOLVN WV10 ... 36 B1
Fords Hospital
COV CV1 ... 8 E5
Forest Glades Leisure Centre
KIDD DY10 ... 138 C7
Forest Hotel
DOR/KN B93 ... 175 K3
Forest Oak School
CBROM B36 ... 92 C4
Forge Mill Needle Museum
REDE B98 ... 194 D7
Forge Trading Estate
RMSLY B62 ... 104 A8
Formans Trading Estate
SPARK B11 ... 126 B2
Fort Industrial Park
ERDE/BCHGN B24 ... 91 K4
The Fort Shopping Park
ERDE/BCHGR B24 ... 91 G4
Forum Health Centre
COVE CV2 ... 156 B1
Fosse Wayside
Industrial Estate
RUGBYN/HIL CV21 ... 187 H1
Foundry Primary School
WSNGN B18 ... 88 B7
Fountain Court Hotel
LDYWD/EDGR B16 ... 106 A4
Four Dwellings High School
RIDG/WDGT B32 ... 104 E4
Four Dwellings Infant School
RIDG/WDGT B32 ... 104 F4
Four Dwellings Junior School
RIDG/WDGT B32 ... 104 F4
Four Oaks J & I School
FOAKS/STRLY B74 ... 56 C1
Four Oaks Medical Centre
MGN/WHC B75 ... 56 C1
Four Oaks Saints Cricket Club
FOAKS/STRLY B74 ... 42 C8
Four Seasons Art Gallery
ERDE/BCHGN B24 ... 72 E8
Foxford School &
Community Arts College
COVN CV6 ... 116 E8
Fox & Goose Shopping Centre
WASH/WDE B8 ... 91 G8
The Fox Hollies Leisure Centre
ACGN B27 ... 126 E4
Fox Hollies Special School
ACGN B27 ... 126 E4
Fox Hotel International
BKHL/PFLD WV2 ... 2 E7
Foxmill Estate
SPARK B11 ... 126 B3
Foxyards Primary School
TPTN/OCK DY4 ... 67 G8
Frank F Harrison
Comprehensive School
WSLW WS2 ... 38 D6
Frank Halfpenny Hall
LICH WS13 ... 21 G5
Frankley Community
High School
RBRY B45 ... 143 K3
Frankley Health Centre
RBRY B45 ... 143 L4
Frankley Industrial Park
RBRY B45 ... 143 M4
Frank Whittle Primary School
COVE CV2 ... 135 K5
Frederick Bird Primary School
COV CV1 ... 134 D8
Friar Park Clinic
DARL/WED WS10 ... 69 H2
Friary Grange Sports Centre
LICH WS13 ... 20 D3
The Friary School
LICH WS13 ... 20 C3
Frogmill Junior School
RBRY B45 ... 143 M3
Fulfen Primary School
BNTWD WS7 ... 19 H6
Fulford Heath Golf Club
HLYWD B47 ... 172 F3
Gainsborough House Hotel
KIDDW DY11 ... 137 M8
Gainsborough Trading Estate
STRBR DY8 ... 119 M1
Gallagher Business Park
RCOVN/BALC/EX CV7 ... 134 C1
Gallagher Retail Park
COVN CV6 ... 134 D5
Galley Common Infant School
NUNW/HART CV10 ... 79 K8
Galley Common Medical Centre
NUNW/HART CV10 ... 97 K1
Gannow Middle School
RBRY B45 ... 143 H6

Garretts Green Trading Estate
STETCH B33 ... 110 A4
Gas Street Basin
CBHAMW B1 ... 6 C6
Gatehouse Trading Estate
BRWNH WS8 ... 26 E4
Gate Medical Centre
OLDBY B69 ... 90 B7
Gay Hill Golf Club
HLYWD B47 ... 146 E5
George Auden School
NFLD/LBR B31 ... 123 K8
George Betts Primary School
SMTHWK B66 ... 87 G6
George Dixon Lower School
HRBN B17 ... 106 A4
George Dixon School &
6th Form
HRBN B17 ... 106 A3
The George Eliot Hospital
NHS Trust
NUNW/HART CV10 ... 98 F3
George Eliot School
NUNW/HART CV10 ... 99 H4
George Fentham J & I School
HIA/OLT B92 ... 129 L7
The George Hotel
BEWD DY12 ... 162 E2
The George Hotel
LICH WS13 ... 20 F5
George Salter High School
WBROM B70 ... 86 E1
Gibbons Industrial Park
KGSWFD DY6 ... 83 L6
The Giffard RC Primary School
DUNHL/THL/PER WV6 ... 35 K8
Gig Mill Primary School
STRBR DY8 ... 119 J2
Gilbertstone Primary School
LGN/SDN/BHAMAIR B26 ... 109 H8
G K Davies Industrial Estate
HAG/WOL DY9 ... 102 E7
Glascote Comprehensive
School
TAM/AM/WIL B77 ... 46 D4
Glascote Health Centre
TAM/AM/WIL B77 ... 46 D3
Glascote Heath
Primary School
TAM/AM/WIL B77 ... 46 D3
Glebe Farm Industrial Estate
RUGBYN/HIL CV21 ... 160 D6
Glebefields Health Centre
TPTN/OCK DY4 ... 67 L5
Glebe Fields Primary School
TPTN/OCK DY4 ... 67 L4
Glendale Infant School
NUNW/HART CV10 ... 98 D3
Glemmead J & I School
PBAR/PBCH B42 ... 71 H5
Glenthorne CP School
GTWY WS6 ... 24 C2
Glynne Primary School
KGSWFD DY6 ... 101 G1
Godiva Trading Estate
COVN CV6 ... 134 D5
Golden Hillock School
SPARK B11 ... 108 B7
The Golden Lion Inn
RRUGBY CV23 ... 159 J1
Goldtel Industrial Estate
ETTPK/GDPK/PENN WV4 ... 50 E8
Goldthorne Medical Centre
ETTPK/GDPK/PENN WV4 ... 50 A7
Goldthorn Park Primary School
ETTPK/GDPK/PENN WV4 ... 50 B8
Good Hope Hospital
MGN/WHC B75 ... 57 H7
Good Shepherd RC
Primary School
COVN CV6 ... 134 D4
Goodyers End Primary School
RCOVN/BALC/EX CV7 ... 116 C5
Gornal Wood Crematorium
SEDC DY3 ... 83 M4
Gorsemoor Primary School
HEDN WS12 ... 17 H4
Goscote Hospital
BLOX/PEL WS3 ... 39 K5
Goscote Industrial Estate
BLOX/PEL WS3 ... 39 J4
Gosford Industrial Estate
COVS CV3 ... 9 K5
Gosford Park Primary School
COVS CV3 ... 9 M6
Gossey Lane J & I School
STETCH B33 ... 110 A3
The GPT Golf Club
COVS CV3 ... 156 B4
Gracechurch Shopping Centre
SCFLD/BOLD B73 ... 56 F8
Grace Mary Primary School
OLDBY B69 ... 86 A6
Grafton Manor House
BRGRVW B61 ... 190 F6
Graiseley Primary School
BKHL/PFLD WV2 ... 2 E9
The Granary Hotel
KIDD DY10 ... 165 H5
Granby Business Park
STETCH B33 ... 110 A4
Grand Theatre
WOLV WV1 ... 3 G4
The Grange Arts & Media Centre
WSL WS1 ... 4 F7
Grange Farm Primary School
COVW CV5 ... 154 F8
Grangehurst Primary School
COVN CV6 ... 134 F1
The Grange Playhouse
DSYBK/YTR WS5 ... 5 M4
The Grange School
HAG/WOL DY9 ... 120 B1
Gravel Hill Surgery
WMBN WV5 ... 64 F7
Gravelly Industrial Park
VAUX/NECH B7 ... 90 C5
Grazebrook Industrial Estate
DUDS DY2 ... 84 E7
Grazebrook Industrial Park
DUDS DY2 ... 84 F7
Great Barr Business Park
PBAR/PBCH B42 ... 70 E8
Great Barr Golf Club
GTB/HAM B43 ... 70 D1
Great Barr Hotel &
Conference Centre
GTB/HAM B43 ... 69 M4
Great Bridge Industrial Estate
TPTN/OCK DY4 ... 68 A6
Great Bridge Primary School
TPTN/OCK DY4 ... 68 A7
Great Central Way
Industrial Estate
RUGBYN/HIL CV21 ... 187 H1
Great Western Industrial Estate
WSNGN B18 ... 88 C7

Great Wyrley High School
GTWY WS6 ... 24 D1
Green Acres Primary School
BILS/COS WV14 ... 51 K7
Greenacres Primary School
TAM/AM/WIL B77 ... 32 F8
Greenfield Primary School
RUSH/SHEL WS4 ... 40 A5
Greenfield Primary School
STRBR DY8 ... 101 K8
Greenfield Surgery
STRBR DY8 ... 101 K8
Greenhill Health Centre
LICH WS13 ... 21 G5
Greenhill Industrial Estate
KIDD DY10 ... 138 E6
Greenholm J & I School
KGSTG B44 ... 71 J6
Green Industrial Estate
HEDN WS12 ... 13 G6
Greenlands Business Centre
REDE B98 ... 202 C1
Green Lane Industrial Estate
BORD B9 ... 108 C3
Green Meadow
Primary School
SLYOAK B29 ... 123 K8
Green Rock J & I School
BLOX/PEL WS3 ... 39 J4
Green Street Trading Estate
KIDD DY10 ... 138 C8
Greet Primary School
SPARK B11 ... 126 B1
Greets Green Road
Industrial Estate
WBROM B70 ... 86 D4
Gregston Industrial Estate
OLDBY B69 ... 86 F5
Grendon Primary School
ALE/KHTH/YWD B14 ... 146 C2
Grestone Primary School
BFLD/HDSWWD B20 ... 88 C4
Greswold Primary School
SOLH B91 ... 127 M7
Greysbrooke CP School
LICHS WS14 ... 28 E7
Griff Clara Industrial Estate
NUNW/HART CV10 ... 98 C6
Griffin Business Park
CHWD/FDBR/MGN B37 ... 111 G8
Griffin Industrial Estate
OLDBY B69 ... 104 D2
Griffins Brook Medical Centre
SLYOAK B29 ... 124 A6
The Griff School
BDWTH CV12 ... 116 F2
Grimstock Country House
Hotel
CSHL/WTROR B46 ... 93 J4
The Grinnall Business Centre
STRPT DY13 ... 188 F4
Grosvenor Hotel
RUGBYN/HIL CV21 ... 186 F2
Grosvenor Shopping Centre
NFLD/LBR B31 ... 144 E1
Grovelands Industrial Estate
RCOVN/BALC/EX CV7 ... 116 F7
Grove Medical Centre
CNCK/NC WS11 ... 16 C7
Grove Park Industrial Estate
CNCK/NC WS11 ... 16 C7
Grove Primary School
BKHL/PFLD WV2 ... 3
Grove School
HDSW B21 ... 88 D5
Grove Vale Primary School
GTB/HAM B43 ... 70 B4
Guardian Angels RC
Primary School
BKDE/SHDE B34 ... 92 B7
Guest Hospital
DUDN DY1 ... 85 J2
Gulson Hospital
COV CV1 ... 9 J5
Gulson Road Clinic
COV CV1 ... 9 J5
Gun Barrel Industrial Centre
CDYHTH B64 ... 103 K6
Gun Hill Infant School
RCOVN/BALC/EX CV7 ... 96 C5
Guns Village Primary School
WBROM B70 ... 86 E2
Gunter Primary School
ERDE/BCHGN B24 ... 91 J1
Gupta Trading Estate
OLDBY B69 ... 86 D4
Guy Motors Industrial Park
WOLVN WV10 ... 36 C8
GWS Industrial Estate
DARL/WED WS10 ... 68 B4
GWS Trading Estate
TPTN/OCK DY4 ... 68 B4
Habberley Golf Club
KIDDW DY11 ... 137 J2
Haden Hill Leisure Centre
CDYHTH B64 ... 103 K5
Hadley Stadium
SMTHWK B66 ... 105 L2
Hagley F & M School
HAG/WOL DY9 ... 119 M8
Hagley Golf & Country Club
HAG/WOL DY9 ... 120 C8
Hagley Hall
HAG/WOL DY9 ... 120 C7
Hagley RC High School
STRBR DY8 ... 119 K7
Haigs Hotel
RCOVN/BALC/EX CV7 ... 151 M6
Halas Industrial Estate
HALE B63 ... 103 M8
Halcyon Gallery
CBHAM B2 ... 6 F6
Halesbury Special School
RMSLY B62 ... 104 C5
Hales Industrial Park
COVN CV6 ... 134 C1
Halesowen CC
HALE B63 ... 121 M3
Halesowen CE Primary School
HALE B63 ... 121 L1
Halesowen College
HALE B63 ... 103 M8
Halesowen FC (The Grove
Recreation Ground)
HALE B63 ... 103 L8
Halesowen Golf Club
RMSLY B62 ... 104 B8
Halesowen Harriers FC
HALE B63 ... 102 F8
Halesowen Health Centre
HALE B63 ... 121 M2
Halesowen Industrial Park
RMSLY B62 ... 103 L8
Halesowen Leisure Centre
HALE B63 ... 121 M2
Halesowen Magistrates Court
HALE B63 ... 121 M2
Hale Trading Estate
TPTN/OCK DY4 ... 67 M8

Hallfield School
 EDG B15 ....106 E6
Hall Green J & I School
 HHTH/SAND B71 ....69 G4
Hall Green J & I School
 HLGN/YWD B28 ....126 C6
Hall Green Little Theatre
 ACGN B27 ....126 E3
Hall Green Secondary School
 HLGN/YWD B28 ....126 C5
Hall Green Stadium
 HLGN/YWD B28 ....126 D4
Hallmoor Special School
 STECH B33 ....109 M2
Hall of Memory
 CBHAMW B1 ....6 D5
Hamd House School
 SMHTH B10 ....108 C5
Ham Dingle Primary School
 HAG/WOL DY9 ....120 A3
Hamilton Special School
 HDSW B21 ....88 B5
Hammerwich Hospital
 BNTWD WS7 ....18 F8
Hammond Business Centre
 NUN CV11 ....99 J2
Hams Hall International
 Freight Terminal
 CSHL/WTROR B46 ....93 L2
Hams Hall National
 Distribution Park
 WALM/CURD B76 ....93 M1
Hamstead Hall School
 BFLD/HDSWWD B20 ....70 C7
Hamstead J & I School
 GTB/HAM B43 ....70 B6
Hanburys Farm Community
 Primary School
 TAM/AM/WIL B77 ....46 B4
Handsworth Boys
 Grammar School
 HDSW B21 ....88 C5
Handsworth Cemetery
 HDSW B21 ....87 M3
Handsworth Golf Club
 BFLD/HDSWWD B20 ....88 B1
Handsworth Leisure Centre
 BFLD/HDSWWD B20 ....88 D5
Handsworth Rugby Club
 DSYBK/YTR WS5 ....70 B1
Handsworth Technical College
 HDSW B21 ....88 E6
Handsworth Wood Girls School
 & Sixth Form Centre
 BFLD/HDSWWD B20 ....88 D3
Hanford Close
 Industrial Estate
 COVN CV6 ....134 C7
Hanover International Hotel
 & Club
 BRGRVW B61 ....191 H3
Harborne Church Farm
 Golf Club
 HRBN B17 ....123 M1
Harborne Golf Club
 RIDG/WDGT B32 ....105 L8
Harborne Hill School
 EDG B15 ....106 C7
Harborne Pool &
 Fitness Centre
 HRBN B17 ....105 M8
Harborne Primary School
 HRBN B17 ....106 A7
Harden Primary School
 BLOX/PEL WS3 ....39 J6
Hargate Primary School
 HHTH/SAND B71 ....87 G1
Harnall Lane Industrial Estate
 COV CV1 ....9 H1
Harnall Lane Medical Centre
 COV CV1 ....9 H1
The Harper Bell School
 BHTH/HG B12 ....107 L5
Harriers Industrial Estate
 KIDD DY10 ....138 D8
Harris CE High School
 RUGBYS/DCH CV22 ....186 D4
Harrisons Institute & Sports Club
 GTWY WS6 ....24 E4
Harry Mitchell Leisure Centre
 SMTHWK B67 ....87 K8
The Harry Taylor First School
 REDW B97 ....202 C4
Hartlebury Castle
 KIDDW DY11 ....189 K2
Hartlebury CE School
 KIDDW DY11 ....189 K2
Hartshill Hayes Country Park
 NUNW/HART CV10 ....79 L4
Hartshill School
 NUNW/HART CV10 ....79 M5
Harvey Road Health Centre
 LGN/SDN/BHAMAIR B26 ....109 J6
Harvey Works
 Industrial Estate
 HALE B63 ....103 K7
Harvills Hawthorn
 Primary School
 WBROM B70 ....68 D6
Harvington Hall
 KIDD DY10 ....165 M4
Hasbury CE Primary School
 HALE B63 ....121 K3
Haslucks Green Junior School
 SHLY B90 ....147 L2
Hastingwood Industrial Park
 ERDE/BCHGN B24 ....90 F4
Hatchford Brook Golf Club
 LGN/SDN/BHAMAIR B26 ....128 C1
Hatchford Brook
 Primary School
 HIA/OLT B92 ....128 A2
Hatchford Gm Primary School
 CHWD/FDBR/MGN B37 ....110 D3
Hateley Heath Primary School
 HHTH/SAND B71 ....68 F6
Hathern Lane Primary School
 WSLW WS2 ....38 D7
Haunchwood Park
 Industrial Estate
 NUNW/HART CV10 ....97 J1
Havergal CE Primary School
 WOLVN WV10 ....23 G3
Hawbush Primary School
 BRLYHL DY5 ....101 M3
Hawkesbury Field School
 COVE CV2 ....135 G2
Hawkesbury Lock
 Industrial Centre
 RCOVN/BALC/EX CV7 ....116 F7
Hawkes Green Medical Centre
 CNCK/NC WS11 ....17 G3
Hawkesley Church
 Primary School
 HWK/WKHTH B38 ....145 J6
Hawkesley Health Centre
 HWK/WKHTH B38 ....145 J6
Hawkins Colliery Sports Club
 GTWY WS6 ....24 B1

Hawkins Sports Club
 GTWY WS6 ....24 B1
Hawksmill Industrial Estate
 BORD B9 ....108 A4
Hawthorne Primary School
 KGSTG B44 ....71 L6
Hawthorns Business Centre
 SMTHWK B66 ....87 L5
Hawthorns Industrial Estate
 SMTHWK B66 ....87 M5
Haybridge High School
 STRBR DY8 ....119 K7
Hayes Trading Estate
 HAG/WOL DY9 ....102 E7
The Hayes Trading Estate
 HAG/WOL DY9 ....102 E7
Hayley Green Hospital
 HALE B63 ....121 H5
Hayward Industrial Park
 ALDR WS9 ....40 E6
Hazelhead Industrial Estate
 COV CV1 ....9 L6
Hazel Way Industrial Estate
 NUNW/HART CV10 ....98 D4
Hazel Oak School
 SHLY B90 ....147 L3
Hazel Slade Primary School
 HEDN WS12 ....13 L7
Hearsall Primary School
 COV CV1 ....8 A6
The Heartlands High School
 VAUX/NECH B7 ....7 M1
Heart of England Crematorium
 NUN CV11 ....99 K2
Heart of England School
 RCOVN/BALC/EX CV7 ....151 M7
Heath Business Park
 KNWTH CV8 ....184 B4
Heath Clinic
 SOLH B91 ....128 B8
Heathcote Industrial Estate
 WWCK CV34 ....206 B8
Heathfield Foundation
 Technology College
 CDYHTH B64 ....103 K3
Heathfield Primary School
 BFLD/HDSWWD B20 ....89 G5
Heathfield School
 KIDD DY10 ....138 D3
Heathfields Infant School
 TAM/AM/WIL B77 ....46 D7
Heath Hayes Primary School
 HEDN WS12 ....17 K3
Heathlands Primary (NC) School
 BKDE/SHDE B34 ....91 K6
Heath Lane Cemetery
 HHTH/SAND B71 ....69 H6
Heath Lane Hospital
 HHTH/SAND B71 ....69 H6
Heath Lodge Hotel
 CHWD/FDBR/MGN B37 ....111 H5
Heath Mount Primary School
 BHTH/HG B12 ....107 J7
Heath Park High School
 WOLVN WV10 ....36 E8
Heath Street Industrial Estate
 SMTHWK B66 ....88 B8
Heath Town Leisure Centre
 WOLVN WV10 ....50 E1
Hebrew Congregation
 CBHAMW B1 ....6 E7
Hedging Lane Industrial Estate
 TAM/AM/WIL B77 ....46 B8
Hednesford Town FC
 (Keys Park)
 HEDN WS12 ....17 H2
Hemdale Business Park
 NUN CV11 ....99 K2
Henley College
 COVN CV6 ....135 G5
Henley Industrial Park
 COVN CV6 ....135 J6
Henry Bellairs CE
 Junior School
 BDWTH CV12 ....117 H2
Henry Hinde Infant School
 RUGBYS/DCH CV22 ....186 A4
Henry Hinde Junior School
 RUGBYS/DCH CV22 ....185 M3
Henry Parkes Primary School
 TLHL/CAN CV4 ....154 A5
Herald Business Park
 COVS CV3 ....156 D6
Herbert Art Gallery &
 Museum
 COV CV1 ....9 G5
Herbert Fowler Junior School
 RCOVN/BALC/EX CV7 ....96 D3
Hereford & Worcester County
 Museum
 KIDDW DY11 ....189 K2
Hereward College of FE
 TLHL/CAN CV4 ....153 K4
Hewell Road Swimming Pool
 REDW B97 ....194 A8
H Hayes Clinic
 HEDN WS12 ....17 J4
Higham Lane School
 NUNW/HART CV10 ....81 J7
Higham on the Hill
 Primary School
 MKTBOS/BARL/STKG CV13 ......81 L1
The High Arcal
 Secondary School
 SEDG DY3 ....66 D7
Highclare St Paul's School
 FOAKS/STRLY B74 ....56 F6
Highclare the Abbey School
 ERDW/GRVHL B23 ....72 E8
Highclare Woodfield School
 CSCFLD/WYGN B72 ....73 G4
Highcroft Hospital
 ERDW/GRVHL B23 ....90 B2
Highfield Primary School
 WASH/WDE B8 ....90 C8
Highfields Primary School
 BILS/COS WV14 ....67 G3
Highfields Primary School
 BLKHTH/ROWR B65 ....104 A5
Highfields Primary School
 BNTWD WS7 ....19 G6
Highfields School
 ETTPK/GDPK/PENN WV4 ....48 F8
Highgate Business Centre
 BHTH/HG B12 ....107 M7
Highgate Medical Centre
 BHTH/HG B12 ....107 K6
Highgate Primary School
 DUDS DY2 ....84 D7
Highgate Retail Park
 BHTH/HG B12 ....107 K6
Highgate Trading Estate
 BHTH/HG B12 ....107 L6
Highgate United FC
 SHLY B90 ....147 J7
High Meadow Infant School
 CSHL/WTROR B46 ....93 K5
Highters Heath J & I School
 ALE/KHTH/YWD B14 ....146 F2

Hillary Primary School
 WSLW WS2 ....4 A9
Hill Avenue Primary School
 ETTPK/GDPK/PENN WV4 ....66 D2
Hillcrest Business Park
 DUDS DY2 ....85 G6
Hillcrest Industrial Estate
 CDYHTH B64 ....103 H5
Hillcrest School &
 Community College
 DUDS DY2 ....84 F8
Hillcrest School &
 6th Form Centre
 RIDG/WDGT B32 ....123 J2
Hill Farm Primary School
 COV CV6 ....133 M6
Hillfields Health Centre
 COV CV1 ....9 H2
Hillmeads Health Centre
 HWK/WKHTH B38 ....145 L4
Hillmorton Manor Hotel
 & Restaurant
 RUGBYN/HIL CV21 ....187 L6
Hillmorton Primary School
 RUGBYN/HIL CV21 ....187 M5
Hillstone Primary School
 BKDE/SHDE B34 ....92 B8
Hill Top Industrial Estate
 WBROM B70 ....68 D5
Hilltop Medical Centre
 LCLYGN/QTN B68 ....105 G3
Hilltop Public Golf Course
 BFLD/HDSWWD B20 ....88 A1
Hill West J & I School
 FOAKS/STRLY B74 ....56 D1
Hilton Cross Business Park
 WOLVN WV10 ....22 F7
Hilton Main Industrial Estate
 WNSFLD WV11 ....23 G8
Hilton Trading Estate
 ETTPK/GDPK/PENN WV4 ....66 D1
Himley Country Hotel
 SEDG DY3 ....82 F2
Himley Hall
 SEDG DY3 ....83 H2
Himley Hall Golf Centre
 SEDG DY3 ....83 J1
Himley Hall & Park
 SEDG DY3 ....83 H1
Himley House Hotel
 SEDG DY3 ....83 G2
Hingley Industrial Park
 DUDS DY2 ....103 G4
Hippodrome Theatre
 DIG/EDG B5 ....6 F8
Hive Industrial Centre
 WSNGN B18 ....88 E6
HM Prison
 REDW B97 ....193 H5
HM Prison
 WOLVN WV10 ....22 D6
HM Prison
 WSNGN B18 ....88 C8
Hob Green Primary School
 HAG/WOL DY9 ....120 C3
Hobmoor Primary School
 YDLY B25 ....109 H5
Hobs Moat Medical Centre
 HIA/OLT B92 ....127 L3
Hockley Brook Trading Estate
 WSNGN B18 ....88 E7
Hockley Heath Pavilion
 (Sports Centre)
 HOCK/TIA B94 ....175 G7
Hockley Heath Primary School
 HOCK/TIA B94 ....174 F7
Hockley Hill Industrial Estate
 WSNGN B18 ....88 F8
Hodge Hill Girls School
 CBROM B36 ....91 G6
Hodge Hill School
 CBROM B36 ....91 G6
The Holborn Shopping Centre
 SEDG DY3 ....66 C6
Holbrook Park
 Industrial Estate
 COVN CV6 ....134 B5
Holbrook Primary School
 COVN CV6 ....134 C4
Holiday Inn
 GTB/HAM B43 ....70 D2
 LGN/SDN/BHAMAIR B26 ....128 E2
 RCOVN/BALC/EX CV7 ....135 M5
Holland House Infant School
 CSCFLD/WYGN B72 ....73 G1
Holland Industrial Park
 DARL/WED WS10 ....52 B3
Holliday Wharf
 CBHAMW B1 ....6 D7
Hollies Business Park
 CNCK/NC WS11 ....16 D4
The Hollies Clinic
 LGLYGN/QTN B68 ....104 F1
Hollies Industrial Estate
 BDMR/CCFT WV3 ....2 D8
Holloway Bank Trading Estate
 DARL/WED WS10 ....68 D4
Holly Bush Medical Centre
 RIDG/WDGT B32 ....105 H6
Holly Farm Business Park
 KNWTH CV8 ....177 M6
Hollyfast Primary School
 COVN CV6 ....133 J6
Hollyfield Primary School
 MGN/WHC B75 ....73 K1
Holly Grove Primary School
 BNTWD WS7 ....18 C4
Holly Hall Clinic
 DUDN DY1 ....84 D7
Holly Hall (GM) School
 DUDN DY1 ....84 D5
Hollyhedge Primary School
 HHTH/SAND B71 ....69 J5
Holly Hill Infant School
 RBRY B45 ....143 K3
Holly Lane Cemetery
 SMTHWK B67 ....87 H8
Holly Lodge High School
 SMTHWK B67 ....87 H6
Holly Park Industrial Estate
 ERDE/BCHGN B24 ....91 G3
Hollywalk Clinic
 RLSN CV32 ....206 E5
Hollywood Primary School
 ALE/KHTH/YWD B14 ....146 E4
Holte School
 LOZ/NWT B19 ....89 H6
Holt Farm Primary School
 RMSLY B62 ....104 C4
Holy Child School
 EDG B15 ....106 C7
Holy Family RC J & I School
 COVN CV6 ....133 M2
Holy Family RC Primary School
 SMHTH B10 ....108 C6
Holyhead Primary School
 DARL/WED WS10 ....68 D2
Holyhead School
 HDSW B21 ....88 B5

Holy Name RC Primary School
 COVN CV6 ....70 C4
Holyoakes Field First School
 REDW B97 ....202 B1
Holy Rosary RC
 Primary School
 WOLV WV1 ....50 E4
Holy Souls RC Primary School
 ACGN B27 ....127 G2
Holy Trinity Catholic
 Primary School
 BILS/COS WV14 ....51 J8
Holy Trinity CE Primary School
 BFLD/HDSWWD B20 ....89 G3
Holy Trinity CE Primary School
 BRWNH WS8 ....26 B7
Holy Trinity CE Primary School
 WBROM B70 ....87 H4
Holy Trinity RC School
 SMHTH B10 ....108 A5
Honiley Court Hotel
 KNWTH CV8 ....138 D7
Hoobrook Industrial Estate
 KIDDW DY11 ....164 B2
Hood Street Industrial Estate
 COV CV1 ....9 J4
Hoo Farm Industrial Estate
 KIDDW DY11 ....164 C4
Hope Aldridge
 Business Centre
 NUNW/HART CV10 ....81 G7
Horeston Grange
 Shopping Centre
 NUN CV11 ....81 L8
Hornchurch Close
 Industrial Estate
 COV CV1 ....8 B7
Horrell Road Health Centre
 LGN/SDN/BHAMAIR B26 ....109 L6
Horse Shoe Associated FC
 SHLY B90 ....147 K7
Hospital of St Cross
 RUGBYS/DCH CV22 ....186 F4
Hotel Clarine
 LDYWD/EDGR B16 ....106 C4
Hotel Du Vin
 CBHAMW B3 ....6 F4
Hotel Ibis
 CBHAMW B1 ....6 E8
 COV CV1 ....9 G7
 COVS CV3 ....155 G7
 DIG/EDG B5 ....7 G4
 SMHTH B10 ....107 M4
Howard Street
 Industrial Estate
 WBROM B70 ....68 D6
Howes Primary School
 COVS CV3 ....155 H8
Howley Grange
 Primary School
 RMSLY B62 ....104 B8
HRS Business Park
 STECH B33 ....109 M4
HRS Industrial Estate
 STECH B33 ....110 A4
Hudson Industrial Estate
 BKHL/PFLD WV2 ....50 D6
Hulbert Industrial Estate
 DUDS DY2 ....84 F7
Hunt End Industrial Estate
 REDW B97 ....202 A8
Hunters Rise
 BRGRVE B60 ....169 K8
Hunters Lane Industrial Estate
 RUGBYN/HIL CV21 ....160 E8
Huntington CP School
 HEDN WS12 ....12 B5
Huntingtree Primary School
 HALE B63 ....121 J1
Hurley Primary School
 ATHST CV9 ....77 H1
Hurst Business Park
 BRLYHL DY5 ....102 D1
Hurstgreen Primary School
 RMSLY B62 ....104 C5
Hurst Hill Primary School
 BILS/COS WV14 ....66 E5
Hydesville Tower School
 RUSH/SHEL WS4 ....5 J2
Hylands Hotel
 COVS CV3 ....8 E9
Ikon Gallery
 CBHAMW B1 ....6 C6
IMAX Cinema
 DIG/EDG B5 ....7 K4
Imex Business Park
 BKHL/PFLD WV2 ....50 A6
Imex Business Park
 BORD B9 ....108 B3
Imex Business Park
 SPARK B11 ....108 D7
Imex Business Park
 STECH B33 ....91 H8
Imex Business Park
 TPTN/OCK DY4 ....85 L2
Imex Industrial Estate
 WSNGN B18 ....106 E1
Indian High Commission
 SMTHWK B66 ....106 C1
Industrial Training Centre
 TLHL/CAN CV4 ....153 D1
Industrial Weston Estate
 SPARK B11 ....126 C1
Infant Welfare Clinic
 GTB/HAM B43 ....70 B3
Inkeeper's Hotel
 DOR/KN B93 ....176 B2
Innisfree House School
 HLYWD B47 ....173 G1
Innkeeper's Lodge
 BRGRVW B61 ....168 F4
Innkeeper's Lodge Hotel
 KGSWFD DY6 ....83 C7
Innkeepers Lodge Hotel
 LGN/SDN/BHAMAIR B26 ....127 M1
Innkeepers Lodge Hotel
 RCOVN/BALC/EX CV7 ....131 G4
Innkeeper's Lodge Hotel
 RIDG/WDGT B32 ....105 G6
The Innkeepers Lodge Hotel
 LICH WS13 ....20 C3
The Innkeeper's Lodge Hotel
 SCFLD/BOLD B73 ....55 L8
International Convention
 Centre
 CBHAMW B1 ....6 C5
International School &
 Community College
 STECH B33 ....110 B2
Ipsley CE Middle School
 REDE B98 ....203 J3
Izons Lane Industrial Estate
 WBROM B70 ....86 D4
Jack o'Watton Business Park
 CSHL/WTROR B46 ....93 H2
Jack o'Watton Industrial Estate
 CSHL/WTROR B46 ....93 H2

Jaguar Daimler
 Heritage Centre
 COVW CV5 132
The James Gilbert
 Rugby Football Museum
 RUGBYN/HIL CV21 186
James Watt Industrial Park
 SMTHWK B66 88
James Watt J & I School
 HDSW B21 88
Jane Lane Special School
 WSLW WS2 52
Janet Shaw Clinic
 CHWD/FDBR/MGN B37 110
Jas Industrial Park
 OLDBY B69 104
Jerome Primary School
 CNCK/NC WS11 17
Jerome Retail Park
 WSL WS1 4
Jervoise J & I School
 SLYOAK B29 123
Jessons CE F & M School
 DUDN DY1 84
Jewellery Quarter
 WSNGN B18 88
The Jewellery Quarter
 Discovery Centre
 WSNGN B18 88
Jewish Cemetery
 AST/WIT B6 71
JFK Memorial
 CBHAMNE B4 6
John Black Day Hospital
 CHWD/FDBR/MGN B37 110
John Gulson Primary School
 COV CV1 134
John Shelton Primary School
 COVN CV6 134
John Willmott School
 WALM/CURD B76 73
John Wood CE Infant School
 CNCK/NC WS11 16
Joseph Cash Primary School
 COVN CV6 134
Joseph Chamberlain
 Sixth Form College
 BHTH/HG B12 107
Joseph Leckie
 Comprehensive School
 WSL WS1 53
Joseph Turner Primary School
 TPTN/OCK DY4 67
Josiah Mason College
 ERDW/GRVHL B23 90
Jubilee Business Park
 HAG/WOL DY9 102
Jubilee Park Primary School
 TPTN/OCK DY4 67
Jubilee Sports Centre
 NUNW/HART CV10 98
Junction 1 Retail Park
 RUGBYN/HIL CV21 184
Junction 2 Industrial Estate
 OLDBY B69 86
Junction 6 Industrial Park
 AST/WIT B6 89
Junction Industrial Estate
 SMTHWK B66 87
Jury's Inn
 CBHAMW B1 6
Karis Medical Centre
 LDYWD/EDGR B16 106
Kates Hill Primary School
 DUDS DY2 85
Kelvin Way Trading Estate
 WBROM B70 86
Kenilworth Business Centre
 KNWTH CV8 197
Kenilworth Castle
 KNWTH CV8 179
Kenilworth Golf Club
 KNWTH CV8 180
Kenilworth RFC
 KNWTH CV8 198
Kenilworth School
 KNWTH CV8 180
Kenilworth Wardens
 Cricket Club
 KNWTH CV8 198
Ken Marriott Leisure Centre
 RUGBYS/DCH CV22 186
Kent Close Primary School
 HHTH/SAND B71 69
Keresley Grange
 Primary School
 COVN CV6 133
Keresley Health Centre
 RCOVN/BALC/EX CV7 115
Keresley Newland
 Primary School
 RCOVN/BALC/EX CV7 115
Key Business Park
 ERDE/BCHGN B24 91
Key Industrial Park
 WLNHL WV13 51
Keyway Retail Park
 WLNHL WV13 51
Khalsa Industrial Estate
 SMTHWK B66 106
Kidderminster College
 KIDD DY10 164
Kidderminster General
 Hospital
 KIDDW DY11 164
Kidderminster Golf Club
 KIDD DY10 138
Kidderminster Harriers FC
 (Aggborough Stadium)
 KIDD DY10 164
Kidderminster Health Centre
 KIDD DY10 138
Kidderminster
 Industrial Estate
 KIDD DY10 165
Kidderminster Railway
 Museum Trust
 KIDD DY10 138
Kineton Green Infant School
 HIA/OLT B92 127
King Charles I High School
 KIDD DY10 138
King Charles Primary School
 WSLW WS2 52
King David Primary School
 MOS/BIL B13 125
King Edward Business Park
 NUN CV11 99
King Edwards School (Boys)
 EDG B15 124
King Edwards VI Aston School
 AST/WIT B6 89
King Edwards VI Handsworth
 School
 HDSW B21 88
King Edward VI Camp Hill
 School for Boys
 ALE/KHTH/YWD B14 71

g Edward VI Camp Hill
chool for Girls
LE/KHTH/YWD B14 ....125 H5
g Edward VI College
NUN CV11 ....99 H1
g Edward VI College
TRBR DY8 ....101 L7
g Edward VI County School
ICHS WS14 ....21 G7
g Edward VI Five Ways
chool
VDG/WDGT B32 ....123 G5
g Edward VI Girls High School
DG B15 ....124 D1
g Edward VI Leisure Centre
ICHS WS14 ....21 G7
gfield Industrial Estate
OVN CV6 ....134 A7
gfield Business Park
EDE B98 ....202 E2
gfisher Industrial Park
VBROM B70 ....86 C1
gfisher Primary School
CBROM B36 ....92 E5
gfisher Shopping Centre
EDW B97 ....202 C1
g George V Primary School
HTH/SAND B71 ....87 J2
g Henry VIII School
COVW CV5 ....8 D1
gsbury Business Park
EDE B98 ....74 C7
gsbury J & I School
OL/KGSB/FAZ B78 ....60 D1
gsbury School
ERDE/BCHGN B24 ....90 D3
gsbury Water Park
OL/KGSB/FAZ B78 ....60 D1
gsbury WABER School
WALM/CURD B76 ....59 M8
gs Business Centre
NUN CV11 ....99 H1
gs Business Park
KGSTG B44 ....71 H2
e Kings CE School
DUNHL/THL/PER WV6 ....34 F8
gs Cinema
VBROM B70 ....87 H2
gs Heath Boys School
MOS/BIL B13 ....125 L7
gs Heath CC
LE/KHTH/YWD B14 ....125 J7
gs Heath J & I School
LE/KHTH/YWD B14 ....125 J4
e Kings High School
or Girls
WWCK CV34 ....205 J6
gs Hill Business Park
DARL/WED WS10 ....68 C1
gs Hill Clinic
DARL/WED WS10 ....52 C8
gs Hill JMI School
DARL/WED WS10 ....52 C8
gshurst City Technology
College
CHWD/FDBR/MGN B37 ....110 F2
gshurst Clinic
CHWD/FDBR/MGN B37 ....92 E8
gshurst J & I School
CHWD/FDBR/MGN B37 ....92 E7
gsland Primary School
KGSTG B44 ....71 K1
gsley College
REDE B98 ....203 G7
gsley Preparatory School
DOR/KN B93 ....175 K1
e Kingsley School
RLSN CV32 ....206 D4
gsmead Technology
College
HEDN WS12 ....17 G1
gs Norton Boys School
BVILLE B30 ....145 J1
gs Norton Business Centre
BVILLE B30 ....145 K1
gs Norton Girls School
BVILLE B30 ....124 C8
gs Norton Golf Club
ALVE B48 ....172 A4
gs Norton High School
WK/WKHTH B38 ....145 K5
gs Norton Primary School
BVILLE B30 ....145 L2
gsrise Community
Primary School
KGSTG B44 ....71 M3
gs Road Industrial Estate
YDLY B25 ....108 D7
gstanding Leisure Centre
KGSTG B44 ....71 M5
gstanding Special School
KGSTG B44 ....71 J4
gsthorne Primary School
KGSTG B44 ....71 L4
gston Court
Shopping Arcade
CNCK/NC CV11 ....16 C4
gston Industrial Estate
BORD B9 ....7 M7
gsway Community
Primary School
RLSS CV31 ....206 C7
e Kingswinford
Secondary School
KGSWFD DY6 ....83 H6
gswood School
SHLY B90 ....147 M3
well J & I School
RIDG/WDGT B32 ....122 E4
rk Industrial Park
KIDDW DY11 ....163 L5
xon Primary School
SPARK B11 ....126 D1
e Knibbs Shopping Centre
WWCK CV34 ....205 K6
ghtlow CE (Aided)
Primary School
RRUGBY CV23 ....183 K6
e Knoll School
KIDDW DY11 ....137 L6
owle CE Primary School
DOR/KN B93 ....150 A6
owle & Dorridge Cricket Club
DOR/KN B93 ....175 L1
owle FC
DOR/KN B93 ....150 A6
owle Village Cricket Club
DOR/KN B93 ....150 A6
dy Katherine Leveson CE
Primary School
RCOVN/BALC/EX CV7 ....150 F8
ypool Primary School
SPARK B11 ....107 M7
ywood Arts &
eisure Centre
LDYWD/EDGR B16 ....106 E3
ywood Middleway
Health Centre
BHAMW B1 ....106 E2

Lakeside Industrial Estate
REDE B98 ....202 F2
Lakeside Industrial Park
POL/KGSB/FAZ B78 ....45 J4
Lakeside JMI School
WLNHL WV13 ....51 J2
Lakeside Medical Centre
DUNHL/THL/PER WV6 ....48 C1
Lakeside Primary School
TAM/AM/WIL B77 ....46 C3
Lakeside Trading Centre
REDE B98 ....202 F2
Lakey Lane Primary School
HLGN/YWD B28 ....126 E1
Lammas Field
WWCK CV34 ....205 L2
Lanchester School
CBROM B36 ....92 C4
Landywood County
Primary School
GTWY WS6 ....24 D5
Lane Green First School
CDSL WV8 ....34 F2
The Lane Medical Centre
BHTH/HG B12 ....107 M8
Lanesfield Primary School
ETTPK/GDPK/PENN WV4 ....66 C2
The Lanes Shopping Centre
SCFLD/BOLD B73 ....72 F6
Langley High School
LGLYGN/QTN B68 ....104 F1
Langley Primary School
HIA/OLT B92 ....127 H1
Langley Primary School
OLDBY B69 ....86 D8
Langley School
HIA/OLT B92 ....127 H1
Langley Special School
MGN/WHC B75 ....57 L1
Langley Swimming Centre
LGLYGN/QTN B68 ....104 F1
Lansdowne Health Centre
WSNGN B18 ....106 D1
Lansdowne Hotel
RLSN CV32 ....206 C4
Lapal Primary School
RMSLY B62 ....122 D1
Lark Hall Infants School
CRTAM B79 ....31 L5
Larkhill Industrial Estate
KIDD DY10 ....138 C6
Lasercare Clinics Birmingham
EDG B5 ....6 B9
Laurie Pike Health Centre
AST/WIT B6 ....89 H1
Lawford Heath
Industrial Estate
RRUGBY CV23 ....185 G6
Lawrence Sheriff School
RUGBYN/HIL CV21 ....186 F2
Lea Marston Hotel &
Leisure Complex
WALM/CURD B76 ....75 L4
Leamington CC
RLSN CV32 ....206 D3
Leamington Museum &
Art Gallery
RLSS CV31 ....206 D5
Leamore Industrial Estate
WSLW WS2 ....38 E6
Leamore Primary School
BLOX/PEL WS3 ....39 G6
Leasowes Community College
RMSLY B62 ....104 C7
Lea Street First School
KIDD DY10 ....138 D7
Leaverstock Industrial Estate
STETCH B33 ....110 A4
Lee Bank Business Centre
CBHAMW B1 ....6 E7
Legg Brothers Industrial Estate
ETTPK/GDPK/PENN WV4 ....50 D8
Leigh CE Primary School
TLHL/CAN CV4 ....153 H4
Leigh JI (NC) School
WASH/WDE B8 ....90 C7
Leighswood Junior School
ALDR WS9 ....40 F4
Leighswood School
ALDR WS9 ....40 E5
Lemar Industrial Estate
BVILLE B30 ....125 G4
Lennon Indoor Market
KGSTG B44 ....71 L2
Leona Industrial Estate
RMSLY B62 ....104 C6
Leviss Industrial Estate
STETCH B33 ....109 H1
Lewisham Industrial Estate
SMTHWK B66 ....87 L6
Leyhill Health Centre
NFLD/LBR B31 ....123 J7
Ley Hill Primary School
NFLD/LBR B31 ....123 H8
Leyland School
BDWTH CV12 ....116 F2
Leys Industrial Estate
BRLYHL DY5 ....101 L2
Lichfield Business Centre
LICH WS13 ....21 H4
Lichfield Cathedral
LICH WS13 ....20 F1
Lichfield Cathedral School
(Bishops Palace)
LICH WS13 ....20 F1
Lichfield Cricket Club
LICH WS13 ....20 E1
Lichfield Magistrates Court
LICH WS13 ....20 F1
Lichfield Road Industrial Estate
CRTAM B79 ....31 K8
Lichfield RUFC
LICHS WS14 ....21 K8
Lichfield Trading Estate
CRTAM B79 ....31 J7
Lickey End First School
BRGRVE B60 ....169 G7
Lickey Hills Country Park
RBRY B45 ....169 L1
Lickey Hills Golf Club
RBRY B45 ....169 L1
Lickey Hills Primary School
RBRY B45 ....169 K3
Lickhill First School
STRPT DY13 ....188 B1
Lickhill Middle School
STRPT DY13 ....188 B1
Lifford Trading Estate
BVILLE B30 ....145 L1
Light Hall School
SHLY B90 ....147 M4
Light House Cinema
WOLV WV1 ....3 G4
Lightwoods Primary School
LGLYGN/QTN B68 ....105 H5
Lillington Primary School
RLSN CV32 ....206 F2
Limbrick Wood Primary School
TLHL/CAN CV4 ....153 K2

Linden Road Instruction
Swimming Pool
BVILLE B30 ....124 D6
Lindens Primary School
FOAKS/STRLY B74 ....55 K7
Lindley Lodge Industrial Estate
ALDR WS9 ....40 C7
Lindsworth North School
ERDW/GRVHL B23 ....72 E7
Lindsworth School
BVILLE B30 ....146 A2
Link One Industrial Park
WBROM B70 ....68 C7
Linkway Retail Park
CNCK/NC CV11 ....15 M7
Linkwood Industrial Estate
STRBR DY8 ....101 K7
Linthurst First School
BRGRVE B60 ....169 L7
Lion Industrial Park
ALDR WS9 ....40 E4
Lisle Court Medical Centre
RLSS CV31 ....206 E7
Little Aston CP School
FOAKS/STRLY B74 ....42 A7
Little Aston Golf Club
FOAKS/STRLY B74 ....55 M1
Little Barrow Hotel
LICH WS13 ....20 E5
Little Heath Industrial Estate
COVN CV6 ....134 E3
Little Heath Primary School
COVN CV6 ....134 D4
Little London JMI School
WLNHL WV13 ....51 L3
Little Sutton Primary School
MGN/WHC B75 ....57 H2
Littleton Business Park
HEDN WS12 ....12 A6
Living Museum
DUDN DY1 ....85 H2
Locarno Primary School
TPTN/OCK DY4 ....67 K7
The Lock Museum
WLNHL WV13 ....51 K4
Lode Heath School
SOLH B91 ....128 A7
Lodge Farm Campsite
RRUGBY CV23 ....185 M3
Lodge Farm Primary School
WSLW WS2 ....52 C1
Lodge Forge Trading Estate
CDYHTH B64 ....103 G6
Lodge Hill Cemetery
SLYOAK B29 ....123 M4
Lodge Hill Crematorium
SLYOAK B29 ....123 M3
Lodge Primary School
WBROM B70 ....86 F2
The Loft Theatre
RLSS CV31 ....206 D6
Long Acre Trading Estate
VAUX/NECH B7 ....89 M6
Longford Industrial Estate
CNCK/NC CV11 ....16 B7
Longford Medical Centre
COVN CV6 ....116 B8
Longford Park
Primary School
COVN CV6 ....134 E2
Longford Primary School
CNCK/NC CV11 ....16 A5
Long Knowle Primary School
WNSFLD WV11 ....37 G5
Long Lane Medical Centre
RMSLY B62 ....104 B4
Long Lane Trading Estate
RMSLY B62 ....104 B4
Long Lawford Primary School
RRUGBY CV23 ....159 L8
Longmoor Special School
SCFLD/BOLD B73 ....71 M1
Longwill Special School
NFLD/LBR B31 ....123 L8
Longwood Primary School
POL/KGSB/FAZ B78 ....45 G4
Lord Leycester Hospital
WWCK CV34 ....205 J7
Lord Leycester Hotel
WWCK CV34 ....205 J7
Lordswood Boys School
HRBN B17 ....105 L5
Lordswood Girls School
HRBN B17 ....105 M5
Lordswood Medical Practice
HRBN B17 ....105 M7
Lower Farm JMI School
BLOX/PEL WS3 ....39 G1
Lower Gornal Health Centre
SEDG DY3 ....83 M3
Low Hill Medical Centre
WOLVN WV10 ....36 C6
Loxdale Industrial Estate
BILS/COS WV14 ....67 J1
Loxdale Primary School
BILS/COS WV14 ....67 K1
Lozells Primary School
LOZ/NWT B19 ....89 H6
Lucy Baldwin Hospital
STRPT DY13 ....163 K8
Lugman Medical Centre
WSL WS1 ....4 C8
Lunt Roman Fort
KNWTH CV8 ....181 K2
Lutley Primary School
HALE B63 ....121 H4
Lye Business Centre
HAG/WOL DY9 ....102 D6
Lye CC
HAG/WOL DY9 ....102 B8
Lye Town FC
HAG/WOL DY9 ....102 B8
Lye Valley Industrial Estate
HAG/WOL DY9 ....102 D7
Lyndon Green JI & I School
LGN/SDN/BHAMAIR B26 ....109 K7
Lyndon School
HIA/OLT B92 ....127 L2
Lyne Hall Industrial Estate
PENK ST19 ....10 C6
Lyng Hall School
COVE CV2 ....135 G7
Lyng Primary School
WBROM B70 ....87 G4
Lythalls Lane Industrial Estate
COVN CV6 ....134 C4
Madinatul Uloom Alislamiya
KIDD DY10 ....165 H5
Magistrates Court
(Victoria Law Courts)
CBHAMNE B4 ....7 G3
Magreal Industrial Estate
LDYWD/EDGR B16 ....106 D2
Maguire Industrial Estate
TLHL/CAN CV4 ....153 J5
Maidensbridge Primary School
KGSWFD DY6 ....82 F4
The Mailbox
CBHAMW B1 ....6 E6

Mainstream Forty Seven
Industrial Park
VAUX/NECH B7 ....90 A8
Mainstream Industrial Park
VAUX/NECH B7 ....108 A1
Malt Mill Lane Trading Estate
RMSLY B62 ....104 B5
Mander Shopping Centre
WOLV WV1 ....2 F5
Manders Industrial Estate
WOLV WV10 ....3 M3
Maney Hill Primary School
CSCFLD/WYGN B72 ....73 H3
Manor CP School
POL/KGSB/FAZ B78 ....45 J8
Manor Farm Community
School
RUSH/SHEL WS4 ....39 M7
The Manor General Hospital
WSLW WS2 ....4 A4
Manor Park School
(Foundation)
DARL/WED WS10 ....69 H2
Manor Hotel
RCOVN/BALC/EX CV7 ....131 H4
Manor House Hotel
RLSS CV31 ....206 D6
Manor Industrial Estate
WSLW WS2 ....4 B4
Manor Park Community School
NUN CV11 ....80 E8
Manor Park Primary School
NUN/HART CV10 ....89 L5
Manor Park Primary School
COVS CV3 ....155 G6
Manor Primary School
BILS/COS WV14 ....66 F3
Manor Primary School
FOAKS/STRLY B74 ....55 L4
Manor Road Industrial Estate
ATHST CV9 ....63 J6
Manor Side Industrial Estate
REDE B98 ....195 J7
Manor Way Primary School
HALE B63 ....122 A2
Manse Business Centre
NUN CV11 ....99 J3
Mansfield Green Primary School
AST/WIT B6 ....89 J3
Mansfield Medical Centre
COVS CV3 ....155 L3
Maple Business Park
VAUX/NECH B7 ....89 M7
Mapledene J & I School
LGN/SDN/BHAMAIR B26 ....110 C7
Maple Hayes Dyslexia School
LICH WS13 ....20 B5
Maple Leaf Industrial Estate
WSLW WS2 ....52 F2
Mappleborough Green CE
J & I School
STUD B80 ....203 M3
Market Hall
BRGRVW B61 ....191 K3
Market Hall
COV CV1 ....8 E5
Market Hall
KIDD DY10 ....138 C7
Market Hall & Museum
WWCK CV34 ....205 H7
Marlborough J & I School
SMHTH B10 ....108 C4
Marlfield Farm First School
REDE B98 ....194 F7
Marlow Estate
BLKHTH/ROWR B65 ....103 H4
The Marlpool First School
KIDDW DY11 ....138 A5
Marmion Junior School
CRTAM B79 ....31 L7
Marriott Forest of Arden Hotel
Golf & Country Club
RCOVN/BALC/EX CV7 ....112 E6
Marshalls Industrial Estate
BKHL/PFLD WV2 ....50 A6
Marshbrook First School
PENK ST19 ....10 C4
Marsh Hill Primary School
ERDW/GRVHL B23 ....89 M1
Marston Farm Hotel
WALM/CURD B76 ....75 K1
Marston Green Clinic
CHWD/FDBR/MGN B37 ....110 C6
Marston Green Infant School
CHWD/FDBR/MGN B37 ....110 D6
Marston Green Junior School
CHWD/FDBR/MGN B37 ....110 E6
Marston Road
Industrial Estate
BKHL/PFLD WV2 ....50 A6
Martindale Trading Estate
CNCK/NC WS11 ....16 E3
Martyr's Memorial
COV CV1 ....9 G7
Mary Ann Evans Hospice
NUNW/HART CV10 ....98 E3
Mary Elliot Special School
WSLW WS2 ....53 J1
Maryvale Catholic Primary School
KGSTG B44 ....71 J3
Maryvale Institute
KGSTG B44 ....71 K3
Matchborough First School
REDE B98 ....203 J4
Maternity Welfare Clinic
BDMR/CCFT WV3 ....49 H7
Matthew Boulton College of
Further & Higher Education
DIG/EDG B5 ....107 H5
Matthew Boulton Community
Primary School
HDSW B21 ....88 C4
Maxstoke Castle
CSHL/WTROR B46 ....94 C6
Maxstoke Park Golf Club
CSHL/WTROR B46 ....94 C6
Maybrook Industrial Estate
BRWNH WS8 ....26 D8
The Mayfair Centre
DIG/EDG B5 ....7 G6
Mayfield Preparatory School
WSL WS1 ....5 J6
Mayfield Special School
BFLD/HDSWWD B20 ....89 G5
Maypole Health Centre
ALE/KHTH/YWD B14 ....146 D2
Meadow Green
Primary School
HLYWD B47 ....172 G2
Meadow Mill Industrial Estate
KIDD DY10 ....138 C6
Meadow View JMI School
GTB/HAM B43 ....55 H8

Meadwood Industrial Estate
BILS/COS WV14 ....51 J8
Meeting Lane Industrial Estate
BRLYHL DY5 ....101 M4
Memorial Clock
WSNGN B18 ....106 D1
Menzies Baron's Court Hotel
ALDR WS9 ....40 C7
Menzies High School
HHTH/SAND B71 ....69 G5
Menzies Leofric Hotel
COV CV1 ....8 F4
Mere Green Combined School
MGN/WHC B75 ....56 F3
Meriden CE Primary School
RCOVN/BALC/EX CV7 ....131 G3
Meriden Green Business Park
COVW CV5 ....131 M5
Merridale Primary School
BDMR/CCFT WV5 ....2 A7
Merry Hill Shopping Centre
BRLYHL DY5 ....102 D3
Merstone School
CHWD/FDBR/MGN B37 ....110 E4
Mesnes Green Industrial Estate
LICHS WS14 ....21 G7
Mesty Croft Primary School
DARL/WED WS10 ....68 C2
Metalloys Industrial Estate
WALM/CURD B76 ....73 M8
Michael Drayton Junior School
NUN/HART CV10 ....79 L5
Middlemarch Business Park
KNWTH CV8 ....181 M4
Middlemarch Business Park
KNWTH CV8 ....182 A2
Middlemarch Middle School
NUNW/HART CV10 ....98 F3
Middlemore Business Park
ALDR WS9 ....40 C7
Middlemore Industrial Estate
HDSW B21 ....87 M4
Middleton Hall
POL/KGSB/FAZ B78 ....59 J2
Middleton Trading Estate
WLNHL WV13 ....51 J3
Middleway Industrial Estate
BHTH/HG B12 ....107 K6
Midland Air Museum
KNWTH CV8 ....181 M2
Midland House Dawley
Trading Estate
KGSWFD DY6 ....83 H5
Midland Institute
CBHAMNE B3 ....6 E1
Midland Oak Industrial Estate
COVN CV6 ....134 C4
Midland Oak Trading Estate
COVN CV6 ....134 C3
Midlands Arts Centre Cinema
BHTH/HG B12 ....125 H1
Midlands Sports Centre for
the Disabled
RCOVN/BALC/EX CV7 ....153 E8
Midland Trading Estate
RUGBYN/HIL CV21 ....160 D7
West Warwickshire
Magistrates Court
RLSN CV32 ....206 D4
Milby F & M Schools
NUN CV11 ....81 K5
Mile Oak Business Park
POL/KGSB/FAZ B78 ....45 G3
Milking Bank Primary School
DUDN DY1 ....84 C3
Millard Industrial Estate
WBROM B70 ....86 E3
Millbuck Industrial Estate
WOLVN WV10 ....36 B6
Millennium Point
CBHAMNE B4 ....7 K4
Millfield CP School
BRWNH WS8 ....26 E6
Millfield Primary School
POL/KGSB/FAZ B78 ....45 L5
Millfields First School
BRGRVW B61 ....191 J5
Millfield Special School
HRTH/SAND B71 ....69 H5
Mill Lodge Primary School
SHLY B90 ....147 J3
Mill Park Industrial Estate
CNCK/NC WS11 ....16 E4
Milverton House
Preparatory School
NUN CV11 ....99 H2
Milverton Primary School
RLSN CV32 ....206 D4
Minster Hall Youth &
Community Centre
LICH WS13 ....20 F5
Minster House Clinic
KIDD DY10 ....138 C7
Minworth Industrial Park
WALM/CURD B76 ....73 M7
Minworth J & I School
WALM/CURD B76 ....74 B8
Mirah Day Hospital
NUN CV11 ....80 E8
Miras Business Estate
HEDN WS12 ....17 H2
Mitton Mill Industrial Estate
STRPT DY13 ....189 G1
Moat Farm J & I School
LGLYGN/QTN B68 ....105 G2
Moat Hall Primary School
GTWY WS6 ....24 D2
Moat House Primary School
COVE CV2 ....135 G7
Mobarak Health Centre
BHTH/HG B12 ....107 J4
Monarch Industrial Estate
SPARK B11 ....108 E8
Monkspath Business Park
SHLY B90 ....148 D5
Monkspath Primary School
SHLY B90 ....148 F7
Monkton Recreation Centre
PENK ST19 ....10 B4
Monmer Close
Industrial Estate
WLNHL WV13 ....51 J2
Monmore Business Park
BKHL/PFLD WV2 ....50 D5
Monmore Green
Greyhound Stadium
WOLV WV1 ....50 C5
Monmore Park
Industrial Estate
BKHL/PFLD WV2 ....50 D6
Montgomery Primary School
SPARK B11 ....108 A6
Montgomery Street
Business Centre
SPARK B11 ....108 A6
Montville Hotel
REDW B97 ....202 B3
Monway Industrial Estate
DARL/WED WS10 ....68 B2

Moons Moat First School
 REDE B98 .....195 G8
The Moore Group
 Business Centre
 WSL WS1 .....4 F7
Moorgate Primary School
 CRTAM B79 .....31 L8
Moor Green FC
 HLGN/YWD B28 .....126 C6
Moor Green J & I School
 MOS/BIL B13 .....125 G4
Moor Green Sports Centre
 MOS/BIL B13 .....125 G3
Moor Hall Golf Club
 MGN/WHC B75 .....57 H4
Moor Hall Hotel
 MGN/WHC B75 .....57 H4
Moor Hall Primary School
 MGN/WHC B75 .....57 H3
Moorhill County Primary School
 CNCK/NC WS11 .....12 C8
Moorhill Primary School
 CNCK/NC WS11 .....16 C1
Moorlands Primary School
 HHTH/SAND B71 .....68 F5
Moor Lane Trading Estate
 AST/WIT B6 .....89 K1
Moor Street Industrial Estate
 BRLYHL DY5 .....102 A3
Moreton Community School
 WOLVN WV10 .....36 D4
Morley Road Shopping Centre
 BNTWD WS7 .....18 F6
Moseley CC
 HIA/OLT B92 .....127 G8
Moseley CE Primary School
 MOS/BIL B13 .....125 K3
Moseley Golf Club
 MOS/BIL B13 .....125 L5
Moseley Hall Hospital
 MOS/BIL B13 .....125 J2
Moseley Park School &
 Technology College
 BILS/COS WV14 .....51 J5
Moseley Primary School
 COVN CV6 .....8 A1
Moseley School
 MOS/BIL B13 .....126 A3
Mossley Clinic
 BLOX/PEL WS3 .....38 D4
Mossley Primary School
 BLOX/PEL WS3 .....38 D3
Mount Carmel RC First School
 REDW B97 .....201 K3
Mount Nod Primary School
 COVW CV5 .....153 L2
Mount Pleasant
 Primary School
 BRLYHL DY5 .....102 C4
Mount School
 BRGRVW B61 .....168 F8
Mount Street Business Centre
 VAUX/NECH B7 .....90 A7
Mount Street Business Park
 VAUX/NECH B7 .....90 B6
Moxley Industrial Centre
 DARL/WED WS10 .....68 A1
Moxley Infant School
 DARL/WED WS10 .....67 M1
Moxley Medical Centre
 DARL/WED WS10 .....52 A7
Mucklow Hill Industrial Estate
 RMSLY B62 .....104 A8
Mucklow Hill Trading Estate
 RMSLY B62 .....104 A8
Municipal Art Gallery
 WOLV WV1 .....2 F4
Munrow Sports Centre
 EDG B15 .....124 D1
Museum of British Road
 Transport
 COV CV1 .....8 F3
The Museum of Cannock Chase
 HEDN WS12 .....13 H7
Myton School
 WWCK CV34 .....205 M7
Nailcote Hall Hotel
 RCOVN/BALC/EX CV7 .....152 E6
The Nancy Doyle Clinic
 BRGRVE B60 .....191 L3
Nansen J & I School
 WASH/WDE B8 .....90 D8
Nathaniel Newton
 Infant School
 NUNW/HART CV10 .....79 M5
Nation Agricultural Centre
 KNWTH CV8 .....198 E1
National Exhibition Centre
 BHAMNEC B40 .....111 J8
National Indoor Arena
 CBHAMW B1 .....6 B5
National Institute of
 Conductive Education
 MOS/BIL B13 .....125 H1
National Motorcycle Museum
 HIA/OLT B92 .....129 L3
National Sea Life Centre
 CBHAMW B1 .....6 B5
The Natural Health Centre
 HWK/WKHTH B38 .....145 K3
Nature Centre
 HHTH/SAND B71 .....70 A7
Nature Park
 WALM/CURD B76 .....73 L8
Nature Reserve
 KIDD DY10 .....167 G6
Nature Reserve
 SEDG DY3 .....82 E2
Neachells Lane
 Industrial Estate
 WLNHL WV13 .....51 H1
Nechells Primary School
 VAUX/NECH B7 .....90 A5
Neilston Street
 Business Centre
 RLSS CV31 .....206 E7
Nelson Mandela
 Primary School
 BHTH/HG B12 .....107 L8
Nelson Primary School
 CBHAMW B1 .....6 A4
Neptune Industrial Estate
 WLNHL WV13 .....51 M5
Netherbrook Primary School
 DUDS DY2 .....103 H3
The Nethersole School
 (CE Controlled Primary)
 POL/KGSB/FAZ B78 .....47 M3
Nether Stowe County
 High School
 LICH WS13 .....20 F4
Netherton Business Park
 DUDS DY2 .....103 H2
Netherton CC
 DUDS DY2 .....102 F1
Netherton CE Primary School
 DUDS DY2 .....84 F8
Network Park Industrial Estate
 VAUX/NECH B7 .....108 A1

The New Art Gallery Walsall
 WSLW WS2 .....4 D3
Newbold Comyn Golf Club
 RLSN CV32 .....207 G4
Newbold Comyn
 Leisure Centre
 RLSS CV31 .....206 F5
Newbold Comyn Park
 RLSN CV32 .....207 H5
Newbold FC
 RUGBYN/HIL CV21 .....160 B7
Newbold Leisure Centre
 RUGBYN/HIL CV21 .....160 B6
Newbold Riverside
 Primary School
 RUGBYN/HIL CV21 .....160 C7
Newbridge Preparatory School
 DUNHL/THL/PER WV6 .....49 J1
New Cross Hospital
 WNSFLD WV11 .....36 F8
New Cross Industrial Estate
 WLNHL WV13 .....51 G2
New Cross Industrial Estate
 WOLV WV1 .....50 E2
Newdigate Primary School
 BDWTH CV12 .....116 A4
Newfield Park Primary School
 HALE B63 .....103 L8
New Hall Hotel
 WALM/CURD B76 .....73 J3
New Hall J & I School
 MGN/WHC B75 .....57 M8
Newhampton Arts Centre
 WOLV WV1 .....2 D3
New Inn Industrial Estate
 COVN CV6 .....134 D3
Newman College of
 Higher Education
 RIDG/WDGT B32 .....123 G5
New Oscott J & I School
 SCFLD/BOLD B73 .....72 A2
New Oxford Medical Centre
 COV CV1 .....8 E3
New Palace Theatre
 REDE B98 .....202 C2
Newshire Industrial Estate
 SPARK B11 .....108 B7
Newton Industrial Estate
 BORD B9 .....108 B3
Newtown Health Centre
 LOZ/NWT B19 .....89 H7
Newtown Primary School
 WBROM B70 .....86 B2
Newtown Shopping Centre
 LOZ/NWT B19 .....89 J7
Nicholas Chamberlaine School
 BDWTH CV12 .....117 H2
Ninestiles School
 ACGN B27 .....126 F4
Nonsuch Primary School
 RIDG/WDGT B32 .....123 H3
Norfolk House School
 EDG B15 .....106 B5
Norman Green Sports Centre
 & Athletics Track
 SOLH B91 .....148 E2
North Birmingham College
 PBAR/PBCH B42 .....71 J6
North Bromsgrove High School
 BRGRVE B60 .....191 L3
Northbrook Health Centre
 SHLY B90 .....127 G8
Northbrook Sports Club
 COVW CV5 .....133 G5
North East Worcestershire
 College
 BRGRVE B60 .....191 M2
 REDW B97 .....202 C1
North East Worcestershire
 Community Health Care
 NHS Trust
 HIA/OLT B92 .....127 G8
 REDW B97 .....202 C1
Northfield Manor
 Primary School
 SLYOAK B29 .....123 L6
Northfield Pool &
 Fitness Centre
 NFLD/LBR B31 .....144 D2
Northfield Road
 Primary School
 DUDS DY2 .....85 H8
Northicote Secondary School
 WOLVN WV10 .....36 C2
Northlands Primary School
 RUGBYN/HIL CV21 .....186 F1
Northmoor Industrial Estate
 BRLYHL DY5 .....102 B2
Northside Business Centre
 WSNGN B18 .....88 C8
North Solihull Sports Centre
 & Track
 CHWD/FDBR/MGN B37 .....110 C2
North Walsall Primary School
 WSLW WS2 .....53 J1
North Warwickshire Golf Club
 RCOVN/BALC/EX CV7 .....130 D5
North Warwickshire &
 Hinckley College
 ATHST CV9 .....63 H5
 NUN CV11 .....81 J7
North Worcestershire
 Golf Club
 NFLD/LBR B31 .....144 B2
Norton Canes
 Business Park
 CNCK/NC WS11 .....25 L1
Norton Canes
 Greyhound Track
 CNCK/NC WS11 .....25 M1
Norton Canes Primary School
 CNCK/NC WS11 .....17 L7
Norton Canes School
 CNCK/NC WS11 .....17 L6
Norwood Hotel
 NFLD/LBR B31 .....144 F1
Novotel
 CBHAMW B1 .....6 B6
 COVN CV6 .....116 D7
 LGN/SDN/BHAMAIR B26 .....129 G1
 WOLV WV1 .....3 H5
Nuneaton Borough AFC
 NUN CV11 .....98 D1
Nuneaton Co-operative
 Sports Club
 NUN CV11 .....98 F1
Nuneaton Indoor Market
 NUN CV11 .....99 G1
Nuneaton Museum &
 Art Gallery
 NUN CV11 .....99 G2
Nuneaton Old Edwardians RFC
 NUNW/HART CV10 .....81 G7

Nuneaton Private Hospital
 NUNW/HART CV10 .....99 G4
Nuneaton RFC
 NUN CV11 .....99 K1
Oak Cottage Primary School
 SOLH B91 .....127 J7
Oakdale Trading Estate
 KGSWFD DY6 .....83 H4
Oakeswell Health Centre
 DARL/WED WS10 .....68 E2
Oakfield Junior School
 ATHST CV9 .....63 J6
Oakham Primary School
 OLDBY B69 .....85 M6
Oakhill First School
 REDE B98 .....202 D3
Oakhill Primary School
 TAM/AM/WIL B77 .....46 D3
Oak House Museum
 WBROM B70 .....86 F3
The Oak Industrial Park
 KGSWFD DY6 .....83 J4
Oakland Industrial Estate
 WNSFLD WV11 .....16 F2
Oaklands Academy of
 Theatre Dance
 BNTWD WS7 .....19 H8
Oaklands Business Park
 KIDDW DY11 .....164 C4
Oaklands Primary School
 ACGN B27 .....127 G3
Oakleigh Trading Estate
 BILS/COS WV14 .....66 F3
Oak Meadow Primary School
 WNSFLD WV11 .....37 L6
Oakridge Golf Club
 NUNW/HART CV10 .....96 F3
The Oaks Primary School
 ALE/KHTH/YWD B14 .....146 B3
Oakstreet Industrial Estate
 CDYHTH B64 .....103 H4
Oak Street Trading Estate
 BRLYHL DY5 .....102 D4
Oakwood Special School
 ALDR WS9 .....40 E2
Ocker Hill J & I School
 TPTN/OCK DY4 .....68 A5
Odeon Cinema
 CBHAM B2 .....7 G6
 COV CV1 .....9 G5
 CSCFLD/WYGN B72 .....72 F2
 NUNW/HART CV10 .....98 E7
Offmore First School
 KIDD DY10 .....138 F7
Ogley Hay Infant School
 BRWNH WS8 .....26 D5
Oil Storage Depot
 POL/KGSB/FAZ B78 .....60 C5
Oken's House & Doll Museum
 WWCK CV34 .....205 J7
Oldbury Business Centre
 LGLYGN/QTN B68 .....104 E3
Oldbury Green Retail Park
 OLDBY B69 .....86 D5
Oldbury Health Centre
 OLDBY B69 .....86 E5
Oldbury Leisure Centre
 OLDBY B69 .....86 C7
Oldbury Road Industrial Estate
 SMTHWK B66 .....87 H6
 WBROM B70 .....86 D3
Oldbury United FC
 BLKHTH/ROWR B65 .....104 C2
Old Bush Trading Estate
 BRLYHL DY5 .....84 B8
 BRLYHL DY5 .....102 A3
 BRLYHL DY5 .....102 C2
Old Church CE Primary School
 DARL/WED WS10 .....52 A7
The Olde Corner House Hotel
 LICHS WS14 .....27 L3
Old Edwardians Sports Club
 HIA/OLT B92 .....127 G8
Oldfield Trading Estate
 CDYHTH B64 .....103 H5
Old Forge Business Centre
 REDE B98 .....203 G5
Old Forge Trading Estate
 HAG/WOL DY9 .....102 C7
Old Halesonians RFC
 HAG/WOL DY9 .....120 D5
Old Hall Industrial Estate
 BLOX/PEL WS3 .....39 G5
Oldhall Special School
 WSLW WS2 .....38 C8
Old Hill CC
 CDYHTH B64 .....103 K5
Old Hill Primary School
 CDYHTH B64 .....103 K4
Oldington Trading Estate
 KIDDW DY11 .....163 M4
Oldknow Junior School
 SMHTH B10 .....108 C3
Old Learningtonians RFC
 RLSN CV32 .....198 C2
Old Limbelost Sports Club
 BFLD/HDSWWD B20 .....88 E2
Old Mill Hotel
 KNWTH CV8 .....181 J2
Old Park Industrial Estate
 DARL/WED WS10 .....52 C1
Old Park Primary School
 DARL/WED WS10 .....52 C8
Old Park Special School
 DUDN DY1 .....84 D5
Old Rep Theatre
 DIG/EDG B5 .....6 F7
The Old Square
 Shopping Centre
 WSL WS1 .....4 E5
Oldswinford CE
 Primary School
 STRBR DY8 .....119 L2
Old Swinford Hospital School
 STRBR DY8 .....119 L1
Old Warwickian
 Sports Ground
 RWWCK/WEL CV35 .....204 B8
Olive Hill Primary School
 RMSLY B62 .....104 B6
Olton Golf Club
 SOLH B91 .....127 L6
Olympia Sports Centre
 CNCK/NC WS11 .....16 C4
One Stop Medical Centre
 COV CV1 .....8 E3
One Stop Retail Park
 PBAR/PBCH B42 .....89 G7
Oratory RC Primary School
 LDYWD/EDGR B16 .....106 D3
Orbital Retail Centre
 CNCK/NC WS11 .....16 D7
Orchard Lane Clinic
 HAG/WOL DY9 .....102 C7
Orchard Retail Park
 COVS CV3 .....182 B1
The Orchard School
 SMTHWK B66 .....87 J6
 SMTHWKW B67 .....87 K8

Orthodontists Surgery
 ACGN B27 .....126 E2
Osborne Primary School
 ERDW/GRVHL B23 .....72 E8
Ounsdale High School
 WMBN WV5 .....64 D6
Ounsdale Sports Centre
 WMBN WV5 .....64 D6
Our Lady of Compassion RC
 Primary School
 HIA/OLT B92 .....127 H6
Our Lady of Fatima RC
 Primary School
 HRBN B17 .....105 K6
Our Lady of Lourdes RC
 Primary School
 MOS/BIL B13 .....126 B8
Our Lady of the Assumption
 RC Primary School
 TLHL/CAN CV4 .....153 J4
Our Lady of the Wayside RC
 Primary School
 WOLVN WV10 .....148 A5
Our Lady & St Chad RC
 Secondary School
 WOLVN WV10 .....36 D5
Our Lady & St Kenelm RC
 Primary School
 HALE B63 .....121 K2
Our Lady & St Rose of Lima
 RC Primary School
 SLYOAK B29 .....123 M4
Our Lady & St Teresas RC
 Combined School
 RLSN CV32 .....199 H8
Our Ladys RC Primary School
 STETCH B33 .....110 B3
The Oval Primary School
 STETCH B33 .....109 K3
Owen Road Industrial Estate
 WLNHL WV13 .....52 A4
Owen Road Trading Estate
 WLNHL WV13 .....52 A4
Oxbarn Social & Sports Club
 BDMR/CCFT WV3 .....49 K6
Oxford Street Industrial Park
 BILS/COS WV14 .....51 K8
Oxley Park Golf Club
 WOLVN WV10 .....36 A6
Packwood House
 HOCK/TIA B94 .....175 L8
Paddox Primary School
 RUGBYS/DCH CV22 .....187 H5
Paddys Wide Water
 Industrial Estate
 BRLYHL DY5 .....84 A8
Paganel J & I School
 SLYOAK B29 .....123 L3
Paget Primary School
 ERDE/BCHGN B24 .....91 G1
Palfrey Girls School
 WSL WS1 .....4 E4
Palfrey Infant School
 WSL WS1 .....4 E8
Palfrey Junior School
 WSL WS1 .....4 D8
Pallasades Shopping Centre
 CBHAM B2 .....6 F6
Palmers Cross Primary School
 DUNHL/THL/PER WV6 .....35 H5
Paper Mill End Industrial Estate
 PBAR/PBCH B42 .....71 H7
Park Attwood Clinic
 BEWD DY12 .....137 H1
Parkbrook Industrial Estate
 HAG/WOL DY9 .....102 D8
Park Clinic
 ERDW/GRVHL B23 .....72 E8
Park Farm Industrial Estate
 REDE B98 .....203 G5
Park Farm Industrial Estate
 REDE B98 .....203 J5
Parkfield Clinic
 BKHL/PFLD WV2 .....50 B7
Parkfield High School
 ETTPK/GDPK/PENN WV4 .....50 C8
Parkfield Primary School
 ETTPK/GDPK/PENN WV4 .....50 C8
 TAM/AM/WIL B77 .....46 A4
 WASH/WDE B8 .....108 C2
Parkgate Primary School
 COVW CV5 .....133 M2
Park Hall Hotel &
 Conference Centre
 ETTPK/GDPK/PENN WV4 .....66 A1
Park Hall Infant School
 DSYBK/YTR WS5 .....54 A6
Park Hall Junior School
 DSYBK/YTR WS5 .....54 A6
Park Hall School
 CBROM B36 .....92 C4
Park Hill Junior School
 KNWTH CV8 .....180 A7
Park Hill Primary School
 COVW CV5 .....153 L1
Park Hill Primary School
 DARL/WED WS10 .....69 G3
Park Hill School
 MOS/BIL B13 .....125 K1
Park Lane Industrial Estate
 HHTH/SAND B71 .....87 L4
Park Lane Industrial Estate
 KIDDW DY11 .....164 B1
Park Lane Primary School
 NUNW/HART CV10 .....97 K2
Park Lane Trading Estate
 OLDBY B69 .....86 E6
Park Lane Trading Estate
 WOLVN WV10 .....36 C8
Park Medical Centre
 SMHTH B10 .....108 C6
Parkrose Industrial Estate
 SMTHWK B66 .....87 M5
Park School
 CRTAM B79 .....31 L6
Parkside Business Park
 COV CV1 .....9 G7
Parkside Industrial Estate
 WOLV WV1 .....3 M7
Parkside Middle School
 BRGRVW B61 .....191 K2
Park Street Industrial Estate
 COVN CV6 .....134 C6
Park Trading Estate
 WSNGN B18 .....88 E7
Park View School
 WASH/WDE B8 .....90 C8
Parkway Industrial Centre
 VAUX/NECH B7 .....7 L1
Pattison College
 COVS CV3 .....155 L3
Pavilions Shopping Centre
 CBHAMNE B4 .....7 H5
PDH Medical Centre
 DARL/WED WS10 .....68 A1
PDH Industrial Estate
 WLNHL WV13 .....51 H2
Pearl Hyde Primary School
 COVE CV2 .....135 L8

Peartree Industrial Park
 DUDS DY2 84
Pedmore CE Primary School
 HAG/WOL DY9 119
Pedmore Road
 Industrial Estate
 BRLYHL DY5 102
The Peel Medical Centre
 CRTAM B79 31
Pegasus Primary School
 CVALE B35 91
Pelsall Clinic
 BLOX/PEL WS3 39
Pelsall Village School
 BLOX/PEL WS3 39
Pendeford Business Park
 COVEN WV9 35
Pendeford Health Centre
 COVEN WV9 35
Pendeford High School
 WOLVN WV10 35
Pendene Complimentary
 Medical Centre
 WOLV WV1 2
Penderford Mill
 Nature Reserve
 COVEN WV9 35
Penkridge Industrial Estate
 PENK ST19 10
Penkridge Leisure Centre
 PENK ST19 10
Penkridge Middle School
 PENK ST19 10
Pennfields Health Centre
 BDMR/CCFT WV3 .....
Penn Fields School
 BDMR/CCFT WV3 .....
Penn Golf Club
 ETTPK/GDPK/PENN WV4 65
Penn Hall Special School
 ETTPK/GDPK/PENN WV4 65
Penn Hospital
 ETTPK/GDPK/PENN WV4 65
Penn Industrial Estate
 DUDS DY2 103
Penn Manor Medical Centre
 ETTPK/GDPK/PENN WV4 65
Penn Road Retail Park
 BKHL/PFLD WV2 2
Penns Primary School
 CSCFLD/WYGN B72 73
Pens Meadow Special School
 STRBR DY8 101
The Pennsett School of
 Technology
 BRLYHL DY5 83
Pensnett Trading Estate
 KGSWFD DY6 83
The Pensnett Trading Estate
 KGSWFD DY6 83
Percy Business Park
 OLDBY B69 .....
Percy Shurmer Primary School
 DIG/EDG B5 107
Perry Barr Greyhound Stadium
 PBAR/PBCH B42 89
Perry Beeches J & I School
 PBAR/PBCH B42 71
Perry Common Primary School
 ERDW/GRVHL B23 71
Perryfields High School
 LGLYGN/QTN B68 104
Perryfields Primary School
 LGLYGN/QTN B68 104
Perry Hall Primary School
 WNSFLD WV11 37
Perry Street Industrial Estate
 BILS/COS WV14 67
Personal & Child Health Centre
 BVILLE B30 124
Perton Clinic
 DUNHL/THL/PER WV6 48
Perton First School
 DUNHL/THL/PER WV6 34
Perton Middle School
 DUNHL/THL/PER WV6 48
Perton Park Golf Club
 DUNHL/THL/PER WV6 48
Peterbrook Primary School
 SHLY B90 147
Peters Hill Primary School
 BRLYHL DY5 102
Pheasey Clinic
 GTB/HAM B43 71
Pheasey Park Farm
 Primary School
 GTB/HAM B43 71
Phillips Street Industrial Estate
 AST/WIT B6 89
Phoenix Business Park
 VAUX/NECH B7 89
Phoenix Industrial Estate
 BILS/COS WV14 67
Phoenix International
 Industrial Estate
 WBROM B70 68
Phoenix Road Industrial Estate
 WLNHL WV13 51
Phoenix Works Industrial Estate
 DARL/WED WS10 52
Piccadilly Cinema
 SPARK B11 107
Pickwick Picture Gallery
 COVN CV6 133
The Picture House
 CNCK/NC WS11 16
 STRBR DY8 119
 WASH/WDE B8 90
 WLNHL WV13 51
Pines Special School
 CBROM B36 91
Pinfold Industrial Estate
 BLOX/PEL WS3 39
Pinfold Street Primary School
 DARL/WED WS10 52
Pingles Leisure Centre
 NUN CV11 99
Pingles Stadium
 NUN CV11 99
Pitcheroak Golf Club
 REDW B97 202
Pitcheroak Special School
 REDW B97 201
Planetary Industrial Estate
 WLNHL WV13 51
Planet Ice Arena
 DIG/EDG B5 .....
Plantsbrook School
 CSCFLD/WYGN B72 73
Playbox Theatre
 KNWTH CV8 197
Pleck Business Park
 WSLW WS2 .....
Pleck Industrial Estate
 WSLW WS2 .....
Plough & Harrow Hotel
 LDYWD/EDGR B16 10
Polesworth High School
 POL/KGSB/FAZ B78 4

esworth Nethersole
  fant School
  OL/KGSB/FAZ B78 ....47 L3
ol Hayes
  omprehensive School
  HHTH WV12 ....37 M8
l Hayes Primary School
  HHTH WV12 ....37 M7
l Meadow Bus Station
  OV CV1 ....9 G4
ol Road Business Centre
  UNW/HART CV10 ....80 D5
l Road Industrial Estate
  UNW/HART CV10 ....80 D8
lar Road Clinic
  LE/KHTH/YWD B14 ....125 K4
lars Trading Estate
  TUD B80 ....203 H7
lar Trading Estate
  ST/WIT B6 ....71 K8
tersfield Industrial Estate
  DYHTH B64 ....103 G5
tland Hotel
  DYWD/EDGR B16 ....106 A4
kway Road Industrial Estate
  LDBY B69 ....86 C7
thouse Hotel
  DIG/EDG B5 ....6 F7
ers Green Primary School
  OVE CV2 ....135 J3
ke Lane Industrial Estate
  LKHTH/ROWR B65 ....103 L3
l Precinct
  ....8 A4
mier Business Centre
  AG/WOL DY9 ....102 D8
mier Business Park
  SLW WS2 ....4 C5
mier Lodge
  DYWD/EDGR B16 ....6 C5
  MGN/WHC B75 ....57 K6
  BRY B45 ....143 M5
  REDW B97 ....201 J2
mier Partnership
  Industrial Estate
  GSWFD DY5 ....101 L1
mier Trading Estate
  VAUX/NECH B7 ....89 K8
sident Kennedy
  omprehensive School &
  ommunity College
  COVN/BALC/EX CV7 ....133 L4
estley Smith Special School
  RDW/GRVHL B23 ....71 M7
mrose Hill Primary School
  WK/WKHTH B38 ....145 K5
mrose Hill Trading Estate
  DUDS DY2 ....103 H1
mrose Lane Health Centre
  OLVN WV10 ....36 E5
ce Albert Primary School
  ST/WIT B6 ....89 J5
ncefield First School
  PENK ST19 ....10 D5
nce of Wales Centre
  CNCK/NC WS11 ....16 C4
nces Drive Industrial Park
  NWTH CV8 ....179 L5
nces End Industrial Park
  BILS/COS WV14 ....67 J4
nces End Primary School
  PTN/OCK DY4 ....67 J6
ncess of Wales Hospital
  BRGRVW B61 ....191 L1
ncethorpe J & I School
  SLYOAK B29 ....123 L5
rs Field CP School
  NWTH CV8 ....179 H6
ory Clinic
  DUDN DY1 ....84 D7
s Priory
  County Record Office)
  WWCK CV34 ....205 J6
ory Courts
  BHAMNW B3 ....7 G4
ory Green Junior &
  nfants School
  COVEN WV9 ....35 L3
ory House Industrial Estate
  VSNGN B18 ....88 F8
ory Infants School
  BLOX/PEL WS3 ....38 F6
ory New Way
  Industrial Estate
  ST/WIT B6 ....89 J8
ory Primary School
  DUDN DY1 ....84 F2
Priory Primary School
  DARL/WED WS10 ....69 H3
ory Theatre
  NWTH CV8 ....179 K8
vate Medical Clinic
  BRGRVW B61 ....191 L2
gress Business Centre
  CNCK/NC WS11 ....16 C6
spect Business Park
  CNCK/NC WS11 ....16 A6
spect Trading Estate
  BHAMW B1 ....6 C4
vidence Industrial Estate
  HAG/WOL DY9 ....102 C7
vost Williams CE
  rimary School
  NWTH CV8 ....182 K4
ley Chase Golf Club
  UNW/HART CV10 ....78 E3
e Green Valley CP School
  HEDN WS12 ....12 G4
e Hayes Golf Club
  WALM/CURD B76 ....73 J7
lcast Road Industrial Estate
  OLV WV1 ....3 L5
lity Hotel
  DMR/CCFT WV3 ....2 D9
  OAKS/STRLY B74 ....57 L2
  EDE B98 ....202 C4
  SLW WS2 ....52 D3
rry Bank Primary School
  RLYHL DY5 ....102 E4
en Alexandra College
  RBN B17 ....105 L7
en Elizabeth Hospital
  DG B15 ....106 C8
en Elizabeth Law Courts
  BHAMNE B4 ....7 H4
en Elizabeth Lower School
  THST CV9 ....63 K6
en Elizabeth
  Psychiatric Hospital
  DG B15 ....124 C1
en Elizabeth's
  rcian School
  RBN B79 ....31 M7
en Elizabeth Upper School
  ST CV9 ....63 J5
n Marys Grammar School
  WS1 ....5 K6

Queen Marys High School
  RUSH/SHEL WS4 ....5 H1
Queensbridge
  MOS/BIL B13 ....125 J3
Queensbury Special School
  ERDE/BCHGN B24 ....90 D2
Queens CE Junior School
  NUN CV11 ....98 E1
Queens College
  EDG B15 ....106 D8
Queens Court Trading Estate
  WBROM B70 ....86 D2
Queens Croft School
  LICH WS13 ....20 E6
Queen Street Industrial Estate
  BNTWD WS7 ....18 D2
Queensway Trading Estate
  DIG/EDG B5 ....7 J4
Queensway Trading Estate
  RLSS CV31 ....206 C7
Queen Victoria Primary School
  SEDG DY3 ....66 B5
Quince Tree Special School
  TAM/AM/WIL B77 ....46 E1
Quinton Business Park
  RIDG/WDGT B32 ....104 E8
Quinton CE Primary School
  RIDG/WDGT B32 ....104 E7
Racecourse Road
  Industrial Estate
  DUNHL/THL/PER WV6 ....35 J3
Race Leys Primary School
  BDWTH CV12 ....116 F1
Racemeadow Primary School
  ATHST CV9 ....63 J4
Racing Club Warwick FC
  WWCK CV34 ....205 G8
Raddlebarn J & I School
  SLYOAK B29 ....124 D4
Radford Primary School
  COVN CV6 ....133 M2
Radford Semele CE
  Primary School
  RLSS CV31 ....207 J8
Radleys Primary School
  RUSH/SHEL WS4 ....40 A6
Radway Industrial Estate
  SHLY B90 ....148 C6
Rainbow Business Park
  WLNHL WV13 ....51 M2
Rake Gate Infant School
  WOLVN WV10 ....35 M4
Rake Gate Junior School
  WOLVN WV10 ....35 M4
Raleigh Industrial Estate
  HDSW B21 ....87 M4
Rathilly School
  ALDR B31 ....144 F2
Ravens Bank First School
  REDE B98 ....195 H7
Ravensdale Primary School
  COVE CV2 ....156 A1
The Rawlett School
  CRTAM B79 ....31 L4
Rea Business Park
  VAUX/NECH B7 ....107 M1
Read Street Industrial Estate
  COV CV1 ....9 K4
Reaside Clinic
  RBRY B45 ....143 L4
Reaside Junior School
  RBRY B45 ....143 L4
Reddal Hill Primary School
  CDYHTH B64 ....103 J4
Red Deeps Special School
  NUNW/HART CV10 ....98 F5
Reddicap Trading Estate
  MGN/WHC B75 ....73 H1
Redditch County Court
  REDW B97 ....202 B1
Redditch Golf Club
  REDW B97 ....201 L5
Redditch Magistrates Court
  REDE B98 ....202 C1
Redditch United FC
  REDW B97 ....202 A1
Red Hall Primary School
  SEDG DY3 ....84 A2
Redhill J & I School
  YDLY B25 ....108 E6
Redhill Primary School
  CNCK/NC WS11 ....12 C8
Redhill Secondary School
  STRBR DY8 ....101 M8
Red Hill Street Clinic
  WOLV WV1 ....2 F1
Redhouse Industrial Estate
  ALDR WS9 ....40 B7
Redhouse JMI School
  ALDR WS9 ....40 C7
Rednal Hill J & I School
  RBRY B45 ....143 M6
Red Rooster Industrial Estate
  ALDR WS9 ....40 C7
Redwood Business Park
  SMTHWK B66 ....87 G6
Reedswood Retail Park
  WSLW WS2 ....52 F1
Reflex Industrial Park
  WLNHL WV13 ....51 K2
Regency Business Centre
  RLSN CV32 ....206 D4
Regency Hotel
  SHLY B90 ....148 C5
Regent Health Centre
  RUGBYN/HIL CV21 ....186 E1
Regents Park
  Primary School
  SMHTH B10 ....108 A5
Regent Special School
  OLDBY B69 ....85 J2
Regis Medical Centre
  BLKHTH/ROWR B65 ....104 A4
Reliance Trading Estate
  BILS/COS WV14 ....50 F8
Renaissance Solihull Hotel
  SOLH B91 ....148 C1
Retail Market Hall
  BDMR/CCFT WV3 ....2 E1
Retail Market Shops
  BKHL/PFLD WV2 ....2 E6
Reynalds Cross School
  HIA/OLT B92 ....127 K6
Richard Lee Primary School
  COVE CV2 ....156 B2
The Ridge Primary School
  STRBR DY8 ....101 G4
Ridgeway Primary School
  BNTWD WS7 ....18 D2
Ridgeway School
  WWCK CV34 ....205 G3
Ridgewood High School
  KINVER DY7 ....101 J2
Ridpool Primary School
  STECH B33 ....109 M2
Rigby Hall Special School
  BRGRVE B60 ....192 A5

Riland Industrial Estate
  MGN/WHC B75 ....57 G8
Ringway Industrial Estate
  LICH WS13 ....21 G2
River Brook Medical Centre
  BVILLE B30 ....124 F5
Riverside Business Centre
  STRPT DY13 ....188 F2
Riverside Industrial Estate
  POL/KGSB/FAZ B78 ....45 M4
Riverside Industrial Estate
  REDE B98 ....203 G5
Riversley Park Clinic
  NUN CV11 ....99 G3
RMW Business Centre
  HAG/WOL DY9 ....102 D8
Robert Clinic
  BVILLE B30 ....124 C8
Roberts Primary School
  SEDG DY3 ....84 C1
Robin Hood Cemetery
  SHLY B90 ....126 F8
Robin Hood Golf Club
  HIA/OLT B92 ....127 G7
Robin Hood Primary School
  HLGN/YWD B28 ....126 F7
Robins Business Park
  TPTN/OCK DY4 ....68 C8
Rocklands Special School
  LICH WS13 ....21 G5
Rocky Lane Trading Estate
  VAUX/NECH B7 ....89 L7
Rokeby Infant School
  RUGBYS/DCH CV22 ....186 E5
Rokeby Junior School
  RUGBYS/DCH CV22 ....186 E5
Rollingmill Business Park
  WSLW WS2 ....4 B5
Roman Way First School
  REDE B98 ....203 H2
Roman Way Hotel
  CNCK/NC WS11 ....15 M6
Romney House
  Industrial Estate
  BILS/COS WV14 ....51 M6
Rood End Primary School
  LCLYGN/QTN B68 ....87 G7
Rookery Primary School
  HDSW B21 ....88 C4
Rosary RC Primary School
  WASH/WDE B8 ....108 C2
Rosedale CE Infant School
  SHHTH WV12 ....38 B8
Rose Theatre
  KIDD DY10 ....138 D5
Rosewood Special School
  DUDN DY1 ....84 C4
Roslyn School
  HLGN/YWD B28 ....126 E8
Rotton Park Medical Centre
  LDYWD/EDGR B16 ....106 B2
Rotunda
  CBHAM B2 ....7 G6
Rough Hay Primary School
  DARL/WED WS10 ....52 A4
Roughwood (Nature Reserve)
  SHHTH WV12 ....38 C7
Round Oak School
  RLSN CV32 ....206 E2
Rounds Green Primary School
  OLDBY B69 ....86 C5
Rovex Business Park
  SPARK B11 ....108 D8
Rowley Hall Primary School
  BLKHTH/ROWR B65 ....104 A1
Rowley Regis Cemetery &
  Crematorium
  BLKHTH/ROWR B65 ....103 L3
Rowley Regis College
  BLKHTH/ROWR B65 ....103 M2
Rowley Regis Hospital
  BLKHTH/ROWR B65 ....103 M2
Rowleys Green
  Industrial Estate
  COVN CV6 ....134 C1
Royal Birmingham
  Society of Arts
  CBHAMNW B3 ....6 D2
Royal Brierley Trading Estate
  BRLYHL DY5 ....102 A2
The Royal Leamington Hotel
  RLSN CV32 ....206 E4
Royal Mail Depot
  WOLVN WV10 ....3 K4
Royal Orthopaedic Hospital
  NFLD/LBR B31 ....123 M7
Royal Priors Shopping Centre
  RLSN CV32 ....206 D5
The Royal Pump Rooms
  RLSS CV31 ....206 E5
Royal Spa Centre Cinema
  RLSN CV32 ....206 E5
Royal Theatre
  CDYHTH B64 ....103 H4
The Royal Wolverhampton
  Junior School
  BDMR/CCFT WV3 ....49 L6
The Royal Wolverhampton
  School
  BDMR/CCFT WV3 ....49 M6
Rubery Clinic
  RBRY B45 ....143 J6
The Rubicon Business Centre
  LOZ/NWT B19 ....89 J2
Ruckleigh School
  SOLH B91 ....149 G1
Rufford Primary School
  HAG/WOL DY9 ....102 A8
Rugby Athletics Track
  RUGBYS/DCH CV22 ....186 F5
Rugby College
  RUGBYN/HIL CV21 ....187 H3
Rugby FC
  RUGBYS/DCH CV22 ....186 C5
Rugby Golf Club
  RUGBYN/HIL CV21 ....187 J1
Rugby High School for Girls
  RUGBYS/DCH CV22 ....186 B7
Rugby School
  RUGBYS/DCH CV22 ....186 E5
Rugby School Museum
  RUGBYN/HIL CV21 ....186 E2
Rugby School Sports Centre
  RUGBYS/DCH CV22 ....186 F5
Rugby Theatre
  RUGBYN/HIL CV21 ....186 D2
Rugby Welsh RFC
  RUGBYN/HIL CV21 ....186 D2
Rumer Hill Business Estate
  CNCK/NC WS11 ....16 C6
Rushall Jm School & Education
  Development Centre
  RUSH/SHEL WS4 ....39 L4
Russell Medical Centre
  DARL/WED WS10 ....68 D3
Russells Hall Hospital
  DUDN DY1 ....84 B6
Russells Hall Primary School
  DUDN DY1 ....84 C4

Ryders Green Primary School
  WBROM B70 ....86 E1
Ryders Hayes JMI School
  BLOX/PEL WS3 ....25 L8
Ryecroft Shopping Centre
  WSL 18 D5
Rylands Sports Centre
  BRGRVE B60 ....191 L4
Ryton Gardens
  KNWTH CV8 ....183 J4
Sacred Heart RC
  Primary School
  BFLD/HDSWWD B20 ....89 H4
Sacred Heart RC
  Primary School
  COVE CV2 ....155 L2
Sacred Heart RC
  Primary School
  TPTN/OCK DY4 ....85 K1
Saddlers Shopping Centre
  WSL 4 E4
Sai Medical Centre
  WSLW WS2 ....4 B3
St Albans CE Primary School
  WNSFLD WV11 ....37 M5
St Albans CE School
  BHTH/HG B12 ....107 K6
St Albans RC Primary School
  ALE/KHTH/YWD B14 ....146 D1
St Alphege CE Infant School
  SOLH B91 ....149 G2
St Alphege CE Junior School
  SOLH B91 ....149 G3
St Ambrose Barlow RC
  Primary School
  HLGN/YWD B28 ....126 E7
St Ambrose RC Primary School
  KIDD DY10 ....138 D7
St Andrews CC Primary &
  Middle School
  RUGBYN/HIL CV21 ....187 H1
St Andrews CE Infant School
  COVW CV5 ....132 A8
  DUNHL/THL/PER WV6 ....49 K1
St Andrews Industrial Estate
  BORD B9 ....108 A3
St Andrews Primary School
  BORD B9 ....107 M3
St Andrews RC
  Primary School
  HIA/OLT B92 ....127 L3
St Andrews RUFC
  RUGBYS/DCH CV22 ....187 H6
St Annes CE Middle School
  BEWD DY12 ....162 D3
St Annes Industrial Estate
  WLNHL WV13 ....51 M2
St Anne's CE JMI School
  FOAKS/STRLY B74 ....55 J5
St Annes RC Primary School
  BHTH/HG B12 ....7 L9
  CHWD/FDBR/MGN B37 ....110 E3
  COVS CV3 ....155 M7
  NUNW/HART CV10 ....80 B6
St Anthonys RC Primary School
  CHWD/FDBR/MGN B37 ....92 E8
  RLSS CV31 ....207 G6
  WOLVN WV10 ....36 B2
St Augustines Catholic
  High School
  REDW B97 ....202 B8
St Augustines Catholic
  Primary School
  HDSW B21 ....88 B3
St Augustines Primary School
  SOLH B91 ....148 E3
St Augustines RC
  Primary School
  COVN CV6 ....133 L6
  KNWTH CV8 ....179 J6
St Barnabas CE First School
  KIDDW DY11 ....137 M4
St Bartholomews CE
  Primary School
  COVS CV3 ....156 C6
  ETTPK/GDPK/PENN WV4 ....65 J2
St Bedes RC Middle School
  REDE B98 ....202 D2
St Benedict Biscop CE
  Primary School
  WMBN WV5 ....64 C6
St Benedicts Infant School
  SMHTH B10 ....108 D6
St Benedicts RC Primary School
  ATHST CV9 ....63 G6
St Bernadette RC JMI School
  BRWNH WS8 ....26 D3
St Bernadettes RC
  Primary School
  SMHTH B10 ....108 F5
  WMBN WV5 ....64 D7
St Bernards RC Primary School
  MOS/BIL B13 ....126 A4
St Brigids RC Primary School
  NFLD/LBR B31 ....144 D2
St Catherine of Siena RC School
  EDG B15 ....6 F9
St Chads CE (VC) Primary School
  LICH WS13 ....21 G5
St Chads Industrial Estate
  LOZ/NWT B19 ....89 J2
St Chad's RC Cathedral
  CBHAM B4 ....6 F2
St Chads RC Primary School
  LOZ/NWT B19 ....89 H8
  SEDG DY3 ....66 B6
St Christopher Primary School
  COVW CV5 ....154 B1
St Christophers RC
  Primary School
  CDSL WV8 ....34 E2
St Clares Primary School
  BFLD/HDSWWD B20 ....88 F4
St Clements CE Primary School
  VAUX/NECH B7 ....89 M6
St Columbas RC
  Primary School
  RBRY B45 ....144 B6
St Cuthberts RC
  Primary School
  WASH/WDE B8 ....109 G1
St Dunstans RC Primary School
  ALE/KHTH/YWD B14 ....125 J5
St Edmund Campion
  Lower School
  ERDE/BCHGN B24 ....73 G7
St Edmund Campion RC School
  ERDE/BCHGN B24 ....72 F7
St Edmund & John CE
  Primary School
  DUDS DY2 ....85 J4
St Edmunds Catholic School
  DUNHL/THL/PER WV6 ....49 H2
St Edwards RC Primary School
  WSNGN B18 ....106 E1
St Edwards RC Primary School
  CSHL/WTROR B46 ....93 L8

St Edwards RC Primary School
  CSHL/WTROR B46 ....111 L2
  SLYOAK B29 ....124 F4
St Elizabeths C Primary School
  COVN CV6 ....134 C6
St Elizabeths RC
  Primary School
  CRTAM B79 ....31 L5
St Francis CE Primary School
  BVILLE B30 ....124 B7
St Francis of Assisi RC School
  ALDR WS9 ....41 G8
St Francis RC Combined School
  BDWTH CV12 ....116 F2
St Francis RC Primary School
  LOZ/NWT B19 ....88 F7
St Francis RC Primary School
  RUSH/SHEL WS4 ....40 A4
St Francis Xavier RC
  Primary School
  OLDBY B69 ....86 E5
St Gabriels RC Primary School
  TAM/AM/WIL B77 ....46 C4
St George & St Teresa RC
  Primary School
  DOR/KN B93 ....175 L1
St Georges CE First School
  KIDD DY10 ....138 D6
  REDE B98 ....202 D2
St Georges CE Primary School
  LDYWD/EDGR B16 ....106 D4
St Georges School Edgbaston
  EDG B15 ....106 F5
St Georges Sixth Form & CE
  Primary School
  LOZ/NWT B19 ....89 H8
St Gerards Orthopaedic
  Hospital
  CSHL/WTROR B46 ....93 L8
St Gerards RC Primary School
  CVALE B35 ....91 M1
St Giles CE Primary School
  WLNHL WV13 ....51 M3
St Giles Junior School
  RCOVN/BALC/EX CV7 ....116 C5
St Gregorys RC Primary School
  COVE CV2 ....156 C2
  SMTHWKW B67 ....105 K3
St Huberts RC
  Primary School
  LGLYGN/QTN B68 ....105 L4
St James CE Junior School
  SHLY B90 ....147 M3
St James CE Primary School
  HDSW B21 ....88 B4
  OLDBY B69 ....86 B8
  STRBR DY8 ....101 H6
St James Medical Centre
  COVS CV3 ....156 A8
  HDSW B21 ....88 B5
St James Primary School
  BRWNH WS8 ....26 D5
St James RC Primary School
  RBRY B45 ....143 L6
St John Bosco RC
  Primary School
  HHTH/SAND B71 ....68 F6
St John Fisher RC
  Primary School
  COVE CV2 ....135 H7
St John Fishers RC
  Primary School
  NFLD/LBR B31 ....144 F1
St John & St Monica RC
  Primary School
  MOS/BIL B13 ....125 J3
St Johns CE First School
  KIDDW DY11 ....137 M7
St Johns CE JMI School
  ALDR WS9 ....40 C2
St Johns CE Middle School
  BRGRVW B61 ....191 J3
  KIDDW DY11 ....137 M7
St Johns CE Primary School
  COVW CV5 ....154 A1
  DARL/WED WS10 ....68 D3
  LDYWD/EDGR B16 ....106 E3
  SEDG DY3 ....82 C3
  SPARK B11 ....126 A1
  WNSFLD WV11 ....37 L1
St John's Hospital
  COV CV1 ....8 F3
St John's Museum
  & Royal Warwickshire
  Regimental Museum
  WWCK CV34 ....205 K6
St Johns Primary School
  KNWTH CV8 ....197 K3
St Johns Retail Park
  BKHL/PFLD WV2 ....2 F7
St John the Baptist RC
  Primary School
  CBROM B36 ....92 E6
St John the Divine CE
  Primary School
  COVS CV3 ....156 A7
St John Vianney RC
  Primary School
  COVW CV5 ....153 M2
St John Wall RC School
  HDSW B21 ....88 B3
St Joseph & St Theresa RC
  Primary School
  BNTWD WS7 ....18 C7
St Josephs Catholic
  Primary School
  DARL/WED WS10 ....52 A4
St Josephs RC Primary School
  MGN/WHC B75 ....57 G8
  STRBR DY8 ....119 K3
St Josephs RC First School
  NUN CV11 ....99 G2
St Josephs RC Primary School
  BVILLE B30 ....124 C8
  DUDS DY2 ....85 J4
  HEDN WS12 ....17 G1
  LICHS WS14 ....21 G6
  VAUX/NECH B7 ....89 M7
St Josephs School
  KNWTH CV8 ....179 K4
St Judes CE Primary School
  BDMR/CCFT WV3 ....49 G7
  ALE/KHTH/YWD B14 ....146 D3
St Kenelms CE First School
  RMSLY B62 ....142 E1
St Laurence CE J & I School
  NFLD/LBR B31 ....144 F1
St Leonards CE Primary School
  CRTAM B79 ....32 A4
St Lukes CE Aided
  Primary School
  BKHL/PFLD WV2 ....49 M6
St Lukes CE First School
  REDW B97 ....202 B3
St Margaret Mary RC
  Primary School
  ERDW/GRVHL B23 ....72 A7
St Margarets CE Primary School
  GTB/HAM B43 ....70 C1

St Margarets Hospital
DSYBK/YTR WS5 ....**54** C5
St Maries Catholic
Infant School
RUGBYS/DCH CV22 ....**186** A6
St Maries RC Junior School
RUGBYS/DCH CV22 ....**186** D3
St Marks CE Primary School
BRLYHL DY5 ....**84** A6
St Marks RC Primary School
PBAR/PBCH B42 ....**70** D6
St Martin de Porres RC
Primary School
MOS/BIL B13 ....**125** L2
St Martins CE Primary School
BILS/COS WV14 ....**67** L3
TPTN/OCK DY4 ....**67** M8
St Martins Industrial Estate
OLDBY B69 ....**86** E7
St Martins Market
DIG/EDG B5 ....**7** H4
St Martins School
SOLH B91 ....**149** H1
St Mary & Johns RC
Primary School
BKHL/PFLD WV2 ....**3** H9
St Mary Magdalene CE
Primary School
HHTH/SAND B71 ....**69** H7
St Mary of the Angels RC
JMI School
ALDR WS9 ....**40** F8
St Mary's Abbey (Remains)
RMSLY B62 ....**122** B3
St Mary & St Benedict RC
Primary School
COV CV1 ....**9** K2
St Mary & St John RC
Primary School
ERDE/BCHGN B24 ....**90** C2
St Mary & St Margarets CE
Primary School
CBROM B36 ....**91** M5
St Marys Catholic
Primary School
WWCK CV34 ....**205** J5
St Marys CE First School
KIDDW DY11 ....**138** C5
St Marys CE Primary School
BFLD/HDSWWD B20 ....**88** F4
KGSWFD DY6 ....**83** H6
SLYOAK B29 ....**124** B4
St Mary's Guildhall
COV CV1 ....**9** G5
St Mary's Priory
COV CV1 ....**8** E4
St Marys RC Primary School
BRLYHL DY5 ....**102** C3
CNCK/NC WS11 ....**16** C5
DARL/WED WS10 ....**68** D1
HRBN B17 ....**106** A8
WOLVN WV10 ....**36** E6
St Marys the Mount RC School
WSL WS1 ....**5** J7
St Matthews Bloxam CE
School
RUGBYS/DCH CV22 ....**186** C3
St Matthews CE Primary School
SMTHWK B66 ....**87** M8
VAUX/NECH B7 ....**7** M1
St Michaels CE First School
PENK ST19 ....**10** C4
St Michaels CE High School
OLDBY B69 ....**86** B8
St Michaels CE Primary School
BLOX/PEL WS3 ....**39** K3
HDSW B21 ....**88** E6
LICH WS13 ....**21** D1
RIDG/WDGT B32 ....**123** G5
St Michael's Hospital
WWCK CV34 ....**205** H5
St Michaels RC Primary School
BDMR/CCFT WV3 ....**49** H4
St Nicholas CE
Combined School
KNWTH CV8 ....**179** L8
St Nicholas CE Vc First School
CDSL WV5 ....**34** D1
St Nicholas Park Leisure Centre
WWCK CV34 ....**205** L6
St Nicholas RC JMI School
SCFLD/BOLD B73 ....**72** D3
St Nicolas CE Primary School
NUN CV11 ....**81** K7
St Osburgs RC Primary School
COV CV1 ....**8** C3
St Oswalds CE First School
KIDD DY10 ....**138** D1
St Oswalds RC Primary School
RUGBYS/DCH CV22 ....**186** B2
St Patricks CE Primary School
HOCK/TIA B94 ....**174** A3
St Patricks Catholic
Primary School
CHWD/FDBR/MGN B37 ..**111** J3
WSLW WS2 ....**4** D1
St Patricks RC
Combined School
RLSS CV31 ....**206** C8
St Patricks RC Primary School
COVE CV2 ....**135** H4
WNSFLD WV11 ....**37** G8
WSNGN B18 ....**106** D1
St Pauls C E First School
COVEN WV9 ....**22** A2
St Pauls Cemetery
COVN CV6 ....**134** A4
St Pauls CE Primary School
NUNW/HART CV10 ....**98** A4
RLSN CV32 ....**206** F4
TPTN/OCK DY4 ....**67** K7
HWK/WKHTH B38 ....**145** L4
St Pauls School
BHTH/HG B12 ....**107** L8
St Pauls School for Girls
LDYWD/EDGR B16 ....**106** C4
St Peter & Paul RC
Primary School
ERDE/BCHGN B24 ....**91** G2
St Peter & St Paul RC
Primary School
COVE CV2 ....**135** J6
LICH WS13 ....**20** F4
St Peters CE Infant School
HRBN B17 ....**123** M1
St Peters CE Junior School
HRBN B17 ....**124** K1
St Peters CE Primary School
ALDR WS9 ....**41** J1
HEDN WS12 ....**17** H1
St Peters C JMI School
BLOX/PEL WS3 ....**38** F3
St Peters Collegiate
Secondary School
DUNHL/THL/PER WV6 ......**49** J2
St Peters RC First School
BRGRVE B60 ....**191** J5

St Peters RC Primary School
RIDG/WDGT B32 ....**123** C4
RLSN CV32 ....**206** D5
St Peters RC School
SOLH B91 ....**148** F3
St Philips Cathedral
CBHAMNW B3 ....**6** F4
St Philips RC Primary School
SMTHWK B66 ....**87** M7
St Philips Sixth Form
College
LDYWD/EDGR B16 ....**106** D5
St Saviours CE Primary School
WASH/WDE B8 ....**90** B8
St Stephens CE First School
REDE B98 ....**194** B8
St Stephens CE Primary School
WOLVN WV10 ....**3** L1
St Teresas RC Primary School
BFLD/HDSWWD B20 ....**88** C3
ETTPK/GDPK/PENN WV4 ..**50** C8
St Thomas Aquinas RC School
HWK/WKHTH B38 ....**145** H2
St Thomas CE Primary School
EDG B15 ....**6** A4
St Thomas CE Primary School
WNSFLD WV11 ....**37** H6
St Thomas More Catholic
School
WLNHL WV13 ....**51** M3
St Thomas More RC School
CNCK/NC WS11 ....**24** E1
COVS CV3 ....**155** H4
LGN/SDN/BHAMAIR B26 **109** M8
St Thomas More RC School
NUNW/HART CV10 ....**98** E2
St Thomas of Canterbury RC
JMI School
BLOX/PEL WS3 ....**39** K7
St Vincents RC Primary School
VAUX/NECH B7 ....**107** M2
St Wilfrids RC Primary School
CBROM B36 ....**91** K5
Salafi Independent School
SMHTH B10 ....**108** B5
Salford Trading Estate
AST/WIT B6 ....**90** A5
Salisbury Place
Industrial Estate
BDMR/CCFT WV3 ....**2** C7
Salisbury Primary School
DARL/WED WS10 ....**52** C6
Saltbrook Trading Estate
HALE B63 ....**102** E6
Salters Meadow
Health Centre
BNTWD WS7 ....**18** D6
Saltley Business Park
WASH/WDE B8 ....**90** B7
Saltley Health Centre
WASH/WDE B8 ....**90** C8
Saltley Industrial Centre
WASH/WDE B8 ....**108** A2
Saltley Leisure Centre
BORD B9 ....**108** E2
Saltley School
BORD B9 ....**108** E2
Saltley Trading Estate
WASH/WDE B8 ....**90** A8
The Samuel Johnson
Birthplace Museum
LICH WS13 ....**20** F6
Sanders Industrial Estate
BRGRVW B61 ....**191** J4
Sandown First School
DUNHL/THL/PER WV6 ......**48** D1
Sandwell Borough FC
OLDBY B69 ....**86** C6
Sandwell Business
Development Centre
OLDBY B69 ....**87** G6
Sandwell Business Park
SMTHWK B66 ....**87** G5
Sandwell Business &
Technology Centre
LGLYGN/QTN B68 ....**104** D3
Sandwell College
DARL/WED WS10 ....**68** C4
Sandwell College of
Further & Higher Education
WBROM B70 ....**87** G2
Sandwell District General
Hospital
HHTH/SAND B71 ....**69** H8
Sandwell Park Golf Club
HHTH/SAND B71 ....**87** K3
Sandwell Park
Industrial Estate
HHTH/SAND B71 ....**87** K4
Sandwell Valley
HHTH/SAND B71 ....**69** L7
Sandyhill Industrial Estate
SHLY B90 ....**147** L1
Sandy Lane Business Park
COV CV1 ....**134** A8
Sandy Lane Industrial Estate
STRPT DY13 ....**188** F4
Sapcote Business Centre
SMTH B10 ....**108** C7
Sapcote Industrial Estate
CDYHTH B64 ....**103** K2
Sapcote Trading Centre
AST/WIT B6 ....**89** L2
Sapcote Trading Centre
CDYHTH B64 ....**103** K2
Sapcote Trading Centre
SMHTH B10 ....**108** C7
Sarehole Mill
MOS/BIL B13 ....**126** B5
Sarepheld Medical Centre
SMTHWK B66 ....**87** L8
Sargent Turner Trading Estate
HAG/WOL DY9 ....**102** D7
Satellite Industrial Park
WLNHL WV13 ....**51** M4
Saxon Hill Special School
LICHS WS14 ....**21** G7
School of Jewellery (UCE)
CBHAMW B1 ....**6** C2
Scotch Orchard County
Primary School
LICHS WS14 ....**21** H4
Scott Arms Shopping Centre
GTB/HAM B43 ....**70** C4
Sears Retail Park
SHLY B90 ....**148** A4
Securehold Business Centre
REDE B98 ....**202** F4
Sedgley Golf Centre
SEDG DY3 ....**65** M7
Selly Manor Museum
BVILLE B30 ....**124** D5
Selly Oak Health Centre
SLYOAK B29 ....**124** C5
Selly Oak Hospital
SLYOAK B29 ....**124** C4
Selly Oak Industrial Estate
SLYOAK B29 ....**124** C4

Selly Oak School
SLYOAK B29 ....**124** C5
Selly Park Technology
College for Girls for Girls
SLYOAK B29 ....**124** F4
Seven Stars Industrial Estate
COVS CV5 ....**155** L6
Severne Primary School
ACGN B27 ....**127** G5
Severnside Business Park
STRPT DY13 ....**188** E2
Severn Valley Railway
BEWD DY12 ....**136** D3
BEWD DY12 ....**163** J3
Shaftmoor Industrial Estate
HLGN/YWD B28 ....**126** D3
Sharmans Cross
Junior School
SOLH B91 ....**148** C1
Shaw Hill Primary School
WASH/WDE B8 ....**108** C1
Shaw Park Business Village
WOLVN WV10 ....**36** B7
The Sheila Godfrey Clinic
DOR/KN B93 ....**175** K2
Sheldon CC
YDLY B25 ....**109** H5
Sheldon Country Park
LGN/SDN/BHAMAIR B26 **110** C7
Sheldon Heath
Community School
STETCH B33 ....**110** A5
Shelfield Clinic
RUSH/SHEL WS4 ....**40** A5
Shelfield Sports &
Community College
RUSH/SHEL WS4 ....**40** A3
Shell Corner Trading Estate
RMSLY B62 ....**104** B5
Shelter Waterside
Industrial Estate
ETTPK/GDPK/PENN WV4 ..**50** E8
Shenley Court School
NFLD/LBR B31 ....**123** K6
Shenley Lane Community
Association Sports Centre
SLYOAK B29 ....**123** L7
Shenstone Lodge Special School
LICHS WS14 ....**42** E2
Shenstone Sports Club
LICHS WS14 ....**28** E7
Shenstone Trading Estate
HALE B63 ....**122** A1
Shepperton Business Park
NUN CV11 ....**99** G4
Sherborne Wharf
LDYWD/EDGR B16 ....**6** A6
Sherbourne Fields
Special School
COVN CV6 ....**133** H8
Sherbourne Medical Centre
RLSN CV32 ....**206** D4
Sheriden House Hotel
BFLD/HDSWWD B20 ....**88** D2
Shireland Hall Primary School
SMTHWK B66 ....**106** A2
Shireland Language College
SMTHWK B66 ....**105** L2
Shire Oak School
BRWNH WS8 ....**26** E8
Shires Gate Trading Estate
RLSS CV31 ....**206** C7
Shires Industrial Estate
LICH WS13 ....**20** E7
Shires Retail Park
RLSS CV31 ....**206** B7
Shirestone Primary School
STETCH B33 ....**110** B3
Shirley Clinic
SHLY B90 ....**147** M2
Shirley Heath Junior School
SHLY B90 ....**148** A4
Shirley Park Sports Club &
Golf Club
SHLY B90 ....**174** E1
Shirley Road Health Clinic
ACGN B27 ....**126** F4
The Shopping Centre
RLSS CV31 ....**206** F8
Short Heath Clinic
SHHTH WV12 ....**38** B7
Short Heath Primary School
ERDW/GRVHL B23 ....**72** B7
Shorth Heath Junior School
SHHTH WV12 ....**38** B8
Showcase Cinemas
DUDN DY1 ....**85** J2
Showcase Cinemas
ERDE/BCHGN B24 ....**91** H3
Showcase Cinemas
RCOVN/BALC/EX CV7 ....**135** M4
Showcase Cinemas
WSLW WS2 ....**52** D4
Showell Road Industrial Estate
WOLVN WV10 ....**36** B7
The Shrubbery School
WALM/CURD B76 ....**73** K6
Shrubland Street Community
Primary School
RLSS CV31 ....**206** E7
Shustoke CE Primary School
CSHL/WTROR B46 ....**94** E3
Sidemoor First School
BRGRVW B61 ....**191** J2
Sidney Stringer Community
Technology College
COV CV1 ....**9** H3
Silhill FC
SOLH B91 ....**148** C1
Silver Birches Business Park
BRGRVE B60 ....**191** L7
Silver End Business Park
BRLYHL DY5 ....**101** M5
Sion Hill Middle School
KIDD DY10 ....**138** D3
Sir Frank Whittle
Business Centre
RUGBYN/HIL CV21 ....**161** H8
Sir Robert Peel Hospital
POL/KGSB/FAZ B78 ....**45** H3
Skydome Leisure Complex
COV CV1 ....**8** D5
Sladefield Infant School
WASH/WDE B8 ....**90** E8
The Sladen CE Middle School
KIDD DY10 ....**138** D5
Slade Primary School
ERDW/GRVHL B23 ....**90** A3
Sledmere Primary School
DUDS DY2 ....**85** H7
Small Heath Business Park
SMHTH B10 ....**108** D6
Small Heath Lower School
SMHTH B10 ....**108** B6
Small Heath Trading Estate
SPARK B11 ....**108** B7
Small Heath Upper School &
Sixth Form Centre
SMHTH B10 ....**108** B5

Smestow Bridge
Industrial Estate
WMBN WV5 ....**64** A7
Smestow Secondary School
BDMR/CCFT WV3 ....**48** A7
Smethwick Medical Centre
SMTHWK B66 ....**87** L7
Smethwick Swimming Centre
SMTHWK B67 ....**105** K3
Smith's Wood School
CBROM B36 ....**92** E7
Sneyd Community School
BLOX/PEL WS3 ....**38** C3
Snow Hill Clinic
BKHL/PFLD WV2 ....**3** G6
Soho Health Centre
HDSW B21 ....**88** D6
Soho House
WSNGN B18 ....**88** E6
Solihull College
SOLH B91 ....**148** E2
Solihull Hospital
SOLH B91 ....**149** H1
Solihull Ice Rink
HIA/OLT B92 ....**127** M2
Solihull Magistrates Court
SOLH B91 ....**149** G2
Solihull Retail Park
SHLY B90 ....**148** B4
Solihull School
SOLH B91 ....**149** H1
Solihull Sixth Form College
SOLH B91 ....**149** H3
Somerville Primary School
SMHTH B10 ....**108** B5
South Birmingham College
HLGN/YWD B28 ....**126** C5
South Birmingham
Mental Health NHS Trust
BVILLE B30 ....**146** B2
South Bromsgrove
Community High School
Technical College
BRGRVE B60 ....**191** K5
Southfield Primary School
COV CV1 ....**9** K4
South Moons Moat
Industrial Estate
REDE B98 ....**203** H1
Southside Business Centre
BHTH/HG B12 ....**107** H4
South Staffordshire Golf Club
DUNHL/THL/PER WV6 ......**35** G7
South Staffs Business Park
CNCK/NC WS11 ....**24** A1
Sovereign Trading Estate
STRBR DY8 ....**101** J8
Sowe Valley Primary School
COVS CV3 ....**156** H5
Sparkbrook Health Centre
SPARK B11 ....**107** M6
Sparkbrook Street
Industrial Estate
COV CV1 ....**9** K3
Sparkhill Pool & Fitness Centre
SPARK B11 ....**126** A1
Sparrowdale Special School
ATHST CV9 ....**62** B1
Spartan Industrial Centre
WBROM B70 ....**68** C7
Speedwell Trading Estate
YDLY B25 ....**108** E2
Spennells First School
KIDD DY10 ....**164** E3
Spines Clinic
WMBN WV5 ....**64** D7
Spinners End Industrial Estate
CDYHTH B64 ....**103** H4
Spon Gate Primary School
COV CV1 ....**8** B4
Spon Lane Industrial Estate
SMTHWK B66 ....**87** H5
Spon Lane Trading Estate
WBROM B70 ....**87** G3
Springdale J & I School
ETTPK/GDPK/PENN WV4 ..**49** G8
Springfield House School
DOR/KN D93 ....
Springfield Infant School
MOS/BIL B13 ....**126** B3
Springfield Junior School
BLKHTH/ROWR B65 ......**103** L1
Springfield Junior School
SPARK B11 ....**126** B3
Springfield Primary School
BLKHTH/ROWR B65 ....**85** L8
Spring Hill Industrial Estate
RCOVN/BALC/EX CV7 ......**96** D5
Spring Hill Industrial Estate
WSNGN B18 ....**106** D1
Springhill Medical Centre
BNTWD WS7 ....**18** E6
Spring Hill Medical Centre
RCOVN/BALC/EX CV7 ......**96** D6
Springhill Primary School
WOLVN WV10 ....**18** F7
Spring Lane Industrial Estate
SHHTH WV12 ....**52** A1
Spring Road Industrial Estate
ETTPK/GDPK/PENN WV4 ..**66** E1
Springvale Business Park
BILS/COS WV14 ....**66** F1
Springvale Industrial Park
BILS/COS WV14 ....**66** F1
Springvale Primary School
CNCK/NC WS11 ....**16** C5
Spring Vale Primary School
ETTPK/GDPK/PENN WV4 ..**66** C1
Sprint Industrial Estate
WOLVN WV10 ....**14** B7
Stafford Road Sports Club
BLOX/PEL WS3 ....**38** C3
Staffordshire College of
Agriculture
PENK ST19 ....**14** C1
Staffordshire Regiment
Museum, Whittington
LICHS WS14 ....**30** A3
Stag Industrial Estate
BILS/COS WV14 ....**67** L1
Stag Industrial Estate
COVN CV6 ....**134** B5
Stambermill Industrial Estate
BRLYHL DY5 ....**102** A7
Stanhope Road Clinic
SMTHWKW B67 ....**105** K2
Stanton Bridge
Primary School
COVN CV6 ....**134** D7
Stanville Primary School
LGN/SDN/BHAMAIR B26 **109** M6
Starbank Primary School
SMHTH B10 ....**108** F5
Star City
VAUX/NECH B7 ....**90** B5
Starcrest Industrial Estate
BRLYHL DY5 ....**102** C4
Star Industrial Park
COVE CV2 ....**135** J8

Start Point Trading Estate
SPARK B11 ....**126**
Station Road Industrial Estate
BLKHTH/ROWR B65 ......**93**
Station Road Industrial Estate
CSHL/WTROR B46 ....**93**
Station Road Industrial Estate
CSHL/WTROR B46 ....**93**
Station Street West
Business Park
COVN CV6 ....**134**
Status Business Centre
COVW CV5 ....**8**
Stechford Cascades
STETCH B33 ....**109**
Stechford Health Centre
STETCH B33 ....**109**
Stechford Primary School
STETCH B33 ....**109**
Stechford Retail Park
STETCH B33 ....**109**
Stechford Trading Estate
STETCH B33 ....**109**
Steetley Industrial Estate
TPTN/OCK DY4 ....**67**
Stephens Industrial Estate
SPARK B11 ....**126**
Stevens Dental Health Centre
STRBR DY8 ....**119**
Stirchley Primary School
BVILLE B30 ....**124**
Stirchley Trading Estate
BVILLE B30 ....**124**
Stivichall Primary School
COVS CV3 ....**154**
Stock Exchange
CBHAMNW B3 ....**6**
Stockingford Clinic
NUNW/HART CV10 ....**98**
Stockingford Primary &
Middle School
NUNW/HART CV10 ....**98**
Stockland Clinic
ERDW/GRVHL B23 ....**90**
Stockland Green Health Centre
ERDW/GRVHL B23 ....**90**
Stockland Green School
ERDW/GRVHL B23 ....**90**
Stoke Aldermoor
Medical Centre
COVS CV3 ....**155**
Stoke Heath J & I School
COVS CV3 ....**134**
Stoke Old Boys RFC
COVS CV3 ....**156**
Stoke Park School and
Community Technology
College
COVE CV2 ....**155**
Stoke Primary School
COVE CV2 ....**155**
Stoke Row Industrial Estate
COVS CV3 ....**155**
Stonebridge Golf Club
RCOVN/BALC/EX CV7 ....**130**
Stonebridge Trading Estate
COVS CV3 ....**181**
Stone CE First School
KIDD DY10 ....**165**
Stone Cross Clinic
HHTH/SAND B71 ....**69**
Stoneleigh Abbey
KNWTH CV8 ....**198**
Stoneleigh Deer Park
Business Village
KNWTH CV8 ....**199**
Stoneleigh Deer Park Golf Club
KNWTH CV8 ....**181**
Stone Manor Hotel
KIDD DY10 ....**165**
Stoneydelph Infants School
TAM/AM/WIL B77 ....**46**
Stoneydelph Primary School
TAM/AM/WIL B77 ....**46**
Stoney Lane Industrial Estate
KIDDW DY11 ....**138**
Stoney Stanton
Medical Centre
COVN CV6 ....**134**
Stourbridge CC
STRBR DY8 ....**101**
Stourbridge Clinic
STRBR DY8 ....**119**
Stourbridge College of
Technology & Art
STRBR DY8 ....**119**
Stourbridge Crematorium
STRBR DY8 ....**119**
Stourbridge FC
STRBR DY8 ....**101**
Stourbridge Golf Club
STRBR DY8 ....**119**
Stourbridge Industrial Estate
STRBR DY8 ....**101**
Stourbridge Lawn Tennis &
Squash Club
KINVER DY7 ....**118**
Stourbridge RFC
KINVER DY7 ....**100**
Stourminster Special School
KIDD DY10 ....**164**
Stourport Health Centre
STRPT DY13 ....**188**
Stourport on Severn
First School
STRPT DY13 ....**188**
Stourport on Severn High School
STRPT DY13 ....**163**
Stourport Sports Centre
STRPT DY13 ....**188**
Stourport Tennis Club
STRPT DY13 ....**188**
Stourside Industrial Estate
KIDD DY10 ....**138**
Stourvale Industrial Estate
HAG/WOL DY9 ....**102**
Stourvale Trading Estate
HALE B63 ....**103**
Stowe CE School
LICH WS13 ....**2**
Stoweheath Industrial Estate &
New Enterprise Centre
WOLV WV1 ....**5**
Stow Heath J & I School
WLNHL WV13 ....**5**
Stowlawn Primary School
BILS/COS WV14 ....**5**
Straits Primary School
SEDG DY3 ....
Stratford Road School Clinic
SPARK B11 ....**108**
The Streetley School
FOAKS/STRLY B74 ....
Streetly Cemetery
ALDR WS9 ....
Streetly Clinic
FOAKS/STRLY B74 ....
Streetly Hockey & Cricket Club
FOAKS/STRLY B74 ....

etly Methodist
ecreation Centre
OAKS/STRLY B74 .....55 K3
etsbrook Infant School
HLY B90 .....148 A1
art Bathurst RC
igh School
ARL/WED WS10 .....52 F8
rt Crystal
TRBR DY8 .....101 J4
ley Cricket Club
UD B80 .....203 J7
merfield Hospital
SNGN B18 .....106 C1
merfield Primary School
SNGN B18 .....106 C1
mer Hill Industrial Park
BHAMW B1 .....6 A3
Summerhill Secondary
chool
SSWFD DY6 .....82 F8
dridge Primary School
GSTC B44 .....71 J1
field School
AG/WOL DY9 .....141 J1
rise Business Park
TRBR DY8 .....101 J6
shine Infant School
LOX/PEL WS3 .....39 G5
erintendent Public Baths
LYOAK B29 .....124 D4
ton Arts Theatre
SCFLD/WYGN B72 .....73 G1
on Coldfield College
OAKS/STRLY B74 .....57 G7
on Coldfield Crematorium
IGN/WHC B75 .....57 L3
on Coldfield Girls School
CFLD/BOLD B73 .....72 F2
on Coldfield Golf Club
OAKS/STRLY B74 .....55 M4
on Coldfield Hospital
CFLD/BOLD B73 .....72 F1
ton Coldfield
Magistrates Court
OAKS/STRLY B74 .....56 F7
on Coldfield Town FC
SCFLD/WYGN B72 .....73 G2
on Coldfield Town Hall
CFLD/BOLD B73 .....56 F7
ton Park First School
DDW DY11 .....163 M1
Sutton Special School
DUDN DY1 .....84 D5
ton Town Sports Club
SCFLD/WYGN B72 .....73 G1
on United FC
IGN/WHC B75 .....57 J8
Swallows
dustrial Estate
HLY B90 .....148 B5
allows Rise Business Park
RLYHL DY5 .....102 C6
n Centre
IDD DY10 .....138 C7
n Corner Shopping Centre
NTWD WS7 .....19 G7
an Lane Industrial Estate
BROM B70 .....68 E8
on Medical Centre
DLY B25 .....109 H6
npool Medical Centre
PTN/OCK DY4 .....67 L5
nshurst Girls School
MOS/BIL B13 .....125 M6
nswell Medical Centre
OV CV1 .....9 G2
rt Valley Industrial Estate
UGBYN/HIL CV21 .....160 D5
nfen Hall Hotel
CHS WS14 .....29 J4
amore Green
rimary School
UDN DY1 .....66 D8
amore House
ledical Centre
VSL WS1 .....5 K7
amore Industrial &
rading Estate
OSW WS2 .....88 B6
enham Industrial Estate
LSS CV31 .....206 F7
enham Primary School
PLSS CV31 .....207 G7
nphony Hall
BHAMW B1 .....6 C5
brook Park
dustrial Estate
WCK CV34 .....206 B8
ots Lane Trading Estate
RLYHL DY5 .....102 C4
man Theatre & Arts Centre
NWTH CV8 .....197 K2
ar Medical Centre
UNHL/THL/PER WV6 .....48 C1
ebridge Industrial Estate
BAR/PBCH B42 .....89 J1
e Road Industrial Estate
ST/WIT B6 .....89 M4
e Valley Industrial Estate
AM/AM/WIL B77 .....46 C6
e Valley Industrial Estate
AM/AM/WIL B77 .....46 C8
e Valley Primary School
RDE/BCHGN B24 .....91 H5
e Valley Small Business
entre
AM/AM/WIL B77 .....46 C7
e View Caravan Site
OL/KGSB/FAZ B78 .....59 M4
worth Assembly Rooms
RTAM B79 .....31 M8
worth Business Centre
AM/AM/WIL B77 .....46 F2
worth Business Park
AM/AM/WIL B77 .....46 F2
worth Castle
RTAM B79 .....45 M1
worth FC (The Lamb)
AM/AM/WIL B77 .....46 A2
worth Leisure Island
nowdome Ski
Peaks Leisure Centre)
AM/AM/WIL B77 .....45 M2
worth & Lichfield College
RTAM B79 .....31 M7
worth Municipal Golf Club
RTAM B79 .....47 G1
worth RUFC
RTAM B79 .....31 K6
worth Sports Stadium
AM/AM/WIL B77 .....46 D4
ton Medical Centre
DG DY3 .....66 C8

Tardebigge CE First School
BRGRVE B60 .....192 F6
Teachers Centre
COV CV1 .....9 G7
Telford Infant School
RLSN CV32 .....199 G8
Telford Junior School
RLSN CV32 .....198 F8
Telsen Industrial Centre
AST/WIT B6 .....89 K7
Templar Industrial Park
TLHL/CAN CV4 .....153 L5
Templars Primary School
TLHL/CAN CV4 .....153 L4
Temple Meadow
Primary School
CDYHTH B64 .....103 K4
Ten Acres First School
REDE B98 .....203 K2
Tenlons Road Industrial Estate
NUNW/HART CV10 .....98 D3
Tenterfields Primary School
HALE B63 .....122 A4
Terrace Industrial Estate
RUGBYN/HIL CV21 .....186 F1
The Terrace School
RLSN CV32 .....206 C6
Terry Business Centre
REDE B98 .....202 D2
Tettenhall College
DUNHL/THL/PER WV6 .....49 H1
Tettenhall Wood
Special School
DUNHL/THL/PER WV6 .....48 F2
Theatre One
COV CV1 .....9 H3
Thinktank Museum
DIG/EDG B5 .....7 K4
Thomas Barnes CP School
POL/KGSB/FAZ B78 .....30 C1
Thornleigh Trading Estate
DUDS DY2 .....84 E6
Thorns Community College
BRLYHL DY5 .....102 B5
Thorns County Infant School
KNWTH CV8 .....197 L1
Thorns Primary School
BRLYHL DY5 .....102 C6
Thornton Junior School
WASH/WDE B8 .....90 F8
Three Crowns Special School
DSYBK/YTR WS5 .....54 D4
Three Spires Industrial Estate
COVN CV6 .....116 E7
Three Spires Shopping Centre
LICH WS13 .....20 F6
Three Spires Special School
COVW CV5 .....133 H7
Tidbury Green
Primary School
SHLY B90 .....173 J1
Tile Cross Trading Estate
STETCH B33 .....110 B4
Tile Hill Wood
Comprehensive School
TLHL/CAN CV4 .....153 H4
Timberley Primary School
BKDE/SHDE B34 .....92 B7
Timbertree Primary School
CDYHTH B64 .....103 J6
Tindal Primary School
BHTH/HG B12 .....107 K8
Tipper Trading Estate
HAG/WOL DY9 .....102 E8
Tipton Green Junior School
TPTN/OCK DY4 .....85 K1
Tipton Sports Academy
TPTN/OCK DY4 .....67 M4
Tiverton J & I School
COVN CV6 .....124 D3
Tiverton Special School
COVN CV6 .....133 H8
Tividale Business Park
TPTN/OCK DY4 .....85 M2
Tividale Comprehensive School
OLDBY B69 .....86 A4
Tividale FC
OLDBY B69 .....85 M4
Tividale Hall Primary School
OLDBY B69 .....85 L4
Tividale Medical Centre
OLDBY B69 .....86 B5
Tividale Primary School
OLDBY B69 .....85 M3
Toffs Country House Hotel
RCOVN/BALC/EX CV7 .....132 C1
Tollgate Shopping Precinct
SMTHWKW B67 .....87 K7
Tolson Industrial Estate
POL/KGSB/FAZ B78 .....45 L5
Tolsons Mill Industrial Estate
POL/KGSB/FAZ B78 .....45 L5
Topcliffe Primary School
CVALE B35 .....91 L2
Touchwood Shopping Centre
SOLH B91 .....149 G1
Tower Hill Health Centre
PBAR/PBCH B42 .....70 E7
Tower Works Industrial Estate
BDMR/CCFT WV3 .....2 A7
Town Gate Retail Park
DUDN DY1 .....85 K3
Town Junior School
CSCFLD/WYGN B72 .....73 G1
Town Wharf Business Park
WSLW WS2 .....4 C3
T P Riley Community School
BLOX/PEL WS3 .....39 G1
Tractor Spares Industrial Estate
WLNHL WV13 .....51 H3
Trading Estate Parkview
HWK/WKHTH B38 .....145 K2
The Trafford Park
Industrial Estate
REDE B98 .....202 D2
Travel Inn
BRGRVE B60 .....191 M2
CBHAMW B1 .....6 D6
CNCK/NC WS11 .....15 M4
COVS CV3 .....156 F5
HAG/WOL DY9 .....120 D6
HOCK/TIA B94 .....174 F6
KGSWFD DY6 .....83 K6
NUNW/HART CV10 .....98 F7
POL/KGSB/FAZ B78 .....45 J3
RCOVN/BALC/EX CV7 .....151 L5
RRUGBY CV23 .....161 G4
SHLY B90 .....147 M2
SHLY B90 .....148 B3
VAUX/NECH B7 .....89 K8
WBROM B70 .....68 C8
WOLVN WV10 .....22 B8
WSLW WS2 .....52 C4
Travelodge
BRLYHL DY5 .....102 C1
CBHAMW B1 .....6 D6
LCN/SDN/BHAMAIR B26 .....109 J7
NUN CV11 .....81 L7
OLDBY B69 .....86 B6

SCFLD/BOLD B73 .....72 D4
STRPT DY13 .....189 L6
TAM/AM/WIL B77 .....47 G6
WNSFLD WV11 .....23 L6
Travelodge Birmingham
RIDG/WDGT B32 .....122 D6
Trent Valley Trading Estate
LICH WS13 .....21 G2
Trescott Primary School
NFLD/LBR B31 .....144 B2
Trevor Street Industrial Estate
VAUX/NECH B7 .....90 A7
Tribune Trading Estate
RUGBYN/HIL CV21 .....160 E7
Trident Business Park
NUN CV11 .....99 H2
Trident Retail Park
BORD B9 .....7 M6
Trident Shopping Centre
DUDN DY1 .....85 G4
Trinity Business Park
HIA/OLT B92 .....129 H2
The Trinity Catholic
Technology College
RLSN CV32 .....206 B3
Trinity CE Primary School
WOLVN WV10 .....50 D1
Trinity High School &
6th Form College
REDE B98 .....202 D1
Trinity RC School
WWCK CV34 .....206 A7
Tripontium Business Centre
RRUGBY CV23 .....161 L1
Tromans Industrial Estate
DUDS DY2 .....103 H2
Truck Stop Business Park
SPARK B11 .....108 F7
Tudor Business Centre
REDE B98 .....202 C2
Tudor Grange School
SOLH B91 .....148 E3
Tudor Grange
Sports Centre & Pool
SOLH B91 .....148 F2
Tudor Industrial Estate
SPARK B11 .....108 F8
Tulip Inn Hotel
KNWTH CV8 .....198 E1
Turves Green Boys School
NFLD/LBR B31 .....144 E5
Turves Green Girls School
NFLD/LBR B31 .....144 E4
Turves Green Primary School
NFLD/LBR B31 .....144 E4
Tuttle Hill Industrial Estate
NUNW/HART CV10 .....80 C7
Twickenham Primary School
KGSTG B44 .....72 A4
Two Gates Primary School
TAM/AM/WIL B77 .....46 A5
Two Gates Trading Estate
TAM/AM/WIL B77 .....46 B6
Two Woods Industrial Estate
BRLYHL DY5 .....102 C4
Two Woods Trading Estate
BRLYHL DY5 .....102 D4
Tyburn Industrial Estate
ERDE/BCHGN B24 .....91 H3
Tyseley Industrial Estate
SPARK B11 .....108 C8
Tyseley Locomotive Works Visitor
Centre
SPARK B11 .....108 D8
UCI Cinema
BRLYHL DY5 .....102 C3
CRTAM B79 .....46 A1
SHLY B90 .....148 C6
Uffcume Clinic
MOS/BIL B13 .....125 J3
Uffcume Special School
MOS/BIL B13 .....125 J4
UGC Cinema
DIG/EDG B5 .....7 G7
UGC Cinema
EDG B15 .....6 B8
Ulverley Primary School
HIA/OLT B92 .....127 M5
Underhill J & I School
WOLVN WV10 .....36 F4
Underhill Primary School
WOLVN WV10 .....36 F4
Union Business Park
WSLW WS2 .....4 D4
Unisant Trading Estate
CDYHTH B64 .....103 K3
University of Birmingham
EDG B15 .....106 E8
University of Birmingham
EDG B15 .....106 D2
University of Central England
PBAR/PBCH B42 .....89 H2
University of Warwick
TLHL/CAN CV4 .....179 M1
University of Warwick
TLHL/CAN CV4 .....180 A2
University of Warwick
Sports Centre
TLHL/CAN CV4 .....154 A8
University of Wolverhampton
WOLV WV1 .....2 F3
University of Wolverhampton
Wulfrun Campus
DUNHL/THL/PER WV6 .....49 J2
Uplands Cemetery
SMTHWKW B67 .....105 J2
Uplands Junior School
BDMR/CCFT WV3 .....49 H5
Uplands Manor Primary School
SMTHWKW B67 .....105 J2
USAM Trading Estate
WOLVN WV10 .....36 B3
Vale Business Park
HIA/OLT B92 .....188 F2
Vale Industrial Estate
KIDDW DY11 .....164 A3
Valley Infant School
HIA/OLT B92 .....128 B2
Valley Park Campus
DUNHL/THL/PER WV6 .....35 K8
Vaughan Trading Estate
TPTN/OCK DY4 .....85 M2
Vauxhall Trading Estate
VAUX/NECH B7 .....107 M1
The Vaynor First School
REDW B97 .....202 A6
Vector Industrial Park
HHTH/SAND B71 .....69 G7
Venkat Medical Centre
STETCH B33 .....110 C2
Ventura Park Shopping Centre
POL/KGSB/FAZ B78 .....45 K2
Ventura Retail Park
POL/KGSB/FAZ B78 .....45 L2
Vernon Trading Estate
RMSLY B62 .....104 A5
Victor Business Centre
REDE B98 .....202 E2
Victoria Business Centre
RLSS CV31 .....206 E6

Victoria Health Centre
SMTHWK B66 .....105 M1
Victoria Infant School
TPTN/OCK DY4 .....67 J8
Victoria Park Primary School
SMTHWK B66 .....87 M8
Victoria School
TLHL/CAN CV4 .....123 L8
Villiers Primary School
BILS/COS WV14 .....51 H6
Villiers Trading Estate
BKHL/PFLD WV2 .....50 A6
Viva! Health & Leisure Club
SOLH B91 .....149 G6
Vulcan House Industrial Estate
SOLH B91 .....128 A7
Vulcan Industrial Estate
WSLW WS2 .....39 G7
Wainbody Wood
Special School
TLHL/CAN CV4 .....180 B3
Wake Green FC
SHLY B90 .....147 J5
Walhouse CE Junior School
CNCK/NC WS11 .....16 A4
Walkmill Business Park
CNCK/NC WS11 .....16 A8
Walkwood CE Middle School
REDW B97 .....202 A5
Wallbrook Primary School
BILS/COS WV14 .....67 J5
The Wallows Industrial Estate
BRLYHL DY5 .....84 B8
Wall Roman Site Museum
LICHS WS14 .....28 B3
Walmley CC
WALM/CURD B76 .....73 J6
Walmley Golf Club
CSCFLD/WYGN B72 .....73 G5
Walmley Junior School
WALM/CURD B76 .....73 L6
Walsall Business Park
ALDR WS9 .....40 F8
Walsall Business Park
ALDR WS9 .....54 C1
Walsall CC
WSL WS1 .....5 J8
Walsall College of Arts
& Technology
WSL WS1 .....4 E2
WSLW WS2 .....4 A5
Walsall FC (Bescot Stadium)
WSL WS1 .....53 H8
Walsall Gala Baths
WSL WS1 .....4 F3
Walsall Golf Club
DSYBK/YTR WS5 .....53 M7
Walsall Leather Museum
WSLW WS2 .....4 E1
Walsall Museum & Library
WSL WS1 .....5 G3
Walsall RFC
WSL WS1 .....53 K7
Walsall Wood Primary School
ALDR WS9 .....40 D1
Walsgrave CE Primary School
COVE CV2 .....135 L7
Walsgrave General Hospital
COVE CV2 .....135 L8
Walsgrave Health Centre
COVE CV2 .....135 K7
Walsgrave Retail Park
COVE CV2 .....135 M6
Walsgrave Triangle
Business Park
RCOVN/BALC/EX CV7 .....135 L4
Ward Arms Hotel
DUDN DY1 .....85 K3
Ward End Medical Centre
WASH/WDE B8 .....90 F8
Ward End Primary School
WASH/WDE B8 .....90 F7
Warley High School
LGLYGN/QTN B68 .....104 E3
Warley Infant School
LGLYGN/QTN B68 .....105 G3
Warley Magistrates Court
OLDBY B69 .....86 E6
Warley Woods Golf Club
SMTHWK B67 .....105 J5
Warren Farm Primary School
KGSTG B44 .....71 M5
Warstones Primary School
ETTPK/GDPK/PENN WV4 .....49 J2
Wartell Bank Industrial Estate
KGSWFD DY6 .....83 H5
Warwick Arms Hotel
WWCK CV34 .....205 J7
Warwick Castle
WWCK CV34 .....205 J7
Warwick CC
WWCK CV34 .....205 H6
Warwick County &
Crown Courts
WWCK CV34 .....205 J7
Warwick Golf Club
WWCK CV34 .....205 H7
Warwick Hospital
WWCK CV34 .....205 J5
Warwick Preparatory School
WWCK CV34 .....205 J7
Warwick Race Course
WWCK CV34 .....205 H5
Warwick Road Trading Estate
SPARK B11 .....126 B1
Warwick School
WWCK CV34 .....205 L7
Warwickshire CCC
(Edgbaston)
DIG/EDG B5 .....107 H8
Warwickshire College
RLSN CV32 .....206 B5
The Warwickshire Golf Club
RWWCK/WEL CV35 .....197 J8
Warwickshire Nuffield Hospital
RLSN CV32 .....198 C8
Warwickshire Racquet &
Health Centre
COVS CV3 .....155 K6
Warwickshire Yeomanry
Museum
WWCK CV34 .....205 J7
Warwick Sports Club
WWCK CV34 .....205 H8
Warwick Technology Park
WWCK CV34 .....205 M8
Waseley Hills Country Park
BRGRVW B61 .....143 G5
Waseley Hills High School
RBRY B45 .....143 H6
Washington Street
Industrial Estate
DUDS DY2 .....103 H2
Washwood Heath
Technology College
WASH/WDE B8 .....91 G2
Waterfall Lane
Trading Estate
CDYHTH B64 .....103 L4

Waterfront Business Park
BRLYHL DY5 .....102 B1
Waterloo Industrial Estate
CBROM B36 .....92 F8
Watermill Primary School
SLYOAK B29 .....124 B2
Water Orton CC
CSHL/WTROR B46 .....92 F2
Water Orton Primary School
CSHL/WTROR B46 .....92 F3
Waterside Industrial Estate
BKHL/PFLD WV2 .....50 D4
BLKHTH/ROWR B65 .....103 K1
Watling Street
Business Park
BLOX/PEL WS3 .....25 L3
Watling Street JMI School
BRWNH WS8 .....26 C4
Wattville Primary School
HDSW B21 .....87 M5
Wattville Road
Industrial Estate
SMTHWK B66 .....87 M6
Waverley School
SMHTH B10 .....108 E5
WCC Sports Ground
WWCK CV34 .....205 M6
Webb Ellis Business Park
RUGBYN/HIL CV21 .....160 F8
Webheath First School
REDW B97 .....201 L3
Webnor Industrial Estate
BKHL/PFLD WV2 .....50 E7
Weddington Industrial Estate
NUNW/HART CV10 .....81 G8
Weddington Primary School
NUNW/HART CV10 .....81 H6
Wedgnock Industrial Estate
WWCK CV34 .....205 G4
Wednesbury Art Gallery
DARL/WED WS10 .....68 D3
Wednesbury Chiropody
Surgery
DARL/WED WS10 .....68 D2
Wednesbury Cricket Club
DARL/WED WS10 .....68 E1
Wednesbury Leisure Centre
DARL/WED WS10 .....68 C2
Wednesbury Medical Centre
DARL/WED WS10 .....68 C3
Wednesbury Oak Primary School
TPTN/OCK DY4 .....67 K4
Wednesbury Rugby Club
DARL/WED WS10 .....68 D4
Wednesbury Town Hall
DARL/WED WS10 .....68 D3
Wednesbury Trading Estate
DARL/WED WS10 .....68 C1
Wednesfield FC
WNSFLD WV11 .....37 G3
Wednesfield High School
WNSFLD WV11 .....37 J3
Wednesfield Village
Primary School
WNSFLD WV11 .....37 H8
Wednesfield Way
Industrial Estate
WNSFLD WV11 .....51 H1
Welfare Clinic
KNWTH CV8 .....197 K1
Welford Primary School
BFLD/HDSWWD B20 .....88 F5
Wellington Industrial Estate
TPTN/OCK DY4 .....67 G6
Welsh House Farm
Primary School
RIDG/WDGT B32 .....123 K1
Welsh RFC
HIA/OLT B92 .....129 L3
Wembrook Primary School
NUN CV11 .....99 G3
Weoley Castle Health Centre
SLYOAK B29 .....123 L4
Weoley Castle Ruins & Museum
SLYOAK B29 .....123 L3
Wergs Golf Club
CDSL WV8 .....34 E4
Westacre Infant School
BDMR/CCFT WV3 .....49 H4
West Bromwich Albion FC
(The Hawthorns)
HHTH/SAND B71 .....87 L4
West Bromwich Dartmouth
Cricket Club
HHTH/SAND B71 .....87 K4
West Bromwich Magistrates
Court
WBROM B70 .....87 G2
West Chadsmoor Clinic
CNCK/NC WS11 .....12 C7
West Croft Special School
WOLVN WV10 .....36 F3
West Cross Shopping Centre
SMTHWK B66 .....87 H6
Western Business Park
RMSLY B62 .....103 M6
Western Business Park
WSNGN B18 .....88 C7
Westfield First School
RUGBYS/DCH CV22 .....186 B3
Westfield Lodge College
RUGBYS/DCH CV22 .....186 D4
Westfield Primary School
WMBN WV5 .....64 D8
West Gate
WWCK CV34 .....205 J7
Westgate Primary School
WWCK CV34 .....205 H7
Westgate Trading Estate
ALDR WS9 .....40 C7
West Heath Hospital
HWK/WKHTH B38 .....145 G5
West Heath J & I School
NFLD/LBR B31 .....145 G4
West Hill Primary School
HEDN WS12 .....12 F7
West House School
EDG B15 .....107 G5
The Westley Hotel
ACGN B27 .....126 F2
Westmead Hotel
ALVE B48 .....170 F7
West Midland Safari &
Leisure Park
BEWD DY12 .....163 J1
West Midlands Hospital
HALE B63 .....103 H8
Westminster Industrial Estate
DUDS DY2 .....103 H3
Westminster Primary School
BFLD/HDSWWD B20 .....89 G4
Westminster School
TPTN/OCK DY4 .....67 G7
Weston Hall Hotel
BDWTH CV12 .....117 M2
West Orchards
Shopping Centre
COV CV1 .....8 E4

West Park Hospital
WOLV WV1 ....2 C4
West Park Primary School
WOLV WV1 ....2 C2
West Side Business Centre
TLHL/CAN CV4 ....153 K5
Westwood Business Park
AST/WIT B6 ....89 M3
TLHL/CAN CV4 ....153 K7
Wharton Park Golf Club
BEWD DY12 ....162 B4
Wharton Street
Industrial Estate
VAUX/NECH B7 ....90 B5
Wheatsheaf Studio Theatre
COVE CV2 ....134 F8
Wheelers Lane J & I School
ALE/KHTH/YWD B14 ....125 K6
Wheelers Lane Technology
College
ALE/KHTH/YWD B14 ....125 K6
Wheeler Street
Shopping Centre
LOZ/NWT B19 ....89 C7
Whetstone Field
Primary School
ALDR WS9 ....54 F1
Whitacre Road Industrial Estate
NUN CV11 ....99 J1
Whitecrest Primary School
GTB/HAM B43 ....70 E3
Whitefriars Friary
COV CV1 ....9 J6
Whitehall Industrial Park
TPTN/OCK DY4 ....68 C8
Whitehall Infant School
WSL WS1 ....4 F9
Whitehall Junior School
WSL WS1 ....5 H9
Whiteheath Clinic
OLDBY B69 ....86 B8
Whitehouse Common
Primary School
MGN/WHC B75 ....57 H6
Whitesmore School
CHWD/FDBR/MGN B37 ....110 D4
Whitestone Clinic
NUN CV11 ....99 L5
Whitestone County
Infant School
NUN CV11 ....99 L5
Whitgreave J & I School
WOLVN WV10 ....36 C5
Whitgreave Primary School
WOLVN WV10 ....22 F6
Whitley Abbey
Community School
COVS CV3 ....155 K7
Whitley Abbey Primary School
COVS CV3 ....155 K7
Whitmore Medical Centre
WOLV WV1 ....2 E2
Whitmore Park J & I School
COVN CV6 ....133 L4
Whitmore Reans
Health Centre
DUNHL/THL/PER WV6 ....2 B1
Whittington Heath Golf Club
LICHS WS14 ....29 M2
Whittington Primary School
LICHS WS14 ....30 C1
Whitworth Industrial Park
BORD B9 ....108 A3
Whoberley Clinic
COVW CV5 ....154 A1
Whoberley Hall
Primary School
COVW CV5 ....154 A2
Wholesale Markets
DIG/EDG B5 ....7 H7
Widney Junior School
SOLH B91 ....148 D4

Wightwick Hall Special School
DUNHL/THL/PER WV6 ....48 C3
Wilden All Saints CE
First School
STRPT DY13 ....164 A8
Wilden Industrial Estate
STRPT DY13 ....164 A7
Wilden Village Cricket Club
STRPT DY13 ....164 B8
Wilkes Green J & I School
HDSW B21 ....88 C4
Wilkinson Primary School
BILS/COS WV14 ....67 K2
Willenhall Industrial Estate
WNHL WV13 ....52 A2
Willenhall Lane
Industrial Estate
BLOX/PEL WS3 ....38 E5
Willenhall Leisure Centre
WLNHL WV13 ....51 M4
Willenhall Town FC
WLNHL WV13 ....51 J2
Willenhall Trading Estate
WLNHL WV13 ....51 K4
Willenhall Wood
Primary School
COVS CV3 ....156 B7
William Baxter Special School
HEDN WS12 ....12 E7
William Cowper Primary School
LOZ/NWT B19 ....89 J7
William Hanke Industrial Estate
BRLYHL DY5 ....102 C4
William Macgregor
Primary School
TAM/AM/WIL B77 ....46 B2
Willingsworth High School
TPTN/OCK DY4 ....67 M3
Willows Primary School
LICH WS13 ....20 F3
Wilnecote Health Centre
TAM/AM/WIL B77 ....46 D6
Wilnecote Junior School
TAM/AM/WIL B77 ....46 D6
Wilnecote School
TAM/AM/WIL B77 ....46 D7
Wilson Stuart Special School
ERDW/CRVHL B23 ....72 A7
Wiltell Road Industrial Estate
LICH WS13 ....20 F6
The Windmill CE Middle School
STRPT DY13 ....188 C4
Windmill Hill (look out)
RBRY B45 ....143 G5
Windmill Industrial Estate
COVW CV5 ....132 D6
Windmill Village Golf &
Leisure Club
COVW CV5 ....132 D6
Windmill Works Industrial Park
DUDS DY2 ....84 F6
Windsor High School
HALE B63 ....121 K1
Windsor Industrial Estate
VAUX/NECH B7 ....89 J2
Windward Way
Industrial Estate
CBROM B36 ....92 D5
Windy Arbor Primary School
CHWD/FDBR/MGN B37 ....111 H2
Winster Grove
Industrial Centre
KGSTG B44 ....71 H3
KGSTG B44 ....71 J3
Winterfold House School
KIDD DY10 ....165 L5
Winyates Health Centre
REDE B98 ....203 J2
Wishaw CC
WALM/CURD B76 ....74 E3
Witherley CE Primary School
ATHST CV9 ....63 M6

Witherley United FC
ATHST CV9 ....63 L5
Withymoor Primary School
BRLYHL DY5 ....102 B4
Withy Road
Industrial Estate
BILS/COS WV14 ....67 G2
Witton Industrial Estate
AST/WIT B6 ....89 L3
Witton Park
Industrial Estate
AST/WIT B6 ....89 L4
Woden Primary School
WOLVN WV10 ....3 J1
Wodensborough Community
Technology College
DARL/WED WS10 ....68 F3
Wodensfield Primary School
WNSFLD WV11 ....36 F7
Wolgarston School
PENK ST19 ....10 E5
Wollescote Business Park
HAG/WOL DY9 ....102 D8
Wollescote Primary School
HAG/WOL DY9 ....120 D1
Wolston Business Park
KNWTH CV8 ....183 L1
Wolverhampton CC
DUNHL/THL/PER WV6 ....35 G7
Wolverhampton Central Baths
WOLV WV1 ....2 D4
Wolverhampton College
(Bilston Campus)
WOLV WV1 ....50 F6
Wolverhampton Girls
High School
DUNHL/THL/PER WV6 ....49 K2
Wolverhampton
Grammar School
BDMR/CCFT WV3 ....49 K3
Wolverhampton Healthcare
NHS Trust
WNSFLD WV11 ....50 F1
The Wolverhampton
Nuffield Hospital
DUNHL/THL/PER WV6 ....49 G1
Wolverhampton Racecourse
DUNHL/THL/PER WV6 ....35 L7
Wolverhampton University
WOLVN WV10 ....36 A7
Wolverhampton Wanderers FC
(Molineux Stadium)
WOLV WV1 ....2 E2
Wolverley High School
KIDDW DY11 ....138 B1
Wolverley Sebright
First School
KIDDW DY11 ....138 B2
Wombourne Cricket Tennis
& Bowling Club
WMBN WV5 ....64 E6
Wombrook Business Centre
WMBN WV5 ....64 C6
Wombrook Industrial Estate
WMBN WV5 ....64 C7
Woodbourne Priory Hospital
HRBN B17 ....106 A4
Woodcock Hill
Primary School
NFLD/LBR B31 ....123 J6
Woodcock Sports Centre
CBHAMNE B4 ....7 K2
Woodcross Clinic
BILS/COS WV14 ....66 E3
Wood End Health Centre
COVE CV2 ....135 G4
Wood End Primary School
COVE CV2 ....135 H4
Wood End Primary School
POL/KGSB/FAZ B78 ....60 F4
Wood End Primary School
WNSFLD WV11 ....37 G6

Woodfield J&ischool
BDMR/CCFT WV3 ....49 K7
Woodfield Middle School
REDE B98 ....202 E3
Woodgate Business Park
RIDG/WDGT B32 ....122 F3
Woodgate Primary School
RIDG/WDGT B32 ....122 F4
Woodgate Valley
RIDG/WDGT B32 ....123 G1
Woodgate Valley
Health Centre
RIDG/WDGT B32 ....123 G3
Wood Green High School
College of Sport
DARL/WED WS10 ....52 F8
Wood Green Junior School
DARL/WED WS10 ....68 D1
Woodhouse High School &
Community Sports Centre
TAM/AM/WIL B77 ....46 D1
Woodhouse J & I School
RIDG/WDGT B32 ....105 J7
Woodlands Cemetery
CSHL/WTROR B46 ....93 G8
Woodlands Infant School
SHLY B90 ....147 M5
Woodlands Primary School
SHHTH WV12 ....38 B7
Woodlands Primary School
TAM/AM/WIL B77 ....46 C1
The Woodlands School
TLHL/CAN CV4 ....153 H2
Woodloes J & I School
WWCK CV34 ....205 J4
Woodrow First School
REDE B98 ....202 F6
The Woodrush High School
HLYWD B47 ....146 E7
Woodrush RFC
HWK/WKHTH B38 ....171 M1
The Woodsbank Industrial Estate
DARL/WED WS10 ....68 D1
The Woodsbank Trading Estate
DARL/WED WS10 ....68 D1
The Woodsetton Special School
SEDG DY3 ....66 D6
Woodside Business Park
RUGBYN/HIL CV21 ....160 E8
Woodside Industrial Estate
BRLYHL DY5 ....84 D8
Woodside Medical Centre
TLHL/CAN CV4 ....153 K3
Woodstock Girls School
BHTH/HG B12 ....125 L1
Woodthorpe Primary School
ALE/KHTH/YWD B14 ....125 J8
Woodview Primary School
EDG B15 ....107 G5
Woodway Park
Community School
COVE CV2 ....135 K3
Worcester Street Surgery
STRBR DY8 ....101 L8
Wordsley Green Health Centre
STRBR DY8 ....101 H3
Wordsley Green
Shopping Centre
STRBR DY8 ....101 H3
Wordsley Hospital
STRBR DY8 ....101 J2
Works Trading Estate
SMTHWK B66 ....87 L6
Worlds End J & I School
RIDG/WDGT B32 ....105 J8
The Worsley School
STRBR DY8 ....101 K2
Wren's Nest National
Nature Reserve
DUDN DY1 ....84 F1
Wrens Nest Primary School
DUDN DY1 ....84 E1

Wribbenhall First School
BEWD DY12 137
Wribbenhall Middle School
BEWD DY12 165
Wrottesley Hall
CDSL WV8 34
Wulfrun Shopping Centre
WOLV WV1 2
Wulfrun Trading Estate
DUNHL/THL/PER WV6 36
Wychall Farm Primary School
NFLD/LBR B31 145
Wyken Croft Primary School
COVE CV2 135
Wyken Medical Centre
COVE CV2 134
Wylde Green Primary School
SCFLD/BOLD B73 72
Wyley Brook Retail Park
CNCK/NC WS11 16
Wyndcliffe Primary School
BORD B9 108
Wyndley Leisure Centre
SCFLD/BOLD B73 56
Wyndley Swimming Baths
SCFLD/BOLD B73 57
Wynford Industrial
Trading Estate
YDLY B25 109
Wynford Road
Industrial Estate
ACGN B27 109
Wyre Forest Golf Club
STRPT DY13 163
Wyrhall Health Centre
HLYWD B47 146
Yardley Cemetery
LGN/SDN/BHAMAIR B26 109
Yardley Green Health Centre
BORD B9 109
Yardley Green Medical Centre
SMHTH B10 108
Yardley J & I School
LGN/SDN/BHAMAIR B26 109
Yardley Medical Centre
YDLY B25 108
Yardleys School
SPARK B11 126
Yardleys Secondary School
SPARK B11 126
Yardley Wood Health Centre
ALE/KHTH/YWD B14 126
Yardley Wood Primary School
ALE/KHTH/YWD B14 147
Yarnfield Primary School
SPARK B11 126
Yenton Infant School
ERDE/BCHGN B24 72
Yenton Junior School
ERDE/BCHGN B24 72
Yew Tree Community
Junior School
AST/WIT B6 89
Yew Tree Primary School
DSYBK/YTR WS5 69
Yew Tree Primary School
SOLH B91 128
York House Medical Centre
STRPT DY13 188
York Mead Primary School
HLGN/YWD B28 126
Yorks Wood Primary School
CHWD/FDBR/MGN B37 92
Zip Theatre
WOLV WV1 2

Acknowledgements

The Post Office is a registered trademark of Post Office Ltd. in the UK and other countries.

Schools address data provided by Education Direct.

Petrol station information supplied by Johnsons

One-way street data provided by © Tele Atlas N.V. *Tele Atlas*

Garden centre information provided by:

Garden Centre Association  Britains best garden centres

Wyevale Garden Centres

Street by Street QUESTIONNAIRE

Dear Atlas User
Your comments, opinions and recommendations are very important to us. So please help us to improve our street atlases by taking a few minutes to complete this simple questionnaire.

You do NOT need a stamp (unless posted outside the UK). If you do not want to remove this page from your street atlas, then photocopy it or write your answers on a plain sheet of paper.

Send to: The Editor, AA Street by Street, FREEPOST SCE 4598, Basingstoke RG21 4GY

ABOUT THE ATLAS...

Which city/town/county did you buy?

Are there any features of the atlas or mapping that you find particularly useful?

Is there anything we could have done better?

Why did you choose an AA Street by Street atlas?

Did it meet your expectations?

Exceeded ☐   **Met all** ☐   **Met most** ☐   **Fell below** ☐

Please give your reasons

MX035z

continued overleaf

Where did you buy it?

For what purpose? (please tick all applicable)

To use in your own local area ☐   To use on business or at work ☐

Visiting a strange place ☐   In the car ☐   On foot ☐

Other (please state)

LOCAL KNOWLEDGE...

Local knowledge is invaluable. Whilst every attempt has been made to make the information contained in this atlas as accurate as possible, should you notice any inaccuracies, please detail them below (if necessary, use a blank piece of paper) or e-mail us at *streetbystreet@theAA.com*

ABOUT YOU...

Name (Mr/Mrs/Ms)
Address

Postcode

Daytime tel no
E-mail address

Which age group are you in?

Under 25 ☐   25-34 ☐   35-44 ☐   45-54 ☐   55-64 ☐   65+ ☐

Are you an AA member?   YES ☐   NO ☐

Do you have Internet access?   YES ☐   NO ☐

Thank you for taking the time to complete this questionnaire. Please send it to us as soon as possible, and remember, you do not need a stamp (unless posted outside the UK).

MX035z